Dietary Reference Intakes: RDA, AI*, (AMDR)

	Macronutrients					
Life-Stage Group	Carbohydrate—Total Digestible (g/d)	Total Fiber (g/d)	Total Fat (g/d)	n-6 polyunsaturated fatty acids (linoleic acid) (g/d)	n-3 polyunsaturated fatty acids (α-linolenic acid) (g/d)	Protein[a]
Infants						
0–6 mo	60* (ND[b])[c]	ND	31*	4.4* (ND)	0.5* (ND)	9.1* (ND)
7–12 mo	95* (ND)	ND	30*	4.6* (ND)	0.5* (ND)	13.5 (ND)
Children						
1–3 y	130 (45–65)	19*	(30–40)	7* (5–10)	0.7* (0.6–1.2)	13 (5–20)
4–8 y	130 (45–65)	25*	(25–35)	10* (5–10)	0.9* (0.6–1.2)	19 (10–30)
Males						
9–13 y	130 (45–65)	31*	(25–35)	12* (5–10)	1.2* (0.6–1.2)	34 (10–30)
14–18 y	130 (45–65)	38*	(25–35)	16* (5–10)	1.6* (0.6–1.2)	52 (10–30)
19–30 y	130 (45–65)	38*	(20–35)	17* (5–10)	1.6* (0.6–1.2)	56 (10–35)
31–50 y	130 (45–65)	38*	(20–35)	17* (5–10)	1.6* (0.6–1.2)	56 (10–35)
51–70 y	130 (45–65)	30*	(20–35)	14* (5–10)	1.6* (0.6–1.2)	56 (10–35)
>70 y	130 (45–65)	30*	(20–35)	14* (5–10)	1.6* (0.6–1.2)	56 (10–35)
Females						
9–13 y	130 (45–65)	26*	(25–35)	10* (5–10)	1.0* (0.6–1.2)	34 (10–30)
14–18 y	130 (45–65)	26*	(25–35)	11* (5–10)	1.1* (0.6–1.2)	46 (10–30)
19–30 y	130 (45–65)	25*	(20–35)	12* (5–10)	1.1* (0.6–1.2)	46 (10–35)
31–50 y	130 (45–65)	25*	(20–35)	12* (5–10)	1.1* (0.6–1.2)	46 (10–35)
51–70 y	130 (45–65)	21*	(20–35)	11* (5–10)	1.1* (0.6–1.2)	46 (10–35)
>70 y	130 (45–65)	21*	(20–35)	11* (5–10)	1.1* (0.6–1.2)	46 (10–35)
Pregnancy						
≤18 y	175 (45–65)	28*	(20–35)	13* (5–10)	1.4* (0.6–1.2)	71 (10–35)
19–30 y	175 (45–65)	28*	(20–35)	13* (5–10)	1.4* (0.6–1.2)	71 (10–35)
31–50 y	175 (45–65)	28*	(20–35)	13* (5–10)	1.4* (0.6–1.2)	71 (10–35)
Lactation						
≤18 y	210 (45–65)	29*	(20–35)	13* (5–10)	1.3* (0.6–1.2)	71 (10–35)
19–30 y	210 (45–65)	29*	(20–35)	13* (5–10)	1.3* (0.6–1.2)	71 (10–35)
31–50 y	210 (45–65)	29*	(20–35)	13* (5–10)	1.3* (0.6–1.2)	71 (10–35)

Source: Reprinted with permission from "Dietary Reference Intakes for Energy, Carbohydrates, Fiber, Fat, Fatty Acids, Cholesterol, Protein, and Amino Acids (Macronutrients)," © 2002 by the National Academy of Sciences, courtesy of the National Academies Press, Washington, DC.

Note: This table is adapted from the DRI reports, see www.nap.edu. It lists Recommended Dietary Allowances (RDAs), with Adequate Intakes (AIs) indicated by an asterisk (*), and Acceptable Macronutrient Distribution Range (AMDR) data provided in parentheses. RDAs and AIs may both be used as goals for individual intake. RDAs are set to meet the needs of almost all (97% to 98%) individuals in a group. For healthy breastfed infants, the AI is the mean intake. The AI for other life stage and gender groups is believed to cover the needs of all individuals in the group, but lack of data prevent being able to specify with confidence the percentage of individuals covered by this intake.

[a] Based on 1.5 g/kg/day for infants, 1.1 g/kg/day for 1–3 y, 0.95 g/kg/day for 4–13 y, 0.85 g/kg/day for 14–18 y, 0.8 g/kg/day for adults, and 1.1 g/kg/day for pregnant (using pre-pregnancy weight) and lactating women.

[b] ND = Not determinable due to lack of data of adverse effects in this age group and concern with regard to lack of ability to handle excess amounts. Source of intake should be from food only to prevent high levels of intake.

[c] Data in parentheses are Acceptable Macronutrient Distribution Range (AMDR). This is the range of intake for a particular energy source that is associated with reduced risk of chronic disease while providing intakes of essential nutrients. If an individual consumes in excess of the AMDR, there is a potential of increasing the risk of chronic diseases and/or insufficient intakes of essential nutrients.

Dietary Reference Intakes: RDA, AI*

Life-Stage Group	Vitamin A (µg/d)[a]	Vitamin D (µg/d)[b]	Vitamin E (mg/d)[c]	Vitamin K (µg/d)	Thiamin (mg/d)	Riboflavin (mg/d)	Niacin (mg/d)[d]	Pantothenic Acid (mg/d)	Biotin (µg/d)	Vitamin B_6 (mg/d)	Folate (µg/d)[e]	Vitamin B_{12} (µg/d)	Vitamin C (mg/d)	Choline (mg/d)
Infants														
0–6 mo	400*	10*	4*	2.0*	0.2*	0.3*	2*	1.7*	5*	0.1*	65*	0.4*	40*	125*
6–12 mo	500*	10*	5*	2.5*	0.3*	0.4*	4*	1.8*	6*	0.3*	80*	0.5*	50*	150*
Children														
1–3 y	300	15	6	30*	0.5	0.5	6	2*	8*	0.5	150	0.9	15	200*
4–8 y	400	15	7	55*	0.6	0.6	8	3*	12*	0.6	200	1.2	25	250*
Males														
9–13 y	600	15	11	60*	0.9	0.9	12	4*	20*	1.0	300	1.8	45	375*
14–18 y	900	15	15	75*	1.2	1.3	16	5*	25*	1.3	400	2.4	75	550*
19–30 y	900	15	15	120*	1.2	1.3	16	5*	30*	1.3	400	2.4	90	550*
31–50 y	900	15	15	120*	1.2	1.3	16	5*	30*	1.3	400	2.4	90	550*
51–70 y	900	15	15	120*	1.2	1.3	16	5*	30*	1.7	400	2.4	90	550*
>70 y	900	20	15	120*	1.2	1.3	16	5*	30*	1.7	400	2.4	90	550*
Females														
9–13 y	600	15	11	60*	0.9	0.9	12	4*	20*	1.0	300	1.8	45	375*
14–18 y	700	15	15	75*	1.0	1.0	14	5*	25*	1.2	400	2.4	65	400*
19–30 y	700	15	15	90*	1.1	1.1	14	5*	30*	1.3	400	2.4	75	425*
31–50 y	700	15	15	90*	1.1	1.1	14	5*	30*	1.3	400	2.4	75	425*
51–70 y	700	15	15	90*	1.1	1.1	14	5*	30*	1.5	400	2.4	75	425*
>70 y	700	20	15	90*	1.1	1.1	14	5*	30*	1.5	400	2.4	75	425*
Pregnancy														
≤18 y	750	15	15	75*	1.4	1.4	18	6*	30*	1.9	600	2.6	80	450*
19–30 y	770	15	15	90*	1.4	1.4	18	6*	30*	1.9	600	2.6	85	450*
31–50 y	770	15	15	90*	1.4	1.4	18	6*	30*	1.9	600	2.6	85	450*
Lactation														
≤18 y	1,200	15	19	75*	1.4	1.4	17	7*	35*	2.0	500	2.8	115	550*
19–30 y	1,300	15	19	90*	1.4	1.4	17	7*	35*	2.0	500	2.8	120	550*
31–50 y	1,300	15	19	90*	1.4	1.4	17	7*	35*	2.0	500	2.8	120	550*

Sources: Reprinted with permission from the Dietary Reference Intakes series, National Academies Press. Copyright 1997, 1998, 2000, 2001, by the National Academy of Sciences. These reports may be accessed via www.nap.edu. Courtesy of the National Academies Press, Washington, DC.

Note: This table is adapted from the DRI reports; see www.nap.edu. It lists Recommended Dietary Allowances (RDAs), with Adequate Intakes (AIs) indicated by an asterisk (*). RDAs and AIs may both be used as goals for individual intake. RDAs are set to meet the needs of almost all (97 percent to 98 percent) individuals in a group. For healthy breastfed infants, the AI is the mean intake. The AI for other life stage and gender groups is believed to cover the needs of all individuals in the group, but lack of data prevent being able to specify with confidence the percentage of individuals covered by this intake.

[a] Given as retinal activity equivalents (RAE).
[b] Also known as calciferol. The DRI values are based on the absence of adequate exposure to sunlight.
[c] Also known as α-tocopherol.
[d] Given as niacin equivalents (NE), except for infants 0–6 months, which are expressed as preformed niacin.
[e] Given as dietary folate equivalents (DFE).

Help your students make **better choices**

Help students become
nutrition savvy

Nutrition and You, **Second Edition** helps students to make healthy nutrition choices and encourages them to become informed consumers of nutrition information.

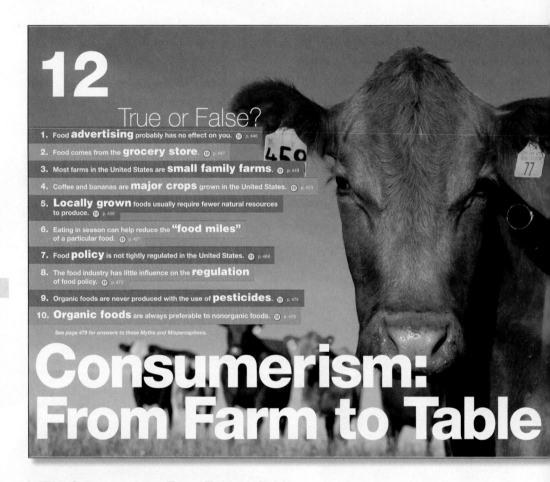

12
True or False?

1. Food **advertising** probably has no effect on you. ⓣ p.446
2. Food comes from the **grocery store**. ⓣ p.447
3. Most farms in the United States are **small family farms**. ⓣ p.449
4. Coffee and bananas are **major crops** grown in the United States. ⓣ p.453
5. **Locally grown** foods usually require fewer natural resources to produce. ⓣ p.456
6. Eating in season can help reduce the **"food miles"** of a particular food. ⓣ p.457
7. Food **policy** is not tightly regulated in the United States. ⓣ p.469
8. The food industry has little influence on the **regulation** of food policy. ⓣ p.472
9. Organic foods are never produced with the use of **pesticides**. ⓣ p.474
10. **Organic foods** are always preferable to nonorganic foods. ⓣ p.475

See page 479 for answers to these Myths and Misperceptions.

Consumerism: From Farm to Table

NEW! Consumerism: From Farm to Table

The new Chapter 12 adds and enhances coverage of topics such as organic foods, biotechnology, food marketing, food policy, and more. This chapter helps students learn how to make good decisions after they get to the grocery store, conveying how to effectively analyze options and determine a better path for their nutritional health.

NEW! "Made Over, Made Better"

Made Over, Made Better appears at the end of Chapters 4-10, helping students make more nutritious decisions.

- In a rich, visual style, this feature illustrates some typical foods students may choose accompanied by an improved, similar food choice.

- The choices presented reinforce chapter concepts such as: What better choice could be made to improve protein intake? Or decrease saturated fat intake?

Made Over, Made Better!

Snacks can be a great way to give your diet a mineral boost. Bananas, for example, are packed with potassium, raisins are naturally high in iron, peanuts are rich in magnesium, and cheese is a ringer for calcium. However, depending upon how these foods are processed, they may be higher in calories, fat, and saturated fat than you bargained for.

Here are some typical mineral-rich snacks made over and made nutritionally better!

Source: USDA National Nutrient Database for Standard Reference.

If you like this...	Try this healthy alternative!
Banana Chips Serving size: 1/2 cup **Calories: 300** **Fat: 14 grams** **Saturated Fat: 12 grams**	**Banana** 1 small **Calories: 90** **Fat: <0.5 grams** **Saturated Fat: 0 grams**
Yogurt Covered Raisins Serving size: 1/2 cup **Calories: 280** **Fat: 12 grams** **Saturated Fat: 9 grams**	**Raisins** Serving size: 1/2 cup **Calories: 123** **Fat: 0 grams** **Saturated Fat: 0 grams**
Trail Mix Serving size: 1/2 cup **Calories: 300** **Fat: 20 grams** **Saturated Fat: 4 grams**	**Peanuts in Shell** Serving size: 1/2 cup **Calories: 170** **Fat: 13 grams** **Saturated Fat: 2 grams**
Cheddar Cheese Serving size: 1 ounce **Calories: 120** **Fat: 10 grams** **Saturated Fat: 6 grams**	**String Cheese** Serving size: 1 ounce **Calories: 80** **Fat: 6 grams** **Saturated Fat: 3 grams**

Made Over, Made Better   325

Two Points of View

Probiotics: Do You Need Them? Probiotics are live microorganisms, usually bacteria, mainly found in cultured dairy foods.[1] Some research indicates that probiotics can have health benefits for the immune and digestive systems. However, the research is not conclusive, and some experts feel adding probiotics to the diet is ineffective at best and possibly harmful at worst. Should you seek out fortified yogurt or probiotic supplements, or can you get along fine without them? Read the arguments below, then consider the critical thinking questions and decide for yourself.

Yes	No
• Regular consumption of certain probiotics helps maintain the normal functioning of the digestive system. Probiotics can help in the prevention or treatment of antibiotic-associated disorders, in the treatment (and to a lesser extent prevention) of gastroenteritis (stomach inflammation) and diarrhea, and in the alleviation of lactose intolerance.[2]	• We do not have sufficient information to say that probiotics are always beneficial and never harmful. Research is promising in several areas of digestive health but more research is needed to confirm their effectiveness, safety, and optimal dosage and duration.[6]
• Some specific strains of probiotics have been shown to increase regularity in some people who have occasional constipation. Other strains have been studied for their effects on decreasing the frequency of irritable bowel syndrome and some inflammatory bowel conditions.[3]	• Some consumers could experience gas or bloating when consuming probiotic products. The microorganisms may also have the potential to cause more serious side effects, especially in people with underlying health conditions.[7]
• Probiotics are generally considered safe. Their safety is somewhat evident by the fact that they have a long history of use in dairy foods like yogurt, cheese, and milk.[4]	• People who have short bowel syndrome, a weakened immune system, a damaged intestinal lining, or are recovering from surgery are at a higher risk for side effects. These individuals should take probiotics only under the advice of a health care provider.
• Though the burden lies with the manufacturer to make sure that the correct probiotic is added to the product and in adequate amounts, there is some regulation of probiotic labeling. The FDA requires that the food label of these products contain accurate and relevant information.[5]	• Due to lack of strict FDA regulation, various probiotic products may not consistently contain the correct type of probiotics or enough of the probiotic to have an effect. Further, probiotics are not always delivered in an effective vehicle (foods versus supplements) and may be of variable quality.[8] Some products have been evaluated in well-controlled human studies, while others have no or not enough research to support their efficacy.

What do you think?

1. Do you think you should add probiotics to your diet? Why or why not? **2.** Which is the most compelling argument for taking probiotics? Which is the most compelling reason not to take them? Explain your rationale. **3.** Do you think we know enough about probiotics to recommend them to the public?

REVISED! Two Points of View

This feature presents the two sides of a controversial or confusing issue in one succinct pro/con format followed by a "What do you think?" section with critical thinking questions about the topic for the student to consider.

Consistency

Each nutrient in a Visual Summary Table is presented using the same categories (forms, functions, daily needs, food sources, toxicity and deficiency symptoms) and headings for **a consistent and easy-to-study format**.

Visual Summary Tables are self-contained spreads (usually two pages) that incorporate photos, illustrations, and text to present each vitamin and mineral. Each micronutrient is discussed using the same categories for a consistent and easy-to-study format. Students can identify at a glance the key aspects of each nutrient.

Vitamin C

You don't have to go out of your way to ensure that your dog's daily chow contains enough vitamin C. Dogs and many other animals possess an enzyme that can synthesize vitamin C from glucose. Humans, however, lack the necessary enzyme for this conversion, and have to rely on food to meet their daily vitamin C needs.[68]

Functions of Vitamin C

Vitamin C Acts as a Coenzyme

Vitamin C, also known as **ascorbic acid,** acts as a coenzyme that is needed to synthesize and use certain amino acids. In particular, vitamin C is needed to make collagen, the most abundant protein in your body. Collagen is plentiful in your connective tissue, which supports and connects all your body parts, so this protein is needed for healthy bones, teeth, skin, and blood vessels.[69] Thus, a vitamin-C–deficient diet would affect your entire body.

Vitamin C Acts as an Antioxidant

Like beta-carotene and vitamin E, vitamin C acts an antioxidant that may help reduce the risk of chronic diseases such

as heart disease and cancer. It also helps you absorb the iron in plant foods such as grains and cereals and break down histamine, the component behind the inflammation seen in many allergic reactions.[70]

White blood cells

Vitamin C Boosts Your Immune System

Vitamin C helps keep your immune system healthy by enabling your body to make white blood cells, like the ones shown in the photo above. These blood cells fight infections, and this immune-boosting role has fostered the belief that high doses of vitamin C can cure the common cold. (The "Gesundheit! Myths and Facts about the Common Cold" box on page 261 takes a look at this theory.)

Daily Needs

Women need to consume 75 milligrams of vitamin C daily, and men need to consume 90 milligrams daily to meet their needs.

Smoking accelerates the breakdown and elimination of vitamin C from the body, so smokers need to consume an additional 35 milligrams of vitamin C every day to make up for these losses.[71]

Food Sources

Americans meet about 90 percent of their vitamin C needs by consuming fruits and vegetables, with orange and/or grapefruit juice being the most popular source in the diet. One serving of either juice will just about meet an adult's daily needs. Tomatoes, peppers, potatoes, broccoli, oranges, and cantaloupe are also excellent sources.

Too Much or Too Little

Brendan, the track athlete introduced at the beginning of this chapter, attempted to ward off a cold by taking vitamin C supplements. His attempt to solve one medical dilemma created another one that impeded his training more than his sniffling and sneezing.

Though excessive amounts of vitamin C aren't known to be toxic, consuming more than 3,000 milligrams daily through the use of supplements has been shown to cause nausea, stomach cramps, and diarrhea. Brendan can attribute the diarrhea he experienced to his daily 3,500-milligram supplement of vitamin C. Once he stopped taking the supplement, his diarrhea ceased.

Awareness

Self Assessments throughout the book ask the student to think about their own diet and behaviors and how well they are meeting their various nutritional needs.

Self-Assessment

Are You Meeting Your Fitness Recommendations and Eating for Exercise?

Now that you know how to plan an effective fitness strategy and eat for optimal fitness and performance, think about your current dietary and exercise habits. Take this brief assessment to find out if your daily habits are as healthful as they could be:

1. Do you participate in 30 minutes of moderately intense physical activity most days of the week?
   Yes ☐ No ☐
2. Do you participate in weight training 2 to 3 times per week?
   Yes ☐ No ☐
3. Do you drink 6 to 12 ounces of fluid every 15 to 20 minutes during exercise?
   Yes ☐ No ☐
4. Do you drink a sports beverage after moderate- or high-intensity exercise lasting longer than 1 hour?
   Yes ☐ No ☐

5. Do you consume carbohydrate and protein within 30 to 45 minutes after stopping exercise?
   Yes ☐ No ☐

Answer

If you answered yes to all of the questions, you are well on your way to optimal fitness. Participating in regular exercise, including aerobic exercise and strength training, helps you maintain optimal health and improves your level of fitness. Eating and drinking adequate nutrients also improves fitness. If you answered no to any of the questions, review this chapter to learn more on fitness and eating for exercise.

Vitamin C

Nutrients-at-a-Glance

Food source diagrams are tied to the design of MyPlate. Students can immediately see how the food sources relate to the food groups in MyPlate, and what the best food sources and daily needs are for the nutrient.

The upper level for vitamin C for adults is set at 2,000 milligrams to avoid the intestinal discomfort that excessive amounts of the vitamin can cause. Too much vitamin C can also lead to the formation of kidney stones in individuals with a history of kidney disease.

Because vitamin C helps to absorb the form of iron found in plant foods, those with a rare disorder called **hemochromatosis** (*hemo* = blood; *chroma* = color; *osis* = condition), which causes the body to store too much iron, should avoid excessive amounts of vitamin C. Iron toxicity is extremely dangerous and can damage many organs in your body, including the liver and heart.

For centuries, **scurvy,** the disease of a vitamin C deficiency, was the affliction of sailors on long voyages. After many weeks at sea, sailors would run out of vitamin-C–rich produce and then develop the telltale signs of scurvy: swollen and bleeding gums, a rough rash on the skin, coiled or curly arm hairs, and wounds that wouldn't heal. Because vitamin C is needed for healthy blood vessels, a deficiency also often causes purple colored spots, a sign of skin hemorrhages, to appear on the skin and in mucus mem-

branes of the body such as the lining of the mouth.

In 1753, a British naval surgeon discovered that orange and lemon juice prevented scurvy. Decades later, the British government added lemon or lime juice to their standard rations for sailors to thwart scurvy. In 1919, vitamin C was discovered as the curative factor in these juices.[72]

Vitamin C–deficiency skin hemorrhages.

Innovation

Eye-catching figures and photos are presented in a visual style that captures student interest and helps them remember key nutrient concepts.

Table Tips

Juicy Ways to Get Vitamin C

Have at least one citrus fruit (such as an orange or grapefruit) daily.

Put sliced tomatoes on your sandwich.

Enjoy a fruit cup for dessert.

Drink low-sodium vegetable juice for an afternoon refresher.

Add strawberries to your low-fat frozen yogurt.

Real-life Applications

Table Tips give practical ideas for incorporating each nutrient into the diet using real foods.

Terms to Know

ascorbic acid · hemochromatosis · scurvy

Help students
visualize nutrition

www.mynutritionlab.com

MyNutritionLab is the online course management system that makes it easy for you to organize your class, personalize your students' educational experience, and push their learning to the next level.

MyDietAnalysis 5.0 is available as a single sign-on from MyNutritionLab.

NEW! **NutriTools**

21 new NutriTools interactive activities are available on MyNutritionLab. These activities address the most important nutrition concepts for students in an engaging and interactive way.

- Students put it all together virtually in some activities—Build-a-Pizza, Build-a-Sandwich, Build-a-Salad, or Build-a-Meal—while other activities reinforce chapter content (such as a drag and drop exercise to evaluate good sources of calcium).
- NutriTools activities are featured within the book's Companion Website and on MyNutritionLab with assignable and gradable questions.

NEW! Author Practical Tips Videos

Joan Salge Blake walks students through making better eating choices in familiar environments, based on a choice related to each chapter topic. Students will be confronted with familiar dilemmas as Joan takes them through a pizza parlor, deli, coffee shop, breakfast choices on-the-go, energy bars, and much more.

The videos will be accompanied by assignable and gradable questions.

It's never been easier to teach nutrition

A unique six-step learning process, MyNutritionLab® includes everything you need to teach introductory nutrition in one convenient place, with content that can be customized for each course.

SEE IT

Students can access more than 50 author and *ABC News* videos, animations, and activities to extend their learning on important nutrition topics.

READ IT

This section contains chapter objectives and RSS news feeds, the Pearson eText, and new pre/post-reading quizzes to better assess student learning.

HEAR IT

Listen to or download MP3s related to the chapter opening case studies with assignable quizzes.

STUDY IT

Access to *Get Ready for Nutrition* gives students extra math and chemistry study assistance and the electronic Study Guide provides extra review and help.

REVIEW IT

Quizzes help check student understanding, and study flashcards used for important key word review are available for download to a mobile phone.

DO IT

Students can apply their learning in real life situations with activities and applications such as the Visual Summary Tables, Made Over, Made Better, Two Points of View and more.

UPDATED!
ABC News Videos

ABC News Videos include 20 new clips. These are now accompanied by assignable and gradable questions.

MyDiet Analysis

www.mydietanalysis.com

MyDietAnalysis was developed by the nutrition database experts at ESHA Research, Inc. and is tailored for use in college nutrition courses. It offers an accurate, reliable, and easy-to-use program for your students' diet analysis needs. MyDietAnalysis features a database of nearly 20,000 foods and multiple reports. The program allows students to track their diet and activity, and generate and submit reports electronically. MyDietAnalysis is also available via single sign-on from MyNutritionLab®.

New features for 5.0 include:

- **A Recipe Builder**, allowing students to input all of the ingredients once, and then call up the recipe for later entries

- **Hundreds of NEW items**, including selections from popular brands and restaurants

- **Improved My Class functionality** for instructors, including the ability to assign certain reports, comment on student reports, and download all student reports

Get a taste of our
outstanding supplements

FOR **INSTRUCTORS**

Teaching Tool Box

978-0-321-72299-7 | 0-321-72299-X

Save hours of valuable planning time with one comprehensive course planning kit. In one handy box, adjunct, part-time, and full-time faculty will find a wealth of supplements and resources that reinforce key learning from the text and suit virtually any teaching style.

The Teaching Tool Box provides all the prepping and lecture tools and instructor needs:

- The **Course-at-a-Glance Quick Reference Guide** to quickly find resources
- *Great Ideas: Active Ways to Teach Nutrition* with suggestions for classroom activities
- **Instructor Resource and Support Manual**
- **Printed Test Bank**
- An **Instructor Resource DVD** including art, tables, selected photos, PowerPoint® Lecture Outlines, PRS Clicker Questions, Quiz Show questions, Video Clips, and Transparency Masters, and the Computerized Test Bank
- A **MyNutritionLab and MyDietAnalysis access kit** so you can get online quickly
- The helpful *Eat Right!* student supplement
- The handy **Food Composition Table** supplement

Pearson Custom Library

The Pearson Custom Library: Health and Nutrition custom publishing program gives you the freedom to create your own customized textbook for courses in nutrition. Select the book chapters you need, in the sequence you want. Delete chapters you don't use: Your students pay only for the material you choose. You're in control. Find out more at www.pearsoncustom.com (keyword search nutrition).

For more information on this text and its resources, please go to our Web Catalog page at **www.pearsonhighered.com/nutrition**

FOR **STUDENTS**

Books à la Carte

978-0-321-72165-5 | 0-321-72165-9

This edition features the exact same content as *Nutrition and You,* **Second Edition** in a convenient, three-hole-punched, loose-leaf version. Books a la Carte also offer a great value for your students— this format costs 35% less than a new textbook.

Pearson eText Student Access Code Card

978-0-321-72302-4 | 0-321-72302-3

Pearson eText gives students access to the text whenever and wherever they can access the Internet. The eText pages look exactly like the printed text, and include powerful interactive and customization functions. This does not include the actual bound book.

CourseSmart eText

978-0-321-72692-6 | 0-321-72692-8

CourseSmart eTextbooks are an exciting new choice for students looking to save money. As an alternative to purchasing the print textbook, students can subscribe to the same content online and save up to 40% off the suggested list price of the print text.

Food Composition Table

978-0-321-66793-9 | 0-321-66793-X

In the Second Edition, the USDA Nutrient Database for Standard Reference will be provided as a new practical supplement, offering the nutritional values of over 1,500 separate foods in an easy-to-follow format.

Companion Website

www.pearsonhighered.com/blake

The Companion Website has been reorganized into six sections: See It, Read It, Hear It, Study It, Review It, and Do It. It includes NutriTools activities, Practical Tips Videos with quizzes, nutrition animations, *ABC News* videos with quizzes, interactive *Get Real, Nutrition Sleuth,* and Visual Summary Table activities, chapter quizzes, Two Points of View analysis questions, eLearn links, web links, flashcards, and glossary. Extra review and study help is available with *Get Ready for Nutrition*, and the Student Study Guide.

Nutrition
and You

MyPlate Edition

Joan Salge Blake, MS, RD, LDN
Boston University

Second Edition

PEARSON

Boston Columbus Indianapolis New York San Francisco Upper Saddle River Amsterdam
Cape Town Dubai London Madrid Milan Munich Paris Montreal Toronto Delhi
Mexico City São Paulo Sydney Hong Kong Seoul Singapore Taipei Tokyo

Senior Acquisitions Editor: *Sandra Lindelof*
Project Editor: *Emily Portwood*
Development Manager: *Barbaras Yien*
Development Editor: *Cheryl Cechvala*
Editorial Assistant: *Meghan Zolnay*
Managing Editor: *Deborah Cogan*
Production Project Managers: *Caroline Ayres and Mary O'Connell*
Production Management: *Mary Tindle and Roxanne Klaas, S4Carlisle Publishing Services*
Copyeditor: *Anna Reynolds Trabucco*

Compositor: *S4Carlisle Publishing Services*
Interior Designer: *Jana Anderson*
Cover Designer: *Jana Anderson*
Illustrator: *Precision Graphics*
Photo Researcher: *Kristin Piljay*
Manufacturing Buyer: *Stacey Weinberger*
Senior Marketing Manager: *Neena Bali*
Text Printer: *Courier Kendallville*
Cover Printer: *Phoenix Color*
Cover Photo Credit: © *Valerie Jansen/Getty*

The Library of Congress has cataloged the earlier edition as follows:
Blake, Joan Salge.
   Nutrition & you / Joan Salge Blake.
     p. cm.
   Includes bibliographical references and index.
   ISBN-13: 978-0-321-69658-8 (student edition)
   ISBN-10: 0-321-69658-1 (student edition)
1. Nutrition—Textbooks. I. Title. II. Title: Nutrition and you.
   RA784.B552 2012
   613.2—dc22

                     2010040860

ISBN 10: 0-321-81371-5 (Student edition)
ISBN 13: 978-0-321-81371-8 (Student edition)
ISBN 10: 0-321-81492-4 (Instructor Review Copy)
ISBN 13: 978-0-321-81492-0 (Instructor Review Copy)

2 3 4 5 6 7 8 9 10—CKV—14 13 12

Manufactured in the United States of America.

PEARSON

Brief Contents

Contents

4

Carbohydrates: Sugars, Starches, and Fiber 92

5

Fats, Oils, and Other Lipids 138

6

Proteins and Amino Acids   180

10

Weight Management and Energy Balance   358

11

Nutrition and Fitness   406

12
Consumerism: From Farm to Table 444

13
Food Safety and Technology 480

14

Hunger at Home and Abroad 516

15

Life Cycle Nutrition: Pregnancy through Infancy 540

16

Life Cycle Nutrition: Toddlers through the Later Years 578

Appendices

Special Features

Nutrition in the Real World

Self-Assessment

Table Tips

 NutriTools

About the Author

Joan Salge Blake is a clinical associate professor and dietetics internship director at Boston University's Sargent College of Health and Rehabilitation Sciences. She teaches both graduate and undergraduate nutrition courses and has been a guest lecturer at both the BU Goldman School of Dental Medicine and BU School of Medicine. She received the Whitney Powers Excellence in Teaching Award from Boston University (BU). Joan completed her MS from BU and is currently working toward her doctorate.

Joan is a member of the American Dietetic Association (ADA) and the Massachusetts Dietetic Association (MDA). She has been a presenter and presiding officer at both the ADA and the MDA annual conventions and she was previously named the MDA's "Young Dietitian of the Year," Outstanding Dietitian (2009), and Outstanding Dietetic Educator (2007). She has served on the MDA board for close to a decade in many roles, including past MDA director of education and nominating committee chairperson.

Joan is also an ADA National Media Spokesperson, responsible for representing the ADA in the media and promoting its initiatives. She conducts over 100 media interviews annually, and her nutrition segments can be seen regularly on Fox25 television in Boston.

In addition to teaching and writing, Joan has a private practice specializing in weight management and lifestyle changes.

Why I Wrote Nutrition and You

"You'll probably finish this class with a whole new outlook on diet and exercise . . . and you'll probably be a lot healthier!"

"Professor Salge Blake makes the material seem like the most interesting material in the universe."

—Excerpts from student comments about my nutrition class at Boston University, courtesy of ratemyprofessor.com

I wrote *Nutrition and You* for you. It is all about you. For more than a decade, I have taught an Introduction to Nutrition course to a packed classroom of almost 200 students, at the unseemly hour of 8 A.M. The students keep coming year after year because I not only deliver accurate nutrition science and information in an easy-to-understand, entertaining format, but more importantly, I personalize the information for them so that they can immediately apply it to their own lifestyles.

As a college student, you are exposed to a steady stream of nutrition and health information from the media, your family and friends, and the Internet. While you may think Google has the answer to your nutrition questions, I have seen students frequently fall victim to misinformation found via a quick Web search and a few glitzy websites. So I designed *Nutrition and You* to be as user friendly as possible, packed exclusively with sound nutrition information. The text goes beyond basic nutrition science and provides realistic advice and strategies to help you easily incorporate what you learn into your busy life. The text is written to meet *your* nutritional concerns and answer *your* questions.

As you read *Nutrition and You,* I want you to feel as though you are sitting in my class being entertained and informed. For this reason, I wrote the text in a conversational tone, and we designed it to visually communicate complex nutrition science and topics in an easy-to-understand way.

The information in this textbook is arranged in a deliberate **"What," "Why,"** and **"How"** format. Each chapter will tell you:

➤ **"What"** the nutrition concept is;
➤ **"Why"** it is important and the role it plays in your body; and then, most importantly,
➤ **"How"** to easily adjust your lifestyle based on what you just learned.

New to This Edition

Nutrition research and applications continue to develop in exciting new ways. To keep pace, a number of updates, additions, and improvements have been made to this edition of *Nutrition and You*. Students will benefit from a variety of new and updated material, including:

➤ **New** coverage of the MyPlate food tool, which is designed to remind Americans to eat healthfully. The Food Source Diagrams have been updated throughout the book to reflect the new MyPlate design.

➤ **New** Consumerism: From Farm to Table chapter, adding and enhancing coverage of organics, biotechnology, and food marketing. Does food spring forth from the grocery store ready to eat? No! Learn where it comes from and the impact various factors have on food choices.

➤ **New** "Made Over, Made Better" and revised "Two Points of View" features—make better, more nutritional food choices, and think critically about topics related to nutrition.

➤ **New** media to enhance learning, including NutriTools interactive online activities and a suite of new ABC News and Practical Tips videos. Expand learning outside the classroom!

➤ **New** daily needs elements in the food source diagrams, helping you compare visually how vitamins and minerals found in nutrient-rich foods stack up in your diet!

What Is the Nutrition Concept?

Each chapter begins with a **Campus Corner,** a short scenario about a college student who is experiencing a common nutrition-related situation pertinent to the chapter topic. Don't be surprised if the student reminds you of yourself, your roommate, or a relative! I want you to be able to immediately relate to the character in the scenario and his or her nutrition problem. As you read, you will learn how to apply the information in the chapter to this person's life situation (and yours) in a practical way.

The popular **Myths and Misperceptions Pretest** is a quiz that will help you recognize misperceptions that you may have about the chapter topic. The answers to these fun pretest questions are woven throughout the chapter (indicated with a T/F symbol) with a complete explanation of the myth. You'll be smarter just by taking this pretest.

Why Is the Nutrition Concept Important to You?

Each chapter contains a **Self-Assessment** that will help you determine whether your current diet and lifestyle habits need a little fine-tuning. The **Visual Summary Tables** are nutrition for your eyes. They visually summarize why each nutrient is invaluable to your health in a consistent and easy-to-study format. **The Top Ten Points to Remember** at the end of each chapter boils down the most important concepts of the entire chapter. Recurring visuals will accompany some of the points to remind you of the information that was initially discussed.

How Can You Easily Adjust Your Lifestyle?

This book is filled with tools and tips to help you make positive diet and lifestyle changes. The **Food Source Diagrams** visually provide you with the most robust food sources of each nutrient and are based on the MyPlate design. No need to memorize a boring list of food sources! The **Table Tips** are short and snappy lists of practical changes that will help you improve your diet. The **Made Over, Made Better** food comparisons at the end of chapters 4 through 10 can help you visually see how to adjust your food choices to improve your health.

The online activities will further allow you to apply what you have learned in a virtual environment. **NutriTools** are interactive activities using real-world food experiences. For example, a Build Your Own Salad activity allows you to create a virtual salad, full of all your favorite toppings, and immediately see the nutritional effects of your choices. Other online, interactive Web tools such as **eLearn** and **Get Real!** help you to make more real-life changes to your diet, while **Be a Nutrition Sleuth** will give you further strategies and tips to apply in the real world.

Finally, the **Two Points of View** at the end of each chapter contains a summary of opposing viewpoints on a timely topic. This feature will encourage you to think critically about pro and con arguments on a given issue and decide for yourself which side you agree with. You will be applying the critical thinking skills that you learned in the chapter as you think through each opposing point of view.

Remember, nutrition matters to *you!* What you eat today and tomorrow will affect you and your body for years to come.

I want to hear what you think of *Nutrition and You.* Feel free to e-mail me with any questions or comments at salge@bu.edu and follow me on Twitter at joansalgeblake. Your feedback will help make future editions of *Nutrition and You* even better.

Acknowledgments

It takes a village, and then some, when it comes to writing a dynamic textbook. *Nutrition & You* is no exception. I personally want to thank all of those who passionately shared their expertise and support to make *Nutrition and You* better than I could have envisioned.

Beginning with the dynamic staff at Benjamin Cummings, I would like to thank Deirdre Espinoza and Sandy Lindelof, who helped make my vision for this textbook a reality. Cheryl Cechvala's on-the-mark developmental editing improved the second edition of *Nutrition and You* and made it even more enjoyable to read. A special thanks to Susan Malloy for her second set of eyes, and for further lending thoughts and edits to the chapters. It takes a project manager to make sure the village runs on a schedule, and Emily Portwood kept me on track, especially when the FedEx packages were arriving daily. Thanks also to editorial assistants Brianna Paulson and Meghan Zolnay for all of their work, especially in commissioning reviewers during the developmental stages of this book.

A very special thanks to Caroline Ayres, production supervisor extraordinaire, and Mary Tindle, production coordinator at Carlisle, for all of their hard work shepherding this book through to publication. My humble appreciation also goes to Kristin Piljay for obtaining the most vivid and unique photos available; to Mark Ong and Jana Anderson, whose design made the text, art, and photos all come alive; to art coordinator Derek Bacchus; and again to Jana Anderson, whose efforts I must thank for the book's gorgeous cover.

Marketing takes energy, and that's exactly what marketing manager Neena Bali and her energetic team seem to generate nonstop. The many instructors who reviewed this book and provided good insights and suggestions are listed on the following pages; I am grateful to all of them for helping to inform the development of the second edition of *Nutrition and You.*

The village also included loyal contributors who lent their expertise to specific chapters. They are: Jennifer Koslo for updating the hunger and "life cycle" chapters; Tara Barber at East Carolina University for revising the weight management and nutrition and fitness chapters. I also thank Jinwon Chung and Cheryl Cechvala for their work on the "Two Points of View" debates.

A heartfelt thank you goes to my research assistant, Sarah Butler, MS, RD, who helped me with the endless research needed to keep the science up-to-date. Lastly, an endless thanks to my family, **A**dam, **B**rendan, and **C**raig, for their love and support when I was working more than I should have been.

Joan Salge Blake

Reviewers

First Edition

Nancy Adamowicz
University of Arizona

Laurie Allen
University of North Carolina, Greensboro

Dawn Anderson
Winona State University

Francine Armenth-Brothers
Heartland Community College

Elizabeth Browne
Tidewater Community College

Nancy Buffum-Herman
Monroe Community College

Joanne Burke
University of New Hampshire

Thomas Castonguay
University of Maryland

Erin Caudill
Southeast Community College

Sai Chidambaram
Cansisius College

Janet Colson
Middle Tennessee State University

Priscilla Connor
University of North Texas

Nancy J. Correa-Matos
University of North Florida

Cathy Hix Cunningham
Tennessee Technological University

Eileen Daniel
State University of New York, Brockport

Carole Dupont
Springfield Technical Community College

Sally Feltner
Western Carolina University

Anna Marie Frank
DePaul University

Bernard Frye
University of Texas, Arlington

Mary Ellen Fydenkevez
Greenfield Community College

Christie Goodner
Winthrop University

Lisa Goodson
Prince George's Community College

Sue Grace
Monroe Community College, Brighton

Donna Hale
Southeastern Oklahoma State University

Charlene Harkins
University of Minnesota Duluth

Nancy Harris
Eastern Carolina University

Beverly Henry
Northern Illinois University

Chris Heuston
Front Range Community College

Thunder Jalili
University of Utah

Lori Kanauss
Western Illinois University

Judy Kaufman
Monroe Community College, Brighton

Danita Kelley
Western Kentucky University

Kathryn Kohel
Alfred University

Claire Kratz
Montgomery County Community College

Laura Kruskall
University of Nevada, Las Vegas

Melody Kyzer
University of North Carolina, Wilmington

Kris Levy
Columbus State Community College

Sue Linnenkohl
Marshall University

Jackie McClelland
North Carolina State University

Katherine Mellen
University of Iowa

Barbara Mercer
University of Louisville

Anna Miller
De Anza College

Kristin Moline
Lourdes College

Maria Montemagni
College of the Sequoias

Gina Marie Morris
Frank Phillips College

Ray Moss
Furman University

Rosemary Mueller
William Rainey Harper College

Katherine Musgrave
University of Maine, Orono

Rosemary O'Dea
Gloucester County College

Millie Owens
College of the Sequoias

Candi Possinger
State University of New York, Buffalo

Lisa Rapp
Springfield Technical Community College

Mike Reece
Ozarks Technical and Community College

Ruth Reilly
University of New Hampshire

Barbara Reynolds
College of the Sequoias

Robert Reynolds
University of Illinois, Chicago

Rebecca Roach
University of Illinois Urbana Champaign

Nancy Rodriguez
Harper College

Beverly Roe
Erie Community College, South Campus

Lisa Sasson
New York University

Donal Scheidel
University of South Dakota

Anne-Marie Scott
University of North Carolina, Greensboro

Anne Semrau
Northeast Texas Community College

Padmini Shankar
Georgia Southern University

Mollie Smith
California State University Fresno

Stasino Stavrianeas
Williamette University

Liane Summerfield
Marymount University

Jo Taylor
Southeast Community College

Norman Temple
Athabasca University

Gabrielle Turner-McGrievy
University of Alabama

Simin Vaghefi
University of North Florida

Amy Vaughan
Radford University

John Warber
Morehead State University

Dana Wassmer
Cosumnes River College

Diana Watson-Maile
East Central University

Beverly Webber
University of Utah

Annie Wetter
University of Wisconsin, Stevens Point

Fred Wolfe
University of Arizona

Maureen Zimmerman
Mesa Community College

Donna Zoss
Purdue University

Second Edition

Barbara Bernardi
Lincoln Land Community College

Tracey Brigman
University of Georgia

Linda Brothers
Indiana University—Purdue

Lisa Duich-Perry
Chaminade University of Honolulu

Jerald C. Foote
University of Arkansas

Boyd Foster
Gonzaga University

Carol Friesen
Ball State University

Krista Jordheim
Normandale Community College

Lorri Kanauss
Western Illinois University

Kathleen M. Laquale
Bridgewater State College

Linda Johnston Lolkus
Indiana University—Purdue

Raymond McCormick
University of South Florida

Owen Murphy
University of Colorado, Boulder

Cheryl Neudauer
Minneapolis Community & Technical College

Patricia Plavcan
Cooking and Hospitality Institute of Chicago

Ramona Rice
Georgia Military College

Lisa Sasson
New York University

Tiffany Shurtz
University of Central Oklahoma

Priya Venkatesan
Pasadena City College

I am nothing without
my ABCs.

Thanks.

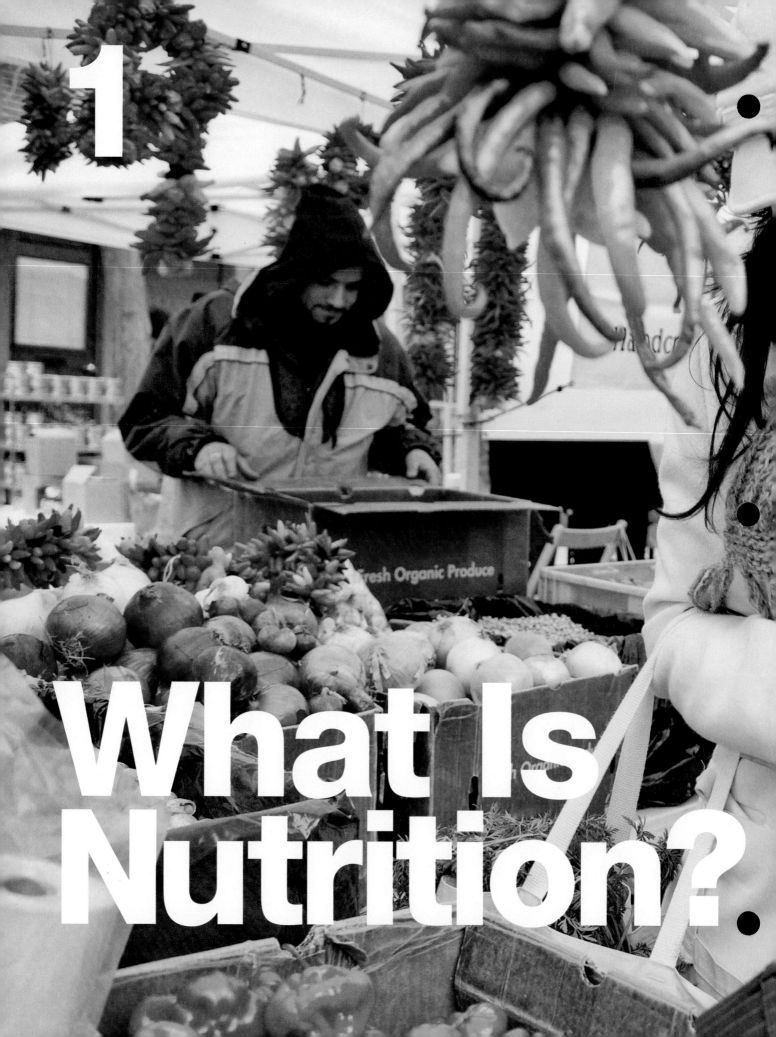

1

What Is Nutrition?

True or False?

1. Factors other than **hunger** drive our food choices. T|F p. 5

2. Heart disease is the leading cause of **death** in the United States. T|F p. 8

3. Carbohydrates, vitamins, and fat all provide you with **energy.** T|F p. 10

4. The energy in food is measured in **calories.** T|F p. 10

5. Water is an essential nutrient. T|F p. 11

6. As long as you take a **vitamin pill,** you don't have to worry about eating healthy foods. T|F p. 11

7. Meats, poultry, and fish contain a lot of **fiber.** T|F p. 12

8. Every year, 40 percent of Americans shell out **money** for daily supplements. T|F p. 13

9. The number of **obese** Americans is lower today than it was ten years ago. T|F p. 14

10. You can get good nutrition advice from anyone who calls himself a **nutritionist.** T|F p. 20

See page 27 for answers to these Myths and Misperceptions.

It's the night before the big biology exam, and Elizabeth, a junior, is in the midst of a down-to-the-wire cram session. She hasn't cracked open her textbook for weeks, so she is in high-stress mode. Elizabeth pours herself a very tall glass of caffeinated cola, opens up a family-size bag of rippled potato chips, and nervously plows through the bag and the book. She snacks and studies to the wee hours of the morning, stuffing as much information as possible into her head, and too many chips into her stomach. After a jittery 3 hours of sleep, Elizabeth heads to her 8 A.M. exam feeling tired, groggy, and still uncomfortably stuffed from her potato chip-and-soda cram session.

Would you be surprised to learn that Elizabeth did not do so well on her exam? Do you, like Elizabeth, sometimes eat snacks or other foods because you're stressed, rather than hungry? What other factors do you think influence your food choices, and how can you make sound nutritional decisions?

Chapter Objectives

After reading this chapter, you will be able to:

1. Discuss the factors that influence food choice.

2. Define the term *nutrition*.

3. Describe how nutrition affects your health.

4. Name and explain the six categories of nutrients found in food and in the body.

5. Differentiate between the three energy nutrients: carbohydrate, protein, and fat.

6. Calculate the calorie content of a food based on the grams of carbohydrate, protein, and fat.

7. Understand the important roles that vitamins, minerals, and water play in your diet.

8. Understand the scientific method that is involved in nutrition research.

9. Identify sources of accurate nutrition information.

10. Discuss the current nutritional state of the American diet.

From the minute you were born, you began performing three automatic behaviors: you slept, you ate, and you expelled your waste products . . . often while you were sleeping. You didn't need to think about these actions, and you didn't have to decide to do them. You also didn't need to make choices about where to sleep, what to eat, or when to go to the bathroom. Life was so easy back then.

Now that you're older, these actions, particularly the eating part, are anything but automatic. You make numerous decisions every day about what to eat, and you make these decisions for reasons that you may not even be aware of. If your dietary advice comes from media sound bites, you may get constantly conflicting information. Yesterday's news flash announced that eating more protein would help you fight a bulging waist. Last week's headline boldly announced you should minimize *trans* fats in your diet to avoid a heart attack. This morning, the TV news lead was a health report advising you to eat more whole grains to live longer, but to hold the line on sodium, otherwise your blood pressure may go up.

Though you may find it frustrating that dietary advice seems to change with the daily news (though it actually doesn't), this bombardment of nutrition news is a positive thing. You are lucky to live in an era when so much is known and being discovered about what you eat and how it affects you. Today's research validates what nutrition professionals have known for decades: Nutrition plays an invaluable role in your health. As with any science, nutrition is not stagnant. Exciting discoveries will continue to be made about the roles that diet and foods play in keeping you healthy.

Let's find out more about nutrition, why it's so important to your health, and how you can identify sound sources of nutrition information. We'll start with the basic concept of why you eat and how this affects your nutrition.

What Drives Our Food Choices?

What did you have for dinner last night? Where did you eat it? Who were you with? How did you feel?

Do you ever think about what drives your food choices? Or are you on autopilot as you stand in line at the sub shop and squint at yet another menu board? Do you adore some foods and eat them often, while avoiding others with a vengeance? Perhaps you have a grandparent who encourages you to eat more (and more!) of her traditional home cooking. You obviously need food to survive, but beyond your basic instinct to eat are many other factors that affect what goes into your stomach. Let's discuss some of these now.

We Need to Eat and Drink to Live

All creatures need fuel in order to function, and humans are no exception. We get our fuel from food in the form of chemical compounds that are collectively known as **nutrients.** These nutrients work together to provide energy, growth, and maintenance, and to regulate numerous body processes. Three of the six classes of nutrients—carbohydrates, fats (part of the larger class of lipids), and protein—provide energy in the form of **kilocalories.** Two other classes of nutrients, vitamins and minerals, help regulate many body processes, including **metabolism.** Some also play other supporting roles. The last class of nutrient, water, is found in all foods and beverages, and is so vital to life that you couldn't live more than a few days without it.

Foods also provide nonnutrient compounds like **phytochemicals** and other substances that help maintain and repair your body in order to keep it healthy. We will explore each of these nutrients in more depth later in this chapter, and in much more depth throughout the book.

Beyond the basic need to replenish our bodies with daily fuel are other factors that drive our food choices.

We Choose Foods for Many Other Reasons

Your favorite foods taste delicious—that's why they're your favorites. You also choose certain other foods because they're staples of your culture, or they've become an important aspect of your social life. Some of your food selections are determined by trends, influenced by media messages, or reflect the amount of time or money you have available (**Figure 1.1**). Sometimes, you choose a food just because it's there. Let's explore each of these factors more closely.

Taste and Culture

Research confirms that when it comes to making food choices, taste is the most important consideration.[1] This shouldn't be too much of a surprise, considering that there are at least 10,000 taste buds in your mouth, mainly on your tongue. Your taste buds tell you that chocolate cheesecake is sweet, fresh lemon juice is sour, and a pretzel is salty.

What you choose to put on your plate is often influenced by your culture. If you were a student in Mexico, you may be feasting on a dinner with corn tortillas and tamales, as maize (corn) is a staple of Mexican cuisine. In India, meals commonly include lentils and other legumes with rice and vegetables, whereas Native Americans often enjoy stews of mutton (sheep), corn, and other vegetables. In China, rice, a staple, would be front and center on your plate.

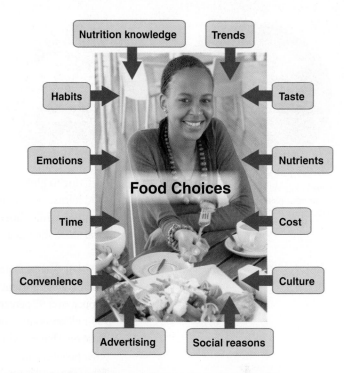

Figure 1.1 Many Factors Influence Your Food Choices

Nutrition knowledge · Trends · Habits · Taste · Emotions · Nutrients · **Food Choices** · Time · Cost · Convenience · Culture · Advertising · Social reasons

nutrients Compounds in foods that sustain your body processes. There are six classes of nutrients: carbohydrates, fats (lipids), proteins, vitamins, minerals, and water.

kilocalories The measurement of energy in foods. Commonly referred to as *calories.*

metabolism The numerous reactions that occur within the cell. The calories in foods are converted to energy in the cells of the body.

phytochemicals Nonnutritive compounds in plant foods that may play a role in fighting chronic diseases.

One in four Americans is of Hispanic, Native American, Asian, or African descent. Cultural food preferences often influence food choices.

A culture's cuisine is greatly influenced by the environment. This includes not only the climate and soil conditions but also the native plants and animals, as well as the distance people live from rivers, lakes, or the sea. People tend to consume foods that are accessible and often have little experience eating foods that are scarce. For example, native Alaskans feast on fish because it is plentiful, but eat less fresh produce, which is difficult to grow locally. For most Americans, this is less of an issue today than in the past, due to global food distribution networks. However, it still rings true for some food items. People living in landlocked states may have less access to fresh fish, for example, while those outside the south may not see collard greens or beignets on local store shelves as often as their Gulf State counterparts do.

Social Reasons and Trends

Eating is an important way to bond with others. Every year, on the fourth Thursday in November, over 95 percent of Americans gather with family and friends to consume close to 700 million pounds of turkey as they celebrate Thanksgiving.[2] A person is likely to eat more on Thanksgiving than on any other Thursday, and this is partly because of all the other people eating with them. Eating dinner with others has been shown to increase the size of the meal by over 40 percent, and the more people present, the more you'll eat.[3] Enjoying your meals in the campus cafeteria also allows you to socialize with your classmates.

For many people, activities like watching a football game with fellow fans or going to a movie with friends often involve particular foods. More pizzas are sold on Super Bowl Sunday than any other day of the year.[4] Movie theatre owners bank on your buying popcorn, candy, and beverages at their concession stands before heading in to watch the picture. Revenue from these snack items can account for up to 50 percent of a theatre's profits. If you're with a group of friends, you're even more likely to buy these snacks. Research shows that movie concession snacks are more often purchased when people are socializing in a group.[5] For instance, chances are that you'll choose a popcorn and soda at the theater, even if you are not hungry, because everyone else is having a snack.

Your food choices are also affected by popular trends. For instance, home cooks in the 1950s bought bags of newfangled frozen vegetables in order to provide healthy meals in less time. A few decades later, vegetables went upscale and consumers bought them as part of ready-to-heat stir-fry mixes. Today, shoppers pay a premium price for bags of fresh veggies, like carrots,

Food, friends, and football . . . a way of life.

Do Outside Factors Influence Your Food Choices?

Rate yourself to see!

1. Whenever I meet friends, we get something to eat or drink, no matter the time of day.
   Yes ☐ **No** ☐
2. I sometimes find myself walking past a coffee shop, fast-food restaurant, or convenience store and am compelled to buy something to eat.
   Yes ☐ **No** ☐
3. When I am bored, stressed, or sad, I snack.
   Yes ☐ **No** ☐
4. I always eat or drink something when I am studying, even if I am not hungry.
   Yes ☐ **No** ☐
5. I always eat when I go out to a movie in a movie theatre.
   Yes ☐ **No** ☐

Answers

If you answered "true" to most of these questions, then you are not alone. Many of our food choices are driven by influences that surround us every day!

that have been prewashed and peeled, sliced, or diced. Similarly, decades ago, the only way to enjoy iced tea was to brew it and chill it yourself. Now most markets provide dozens of choices in flavored and enhanced bottled teas, a popular beverage for many college students. As food manufacturers pour more money into research and development, who knows what tomorrow's trendy food item will be?

Cost, Time, and Convenience

According to the United States Department of Agriculture, almost 15 percent of American households experienced food insecurity in 2008. That is, the people living in these households are not able to meet their nutrient needs every day (you'll learn more about hunger and food insecurity in Chapter 14).[6] It's not surprising, then, that many people may be forced to base their food choices on cost. The large, store-brand bag of potato chips, on sale, may be an economically appealing way for a struggling family on a tight budget to fill a dinner plate, rather than with more nutritious fresh or frozen vegetables, which tend to cost more. The good news is that cheaper food doesn't have to always mean junk food or fast food. When healthy foods are offered at lower prices, people do buy them. Researchers found that lowering the cost of fresh fruits, vegetables, and lower-fat snacks improves the consumption of these nutritious foods.[7]

For those with adequate food budgets, time is often at a premium. Because of this, the types of foods that many people choose have changed. Research shows that Americans, especially working women with families, want to spend less than 15 minutes preparing a meal.[8] Consequently, supermarkets have changed the types of foods they sell as well as how the food is presented.

If chicken is on the menu tonight, you can go to the poultry section in the store and buy it uncooked. Or you can go to the take-out section of the store and buy it hot off the rotisserie, precooked and stuffed with bread crumbs, or grilled with teriyaki sauce. You can also probably get the cooked vegetables and rice side dishes to take home and reheat with the chicken.

Convenience also influences food choices. Foods that are easily accessible to you are more likely to be eaten. Let's say you have a long walk back to your dorm building after your last class of the day. On the way, you pass a food stand selling slices of delicious-looking pizza. The wonderful smell reminds you that you are hungry, so you buy a slice, or two. Or consider coffee. Decades ago, the most convenient way to get a hot cup of coffee was to brew it yourself. Americans today are more likely to get their java from one of the 17,000 coffee shops, carts, and kiosks across the United States.[9] Pizza and coffee are just two examples of a broad trend of Americans spending more of their household food budget on eating out.

Habits and Emotions

Many people start their day with a bowl of cereal and a glass of orange juice. In fact, ready-to-eat cereals are the number-one breakfast food choice among Americans, and citrus juice is the top juice choice for most people in the morning.[10] Why? For many, the only answer is habit.

Your daily routine and habits can dictate not only what you eat but also *when* you eat. When you get home from work or school, do you head straight for the refrigerator, whether or not you're hungry? Do you always snack when you watch television at night? Or when you're studying?

Emotions also influence your food choices. Recall that Elizabeth from earlier in the chapter nervously ate her way through a large bag of chips before her exam. Does this sound familiar? When the going gets tough, the tough often eat. For many, food is used as an emotional crutch during times of stress, sadness, or joy. Happiness can also trigger eating. Many people celebrate their end-of-term good grades or a promotion at work with a celebratory meal with friends or family. On vacation,

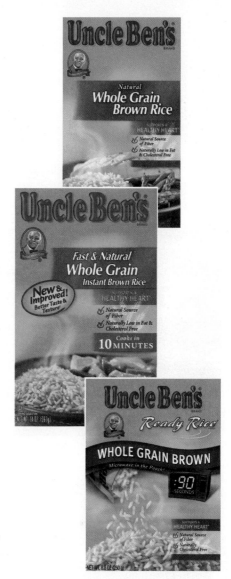

While brown rice is a healthy whole-grain addition to any meal, it can take close to an hour to cook. For time-strapped consumers, food manufacturers have developed instant brown rice that cooks in 10 minutes, and a precooked, microwavable variety that reheats in less than 2 minutes.

you likely reward yourself with fun, relaxation, and, of course, good food. No matter your mood, food is often part of how you express your emotions.

The Take-Home Message Food provides the nutrients that your body needs to function, and the foods that you choose are influenced by many factors. Taste is the primary reason why certain foods have become your favorites. The availability of certain foods has made them a part of your culture and a habitual part of your day. Food trends, cost, limits on your time, convenience, and your emotions all can influence your food choices.

What Is Nutrition and Why Is Good Nutrition So Important?

A well-balanced, healthy diet can help reduce the risk of heart disease, cancer, stroke, and diabetes, which are leading causes of death among Americans.

Whereas food is the source of nutrients that your body needs, **nutrition** is about more than just food. Nutrition is the science that studies how the nutrients and compounds in foods nourish you, help you function, and affect your health.

Your body needs all the nutrients to function properly. A chronic deficiency of even one nutrient will negatively affect your body's ability to function in the short term. Chronic deficiencies, excesses, and imbalances of many nutrients can also affect your long-term health.

Good nutrition plays a role in reducing the risk of four of the top ten leading causes of death in the United States, including the top three—heart disease, cancer, and stroke—as well as diabetes (Table 1.1). Nutrition also plays an important role in preventing other diseases and conditions that can impede your lifestyle. A healthy diet can help keep your bones strong and reduce your risk of osteoporosis. Eating right will help you better manage your body weight, which in turn will reduce your risk of developing obesity, diabetes mellitus, and high blood pressure.

nutrition The science that studies how the nutrients and compounds in foods that you eat nourish and affect your body functions and health.

Table 1.1
Leading Causes of Death in the United States

Disease/Cause of Death	Nutrition Related	Other
Heart Disease	X	
Cancer	X	
Stroke	X	
Respiratory Diseases		X
Accidents		X
Alzheimer's Disease		X
Diabetes	X	
Influenza/Pneumonia		X
Kidney Disease		X
Blood Poisoning		X

Source: Centers for Disease Control. 2010. "Leading Causes of Death in the United States." www.cdc.gov/nchs/fastats/deaths.htm.

You are a product of what you eat, what you *don't* eat, or what you may eat *too much* of. You want to eat the best combination of a variety of foods to meet your nutritional needs and to be healthy. To do that, you need to understand the roles of the essential nutrients in your body and which foods to eat to get them.

The Take-Home Message Nutrition is the scientific study of how the nutrients and compounds in foods nourish your body. Good nutrition plays a role in reducing the risk of many chronic diseases and conditions. Long-term imbalances of many nutrients will affect your health.

What Are the Essential Nutrients and Why Do You Need Them?

The classes of nutrients that we introduced earlier are all *essential* because you must have them in order to function. (Alcohol, in contrast, is not an essential nutrient; even though it provides energy in the form of kilocalories, your body does not need it to function.) Your body is, in fact, made up of the same essential nutrients that are found in foods (see **Figure 1.2**).

Carbohydrates, lipids (fats), and proteins are called **macronutrients,** because you need higher amounts of them in your diet. Vitamins and minerals, though equally important to your health, are considered **micronutrients** because you need them in lesser amounts. You need to consume the final nutrient, water, in copious amounts daily so that you are well hydrated.

Kilocalories (commonly referred to as calories, which is the term we will use throughout this book) from the macronutrients are used as energy during the process of metabolism, and many vitamins and minerals are essential to this process. Vitamins and minerals are also needed for growth and reproduction and to help repair and maintain your body (**Figure 1.3**).

Although each nutrient is unique, they are all equally important, as they work together in numerous ways to keep you healthy. An imbalance of just one will affect your health. Let's take a closer look at the macro- and micronutrients, and water.

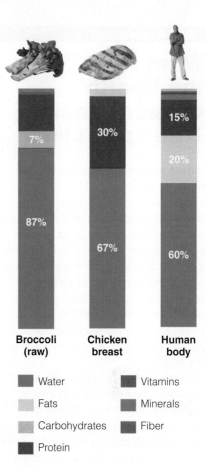

Figure 1.2 Nutrients in Foods and in the Body
The nutrients found in the foods that you eat are the same ones that provide structure for your body and allow your normal body processes to occur.

Figure 1.3 Nutrients and Their Functions
Nutrients work closely together to provide energy, structure, and support, and to regulate body processes.

macronutrients The energy-containing essential nutrients that you need in higher amounts: carbohydrates, lipids (fats), and proteins.

micronutrients Essential nutrients that you need in smaller amounts: vitamins and minerals.

What Does the Health of Your Family Tree Look Like?

Is there a history of heart disease, diabetes, or obesity in your family? What about other chronic diseases or conditions? Before you read this textbook and learn about the role that good nutrition plays in preventing chronic diseases and maintaining overall good health, ask your parents and grandparents about your family's health history. If there are certain diseases or conditions that run in your family, you'll want to pay particular attention to these as you read about them in this book.

An easy way to gather information about your family's health history is by visiting My Family Health Portrait at http://familyhistory.hhs.gov. When you input your family medical history, it provides a family tree report. Save a copy of this family health history for future reference.

organic Containing carbon.

enzymes Substances that speed up reactions in your body.

inorganic Not containing carbon. Inorganic compounds include minerals, water, and salts.

Carbohydrates, Fats, and Proteins Provide Energy

Carbohydrates, fats (lipids), and proteins are the energy-providing nutrients, because they contain calories. When we talk about energy, we mean that your body breaks down these nutrients and "burns" them to fuel your activities and internal functioning. One kilocalorie equals the amount of energy needed to raise the temperature of 1 kilogram (a liter) of water 1 degree Celsius. (Note that *kilocalories* are commonly referred to as *calories,* which is the term used in this book.) Carbohydrates and protein provide 4 calories per gram, and fats provide 9 calories per gram. The number of calories in a given food can be determined by measuring the weight, in grams, of each of the three nutrients in one serving of the food.

The amount of calories that you need daily to maintain your weight is estimated based on your age, gender, and activity level. However, you need these nutrients for many reasons beyond their providing energy. You must consume a healthy combination of carbohydrates, fats, and protein so that excesses, deficiencies, and imbalances don't occur that may increase your risk of chronic diseases.

Carbohydrates supply the simple sugar, called glucose, that your cells use as the major energy source to fuel your body. Most of your daily calories should come from carbohydrates. Fats are another major fuel source. They also help cushion your organs to prevent damage and act as insulation under your skin to help maintain your body temperature. Proteins can be used as energy, but are better used to build and maintain your tissues, muscles, and organs. You also need protein to make most enzymes and some hormones, to help transport other nutrients, and for a healthy immune system. A healthy diet should provide adequate amounts of carbohydrates and fats for energy, and enough protein to maintain and repair your body.

Carbohydrates, fats, and proteins are all **organic** because they contain the element carbon. They also contain two other elements, hydrogen and oxygen. Proteins also contain nitrogen, while carbohydrates and fats do not.

Vitamins and Minerals Are Essential for Metabolism

You need vitamins and minerals to use carbohydrates, fats, and proteins and to sustain numerous chemical reactions. A deficiency of vitamins and minerals can cause ill effects ranging from fatigue to stunted growth, weak bones, and organ damage.

Many vitamins and minerals aid **enzymes,** which are substances that speed up reactions in your body. For example, many of the B vitamins function as coenzymes in the metabolism of carbohydrates and fats. Many minerals, such as calcium and phosphorus, work with protein-containing hormones and enzymes to maintain and strengthen your teeth and bones. The fate of carbohydrates, protein, and fats in your body is very much dependent upon your consuming enough vitamins and minerals in your daily diet.

Vitamins are organic compounds that usually have to be obtained from your foods. Your body is able to make some vitamins, such as vitamin D, but sometimes cannot make enough of it to maintain good health. In these situations, your diet has to supplement your body's efforts.

Minerals are **inorganic** substances that play a role in body processes and are key to the structure of some tissues, such as bone. A deficiency of any of the minerals can cause disease symptoms. Anyone who has ever suffered from iron-deficiency anemia can tell you that falling short of your daily iron needs, for example, can cause fatigue and interfere with your ability to function.

Water Is Vital for Many Processes in Your Body

Although plain water does not provide energy or calories, it is vital to many key body functions, and staying hydrated is therefore an important part of staying healthy. As part of the fluid medium inside your cells, water helps chemical reactions, such as those involved in the production of energy, take place. Water also bathes the outside of your cells, playing a key role in transporting vital nutrients and oxygen to, and removing waste products from, your cells. Water helps maintain your body temperature and acts as a lubricant for your joints, eyes, mouth, and intestinal tract. It surrounds your organs and cushions them from injury.

The Take-Home Message Your body needs carbohydrates, fats (lipids), protein, vitamins, minerals, and water to survive. These six classes of nutrients have specific roles in your body, and you need them in specific amounts for good health. While carbohydrates, fats, and protein provide energy, vitamins, minerals, and water are needed to use the energy-producing nutrients and to maintain good health. Water is part of the medium inside and outside your cells that carries nutrients to, and waste products from, your cells. Water also helps maintain your body temperature and acts as a lubricant and protective cushion.

How Should You Get These Important Nutrients?

There is no question that you need all six classes of nutrients to function properly. But is there an advantage to consuming them through food rather than taking them as supplements? Is there more to a healthy diet than just meeting your basic nutrient needs? Let's look at these questions in more detail.

The Best Way to Meet Your Nutrient Needs Is with a Well-Balanced Diet

Many foods provide a variety of nutrients. For example, low-fat milk is high in carbohydrates and protein and provides a small amount of fat. Milk is also a good source of the vitamins A, D, and riboflavin, as well as the minerals potassium and calcium, and is approximately 90 percent water by weight. Whereas milk contains a substantial variety of all six classes of nutrients, a single food item doesn't have to provide all nutrients in order to be good for you. Rather, a well-balanced diet composed of a variety of foods can provide you with all of these important nutrients.

A well-balanced diet will also provide other dietary compounds, such as phytochemicals and **fiber,** that have been shown to help fight many diseases. At least 900 different phytochemicals have been identified in foods and more are likely to be discovered. Don't assume that these compounds can be extracted from foods, put in a pill, and still produce the same positive effect on your health. The disease-fighting properties of phytochemicals likely go beyond the compounds themselves, and work

fiber The portion of plant foods that isn't digested in the small intestine.

with fiber, nutrients, or unknown substances in foods to provide a synergistic, positive effect on your health.

Fiber is the portion of plant foods that isn't digested in the stomach and small intestine. Some foods, such as whole grains, fruits, and vegetables that are high in fiber, are also phytochemical powerhouses. Studies have shown that diets rich in these foods fight many diseases. ⓉⒻ

Also, let's not forget some of the obvious benefits of getting your nutrients from food. The delicious texture and aroma of foods, coupled with the social interaction of meals, are lost when you pop a pill to meet your nutrient needs. That said, some individuals *should* take a supplement if food alone can't meet their needs.

You Can Meet Some Nutrient Needs with a Supplement

Although many people can get all their nutrients through their diet, others have diet restrictions or higher nutrient needs such that they would benefit from taking a supplement in addition to consuming a healthy diet. For example, someone who is lactose intolerant (meaning they have difficulty digesting milk products) may have to meet his or her calcium needs from other sources. A calcium supplement could be an option for these individuals. Pregnant women should take an iron supplement because their increased need for this mineral is unlikely to be met through the diet alone. As you can see, a well-balanced diet and dietary supplements aren't mutually exclusive. In some situations, they should be partnered as the best nutritional strategy for good health.

Even with an abundance of foods and the availability of supplements for those who may need them, the diets of Americans aren't as healthy as they could be. Let's find out why this is the case.

The Take-Home Message **A well-balanced diet will likely meet all of your nutrient needs and also provide a variety of compounds that may help prevent chronic diseases. People who cannot meet their nutrient needs through food alone may benefit from taking a supplement.**

How Does the Average American Diet Stack Up?

The food supply in the United States provides an array of nutritious choices to meet the dietary needs of most Americans. Fresh fruits and vegetables, whole grains, and lean meats, fish, and poultry are usually easily accessible and affordable through grocery stores and farmers' markets. Yet, with such an abundance of healthy foods to choose from, are Americans adopting healthy diets?

The Quality of the American Diet

In general, Americans eat too much added sugar, sodium, and saturated fat, and too little fiber and some vitamins and minerals. Our low fiber intake is partly due to our inadequate consumption of fruits and vegetables, and our overconsumption of refined rather than whole grains.[11] At the same time, while dietary fiber intakes are below recommended levels, added sugars account for an average of 16 percent of Americans' daily

This isn't exactly what's meant by the phrase "You are what you eat," but it's close.

calories. This is largely due to Americans' love of soft drinks and other sugary beverages, as well as sweets and treats.[12] For most of us, our fat intake is at the higher end of the recommended range, at about 34 percent. We eat too much saturated fat, and many of us exceed the recommended dietary cholesterol intake of less than 300 milligrams per day.[13]

With regard to the micronutrients, American men meet their recommendations for most vitamins and minerals but women often fall short of many—including iron, for example. Americans, in general, eat too much sodium, but not enough vitamin D, potassium, and calcium. In an attempt to balance our lack of healthy food choices, 50 percent of Americans take at least one dietary supplement per day.[14]

The lack of a healthy diet may also be due to *where* we eat. Americans spend over 40 percent of their food budget consuming food outside the home.[15] As mentioned earlier, many of us buy prepared foods from the supermarket or take-out meals from restaurants. If you don't prepare a meal yourself, it can be more difficult to keep track of how much sugar, sodium, or saturated fat you're consuming. Research shows that these prepared foods purchased outside the home tend to be less nutritious than those foods prepared in the home.[16] Eating one or more fast-food meals a week can increase the risk of weight gain, overweight, and obesity.[17]

Skipping breakfast may also be a hindrance to the waistline. Research suggests that children and adolescents who do not eat breakfast are at a higher risk for overweight and obesity.[18]

Rates of Overweight and Obesity in Americans

Americans have been battling the bathroom scale for decades, and the scale is winning. The prevalence of both **overweight** and **obesity** has become epidemic in the United States (see **Figure 1.4**). As people take in more calories than they burn, usually due to more sedentary lifestyles, they create a recipe for poor health. Over 65 percent of American adults are overweight and of those, 34 percent are considered obese.[19] Whereas the latest statistics indicate that the epidemic of obesity may be slowing, rates are still too high, and reducing them is a top health care priority.

Unfortunately, the rate of excessive weight gain is increasing for younger Americans. Currently, over 10 percent of children aged 2 to 5 years and approximately 17 percent of those aged 6 to 19 are considered obese.[20] Along with the weight gain have come higher rates of type 2 diabetes, particularly among children, and increased rates of heart disease, cancer, and stroke.

Ironically, being overweight doesn't necessarily mean being well fed. In fact, many of the poorest Americans are obese and malnourished. The feature box "Poor, Obese, and Malnourished: A Troubling Paradox" looks at this growing problem among Americans.

Improving Americans' Diets Is One Goal of *Healthy People 2020*

The U.S. Surgeon General has issued calls for a nationwide health improvement program since 1979. The latest edition of this report, *Healthy People 2020,* contains a set of health goals and objectives for the nation to achieve over the second decade of the twenty-first century.[21]

Healthy People 2020 focuses on several overarching goals:

➤ Attain high-quality, longer lives free of preventable disease, disability, injury, and premature death.

➤ Achieve health equity, eliminate disparities, and improve the health of all groups.

1990

2000

2009

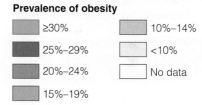

Prevalence of obesity

≥30%   10%–14%

25%–29%   <10%

20%–24%   No data

15%–19%

Figure 1.4 Obesity Trends among U.S. Adults
Over the last two decades, rates of overweight and obesity have risen significantly in the United States.

Source: Centers for Disease Control. 2010. "Overweight and Obesity: Obesity Trends." www.cdc.gov/obesity/data/trends.html.

overweight Carrying extra weight on your body in relation to your height. (See Chapter 10 for the clinically defined weight range.)

obesity Carrying an excessive amount of body fat above the level of being overweight. (See Chapter 10 for the clinically defined level.)

Healthy People 2020 A set of disease prevention and health promotion objectives for Americans to meet during the second decade of the new millennium.

Poor, Obese, and Malnourished: A Troubling Paradox

Food costs money, so people who are poor have less money to buy food. Therefore, people who are poor are less likely to be overweight or obese—right? Makes sense, but the conclusion is wrong. In survey after survey, rates of obesity turn out to be highest among people with the lowest incomes. The numbers are greater for women than for men, but for both genders Americans living near or below the poverty level have much higher rates of obesity than affluent Americans.[1] And despite their obesity, these lowest-income Americans are also malnourished. How can this be so?

In 1995, a pediatrician named William Dietz, now considered a leading expert on obesity, published an account of a 7-year-old patient: a girl weighing more than twice her ideal body weight and living in poverty. Dietz entitled his case study "Does Hunger Cause Obesity?" and proposed two possible scenarios in which it might:[2]

➤ When a family lacks money, its members choose foods that provide them with the greatest number of calories at the lowest cost. These foods tend to be high in fat and sugar and low in nutrients, such as vitamins, minerals, and fiber. Thus, although overfed, individuals on this kind of diet can be significantly malnourished.

➤ When a person experiences hunger, the body adapts by slowing energy expenditure and "hoarding" calories: In other words, episodes of food shortages might cause increased body fat.

More recently, Angie Tagtow, head of the Hunger and Environmental Nutrition group, identified another possible link among hunger, malnutrition, and obesity: the family's living environment.[3] Economics influences not only what a family can afford to buy but also where it can afford to live, and this affects its proximity to quality food stores and farmers' markets versus fast-food restaurants and convenience stores. Economics also affects access to trans-portation, social services, and nutrition education and assistance.

Adam Drewnowski, director of the Center for Public Health Nutrition of the University of Washington, adds one more factor: the greater palatability of low-cost foods. In other words, chips and cookies tend to satisfy our taste buds more than peppers and pears. He cites laboratory studies suggesting that we're more likely to overeat cheap junk foods, and contends that limited money for food may shift a poor family's purchases toward more palatable foods that fill people up with the maximum calories at the minimum cost.[4] Drewnowski points out that a low-income family of four gets $104 a week in food assistance, which breaks down to $3.71 per person per day.[5] Think about it: If you had just $3.71 to buy a day's worth of food, how would you spend it? Would you be more concerned with getting the right balance of nutrients or purchasing high-volume, less nutritious foods that keep hunger at bay throughout the day?

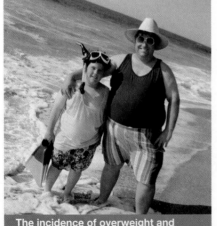

The incidence of overweight and obesity among adults and children is becoming more prevalent in the United States.

➤ Create social and physical environments that promote good health for all.
➤ Promote quality of life, healthy development, and healthy behaviors across every stage of life.

There are more than 35 topic areas in *Healthy People 2020*, ranging from ensuring that Americans have adequate access to health services to improvements in their diets and physical activity. Objectives are developed within each topic area.

For example, current research indicates that Americans body weights are increasing rather than decreasing. Thus, "Nutrition and Weight Status" is one topic area. Its goal is to promote health and reduce chronic diseases associated with diet and weight. There are numerous objectives developed within this topic area that, if fulfilled, will help Americans improve their diet and reduce their weight. See Table 1.2 for the list of a few objectives in this area of focus.

As you can see from the table, consuming adequate amounts of fruits and vegetables are beneficial to managing one's weight. Americans should increase their intake of both of these food sources to help them improve their nutrition and weight status.

Table 1.2		
***Healthy People 2020* Nutrition and Weight Status Objectives**		
Objectives		
Increase the proportion of adults who are at a healthy weight		
Reduce the proportion of adults who are obese		
Reduce the proportion of children and adolescents who are considered obese		
Increase the contribution of fruits to diets of the population age 2 years and older		
Increase the variety and contribution of vegetables to the diets of the population aged 2 and older		

The Take-Home Message Incidences of overweight and obesity among Americans are prevalent, yet many people are falling short of some nutrient needs. *Healthy People 2020* is a set of health objectives for the nation to achieve over the second decade of the twenty-first century.

What's the Real Deal When It Comes to Nutrition Research and Advice?

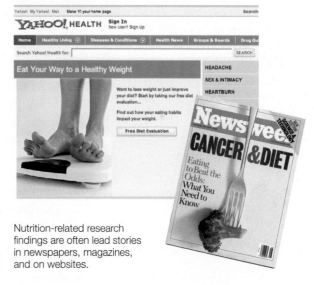

Nutrition-related research findings are often lead stories in newspapers, magazines, and on websites.

If you "Google" the word *nutrition*, you will get a list of about 103,000,000 entries in 0.25 seconds. Obviously, the world is full of nutrition information.

Just ask anyone who is trying to lose weight and that person will probably tell you how hard it is to keep up with the latest diet advice—because it seems to keep changing. In the 1970s, waist watchers were told that carbohydrates were the bane of their existence and that a protein-rich, low-carbohydrate diet was the name of the game when it came to shrinking their waistlines. A decade later, avoiding fat was the key to winning the battle of the bulge. By 2000, carbohydrates were being ousted yet again, and protein-rich diets were back in vogue. But now protein-heavy diets seem to be fading out of the limelight and higher carbohydrate diets—with plenty of fiber—are becoming the way to fight weight gain. So . . . are you frustrated yet?

Even though popular wisdom and trends seem to change with the wind, scientific knowledge about nutrition doesn't change this frequently. While the media publicizes results from studies deemed newsworthy, in reality it takes many, many affirming research studies before a **consensus** is reached about nutrition advice. News of the results of one study is just that: news. In contrast, advice from an authoritative health organization or committee, such as the American Heart Association or the Dietary Guidelines

consensus The opinion of a group of experts based on a collection of information.

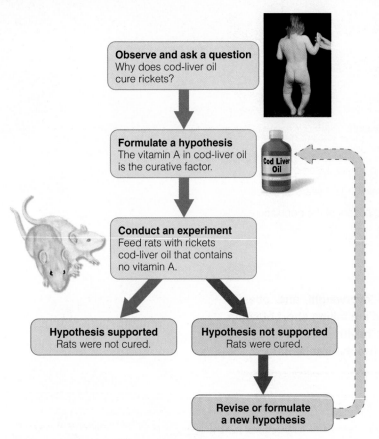

Observe and ask a question
Why does cod-liver oil
cure rickets?

Formulate a hypothesis
The vitamin A in cod-liver oil
is the curative factor.

Conduct an experiment
Feed rats with rickets
cod-liver oil that contains
no vitamin A.

Hypothesis supported
Rats were not cured.

Hypothesis not supported
Rats were cured.

**Revise or formulate
a new hypothesis**

Figure 1.5 Steps of the Scientific Method
The scientific method is used to conduct credible research in nutrition and other
scientific fields.

Committee, which is based on a consensus of research information, is sound information that can be trusted for the long term. Headlines in newspapers, lead articles on websites, and the sound bites on television often report the results of a single, recent research study. The boxed feature "Evaluating Media Headlines with a Critical Eye" discusses how to scrutinize information about current research findings and not get caught up in the media hype.

Sound Nutrition Research Begins with the Scientific Method

Research studies that generate enough information are based on a process called the **scientific method.** Scientists are like detectives. They observe something in the natural world, ask questions, come up with an idea (or **hypothesis**) based on their observations, test their hypothesis, and then see if their idea is correct. There are many steps in the scientific method and many adjustments made along the way before a scientist has gained enough information to support his or her hypothesis. In fact, the entire process can take years to complete.

Let's walk through a nutrition-related study in which scientists used the scientific method to study rickets. Rickets is a potentially severe and even fatal disease in children, whereby the bones throughout the body weaken. For instance, the spine and rib cage can become so distorted that breathing is impaired. The leg bones can become so weakened that they are unable to hold up the child's body weight, and they curve outward ("bow legs"). In the nineteenth century, parents often relied on folk remedies to treat diseases; in the case of rickets, they used cod-liver oil because it seemed to prevent the disorder as well as cure it, although no one knew how.

The first steps of the scientific method are to make an observation and ask questions (**Figure 1.5**). Originally, scientists were piqued by the cod-liver oil curing phenomenon. They asked themselves why cod-liver oil cured rickets. In the second step of the scientific method, a hypothesis is formulated. Because cod-liver oil is very rich in vitamin A, scientists initially thought that this vitamin must be the curative factor. To confirm this, scientists proceeded to the next step in the scientific method, which was to conduct an experiment.

The scientists altered the cod-liver oil to destroy all of its vitamin A. The altered oil was given to rats that had been fed a diet that caused rickets. Surprisingly, the rats were still cured of rickets. This disproved the scientists' original hypothesis that vitamin A was the curative factor. They then needed to modify their hypothesis, as it was obvious that there was something else in the cod-liver oil that cured rickets. They next hypothesized that it was the vitamin D that cured the rats, and conducted another experiment to confirm this hypothesis, which it did.

The next step in the scientific method involves sharing these findings with the scientific community. What good would it be to make this fabulous discovery if other scientists couldn't find out about it? To do this, scientists summarize and submit their

scientific method A stepwise process used by scientists to generate sound research findings.

hypothesis An idea generated by scientists based on their observations.

Evaluating Media Headlines with a Critical Eye

Based on this headline, you may be tempted to run out immediately and get yourself a couple of chocolate bars. However, you would be doing a disservice to your health if you didn't read below this tantalizing headline, to assimilate and analyze the evidence on which the headline is based.

February 11, 2010

Sweet Science: The Health Benefits of Chocolate

Rachael Rettner, *LiveScience*

The media are routinely bombarded by press releases sent from medical journals, food companies, organizations, and universities about research being conducted and/or conferences being sponsored by these institutions. These releases are sent for one reason: to gain publicity. Reputable news organizations that report these findings will seek out independent experts in the field to weigh in on the research and, just as importantly, explain how these findings relate to the public. If you don't read beyond the headlines, you are probably missing important details of the story. Even worse, if you begin making dietary and lifestyle changes based on each news flash, you become a scientific guinea pig.

When a headline piques your interest, read the article with a critical eye, and ask yourself the following questions.

1. Was the Research Finding Published in a Peer-Reviewed Journal?

You can be confident that studies published in a peer-reviewed journal have been thoroughly reviewed by experts in this area of research. If the research isn't published in a peer-reviewed journal, you have no way of knowing if the study was conducted in an appropriate manner and whether the findings are accurate. A study about the possible virtues of chocolate in fighting heart disease that is published in the *New England Journal of Medicine* has more credibility than a similar article published in a baking magazine.

2. Was the Study Done Using Animals or Humans?

Animals are animals and humans are humans. Experiments with animals are often used to study how a particular substance affects a health outcome. But if the study is conducted in rats, it doesn't necessarily mean that the substance will have the same effect if consumed by humans. This doesn't mean that animal studies are frivolous. They are important stepping stones to designing and conducting similar experiments involving humans.

3. Do the Study Participants Resemble Me?

When you read or hear about studies involving humans, you should always seek more information about the individuals who took part in the research. For example, were the people in the chocolate studies college-aged subjects or older individuals with heart disease and high blood pressure? If older adults were studied, then would these findings be of any benefit to young adults who don't have high blood pressure or heart disease?

4. Is This the First Time I've Heard about This?

A single study in a specific area of research is a lonely entity in the scientific world. Is this the first study regarding the health benefits of chocolate? If the media article doesn't confirm that other studies have also supported these findings, this one study may be the *only* study of its kind. Wait until you hear that these research findings have been confirmed by a reputable health organization, such as the American Heart Association, before considering making any changes in your diet. Reputable organizations will only change their advice based on a consensus of research findings.

In your lifetime, you are going to read thousands of newspaper and website headlines, as well as watch and listen to who-knows-how-many similar television and radio reports. Your critical thinking skills in evaluating the sources and information presented will be your best friend when it comes to deciding which blurbs to believe. These skills may also save you considerable money by helping you avoid nutrition gimmicks. When it comes to assessing nutrition information in the media, it's worth your time and effort to find out where it came from and why (or if) you should care.

Figure 1.6 A Hypothesis Can Lead to a Scientific Consensus
When a hypothesis is supported by research, the results are published in peer-reviewed journals. Once a theory has been developed and supported by subsequent experiments, a consensus is reached in the scientific community.

peer-reviewed journal A research journal in which fellow scientists (peers) review studies to assess if they are accurate and sound before they are published.

laboratory experiment A scientific experiment conducted in a laboratory. Some laboratory experiments involve animals.

observational research Research that involves looking at factors in two or more groups of subjects to see if there is a relationship to certain outcomes.

epidemiological research Research that looks at populations of people; it is often observational.

experimental research Research involving at least two groups of subjects.

experimental group The group given a specific treatment.

control group The group given a placebo.

placebo A sugar pill that has no impact on the individual's health when ingested.

double-blind placebo-controlled study When the scientists and subjects in a research experiment can't distinguish between the treatments given to the subjects and don't know which group of subjects received which treatment.

research findings to a **peer-reviewed journal** (Figure 1.6). Other scientists (peers) then look at the researchers' findings to make sure that they are sound. If so, the research study is published in the journal. (If this relationship between vitamin D and rickets was discovered today, it would probably be the lead story on CNN.)

As more and more studies were done that confirmed that vitamin D can cure and prevent rickets, a theory developed. We now know with great certainty that vitamin D can prevent rickets and that a deficiency of vitamin D will cause this type of deformed bones in children. Because of this, there is a consensus among health professionals as to the importance of vitamin D in the diets of children.

Research Studies and Experiments Confirm Hypotheses

Scientists can use different types of experiments to test hypotheses. The rickets experiment just described is called a **laboratory experiment**, as it was done in the confines of a lab. In the fields of nutrition and health, laboratory experiments are often conducted using animals, such as rats. Research conducted with humans is usually observational or experimental.

Observational Research

Observational research involves looking at factors in two or more groups of subjects to see if there is a relationship to a certain disease or another health outcome. For example, researchers might study rates of breast-feeding in infants with and without rickets, to see if breast-feeding influences the incidence of the disease.

One type of observational research is **epidemiological research,** which looks at populations of people. For example, scientists may look at people who live in Norway and notice that there is a higher incidence of rickets among children there than in Australia. Through their observation, they may find a relationship between the lack of sun exposure in Norway and the high incidence of rickets there compared with sunny Australia. However, the scientists can't rule out the possibility that the difference in the incidence of rickets in these two populations may also be due to other factors in the subjects' diet or lifestyle.

Experimental Research

Experimental research involves at least two groups of subjects. One group, the **experimental group,** is given a specific treatment, and another group, the **control group,** isn't. For instance, after hypothesizing that vitamin D cures rickets, scientists would have randomly assigned children with rickets to two groups. They would have given the children in the experimental group a vitamin D supplement but would have given the children in the control group a substance, called a **placebo,** that looked just like the vitamin D supplement but contained only sugar or some other nonactive ingredient. If neither of the two groups of subjects knew which substance they received, then they were "blind" to the treatment. If the scientists who were giving the placebo and the vitamin D supplement also couldn't distinguish between the two treatments and didn't know which group received which, this would be called a **double-blind, placebo-controlled study.**

The scientists would also have to make sure that all other significant factors were the same for both groups during the experiment. For example, since the scientists knew that sun exposure has a therapeutic effect on rickets, they couldn't let the children in the control group go outside in the sunshine while keeping the children in the experimental group inside. The exposure to sunshine would change the outcome of the experiment. Similarly, they'd have to ensure that the children were eating exactly the same diet for the duration of the study.

A double-blind, placebo-controlled study is considered the "gold standard" of research, because all of the factors that might influence the study results are kept the same for the groups of subjects, and neither the subjects nor the researchers are biased, as they don't know which group has received which treatment (**Figure 1.7**).

Although the results of many experiments fail to support the initial hypotheses, a great many discoveries are made. With continuing research, one discovery builds upon another. Though it may seem frustrating when the findings of one research study dispute the results of another from just a few months before, even contradictory findings help advance scientific knowledge, in part because of the questions they raise. Why did the first study show one result and a second study something different? In tackling such questions, scientists continue to advance our understanding of the world around us, and within us. For example, scientists are asking intriguing research questions about nutritional genomics. The feature box, "What Is Nutritional Genomics?" discusses this fascinating area of nutritional science.

You Can Trust the Advice of Nutrition Experts

Figure 1.7 Controlled Scientific Experiments
Scientists use experimental research to test hypotheses.

If you want legal advice, you seek the expertise of a lawyer. If you need a knee operation, you should visit an orthopedic surgeon. If you want nutrition advice, to whom should you turn? Of course you want to speak with a credible expert who has training in the field of nutrition. So, who are these people and where do you find them?

One option is to seek the expertise of a **registered dietitian (RD)**. The RD has completed at least a bachelor's degree at an accredited university or college in the United States that has incorporated specific coursework and supervised practice that have been approved by the accrediting body of the American Dietetic Association (ADA). RDs have also passed a national exam administered by the ADA. They have an understanding of **medical nutrition therapy,** which is an integration of nutrition counseling and dietary changes based on an individual's medical history and current health needs to improve that person's health.

RDs work with their patients to make dietary changes that can help prevent diseases such as heart disease, diabetes, stroke, and obesity. Many physicians, based on the diagnoses of their patients, refer them to RDs for nutrition advice and guidance.

registered dietitian (RD) A health professional who has completed at least a bachelor's degree in nutrition from an accredited university or college in the United States, completed a supervised practice, and passed an exam administered by the American Dietetic Association (ADA).

medical nutrition therapy The integration of nutrition counseling and dietary changes based on an individual's medical and health needs to treat a patient's medical condition.

What Is Nutritional Genomics?

As we learn more about nutrition from on-going research, we are likely to find even more ways in which what we eat affects our personal health. One exciting area of research now is **nutritional genomics.** Genomics is the study of genes, their functions in your body, and how the environment may influence **gene expression.** Your genes determine your inherited, specific traits. With the completion of the **Human Genome Project,** the complete sequencing of **deoxyribonucleic acid (DNA)** in your cells is now known. Your DNA contains the genetic instructions needed to develop and direct the activities of your body.

Nutritional genomics is concerned with how the specific components in foods that you eat interact on a cellular level with the expression of your genes. Certain dietary components can cause different effects on your genes, and thus, initiate a very specific response in your body that could be different from the response it initiates in another person. For example, nutritional genomics will help determine the specific dietary combination of types of fats that you should consume to lower your risk of heart disease based on your genetic makeup.[6] As more becomes known about the application of nutritional genomics, you will have more control over how your diet affects your long-term health.

nutritional genomics A field of study that researches the relationship between nutrition and genomics (the study of genes and gene expression).

gene expression The processing of genetic information to create a specific protein.

Human Genome Project A project sponsored by the United States government to determine the complete set and sequencing of DNA in human cells and identify all human genes.

deoxyribonucleic acid (DNA) Genetic material within cells that directs the synthesis of proteins in the body.

RDs must participate in continuing professional education in order to remain current in the fast-changing world of nutrition, medicine, and health and maintain their registration. RDs work in hospitals and other health care facilities, private practice, universities, medical schools, professional athletic teams, food companies, and other nutrition-related businesses.

Individuals with advanced degrees in nutrition can also provide credible nutrition information. Sometimes physicians may have taken a nutrition course in medical school and gone on to get a master of science in public health (MPH), which involves some nutrition courses, or an MS in nutrition at an accredited university or college.

Some **public health nutritionists** may have an undergraduate degree in nutrition but didn't complete a supervised practice, so are not eligible to take the RD exam. These individuals can work in the government organizing community outreach nutrition programs, such as programs for the elderly.

In order to protect the health of the public receiving nutrition information, more than 30 states in the United States currently license nutrition professionals who must meet specified educational and experience criteria to be considered experts in the field of nutrition. A person who meets these qualifications is a **licensed dietitian (LD)** and so will have the letters "LD" after his or her name. Because RDs have completed the rigorous standards set forth by the ADA, they automatically meet the criteria for LD and often will have both "RD" and "LD" after their names.

Be careful when taking nutrition advice from a trainer at the gym or the person who works at the local health food store. Whereas some of these people may be credible, many are not, and thus, less likely to give you valid information that's based on solid scientific evidence. Anyone who calls himself or herself a **nutritionist** may have taken few or no accredited courses in nutrition.

public health nutritionist An individual who may have an undergraduate degree in nutrition but isn't an RD.

licensed dietitian (LD) An individual who has met specified educational and experience criteria deemed necessary by a state licensing board to be considered an expert in the field of nutrition. An RD would meet all the qualifications to be an LD.

nutritionist A generic term with no recognized legal or professional meaning. Some people may call themselves nutritionists without having any credible training in nutrition.

You also need to beware of individuals who specialize in health **quackery** or fraud. Such scammers will try to persuade you with false nutrition claims and anecdotal stories that aren't backed up by sound science and research. Americans spend billions of dollars annually on fraudulent health products, an injustice that Stephen Barrett, MD, a nationally known author and consumer advocate, has been trying to fight for decades. His website, quackwatch.org, helps consumers identify quackery and health fraud and make educated decisions about health-related information and products. Dr. Barrett's list of common deceptive statements made by health quacks is in the boxed feature "Quackwatchers."

Identifying quackery and fraud is important not only when you are seeking out an expert for advice, but also when you read about nutrition on the Internet. The Web is overflowing with nutrition information and *mis*information.

You Can Obtain Accurate Nutrition Information on the Internet

Mark Twain once said, "Be careful about reading health books. You could die of a misprint." If he was alive today, he probably would have included websites that dole out health advice. More than 60 percent of American adult Internet users have surfed millions of websites looking for health and medical information.[22]

Don't assume that a slick website is a sound website. Although many websites, such as Shape Up America! (www.shapeup.org) and the Tufts Health & Nutrition Newsletter (www.healthletter.tufts.edu) provide credible, reliable, up-to-date nutrition information, many, many others do not. Remember, anyone with computer skills can put up a website. The National Institutes of Health (NIH) has developed 10 questions that you should consider when viewing a nutrition- or health-related website:[23]

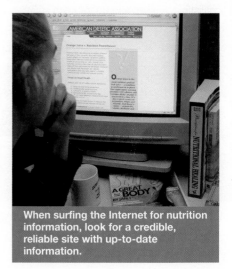

When surfing the Internet for nutrition information, look for a credible, reliable site with up-to-date information.

1. Who Runs the Site?

Credible websites are willing to show their credentials. For example, the National Center for Complementary and Alternative Medicine (www.nccam.nih.gov) provides information about its association with the NIH and its extensive ongoing research and educational programs. If you have to spend more than a minute trying to find out who runs the website, you should click to another site.

2. Who Pays for the Site?

Running a website is expensive, and finding out who's paying for a particular site will tell you something about the reliability of its content. Websites sponsored by the government (with URL ending in .gov), or an academic institution (.edu) are more reliable than many commercial websites (.com or .net). Some commercial websites, such as *Web*MD, carry articles that can be reliable if they are written by credible health professionals, but other websites may be promoting information to suit a company's own purposes.

For example, if the funding source for the website is a vitamin and mineral supplement company, are all the articles geared toward supporting the use of supplements? Does the website have advertisers, and do their products also influence the content on the website? You need to investigate whether the website content may be biased based on the funding source.

quackery The promotion and selling of health products and services of questionable validity. A quack is a person who promotes these products and services in order to make money.

Quackwatchers

Consumers beware. The snake oil salespeople of yesteryear never left the building. They just left the oil behind and moved on to selling nutrition supplements and other products that are not based on science. These skilled salespeople introduce health fears into your mind and then try to sell services and products to allay these newly created fears. They make unrealistic promises and guarantees.

To avoid falling for one of their shady schemes, you should be leery of infomercials, magazine ads, and websites that try to convince you that:

➤ Most Americans are not adequately nourished.
➤ Everyone needs to take vitamin supplements.
➤ You need supplements to relieve stress or give you energy.

➤ You can lose a lot of weight in a short amount of time.
➤ Their products can produce amazing results and cure whatever ails you.
➤ Your behavior is caused by your diet.
➤ Herbs are safe because they are natural.
➤ Sugar will poison you.
➤ A hair sample can identify nutrient deficiencies.
➤ Your MD or RD is a quack to whom you should not listen.
➤ There is no risk, as there is a money-back guarantee. (Good luck getting your money back!)

Source: S. Barrett, Signs of a 'Quacky' Web Site and Twenty-Five Ways to Spot Quacks and Vitamin Pushers. Available at http://quackwatch.org.

3. What Is the Purpose of the Site?

After you answer the first two questions, look for the "About This Site" link. This will help you understand the website's purpose. For example, at Nutrition.gov, the purpose is to "provide easy access to the best food and nutrition information across the federal government." This website doesn't exist to sell you anything, but to help you find reliable information.

4. Where Does the Information Come From?

You should always know who wrote what you are reading. Is the author a qualified nutrition expert, or did she or he interview qualified individuals? If the site obtained information from another source, was that source cited?

5. What Is the Basis of the Information?

Is the article's information based on medical facts and figures that have references? For example, any medical news items released on the American Heart Association website (www.americanheart.org) will include the medical journal from which the information came. In fact, the website will often include the opinion of experts regarding the news items.

6. How Is the Information Selected?

A physician who is a well-known medical expert for a major television network once commented that he spends most of his time not delivering medical advice, but trying to stop the networks from publicizing health news that isn't credible. Always look to see if the website has an editorial board of medical and health experts and if qualified individuals review or write the content before it is released.

7. How Current Is the Information?

Once a website is on the Internet, it will stay there until someone removes it. Consequently, the health information that you read may not be the most up to date. Always check to see when the content was written, and if it is over a year old, whether it has been updated.

8. How Does the Site Choose Links to Other Sites?

Some medical sites don't like to link to other sites, as they don't have control over other sites' credibility and content. Others do link, if they are confident that these sites meet their criteria. Some sites receive financial reimbursement from the links that they post. Don't always assume that the link is credible.

9. What Information Is Collected about You and Why?

Websites track the pages that you click on in order to analyze their more popular topics. Sometimes, they elicit personal information such as your gender, age, and health concerns. After collecting data on your viewing selections and your personal information, they can sell this information to interested companies. These companies can create promotional materials about their goods and services targeted to your needs. Credible sites should tell you about their privacy policy and if they will or will not give this information to other sources. A website's privacy policy is often found in a link at the bottom of its screens.

10. How Does the Site Manage Interactions with Visitors?

You should always be able to easily find the contact information of the website's owners should you have any concerns or questions that you want answered. If the site has a chat room or ongoing discussion group, you should know how it is moderated. Read the discussion group dialogue before you jump in.

The Take-Home Message Sound nutrition advice is based on years of research using the scientific method. You should only take nutrition advice from a credible source, such as a registered dietitian or other valid nutrition expert. When obtaining nutrition information from the Internet, you need to carefully peruse the site to make sure that it is credible, it contains up-to-date information, and its content isn't influenced by those that fund and support the website.

Two Points of View

Does Food Advertising Contribute to an Unhealthy Diet? The food industry spends billions of dollars per year to market and advertise products; in fact, the Federal Trade Commission found that in 2006, $1.6 billion was spent on marketing to children and adolescents alone. Unfortunately, most of that amount is used to promote highly processed, highly packaged foods[1] and much of it involves cross-promotional campaigns that tie products to movies, television shows, and animated characters.[2]

Do food ads compel consumers to eat junk food? Do food companies and advertising agencies have a responsibility to help people eat a healthy diet? After you've read the arguments for and against, answer the critical thinking questions and decide for yourself.

Yes

- Food advertising, particularly ads targeted at children, is pervasive. Every day, children view, on average, 15 TV food advertisements,[3] and an overwhelming 98 percent of these ads promote products high in fat, sugar, and/or sodium.[4]

- Sugar-sweetened breakfast cereals, soft drinks, confectionery items, and savory snacks are the most frequently advertised categories, with fast-food promotion continuing to gain marketing share. Promotion of unprocessed foods, such as fruit and vegetables, whole grains, and milk, is found to be almost zero.[5]

- There is evidence that limiting children's exposure to food advertising will reduce the prevalence of childhood obesity.[6]

- Food ads cause people to consume more than just those foods that are advertised. In one study, adults consumed more of both healthy and unhealthy snack foods following exposure to snack food advertising. These effects were not related to reported hunger or other conscious influences.[7]

No

- Children and adults are active consumers of advertising from an early age and they interpret critically what they see and hear rather than being passive recipients of advertising messages.[8] Further, most people are smart enough to know that fruits and vegetables are better for them than cookies and chips. If they've made the conscious decision to eat healthfully, television commercials aren't going to bring them back to pizza and doughnuts.

- Regions like Quebec and Sweden that have banned all advertising to children still have high obesity rates.[9]

- Americans are actually very healthy. Our life expectancy continues to reach all-time highs.[10] Deaths from heart disease, cancer, and stroke—the country's three biggest killers—have been in decline for 15 years.[11]

- If Americans truly want to eat a healthy diet, companies that produce healthy food will flourish.

- In recent years, many major food manufacturers have significantly re-formulated their products to reduce salt, fat, or sugar content. In many cases, the product being advertised is very different from previous versions.[12]

What do you think?

1. Do you think people are more likely to buy less-healthy foods because of food advertising? **2.** Has an ad recently influenced your own purchasing habits? **3.** Are food companies ethically obligated to help us eat healthfully? **4.** Why are fruits and vegetables less advertised than processed food?

Chapter Review

 Be a Nutrition Sleuth

Spotting a Bogus Weight-Loss Product

When a miraculous weight-loss product sounds a little too good to be true, it probably is! Identify the signs of a bogus product at **www.pearsonhighered.com/blake.**

 Get Real!

Find Online Information You Can Use

Don't know where to begin to find credible nutrition information on the Internet? Visit **www.pearsonhighered.com/blake** for a reliable starting point.

The Top Ten Points to Remember

1. Food choices are influenced by personal taste, culture, social life, accessibility, cost, and time constraints. You eat out of habit, in response to your emotions, and, of course, because food is delicious.

2. There are six categories of nutrients: carbohydrates, lipids (fats), proteins, vitamins, minerals, and water. Your body needs a mixture of these nutrients in specific amounts to stay healthy.

	Energy
Carbohydrates	⚡
Protein	⚡
Fats	⚡
Vitamins	
Minerals	
Water	

3. Nutrition plays an important role in preventing many of the leading causes of death in the United States, including heart disease, cancer, stroke, and a certain type of diabetes.

4. Carbohydrates, fats, and proteins provide the energy (calories) that your body needs. The majority of your daily calories should come from carbohydrates. You also need adequate amounts of both fats and proteins. Most of the proteins that you eat should be used to build and maintain your body tissues, muscles, and organs, rather than for energy.

5. Vitamins and minerals are important for metabolism and to properly utilize carbohydrates, fats, and protein. Many vitamins aid enzymes in your body.

6. Water is an essential nutrient that is vital for many functions. It bathes the inside and outside of your cells, helps maintain your body temperature, and acts as a lubricant and protective cushion.

7. Eating a well-balanced diet is the best way to meet your nutrient and health needs. Vitamin and mineral supplements can help complete a healthy diet but should not replace foods.

8. Nutrition is a science and new discoveries are continually made. Nutritional genomics is the integration of nutrition and genomics. Genomics is the study of genes, their functions in your body, and how the environment, including the foods and nutrients that you eat, influences the expression of your genes and, therefore, your health.

9. Sound nutrition information is the result of numerous scientific studies that are based on the scientific method. These research findings should be reviewed by and shared with the medical and scientific community. You should never change your diet or lifestyle based upon the findings of just one or a few studies.

10. Nutritional advice should come from credible sources. Individuals who call themselves nutritionists may or may not have a credible nutrition education. Always assess the source of nutrition information to make sure that it is credible.

Test Your Knowledge

1. Which of the following can influence your food choices?
   a. your ethnic background
   b. your busy schedule
   c. your emotions
   d. all of the above
2. Nutrition is
   a. the study of genes, how they function in your body, and how the environment can influence your genes.
   b. the study of how your body functions.

c. the scientific study of how nutrients and compounds in foods that you eat nourish and affect your body functions and health.

d. the study of hormones and how they function in your body.

3. The energy in foods is measured in carbohydrates.
   a. true
   b. false

4. The majority of your daily calories should come from
   a. fats.
   b. minerals.
   c. vitamins.
   d. carbohydrates.
   e. water.

5. Which nutrients may help enzymes function in your body?
   a. carbohydrates
   b. vitamins
   c. minerals
   d. all of the above
   e. b and c only

6. Everyone needs to take vitamin and mineral supplements to be healthy.
   a. true
   b. false

7. Which of the following are overarching goals for *Healthy People 2020*?
   a. attain high-quality, longer lives free of preventable disease, disability, injury, and premature death
   b. achieve health equity, eliminate disparities, and improve the health of all groups
   c. create social and physical environments that promote good health for all
   d. all of the above

8. The first step in the scientific method is to
   a. make observations and ask questions.
   b. form a hypothesis.
   c. do an experiment.
   d. develop a theory.

9. You decide to have your diet assessed and be counseled by a nutrition professional because you want to lose weight. Which of the following individuals would be the most credible source of information?
   a. an employee of your local health food store
   b. your personal trainer at the gym
   c. a licensed dietitian
   d. your aunt
   e. your roommate, who runs for the campus track team

10. When exploring a website that provides nutrition and health information, which of the following should you look at to assess its content?
    a. who wrote it
    b. when it was written
    c. when it was last updated
    d. a and b only
    e. a, b, and c

Answers

1. (d) Your food choices are influenced by many factors, including your ethnic background, the limited time you may have to devote to food preparation, and your emotions.

2. (c) Nutrition is about how nutrients affect your body and health. The study of genes is called genomics. Physiology is the study of how your body functions. The study of hormones and their function in your body is called endocrinology.

3. (b) False. Carbohydrates are a source of energy in your foods. The energy in your foods is measured in units called calories.

4. (d) The majority of your daily calories should come from carbohydrates. Vitamins, minerals, and water don't provide calories. Fats do contain calories, but these shouldn't be the main source of energy in your diet.

5. (e) Certain vitamins and minerals may aid enzymes in your body. Carbohydrates don't aid enzymes, but these nutrients need enzymes to be properly metabolized.

6. (b) False. Many people can meet their vitamin and mineral needs from a well-balanced diet. Those who can't should take a supplement in addition to eating a healthy diet.

7. (d) All are goals for *Healthy People 2020*.

8. (a) The scientific method begins with scientists observing and asking questions. From this step, a hypothesis follows. The scientists will then test their hypothesis using an experiment. After many experiments confirm their hypothesis, a theory will be developed.

9. (c) Unless the salesperson, personal trainer, your aunt, and your roommate are all licensed dietitians, they are not qualified to provide nutrition counseling.

10. (e) When reading nutrition and health information on the Internet, it is very important to make sure the source is qualified to provide this information. Because you also need to assess if the information is current, you should find out when it was written and if it has been or needs to be updated.

Web Resources

Examples of reliable nutrition and health websites include:

- Agricultural Research Service: www.ars.usda.gov/ba/bhnrc/ndl
- American Cancer Society: www.cancer.org
- American College of Sports Medicine: www.acsm.org
- American Diabetes Association: www.diabetes.org
- American Dietetic Association: www.eatright.org
- American Heart Association: www.heart.org/HEARTORG/
- American Institute for Cancer Research: www.aicr.org
- American Medical Association: www.ama-assn.org
- Center for Science in the Public Interest: www.cspinet.org
- Centers for Disease Control: www.cdc.gov
- Food Allergy Network: www.foodallergy.org
- Food and Drug Administration: www.fda.gov
- Food and Nutrition Information Center: www.nal.usda.gov/fnic
- National Cholesterol Education Program: www.nhlbi.nih.gov/about/ncep
- National High Blood Pressure Program: www.nhlbi.nih.gov/hbp
- National Institutes of Health: www.nih.gov
- National Osteoporosis Foundation: www.nof.org
- Shape Up America!: www.shapeup.org
- Tufts University Health & Nutrition Newsletter: www.tuftshealthletter.com
- U.S. Department of Agriculture: www.nutrition.gov
- Vegetarian Resource Group: www.vrg.org
- Weight Control Information Network: www.win.niddk.nih.gov/index.htm

Answers to Myths and Misperceptions

1. **True.** There are many outside factors that stimulate and motivate you to eat. To find out what they are, turn to page 5.

2. **True.** Heart disease is the leading cause of death among Americans. The good news is that your diet can play an important role in preventing it. For more information, turn to page 8.

3. **False.** Carbohydrates and fat provide energy, but vitamins are not an energy source. They do play important roles in helping your body use both carbohydrates and fat. To find out more, turn to page 10.

4. **True.** Calories are the measure of energy in foods. Turn to page 10.

5. **True.** Although water is often overlooked as an essential nutrient, it shouldn't be. To learn about the important roles water plays in your body, turn to page 11.

6. **False.** A supplement can augment a healthy diet, but it can't replace it. To find out why, turn to page 11.

7. **False.** Although lean meats, poultry, and fish are excellent sources of protein, they don't contain fiber. To find out how to get your fill of fiber, turn to page 12.

8. **True.** Shocked? Americans spend an enormous amount of money shopping for supplements. Turn to page 13.

9. **False.** Currently, obesity is at epidemic proportions in the United States, and it isn't just affecting adults. Turn to page 14 for more information.

10. **False.** Anyone can call himself or herself a nutritionist. To find out whose advice you can trust, turn to page 20.

2

True or False?

1. The **Dietary Reference Intakes** for vitamins and minerals tell you how much of each nutrient you need to eat to avoid a deficiency. **TF** p. 32

2. To be healthy, you should be **physically active** twice a week. **TF** p. 36

3. If you follow the advice in the *Dietary Guidelines for Americans* you can reduce your risk of dying from heart disease, high blood pressure, and diabetes mellitus. **TF** p. 36

4. The concepts of proportionality, moderation, and variety are all depicted in **MyPlate**. **TF** p. 39

5. You can use your hands to estimate a single **portion size** of many foods. **TF** p. 42

6. **Solid fats** should be increased in your diet. **TF** p. 42

7. All packaged foods must contain a **food label**. **TF** p. 48

8. A **nutrient claim** describes how much of that nutrient is in one serving of the food. **TF** p. 52

9. A **health claim** must state the beneficial component that the food contains and the disease or condition that it can improve. **TF** p. 52

10. **Functional foods** can cure a variety of health problems. **TF** p. 58

See page 63 for answers to these Myths and Misperceptions.

Tools for Healthy Eating

Jessie, a 21-year-old biology major, has been told by her doctor to watch her sodium intake so as to keep her borderline high blood pressure from becoming full-fledged high blood pressure (hypertension). Although Jessie takes care to make sodium-conscious food choices at her meals, she also likes to microwave a mug of canned soup in her dorm room at night. Since the soups usually contain lots of meat and vegetables, Jessie assumes that they're a healthy choice. However, if she looked at the labels, she might be surprised to discover that her frequent soup snacks are providing more sodium than her meals.

Would it surprise you to learn that Jessie's canned soup habit has her consuming too much sodium? What tools could she use to monitor the sodium content of her foods, and reduce her overall intake? In this chapter, we'll discuss the various guidelines that exist to help you construct a healthy diet, as well as the tools, including food guidance systems and food labels, you can use to make the best food choices. At first, deciphering the information on the food label might seem confusing. But once you've cracked the code, you'll be able to confidently decide which foods to buy and which to leave on the store shelf.

Chapter Objectives

What Is Healthy Eating and What Tools Can Help?

Healthy eating involves the key principles of balance, variety, and moderation. As a student, you are probably familiar with these principles from other areas of your life. Think about how you balance your time between work, school, and your family and friends. You engage in a variety of activities to avoid being bored, and you enjoy each in moderation, since spending too much time on one activity (such as working) would reduce the amount of time you could spend on others (such as studying, socializing, or sleeping). An unbalanced life soon becomes unhealthy and unhappy.

Likewise, your diet must be balanced, varied, and moderate in order to be healthy.

➤ A balanced diet includes healthy proportions of all nutrients. For instance, a student subsisting largely on bread, bagels, muffins, crackers, chips, and cookies might be eating too much carbohydrate and fat but too little protein, vitamins, and minerals.

➤ A varied diet includes many different foods. A student who habitually chooses the same foods for breakfast, lunch, and dinner is not likely to be consuming the wide range of phytochemicals, fiber, and other benefits that a more varied diet could provide.

➤ A moderate diet provides adequate amounts of nutrients and energy. Both crash diets and overconsumption are immoderate.

In short, you need to consume a variety of foods, some more moderately than others, and balance your food choices to meet your nutrient and health needs.

A diet that lacks variety and is unbalanced can cause **undernutrition,** a state in which you are not meeting your nutrient needs. If you were to consume only grains like white bread and pasta, and avoid other foods such as milk products, fruits, vegetables, and meats, your body wouldn't get enough fiber, calcium, protein, and other important nutrients. You would eventually become **malnourished.**

In contrast, **overnutrition** occurs when a diet provides too much of a nutrient such as iron, which can be toxic in high amounts, or too many calories, which can lead

Figure 2.1
The science-based DRIs serve as the basis for information found in the *Dietary Guidelines*, MyPlate, and the Nutrition Facts panel.

to obesity. A person who is overnourished can also be malnourished. For example, a person can be overweight on a diet laden with less nutritious snack foods and sweets—foods that should be eaten in moderation—because he or she is taking in more calories than needed. These foods often displace more nutrient-rich choices, leaving the person malnourished.

Fortunately, the United States government provides several tools that can help you avoid both under- and overnutrition, including:

> The *Dietary Reference Intakes (DRIs)*, which provide recommendations regarding your nutrient needs
> The *Dietary Guidelines for Americans*, which provide broad dietary and lifestyle advice
> *MyPlate*, part of the ChooseMyPlate.gov web-based initiative, which is designed to help you eat healthfully and implement the recommendations in the DRIs and the advice in the *Dietary Guidelines*. MyPlate illustrates the five food groups using a friendly, mealtime visual of a place setting.
> The *Nutrition Facts panel* on food labels contains the Daily Values, and can help you decide which foods to buy.

Together, these tools help you plan a balanced, moderate, and varied diet that meets your nutrient and health needs (**Figure 2.1**).

Let's look at each of these tools, beginning with the DRIs.

The Take-Home Message A healthy diet is balanced, moderate, and varied. The United States government provides several tools to assist you in planning a healthy diet. These include the Dietary Reference Intakes, the *Dietary Guidelines for Americans*, and ChooseMyPlate.gov, the focal point for a multi-level, web-based initiative that includes the MyPlate food guidance system.

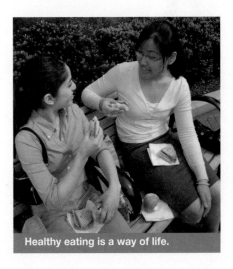

Healthy eating is a way of life.

undernutrition A state of inadequate nutrition whereby a person's nutrient and/or calorie needs aren't met through the diet.

malnourished The long-term outcome of consuming a diet that doesn't meet nutrient needs.

overnutrition A state of excess nutrients and calories in the diet.

What Are the Dietary Reference Intakes?

The **Dietary Reference Intakes (DRIs)** are specific reference values for each nutrient issued by the United States' National Academy of Sciences' Institute of Medicine. The DRIs are the specific amounts of each nutrient that one needs to consume to maintain good health, prevent chronic diseases, and avoid unhealthy excesses.[1] The Institute of Medicine periodically organizes committees of U.S. and Canadian scientists and health experts to update these recommendations based on the latest scientific research.

DRIs Tell You How Much of Each Nutrient You Need

Since the 1940s, the Food and Nutrition Board, part of the Institute of Medicine, has recommended amounts of essential nutrients needed daily to prevent a deficiency and promote good health. Because nutrient needs change with age, and because needs are different for men and women, different sets of recommendations were developed for each nutrient based on an individual's age and gender. In other words, a teenager may need more of a specific nutrient than a 55-year-old (and vice versa) and women need more of certain nutrients during pregnancy and lactation, so they all have different DRIs. Since the 1940s the DRIs have been updated ten times.

In the 1990s, nutrition researchers identified expanded roles for many nutrients. Though nutrient deficiencies were still an important issue, research suggested that higher amounts of some nutrients could play a role in disease prevention. Also, as consumers began using more dietary supplements and fortified foods, committee members grew concerned that excessive consumption of some nutrients might be as unhealthy as, or even more dangerous than, not consuming enough. Hence, the Food and Nutrition Board convened a variety of committees between 1997 and 2004 to take on the enormous task of reviewing the research on vitamins, minerals, carbohydrates, fats, protein, water, and other substances such as fiber and developing the current DRI reference values for all the nutrients. As research evolves, changes are made in the DRIs.

DRIs Encompass Several Reference Values

The DRIs comprise five reference values: Estimated Average Requirement (EAR), Recommended Dietary Allowance (RDA), Adequate Intake (AI), the Tolerable Upper Intake Level (UL), and the Acceptable Macronutrient Distribution Range (AMDR) (**Figure 2.2**). Each of these values is unique, and serves a different need in planning a healthy diet. It may seem like a lot to remember, but you will use only the RDA or AI (not both), the AMDR, and the UL to assess whether your diet is meeting your nutrient needs. The EAR is the starting point in the process of determining the other values. Let's look at how the values are determined.

The DRI committee members begin by reviewing a variety of research studies to determine the **Estimated Average Requirement (EAR)** for the nutrient. They may look at studies that investigate the consequences of eating a diet too low in the nutrient and the associated side effects or physical changes that develop, as well as how

Figure 2.2 The Dietary Reference Intakes
When planning your diet, focus on the RDAs or AIs and the AMDR. Avoid consuming the UL of any nutrient.

Dietary Reference Intakes (DRIs) Reference values for the essential nutrients needed to maintain good health, to prevent chronic diseases, and to avoid unhealthy excesses.

Estimated Average Requirement (EAR) The average amount of a nutrient that is known to meet the needs of 50 percent of the individuals in a similar age and gender group.

Figure 2.3 The DRIs in Action
(a) The EAR is the average amount of a nutrient that is likely to meet the daily needs of half of the healthy individuals in a specific age and gender group. **(b)** The RDA, which is higher than the EAR, will meet the needs of approximately 97 to 98 percent of healthy individuals in a specific group. Consuming more than the RDA but less than the UL is safe for individuals. **(c)** The UL is the highest amount of a nutrient that is unlikely to pose any risk of adverse health effects even if consumed daily. As the intake of a nutrient increases above the UL, the risk of toxicity increases.

much of the nutrient should be consumed to correct the deficiency. They may also review studies that measure the amount a healthy individual absorbs, stores, and maintains daily. Additionally, they look at research studies that address the role the nutrient plays in reducing the risk of associated chronic diseases, such as heart disease. After a thorough review process, the EAR for the nutrient is determined.

The EAR is the average amount of a nutrient that is known to meet the needs of 50 percent of the individuals in a similar age and gender group (**Figure 2.3**). The EAR is a starting point to determine the amount of a nutrient individuals should consume daily for good health.

Let's use Figure 2.3 to locate the EAR for Nutrient X. As you can see from the figure, the EAR for Nutrient X is about 40 units. If the recommended reference value for Nutrient X was set at 40 units, then half of the individuals would be able to either meet or exceed their needs. However, the other 50 percent of the individuals would need more than the EAR to be healthy.

This is where the **Recommended Dietary Allowance (RDA)** comes in. The RDA is based on the EAR, but it is set higher. It represents the average amount of a nutrient that meets the needs of nearly all (97 to 98 percent) of the individuals in a similar group. The RDA for Nutrient X in Figure 2.3 is 75 units. So, by setting the reference value at 75 units, nearly all of the individuals in this group will meet their needs for this nutrient.

If there is insufficient scientific information to determine the EAR for a nutrient, the RDA can't be developed. When this happens, an **Adequate Intake (AI)** is determined instead. The AI is the next best scientific estimate of the amount of a nutrient that groups of similar individuals should consume to maintain good health.

Because consuming too much of some nutrients can be harmful, the committees developed the **Tolerable Upper Intake Level (UL)**. The UL refers to the highest amount of a nutrient that is unlikely to cause harm if the amount is consumed daily. The higher the consumption above the UL, the higher the risk of **toxicity.** You should not try to consume the UL of a nutrient. There isn't any known benefit from consuming a higher amount, and it may cause health problems.

The DRI committee also developed a range of intakes for the energy-containing nutrients, carbohydrates, proteins, and fats. These ranges are called the **Acceptable Macronutrient Distribution Ranges (AMDR)** and are as follows:

➤ Carbohydrates should comprise 45 to 65 percent of your daily calories.
➤ Fat should comprise 20 to 35 percent of your daily calories.
➤ Proteins should comprise 10 to 35 percent of your daily calories.

Recommended Dietary Allowance (RDA) The average amount of a nutrient that meets the needs of 97 to 98 percent of individuals in a similar age and gender group. The RDA is higher than the EAR.

Adequate Intake (AI) The *approximate* amount of a nutrient that groups of similar individuals are consuming to maintain good health.

Tolerable Upper Intake Level (UL) The highest amount of a nutrient that can be consumed daily without harm in a similar age and group of individuals.

toxicity The level at which exposure to a substance becomes harmful.

Acceptable Macronutrient Distribution Range (AMDR) A healthy range of intakes for the energy-containing nutrients—carbohydrates, proteins, and fats—in your diet, designed to meet your nutrient needs and help reduce the risk of chronic diseases.

Table Tips

Tip-Top Nutrition Tips

Use traffic light colors to help you vary your lunchtime veggie choices. Add tomato slices (red) to your sandwich and carrots (yellow/orange) to your tossed salad (green).

Pop a snack-pack size of light microwave popcorn for a portion-controlled whole-grain snack.

Say "so long" to the elevator and hoof it up the stairs to work some extra physical activity into your day.

To keep your sweets to a discretionary amount, read the nutrition label and stick to a single serving that is no more than about 100 calories. Note that many big bars and bags contain more than double this amount.

Plan your dinner using at least one food from each of the food groups. Add tomato-pepper salsa (fruits and vegetables) and a can of rinsed black beans (meat and beans) to your macaroni (bread) and cheese (dairy) for a complete Mexican meal.

Estimated Energy Requirement (EER) The amount of daily energy needed to maintain a healthy body weight and meet energy (calorie) needs based on age, gender, height, weight, and activity level.

Table 2.1

How Many Calories Do You Need Daily?

The amount of calories that you need daily is based upon your age, gender, and activity level.*

| | Males | | | | Females | | |
| | | Moderately | | | | | Moderately | |
Age	Sedentary	Active	Active	Age	Sedentary	Active	Active
16–18	2,400	2,800	3,200	16–18	1,800	2,000	2,400
19–20	2,600	2,800	3,000	19–20	2,000	2,200	2,400
21–25	2,400	2,800	3,000	21–25	2,000	2,200	2,400
26–30	2,400	2,600	3,000	26–30	1,800	2,000	2,400
31–35	2,400	2,600	3,000	31–35	1,800	2,000	2,200
36–40	2,400	2,600	2,800	36–40	1,800	2,000	2,200
41–45	2,200	2,600	2,800	41–45	1,800	2,000	2,200
46–50	2,200	2,400	2,800	46–50	1,800	2,000	2,200

Source: U.S. Department of Agriculture, *Dietary Guidelines for Americans*, *2010*. Available at www.health.gov/dietaryguidelines.
*These calorie levels are based on the Institute of Medicine's Estimated Energy Requirements from the *Dietary Reference Intakes: Macronutrients Report,* 2002.
Sedentary: Partaking in less than 30 minutes a day of moderate physical activity in addition to daily activities.
Moderately Active: Partaking in at least 30 minutes and up to 60 minutes a day of moderate physical activity in addition to daily activities. Active: Partaking in 60 or more minutes a day of moderate physical activity in addition to daily activities.

Consuming these nutrient types in these ranges will ensure that you meet your calorie and nutrient needs, and reduce your risk of developing chronic diseases such as heart disease and obesity.

Although dietary recommendations have been established for carbohydrate, fat, protein, vitamins, and minerals that meet the optimal intake of nutrients, no DRI has been established for your energy (calorie) intake. The method used to determine the amount of energy you need, or your **Estimated Energy Requirement (EER),** uses a different approach than the RDAs or AIs. In addition to taking into account your age and gender, the EER is calculated based on your height, weight, and activity level, and indicates the amount of energy *you* need daily to maintain energy balance. Individuals who consume more energy than they need will gain weight. Equations have been designed for men and women to provide a general estimate of energy needs. You can find the approximate amount of energy you require daily in Table 2.1. We will cover this in greater detail in Chapter 10.

How to Use the DRIs

You can use the DRIs to make healthy food choices and plan a quality diet. To meet your needs, your goal should be to meet the RDA or the AI of all nutrients, but not exceed the UL. Table 2.2 summarizes the DRIs for you. On the inside cover of your textbook, you will find the DRIs for all the nutrients that you need daily.

Each chapter in this textbook will further explain what each nutrient is; why it is important; how much, based on the DRIs, you need to consume; and how to get enough, without consuming too much, in your diet.

Whereas the DRIs were released to prevent undernutrition, the *Dietary Guidelines for Americans* were developed out of concern over the incidence of overnutrition among Americans. Let's now look at the second tool that can help you attain a healthy diet and lifestyle, the *Dietary Guidelines for Americans.*

Table 2.2

The Do's and Don'ts of the DRIs

The Reference Values and Their Meaning	When Planning Your Diet
Estimated Average Requirement (EAR)	**Don't** use this amount.
Recommended Dietary Allowance (RDA)	**Do** aim for this amount!
Adequate Intake (AI)	**Do** aim for this amount if an RDA isn't available.
Tolerable Upper Intake Level (UL)	**Don't** exceed this amount on a daily basis.
Acceptable Macronutrient Distribution Range (AMDR)	**Do** follow these guidelines regarding the percentage of carbohydrates, protein, and fat in your diet.

Source: "The Do's and Don'ts of the DRIs" from Dietary Reference Intakes: Applications in Dietary Planning by Institute of Medicine of the National Academies. Reprinted with permission from the National Academies Press. Copyright © 2003, National Academy of Sciences.

The Take-Home Message The Dietary Reference Intakes (DRIs) are specific reference values that help you determine your daily nutrient needs to maintain good health, prevent chronic diseases, and avoid unhealthy excesses. The reference values include the EAR, RDA, AI, UL, and AMDR. Try to meet your RDA or AI and consume below the UL for each nutrient daily. The EER is calculated according to your height, weight, and activity level, in addition to your age and gender.

What Are the *Dietary Guidelines for Americans?*

By the 1970s, research had shown that Americans' overconsumption of foods rich in fat, saturated fat, cholesterol, and sodium was increasing their risk for chronic diseases, such as heart disease and stroke.[2] In 1977, the U.S. government released the *Dietary Goals for Americans,* which were designed to improve the nutritional quality of Americans' diets and to try to reduce the incidence of overnutrition and its associated health problems.[3]

Amid controversy over the scientific validity of the goals, the government asked scientists to lend credence to the goals and provide dietary guidance. Their work culminated in the 1980 *Dietary Guidelines for Americans,* which emphasized eating a variety of foods to obtain a nutritionally well-balanced daily diet. Since 1990, the U.S. Department of Agriculture (USDA) and the Department of Health and Human Services (DHHS) have been mandated by law to update the guidelines every five years. The guidelines serve as one governmental voice to shape all federally funded nutrition programs in areas such as research and labeling, and to educate and guide consumers about healthy diet and lifestyle choices.[4]

The ***Dietary Guidelines for Americans, 2010*** reflect the most current nutrition and physical activity recommendations based on science for good health. They are designed to help individuals aged 2 and older improve the quality of their diet and lifestyle to lower their risk of chronic diseases and conditions, such as high blood pressure,

Dietary Guidelines for Americans Guidelines published every five years that provide dietary and lifestyle advice to healthy individuals aged 2 and older to maintain good health and prevent chronic diseases.

The *Dietary Guidelines for Americans* at a Glance

Whereas past versions of these dietary guidelines were intended for *healthy* Americans aged 2 and older, this edition was released during a time when a poor diet and the sedentary habits of Americans have become associated with chronic poor health and reduced longevity. The science-based *Dietary Guidelines for Americans, 2010* are intended for those who are 2 years of age and older, *including* those who may also be at risk for chronic diseases. The following is a short overview of the recommendations. The complete guidelines and more information are available at http://health.gov/dietaryguidelines/.

There are two overarching concepts in the *Dietary Guidelines for Americans, 2010*:

1. **Maintain calorie balance over time to achieve and sustain a healthy weight**
   The Health Concern in a Nutshell: Many Americans are in calorie imbalance, consuming more calories than they are expending daily.
   It's Recommended that You: Eat a well-balanced, calorie-appropriate diet, coupled with regular physical activity, to achieve and maintain a healthy body weight.

2. **Consume more nutrient-rich foods and beverages**
   The Health Concern in a Nutshell: Many Americans are consuming too much sodium and too many calories from solid fats (which are sources of saturated and *trans* fats), as well as added sugars and refined grains, such as those in cakes and cookies. At the same time, they are not consuming enough fiber, vitamin D, calcium, and potassium.
   It's Recommended that You: Routinely follow a healthy, well-balanced, plant-based eating pattern rich in vegetables, fruits, and whole grains. You should consume adequate amounts of lean dairy and protein-rich foods (lean meat, poultry, fish, eggs, nuts, seeds, and dried peas), along with some heart-healthy unsaturated fats. This eating pattern will help you meet nutrient needs without exceeding daily calorie needs.

There are key recommendations provided in the *Dietary Guidelines* to help you do the above:

Balance Calories to Manage Weight

➤ Prevent and/or reduce becoming overweight and/or obese through improved eating and physical activity behaviors.

➤ Control total calorie intake to manage body weight. For those overweight or obese, this means consuming fewer calories from foods and beverages.

➤ Increase physical activity and reduce the time spent in sedentary behaviors.

➤ Maintain appropriate calorie balance during each stage of life—childhood, adolescence, adulthood, pregnancy and breast-feeding, and older ages.

Foods Components to Reduce

➤ Daily sodium intake should be less than 2,300 milligrams (mg). Intake should be further reduced to 1,500 mg among people who are 51 and older, and those of any age who are African-American or

high blood cholesterol levels, diabetes mellitus, heart disease, certain cancers, and osteoporosis. These recent guidelines are different from previous reports, as they address the obesity epidemic that is occurring among Americans.[5] The feature box "The *Dietary Guidelines for Americans* at a Glance" provides an overview of the current guidelines, along with helpful dietary and lifestyle recommendations.

The final resource provided by the government to help you eat healthfully is the web-based initiative ChooseMyPlate.gov, featuring the MyPlate tool.

The Take-Home Message The *Dietary Guidelines for Americans, 2010* provide dietary and lifestyle advice to individuals aged 2 and older. The goal of the guidelines is to help individuals maintain good health and prevent chronic diseases.

have hypertension, diabetes, or chronic kidney disease. This 1,500-mg recommendation applies to about half of the U.S. population.

➤ Consume less than 10 percent of your daily calories from saturated fatty acids by replacing them with monounsaturated and polyunsaturated fatty acids.

➤ Consume less than 300 mg of dietary cholesterol daily.

➤ Keep *trans* fatty acid as low as possible by limiting foods that contain synthetic sources of *trans* fats, such as partially hydrogenated oils, and by limiting other solid fats.

➤ Reduce the calories from solid fats* and added sugars.

➤ Limit the consumption of foods that contain refined grains, and especially of refined-grain foods that contain solid fats, added sugars, and sodium.

➤ Consume alcohol in moderation, if at all—up to one drink per day for women and two drinks per day for men—and only if you are an adult of legal drinking age**.

Foods and Nutrients to Increase

In order to consume a well-balanced, healthy eating pattern that meets your daily calorie needs:

➤ Increase your vegetable and fruit intake.

➤ Eat a variety of vegetables, especially dark-green and red and orange vegetables and beans and peas.

➤ Consume at least half of all your grain choices as whole grains.

➤ Increase the intake of fat-free or low-fat milk and milk products such as milk, yogurt, cheese, or fortified soy beverages (soy milk).

➤ Choose a variety of protein foods, including seafood, lean meat and poultry, eggs, beans and peas, soy products, and unsalted nuts and seeds.

➤ Increase the amount and variety of seafood consumed by choosing seafood in place of some meat and poultry.

➤ Replace protein foods higher in solid fats with choices lower in these solid fats and calories.

➤ Use oils to replace solid fats where possible.

➤ Choose foods that provide more potassium, dietary fiber, calcium, and vitamin D. These foods include vegetables, fruits, whole grains, and milk and milk products.

Note: There are recommendations for specific groups such as women capable of being

pregnant, pregnant and breast-feeding women, and individuals who are 50 years of age and older. (See Chapters 15 and 16.)

Build Healthy Eating Patterns

➤ Select an eating pattern that meets nutrient needs over time at an appropriate calorie level.

➤ Account for all foods and beverages consumed and assess how they fit within a healthy eating pattern.

➤ Follow food safety recommendations when preparing and eating foods to reduce the risk of foodborne illness.

While the above may seem like a "mouthful," the good news is that the chapters in this textbook have been written to help you meet these dietary guidelines, *one bite at a time.*

*Solid fats are not liquid at room temperature; these contain more saturated and *trans* fatty acids. Solid fats include: butter, meat fat, coconut and palm oils, shortening, and margarine. Common food sources of solid fats include: full-fat cheese, whole milk, fatty cuts of meat, poultry skin, and many baked goods. **See Chapter 9 for additional guidance, as there are many circumstances in which individuals should avoid alcohol consumption entirely.

What Are MyPlate and ChooseMyPlate.gov?

With so many nutrient and dietary recommendations in the DRIs and the *Dietary Guidelines,* you may be wondering how to keep them straight and plan a balanced diet that meets all of your nutritional needs. Luckily, there are several carefully designed **food guidance systems** to help you select the best foods for your diet. These illustrated systems picture healthy food choices from a variety of food groups from which you can select, and show you how to proportion your food choices. Many countries have developed food guidance systems based on their food supply, cultural food preferences, and the nutritional needs of their population (**Figure 2.4**).[6]

Some researchers have also developed food guidance systems to help individuals reduce their risk of certain diseases. For example, the DASH (Dietary Approaches to Stop

food guidance systems Visual diagrams that provide a variety of food recommendations to help create a well-balanced diet.

Figure 2.4 Healthy Eating Around the World
Many countries have developed their own food guidance systems. Although these food guides look very different, they have a lot in common. They all recommend a plant-based diet with plenty of grains, fruits, and vegetables, and moderate amounts of milk products, meat, poultry, and fish. Even though the foods pictured vary to reflect the cultural preferences and foods available in each country, the overall health and nutrition messages are the same around the world.

Source: Reprinted from *Journal of the American Dietetic Association,* Vol. 102, Issue 4, J. Painter, J. Rah, and Y. Lee, "Comparison of International Food Guide Pictorial Representations," pp. 483–489, © 2002, with permission from Elsevier. www.sciencedirect .com/science/journal.

Korea

Great Britain

Canada

Portugal

Puerto Rico

Hypertension) diet is based on an eating style that has been shown to significantly lower a person's blood pressure. High blood pressure is a risk factor for heart disease and stroke. The DASH diet will be discussed in Chapter 8. The Mediterranean-style eating pattern is another food guidance system that emphasizes a plant-based diet rich in vegetables and fruits, nuts, olive oil, grains, and smaller amounts of meats and dairy. A Mediterranean-style eating pattern (discussed in Chapter 5) has been associated with a lower risk of heart disease.

MyPyramid was a food guidance system previously released by the USDA. Using a pyramid-based visual model, it depicted the recommendations in the 2005 *Dietary Guidelines for Americans.* In 2011, the USDA released the website www.ChooseMyPlate .gov and the tool MyPlate to reflect the new recommendations in the 2010 *Dietary Guidelines for Americans.*

MyPlate serves as an icon to remind consumers to eat healthfully. It depicts the five food groups using a familiar mealtime visual, a place setting

MyPlate A tool that depicts five food groups using the familiar mealtime visual of a place setting. It is part of a USDA web-based initiative to provide consumer information with a food guidance system to help you build a healthy diet based on the current *Dietary Guidelines for Americans.*

(see **Figure 2.5**). MyPlate is the focal point for a larger, web-based communication and education initiative at ChooseMyPlate.gov that provides information, tips, and tools to help you build a healthier diet based on the *Dietary Guidelines for Americans, 2010*. Also available at ChooseMyPlate.gov is an interactive food guidance system that is based on the USDA Food Patterns, which will provide you with a personalized food plan based on the latest nutrition and health recommendations. Consuming a calorie-appropriate, balanced diet that includes a variety of foods in moderation will also allow you to meet the DRIs for your nutrient needs and better manage your health and weight.

MyPlate and ChooseMyPlate.gov Emphasize Changes in Diet, Eating Behaviors, and Physical Activity

In addition to showing a variety of food groups that can make up a healthy diet, the tool MyPlate and the supporting information at ChooseMyPlate.gov promote proportionality, moderation, variety, and personalization.

As you can see from Figure 2.5, MyPlate shows a place setting split into sections, with each colored section representing one of five food groups: fruits, vegetables, grains, protein foods, and dairy. While oils are an important part of a healthy diet, they are not represented on the plate, as they are not considered a food group.

You can now easily see **proportionality** in how these food groups should dominate your diet. Half of your plate should be devoted to waist- and heart-friendly vegetables and fruit with a smaller portion for grains (preferably whole grains), and lean protein foods such as fish, skinless poultry, lean meats, dried beans, and peas. The blue circle next to the plate is a visual reminder to make sure that fat-free and low-fat dairy foods such as milk should not be forgotten at mealtimes. With the majority of Americans overweight, this shift of food proportionality on your plate can have a dramatic effect on your calorie intake. Devoting more than half of the surface of the plate to low-calorie fruits and vegetables should crowd out higher calorie grains and protein food choices. Take the following Self-Assessment to see how well-proportioned your diet is.

There are several important nutrition messages at ChooseMyPlate.gov based on the current *Dietary Guidelines*, which emphasize moderation in your diet and eating behaviors. The messages are based on three general areas of recommendation:

1. Balance Calories
   - Enjoy your food, but eat less.
   - Avoid oversized portions.
2. Foods to Increase
   - Make half your plate fruits and vegetables.
   - Make at least half your grains whole grains.
   - Switch to fat-free or low-fat (1%) milk.

Figure 2.5 MyPlate
The MyPlate icon reinforces important concepts of meal planning, healthful choices, proportionality, and moderation to be used in planning a healthful diet.

Source: U.S. Department of Agriculture. Available at www.ChooseMyPlate.gov.

proportionality The relationship of one entity to another. Vegetables and fruits should be consumed in a higher proportion than dairy and protein foods in the diet.

Does Your Diet Have Proportionality?

Answer yes or no to the following questions.

1. Are grains the main food choice at all your meals?
   Yes ☐ **No** ☐
2. Do you often forget to eat vegetables?
   Yes ☐ **No** ☐
3. Do you typically eat fewer than three pieces of fruit daily?
   Yes ☐ **No** ☐
4. Do you often have fewer than three cups of milk daily?
   Yes ☐ **No** ☐
5. Is the portion of meat, chicken, or fish the largest item on your dinner plate?
   Yes ☐ **No** ☐

Answers

If you answered yes to three or more of these questions, it is very likely that your diet lacks proportionality. This section explains how to improve your diet.

---

3. Foods to Reduce
   • Compare sodium in foods like soup, bread, and frozen meals—and choose the foods with lower numbers.
   • Drink water instead of sugary drinks.

These messages not only emphasize that you should balance your calories daily to better manage your weight but also that you should choose mostly nutrient-dense foods from each food group. **Nutrient density** refers to the amount of nutrients a food contains in relationship to the number of calories it contains. More nutrient-dense foods provide more nutrients per calorie (and in each bite) than less nutrient-dense foods, and so are better choices for meeting your DRIs without exceeding your daily calorie needs.

The foundation of your diet should be nutrient-dense foods with little solid fats and added sugars. Solid fats are solid at room temperature and contain a high percentage of heart-unhealthy saturated and/or *trans* fatty acids. Solid fats include butter, beef fat, chicken fat, pork fat (lard), stick margarine, and shortening. The fat in milk is also considered a solid fat, as it is solid at room temperature. Because of the homogenization process involved in processing milk, the solid fat is evenly dispersed and suspended in fluid milk, which masks its solid density. Saturated fat–laden coconut, palm, and palm kernel oils, as well as partially hydrogenated oils, which contain *trans* fatty acids, are also considered solid fats. Added sugars include sources such as brown sugar, corn syrup, molasses, and table sugar (you will learn about other sources in Chapter 4). Foods within each food group that contain solid fats and added sugars should be eaten in moderation because they add calories that are less nutrient dense to your diet.

Let's compare the nutrient density of two versions of the same food: a medium baked potato and an ounce of potato chips (**Figure 2.6**). Both have about the same number of calories, but the baked potato provides much more folate, potassium, and vitamin C, and is therefore much more nutrient dense, than the deep-fried chips. If you routinely choose foods with a lot of added sugar and solid fats, you will have to reduce your food intake elsewhere to compensate for the extra calories. This could cause you to displace healthier foods in your diet. If you don't adjust for these extra calories, but eat them in addition to your normal diet, you will soon experience weight gain.

In contrast to nutrient density, **energy density** refers to foods that are high in energy but low in weight or volume, such as that potato chip. A serving of deep-fried chips weighs much less than a plain baked potato, but is considerably higher in solid fats and calories. Therefore, the chip contains more calories per gram. A big, leafy green salad, on

Figure 2.6 Which Is the Healthier Way to Enjoy Your Potatoes?
While one ounce of potato chips and one medium baked potato have similar amounts of calories, their nutrient content is worlds apart. A baked potato is more nutrient dense than potato chips.

*Note: Based on the percentage of the DRI for 19–50-year-old males. All these percentages apply to females in the same age range except for vitamin C. Females have lower vitamin C needs than males, so a baked potato provides more than 20 percent of the DRI for this vitamin for women.

nutrient density The amount of nutrients per calorie in a given food. Nutrient-dense foods provide more nutrients per calorie than less nutrient-dense foods.

energy density A measurement of the calories in a food compared with the weight (grams) or volume of the food.

	Vegetables	Fruits	Grains	Protein	Dairy	Oils	
Foods with high amounts of added sugars and heart-unhealthy solid fats. These are less nutrient dense.	French fries, potato chips	Fruit canned in syrup, fruit drinks, sweetened dried fruit	Buttered popcorn, cake, cookies, donuts, pastries	Fatty cuts of meat and luncheon meats, fried chicken or fish, poultry with skin	Full-fat cheeses, fried mozzarella sticks, high-fat ice cream	Butter, hydrogenated oils	Eat **less** of these
Foods that are more nutrient dense.	Fresh, frozen and canned vegetables, dried beans and peas	Dried fruit, whole fruit, 100% fruit juice	Brown rice, bulgur, couscous, oats, pasta, popcorn, rice, whole-grain cereals, bread, crackers	Dried beans and peas, eggs, fish, lean meat, nuts, skinless poultry, seeds	Low-fat or nonfat cheese, milk or yogurt, low-fat ice cream or frozen yogurt	Vegetable oils	Eat **more** of these

Figure 2.7 Nutrient-Dense Food Choices
Nutrient-dense foods provide more nutrition per calorie and less solid fats and added sugars. Choose nutrient-dense food more often to build a well-balanced diet.

the other hand, is large in volume but low in energy density, due to its high water content. Most higher-fat foods and sweets and treats, such as fried foods and candy, are considered energy dense.

Individuals who choose low-energy-dense and high-nutrient-dense foods will generally have diets that are lower in solid fats and added sugars and higher in nutrient content. **Figure 2.7** helps you compare some nutrient-dense food choices to less healthy food choices in each food group.

Eating a variety of foods among and within the food groups highlighted in MyPlate will increase your chances of consuming all 40 of the nutrients your body needs. Because no single food or food group provides all the nutrients, a varied diet of nutrient-dense foods is the savviest strategy. **Figure 2.8** on page 42 provides tips on how to choose a variety of foods from each food group.

The interactive website ChooseMyPlate.gov is designed to help you plan a personalized food plan based on your dietary and lifestyle needs. We will discuss this in more detail later in the chapter.

Lastly, physical activity is an important component in the *Dietary Guidelines*. Being physically active helps you stay fit and reduce your risk of chronic diseases such as heart disease and cancer. Advice regarding physical activity can also be found at ChooseMyPlate.gov.

Remember, "Rome wasn't built in a day." Adopting a healthier diet and lifestyle, and changing long-term eating habits, takes time. Taking small steps of improvement every day can be less overwhelming and will ultimately be beneficial to your health.

Let's next look at the foods of each food group, and why each group is uniquely important to you.

Full-fat cheese is the number-one source of solid fats in the diets of Americans.

How to Use MyPlate and ChooseMyPlate.gov

You now know to eat a variety of nutrient-dense foods to be healthy, and that MyPlate reminds you to eat a diverse group of foods, but you may be wondering how much from each food group *you*, personally, should be eating. The ChooseMyPlate.gov interactive website will give you the exact numbers of servings to eat from each food group based on your daily calorie needs.

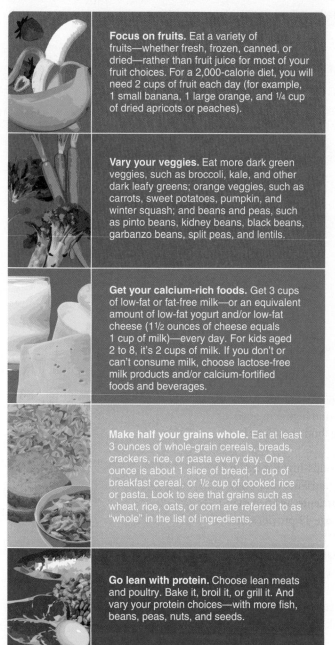

Focus on fruits. Eat a variety of fruits—whether fresh, frozen, canned, or dried—rather than fruit juice for most of your fruit choices. For a 2,000-calorie diet, you will need 2 cups of fruit each day (for example, 1 small banana, 1 large orange, and ¼ cup of dried apricots or peaches).

Vary your veggies. Eat more dark green veggies, such as broccoli, kale, and other dark leafy greens; orange veggies, such as carrots, sweet potatoes, pumpkin, and winter squash; and beans and peas, such as pinto beans, kidney beans, black beans, garbanzo beans, split peas, and lentils.

Get your calcium-rich foods. Get 3 cups of low-fat or fat-free milk—or an equivalent amount of low-fat yogurt and/or low-fat cheese (1½ ounces of cheese equals 1 cup of milk)—every day. For kids aged 2 to 8, it's 2 cups of milk. If you don't or can't consume milk, choose lactose-free milk products and/or calcium-fortified foods and beverages.

Make half your grains whole. Eat at least 3 ounces of whole-grain cereals, breads, crackers, rice, or pasta every day. One ounce is about 1 slice of bread, 1 cup of breakfast cereal, or ½ cup of cooked rice or pasta. Look to see that grains such as wheat, rice, oats, or corn are referred to as "whole" in the list of ingredients.

Go lean with protein. Choose lean meats and poultry. Bake it, broil it, or grill it. And vary your protein choices—with more fish, beans, peas, nuts, and seeds.

Know the limits on fats, salt, and sugars. Read the Nutrition Facts label on foods. Look for foods low in saturated fats and *trans* fats. Choose and prepare foods and beverages with little salt (sodium) and/or added sugars (caloric sweeteners).

Figure 2.8 Mix Up Your Choices within Each Food Group

Source: USDA Consumer Brochure, Finding Your Way to a Healthier You. Based on the *Dietary Guidelines for Americans*.

Recall that your calorie needs (your EER) are based upon your age and gender (two factors beyond your control) and your activity level (a factor you can control). As you just read, the more active you are, the more calories you burn to fuel your activities, and the more calories you can (and need to) consume in foods.

At the website, you will enter your age, gender, and activity level. Based on this information, your daily calorie needs will be determined and your personalized eating plan, specifying the exact number of servings from each of the five food groups, will be provided. With this information, you can plan your meals and snacks for the day. If you cannot go to the website, you can obtain similar information by using Tables 2.1 and 2.3 in this chapter. Let's use the tables to obtain your recommendations.

The first step in creating your personalized daily food plan is to figure out how many calories you should be eating daily. To do this, you need to find out how active you are. If you participate in activities such as water aerobics, play doubles tennis, enjoy ballroom dancing, garden at home, or walk briskly, you are likely moderately active. You could consider yourself vigorously active if, for example, you race-walk, jog, run, swim laps, play singles tennis, or bicycle 10 miles per hour or faster. Based on these examples, are you moderately or vigorously active? Refer back to Table 2.1 on page 34 for the number of calories you need based on your activity level, age, and gender. When you know the number of calories you need daily, Table 2.3 will tell you how many servings from each food group you should consume to healthfully obtain those calories. This is the equivalent of *your* personalized daily food plan.

Let's say that you are a moderately active female who needs 2,000 calories daily. To healthfully meet this level, you should consume each day:

➤ 6 servings from the grains group
➤ 2½ cups of dark green, orange, starchy, and other vegetables, and some legumes
➤ 2 cups of fruits
➤ 3 cups of fat-free or low-fat milk and yogurt
➤ 5½ ounces of lean meat, poultry, and fish or the equivalent in meat alternatives such as beans
➤ You should also add 6 teaspoons (3 tablespoons) of vegetable oils to your diet over the course of the day.

If you are having difficulty figuring out what 1 cup of vegetables, 3 ounces of meat, or 1 tablespoon of salad dressing looks like, use **Figure 2.9**. It provides an easy way to eyeball your serving sizes. Keep in mind that if you consistently eat oversized portions that are larger than those suggested in your daily food plan, you will consume too many calories and may gain weight. The feature box "When a Portion *Isn't* a Portion" on page 46 takes a look at how portion sizes have changed over the years, and how portion distortion can adversely affect our health.

If all of your food selections are low in solid fat and added sugars, the above menu will provide a total of about 1,740 calories. This means that, after meeting your nutrient requirements, you have a maximum of about 260 of your 2,000 calories left (see **Figure 2.10**). You can "spend" these calories on extra servings

Table 2.3

How Much Should You Eat from Each Food Group?

The following are suggested amounts to consume daily from each of the basic five food groups and healthy oils based on your daily calorie needs. Remember that most of your choices should contain little solid fats and added sugar.

Calorie Level	Vegetables (cups)	Fruits (cups)	Grains (oz eq)	Protein (oz eq)	Dairy (cups)	Oil (tsp)
1,600	2	1.5	5	5	3	5
1,800	2.5	1.5	6	5	3	5
2,000	2.5	2	6	5.5	3	6
2,200	3	2	7	6	3	6
2,400	3	2	8	6.5	3	7
2,600	3.5	2	9	6.5	3	8
2,800	3.5	2.5	10	7	3	8
3,000	4	2.5	10	7	3	10
3,200	4	2.5	10	7	3	11

Vegetables: Includes all fresh, frozen, canned, and dried vegetables, and vegetable juices. In general, 1 cup of raw or cooked vegetables or vegetable juice, or 2 cups of raw leafy greens, is considered 1 cup from the vegetable group.
Fruits: Includes all fresh, frozen, canned, and dried fruits, and fruit juices. In general, 1 cup of fruit or 100% fruit juice, or 1/2 cup of dried fruit, is considered 1 cup from the fruit group.
Grains: Includes all foods made with wheat, rice, oats, cornmeal, or barley, such as bread, pasta, oatmeal, breakfast cereals, tortillas, and grits. In general, 1 slice of bread, 1 cup of ready-to-eat cereal, or ½ cup of cooked rice, pasta, or cooked cereal is considered 1 ounce equivalent (oz eq) from the grains group. *At least half of all grains consumed should be whole grains such as whole-wheat bread, oats, or brown rice.*
Protein: In general, 1 ounce of lean meat, poultry, or fish, 1 egg, 1 tablespoon peanut butter, ¼ cup cooked dry beans, or ½ ounce of nuts or seeds is considered 1 ounce equivalent (oz eq) from the protein foods group.
Dairy: Includes all fat-free and low-fat milk, yogurt, and cheese. In general, 1 cup of milk or yogurt, 1½ ounces of natural cheese, or 2 ounces of processed cheese is considered 1 cup from the dairy group.
Oils: Includes vegetable oils such as canola, corn, olive, soybean, and sunflower oil, fatty fish, nuts, avocados, mayonnaise, salad dressings made with oils, and soft margarine.
Source: U.S. Department of Agriculture, www.ChooseMyPlate.gov.

of foods such as grains, fruits, and/or vegetables, or on occasion, on a food such as a sweet or dessert that has added solid fats or added sugars. The calorie levels and distribution of food groups in daily food plans are calculated using the leanest food choices with no added sugars. So if you pour whole milk (high in solid fats) over your sweetened cereal (added sugars) instead of using skim milk (fat free and low in solid fats) to drench your shredded wheat (no added sugars), you will have added a fair amount of calories from solid fats and added sugars. As you can see from Table 2.4, your food choices could quickly provide less healthy calories from solid fats and added sugars and cause your diet to be less nutrient rich per bite.

Table 2.4

Choose Right!

As you can see, your daily food plan could provide a fair amount of solid fats and added sugars, depending on your food selections.

Choosing . . .	Over . . .	Will Cost You
Whole milk (1 cup)	Fat-free milk (1 cup)	65 calories of solid fats
Roasted chicken thigh with skin (3 oz)	Roasted chicken breast, skinless (3 oz)	70 calories of solid fats
Glazed donut, yeast type (3¾" diameter)	English muffin (1 muffin)	165 calories of sold fats and added sugars
French fries (1 medium order)	Baked potato (1 medium)	299 calories of solid fats
Regular soda (1 can, 12 fl oz)	Diet soda (1 can, 12 fl oz)	150 calories of added sugars

Source: U.S. Department of Agriculture, MyPyramid: How Do I Count the Discretionary Calories I Eat? Available at www.ChooseMyPlate.gov.

A woman's palm is approximately 3 ounces of cooked meat, chicken, or fish

a

A woman's fist is about 1 cup of pasta or vegetables (a man's fist is the size of about 2 cups)

b

About 1 tablespoon of vegetable oil

c

Figure 2.9 What's a Serving? Eat with Your Hands!
Your hands can guide you in estimating portion sizes.

Let's now use these recommended amounts of servings from each food group and plan a 2,000-calorie menu. **Figure 2.11** shows how servings from the various food groups can create well-balanced meals and snacks throughout the day.

Although this particular menu is balanced and the foods are nutrient dense, it is unlikely that every day will be this ideal. The good news is that your nutrient needs are averaged over several days, or a week, of eating. If one day you eat insufficient servings of one food group or a specific nutrient, you can make up for it the next day. For example, let's say that you don't eat enough fruit one day but do eat an extra serving of grains. The next day you can adjust your diet by cutting back on your grain servings and adding an extra serving of fruit.

If the foods at your meals are sometimes mixed dishes that contain a combination of foods, such as pizza, then they probably contribute servings to more than one food group. Table 2.5 provides examples of foods that contribute servings from multiple groups.

Now that you know what constitutes a healthy diet, the next step is to go food shopping. As you shop, you'll want to make sure you know the nutrient and calorie contents of the foods you buy. The food label will give you this information, and more.

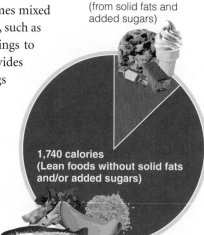

260 calories (from solid fats and added sugars)

1,740 calories (Lean foods without solid fats and/or added sugars)

2,000 total daily calories

Figure 2.10 How Solid Fats and Added Sugars Fit into a Healthy Diet
If you select mostly nutrient-dense, lean foods that contain few solid fats and added sugars, you may have leftover calories to "spend" on extra helpings or a small sweet dessert.

Table 2.5

A Combination of Good Food

Many of the foods you eat are probably mixed dishes that contain servings from multiple food groups. The following list should help you estimate the servings from each food group for some popular food items. Because the preparation process can vary greatly among recipes, these are only estimates.

Food and Sample Portion	Vegetable Group (cups)	Fruit Group (cups)	Grains Group (oz eq)	Protein Group (oz eq)	Dairy Group (cups)	Estimated Total Calories
Cheese pizza, thin crust (1 slice from medium pizza)	⅛	0	1	0	½	215
Macaroni and cheese (1 cup, made from packaged mix)	0	0	2	0	½	260
Bean and cheese burrito (1)	⅛	0	2½	2	1	445
Chicken fried rice (1 cup)	¼	0	1½	1	0	270
Large cheeseburger	0	0	2	3	⅓	500
Turkey sub sandwich (6 inch)	½	0	2	2	¼	320
Peanut butter and jelly sandwich (1)	0	0	2	2	0	375
Apple pie (1 slice)	0	¼	2	0	0	280

Source: U.S. Department of Agriculture, Mixed Dishes in MyPyramid. Available at www.ChooseMyPlate.gov.

	Vegetables	Fruits	Grains	Protein	Dairy	Oils
Breakfast		Banana, 1 small Orange juice, 1 cup	Bran flakes, 1 cup Whole-wheat English muffin, ½		Fat-free milk, 1 cup	Soft margarine, 1 tsp
Lunch	Diced celery, 1 tbs Romaine lettuce, ½ cup Tomatoes, 2 slices	Pear, 1 medium	Whole-wheat bread, 2 slices	Tuna (packed in water), 2.5 oz	Fat-free milk, 1 cup	Mayonnaise, 2 tsp
Dinner	Baked sweet potato, 1 large Peas and onions, ½ cup Leafy green salad, 1 cup		Dinner rolls, 2 1 oz each	Roasted chicken breast (boneless and skinless), 3 oz		Soft margarine, 1 tsp Sunflower oil, 3 tsp
Snack		Dried apricots, ¼ cup			Low-fat vanilla yogurt, 1 cup	

Figure 2.11 A Healthy Daily Food Plan
A variety of foods from each group creates a well-balanced diet.

The Take-Home Message MyPlate depicts the five food groups using the familiar mealtime visual of a place setting. It is part of the USDA web-based initiative at ChooseMyPlate.gov, providing information, a food guidance system, and a personalized daily food plan to help you build a healthy diet based on the 2010 *Dietary Guidelines for Americans*. The concepts of nutrient density and energy density refer to the amount of nutrients per bite of food and the number of calories per gram of food. You want to consume nutrient-dense foods fruits, vegetables, whole grains, and lean dairy and protein foods, but limit energy-dense foods which provide calories from solid fats and added sugars but little nutrition. Daily physical activity is encouraged to better manage your weight and health.

When a Portion *Isn't* a Portion

What is a portion of pasta? The answer depends on who is serving you the pasta. A **portion** is the amount of food eaten at one sitting. At home, a portion of pasta would be the amount that you heap on your plate. In a restaurant, it's the amount that they serve you, which can vary enormously among eating establishments.

On the other hand, the FDA defines a **serving size** as a standard amount of food that is customarily consumed. The FDA groups foods together into similar categories and standardizes the serving sizes of the foods within each group. These reference serving sizes are used on the Nutrition Facts panel of the food label. For example, the serving size for pasta is one cup, no matter what brand of pasta you purchase. Standardizing serving sizes among similar foods not only allows for consistency when choosing foods in the supermarket, but also helps the consumer get a ballpark idea of what a typical serving should be.

However, when following the online MyPlate recommendations, the portion size for pasta is only half a cup. Why the difference between the food label and this tool for healthy eating? The MyPlate materials set portion sizes based on many

Comparison of Portion Sizes of Common Foods

Food	Typical Portion	Recommended Serving Size	FDA Label
Cooked pasta	2.9 cups	0.5 cup	1.0 cup
French fries	5.3 oz	10 fries	2.5 oz
Bagel	4.4 oz	1.0 oz	2.0 oz
Muffin	6.5 oz	1.5 oz	2.0 oz
Cookie, chocolate chip	4.0 oz	0.5 oz	1.1 oz

Source: Adapted from L. R. Young and M. Nestle, "Expanding Portion Sizes in the U.S. Marketplace: Implications for Nutrition Counseling," *Journal of the American Dietetic Association* 103 (2003): 231–234.

different factors, one of which is the nutrient and calorie content of the foods in each group. All the foods in the grain group, which contains foods such as pasta, bread, and rice, provide similar amounts of nutrients and calories. The calories in half a cup of pasta are similar to the calories of the other foods in the group, such as a slice of bread.[1]

As you can see from the table, most times, the portions of the foods that you eat don't coincide with the standard serving size on the food label or the portion sizes recommended. A generous helping of

A Few Words About the Exchange Lists

The **Exchange Lists for Meal Planning** were designed in 1950 to give people with diabetes a structured eating plan. The lists are still in use. The Exchange Lists group foods together according to their carbohydrate, protein, and fat composition and provide specific portion sizes for each food. This assures that each food in the group contributes a similar amount of calories per serving.

Some weight-loss programs have adopted a similar meal planning tool to help their members manage their weight by controlling the number of calories that they consume. Because of the similarity of the foods within each group, foods can be exchanged or swapped with each other at meals and snacks. This flexible meal plan is a useful tool to control calorie, carbohydrate, protein, and fat intakes. Appendix B provides more information on the Exchange Lists.

Exchange Lists for Meal Planning A grouping of foods, in specific portions, according to their carbohydrate, protein, and fat composition to ensure that each food in the group contributes a similar amount of calories per serving.

cooked pasta that spills over the edge of a plate is probably equal to about 3 cups, which is triple the amount listed on the food label and six times the recommended serving size.

How Have Portion Sizes Changed?

The restaurant industry has appealed to your desire to get the most food for your money by expanding restaurant portion sizes, especially of inexpensive foods, such as potatoes and coffee.[2] When McDonalds first introduced french fries in 1954, the standard serving weighed 2.4 ounces. Although a small 2.5-ounce size (230 calories) is available on the menu today, you can also choose the medium french fries weighing 4.1 ounces (380 calories) or the large at 5.4 ounces (500 calories). Twenty years ago, a cup of coffee was 8 ounces and a mere 45 calories with added milk and sugar. Today, consumers enjoy 16-ounce lattes on their way to work, to the tune of 350 calories.[3] The difference in costs to the restaurants for the larger sizes is minuscule compared with the perceived "value" of the larger portion to the consumers.[4] Customers will frequent a restaurant more often if they think they are getting a bargain for their buck.

Unfortuantely, from a health standpoint, research shows that even slight changes in the portion sizes of foods can lead to increased calorie intake and weight gain.[5] As you have read, being overweight increases the risk of developing heart disease, diabetes, joint problems, and even some types of cancers.[6] Downsizing your portions could downsize your health risks.

Here are some tips to help you control your portion sizes:

Controlling Portion Size

When You Are:	Do This:
At Home	Measure your food until you develop an "eye" for correct portion sizes.
	Use smaller plates so portions appear larger.
	Plate your food at the counter before sitting down at the table or in front of the television.
	Store leftover foods in portion-controlled containers.
	Don't eat snacks directly from the box or bag; measure a portion first, then eat only that amount.
	Cook smaller quantities of food so you don't pick at the leftovers.
Eating Out	Ask for half orders when available.
	Order an appetizer as your main entrée.
	Don't be compelled to "clean your plate"; stop eating when you're full and take the rest home.
Food Shopping	Divide a package of snacks into individual portion sizes and consume only that amount at any one sitting.
	Be aware of the number of servings in a package; read the labels.
	Buy foods in pre-portioned servings such as a 1-ounce sliced cheese or snack and 100-calorie microwave popcorn.

The Take-Home Message The Exchange Lists for meal planning group foods according to their macronutrient content and are used to plan diets for individuals with diabetes and in some weight-loss programs.

What Is a Food Label and Why Is It Important?

Imagine walking down the supermarket aisle and finding that all the foods on the shelves are packaged in plain cardboard boxes and unmarked aluminum cans. How would you know if a brown box contained one pound of pasta or 100 dog biscuits? Do the blank cans hold chicken noodle soup or crushed pineapple?

Food labels don't just make food shopping easier, they also serve important functions that make them helpful tools for anyone who wants to eat a healthy diet. First and foremost, they tell you what's inside the package. Second, they contain a Nutrition Facts panel, which identifies the calories and nutrients in a serving of the food. Third, they list Daily Values (DVs), which help you determine how those calories and nutrients will fit into your overall diet.

The Food Label Tells You What's in the Package

To help consumers make informed food choices, the Food and Drug Administration (FDA) regulates the labeling of all packaged foods in the United States.[7] Currently, the FDA has mandated that every packaged food be labeled with:[8]

- The name of the food
- The net weight of the food (the weight of the food in the package, excluding the weight of the package or packing material)
- The name and address of the manufacturer or distributor
- A list of ingredients in descending order by weight, with the heaviest item listed first
- Nutrition information, which lists total calories, calories from fat, total fat, saturated fat, *trans* fats, cholesterol, sodium, total carbohydrate, dietary fiber, sugars, vitamin A, vitamin C, calcium, and iron
- Serving sizes that are uniform among similar products, which allows for easier comparison shopping by the consumer
- An indication of how a serving of the food fits into an overall daily diet
- Uniform definitions for descriptive label terms such as "light" and "fat-free"
- Health claims that are accurate and science based, if made about the food or one of its nutrients
- The presence of any of eight common allergens that might be present in the food, including milk, eggs, fish, shellfish, tree nuts (cashews, walnuts, almonds, etc.), peanuts, wheat, and soybeans

Very few foods are exempt from carrying a Nutrition Facts panel on the label. Such foods include plain coffee and tea; some spices, flavorings, and other foods that don't provide a significant amount of nutrients; deli items, bakery foods, and other ready-to-eat foods that are prepared and sold in retail establishments; restaurant meals; and foods produced by small businesses (companies that have total sales of less than $500,000).[9]

Compare the two food labels in **Figure 2.12**. Note that the amount and type of nutrition information on the 1925 box of cereal is vague and less informative than the more recent version, which meets the FDA's current labeling requirements. Whereas raw fruits and vegetables and fresh fish typically don't have a label, these foods fall under the FDA's voluntary, point-of-purchase nutrition information program. Under the guidelines of this program, at least 60 percent of a nationwide sample of grocery stores must post the nutrition information of the most commonly eaten fruits, vegetables, and fish near where the foods are sold.[10] Nutrition labeling is mandatory for meat and poultry, which is regulated by the USDA. Meat and poultry items that are prepared and sold at the supermarket, such as take-out cooked chicken, do not have a nutrition label.[11]

eLearn

Virtual Food Label Fun

Take this virtual shopping trip challenge to see how food-label savvy you really are. Visit www.accessdata.fda.gov/videos/CFSAN/HWM/hwmintro.cfm for some comparison-shopping fun!

The Food Label Can Help You Make Healthy Food Choices

Suppose you're in the dairy aisle of a supermarket trying to select a carton of milk. You want to watch your fat intake, so you have narrowed your choices to reduced-fat 2% milk or nonfat milk. How do they compare in terms of calories, fat, and other nutrients per serving? How do you decide which is more healthful? The answer is simple: Look at the labels. All the information that you need to make a smart choice is provided on one area of the label, the **Nutrition Facts panel.**

On the Label: The Nutrition Facts Panel

The Nutrition Facts panel provides a nutritional snapshot of the food inside a package. By law, the panel must list the following per serving of the food:

- ➤ Calories and calories from fat
- ➤ Total fat, saturated fat, and *trans* fat
- ➤ Cholesterol
- ➤ Sodium
- ➤ Total carbohydrate, dietary fiber, and sugars
- ➤ Protein
- ➤ Vitamin A, vitamin C, calcium, and iron

If an additional nutrient, such as vitamin E or vitamin B_{12}, has been added, or if the product makes a claim about a nutrient, then that nutrient must also be listed. Other nutrients, such as additional vitamins and minerals, can be listed by the manufacturer on a voluntary basis. The majority of the packaged foods you purchase will contain this nutrition information.

The **Nutrition Facts panel** lists standardized serving sizes, specific nutrients, and shows how a serving of the food fits into a healthy diet by stating its contribution to the percentage of the Daily Value for each nutrient. The old cereal box doesn't contain this information.

The **name** of the product must be displayed on the front label.

The **ingredients** must be listed in descending order by weight. This format is missing in the old box. Whole-grain wheat is the predominant ingredient in the current cereal box.

The **net weight** of the food in the box must now be located at the bottom of the package.

Let's learn how to decipher the Nutrition Facts panel (**Figure 2.13**). At the top of the panel is the serving size. By law, the serving size must be listed both by weight in grams (less useful to you) and in common household measures, such as cups and ounces (more useful to you). Because serving sizes are standardized among similar food products, you can compare one brand of macaroni and cheese with a different brand to assess which one better meets your needs.

The rest of the information on the panel is based on the listed serving size (in this case, one cup) of the food. For example, if you ate two servings (two cups) of this macaroni and cheese, which is the number of servings in the entire box, you would double the nutrient information on the label to calculate the calories as well as the fat and other nutrients. The servings-per-container information is particularly useful for portion control.

Below the serving size is listed the calories per serving. The calories from fat give you an idea of what proportion of the food's calories comes from fat. In this box of macaroni and cheese, 110 out of a total of 250 calories—that is, nearly half—are from fat.

Next are the nutrients that you should limit or add to your diet. Americans typically eat too much fat, including saturated fat, *trans* fat, and cholesterol, and too

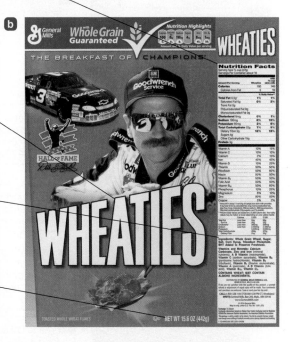

Figure 2.12 Out with the Old and In with the New
(a) A cereal box from the 1920s carried vague nutrition information. **(b)** Today, manufacturers must adhere to strict labeling requirements mandated by the FDA.

Nutrition Facts panel The area on the food label that provides a uniform listing of specific nutrients obtained in one serving of the food.

Figure 2.13 Understanding the Nutrition Facts Panel

Source: Center for Food Safety and Applied Nutrition, How to Understand and Use the Nutrition Facts Label. 2009.

a Serving sizes are standardized, making comparison shopping easier.

b Calories per serving are listed as well as the number of servings in the box.

c This section contains nutrients that should be limited in your diet.

d This section contains dietary components and nutrients most individuals need more of in their diets.

e Daily Values (DV) are general reference values.

f The footnotes provide a summary of the DV for a 2,000-calorie and a 2,500-calorie diet.

g The % DV can tell you if a food is high or low in a nutrient or dietary substance.

Daily Values (DVs) Established reference levels of nutrients, based on a 2,000-calorie diet, that are used on food labels.

much sodium. In contrast, they tend to fall short in dietary fiber, vitamins A and C, and iron. These are on the label to remind you to make sure to eat foods rich in these substances. The Nutrition Facts panel can be your best shopping guide when identifying and choosing foods that are low in the nutrients you want to limit (like saturated fat) and high in the nutrients that you need to eat in higher amounts (like fiber).

Are you wondering what determines if a food contains a "high" or "low" amount of a specific nutrient? That's where the Daily Values come into play.

On the Label: The Daily Values

Unlike the DRIs, which are precise recommended amounts of each nutrient that you should eat, the **Daily Values (DVs)** listed on the Nutrition Facts panel are general reference levels for the nutrients listed on the food label. The DVs give you a ballpark idea of how the nutrients in the foods you buy fit into your overall diet.

For example, if calcium is listed at 20 percent, a serving of that food provides 20 percent of most adults' daily requirement for calcium. However, if you are under 19 years of age or older than 70, your calcium needs are higher than the reference number used on the DV. Since the DVs on the food label are based on a 2,000-calorie diet, if you need more or fewer than 2,000 calories daily, some of your DV numbers may be higher or lower than those listed on the Nutrition Facts panel.

The DVs are based on older reference levels and are not as current as the DRIs. For example, whereas the DRIs recommend an upper level of dietary sodium of no more than 2,300 milligrams (daily), the DVs use less than 2,400 milligrams as the reference level.

There are no DVs listed on the label for *trans* fat, sugars, and protein. This is because there isn't enough information available to set reference values for *trans* fat and sugars. Although there are reference values for protein, consuming adequate amounts of protein isn't a health concern for most Americans over age 4, so listing the percent of the DV for this nutrient isn't warranted on the label. The DV for protein will only be listed if the product is being marketed for children under the age of 4, such as a jar of baby food, or if a claim is made about the food, such as that it is "high in protein."[12]

If a serving provides 20 percent or more of the DV, it is considered high in that nutrient. For example, a serving of this macaroni and cheese is high in sodium (not a healthy attribute) and is also high in calcium (a healthy attribute). If you eat this entrée for lunch, you'll need to eat less sodium during the rest of the day. However, the good news is that a serving of this pasta meal also provides 20 percent of the DV for calcium.

If a nutrient provides 5 percent or less of the DV, it is considered low in that nutrient. A serving of macaroni and cheese doesn't provide much fiber, vitamin A, vitamin C, or iron. You will need to add other foods to supply these nutrients to your diet on the days that you eat macaroni and cheese.

Lastly, depending on the size of the food package, there may be a footnote at the bottom of the label. This provides a summary of the DVs for a 2,000-calorie diet as

Reduced Fat 2% Milk

Nutrition Facts
Serving Size 1 cup (236ml)
Serving Per Container 1

Amount Per Serving

Calories 120   Calories from Fat 45

	% Daily Value*
Total Fat 5g	8%
Saturated Fat 3g	15%
Trans Fat 0g	
Cholesterol 20g	7%
Sodium 120mg	5%
Total Carbohydrate 11g	4%
Dietary Fiber 0g	0%
Sugars 11g	
Protein 9g	17%

Vitamin A 10%   •   Vitamin C 4%
Calcium 30%   •   Iron 0%   •   Vitamin D 25%

* Percent Daily Values are based on a 2,000 calorie diet. Your daily values may be higher or lower depending on your calorie needs:

Nonfat Milk

Nutrition Facts
Serving Size 1 cup (236ml)
Serving Per Container 1

Amount Per Serving

Calories 80   Calories from Fat 0

	% Daily Value*
Total Fat 0g	0%
Saturated Fat 0g	0%
Trans Fat 0g	
Cholesterol Less than 5mg	0%
Sodium 120mg	5%
Total Carbohydrate 11g	4%
Dietary Fiber 0g	0%
Sugars 11g	
Protein 9g	17%

Vitamin A 10%   •   Vitamin C 4%
Calcium 30%   •   Iron 0%   •   Vitamin D 25%

* Percent Daily Values are based on a 2,000 calorie diet. Your daily values may be higher or lower depending on your calorie needs:

Figure 2.14 Using the Nutrition Facts Panel to Comparison Shop
The Nutrition Facts panel makes comparison shopping between types and brands of foods easier for the consumer.

Source: U.S. Food and Drug Administration, Center for Food Safety and Applied Nutrition, How to Understand and Use the Nutrition Facts Label. 2009.

well as a 2,500-calorie diet. This area of the panel provides you with a little "cheat sheet" to help you when you are shopping so that you don't have to memorize the values. As you can see from the footnote, you should try to keep your sodium intake to less than 2,400 milligrams daily. Since you know that this macaroni and cheese is high in sodium, providing 20 percent of the DV, or 470 milligrams, of sodium, you should try to keep the sodium in your remaining food choices during the day to less than 2,000 milligrams.

Now that you know how to read the Nutrition Facts panel, let's return to the milk question posed at the beginning of this section and use what you've learned to compare the reduced-fat 2% and nonfat milk labels in **Figure 2.14**.

Let's start at the top:

a. Both cartons have the same standardized one-cup serving, which makes the comparison easy.

b. The reduced-fat milk has 50 percent more calories than the nonfat milk; almost 40 percent of the calories in the reduced-fat milk are from fat.

c. Use the percent of the DV to assess whether the milk is considered "high" or "low" in a given nutrient. For instance, a serving of reduced-fat milk provides more than 5 percent of the DV for both total and saturated fat (as well as cholesterol), so it isn't considered "low" in these nutrients. In fact, the saturated fat provides 15 percent of the DV, which is getting close to the definition of "high" (20 percent of the DV). In contrast, the nonfat milk doesn't contain any fat, saturated fat, or cholesterol, so it appears so far to be the healthier choice.

d. However, since being low in fat doesn't necessarily mean being healthier, let's make sure that the nonfat milk is as nutritious as the reduced-fat variety. Comparing the remaining nutrients, especially calcium and vitamin D, confirms that the nonfat milk has all the vitamins and minerals that reduced-fat milk does, but with fewer calories and less fat, saturated fat, and cholesterol. In fact, both milks provide a "high" amount of calcium and vitamin D. So, when it comes to choosing milk, the nonfat version is the smarter choice.

 NutriTools

What's Missing on This Label?

Test your label know-how! Visit www.pearsonhighered.com/blake and complete this interactive NutriTools activity.

While the Nutrition Facts panel on the side or back of the package can help you make healthier food choices, some foods carry claims on their front labels that may also influence your decision to buy. Let's look at these next.

On the Label: Label Claims

In the 1980s, the savvy Kellogg Company ran an ad campaign for its fiber-rich All Bran cereal reminding the public of the National Cancer Institute's recommendation to eat low-fat, high-fiber foods, fresh fruits, and vegetables to maintain a healthy weight. According to the FDA, sales of high-fiber cereals increased over 35 percent within a year.[13] Manufacturers realized that putting nutrition and health claims on labels was effective in influencing consumer purchases. Supermarket shelves were soon crowded with products boasting various claims.

So, can you feel confident that the jar of light mayonnaise is really lighter in calories and fat than regular mayonnaise? Yes, you can. The FDA mandates that all claims on labels follow strict guidelines.

Currently, the FDA allows the use of three types of claims on food products: (1) **nutrient content claims,** (2) **health claims,** and (3) **structure/function claims.** All foods displaying these claims on the label must meet specified criteria. Let's look at each of these claims closely.

Nutrient Content Claims

A food product can make a claim about the amount of a nutrient it contains (or doesn't contain) by using descriptive terms such as *free* (fat-free yogurt), *high* (high-fiber crackers), *low* (low saturated fat cereal), *reduced* (reduced-sodium soup), and *extra lean* (extra lean ground beef) as long as it meets the strict criteria designated by the FDA. These terms can help you identify at a glance the food items that best meet your needs.

Jessie, the student with borderline high blood pressure from the beginning of this chapter, could look for low-sodium claims on labels to help limit the amount of sodium in her diet. As you may remember, Jessie enjoys a mug of hot soup during her late-night studying. But she's probably sipping more sodium than she thinks.

Look at the labels of the canned soups in **Figure 2.15.** Jessie should be looking for the "low sodium" label on her chicken soup, as that soup cannot contain more than 140 milligrams of sodium per serving. A next best choice would be the soup with the term "less sodium" on the label, which means that it must contain at least 25 percent less sodium than the regular variety. The classic can of chicken soup contains almost 900 milligrams for a serving, which is likely the same or even more sodium than Jessie consumed at dinner. Table 2.6 provides some of the most common nutrient claims on food labels, the specific criteria that each claim must meet as mandated by the FDA, and examples of food products that carry these nutrient claims.

Health Claims

Suppose you are sitting at your kitchen table eating a bowl of Cheerios in skim milk, and staring at the front of the cereal box. You notice a claim on the front of the box that states: "The soluble fiber in Cheerios, as part of a heart healthy diet, can help you lower your cholesterol." Do you recognize this as a health claim that links Cheerios with better heart health?

A health claim must contain two important components: (1) a food or a dietary compound, such as fiber, and (2) a corresponding disease or health-related condition that is associated with the claim.[14] In the Cheerios example, the soluble fiber (the dietary compound) that naturally occurs in oats has been shown to lower blood

nutrient content claims Claims on the label that describe the level or amount of a nutrient in a food product.

health claims Claims on the label that describe a relationship between a food or dietary compound and a disease or health-related condition.

structure/function claims Claims on the label that describe how a nutrient or dietary compound affects the structure or function of the human body.

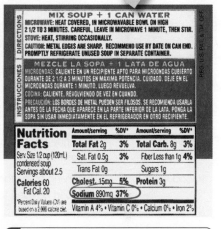

a Because this can of chicken noodle soup displays the "low sodium" nutrient claim, it can't provide more than 140 milligrams of sodium in a serving.

b This can of soup has more than 25 percent less sodium than the classic version, so the term "less" can be displayed on its label.

c The classic variety of chicken noodle soup has the most sodium per serving.

Figure 2.15 Soup's On!
Nutrient claims on the food label must meet strict FDA criteria.

cholesterol levels (the corresponding health-related condition), which can help reduce the risk of heart disease.

There are three types of health claims: (1) authorized health claims, (2) health claims based on authoritative statements, and (3) qualified health claims. The differences between them lie in the amount of supporting research and agreement among scientists about the strength of the relationship between the food or dietary ingredient and the disease or condition. See Table 2.7 for a definition of these claims and examples of each.

Structure/Function Claims
The last type of label claim is the structure/function claim, which describes how a nutrient or dietary compound affects

Cereal-box readers will read the information on the box as many as 12 times before they consume the last spoonful!

Table 2.6

What Does That Labeling Term Mean?

Nutrient	Free	Low	Reduced/Less	Light
Calories	<5 calories (cal) per serving	≤40 cal per serving	At least 25% fewer calories per serving	If the food contains 50% or more of its calories from fat, then the fat must be reduced
Fat	<0.5 grams (g) per serving	≤3 g per serving	At least 25% less fat per serving	Same as above
Saturated Fat	<0.5 g per serving	≤1 g per serving	At least 25% less saturated fat per serving	N/A
Cholesterol	<2 milligrams (mg) per serving	≤20 mg per serving	At least 25% less cholesterol per serving	N/A
Sodium	<5 mg per serving	<140 mg per serving	At least 25% less sodium per serving	If the sodium is reduced by at least 50% per serving
Sugars	<0.5 g	N/A	At least 25% less sugar per serving	N/A

Other Labeling Terms

Term	Definition
"High," "Rich in," or "Excellent source of"	The food contains 20% or more of the DV of the nutrient in a serving. Can be used to describe protein, vitamins, minerals, fiber, or potassium.
"Good source of"	A serving of the food provides 10–19% of the DV. Can be used to describe meals or main dishes.
"More," "Added," "Extra," or "Plus"	A serving of the food provides 10% of the DV. Can only be used to describe vitamins, minerals, protein, fiber, and potassium.
"Lean"	Can be used on seafood and meat that contains less than 10 g of fat, 4.5 g or less of saturated fat, and less than 95 mg of cholesterol per serving.
"Extra lean"	Can be used on seafood and meat that contains less than 5 g of fat, less than 2 g of saturated fat, and less than 95 mg of cholesterol per serving.

N/A = not applicable

the structure or function of the human body (see **Figure 2.16**).[15] The claims "calcium (nutrient) builds strong bones (body structure)" and "fiber (dietary compound) maintains bowel regularity (body function)" are examples of structure/function claims. Structure/function claims cannot state that the nutrient or dietary compound can be used to treat a disease or a condition.[16] These claims can be made on both foods and dietary supplements. Unlike the other health claims, structure/function claims don't have to be preapproved by the FDA. They do have to be truthful and not misleading, but the manufacturer is responsible for making sure that the claim is accurate. These claims can be a source of confusion. Shoppers can easily fall into the trap of assuming that one brand of a product with a structure/function claim on its label is superior to another product without the claim. For instance, a yogurt that says "calcium builds strong bones" on its label may be identical to

Table 2.7

Sorting Out the Label Claims

Type of Claim	Definition	Examples (Claims of links between . . .)
Authorized health claims (well-established)	Claims based on a well-established relationship between the food or compound and the health benefit. Food manufacturers must petition the FDA and provide the scientific research that backs up the claim. If there is significant agreement among the supporting research and a consensus among numerous scientists and experts in the field that there is a relationship between the food or dietary ingredient and the disease or health condition, the FDA will allow an authorized health claim. Specified wording must be used. The FDA has approved 12 authorized health claims.	• Calcium and osteoporosis • Sodium and hypertension • Dietary fat and cancer • Dietary saturated fat and cholesterol and risk of coronary heart disease • Fiber-containing grain products, fruits, and vegetables and cancer • Fruits, vegetables, and grain products that contain fiber, particularly soluble fiber, and the risk of coronary heart disease • Fruits and vegetables and cancer • Folate and neural tube defects • Dietary noncarcinogenic carbohydrate sweeteners and dental caries • Soluble fiber from certain foods and risk of coronary heart disease • Soy protein and risk of coronary heart disease • Plant sterol/stanol esters and risk of coronary heart disease
Health claims based on authoritative statements (well-established)	Claims based on statements made by a U.S. government agency, such as the Centers for Disease Control and Prevention (CDC) and the National Institutes of Health (NIH). If the FDA approves the claim submitted by the manufacturer, the wording of these claims must include "may," as in "whole grains may help reduce the risk of heart disease," to illustrate that other factors in addition to the food or dietary ingredient may play a role in the disease or condition. This type of health claim can only be used on food and cannot be used on dietary supplements.	• Whole-grain foods and risk of heart disease and certain cancers • Potassium and the risk of high blood pressure • Fluoridated water and the reduced risk of dental caries • Saturated fat, cholesterol, and *trans* fat and reduced risk of heart disease
Qualified health claims (less well-established)	Claims based on evidence that is still emerging. However, the current evidence to support the claim is greater than the evidence suggesting that the claim isn't valid. These are allowed in order to expedite the communication of potentially beneficial health information to the public. They must be accompanied by the statement "the evidence to support the claim is limited or not conclusive" or "some scientific evidence suggests. . . ." Qualified health claims can be used on dietary supplements if approved by the FDA.	• Selenium and cancer • Antioxidant vitamins and cancer • Nuts and heart disease • Omega-3 fatty acids and coronary heart disease • B vitamins and vascular disease • Monounsaturated fatty acids from olive oil and coronary heart disease • Unsaturated fatty acids from canola oil and reduced risk of coronary heart disease • 0.8 mg folic acid and neural tube birth defects • Green tea and cancer • Chromium picolinate and diabetes • Calcium and colon/rectal cancer and calcium and recurrent colon/rectal polyps • Calcium and hypertension, pregnancy-induced hypertension, and preeclampsia • Tomatoes and/or tomato sauce and prostate, ovarian, gastric, and pancreatic cancers • Corn oil and corn oil-containing products and reduced risk of heart disease

Figure 2.16 A Structure/Function Label Claim
The structure/function claim is that the antioxidants added to this cereal support the immune system. The manufacturer cannot claim that the food lowers a consumer's risk of a chronic disease or health condition.

another yogurt without the flashy label claim. The consumer has to recognize the difference between claims that are supported by a significant amount of solid research and approved by the FDA, and structure/function claims that don't require prior approval for use.

If a dietary supplement such as a multivitamin is to contain a structure/function claim, its manufacturer must notify the FDA no later than 30 days after the product has been on the market. Dietary supplements that use structure/function claims must display a disclaimer on the label that the FDA did not evaluate the claim and that the dietary supplement is not intended to "diagnose, treat, cure, or prevent any disease." Manufacturers of foods bearing structure/function claims do not have to display this disclaimer on the label, just on dietary supplements.

All foods that boast a health claim and/or a structure/function claim can also be marketed as "functional foods." The feature box "Functional Foods: What Role Do They Play in Your Diet?" on page 58 discusses this trendy category of foods.

Although keeping the types of health and structure/function claims straight can be challenging, here's one way to remember them:

➤ Authorized health claims and health claims based on authoritative statements are the strongest, as they are based on years of accumulated research or an authoritative statement.
➤ Qualified health claims are less convincing. They are made on potentially healthful foods or dietary ingredients, but, because the evidence is still emerging, the claim has to be "qualified" as such.
➤ Structure/function claims are the weakest claims, as they are just statements or facts about the role the nutrient or dietary ingredient plays in your body. They can't claim that the food or dietary ingredient lowers your risk of developing a chronic disease such as heart disease or cancer. As you read the claims on the labels, you will quickly see that those with less established scientific evidence behind them have the weakest wording.

Table 2.8 summarizes the various areas of information you can use to help you achieve a healthful diet.

The Take-Home Message The FDA regulates the labeling on all packaged foods. The Nutrition Facts Panel and the Daily Values are found on all food labels. Every food label must include the name of the food, its net weight, the name and address of the manufacturer or distributor, a list of ingredients, and standardized nutrition information. The FDA allows and regulates the use of nutrient content claims, health claims, and structure/function claims on food labels. Any foods or dietary supplements displaying these claims on the label must meet specified criteria and be truthful.

Table 2.8

A Summary of Tools for Healthy Eating

Putting It All Together: Tools for Healthy Eating

	DRIs	*Dietary Guidelines for Americans, 2010*	MyPlate	Nutrition Facts Panel	Label Claims
What Are They?	Specific reference values, for each nutrient by age and gender	Reflect the most current nutrition and physical activity recommendations for good health	A representational icon that depicts five food groups using the familiar mealtime visual of a place setting.	Contains important nutrition information to be used to compare food products	There are three types of claims: 1. Nutrient content claims 2. Health claims 3. Stucture/ function claims
How Do They Guide You in Healthy Eating?	DRIs provide recommendations to prevent malnutrition and chronic diseases for each nutrient. The upper level is designed to prevent overnutrition or toxicity.	The *Dietary Guidelines* emphasize healthy food choices, maintaining healthy weight, and physical activity. Guidelines for types of foods, moderate alcohol intake, and food safety are also included.	MyPlate is the focal point for the web-based ChooseMyPlate.gov initiative, which provides information to build a healthy diet based on the *Dietary Guidelines for Americans, 2010.*	You can use the Nutrition Facts panel to compare the nutrient density of foods.	You can use these label terms to help you choose foods that may contain a specific amount of a nutrient or compound to improve your diet.
What Are They Made Up Of?	EARs, RDAs, AIs, ULs, and AMDRs	The recommendations are guided by two overarching concepts: 1. Maintain calorie balance over time to achieve and sustain a healthy weight. 2. Consume more nutrient-rich foods and beverages.	Recommendations are made for physical activity as well as five food groups, plus oils: 1. Vegetables 2. Fruits 3. Grains 4. Protein 5. Dairy 6. Oils	Information is presented about: Serving size Servings per package Total calories and calories from fat Macronutrients Vitamins and minerals % Daily Values	1. Nutrient content claims describe the level or amount of a nutrient in a food product. 2. Health claims describe a relationship between a food or dietary compound and a disease or health-related condition. 3. Structure/ function claims describe how a nutrient or dietary compound affects the structure or function of the body.

Functional Foods: What Role Do They Play in Your Diet?

Have you ever eaten broccoli? Odds are that you have, but you may not have known that you were eating a functional food. In fact, some people have even called broccoli a superfood. Although there isn't a legal definition for either of these terms, a commonly used definition for a **functional food** is one that has been shown to have a positive effect on your health beyond its basic nutrients ("superfood" is a more trendy term often used in the media to highlight that a food has functional and healthy properties).[7] Broccoli is a functional food because it is rich in beta-carotene, which, in addition to being a key source of vitamin A, helps protect your cells from damaging substances that can increase your risk of some chronic diseases, such as heart disease. In other words, the beta-carotene's function goes beyond its basic nutritional role as a source of vitamin A, because it may also help fight heart disease. Broccoli is also a cruciferous vegetable, which, along with cauliflower and brussels sprouts, is part of the cabbage family. These vegetables contain compounds such as isothiocyanates, which may also be "super" at fighting cancer. Oats are also a functional food and sometimes also referred to as a superfood, because they contain the soluble fiber beta-glucan, which has been shown to lower blood cholesterol levels. This can play a positive role in lowering the risk for heart disease.[8]

functional foods Foods that have a positive effect on health beyond providing basic nutrients.

phytochemicals Plant chemicals that have been shown to reduce the risk of certain diseases such as cancer and heart disease. Beta-carotene is a phytochemical.

zoochemicals Compounds in animal food products that are beneficial to human health. Omega-3 fatty acids are an example of zoochemicals.

If the beneficial compound in the food is derived from plants, such as in the case of beta-carotene, isothiocyanates, and beta-glucan, it is called a **phytochemical** (*phyto* = plant). If it is derived from animals it is called a **zoochemical** (zoo = animal). Heart-healthy, omega-3 fatty acids, found in fatty fish such as salmon and sardines, are considered zoochemicals. The accompanying table provides a list of currently known compounds in foods that have been shown to provide positive health benefits. Manufacturers are promoting foods containing naturally occurring phytochemicals and zoochemicals and have also begun fortifying other food products with these compounds. You can buy margarine with added plant sterols and a cereal with the soluble fiber, psyllium, which both help to lower blood cholesterol levels, as well as pasta and eggs that have had omega-3 fatty acids added (see table).

Are People Buying Functional Foods?

Yes, people are buying them. Americans spent more than $31 billion in 2008 on functional foods and beverages, and the market is predicted to grow to more than $40 billion through 2013 as more consumers take a self-care approach to their health.[9] In one survey of 1,000-plus American adults, more than 55 percent were changing the types of foods they eat in order to improve their health.[10]

Baby boomers, in particular—the generation of people born between 1946 and 1964—are eager not only to live longer than their parents, but also, to live better. They are turning to functional foods to fight heart disease, aid in diminishing joint pain, prevent memory loss, and help them keep their eyesight healthy.[11]

What Are the Benefits of Functional Foods?

Functional foods are being used by health care professionals to thwart patients' chronic diseases and, in some situations, as an economical way to treat a disease. For example, many doctors send their patients to a registered dietitian (RD) for diet advice to treat specific medical conditions, such as an elevated blood cholesterol level, rather than automatically prescribing cholesterol-lowering medication. Eating a diet that contains a substantial amount of cholesterol-lowering oats or plant sterols is less expensive, and often more appealing, than taking costly prescription medication. Ideally, the RD, who is trained in the area of nutrition, can recommend the addition of functional foods to the diet based on the person's own medical history and nutritional needs.

However, problems can arise when consumers haphazardly add functional foods to their diets.

Your Guide to Functional Foods

This Compound	Found in This/These Functional Food(s)	May Have This Health Benefit
Beta-carotene	Carrots, pumpkin, cantaloupe, broccoli	Functions as an antioxidant in the body
Lycopene	Tomatoes, tomato sauce	May lower risk of prostate cancer
Soy protein	Tofu, soy milk	Lowers risk of heart disease
Beta-glucan	Oatmeal, oats, oat bran	Lowers blood cholesterol
Plant sterol and stanol esters	Fortified margarines, like Benecol spreads	Lowers blood cholesterol
Omega-3 fatty acids	Salmon, sardines, tuna	May reduce the risk of heart disease
Whole grains	Whole-wheat bread, brown rice, popcorn	May reduce the risk of some cancers
Flavanols	Dark chocolate, green apples	May contribute to heart health
Anthocyanins	Berries, red grapes, cherries	Act as antioxidants, may contribute to brain function
Probiotics	Active cultures in fermented dairy products such as yogurt	Supports intestinal health

Source: Adapted from IFIC, Functional Foods. Available at www.ific.org. Accessed April 2010.

What Concerns Are Associated with Functional Foods?

With so many labeling claims now adorning products on supermarket shelves, consumers have an array of enhanced functional foods from which to choose. Having so many options can be confusing. Consumers often cannot tell if a pricey box of cereal with added "antioxidants to help support the immune system" is really better than an inexpensive breakfast of oatmeal and naturally antioxidant-rich orange juice. There is also a concern that after eating a bowl of this antioxidant-enhanced cereal, consumers may think they are "off the hook" about eating healthfully the rest of the day. Often, more than one serving of a functional food is needed to reap the beneficial effect of the food compound, but the consumer hasn't been educated appro-

priately about how much of such a food to consume. Finally, while functional foods do convey health benefits, they are not magic elixirs that can negate a poor diet. The best way to use functional foods is as part of a healthy diet that can help *prevent* adverse health conditions from occurring in the first place.

As with most dietary substances, problems may arise if too much is consumed. For example, whereas consuming some omega-3 fatty acids can help reduce the risk of heart disease, consuming too much can be problematic for people on certain medications or for those at risk for a specific type of stroke.[12] A person can unknowingly overconsume a dietary compound if his or her diet contains many different functional foods enhanced with the same compound. Also, functional beverages, such as herbal beverages or vitamin-

enhanced water, can have more calories and added sugar than cola.[13]

How to Use Functional Foods

Functional foods can be part of a healthy, well-balanced diet. Keep in mind that whole grains, fruits, vegetables, healthy vegetable oils, lean meat and dairy products, fish, and poultry all contain varying amounts of naturally occurring phytochemicals and zoochemicals and are the quintessential functional foods. If you consume other, packaged functional foods, take care not to overconsume any one compound. Seek out an RD for sound nutrition advice on whether you would benefit from added functional foods, and, if so, how to balance them in your diet.

Two Points of View

What Were the Problems with the Design of MyPyramid? For many consumers, nutrition students, and educators, MyPyramid was a useful guide for assembling a complete, healthy diet. However, when it was first published in 2005, there were many nutrition experts who felt it didn't convey the most important dietary messages, and/or that it reflected the interests of certain groups over the health of consumers.

Was MyPyramid the most effectively designed symbol for planning a healthy diet? Or do its shortfalls outweigh the benefits? After you've read the arguments for and against, answer the critical thinking questions and decide for yourself.

Yes

- Much of the information available for MyPyramid is contained on the website mypyramid.gov, rather than in the symbol itself. However, the information is not likely to be accessed by the populations that need it most: the underprivileged and/or the elderly, who may not have easy access to a computer, are not computer literate, or cannot afford Internet access.[1]

- The pyramid only hints about the necessity for eating fewer foods (such as fats, sugars, and salt), and the concept of replacing unhealthy food (fast food, junk food, soda) with more desirable food is difficult to discern.[2] It makes no mention of added sugars, or that there is no safe level of *trans* fats.

- MyPyramid.gov does not address the concept of healthy body weight; most individuals do not know their healthy weight range.[3]

- Some members of the 2005 Dietary Guidelines Advisory Committee, sometimes received food industry funding to support their research, or have been paid by food companies as consultants. Critics contend that this also represents a conflict of interest.[4]

No

- MyPyramid is intended primarily as a symbol for nutrition policy; the accompanying slogan directs consumers to a website where they can access educational messages and information.[5]

- Given the widespread availability of the Internet in homes and through schools and public libraries, and the Internet's ability to deliver quantities of information efficiently, it was determined to be an effective dissemination tool for the additional information of MyPyramid.[6]

- MyPyramid incorporates an icon to convey the importance of physical activity (via the figure running up the steps on the side) and it provides personalized advice via the website.[7]

- USDA conducted extensive consumer research, including focus groups, user testing, and a call for general review, to develop a symbol that conveys the primary messages necessary for a healthy diet.[8]

- Respondents generally felt that site text was written at an appropriate reading level. (It was designed to be at a 7th to 8th grade reading level.)[9]

MyPyramid.gov
STEPS TO A HEALTHIER YOU

What do you think?

1. Is MyPyramid the optimal means of communicating the basics of a healthy diet? How would you change or improve it? **2.** Do you think the development of MyPyramid was influenced by the food industry? Is there evidence to support your opinion? **3.** Is MyPlate an effective replacement?

Chapter Review

Be a Nutrition Sleuth
More on Portion Distortion

Years ago, a standard bagel could fit in the palm of your hand. Today, a typical bagel is likely larger than your entire hand. Today's supersized hamburger dwarfs the average burger of the 1950s. Over the past few decades, the portion sizes of many commercially prepared and fast foods have increased greatly, and so have the number of calories from a serving. Can you guess the calorie differences between the servings of yesteryear and those of today? Go online at **www.pearsonhighered.com/blake** to find out.

The Top Ten Points to Remember

1. The Dietary Reference Intakes (DRIs) are specific reference values, based on your age and gender, for the essential nutrients you need daily. The DRIs are designed to prevent nutrient deficiencies, maintain good health, prevent chronic diseases, and avoid unhealthy excesses. The DRIs consist of the Estimated Average Requirement, Recommended Dietary Allowance, Adequate Intake, Tolerable Upper Intake Level, and the Acceptable Macronutrient Distribution Ranges.

2. The *Dietary Guidelines for Americans* are the current nutrition and physical activity recommendations for healthy Americans aged 2 and older. These guidelines are designed to help individuals improve their diet to lower their risk of chronic diseases and conditions such as diabetes mellitus, heart disease, certain cancers, osteoporosis, high blood pressure, high blood cholesterol levels, and most importantly, obesity.

3. MyPlate is the USDA's latest tool that visually represents the five food groups and many of the recommendations in the *Dietary Guidelines for Americans.* Together MyPlate and ChooseMyPlate.gov help you meet your daily DRIs and the recommendations for the number of servings that you should eat every day from each food group based on your

calorie needs. The new recommendations emphasize daily physical activity, proportionality among the food groups, and variety within the food groups, as well as moderation when consuming foods with unhealthy solid fats and added sugars. ChooseMyPlate.gov provides a personalized eating plan based on your needs and encourages improvements in your diet and lifestyle choices to improve your health.

4. Nutrient density refers to the amount of nutrients per calorie in a given food; energy density refers to the number of calories per gram of the food. Whole fruits and vegetables, whole grains, and lean meat and dairy products tend to be nutrient dense (a desirable attribute), whereas high-calorie fried foods and sweets are energy dense (a less desirable attribute). The discretionary calorie allowance is the amount of calories left over in the diet if the food choices within each food group are lean and don't have added sugar.

5. The FDA regulates all packaged foods to ensure that they are accurately labeled. The Nutrition Facts panel on the food label must list the serving size of the food. It must also show the corresponding amount of calories, fat, saturated fat, *trans* fat, cholesterol, sodium, sugars, protein, vitamins A and C, calcium, and iron that are contained in a serving of the food. Other nutrients can be listed by the manufacturer voluntarily. If a food product makes a claim about a nutrient, that nutrient must be listed in the Nutrition Facts panel.

6. The Daily Values are reference levels of intakes for the nutrients listed on the food label. Unlike the DRIs, they are

not specific, individualized recommended intakes, but rather reference points that allow you to assess how the nutrients in the foods you buy can fit into your overall diet.

7. A food product label can carry a nutrient content claim about the amount of a nutrient the food contains by using descriptive terms such as *free, high, low, reduced,* and *extra lean,* as long as the claim meets the strict criteria for each item designated by the FDA.

8. A health claim must contain a food compound or a dietary ingredient and a corresponding disease or health-related condition that is associated with the claim. All health claims must be approved by the FDA.

9. Structure/function claims describe how a food or dietary compound affects the structure or function of the body. These claims must be truthful and accurate and do not require FDA approval before use. They cannot be tied to a disease or health-related condition.

10. Functional foods have been shown to have a positive effect on health beyond providing basic nutrients. Some foods are deliberately enhanced with compounds and marketed as functional foods.

Test Your Knowledge

1. The *Dietary Guidelines for Americans* recommend that you
   a. maintain calorie balance over time and sustain a healthy weight.
   b. stop smoking and walk daily.
   c. sleep eight hours a night and jog every other day.
   d. consume adequate nutrients within your calorie needs and stop smoking.

2. The Dietary Reference Intakes (DRIs) are reference values for nutrients and are designed to
   a. only prevent nutritional deficiency.
   b. provide a ballpark range of your nutrient needs.
   c. prevent nutritional deficiencies by meeting your nutrient needs as well as prevent the consumption of excessive and dangerous amounts of nutrients.

3. The Estimated Average Intake (EAR) is
   a. the estimated amount of a nutrient that you should consume daily to be healthy.
   b. the amount of a nutrient that meets the average needs of 50 percent of individuals in a specific age and gender group.
   c. the maximum safe amount of a nutrient that you should consume daily.

4. MyPlate is part of the web initiative ChooseMyPlate .gov that
   a. can help you implement the recommendations in the DRIs.
   b. can help you use the advice in the *Dietary Guidelines for Americans, 2010.*
   c. provides personalized food choices among a variety of food groups to help you create a balanced diet.
   d. does all of the above.

5. Which of the following are the food groups in MyPlate?
   a. grains, vegetables, dairy, sweets, protein
   b. grains, fruits, alcohol, sweets, protein
   c. grains, vegetables, fruits, dairy, protein
   d. grains, vegetables, oils, dairy, protein

6. Which of the following foods is most nutrient dense?
   a. an orange ice pop
   b. an orange
   c. orange-flavored punch
   d. orange sherbet

7. By law, which of the following MUST be listed on the food label?
   a. calories, fat, and potassium
   b. fat, saturated fat, and vitamin E
   c. calories, fat, and saturated fat
   d. calories, sodium, and vitamin D

8. The bran cereal that you eat in the morning carries a "high-fiber" claim on its label. This is an example of a
   a. nutrient claim.
   b. structure/function claim.
   c. health claim.

9. The yogurt that you enjoy as a morning snack states that a serving provides 30 percent of the Daily Value for calcium. Is this a high or low amount of calcium?
   a. high
   b. low

10. Oatmeal contains a soluble fiber that can help lower your cholesterol. Oatmeal is considered a functional food.
    a. true
    b. false

Answers

1. (a) The *Dietary Guidelines for Americans, 2010* recommend that you maintain calorie balance over time and sustain a healthy weight. Though the *Dietary Guidelines* do not specifically address stopping smoking, this is a habit worth kicking. Walking or jogging daily are wonderful ways to be physically active. Sleeping eight hours a night isn't mentioned in the *Dietary Guidelines* but is another terrific lifestyle habit.

2. (c) The DRIs tell you the amount of nutrients you need to prevent deficiencies, maintain good health, and avoid toxicity.

3. (b) The EAR is the amount of a nutrient that would meet the needs of half of the individuals in a specific age and gender group. The EAR is used to obtain the Recommended Dietary Allowance, which is the amount of a nutrient that you should be consuming daily to maintain good health. The Tolerable Upper Intake Level is the maximum amount of a nutrient that you can consume on a regular basis that is unlikely to cause harm.

4. (d) MyPlate and ChooseMyPlate.gov together can help you to create a balanced diet so that you can eat healthfully. They are designed to help you meet the nutrient needs recommended in the DRIs and also implement the advice in the *Dietary Guidelines for Americans, 2010.*

5. (c) Vegetables, fruits, grains, protein, and dairy are the five basic food groups in MyPlate. Sweets and alcohol are not food groups and should be limited in the diet.

6. (b) While an orange ice pop and orange sherbet may be refreshing treats on a hot day, the orange is by far the most nutrient-dense food among the choices because it provides the most nutrients for the fewest calories. The orange-flavored punch is a sugary drink with orange flavoring.

7. (c) The Nutrition Facts panel on the package must contain the calories, fat, and saturated fat per serving. Vitamins E and D do not have to be listed unless they have been added to the food and/or the product makes a claim about them on the label.

8. (a) This high-fiber cereal label boasts a nutrient claim and is helping you meet your daily fiber needs.

9. (a) If you consume 20 percent or more of the Daily Value for a nutrient, it is considered "high" in that nutrient. If a nutrient provides 5 percent or less of the Daily Value, it is considered "low" in that nutrient.

10. (a) Functional foods go beyond providing basic nutrients and also provide other health benefits. Oats contain the soluble fiber beta-glucan, which has been shown to help reduce blood cholesterol levels. Because of this, oatmeal is considered a functional food.

Web Resources

➡ For more tips and resources for MyPlate, visit: ChooseMyPlate.gov

➡ For more on functional foods, visit: www.foodinsight.org/Content/6/functionalfoodsbackgrounder.pdf

➡ For more on food labels, visit: www.fda.gov/Food/default.htm

Answers to Myths and Misperceptions

1. **True.** The DRIs are set at a level higher than the minimum amount needed to prevent a deficiency. To find out why, turn to page 32.

2. **False.** You should be physically active *regularly,* not just twice a week. To find out why, turn to page 36.

3. **True.** The *Dietary Guidelines* are designed to help reduce your risk of the leading causes of death in the United States. To learn more, turn to page 36.

4. **True.** MyPlate visually depicts the basic rules for a healthy diet, and moderation, variety, and proportionality are three of the most important. To learn more, turn to page 39.

5. **True.** Downsizing your portion sizes to mirror a standard serving size is an important strategy for reducing calorie consumption. Fortunately, you can use your palm, fist, and fingers to estimate the serving sizes of many foods. Turn to page 42 to find out how this works.

6. **False.** Solid fats are less nutrient dense so should be reduced in your diet. Turn to page 42 to find out the sources of solid fats that you may be consuming.

7. **True.** The FDA requires a food label on all packaged food items, and specific information must be included. To find out exactly what must be disclosed on the food label, turn to page 48.

8. **True.** Specific descriptive terms approved by the FDA must be used. To find out what these terms are and what they mean, turn to page 52.

9. **True.** However, more than one type of health claim is allowed on a label. Turn to page 52 to learn about the types of claims that food manufacturers may use.

10. **False.** Eating functional foods and "superfoods" can have numerous health benefits, but they are not a magic potion. Find out which foods are functional foods, and why they are beneficial, on page 58.

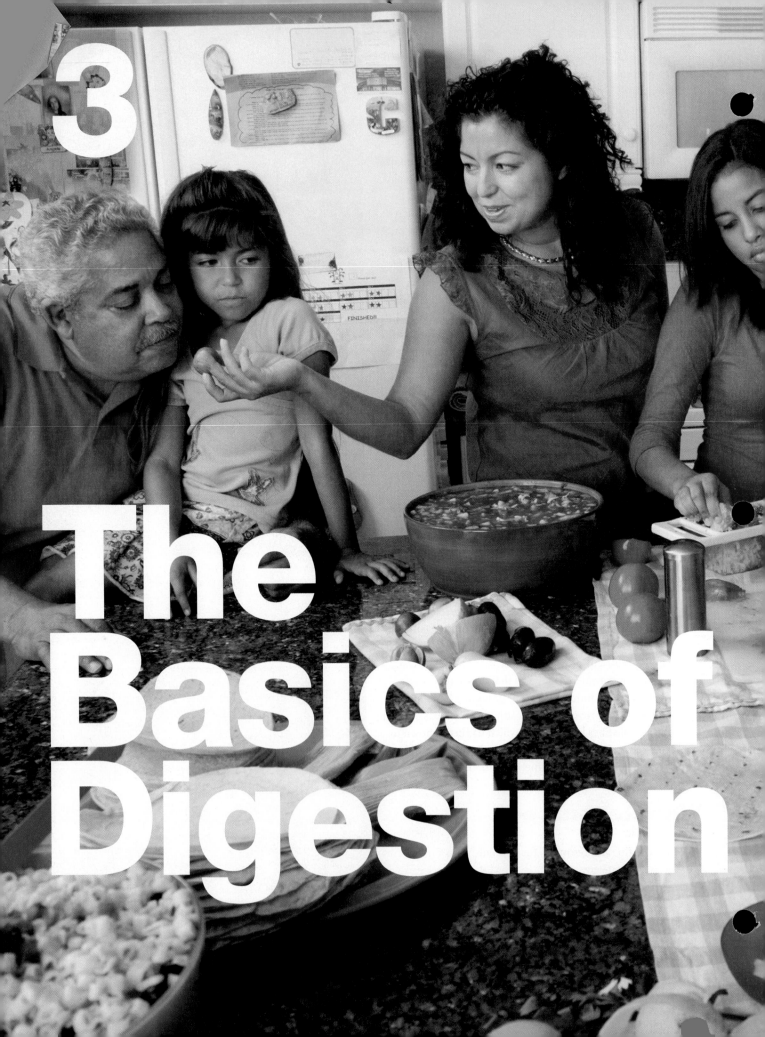

3

The Basics of Digestion

True or False?

1. You cannot fully enjoy food without your sense of **smell.** T/F p. 67

2. The **GI tract** is essentially a long tube. T/F p. 68

3. You absorb only **75 percent** of the nutrients in your food. T/F p. 69

4. Food enters your stomach from the **trachea.** T/F p. 70

5. Hydrochloric acid is produced in the **esophagus.** T/F p. 71

6. Protein, fat, and carbohydrates are all digested at the same **rate.** T/F p. 71

7. All nutrients are **absorbed** in the small intestine. T/F p. 73

8. **Stool** is mostly made up of food remnants and bacteria. T/F p. 75

9. Few people experience **heartburn.** T/F p. 81

10. Dietary **fiber** is useless. T/F p. 84

See page 91 for answers to these Myths and Misperceptions.

Twenty-one-year-old Rachel usually eats a breakfast of cereal and milk right before her morning nutrition class. However, recently, as she listened to her instructor's gripping lecture on digestive enzymes, she noticed a bloating feeling in her stomach, followed by an urgent need to run to the bathroom. On her way out of the classroom, she suddenly had severe cramping, which caused her to double over in pain. She initially thought that the cramps must be caused by something "bad" that she ate, or a bout of stomach flu. She thought it would pass as a temporary problem. But over time, she noticed it happening more often, particularly after a lunchtime sandwich or when she has pasta for dinner.

Can you guess the reason for Rachel's discomfort after she eats? Would you be surprised to learn that Rachel is not alone in her post-meal digestive issues? In this chapter, we'll discuss several common ailments of the digestive tract; we'll also explore the process of digestion and the organs involved.

Chapter Objectives

After reading this chapter, you will be able to:

1. Define digestion, absorption, and nutrient transport.

2. Describe the organs involved in digestion and their primary functions.

3. Explain the roles of the gallbladder, liver, and pancreas in digestion.

4. Explain the function of peristalsis and segmentation in the movement of food through the GI tract.

5. Explain the role of enzymes in digestion.

6. List the main carbohydrate-, protein-, and fat-digesting enzymes and the tissues that secrete them.

7. Identify the hormones involved in digestion, including their primary action and their source of origin.

8. Explain the role of the small intestine, villi, and microvilli in digestion.

9. Explain how the circulatory and lymphatic systems transport absorbed nutrients throughout the body.

10. Describe the symptoms and causes of the most common digestive disorders.

What Makes Eating So Enjoyable?

As much fun as it is to eat, you're not just taking in food for fun. Food satisfies a genuine physical need. Eating food and drinking fluids often begins with the sensation of either **hunger** or **thirst.** The amount of food that we eat and the timing of our meals are driven by physical needs. **Appetite** is another powerful drive, but it is often unreliable. Appetite is influenced by our food preferences and the psychological stimulation to eat. In other words, you can become interested in food, pursue food, and experience the desire to eat too much food without actually needing nourishment or being hungry.

Chapter 1 discussed many factors that affect how, when, and why you eat, so you know that everything from your social situation to your cultural heritage will influence what you put on your plate. Beyond these external factors, there are qualities in foods that affect your desire to eat them. *Taste* and *aroma* are two of these qualities.

We Develop a Taste for Certain Foods

Everyone enjoys eating food that tastes delicious, but what exactly *is* taste? There are five basic categories of taste: sweet, salty, sour, bitter, and savory ("umami"). Most taste buds are located on the tongue, but additional taste buds are found in the throat and elsewhere in the mouth. Food scientists estimate that each of us has at least 10,000 taste buds.

Even though we each have our own favorite foods, we share some taste traits. In general, we all have an innate preference for sweet, salty, and fatty foods. There is a scientific explanation for these preferences. Sugar seems to elicit universal pleasure (even among infants), and the brain seeks pleasure.[1] Salt provides two important **electrolytes** (sodium and chloride) that are essential to your body and can stimulate the appetite. Your liking of both sugar and salt makes carbohydrate-rich foods appealing to you. Foods rich in carbohydrates provide the fuel that your body needs daily. High-fat foods not only have rich textures and aromas that round out the flavors of food, but also provide essential nutrients that are critical to your health.[2] Thus, while we tend to enjoy rich sauces, gravies, and salad dressings, we are, at the same time, meeting our nutritional needs.

Sometimes, our food preferences and our nutritional needs conflict. We may eat too much because the food is so pleasurable. When there is a reason to change our food habits, such as a need to lose weight or reduce salt or fat intake, we realize how challenging it can be to control our food choices.

How does the brain recognize taste? When food is consumed, portions of the food are dissolved in saliva. These fluids then make contact with the tongue's surface. The taste (gustatory) cells send a message to the brain. The brain then translates the nerve impulses into taste sensations that you recognize.

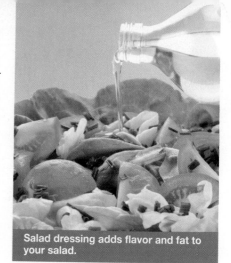
Salad dressing adds flavor and fat to your salad.

Aromas and Flavors Enhance the Pleasure of Eating

The word *umami* means "delicious" in Japanese.

The sensing structures in the nose are also important to the ability to taste foods. The average person is capable of distinguishing 2,000 to 4,000 aromas.[3] We detect food aroma through the nose when we smell foods and, as we eat, when food odors enter the mouth and migrate to the back of the throat and into the nasal cavities.[4] The average person has about 10 million to 20 million olfactory cells (odor cells) in the nasal cavity. Therefore, both your mouth and your nose contribute to the tasting of foods. This explains why you lose interest in eating when you have a cold or other forms of nasal congestion. Food loses some of its appeal when you can't smell it.

Both the taste and the aroma of a food contribute to its flavor. The term *flavor* also refers to the complete food experience. For example, when you eat a candy bar, you sense a sweet taste, but the flavor is chocolate.

The presence of fat tends to enhance the flavor of foods. When the fat content increases, the intensity of the flavor also increases, as many aromatic compounds are soluble in fat. Increased fat content causes the flavor of food to last longer compared with flavor compounds dissolved in water. Flavors dissolved in water are quickly detected, but also quickly dissipated.[5] This explains why most people prefer premium ice cream over frozen popsicles. It also explains why several low-fat foods have an acceptable flavor, but they are not as delicious as their high-fat counterparts.

The Take-Home Message The five categories of taste are sweet, salty, sour, bitter, and savory (umami). Humans have an innate taste for salty, sugary, and fatty foods. The tastes and aromas of foods are a big part of what makes eating pleasurable. Flavor includes both taste and aroma. In general, the higher the fat content, the more intensely flavored the food.

hunger The physical need for food.

thirst The physical need for water.

appetite The psychological desire to eat or drink.

electrolytes Charged particles (positive or negative ions). Vomiting and diarrhea cause the loss of electrolytes from your body.

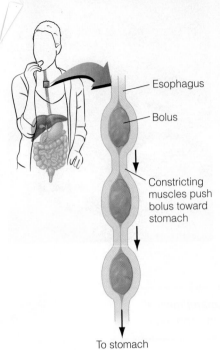

Figure 3.1 Peristalsis
Muscles around the organs of the GI tract constrict in a wavelike manner to help move food along.

Esophagus

Bolus

Constricting muscles push bolus toward stomach

To stomach

What Is Digestion and Why Is It Important?

The simple definition of digestion is the breaking down of foods into absorbable components in the **gastrointestinal (GI) tract.** Through a multistep **digestive process,** food is softened with moisture and heat, and then broken down into smaller particles by chewing and exposure to **enzymes.**

Digestion Occurs in the GI Tract

The GI tract consists of the mouth, esophagus, stomach, small intestine, large intestine, and other organs. The main roles of the GI tract are to (1) break food down into its smallest components; (2) absorb the nutrients; and (3) prevent microorganisms or other harmful compounds consumed with food from entering the tissues of the body.[6]

The GI tract is a tube about 23 feet long beginning with the mouth and ending with the anus. Stretched vertically, this would be about as high as a two-story building. The many circular folds, grooves, and projections in the stomach and intestines provide an extensive surface area over which absorption can occur. The cells lining your GI tract have a very brief life span. They function for three to five days and then they are shed into the **lumen** (interior of the intestinal tract) and are replaced with new, healthy cells.

Digestion Is Mechanical and Chemical

There are two forms of digestion: mechanical and chemical. **Mechanical digestion** involves chewing, grinding, and breaking food apart in the mouth so that it can be comfortably swallowed. The muscular activity and rhythmic contractions, or **peristalsis** (**Figure 3.1**), that move food through the GI tract and mix it with enzymes are also part of mechanical digestion.

gastrointestinal (GI) tract
Body area containing the organs of the digestive tract. It extends from the mouth to the anus.

digestive process The breakdown of foods into absorbable components using mechanical and chemical means.

enzymes Substances that produce chemical changes or catalyze chemical reactions.

lumen The interior of the digestive tract, through which food passes.

mechanical digestion Breaking food down through chewing and grinding, or moving it through the GI tract with peristalsis.

peristalsis The forward, rhythmic motion that moves food through the digestive system. Peristalsis is a form of mechanical digestion because it influences motion, but it does not add chemical secretions.

Digestion converts whole foods into individual nutrients that can be used by the body's cells.

Chemical digestion involves digestive juices and enzymes breaking down food into absorbable nutrients that are small enough to enter the cells of the GI tract, blood, or lymph tissue.

Digestion Allows Us to Absorb Nutrients from Foods

Digestion is the forerunner to **absorption.** Once the nutrients have been completely broken down, they are ready to be used by the cells of the body. In order to reach the cells, however, they have to leave the GI tract and move to the other parts of the body. To accomplish this, nutrients are absorbed through the walls of the intestines and into the body's two transport systems: the circulatory and lymph systems. They are then taken to the liver for processing before moving on to their destination. The body is remarkably efficient when it comes to absorbing nutrients. Under normal conditions, you digest and absorb 92 to 97 percent of the nutrients from your food.[7]

The Take-Home Message Digestion is the chemical or mechanical breaking down of food into smaller units until it can be absorbed for use by the body. Digestion takes place in the gastrointestinal tract, which includes the mouth, esophagus, stomach, small intestine, large intestine, and other organs. Absorption is the process by which the digested nutrients move into your tissues. You absorb more than 90 percent of the nutrients that you take in from foods.

The smell of food, such as freshly baked bread, often triggers the appetite. As you eat a piece of bread, its aroma will also contribute to its flavor.

What Are the Organs of the GI Tract and Why Are They Important?

The organs of the GI tract each play a unique and crucial role in digestion. Before we examine the individual roles of the organs, take a look at **Figure 3.2** and refresh your memory of how organs are built from cells and tissues and how they work together in various body systems. Understanding how cells build tissues will help you understand how digestion and absorption happen in the body.

> You produce 1 to 1.5 liters of saliva every day.

Digestion Begins in the Mouth

The process of digestion begins when you first see, smell, or think about a food that you want to eat. Glands in your mouth release **saliva,** a watery fluid that will help soften the food you are about to eat. Once you take a bite and begin to chew, your teeth, powered by your jaw muscles, cut and grind the food into smaller pieces and with your tongue mix it with saliva. Saliva helps dissolve small food particles and allows us to comfortably swallow dry food. In addition to water, saliva contains electrolytes, a few enzymes (including amylase, which begins to break down carbohydrate), and **mucus.** The mucus helps lubricate the food, helps it stick together, and

chemical digestion Breaking down food with enzymes or digestive juices.

absorption The process by which digested nutrients move into the tissues where they can be transported and used by the body's cells.

saliva Watery fluid secreted by the salivary glands in the mouth. Saliva moistens food and makes it easier to swallow.

mucus Viscous, slippery secretions found in saliva and other digestive juices.

Figure 3.2 From Cells to Organs and Organ Systems

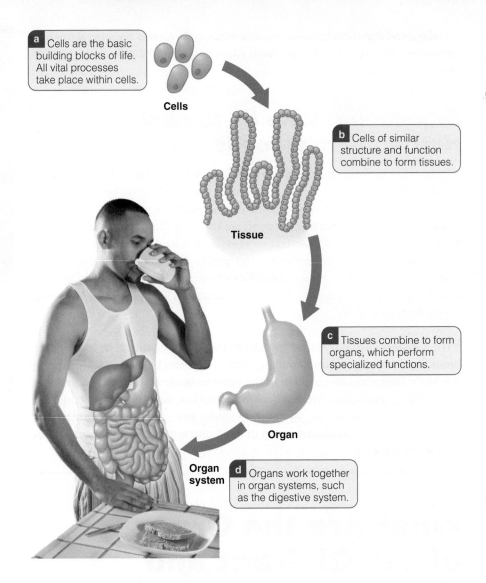

a Cells are the basic building blocks of life. All vital processes take place within cells.

Cells

b Cells of similar structure and function combine to form tissues.

Tissue

c Tissues combine to form organs, which perform specialized functions.

Organ

Organ system

d Organs work together in organ systems, such as the digestive system.

---

protects the inside of the mouth. Once food has been adequately chewed, it's pushed to the back of the mouth and into the **pharynx** by the tongue.

Swallowing seems simple because we do it hundreds of times a day, but it is actually a complicated process. Pushing chewed food to the pharynx is a voluntary act—that is, you control it. Once the food mass (now called a **bolus**) enters the pharynx, the swallowing reflex kicks in, and you no longer control the action.

You have probably experienced an episode of "swallowing gone wrong" in which you've accidentally propelled food down the wrong pipe. When this happens (and you find yourself in a coughing fit trying to expel the item), it is because the normal mechanism that protects your trachea (or windpipe) didn't engage properly. Usually, a small flap called the **epiglottis** closes off your trachea during swallowing (**Figure 3.3**). The epiglottis ensures that food and drink go down the correct pipe—the **esophagus**—rather than down the windpipe. When the epiglottis doesn't work properly, food can get lodged in the trachea, which can potentially result in choking.

Once swallowed, a bolus of food is pushed down your esophagus by *peristalsis* (refer again to Figure 3.1). When the bolus of food reaches the stomach, the lower part of the esophagus relaxes, allowing the bolus to enter the stomach. Solid or partially chewed food passes through the esophagus in about 8 seconds. Soft food and liquids pass through in about 1 to 2 seconds.[8]

The esophagus narrows at the bottom (just above the stomach) and ends at a sphincter, called the **lower esophageal sphincter (LES).** Under normal conditions,

pharynx The throat. Passageway for the respiratory (air) and digestive tracts (food and beverages).

bolus Chewed mass of food.

epiglottis Flap of tissue that protects the trachea while swallowing.

esophagus Tube that extends from the throat to the stomach.

lower esophageal sphincter (LES) A circular band of muscle between the esophagus and the stomach that opens and closes to allow food to enter the stomach.

when we swallow food, the LES relaxes and allows food to pass into the stomach. The stomach also relaxes to comfortably receive the food.[9] After food enters the stomach, the LES should close. If it doesn't, hydrochloric acid from the stomach may flow back into the esophagus and irritate its lining. This is called *heartburn* because it causes a burning sensation in the middle of the chest.

Chronic heartburn and the reflux of stomach acids are symptoms of gastro-esophageal reflux disease (GERD). The condition, GERD, and the treatment for it will be discussed later in this chapter.

The Stomach Stores, Mixes, and Prepares Food for Digestion

The **stomach** is a muscular organ that continues mechanical digestion by churning and contracting to mix food with digestive juices (see **Figure 3.4**). The food is continuously mixed for several hours. The stomach also has a role in chemical digestion in that it produces powerful digestive secretions. These secretions include **hydrochloric acid (HCl),** various enzymes, mucus, intrinsic factor (needed for vitamin B_{12} absorption), and the stomach hormone, **gastrin.** The swallowed bolus of food soon becomes **chyme,** a semiliquid substance that contains digestive secretions plus the original food. The stomach can expand to hold 2 to 4 liters of chyme.

Hydrochloric acid has important digestive functions. These include activation of the protein-digesting enzyme **pepsin,** enhanced absorption of minerals, breakdown of connective tissue in meat, and the destruction of some ingested microorganisms.[10] You might think that such a strong chemical would "digest" the stomach itself, but mucus produced in the stomach acts as a barrier between the HCl and the stomach lining, protecting the lining from irritation or damage.

Enzymes in the stomach, including pepsin and gastric lipase, begin breaking down protein into polypeptides and a few triglycerides into shorter-chain fatty acids. (The majority of triglycerides are broken down in the small intestine with the help of another enzyme.) The hormone gastrin stimulates the secretion of HCl, among other functions.

Have you ever noticed that some foods keep you feeling full longer than others? Foods high in carbohydrate exit the stomach faster, and therefore make you feel less full, than foods high in protein, fat, or fiber. Most liquids, carbohydrates, and low-fiber foods require minimal digestive activity, are easier to absorb, and have less surface area due to low fiber content.

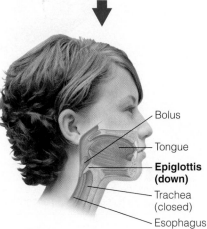

Figure 3.3 The Epiglottis
The epiglottis prevents food from entering the trachea when you swallow.

stomach Digestive organ that holds food after it's moved down the esophagus and before it is propelled into the small intestine.

hydrochloric acid (HCl) A powerful acid made in the stomach that has digestive functions. It also helps to kill microorganisms and lowers the pH in the stomach.

gastrin A digestive hormone produced in the stomach that stimulates digestive activities and increases motility and emptying.

chyme A liquid combination of partially digested food, water, HCl, and digestive enzymes.

pepsin A digestive enzyme produced in the stomach that breaks down protein.

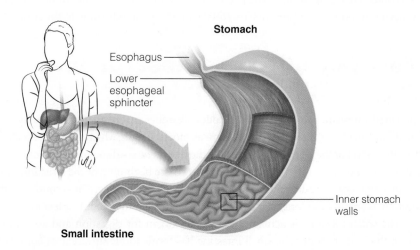

Figure 3.4 Anatomy of the Stomach

Small intestine

Fingerlike structure of the villi

Cells of the intestinal lining

Villi

Microvilli (brush border)

Nutrients

Blood capillaries

Lymph vessel

a The multifolded arrangement and villi provide an immense surface area over which nutrients can be absorbed.

b Blood and lymph vessels pick up nutrients through the brush border and transport them throughout the body.

c Microvilli on the surface of intestinal cells further increase the surface area.

Figure 3.5 Surface Area in the Small Intestine
The small intestine is a long, narrow, tightly coiled chamber in which most digestive absorption takes place.

Similarly, low-calorie foods exit the stomach faster than concentrated, high-calorie foods. This is because low-calorie foods frequently require minimal digestion. For example, a lightly sweetened cup of tea, a lower calorie beverage, requires less digestion than a higher-calorie, nutrient-dense milkshake. Digesting the tea involves only the breakdown of the sugar, sucrose, into fructose and glucose (you'll learn more about all of these sugars in Chapter 4). In contrast, digesting the milkshake involves breaking down fat, protein, and carbohydrates.

As digestion continues, peristaltic contractions push the chyme toward the lower part of the stomach. As the chyme accumulates near the **pyloric sphincter,** the muscular sphincter relaxes and the chyme gradually enters the small intestine. Approximately 1 to 5 milliliters (1 teaspoon) of chyme are released into the small intestine every 30 seconds during digestion.[11] The pyloric sphincter prevents chyme from exiting the stomach too soon, and it prevents intestinal contents from returning to the stomach.

Most Digestion and Absorption Occur in the Small Intestine

The **small intestine** is a long, narrow, coiled chamber in the abdominal cavity. The "small" in "small intestine" refers to its diameter, not its length, which accounts for about 20 of the 23 feet of the GI tract. It consists of three segments—duodenum, jejunum, and ileum—and extends from the pyloric sphincter to the beginning of the large intestine. The first segment, the duodenum, is approximately 10 inches long. The second area, the jejunum, is about 8 feet long, and the final region, the ileum, is about 12 feet long.

The small intestine is actually the primary organ for digestion and absorption within the human body. The small intestine has tremendous surface area compared with the stomach (**Figure 3.5**), and its digestive secretions do most of the work when

pyloric sphincter Sphincter in the bottom of the stomach that separates the pylorus from the duodenum of the small intestine.

small intestine Comprised of the duodenum, jejunum, and ileum, the small intestine is the longest part of the GI tract. Most of the digestion and absorption of food occurs in the small intestine.

it comes to breaking down food into absorbable nutrients. Both mechanical and chemical digestion occur in the small intestine. Mechanical digestion occurs through peristalsis, segmentation, and pendular movement. You already know that peristalsis is a mechanical, muscular movement that helps propel the contents through the GI tract. **Segmentation** is a "sloshing" motion that thoroughly mixes the chyme with the chemical secretions of the intestine. **Pendular movement** is a constrictive wave that involves both forward and reverse movements and enhances nutrient absorption. Together, these three actions move the chyme through the small intestine at a rate of 1 centimeter per minute.[12] Depending on the amount of food and the type of food consumed, the contact time in the small intestine is about 3 to 10 hours.[13] Chemical digestion in the small intestine occurs as enzymes in intestinal secretions continue to break down nutrients to prepare them for absorption. All macronutrients—carbohydrates, fats, and proteins—are broken down into their component parts by their specific enzymes. Vitamins and minerals are absorbed intact. This process of chemical breakdown and absorption can be interrupted. For example, the weight-loss drug orlistat, sold over the counter as Alli, interferes with the chemical digestion of fat (see the box "Tinkering with Your Body's Digestive Process" on page 74).

The interior of the small intestine is covered with thousands of small projections called **villi.** The villi increase the surface area of the small intestine's lining and mix the partially digested chyme with the intestinal secretions. Each individual villus is adjacent to a cluster of blood capillaries, lymph vessels, and nerve fibers.

The villi are covered by even smaller projections called **microvilli,** which provide additional surface area through which nutrients are absorbed into the blood and lymph (see Figure 3.5). The lining of the small intestine is also arranged in unique, circular folds, which further increase the absorptive surface area. The circular folds cause the chyme to spiral forward through the small intestine, rather than merely move in a straight line.

Thousands of fingerlike projections called villi cover the walls of the small intestine to increase its surface area.

There are more microorganisms than human cells in your body, and many of them are located in your large intestine.

The Large Intestine Absorbs Water and Some Nutrients

Once the chyme has passed through the small intestine, it comes to the **ileocecal sphincter,** which serves as the gateway to its next digestive destination, the **large intestine.** The primary purpose of the ileocecal sphincter is to prevent backflow of fecal contents from the large intestine into the ileum. In general, this sphincter is quite strong and resists reverse pressure. About 750 milliliters (approximately 3 cups) of unabsorbed residue enters the large intestine each day. The slow entry of this residue from the small to the large intestine enables the body to maximize nutrient absorption.[14]

By the time food enters the large intestine, it has been digested and the majority of the nutrients have been absorbed. But the large intestine serves some important functions, including the absorption of water, production of a few vitamins, absorption of important electrolytes, and the formation and storage of fecal material.

The large intestine is about 5 feet long and 2½ inches in diameter. It looks and acts much differently than the small intestine in that it does not contain villi or microvilli, and is not tightly coiled. Further, the large intestine does not secrete or use digestive enzymes and hormones. Rather, the chemical digestion that takes place in the large intestine is due to the efforts of bacteria. The large intestine produces mucus that protects the cells and acts as a lubricant for fecal matter. The cells of the large intestine absorb water and electrolytes much more efficiently than do the cells of the small intestine.

segmentation A "sloshing" motion that thoroughly mixes chyme with the chemical secretions of the intestine.

pendular movement A constrictive wave that involves both forward and reverse movements of chyme and enhances nutrient absorption.

villi Projections on the walls of the small intestine that increase the surface area over which nutrients can be absorbed. Villi are in turn covered with **microvilli,** which increase the surface area even more.

ileocecal sphincter Gateway between the end of the small intestine and the beginning of the large intestine. The sphincter prevents backflow of fecal contents from the large intestine into the small intestine.

large intestine Final organ of the GI tract. It consists of the cecum, appendix, colon, and rectum.

Tinkering with Your Body's Digestive Process

If you're like a lot of people, you may have considered using a weight-loss aid at some point. One of those aids, Alli, has popped up in many drugstores in recent years. How does this drug work, and will it help you lose weight? Is the potential for weight loss worth the side effects and costs?

Let's find out. Alli (pronounced al-eye) is the first Food and Drug Administration (FDA) approved, over-the-counter drug containing orlistat. When taken with a meal, orlistat helps prevent some dietary fat from being absorbed into your body. Orlistat works its magic by preventing enzymes in the intestines from breaking down dietary fat. If the fat isn't broken down, your body can't absorb it, and it will pass through the GI tract and be eliminated in stool. Alli blocks the absorption of about 25 percent of the fat at a meal. If you are taking Alli and eat a slice of pepperoni pizza containing 189 calories from fat for lunch, you will only absorb about 140 of them. Since fat—a hefty source of calories—isn't absorbed by your body, your body can end up with sig-

nificantly fewer calories to potentially store as body fat.

Unfortunately, because this unabsorbed fat has to be eliminated from your body, there may be some not-so-pleasant side effects, including oily spotting, gas with discharge, the feeling of having to go to the bathroom immediately, fatty/oily stools, and frequent bowel movements. Interestingly, because these side effects are so unpleasant, they may actually help an individual adhere to a well-balanced, low-fat diet (approximately 30 percent of calories from fat) when taking the drug. Orlistat taken with a very high-fat meal will make these side effects more pronounced.

Orlistat also reduces the absorption of some fat-soluble vitamins as well as beta-carotene. Consequently, individuals taking the drug are advised to take a supplement that contains the fat-soluble vitamins A, D, E, and K and the antioxidant beta-carotene.

According to the FDA, Alli is indicated for obese individuals or for people who are overweight and have other risk factors such as diabetes, high cholesterol, and elevated blood pressure. However, taking the drug won't let you off

the hook when it comes to managing your weight. If you replace the unabsorbed fat calories with excess nonfat calories, such as from sweets, pretzels, and soda, or with hefty snacks between meals, you'll end up getting nowhere fast. There is also a cost factor. A month's supply of Alli costs approximately $50.

There isn't any quick fix when it comes to weight loss. Although Alli has been approved to help those who are obese, in the long term, eating healthfully, changing eating habits and behaviors, and exercising regularly are still, and always will be, the cornerstones and the *least expensive* methods of long-term weight management—for everyone.

REFILL PACK SEE SIDE OF PACKAGE FOR LISTING OF CONTENTS

alli®

Orlistat 60mg Capsules
Weight Loss Aid

FDA approved
non-prescription
weight loss aid

*Helps you lose more
weight than dieting alone*

120 CAPSULES

There are three segments of the large intestine: the cecum, colon, and rectum (**Figure 3.6**). The cecum is a small, pouchlike area that has the appendix hanging from one end. The middle section, or colon, is the largest portion of the large intestine. (Note that though the terms "colon" and "large intestine" are often used interchangeably, they're not technically the same thing.) The colon includes the ascending, transverse, descending, and sigmoid regions. These regions are relatively long and straight. Most of the vitamin production and absorption of water and electrolytes occur within the first half of the colon. The last half of the colon stores fecal matter.

The colon receives about 1 liter (about 1 quart) of fluid material each day from the cecum, consisting of water, nondigested or unabsorbed food particles, indigestible residue, and bacteria. It slowly and gently mixes these intestinal contents and absorbs the majority of the fluids presented to it. The colon gradually produces a semisolid material that is reduced to about 200 grams (about 7 ounces) of fecal matter (**stool**, or **feces**). The intestinal matter passes through the colon within 12 to 70 hours, depending on a person's age, health, diet, and fiber intake.[15]

Bacteria in the colon play a role in producing some vitamins, including the B vitamin biotin and vitamin K.[16] Bacteria also ferment some of the undigested and unabsorbed dietary carbohydrates into simpler compounds, including methane gas, carbon dioxide, and hydrogen. Similarly, some of the colon's bacteria break down undigested fiber and produce various short-chain fatty acids. Amino acids that reach the colon are converted to hydrogen, sulfide, some fatty acids, and other chemical compounds.

As in the small intestine, the colon moves contents via peristalsis and segmentation. Peristalsis occurs within the ascending colon, but the waves of contraction are quite slow. The mixing motion of segmentation allows the organ to progressively absorb fluids.[17]

The stool is propelled forward until it reaches the **rectum,** the final eight-inch portion of the large intestine, where it is stored. When stool distends the rectum, the action stimulates stretch receptors, which in turn stimulate the defecation reflex. This causes nerve impulses of the rectum to communicate with the rectum's muscles. The end result is relaxation of the internal sphincter of the anus.

The **anus** is connected to the rectum and controlled by two sphincters: an internal and an external sphincter. Under normal conditions, the anal sphincters are closed. Periodically, the anal sphincters will relax, stool will enter the anal canal, and defecation will occur. The final stage of defecation is under our voluntary control and influenced by age, diet, prescription medicines, health, and abdominal muscle tone. See **Figure 3.7** for a summary of the digestive organs and their functions.

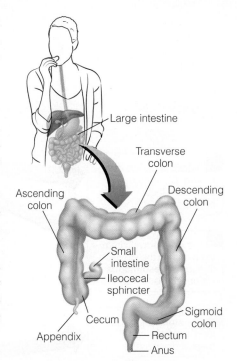

Figure 3.6 Anatomy of the Large Intestine
By the time chyme reaches the large intestine, most of its nutrients have been absorbed. However, water and some electrolytes are absorbed in the colon. The final waste products of digestion pass out of the body as stool through the anus.

Enzymes, Hormones, and Bile Aid Digestion

The complete digestion of chyme requires chemical secretions, including enzymes, hormones, and bile. Supportive digestive organs such as the pancreas, liver, and gallbladder contribute or concentrate many of these fluids. The stomach and small intestine also produce digestive enzymes. The purpose of the enzymes is to break apart food particles into small, unbound nutrients that can be efficiently absorbed.

There are several **hormones,** such as *gastrin, insulin,* and *glucagon,* that regulate digestion. Some hormones are produced in the stomach and the small intestine. Hormones don't digest food, but they regulate the activity of other cells, such as by controlling digestive secretions (gastric and pancreatic secretions) and regulating enzymes. They are stimulated by various dietary factors and their activity varies according to the digestive function required. Hormones influence gastrointestinal motility, stomach emptying, gallbladder contraction, insulin release, cell growth, intestinal absorption, and even hunger.

The hormones insulin and glucagon are produced in the pancreas and play important roles in your body. You will learn more about these two hormones in Chapter 4. The hormone gastrin stimulates the secretion of HCl, increases gastric motility and emptying, and increases the tone of the LES.[18] Gastrin also causes the release of gastric secretions that contain the enzyme gastric lipase. Gastric lipase contributes to the digestion of short- and medium-chain fatty acids, which are primarily found in human milk (consumed by infants) or in other dairy foods. These types of fatty acids are found less often in the diets of adults, as most of the dietary fats we consume contain long-chain fatty acids. Thus, gastric lipase is not a particularly important enzyme in adulthood. Table 3.1 summarizes the functions of digestive secretions.

stool (feces) Waste products that are stored in the large intestine and then excreted from the body. Consists mostly of bacteria, sloughed-off gastrointestinal cells, inorganic matter, water, unabsorbed nutrients, food residue, undigested fibers, fatty acids, mucus, and remnants of digestive fluids.

rectum The lowest part of the large intestine, continuous with the sigmoid colon and the **anus.**

hormones Chemical substances that regulate, initiate, or direct cellular activity.

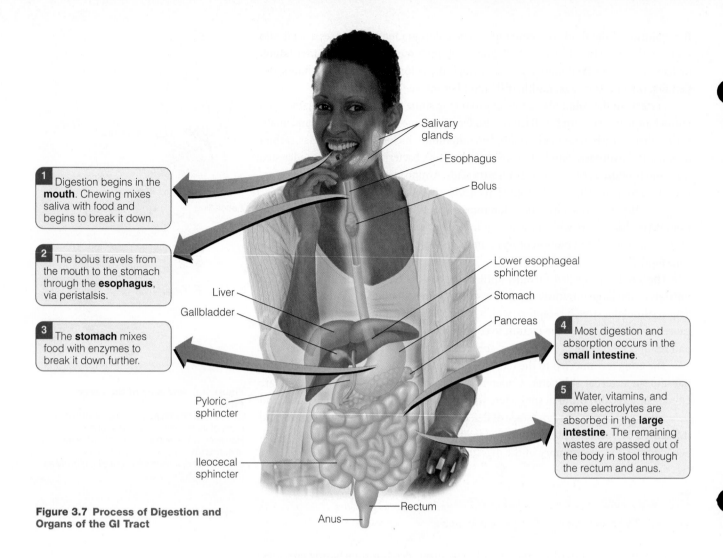

1 Digestion begins in the **mouth**. Chewing mixes saliva with food and begins to break it down.

2 The bolus travels from the mouth to the stomach through the **esophagus**, via peristalsis.

3 The **stomach** mixes food with enzymes to break it down further.

4 Most digestion and absorption occurs in the **small intestine**.

5 Water, vitamins, and some electrolytes are absorbed in the **large intestine**. The remaining wastes are passed out of the body in stool through the rectum and anus.

Salivary glands
Esophagus
Bolus
Lower esophageal sphincter
Stomach
Pancreas
Liver
Gallbladder
Pyloric sphincter
Ileocecal sphincter
Rectum
Anus

Figure 3.7 Process of Digestion and Organs of the GI Tract

Take a Ride through the GI Tract

Want to learn even more about the organs of the GI tract? Visit www.pearsonhighered.com/blake and slide through the organs and their functions.

bile A greenish-yellow fluid made in the liver and concentrated and stored in the gallbladder. It helps emulsify fat and prepare it for digestion.

liver The largest gland of the body. It aids in digestive activity and is responsible for metabolism of nutrients, detoxification of alcohol, and some nutrient storage.

The Liver, Gallbladder, and Pancreas Are Accessory Organs

Although food doesn't pass through the liver, gallbladder, or pancreas during digestion, these three accessory organs are still essential to the process (see **Figure 3.8**). The liver, for example, makes **bile,** a greenish-yellow liquid that is important for fat digestion, and the gallbladder concentrates and stores the bile. As mentioned, the pancreas makes the hormones insulin and glucagon, as well as some important digestive enzymes.

Weighing in at about three pounds, the **liver** is the largest gland in the body. It is so important that you couldn't survive without it. In addition to its key role of producing bile, the liver helps regulate the metabolism of carbohydrates, fats, and protein. The liver also stores several nutrients, including vitamins A, D, and E; the minerals iron and copper; and glycogen, the storage form of glucose. The liver is also essential for processing and detoxifying alcohol. You'll learn about each of these functions in more depth in later chapters of this book. For our overview of digestion, we'll focus on the liver's role in bile production.

The liver produces about 500 to 1,000 milliliters (about 2 pints) of bile each day.[19] Bile consists of water, bile acids (and/or salts), cholesterol, phospholipids, pigments, and several ions. Bile has two main functions:

1. It breaks up large fat globules into small, suspended fat droplets. This action enhances the absorption of fats because it increases the surface area exposed

Table 3.1

Functions of Digestive Secretions

Secretion	Secreted From	Function
Saliva	Glands in the mouth	Moistens food, eases swallowing, contains the enzyme salivary amylase
Mucus	Stomach, small and large intestines	Lubrication and coating of the internal mucosa to protect it from chemical or mechanical damage
Hydrochloric acid (HCl)	Stomach	Activation of enzymes that begin protein digestion
Bile	Liver (stored in the gallbladder)	Emulsifies fat in the small intestine
Bicarbonate	Pancreas	Raises pH and neutralizes stomach acid
Enzymes (amylases, proteases, and lipases)	Stomach, small intestine, pancreas	Chemicals that break down food into nutrient components that can be absorbed
Hormones (gastrin, secretin, cholecystokinin, and gastric inhibiting peptide)	Stomach, small intestine	Chemicals that regulate digestive activity, increase or decrease peristalsis, and stimulate various digestive secretions

to fat-digesting enzymes. The breakdown of fat also increases the rate of fat digestion.

2. Bile also functions as an emulsifier, dispersing fat throughout the chyme, thus helping enzymes to make contact with it and digest it. *Emulsification* is the dispersion of fat or the surrounding of fat with hydrophilic (water-soluble) and hydrophobic (fat-soluble) portions. This action is similar to the detergent activity of dishwashing soap on greasy dishes.

Bile is collected, drained, and released into the gallbladder. The gallbladder is attached to the liver and stores approximately 30 to 50 milliliters (1 to 2 ounces) of concentrated bile at a time. Bile is released into the GI tract in response to the ingestion of fat. Bile aids in fat digestion but isn't digested itself. Whereas some compounds of bile leave the body in stool, the bile acids are reabsorbed and return to the liver to be reused in new bile.

The **pancreas** is an organ about the size and shape of your hand that produces hormones, including the two blood-regulating hormones, insulin and glucagon. It also produces digestive enzymes that are delivered into the duodenum. The pancreas has a duct that merges with the bile duct (from the gallbladder) and enters the duodenum through the common bile duct.

Sodium bicarbonate and several powerful, specific enzymes essential for the final stages of food digestion are produced in the pancreas. Sodium bicarbonate neutralizes the acidic chyme (raises the pH), creating a neutral environment. This protects certain enzymes that would otherwise become inactivated in an acidic environment.

Some of the most important enzymes produced by the pancreas are *amylase*, which digests carbohydrate; *lipase*, which digests fat; and *trypsin*, *chymotrypsin*, and *carboxypeptidase*, which digest protein. The enzymes from the pancreas are responsible for the digestion of almost all (90 percent) of ingested fat, about half (50 percent) of all ingested protein, and half (50 percent) of all carbohydrates.[20]

Pancreatic secretion is regulated by various hormones. When acidic chyme enters the small intestine, the hormone secretin is produced by intestinal cells. Secretin stimulates the pancreas to secrete copious amounts of sodium bicarbonate and various digestive enzymes. When partially digested protein and fat enter the small intestine, the intestinal cells secrete the hormone cholecystokinin. This powerful hormone also

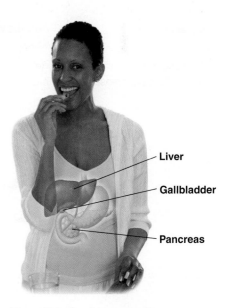

Liver

Gallbladder

Pancreas

Figure 3.8 The Accessory Organs
The liver, gallbladder, and pancreas produce digestive secretions that flow into the small intestine through various ducts.

pancreas Accessory organ of digestion that produces hormones and enzymes. It's connected to the duodenum via the bile duct.

Table 3.2

Organs of the GI Tract and Their Functions

Organ	Function	How They Work Together to Digest a Peanut Butter Sandwich
Mouth	Begins breaking down food into components through chewing	Saliva moistens the sandwich as your teeth grind the food. Amylase begins to break down the carbohydrate in the bread.
Esophagus	Transfers food from the mouth to the stomach	Bolus of sandwich moves through the esophagus to the stomach.
Sphincters (LES, pyloric, ileocecal)	Keep swallowed food from returning to the esophagus, stomach, or small intestine	The LES makes sure that the sandwich stays in the stomach once it gets there.
Stomach	Mixes food with digestive juices; breaks down some nutrients into smaller components	The HCl activates pepsin to begin digesting the protein in the sandwich. Gastric lipase starts breaking down the triglycerides in the peanut butter.
Small intestine	Completes digestion of food and absorbs nutrients through its walls	The carbohydrates, proteins, and fat are broken down further with the help of bile and other enzymes so they can be absorbed.
Large intestine	Absorbs water and some nutrients; passes waste products out of the body	The fiber in the bread leaves the body in the stool.
Accessory organs (liver, gallbladder, pancreas)	Release hormones and enzymes, and help break down food or direct digestive activity	Hormones cause the release of gastric lipase as well as cause the gallbladder to release the stored bile into the small intestine to help emulsify the fat in the peanut butter sandwich. The liver produces the bile and also regulates the metabolism of the absorbed nutrients. The pancreas produces the two important blood-regulating hormones, insulin and glucagon.

stimulates the pancreas to secrete digestive enzymes, slows down gastric motility (which controls the pace of digestion), and contributes to meal satisfaction.

Table 3.2 not only summarizes the organs of the GI tract and their functions but also shows you how these organs work together to digest a peanut butter sandwich. The next several chapters will further illustrate how the specific nutrients in foods that you eat, such as pasta and pizza, travel through your GI tract and are digested, absorbed, and or/eliminated from your body.

Your Body Can Store Some Surplus Nutrients

While you now know how the body digests and absorbs the nutrients from foods, you might be wondering what happens to the nutrients once they are absorbed. Whereas some nutrients are used immediately for energy and other functions, your body can store other, surplus nutrients to be used in times of need. For example, some excess glucose is stored in your liver and muscles in a form called glycogen, to be readily available when you don't eat, such as between meals. Other excess energy (calories) is stored in the form of fat cells. Some vitamins and minerals can also be stored. For example, storing calcium in your bones will help keep them strong. However, storing excessive amounts of fat-soluble vitamins, such as vitamin A, and some minerals, such as iron, can be toxic.

 NutriTools

Build-a-Sandwich

Can you put together a healthy meal between slices of bread? Visit www.pearsonhighered.com/blake and complete this interactive NutriTools activity to find out.

The Take-Home Message In the mouth, saliva mixes with food during chewing, moistening it and making it easier to swallow. Swallowed food that has mixed with digestive juices in the stomach becomes chyme. Maximum digestion and absorption occur through the villi and microvilli in the small intestine. Undigested residue next enters the large intestine, where additional absorption of water and electrolytes occurs. Eventually, the remnants of digestion reach the anus and exit the body in stool. Enzymes, hormones, and bile help break down food and regulate digestion. The liver, gallbladder, and pancreas are important accessory organs. The liver produces bile and the gallbladder concentrates and stores it. The pancreas produces enzymes and hormones. Some excess nutrients can be stored in your body.

What Other Body Systems Affect Your Use of Nutrients?

The human body is a well-coordinated organism. Each of us eats, drinks, sleeps, and lives a normal existence without too much thought about what we are consuming. We don't have to constantly worry about keeping ourselves nourished, or distributing nutrients to our cells, because numerous body systems are doing this work for us. Among the systems that remind us to eat, distribute nutrients in our bodies, and excrete waste products are the nervous system, the circulatory and lymphatic systems, the endocrine system, and the excretory system.

The Nervous System Stimulates Your Appetite

The main role of the nervous system in keeping you nourished is to let you know when you need to eat and drink and when to stop. Your brain, with the help of hormones, has a central role in communicating and interpreting the message of hunger and encouraging you to seek food. For example, when your stomach is empty, the hormone ghrelin signals your brain to eat. If you ignore the signals of hunger or thirst sent by your nervous system, you may experience a headache, dizziness, or weakness. The nervous system helps each of us make daily decisions regarding what to eat, when to eat, where to eat, and, perhaps most important, when to stop eating.

The Circulatory System Distributes Nutrients through Your Blood

The blood is the body's primary transport system, shuttling oxygen, nutrients, hormones, and waste products throughout the body. The oxygen-rich blood that the heart receives from the lungs is pumped from the right side of the heart out to the body for its use (**Figure 3.9**). During digestion, the blood picks up nutrients through the capillary walls in the GI tract, transports them to your liver, and eventually delivers them to the cells of your body. Without the circulatory system,

Figure 3.9 The Circulatory and Lymphatic Systems
Blood and lymph are fluids that circulate throughout the body. They both distribute nutrients to cells and blood also picks up waste products from cells and delivers them to the kidneys for eventual excretion.

nutrients that you eat would not reach your cells. Equally important, the blood removes carbon dioxide, excess water, and waste products from the cells and brings these substances to the lungs (carbon dioxide) and kidneys (water, waste products) for excretion (see below).

The Lymphatic System Distributes Some Nutrients through Your Lymph

The lymphatic system is a complex network of capillaries, small vessels, valves, nodes, and ducts that helps maintain the internal fluid environment. Some absorbed nutrients, such as the products of fat digestion, must pass through the lymphatic system before they enter the bloodstream because they are too large to enter the bloodstream directly. Lymph also transports digested fat-soluble vitamins from the intestinal tract to your blood. The lymph eventually connects with the blood near the heart. Lymph also contains white blood cells that aid your immune system.

The Endocrine System Releases Hormones That Help Regulate the Use of Nutrients

The endocrine system consists of a series of glands, including the pancreas, the pituitary, the thyroid, and the adrenal glands, that release hormones into the bloodstream. The hormones regulate growth, reproduction, metabolism, and the cells' use of nutrients. For example, the hormones insulin and glucagon help regulate blood levels of glucose. When blood glucose levels get too high, the pancreas releases insulin, which directs the glucose out of the blood and into cells. On the flip side, if blood glucose levels dip too low, the body releases glucagon, which directs the release of the body's stored glucose to increase the levels in blood. We will learn more about the important roles of hormones in future chapters.

The Excretory System Passes Urine Out of the Body

The excretory system eliminates wastes from the circulatory system. After the cells have gleaned the nutrients and other useful metabolic components they need, waste products accumulate. For example, the breakdown of proteins creates nitrogen-containing waste, such as urea, that must be eliminated. The kidneys filter the blood, allowing these waste products to be concentrated in urine and excreted out of your body (**Figure 3.10**). Excess water-soluble vitamins are also excreted in urine. Finally, the kidneys play an important role in helping the body maintain water balance.

The Take-Home Message In addition to the digestive system, other body systems help us use the nutrients we take in from foods. The nervous system lets us know when we need to eat or drink, the blood and lymph systems deliver absorbed nutrients to cells, the endocrine system releases hormones that regulate nutrient use in cells, and the excretory system helps filter and eliminate waste products from the blood.

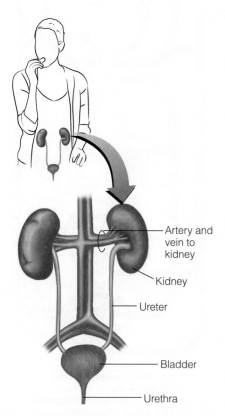

Artery and vein to kidney

Kidney

Ureter

Bladder

Urethra

Figure 3.10 The Excretory System
Water and waste products from cells are filtered from your blood in the kidneys and expelled from your body in urine.

What Are Some Common Digestive Disorders?

Generally, the digestive tract works just fine. As a matter of fact, it doesn't usually require tinkering or medications to be healthy. But sometimes the digestive tract gets "off track" and the resulting symptoms can quickly catch your attention. Some of the problems are minor, like occasional heartburn or indigestion. Other problems such as ulcers or colon cancer are very serious.

Disorders of the Mouth and Esophagus

Oral health involves healthy teeth, gums, and supporting tissue. Maintaining a healthy oral environment is important because these tissues are used to bite, chew, taste, speak, smile, swallow, and communicate through facial expressions. Properly nourishing yourself can be difficult if you have chronic oral disease or extensive dental problems. There are many oral diseases, but we will only review some of the most common ones in this section.

Gingivitis and Periodontal Disease

In addition to tooth decay, which we'll discuss in depth in Chapter 4, common oral health problems include gingivitis and periodontal disease. Gingivitis is an early form of periodontal disease that involves gum swelling, bleeding, and oral pain. Periodontal disease is an inflammation of the gums that leads to multiple dental diseases. It is caused by infections or by plaque that adheres to the surface of the teeth, and is a common problem for adults over age 35.[21] Periodontitis results in a gradual loss of teeth as they loosen or partially separate from the gums and jawbone. Even though these conditions are serious, they are treatable with various dental procedures, optimal food choices, and excellent oral hygiene. Other oral health problems include dry mouth, inflamed oral tissue, cold sores, soft tissue ulceration, oral cancers, fungal infections, or various abnormalities of the tongue.

Swallowing Problems

Under some circumstances the ability to swallow is compromised. Difficult swallowing, or **dysphagia,** can have mechanical causes such as tumors, scar tissue, obstruction, cancer, trauma, or other barriers in the throat. Dysphagia can also result from nerve damage or a stroke.

Swallowing problems can lead to malnutrition, respiratory problems, tooth decay, nasal regurgitation, and compromised health. Various health care professionals are trained to help a person overcome swallowing difficulties.

Esophageal Problems

Several esophageal problems can lead to annoying symptoms such as belching, hiccups, burning sensations, or uncomfortable feelings of fullness. Some serious esophageal problems include cancer, obstruction from tumors, faulty nerve impulses, severe inflammation, and abnormal sphincter function.

One of the most common problems involving the esophagus is **heartburn,** or *reflux disease.* About 7 percent of the population experiences daily heartburn, about 20 percent of adults report frequent heartburn, and 25 to 35 percent of adults have

dysphagia Difficult swallowing.

heartburn A burning sensation originating in the esophagus. Heartburn is usually caused by the reflux of gastric contents from the stomach into the esophagus. Chronic heartburn can lead to **gastroesophageal reflux disease (GERD).**

occasional symptoms.[22] Collectively, this adds up to millions of people experiencing heartburn symptoms.

Heartburn, also known as indigestion or acid reflux, is caused by hydrochloric acid flowing from the stomach back into the esophagus or even the throat. The acid causes a lingering, unpleasant, sour taste in the mouth. Other symptoms include nausea, bloating, belching, a vague burning sensation, or an uncomfortable feeling of fullness. Chronic heartburn can lead to a condition called **gastroesophageal reflux disease,** or **GERD.**

A weak LES is often the culprit in HCl reflux, because it sometimes permits this backflow of stomach fluids into the esophagus. Certain foods, including chocolate, fried or fatty foods, coffee, soda, onions, and garlic, seem to be associated with this condition.[23] Lifestyle factors also play a role. For example, smoking cigarettes, drinking alcohol, wearing tight-fitting clothes, being overweight or obese, eating large evening meals, and reclining after eating tend to cause or worsen the condition. If dietary changes and behavior modification are insufficient to relieve the heartburn, over-the-counter antacids or prescription drugs may help. In rare circumstances, surgical intervention is required to treat severe, unrelenting heartburn.

Esophageal cancer is another medical condition that has serious consequences. According to the National Cancer Institute, esophageal cancer is one of the most common cancers of the digestive tract, and the seventh leading cause of cancer-related deaths worldwide. In the United States, this type of cancer is typically found among individuals older than 50 years, men, those who live in urban areas, long-term smokers, and heavy drinkers.[24] Treatments include surgery, radiation, and chemotherapy.

Disorders of the Stomach

Does your stomach ever "growl"? A rumbling stomach, or *borborygmus,* isn't really a disorder (though if it's accompanied by pain or vomiting, it can be a sign of a larger problem, such as a mechanical obstruction).[25] Rather, the gurgling is due to the gas and air pockets that form as the stomach contents are pushed through the GI tract. The best way to quiet the noise is to eat or drink something, or to apply mild pressure to the abdomen. Other stomach problems can range from the trivial, like an occasional stomachache, to life-threatening complications such as bleeding ulcers or stomach cancer.

At some point in time, everyone has had a stomachache. Common causes include overeating, gastric bloating, or eating too fast. Other possible causes include eating foods that are high in fat or fiber, eating spicy foods, lactose intolerance, or swallowing air while eating. More serious causes of a stomachache include the flu or consuming food or water that is contaminated with bacteria. Stomach flu or **gastroenteritis** is an inflammation of the stomach or intestines caused by a virus or bacteria. Flu symptoms include nausea, vomiting, diarrhea, and abdominal cramping. Sometimes the problem requires medical intervention, but usually rest, oral rehydration therapy, and a soft-food diet will help with the symptoms of this type of flu. (*Note:* The stomach flu is not the same as influenza (flu), which is a respiratory illness caused by the influenza virus.)

Peptic ulcers occur in the lower region of the stomach.[26] Ulcers are a sore or erosion in the stomach or intestinal lining caused by drugs, alcohol, or, more often, the *Helicobacter pylori* bacterium. Symptoms of an ulcer include abdominal pain, vomiting, fatigue, bleeding, and general weakness. Medical treatments may consist of prescription drugs and dietary recommendations, such as limiting alcohol and caffeine-containing beverages, and/or restricting spices and acidic foods.

Certain foods and lifestyle factors contribute to heartburn.

gastroenteritis Formal term for "stomach flu." Caused by a virus or bacteria and results in inflammation of the stomach and/or intestines.

peptic ulcers Sores, erosions, or breaks in the mucosal lining of the stomach.

(Left) An ulcer is created when the mucosal lining of the GI tract erodes or breaks. (Right) Gallstones result from the crystallization of salts and other compounds in bile.

Gallbladder Disease

One common problem of an unhealthy gallbladder is the presence of **gallstones.** Most people with gallstones have abnormally thick bile, and the bile is high in cholesterol and low in bile acids. Over an extended period of time, the high-cholesterol bile forms crystals, then sludge, and finally gallstones. Some individuals with gallstones experience no pain or mild pain. Others have severe pain accompanied by fever, nausea, vomiting, cramps, and obstruction of the bile duct.

Medical treatment for gallstones may involve surgery to remove the gallbladder, prescription medicine to dissolve the stones, shock-wave therapy (a type of ultrasound treatment) to break them up, or a combination of therapies. If surgery is required to remove the gallbladder, patients typically recover quickly. After gallbladder removal surgery, the anatomy of the biliary tract adapts. The liver continues to produce the bile and secrete it directly into the duodenum. Interestingly, the remaining bile duct dilates, forming a "simulated pouch" that works in a manner very similar to the original gallbladder.

Disorders of the Intestines

Disorders of the intestines can occur anywhere along the length of the small and large intestines. Common, temporary problems can include gassiness, diarrhea, constipation, and hemorrhoids; more serious disorders include celiac disease and Crohn's disease.

Flatulence

Flatulence is the release of intestinal gas from the rectum. It can be uncomfortable and sometimes embarrassing (but normal). Intestinal gas is produced for a variety of reasons, and most adults release it 10 to 20 times a day! Eating too fast, or drinking beverages with added air, such as beer and carbonated beverages, can result in the intake of air that makes its way through the GI tract. Legumes such as beans and lentils can lead to gas production because they contain indigestible carbohydrates that are fermented by intestinal bacteria. The bacteria produce the gas as a by-product. The gas is a mixture of carbon dioxide, hydrogen, nitrogen, oxygen, and methane. The offending odor comes from the gases that contain sulfur. Using products such as Beano, eating smaller meals, adding fiber gradually in your diet, and increasing your fluid intake can all help you help reduce the amount of gas produced.

Constipation and Diarrhea

Constipation is caused by excessively slow movements of the undigested residue through the colon, and is often due to insufficient fiber or water intake. Consuming an

gallstones Small, hard, crystalline structures formed in the gallbladder or bile duct due to abnormally thick bile.

flatulence Production of excessive gas in the stomach or the intestines.

constipation Difficulty in passing stools.

Celiac Disease: An Issue of Absorption

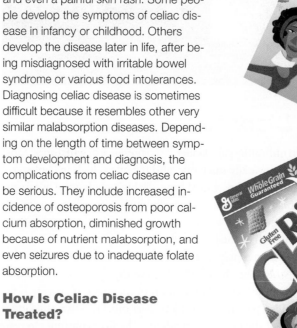

One of the more serious malabsorption conditions to occur in the small intestine is celiac disease. A healthy small intestine contains the numerous villi and microvilli that efficiently and exhaustively absorb nutrients from food. In some people (about 1 in 133 Americans), the lining of the small intestine flattens out due to an autoimmune reaction to gluten, a protein found in wheat and other grains. This reduces the intestine's ability to absorb nutrients.

What Causes Celiac Disease?

The exact cause of celiac disease is unknown, but it is believed to be genetic, and is more common among people of European descent. The risk for the disease may be decreased by breast-feeding rather than bottle-feeding infants. Celiac disease is sometimes detected or caused by surgery, pregnancy, a viral infection, or severe emotional stress.

What Are the Symptoms of Celiac Disease?

The classic celiac symptoms include reoccurring abdominal bloating, cramping, diarrhea, gas, fatty and foul-smelling stools, weight loss, anemia, fatigue, bone or joint pain, and even a painful skin rash. Some people develop the symptoms of celiac disease in infancy or childhood. Others develop the disease later in life, after being misdiagnosed with irritable bowel syndrome or various food intolerances. Diagnosing celiac disease is sometimes difficult because it resembles other very similar malabsorption diseases. Depending on the length of time between symptom development and diagnosis, the complications from celiac disease can be serious. They include increased incidence of osteoporosis from poor calcium absorption, diminished growth because of nutrient malabsorption, and even seizures due to inadequate folate absorption.

How Is Celiac Disease Treated?

The only treatment for celiac disease is a gluten-free diet. This should stop the symptoms from progressing, allow the intestines to heal, and prevent further damage. The symptoms often improve within a few days after beginning the gluten-free diet.

Within three to six months, the absorption area of the intestinal tract often returns to normal status, if the diet is faithfully followed. Depending on the age at diagnosis and the severity of the disease, there may be some permanent health problems such as delayed or stunted growth.

Adhering to a gluten-free diet, which means avoiding breads, pasta, and cereals, among other foods, can be challenging. However, there are many gluten-free foods to choose from, such as meat,

---

adequate amount of dietary fiber daily can help prevent constipation. Stress, inactivity, or various illnesses can also lead to constipation. It is usually treated with increasing the fiber and fluids in the diet. Daily exercise, establishing eating and resting routines, and using over-the-counter stool softeners are usually recommended to treat this condition.

Diarrhea is the passage of frequent, watery, loose stools. It is considered more serious than constipation because of the loss of fluids and electrolytes. If the diarrhea continues for an extended period of time, you may malabsorb additional nutrients, which can lead to malnutrition. There are many causes of diarrhea, including con-

diarrhea Frequent, loose, watery stools.

Gluten-Free Diets

Allowed Foods	Foods to Avoid	Processed Foods That May Contain Wheat, Barley, or Rye
Amaranth	Wheat, including:	Bouillon cubes
Arrowroot	Einkorn	Brown rice syrup
Buckwheat	Emmer	Candy
Cassava	Spelt	Chips/potato chips
Corn	Kamut	Cold cuts, hot dogs, salami, sausage
Flax	Wheat starch	Communion wafer
Indian rice grass	Wheat bran	French fries
Job's tears	Wheat germ	Gravy
Legumes	Cracked wheat	Imitation fish
Millet	Hydrolyzed wheat protein	Matzo
Nuts	Bromated flour	Rice mixes
Potatoes	Durum flour	Sauces
Quinoa	Semolina	Seasoned tortilla chips
Rice	White, wheat, graham flour	Self-basting turkey
Sago	Barley	Soups
Seeds	Rye	Soy sauce
Soy	Triticale (a cross between wheat and rye)	Vegetables in sauce
Sorghum		
Tapioca		
Wild rice		
Yucca		

Adapted from T. Thompson. *Celiac Disease Nutrition Guide*, 2nd ed. (Chicago: American Dietetic Association, 2006), used with permission. For a complete copy of this guide, visit www.eatright.org.

milk, eggs, fruit, and vegetables. These foods are permissible in any quantity. Rice, potatoes, corn, and beans are also acceptable because they do not contain gluten (see the table Gluten-Free Diets). Specially formulated gluten-free breads, pasta, and cereal products are also available in many supermarkets. The most problematic feature of the diet is avoiding the multiple foods that contain "latent," or hidden, sources of gluten. Individuals with celiac disease need to read food labels.

Celiac disease is a manageable condition. Individuals with celiac disease can live normal lives. They can learn about their condition by talking to health care professionals. Researchers are currently working to determine the exact component in gluten that causes celiac disease, and to develop enzymes that would destroy these immunotoxic peptides.

taminated water, various microorganisms, stress, or excessive fiber intake. Diarrhea is generally treated with fluid and electrolyte replacement. Most physicians identify the cause(s) of the diarrhea in addition to treating the symptoms.

Hemorrhoids

Hemorrhoids are a condition in which pressure in the veins in the rectum and anus causes swelling and inflammation. The walls of the veins dilate, become thin, and bleed. As the pressure builds, the vessels protrude. Straining to pass dry stools,

hemorrhoids Swelling in the veins of the rectum and anus.

Polyp

Polyps, or abnormal growths, on the lining of the large intestine may indicate early stages of colon cancer.

pregnancy, chronic constipation or diarrhea, and aging are all factors that can contribute to hemorrhoids. You may never know that you have hemorrhoids unless they begin to bleed (following a bowel movement), itch, or become painful. As with constipation, increasing both your fiber and fluid intake can treat hemorrhoids. Sometimes surgery may be necessary to remove hemorrhoids.

More Serious Intestinal Disorders

The more serious small intestine and large intestine problems, such as irritable bowel syndrome, celiac disease, Crohn's disease, and colon cancer, tend to involve nutrient malabsorption, which can cause severe health consequences. The symptoms of these diseases vary, but they include abdominal pain, nausea, vomiting, bloating, loss of appetite, diarrhea, anxiety, weight loss, and fatigue. The medical problems that have to be addressed include various anemias, gastrointestinal blockages, inflammation, malnutrition, growth failure, vitamin and mineral deficiencies, and other medically complicated challenges.

Irritable Bowel Syndrome (IBS)

Approximately 20 percent, or one in five, American adults have symptoms of **irritable bowel syndrome (IBS).** In fact, it is one of the most common disorders diagnosed and treated by doctors.[27] IBS is a functional disorder that involves changes in colon rhythm; it is not an actual disease. People with IBS overrespond to colon stimuli. This results in alternating patterns of diarrhea, constipation, and abdominal pain. The exact cause of IBS is unknown, but low-fiber diets, stress, consumption of irritating foods, and intestinal motility disorders are all suspected factors. Medical management includes dietary modification, stress management, and occasional use of prescription drugs.

Celiac Disease

Celiac disease is an autoimmune, genetic disorder that causes a person's own immune system to damage the small intestine when gluten, a protein in wheat and other grains, is consumed. Rachel, the person you read about in the beginning of this chapter, has celiac disease and needs to make many dietary adjustments. The boxed feature "Celiac Disease: An Issue of Absorption" explains this intestinal disorder in greater detail. Note that celiac disease is not the same thing as **gluten intolerance,** which does not involve the immune system or damage the wall of the small intestine. However, individuals with gluten intolerance can experience symptoms such as stomachaches, diarrhea, bloating, and tiredness if gluten is consumed.

Crohn's Disease

Crohn's disease, or inflammatory bowel disease, is the general name for diseases that cause swelling in the intestines. Crohn's disease can affect any area of the GI tract, from the mouth to the anus, but it typically affects the ileum. The swelling can cause pain and diarrhea. Bleeding from the rectum, weight loss, and anemia are just some of the symptoms that can occur. Though there isn't a cure for Crohn's disease, medication, nutritional and dietary supplements, and/or surgery are currently used to manage the disease.[28]

Colon Cancer

Colon cancer is one of the leading forms of cancer and the second leading cause of cancer deaths. Fortunately, colon cancer is one of the most curable forms of cancer, if it is detected in the early stages.

irritable bowel syndrome (IBS) A functional disorder that involves changes in colon rhythm.

celiac disease An illness of the small intestine that involves the inability to digest the protein gluten.

gluten intolerance A sensitivity to the protein gluten, which is found in wheat and other grains. Symptoms incude stomachaches, diarrhea, bloating, and tiredness.

Crohn's disease An inflammatory bowel disease.

Table 3.3

Common Digestive Disorders

Site	Disorder	Symptoms	Causes	Treatment
Esophagus and stomach	Gastrointestinal reflux disease (GERD)	Sore throat, burning sensation in the chest (heartburn)	Poor eating habits; overeating; other lifestyle choices	Eat smaller meals; eat more slowly; decrease fat and/or alcohol intake; quit smoking
Stomach or small intestine	Gastric and duodenal ulcers	Bleeding, pain, vomiting, fatigue, weakness	Multiple causes	Prescription drugs and an as-tolerated diet
Gallbladder	Gallstones	Cramps, bloating, intense abdominal pain, diarrhea	The concentration of high-cholesterol-containing bile that crystallizes and forms stones in the duct	Gallbladder removal, medication, or shock-wave therapy
Small intestine	Celiac disease	Malabsorption	Error of gluten metabolism	Gluten-free diet
Small intestine	Crohn's disease	Pain, diarrhea, rectal bleeding, weight loss, anemia	Swelling of the intestines	Medication, nutritional or dietary supplements, surgery
Large intestine	Constipation	Cramping, bloated uncomfortable feeling in abdomen	Too little water or too little fiber; inactivity	More water, fiber, and exercise
Large intestine	Diarrhea	Too-frequent bowel movements	Multiple causes	Water and electrolyte replacement
Large intestine	Irritable bowel syndrome (IBS)	Diarrhea and constipation in alternating sequence; pain	Unknown cause(s); stress worsens the condition	Self-management with fiber therapy, stress relief, and good sleep habits
Large intestine	Colon cancer	Symptoms are often silent; may include weight loss, internal bleeding, iron-deficiency anemia, fatigue	Multiple causes (genetics, various colon diseases, smoking, exposure to dietary carcinogens)	Radiation therapy, chemotherapy, surgery

Colon cancer often begins with polyps on the lining of the colon. They vary in size from that of a small pea to that of a mushroom or plum. The good news is that polyps can be removed surgically, and they are often small and benign. If the polyps are not removed or change to cancerous tumors, colon cancer can be more difficult to cure.

Individuals diagnosed with colon cancer may require radiation therapy, chemotherapy, and surgery to remove part of the colon or the entire colon. After surgery, patients are given dietary advice regarding the foods that would be the most comfortable to eat. Survival rates vary depending on the individual's age, health, treatment response, and stage of cancer diagnosis.

Table 3.3 summarizes common digestive disorders.

The Take-Home Message Gastrointestinal diseases and digestive disorders include less serious conditions, like heartburn (GERD), indigestion, stomach flu, flatulence, constipation, diarrhea, and hemorrhoids, and more serious conditions, such as esophageal cancer, gastric ulcers, irritable bowel syndrome, celiac disease, Crohn's disease, and colon cancer. Disorders of the small intestine may result in malnutrition.

Two Points of View

Probiotics: Do You Need Them? Probiotics are live microorganisms, usually bacteria, mainly found in cultured dairy foods.[1] Some research indicates that probiotics can have health benefits for the immune and digestive systems. However, the research is not conclusive, and some experts feel adding probiotics to the diet is ineffective at best and possibly harmful at worst. Should you seek out fortified yogurt or probiotic supplements, or can you get along fine without them? Read the arguments below, then consider the critical thinking questions and decide for yourself.

Yes

- Regular consumption of certain probiotics helps maintain the normal functioning of the digestive system. Probiotics can help in the prevention or treatment of antibiotic-associated disorders, in the treatment (and to a lesser extent prevention) of gastroenteritis (stomach inflammation) and diarrhea, and in the alleviation of lactose intolerance.[2]

- Some specific strains of probiotics have been shown to increase regularity in some people who have occasional constipation. Other strains have been studied for their effects on decreasing the frequency of irritable bowel syndrome and some inflammatory bowel conditions.[3]

- Probiotics are generally considered safe. Their safety is somewhat evident by the fact that they have a long history of use in dairy foods like yogurt, cheese, and milk.[4]

- Though the burden lies with the manufacturer to make sure that the correct probiotic is added to the product and in adequate amounts, there is some regulation of probiotic labeling. The FDA requires that the food label of these products contain accurate and relevant information.[5]

No

- We do not have sufficient information to say that probiotics are always beneficial and never harmful. Research is promising in several areas of digestive health but more research is needed to confirm their effectiveness, safety, and optimal dosage and duration.[6]

- Some consumers could experience gas or bloating when consuming probiotic products. The microorganisms may also have the potential to cause more serious side effects, especially in people with underlying health conditions.[7]

- People who have short bowel syndrome, a weakened immune system, a damaged intestinal lining, or are recovering from surgery are at a higher risk for side effects. These individuals should take probiotics only under the advice of a health care provider.

- Due to lack of strict FDA regulation, various probiotic products may not consistently contain the correct type of probiotics or enough of the probiotic to have an effect. Further, probiotics are not always delivered in an effective vehicle (foods versus supplements) and may be of variable quality.[8] Some products have been evaluated in well-controlled human studies, while others have no or not enough research to support their efficacy.

What do you think?

1. Do you think you should add probiotics to your diet? Why or why not? **2.** Which is the most compelling argument for taking probiotics? Which is the most compelling reason not to take them? Explain your rationale. **3.** Do you think we know enough about probiotics to recommend them to the public?

Chapter Review

 Be a Nutrition Sleuth

Diving into Digestion

You just ate a hamburger on a whole-wheat bun for lunch. What happens to the food during the digestive process? Visit **www.pearsonhighered.com/blake** and trace the path of your meal through your digestive system!

 Get Real!

How Do Your Eating Habits Stack Up?

What are your less-than-healthy eating habits? Visit **www.pearsonhighered.com/blake** and learn how your eating habits measure up.

The Top Ten Points to Remember

1. There are five categories of taste—sweet, salty, sour, bitter, and savory (umami)—but there are thousands of aromas and flavors. Hunger and thirst alert you to your basic physical need to take in food and fluid. Appetite is less about physical need and more about the psychological desire to take in foods.

2. Digestion is the process of breaking down food into absorbable nutrients. Digestion takes place in the organs of the GI tract—particularly in the stomach, small intestine, and large intestine.

3. There are both mechanical and chemical aspects of digestion. Mechanical digestion includes chewing and peristalsis. Chemical digestion involves mixing consumed food with enzymes and gastric juices to break it down.

4. Digestion begins in the mouth as chewing breaks down food and mixes it with saliva. Swallowing is a coordinated process that involves the mouth, throat, and esophagus. The stomach mixes food with enzymes and stores it before propelling it into the small intestine, where most digestion and absorption occur. The walls of the small intestine are covered with villi, which greatly increase its surface area and facilitate absorption. The large intestine absorbs water and some nutrients, before pushing waste through the colon and out of the body via the anus. Several sphincters control the entry and exit of food and chyme through the organs of the GI tract.

5. Hydrochloric acid, hormones, enzymes, bile, and bicarbonate are all necessary for efficient digestion. Hydrochloric acid is a gastric juice that helps prepare the food for further digestion. Hormones are chemical messengers that direct activities in the body. Hormones direct enzymes that do the actual work of facilitating

reactions. Bile is produced in the liver and stored in the gallbladder and is particularly important for fat digestion.

6. In addition to producing bile, the liver processes and metabolizes several nutrients after they have been digested and absorbed. The liver also stores several nutrients, and plays an important role in detoxifying alcohol. The gallbladder stores concentrated forms of bile. The pancreas produces both hormones and enzymes that play roles in digestion.

7. Body systems other than the digestive system help you use the nutrients you eat. Your nervous system lets you know when you are hungry or thirsty. Your circulatory and lymph systems distribute nutrients to all your cells. The endocrine system releases hormones that regulate the cells' use of nutrients, and the excretory system filters waste products, such as urea, from the blood and passes them out of the body in urine.

8. Flatulence is the release of intestinal gas from the rectum.

9. Digestive disorders can range from the trivial, such as occasional stomachaches, heartburn, diarrhea, constipation, or hemorrhoids, to the serious conditions of irritable bowel syndrome (IBS), Crohn's disease, ulcers, and cancer. Heartburn is the layman's term for the uncomfortable sensation of stomach acid returning to the esophagus or throat. A primary cause of heartburn is poor eating habits and other lifestyle choices. Constipation is a generally benign condition of sluggish colon movements commonly caused by a low-fiber, low-fluid diet. Diarrhea is a potentially serious and distressing condition characterized by frequent, loose, and watery stools. It is often caused by exposure

to microorganisms in food or water. IBS and Crohn's disease can lead to malabsorption and malnutrition. Peptic ulcers are sores or breaks in the lining of the stomach or upper part of the small intestine. Colon cancer begins with polyps on the intestinal lining and is very treatable if caught early.

10. Celiac disease is an autoimmune disorder of the small intestine that can be treated with a gluten-free diet. Celiac disease is not the same thing as gluten intolerance, which does not involve the immune system or damage the wall of the small intestine.

Test Your Knowledge

1. You have an innate preference for sweet and salty foods because
   a. your friends prefer these types of foods.
   b. these foods provide plenty of calories and nutrients, which you need for energy and health.
   c. these foods are less dangerous than sour or bitter foods.
   d. none of the above
2. _____ is the process that breaks down food into absorbable units.
   a. Circulation
   b. Digestion
   c. Absorption
   d. Excretion
3. Digestion begins in the
   a. liver.
   b. stomach.
   c. mouth.
   d. colon.
4. The name of the protective tissue that covers the trachea when you swallow is the
   a. esophagus.
   b. tongue.
   c. pharynx.
   d. epiglottis.
5. What causes heartburn?
   a. improper relaxation of the lower esophageal sphincter
   b. improper contraction of the lower esophageal sphincter
   c. improper and rapid swallowing
   d. improper breathing and chest congestion
6. The name of the secretion produced in the stomach that helps break down protein and activates pepsin is
   a. hydrochloric acid (HCl).
   b. amylase.

   c. bile.
   d. gastrin.
7. The sphincter that separates the stomach from the duodenum is the
   a. lower esophageal sphincter.
   b. ileocecal sphincter.
   c. pyloric sphincter.
   d. colon sphincter.
8. The compounds that help break down foods during digestion are
   a. enzymes.
   b. hormones.
   c. proteins.
   d. digestive organs.
9. What is the purpose of the gallbladder?
   a. to make bile
   b. to modify bile so it becomes liquid
   c. to digest bile
   d. to concentrate and store bile
10. Which of the following is true regarding the small intestine?
   a. The small intestine has a vast digestive surface area.
   b. The small intestine has minimal digestive surface area.
   c. The small intestine has access to lymph tissue, but not to the bloodstream.
   d. The small intestine is unimportant in the process of digestion.

Answers

1. (b) Sweet and salty foods provide sugar and electrolytes, which are important sources of energy and overall health. Too much of these types of foods, however, can lead to overconsumption of calories and therefore be unhealthy.
2. (b) Digestion. Circulation is the process of distributing blood or lymph throughout the body. Absorption is the process of pulling nutrients from the GI tract into the body. Excretion is the passing of waste products out of the body.
3. (c) Digestion begins in the mouth, where chewing starts breaking food down and mixing it with saliva and enzymes. The liver is an accessory organ to digestion. The stomach and colon (part of the large intestine) are organs in the GI tract.
4. (d) Epiglottis. The esophagus is a tube that connects your mouth with your stomach. The tongue is a muscle that pushes food to the back of the mouth into the pharynx. The pharynx is a chamber that food passes through just before being swallowed.

5. (a) Heartburn occurs when the lower esophageal sphincter allows acid from the stomach back into the esophagus.

6. (a) Hydrochloric acid (HCl) is part of the gastric juices produced in the stomach; it activates pepsin, breaks down connective tissue in meat, and destroys some ingested microorganisms. Amylase is an enzyme in the mouth that begins breaking down carbohydrates. Bile is made by the liver and emulsifies fat. Gastrin is a hormone in the stomach that stimulates digestive activity.

7. (c) The pyloric sphincter allows chyme to pass from the bottom of the stomach to the beginning of the duodenum, the first part of the small intestine. The lower esophageal sphincter is between the mouth and the stomach. The ileocecal sphincter separates the ileum from the colon. The colon sphincter is also called the anal sphincter and it is the last part of the GI tract.

8. (a) Enzymes. Enzymes such as amylase and lipase break down the individual nutrients during digestion. Hormones are chemical messengers that regulate activities such as metabolism and the cells' use of nutrients. Protein is a macronutrient, and the digestive organs include the stomach, small intestine, and large intestine.

9. (d) Bile is concentrated and stored in the gallbladder. The liver makes the bile in dilute, liquid form. Bile is not digested; rather, it circulates through the digestive tract.

10. (a) With numerous villi and microvilli along its interior wall, the small intestine indeed has a vast surface area that enhances digestion. Nutrients are absorbed through these projections and are transported through the blood and lymph throughout the body. The small intestine is critical to the process of digestion.

Web Resources

➡ To find out more about celiac's disease, visit www.celiac.org
➡ To learn about numerous types of cancer, cancer treatments, and preparation for treatment, visit www.cancer.gov
➡ Go to www.medicinenet.com to learn more about GI concerns, diseases, conditions, medicines, procedures, and treatments
➡ The National Library of Medicine is an abundant Internet resource for health care professionals, the public, researchers, and librarians; visit it at www.nlm.nih.gov
➡ To learn more about various digestive diseases, go to http://digestive.niddk.nih.gov

Answers to Myths and Misperceptions

1. **True.** Smell is a big part of taste. Turn to page 67 to find out more.

2. **True.** The gastrointestinal, or GI, tract runs through the body and connects the mouth to the anus. Turn to page 68 to find out more about the organs that make up the GI tract.

3. **False.** Your body is very efficient and absorbs more than 90 percent of the nutrients in food. To find out how this happens, turn to page 69.

4. **False.** The trachea is the windpipe. To find out what happens if food mistakenly enters it, turn to page 70.

5. **False.** Hydrochloric acid is only produced in the stomach. For more about digestive juices, turn to page 71.

6. **False.** Fats and protein take longer to digest than carbohydrates. Turn to page 71 to find out why.

7. **False.** Though most absorption does take place in the small intestine, some nutrients, particularly water, are absorbed in the large intestine. Turn to page 73 to learn more.

8. **True.** Stool (or feces) contains leftover food residue, nondigestible fibers, bacteria, gases, and sloughed-off intestinal cells. Turn to page 75 to find out more about the waste products of digestion.

9. **False.** Approximately 20 percent of adults experience heartburn every day. Turn to page 81 to learn what causes it.

10. **False.** Fiber helps keep you "regular." To find out more, turn to page 84.

4

Carbo

True or False?

1. You don't **need** to eat carbohydrates. ⓉⒻ p. 94

2. There is more fiber in dark-colored **wheat bread** than in white bread. ⓉⒻ p. 98

3. Americans do not consume **enough fiber.** ⓉⒻ p. 98

4. People who are **lactose intolerant** need to avoid all dairy products. ⓉⒻ p. 101

5. Carbohydrates make you **fat.** ⓉⒻ p. 107

6. Sugar causes **cavities.** ⓉⒻ p. 111

7. **Honey** is more nutritious than sugar. ⓉⒻ p. 111

8. Sugar free equals **calorie free.** ⓉⒻ p. 118

9. Saccharin causes **cancer** in humans. ⓉⒻ p. 118

10. Obesity increases your risk for **diabetes.** ⓉⒻ p. 128

See page 137 for answers to these Myths and Misperceptions.

hydrates
Sugars, Starches, and Fiber

Adam is nineteen and the star on his university's Division I hockey team. He spends about twice as much time in practice now as he did when he played for his high school team. When not on the ice, Adam is in the library maintaining a 3.7 GPA. Because of a grueling hockey and school schedule, he often doesn't eat a full meal until late in the evening. During his first semester, Adam lost some weight, but attributed it to the skating demands of the team. He was also feeling uncommonly irritable most days, and having more difficulty concentrating while studying. When his vision started to get blurry, the team trainer told him to go to the student health center to get his eyesight checked. The doctor at the center ordered a blood test and sent Adam home, after asking him to come back in the morning to repeat the blood test.

Do you have any idea why Adam's symptoms may have prompted the doctor to have his blood analyzed? What do you think the doctor suspects is happening to Adam?

In this chapter, you will learn about the condition that's likely causing Adam's symptoms and how it relates to the body's use of carbohydrate. We will also discuss the unique role that carbohydrates play in your body, the nutritional differences between simple and complex carbohydrates, the significance of high-fiber foods in fighting diseases such as obesity, heart disease, cancer, and diabetes, and, most importantly, how to change your diet to take advantage of all the wonderful attributes of carbohydrates.

Chapter Objectives

After reading this chapter, you will be able to:

1. Compare and contrast the monosaccharides, disaccharides, and polysaccharides.

2. List the functions of carbohydrates in the body.

3. Describe the differences between insoluble and soluble fibers and their role in promoting health.

4. Explain the process of digesting and absorbing dietary carbohydrates.

5. Explain how the body regulates blood glucose levels, and the hormones involved in the process.

6. Describe the guidelines for carbohydrate intake, including the AMDR for carbohydrates, the DRI for fiber, and the recommendation for consuming simple sugars.

7. Identify good food sources for each type of carbohydrate.

8. Describe the potential health implications of consuming too much or too little added sugar.

9. Define type 1 and type 2 diabetes and describe how diabetes differs from hypoglycemia.

10. List alternative sweeteners used as sugar substitutes.

What Are Carbohydrates and Why Do You Need Them?

Carbohydrates are essential nutrients that make up the foundation of diets the world over. They are predominant in plant-based foods such as grains (rice and pasta), fruits, vegetables, nuts, and legumes (dry beans and peas), but are also found in dairy products such as milk and yogurt. These foods are staples in cuisines from Asia to Latin America, the United States to the Mediterranean. In Asia, rice accounts for 80 percent of people's daily calories. In Latin America, carbohydrate-laden bananas and nuts adorn most dinner plates. In the Mediterranean, grain-based pastas, breads, and couscous are plentiful, and here in the United States, many people consume the good old potato on a daily basis.[1]

You need carbohydrates because they are the most desirable source of energy for your body. Providing four calories of energy per gram, their main role is to supply fuel, primarily in the form of **glucose** (*ose*= carbohydrate), the predominant sugar in high-carbohydrate foods, to your cells. Your brain in particular relies on glucose to function, as do your red blood cells.

The carbohydrates you eat come mostly from plant foods. Plants make carbohydrates to store energy and to build their root and stem structures. Animals, including humans, also store energy as carbohydrates, but in limited amounts. The storage form of carbohydrates in animals breaks down when the animal dies, so eating meat and poultry will not supply carbohydrates to our diets. Plants form the basic carbohydrate, glucose, in a process called **photosynthesis** (**Figure 4.1**). During photosynthesis, plants use the **chlorophyll** in their leaves to absorb the energy in sunlight. The absorbed energy splits water in the plant into its component parts: hydrogen and oxygen. Glucose is formed when the hydrogen joins with carbon dioxide that the plant has taken in from the air. The oxygen is released as a waste product.

Glucose is the most abundant carbohydrate in nature, and plants use it as energy, or combine it with minerals from the soil to make other compounds, such as protein and vitamins. They also link glucose units together and store them in the form of starch. Plants synthesize an estimated 140 billion tons of carbohydrates a year. This equals about 20 tons per person in the world.[2]

The Take-Home Message Carbohydrates are found most abundantly in plant-based foods. Your body cells, including brain cells and red blood cells, use them for energy. Many cultures around the world rely on carbohydrate-based foods as staples in their diets. Glucose is created in plants through the process of photosynthesis, and it is the most abundant carbohydrate in nature.

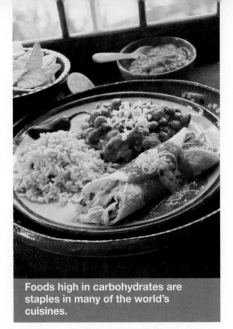
Foods high in carbohydrates are staples in many of the world's cuisines.

Figure 4.1 Photosynthesis: How Glucose Is Made
During photosynthesis, the leaves of green plants absorb the energy from sunlight. This energy splits six molecules of water (H_2O) into hydrogen and oxygen. The hydrogen joins with carbon dioxide in the plant to create glucose. In this process, six molecules of oxygen are released into the air. Glucose is the most abundant sugar in nature and the optimal fuel for your body.

glucose The most abundant sugar in foods and the primary energy source for your body.

photosynthesis A process by which green plants create carbohydrates using the energy from sunlight.

chlorophyll The green pigment in plants that absorbs energy from sunlight to begin the process of photosynthesis.

What Are Simple and Complex Carbohydrates?

Carbohydrates are divided into two categories based on the number of units that are joined together. **Simple carbohydrates** include **monosaccharides** (*mono* = one, *saccharide* = sugar) and **disaccharides** (*di* = two), and **complex carbohydrates** include **polysaccharides** (*poly* = many).

Simple Carbohydrates Contain One or Two Sugar Units

Three monosaccharides are found in foods. In addition to glucose, which we just discussed, there are **fructose** and **galactose** (**Figure 4.2**). Fructose is the sweetest of the simple sugars and is found abundantly in fruit. For this reason, it is often referred to as fruit sugar. Galactose is found in dairy foods. From these three sugars, the disaccharides can be created:

➤ When glucose and fructose join together, the disaccharide **sucrose,** or table sugar, is formed.
➤ When two glucose units join together, the disaccharide **maltose** is created. Maltose is the sugar found in grains, such as barley. It is used in the process of brewing beer.
➤ When glucose and galactose join together, the disaccharide **lactose** is created. Lactose is often called *milk sugar*, as it is found in dairy foods.

Polysaccharides Are Complex Carbohydrates

Polysaccharides consist of long chains of monosaccharides linked together. As you can see in Figure 4.2c, these chains contain many combined glucose units, which is why they are called complex carbohydrates. **Starch, fiber,** and **glycogen** are the three groups of polysaccharides.

Starch Is the Storage Form in Plants

Plants can store thousands of straight or branched glucose units strung together as starch. The straight chains of glucose units in starch are called amylose, whereas branched chains are called amylopectin. The many branches in amylopectin enable the body to break it down quickly and easily compared with amylose because there are so many sites where the enzymes can attach (Figure 4.2c). Starchy foods with highly branched amylopectin, such as potatoes, rice, bread, pasta, and cereals, are digested more rapidly than foods rich in amylose, such as legumes (dried peas, beans, and lentils).

Fiber Is Nondigestible but Important

Humans lack the digestive enzyme needed to break down fiber, so for the most part, fiber is the part of the plant that we eat but cannot digest. Plant components like cellulose, hemicellulose, lignins, gums, and pectin are all types of fibers. **Dietary fiber** is found naturally in foods and **functional fiber** is added to food for a specific, beneficial effect. For example, psyllium is a functional fiber derived from wheat husks. It can be added to breakfast cereals to help promote regular bowel moments. Together, dietary and functional fibers account for the *total fiber* that you eat.

---

simple carbohydrates A category of carbohydrates that contain a single sugar unit or two sugar units combined. Monosaccharides and disaccharides are simple carbohydrates.

monosaccharide One sugar unit. There are three monosaccharides: glucose, fructose, and galactose.

disaccharide Two sugar units combined. There are three disaccharides: sucrose, lactose, and maltose.

complex carbohydrates A category of carbohydrates that contain many sugar units combined. A polysaccharide is a complex carbohydrate.

polysaccharide Many sugar units combined. Starch, glycogen, and fiber are all polysaccharides.

fructose The sweetest of the monosaccharides; also known as fruit sugar.

galactose A monosaccharide that links with glucose to create the sugar found in dairy foods.

sucrose A disaccharide composed of glucose and fructose. Also known as table sugar.

maltose A disaccharide composed of two glucose units joined together.

lactose A disaccharide composed of glucose and galactose; also known as milk sugar.

starch The storage form of glucose in plants.

fiber A nondigestible polysaccharide.

glycogen The storage form of glucose in humans and animals.

dietary fiber Nondigestible polysaccharides found in foods.

functional fiber The nondigestible polysaccharides that are added to foods because of a specific desired effect on health.

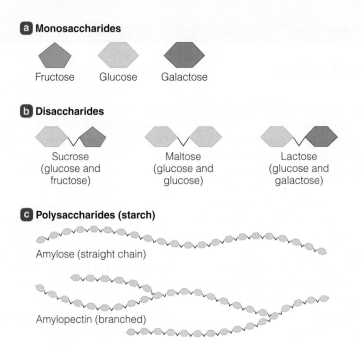

a Monosaccharides

Fructose Glucose Galactose

b Disaccharides

Sucrose
(glucose and
fructose)

Maltose
(glucose and
glucose)

Lactose
(glucose and
galactose)

c Polysaccharides (starch)

Amylose (straight chain)

Amylopectin (branched)

Figure 4.2 Creating Monosaccharides, Disaccharides, and Polysaccharides **(a)** Fructose, glucose, and galactose are the three monosaccharides that are found in nature. **(b)** The disaccharides sucrose, maltose, and lactose are created from the monosaccharides. **(c)** The polysaccharide, starch, is composed of many glucose units joined together.

Many compounds can be classified as both dietary fiber and functional fiber, depending on how they are used. Pectin occurs naturally in foods such as apples and citrus fruits and would be considered a source of dietary fiber. However, pectin can also be isolated and added to foods, such as nonfat yogurt, to add texture. In this situation, pectin is considered a functional fiber.

Fiber is sometimes also classified by its properties when combined with water. **Soluble fiber** dissolves in water, whereas **insoluble fiber** does not. Soluble fiber can be viscous (though not all soluble fibers are viscous); that is, it can have gummy or thickening properties. For example, the viscous soluble fiber in oats and beans thickens cooked oatmeal and bean chili. When you eat such foods, their soluble fiber is fermented (or digested) by bacteria in your large intestine. In contrast, insoluble fiber, found in foods such as bran flakes, is not viscous and is fermented less readily by bacteria.

A fiber's solubility affects how quickly it moves through the digestive tract. This classification system isn't exact, as most foods typically contain both types of fiber (**Figure 4.3**) and some fibers can have multiple effects in your body. In general, insoluble fibers include cellulose, hemicellulose, and lignins and are found in the bran portion of whole grains, cereal fiber, seeds, and in many fruits and vegetables (see the boxed feature "Grains, Glorious Whole Grains"). They typically move more quickly through your intestinal tract, so can have a laxative effect. Soluble fiber—like pectin in fruits and vegetables, beta-glucan in oats and barley, gums in legumes, and psyllium—is more viscous and moves slowly through your digestive system. Meat and dairy products do not contain fiber. Even though fiber is mostly nondigestible, it can have powerful health effects. We will discuss some of its effects in depth later in the chapter.

Unripe fruit tastes more starchy than sweet. As fruit ripens, its complex carbohydrates are broken down into simple sugars, including fructose. The more it ripens, the more fructose it has.

Cellulose:
insoluble
fiber

Pectin:
soluble fiber

Figure 4.3 Most Plant Foods Contain Both Soluble and Insoluble Fibers The skin of an apple is high in cellulose, an insoluble fiber, while the pulp is high in pectin, a soluble fiber.

soluble fiber A type of fiber that dissolves in water and is fermented by intestinal bacteria. Many soluble fibers are viscous and have gummy or thickening properties.

insoluble fiber A type of fiber that doesn't dissolve in water and is not fermented by intestinal bacteria.

Glycogen Is the Storage Form in Animals

Glycogen is the storage form of glucose in humans and animals and is found in the liver and in muscle cells. Glycogen is branched glucose similar to amylopectin. Humans store only limited amounts of glycogen in their bodies, but it can be an important source of glucose for the blood. People can't access the carbohydrates stored in meats and poultry because the glycogen stored in animals breaks down when the animals die.

Grains, Glorious Whole Grains

Grains are not only an important staple in the diet but also a wonderful source of nutrition. Americans' consumption of wheat, corn, oats, barley, and rye products has increased by nearly 50 percent since the 1970s. The consumption of starchy flour and cereal products is estimated to be approximately 140 pounds per person each year.[1]

There are three edible parts in a kernel of grain: the bran, the endosperm, and the germ (see figure). The **bran** or outer shell of the wheat kernel is rich in fiber, B vitamins, phytochemicals, and trace minerals such as chromium and zinc. The **germ** or seed of the kernel is a nutritional

powerhouse providing vitamin E, heart-healthy fats, phytochemicals, and plenty of B vitamins. The **endosperm,** or starchy component of the grain, contains protein, B vitamins, and some fiber, although not as much as the bran.

Depending upon which parts of the kernel are used, grain products can be divided into two main categories: **refined grains** and **whole grains.** In refined grains, such as wheat or white bread and white rice, the grain kernel goes through a milling process that strips out the bran and germ, leaving only the endosperm of the kernel in the end product. As a result, some, though not all, of the B vitamins, iron, phytochemicals, and dietary fiber are removed.

To restore some of the nutrition lost from refined grains, **enriched grains** have folic acid, thiamin, niacin, riboflavin, and iron added to them. This improves their nutritional quality somewhat, but the fiber and the phytochemicals are lost. Though refined grains can still be a good source of complex carbohydrates, you can think of *refined* as having left some of the nutrition *behind*. From a health standpoint, what was left behind may end up being the most important part of the kernel.

Whole-grain foods, such as whole-wheat bread, white whole-wheat bread, brown rice, and oatmeal, contain all three parts of the kernel. (Note: White whole-wheat bread *is* a whole grain. It is made from a lighter variety of wheat, so while the bread is lighter in color, it has the same whole-grain nutrition as darker

whole-wheat bread.) Whole grains are potential disease-fighting allies in the diet.[2] Research has shown that as little as one serving of whole grains daily may help lower the risk of dying from heart disease or cancer and reduce the risk of stroke.[3] Several research studies have also shown that the fiber in whole grains may help reduce the risk of diabetes.[4] Because whole grains are abundant in vitamins, minerals, fiber, and phytochemicals, it is uncertain which of these substances are the disease-fighting heroes, or if some or all of them work in a complementary fashion to provide the protection.[5]

Over 85 percent of Americans' grain choices are not whole grains, but refined grains. Whereas the current recommendation is to consume at least three servings of whole-grain products every day, Americans eat less than one serving of whole grains daily, on average.[6]

The good news is that it's easy to incorporate more grains into your diet. When it comes to whole grain, you have a lot of choices:

- ➤ Brown rice
- ➤ Bulgur (cracked wheat)
- ➤ Graham flour
- ➤ Oatmeal
- ➤ Popcorn
- ➤ Pearl barley
- ➤ Whole-grain cornmeal
- ➤ Whole oats
- ➤ Whole rye
- ➤ Whole wheat

bran The indigestible outer shell of the grain kernel.

germ In grains, the seed of the grain kernel.

endosperm The starchy part of the grain kernel.

refined grains Grain foods that are made with only the endosperm of the kernel. The bran and germ are not included.

whole grains Grain foods that are made with the entire edible grain kernel: the bran, the endosperm, and the germ.

enriched grains Refined grain foods that have folic acid, thiamin, niacin, riboflavin, and iron added.

The Take-Home Message Carbohydrates are divided into two categories: simple and complex. Simple carbohydrates include the monosaccharides and disaccharides; complex carbohydrates include polysaccharides. Glucose, fructose, and galactose are the three monosaccharides. Sucrose, lactose, and maltose are the three disaccharides. Starch, fiber, and glycogen are all polysaccharides. Dietary fiber occurs naturally in plant-based foods. Functional fiber has been added to foods

a A kernel of wheat

Bran
• High fiber
• B vitamins
• Phytochemicals
• Minerals

Germ
• Vitamin E
• Healthy unsaturated fats
• Antioxidants
• Phytochemicals
• Minerals
• B vitamins

Endosperm
• Starch
• Protein
• B vitamins

b Whole kernel used

c Only endosperm used

d Only endosperm used

Whole-Wheat Flour

Enriched Wheat Flour
Folic acid, thiamin, niacin, riboflavin, and iron added

Wheat Flour (not enriched)

Missing ingredients:
• Enriched folic acid

Missing ingredients:
• Bran (fiber)
• Phytochemicals
• Calcium
• Vitamin E
• Heart-healthy fats
• Antioxidants

Missing ingredients:
• Bran (fiber)
• Phytochemicals
• Calcium
• Vitamin E
• Heart-healthy fats
• Antioxidants
• Folic acid
• Thiamin
• Niacin
• Riboflavin
• Iron

From Wheat Kernel to Flour
(a) The wheat grain kernel has three parts: the bran, germ, and endosperm. **(b)** Whole-wheat flour is made using the entire grain kernel. It is not enriched. **(c)** Enriched wheat flour doesn't contain the bran and germ, so it is missing nutrients and phytochemicals. The nutrients, including folic acid, thiamin, niacin, riboflavin, and iron, are added back to the flour during an enrichment process. **(d)** Wheat flour that is not enriched lacks not only the bran and germ, but also many nutrients and phytochemicals.

because it has been shown to have a specific, functional effect. The total fiber in your diet is a combination of dietary and functional fiber. Viscous, soluble fiber has thickening properties and can be fermented by intestinal bacteria and moves slowly through your intestinal tract. Insoluble fiber typically moves more quickly through your digestive system, so it can have a laxative effect.

What Happens to the Carbohydrates You Eat?

When you eat plant foods, your body breaks down the carbohydrates for energy. Let's look at how your body digests a meal of pasta (starch), milk (lactose), and a handful of cherries (sucrose and fiber).

You Digest Carbohydrates in Your Mouth and Intestines

The digestion of carbohydrates starts in your mouth (**Figure 4.4**, step 2). The act of chewing mixes the saliva in your mouth with the food. Your saliva delivers a powerful enzyme called amylase (*ase* = enzyme), which starts breaking down the starch, specifically the amylose and amylopectin, in the pasta into smaller starch units. Some of the starch is broken down to the disaccharide, maltose.

This mixture of starch and amylase, along with the disaccharides maltose, lactose (in the milk), and sucrose (in the cherries), and the fiber (in the cherries) travels down to your stomach (Figure 4.4, step 3). The amylase continues to break down the starch until your stomach acids deactivate this enzyme. Once the food leaves your stomach, it moves through your small intestine (Figure 4.4, step 4). The arrival of the food in the small intestine signals the pancreas to release another enzyme, pancreatic amylase. The pancreatic amylase breaks down the remaining starch units into maltose.

All the disaccharides—maltose, lactose, and sucrose—are absorbed in your small intestine. The disaccharides brush up against the lining of your digestive tract. A variety of enzymes such as maltase, lactase, and sucrase, called brush border enzymes, are housed in the microvilli in your small intestine. These enzymes break down the disaccharides into monosaccharides, specifically glucose, fructose, and galactose. The monosaccharides are now ready to be absorbed into the blood.

Figure 4.4 From Carbohydrates to Glucose in Your Body

1. Sucrose and fiber / Starch / Lactose

2 **Mouth**
Starch breaks down to smaller units

3 **Stomach**
Starch, disaccharides, and fiber

4 **Small intestine**
Dissaccharides broken down to monosaccharides

5 **Liver**
Monosaccharides converted to glucose

6 **Blood**
Glucose distributed throughout body

7 Fiber leaves body

These absorbed monosaccharides travel in your blood to the liver (Figure 4.4, step 5). There the fructose and galactose are converted to glucose. The glucose is either stored in the liver or shipped back out into the blood for delivery to your cells (Figure 4.4, step 6).

The fiber continues down to the large intestine, where some of it is metabolized by bacteria in your colon. However, the majority of the fiber is eliminated from your body in stool (Figure 4.4, step 7).

Some People Cannot Digest Milk Sugar

Lactose, or milk sugar, is the principal carbohydrate found in dairy products such as milk, yogurt, and cheese. People with a deficiency of the brush border enzyme lactase cannot properly digest lactose.

Lactose maldigestion is a natural part of the aging process. In fact, as soon as a child stops nursing, his body makes less lactase. Some lucky individuals of specific ethnic origins, such as those from northern Europe, central Africa, and the Middle East, aren't as prone to developing lactose maldigestion. They appear to have a genetic predisposition to maintaining higher levels of lactase throughout their adult life.[3]

Though the term lactose maldigestion may sound serious, it doesn't mean that dairy foods have to be eliminated from the diet. In fact, the latest consensus is that people with lactose maldigestion can enjoy a serving of milk, yogurt, or cheese, especially with a meal or snack, without any problems or unpleasant side effects.[4] This is good news, as dairy products are an important source of calcium in the diet.[5]

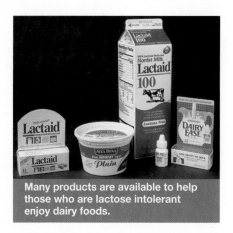

Many products are available to help those who are lactose intolerant enjoy dairy foods.

However, in some individuals the amount of lactase in the digestive tract decreases so much that they start to experience distressing symptoms. The undigested lactose draws water into the digestive tract, causing diarrhea. To make matters worse, once the lactose reaches the colon, the bacteria that normally live in the colon ferment this sugar and produce various gases. For some lactose-sensitive individuals, bloating, flatulence (gassiness), and cramps can sometimes be an unpleasant reminder that they ate lactose-containing foods. When these symptoms occur within two hours after eating or drinking foods that contain lactose, these people may be **lactose intolerant.**[6]

You should never self-diagnose lactose intolerance, or any other medical condition. This could not only cause you to inflict unnecessary dietary restrictions, it could delay you from receiving an accurate diagnosis of a potentially more serious medical condition. There are many documented cases of individuals who thought that they were lactose intolerant but discovered they weren't once the proper testing was done.[7] It is best to leave medical diagnosis to your physician.

People with lactose intolerance have varying thresholds for tolerating lactose-containing foods and beverages. These thresholds can be raised depending upon how much of a lactose-containing food one eats at a time (Table 4.1). Consuming smaller amounts of dairy foods throughout the day can be better tolerated than having a large amount at one time. Eating these foods with a meal or snack, rather than by themselves, can also influence how much can be tolerated.[8] Including dairy foods regularly in your diet may also improve your tolerance. The continuous exposure to undigested lactose promotes an acidic environment created by the fermenting of lactose by the bacteria in the colon, which inhibits further fermentation. Also, the constant presence of lactose in the colon perpetuates an increase in the growth of nongaseous bacteria and subsequent displacement of the gas-producing bacteria.[9]

People tend to respond differently to various dairy foods.[10] Whole milk tends to be better tolerated than skim milk. Cheeses (especially hard, aged cheeses, such as Swiss and cheddar) typically have less lactose than milk, and so are better tolerated. Yogurts that contain active cultures are better tolerated than skim or low-fat milk.

lactose maldigestion The inability to digest lactose in foods due to low levels of the enzyme lactase.

lactose intolerant When maldigestion of lactose results in symptoms such as nausea, cramps, bloating, flatulence, and diarrhea.

Table 4.1

How Much Lactose Is in Your Foods?

Food	Amount	Lactose (grams)
Yogurt, low fat	1 cup	11–17 grams
Milk, whole, 1%, or skim	1 cup	11
Lactaid milk	1 cup	< 1
Soy milk	1 cup	0
Ice cream	½ cup	6
Sherbet	½ cup	2
Cottage cheese	½ cup	2
Swiss, Blue, Cheddar, Parmesan cheese	1 oz	1
Cream cheese	1 oz	1

Don't Forget These Hidden Sources of Lactose

Baked goods

Baking mixes for pancakes, biscuits, and cookies

Bread

Breakfast drinks

Candies

Cereals, processed

Instant potatoes

Lunch meats (other than kosher meats)

Margarine

Salad dressings

Soups

Source: Adapted from the American Dietetic Association, *Manual of Clinical Dietetics 2000*; food manufacturers; and the National Digestive Diseases Information Clearinghouse, *Lactose Intolerance* (National Institutes of Health Publication No. 02-2751, 2002); National Institutes of Health. 2010. NIH Consensus Development Conference: Lactose Intolerance and health. Available at: http://consensus.nih.gov/2010/lactosestatement.htm. Accessed May 2010.

Table Tips

Tolerating Lactose

Gradually add some dairy or lactose-containing foods to your diet.

Eat smaller amounts of lactose-containing foods throughout the day rather than eating a large amount at one time.

Enjoy your dairy foods with a meal or snack.

Try reduced-lactose milk and dairy products such as cottage cheese.

Lactase pills can help with a lactose-laden meal or snack.

For those who want to enjoy dairy foods without worrying about developing the unpleasant side effects, lactose-reduced dairy products such as milk, cottage cheese, ice cream, and other items are available in many supermarkets. Lactase pills are available that can be consumed with meals containing lactose. See the Table Tips for some more ideas on how to develop a tolerance for lactose.

The Take-Home Message The digestion of carbohydrates begins in your mouth and continues in your stomach and small intestine. Enzymes help break down the carbohydrates into disaccharides and then monosaccharides so that they can be absorbed. All the monosaccharides are converted to glucose in your liver to be used as energy by your cells or stored as glycogen or fat. Fiber travels to your colon and then most of it is eliminated from your body. Lactose maldigestion is the inability to properly absorb the milk sugar lactose due to a decrease in the amount of lactase in your digestive tract.

How Does Your Body Use Carbohydrates?

Your body uses carbohydrates—specifically glucose—for energy, and there are chemical messengers called **hormones** that regulate the amount of glucose in your blood. Hormones are like traffic cops, directing specific actions in your body. Let's take a closer look at how this works.

Insulin Regulates Glucose in Your Blood

After you eat a carbohydrate-heavy meal, your blood is flooded with glucose. To lower your blood glucose level, your pancreas releases the hormone **insulin** into the blood. Insulin helps direct the uptake of glucose by cells and also determines whether it will be used immediately as energy or stored for later use. When your cells need fuel, insulin stimulates the conversion of glucose to energy (**Figure 4.5**). If the amount of glucose in your blood exceeds your body's immediate energy needs, insulin directs it to be stored.

As mentioned, the surplus of glucose is stored in long, branched chains called glycogen. (Recall that plants store glucose as starch. Animals and humans store glucose as glycogen.) This process of generating glycogen for later use is called **glycogenesis** (*glyco* = sugar/sweet, *genesis* = origin) (**Figure 4.6a**). Glycogenesis occurs only in your liver and muscle cells. Whereas plants have an unlimited capacity to store glucose as starch, you can't squirrel away unlimited extra energy in the form of glycogen.

However, your body can store energy in another form: fat! Insulin can direct the conversion of the excess glucose to fat. In fact, most of the energy stored in your body is in the form of fat. Very little of it is in the form of glycogen. Fat is covered in detail in Chapter 5.

NutriTools

Digestion and Absorption: Carbohydrates

How and where in the digestive process are different types of carbohydrates digested and absorbed by your body? Visit www.pearsonhighered.com/blake and complete this interactive NutriTools activity to check your understanding.

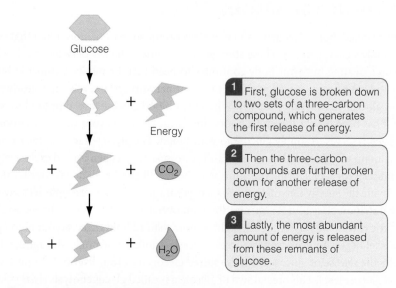

Glucose

Energy

CO_2

H_2O

1 First, glucose is broken down to two sets of a three-carbon compound, which generates the first release of energy.

2 Then the three-carbon compounds are further broken down for another release of energy.

3 Lastly, the most abundant amount of energy is released from these remnants of glucose.

Figure 4.5 Generating Energy from Glucose
When your body needs to break down glucose for energy, it begins a three-step process in your cells.

hormones Protein- or lipid-based chemical substances that act as "messengers" in the body to initiate or direct actions or processes. Insulin, glucagon, and estrogen are examples of hormones.

insulin The hormone, produced in and released from the pancreas, that directs the glucose from the blood into cells.

glycogenesis The process of converting excess glucose into glycogen in your liver and muscle.

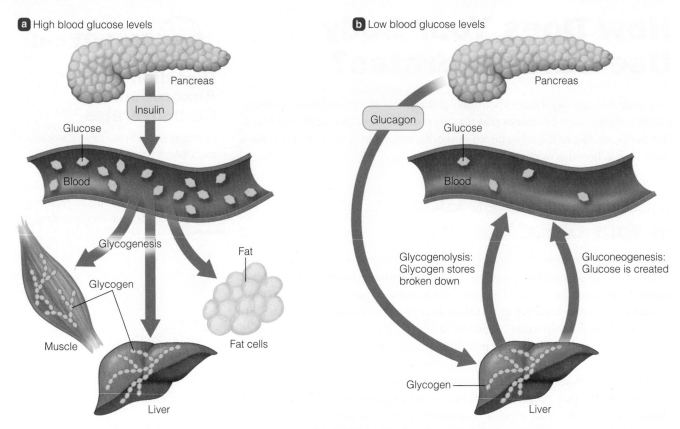

a High blood glucose levels

Pancreas

Insulin

Glucose

Blood

Glycogenesis

Fat

Glycogen

Muscle

Fat cells

Liver

b Low blood glucose levels

Pancreas

Glucagon

Glucose

Blood

Glycogenolysis:
Glycogen stores
broken down

Gluconeogenesis:
Glucose is created

Glycogen

Liver

Figure 4.6 Hormones Help Maintain Healthy Blood Glucose Levels in Your Body
(a) When your blood glucose levels are too high, the pancreas releases the hormone insulin into your blood to direct glucose. Excess glucose will be stored in your muscles and liver as glycogen and in your fat cells as fat. **(b)** When your blood glucose levels drop too low, the pancreas releases the hormone glucagon, which directs the release of glucose from stored glycogen and the creation of glucose from gluconeogenesis in your liver.

Carbohydrates Fuel Your Body between Meals and Help Spare Protein for Other Uses

As mentioned, both glycogen and fat are important sources of stored fuel that meet your body's energy needs. These storage forms come in handy between meals when you aren't eating but your body continues to need fuel. Remember, your red blood cells and your brain, as well as the rest of your nervous system, rely on a steady supply of glucose to function properly. When your blood glucose level dips too low, such as if it has been longer than four hours since your last meal, your body calls upon its glycogen reserves to supply glucose to your blood. The glycogen in your liver is used to maintain your blood glucose level, and your muscle glycogen is used exclusively by the muscles for fuel. During this time, your body will also break down your fat stores to provide the energy for your tissues, such as your muscles. For example, let's say that your nutrition class is at 8 a.m. and that you overslept and didn't eat breakfast. The last time you ate was at dinner last night—more than 12 hours ago. As your blood glucose level begins to drop, your pancreas releases another hormone, **glucagon,** which directs the release of glucose from the stored glycogen in your liver to help raise your blood glucose level. This breakdown of glycogen is called **glycogenolysis** (*lysis* = loosening) (Figure 4.6b).

In addition to directing the breakdown of glycogen, glucagon signals the liver to start **gluconeogenesis** (*gluco* = sugar/sweet, *neo* = new, *genesis* = origin). This is the

glucagon The hormone that directs glycogenolysis and gluconeogenesis to increase glucose in the blood. Glucagon is produced in and released from the pancreas.

glycogenolysis The breakdown of glycogen to release glucose.

gluconeogenesis The creation of glucose from noncarbohydrate sources, predominantly protein.

creation of glucose from noncarbohydrate sources, mostly from protein. Gluconeo-genesis can only occur in your liver and kidneys, as these are the only organs that have all the enzymes needed. Most of the time, this glucose-generating process occurs in your liver. Gluconeogenesis kicks in from the kidney only after long periods of fasting. In times of deprivation, your body dismantles protein, using specific remnants (amino acids, which we will discuss in Chapter 6) to generate the glucose that it needs. If you don't feed your blood with glucose, your body will attempt to feed it. Thus, consuming adequate amounts of carbohydrates is important to *spare* protein from being broken down to make glucose. You will learn in Chapter 6 that protein has so many other important functions in your body that you want to preserve it, rather than use it to make glucose. Once your blood glucose returns to normal, glucagon will no longer be released.

In addition to glucagon, other hormones can increase your blood glucose level. Epinephrine, also known as adrenaline, acts on the liver and muscle cells to stimulate glycogenolysis to quickly flood your blood with glucose. Emotional and physical forms of stress, such as fear, excitement, and bleeding, will increase your body's output of epinephrine. For example, if an aggressive dog was chasing you down the street, your body would be pumping out epinephrine to help provide the fuel you need to run. For this reason, epinephrine is also referred to as the "fight-or-flight" hormone.

A low blood glucose level can also trigger the release of epinephrine. In fact, some of the symptoms that you may experience when your blood glucose level dips too low, such as anxiety, rapid heart-beat, turning pale, and shakiness, are caused by the release of epinephrine.

Carbohydrates Fuel Your Body during Fasting and Prevent Ketosis

Skipping breakfast is one thing; fasting, or not eating for long periods of time, is quite another. After about 18 hours of fasting, your liver's glycogen stores are depleted, so your body must rely solely on fat and protein for fuel.

To burn fat thoroughly, you need adequate amounts of glucose. Without it, **ketone bodies,** by-products of the incomplete breakdown of fat, are created and spill out into your blood. Because most ketone bodies are acids, they can cause your blood to become slightly acidic. After about two days of fasting, the number of ketone bodies in your blood is at least doubled, and you are in a state of **ketosis.** Individuals who fast or follow strict low-carbohydrate diets are often in ketosis because they consume inadequate amounts of carbohydrates. Although the term *ketosis* sounds scary, the condition is not necessarily harmful as long as you are otherwise healthy.

As mentioned above, while your body continues to break down fat for fuel, it also uses protein to generate glucose. You can't store extra protein for this, so protein from your muscles and organs is broken down and some of its parts are used to make glucose. If you continue to fast, your body's protein reserves will reach a dangerously low level, causing death.

The Take-Home Message After a meal, when your blood glucose level begins to rise, the hormone insulin is released from the pancreas, directing glucose into your cells to be used for energy. Excess glucose is stored as glycogen or as fat. When your blood glucose drops too low, the hormone glucagon directs the release of glucose from glycogen in your liver to increase the glucose in your blood. Glucagon will also signal the start of gluconeogenesis in the liver, which is the creation of glucose from noncarbohydrate sources, such as protein. Epinephrine also plays a role

ketone bodies The by-products of the incomplete breakdown of fat.

ketosis The condition of increased ketone bodies in the blood.

in increasing your blood glucose level. When you fast, stored fat and ketone bodies become the primary source of energy to fuel your body. This spares your protein-rich tissues by reducing the amount of protein that needs to be broken down to generate glucose. If the fasting continues, death is inevitable.

How Much Carbohydrate Do You Need and What Are the Best Food Sources?

Although your body has mechanisms in place to provide the energy it needs on demand, you have to feed it the proper fuel to keep it running efficiently. Consequently, the question of how much carbohydrate you should consume daily has two answers. The first refers to the minimum amount of carbohydrates that you should eat to provide adequate fuel for your body, specifically your brain, to function efficiently. The longer, and more challenging, answer relates to the best type and source of carbohydrates that you should eat daily for long-term health. First, let's look at the amount of carbohydrates that you should eat daily.

You Need a Minimum Amount of Carbohydrates Daily

The latest Dietary Reference Intakes (DRIs) for carbohydrates recommend that adults and children consume a minimum of 130 grams daily. This is based on the estimated minimum amount of glucose your brain needs to function efficiently. This may sound like a lot, but 130 grams is less than the amount you would consume by eating the minimum recommended daily servings for each food group in MyPlate, that is, 6 servings from the grain group, 3 servings each from the vegetable and dairy groups, and 2 servings from the fruit group (**Figure 4.7**).

If your diet is well balanced, feeding your brain should be a no-brainer. In the United States, adult males consume, on average, over 300 grams of carbohydrates daily, whereas adult females eat over 200 grams daily, well over the minimum DRI.[11]

Recall from Chapter 2 that the AMDR for carbohydrates is 45 to 65 percent of your total daily calories. Adults in the United States consume about half of their calories from carbohydrate-rich foods, so they are easily meeting this optimal range.

For fiber, the current DRIs recommend that you consume 14 grams for every 1,000 calories you eat, to promote heart health. For example, individuals who need 2,000 calories daily to maintain their weight should consume 28 grams of fiber daily. Because few people know the exact number of calories they consume daily, the recommendations for fiber are categorized by both age and gender so that your estimated needs can be determined (Table 4.2). Unfortunately, most Americans fall short of this goal and consume approximately 15 grams of fiber a day, on average.[12]

Table 4.2

What Are Your Fiber Needs?

	Grams of Fiber Daily*	
	Males	Females
14 through 18 years old	38	36
19 through 50 years old	38	25
51 through 70+ years old	30	21
Pregnancy		28
Lactation		29

*Based on an Adequate Intake (AI) for fiber.
Source: Institute of Medicine, *Dietary Reference Intakes for Energy, Carbohydrate, Fiber, Fat, Fatty Acids, Cholesterol, Protein, and Amino Acids* (Washington, D.C.: The National Academies Press, 2002).

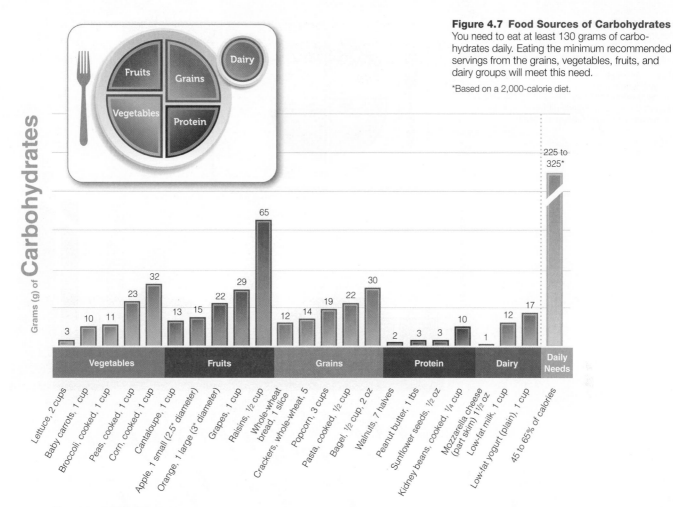

Figure 4.7 Food Sources of Carbohydrates
You need to eat at least 130 grams of carbohydrates daily. Eating the minimum recommended servings from the grains, vegetables, fruits, and dairy groups will meet this need.

*Based on a 2,000-calorie diet.

*Based on a 2,000 calorie diet

The Best Carbohydrates Are Found in These Foods

Now let's turn to the second part of our answer and look at the best type and source of carbohydrates to choose for long-term health. As with other nutrients, not all carbohydrate-laden foods are created equal. For example, eating high-sugar foods containing lots of calories and saturated fat, but few other nutrients, can lead to weight gain and promote heart disease. It's best to choose carbohydrates from a variety of nutrient-dense, low-saturated-fat foods whenever possible. In general, the best strategy for long-term health is to eat a diet with fewer (low to moderate amounts of) simple carbohydrates and more complex carbohydrates.

Whole Grains Can Help Meet Starch and Fiber Needs
Starch is the primary complex carbohydrate found in refined grains, while fiber is found in whole grains. Select whole-grain breads and cereals that have at least 2 to 3 grams of total fiber per serving, such as quinoa, whole-wheat bread, bulgur, brown rice, and whole-wheat pasta.

Fruits and Vegetables Provide Simple Sugars, Starch, and Fiber
Whole fruits, 100-percent fruit juices, and vegetables are naturally good sources of simple carbohydrates. The flesh of fruit, for example, is rich in simple sugars, including fructose and glucose. Though you can also get simple sugars from processed foods and sweets, the higher calorie and lower nutrient levels in these foods make them a less

 NutriTools

Know Your Carbohydrate Food Sources

Can you identify the food sources of different types of carbohydrates? Visit www.pearsonhighered.com/blake and complete this interactive NutriTools activity.

Figure 4.8 Food Sources of Fiber

Adults need to consume about 20 to 38 grams of fiber daily. Foods are a combination of soluble and insoluble fiber.

Source: Anderson, J., and S. Bridges, "Dietary Fiber Content of Selected Foods," *The American Journal of Clinical Nutrition* 47 (1988): 440–447. USDA National Nutrient Database for Standard Reference, Release 14, www.nal.usda.gov/foodcomp/search.

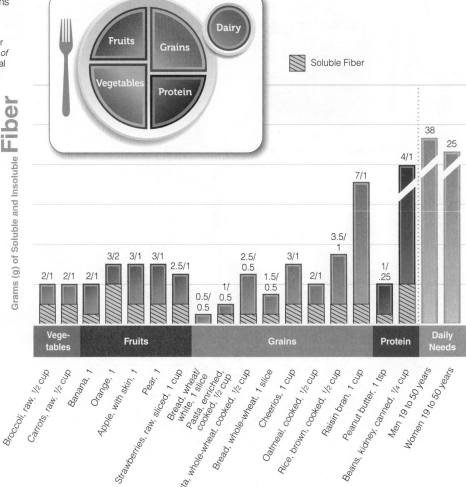

healthy option (you'll learn more about the pros and cons of natural and added sugars in the next section). The skins of many fruits contain cellulose (a type of insoluble fiber; see **Figure 4.8**), so eat unpeeled (but cleaned and scrubbed) fruit more often. Another type of fiber, pectin, is found in the flesh of fruit, and makes up about 15 percent to 30 percent of the fiber in fruit. Fruit overall contains about 2 grams of dietary fiber per serving. When selecting fruit, choose fresh or frozen versions over canned, but if canned is your only option, choose fruit packed in fruit juice rather than heavy syrup, to cut down on added sugar.

An orange has four times the fiber of six ounces of orange juice.

Vegetables contain abundant amounts of complex carbohydrates, including starch and fiber. A serving of vegetables contains approximately 2 grams of fiber. In general, starchy vegetables, such as corn and potatoes, contain more carbohydrate per serving than nonstarchy vegetables like green beans or carrots (see Figure 4.7).

Legumes, Nuts, and Seeds Are Excellent Sources of Carbohydrates and Fiber

Legumes, such as kidney beans and chickpeas, are rich sources of both carbohydrates and fiber. Nuts and seeds are also good sources of fiber, providing over 1 gram in a 1/2 ounce or small handful. A 1/2 ounce of nuts is about 15 peanuts, 7 walnut halves, or 24 shelled pistachios. See the High Five! Table Tips for some ways to add legumes and other fiber-rich foods to your diet.

Low-Fat and Fat-Free Dairy Products Provide Some Simple Sugars

Milk and milk products, including cheese and yogurt, contain 1 to 17 grams of lactose per serving. Choose low-fat or fat-free dairy products whenever possible, for the sake of your heart health. The lactose content is the same regardless of the fat content.

Packaged Foods Can Also Provide Carbohydrates

Packaged and processed foods, such as ready-to-eat cereals, crackers, and savory snacks, can be good sources of carbohydrate, but can also contain fair amounts of added sugar, salt, and fat. When selecting these packaged foods, choose products that contain at least 2 grams of dietary fiber per serving and be aware of the amounts of added sugar, salt, fat, and total calories. Choose whole-grain cereals with lower amounts of added sugar, whole-grain crackers, and baked rather than fried snacks. The Nutrition Facts panel and ingredients listings on the product can help you to choose healthier packaged foods.

The Take-Home Message You need to consume a minimum of 130 grams of carbohydrates daily to provide adequate glucose for your brain. It is recommended that 45 to 65 percent of your daily calories come from carbohydrates. You should consume 14 grams of fiber for every 1,000 calories you eat. Whole grains, whole fruits and vegetables, legumes, and lean dairy products are the best food sources of simple carbohydrates and starch. Whole grains, fruits, vegetables, legumes, nuts, and seeds are excellent sources of fiber. Packaged foods can be good sources of carbohydrate, but the added sugars, fat, and total calories in such foods should be monitored.

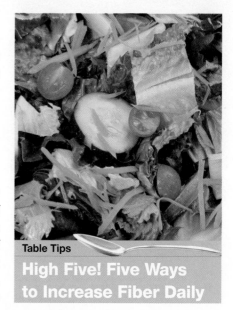

Table Tips

High Five! Five Ways to Increase Fiber Daily

Choose only whole-grain cereals for breakfast.

Eat two pieces of whole fruit daily as snacks.

Use only 100% whole-wheat bread for your lunchtime sandwich.

Layer lettuce, tomatoes, or other vegetables on your sandwich.

Eat a large salad topped with chickpeas with dinner nightly.

What's the Difference between Natural and Added Sugars?

Finding the taste of sweet foods pleasurable is an innate response. A child being fed puréed applesauce for the first time will probably show his pleasure with a big smile. You're not likely to see the same smile when Junior is eating plain oatmeal.

You don't have to fight this taste for sweetness. A modest amount of sweet foods can easily be part of a well-balanced diet. However, some sources of sugar provide more nutrition than others.

Your taste buds can't distinguish between **naturally occurring sugars,** which are found in foods such as fruit and dairy products, and **added sugars,** which are added by manufacturers to foods such as soda or candy. From a nutritional standpoint, however, there is a big difference between these sugar sources. Foods that contain naturally occurring sugar tend to be nutrient dense and thus provide more nutrition per bite. In contrast, foods that contain a lot of added sugar tend to give little else. The calories in sugar-laden foods are often called **empty calories** because they provide so little nutrition.

naturally occurring sugars Sugars such as fructose and lactose that are found naturally in fruit and dairy foods.

added sugars Sugars that are added to processed foods and sweets.

empty calories Calories that come with little nutrition. Jelly beans are an example of a food that provides lots of calories from sugar but few nutrients.

Foods with Natural Sugars Usually Contain More Nutrients for Fewer Calories

Just one bite into a ripe peach, a crisp apple, or some chilled grapes will confirm that fruit can taste sweet, and not surprisingly, can contain more than 15 percent sugar by weight. There are many nutritional advantages of satisfying your sweet tooth with fruit rather than sweets with added sugar. Let's compare slices from a fresh navel orange with candy orange slices (**Figure 4.9**).

Six slices of a navel orange provides about 65 calories, more than 100 percent of the daily value for vitamin C, and 3.5 grams of fiber, which is more than 10 percent of the amount of fiber that many adults should consume daily. These juicy slices also provide fluid. In fact, more than 85 percent of the weight of the orange is water. The hefty amounts of fiber and water make whole fruits such as oranges a hearty, sweet snack that provides bulk. This bulk can increase eating satisfaction, or satiation. When you eat fruit, you not only satisfy your urge for a sweet, but you will also feel full before you overeat.

In contrast, six candy orange slices provide 300 calories of added sugar and little else. The candy is quite energy dense. It provides more than four times as many calories as the fresh orange. However, as it provides no fiber and only negligible amounts of water, it contains a concentrated amount of calories in relationship to the volume of food in the serving. You wouldn't likely feel satiated after consuming six candy orange slices. To consume close to the 300 calories found in the six pieces of candy, you would have to eat more than four oranges. It would be easier to overeat candy orange slices than fresh oranges.

Fiber-abundant whole fruits (and vegetables, for that matter) are not only very nutritious, but they are also kind to your waist, as their bulk tends to fill you up before they fill you out. In other words, it is more difficult to overconsume calories from fruits and vegetables because you will feel full and stop eating before you take in too many calories. In fact, researchers at the USDA reviewed the diets of Americans and found that adults who ate more fruit had healthier body weights. According to the researchers, this finding may be due to lower-calorie fruit being substituted for higher-calorie cake or other sweets on the dessert plates of Americans.[13]

Figure 4.9 Slices of an Orange versus Orange Slices
A fresh orange provides more nutrition for fewer calories and without any added sugars compared with candy orange slices.

Fresh orange

Calories	65
Vitamin C	130% DV
Fiber	🌾🌾🌾½
Added sugar	0

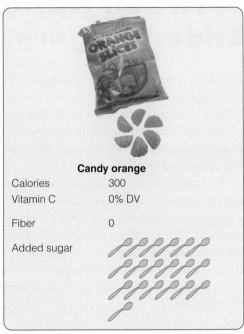

Candy orange

Calories	300
Vitamin C	0% DV
Fiber	0
Added sugar	

🌾 = 1 gram of fiber

🥄 = 1 tsp of added sugar

Processed Foods and Sweets Often Contain Added Sugars

Between 1970 and 2005, our yearly consumption of added sugars increased by 19 percent.[14] Sugars are added to foods for many reasons. In baked goods, they can hold onto water, which helps keep the product moist and soft. They help provide a golden brown color to the finished product. Sugars function as preservatives and thickeners in foods such as sauces. Fermenting sugars in dough produce the carbon dioxide that makes yeast breads rise. And of course, sugars make foods taste sweet.

Are Added Sugars Bad for You?

Sugar has been blamed for everything from hyperactive children to diabetes, but are these claims myths or facts? Let's look at the most common claims:

- "Sugar causes hyperactivity in kids." Adults often point to sugary foods as the culprit behind the overly excited behavior of children at parties and holidays. However, research does not support the theory that sugar makes kids hyperactive.[15] The excitable behavior in the kids is more likely due to the festivities of the day rather than the sweets being consumed.
- "Eating too much sugar causes diabetes." Contrary to popular thought, sugar doesn't necessarily cause diabetes mellitus, as discussed in the section, "What Is Diabetes Mellitus?"
- "Too much sugar can contribute to dental caries." This is certainly true, but so can other sources of carbohydrates. See the boxed feature, "Avoiding a Trip to the Dentist" on page 112 for information on how to prevent tooth decay.

Though these claims don't hold up, a high-sugar diet has been associated with some real health risks:

- Too much sugar in the diet can increase your blood level of triglycerides, the primary form of fat in your body. At the same time, it can lower the level of your "good" HDL cholesterol. Together, these changes may increase your risk for heart disease.[16] (This will be discussed in Chapter 5.) Luckily, a reduction in dietary sugar coupled with an increase in dietary fiber can typically alleviate this problem.
- Consuming too much sugar can make weight management challenging. Eating sugar won't cause you to gain weight as long as you do not exceed the number of total calories that you need daily. However, it is easy to overeat high-calorie, sugary foods and quickly add excess calories to your diet. Added sugars are considered "empty calories" as they add calories to food but add few or no nutrients.

Finding the Added Sugars in Your Foods

While sucrose and fructose are the most common added sugars in our foods, sugars can appear on the food label under numerous different names. **Figure 4.10** includes some of the most common added sugars in foods.

Over the years, honey has been publicized in the popular press as being more nutritious than table sugar. This is an exaggeration. Honey provides a negligible amount of potassium, and it actually has more calories than sugar. A teaspoon of honey contains 21 calories. The same amount of sugar provides only 16 calories. High-fructose corn syrup (HFCS), a sweetener produced from modified corn and composed of glucose and fructose, has also made media headlines because it has been blamed as a culprit in obesity. HFCS is less expensive than sucrose, and

Honey should never be given to children younger than one year of age, as it may contain spores of *Clostridium botulinum*. These spores can germinate in the immature digestive tracts of babies and cause deadly botulism. Adults do not face this risk.

Table Tips

Lowering Your Added Sugars

Mix chocolate milk with an equal amount of regular low-fat milk.

Mix equal amounts of sweetened cereal with an unsweetened variety for a breakfast cereal with half the added sugar.

Drink water rather than soda or sweetened beverages throughout the day.

Buy sweets such as candy and cookies in individual serving sizes rather than large packages. The less you buy, the less you'll eat.

Choose canned fruit packed in juice rather than syrup.

Avoiding a Trip to the Dentist

Carbohydrates play a role in the formation of dental caries. Over the past 30 years, the incidence of **dental caries** (tooth decay) in the United States has decreased as the use of fluoride has increased.[7] (The mineral fluoride will be covered in more detail in Chapter 8.) Though things are improving in the world of dental health, an estimated 20 percent of children age 2 to 4 still have dental caries, and by the time these children reach age 17, almost 80 percent will have experienced a cavity, the later stage of dental caries. Dental caries are the cause of tooth loss in more than two-thirds of adults aged 35 to 44 years.[8] To avoid dental caries, you need to understand the role your diet plays in tooth decay.

Feeding into Dental Caries

If you constantly eat carbohydrate-heavy foods, such as cookies, candy, and crackers, you are providing a continual buffet of easily fermentable sugars and starches to the bacteria that bathe your teeth. A study of American diets found that adults who drank sugary sodas three or more times daily had 60 percent more dental caries than those who didn't drink any soda. To make matters worse, soft drinks often contain phosphoric acid and citric acid, which can also erode teeth if consumed over a prolonged time.[9] Soft drinks are not the only beverage that may damage your teeth. Sports drinks, includ-

dental caries The decay or erosion of teeth.

baby bottle tooth decay The decay of baby teeth in children due to continual exposure to fermentable sugary liquids.

remineralization The repairing of teeth by adding back the minerals lost during tooth decay. Saliva can help remineralize teeth.

ing energy drinks and vitamin waters, if consumed often, have been shown to be even more damaging to your teeth than soft drinks.[10]

Eating three balanced meals daily is best for minimizing tooth decay. Snacks should be kept to a minimum, and you should choose fruit or vegetables over candies or pastries. Whole fruits and raw vegetables tend not to cause tooth decay, so snack on these to your teeth's content.

Sticky foods like dried fruits, such as raisins and figs, can adhere to your teeth, so their fermentable sugars hang onto the tooth for longer periods. The longer the carbohydrate is in contact with your tooth, the more opportunity there is for the acids to do damage. Eating sticky foods in combination with other foods will discourage their adherence to your teeth. Drinking water after you eat will help by rinsing your teeth.

Fruit juice, even unsweetened juices, may be a problem for teeth, especially in small children. A child who routinely falls asleep with a bottle in his mouth that contains carbohydrate-containing beverages is at risk for developing **baby bottle tooth decay** because the baby's teeth are continually exposed to fermentable sugars during sleep.[11] Children need adequate amounts of fluids, such as water, but they should not be given a continual supply of sweetened beverages.

Foods That Fight Dental Caries

There are actually some foods that may help reduce this risk of acid attacks on your teeth. The texture of cheese stimulates the release of cleansing saliva.

Cheese is also rich in protein, calcium, and phosphorus, all of which can help buffer the acids in your mouth following a meal or snack. The calcium can also assist in **remineralization** of your teeth. Eating as little as half an ounce of cheese after a snack, or eating cheese with a meal, has been shown to protect your teeth.[12] Chewing sugarless gum can also be a healthy ending to a meal or snack if you can't brush your teeth. It encourages the production of saliva and provides a postmeal bath for your teeth. Xylitol, a sugar substitute often found in sugarless chewing gum, may even help with remineralization.[13]

With regular visits to your dentist, good dental hygiene, and a healthy diet, you can reduce the risk of dental caries. Follow these Do's and Don'ts to keep your teeth healthy:

DO eat three solid meals daily but keep snacks to a minimum.

DON'T graze all day long!

DO snack, if necessary, on whole fruit, raw vegetables, and low-fat cheese, which tend to be friendlier to your teeth.

DON'T munch on sugary foods such as candy, cookies, and other sweets.

DO drink plenty of water.

DON'T drink a lot of sugar-sweetened beverages.

DO chew sugarless gum or eat a piece of low-fat cheese after meals and snacks when you can't brush your teeth.

DON'T think that sugarless gum and cheese can replace a routine of brushing and flossing.

DO brush your teeth at least twice a day and floss daily.

DON'T forget this!

a The many aliases of added sugar

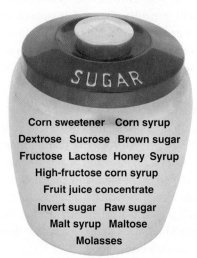

Corn sweetener   Corn syrup
Dextrose   Sucrose   Brown sugar
Fructose   Lactose   Honey   Syrup
High-fructose corn syrup
Fruit juice concentrate
Invert sugar   Raw sugar
Malt syrup   Maltose
Molasses

Ingredients: Granola (whole grain rolled oats, sugar, rice flour, whole grain rolled wheat, partially hydrogenated soybean and cottonseed oils* with TBHQ and citric acid added to preserve freshness and/or sunflower oil with natural tocopherol added to preserve freshness, whole wheat flour, molasses, sodium bicarbonate, soy lecithin, caramel color, barley malt, salt, nonfat dry milk), corn syrup, crisp rice (rice, sugar, salt, barley malt), semisweet chocolate chunks (sugar, chocolate liquor, cocoa butter, soy lecithin, vanillin [an artificial flavor]), sugar, corn syrup solids, glycerin, high-fructose corn syrup, partially hydrogenated soybean and/or cottonseed oil*, sorbitol, fructose, calcium carbonate, natural and artificial flavors, salt, soy lecithin, molasses, water, BHT (a preservative), citric acid.

* Adds a dietarily insignificant amount of *trans* fat.

b

Nutrition Facts

Serving Size 1 Bar (24g)
Servings Per Container 10

Amount Per Serving	
Calories 90	Calories from Fat 20

	% Daily Value*
Total Fat 2g	3%
Saturated Fat 0.5g	3%
Trans Fat 0g	
Sodium 80 mg	3%
Total Carbohydrate 19g	6%
Dietary Fiber 1g	3%
Sugars 7g	
Protein 1g	

Calcium	8%	•	Iron	4%

Not a significant source of Cholesterol, Vitamin A, Vitamin C

* Percent Daily Values are based on a 2,000 calorie diet. Your Daily Values may be higher or lower depending on your calorie needs:

	Calories:	2,000	2,500
Total Fat	Less than	65g	80g
Sat Fat	Less than	20g	25g
Cholesterol	Less than	300mg	300mg
Sodium	Less than	2,400mg	2,400mg
Total Carbohydrate		300g	375g
Dietary Fiber		25g	30g

Figure 4.10 Finding Added Sugars on the Label
(a) Sugar can be called a number of different names on ingredients lists and labels. **(b)** A food is likely to contain a large amount of sugar if added sugars appear first or second on the ingredients list and/or if many varieties of added sugars are listed. You can also look on the Nutrition Facts panel to see the total grams of sugar.

thus has replaced sucrose as the most common sweetener in processed foods such as sugars, sweets, and soft drinks. Based on current research, the American Medical Association and other major health organizations suggest that it is unlikely that HFCS contributes more to obesity than any other sweetener in the diet.[17]

To find the amount and type of added sugars in the foods that you eat, read the ingredients on the food label. If added sugars appear first or second on the list or if the product contains many varieties of added sugars, it is likely to be high in sugar.

The Nutrition Facts panel that is currently used on food labels doesn't distinguish between naturally occurring and added sugars. For example, the nutrition labels on ready-to-eat cereals such as raisin bran and dairy products such as milk list 21 grams of sugars for raisin bran and 12 grams for low-fat milk. This can be misleading, as the grams of sugars listed for the raisin bran cereal include both the amount of naturally occurring sugars from the raisins and the sugars added to sweeten the cereal. For the milk, the sugar listed on the Nutrition Facts panel includes the naturally occurring sugar, lactose. With the growing concern about the rising levels of added sugars in the diets of Americans, various health professionals and organizations have pressured the FDA to require that all *added* sugars be disclosed on the food label. A final decision by the FDA is pending.

As you know, added sugars come from many sources and are found in many products. In fact, most Americans don't eat the majority of the added sugars in their diets—they drink them. The number-one source of added sugars in the United

Food Label: Find the Carbohydrates

What is a carbohydrate? Can you find them on food labels? Visit www.pearsonhighered.com/blake and complete this interactive NutriTools activity.

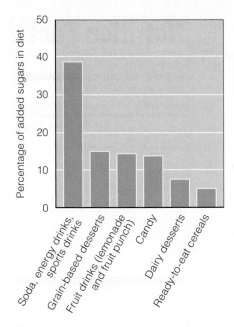

Figure 4.11 Where Are All These Added Sugars Coming From?
Sodas, energy drinks, and sports drinks are the number-one source of added sugars in American diets. Desserts, candy, fruit drinks, and some grains are also sources of added sugars.

Source: *Dietary Guidelines for Americans,* 2010.

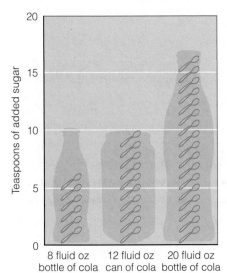

Figure 4.12 The Many Sizes of Soft Drinks
A bottle or can of soda can provide from 6 to 17 teaspoons of added sugars, depending on the size of the container.

States is sweetened sodas, energy drinks, and sports drinks (**Figure 4.11**). This fact isn't too surprising when you look at the size of the sweetened beverages that Americans consume. A classic 8-ounce bottle of cola provides almost 7 teaspoons of added sugars. In today's vending machine, you are more likely to find a 12-ounce can or a 20-ounce bottle. People typically consume the entire can or bottle, regardless of its size, so they consume more sugar (**Figure 4.12**). In addition to beverages, added sugars are hidden in many other foods (Table 4.3).

How Much Added Sugar Is Too Much?

The DRI recommends that added sugars make up no more than 25 percent of your daily calories, but the *Dietary Guidelines for Americans, 2010* suggest that no more than 5 to 15 percent of your daily calories come from a combination of added sugars *and* solid fats. Americans, on average, consume 16 percent of their daily calories from added sugars alone![18] Many Americans, especially women, sedentary individuals, and older adults who have lower daily calorie needs would benefit from reducing the amount of added sugars i n their diet. These individuals need to make sure that they are getting a substantial amount of nutrition from each bite of food.

Table 4.3
Sugar Smacked!

Food Groups	Teaspoons of Added Sugar
Bread, Cereal, Rice, Pasta	
Bread, 1 slice	0
Cookies, 2 medium	1
Doughnut, 1 medium	1
Cereal, Frosted Flakes	4
Cake, frosted, 1/16 average	6
Pie, fruit, 2 crust, 1/6, 8" pie	6
Fruit	
Fruit, canned in juice, 1/2 cup	0
Fruit, canned in heavy syrup, 1/2 cup	4
Milk, Yogurt, and Cheese	
Milk, plain, 1 cup	0
Chocolate milk, 2% fat, 1 cup	3
Yogurt, low fat, plain, 8 oz	0
Yogurt, fruit, sweetened, 8 oz	7
Chocolate shake, 10 fl oz	9
Other	
Energy drink, 8 oz	6
Chocolate bar, 2 oz	6
Fruit drink, ade, 12 fl oz	12

= 1 teaspoon of sugar

Source: USDA, *Dietary Guidelines for Americans,* 5th ed. (Home and Garden Bulletin No. 232, 2000); Manufacturers labels.

What Can You Get for a Quarter These Days?

As you read earlier in the chapter, sweetened beverages can provide 6 teaspoons or more of added sugar in each 8-ounce serving. Soft drinks not only provide a sugary punch and few to no nutritional benefits, but they can also be quite a drain on your wallet. Let's compare what a quarter ($0.25) spent on each of the following beverages actually "buys" for you:

Wow! A quarter will buy you a full, 8-ounce glass of fat-free milk and delivers 9 essential nutrients. Compared with the milk, a quarter's worth of a sports drink, energy drink, vitamin water, or iced tea doesn't provide much volume or nutrition. None of these beverages provides the good nutrition that fat-free or low-fat milk

will provide at a reasonable price. Further, drinking milk, which is high in the mineral calcium, today will lead to better bone health tomorrow (see Chapter 8). So, when it comes to choosing a healthy beverage for your money, which one would you choose?

Fat Free Milk 1 glass

- ✓ Calcium
- ✓ Vitamin D
- ✓ Vitamin A
- ✓ Protein
- ✓ Potassium
- ✓ Riboflavin
- ✓ Niacin
- ✓ Vitamin B12
- ✓ Phosphorus

9 nutrients

Sports Drink 3/4 glass

- ✓ Riboflavin
- ✓ Vitamin B12

2 nutrients

Energy Drink 1 swig

- ✓ Riboflavin
- ✓ Niacin

2 nutrients

Ready-to-Drink Sweetened Iced Tea 3/4 glass

0 nutrients

Vitamin Enhanced Water 3/8 glass

- ✓ Vitamin C

1 nutrient

Source: Used with permission from the National Milk Mustache "got milk?"® Campaign. Costs were calculated based on national averages in 2008 and may vary.

The World Health Organization and the Food and Agriculture Organization recently commissioned an expert report, which recommends that individuals lead an active lifestyle and consume a diet that is abundant in fruits and vegetables and low in saturated fat, sugar, and energy-dense foods. The report recommends keeping calories from added sugars* to less than 10 percent of the diet. These two agencies maintain that this type of diet is among the best strategies to fight chronic diseases such as heart disease, diabetes, and obesity.[19]

This more conservative limit for consumption of sugars would mean that a person who consumes 2,200 calories (about the number of calories needed daily for active women) should keep added sugar to about 8 teaspoons daily (128 calories), or 9 percent of total calories. Those consuming 2,800 calories daily (approximately the amount of calories needed daily for active men) should consume no more than about 18 teaspoons of added sugar daily (288 calories), or 10 percent of total calories.

> A super-large soda at the movie theatre can be as large as 64 ounces! This giant beverage contains more than 800 calories and 50-plus teaspoons of added sugars.

* This report includes the sugars that naturally occur in fruit juice as "added sugars." The *Dietary Guidelines for Americans* do not include fruit juice sugars in the category of added sugars.

Concerned with the prevalence of obesity in Americans, the American Heart Association has recommended even more conservative limits for added sugars in the diet.[20]

American adults consume approximately 20 teaspoons of added sugars daily.[21] Eating this much added sugar can have a major impact on daily nutrition and is one of the many reasons Americans are overweight. The Table Tips can help you trim some added sugars from your diet.

The Take-Home Message Your taste buds can't distinguish between naturally occurring and added sugars. Foods with naturally occurring sugars, such as whole fruit, tend to provide more nutrition and satiation than empty-calorie sweets such as candy. Sugar can contribute to dental caries, an elevated level of fat in your blood, and a lowering of the "good" HDL cholesterol. Foods with added sugars may displace more nutritious foods and quickly add excess calories to your diet. The current recommendation is to lower consumption of added sugars in the diet as they are considered empty calories.

What Are Sugar Substitutes and What Forms Can They Take?

sugar substitutes Alternatives to table sugar that sweeten foods for fewer calories.

Because eating too much sugar can be unhealthy, what's a person with a sweet tooth to do? Americans have looked to sugar-free beverages and foods over the years to limit their sugar intake while satisfying their yen for sugar (**Figure 4.13**). Such items contain **sugar substitutes** that are as sweet as—or sweeter than—sugar but contain fewer calories.

All sugar substitutes must be approved by the FDA and deemed safe for consumption before they are allowed in food products sold in the United States.[22] Several sugar substitutes are presently available to consumers, including polyols, saccharin, aspartame, acesulfame-K, sucralose, rebaudioside A, and neotame. Alitame and cyclamate are two other sugar substitutes that are not yet approved for use in the United States but are on the horizon. Polyols don't promote dental caries and cause a slower rise in blood glucose than sugar does. Saccharin, aspartame, acesulfame-K, sucralose, rebaudioside A, and neotame also won't promote dental caries and have the added advantage of not affecting blood glucose levels. These sugar substitutes are a plus for people with diabetes, who have a more challenging time managing their blood glucose levels. All these sugar substitutes are either reduced in calories or are calorie free. See Table 4.4 for a comparison of available sweeteners.

Figure 4.13 Growing Interest in Sugar-Free Foods and Beverages
The use of sugar-free products has more than doubled since 1986.
Source: Calorie Control Council, Trends and Statistics. 2007.
www.caloriecontrol.org.

Polyols Are Sugar Alcohols

Polyols are often called sugar alcohols because they have the chemical structure of sugar with an alcohol component added.

Table 4.4

Oh So Sweet!

Sweetener	Calories/ Gram	Trade Names	Sweetening Power	The Facts
Sucrose	4	Table Sugar	—	Sweetens food, enhances flavor, tenderizes, and contributes browning properties to baked goods
Reduced-Calorie Sweeteners				
Sorbitol	2.6	Sorbitol	50–70% as sweet as sucrose	Found in foods such as sugarless chewing gum, jams, baked goods, and candy. May cause diarrhea when 50 grams (about 15 sugar-free candies) are consumed.
Mannitol	1.6	Mannitol	50–70% as sweet as sucrose	Found in foods such as chewing gum, jams, and as a bulking agent in powdered foods. Excessive amounts may cause diarrhea.
Xylitol	2.4	Xylitol	Equally sweet as sucrose	Found in foods such as chewing gum, candies; also in pharmaceuticals and hygiene products
Hydrogenated Starch Hydrolysates (HSH)	3.0	HSH	50–70% as sweet as sucrose	Found in confections and can be used as a bulking agent
Calorie-Free Sweeteners				
Saccharin	0	Sweet'N Low	200–700% sweeter than sucrose	Retains its sweetening power at high temperatures such as baking
Aspartame	4*	Nutrasweet, Equal	Approximately 200% sweeter than sucrose	Sweetening power is reduced at high temperatures such as baking. Can be added at end stages of recipes such as cooked puddings if removed from heat source. Individuals with PKU need to monitor all dietary sources of phenylalanine, including aspartame.
Acesulfame-K	0	Sunette	200% sweeter than sucrose	Retains its sweetening power at high temperatures
Sucralose	0	Splenda	600% sweeter than sucrose	Retains its sweetening power at high temperatures
Rebaudioside A	0	Truvia, PureVia	200% sweeter than sucrose	Retains its sweetening power at high temperatures
Neotame	0	Neotame	7,000–13,000% sweeter than sucrose	Retains its sweetening power at high temperatures

*Since so little aspartame is needed to sweeten foods, it provides negligible calories.

Whereas polyols such as sorbitol, mannitol, and xylitol are found naturally in plants, they are also produced synthetically and are used as sweeteners in foods such as chewing gum and candies. They can be used tablespoon for tablespoon to substitute for sucrose. Sorbitol and mannitol are also less likely to promote dental caries because the bacteria on your teeth metabolize them so slowly. (Humans lack the enzyme needed

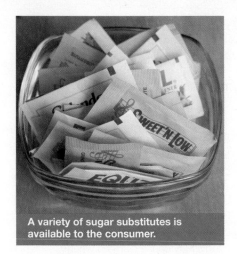
A variety of sugar substitutes is available to the consumer.

to ferment xylitol.) Their slower absorption means that they do not produce a spike in blood glucose, which is a benefit for those with diabetes.

Chewing gums and candies that contain sugar alcohols can be labeled "sugar free" and boast that they don't promote tooth decay. Keep in mind, though, that even though these products are sugar free, they are not necessarily calorie free. Even more importantly, because polyols are incompletely absorbed in your digestive tract, they can cause diarrhea. For this reason, they should be used in moderation.

Another type of polyol is hydrogenated starch hydrolysates (HSH), which are made by partially breaking down corn, wheat, or potato starch into smaller pieces and then adding hydrogen to these pieces. The end product is a wide range of polyols, including those that can be strung together and used commercially. HSH adds sweetness, texture, and bulk to many sugarless products such as baked goods and candies.[23]

Saccharin Is the Oldest Sugar Substitute

Saccharin was first discovered in 1879, and during the two World Wars, when sugar was being rationed, it was used as a sugar substitute in the United States and Europe. Today, you probably know saccharin as those little pink packets often found on coffee shop counters or diner tables. It has been used in foods, beverages, vitamins, and pharmaceuticals. Because saccharin is not metabolized in your body, it doesn't provide any calories.

In 1977, the FDA banned saccharin due to reports from the research community that it could cause bladder cancer in rats. Congress immediately implemented an 18-month moratorium on this ban through the Saccharin Study and Labeling Act. This allowed the continued commercial use of saccharin, but required that any saccharin-containing products bear a warning label stating that saccharin was potentially hazardous to your health, as it caused cancer in laboratory animals.

In 2000, the National Toxicology Program (NTP) removed saccharin from the list of substances that could potentially cause cancer. After extensive review, the NTP determined that the observed bladder tumors in rats were actually from a mechanism that wasn't relevant to humans.[24] The lesson learned from this is that though you can safely consume saccharin in moderation, you shouldn't feed it to your pet rat. Saccharin is used in more than 100 countries in the world today.

Aspartame Is Derived from Amino Acids

In 1965, a scientist named James Schlatter was conducting research on amino acids in his quest to find a treatment for ulcers. To pick up a piece of paper in his laboratory, he licked his finger and stumbled upon a sweet-tasting compound.[25] It was the "lick" that was soon to be "tasted" around the world. Schlatter had just discovered aspartame, a substance that would change the world of sugar substitutes.

Aspartame is composed of two amino acids: a modified aspartic acid and phenylalanine. Enzymes in your digestive tract break down aspartame into its components, and the amino acids are absorbed, providing 4 calories per gram. Consequently, aspartame has the potential to provide calories to foods as an added sweetener. However, as aspartame is 200 times sweeter than sucrose, only a small amount is needed to sweeten a food.

In 1981, the FDA approved aspartame for use in tabletop sweeteners such as Equal and Nutrasweet, and for various other uses, such as to sweeten breakfast cereals, chewing gums, and carbonated beverages. The majority of the aspartame that is consumed in the United States is in soft drinks. In 1996, the FDA gave the food industry carte blanche to use aspartame in all types of foods and beverages. It is currently used as a sweetener in more than 100 countries, and can now be found in more than 6,000 foods, as well as pharmaceuticals and personal care products, sold in the United States.

Aspartame has undergone continual, vigorous reviews to ensure that it is safe for human consumption. The FDA considers it one of the most thoroughly studied and tested food additives approved by the agency. The FDA has reevaluated the safety of aspartame more than 25 times since it first came on the market and each time has concluded that it is safe to consume.[26]

Major health organizations such as the American Dietetic Association, the American Medical Association, and the American Diabetes Association all support aspartame's use by healthy adults, children, and pregnant women in moderation as part of a well-balanced diet.[27] The FDA has set an Acceptable Daily Intake (ADI) for aspartame at 50 milligrams per kilogram (mg/kg) of body weight. To exceed this ADI, a 150-pound person would need to consume almost sixteen 12-ounce cans of a "diet" (aspartame-containing) soda daily for a lifetime. Currently the general public consumes an estimated 4 to 7 percent of the ADI, or 2 to 3.5 mg/kg body weight daily.[28]

Individuals with a rare, inherited disorder known as phenylketonuria (PKU) are unable to metabolize one of the amino acids in aspartame, phenylalanine, and must adhere to a special diet. PKU affects about 1 out of every 15,000 infants in the United States. It is usually the result of a deficiency of phenylalanine hydroxylase, an enzyme needed to properly metabolize phenylalanine.[29]

People with PKU need to control all dietary sources of this amino acid, including aspartame as well as protein-rich foods such as meat, milk, eggs, and nuts. These individuals do not necessarily have to avoid aspartame, but they need to monitor it as an additional source of phenylalanine in their diet. Because of the seriousness of this disorder, the FDA mandates that all food products that contain phenylalanine carry a label declaring its content.

Foods and beverages that contain aspartame must carry a warning label that says phenylalanine is present.

Substituting sweeteners for sugar isn't shaving off the pounds. Although the consumption of low-calorie sweeteners has tripled since 1980, the prevalence of overweight and obese Americans has increased by 60 percent.

Neotame Is Also Derived from Amino Acids

Neotame, which the FDA approved in 2002, comprises the same two amino acids—aspartic acid and phenylalanine—as aspartame, but they are joined together in such a way that the body cannot break them apart. So, individuals with PKU can use neotame without concern. Neotame is completely eliminated in either the urine or stool. It has been approved as a sweetener and for a variety of uses, such as chewing gum, frostings, frozen desserts, puddings, fruit juices, and syrups.[30]

Acesulfame-K Contains Potassium

While less than sweet sounding, acesulfame-K (the K refers to the potassium component) is about 200 times sweeter than sucrose. It is available as a tabletop sweetener, called Sunette, and is currently used in chewing gum, candy, desserts, yogurt, and alcoholic beverages. Your body does not metabolize acesulfame-K.

Sucralose Is Made from Sucrose

Sucralose was developed in 1976 by slightly changing the structure of the sucrose molecule. Unlike sucrose, sucralose isn't absorbed by your body—it is excreted in your urine. In 1998, sucralose was approved as a tabletop sweetener, and it's available commercially as Splenda.

Rebaudioside A Is Derived from the Stevia Plant

The newest addition to the world of sugar substitutes is rebaudioside A, which is a combination of a sugar alcohol with an extract from the stevia plant. Extracts from the stevia plant, which is native to Brazil and Paraguay, are currently used in Brazil and Japan as a table-top sweetener and in some products, such as teas and yogurt. This zero-calorie sweetener is approximately 200 times sweeter than sugar and is available under trade names such as Truvia, Sun Crystals, and PureVia. It doesn't affect blood glucose levels, so it could be used by those with diabetes.

The Take-Home Message **Millions of Americans consume reduced-calorie or calorie-free sugar substitutes. The FDA has approved polyols, saccharin, aspartame, acesulfame-K, sucralose, neotame, and rebaudioside A to be used in a variety of foods. These sugar substitutes do not promote dental caries and can benefit those with diabetes who are trying to manage their blood glucose.**

Why Is Fiber So Important?

Even though fiber is a nondigestible substance that is resistant to being broken down in your small intestine, it can have many powerful health effects in your body. Fiber has been shown to help lower your risk of developing constipation, diverticulosis, obesity, heart disease, cancer, and diabetes mellitus (Table 4.5). Let's look closely at how this works.

Fiber Helps Prevent Constipation and Diverticulosis

More than 4 million Americans complain about being constipated, with women, especially pregnant women and adults 65 years of age and older, experiencing it more often than others. The uncomfortable, bloated, and sluggish feelings of constipation compel Americans to spend more than $700 million each year on laxative products.[31] Because a diet lacking sufficient high-fiber whole grains, fruits, and vegetables and abounding in cheese, eggs, and meats is a recipe for constipation, many people would

A Pizza That Really Delivers

According to the USDA, over 50 percent of Americans eat outside the home on any given day, with pizza being one of the most popular food choices. Visit www.pearsonhighered.com/blake and create a custom-made, *healthier* pizza that is higher in fiber. *Hint:* Hold the pepperoni and go wild with the peppers and mushrooms!

Table 4.5

Type-Casting Fiber

Type	Found in	Can Help Reduce the Risk of
Insoluble Fiber		
Cellulose	Whole grains, whole-grain cereals, bran, oats, fruit, and vegetables	Constipation
Hemicellulose		Diverticulosis
Lignins		Certain cancers
		Heart disease
		Obesity
Soluble, Viscous Fibers		
Pectin	Citrus fruits, prunes, legumes, oats, barley, brussels sprouts, carrots	Constipation
Beta-glucan		Heart disease
Gums		Diabetes mellitus
Psyllium		Obesity

be better off spending time in the produce and whole-grain aisles of the supermarket rather than shopping for laxatives.

A diet plentiful in insoluble fibers such as bran, whole grains, and many fruits and vegetables will help keep things moving along in your digestive tract and decrease your likelihood of becoming constipated. As remnants of food move through your colon, water is absorbed, which causes the formation of solid waste products (stool). The contractions of the muscles in your colon push the stool toward your rectum to be eliminated. If these muscle contractions are sluggish, the stool may linger too long in your colon, which can cause too much water to be reabsorbed. This can create hard, dry stools that are more difficult and painful to expel. (Note: Some soluble fibers, such as psyllium, can also be an aid in relieving constipation, as its water-attracting capability allows the stool to increase in bulk and form a gel-like, soft texture, which makes it easier to pass.)

Constipation can become more frequent during different stages of your life. During pregnancy, hormonal changes as well as the pressure of the growing baby on the intestine can make regular bowel movements more difficult. As you age, your metabolism slows, which results in a slower-moving digestive tract as well as loss of intestinal muscle tone. Unfortunately, abusing laxatives can damage the nerve cells in the colon and disrupt the colon's natural movements. This can cause you to depend on laxatives in order to bring on a normal bowel movement.[32]

Long-term constipation can lead to a disorder called **diverticulosis** (*osis* = condition). Constipation is the main cause of increased pressure in the colon and may cause the weak spots along your colon wall to bulge out, forming **diverticula** (**Figure 4.14**).

Infection of the diverticula, a condition known as **diverticulitis** (*itis* = inflammation), can lead to stomach pain, fever, nausea, vomiting, cramping, and chills. Though not proven, it is believed that the stool and its bacteria in the colon may get stuck in the diverticula and cause the infection in approximately 50 percent of Americans over age 60.[33] The disorder is more common in developed countries, such as the United States and England, and is rarely found in areas where high-fiber diets are more commonplace, such as Asia and Africa. Consuming a diet with adequate fiber may reduce the symptoms associated with diverticulosis. The best way to prevent both diverticulosis and diverticulitis is to eat a diet that is generous in fiber to avoid constipation and to keep things moving through your system.

diverticulosis The existence of diverticula in the lining of your intestine.

diverticula Small bulges at weak spots in the colon wall.

diverticulitis Infection of the diverticula.

Figure 4.14 Diverticula
Diverticula are small pouches that can occur along your colon. When stool gets trapped in them, they can become inflamed, and this can lead to diverticulitis.

Colon

Diverticula

Stool

Fiber Helps Prevent Obesity

A fiber-rich diet can also be kind to your waistline. As mentioned earlier, high-fiber foods, such as whole grains, fruits, and vegetables, can add to satiation so that you need to eat fewer calories to feel full. Research studies have shown that obese men and women tend to consume lower amounts of dietary fiber daily than their leaner counterparts. This lends credence to the concept that fiber plays a role in weight management.[34] Whereas some weight-loss diets restrict carbohydrates, these plans would work better if they *increased* high-fiber carbohydrates.

Fiber Helps Prevent Heart Disease, Diabetes, and Cancer

Viscous, soluble fibers have been shown to help lower elevated blood cholesterol levels. A high blood cholesterol level can increase the risk of heart disease. It is believed that viscous fiber interferes with the reabsorption of bile acids in the intestines. Bile acids are high in cholesterol and are released into your intestine by your gallbladder to help with the digestion of fat. The bile acids are likely "grabbed" by the fiber before they can be reabsorbed by the body. They then end up being excreted along with the fiber in your waste products. Your body replaces these lost bile acids by removing cholesterol from the blood to generate new bile acids in the liver. Blood cholesterol levels are lowered as a result.

Slow-moving, viscous, soluble fibers may reduce the rate at which fat and carbohydrates are absorbed from your meals. Delayed absorption can lower the surge of fat in your blood after a meal, and may help improve sensitivity to the hormone insulin. Both high levels of fat in the blood and a decreased sensitivity to insulin are considered risk factors for heart disease.

Viscous, soluble fiber may not be the only type of fiber that can promote heart health. Several research studies have shown that cereal and grains, which contain insoluble fiber, may help to lower the risk of heart disease.[35] A study looking at the dietary habits of over 65,000 women for a period of 10 years found that the risk of developing heart disease was more than 30 percent lower in those consuming the highest amount of cereal fiber.[36]

Viscous, soluble fibers have also been shown to help individuals with diabetes mellitus. They slow the release of food from your stomach, and thus slow down the digestion and absorption of glucose. This could help avoid a large spike in blood glucose after eating and help those with diabetes improve the long-term control of their blood glucose level.[37] Fiber may also play a role in preventing diabetes. Research studies involving both men and women have shown that a higher consumption of fiber from cereals helped reduce the risk of a certain type of diabetes.[38]

Fiber is thought to have many positive and protective effects in the fight against certain cancers. Fiber from cereals has been shown to help lower the risk of breast cancer.[39] Research also suggests that as fiber consumption increases, the incidence of colorectal cancer is reduced.

Four mechanisms may account for fiber's role in fighting cancer:

➤ Fiber increases the bulk of stool, which can dilute cancer-promoting substances in the colon.
➤ Fiber helps keep things moving through the digestive tract so that potential cancer-promoting substances spend less time in contact with the intestinal lining.

➤ Fiber encourages the growth of friendly bacteria in the colon and their fermentation by-products, both of which may have cancer-fighting potential.

➤ Fiber binds with acids in bile, a substance produced by the liver and important in fat breakdown. This causes the acids to be expelled from the body in the stool, rather than being reabsorbed. Because an increased amount of bile acids in the colon is thought to be associated with colon and rectal cancer, fiber's ability to reduce the concentration of these acids is viewed as a cancer deterrent.[40]

Over the years, some studies have challenged fiber's protective role against colorectal cancer. Several short-term research studies failed to show an anticancer effect of fiber. These findings may have been due to several factors. The amount of fiber consumed in the studies may not have been large enough to make a difference; the studies may have been too short in length to show an effect; and the fiber that was used in these studies wasn't from a variety of sources.[41]

Current research supports the cancer-fighting potential of fiber. A large research study involving over 500,000 individuals recruited from 10 European countries showed that individuals who consumed the most fiber (35 grams of fiber daily, on average), compared with those eating the least amount of fiber daily (15 grams, on average), reduced their risk of colorectal cancer by about 40 percent.[42] The dietary sources of fiber were varied among the countries and included fiber from cereal, vegetables, fruits, and legumes.

Because this large study was done with high-fiber foods and not fiber supplements, it is difficult to tease out if the potential cancer-fighting substance in these foods is only the fiber, or the other nutrients and phytochemicals in these plant-based foods operating in concert with the fiber. Once again, the best advice is to eat a varied, balanced, plant-based diet rich in whole grains, fruits, vegetables, and legumes.

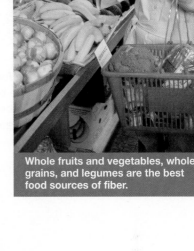

Whole fruits and vegetables, whole grains, and legumes are the best food sources of fiber.

Too Much Fiber Can Cause Health Problems

Dark bread is not necessarily whole-grain bread. Bread made with refined wheat flour can have caramel coloring added to give it a darker brown appearance.

A word of caution: Initially, a high-fiber diet can have negative side effects (flatulence and bloating). Consuming too much fiber can reduce the absorption of some vitamins and minerals and may cause diarrhea in some individuals.[43] Gradually increasing the fiber in your diet, rather than suddenly adding large amounts, will allow your body to adjust to the increased amount of fiber and minimize the side effects. A small, steady increase of fiber will be easier on your colon and on those around you. As you add more fiber to your diet, you should also drink more fluids.

The Take-Home Message Fiber is a nondigestible substance that can help reduce the risk of constipation, diverticulosis, heart disease, obesity, diabetes mellitus, and certain cancers. Increasing fiber intake too quickly can cause diarrhea, constipation, and gassiness, so consumption should be increased gradually and be accompanied by plenty of fluids.

What Is Diabetes Mellitus and Why Is It an Epidemic?

Diabetes mellitus, or *diabetes*, is becoming so common that it would be rare if you *didn't* know someone who has it. An estimated 23.6 million American adults—more than 7.8 percent of the population—have diabetes. [44]

Mellitus is Latin for "honey-sweet," which is what the blood and urine of a person with diabetes might be, due to the increased amount of glucose.

Recall that the hormone insulin directs glucose into the cells to be used as immediate energy or stored in another form for later use. Individuals develop diabetes because they aren't producing enough insulin and/or they have developed **insulin resistance,** such that their cells do not respond to the insulin when it arrives. [45] In essence, insulin is available in the blood, but the cells' decreased sensitivity interferes with its ability to work properly. Hence, the bloodstream is flooded with glucose that can't get into the cells. In this situation, the body thinks that it must be fasting and shifts into fasting mode. The liver begins the process of breaking down its glycogen stores (glycogenolysis) and making glucose from noncarbohydrate sources (gluconeogenesis) in an attempt to provide the glucose for its cells. This floods the blood with even more glucose. Eventually, the level of glucose builds up in the blood and some of it spills over into the urine and leaves the body.

At the same time, the body has called on its energy reserve, fat, to be used as fuel. The body needs glucose in order to thoroughly burn fat; otherwise, it makes ketone bodies. In poorly managed diabetes, when glucose is unable to get into the cells, acidic ketone bodies build up in the blood to dangerous levels, causing diabetic **ketoacidosis.** Diabetic ketoacidosis can cause nausea and confusion, and in some cases, if left untreated, could result in coma or death. (Note: Although ketosis can develop in individuals who are fasting or consuming a low-carbohydrate diet, ketoacidosis only occurs when insulin is lacking in the body. Ketosis is not the same as diabetic ketoacidosis, nor is it life-threatening.)

Supreme Court Justice Sonia Sotomayor has type 1 diabetes and maintains good control by following a proper diet.

diabetes mellitus A medical condition whereby an individual either doesn't have enough insulin or is resistant to the insulin available. This will cause the blood glucose level to rise. Diabetes mellitus is often called diabetes. **Type 1 diabetes** is an autoimmune disease and is rarer than **type 2 diabetes**, which is seen in those with insulin resistance.

insulin resistance The inability of the cells to respond to insulin.

ketoacidosis The buildup of ketone bodies to dangerous levels, which can result in coma or death.

There Are Several Forms of Diabetes

All forms of diabetes involve insulin and unregulated blood glucose levels. Some are due to insulin resistance, as just described, and others are due to a lack of insulin production. Still another form occurs only during pregnancy. The most prevalent types of diabetes are type 1 and type 2.

Type 1 Diabetes

Type 1 diabetes is considered an *autoimmune* disease and is the rarer of the two forms. It usually begins in childhood and the early adult years and is found in 5 to 10 percent of the individuals with diabetes in the United States. [46] The immune system of type 1 diabetics actually destroys the insulin-producing cells in the pancreas. Symptoms such as increased thirst, frequent urination, constant blurred vision, hunger, weight loss, and fatigue are common, as the glucose can't get into the cells of the body. These were many of the symptoms that Adam, the hockey player that you read about in the beginning of the chapter, was experiencing and are what prompted the doctor to have his blood analyzed. If not treated with insulin, the person is susceptible to the dangers of ketoacidosis. Individuals with type 1 diabetes must inject insulin every day in order to live a normal life.

Type 2 Diabetes

Type 2 diabetes is the more common form of diabetes and is seen in people who have become insulin resistant. It accounts for 90 to 95 percent of diagnoses of the disease. Being overweight increases the risk of type 2 diabetes.[47] People with type 2 diabetes typically produce insulin but have become insulin resistant. After several years of exhausting their insulin-producing cells in the pancreas, their production of insulin decreases to the point where they have to take medication and/or insulin to manage their blood glucose level.

One of the major problems with type 2 diabetes is that this condition can go undiagnosed for some time. While some people may have symptoms such as increased thirst, others may not. Consequently, diabetes can silently damage a person's vital organs without his or her being aware of it. Because of this, the American Diabetes Association (ADA) recommends that everyone 45 years of age and older undergo testing for diabetes. However, if a person is at a higher risk for developing diabetes, he or she shouldn't wait until age 45 to be tested. Take the following Self-Assessment to see if you are at risk.

Because the hormone insulin is derived from the components of protein, it can't be taken orally, as it would be broken down in the same manner that other protein-containing foods are digested. Therefore, most individuals who need to take insulin have

---

Self-Assessment

Are You at Risk for Type 2 Diabetes?

Take the following quiz to assess if you are at a higher risk for developing type 2 diabetes. Whereas this list contains the presently known risk factors for type 2 diabetes, there may be others. If you have questions or doubts, check with your doctor.

Do you have a body mass index (BMI) of 25 or higher*?

Yes ☐ **No** ☐

If you answered no, you don't need to continue. If you answered yes, continue.

1. Does your mom, dad, brother, or sister have diabetes?
   Yes ☐ **No** ☐
2. Do you typically get little exercise?
   Yes ☐ **No** ☐
3. Are you of African-American, Alaska Native, Native American, Asian-American, Hispanic-American, or Pacific Islander-American descent?
   Yes ☐ **No** ☐
4. Have you ever delivered a baby that weighed more than 9 pounds at birth?
   Yes ☐ **No** ☐
5. Have you ever had diabetes during pregnancy?
   Yes ☐ **No** ☐
6. Do you have a blood pressure of 140/90 millimeters of mercury (mmHg) or higher?
   Yes ☐ **No** ☐

7. Have you been told by your doctor that you have too much fatty triglycerides (fat) in your blood (more than 250 mg/dl) or too little of the "good" HDL cholesterol (less than 35 mg/dl)?
   Yes ☐ **No** ☐
8. Have you ever had blood glucose test results that were higher than normal?
   Yes ☐ **No** ☐
9. Have you ever been told that you have vascular disease or problems with your blood vessels?
   Yes ☐ **No** ☐
10. Do you have polycystic ovary syndrome[†]?
    Yes ☐ **No** ☐

Answers

If you are overweight and answered yes to any of the above questions, you could benefit from speaking with your doctor.

*BMI is a measure of your weight in relationship to your height. See Chapter 10 for a chart to determine your BMI.

[†]Polycystic ovary syndrome is a disorder in women due to an abnormal level of hormones, including insulin. This disorder increases your risk of diabetes as well as heart disease and high blood pressure.

Table 4.6

Interpreting Blood Glucose Levels

If a Fasting Blood Glucose Level Is	The Level Is Considered
100 mg/dl	Normal
100 to 125 mg/dl	Prediabetic
≥126 mg/dl*	Diabetic

*There must be two "positive" tests, done on separate days, for an official diagnosis of diabetes. Source: American Diabetes Association, "Diagnosis and Classification of Diabetes Mellitus," *Diabetes Care* 82 (2009): S62–S67.

There are many ways for an individual to monitor his or her blood glucose levels.

impaired glucose tolerance
A condition whereby a fasting blood glucose level is higher than normal (>100 mg/dl), but not high enough (≤126 mg/dl) to be classified as diabetes mellitus. Also called prediabetes.

to inject themselves with a syringe. Researchers are continually testing alternative ways for those with diabetes to self-administer insulin. New methods include insulin pens, insulin jet injectors, and insulin pumps. Researchers hope that someday those with diabetes will no longer have to use needles to obtain the insulin they critically need.

Prediabetes

A simple blood test at a physician's office can reveal if a person's blood glucose is higher than normal and whether he or she has **impaired glucose tolerance,** or *prediabetes*. The blood is typically drawn first thing in the morning after fasting overnight for 8 to 12 hours. A fasting blood glucose level of under 100 milligrams per deciliter (mg/dl) is considered "negative" and a fasting blood glucose of 126 mg/dl or higher is considered a "positive" test for diabetes (Table 4.6). A reading between 100 mg/dl and 126 mg/dl is classified as prediabetes. Individuals with prediabetes have a blood glucose level that is higher than it should be but not yet high enough to be classified as diabetic. About 57 million people age 20 years and older have prediabetes and are at a higher risk of developing not only diabetes, but also heart disease.[48] When a person is in this prediabetic state, damage may already be occurring to the heart and circulatory system.

Diabetes Can Result in Long-Term Damage

Constant exposure to high blood glucose levels can damage vital organs over time. Diabetes, especially if it is poorly managed, increases the likelihood of a multitude of dire effects, such as nerve damage, leg and foot amputations, eye diseases, including blindness, tooth loss, gum problems, kidney disease, and heart disease.[49]

Nerve damage occurs in an estimated 50 percent of individuals with diabetes, and the longer the person has diabetes, the greater the risk for the damage. Numbness in the toes, feet, legs, and hands, as well as changes in bowel, bladder, and sexual function, are all signs of damage to nerves. This nerve damage can affect the ability to feel a change in temperature or pain in the legs and feet. A cut or sore on the foot could go unnoticed until it becomes infected. The poor blood circulation common in those with diabetes can also make it harder for sores or infections to heal. The infection could infiltrate the bone, causing the need for an amputation.

Diabetes can also damage the tiny blood vessels in the retina of the eye, which can cause bleeding and cloudy vision, and eventually destroy the retina and cause blindness. A high blood glucose level can cause tooth and gum problems, including the loss of teeth, and damage to the kidneys. If the kidneys are damaged, protein can leak out into the urine, and at the same time, cause a backup of wastes in the blood. Kidney failure could result.

Diabetes is a risk factor for heart disease. The excess amount of fat often seen in the blood in poorly managed diabetes is most probably an important factor in the increased risk of heart disease in those with diabetes. Fortunately, good nutrition habits play a key role in both the prevention and management of diabetes.

Control Is Key

For years, people with diabetes have been advised to keep their blood glucose level under control. In the early 1990s, the research community gathered the evidence to back up that advice. The groundbreaking Diabetes Control and Complications Trial (DCCT), conducted from 1983 to 1993, involved more than 1,400 people with type 1 diabetes. It showed that controlling the level of blood glucose with an intense regimen of diet, insulin, and exercise, along with monitoring blood sugar levels and routinely visiting health care professionals, slowed the onset of some of the complications of diabetes. In this study, it was shown that reducing high blood glucose helped lower the risk of eye disease by 76 percent and the risk of kidney and nerve disease by at least 50 percent. However, because some of the individuals in this study experienced bouts of hypoglycemia, this type of intense regimen is not recommended for children under age 13, people with heart disease or advanced complications of heart disease, older people, and those prone to frequent bouts of severe hypoglycemia.[50] For all others, diligent and conscientious management of their blood glucose can minimize the devastating complications of diabetes often seen later in life.

The nutrition and lifestyle goals for individuals with type 1 or type 2 diabetes are the same: to minimize the complications of diabetes by adopting a healthy, well-balanced diet and participating in regular physical activity that maintains a blood glucose level in a normal or close to normal range. The ADA recommends that individuals with diabetes consume a diet that includes a combination of predominantly high-fiber carbohydrates from whole grains, fruits, and vegetables, along with low-fat milk, adequate amounts of lean protein sources, and unsaturated fats.[51]

The glycemic index (GI) and glycemic load (GL) can be used to classify the effects of carbohydrate-containing foods on blood glucose. The GI refers to the measured upward rise, peak, and eventual fall of blood glucose following the consumption of a carbohydrate-intense food. Some foods cause a sharp spike and rapid fall in blood glucose levels compared with others that cause less of a spike and a more gradual decline.[52] The index ranks high-carbohydrate foods according to their effect on blood glucose levels compared with that of an equal amount of white bread or pure glucose.

If a carbohydrate-rich food causes your blood glucose level to produce a curve with a larger area than the standard curve of white bread, the food is considered a high-GI food. A carbohydrate-containing food that produces a smaller blood glucose level curve than that of white bread would be considered a low-GI food. For example, 50 grams of white bread have a glycemic index of 100. A 50-gram portion of kidney beans has a GI of 42, whereas the same amount of puffed wheat cereal has a GI of 105. Consequently, the kidney beans are considered a low-GI food compared with the white bread, while puffed wheat is considered a high-GI food (**Figure 4.15**). The problem with use of the GI is that 50 grams of puffed wheat would be more than 4 cups of cereal, an amount that is unlikely to be eaten in one sitting. The glycemic load (GL) adjusts the GI to take into account the amount of carbohydrate consumed in a typical serving of a food, and in the case of puffed wheat cereal would lower its effect on blood glucose dramatically.

Other factors can also affect the GI of a food. Overripe fruits have more easily digested sugar and a higher GI than underripe ones. Both cooking and food processing change the structure of foods and make them more easily digested, increasing the GI compared with raw, unprocessed equivalents. Larger chunks or bigger particle sizes of food contribute to slower digestion and lower GI than the same foods chopped into smaller pieces. Foods with viscous, soluble fiber tend to be absorbed more slowly so will have a lower GI than refined carbohydrates. In general, whole grains, vegetables, whole fruit, and legumes tend to have a low GI.[53] Lastly, eating carbohydrate-heavy foods with protein and/or fat can also lower the GI.[54]

Whereas monitoring the overall amount of carbohydrate within a healthy diet along with weight management are key factors in managing diabetes, the GI and GL may also modestly help those with diabetes, according to the American Diabetes Association. The ADA recommends that individuals with diabetes consume a diet that includes a combination of predominantly high-fiber carbohydrates from whole grains, fruits, and vegetables, along with low-fat milk, monounsaturated fat, and adequate amounts of lean protein sources, which also help control GI.[55]

Though sugar was once thought of as a "diabetic no-no," it can now be part of a diabetic's diet. Research has found that eating sucrose doesn't cause a rise in a person's

The Glycemic Index Of Foods

Foods	GI*
Rice, low amylose	126
Potato, baked	121
Cornflakes	119
Jelly beans	114
Green peas	107
Cheerios	106
Puffed wheat	105
Bagel, plain	103
White bread	100
Angel food cake	95
Ice cream	87
Bran muffin	85
Rice, long grain**	80
Brown rice	79
Oatmeal	79
Porpcorn	79
Corn	78
Banana, overripe	74
Chocolate	70
Baked beans	69
Sponge cake	66
Pear, canned in juice	63
Custard	61
Spaghetti	59
Rice, long grain***	58
Apple	52
Pear	47
Banana, underripe	43
Kidney beans	42
Whole milk	39
Peanuts	21

*GI = Glycemic Index
**Boiled for 25 minutes.
***Boiled for 5 minutes.

Figure 4.15 The Glycemic Index of Commonly Eaten Foods

blood glucose level to any greater extent than does eating starch, so avoidance of sugar isn't necessary. However, because weight management is often a concern, especially for type 2 diabetics, there isn't room for a lot of sweets and treats in a diabetic diet (or *anyone's* diet, for that matter).

Cases of Diabetes Are on the Rise

The incidence of adults being diagnosed with diabetes in the United States has more than doubled since the early 1990s.[56] According to the CDC, if this trend continues, it is likely that one-third of Americans will develop diabetes in their lifetime, reducing their life expectancy, on average, by 10 to 15 years.[57] More than 200,000 Americans die from diabetic complications annually, and diabetes is one of the leading causes of death in the United States. Diabetes is not only a deadly disease but also an extremely costly one. Disability insurance payments, time lost from employment, and the medical costs associated with diabetes cost the United States $174 billion annually.[58]

The number of people who have diabetes is not only strikingly high, but it's rising, particularly among children. Whereas the disease used to be common only in adults, in the last couple of decades there's been a steady increase among those under age 20.

Children and Diabetes

The rising incidence of overweight and obesity is happening among younger and younger children. Almost 1 in 5 children and adolescents between the ages of 6 and 19 is obese.[59] Obesity increases the risk factor for type 2 diabetes in children.

Type 1 diabetes was formerly the only type of diabetes prevalent in children. In fact, in 1990, less than 4 percent of diabetic children had type 2 diabetes. However, up to 45 percent of the new cases of diabetes in children are the type 2 variety, and of those children, as many as 85 percent are also overweight or obese.[60] Developing diabetes at a younger age means longer exposure to the disease and its medical complications. Early detection is important for effective treatment, and all children who are at risk for developing type 2 diabetes should be screened (Table 4.7).

Table 4.7

Red Flags for Type 2 Diabetes in Children and Adolescents

The following risk factors may increase the risk of childhood type 2 diabetes in children and adolescents:

⚑ Being overweight

AND any two of the following:

⚑ Having a parent or grandparent with type 2 diabetes

⚑ Being of Native American, African-American, Hispanic-American, Asian-American, or Pacific Islander-American descent

⚑ Showing signs of being resistant to insulin or having conditions associated with insulin resistance, such as high blood pressure or too much fat and/or cholesterol in the blood, and polycystic ovary syndrome

Copyright © 2004 American Diabetes Association. From *Diabetes Care* 27(2004): 1798–1811. Reprinted with permission from the American Diabetes Association.

Preventing Type 2 Diabetes

Recent research has suggested that shedding some excess weight, exercising regularly, and eating a balanced, high-fiber, healthy diet may be the best strategy to lower the risk of developing diabetes. A landmark study by the Diabetes Prevention Program of more than 3,000 individuals with prediabetes showed that those who made changes in their lifestyle, such as losing weight, exercising 2.5 hours a week, eating a plant-based, heart-healthy diet, and meeting with a health professional for ongoing support and education, were 58 percent less likely to develop type 2 diabetes than those who did not partake in such intervention.[61] When it comes to winning the battle against diabetes, a healthful diet and lifestyle is the best game plan.

The Take-Home Message Diabetes is a condition involving inadequate regulation of blood glucose levels. Individuals with type 1 diabetes produce inadequate amounts of insulin. Those with type 2 diabetes have developed insulin resistance. Chronic high blood glucose levels can damage the vital organs of the body, including the heart. Individuals with diabetes need to take medications and/or insulin to manage their blood glucose. A high-fiber diet and routine exercise play important roles in managing and preventing diabetes. Diabetes is becoming more common in children, especially those who are overweight and inactive.

What Is Hypoglycemia?

Whereas a high level of glucose in your blood on a regular basis isn't healthy, a blood glucose level that is too low, or **hypoglycemia,** can be unpleasant for many of us and downright dangerous for some with diabetes. Individuals who experience hypoglycemia may feel hungry, nervous, dizzy, light-headed, confused, weak, or shaky, and even begin to sweat. Eating or drinking carbohydrate-rich foods, such as hard candies, juice, or soda, can relieve these symptoms quickly and raise the blood glucose level to a normal range.

Those with diabetes who need to use insulin and/or blood glucose–lowering medications daily are at risk of hypoglycemia if they skip meals and snacks or if they don't eat enough to cover the effects of the medication. If these individuals ignore their symptoms, their blood glucose level can drop so low that they could faint, or slip into a coma (see **Figure 4.16**).[62] Those with diabetes need to eat regularly to maintain blood glucose levels that coincide with their medication. A change in their activities or exercise level can also lower the blood glucose level. Diabetics need to check their blood glucose level before they exercise to determine if a snack is needed.

Though not common, people without diabetes may also experience bouts of hypoglycemia after meals, better known as reactive hypoglycemia, which may be hormone related. This can occur within four hours after a meal and cause the similar hypoglycemic symptoms: shakiness, dizziness, hunger, and perspiration. A doctor can diagnose this condition by testing the blood glucose level while the person is having these symptoms. Though the cause of reactive hypoglycemia is not known, one thought is that some people may be overly sensitive to epinephrine, one of the hormones normally released when the blood glucose level begins to drop. The hormone glucagon may also play a role. Eating smaller, well-balanced meals throughout the day can help avoid hypoglycemia.

Drinking juice can help restore one's blood glucose level to a normal range.

hypoglycemia A blood glucose level that drops to lower than 70 mg/dl. Hunger, shakiness, dizziness, perspiration, and light-headedness are some signs of hypoglycemia.

Figure 4.16 Change in Blood Glucose after Eating a High-Carbohydrate Meal
An individual with hypoglycemia experiences a more rapid decline in blood glucose after a carbohydrate-rich meal.

Another type of hypoglycemia, called fasting hypoglycemia, can occur in the morning, after fasting throughout the night. It can also occur during long stretches between meals or after exercise. Some medications, illnesses, certain tumors, hormone imbalances, or drinking too much alcohol may cause this type of hypoglycemia.

The Take-Home Message Symptoms of hypoglycemia include feeling hungry, nervous, light-headed, shaky, and sweaty. Those who take medication and/or insulin to manage their diabetes but don't eat properly are at a greater risk of experiencing hypoglycemia. Individuals without diabetes may experience reactive hypoglycemia several hours after a meal. Fasting hypoglycemia can occur in the morning upon awakening and can be caused by some medications, illnesses, hormone imbalances, or excessive consumption of alcohol.

Made Over, Made Better!

Americans, on average, are consuming only about half of the amount of fiber recommended daily. Making some easy food substitutions can quickly bump up your daily fiber intake. Here are some typical foods made over and made nutritionally better!

If you like this. . .	Try this to boost your fiber intake!

Special K cereal
Serving size: 1 cup
Total Fiber: 1 gram

Wheaties cereal
Serving size: 1 cup
Total Fiber: 4 grams

Cheez-It
Serving size: 27 crackers
Total Fiber: 1 gram

Triscuit
Serving size: 6 crackers
Total Fiber: 3 grams

White bread
Serving size: 2 slices
Total Fiber: 1.2 grams

100% Whole-wheat bread
Serving size: 2 slices
Total Fiber: 8 grams

Pretzels
Serving size: 10 pretzels
Total Fiber: 0.9 grams

Popcorn
Serving size: 100 calorie microwave popcorn bag
Total Fiber: 4 grams

Source: USDA National Nutrient Database for Standard Reference, www.nal.usda.gov/fnic and manufacturers.

Carbohydrates

What Are Carbohydrates?

Carbohydrates are essential nutrients that are predominant in plant-based foods, and they make up the foundation of many diets around the world. You need carbohydrates on a daily basis because they are the most desirable source of energy for your body. Their main role is to supply fuel to your cells, primarily in the form of **glucose** (*ose* = carbohydrate), the predominant sugar in carbohydrate-rich foods. Plants form glucose in a process called **photosynthesis.**

Glucose

Simple and Complex Carbohydrates

Carbohydrates are divided into two categories based on the number of sugar units that are joined together. **Simple carbohydrates,** or sugars, include **monosaccharides** (*mono* = one, *saccharide* = sugar) and **disaccharides** (*di* = two), and **complex carbohydrates** include **polysaccharides** (*poly* = many).

a Monosaccharides

Fructose   Glucose   Galactose

b Disaccharides

Sucrose   Maltose   Lactose
(glucose and   (glucose and   (glucose and
fructose)   glucose)   galactose)

c Polysaccharides (starch)

Amylose (straight chain)

Amylopectin (branched)

Three monosaccharides are found in foods: glucose, **fructose,** and **galactose.** Fructose is the sweetest of the simple sugars and is found abundantly in fruit. For this reason, it is often referred to as fruit sugar. Galactose is found in dairy foods. From these three sugars, the other simple and complex carbohydrates can be created.

When two glucose units join together, the disaccharide **maltose** is created. Maltose is the sugar found in grains. When glucose and fructose pair up, the disaccharide **sucrose,** or table sugar, is formed. Galactose is joined with glucose to create lactose (often called milk sugar, as it is found in dairy foods).

Polysaccharides contain the most sugars, so it makes sense that they are called complex carbohydrates. **Starch, fiber,** and **glycogen** are all polysaccharides.

Functions of Carbohydrates

Your body uses carbohydrates, specifically glucose, for energy, and there are chemical messengers called **hormones** that regulate the amount of glucose in your blood. To lower your blood glucose level, your pancreas releases the hormone **insulin** into the blood.

Surplus glucose is stored in long chains of glycogen. The process of generating glycogen for later use is called **glycogenesis** (*glyco* = sugar/sweet, *genesis* = origin). Glycogenesis occurs only in your liver and muscle cells. You can't squirrel away unlimited extra energy reserves in the form of glycogen. However, you can store excess energy in the form of fat.

Your pancreas releases another hormone, **glucagon,** when the body needs to direct the release of glucose from the stored glycogen in your liver to help raise your blood glucose level. This breakdown of glycogen is called **glycogenolysis** (*lysis* = loosening).

Fiber Has Many Health Benefits

Fiber has been shown to help lower your risk of developing constipation, diverticulosis, obesity, heart disease, cancer, and diabetes mellitus.

Meals high in fiber are typically digested more slowly, which allows the absorption of the nutrients to be extended over a longer period of time. Foods high in fiber, such as whole grains, fruits, and vegetables, can add to satiation so that you need to eat fewer calories to feel full.

Viscous, soluble fibers have been shown to help lower elevated blood cholesterol levels. A high blood cholesterol level can increase the risk of heart disease.

Daily Needs

The latest Dietary Reference Intakes (DRIs) for carbohydrates recommend that adults and children consume a minimum of 130 grams daily. This is based on the estimated minimum amount of glucose your brain needs to function efficiently. A quick look at MyPlate shows that 130 grams is less than the amount you would consume by eating the minimum recommended daily servings from the grain group (6 servings), vegetable group (3 servings), fruit group (2 servings), and milk group (3 servings).

In the United States, adult males consume, on average, 220 grams to 330 grams of carbohydrates daily, whereas adult females eat 180 grams to 230 grams daily, well over the minimum DRI.

The latest DRIs indicate that 45 to 65 percent of your total daily calories should come from carbohydrates. Adults in the United States consume about half of their calories from carbohydrate-laden foods, so they are easily meeting this optimal range.

Food Sources

In general, you want your diet to contain low to moderate amounts of simple carbohydrates and be high in fiber and other complex carbohydrates. This is the best strategy for long-term health.

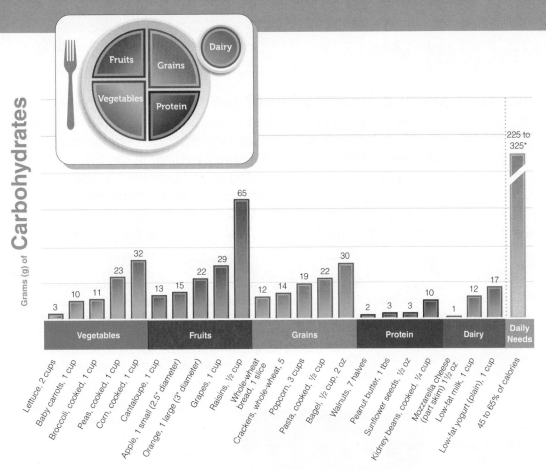

Grams (g) of Carbohydrates

Vegetables
- Lettuce, 2 cups: 3
- Baby carrots, 1 cup: 10
- Broccoli, cooked, 1 cup: 11
- Peas, cooked, 1 cup: 23
- Corn, cooked, 1 cup: 32

Fruits
- Cantaloupe, 1 cup: 13
- Apple, 1 small (2.5" diameter): 15
- Orange, 1 large (3" diameter): 22
- Grapes, 1 cup: 29
- Raisins, 1/2 cup: 65

Grains
- Whole-wheat bread, 1 slice: 12
- Crackers, whole-wheat, 5: 14
- Popcorn, 3 cups: 19
- Pasta, cooked, 1/2 cup: 22
- Bagel, 1/2 cup, 2 oz: 30

Protein
- Walnuts, 7 halves: 2
- Peanut butter, 1 tbs: 3
- Sunflower seeds, 1/2 oz: 3
- Kidney beans, cooked, 1/4 cup: 10

Dairy
- Mozzarella cheese (part skim) 1 1/2 oz: 1
- Low-fat milk, 1 cup: 12
- Low-fat yogurt (plain), 1 cup: 17

Daily Needs
- 45 to 65% of calories: 225 to 325*

*Based on a 2,000 calorie diet

Simple carbohydrates are found naturally in fruits, vegetables, and dairy foods. Though you can also get simple sugars from processed foods and sweets, the higher calorie and lower nutrient levels in these foods make them a less healthy option.

Complex carbohydrates, including starch and fiber, are found abundantly in grains, whole fruits, and vegetables. Starch is the primary complex carbohydrate found in grains and potatoes, while fiber is found in whole grains, whole fruits, vegetables, legumes, nuts, and seeds.

Too Much or Too Little?

Adding too much carbohydrate in the diet can displace other essential nutrients, whereas consuming too little carbohydrate can create a diet that falls short of many vitamins, minerals, fiber, and phytochemicals. Both extremes will produce an unbalanced diet. Individuals with diabetes need to monitor their carbohydrate intake to maintain a healthy blood glucose level. Chronic, poor regulation of blood glucose levels can damage the body.

What Is Diabetes?

Individuals develop **diabetes** because they aren't producing enough insulin (type 1 diabetes) and/or they have developed **insulin resistance,** such that their cells do not respond to the insulin when it arrives (type 2 diabetes).

Type 1 diabetes is an autoimmune disease and is the rarer of the two forms. Type 2 is the more common form and is seen in people who have become insulin resistant. Type 2 diabetes accounts for 90 to 95 percent of diagnoses of the disease.

Diabetes, especially if it is poorly managed, increases the likelihood of a multitude of dire effects such as nerve damage, leg and foot amputations, eye diseases, including blindness, tooth loss, gum problems, kidney disease, and heart disease. Diabetes can also damage the tiny blood vessels in the retina of the eye, which can cause bleeding and cloudy vision, and eventually destroy the retina and cause blindness.

Good nutrition habits play a key role in both the prevention and management of diabetes. The ADA (American Diabetes Association) recommends that individuals with diabetes consume a diet that includes a combination of predominantly high-fiber carbohydrates from whole grains, fruits, and vegetables, along with low-fat milk, adequate amounts of lean protein sources, and unsaturated fats.

Terms to Know

glucose • photosynthesis • simple carbohydrates • monosaccharides • disaccharides • complex carbohydrates • polysaccharides • fructose • galactose • maltose • sucrose • starch • fiber • glycogen • hormones • insulin • glycogenesis • glucagon • glycogenolysis • diabetes • insulin resistance

Two Points of View

Can Soft Drinks Be Part of a Healthy Diet?

Soft drinks are nonalcoholic beverages, including carbonated versions like sodas, as well as fruit drinks and sports drinks. In addition to water and fruit juice, they can contain low-calorie sweeteners, high-fructose corn syrup, and caffeine.[1] While many nutrition experts feel that soft drinks are a primary culprit in the overconsumption of calories and the rise in obesity that's occurred in the United States over the last few decades, other individuals argue that soft drinks can be part of a healthy diet. Can you consume soft drinks and still be healthy? Or do these drinks just provide empty calories and contribute to weight gain? Read the arguments, then consider the critical thinking questions and decide for yourself.

Yes

- Soda, along with sweetened waters, sports drinks, and energy drinks, contribute only 5.5 percent of the calories in the American diet.[2]

- Beverages that have no calories, including diet soft drinks, are useful for hydration, particularly for people who may not like to drink milk or water.

- Science shows that, when it comes to tackling obesity, what matters most is balancing the calories from all the foods and beverages we eat and drink with those we burn through regular physical activity.[3]

- The beverage industry is producing more good-tasting, lower-calorie choices that are popular with consumers. In fact, since 1998, there has been a 21 percent reduction in calories in beverages in the marketplace.[4]

- Diet soft drinks can be helpful for consumers who are hooked on regular sodas and trying to wean themselves off the sugary beverages.[5]

No

- Studies consistently show that increased consumption of soft drinks is associated with increased energy intake. Fluids don't provide the same feeling of fullness or satisfaction that solid foods do, which might prompt you to keep eating. This would mean that soda calories are added on top of calories from the rest of the diet.[6]

- Strong evidence indicates that sugar-sweetened soft drinks contribute to the development of diabetes. In the well-known Nurses' Health Study, the nurses who said they had one or more servings a day of a sugar-sweetened soft drink or fruit punch were twice as likely to have developed type 2 diabetes than those who rarely had these beverages.[7]

- The Nurses' Health Study also found that women who drank more than two servings of sugary beverage each day had a 40 percent higher risk of heart attacks or death from heart disease than women who rarely drank sugary beverages.[8]

What do you think?

1. Do you think soft drinks can be part of a healthy diet? **2.** Do you consume soda or other bottled (nonwater) beverages? If so, what effect is this consumption having on the quality of your diet? **3.** Should the government impose a "soda tax" to discourage the consumption of soft drinks?

Chapter Review

Be a Nutrition Sleuth

Sweet on Sweets

Go to **www.pearsonhighered.com/blake** to see one student's typical daily diet—high in added sugars and low in fiber. Use Table 4.3 and Figure 4.8 to see if you can come up with healthier choices that will satisfy a sweet tooth and provide the fiber this student needs.

Get Real!

How Much Fiber Are You Eating?

Do you think you have enough fiber in your diet? You may be surprised. Go to **www.pearsonhighered.com/blake** and fill out the daily food record. Use the Food Composition Table supplement or the MyDietAnalysis program to complete the record and see how you are really doing!

The Top Ten Points to Remember

1. Glucose, fructose, and galactose are monosaccharides. Glucose is the most abundant monosaccharide and the preferred fuel for the body. When two monosaccharides are joined, a disaccharide is formed. The best-known disaccharide, sucrose (table sugar), is made of fructose and glucose. Lactose, or milk sugar, is made up of glucose and galactose. Maltose is two glucose units joined together. When many glucose units are joined together, starch, a polysaccharide, is formed. Glycogen is the polysaccharide storage form of glucose in your body. Fiber is a nondigestible polysaccharide.

   a Monosaccharides — Fructose, Glucose, Galactose

2. Carbohydrate digestion begins in the mouth, where the enzyme amylase begins to break down starch. In the small intestine, enzymes such as pancreatic amylase, maltase, lactase, and sucrase continue to break down starch and the disaccharides into monosaccharides, which are then absorbed through the intestinal wall. The absorbed monosaccharides travel in the blood to the liver, where fructose and galactose are converted to glucose. Glucose is then either stored or shipped back out to the cells. Lactose maldigestion and lactose intolerance are two conditions experienced by people who cannot digest the milk sugar, lactose.

3. The major functions of glucose are to provide fuel for the body, particularly the brain and red blood cells, and to spare protein for other uses. Your blood glucose level is maintained in a healthy range with the help of hormones. Insulin directs glucose into cells. When your blood glucose level drops too low, the hormone glucagon is released to increase the blood glucose level. When your diet is deficient in carbohydrates, your body will not be able to break down fat completely. Ketone bodies are created.

4. A minimum of 130 grams of dietary carbohydrates is needed daily. It's recommended that 45 to 65 percent of your daily calories come from carbohydrates. Adults should consume 20 to 35 grams of fiber daily, depending on their age and gender. The best food sources of carbohydrates are fruits and vegetables, whole grains, and low-fat dairy products.

5. Your body can't distinguish between naturally occurring and added sugar. Food sources of naturally occurring sugars tend to be more nutritious than foods with a lot of added sugar. The major source of dietary added sugar is soft drinks. Sugary foods contain calories but little else and can crowd out more nutritious food choices in the diet. Frequently exposing your teeth to starchy and sugary foods, especially sticky foods, can increase your risk of dental caries.

6. Polyols, saccharin, aspartame, acesulfame-K, sucralose, rebaudioside A, and neotame are sugar substitutes currently deemed safe by the FDA. Because aspartame contains the amino acid phenylalanine, individuals with phenylketonuria (PKU) must limit all dietary sources of this amino acid.

7. Soluble fiber is important to a healthy diet because it provides bulk to stool and helps food move along the GI tract. Adequate fiber intake has been shown to help lower the risk of constipation, diverticulosis, obesity, heart disease, cancer, and diabetes mellitus. Increasing fiber intake too quickly can lead to intestinal gas, so changes should be made gradually and be accompanied by plenty of fluids.

8. Whole grains contain vitamins, minerals, fiber, and phytochemicals. Whereas refined grains can be "enriched" with some of the vitamins and minerals that were lost during processing, the fiber and phytochemicals are not added back. At least half of your daily servings of grains should be whole grains.

9. Diabetes mellitus, particularly type 2 diabetes, is becoming more prevalent in the United States, especially among children. Those with diabetes should consume a well-balanced diet and exercise regularly to help maintain a blood glucose level within a healthy range. Medication and/or insulin as well as regular blood tests may also be needed to manage blood glucose.

10. Hypoglycemia or low blood sugar can occur in individuals with diabetes, especially if they are taking medication and/or insulin and are not eating properly. Individuals without diabetes can also experience hypoglycemia, but the incidence is less common.

Test Your Knowledge

1. _____ is the storage form of glucose in your body.
   a. Glucagon
   b. Glycogen
   c. Gluconeogenesis
   d. Glucose

2. Sucrose is a
   a. monosaccharide.
   b. disaccharide.
   c. polysaccharide.
   d. starch.

3. The hormone that directs the breakdown of glycogen is
   a. galactose.
   b. glucagon.
   c. insulin.
   d. none of the above.

4. The minimum amount of carbohydrates needed daily is
   a. 75 grams.
   b. 100 grams.
   c. 120 grams.
   d. 130 grams.
   e. 150 grams.

5. Which of the following can help someone who's lactose intolerant to enjoy dairy products?
   a. drinking Lactaid milk
   b. pouring milk over a cup of bran cereal
   c. enjoying cheese a little at a time, and building up to larger servings
   d. all of the above
   e. none of the above

6. Reducing consumption of which item would have the biggest impact on decreasing the amount of added sugars that Americans consume?
   a. watermelon
   b. candy
   c. soda
   d. apples

7. Your blood cholesterol level is too high, so you would like to eat additional viscous, soluble high-fiber foods to help lower it. A good choice would be
   a. low-fat milk.
   b. chocolate chip cookies.
   c. bananas.
   d. oatmeal.

8. Which of the following nutrients are added to enriched grains?
   a. folic acid, thiamin, B_{12}, niacin, and calcium
   b. folic acid, thiamin, riboflavin, B_{12}, and iron
   c. fiber, thiamin, riboflavin, niacin, and iron
   d. folic acid, thiamin, riboflavin, niacin, and iron

9. The small bulging pouches that are sometimes found along the intestinal lining are called
   a. diverticulosis.
   b. diverticulitis.
   c. diverticula.
   d. diabetes.

10. Which of the following can help reduce your risk of type 2 diabetes?
    a. avoiding sugar
    b. eating a high-fiber, plant-based diet
    c. exercising regularly
    d. all of the above
    e. b and c only

Answers

1. (b) glycogen. Glycogen is stored in your liver and muscles and provides a ready-to-use form of glucose for your body. Glucagon is the hormone that directs the release of glucose from the stored glycogen. Gluconeogenesis is the creation of glucose from noncarbohydrate sources.

2. (b) Sucrose contains the two monosaccharides glucose and fructose, and is therefore a disaccharide. Starch contains many units of glucose linked together and is therefore a polysaccharide.

3. (b) When your blood glucose level drops too low, glucagon is released from your pancreas to direct the breakdown of glycogen in your liver to raise your blood level of glucose. Insulin is a hormone that directs the uptake of glucose by your cells. Galactose is a monosaccharide found in dairy foods.

4. (d) You should consume at least 130 grams of carbohydrates daily to supply your body, particularly your brain, with the glucose needed to function effectively.

5. (d) All of these can help improve lactose absorption. The Lactaid milk is pretreated to facilitate the breakdown of the lactose in the milk. Consuming lactose-containing foods, such as milk, with a meal or snack will improve the digestion of lactose. Gradually adding dairy foods to the diet will lessen the symptoms of lactose intolerance.

6. (c) Sodas are the number-one source of added sugars in the American diet, so reducing the intake of these sugary beverages would go a long way in reducing the amount of added sugars that Americans consume. Reducing the amount of candy that Americans consume would also help reduce the added sugars in the diet but not as much as cutting back on soda. Watermelon and apples contain naturally occurring sugars.

7. (d) oatmeal. Oatmeal is rich in beta-glucan, a viscous fiber that can help lower your cholesterol when eaten as part of a heart-healthy diet. Though nutrient dense, the bananas and milk do not contain fiber. Cookies won't help lower your cholesterol.

8. (d) These nutrients are added to enriched grains.

9. (c) Diverticula are a condition of diverticulosis. When these pouches become inflamed, diverticulitis occurs. Diabetes is a chronic disease that results from poor regulation of blood glucose.

10. (e) Eating a high-fiber, plant-based diet and getting regular exercise, both of which will help you maintain a healthy weight, is the best approach, at present, to help reduce your risk of developing type 2 diabetes. Eating sugar doesn't cause diabetes.

Web Resources

➡ For more on fiber, visit the American Heart Association at www.heart.org/HEARTORG/

➡ For more on diabetes, visit the National Diabetes Education Program (NDEP) at www.ndep.nih.gov/

➡ For more on lactose intolerance, visit the National Institute of Diabetes and Digestive and Kidney Disease (NIDDK) at http://digestive.niddk.nih.gov/ddiseases/pubs/lactoseintolerance

Answers to Myths and Misperceptions

1. **False.** You need a *minimum* amount of carbohydrates daily to fuel your brain. See page 94 to find out how much you need to eat.

2. **False.** Dark bread doesn't necessarily have more fiber than white bread. Learn why on page 98.

3. **True.** The average American consumes about half the amount of fiber that's recommended daily. Turn to page 98 to learn more about the potential problems associated with this shortfall.

4. **False.** Many people who are lactose intolerant may still be able to enjoy some dairy products, especially if they are eaten with meals. In fact, dairy foods may be just what the doctor ordered. Turn to page 101 to learn why.

5. **False.** Calories, not carbs, are what you need to monitor to avoid weight gain. In fact, some high-fiber carbohydrates can actually help you lose weight. Turn to page 107 to find out why.

6. **True.** The more sugar you eat, the more likely you are to have tooth decay. Turn to page 111 to find out why this is the case.

7. **False.** Honey contains a small amount of nutrients but not enough to make it nutritionally superior to sugar. Turn to page 111 to learn more.

8. **False.** Foods that contain sugar alcohols, such as sorbitol, can be labeled "sugar free" because they are carbohydrates but not sugars. But they still provide calories. Turn to page 118 to learn more.

9. **False.** Though saccharin once bore the stigma of being a cancer causer, it's no longer thought to cause cancer in humans. Turn to page 118 to learn more about this turnaround.

10. **True.** Being overweight or obese can increase your chances of developing type 2 diabetes. Turn to page 128 to learn more.

5

True or False?

1. You need to eat **cholesterol** daily to meet your needs. ⓉⒻ p. 145

2. A high amount of **HDL** cholesterol in your blood is good for you. ⓉⒻ p. 148

3. Americans today eat a **lower percentage** of their daily calories from fat than they did 50 years ago. ⓉⒻ p. 151

4. A healthy diet is very low in **fat**. ⓉⒻ p. 151

5. **Saturated fat** is a major dietary culprit behind an elevated blood cholesterol level. ⓉⒻ p. 153

6. You can eat as many fat-free **cookies** as you want without gaining weight. ⓉⒻ p. 160

7. Butter is better for you than **margarine**. ⓉⒻ p. 167

8. **Peanut butter** is high in cholesterol. ⓉⒻ p. 168

9. If you don't eat **fish,** you should take a fish oil supplement. ⓉⒻ p. 169

10. **Vegetarian** baked beans can help lower your cholesterol. ⓉⒻ p. 170

See page 179 for the answers to these Myths and Misperceptions.

Fats, Oils, and Other Lipids

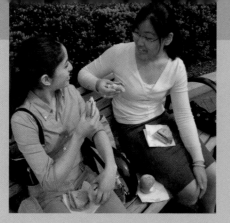

esiree loves her grandmother's homemade salad dressing of balsamic vinegar, canola oil, and basil. She uses it every night on her dinner salad, and every night, her friend Diane chides her for using oil. "It adds calories and nothing else to your diet," Diane claims. "I don't go near the stuff. Fat makes you fat."

Is Diane right to advise her friend to skip the oil? Does eating fat really make you fat? Do you know what fats are, how they affect your heart, and the roles they play in your overall health? Do you know which types of fats are more healthy, and why? In this chapter, we answer these questions as well as debunk some popular myths about fat. We'll also discuss the different types of fats, the foods in which they're found, and which of them you should aim to eat during meals and snacks.

Chapter Objectives

After reading this chapter, you will be able to:

1. Describe the three classifications of lipids.

2. Explain the differences in the structure of triglycerides, phospholipids, and cholesterol.

3. Describe how fat is digested and absorbed in the body.

4. Explain how fat is transported in the blood.

5. Describe the functions of fat in the body.

6. Define the dietary recommendations for total fat, the essential fatty acids, cholesterol, and *trans* fat.

7. Identify the major food sources of the different types of fats, including the essential fatty acids, saturated fats, and *trans* fats.

8. Compare the different fat substitutes currently used in food products.

9. Describe the development of atherosclerosis, including its role in the risk of heart disease.

10. Explain how lifestyle factors can affect the risk for heart disease.

What Are Fats and Why Do You Need Them?

When you see the word *fat*, you may think of butter, mayonnaise, the cholesterol in meats and eggs, and even the fatty tissues in your own body. But technically speaking, these aren't all fats. Instead, they're examples of a broader category of substances known as **lipids**—compounds that contain carbon, oxygen, and hydrogen and which are **hydrophobic** (*hydro* = water, *phobic* = fearing), meaning they don't dissolve in water. If you were to drop lipids, such as butter or olive oil, into a glass of water, you would see them rise to the top and sit on the water's surface. This repelling of water enables lipids to play a unique role in foods and in your body.

To answer our original question, *fat* is the common name for just one type of lipid, known as a triglyceride. Because this is the type of lipid found most abundantly in foods, food labels and nutrition sources refer generally to this category as dietary *fat*—not dietary *lipid*—so fat is the term we'll use in this chapter.

Fats Serve Multiple Functions in Foods and in Your Body

Fats perform a variety of functions in cooking. They give a flaky texture to pie crusts and other baked goods, and they make meat tender and soups and puddings creamy. The flavors and aromas that fats provide can make your mouth water as you eye crispy fried chicken or smell baking cookies. Foods that are higher in fats contribute to satiety, that feeling of fullness you experience after eating.

In your body, fats are essential for energy storage and insulation. Two other types of lipids are also important as components of the membranes surrounding your cells and play a key role in transporting proteins in your blood.

Three types of lipids are found in foods and in your body: triglycerides (*fats*), phospholipids, and sterols. Two of the three, triglycerides and phospholipids, are built from a basic unit called a fatty acid. So let's start our discussion of the structure of lipids with the fatty acids.

Fatty Acids Are Found in Triglycerides and Phospholipids

All **fatty acids** (**Figure 5.1**) consist of a chain of carbon and hydrogen atoms, with an acid group (COOH) at one end. There are more than 20 different fatty acids. They can vary by (1) the length of the chain, (2) whether the carbons have a single or a double bond between them (C — C or C = C), and (3) the total number of double bonds. The way carbon bonds occur in different types of fatty acids is what makes some fatty acids healthier than others.

There are three main types of fatty acids:

Figure 5.1 Structure of a Fatty Acid
Fatty acids are the building blocks of some lipids.

➤ *Saturated fatty acids.* When each carbon in a fatty acid chain is bonded with two atoms of hydrogen, as we saw in Figure 5.1, the chain is considered *saturated* with hydrogen. It cannot hold any more. We therefore call such a fatty acid a **saturated fatty acid.** For example, stearic acid is a saturated fatty acid (**Figure 5.2a**). It has 18 carbons, all of which are bound, or saturated, with hydrogen. Long fatty acids, such as stearic acid, are strongly attracted to one another, and are relatively straight, so they are able to pack tightly together in food, and thus become solid fats at room temperature. Stearic acid can be found in cocoa butter (in chocolate) and in the fatty part of meat. Shorter saturated fatty acids (with fewer than 12 carbons) have a weaker attraction to one another, and so do not pack tightly together. Because of this, foods that contain them are liquid at room temperature. Whole milk contains short-chain saturated fatty acids. Fats made up of mostly saturated fatty acids are called **saturated fats.** As you will learn later on in the chapter, saturated fats and other solid fats should be minimized in the diet, as they are not healthy for your heart.

Cocoa butter melts at body temperature. This is why solid milk chocolate melts in your mouth.

➤ *Monounsaturated fatty acids (MUFAs).* Take a look at the fatty acid shown in **Figure 5.2b**. Do you notice that, at one place in the chain, two carbons are each bound to only one atom of hydrogen, and are joined twice to each other? This double carbon bond means that the carbons are not "saturated" with hydrogen atoms at that point in the chain. This makes the chain unsaturated. Because a double bond occurs at just one point in the chain, the molecule is called a **monounsaturated fatty acid** (recall that *mono-* means one). The example shown in Figure 5.2b is oleic acid. Like stearic acid, oleic acid contains 18 carbons, but two of them are paired with each other rather than hydrogen, so it has one double bond. This one double bond makes oleic acid a monounsaturated fatty acid. It also makes it crooked. That is, double bonds cause a kink in the chain of the fatty acid. This kink keeps **unsaturated fatty acids** from packing together tightly. Thus, unsaturated fatty acids are liquid at room temperature. For instance, oleic acid is found in olive oil. You can see the effect of straight versus kinked fatty acid chains on foods in **Figure 5.3**. As you might expect, fats made up of mostly unsaturated fatty acids are called **unsaturated fats.** Whereas saturated fats are unhealthy, unsaturated fats are considered important to your health.

➤ *Polyunsaturated fatty acids (PUFAs).* A **polyunsaturated fatty acid** (*poly* = many) contains more than one double bond and is even less saturated with hydrogen than a monounsaturated fatty acid. For instance, linoleic acid contains two double bonds and is polyunsaturated (**Figure 5.2c**). It is found in soybean oil. Like monounsaturated fats, polyunsaturated fats are considered healthy. Incidentally, your body can make most of the fatty acids it needs, but there are two

lipid A category of carbon, hydrogen, and oxygen compounds that are insoluble in water.

hydrophobic Having an aversion to water.

fatty acid The basic unit of triglycerides and phospholipids.

saturated fatty acid A fatty acid that has all of its carbons bound with hydrogen.

saturated fats Fats that contain mostly saturated fatty acids.

monounsaturated fatty acid (MUFA) A fatty acid that has one double bond.

unsaturated fatty acid A fatty acid that has one or more double bonds between carbons.

unsaturated fats Fats that contain mostly unsaturated fatty acids.

polyunsaturated fatty acid (PUFA) A fatty acid with two or more double bonds.

Figure 5.2 Saturated and Unsaturated Fatty Acids

Fatty acids differ by the length of the fatty acid chain, whether or not there are double bonds between the carbons, and (if there are double bonds) how many double bonds they contain.

a Stearic acid, a saturated fatty acid

b Oleic acid, a monounsaturated fatty acid

Double bond in carbon chain creates a bend

c Linoleic acid, a polyunsaturated, omega-6 fatty acid

2 double bonds create 2 bends

d Alpha-linolenic acid, a polyunsaturated, omega-3 fatty acid

3 double bonds create 3 bends

Figure 5.3 Saturated and Unsaturated Fatty Acids Help Shape Foods

Saturated fatty acids are able to pack tightly together and are solid at room temperature. The double bonds in unsaturated fatty acids cause kinks in their shape and prevent them from packing tightly together, so they tend to be liquid at room temperature.

a Saturated fatty acids

b Unsaturated fatty acids

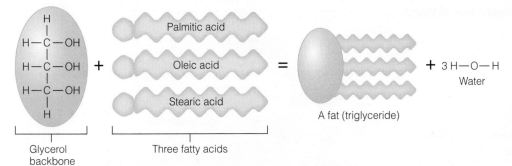

Figure 5.4 Structure of a Triglyceride
A triglyceride consists of three fatty acids attached to a glycerol backbone. Note that a single triglyceride can contain different fatty acids.

Source: Adapted from J. L. Smith, S. S. Gropper, and J. L. Groff. 2005. *Advanced Nutrition and Human Metabolism.* 4th ed. Thomson Wadsworth.

that it cannot make, and both are polyunsaturated. Because you must consume them in your diet, they're known as **essential fatty acids.** They are **linoleic acid,** shown in Figure 5.2c, and **alpha-linolenic acid,** shown in **Figure 5.2d.** We'll discuss these essential fatty acids in more detail later in this chapter.

Triglycerides Contain Three Fatty Acid Chains

Triglycerides are the most common lipid found in foods and in your body. Each **triglyceride** compound is made up of three fatty acid chains (*tri* = three) connected to a **glycerol** "backbone." Glycerol is a compound containing carbon, hydrogen, and a type of alcohol. The three fatty acids join to the glycerol backbone to form the triglyceride (**Figure 5.4**). Any triglyceride can contain a variety of different fatty acids.

The more common name for triglycerides is **fat,** and this is the term we'll use throughout this chapter and the rest of the book. Most of the lipids that you eat and that are in your body are in the form of fat. Many fatty foods, such as butter, lard, and the fat in meats, are solid at room temperature so are often referred to as solid fats. **Oils** are lipids that are liquid at room temperature.

Phospholipids Contain Phosphate

Like fats, **phospholipids** contain a glycerol backbone, but instead of being made up of three fatty acids, they contain two fatty acids and a phosphate group (a compound containing the mineral phosphorus) (**Figure 5.5**). The portion where the phosphate is attached to the glycerol is referred to as the head, which is *hydrophilic*

essential fatty acids The two polyunsaturated fatty acids that the body cannot make and therefore must be eaten in foods: linoleic acid and alpha-linolenic acid.

linoleic acid A polyunsaturated essential fatty acid; part of the omega-6 fatty acid family.

alpha-linolenic acid A polyunsaturated essential fatty acid; part of the omega-3 fatty acid family.

triglyceride Three fatty acids that are attached to a glycerol backbone. Also known as **fat.**

glycerol The three-carbon backbone of a triglyceride.

oils Lipids that are liquid at room temperature.

phospholipids Lipids made up of two fatty acids and a phosphate group attached to a glycerol backbone.

Figure 5.5 Structure of a Phospholipid
Phospholipids are similar to triglycerides but they have only two fatty acids and a phosphate group connected to the glycerol backbone. This configuration allows phospholipids, such as lecithin, to be attracted to both water and fat.

Figure 5.6 Phospholipids' Role in Your Cell Membranes

Cell

Outside of cell (watery extracellular fluid)

1 Because the phosphorus–containing head is polar, it attracts charged particles, such as water located both outside and inside your cells.

2 Its fatty acid–containing tail is nonpolar, so it mingles and lines up with other nonpolar molecules such as the fatty acid–containing ends of other phospholipids.

3 This creates a two-layer membrane that surrounds the cell and acts as a barrier, allowing certain substances to enter the cell but keeping others from leaving.

Cell membrane

Protein

Inside of cell (watery cytoplasm)

Phospholipid head
Phospholipid tails
Phospholipid tails
Phospholipid head

Cholesterol

Water

Fat droplet

Emulsifier (lecithin, a phospholipid)

Figure 5.7 Keeping a Salad Dressing Blended

To prevent the fat from separating out in a salad dressing, an emulsifier is added. The emulsifier's fat-attracting tails surround the droplets of fat, whereas the water-attracting heads remain oriented toward the watery portion of the solution or dressing. This allows the fat droplet to stay suspended and blended in the dressing.

(*philic* = loving), so it is able to attract water. In contrast, phospholipids' fatty acid tails are hydrophobic.

Phospholipids make up the phospholipid bilayer in cell membranes. Their water-loving heads face outward to the watery areas both outside and inside your cells, and their fat-loving tails line up with each other in the center, creating a phospholipid membrane that surrounds the cell and acts as a barrier (**Figure 5.6**). The cell membrane allows certain substances, such as water, to enter the cell but keeps others, like protein, from leaking out. You can visualize this phospholipid layer as being like a picket fence, acting as a barrier surrounding each cell.

The major phospholipid in your cell membranes is lecithin. Even though lecithin plays an important role in your body, you don't have to worry about eating large amounts of lecithin in foods. As with all phospholipids, your body is able to make all the lecithin it needs. Because of its unique water- and fat-loving attributes, lecithin is used in many foods as an **emulsifier,** which helps keep incompatible substances, such as water and oil, mixed together. For example, an emulsifier is sometimes added to commercially made salad dressings to prevent the fat from separating and rising to the top of the dressing (**Figure 5.7**). The emulsifier's nonpolar, fat-attracting tail surrounds the droplets of fat, which orients the polar, water-attracting head of the emulsifier toward the watery solution of the dressing. This keeps the fat droplet suspended in the dressing and allows these two incompatible substances to stay blended together. We'll see the process of emulsification again when we discuss how the body uses fat.

Sterols Have a Unique Ring Structure

Unlike phospholipids, **sterols** are lipids that do not contain glycerol or fatty acids. Instead, they are composed mainly of four connecting rings of carbon and hydrogen

Figure 5.8 Structure of a Sterol
Rather than being made from fatty acids attached to a glycerol backbone, sterols have a carbon ring configuration with hydrogens and an oxygen attached. Cholesterol is the best-known sterol.

Lipid	Structure		Examples
Triglycerides	Glycerol	Fatty acids	Saturated fat Unsaturated fat *Trans* fat
Phospholipids	Phosphate head	Fatty acids	Lecithin
Sterols	HO		Cholesterol

Figure 5.9 Three Types of Lipids
The three types of lipids vary in structure. Triglycerides and phospholipids are built from fatty acids, whereas sterols are composed of carbon rings.

(**Figure 5.8**). The best known sterol is cholesterol. Though cholesterol's association with heart disease has blemished its reputation, it plays an important role in your cell membranes and is the **precursor** of some very important compounds in your body. As with lecithin, don't be concerned about meeting your daily need for this important substance through your diet, since your body manufactures all the cholesterol you need. **Figure 5.9** summarizes the structures of the three types of lipids.

The Take-Home Message Lipids are hydrophobic compounds made up of carbon, hydrogen, and oxygen. The three types of lipids are triglycerides, phospholipids, and sterols. Fatty acids, which consist of a carbon and hydrogen chain and an alcohol group, are the basic structural units of triglycerides and phospholipids. Triglycerides are formed from three fatty acids connected to a glycerol backbone and are the most prevalent lipids in your food and body. Phospholipids are made of two fatty acids and a phosphate-containing group attached to a glycerol backbone. Phospholipids are an important part of the structure of cell membranes. Cholesterol is an important sterol in your cell membranes and is the precursor to other essential compounds.

What Happens to the Fat You Eat?

As with all nutrients, the digestion of fat begins in your mouth (see **Figure 5.10**, step 1). Chewing mechanically breaks down the food—in this case, a slice of pizza. The enzyme lingual lipase in the mouth plays a minor role in breaking down some fat. Once food is swallowed, the stomach begins to breaks down fat further. Let's follow the fat in the cheese pizza through the rest of the GI tract.

You Digest Most Fat in Your Stomach and Small Intestine

In the stomach, fat mixes with gastric lipase, an enzyme that breaks down some of it into a fatty acid and a **diglyceride** (the remnant of fat digestion when only two fatty

emulsifier A compound that keeps two incompatible substances, such as oil and water, mixed together.

sterol A lipid that contains four connecting rings of carbon and hydrogen.

precursor A substance that is converted into or leads to the formation of another substance.

diglyceride A glycerol with only two attached fatty acids.

Figure 5.10 Digesting and Absorbing Fat

1 Mouth
Chewing or mechanically breaking down fatty foods begins in your mouth.

Esophagus

2 Stomach
Fat digestion continues in the stomach with the aid of the enzyme gastric lipase.

Liver

Gallbladder

Stomach

Pancreas

Enzyme

Small intestine

3 Small intestine
Bile acids in bile secreted from the gallbladder help emulsify the fat into smaller globules, enabling pancreatic lipase to break it down more easily.

Micelles (free fatty acids and bile salts)

Inside of small intestine

Intestinal cells

Chylomicrons

4 Absorption
By-products of fat digestion travel through your intestinal cells. Short-chain fatty acids enter your bloodstream directly. Long-chain fatty acids are reformulated into fats and need transport carriers, called chylomicrons, which travel in your lymph before entering your blood.

Blood vessel

Lymph vessel

monoglyceride A glycerol with only one attached fatty acid.

bile A secretion that's squirted into the small intestine to emulsify fat into smaller globules, which allows enzymes to break the fat down. Bile is made in the liver and stored in the gallbladder.

acids are left joined to the glycerol backbone) (Figure 5.10, step 2). The majority of fat digestion occurs in your small intestine, where an enzyme released from your pancreas, pancreatic lipase, continues to break down the fat into two fatty acids and a **monoglyceride** (the remnant of fat digestion when only one fatty acid is left joined to the glycerol backbone).

Just as oil and water don't mix, fat can't mix with the watery fluids in your digestive tract. The fat globules tend to cluster together rather than disperse throughout the fluids. Mixing fats with watery fluids requires the addition of **bile,** which is made in your liver and stored in your gallbladder. When the fat from the pizza arrives in your intestines, your gallbladder releases bile. Bile contains bile acids that help to emulsify the fat into smaller globules within the watery digestive solution (Figure 5.10, step 3). This keeps the smaller fat globules dispersed throughout the fluids, and provides more surface area so that the pancreatic lipase can more easily break down the fat.

Monoglycerides and fatty acids are next packaged with lecithin, which is in the bile, and other substances to create **micelles** (small transport carriers). Once close to the mucosa of your small intestine, micelles travel through your intestinal cells.

The length of the fatty acid chain determines what happens next. Short-chain fatty acids will enter your bloodstream and go directly to your liver. The long-chain fatty acids can't enter your bloodstream directly. They enter your **lymph** and need transport carriers (Figure 5.10, step 4).

Lipoproteins Transport Fat through the Lymph and Blood

Long-chain fatty acids are reformulated into a fat within the wall of your intestines as they are absorbed. These reformulated fats (as well as other lipids, such as cholesterol) are not soluble in your watery blood. They need to be packaged inside protein-containing carriers called **lipoproteins.** These capsule-shaped fat "carriers" have an outer shell high in protein and phospholipids and an inner compartment that carries the insoluble fat, as well as cholesterol, through your lymph and bloodstream. One example of a lipoprotein carrier that transports these lipids is a **chylomicron** (**Figure 5.11**).

Chylomicrons are too large to be absorbed directly into your bloodstream, so they travel through your lymph system first and then enter your blood. Once in the blood, the fat is broken down into fatty acids and glycerol with the help of the enzyme lipoprotein lipase, which is located in the walls of the capillaries. After the fat is removed from the chylomicrons, the remnants of these lipoproteins go to your liver to be dismantled.

The liver produces other lipoproteins with different roles in your body:

> ➤ **very low-density lipoprotein (VLDL)**
> ➤ **low-density lipoprotein (LDL)**
> ➤ **high-density lipoprotein (HDL)**

Although all lipoproteins contain fat, phospholipids, cholesterol, and protein, the proportion of the protein in these substances differs in the various types. Protein is denser than fat, so the proportion of protein in the lipoproteins determines their overall density (**Figure 5.12**).

For example, VLDLs are composed mostly of triglycerides and have very little protein, so they are considered to be of very low density. The LDLs, which are mostly made of cholesterol, have more protein than the VLDLs but less than HDLs, which have the highest density. The protein in the lipoproteins helps them to perform their functions in your body. For example, the high protein content in HDLs not only helps remove cholesterol from your cells, but also enables the carrier to expand and contract, depending on the amount of fat and cholesterol it is carrying.

Why is the proportion of protein in a lipoprotein carrier important? Each lipoprotein has a different role. The main role of the VLDLs is to deliver fat that is made in the liver to your tissues. Once the fat is delivered, the VLDL remnants are converted into LDLs. The LDLs deliver cholesterol to your cells and are often referred to as the "bad" cholesterol carriers because they deposit cholesterol in the walls of your arteries, which can lead to heart disease. To help you remember this, you may want to think of the "**L**" in LDL as being of "Little" health benefit.

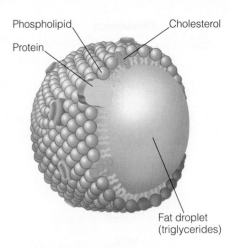

Figure 5.11 Chylomicron
Chylomicrons are one type of lipoprotein.

micelles Small transport carriers in the intestine that enable fatty acids and other compounds to be absorbed.

lymph Watery fluid that circulates through the body in lymph vessels and eventually enters the blood.

lipoproteins Capsule-shaped transport carriers that enable fat and cholesterol to travel through the lymph and blood.

chylomicron A type of lipoprotein that carries digested fat and other lipids through the lymph system into the blood.

very low-density lipoprotein (VLDL) A lipoprotein that delivers fat made in the liver to the tissues. VLDL remnants are converted into LDLs.

low-density lipoprotein (LDL) A lipoprotein that deposits cholesterol in the walls of the arteries. Because this can lead to heart disease, LDL is referred to as the *bad* cholesterol carrier.

high-density lipoprotein (HDL) A lipoprotein that removes cholesterol from the tissues and delivers it to the liver to be used as part of bile and/or to be excreted from the body. Because of this, it is known as the *good* cholesterol carrier.

Chylomicron

Protein 2%
Phospholipids 3%
Cholesterol
5%
Triglycerides
90%

VLDL

Phospholipids
Protein
10%
18%
Triglycerides
60%
Cholesterol
12%

LDL

Triglycerides
10%
Protein
25%
Phospholipids
15%
Cholesterol
50%

HDL

Triglycerides
5%
Cholesterol
20%
Protein
50%
Phospholipids
25%

Figure 5.12 Lipoproteins
The various types of lipoproteins and their composition.

The HDLs, as mentioned earlier, are mostly protein. They remove cholesterol from your cells and deliver it to your liver to be used to make bile or to be excreted from your body. For this reason, the HDLs are often referred to as the "good" cholesterol carriers, as they help remove cholesterol from your arteries. An easy way to remember this is to think of the "**H**" in HDL as referring to "Healthy" (**Figure 5.13**).

The Take-Home Message The digestion of fat begins in your mouth, and with the help of enzymes and emulsifying bile acids, most of it is digested and then absorbed in your small intestine. Fat is generally packaged as part of a chylomicron lipoprotein carrier, and travels in the lymph before entering your bloodstream. The other lipoproteins are VLDLs, LDLs, and HDLs. The VLDLs are converted to the "bad" LDL cholesterol carriers, which can deposit cholesterol in the walls of your arteries. The "good" HDL cholesterol carriers remove cholesterol from your arteries and deliver it to your liver to be excreted from your body.

How Does Your Body Use Fat and Cholesterol?

Some people, like Diane, whom you read about in the beginning of the chapter, try to avoid fat in their diets, as they think it is unhealthy. This can actually be counterproductive, because fat plays many key roles in your body. Fat is an important source of energy and helps the absorption of some compounds. Fat also insulates your body and cushions your major organs. Some fats are essential for your good health. There are differences among the types of fat that you eat. Different fats can have different effects on your health, specifically your heart. Let's look at the roles that fats play in your body.

Fat Is Used as Energy

At 9 calories per gram, compared with 4 calories per gram for both carbohydrates and protein, fat is a major fuel source for your body. Your body has an *unlimited* ability to store excess energy (calories) as fat. In fact, your fat reserves have the capacity to enlarge as much as 1,000 times their original size, as more fat is added. If your cells fill to capacity, your body can add more fat cells.

Remember from Chapter 4 that your body only has a limited ability to store glucose, which is needed for the brain and red blood cells to function. When your blood glucose level begins to decline, the hormone glucagon promotes the release of glucose from the liver in order to supply the blood with glucose. Glucagon simultaneously promotes the release of fat from fat cells to provide additional energy for your body. Your heart, liver, and resting muscles prefer fat as their fuel source, which spares glucose to be used for your nervous system and red blood cells. In fact, fat is your main source of energy throughout the day. This fat stored in your fat cells provides a backup source of energy between meals. In a famine situation, some individuals could last months without eating, depending upon the extent of their fat stores and the availability of adequate fluids.

Liver

c HDLs transport cholesterol from the body cells and deliver it to the liver for disposal.

HDL

a VLDLs deliver fatty acid made in the liver to the cells.

VLDL

LDL

b LDLs transport cholesterol to the cells, in some cases into the arterial lining.

Body cells

Body cells (including arteries)

Fat Helps You Absorb Certain Compounds and Insulates the Body

Fat allows you to absorb the fat-soluble vitamins A, D, E, and K, as well as carotenoids, compounds that can have antioxidant properties in your body.[1] Consuming inadequate amounts of fat may impede your absorption of these fat-soluble vitamins and compounds. The fat that is located just under your skin helps to insulate your body and maintain your body temperature. Fat also acts as a protective cushion for your bones, organs, and nerves.

Essential Fatty Acids Help Keep Cells Healthy

Two polyunsaturated fatty acids, *linoleic acid* and *alpha-linolenic acid*, are essential, which means that your body can't make them; thus, you need to obtain them from your diet. Linoleic acid is also referred to as an *omega-6 fatty acid*, and alpha-linolenic acid is commonly called an *omega-3 fatty acid*. If this sounds like Greek to you, it should. The letters of the Greek alphabet help identify the placement of the carbons in fatty acids. Omega is the last letter of the Greek alphabet. Because the numbering of the carbons in a fatty acid starts from the acid end and is counted outward, the omega carbon is the *last* carbon of the fatty acid. In alpha-linolenic acid, the first double bond occurs at the third carbon from the omega end. Hence, it is referred to as an omega-3 fatty acid (refer again to Figure 5.2d).

The essential fatty acids help maintain healthy skin cells, nerves, and cell membranes. For example, a deficiency of linoleic acid can interfere with normal growth and result in inflammation of the skin. A deficiency in alpha-linolenic acid can affect the functioning of the brain and nervous system. Essential fatty acids are also necessary to make other substances your body needs. Linoleic acid is used to make another polyunsaturated fatty acid, called arachidonic acid (**Figure 5.14**). This fatty acid is important for your cells and for making **eicosanoids,** which are hormone-like substances. Among other roles, eicosanoids help with blood pressure, inflammation, and blood clotting.

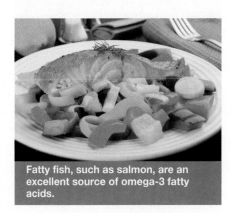

Fatty fish, such as salmon, are an excellent source of omega-3 fatty acids.

eicosanoids Hormone-like substances in the body. Prostaglandins, thromboxanes, and leukotrienes are all eicosanoids.

Figure 5.14 Essential Fatty Acids

Both linoleic acid (an omega-6 fatty acid) and alpha-linolenic acid (an omega-3 fatty acid) are essential fatty acids that you have to obtain from your diet. Other fatty acids can be made from these fatty acids.

A limited amount of alpha-linolenic acid can be converted to two other important omega-3 fatty acids: **eicosapentaenoic acid (EPA)** and **docosahexaenoic acid (DHA)**. EPA and DHA have been shown to reduce the risk of heart disease, stroke, and diabetes.[2] All fish contain EPA and DHA, although fatty fish such as salmon, herring, and sardines are especially rich sources. Cod-liver oil is abundant in EPA and DHA, but also in the fat-soluble vitamins A and D, which can both be toxic if consumed in high amounts. Eating fish is a safer way to obtain EPA and DHA, and it can also be very healthy for your heart, as discussed later in the chapter.

Omega-6, linoleic acid, and omega-3, alpha-linolenic acid, must be consumed in a proper ratio. Some research suggests that a diet that has too much omega-6 fatty acids in comparison with omega-3 fatty acids may be unhealthy. Too much linoleic acid in relationship to alpha-linolenic acid can inhibit the conversion of alpha-linolenic acid to DHA, while the inverse (too much alpha-linolenic acid and not enough linoleic acid) can inhibit the conversion of linoleic acid to arachidonic acid.[3]

Cholesterol Has Many Important Roles

Your body needs cholesterol both as a part of your cell membranes and as the precursor for vitamin D and bile acids. Cholesterol is also the precursor for the sex hormones such as estrogen and testosterone, which help to determine sexual characteristics.

The confusion over cholesterol persists. Though dietary cholesterol has been proclaimed as unhealthy, the cholesterol in your blood can be either "good" or "bad" cholesterol. How can one substance be both Dr. Jekyll and Mr. Hyde? Later in this chapter, we will look at the health effects of cholesterol, and try to clear up this confusion. During the discussion, keep in mind that the cholesterol in your diet isn't the only factor that determines the levels of cholesterol in your blood.

The Take-Home Message Fat contains 9 calories per gram and is an energy-dense source of fuel for your body. Fat cushions and protects your bones, organs, and nerves and insulates you to help maintain your body temperature. Fat also provides essential fatty acids and is needed for the absorption of fat-soluble vitamins and carotenoids. The essential fatty acids, linoleic acid (an omega-6 fatty acid) and alpha-linolenic acid (an omega-3 fatty acid), are necessary to keep cells healthy. Linoleic acid

A deficiency of linoleic acid can interfere with normal growth and result in inflammation of the skin. Scaly skin can be a sign of inadequate amounts of alpha-linolenic acid.

eicosapentaenoic acid (EPA) and **docosahexaenoic acid (DHA)** Two omega-3 fatty acids that are heart healthy. Fatty fish such as salmon are good sources.

is necessary to make arachidonic acid and eicosanoids. A limited amount of alpha-linolenic acid can be converted to two other omega-3 fatty acids, EPA and DHA, which are also found in fish. Cholesterol is part of your cell membranes and is needed to make vitamin D, bile acids, and sex hormones.

How Much Fat Do You Need Each Day?

At first glance, it looks as though Americans' fat consumption has gone up and down over the last century. In the 1930s, Americans were consuming about 34 percent of their calories from fat; this number climbed to 42 percent in the mid 1960s. By 1984, fat consumption had declined to 36 percent of total calories, and current consumption is about 34 percent of calories. However, while today's consumption levels are in line with the current recommendations, we can't break out the hot fudge sundaes just yet. Measuring fat consumption only as a percentage of total calories, and not including the absolute grams of fat, can be misleading.

Looking at the latest patterns of food intake by Americans, we find that the grams of fat we consume daily have not only increased about 12 percent since the early 1990s, but the number of *calories* has also increased about 15 percent. In other words, Americans are eating more of both fat and calories, and the reason that the percentage of fat in their diets has gone down is because the number of calories has gone up. The main source of this increase in calories is sweetened beverages, such as soft drinks, which are high in refined carbohydrates.[4]

As you can see, the overall consumption of fat (and calories) in the United States is higher than it should be. But dietary fat is still essential for health. So, how much should you eat?

You Need to Consume a Specific Percentage of Your Daily Calories from Fat

The current AMDR (Acceptable Macronutrient Distribution Range) recommendation is that 20 to 35 percent of your daily calories should come from fat. For some individuals, especially sedentary, overweight folks, a very low-fat diet (providing less than 20 percent of daily calories from fat) that is consequently high in carbohydrates may cause an increase in fat in the blood and a lowering of the good HDL cholesterol—not exactly a healthy combination for the heart. For others, consuming more than 35 percent of their total daily calories from fat could perpetuate obesity, which is a risk factor for heart disease.[5]

Although consuming fat won't increase your weight unless you consistently consume more calories than you need, remember that dietary fat has more than twice the calories per gram of carbohydrates or protein. Therefore, eating too many fatty foods could perpetuate a weight management problem. Numerous research

Table 5.1

Capping Your Fat Intake

If You Need This Many Calories to Maintain Your Weight	You Should Eat No More Than This Much	
	Fat (grams) (20% to 35% of total calories)	Saturated Fat (grams) (<7 to 10% of total calories)
1,600	36–62	12–18
1,700	38–66	13–19
1,800	40–70	14–20
1,900	42–74	15–21
2,000	44–78	16–22
2,100	47–82	16–23
2,200	49–86	17–24
2,300	51–89	18–26
2,400	53–93	19–27
2,500	56–97	19–28
2,600	58–101	20–29
2,700	60–105	21–30
2,800	62–109	22–31

Sedentary women should consume approximately 1,600 calories daily. Teenage girls, active women, and many sedentary men need approximately 2,200 calories daily. Teenage boys, many active men, and some very active women need about 2,800 calories daily.

The percentage of calories from fat and the corresponding grams of fat can be calculated by multiplying your number of daily calories by 20 percent and 35 percent and then dividing those numbers by 9. (Fat provides 9 calories per gram.) To determine the amount of calories you should be eating daily, turn to Table 2.3 in Chapter 2.

For example, if you consume 2,000 calories daily:

$$\underline{2,000} \times 0.20 \text{ (20 percent)} = \underline{400} \text{ calories} \div 9 = \underline{44} \text{ grams}$$

$$\underline{2,000} \times 0.35 \text{ (35 percent)} = \underline{700} \text{ calories} \div 9 = \underline{78} \text{ grams}$$

Your range of fat intake should be 44 to 78 grams daily.

To find the maximum grams of saturated fat that you should be consuming daily, repeat the process:

$$\underline{2,000} \times 0.07 \text{ (7 percent)} = \underline{140} \text{ calories} \div 9 = \underline{16} \text{ grams}$$

$$\underline{2,000} \times 0.10 \text{ (10 percent)} = \underline{200} \text{ calories} \div 9 = \underline{22} \text{ grams}$$

The total amount of saturated fat intake should be no more than 22 grams daily.

studies have shown that reducing dietary fat can also reduce dietary calories, which can result in weight loss.[6] Consequently, controlling one's fat intake may help control one's weight.

According to the AMDR recommendation, if you need 2,000 calories daily to maintain your weight, you can consume between 44 and 74 grams of fat daily (Table 5.1). For your heart health, you should consume less than 10 percent (and ideally less than 7 percent) of your calories, or 16 to 22 grams, from saturated fats.

You Need to Consume a Specific Amount of Essential Fatty Acids Daily

To ensure that you consume enough linoleic acid and alpha-linolenic acid, a recommended amount has been set for each of these important nutrients. A minimum of 5 percent and up to 10 percent of the total calories in your diet should come from linoleic acid, and alpha-linolenic acid should make up 0.6 percent to 1.2 percent of your total calories.[7] These recommended amounts are based on the estimated daily caloric needs according to your gender and age. For example, men aged 19 to 50 need 17 grams of linoleic acid daily, and women aged 19 to 50 who aren't pregnant or lactating need 12 grams daily. For alpha-linolenic acid, men aged 14 to 70 need 1.6 grams daily, whereas women of the same age need 1.1 grams daily.

Minimize Solid Fats: Saturated and *Trans* Fats in Your Diet

While your diet should include essential fatty acids, some types of fats should be avoided. Solid fats—like butter, chicken fat, cream, coconut oil, palm kernel and palm oils, and partially hydrogenated oils—are major sources of heart-unhealthy saturated and/or *trans* fat in the diet (as mentioned in Chapter 2). These solid fats are often found in grain-based desserts, pizza, full-fat cheese, sausages, and franks.[8] Research has confirmed that saturated fat plays a role in increased risk of heart disease. Consuming too much saturated fat can lead to higher levels of the "bad" LDL cholesterol carrier (you'll learn more about how these lipoproteins affect heart disease risk later in the chapter).

The majority of *trans* fats in foods are created by food manufacturers through the process of **hydrogenation.** Hydrogenation involves heating an oil and exposing it to hydrogen gas, which causes some of the double bonds in the unsaturated fatty acid to become saturated with hydrogen. Typically, the hydrogens of a double bond are lined up in a *cis* (*cis* = same) configuration, that is, they are all on the same side of the carbon chain in the fatty acid. During hydrogenation, some hydrogens cross to the opposite side of the carbon chain, resulting in a *trans* (*trans* = cross) configuration (**Figure 5.15**). The newly configured fatty acid is now a synthetic ***trans* fatty acid.** These ***trans* fats** are actually worse for heart health than saturated fat because they not only raise the LDL cholesterol levels, but they also lower HDL cholesterol in the body.

Trans fats were initially used in many processed foods because they provide a richer texture, a longer shelf life, and better resistance to **rancidity** than unsaturated fats. After saturated fat fell out of favor in the 1980s, because of research that confirmed its association with heart disease, *trans* fats came into widespread commercial use. Everything from cookies, cakes, and crackers to fried chips and doughnuts used *trans* fats to maintain their texture and shelf life. *Trans* fats were also frequently used for frying at fast-food restaurants.

To make consumers more aware of *trans* fat, the FDA mandated in 2006 that most foods, and even some dietary supplements such as energy bars, list the grams of *trans* fats per serving on the Nutrition Facts panel on the food label. The label allows you to quickly add up the saturated and *trans* fats listed and makes it easier for you to monitor the amount of these fats that you consume.[9] Because of this labeling requirement, many food manufacturers reformulated their products to remove or reduce the amount of *trans* fats made with hydrogenation. However, you may still find them in commercially made cakes, cookies, crackers, margarines, and other foods. Reducing the amount of food sources of solid fats in your diet will help you reduce your consumption of both saturated fats and *trans* fats (see **Figure 5.16**).

Figure 5.15 Creating *Trans* Fatty Acids Hydrogenating, or adding hydrogen to, an unsaturated fatty acid will create a more saturated fatty acid. This process will also cause some of the double bonds to twist from a *cis* position to a trans position. This creates a *trans* fatty acid.

hydrogenation Adding hydrogen to an unsaturated fatty acid to make it more saturated and solid at room temperature.

***trans* fatty acids** Substances that result from the hydrogenating of an unsaturated fatty acid, causing a reconfiguring of some of its double bonds. A small amount of *trans* fatty acids occurs naturally in animal foods.

***trans* fat** Substance that contains mostly *trans* fatty acids.

rancidity The decomposition, or spoiling, of fats through oxidation.

Figure 5.16 Major Food Sources of Saturated and *Trans* Fats for Americans
Reducing the amount of food sources containing solid fats will help you reduce saturated and *trans* fats in your diet.

Source: USDA and HHS. *Dietary Guidelines for Americans, 2010.* Available at www.health.gov/dietaryguidelines.

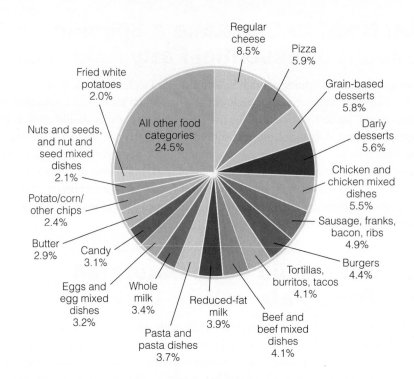

Table 5.2	
How Much Cholesterol Is in Your Foods?	
	Cholesterol (mg)
Liver, 3 oz	324
Breakfast biscuit with egg and sausage, 1	302
Egg, 1 large	186
Shrimp, 3 oz, canned	147
Fast-food hamburger, large, double patty	122
Ice cream, soft serve, vanilla, ½ cup	78
Beef, ground, cooked, 3 oz	77
Salmon, cooked, 3 oz	74
Chicken or turkey, breast, cooked, 3 oz	72
Lobster, cooked, 3 oz	61
Turkey, light meat, cooked, 3 oz	59
Egg noodles, 1 cup	53
Butter, 1 tbs	31
Cheddar cheese, 1 oz	30
Frankfurter, beef, 1	24
Milk, whole, 1 cup	24
Cheddar cheese, low fat, 1 oz	6
Milk, skim, 1 cup	4

Source: USDA National Nutrient Database for Standard Reference, Release 16, Available at www.ars.usda.gov. Accessed March 2011.

Minimize Cholesterol in Your Diet

As mentioned earlier, your body can make all the cholesterol it needs. Therefore, you do not need to consume it in your diet, and in fact, you should limit the amount of cholesterol you take in for the sake of your heart and arteries. Healthy individuals over the age of 2 are advised to limit their dietary cholesterol to less than 300 milligrams (mg) daily, on average. Adult males in the United States currently consume about 358 milligrams daily, whereas adult females eat slightly more than 237 milligrams of cholesterol daily, on average.[10] Table 5.2 lists a variety of foods and their cholesterol content.

Keeping the types of lipids straight, and remembering how much of each to consume or avoid, can be a challenge. The following summary should help you remember what you have learned thus far:

➤ **DO** be sure to get enough of the two heart-healthy essential fatty acids, linoleic acid and alpha-linolenic acid, in your diet by consuming plenty of polyunsaturated fats in your daily meals.

➤ **DO** choose mono- and polyunsaturated fats over saturated fats when possible, as these unsaturated fats are better for you. Saturated fats should be kept to less than 10 percent of your total calories, because they aren't good for your heart or your blood cholesterol levels.

➤ **DON'T** add *trans* fats to your diet. These are unhealthy for your heart and blood cholesterol levels and should be consumed as little as possible.

➤ **DON'T** worry about eating enough cholesterol, because your body makes all it needs.

When it comes to keeping track of your fat intake, counting grams of fat in your foods is the best strategy. Table 5.1 provided you with a healthy range of recommended fat intake based on your daily caloric needs. (To figure out your approximate daily caloric needs, see Chapter 2.) Use the following Self-Assessment to estimate how much fat and saturated fat you consume daily.

How Much Fat Is in Your Diet?

Is your diet too overloaded with fat, and/or saturated fat? Use the diet analysis program, the Food Composition Table, and/or food labels to track your fat consumption for a day. How does your actual intake compare to the amount recommended for you in Table 5.1?

Vegetable oils are good sources of essential fatty acids.

Food Log

	Food/Drink	Amount	Fat (g)	Saturated Fat (g)
Breakfast				
Snack				
Lunch				
Snack				
Dinner				
Snack				
Total				

The Take-Home Message You need to consume some fat in your diet, particularly the essential fatty acids, but you should limit other fats, like saturated fats and *trans* fats. Your fat intake should range from 20 to 35 percent of your total calories. To meet your essential fatty acid needs, 5 to 10 percent of your calories should come from linoleic acid and 0.6 to 1.2 percent of your daily calories should come from alpha-linolenic acid. No more than 10 percent of your fat intake should come from saturated fat and *trans* fats should be limited in your diet. You do not need to eat cholesterol in foods, as your body makes all the cholesterol it needs.

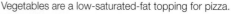

Vegetables are a low-saturated-fat topping for pizza.

What Are the Best Food Sources of Fats?

Foods that contain unsaturated fats (both monounsaturated and polyunsaturated fats) are better for your health than foods high in saturated fat, cholesterol, and/or *trans* fat (see **Figure 5.17**). So, where can you find the healthier fats in foods? Unsaturated fats are abundant in vegetable oils, such as soybean, corn, and canola oils, as well as soybeans, walnuts, peanut butter, flaxseeds, and wheat germ. Vegetable oils, nuts and flaxseeds are also good sources of the essential fatty acids. In fact, all the foods listed in Figure 5.17 are excellent sources of both unsaturated fats and essential fatty acids.

Most saturated fat in the diet comes from animal foods, such as fatty cuts of meat, whole-milk dairy products like cheese, butter, and ice cream, and the skin on poultry (**Figure 5.18**). Choosing lean meats and dairy foods, skinless poultry, and oil-based spreads will help you minimize the saturated fat in your diet. Certain vegetable oils, such as coconut, palm, and palm kernel oils, are very high in saturated fat. Although food manufacturers now use these highly saturated tropical oils less often, they may still be found in foods such as candies, commercially made baked goods, and gourmet ice cream. Checking the ingredient label on food packages is the best way to find out if these oils are in the foods that you eat.

Because all fats and oils are a combination of fatty acids, however, it's not only impossible to eliminate saturated fat entirely from your diet, it is unhealthy for you to do so (see **Figure 5.19**). Extreme trimming of fats and oils could lead to the unnecessary elimination of certain foods, such as soybean and canola oils, lean meats, fish, poultry, and low-fat dairy foods, which could cause you to fall short of important nutrients such as essential fatty acids, protein, and calcium. Just remember to keep your dietary intake of saturated fat to less than 10 percent of your daily total calories.

Americans on average consume about 11 percent of their daily calories from saturated fat, so it's likely that you need to reduce your intake.[11] You can use Figure 5.18 to make low-saturated-fat food choices at some of your meals and snacks.

> The cheddar cheese on the top of a cheeseburger has more fat and saturated fat per ounce than the burger.

The Take-Home Message Eating lean meats, skinless poultry, lean dairy products, and vegetable oils while limiting commercially prepared baked goods and snack items is a good strategy for overall good health. These foods will provide you with enough healthy unsaturated fats, with plenty of essential fatty acids, while limiting your intake of unhealthy, saturated fats.

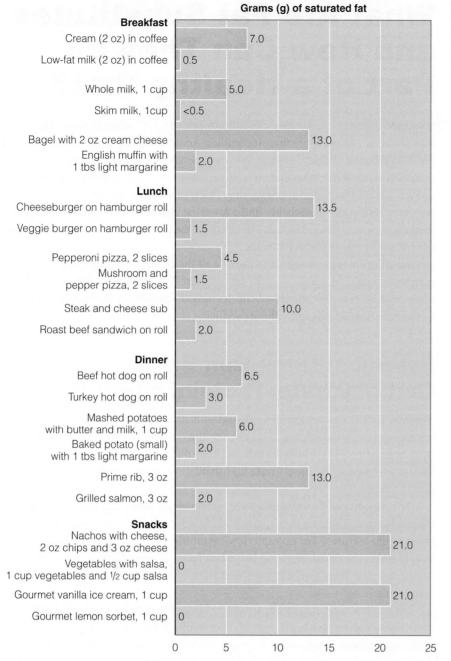

Grams (g) of saturated fat

Breakfast

Cream (2 oz) in coffee — 7.0
Low-fat milk (2 oz) in coffee — 0.5

Whole milk, 1 cup — 5.0
Skim milk, 1cup — <0.5

Bagel with 2 oz cream cheese — 13.0
English muffin with
1 tbs light margarine — 2.0

Lunch

Cheeseburger on hamburger roll — 13.5
Veggie burger on hamburger roll — 1.5

Pepperoni pizza, 2 slices — 4.5
Mushroom and
pepper pizza, 2 slices — 1.5

Steak and cheese sub — 10.0
Roast beef sandwich on roll — 2.0

Dinner

Beef hot dog on roll — 6.5
Turkey hot dog on roll — 3.0

Mashed potatoes
with butter and milk, 1 cup — 6.0
Baked potato (small)
with 1 tbs light margarine — 2.0

Prime rib, 3 oz — 13.0
Grilled salmon, 3 oz — 2.0

Snacks

Nachos with cheese,
2 oz chips and 3 oz cheese — 21.0
Vegetables with salsa,
1 cup vegetables and ½ cup salsa — 0

Gourmet vanilla ice cream, 1 cup — 21.0
Gourmet lemon sorbet, 1 cup — 0

0   5   10   15   20   25

Figure 5.18 Where's the Saturated Fat in Your Foods?
Choosing less-saturated-fat versions of some of your favorite foods at meals and snacks can dramatically lower the amount of "sat" fat you consume in your diet.

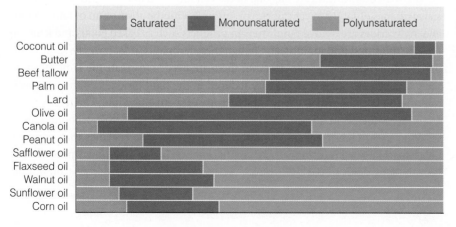

Saturated   Monounsaturated   Polyunsaturated

Coconut oil
Butter
Beef tallow
Palm oil
Lard
Olive oil
Canola oil
Peanut oil
Safflower oil
Flaxseed oil
Walnut oil
Sunflower oil
Corn oil

Figure 5.19 Composition of Various Fats
Foods vary in their composition of fat.

What Are the Best Food Sources of Fats?   **157**

What Are Fat Substitutes and How Can They Be Part of a Healthy Diet?

If you adore the taste and texture of creamy foods but don't adore the extra fat in your diet, you're not alone. More than 160 million Americans (79 percent of the adults in the United States) choose lower-fat foods and beverages for health reasons.[12] To meet this demand, food manufacturers introduced more than 1,000 reduced-fat or low-fat products, from margarine to potato chips, each year during the 1990s.[13] Today, with few exceptions you will probably find a lower-fat alternative for almost any high-fat food on the grocery store shelves. The keys to these products' containing less fat than their counterparts are **fat substitutes.**

Fat substitutes are designed to provide all the creamy properties of fat for fewer calories and total fat grams. Because fat has more than double the calories per gram of carbohydrates or protein, fat substitutes have the potential to reduce calories from fat by more than 50 percent without sacrificing taste and texture.

Fat Substitutes Can Be Carbohydrate, Protein, or Fat Based

No single substitute works in all foods and with all cooking preparations, so there are several types of fat substitutes. They fall into three categories depending on their primary ingredient: (1) carbohydrate-based substitutes, (2) protein-based substitutes, and (3) fat-based substitutes.[14] Table 5.3 lists all three types of fat substitutes and their uses in foods.

The majority of fat substitutes are carbohydrate based and use plant polysaccharides such as fiber, starches, gums, and cellulose to help retain moisture and provide a fatlike texture.[15] For example, low-fat muffins might have fiber added to them to help retain the moisture that is lost when fat is reduced. Carbohydrate-based fat substitutes have been used for years and work well under heat preparations other than frying.

Protein-based fat substitutes are created from the protein in eggs and milk. The protein is heated and broken down into microscopic balls that tumble over each other when you eat them, providing a creamy mouthfeel that's similar to that of fat. Because these are protein based, they break down under high temperatures and lose their creamy properties. Therefore, they are not suitable for frying and baking.[16]

Fat-based substitutes are fats that have been modified to either provide the physical attributes of fat for fewer calories or interfere with the absorption of fat.[17] Mono- and diglycerides are used as emulsifiers in products such as baked goods and icings to provide moistness and mouthfeel. Though these remnants of fat have the same number of calories per gram as fat, fewer of them are needed to create the same effect, so the total levels of calories and fat are reduced in the food product.[18] One fat substitute, olestra (also known as Olean), is a mixture of sucrose and long-chain fatty acids. Unlike fat, which contains three fatty acids connected to a glycerol backbone, olestra contains six to eight fatty acids connected to sucrose. The enzymes that normally break apart fatty acids from their glycerol backbones during digestion cannot disconnect the fatty acids in olestra. Instead, olestra moves through your gastrointestinal

Commercially made peanut butter doesn't have any detectable levels of *trans* fatty acids. Even though partially hydrogenated oil is used as a stabilizer in many peanut butter brands, the amount is so small that it is insignificant.

fat substitutes Substances that replace added fat in foods by providing the creamy properties of fat for fewer calories and fewer total fat grams.

Table 5.3

The Lighter Side of Fat: Fat Substitutes

Name (trade names)	Calories per Gram	Properties	How It's Used
Carbohydrate-Based			
Fibers from Grains (Betatrim)	1–4	Gelling, thickener	Baked goods, meats, spreads
Fibers, Cellulose (Cellulose Gel)	0	Water retention, texture, mouthfeel	Sauces, dairy products, frozen desserts, salad dressings
Gums	0	Thickener, texture, mouthfeel, water retention	Salad dressings, processed meats
Polydextrose (Litesse)	1	Water retention, adds bulk	Baked goods, dairy products, salad dressings, cookies, gum
Modified Food Starch (Sta Slim)	1–4	Thickener, gelling, texture	Processed meats, salad dressings, frostings, fillings, frozen desserts
Protein-Based			
Microparticulated Protein (Simplesse)	1–4	Mouthfeel	Dairy products, salad dressings, spreads
Fat-Based			
Mono- or Diglycerides (Dur-Lo)	9*	Mouthfeel, moisture retention	Baked goods
Short-chain Fatty Acids (Salatrim)	5	Mouthfeel	Confections, baked goods
Olestra (Olean)	0	Mouthfeel	Savory snacks

*Less of this fat substitute is needed to create the same effect as fat, so the calories are reduced in foods using this product.
R. D. Mattes, "Fat Replacers," *Journal of the American Dietetic Association* 98 (1998): 463–468; J. Wylie-Rosett, "Fat Substitutes and Health: An Advisory from the Nutrition Committee of the American Heart Association," *Circulation* 105 (2002): 2800–2804.

tract intact and unabsorbed. Thus, it doesn't provide calories. Olestra is very heat stable, so it can be used in baked and fried foods.

In 1996, the FDA approved olestra for use in salty snacks such as potato and corn chips. An ounce of potato chips made with olestra can trim half the calories and all the fat from regular chips. Because of its inability to be absorbed, there was concern about olestra's interference with the absorption of fat-soluble vitamins and carotenoids.[19] (Absorption of water-soluble vitamins is not affected by olestra.) Consequently, the FDA has mandated that fat-soluble vitamins be added to olestra to offset these losses.[20] Because olestra travels through your digestive tract untouched, there was also a concern that it may cause stomach cramps and loose stools. Though there have been anecdotal studies of individuals experiencing bouts of diarrhea and cramps after consuming olestra-containing products, controlled research studies don't seem to support this phenomenon.[21]

Reduced-Fat Products Aren't Calorie Free

The use of fat substitutes doesn't seem to be helping Americans curb their calories or weight, and one reason for this may be people's overeating of low-fat and fat-free foods. Another reason may be that many reduced-fat products have close to the same

Foods made with fat substitutes aren't calorie free.

What Are Fat Substitutes and How Can They Be Part of a Healthy Diet? **159**

Table 5.4

Fat Free Doesn't Equal Calorie Free

	Serving Size	Calories	Fat (g)	Carbohydrates (g)	Calories Saved
Fudgsicle Pop (Popsicle)	1 (1.65 fl oz)	60	1.5	12	
Fat-Free Fudgsicle Bar (Popsicle)	1 (1.75 fl oz)	60	0	13	0
Oatmeal Raisin Cookies (Archway)	1 (28 g)	120	3.5	20	
Fat-Free Oatmeal Raisin Cookies (Archway)	1 (31 g)	110	0	25	10
Fig Newtons (Nabisco)	2 (31 g)	110	2	22	
Fat-Free Fig Newtons (Nabisco)	2 (29 g)	90	0	22	20

Source: Food manufacturers.

number of calories as their regular counterparts. Also, research indicates that people who snack on fat-reduced products may be reducing their overall fat intake, but not their overall intake of calories.[22] As with sugar substitutes, consumers need to recognize that using reduced-fat or fat-free products is not a blank check for eating unlimited amounts of those foods. The foods still contain calories, and overconsuming calories leads to weight gain.

Also, some fat-free foods, especially baked goods, may have a reduced fat content but added carbohydrates, which will add back some calories. The fat-free version may actually be a smaller serving size compared to the original food item. Consequently, the savings in fat calories isn't always much of a savings in total calories (Table 5.4). Consumers should be careful not to assume that fat-free foods are healthy, because they often aren't. Jelly beans are fat free, but they don't provide the vitamins and minerals found in, for example, naturally fat-free green beans. Similarly, while choosing 4 ounces of fat-free chips will spare you half of the 600 calories found in the same amount of regular chips, those fat-free chips are also displacing 300 calories of more nutritious foods, such as fruits, vegetables, and whole grains, elsewhere in your diet. If you want chips, enjoy a handful rather than a large bag full, alongside your whole-grain sandwich and large salad at lunch.

Fats affect more than your weight and waistline. They also affect the health of your heart. Let's take a closer look at how lipids in your diet can affect your risk for heart disease.

The Take-Home Message Fat substitutes are used in foods to provide the properties of fat for fewer calories and grams of fat. Fat substitutes can be carbohydrate-based, protein-based, or fat-based. Though some fat substitutes provide fewer calories and fat grams than regular fat, others, such as olestra, aren't absorbed, so they are fat and calorie free. Reduced-fat or fat-free foods may help reduce the calories and fat in some foods, but shouldn't displace naturally low-fat and healthy foods such as fruits and vegetables.

What Is Heart Disease and What Increases Your Risk?

Cardiovascular disease is a name that encompasses several disorders affecting the heart, including problems with heart valves, heartbeat irregularities, infections, and other problems. But the most common type of heart disease is *coronary heart disease*, which affects the blood vessels that serve the heart muscle, and can lead to a heart attack. That's the type we focus on in this chapter.

Heart disease has been the number-one killer of adults in the United States since 1918. Currently, one of every five deaths among Americans is caused by heart disease. More than 213,500 American women and 232,000 men lose their lives to heart disease annually.[23] Let's look at how heart disease develops, and the types of lipids that can accelerate it.

Heart Disease Begins with a Buildup in the Arteries

Heart disease develops when the coronary arteries, the large blood vessels that supply oxygen and other nutrients to the heart, accumulate a buildup of substances such as fat and cholesterol along their walls. As the artery gets narrower, blood flow is impeded, and less oxygen and nutrients are delivered to the heart. If the heart doesn't receive enough oxygen, chest pains can result. A narrowed artery also increases the likelihood that a blood clot can block the vessel, leading to a **heart attack.** If the artery leads to the brain, a **stroke** can occur. Approximately 8 million Americans suffer a heart attack every year.[24]

The exact cause of the narrowed arteries, also known as **atherosclerosis** (*athero* = paste, *sclera* = hardness, *sis* = condition), is unknown, but researchers think it begins with an injury to the lining of the arteries. High blood levels of cholesterol and fat, high blood pressure, diabetes, and smoking likely contribute to this damage.

Over time, LDLs and other substances are deposited along an injured artery wall. The LDLs that accumulate become oxidized and attract macrophages (white blood cells), which become enlarged with cholesterol-laden LDL and develop into foam cells. The foam cells stick to the walls of the artery and build up, along with platelets (fragments of cells in the blood) and other substances, into **plaque.** The plaque narrows the passageway of the artery (**Figure 5.20**).

Risk Factors for Heart Disease

While the primary risk factor for heart disease is an elevated LDL cholesterol level, other risk factors also exist (Table 5.5). Some of these you can control, others you cannot.

Risk Factors You Can't Control

As your blood cholesterol increases, so does your risk of developing heart disease and experiencing a heart attack. Your blood cholesterol level tends to rise with age until it stabilizes around the age of 65. Your gender will also play a role. Up until menopause, which is around the age of 50, women tend to have a lower blood cholesterol level than

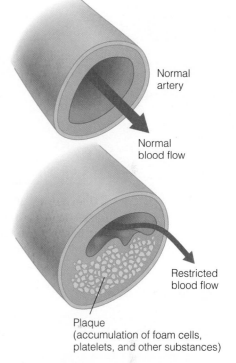

Normal artery

Normal blood flow

Restricted blood flow

Plaque (accumulation of foam cells, platelets, and other substances)

Figure 5.20 Atherosclerosis
When plaque builds up in the coronary arteries, it narrows the passageway and causes a decreased flow of oxygen-rich blood to the heart. A blood clot, traveling in the blood, can partially or totally block the arteries to the heart, leading to a heart attack.

heart attack Permanent damage to the heart muscle that results from a sudden lack of oxygen-rich blood.

stroke A condition caused by a lack of oxygen to the brain that could result in paralysis and possibly death.

atherosclerosis Narrowing of the coronary arteries due to buildup of debris along the artery walls.

plaque The hardened buildup of cholesterol-laden foam cells, platelets, cellular waste products, and calcium in the arteries that results in atherosclerosis.

Table 5.5

Risk Factors for Heart Disease

Factors You Cannot Control	Factors You Can Control
Your age and gender	Type 2 diabetes mellitus
Your family history of heart disease	High blood pressure
Type 1 diabetes mellitus	Smoking
	Physical inactivity
	Excess weight
	A low HDL "good" cholesterol level
	A high LDL "bad" cholesterol level

men and a reduced risk of heart disease. After menopause, the blood cholesterol level in women tends to catch up and even surpass that of a man of the same age.[25] About one in eight American women between 45 and 64 years of age has heart disease, but this jumps to one out of every four women over the age of 65. The decrease in the level of the hormone estrogen in postmenopausal women plays a part in the increased risk of heart disease that occurs in older women.[26]

> One in every 30 American women dies each year of breast cancer, but one in every two female adult deaths is from either heart disease or stroke.

Because high blood cholesterol levels can be partly determined by your genes, such levels can sometimes run in families.[27] If your father or brother had early signs of heart disease before age 55, or your mother or sister had them before the age of 65, then you are at a greater risk of getting heart disease. Having diabetes increases the risk of heart disease. Though the less common form of diabetes, type 1, is not preventable, the more prevalent form, type 2 diabetes, can be controlled.

Risk Factors You Can Control

Controlling diabetes can help dramatically lower the risk of heart disease for those with this condition. Type 2 diabetes can be managed and, as you read in the last chapter, possibly even prevented, through diet and lifestyle changes. Sometimes, the use of doctor-prescribed medication is also needed to control type 2 diabetes. Diseases of the heart and blood vessels are the cause of death of an estimated 65 percent of adults with diabetes.[28]

Because chronic high blood pressure can damage your arteries, maintaining a healthy blood pressure is another factor you can control. Blood pressure is the force of your blood against the walls of your arteries. A blood pressure reading consists of two numbers. The top number, called the *systolic pressure*, is the pressure within your arteries when your heart contracts. The bottom number, called the *diastolic pressure*, is the pressure in your arteries a moment later, when your heart is relaxed. A **normal blood pressure** is considered less than 120 millimeters of mercury (Hg) for the systolic pressure and less than 80 millimeters Hg for the diastolic pressure. You might hear this referred to as "120 over 80." A blood pressure reading of 140/90 or higher is considered **hypertension,** or high blood pressure. People with hypertension constantly have a higher than normal force pushing against the walls of their arteries. This is thought to damage the artery lining and accelerate the buildup of plaque. Chronic high blood pressure also causes the heart to work harder than normal and can lead to an enlarged heart. (Chapter 8 contains a detailed discussion of hypertension and how a healthy diet can help lower high blood pressure.)

normal blood pressure Less than 120 mm Hg (systolic—the top number) and less than 80 mm Hg (diastolic—the bottom number). Referred to as 120/80.

hypertension High blood pressure.

Smoking damages the walls of the arteries and accelerates atherosclerosis and heart disease. In fact, individuals who smoke are up to three times more likely to have heart disease and, compared to nonsmokers, their likelihood of experiencing a heart attack doubles.[29]

Because regular exercise can help lower your LDL cholesterol and raise your good HDL cholesterol, being inactive is a risk factor for heart disease. Since a high HDL cholesterol level can help protect you from heart disease, having an HDL level of less than 40 milligrams per deciliter (mg/dl) increases your risk of heart disease, as you don't have enough of this "good" cholesterol carrier in your body. In contrast, having a high level of HDL cholesterol, 60 mg/dl or higher, is considered a "negative" risk factor. In other words, there is so much of this "good" cholesterol in your body helping to protect against heart disease that it allows you to "erase" a risk factor from your list.

In addition to exercising regularly, losing excess weight and quitting smoking can help increase your HDL cholesterol. Exercise can also help you better manage your weight. Being overweight can raise your LDL cholesterol and increase your risk of heart disease. Whereas drinking modest amounts of alcohol has also been shown to raise HDL cholesterol, other problems can outweigh this benefit. In fact, for some individuals, drinking alcohol is not advised.[30]

You can find out more about diet and lifestyle habits that may lead to lower risk for heart disease in the boxed feature "The Mediterranean Diet."

Every pack of cigarettes smoked in the United States costs the nation about $7.18 in medical care and lost job productivity. Whereas the average pack of cigarettes may cost $5, it costs 1½ times that to keep the smoker healthy and productive.

Other Potential Risk Factors

There are some individuals who don't have an elevated level of LDL cholesterol in their blood, yet still experience a heart attack and heart disease, which points to other factors that must be affecting their heart health. These other potential risk factors are referred to as *emerging risk factors*.

Researchers are continually searching for clues or "markers" in the blood, other than cholesterol levels, that are signs of the presence of heart disease. Here are some:

➤ A high level of the amino acid homocysteine may injure arteries and promote the development of atherosclerosis.

➤ A high level of a protein called C-reactive protein can indicate that there is inflammation in the walls of the arteries, which can lead to plaque formation.[31]

➤ A lipid-protein compound called Lp(a) is being investigated for its role in promoting heart disease.

➤ Apolipoprotein B (ApoB) is a measure of the amount of "bad" LDL cholesterol in the blood. A high ApoB level indicates a higher risk for heart disease.

Though the name sounds mysterious, *syndrome X*, also called *metabolic syndrome*, refers to a cluster of many factors that increase the risk for heart disease. These include abdominal obesity (too much weight around the middle), insulin resistance, high blood pressure, elevated blood levels of triglycerides and the slower clearance of this fat from the blood, a low level of HDL cholesterol, smaller and more dense LDL cholesterol particles, the higher likelihood of forming and maintaining blood clots, too much insulin, and, possibly, too much glucose in the blood. Being overweight and inactive increases the risk for insulin resistance. Exercise and weight reduction can help reduce all of the risk factors associated with this syndrome.[32]

The Mediterranean Diet: What Do People Living in the Mediterranean Do Differently?

The Mediterranean diet doesn't refer to the diet of a specific country but to the dietary patterns found in several areas of the Mediterranean region, specifically Crete (a Greek island), other areas of Greece, and southern Italy, circa 1960. Researchers were drawn to these areas because the adults living there had very low rates of chronic diseases, such as heart disease and cancer, and a very long life expectancy. For example, the natives of Greece had a rate of heart disease that was 90 percent lower than that of Americans at that time.[1] Ironically, the people in Crete, in particular, were less educated and affluent, and less likely to obtain good medical care than were Americans, so their health successes could not be explained by education level, financial status, or a superior health care system.

Researchers found that compared with the diets of affluent Americans, the Cretans' diet was dramatically lower in foods from animal sources, such as meat, eggs, and dairy products, and higher in fat (mostly from olive oil and olives) and inexpensive grains, fruits, and vegetables.

Research continues to support the benefits of a Mediterranean-style diet. A study in Greece showed that greater adherence to a traditional Mediterranean diet was associated with greater longevity. In another study, individuals who had experienced a heart attack, and then adopted a Mediterranean-style diet, had a 50 to 70 percent lower risk of recurrent heart disease compared with those following a more classic low-saturated-fat, low-cholesterol diet.[2]

The newly updated Mediterranean Diet Pyramid shown here was designed to reflect these dietary patterns and lifestyle habits (see figure).[3] Let's look a little closer at this pyramid, the dietary and lifestyle changes that augment it, and some potential changes that you can make in your diet and lifestyle to reap similar benefits.

The Mediterranean Lifestyle

First, notice that there are no portion recommendations in the Mediterranean Diet Pyramid. This purposeful omission portrays the relative importance and frequency of each grouping of foods as it contributes to the whole diet, rather than to a strict diet plan. It was designed to

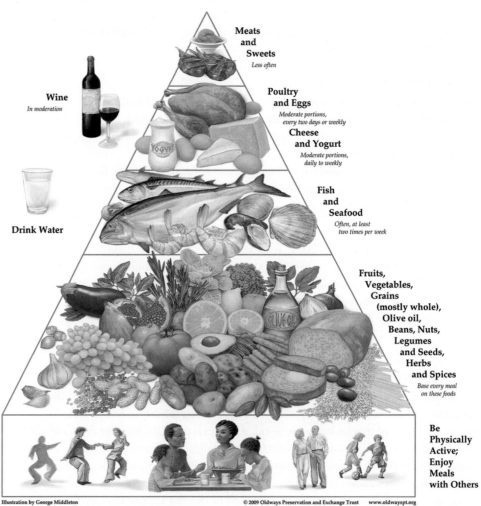

The Healthy Mediterranean Diet Pyramid
A plant-based diet with minimal amounts of high-saturated-fat, high-sugar foods, coupled with daily physical activity, reflects the healthy habits of the Mediterranean lifestyle.

provide an overview of healthy food choices rather than dictate rigid amounts from each food group.[4]

Next, note that physical activity is front and center, at the base of this pyramid, reflecting the foundation for the Mediterranean way of life. This is an important concept, as the Mediterranean residents in the 1960s were very active and, not surprisingly, much leaner than Americans at that time. In addition to exercise, Mediterranean citizens enjoyed other lifestyle habits that have been known to promote good mental and physical health. They had a supportive community of family and friends, long relaxing family meals, and afternoon siestas (naps).[5] Exercising daily, resting, and relaxing with family and friends is good health advice for all, no matter what food pyramid you follow.

A Diet of Well-Seasoned Plant Foods, Olive Oil, Fish, and Dairy

Plant-based foods such as whole grains, fruits, vegetables, legumes, and nuts are the focus of the Mediterranean diet. In fact, more than 60 percent of the calories of the Cretans' diets in the 1960s were supplied by these high-fiber, nutritionally dense plant foods. In traditional Mediterranean-style eating, a combination of plant foods, such as vegetables and legumes ladled over couscous or

pasta, was the focus of the meal.[6] Fresh bread, without margarine or butter, often accompanied the meal, and fruit was served as dessert.

More than 75 percent of the fat in the diets of the Cretans was supplied by olives and olive oil.[7] As previously discussed, vegetable oils are low in saturated fat, and olive oil in particular is high in monounsaturated fat. Heart-healthy meals featuring fish and seafood should be enjoyed at least twice a week, following the example of the Mediterraneans.

Nonfat milk and yogurt, and low- or reduced-fat cheeses can be enjoyed on a daily basis when eating a Mediterranean-style diet. A small amount of grated Parmesan cheese sprinkled over vegetables and a grain-based meal can provide a distinct Mediterranean flavor.

Occasional Poultry, Eggs, and Meat

Foods from animal sources were limited in the Cretan diet; local people consumed less than 2 ounces of meat and poultry daily.[8] No more than four eggs were eaten weekly, which included those used in cooking and baking. Following this trend, the Mediterranean Diet Pyramid suggests eating limited amounts of poultry and eggs weekly, but relegates red meat consumption to only occasionally.

Sweets, Water, and Wine

Historically, sweets were more prevalent during the holidays and fruit was the standard daily dessert.[9] Consequently, this pyramid recommends that consumption of honey- or sugar-based sweets remain modest. Water is recommended daily. The Cretans drank it all day long and with their meals. They also drank low to moderate amounts of wine, typically only with meals. Sometimes the wine was mixed with water, and many times women did not consume any alcohol. Though the pyramid depicts wine on a daily basis, it is actually considered optional and based on personal preferences, family and medical history, and social situations.

How Does the Mediterranean Diet Pyramid Compare with MyPlate?

There are many similarities between the Mediterranean Diet Pyramid and MyPlate. Both emphasize the importance of regular physical activity, and both encourage a plant-based diet rich in whole grains, fruits, and vegetables, and daily consumption of dairy products. Mediterranean-style eating encourages the use of olive oil, a fat source that is rich in heart-healthy, unsaturated fat, and fish and seafood. Vegetable oils are also encouraged on MyPlate, but more modestly. Whereas poultry, eggs, and meat are recommended more modestly in the Mediterranean Diet Pyramid than in MyPlate, both advise minimizing intake of sweets. Both tools can be used as a foundation for a healthy diet. The key is to stick to the recommendations.

The Take-Home Message Heart disease, the leading cause of death in the United States, develops when atherosclerosis causes a narrowing of the coronary arteries and a decreased flow of nutrient-rich blood to the heart. An elevated blood LDL cholesterol level is the major risk factor for heart disease. Risk factors that you can't control are your age, gender, family history of heart disease, and having type 1 diabetes. Risk factors that you can control include preventing and controlling type 2 diabetes, high blood pressure, smoking, physical inactivity, excess weight, a low HDL cholesterol level, and an elevated LDL cholesterol level. A low HDL cholesterol level may be raised by losing excess weight, getting regular exercise, and quitting smoking. Syndrome X is a group of risk factors that collectively increase the risk of heart disease.

What Can You Do to Maintain Healthy Blood Cholesterol Levels?

Numerous research studies have shown that reducing the amount of LDL cholesterol in your blood will reduce your risk for heart disease.[33] Starting at age 20, you should have your blood tested at least once every five years to obtain your "lipoprotein profile." This profile shows the total cholesterol, LDL cholesterol, and HDL cholesterol levels in your blood. Table 5.6 provides the recommended goals for total cholesterol,

Table 5.6

What Your Cholesterol Level* Can Tell You

If Your Total Cholesterol Level Is	That Is Considered
<200	Fabulous! Keep up the good work!
200–239	Borderline high
≥240	High

If Your LDL Cholesterol Level Is	That Is Considered
<100	Fabulous! Congratulations!
100–129	Near or above optimal
130–159	Borderline high
160–189	High
190	Much too high!

If Your HDL Cholesterol Is	That Is Considered
≥60	Fabulous!
40–60	Good
<40	Too low

*All lipoprotein levels are measured in milligrams of cholesterol per deciliter of blood (mg/dl).
Source: Detection, Evaluation, and Treatment of High Blood Cholesterol in Adults (Adult Treatment Panel III). May 2001. National Cholesterol Education Program. National Institutes of Health Publication No. 01-3290.

LDL cholesterol, and HDL cholesterol. The good news is that there are several diet and lifestyle changes you can make to help lower your LDL cholesterol level.

Minimize Saturated Fats, *Trans* Fats, and Cholesterol in Your Diet

In general, saturated fats raise your LDL cholesterol level, while unsaturated fats, when they replace saturated fats in your diet, will have a cholesterol-lowering effect. (Note that saturated fats in your diet will raise your blood cholesterol level more than cholesterol in your diet will.) Typically, the higher your consumption of saturated fats, the higher the LDL cholesterol levels in your blood.[34] Refer back to Figure 5.18 on page 157 for ways to choose foods that are lower in saturated fat.

Americans consume about five times more saturated fat than *trans* fat. A food that is low in *trans* fats can still be heart unhealthy if it is high in saturated fat. For example, years ago, some consumers switched from using stick margarine, which is high in *trans* fat, to butter, thinking that butter was better for their blood cholesterol. As shown in Table 5.7, although butter has less *trans* fat than stick margarine, if you combine both the saturated fat and *trans* fat in each spread, margarine would still be better for your blood cholesterol. Decreasing the *trans* fats in your diet at the expense of increasing the saturated fat won't be healthy for your heart.[35] When it comes to lowering your LDL cholesterol level, you need to limit both types of fats in your diet. For your heart's sake, cholesterol-raising saturated fat should contribute less than 10 percent of your daily calories and *trans* fats should be as low as possible.[36]

Dietary cholesterol raises your LDL cholesterol level, although saturated fats and *trans* fats will raise it more.[37] The less cholesterol in your diet, the better for your heart. Dietary cholesterol is found in foods from animal sources, with egg yolks being a

Eggs are an excellent source of protein, but egg yolks are high in cholesterol.

Table 5.7

The Cholesterol-Raising Effects of Popular Foods

Food	Total Fat	Saturated Fat	*Trans* Fat	Total Cholesterol-Raising Fats (Saturated fats + *trans* fats)
Spreads				
Butter, 1 tbs	**11**	**7.0**	0.5	7.5
Margarine (stick), 1 tbs	**11**	**2.0**	3.0	5.0
Margarine (tub), 1 tbs	**6.5**	**1.0**	0.5	1.5
Commercially Prepared Foods and Snacks				
French fries, medium (fast food)	**27**	**6.5**	8.0	14.5
Doughnut, 1	**18**	**4.5**	5.0	9.5
Potato chips, small bag	**11**	**2.0**	3.0	5.0
Cookies, 3	**6**	**1.0**	2.0	3.0

Source: Adapted from Center for Food Safety and Applied Nutrition. Updated 2006. Questions and Answers about *Trans* Fat Nutrition Labeling. CFSAN Office of Nutritional Products, Labeling and Dietary Supplements. Available at www.cfsan.fda.gov/~dams/qatrans2.html. Accessed 2006; U.S. Department of Agriculture. 2002. National Nutrient Database for Standard Reference, Release 15. Available at www.nal.usda.gov/fnic/foodcomp/search.

Easy Ways to Add Fish to Your Diet

Flake canned salmon over your lunch or dinner salad.

Add tuna to cooked pasta and vegetables and toss with a light salad dressing for a quick pasta salad meal.

Order baked, broiled, or grilled fish when dining out.

Try a shrimp cocktail on your next restaurant visit.

significant contributor in the diet.[38] Limiting the amount of these foods and choosing low-fat dairy products will cut down fat and trim dietary cholesterol.

The cholesterol in an egg is contained entirely in the yolk—the egg white is cholesterol free. Because egg yolks tend to be a significant source of cholesterol in Americans' diets, the National Institutes of Health (NIH) recommends consuming no more than four egg yolks per week to help prevent heart disease. However, research now suggests that consuming up to an egg daily may not be associated with an increased risk of heart disease. Given that eggs are also a source of many healthy nutrients, such as protein and vitamin B_{12}, some health professionals have suggested lifting the weekly cap on egg yolks for healthy individuals and focusing on keeping dietary cholesterol to no more than 300 milligrams daily, regardless of the source.[39] Hence, egg yolks can be eaten more often if other sources of dietary cholesterol are low. (However, if you eat an egg a day, you don't have a lot a leeway in your diet.)

Some shellfish, such as shrimp, are also high in cholesterol; however, these are very low in saturated fat and contain some heart-healthy omega-3 fatty acids. Lobster has less than one-third the amount of cholesterol of shrimp and is also very low in total fat. Unfortunately, the high price of shrimp and lobster limits their consumption for many people.

Because cholesterol is not found in foods from plant sources, you won't find it in vegetables, fruits, pasta, nuts, peanut butter, or vegetable oils. The best way to minimize dietary cholesterol intake is to keep your portions of lean meat, skinless poultry, and fish to about 6 ounces daily; use only low-fat or nonfat dairy foods; use vegetable oils more often than butter; keep the consumption of baked goods to a minimum; and fill up on cholesterol-free fruits, vegetables, and whole grains.

Eat More Fish

More than a decade ago, researchers suggested that the Greenland Eskimos' regular consumption of fatty fish (approximately 14 ounces a day), which is rich in EPA and DHA, played a key role in their low incidences of death from heart disease.[40] Ongoing research continues to support the protective roles EPA and DHA may play in reducing the risk of heart disease and stroke. These omega-3 fatty acids may prevent irregular heart-beats, reduce atherosclerosis, mildly lower blood pressure, decrease the clustering or clumping of platelets, lower the level of fat in the blood, and modestly increase the amount of good HDL cholesterol in the blood, to name a few protective actions.[41] In fact, research studies have shown that eating a little over an ounce or more of fish daily may help to reduce your risk of dying from heart disease, and that consuming even one fish meal per week may help reduce your risk of heart attack.[42]

The American Heart Association (AHA) recommends that you consume at least two servings of fish (especially fatty fish such as salmon, sardines, or herring) per week, which is approximately 0.5 gram daily, to obtain these omega-3 fatty acids (see **Figure 5.21** for food sources).[43] However, don't try to meet this quota at the fast-food drive-through. Fried fish that is commercially prepared tends to have few of these fatty acids and is often fried in unhealthy fat. Note some cautions regarding fish consumption in the boxed feature "Mercury and Fish."

Figure 5.21 Food Sources of Omega-3 Fatty Acids
Several types of fish, particularly fatty fish, are high in the heart-healthy omega-3 fatty acids.

Mercury and Fish

Although the health benefits of eating fish are well established, not everyone should be eating unlimited amounts of *all* types of fish. In fact, pregnant and nursing women, women of childbearing age who may become pregnant, and young children should avoid certain types of seafood that may contain high amounts of methylmercury. This form of mercury can be harmful to the nervous systems of unborn children, especially during the first trimester of pregnancy, a time when women may not even realize that they are pregnant.[10]

Though mercury occurs naturally in nature, it is also a by-product of industrial processes and pollution. The airborne form of mercury accumulates on the surface of streams and oceans and is transformed by the bacteria in the water into the toxic form of methylmercury.[11] The fish absorb the methylmercury from the water, or get it by eating the organisms that live in the water. Because the ingested methylmercury accumulates over time, larger fish, such as swordfish, shark, king mackerel, and tilefish (golden bass or golden snapper), will have the

Large fish such as swordfish, shark, king mackerel, and tilefish are likely to contain high levels of methylmercury.

highest concentration of methylmercury, as they have a longer life span and feed on other, smaller fish.

The Food and Drug Administration (FDA) recommends that women of childbearing age and young children avoid eating these four types of fish. Pregnant women and women of childbearing age can eat up to 12 ounces weekly of other types of cooked fish, including shellfish, and should choose from a variety of fish. Luckily, the ten most popular types of seafood (canned *light* tuna, shrimp, pol-

lock, salmon, cod, catfish, clams, flatfish, crabs, and scallops) contain only low amounts of methylmercury. Canned albacore (white) tuna has more mercury than the light variety, so should be limited to no more than 6 ounces weekly.[12]

While the FDA regulates all commercial fish, the Environmental Protection Agency (EPA) oversees all freshwater fish caught recreationally, such as by family members and friends. This agency recommends that all women who are or may become pregnant, nursing mothers, and young children should limit their consumption of freshwater fish to six ounces of cooked fish weekly for adults and two ounces of cooked fish weekly for children. If you eat noncommercial fish from local waters, you should always check with your state or local health department for specific advice, as there could be additional fish consumption advisories based on your local waters. The EPA recommends that if you want to eat coastal and ocean fish that is caught recreationally, you should check with your local or state health department and follow the FDA advice referenced earlier.[13]

Though consuming some omega-3 fatty acids is good, more may not be better. Because EPA and DHA interfere with blood clotting, consuming more than 3 grams, which typically only happens by taking supplements, could raise both blood glucose and LDL cholesterol levels, increase the risk of excessive bleeding, and cause other related problems such as hemorrhagic stroke (*hemo* = blood, *rhagic* = ruptured flow) in certain people.[44] Because of these potential adverse side effects, omega-3 fatty acid supplements (fish oil supplements) should only be consumed with the advice and guidance of a doctor. (Consuming large amounts of fish oil supplements can also leave a less-than-appealing fishy aftertaste in your mouth.) However, eating approximately one gram of EPA and DHA daily from fish may provide some protection against heart disease without any known adverse effects.[45]

Americans are currently consuming only about 0.1 to 0.2 grams (as compared with the 0.5 grams recommended) of EPA and DHA daily.[46] Figure 5.21 listed the omega-3 fatty acid content of some popular fish, and the Table Tips provide a few quick ways to add fish to your diet. Think of fish as food for your heart.

While fish oil supplements contain omega-3 fatty acids, excessive amounts can be unhealthy for some individuals.

Eat More Plant Foods

In addition to fish, the AHA also recommends that you consume plant-based foods such as walnuts and flaxseeds, as well as soybean and canola oils, which are all high in alpha-linolenic acid.[47] As mentioned, some alpha-linolenic acid is converted in the body to these heart-healthy omega-3 fatty acids.

Eating more plant foods high in viscous, soluble fiber may be one of the easiest ways to decrease your LDL cholesterol level. In reviewing more than 65 studies, researchers found that each gram of viscous, soluble fiber consumed, in the range of 2 to 10 grams daily, from oatmeal, oat bran, legumes such as dried beans, psyllium, and/or pectin, lowered LDL cholesterol levels by more than 2.0 mg/dl on average.[48] Although the DRI for fiber ranges from consuming 20 to 38 grams daily, consuming about half of this amount, or 10 to 25 grams of viscous, soluble fiber, can help decrease high LDL cholesterol levels.[49] Increasing the soy in your diet may also help reduce the risk of heart disease.

Although all plant foods are cholesterol free, they do contain **phytosterols,** which are plant sterols similar to cholesterol that are found in the plant's cell membranes. Plant sterols can help lower LDL cholesterol levels by competing with cholesterol for absorption in the intestinal tract.[50] With less cholesterol being absorbed, there will be less in the blood. Plant sterols occur naturally in soybean oil, many fruits, vegetables, legumes, sesame seeds, nuts, cereals, and other plant foods.[51]

In a study of more than 150 individuals with mildly high cholesterol levels, a margarine containing a plant sterol was shown to reduce LDL cholesterol levels by approximately 14 percent after one year of use.[52] Products such as margarines, cream cheese, cereals, and soft-gel tablets that contain plant sterols are now available.

> Grind whole flaxseeds before eating them to best reap their nutritional benefits. Whole flaxseeds can pass through your gastrointestinal tract intact, keeping their essential fatty acids and vitamin E enclosed in the shell.

Spreads and soft-gel tablets containing plant sterols and stanols can be used as part of a heart-healthy diet to lower LDL cholesterol.

Load Up on Foods Rich in Antioxidants and Phytochemicals

You might think that a substance that starts with the prefix "anti" couldn't be good for you. However, the antioxidants vitamins C and E and beta-carotene appear to be "pro" heart health. Antioxidants may help LDL cholesterol become more resistant to oxidants.[53] Antioxidants appear to protect LDL cholesterol from being oxidized by inhibiting the formation of oxidants, intercepting them once they are created, or helping to repair any injury to cells due to these substances. However, when there are more oxidants than antioxidant defense mechanisms occurring in the body, an imbalance occurs. This can cause adverse effects, such as heart disease.

Antioxidant-rich plant foods such as fruits and vegetables contain many other vitamins and minerals, which are not only healthy for your heart in their own right, but may also work with antioxidants. These foods are naturally low in saturated fat and *trans* fat and are cholesterol free, so they can displace heart-unhealthy foods in your diet. Plant foods are also full of fiber, particularly soluble fiber. For all of these reasons, your heart will benefit if you eat plant foods high in antioxidants at each meal.

Nuts are one type of food that is rich in antioxidants and fiber, and they can have a positive effect on LDL cholesterol levels for other reasons. Research involving healthy men showed that a diet with 20 percent of the calories coming from walnuts lowered LDL cholesterol by a little over 15 percent. A study of more than 80,000 women showed that those who ate nuts frequently—an ounce of nuts at least five times a week—had an approximately 35 percent reduction in the risk of heart disease compared with

phytosterols Naturally occurring sterols found in plants. Phytosterols lower LDL cholesterol levels by competing with cholesterol for absorption in the intestinal tract.

women who hardly ever ate nuts.[54] The FDA now allows the food label on certain nuts and nut products to claim that the product potentially helps fight heart disease.[55]

The only downside to nuts is that they're high in calories. A mere ounce of nuts (about 24 almonds or 28 peanuts) can contribute a hefty 160 to 200 calories to your diet. Routinely sitting down with a jar of peanuts while studying can quickly have you overconsuming calories. The Table Tips on this page provide ideas on how to enjoy a modest amount of nuts in your diet.

There are other substances that may provide an extra boost to your heart health. Garlic may not be perfume to your breath, but it may be slightly protective for your heart. Although not definite, garlic has been found in some studies to reduce high blood cholesterol levels by inhibiting cholesterol synthesis in the body, decreasing the clustering of platelets, interfering with blood clotting, and helping to lower blood pressure. Sulfur-containing compounds, specifically allicin, that are abundant in garlic are believed to be the protective factor.[56] However, a more recent review of clinical studies questions whether adding garlic as part of a low-fat, low-cholesterol diet has a substantial cholesterol-lowering benefit.[57] Until more is known about garlic, your best bet is to enjoy it as part of your heart-healthy meals.

Tea may also reduce your risk of heart disease. Black and green tea are high in **flavonoids,** phytochemicals similar to antioxidants that are believed to prevent LDL cholesterol from becoming oxidized in the body. In a study of more than 800 elderly men, those who consumed the most flavonoids, predominantly from tea, cut their risk of dying from heart disease by about half compared with those who had low flavonoid consumption.[58] Drinking tea may be beneficial even if a person has had a heart attack. In a study of 1,900 heart attack victims, researchers found that those who consumed large amounts of tea (>14 cups weekly) had a 44 percent lower risk of dying from a heart attack during the 3½-year follow-up period compared with those who didn't consume any tea. Even those who drank moderate amounts of tea (<2 cups weekly) fared better than the tea abstainers, reducing their risk by 28 percent.[59]

Get Plenty of Exercise and Manage Your Weight

Routine exercise can help reduce LDL cholesterol levels, high blood pressure, insulin resistance, and excess weight, and improve HDL cholesterol levels.[60] A review of more than 50 studies involving more than 4,500 people found that exercise training for more than 12 weeks increased HDL cholesterol levels by about 4.5 percent. Currently, the AHA recommends that healthy individuals 18 to 65 years old partake in 30 minutes or more of moderate-intensity exercise, such as brisk walking, at least five days a week.[61] This amount of physical activity is considered sufficient to help reduce the risk of heart disease, but exercising longer than 30 minutes or at higher intensity could offer greater protection, especially when it comes to maintaining a healthy body weight.[62]

Regular physical activity can also help accelerate weight loss. Losing excess weight can help not only to lower LDL cholesterol levels, high blood pressure, and the risk of developing type 2 diabetes, but also to raise HDL cholesterol levels. Hence, sedentary individuals should "move" and sedentary, overweight individuals should "move and lose" to lower their risk of heart disease. Table 5.8 summarizes the diet and lifestyle changes you can make to reduce your LDL cholesterol and risk for heart disease.

Table Tips

Nuts about Nuts?

Have some mixed nuts as an afternoon snack. Though high in calories, they are an excellent source of antioxidants and fiber, have zero cholesterol, and are low in saturated fat.

Toss some nuts into your mealtime salad. Use less oil or salad dressing and more nonfat vinegar to adjust for the added calories.

Swap nuts for meat, like chicken or beef, in dishes such as stir-fries. A third of a cup of nuts is equal to an ounce of red meat or chicken.

Add a tablespoon of nuts to your morning cereal, and use skim rather than reduced-fat milk to offset some of the extra calories.

Add a tablespoon of chopped nuts to your afternoon yogurt.

Add a handful of peanuts to your air-popped popcorn the next time you need a snack.

Table 5.8

To Decrease Excess LDL Cholesterol

Dietary Changes	Lifestyle Changes
Consume less saturated fat	Lose excess weight
Consume less *trans* fats	
Consume less dietary cholesterol	
Consume more soluble fiber–rich foods	Exercise more
Consume a more plant-based diet	

flavonoids Phytochemicals found in fruits, vegetables, tea, nuts, and seeds.

A Word about the Protective Effects of Red Wine

Drinking alcohol in moderate amounts can reduce the risk of heart disease.[63] Alcohol can increase the level of the heart-protective HDL cholesterol. In fact, approximately 50 percent of alcohol's heart-protective effect is probably due to this positive effect on HDL cholesterol. Studies have also suggested that alcohol may decrease blood clotting by affecting the coagulation of platelets or by helping the blood to break up clots.[64]

Other studies have suggested that the antioxidants in wine as well as dark beer also contribute to the heart-protective aspects of alcohol.[65] However, these heart-health benefits of alcohol consumption are reaped mainly by middle-aged and older adults. We will talk more about alcohol consumption in younger individuals in Chapter 9. Though some alcohol may be good, more is definitely not better. Individuals who consume three or more drinks per day *increase* their risk of dying prematurely.[66]

The Whole Is Greater Than the Sum of Its Parts

When it comes to reducing the risk of heart disease, the whole diet may be greater than the sum of its parts. A study of more than 45 adults with elevated total and LDL cholesterol levels illustrated that a diet "portfolio" consisting of a diet low in saturated fat and cholesterol that was also high in soluble fiber, soy protein, plant sterols, and nuts lowered LDL cholesterol levels by almost 30 percent. This impressive reduction was similar to that observed in the group that was given a cholesterol-lowering drug but was limiting *only* the saturated fat and cholesterol in their diet. The latter group's diet did not include the other items in the portfolio diet.[67] Hence, a dietary portfolio approach to eating may be a viable way for individuals to lower high cholesterol levels and avoid taking medication that could have potential side effects.[68] The Table Tips on this page provide eating tips for a heart-healthy diet.

The Take-Home Message Limiting saturated fat, cholesterol, and *trans* fat, and increasing fish consumption, as well as consumption of antioxidant-rich fruits, vegetables, whole grains, and nuts, are associated with a reduction in the risk of heart disease. Regular exercise and weight loss can also help lower LDL cholesterol levels and raise HDL cholesterol levels. Drinking a moderate amount of alcohol may help reduce the risk of heart disease. Some individuals should avoid alcoholic beverages.

Table Tips

Eating for a Healthy Heart

Choose only lean meats (round, sirloin, and tenderloin cuts) and skinless poultry and keep your portions of meat to about 6 ounces daily. Eat fish at least twice a week.

Use two egg whites in place of one whole egg when baking.

Use reduced-fat or nonfat dairy products, such as low-fat or skim milk, reduced-fat cheese, and low-fat or nonfat ice cream. Sprinkle cheese on top of your food rather than mix it in so you use less. Be sure to keep ice cream servings small.

Substitute cooked beans for half the meat in chili, soups, and casseroles.

Use canola, olive, soybean, or corn oil, and *trans* fat–free margarine instead of butter or shortening.

Made Over, Made Better!

Many Americans' diets are too high in fat and heart-unhealthy saturated fat. A few tweaks in your diet selections can help you keep your fat intake within a healthy range of 20 to 35 percent of your daily calories and your saturated fat intake to no more than 7 to 10 percent of your calories every day. Here are some typical fat-rich foods made over and made nutritionally better!

If you like this. . .	Try this to control your fat intake!

Mocha, 2% milk, whipped cream
Serving size: 16 oz
Total Fat: 15 grams
Saturated Fat: 8 grams

Coffee, brewed
Serving size: 16 oz
Total Fat: 0 grams
Saturated Fat: 0 grams

Butter
Serving size: 1 pat
Total Fat: 3.8 grams
Saturated Fat: 2.4 grams

Jelly
Serving size: 1 tbs
Total Fat: 0 grams
Saturated Fat: 0 grams

Cheddar cheese
Serving size: 1.5 ounces
Total Fat: 14.1 grams
Saturated Fat: 9 grams

Reduced-fat cheddar cheese
Serving size: 2 ounces
Total Fat: 9 grams
Saturated Fat: 6 grams

Chocolate ice cream
Serving size: 1/2 cup
Total Fat: 14 grams
Saturated Fat: 9 grams

Low-fat frozen yogurt
Serving size: 1/2 cup
Total Fat: 1.5 grams
Saturated Fat: 1 gram

Source: USDA National Nutrient Database for Standard Reference, www.nal.usda.gov/fnic

Lipids

What Are Lipids?

The term *lipids* refers to a category of carbon, oxygen, and hydrogen compounds that are all **hydrophobic** (*hydro* = water, *phobic* = fearing). In other words, they don't dissolve in water. There are three types of lipids: triglycerides (fats), phospholipids, and sterols. Two of these, triglycerides and phospholipids, are built from a basic unit called a fatty acid.

Fatty Acids Vary in Length and Structure

All **fatty acids** consist of a chain of carbon and hydrogen atoms, with an acid group (OH) at one end. There are more than 20 different fatty acids. They can vary by (1) the length of the chain, (2) whether the carbons have a single or double bond between them (C—C or C=C), and (3) the total number of double bonds.

If all the carbons have single bonds between each other in a fatty acid, they are also all bonded to hydrogen. When all of the carbons on a fatty acid are bound with hydrogen, it is called a **saturated fatty acid.** In contrast, if a fatty acid has carbons that are not bound to hydrogen, but rather to each other, which creates a double bond, it is called an **unsaturated fatty acid.** Saturated fats are made up of primarily saturated fatty acids, whereas unsaturated fats contain mostly unsaturated fatty acids, such as MUFAs and PUFAs. Two particular fatty acids, **linoleic acid** (an omega-6 fatty acid) and **alpha-linolenic acid** (an omega-3 fatty acid), are essential for health and must be consumed in the diet.

Triglycerides Are More Commonly Known as Fat

Three fatty acids connected to a **glycerol** backbone create a **triglyceride**, more commonly known as **fat,** which is the most common lipid found in foods and in your body. Glycerol is a three-carbon compound that contains three alcohol (OH) groups. The fatty acids join to each of the alcohol groups.

Phospholipids and Sterols Are More Complex

Like fats, **phospholipids** contain a glycerol backbone, but instead of being made up of three fatty acids, they contain two fatty acids and a phosphate group. The phosphate-containing head is polar, which attracts charged particles, such as water, and the fatty acid–containing tail is nonpolar, so it mingles with other nonpolar molecules such as fats.

Unlike phospholipids, **sterols** do not contain glycerol or fatty acids. Sterols are comprised mainly of four connecting rings of carbon and hydrogen. The best known sterol is cholesterol.

Functions of Lipids

Fat provides essential fatty acids and allows you to absorb the fat-soluble vitamins, A, D, E, and K. Fat is also an important source of energy, helps insulate you, keeps you at a constant body temperature, and cushions your major organs.

Phospholipids make up the phospholipid bilayer in cell membranes. Lipoproteins, made of protein and phospholipids, are transport carriers that shuttle insoluble fat and cholesterol through your bloodstream and lymph to be used throughout the body.

Cholesterol is also an important part of your cell membranes. It is a precursor for vitamin D, bile acids, and sex hormones, such as estrogen and testosterone.

Daily Needs

The current AMDR recommendation is for 20 to 35 percent of your daily calories to come from fat. For some individuals, especially sedentary, overweight folks, a very low-fat diet (providing less than 20 percent of daily calories from fat) that's high in carbohydrates may cause an increase in fat in the blood and a lowering of the good HDL cholesterol. For others, consuming more than 35 percent of their total daily calories from fat could perpetuate obesity, which is a risk factor for heart disease.[69]

You Need to Consume at Least the Minimum Amounts of the Essential Fatty Acids

A minimum of 5 percent and up to 10 percent of the total calories in your diet should come from linoleic acid, and alpha-linolenic acid should make up 0.6 percent to 1.2 percent of your total calories.[70]

Men aged 19 to 50 need 17 grams and women aged 19 to 50 who aren't pregnant or lactating need 12 grams of linoleic acid daily. For alpha-linolenic acid, men aged 14 to 70 need 1.6 grams daily, and women of the same age need 1.1 grams daily.

Linoleic and alpha-linolenic acids must also be consumed in the proper ratio. Too much linoleic acid in relationship to alpha-linolenic acid can inhibit the conversion of alpha-linolenic acid to DHA, while the inverse (too much alpha-linolenic acid and not enough linoleic acid) can inhibit the conversion of linoleic acid to arachidonic acid.

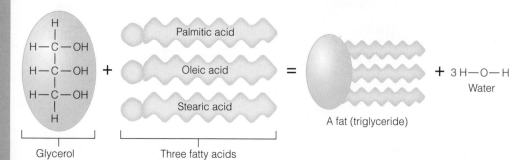

Glycerol backbone + Three fatty acids (Palmitic acid, Oleic acid, Stearic acid) = A fat (triglyceride) + 3 H—O—H Water

Grams (g) of **Linoleic** and **Alpha-linolenic acid**

Legend:
- Linoleic acid
- Alpha-linolenic acid

Chart values:
- Flaxseeds, 1/4 cup: 1.5 / 7.0
- Soybeans, roasted, 1/4 cup: 4.5
- Almonds, 1/4 cup: 4.5
- Walnuts, 1/4 cup: 10.0 / 2.0
- Canola oil, 1 tbs: 3.0 / 1.0
- Soybean oil, 1 tbs: 7.0 / 1.0
- Adults 19 to 50 years: 5–10g
- Adults 19 to 50 years: 0.6–1.2g

Categories: Protein | Oils | Daily Needs

You Do Not Need to Consume Cholesterol or *Trans* Fat

Your body can make all the cholesterol it needs, so you do not need to consume it in your diet, and you should limit your cholesterol intake for the sake of your heart and arteries. Healthy individuals over the age of 2 are advised to limit their dietary cholesterol to less than 300 milligrams daily, on average.[71]

Trans fats are worse for heart health than saturated fat because they not only raise the LDL cholesterol levels, but also lower HDL cholesterol in the blood. Therefore, *trans* fats should be avoided or limited in foods.

Food Sources

Unsaturated fats are abundant in vegetable oils, such as soybean, corn, and canola oils, as well as soybeans, walnuts, flaxseeds, and wheat germ, and these are also all good sources of essential fatty acids.

Foods high in cholesterol and saturated fat should be limited. Dietary cholesterol is found only in foods from animal sources, with egg yolks being a significant contributor. Because cholesterol is not found in foods from plant sources, you won't find it in vegetables, fruits, pasta, nuts, peanut butter, or vegetable oils.

Most dietary saturated fat comes from animal foods such as fatty cuts of meat, whole-milk dairy products like cheese, butter, and ice cream, and the skin on poultry. Certain vegetable oils, such as coconut, palm, and palm kernel oils, are very high in saturated fat. Although food manufacturers now use these oils less often, they may still be found in foods such as candies, commercially made baked goods, and gourmet ice cream.

The best way to minimize both dietary cholesterol and saturated fat intake is to keep your portions of lean meat, skinless poultry, and fish to about 6 ounces daily; use only low-fat or nonfat dairy foods; use vegetable oils more often than butter; keep consumption of baked goods to a minimum; and fill up on fruits, vegetables, and whole grains.

Too Much or Too Little

Overweight and Obesity

Your body has an *unlimited* ability to store excess energy (calories) as fat. In fact, your fat reserves have the capacity to enlarge as much as 1,000 times their original size, as more fat is added. If your cells fill to capacity, you can add more fat cells.

Heart Disease

Blood cholesterol levels are one of several factors that can affect your risk of heart disease. Eating foods low in saturated fat, dietary cholesterol, and *trans* fat, exercising regularly, and maintaining a healthy weight can help control your blood cholesterol levels and reduce your risk of heart disease. Quitting smoking, lowering high blood pressure, and controlling diabetes (if you have it) can also reduce your risk of heart disease.

In general, you want to lower your "bad" LDL cholesterol levels and raise your "good" HDL cholesterol levels. Having an LDL level of less than 100 milligrams per deciliter (mg/dl) is optimal. An HDL level of less than 40 mg/dl increases your risk of heart disease, whereas a high level of HDL cholesterol, 60 mg/dl or higher, is considered a "negative" risk factor.

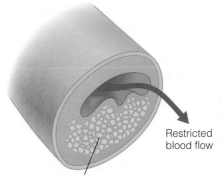

Restricted blood flow

Plaque (accumulation of foam cells, platelets, and other substances)

Too Little of the Essential Fatty Acids Can Result in These Symptoms

A deficiency of the essential fatty acids can interfere with normal cell membranes and growth and result in scaly skin.

Terms to Know

hydrophobic • fatty acids • saturated fatty acid • unsaturated fatty acid • linoleic acid • alpha-linolenic acid • glycerol • triglyceride • fat • phospholipids • sterols

Two Points of View

Is Wild Salmon a Better Choice Than Farmed Salmon? Salmon has long been touted as an excellent source of omega-3 fatty acids. Both farmed and wild-caught salmon contain this essential nutrient; however, farmed salmon may also contain toxins such as methylmercury and Polychlorinated biphenyls (PCBs).

Is the nutritional benefit of consuming high amounts of omega-3 fatty acids worth the risk of ingesting toxins? Should you avoid farmed salmon and eat only wild-caught salmon? After you've read the arguments for and against, answer the critical thinking questions and decide for yourself.

Yes

- Farmed salmon have much higher levels of toxic chemicals such as PCBs, dioxins, and certain pesticides than their wild-caught counterparts.[1] The contamination source in farmed fish is fish oil and fishmeal in their feed. However, PCB levels vary greatly from farm to farm.

- There are some environmental concerns associated with farm-raised salmon. For instance, most salmon are farmed in open pens and cages in coastal waters. Waste from these farms is released directly into the ocean and can harm wild fish populations.[2]

- Salmon farms can be incubators of disease. One study found that reoccurring sea lice outbreaks killed up to 80 percent of young wild pink salmon whose migration paths crossed salmon farms.[3]

- Farmed salmon feed can contain high amounts of antibiotics and other chemicals, some of which are outlawed in the U.S. for threats to human and marine health.[4]

No

- Farmed and wild salmon are both low in saturated fat and calories. Both are high in protein, and both are excellent sources of omega-3 fatty acids.[5]

- A study in 2004 found that farmed salmon had PCB levels 10 times as high as wild salmon,[6] but those levels were still very low[7] — well below those the Food and Drug Administration says are safe. And since then, PCB levels in farmed salmon have come down quite a bit.

- The Institute of Medicine found that the benefits of eating oily fish outweighed the risk, even for the most sensitive parts of the population.[8]

- Most farm-raised salmon are Atlantic salmon and are readily available year-round. Wild populations of Atlantic salmon are generally at very low levels and their commercial harvest is limited.[9]

- Wild-caught salmon is often higher priced than farmed salmon.[10]

What do you think?

1. What is the most compelling argument for consuming wild rather than farm-raised salmon? Is this argument strong enough to influence your food choice? **2.** Do the benefits of eating farmed salmon outweigh the risks? **3.** How can consumers make the best choices when it comes to eating fish?

Chapter Review

Be a Nutrition Sleuth

Assessing the Fat Content of Fast Foods

What has more saturated fat: a chocolate doughnut or a bagel with cream cheese? How much heart-unhealthy fat is in a large mocha coffee? Visit **www.pearsonhighered.com/blake** to test your assumptions—the answers may surprise you!

Get Real!

Eating Right and Light

Your challenge: Plan a lower-fat fast-food meal (from restaurants like McDonald's, Taco Bell, and KFC) that will include at least one serving from four out of five food groups found in MyPlate. Can it be done? Visit **www.pearsonhighered.com/blake** to find out.

The Top Ten Points to Remember

1. A fatty acid is a carbon and hydrogen chain with an acid group at one end. A triglyceride, also known as a fat, contains three fatty acids joined to a glycerol backbone and is the most abundant type of lipid in your body and in foods. A fatty acid without any double bonds is called a saturated fatty acid. If one or more double bonds is present, it is called an unsaturated fatty acid. A saturated fat contains mostly saturated fatty acids and tends to be solid at room temperature. An unsaturated fat has mostly unsaturated fatty acids, is liquid at room temperature, and is also known as an oil.

2. Phospholipids contain two fatty acids at their tail end and have a phosphate-containing head. Their polar heads and nonpolar tails cause them to be attracted to both water and fat. Lecithin is the major phospholipid in your cell membranes. Lecithin is often used as an emulsifier in foods. Cholesterol is the major sterol in your body and in foods. Cholesterol is the precursor of vitamin D, bile acids, and sex hormones. Your body makes all the cholesterol it needs.

3. The majority of fat in your diet is digested and absorbed in your small intestine with the help of bile acids and pancreatic lipase. The digested fat is predominantly packaged in protein- and phosphorus-containing lipoproteins called chylomicrons, which travel in your lymph to your bloodstream.

4. Other lipoproteins include the "bad" LDL cholesterol carrier and the "good" HDL cholesterol carrier. LDL deposits cholesterol along your artery walls and contributes to atherosclerosis. HDL removes cholesterol from arteries and brings it to the liver to be used or excreted from your body.

5. In your body, fat is used as a protective cushion for your bones, organs, and nerves and as insulation to maintain your body temperature. In food, fat provides texture and flavor, and contributes to satiety. Fat in food also aids in the absorption of fat-soluble vitamins.

6. Fat provides the essential fatty acids, linoleic acid and alpha-linolenic acid. A minimum of 5 percent and up to 10 percent of your total calories should be from linoleic acid, and 0.6 percent to 1.2 percent of total calories should be from alpha-linolenic acid. Soybean oil, walnuts, flaxseeds, and flaxseed oil are good sources of these essential fatty acids. A limited amount of alpha-linolenic acid can be converted to the omega-3 fatty acids, eicosapentaenoic acid (EPA) and docosahexaenoic acid (DHA), which have been shown to reduce the risk of heart disease and stroke. Because fish, especially fatty fish, are good sources of EPA and DHA, you should consume at least two servings of fish weekly.

7. Approximately 20 to 35 percent of your total calories should come from fat. Saturated fat, which raises LDL cholesterol, and *trans* fatty acids, which are created by

hydrogenating unsaturated fatty acids, should be limited in your diet. Your intake of saturated fat should be no more than 10 percent of your total calories.

8. Eating a well-balanced plant-based diet that contains lean meats and dairy foods with moderate amounts of heart-healthy unsaturated fat is the best strategy to lower your LDL cholesterol level and your risk of heart disease. Commercially prepared baked goods, snack items, and fried foods should be limited to decrease *trans* fats. Your diet should contain no more than 300 milligrams of cholesterol daily, on average. Soluble fiber-containing foods such as oats, legumes, and psyllium-containing cereal, soy protein, and plant sterols can also help lower your LDL cholesterol level. Exercising and losing excess weight can help lower your LDL cholesterol level and increase your HDL cholesterol level.

9. Heart disease occurs when atherosclerosis causes narrowing of the passageways of the coronary arteries. A high level of LDL cholesterol is the major risk factor for heart disease. A high level of HDL cholesterol is protective against heart disease. A family history of heart disease, being a man or a postmenopausal woman, having diabetes, smoking, being physically inactive, having high blood pressure, being overweight, and having a low HDL cholesterol level can all increase the risk of heart disease.

10. Fat substitutes are designed to provide all the properties of fat but for fewer calories. Fat substitutes can reduce calories from fat in a food by more than 50 percent. Some fat-free foods, especially baked goods, may have reduced fat content but not necessarily a reduction in calories, as carbohydrates have been added to these foods. Consequently, fat-free foods may not be lower in calories.

Test Your Knowledge

1. The primary lipid in your body is
   a. cholesterol.
   b. lecithin.
   c. triglycerides.
   d. chylomicrons.
2. Fat in foods is a source of
   a. flavor.
   b. calories.
   c. fat-soluble vitamins.
   d. all of the above.

3. The type of lipoprotein that carries absorbed fat and other lipids through your lymph system is called
   a. VLDL.
   b. LDL.
   c. bile acid.
   d. a chylomicron.
4. Donald has heart disease. To obtain heart-healthy omega-3 fatty acids, he should eat
   a. a tuna fish sandwich at lunch and a Burger King fish sandwich for dinner.
   b. shrimp for lunch and salmon for dinner.
   c. fish and chips for lunch and flounder at dinner.
   d. fried fish sticks at lunch and steamed lobster for dinner.
5. Which of following does *not* provide dietary cholesterol?
   a. steak
   b. skinless chicken
   c. low-fat milk
   d. margarine
6. You should keep your dietary fat intake between
   a. 8 and 10 percent of your daily calories.
   b. 20 and 35 percent of your daily calories.
   c. 35 and 40 percent of your daily calories.
   d. under 300 milligrams to 500 milligrams daily.
7. The major dietary component that raises your LDL cholesterol is
   a. viscous soluble fiber.
   b. dietary cholesterol.
   c. saturated fat.
   d. plant sterols.
8. Which of the following are good sources of the essential fatty acids linoleic acid and alpha-linolenic acid?
   a. flaxseeds
   b. walnuts
   c. soybean oil
   d. all of the above
9. To raise your level of HDL cholesterol, you can
   a. increase the viscous, soluble fiber in your diet.
   b. exercise more.
   c. lose excess weight.
   d. do b and c only.
10. *Trans* fats are unhealthy for your heart because they
    a. lower LDL cholesterol levels.
    b. raise HDL and LDL cholesterol levels.
    c. raise LDL cholesterol and lower HDL cholesterol levels.
    d. have no effect on LDL cholesterol.

Answers

1. (c) The major lipid in your body is triglycerides, also known as fat. Cholesterol is another type of lipid but is not as abundant as fat. Lecithin is a phospholipid found in your cell membranes and is used as an emulsifier in some foods. Chylomicrons are lipoproteins that transport fat and other lipids to your liver.
2. (d) Fat provides flavor, calories, and fat-soluble vitamins.
3. (d) Chylomicrons enable insoluble fat as well as cholesterol and phospholipids to travel through the lymph system. Bile acids help emulsify fat in your GI tract. VLDLs and LDLs transport fat and other lipids through your blood.
4. (b) Though tuna fish is a wonderful way to enjoy fish at lunch, the commercially prepared fried fish sandwich, fish and chips, and fish sticks have little of the omega-3 fatty acids that would help Donald's heart. Shrimp and salmon are much better choices.
5. (d) Because dietary cholesterol can only be found in foods from animal sources, margarine, which is made from vegetable oils, is free of dietary cholesterol.
6. (b) Your daily fat intake should be between 20 and 35 percent of your daily calories.
7. (c) Whereas dietary cholesterol raises LDL cholesterol, saturated fat is the bigger culprit behind an elevated LDL cholesterol in the blood. Viscous, soluble fiber and plant sterols can help lower LDL cholesterol.
8. (d) Flaxseeds, walnuts, and soybean oil are all good sources of essential fatty acids.
9. (d) Increasing your exercise and losing excess weight can help increase your HDL cholesterol level. Increasing soluble fiber does not affect your level of HDL cholesterol.
10. (c) *Trans* fats provide a double whammy for your heart because they raise the "bad" LDL cholesterol and lower the "good" HDL cholesterol in your body.

Web Resources

To learn more about heart disease and how to lower your risk, visit the
➡ National Cholesterol Education Program at www.nhlbi.nih.gov/chd
➡ American Heart Association at www.heart.org/HEARTORG/
➡ Centers for Disease Control and Prevention, at www.cdc.gov/physicalactivity/

Answers to Myths and Misperceptions

1. **False.** Your body *does* need cholesterol for important functions. However, you don't need to eat any to meet your needs. See page 145.

2. **True.** High levels of HDL cholesterol can help reduce your risk of heart disease. See page 148.

3. **True.** However, this isn't necessarily good news; the percentage is only lower because the amount of total calories consumed has increased. See page 151.

4. **False.** Whereas too much dietary fat may cause you to gain weight, eating too little isn't healthy either. A diet low in fat but high in added sugars may increase the level of fat in your blood. See page 151.

5. **True.** A diet high in saturated fat can raise your cholesterol. See page 153.

6. **False.** Fat-free foods are not necessarily calorie free. See page 160.

7. **False.** Although stick margarines can contain heart-unhealthy *trans* fats, butter has more total cholesterol-raising fats than margarine, and so is ultimately less healthy. See page 167.

8. **False.** Because peanut butter doesn't come from an animal, it does not contain cholesterol. See page 168.

9. **False.** Consuming too much fish oil can be unhealthy. See page 169.

10. **True.** The viscous, soluble fiber found in beans and other foods can lower your blood cholesterol. See page 170.

6

True or False?

1. With a healthy, well-balanced diet, **your body** can make all the proteins it needs. (T|F) p. 188

2. Proteins provide **structural** support. (T|F) p. 190

3. Most **enzymes** are proteins. (T|F) p. 191

4. Your body can use protein as an **energy source**. (T|F) p. 193

5. Growing children are in a state of negative **nitrogen balance**. (T|F) p. 195

6. You can digest the protein in **pasta** as easily as the protein in a **chicken breast**. (T|F) p. 196

7. Approximately **one-half** of your daily calories should come from protein. (T|F) p. 197

8. Active people need to eat **protein bars**. (T|F) p. 202

9. Eating too much protein-rich food may increase your blood **cholesterol** level. (T|F) p. 204

10. **Soy** is a good source of dietary protein. (T|F) p. 214

See page 223 for answers to these Myths and Misperceptions.

Proteins and Amino Acids

Melissa Cone, a 35-year-old college student, started struggling with her weight when she went back to school and had to juggle class time and homework with her family's needs. She often found herself eating on the run between classes or family errands. After reading an article in a health magazine that said a high-protein diet would help her lose weight, Melissa cut back on eating grains, fruits, and vegetables and started eating more hamburgers, steaks, cheese, and fried foods. Though she dropped a few pounds in the first week, the bathroom scale didn't budge much thereafter. After about eight weeks of eating high-protein foods, she began to have stomach pains.

When she visited her family doctor, a blood test revealed that she had higher than normal levels of some substances in her blood.

Do you think Melissa's high-protein diet is a healthy way for her to lose weight? Can you guess what problems Melissa was having as a result of this diet? In this chapter, we will introduce and discuss the concept of proteins—how they're structured, the roles they play in the body, and the best dietary sources. We'll also discuss the potential health effects of consuming too many high-protein foods, and why Melissa's steady menu of fatty beef, cheese, and fried foods is unhealthy for both her bowels and her heart.

Chapter Objectives

After reading this chapter, you will be able to:

1. Explain how proteins are different from carbohydrates and lipids.

2. Describe the basic structure of an amino acid.

3. Explain the difference between essential and nonessential amino acids.

4. Identify the key steps in digesting protein.

5. Identify the functions of protein in the body.

6. Identify sources of lean protein in the diet.

7. Create a diet plan that achieves the Recommended Dietary Allowance for protein.

8. Calculate the recommended protein intake for an individual based on the Dietary Reference Intakes.

9. Explain the health consequences of consuming too little or too much protein.

10. Describe the benefits and risks of a vegetarian diet.

What Are Proteins and Why Are They Important?

Proteins are the predominant structural and functional materials in every cell, and you have thousands of unique proteins in your body. Your protein-rich muscles enable you to swim, walk, stand, and hold your head up so you can read this textbook. Without adequate protein, your immune system wouldn't be able to fight off infections, your hair wouldn't grow, your fingernails would be mere stubs, and you wouldn't digest your food. In fact, proteins are involved in most of your body's functions and life processes, and without them, you wouldn't survive.[1]

We'll begin our discussion of protein with a look at how they're structured. Specifically, we'll start by looking at the amino acids.

The Building Blocks of Proteins Are Amino Acids

All proteins consist of some combination of 20 unique **amino acids,** and they are classified according to the number of amino acids in the chain. If the chain contains fewer than 50 amino acids linked together, it is called a peptide. Two joined amino acids form a *dipeptide*; three joined amino acids form a *tripeptide;* and a *polypeptide* is more than 10 amino acids joined together. A chain with more than 50 amino acids is called a protein. Proteins typically contain between 100 and 10,000 amino acids in a sequence. For instance, the protein that forms the hemoglobin in red blood cells consists of close to 300 amino acids, as compared with collagen, which contains approximately 1,000 amino acids.

Amino acids are like numeric digits, in that their specific sequence will determine a specific function. Consider that telephone numbers, Social Security numbers, and bank PIN numbers are all made up of the same digits (0 to 9) arranged in different sequences of varying lengths. Each of these numbers has a specific purpose. Similarly,

Figure 6.1 The Structure of an Amino Acid

Side chain

Amine group — NH₂ — C — C — OH — Acid group

a **Amino acid structure.** All amino acids contain carbon, hydrogen, and oxygen, similar to carbohydrates and fat. They also contain a nitrogen-containing amine group and an acid group.

Aspartic acid (Asp)

Glycine (Gly)

Phenylalanine (Phe)

b **Different amino acids showing their unique side chains.** A unique side chain (shown in yellow) distinguishes the various amino acids.

amino acids can be linked together to make unique sequences of varying lengths, each with a specific function.

Anatomy of an Amino Acid

As illustrated in **Figure 6.1a**, each amino acid contains a central carbon (C) surrounded by four parts: an **acid group** (COOH) (which is why it is called an amino "acid"), an **amine group** (NH₂) that contains the nitrogen, a hydrogen atom, and a unique **side chain.** Whereas all 20 nutritionally important amino acids contain the same four parts, it is the side chain that makes each amino acid different.

The side chain can be as simple as a single hydrogen atom, as in the amino acid glycine; or it can be a collection of atoms, as in aspartic acid and phenylalanine (see Figure 6.1b). (Do these last two amino acids sound familiar? Recall that they are the major components of the sugar substitute aspartame, which we discussed in Chapter 4.)

Now let's look at how amino acids are linked together to build proteins.

Peptide Bonds and Side Chains Determine a Protein's Shape and Function

Amino acids are joined to each other by **peptide bonds** to build proteins. A peptide bond is created when the acid group (COOH) of one amino acid is joined with the amine group (NH₂) of another amino acid (**Figure 6.2**). The unique nature of each amino acid side chain prevents a protein from remaining in an orderly straight line. Rather, each polypeptide folds into a precise three-dimensional shape, such as a coil, based on the interactions of its amino acid side chains with each other and the environment. Some side chains are attracted to other side chains; some are neutral; and some repel each other.

proteins Compounds in your body that consist of numerous amino acids and are found in all living cells.

amino acids The building blocks of protein. Amino acids contain carbon, hydrogen, oxygen, and nitrogen. All amino acids are composed of an acid group, an amine group, and a unique side chain.

acid group The COOH group that is part of every amino acid; also called the *carboxyl group.*

amine group The nitrogen-containing part (NH₂) of an amino acid.

side chain The side group of an amino acid that provides it with its unique qualities; also referred to as the R group.

peptide bonds The bonds that connect amino acids, created when the acid group of one amino acid is joined with the nitrogen-containing amine group of another amino acid.

Figure 6.2 The Making of a Protein

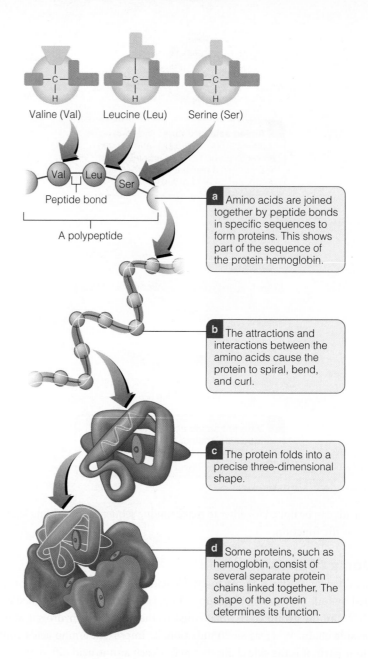

Valine (Val)   Leucine (Leu)   Serine (Ser)

Peptide bond

A polypeptide

a Amino acids are joined together by peptide bonds in specific sequences to form proteins. This shows part of the sequence of the protein hemoglobin.

b The attractions and interactions between the amino acids cause the protein to spiral, bend, and curl.

c The protein folds into a precise three-dimensional shape.

d Some proteins, such as hemoglobin, consist of several separate protein chains linked together. The shape of the protein determines its function.

Additionally, side chains can be *hydrophilic* ("water-loving") or *hydrophobic* ("water-fearing"), and this affects how they react with their environment. The hydrophobic side chains tend to cluster together in the interior of the protein, causing the protein to be globular in shape. The hydrophilic side chains assemble on the outside surface of the protein, closer to the watery environments of blood and other body fluids. The shape of a protein determines its function in your body. Therefore, anything that alters the bonds between the side chains will alter its shape and thus its function.

Essential, Nonessential, and Conditional Amino Acids

There are nine amino acids that your body cannot make and that you must therefore obtain from foods. These are the **essential amino acids,** and you can find them in foods such as meat and milk. It is *essential* that you obtain them from your diet.

The remaining 11 amino acids are **nonessential amino acids** because they can be synthesized, or created, in your body. It is *not essential* to consume them in the diet. Your body creates nonessential amino acids as needed by adding nitrogen to a carbon-

essential amino acids The nine amino acids that the body cannot synthesize; they must be obtained through dietary sources.

nonessential amino acids The 11 amino acids that the body can synthesize.

Table 6.1

The Mighty Twenty

Essential Amino Acids	Nonessential Amino Acids
Histidine (His)[a]	Alanine (Ala)
Isoleucine (Ile)	Arginine (Arg)[b]
Leucine (Leu)	Aspartic acid (Asp)
Lysine (Lys)	Asparagine (Asn)
Methionine (Met)	Cysteine (Cys)[b]
Phenylalanine (Phe)	Glutamic acid (Glu)
Threonine (Thr)	Glutamine (Gln)[b]
Tryptophan (Trp)	Glycine (Gly)[b]
Valine (Val)	Proline (Pro)[b]
	Serine (Ser)
	Tyrosine (Tyr)[b]

a. Histidine was once thought to be essential only for infants. It is now known that small amounts are also needed for adults.
b. These amino acids can be "conditionally essential" if there are either inadequate precursors or inadequate enzymes available to create them in the body. This can happen in certain illnesses and in premature infants.

containing structure. Some nonessential amino acids can also be made from other amino acids. This process occurs primarily in the liver. Table 6.1 lists these 20 amino acids by their classification.

Some nonessential amino acids may become **conditionally essential** if the body cannot make them because of illness, or because the body lacks the necessary **precursors** or enzymes. In such situations, they are considered essential and must be consumed through food. An example of this is when premature infants are not able to make enough of the enzymes needed to create arginine, so they need to get this amino acid in their diet.[2]

Denaturation of Proteins Changes Their Shape

Proteins can be unfolded or **denatured** (**Figure 6.3**) by heat, acids, bases, salts, or mechanical agitation. **Denaturation** doesn't alter the primary structure of the protein (amino acids will still be in the same sequence), but it does change the shape. As mentioned earlier, changing the protein's shape will alter its function, sometimes permanently.

The protein found in eggs can be used to illustrate denaturation. When you apply heat to a raw egg, such as by frying it, the heat denatures the protein in both the yolk and the egg white. Heat disrupts the bonds between the amino acid side chains, causing the protein in the egg to uncoil. New bonds then form between the side chains, changing the shape and structure of the protein and the texture of the egg. As the egg cooks, it solidifies, illustrating the permanent change in the protein's shape and structure.

Similarly, mechanical agitation, such as beating egg whites when you prepare a meringue, can denature protein. Beating an egg white uncoils the protein, allowing the hydrophilic side chains to react with the water in the egg white, while the hydrophobic portions of the side chains form new bonds, trapping the air from the whipping. The stiffer the peaks of egg white, the more denatured the protein.[3]

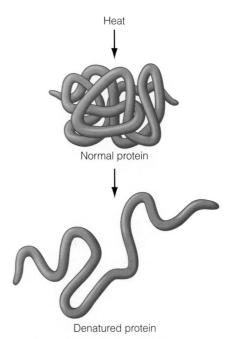

Heat

Normal protein

Denatured protein

Figure 6.3 Denaturing a Protein
A protein can be denatured, or unfolded, by exposure to heat, acids, bases, or salts. Any change in a protein's shape will alter its function.

conditionally essential amino acids Nonessential amino acids that become essential if the body cannot make them, such as during bouts of illness.

precursor A substance that is converted to another substance in the body.

denaturation The alteration of a protein's shape, which changes the structure and function of the protein.

Cooking denatures protein and will often improve the quality, structure, and texture of the protein-rich foods you eat. Raw eggs, meat, and poultry are basically inedible, but cooking these foods greatly increases their palatability.

Salts and acids can also denature proteins. For example, when you marinate a chicken breast or a steak before cooking, you might use salt (such as in soy sauce) or acid (such as wine or vinegar) to denature its protein. The end result is juicier, more tender meat.[4] During digestion, acidic stomach juices help denature and untangle proteins to reveal the peptide bonds. This allows digestive enzymes to break them apart.

The Take-Home Message An amino acid is made up of carbon, oxygen, hydrogen, a nitrogen-containing amine group, and a unique side chain. There are 20 side chains and so 20 unique amino acids. Whereas all 20 amino acids are needed to make proteins, 11 of these can be synthesized in your body and are thus nonessential. The remaining nine amino acids are the essential amino acids that your body cannot synthesize. Essential amino acids must be obtained in your diet. Amino acids are joined together by peptide bonds to create proteins. The attractions and interactions between the side chains cause the protein to fold into a precise three-dimensional shape. The protein's shape determines its function. Heat, acids, bases, and salts can break, or denature, a protein and alter its shape and function.

What Happens to the Protein You Eat?

When you enjoy a tasty peanut butter sandwich, what happens to the protein from the peanut butter once it's in your body? How is the protein in the peanuts broken down so that the valuable amino acids can be efficiently digested, absorbed, and used to synthesize other proteins?

You Digest and Absorb Dietary Proteins in Your Stomach and Small Intestine

Protein digestion begins after chewed food enters your stomach (**Figure 6.4**). Stomach acids denature the protein strands, untangling their bonds. This allows the digestive enzyme pepsin, which is produced in your stomach lining and activated by its acidic environment, to begin breaking the proteins down and preparing them for absorption. Pepsin splits the protein into shorter polypeptide strands, and these strands are propelled into the small intestine.

In the small intestine, other enzymes further break down the strands into tripeptides and dipeptides, as well as some amino acids. The protein remnants are then absorbed into the cells of the small intestine lining, where the remaining tripeptides and dipeptides are broken down into single amino acids, which enter the blood and travel to the liver.

How the liver uses these amino acids depends on the needs of your body. For example, they might be used to make new proteins or, if necessary, as an energy source. They can also be converted to glucose if you are not getting enough carbohydrate in your diet. Some of these amino acids also travel back out to the blood to be picked up and used by your cells.

Figure 6.4 Digesting and Absorbing Proteins

Stomach

Acidic juices

Proteins

Pepsin

Small intestine

Polypeptides

Other enzymes

Tripeptides and dipeptides, amino acids

Small intestine lining

Blood

Amino acids

To liver

1 In the stomach, acidic juices denature the protein and activate the enzyme pepsin, which breaks the protein into shorter strands.

2 These strands enter the small intestine. Pepsin is inactivated. Other enzymes further break down the polypeptide strands into tripeptides and dipeptides and single amino acids.

3 These protein remnants are absorbed through the small intestine lining. They are further broken down to single amino acids, which enter the blood and travel directly to the liver.

4 The liver uses some of the amino acids to make new proteins, or glucose, or for other purposes. Other amino acids will pass through the liver and return to the blood to be picked up and used by the cells.

Your Body Degrades and Synthesizes Proteins

Your diet provides essential and nonessential amino acids. Your body stockpiles a limited amount of all these in **amino acid pools** in your blood and inside your cells. Because your body can't make the essential amino acids, the pools need to be constantly restocked.

Your body is also constantly degrading its proteins, that is, breaking them down into their component parts, to synthesize other needed proteins. Hence, amino acids are continually being removed from your amino acid pools to create proteins on demand. This process of continually degrading and synthesizing protein is called **protein turnover** (see **Figure 6.5**). In fact, more than 200 grams of protein are turned over daily. The proteins in your intestines and liver—two active areas in your body—account for as much as 50 percent of this turnover.[5] The cells that make up the lining of your intestines are continually being sloughed off and replaced. The proteins in these sloughed-off cells are degraded, and most of the resulting amino acids are absorbed and recycled in your body, although some are lost in your stool and urine. Proteins and amino acids are also lost daily through sloughed-off skin, hair, and nails. Replacements for these proteins must be synthesized, and the amino acid pools provide the building materials to do this. Some of the amino acids in the pools are used to synthesize nonprotein substances, including thyroid hormones and melanin, the pigment that gives color to dark skin and hair.

Amino acids are also broken down into their component parts for other uses or stored in another form. To begin the breakdown process, the amino acids lose their amine groups. The nitrogen in the amine groups forms ammonia (NH_2), which can be toxic to your cells in high amounts. Your liver converts the ammonia to **urea,** a waste product that is excreted in your urine via the kidneys.

amino acid pools A limited supply of amino acids stored in your blood and cells and used to build new proteins.

protein turnover The continual process of degrading and synthesizing protein. When the daily amount of degraded protein is equivalent to the amount that is synthesized, you are in protein balance.

urea A nitrogen-containing waste product that is excreted in urine.

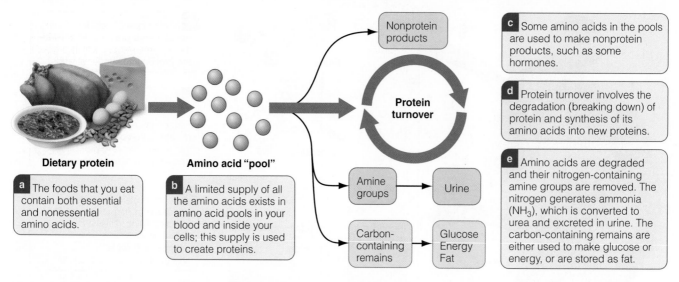

Figure 6.5 The Fate of Amino Acids in Your Body

The carbon-containing remnants of the amino acids are then converted to glucose, used as energy, or stored as fat, depending on the needs of your body. When your diet is too low in carbohydrates, the amino acids will be used to make glucose. When calories are inadequate, the amino acids can be sacrificed for energy. Surplus amino acids (beyond what is needed in the amino acid pools) from excess dietary protein can't be stored as protein in your body and so must be stored predominantly as fat. Hence, as you know from the last two chapters, *all* excess calories—whether from carbohydrates, proteins, or fats—will be stored as fat in your body.

Proteins don't have a mind of their own. How does your body know when to create or synthesize more proteins? Let's look at how proteins are synthesized in your body.

DNA Directs the Synthesis of New Proteins

Protein synthesis is directed by a molecule in the nucleus of your cells called **DNA** (**d**eoxyribo**n**ucleic **a**cid). DNA is the blueprint for every cell in your body.

Each DNA molecule carries the code to synthesize every protein that you need. However, your cells' protein-producing capabilities are specialized. For example, only cells in the pancreas make the hormone insulin, because no other cell in the body expresses the **gene** (a DNA segment that codes for a specific protein) to make insulin. Several hormones prompt DNA to synthesize proteins as needed.

As with any blueprint, DNA doesn't do the actual building or synthesizing; it only provides the instructions. DNA can't leave the nucleus of the cell, so it directs another important molecule within the cell, called **RNA** (**r**ibo**n**ucleic **a**cid), to carry out its instructions for building a protein. There are two specialized RNAs, called **messenger RNA (mRNA)** and **transfer RNA (tRNA),** which perform very specific roles during protein synthesis. See **Figure 6.6** to view how protein synthesis takes place in a cell.

When abnormalities occur during protein synthesis, serious medical conditions may result. One such condition is **sickle-cell anemia.** The most common inherited blood disorder in the United States, sickle-cell anemia is caused by the abnormal formation of the protein hemoglobin. According to the National Institutes of Health

DNA The blueprint in cells that stores all genetic information. DNA remains in the nucleus of the cell and directs the synthesis of proteins.

gene A DNA segment that codes for a specific protein.

RNA A molecule that carries out the orders of DNA.

messenger RNA (mRNA) A type of RNA that copies the genetic information encoded in DNA and carries it out of the nucleus of the cell to synthesize the protein.

transfer RNA (tRNA) A type of RNA that collects the amino acids within the cell that are needed to make a specific protein.

sickle-cell anemia A blood disorder caused by a genetic defect in the development of hemoglobin. Sickle-cell anemia causes the red blood cells to distort into a sickle shape and can damage organs and tissues.

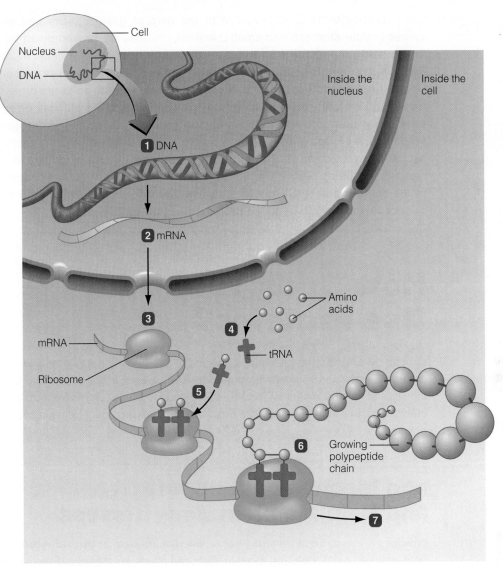

1 Each strand of DNA holds the code to create specific proteins. Because the DNA can't leave the nucleus of the cell, a copy of the code, called messenger RNA (mRNA), is made.

2 The mRNA takes this information outside the nucleus and brings it to the ribosome.

3 The ribosome moves along the mRNA, reading the code.

4 Another type of RNA, called transfer RNA (tRNA), collects the specific amino acids that are needed to make the protein. There are 20 different tRNAs, one for each amino acid.

5 The tRNA brings the amino acid to the ribosome.

6 The ribosome then builds a chain of amino acids (the protein) in the proper sequence, based on the code in the mRNA.

7 The ribosome continues to move down the mRNA strand until all the appropriate amino acids are added and the protein is complete.

Figure 6.6 Protein Synthesis

(NIH), approximately one in 12 African-Americans and one in 100 Hispanics are carriers of the mutated gene that causes the disease.[6]

The mutation in the gene causes a change in the amino acid sequence in the hemoglobin molecule. In sickle-cell anemia, there is a displacement of just *one* amino acid, glutamine, with another amino acid, valine, in the polypeptide chains of hemoglobin. This causes the chains to stick to one another and form crescent-shaped structures rather than the normal globular ones. Whereas red blood cells with normal hemoglobin are smooth and round, those with this mutation are stiff and form a sickle or half-moon shape under certain conditions, such as after vigorous exercise, when oxygen levels in the blood are low. These abnormal sickle cells are easily destroyed, which can lead to anemia, and they can build up in blood vessels, causing painful blockages and damage to tissues and organs.

Another rare genetic disorder, phenylketonuria (PKU), is caused by the body's inability to properly degrade phenylalanine, causing a buildup of this amino acid in the blood. If not identified and treated early in life, PKU can cause mental retardation. To prevent this, infants are screened for PKU at birth.

Red blood cells with normal hemoglobin, like the three similar ones, are smooth and round. A person with sickle-cell anemia has red blood cells like the one on the right; these cells are stiff and form a sickle (half-moon) shape when blood oxygen levels are low.

The Take-Home Message With the help of gastric juices and enzymes in your stomach and small intestine, proteins are broken down into amino acids and absorbed into your blood to be used by your cells. A limited supply of amino acids exists in pools in your body, which act as a reservoir for the synthesis of proteins as needed. Surplus amino acids are broken down, and the carbon-containing remains can be used for glucose or energy, or can be stored as fat, depending on your body's needs. The nitrogen in the amine groups is eventually converted to the waste product urea and excreted in your urine. Amino acids can be used to create nonprotein substances, including certain hormones. The synthesis of proteins is directed in the cell nucleus by DNA, which carries the code for the amino acid sequences necessary to build the proteins that you need.

How Does Your Body Use Proteins?

Proteins play many important roles in the body, from providing structural and mechanical support and maintaining your body's tissues to creating enzymes and hormones and helping maintain acid-base and fluid balance. They also transport nutrients, assist your immune system, and, when necessary, become a source of energy.

Proteins Provide Structural and Mechanical Support and Help Maintain Body Tissues

Proteins provide much of the structural and mechanical support that keeps you upright, moving, and flexible. Just as wood, nails, and plaster are the behind-the-scenes materials holding up the room around you, several fibrous proteins in your bones, muscles, and other tissues help hold up your body.

Collagen, the most abundant protein in your body, is found in all of your **connective tissues,** including the bones, tendons, and ligaments, that support and connect your joints and other body parts. This fibrous protein is also responsible for the elasticity in your skin and helps form scar tissue to repair injuries such as wounds. Two other proteins, actin and myosin, provide mechanical support by helping your muscles contract so you can run, walk, sit, and lie down.

The daily wear and tear on your body causes the breakdown of hundreds of grams of proteins each day. For example, the protein-rich cells of your skin are constantly sloughing off, and proteins help create a new layer of outer skin every 25 to 45 days.[7] Because your red blood cells have a short life span—only about 120 days—new red blood cells must continually be regenerated. The cells that line the inner surfaces of your organs, such as your lungs and intestines, are also constantly sloughed off, excreted, and replaced.

In addition to regular maintenance, extra protein is sometimes needed for "emergency repairs." Protein is essential in healing, and a person with extensive wounds, such as severe burns, may have dietary protein needs that are more than triple his or her normal needs.

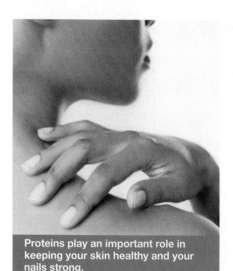
Proteins play an important role in keeping your skin healthy and your nails strong.

collagen A ropelike, fibrous protein that is the most abundant protein in your body.

connective tissue The most abundant tissue type in the body. Made up primarily of collagen, it supports and connects body parts as well as providing protection and insulation.

Proteins Build Most Enzymes and Many Hormones

When your body needs a reaction to take place promptly, such as breaking down carbohydrates after a meal, it calls upon **enzymes,** biological **catalysts** that speed up reactions. Without enzymes, reactions would occur so slowly that you couldn't survive. Most enzymes are proteins, although some may also have a **coenzyme,** such as a vitamin, that aids in initiating a reaction.

Each of the thousands of enzymes in your body catalyzes a specific reaction. Some enzymes, such as digestive enzymes, break compounds apart. (Recall from Chapter 4 that the enzyme lactase is needed to break down the milk sugar lactose.) Other enzymes, such as those used to synthesize proteins, help compounds combine. Enzymes aren't changed, damaged, or used up in the process of speeding up a particular reaction. **Figure 6.7** shows how an enzyme breaks apart two compounds, yet isn't changed in the process. Thus, the enzyme is available to catalyze additional reactions.

While enzymes expedite reactions, hormones direct them. Many **hormones** are proteins that direct or signal an activity, often by turning on or shutting off enzymes. (Recall from Chapter 5 that some hormones can also be lipids.) Hormones are released from tissues and organs and travel to target cells in another part of your body to direct an activity. There are more than 70 trillion cells in your body, and all of these cells interact with at least one of more than 50 known hormones.[8]

Let's consider an example of one hormone in action. When your blood glucose level rises after a meal or snack, your pancreas (an organ) releases insulin (a hormone) into your blood, which in turn directs the uptake of glucose in your cells (the activity). If your blood glucose level drops too low, such as between meals, your pancreas (an organ) releases glucagon (a hormone), which promotes the release of glucose from the glycogen stored in your liver (the activity), which in turn raises your blood glucose level.

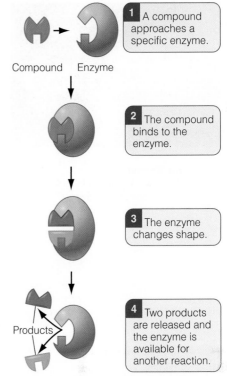

Compound Enzyme

1 A compound approaches a specific enzyme.

2 The compound binds to the enzyme.

3 The enzyme changes shape.

4 Two products are released and the enzyme is available for another reaction.

Products

Figure 6.7 An Enzyme in Action
Enzymes speed up reactions in your body, yet they aren't changed, damaged, or used up in the process.

Proteins Help Maintain Fluid Balance

Your body is made up predominantly of water, which is distributed throughout various body compartments. Proteins help ensure that all this water is dispersed evenly, keeping you in a state of **fluid balance.**

Normally, your blood pressure forces the nutrient- and oxygen-rich fluids out of your capillaries and into the spaces between your cells. Whereas fluids can flow easily in these spaces, proteins can't, because they are too big to cross the cell membranes. Proteins attract water, so the proteins remaining in the capillaries eventually draw the fluids back into the capillaries. Hence, protein plays an important role in the movement of fluids and in keeping the fluids balanced among these compartments. (Note: The mineral sodium also plays a major role in fluid balance.)

When fewer proteins are available to draw the fluid from between the cells back into the bloodstream, as during severe malnutrition, a fluid imbalance results. The spaces between the cell become bloated and the body tissue swells, a condition known as **edema** (**Figure 6.8**).

Proteins Help Maintain Acid-Base Balance

Proteins can alter the pH (the concentration of hydrogen ions) of your body fluids. Normally, your blood has a pH of about 7.4, and the fluid in your cells has a pH of about 7.0. Even a small change in the pH of your blood in either direction can be

enzymes Substances that act as catalysts and speed up reactions.

catalysts Substances that aid and speed up reactions without being changed, damaged, or used up in the process.

coenzyme Substances, often vitamins, that are needed by enzymes to perform many chemical reactions in your body.

hormones Protein- or lipid-based chemical messengers that initiate or direct a specific action. Insulin, glucagon, and estrogen are examples of hormones.

fluid balance The equal distribution of water throughout your body and within and between cells.

edema The accumulation of excess fluid in the spaces surrounding your cells, which causes swelling of the body tissue.

Figure 6.8 Edema
Inadequate protein in the blood can cause fluid retention within body tissue, also known as edema.

harmful or even fatal. With a blood pH below 7.35, a condition called acidosis sets in, which can result in a coma. A blood pH above 7.45, known as alkalosis, can result in convulsions.

Proteins act as **buffers** and minimize the changes in acid-base levels by picking up or donating hydrogen ions in the blood. Should your blood become too acidic, some of the amino acid side chains in the proteins will pick up excess hydrogen ions. Other side chains can donate hydrogen ions to your blood if it becomes too basic.

Proteins Transport Substances throughout the Body

Transport proteins shuttle oxygen, waste products, lipids, some vitamins, and sodium and potassium through your blood and into and out of cells through cell membranes. Hemoglobin acts as a transport protein that carries oxygen to cells from the lungs. Hemoglobin also picks up carbon dioxide waste products from cells for transport to your lungs to be exhaled from your body. Once in your blood, vitamin A travels to your liver and is bound to yet another protein to be transported to your cells.

Transport proteins in cell membranes form a "doorway" that allows substances such as sodium and potassium to pass in and out of cells (**Figure 6.9**). Substances that are not lipid-soluble or that are simply too big to pass through the lipid-rich membrane have to enter the cell through a protein channel.

Proteins Contribute to a Healthy Immune System

Your immune system works like an army to protect your body from foreign invaders, such as disease-causing bacteria and viruses. Specialized protein "soldiers" called **antibodies** eliminate these potentially harmful substances.

buffers Substances that help maintain the proper pH in a solution by attracting or donating hydrogen ions.

transport proteins Proteins that carry lipids (fat and cholesterol), oxygen, waste products, and vitamins through the blood to various organs and tissues. Proteins can also act as channels through which some substances enter cells.

antibodies Proteins made by your body to bind to and neutralize foreign invaders, such as harmful bacteria, fungi, and viruses, as part of the body's immune response.

Outside cell

Transport protein

Potassium

Sodium

Sodium binds to transport protein

Transport protein releases sodium outside of cell

Potassium binds to transport protein

Transport protein releases potassium inside the cell

Inside cell

Figure 6.9 Proteins as Transport Channels
Transport proteins form a channel, or doorway, through which substances such as sodium and potassium can move from one side of the cell membrane to the other.

Once your body knows how to create antibodies against a specific invader, such as a virus, it stores that information and you have **immunity** to that pathogen. The next time the invader enters your body, you can respond very quickly (producing up to 2,000 precise antibodies per second!) to fight it. When this rapid immune response works efficiently, it prevents the virus or other invader from multiplying to levels high enough to make you sick.

Sometimes, your body incorrectly perceives a nonthreatening substance as an invader and attacks it. This perceived invader is called an *allergen*. Food allergens are proteins in a food that are resistant to being broken down by heat during cooking or by the gastric juice and enzymes in the body.[9] Individuals who react to these allergens are diagnosed with food allergies. You will learn more about food allergies in Chapter 15.

Proteins Can Provide Energy

(T)(F) Because proteins provide 4 calories per gram, they can be used as an energy source. However, the last thing you want to do is use this valuable nutrient, which plays so many important roles in your body, as a regular source of fuel, especially since carbohydrates and fats are far better suited for providing energy. When your diet contains adequate amounts of calories from carbohydrates and fat, proteins are used for their other important roles.

When your diet doesn't provide adequate amounts of calories—for example, in times of starvation—your body begins to break down its protein, mainly from muscles, into its amino acid components. The carbon skeletons of the amino acids are used for energy and for gluconeogenesis, the creation of glucose from noncarbohydrate sources. (Remember that your brain and nervous system need a minimum amount of glucose to function properly.) However, when proteins are used for energy, they create waste products that must be eliminated from your body, which is particularly burdensome for your liver and kidneys.

Protein Improves Satiety and Appetite Control

In addition to the structural and functional roles protein plays in the body, protein also helps increase satiety, the feeling of fullness, after a meal more than either carbohydrate or fat.[10] Eating a meal that contains a good source of protein will leave you more satisfied than a meal containing the same amount of calories but with the majority of them coming from carbohydrate. Although the mechanism behind protein's effect on your appetite is not yet known, some research studies suggest that it may be due to several factors, such as changes in appetite-suppressing hormones in the body, how the body metabolizes protein, and the levels of the amino acids in the blood.[11] Including protein in each meal can help control your appetite, which in turn can help you maintain a healthy weight.

Table 6.2 summarizes the many roles that proteins play in your body.

The Take-Home Message Proteins play many important roles in the body, including: (1) structural and mechanical support, (2) building enzymes and some hormones, (3) maintaining fluid balance, (4) maintaining acid-base balance, (5) transporting substances throughout the body, (6) providing antibodies for a strong immune system, (7) providing energy, and (8) promoting satiety.

immunity The state of having built up antibodies to a particular foreign substance so that when particles of the substance enter the body, they are destroyed by the antibodies.

Table 6.2

The Many Roles of Proteins

Role of Proteins	How It Works
1. Provide structural and mechanical support and maintenance	Proteins are your body's building materials, providing strength and flexibility to your tissues, tendons, ligaments, muscles, organs, bones, nails, hair, and skin. Proteins are needed for the ongoing maintenance of your body.
2. Build enzymes and hormones	Proteins are needed to make most enzymes that speed up reactions in your body and many hormones that direct specific activities, such as regulating your blood glucose level.
3. Maintain fluid balance	Proteins play a major role in ensuring that your body fluids are evenly dispersed in your blood and inside and outside your cells.
4. Maintain acid-base balance	Proteins act as buffers to help keep the pH of your body fluids balanced within a tight range. A drop in pH will cause your body fluids to become too acidic, whereas a rise in pH can make them too basic.
5. Transport substances	Proteins shuttle substances such as oxygen, waste products, and nutrients (such as sodium and potassium) through your blood and into and out of your cells.
6. Affect antibodies and the immune response	Proteins create specialized antibodies that attack pathogens in your body that can make you sick.
7. Provide energy	Because proteins provide 4 calories per gram, they can be used as fuel or energy in your body.
8. Improves satiety	Protein increases satiety, which can help control your appetite and weight.

How Much Protein Do You Need?

Healthy adults should consume enough dietary protein to replace the amount they use each day, whereas pregnant women, people recovering from surgery or an injury, and growing children need more protein to supply the necessary amino acids and nitrogen to build new tissue. **Nitrogen balance** studies have been used to determine how much protein individuals need to replace or build new tissue.

Healthy Adults Should Be in Nitrogen Balance

nitrogen balance The state in which an individual is consuming the same amount of nitrogen (from protein) in the diet as he or she is excreting in the urine.

A person's daily protein requirement can be estimated by using what we know about the structure of an amino acid. We know that 16 percent of every dietary protein molecule is nitrogen, and we also know that this nitrogen is retained by the body during protein synthesis. With this information, we can assess a person's protein status by

Figure 6.10 Nitrogen Balance and Imbalance

Pregnant women, growing children and adolescents, and some athletes tend to be in positive nitrogen blanace.

A healthy adult is typically in nitrogen balance.

An individual who is experiencing a medical trauma or not eating a healthy diet is often in negative nitrogen balance.

measuring the amount of nitrogen consumed and subtracting the amount of nitrogen excreted. The goal is to achieve nitrogen balance.

If the nitrogen intake from dietary protein is equivalent to the amount of nitrogen excreted (mostly as urea) in the urine, then a person is in nitrogen balance. Such an individual is consuming a balanced diet with adequate amounts of protein and excreting an equally balanced amount of nitrogen. Healthy, nonpregnant adults are typically in nitrogen balance.

A body that retains more nitrogen than it excretes is in positive nitrogen balance. Rapidly growing babies, children, or teenagers are all in positive nitrogen balance because their bodies use nitrogen to build new tissues that aid growth, build muscles, and expand the supply of red blood cells. They therefore excrete less nitrogen in their urine. When your mother was pregnant with you, she was in positive nitrogen balance because she was building a robust baby.

Negative nitrogen balance occurs when the body excretes more nitrogen than is consumed due to some physical impairment, such as a serious injury, infection, malnutrition, or other trauma, where the body cannot synthesize protein as quickly as it's broken down. These situations all increase the body's need for both calories and protein. If the calories and protein in the diet are inadequate to cover the increased demands, then proteins from tissues are broken down to meet the body's needs. **Figure 6.10** lists some of the situations that lead to nitrogen balance or imbalance in the body.

While it is important to eat a sufficient quantity of protein to meet your needs, the quality of protein also matters.

Not All Protein Is Created Equal

A high-quality protein is digestible, contains all the essential amino acids, and provides sufficient protein to be used to synthesize the nonessential amino acids. **Protein quality** is determined by two factors: your body's ability to digest the protein (the protein's **digestibility**) and the types and amounts of amino acids (essential, nonessential, or both) that the protein contains. Proteins that are more easily digested and that contain both essential and nonessential amino acids are of higher quality.

protein quality The measure of a protein's digestibility and how its amino acid pattern compares with your body's needs. Proteins that are more easily digested and have a complete set of amino acids are of higher quality.

digestibility A food's capacity to be broken down so that it can be absorbed.

Chickpeas are short of the limiting amino acid methionine. The addition of sesame seed paste, which has an abundance of methionine, completes the protein. Add garlic and lemon as seasonings for a completely delicious hummus.

amino acid profile The types and amounts of amino acids in a protein.

complete protein A protein that provides all the essential amino acids that your body needs, along with some nonessential amino acids. Soy protein and protein from animal sources, in general, are complete.

incomplete protein A protein that is low in one or more of the essential amino acids. Protein from plant sources tends to be incomplete.

limiting amino acid The amino acid that is in the shortest supply in an incomplete protein.

complemented proteins Incomplete proteins that are combined with modest amounts of animal or soy proteins or with other plant proteins that are rich in the limiting amino acids to create a complete protein.

protein digestibility corrected amino acid score (PDCAAS) A score measured as a percentage that takes into account both digestibility and amino acid profile and gives a good indication of the quality of a protein.

Digestibility

The digestibility of proteins varies, depending on their source. In general, animal proteins are more digestible than plant proteins. Some of the plant proteins, especially when consumed raw, are protected by the plant's cell walls and cannot be broken down by the enzymes in your intestinal tract. While 90 to 99 percent of the proteins from animal sources (cheese and other dairy foods, meat, poultry, and eggs) are digestible, only 70 to 90 percent of plant proteins, such as from chickpeas and other legumes, are typically digestible.[12]

Amino Acid Profile

The second factor that affects protein quality concerns the types and amounts of amino acids that the protein contains, or its **amino acid profile.** A protein that provides all nine of the essential amino acids, along with some of the 11 nonessential amino acids, is considered a **complete protein.** A protein that is low in one or more of the essential amino acids is considered an **incomplete protein.** A complete protein is considered of higher quality than an incomplete protein. Protein from animal sources is typically complete protein, whereas protein from plant foods tends to be incomplete.

Two exceptions to this generalization are gelatin and soy. Gelatin, an animal protein, is not a complete protein because it is missing the amino acid tryptophan. Soy, a plant protein, has an amino acid profile that resembles the protein needs in your body, making it a complete protein.

Any protein chain is only as strong as its weakest amino acid link. If a single essential amino acid is in low supply in your diet, and thus in your body, your ability to synthesize the proteins that you need will be limited. The amino acid that is in the shortest supply in an incomplete protein is known as the **limiting amino acid.**

Imagine a jeweler trying to create a necklace. If the jeweler attempts to make a necklace using a diamond-ruby-emerald pattern with unlimited numbers of diamonds and rubies but only three emeralds, the emeralds are the limiting jewels in the pattern. After the third round of sequencing, the jeweler has run out of emeralds, and the necklace can't be completed as designed. Because the full chain can't be completed, the jewels have to be dismantled.

Similarly, when proteins are being synthesized in your body, all the amino acids have to be available at the same time to complete the protein. A half-synthesized protein can't wait for the needed amino acids to come along to complete the process. Rather, the unfinished protein will be degraded, and the amino acids will be used to make glucose, be used as energy, or be stored as fat.

Does that mean that plant proteins are of less value in the diet? Absolutely not. When incomplete proteins are coupled with modest amounts of animal proteins or soy, which have all the essential amino acids, or combined with other plant proteins that are rich in the incomplete protein's limiting amino acids, the incomplete protein is **complemented.** In other words, its amino acid profile is upgraded to a complete protein. You don't have to eat the two food sources of the complementing plant proteins at the same meal to improve the quality of the protein source. As long as the foods are consumed in the same day, all the essential amino acids will be provided to meet your daily needs.

Once the digestibility and the amino acid profile of a protein are known, the quality of a protein can be determined.

Protein Scoring

The **protein digestibility corrected amino acid score (PDCAAS),** which is measured as a percentage, takes into account both the amino acid profile and digestibility of a protein to give a good indication of its quality. Milk protein, which is easily digested and meets essential amino acid requirements, has a PDCAAS of 100 percent. In comparison, chickpeas garner a PDCAAS of 87 percent, and wheat has a score of only 44 percent. If your only dietary source of protein is wheat, you are not meeting your essential amino acid needs.

The Food and Drug Administration (FDA) uses the PDCAAS to assess the quality of dietary proteins. On a food label, when protein is listed as a percentage of the daily value, this percentage is determined based on its PDCAAS.

You Can Determine Your Personal Protein Needs

There are two ways to determine protein intake in the diet. It can be measured as a percentage of total calories or as grams of protein eaten per day. The latest dietary recommendation, based on data from numerous nitrogen balance studies, is to consume from 10 to 35 percent of your total daily calories from protein. Currently, adults in the United States consume about 15 percent of their daily calories from protein, which falls within this range.[13]

The current recommendation for the grams of protein that you need daily is based on your age and your weight (Table 6.3). Adults age 19 and older should consume 0.8 gram (g) of protein for each kilogram (kg) of body weight. For example, a person who weighs 176 pounds (lb) would weigh 80 kg (176 lb ÷ 2.2 = 80 kg) and should consume 80 kg × 0.8 g, or 64 g of protein a day. A person who weighs 130 lb should consume approximately 47 g of protein daily (130 lb ÷ 2.2 = 59 kg × 0.8 g = 47 g). In the United States, men age 20 and older consume, on average, more than 100 grams of protein daily, while women of the same age consume, on average, 70 grams every day.[14] As you can see, Americans are typically meeting, and even exceeding, their dietary protein needs.

Even though most Americans consume more protein than they need, their percentage of daily calories contributed by protein (approximately 15 percent) falls within the recommended range. This is because they consume an abundant amount of calories from carbohydrates and fats, which lowers the percentage of their total calories coming from protein.

An overweight individual's protein needs are not much greater than those of a normal-weight person of similar height. This is because the Recommended Dietary Allowance (RDA) for dietary protein is based on a person's need to maintain protein-dependent tissues like lean muscle and organs and to perform protein-dependent

Table 6.3
Calculating Your Daily Protein Needs

If You Are	You Need
14–18 years old	0.85 g/kg
≥19 years old	0.80 g/kg

To calculate your needs, first convert your body weight from pounds (lb) to kilograms (kg) by dividing by 2.2, like this:

Your weight in pounds: _____ lb ÷ 2.2 = _____ kg

Then, multiply your weight in kilograms by 0.8 or 0.85:

Your weight in kilograms: _____ kg × 0.8 g = _____ g/day

Source: Institute of Medicine, *Dietary Reference Intakes for Energy, Carbohydrate, Fiber, Fat, Fatty Acids, Cholesterol, Protein, and Amino Acids* (Washington, D.C.: The National Academies Press, 2002).

Table 6.4 Protein Supplements

Protein Shakes and Powders

Sometimes used by athletes in the belief that they'll help build muscle, or as meal replacers by those looking to lose weight. In both cases, they are expensive, and unnecessary. Athletes and bodybuilders can obtain adequate protein through a healthy diet, and don't need extra shakes to bulk up. In fact, excessive amounts of protein can be unhealthy and produce undesirable results (see Chapter 11). While dieters may lose weight using a high-protein meal replacer, the same results can occur with a calorie-controlled meal of whole foods. When it comes to losing weight, it's the calories that count.

Amino Acid Supplements

Including those for individual amino acids such as trytophan and lysine, these are marketed as remedies for a range of health issues, including pain, depression, insomnia, and certain infections, even though there are conflicting results from research studies. The reality is that consuming too much of any one amino acid can impede absorption of other amino acids in the intestinal tract. Further, overconsuming specific amino acids can lead to side effects, such as nausea, light-headedness, vomiting, and drowsiness. Your diet can provide all the amino acids you need.

Digestive Enzyme Supplements

Useless because they are broken down in the intestinal tract, and thus made ineffective. Your body manufactures all the enzymes needed to efficiently aid in the digestion of your foods. Spending money on these items is literally akin to flushing your hard-earned money down the toilet.

A variety of protein-related products are heavily marketed and sold to young adults as the key to building muscle, losing weight, or curing a host of health problems. With very few exceptions, purchasing and consuming these products is, at best, a waste of money, and at worst, potentially harmful.

Source: SCAN, "Eating for Recovery, Nutrition Fact Sheet." 2009. Available at www.scandpg.org/files/2009/SD-USA_Fact_Sheet_Eating_for_Recovery_Apr09.pdf; SCAN, "Gaining Weight and Building Muscle." 2010. Available at www.scandpg.org/files/2010/SD-USA_Fact_Sheet_Gaining_Weight_Building_Muscle_Jan_2010.pdf; H. Seagle, F. Witt Strain, A. Makris, and R. Reeves, "Position of the American Dietetic Association: Weight Management." *Journal of the American Dietetic Association* 109 (2009): 330–346; A. Fragakis and C. Thomson, *The Health Professional's Guide to Popular Dietary Supplements*. (Chicago: The American Dietetic Association, 2007); Institute of Medicine, *Dietary Reference Intakes for Energy, Carbohydrate, Fiber, Fat, Fatty Acids, Cholesterol, Protein, and Amino Acids*. (Washington, D.C.: The National Academies Press, 2002).

body functions. Because most overweight people carry their extra body weight predominantly as fat, not muscle, they do not need to consume significantly more protein than normal-weight people.

The American College of Sports Medicine, the American Dietetic Association, and other experts have advocated an increase of 50 to 100 percent more protein for competitive athletes participating in endurance exercise (marathon runners) or resistance exercise (weight lifters) to meet their needs.[15] However, because of their active lifestyles, athletes typically have a higher intake of food and thus already consume higher amounts of both calories and protein. Protein supplements are not needed. Table 6.4 provides you with the facts about protein supplements and shakes. Now let's look at how you can meet your daily protein needs through a well-balanced diet.

The Take-Home Message Protein quality is determined by the protein's digestibility and by the types and amounts of amino acids (essential versus nonessential) it contains. Protein from animal foods is more easily digested than protein from plant foods. A complete protein, which is typically found in animal foods and soy, provides a complete set of the essential amino acids along with some nonessential amino acids. Plant proteins are typically incomplete, as they are missing one or more of the essential amino acids. Plant proteins can be complemented with protein from other plant sources or animal food sources to improve their protein quality. Adults should consume 0.8 gram of protein for each kilogram of body weight. In the United States, men, on average, consume more than 100 grams of protein daily, while women, on average, are consuming more than 70 grams—in both cases, far more than is needed.

Figure 6.11 **What Americans Are Eating**
Americans' consumption of red meat has been declining, and they are eating more poultry and fish.

What Are the Best Food Sources of Protein?

Although some amount of protein is found in many foods, it is particularly abundant in meat, fish, poultry, and meat alternatives such as dried beans, peanut butter, nuts, and soy. Americans, on average, not only consume more than the recommended servings of the protein-rich foods in the meat and beans group, but also eat approximately 10 percent more than they did in the 1970s.[16] A 3-ounce serving of cooked meat, poultry, or fish, which is about the size of a woman's palm or a deck of cards, provides approximately 21 to 25 grams of protein, or about 7 grams per ounce, and is plenty of protein for one meal.

While red meat is still the most popular food in the meat and beans group, Americans' love of meat has declined over the last four decades. In contrast, Americans currently eat more than double the amount of poultry, and over 25 percent more fish, than they did in 1970 (see **Figure 6.11**).[17] Dried beans such as kidney beans, pinto beans, and black beans not only provide an excellent source of protein, but are also a potent source of fiber (as you saw in Chapter 4). Dairy foods are also an excellent source of protein, and though grains and vegetables are less robust protein sources, as part of a varied, balanced diet they can aid significantly in meeting your daily needs.

More than half of the protein in an egg is in the white. In fact, two egg whites provide 7 grams of protein, compared with only 6 grams in a whole egg.

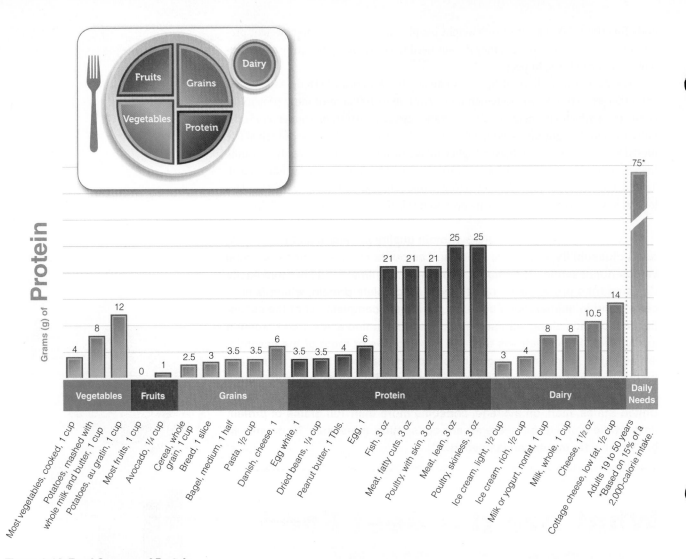

Figure 6.12 Food Sources of Protein
Food choices from the meat, poultry, fish, meat alternative, and milk groups are the most abundant sources of dietary protein. Grains and vegetables provide less protein per serving but as part of a varied, balanced diet can add significantly to your daily needs.

Source: USDA National Nutrient Database for Standard Reference (www.nal.usda.gov/fnic).

Eating a wide variety of foods is the best approach to meeting your protein needs (**Figure 6.12**). A diet that consists of the recommended servings from the five food groups based on 1,600 calories, which is far less than most adults consume daily, will supply the protein needs for adult women and most adult men (see Table 6.5). In fact, many people have already met their daily protein needs before they even sit down to dinner! How does your diet stack up when it comes to protein? Take the Self-Assessment to find out.

Though most Americans are getting plenty of protein in their diets, there has recently been a boom in the consumption of high-protein energy bars. Are these a bargain? Are they necessary? The feature box "Protein Bars: Are They a Health Bargain?" on page 202 takes a look at this hot topic.

The Take-Home Message A well-balanced diet can easily meet your daily protein needs. Meat, fish, poultry, and meat alternatives such as dried beans, peanut butter, nuts, and soy are particularly abundant in protein. Dairy products and some vegetables can also be good sources.

Do You Have a Protein-Friendly Diet?

Take this brief self-assessment to see if you have adequate amounts of protein-rich foods in your diet.

1. Do you eat at least 5 to 7 ounces of meat, fish, and/or poultry on most days of the week?
   Yes ☐ **No** ☐

2. Do you have at least 2 to 3 cups of milk, yogurt, soy milk, and/or soy yogurt daily?
   Yes ☐ **No** ☐

3. Do you enjoy at least 6 ounces of grains every day? (An ounce is considered 1 slice of bread, 1 cup of ready-to-eat cereal, or ½ cup of pasta or rice.)
   Yes ☐ **No** ☐

4. Do you eat at least 1 ounce of cheese or soy cheese daily?
   Yes ☐ **No** ☐

5. Do you eat at least 1 tablespoon of peanuts daily?
   Yes ☐ **No** ☐

6. Do you eat at least ½ cup of dried beans or peas, such as kidney beans or chickpeas, every day?
   Yes ☐ **No** ☐

7. Do you eat soy-based foods such as soy burgers and tofu daily?
   Yes ☐ **No** ☐

Answers

If you answered yes to at least the first three questions and are also meeting your calorie needs on a daily basis, you have a *very* protein-friendly diet! If you answered no to question 1 but yes to most of the other questions, you are also likely meeting your protein needs if your daily calories are adequate. If you have more no than yes answers, your diet may be in need of a protein makeover. Read on in the chapter to learn how you can easily add healthy sources of protein to your diet.

Table 6.5
A Typical Day in the Life

Food	Amount	Calories	Protein (g)	Vegetable Group (servings)	Fruit Group (servings)	Grain Group (servings)	Protein Group (oz)	Dairy Group (servings)	Oil Group (tsp)
Breakfast									
Bran flakes	2 cups	256	7.5			2			
Milk, nonfat	1 cup	86	8					1	
Orange juice	8 oz	112	2		1				
Lunch									
Turkey and cheese sandwich:									
Turkey breast	2 oz	94	11				2		
Cheese, low fat	2 oz	98	14					1	
Whole-wheat bread	2 slices	138	5			2			
Tossed salad	3 cups	30	2	1.5					
Italian dressing	1 tbs	69	0						3
Snack									
Yogurt, vanilla	8 oz	160	8					1	
Banana	1	109	1		1				
Dinner									
Chicken breast, skinless	3 oz	189	25				3		
Brown rice	1 cup	216	5			2			
Broccoli, cooked	1 cup	52	6	1					
Margarine	2 tsp	68	0						2
Totals:		1,677	94.5	2.5	2	6	5	3	5

Note: A 140-pound adult needs 51 g of protein daily. A 180-pound adult needs 65 g of protein daily.
Source: MyPlate.gov; J. Pennington and J. S. Douglass, *Bowes & Church's Food Values of Portions Commonly Used,* 18th ed. (New York: Lippincott Williams & Wilkins, 2005).

Protein Bars: Are They a Health Bargain?

The sales of protein and energy bars have skyrocketed over the last decade, fueling an industry that now generates over a billion dollars annually.[1] There are bars advertised for women, bars for men, bars for the elderly, and junior bars for children. When they emerged in the 1980s, these bars were marketed as a portable snack to keep athletes fueled for long-distance or endurance outings. Manufacturers often claim that the bars are needed to fuel daily activities and build strong muscles or that they serve as a quick meal in a cellophane wrapper.

As you learned from the previous two chapters, all foods provide calories and therefore energy. Whether your calories come from a balanced meal or a "balanced bar," your body will either use them as fuel or store them if they're not immediately needed. You also just learned that you can easily meet your daily protein needs by making wise food choices. Given this knowledge, what advantage, if any, do you think protein and energy bars provide?

If convenience and portability are the main attractions of protein and energy bars, then consider another classic, convenient, and portable food, the peanut butter sandwich. It can be made in a snap, and since it doesn't have to be refrigerated, it can travel anywhere. The

Bar Hopping

Product	Price ($)	Calories	Protein (g)	Total Carb (g)	Total Fat (g)	Sat. Fat (g)	Sugars (tsp)	Fiber (g)
Peanut butter (1 tbs) on 2 slices whole-wheat bread	**0.22**	**234**	**9**	**29**	**11**	**2**	**<1 (5%)***	**5**
Dr Soy Double Chocolate	1.40	180	12	27	3	2.5	2.5 ½ (22%)	1
Balance Chocolate	1.28	200	14	22	6	3.5	4.5 ½ (36%)	
Zoneperfect Chocolate Peanut Butter	1.31	210	16	20	7	3	3.5 ½ (25%)	1
EAS AdvantEdge Chocolate Peanut Crisp	1.10	220	13	32	6	3	5 (26%)	1
Atkins Advantage Chocolate Decadence	2.29	220	17	25	11	7	0	11
Genisoy Ultimate Chocolate Fudge Brownie	1.15	230	14	33	4.5	3	7 (49%)	2
Carb Solutions Creamy Chocolate Peanut Butter	2.24	240	24	14	10	3.5	0.5 (3%)	1

table in this box lets us do some comparison shopping to see how a peanut butter sandwich stacks up to a protein bar.

From a price standpoint, a peanut butter sandwich is a bargain compared with bars that can cost more than $2.50 each, or ten times as much as the sandwich. While the calories and protein content of the sandwich are similar to that in many bars, the saturated fat and sugar contents are not. Some bars provide up to 7 grams of saturated fat, which is about one-third of the upper limit recommended for many adults daily. In contrast, the sandwich contains less saturated fat than all the bars listed. Since these bars can contain up to 7 teaspoons of sugar, which supplies up to 50 percent of the calories in the bar, much of the "energy" in an energy bar is simply sugar. The bars with the most sugar tend to have the least amount of fiber. Ironically, most consumers need more fiber in their diet. Because the peanut butter sandwich has lower amounts of sugar and a higher amount of fiber than almost all of the bars, it's actually the healthier food choice.

Product	Price ($)	Calories	Protein (g)	Total Carb (g)	Total Fat (g)	Sat. Fat (g)	Sugars (tsp)	Fiber (g)
PowerBar ProteinPlus Chocolate Fudge Brownie	1.99	270	24	36	5	3	5 (38%)	2
Met-Rx Protein Plus Chocolate Roasted Peanut	2.57	320	31	29	9	4.5	0.5 (3%)	1
PowerBar Pria Double Chocolate Cookie	0.94	110	5	16	3	2.5	2.5 ½ (36%)	0
Clif Luna Nutz Over Chocolate	1.40	180	10	24	4.5	2.5	3 (27%)	2
Kellogg's Krave Chocolate Delight	0.53	200	7	31	6	3.5	5.5 ½ (44%)	2
Slim-Fast Meal Options Rich Chocolate Brownie	1.02	220	8	35	5	3	6 (44%)	2
Ensure Chewy Chocolate Peanut	1.13	230	9	35	6	4	6 (42%)	1

Key: ⁄ = 1 tsp sugar
⌇ = 1 g fiber
* = % of calories

Source: Adapted from *Consumer Reports* 68 (June 2003): 19–21.

What Happens If You Eat Too Much or Too Little Protein?

While protein is essential to health and normal body function, eating too much or too little can be unhealthy. Let's look at what happens to the human body when it gets too much or too little protein.

Eating Too Much Protein Can Mean Too Much Heart-Unhealthy Fat and Weaker Bones

As you read in the beginning of the chapter, Melissa, the college student, had switched to a high-protein diet to help her slim down. Unfortunately, her steady diet of low-fiber, fat-rich cheeses, hamburgers, and fried foods was affecting her health. The lack of fiber-rich whole grains, fruits, and vegetables was causing her to become extremely constipated and giving her bellyaches. As you remember from Chapter 5, a diet high in saturated fat can raise the LDL ("bad") cholesterol level in the blood. Before Melissa switched to a high-protein diet, her LDL cholesterol was in the healthy range. But her steady diet of fatty foods caused her LDL cholesterol to climb into the dangerously high range. Her doctor sent her to a registered dietitian (RD), who advised her to trim the fatty foods from her diet and add back the fiber-rich whole grains, fruits, and vegetables. Melissa's cholesterol dropped to a healthy level within months, and the high-fiber foods helped to "keep things moving" in her intestinal tract and eliminate the constipation. The RD also recommended that Melissa walk on campus between classes daily to help her better manage her weight.

Figs are a sweet way to get some calcium. Five large figs provide more than 10 percent of many adults' daily calcium needs.

Although consuming protein is a key to good health, eating more is clearly not necessarily eating better. In fact, a diet that is too high in protein is associated with the following risks:

➤ *Heart disease.* A high-protein diet may increase your risk for heart disease and dying prematurely from heart disease. Many foods rich in protein are also rich in heart-unhealthy saturated fats. Although lean meats and skinless poultry contain less saturated fat than some other cuts of meat, they are not completely free of saturated fat. Hence, a high protein intake can make a low saturated fat intake a challenge (see **Figure 6.13**). Lowering the saturated fat in your diet is important in lowering your risk for heart disease.

➤ *Kidney stones.* A high-protein diet may also increase your risk for kidney stones, which commonly contain calcium. More than 10 percent of Americans will likely suffer from a kidney stone at least once in their lives.[18]

➤ *Osteoporosis.* A high-protein diet may also increase your risk of osteoporosis (poor bone density). Although still a controversial issue, numerous research studies have shown that bones lose calcium when a person's diet is too high in protein. The loss seems to occur because calcium is taken from bone to act as a buffer, offsetting the acid generated when specific amino acids are broken down.[19] Other research has attempted to determine if calcium loss leads to

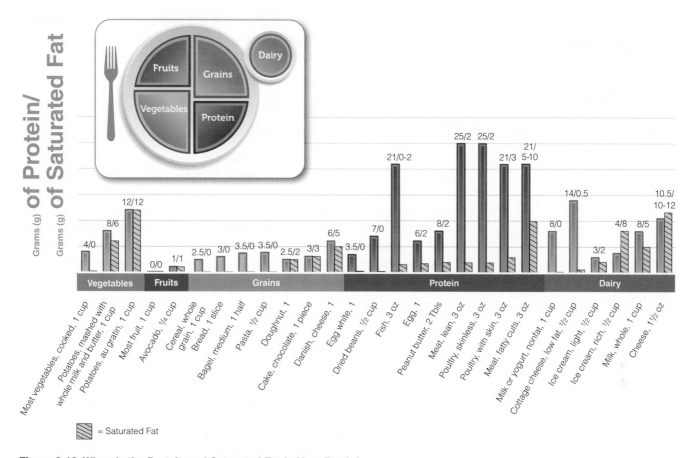

Figure 6.13 Where's the Protein and Saturated Fat in Your Foods?
While many foods, in particular dairy foods and meats, can provide a hefty amount of protein, they can also provide a large amount of saturated fat. Choose nonfat and low-fat dairy foods and lean sources of meats and skinless poultry to enjoy your protein without consuming too much saturated fat.

osteoporosis when there is an adequate amount of calcium in a high-protein diet. If a higher dietary protein intake is coming from foods such as low-fat milk, yogurt, and cheese, it can add calcium to the diet.[20] Unfortunately, many American adults are falling short of their recommended calcium intake. If their diets are also high in protein, this isn't a healthy combination for their bones.

➤ *Cancer.* A high-protein diet may increase your risk for cancer; however, this relationship is also less than clear. While large amounts of meat, especially red and processed meats, may increase the risk for colon cancer, research doesn't necessarily support a connection between high amounts of total protein and increased colon cancer risk.[21]

One final health concern surrounding a high-protein diet is the displacement of other foods. If your diet is overloaded with protein-rich foods, such as meat, fish, and poultry, they will likely crowd out other nutrient- and fiber-rich foods. As you know, a diet that contains high fiber and a wide variety of nutrient-dense foods can help you reduce your risk for several chronic diseases, such as cancer, heart disease, diabetes, and stroke. If you fill up on meat and milk at meals, you might be short-changing yourself on foods, such as whole grains, fruits, and vegetables, that contain disease-fighting compounds.

While many individuals have the luxury of worrying about consuming too much protein, others are desperately trying to meet their daily needs. Let's look at the serious health implications of chronically eating too little dietary protein.

Eating Too Little Protein Can Lead to Poor Bone Health and Malnutrition

Eating too little protein can lead to many health problems, including compromised bone health. In fact, eating too little protein has been shown to lead to loss of bone mass. A study of more than 500 women over age 55 showed that higher dietary protein consumption was associated with more dense bone. Another study of more than 2,000 males and females ranging in age from 50 to 89 showed that those under the age of 70 who had a diet higher in protein had 65 percent fewer hip fractures compared with those with the lowest protein intake. When it comes to our bones, too much protein or too little can both be unhealthy.[22]

Protein-Energy Malnutrition

Every day, almost 17,000 children around the world—approximately 6 million annually—die because they don't have access to enough food.[23] These children's diets are inadequate in either protein or calories or both, a condition known as **protein-energy malnutrition (PEM).** When calories and protein are inadequate, dietary protein is used for energy rather than reserved for its numerous other roles in the body. Moreover, other important nutrients, such as vitamins and minerals, also tend to be in short supply, which further compounds PEM.

Many factors can lead to PEM, including poverty, poor food quality, insufficient food intake, unsanitary living conditions, ignorance regarding the proper feeding of children, and stopping lactation (nursing) too early.[24] Because they are growing, infants and children have higher nutritional needs for their size than adults. They are also dependent on others to provide them with food. For these reasons, PEM is more frequently seen in infants and children than in adults.

Because protein is needed for so many functions in the body, it isn't surprising that a chronic protein deficiency can lead to many health problems. For example, without adequate dietary protein, the cells in the lining of the gastrointestinal tract aren't adequately replaced when they are routinely sloughed off. The inability to regenerate these cells inhibits their function. Absorption of the little amount of food that may be available is reduced, and bacteria that normally stay in the intestines can get into the blood and poison it, causing septicemia. Malnourished individuals frequently have a compromised immune system, which can make fighting even a minor infection, such as a respiratory infection or diarrhea, impossible. Malnourished children have died after exposure to measles as well as after bouts of diarrhea.[25]

While deficiencies of both calories and protein often occur simultaneously, sometimes one condition may be more prevalent than the other. A severe deficiency of protein is called **kwashiorkor,** whereas a severe deficiency of calories is called **marasmus.** A condition that is caused by a chronic deficiency of both calories and protein is called marasmic kwashiorkor.

Kwashiorkor

Kwashiorkor was first observed in the 1930s in tribes in West Africa: often the first-born child became sick when a new sibling became part of the family. Typically, the newborn displaced the first child, usually around 18 months of age, from his or her

protein-energy malnutrition (PEM) A lack of sufficient dietary protein and/or calories.

kwashiorkor A state of PEM where there is a severe deficiency of dietary protein.

marasmus A state of PEM where there is a severe deficiency of calories that perpetuates wasting; also called starvation.

lactating mother and her nutritionally balanced breast milk. The first child was then relegated to an inadequate and unbalanced diet high in carbohydrate-rich grains but severely deficient in protein. This sets the stage for serious medical complications.

A classic symptom of severe kwashiorkor is edema in the legs, feet, and stomach (see **Figure 6.14**). As we discussed earlier, protein plays an important role in maintaining fluid balance in the blood and around the cells. With protein deficiency, fluid accumulates in the spaces surrounding the cells, causing swelling. The body wastes away as the muscle proteins are broken down to generate the amino acids needed to synthesize other proteins. Consequently, muscle tone and strength diminish. Those with kwashiorkor often have skin that is dry and peeling. Rashes or lesions can also develop. Their hair is often brittle and can be easily pulled out. These children often appear pale, have facial expressions that display sadness and apathy, and cry easily. They are prone to infections, rapid heart-beats, excess fluid in the lungs, pneumonia, septicemia, and water and electrolyte imbalances—all of which can be deadly.[26]

Marasmus and Marasmic Kwashiorkor

The bloating seen in kwashiorkor is the opposite of the frail, emaciated appearance of marasmus (**Figure 6.15**). Because they are not consuming enough calories, marasmic individuals are starving. They are often not even at 60 percent of their desirable body weight. Marasmic children's bodies use all available calories to stay alive; thus, growth is interrupted. These children are weakened and appear apathetic. Many can't stand without support. They look old beyond their years, as the loss of fat in the face—one of the last places that the body loses fat during starvation—causes the disappearance of a robust childlike appearance. Their hair is thin and dry and lacks the sheen seen in the hair of healthy children. Their body temperature and blood pressure are both low, and they are prone to dehydration, infections, and unnecessary blood clotting.[27]

Individuals with marasmic kwashiorkor have the worst of both conditions. They often have edema in their legs and arms, yet have a "skin and bones" appearance in other parts of the body. When these individuals are provided with medical and nutritional treatment, such as receiving adequate protein, the edema subsides and their clinical symptoms more closely resemble that of a person with marasmus.

Appropriate medical care and treatment can dramatically reduce the 20 to 30 percent mortality rate seen among children with severe PEM worldwide.[28] The treatment for PEM should be carefully and slowly implemented using a three-step approach. The first step addresses the life-threatening factors, such as severe dehydration and fluid and nutrient imbalances. The second step is to restore the individual's depleted tissues by gradually providing nutritionally dense calories and high-quality protein. The third step involves transitioning the person to foods and introducing physical activity. The only successful way to cure PEM is to eradicate it.[29]

The Take-Home Message A high-protein diet may play a role in increasing the risk of heart disease, kidney problems, and calcium loss from bone. Consuming too much protein from animal sources can increase the amount of heart-unhealthy saturated fat in your diet. Too many protein-rich foods in the diet can displace whole grains, fruits, and vegetables, which have been shown to help reduce many chronic diseases. A low-protein diet has also been shown to lead to loss of bone mass. PEM is caused by an inadequate amount of protein and/or calories in the diet. A severe deficiency of protein is called kwashiorkor; a deficiency of calories is called marasmus. These conditions can be improved with proper food and treatment.

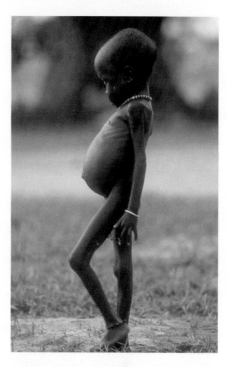

Figure 6.14 Kwashiorkor
The edema in this child's belly is a classic sign of kwashiorkor.

Figure 6.15 Marasmus
The emaciated appearance of this child is a sign (symptom) of marasmus.

How Do Vegetarians Meet Their Protein Needs?

What do spaghetti topped with marinara sauce, cheese pizza, and macaroni and cheese all have in common? These common, classic **vegetarian** meals all lack meat.

For many people, being a vegetarian is a lifestyle choice made for a particular reason. While some vegetarians avoid foods from animal sources for ethical, religious, or environmental reasons, others choose a vegetarian lifestyle because they believe it's better for their health.[30] An estimated 3 percent of American adults, or about 6 million people, follow a vegetarian diet.[31]

Because vegetarians avoid meat, which is high in protein, they need to be sure to get adequate protein from other food sources. Vegetarians can meet their daily protein needs by consuming a varied plant-based diet that contains protein-rich meat alternatives such as soy, dried beans and other legumes, and nuts. Some vegetarians include protein-rich eggs, dairy foods, and fish as part of their diet. There are several types of vegetarians and associated ranges of acceptable foods. See Table 6.6 for a description of vegetarian diets and the foods associated with each.

In the United States, the vegetarian food market has grown to be a $1.1 billion-plus industry as manufacturers accommodate growing consumer demand with an array of new vegetarian products each year.[32] More than 70 percent of sit-down restaurants offer a vegetarian entrée on their menus, and even some fast-food restaurants now offer veggie burgers. University food services are increasingly making vegetarian options available to meet growing student demand.

vegetarian A person who doesn't eat meat, fish, or poultry or (sometimes) foods made from these animal sources.

Table 6.6
The Many Types of Vegetarians

Type	Dietary Patterns	
	Does Eat	**Doesn't Eat**
Semivegetarian	A vegetarian diet that occasionally includes meat, fish, and poultry	Meat, fish, and poultry on occasion
Lacto-ovo-vegetarian	Grains, vegetables, fruits, legumes, seeds, nuts, dairy foods, eggs	Meat, fish, and poultry
Lacto-vegetarian	Grains, vegetables, fruits, legumes, seeds, nuts, dairy foods	Meat, fish, poultry, and eggs
Ovo-vegetarian	Grains, vegetables, fruits, legumes, seeds, nuts, eggs	Meat, fish, poultry, dairy foods
Vegan	Grains, vegetables, fruits, legumes, seeds, nuts	Any animal foods, meat, fish, poultry, dairy foods, eggs

The Potential Benefits and Risks of a Vegetarian Diet

A plant-based diet can be rich in high-fiber whole grains, vegetables, fruits, legumes, and nuts and thus naturally lower in saturated fat and cholesterol. This type of diet contains the fundamentals for reducing the risk of the following diseases:

➤ *Heart disease.* Vegetarian food staples, such as soy, nuts, and soluble fiber–rich foods, such as beans and oats, have been shown to reduce blood cholesterol levels. Numerous studies have shown that the rates of deaths from heart disease are about 25 percent lower among vegetarians than among nonvegetarians.[33]

➤ *High blood pressure.* Vegetarians tend to have lower blood pressure than meat eaters. The incidence of high blood pressure has been shown to be more than two times higher in nonvegetarians.[34] High blood pressure is a risk factor not only for heart disease but also for stroke.

➤ *Type 2 diabetes.* You know from Chapter 4 that a plant-based diet can help reduce the risk for type 2 diabetes, so it shouldn't surprise you that vegetarians tend to have a lower risk for diabetes. Diabetes is also a risk for heart disease. For people with diabetes, consuming foods rich in fiber and low in saturated fat and cholesterol makes eating a vegetarian diet an attractive strategy to better manage this disease.[35]

➤ *Certain types of cancer.* Vegetarian diets have been shown to reduce the risk for both prostate and colon cancer. Respected health organizations, such as the American Institute for Cancer Research and the American Cancer Society, advocate a plant-based diet to reduce the risk for cancer.[36]

➤ *Obesity.* A plant-based diet containing mostly fiber-rich whole grains and low-calorie, nutrient-rich vegetables and fruits tends to "fill you up before it fills you out," making you more likely to eat fewer calories overall. Hence, the plant-based foods of a vegetarian diet can be a healthy, satisfying strategy for those fighting the battle against obesity.

In addition to diet, other lifestyle habits such as not smoking, abstaining from alcohol and recreational drugs, and enjoying daily physical activity, which are all common among vegetarians, may also contribute to their lower risk of the above conditions.

The biggest risk of a vegetarian diet is in not consuming enough of the nutrients, such as protein and vitamin B_{12}, that are found in abundance in animal foods. Strictly avoiding meat, fish, poultry, and foods derived from animal sources can be *unhealthy* if you don't replace these foods with healthy, nutrient-dense, nonmeat alternatives. Also, vegetarian meals may not always be low in saturated fat if full-fat dairy products are heavily used. Planning is needed to be a healthy vegetarian.

Hungry for More Vegetarian Advice?

Need some more help in planning a vegetarian diet? Click your way through a menu of more delicious vegetarian tips at http://people.bu.edu/salge.

How You Can Be a Healthy Vegetarian

To avoid nutrient deficiencies, vegetarians must consume adequate amounts of all nutrients by eating a wide variety of foods (see **Figure 6.16** on page 212). Some nutrients found in abundance in animal foods, including protein, iron, zinc, calcium, vitamin D, riboflavin (a B vitamin), vitamin B_{12}, vitamin A, and omega-3 fatty acids, are particularly important to monitor. The tips in Table 6.7 can help you easily incorporate these

Table 6.7

Nutrients That Could Be MIA (Missing in Action) in a Vegetarian Diet

Vegetarians need to take care in planning a diet that meets all their nutritional needs. Here are the nutrients that a vegetarian diet could fall short of, some vegetarian food sources for these nutrients, and tips on how to enjoy these foods as part of a balanced diet.

Nutrient	Risks	Vegetarian Food Sources	Table Tips
Protein	A vegetarian's protein needs can be met by consuming a *variety* of plant foods. A combination of protein-rich soy foods, legumes, nuts, and/or seeds should be eaten daily.	Soybeans, soy burgers, tofu, tempeh, nuts, peanuts, peanut butter, legumes, sunflower seeds, milk, soy milk, yogurt, cheese	• Add nuts to your morning cereal. • Add beans to your salads, soups, and main entrées. • Have a soy burger for lunch. • Use tofu in stir-fries, rice and pasta dishes, and casseroles. • Snack on a soy milk and banana or berry shake.
Iron	The form of iron in plants is not as easily absorbed as the type in meat, milk, and poultry. Also, phytate in grains and rice and polyphenols in tea and coffee can inhibit iron absorption. The iron needs of vegetarians are about 1½ times higher than those of nonvegetarians. Vitamin C enhances the absorption of the iron in plant foods.	Iron-fortified cereals, enriched grains, pasta, bread, oatmeal, potatoes, wheat germ, cashews and other nuts, sunflower seeds, legumes, soybeans, tofu, bok choy, broccoli, mushrooms, dried fruits	• Make sure your morning cereal is iron fortified. • Add soybeans to your lunchtime salad. • Eat bread with your salad lunch or make a sandwich. • Pack a trail mix of dried fruits and nuts for a snack. • Add vitamin C–rich foods (broccoli, tomatoes, citrus fruits) to all your meals.
Zinc	The absorption of zinc is enhanced by animal protein. Eating a vegetarian diet means that you lose out on this benefit and are more likely to develop a deficiency. Phytate also binds zinc, making it unavailable to your body. A vegan's zinc needs may be as much as 50 percent higher than a nonvegetarian's.	Soybeans, soy milk, tofu, tempeh, fortified soy burgers, legumes, nuts, sunflower seeds, wheat germ, fortified ready-to-eat cereals, mushrooms, low-fat or nonfat milk, yogurt, and cheese	• Douse your morning cereal with low-fat milk. • Add low-fat cheese and soybeans to your lunchtime salad. • Snack on sunflower seeds. • Top an afternoon yogurt with wheat germ. • Add soybeans to your dinner rice.
Calcium	Calcium is abundant in lean dairy foods such as nonfat or low-fat milk, yogurt, and cheese, so obtaining adequate amounts shouldn't be difficult if you consume these foods. Calcium-fortified soy milk and orange juice, as well as tofu, can provide about the same amount of calcium per serving as is found in dairy foods.	Low-fat or nonfat milk, yogurt, and cheese, fortified soy milk, soy yogurt, and soy cheese, calcium-fortified orange juice, legumes, sesame tahini, tofu processed with calcium, bok choy, broccoli, kale, collard greens, mustard greens, okra	• Add milk to your morning cereal and coffee. • Have at least one yogurt a day. • Have a glass of calcium-fortified orange juice with lunch. • Snack on low-fat cheese or yogurt in the afternoon. • Eat green vegetables often at dinner.

Table 6.7 continued

Nutrients That Could Be MIA (Missing in Action) in a Vegetarian Diet

Nutrient	Risks	Vegetarian Food Sources	Table Tips
Vitamin D	Some vegetarians will need to consume vitamin D–fortified milk or soy products.	Low-fat or nonfat milk, egg yolk, fortified yogurt, soy milk, soy yogurt, ready-to-eat cereals; a vitamin supplement	• Have a glass of milk or soy milk at breakfast every day. • Make sure your morning cereal is vitamin D fortified. • Use fortified evaporated skim milk as a base for cream sauces. • Snack on fortified cereals. • Have a fortified yogurt each day.
Vitamin B_{12}	Animal foods are the only naturally occurring food source of B_{12}, so it is extremely important that vegetarians, especially strict vegans, look to fortified cereals and soy milk or a supplement to meet their daily needs.	Low-fat and nonfat milk, yogurt, or cheese, eggs, fortified soy milk, ready-to-eat cereals, soy burgers, egg substitutes; vitamin supplement	• Make sure your morning cereal is fortified with vitamin B_{12}. • Drink a cup of milk or fortified soy milk with your meals. • Top an afternoon yogurt snack with a fortified cereal. • Try an egg-substitute omelet for lunch. • Use fortified soy "meat" alternatives at dinner.
Vitamin A	Vitamin A is found only in animal foods. However, vegetarians can meet their needs by consuming the vitamin A precursor, beta-carotene.	Fortified low-fat or nonfat milk and soy milk, apricots, cantaloupe, mangoes, pumpkin, kale, spinach	• Enjoy a slice or bowl of cantaloupe in the morning. • Snack on dried apricots. • Add spinach to your lunchtime salad. • Drink a glass of fortified milk or soy milk with dinner. • Try mangoes for a sweet dessert.
Omega-3 fatty acids	If your vegetarian diet doesn't include fish, you may not be consuming enough of the essential omega-3 fatty acid called alpha-linolenic acid.	Fish, especially fatty fish such as salmon and sardines, walnuts, flaxseed and flaxseed oil, soybean and canola oil	• Add walnuts to baked breads and muffins. • Try canned salmon on top of your lunchtime salad. • Top your yogurt with ground flaxseeds. • Have fish regularly for dinner. • Cook with canola and flaxseed oil.

Figure 6.16 Vegetarian Food Guide Pyramid
Vegetarians should eat a variety of foods from each food group, especially legumes, nuts, and oils, to obtain essential fatty acids, and adequate protein, calcium, and vitamin B$_{12}$.

Source: Reprinted from *Journal of the American Dietetic Association.* Vol. 103, Issue 6, Messina et al., "A new food guide for North American vegetarians," pp. 771–775. © 2003, with permission from Elsevier. www.sciencedirect.com/science/journal.

nutrients in a vegetarian diet, and the feature box on page 214 gives an overview of the abundance of soy products available on the market. Table 6.8 compares the nutrient composition of a traditional meat-based meal and a similar meal made solely from plant foods. Comparing these nutrient profiles may surprise you! Finally, when following a vegetarian diet, a vitamin and mineral supplement may be necessary.

Athletes Can Follow a Vegetarian Diet

Sports dietitians agree that athletes consuming a vegetarian diet can keep their competitive edge—with careful planning. Soy products, eggs, yogurt, cow's milk, cheese, and protein shakes can help a vegetarian athlete get needed amounts of protein, vitamin B$_{12}$, calcium, and vitamin D. Iron is a critical nutrient for athletes, because it carries oxygen to working muscles. Zinc is important to help tissues recover from the stress of training. Fortified foods can help increase the level of these minerals in a vegetarian diet, and a daily multivitamin/mineral supplement can provide added insurance. For athletes who don't consume fish, soy products, walnuts, flaxseeds, soybean oil, and canola oil provide omega-3 fatty acids. Vegetarian athletes should consult a registered dietitian to plan a nutritionally complete diet.

Table 6.8

How Does a Vegetarian Meal Compare?

Similar to meat meals, vegetarian meals can provide a robust amount of protein and iron with less heart-unhealthy saturated fat and cholesterol. While a tofu stir-fry doesn't provide as much zinc or vitamin B$_{12}$ as meat, it is a fabulous source of calcium, a mineral many adults are falling short of.

	Beef Stir-Fry (per Serving)	vs.	Tofu Stir-Fry (per Serving)
Protein	38 grams		26 grams
Saturated Fat	3.3 grams		1.8 grams
Dietary Cholesterol	105 milligrams		0
Iron	3.9 milligrams		5.1 milligrams
Calcium	34 milligrams		450 milligrams
Zinc	6.8 milligrams		2.9 milligrams
Vitamin B$_{12}$	2.5 micrograms		0

NutriTools

Build a Salad

Can you create a healthy, protein-filled salad? Visit www.pearsonhighered.com/blake and complete this interactive NutriTools activity to find out.

The Take-Home Message Vegetarian diets can be a healthy eating style that may help reduce the risk of some chronic diseases. Some vegetarians abstain from all animal foods, while others may eat animal foods (such as eggs and dairy products) in limited amounts. All vegetarians must take care in planning a varied diet that meets their nutrient needs, especially for protein, iron, zinc, calcium, vitamin D, riboflavin (a B vitamin), vitamin B$_{12}$, vitamin A, and omega-3 fatty acids.

The Joy of Soy

Soy has been used as a dietary staple for centuries in Asia. Soy consumption in the United States, in foods ranging from soy milk to soy bars, has been increasing since the early 1990s. From 1992 to 2008, the market for soy products has grown from $300 million to $4 billion.[2] According to a survey conducted by the United Soybean Board, 84 percent of U.S. consumers perceive soy foods as being healthy and one-third of consumers intentionally seek out soy products on a regular basis.[3]

The popularity of soy foods is increasing among many age groups and ethnic groups, including baby boomers, who are more interested in good health and longevity than their parents' generation was; Asian populations in the United States looking for traditional soy-based foods; and young adults with an increasing interest in vegetarian diets.[4]

Soy is a high-quality protein source that is low in saturated fat and that contains **isoflavones,** which are naturally occurring phytoestrogens (*phyto* = plant). These plant estrogens have a chemical structure similar to human **estrogen.** While they are considered weak estrogens (they have less than a thousandth of the potential activity of estrogen), they may interfere with or mimic some of estrogen's activities in certain cells in the body.[5] Although isoflavones can also be found in other plant foods, such as grains, vegetables, and legumes, soybeans contain the largest amount found in food.

Soy and Your Health

Epidemiological studies, which look at health and disease in populations, have suggested that isoflavones may reduce the risk of chronic diseases, including heart disease and certain cancers. Some other studies suggest that isoflavones may help relieve menopausal symptoms.[6] At the same time, because isoflavones act as weak estrogens in the body, some concern exists that they may be harmful for diseases such as breast cancer.[7]

Eating soy protein as part of a heart-healthy diet may reduce the risk of heart

isoflavones Naturally occurring phytoestrogens, or weak plant estrogens, that function in a fashion similar to the hormone estrogen in the human body.

estrogen The hormone responsible for female sex characteristics.

What's on the Soy Menu?

Tofu

➤ Cooked, puréed soybeans that are processed into a silken, soft, or firm texture; has a neutral flavor, which allows it to blend well

➤ Use the silken version in dips, soups, and cream pies. Use the firm variety in stir-fries or on salads, or marinate it and then bake or grill it.

Edamame

➤ Tender young soybeans; can be purchased fresh, frozen, or canned

➤ Use in salads, grain dishes, stir-fries, and casseroles.

Soy Flour

➤ Made from ground, roasted soybeans

➤ Use it in baked goods such as pancakes, muffins, and cookies. It can also substitute for eggs in baked goods:

Use 1 tbs soy flour combined with 1 tbs of water for each whole egg.

Soy Milk

➤ A soy beverage made from a mixture of ground soybeans and water

➤ Use it in place of cow's milk. Combine soy milk with ice and fruit in a blender for a soy shake.

disease by lowering cholesterol levels. A review of more than 35 research studies showed that soy protein lowered the "bad" LDL cholesterol by about 10 percent.[8] However, recent findings suggest that the lowering effect may be a more modest 3 percent.[9]

Interest in soy as a cancer fighter was sparked after researchers observed that Asian countries had lower rates of breast cancer than Western countries, including the United States. Numerous studies suggest that the isoflavones in soy may help reduce the risk of cancer, as these weak estrogens may have anticancer functions in the body. One of the functions of isoflavones is that they compete with the hormone estrogen for its binding site on specific cells. The isoflavone latches onto the cell and blocks the binding of the hormone. Because estrogen may increase the risk of breast cancer, inhibiting or blocking the actions of estrogen may help reduce the risk.[10]

Timing may be an important part in the preventive role that soy plays in breast cancer. A study of Chinese women found that those who ate the most soy during their adolescent years had a reduced risk of breast cancer in adulthood. The early exposure to soy foods may be protective by stimulating the growth of cells in the breast, enhancing the rate at which the glands mature, and altering the tissues in a beneficial way.[11]

The anticancer role of isoflavones may also be a detriment. There is some concern that once the isoflavones are bound to the estrogen receptors, they can initiate the production of cancer cells, which can *raise* the risk of breast cancer.[12] A review of more than 200 research studies supports the safety of soy isoflavones when consumed as soy and soy products.[13] However, this issue of potentially increasing the risk of breast cancer, especially for those who are at high risk of developing it or who presently have breast cancer, isn't resolved as yet. According to the American Cancer Society, women with breast cancer should consume a healthy, plant-based diet with only moderate amounts of soy foods and should avoid soy-containing pills, powders, and supplements with high levels of isoflavones.[14]

Soy can be an inexpensive, heart-healthy protein source that may also help modestly lower your blood cholesterol. While soy may help lower the risk of certain cancers, it is currently unclear if it is beneficial or harmful for individuals at high risk of developing breast cancer.

Tempeh

➤ Made from cooked whole soybeans that are condensed into a solid block

➤ Can be seasoned and used as a meat substitute.

Miso

➤ A flavorful paste of fermented soybeans used to season foods

➤ Use in soups, stews, and sauces.

Soy Meat Analogs

➤ Products such as hot dogs, sausages, burgers, cold cuts, yogurts, and cheese that are made using soy

➤ Use as a meat substitute at meals and snacks.

Textured Soy Protein

➤ Created from defatted soy flour that has been compressed and dehydrated

➤ Use it as a meat substitute in foods such as meatballs, meatloaf, chili, tacos, and spaghetti sauce.

Protein

What Are Proteins?

Proteins are the predominant structural and functional materials in every cell in your body. Proteins are made up of **amino acids.**

As with carbohydrates and fats, amino acids are made up of carbon, hydrogen, and oxygen atoms. Unlike carbohydrates and fats, amino acid molecules also contain nitrogen.

The atoms that make up every amino acid molecule are clustered into three groups. The **acid group** contains carbon, hydrogen, and oxygen atoms (COOH), which is why it is called an amino "acid." The **amine group** (NH_2) contains the nitrogen. These two groups are the same for every amino acid. The third group, a unique **side chain,** varies from amino acid to amino acid and gives each its distinguishing qualities.

There are 20 different amino acids, nine of which are **essential** and 11 of which are **nonessential.** Essential amino acids are not made in the body and need to be obtained through foods. Nonessential amino acids are synthesized in the body.

Peptide Bonds Link Amino Acids into Protein Chains

Amino acids are joined to each other by **peptide bonds** to build proteins.

Two amino acids joined together form a *dipeptide*. Three amino acids joined together form a *tripeptide*. And a *polypeptide* consists of many amino acids joined together.

Shapes of Proteins Are Altered by Denaturation

The shape of a protein determines its function. The weak bonds between the side chains on the amino acids can be **denatured,** or broken apart, by temperature change or acids, bases, or salts. Although denaturation doesn't alter the sequence of amino acids in the protein strand, changing the protein's shape can alter its function, sometimes permanently.

Functions of Protein

➤ Proteins provide structural and mechanical support and help maintain body tissues.
➤ Proteins build enzymes and hormones.
➤ Proteins help maintain acid-base balance.
➤ Proteins transport substances throughout the body and act as channels in membranes.
➤ Proteins are needed for antibodies and the immune response.
➤ Proteins can provide energy.

Daily Needs

If you are 14 to 18 years old, you need 0.85 gram of protein per kilogram of body weight (g/kg) per day. If you are 19 years

of age or older, you need 0.80 gram per kilogram daily.

Not all proteins are created equal. **Protein quality** is determined by two factors: your body's ability to digest the protein, which is unique to each person, and the types of amino acids (essential, nonessential, or both) that the protein contains.

Proteins that are more easily digested and that contain both essential and nonessential amino acids are of higher quality.

Food Sources

Protein is particularly abundant in meat, fish, poultry, and meat alternatives such as peanut butter and soy. A 3-ounce serving of cooked meat, poultry, or fish provides approximately 21 to 25 grams of protein, or about 7 grams per ounce. Dried beans are not only a good source of protein, but also of fiber. Dairy foods are excellent protein sources and grains and vegetables can also add to your daily protein intake.

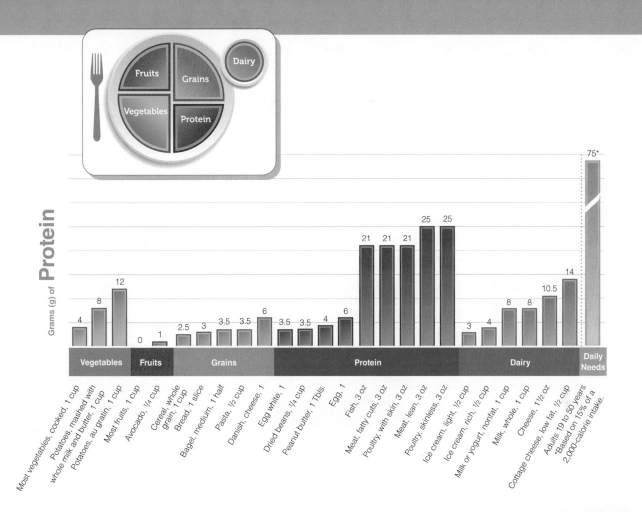

Grams (g) of Protein

Category	Item	Grams
Vegetables	Most vegetables, cooked, 1 cup	4
	Potatoes, mashed with whole milk and butter, 1 cup	8
	Potatoes, au gratin, 1 cup	12
Fruits	Most fruits, 1 cup	0
	Avocado, 1/4 cup	1
Grains	Cereal, whole grain, 1 cup	2.5
	Bread, 1 slice	3
	Bagel, medium, 1 half	3.5
	Pasta, 1/2 cup	3.5
	Danish, cheese, 1	6
Protein	Egg white, 1	3.5
	Dried beans, 1/4 cup	3.5
	Peanut butter, 1 Tbls.	4
	Egg, 1	6
	Fish, 3 oz	21
	Meat, fatty cuts, 3 oz	21
	Poultry, with skin, 3 oz	21
	Meat, lean, 3 oz	25
	Poultry, skinless, 3 oz	25
Dairy	Ice cream, light, 1/2 cup	3
	Ice cream, rich, 1/2 cup	4
	Milk or yogurt, nonfat, 1 cup	8
	Milk, whole, 1 cup	8
	Cheese, 1 1/2 oz	10.5
	Cottage cheese, low fat, 1/2 cup	14
Daily Needs	Adults 19 to 50 years	75*

*Based on 15% of a 2,000-calorie intake.

Too Much or Too Little

A diet that is too high in protein has been linked to health problems such as cardio-vascular disease, kidney stones, osteoporosis, and some types of cancer. Eating too little protein can also lead to compromised bone health.

Diets that are inadequate in protein, calories, or both lead to **protein-energy malnutrition (PEM).** Two forms of PEM are kwashiorkor and marasmus.

Kwashiorkor occurs when a person consumes sufficient calories but not sufficient protein. A classic symptom of severe kwashiorkor is edema in the legs, feet, and stomach. Other symptoms include dry and peeling skin, rashes or lesions, and brittle hair that can be easily pulled out. Marasmus is a disease caused by insufficient intake of energy. Marasmic individuals are starving and are often not even at 60 percent of their desirable body weight for their height.

Kwashiorkor

Marasmus

Terms to Know

amino acid • acid group • amine group • side chain • essential amino acid • nonessential amino acid • peptide bonds • denatured • protein quality • protein-energy malnutrition (PEM)

Made Over, Made Better!

Although protein is an important nutrient in your diet, you don't want to consume protein-rich sources at the expense of your heart. Your best bet is to choose leaner protein foods, as they contain less heart-unhealthy saturated fat.

Here are some typical protein-rich foods made over and made nutritionally better!

If you like this. . .

Try these healthier proteins!

Fried Chicken
3 oz = 246 calories
Protein: 19 grams
Fat: 15 grams
Saturated Fat: 4 grams

Roasted Chicken
3 oz = 147 calories
Protein: 26 grams
Total Fat: 4 grams
Saturated Fat: 1 grams

Hamburger
3 oz = 230 calories
Protein: 22 grams
Fat: 15 grams
Saturated Fat: 6 grams

Veggie Burger
3 oz = 119 calories
Protein: 12 grams
Fat: 4 grams
Saturated Fat: 1 grams

Bologna
3 oz = 261 calories
Protein: 12 grams
Fat: 24 grams
Saturated Fat: 10 grams

Turkey
3 oz = 72 calories
Protein: 13 grams
Fat: 1 grams
Saturated Fat: 0 grams

Fried Fish
3 oz = 195 calories
Protein: 15 grams
Fat: 11 grams
Saturated Fat: 3 grams

Grilled Fish
3 oz = 129 calories
Protein: 16 grams
Fat: 1 grams
Saturated Fat: 0 grams

Source: USDA National Nutrient Database for Standard Reference, www.nal.usda.gov/fnic.

Two Points of View

Are Protein Shakes and Supplements Beneficial? As you've learned in this chapter, our bodies need protein to build muscle, among other functions. But in addition to the protein we get from food, extra protein, in the form of powders and shakes, is frequently touted as a means to build muscle, lose weight, or help the body recover after exercise, especially among athletes and bodybuilders.

Does the average person need these types of specially formulated products? Is more protein always better? Read the arguments for and against and draw your own conclusions.

Yes

- Older adults, who may have limited appetites and be less likely to consume adequate nutrients in foods, as well as people suffering from fatigue or certain other physical ailments, can benefit from a liquid protein supplement.[1]

- High-level strength and endurance athletes can require twice as much protein as nonathletes to repair muscle tissue after bouts of strenuous exercise. Although most can get enough protein through their diet, some may need supplements.[2]

- A supplement containing carbohydrates and a small amount of protein has proven effective, immediately after exercise, in improving muscle protein synthesis, which helps athletes, as well as anyone who exercises, recover faster postworkout and build muscle.[3]

No

- The average American already consumes enough protein to build muscle. Excess calories from additional protein will be stored in the body as fat.[4]

- The claims made on supplement labels, and the purity of the supplements themselves, are not regulated by the FDA.[5]

  - Consuming too much protein, such as from shakes or supplements, can lead to loss of appetite, diarrhea, dehydration, and undue stress on the kidneys.[6]

  - Excess protein can also lead to a loss of calcium through the urine. Chronic calcium loss can increase the risk of osteoporosis, especially in women.[7]

  - While replacing certain meals with protein shakes may help reduce daily calories, thus helping you lose weight, you would miss out on the nutritional benefits of whole foods.[8]

  - Protein supplements tend to be expensive. Recall from the chapter that the average bar will cost about $1–3 each, and the average shake about $1.50, while a just-as-effective peanut butter sandwich costs about $0.22.

What do you think?

1. Do you think most people would benefit from consuming protein bars or shakes? Why or why not? **2.** Are there any benefits of protein supplements that cannot be achieved by consuming protein-rich foods? If yes, what are they? **3.** What role does marketing play in promoting protein shakes and supplements?

Chapter Review

Be a Nutrition Sleuth

Where's the Protein?

After reading this chapter, let's see if you can accurately guess how much protein is in the foods you eat. Go to www.pearsonhighered.com/blake to match the foods with the amount of protein that they provide.

Get Real!

The Real Deal When It Comes to Dietary Protein

Go to www.pearsonhighered.com/blake to plan a realistic day of food choices that will allow you to meet your protein needs without exceeding your upper limits for saturated fat. (Note: You can use the Food Composition Table or the MyDietAnalysis program to help you plan your meals.)

The Top Ten Points to Remember

1. Proteins are made of amino acids, which contain an acid group, an amine group, and a unique side chain. Each group is made of carbon, hydrogen, oxygen, and, in the case of the amine group, nitrogen. There are 20 unique side chains and therefore 20 unique amino acids. Amino acids are joined together by peptide bonds to form proteins.

2. The interactions between the amino acids cause individual proteins to fold into precise three-dimensional shapes. The shape of a protein determines its function. Heat, acids, bases, and salts denature these bonds and disrupt the shape and function of a protein.

3. Of the 20 amino acids, 9 are essential, so you need to obtain them through your diet. Your body can synthesize the remaining 11 amino acids, so they are nonessential.

4. With the help of stomach juices and enzymes, your body digests and breaks down proteins into amino acids to make them available for use. A limited amount of amino acids exists in pools in your body. The DNA in your cells directs the synthesis of proteins. Excess amino acids are also broken down and either stored in another form or used as energy, depending on your needs. The nitrogen is converted to the waste product urea and excreted in your urine.

5. Proteins play many roles in your body. They provide structural and mechanical support, supply materials for ongoing maintenance, form enzymes and hormones, maintain acid-base and fluid balance, transport nutrients, and aid your immune system. Proteins can provide energy, be used to make glucose, and increase satiety at meals. Calories from excess protein will be stored as fat.

6. Healthy adults are usually in a state of nitrogen balance, which means they excrete as much nitrogen as they consume. Pregnant and lactating women and growing children are in a state of positive nitrogen balance because they use additional nitrogen to grow new tissues. People who are malnourished or experiencing medical trauma may be in negative nitrogen balance.

7. Protein quality is determined by the protein digestibility corrected amino acid score (PDCAAS), which is based on the protein's digestibility and its amino acid profile. Protein from animal foods is more easily digested than protein from plant foods. Proteins from animal foods and soy are typically complete proteins and provide all of the essential amino acids along with some nonessential amino acids. Plant proteins are typically incomplete, as they are missing one or more essential amino acids.

8. Adults should consume 0.8 gram of protein for each kilogram of body weight. A varied diet provides most Americans with far more protein than they need. Consuming too much protein from animal sources can increase the amount of heart-unhealthy saturated fat in your diet. A high-protein diet has been associated with the loss of calcium from the body and the development of kidney stones. An excess of protein-rich foods in the diet can displace whole grains, fruits, and vegetables.

9. Protein-energy malnutrition (PEM) is caused by an inadequate amount of protein and/or calories in the diet. Kwashiorkor is a severe deficiency of protein; marasmus is a severe deficiency of calories. A deficiency of both calories and protein is known as marasmic kwashiorkor.

10. Healthy vegetarian diets can reduce the risk of certain chronic diseases. Some vegetarians abstain from all animal foods, while others may eat a limited amount. All vegetarians must take care to eat a varied diet that meets all of their nutrient needs.

Test Your Knowledge

1. A protein's shape, and therefore its function in your body, is determined by the interactions of amino acids in the protein with each other and their environment.
   a. true
   b. false
2. Essential amino acids can be made by the body.
   a. true
   b. false
3. Which of the following will *not* denature a protein?
   a. grilling a chicken breast
   b. frying an egg
   c. marinating a steak in red wine
   d. refrigerating milk
4. Limited amounts of surplus amino acids are stored in your body in your
   a. muscles.
   b. fat stores.
   c. amino acid pools.
   d. stomach.

5. Proteins play important roles in your body, such as
   a. helping you fight the flu.
   b. allowing you to walk, run, sit, and lie down.
   c. aiding in digesting the pizza that you ate for lunch.
   d. transporting fat and cholesterol through your blood.
   e. all of the above.
6. Proteins can be used to make glucose.
   a. true
   b. false
7. Protein is found abundantly in the
   a. dairy group and the fat group.
   b. protein group and the fruit group.
   c. fruit group and the dairy group.
   d. dairy group and the protein group.
   e. vegetable group and the fruit group.
8. Which of the following is a source of complete protein?
   a. kidney beans
   b. peanut butter
   c. soy milk
   d. pasta
9. Kwashiorkor is a type of PEM that develops when
   a. there is a severe deficiency of protein in the diet but an adequate amount of calories.
   b. there are inadequate amounts of both protein and calories in the diet.
   c. there is an inadequate amount of animal protein in the diet.
   d. there are adequate amounts of both protein and calories in the diet.
   e. there is an imbalance of animal and plant proteins in the diet.
10. A lacto-ovo-vegetarian is coming to your house for dinner. You need to make a meal that she will enjoy. An acceptable entrée would be
   a. stir-fried tofu and vegetables over brown rice.
   b. a cheese and broccoli omelet.
   c. baked ziti with ricotta cheese, spinach, and tomato sauce.
   d. a mushroom pizza.
   e. all of the above.

Answers

1. (a) The interactions of the amino acids with each other and with their environment determine the shape, and thus the function, of the proteins in your body.

2. (b) Essential amino acids cannot be made in the body and have to be obtained from foods.

3. (d) Heat and acids will denature proteins. Refrigeration does not alter the bonds between the amino acid side chains and so does not denature proteins.

4. (c) Limited amounts of all the amino acids exist in amino acid pools in your blood and inside your cells, not your stomach. Your muscles contain protein but don't store surplus amino acid. Your fat stores are the result of excess calories from carbohydrates, proteins, and/or fats.

5. (e) You need adequate amounts of protein to fight infections such as the flu, to provide structural and mechanical support when you're moving or lying down, to build enzymes that help you digest your foods, and to transport substances such as fat and cholesterol through your blood.

6. (a) If you don't eat an adequate amount of carbohydrates, your body can break down proteins to create glucose.

7. (d) Both the dairy group and the protein foods group are full of protein-rich food sources. While there is some protein in vegetables, there is little in fruits. Fats do not contain protein.

8. (c) Soy foods such as soy milk provide all the essential amino acids that you need, along with some nonessential amino acids, and thus are a source of complete protein. Kidney beans, peanut butter, and pasta are missing adequate amounts of the essential amino acids.

9. (a) Kwashiorkor occurs when protein is deficient in the diet even though calories may be adequate. Marasmus occurs when calories are inadequate in a person's diet and thus he or she is starving. Protein from animal sources is not necessary because people can meet their protein needs from a combination of plant proteins, such as soy, legumes, grains, and vegetables, as part of a well-balanced diet. There need not be a balance between animal and plant proteins.

10. (e) Because a lacto-ovo-vegetarian avoids meat, poultry, and fish but eats a predominantly plant-based diet with dairy foods and eggs, the tofu stir-fry, cheese omelet, baked ziti, and pizza with any vegetable topping are all fine.

Web Resources

➡ For information on specific genetic disorders, including those that affect protein use in the body, visit the National Human Genome Research Institute at www.genome.gov

➡ For more information on vegetarian diets, visit the Vegetarian Research Group at www.vrg.org

➡ For more information on soy foods, visit the United Soy Board at www.soybean.org

Answers to Myths and Misperceptions

1. **True.** If you make the correct food choices, your body can extract all the building materials it needs to create all of the proteins that it needs. For more on how your body builds proteins, turn to page 188.

2. **True.** Protein also plays other important roles in your body. Turn to page 190 to learn why.

3. **True.** There are thousands of unique enzymes in your body, and the majority are made of protein. Turn to page 191 to discover why you need so many specialized enzymes.

4. **True.** However, burning proteins, rather than carbohydrates or fat, for energy is an inefficient way to use this precious nutrient. To learn why, turn to page 193.

5. **False.** Growing children are in a state of positive nitrogen balance, which means that more nitrogen is being retained by the body (to be incorporated into new body proteins) than is excreted in the urine. Turn to page 195 to learn more.

6. **False.** Although both pasta and chicken can contribute to your daily protein needs, the protein in poultry is more easily digested than the protein found in grains. Turn to page 196 to learn why.

7. **False.** Proteins do play a vital role in your body, but a little can go a long way. For most healthy adults, less than one-fifth of their daily calories should come from dietary protein. For more on how to meet your protein needs, see page 197.

8. **False.** Even an extremely active person or competitive athlete can easily meet his or her protein needs through a well-balanced diet. To learn more about protein bars, turn to page 202.

9. **True.** A high-protein diet that contains artery-clogging saturated fat and low amounts of whole grains, fruits, and vegetables is not heart friendly and may raise your blood cholesterol. To learn more, turn to page 204.

10. **True.** Soy foods are excellent sources of protein, and they help fight certain chronic diseases. Turn to page 214 and find out more.

7
Vitamins

True or False?

1. Vitamins provide your body with **energy**. ⓉⒻ p. 226

2. Taking **vitamin supplements** is *never* harmful because your body eliminates any excesses that you don't need. ⓉⒻ p. 228

3. Carrots, winter squash, and broccoli are good sources of **vitamin A**. ⓉⒻ p. 235

4. Vitamin E is an **antioxidant**. ⓉⒻ p. 238

5. Vitamin K helps keep your **bones** healthy. ⓉⒻ p. 240

6. Your body makes vitamin D with the help of **sunlight**. ⓉⒻ p. 242

7. Folate reduces the risk of certain **birth defects**. ⓉⒻ p. 254

8. Taking vitamin C supplements can help you ward off the **common cold**. ⓉⒻ p. 261

9. **Fortified foods** can help you meet your vitamin needs. ⓉⒻ p. 265

10. Everyone can meet their vitamin needs through **food**, so taking supplements is never necessary. ⓉⒻ p. 267

See page 275 for answers to these Myths and Misperceptions.

Brendan is a college freshman and future track star at a state university. In addition to carrying a full course load and working part-time at the campus bookstore, Brendan works out at least two hours a day on the outdoor track. Within the first few weeks of school, Brendan caught a cold and had a stuffy nose and headache for a few days. As soon as he recovered, a second cold set in and lingered for more than a week.

Hoping to ward off another bout of illness, Brendan went online to find out what he could do to build up his immune system. He found websites that claimed that vitamin C would help protect against colds. After a visit to his local health food store, Brendan began to take vitamin C tablets, and soon his daily intake was 3,500 milligrams, more than

35 times his daily needs. Within a week, his long training runs were interrupted with bouts of diarrhea. He visited the student health center and complained to the staff doctor that the only training he was getting was running to the bathroom. The doctor recognized Brendan's symptoms as common in runners who take particular supplements. Can you guess what caused Brendan's intestinal discomforts? What do you think he needs to do to alleviate his symptoms? In this chapter, we'll discuss the numerous roles of vitamins in the body, as well as the consequences of consuming too little or too much of any one of them. We'll also discuss the best ways to preserve vitamins in your foods when cooking and storing them, and introduce the concept of antioxidants.

Chapter Objectives

After reading this chapter, you will be able to:

1. Describe the characteristics of vitamins.

2. Explain the differences between fat-soluble and water-soluble vitamins, and classify each vitamin according to its solubility.

3. Define the term *antioxidant* and explain which vitamins perform this function.

4. List at least one good food source for each of vitamins A, D, E, and K.

5. List at least one major role in the body for vitamins A, D, E, and K.

6. Name at least one toxicity symptom for a fat-soluble vitamin.

7. List at least one good food source for each of the water-soluble vitamins.

8. Name at least one disease associated with a water-soluble vitamin deficiency.

9. Explain the role of vitamin supplements in the diet.

While vitamins (*vita* = vital) have always been in foods, they remained nameless and undiscovered substances as recently as 100 years ago. If you were to flash back to the early part of the twentieth century, you would find scientists hard at work searching for substances to cure diseases such as beriberi, scurvy, and rickets.[1] These may sound like the names of rock bands to you, but they're actually the devastating diseases caused by deficiencies of thiamin (for beriberi), vitamin C (for scurvy), and vitamin D (for rickets). Throughout the twentieth century, scientists received Nobel Prizes for their discoveries of the vitamins that cured these and other diseases. By the 1940s, the U.S. government mandated that specific vitamins be added to grains and milk to improve the nation's health by improving people's diet.

Now flash forward to the latter part of the twentieth century, when an improved diet meant that vitamin deficiencies became less of an issue for most Americans. Scientists shifted their focus from using vitamins to cure disease to using them to prevent disease. Today, research is being done to find out how vitamins affect and prevent everything from birth defects to heart disease and cancer.

What Are Vitamins?

Vitamins are tasteless organic compounds that you need in small amounts for growth, reproduction, and overall good health. Although they don't provide energy (calories) for your body, they are essential nutrients for your well-being. A deficiency of any one will cause physiological symptoms. There are 13 vitamins, and you get most of them by eating a variety of foods from each of the food groups (see **Figure 7.1**), though the vitamins D, K, niacin, and biotin can also be synthesized in your body or by microorganisms in the intestinal tract.

A chronic deficiency of any of the essential vitamins can cause a cascade of symptoms from scaly skin to blindness. However, consuming too much of some vitamins can also cause adverse effects that can be as damaging as consuming too little. Balance is always your best bet when it comes to meeting your vitamin needs.

Vegetables	Fruit	Grains	Protein	Dairy
Folate	Folate	Folic acid	Niacin	Riboflavin
Vitamin A	Vitamin C	Niacin	Thiamin	Vitamin A
Vitamin C		Vitamin B_6	Vitamin B_6	Vitamin B_{12}
Vitamin E		Vitamin B_{12} (if fortified)	Vitamin B_{12}	Vitamin D
		Riboflavin		
		Thiamin		

Vitamins Are Either Fat Soluble or Water Soluble

A vitamin is either fat soluble or water soluble, depending on how it is absorbed and handled in your body. Fat-soluble vitamins need dietary fat to be properly absorbed, whereas water-soluble vitamins are absorbed with water. Vitamins A, D, E, and K are fat soluble; the B vitamins and vitamin C are water soluble (**Figure 7.2**).

The fat-soluble vitamins are absorbed at the beginning of your small intestine (**Figure 7.3**). They are packaged with fatty acids and bile in micelles, small transport carriers that shuttle them close to the intestinal wall. Once there, the fat-soluble vitamins travel through the cells in the intestinal wall and are packaged with fat and other

Fat-soluble vitamins	Water-soluble vitamins

Figure 7.2 Categorizing the Vitamins: Fat Soluble and Water Soluble
Fat-soluble vitamins need dietary fat to be properly absorbed, whereas water-soluble vitamins are absorbed with water.

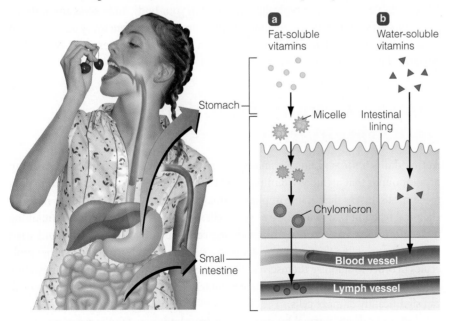

Figure 7.3 Digesting and Absorbing Vitamins
(a) Once in the small intestine, the fat-soluble vitamins are packaged with fatty acids and bile in micelles that transport them to the intestinal wall. The fat-soluble vitamins travel through the cells in the intestinal wall and are packaged with fat and other lipids in chylomicrons. The chylomicrons travel through the lymph system and into the bloodstream. **(b)** The water-soluble vitamins are absorbed directly into the bloodstream from the small intestine.

vitamins Essential nutrients that your body needs in small amounts to grow, reproduce, and maintain good health.

Table 7.1

Fat-Soluble vs Water-Soluble Vitamins

	Fat Soluble: A, D, E, K	Water Soluble: Bs and C
Requirements	Needed in small amounts	Needed in small amounts
Absorption	Need fat to be absorbed	Absorbed with water
	Absorbed in upper part of small intestine	Most absorbed in upper part of the small intestine
		Vitamin B_{12} absorbed in the lower part of the small intestine
Transport through Body	Packed in micelles and chylomicrons in lymph	Enter bloodstream directly
Storage in Body	Stored in liver, fat, and muscle tissue	Not stored in body
		Excess amounts excreted in the urine
Toxicity	Can be toxic in high doses	Not toxic, *but* excesses can be harmful
Major Food Sources	Fortified milk, oils	Fortified grains, whole fruits and vegetables

 NutriTools

Let's Go to Lunch: Water-Soluble Vitamins

What water-soluble vitamins are in your lunch? Visit www.pearsonhighered.com/blake and complete this interactive NutriTools activity.

antioxidants Substances that neutralize free radicals. Vitamins A, C, and E and beta-carotene are antioxidants.

oxidation The process during which oxygen combines with other molecules.

free radicals Unstable oxygen-containing molecules that can damage the cells of the body and possibly contribute to the increased risk of chronic diseases.

lipids in chylomicrons (one of the lipoprotein carriers discussed in Chapter 5). The vitamins then travel through your lymph system before they enter your bloodstream.

Fat-soluble vitamins are stored in your body and used as needed when your dietary intake falls short. Your liver is the main storage depot for vitamin A and to a lesser extent vitamins K and E, whereas vitamin D is mainly stored in your fat and muscle tissues. Because they are stored in the body, large quantities of some of the fat-soluble vitamins, particularly A and D, can build up to the point of toxicity, causing harmful symptoms and conditions.

Water-soluble vitamins are absorbed with water and enter your bloodstream directly. Most water-soluble vitamins are absorbed in the upper portion of your small intestine, although vitamin B_{12} is absorbed in the lower part of your small intestine. Water-soluble vitamins are typically not stored in your body, and excess amounts are excreted, so it's important to consume adequate amounts of them every day. Note that even though most water-soluble vitamins aren't stored, dietary excesses can still be harmful. Table 7.1 provides a summary of the two categories of vitamins.

Some Vitamins Function as Antioxidants

Antioxidants (*anti* = against; *oxidants* = oxygen-containing substances) are a group of compounds that includes vitamins E and C, the mineral selenium, and certain phytochemicals. Just as their name implies, antioxidants counteract **oxidation,** a harmful chemical reaction that takes place in your cells. During oxidation, oxygen-containing molecules called **free radicals** can damage cell structure, cell proteins, and even DNA.[2] Like prowling thieves, the unstable free radicals steal electrons from other molecules in order to stabilize themselves. The robbed molecule then itself becomes a free radical, and looks for another molecule to attack. This chain reaction, if not stopped, can significantly damage cells.

Free radicals are normal by-products of your body's metabolic reactions, which release energy from food. They can also result from exposure to chemicals in the environment (such as cigarette smoke and air pollution) and from the damaging effects of the sun's ultraviolet rays on unprotected skin.

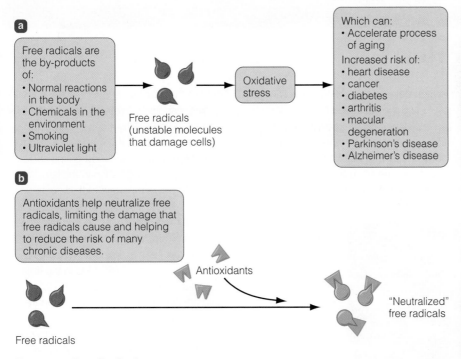

a Free radicals are the by-products of:
- Normal reactions in the body
- Chemicals in the environment
- Smoking
- Ultraviolet light

Free radicals (unstable molecules that damage cells)

Oxidative stress

Which can:
- Accelerate process of aging

Increased risk of:
- heart disease
- cancer
- diabetes
- arthritis
- macular degeneration
- Parkinson's disease
- Alzheimer's disease

b Antioxidants help neutralize free radicals, limiting the damage that free radicals cause and helping to reduce the risk of many chronic diseases.

Free radicals

Antioxidants

"Neutralized" free radicals

Figure 7.4 Free Radicals

a Normal vision and the ability to clearly see the world around you is often taken for granted.

b People with age-related macular degeneration (AMD) have difficulty seeing things directly in front of them.

c Cataracts cause vision to become cloudy.

Figure 7.5 Normal and Impaired Vision

Source: National Institutes of Health, National Eye Institute.

Antioxidants are part of your body's natural defense system to harness free radicals and stop them from damaging cells (**Figure 7.4**). If free radicals accumulate faster than your body can neutralize them (a condition known as *oxidative stress*), their effects can contribute to various health problems, including heart disease, cancer, type 2 diabetes, arthritis, and Alzheimer's disease.[3]

Free radicals can also damage your eyes by contributing to age-related macular degeneration (AMD) and cataracts. **Age-related macular degeneration (AMD)** results from damage to the macula, a tiny area of the retina that is needed for central vision (the ability to see things that are directly in front of you). AMD can make activities such as reading, driving, and watching television impossible (compare **Figure 7.5a** with **Figure 7.5b**). It is usually the culprit when Americans 60 years of age or older experience blindness.[4] A study conducted by the National Eye Institute (NEI) discovered that supplements containing large amounts of antioxidants (vitamin C, vitamin E, and beta-carotene), with the minerals zinc and copper, are effective in reducing the risk for AMD, as well as the extent of vision loss.[5]

A **cataract** is a disorder in which the lens of the eye becomes cloudy, resulting in blurred vision (see **Figure 7.5c**). More than half of all Americans have experienced cataracts by the time they reach 80 years of age, and many undergo surgery to remove them.[6] The NEI recommends consuming antioxidant- and carotenoid-rich fruits and vegetables, such as citrus fruits, broccoli, and leafy dark green vegetables, for the health of your eyes.[7]

There is no question that diets high in antioxidant-rich fruits, vegetables, and whole grains are associated with a lower incidence of some diseases. However, these foods contain other compounds that may work with antioxidants to provide protection. For example, **phytochemicals** (*phyto* = plant), naturally occurring plant compounds that give fruits and vegetables their vibrant colors, have many beneficial functions in the body, such as acting as antioxidants, stimulating the immune system, and interacting with hormones that may help prevent certain cancers.[8]

age-related macular degeneration (AMD) A disease that affects the macula of the retina, causing blurry vision.

cataract A common eye disorder that occurs when the lens of the eye becomes cloudy.

phytochemicals Naturally occurring substances in fruits, vegetables, and whole grains that protect against certain chronic diseases.

B Vitamins for Your Heart

In the late 1970s, researchers made a curious discovery. They noticed that individuals with a very rare genetic disorder, whereby they have too much of the amino acid homocysteine in their blood, suffer from a higher than average incidence of heart disease. Since then, approximately 80 research studies have found an association between high levels of homocysteine and the increased risk for heart disease. Though it isn't known exactly how this amino acid contributes to heart disease, it may be that excessive amounts of homocysteine injure the arteries, decrease the flexibility of the blood vessels, or increase the likelihood of clots forming in the blood. Because vitamin B_6, folate, and vitamin B_{12} are all involved in breaking down homocysteine in the body, researchers began studying the effect of these vitamins on this amino acid.[1]

Numerous studies have suggested that low blood levels of these B vitamins, especially folate, are associated with an increased level of homocysteine in the body. In fact, the mandatory addition of folic acid to enriched grains and grain products that began in the late 1990s to prevent certain birth defects may also be fighting heart disease. In a study of more than 1,000 individuals, the average blood level of folate was higher and the level of the amino acid homocysteine lower in individuals seen in the time period after implementation of the folic acid enrichment program than compared with before the program began.[2]

Studies are currently under way to determine if taking supplements of these B vitamins will lower the risk of heart disease. Some studies have shown promise, but others have not.[3] Until more is known, you should eat a diet that is naturally rich in these B vitamins.

Salad Bar Savvy

A trip to your local salad bar can be a wonderful way to add vitamin-rich vegetables to your diet. However, some of the food choices at a salad bar may also be high in heart-unhealthy saturated fat. To learn how to build a heart-friendly, vitamin-rich salad at the salad bar, visit www.pearsonhighered.com/blake.

bioavailability The degree to which a nutrient is absorbed from foods and used in the body.

The big question that remains is if antioxidant *supplements* provide the same health protection as antioxidants consumed in foods. As you will soon read, too much of vitamins C and E, as well as beta-carotene supplements—all of which are antioxidants—can cause health problems. At this time, the American Heart Association, National Cancer Institute, and United States Preventive Services Task Force do not advocate taking supplements to reduce the risk of specific diseases, but encourage eating a phytochemical- and antioxidant-rich, well-balanced diet.[9] Filling your plate with a colorful variety of plant-based foods is currently one of the best-known strategies to fight chronic diseases. Table 7.2 provides you with a list of disease-fighting phytochemicals and their food sources.

Vitamins Differ in Bioavailability

Not all of the vitamins consumed in foods are available to be used in the body. In other words, they are not 100 percent bioavailable. The **bioavailability** of individual vitamins varies according to several factors, including the amount of the vitamin in the food; whether the food is cooked, raw, or refined; how efficiently the food is digested and absorbed; the individual's nutritional status; and whether or not the vitamin is natural or synthetic. In general, if the body needs more vitamins, a greater percentage will be absorbed. For example, a young child or pregnant woman will absorb more ingested vitamins than will a nonpregnant adult.

Table 7.2

The Phytochemical Color Guide

The National Cancer Institute recommends eating a variety of colorful fruits and vegetables daily to provide your body with valuable vitamins, minerals, fiber, and disease-fighting phytochemicals. Whole grains also have phytochemicals and have been added to this list.

Color	Phytochemical	Found In
Red	Anthocyanins	Apples, beets, cabbage, cherries, cranberries, red cabbage, red onion, red beans
	Lycopene	Tomatoes, watermelon, pink grapefruit
Yellow/Orange	Beta-carotene	Apricots, butternut squash, cantaloupe, carrots, mangoes, peaches, pumpkin, sweet potatoes
	Flavonoids	Apricots, clementines, grapefruits, lemons, papaya, pears, pineapple, yellow raisins
White	Alliums/allicin	Chives, garlic, leeks, onions, scallions
Green	Lutein, zeaxanthin	Broccoli, collard greens, honeydew melon, kale, kiwi, lettuce, mustard greens, peas, spinach
	Indoles	Arugula, broccoli, bok choy, brussels sprouts, cabbage, cauliflower, kale, Swiss chard, turnips
Blue/Purple	Anthocyanins	Blackberries, black currants, elderberries, purple grapes
	Phenolics	Eggplant, plums, prunes, raisins
Brown	Beta-gluton, lignans, phenols, plant sterols, phytoestrogens, saponins, tocotrienols	Barley, brown rice, oats, oatmeal, whole grains, whole-grain cereals, whole wheat

Source: Adapted from the National Cancer Institute, "The Color Guide."

The bioavailability of fat-soluble vitamins is usually less than that of water-soluble vitamins because fat-soluble vitamins require bile salts and the formation of a micelle to be absorbed. Vitamins in plant foods are typically less bioavailable than those in animal foods because plant fiber can trap vitamins.

Vitamins Can Be Destroyed by Air, Water, or Heat

Water-soluble vitamins can be destroyed by exposure to air, water, or heat. In fact, vegetables and fruits begin to lose their vitamins almost immediately after being harvested, and some preparation and storage methods can accelerate vitamin loss. Although the fat-soluble vitamins tend to be more stable than water-soluble vitamins, some food preparation techniques can cause the loss of these vitamins as well.

Don't Expose Your Produce to Air

Air (oxygen) exposure can destroy the water-soluble vitamins and the fat-soluble vitamins A, E, and K. For this reason, fresh vegetables and fruits should be stored in airtight, covered containers and used soon after being purchased. Cutting vegetables and fruits increases the amount of surface exposed to air, so cut your produce close to the cooking and serving time to minimize vitamin loss.

Vitamins were originally called vitamines. Casimir Funk, a chemist and early vitamin researcher, believed that vitamins were vital to life (he was correct) and were probably also a nitrogen-containing amine (he was incorrect). When later discoveries found that an amine wasn't present, the *e* was dropped from the word.

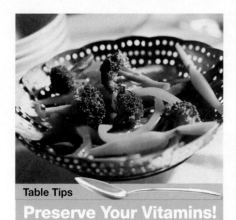

Preserve Your Vitamins!

Cook your vegetables in a small amount of water. If you have to boil vegetables, use the leftover cooking liquid as a soup or gravy base.

Don't rinse rice before cooking it or pasta after cooking it. You'll wash away water-soluble vitamins.

Steam, microwave, or stir-fry vegetables instead of boiling them to reduce the amount of time they are exposed to heat and therefore the amount of vitamins that are lost.

Store produce in a refrigerator and eat it soon after purchase.

Cut vegetables and fruits close to the time that they are going to be cooked and/or served.

Source: Adapted from U.S. Department of Agriculture Food and Nutrition Services, 2002.

toxicity The accumulation of a substance to the level of being poisonous.

megadose A very large dose or amount.

provitamins Substances found in foods that can be converted into an active form once they are absorbed.

A Little Water Is Enough

When you toss out the water that cooks your vegetables, you are also tossing out some water-soluble vitamins. Soaking foods will cause water-soluble vitamins to leach out of the food and into the liquid. To reduce vitamin loss, cook vegetables in a minimal amount of liquid—just enough to prevent the pot from scorching and to keep your vegetables crisp. Although cooking rice in water doesn't diminish its nutrient content (because the water is absorbed by the grain rather than discarded), washing rice before cooking it will wash away the B vitamins that were sprayed on during the enrichment process.[10]

Reduce Cooking Time

Heat, especially prolonged heat from cooking, will also destroy water-soluble vitamins, especially vitamin C. Because they are exposed to less heat, vegetables cooked by microwaving, steaming, or stir-frying can have approximately 1½ times more vitamin C after cooking than if they were boiled, which involves longer heat exposure.[11] The first three cooking methods are faster than boiling, reducing the length of time the food is in direct contact with the heat, and they all use less added water. (Stir-frying typically uses only oil.) Cooking vegetables until "just tender" is best, as it reduces the cooking time and heat exposure and preserves the vitamins. If you find yourself with a plate full of limp and soggy vegetables, this is a sure sign that vitamins have been lost.

Keep Your Food Cool

Whereas heat causes foods to lose vitamins, cooler temperatures help preserve them. For this reason, produce should be stored in your refrigerator rather than on a counter or in a pantry. A package of fresh spinach left at room temperature will lose more than half of its folate, a B vitamin, after four days. Keeping the spinach in the refrigerator delays that loss until eight days.[12] See the Table Tips for ways to preserve the vitamins in your foods.

Overconsumption of Some Vitamins Can Be Toxic

Vitamin **toxicity,** or *hypervitaminosis,* is very rare. This condition results from ingesting more of the vitamin than the body needs, to the point where tissues become saturated. The excess vitamin can damage cells, sometimes permanently. Vitamin toxicity does not occur by eating a normal balanced diet. It can result when individuals consume **megadose** levels of vitamin supplements, usually in the mistaken belief that "more is better." Many individuals, for example, overload on vitamin C tablets to ward off a cold, despite the fact that there is no evidence showing that vitamin C prevents the common cold, and despite the fact that too much vitamin C in the body can lead to unpleasant side effects.

To prevent excessive intake, the Dietary Reference Intakes include a tolerable upper intake level for most vitamins. Even though some vitamins lack sufficient evidence to establish a UL, there still may be risks in taking them in megadose amounts.

Provitamins Can Be Converted to Vitamins by the Body

Provitamins are substances found in foods that are not in a form directly usable by the body, but that can be converted into an active form once they are absorbed. The

Are You Getting Enough Fat-Soluble Vitamins in Your Diet?

Take this brief self-assessment to see if your diet contains enough food sources of the four fat-soluble vitamins.

1. Do you eat at least 1 cup of deep yellow or orange vegetables, such as carrots and sweet potatoes, or dark green vegetables, such as spinach, every day?
   Yes ☐ **No** ☐

2. Do you consume at least 2 glasses (8 ounces each) of milk daily?
   Yes ☐ **No** ☐

3. Do you eat a tablespoon of vegetable oil, such as corn or olive oil, daily? (Tip: Salad dressings, unless they are fat free, count!)
   Yes ☐ **No** ☐

4. Do you eat at least 1 cup of leafy green vegetables in your salad and/or put lettuce in your sandwich every day?
   Yes ☐ **No** ☐

Answers

If you answered yes to all four questions, you are on your way to acing your fat-soluble vitamin needs! If you answered no to any one of the questions, your diet needs some fine-tuning. Deep orange and dark green vegetables are excellent sources of vitamin A, and milk is an excellent choice for vitamin D. Vegetable oils provide vitamin E, and if you put them on top of your vitamin K–rich leafy green salad, you'll hit the vitamin jackpot.

best-known example of this is beta-carotene, which is split into two molecules of vitamin A in the small intestinal cell wall or in the liver cells. Vitamins found in foods that are already in the active form, called **preformed vitamins,** do not undergo conversion.

Now that we've discussed the general characteristics of vitamins, let's review them individually. Before we begin our discussion of the fat-soluble vitamins, take the Self-Assessment to see if your diet is rich in foods containing these important nutrients.

The Take-Home Message Vitamins are essential nutrients needed in small amounts for growth, reproduction, and overall good health. All vitamins are either fat soluble or water soluble. The fat-soluble vitamins, A, D, E, and K, require fat for absorption and are stored in your body. For this reason, chronic dietary excesses of some fat-soluble vitamins can be toxic. The water-soluble B and C vitamins are absorbed with water. Excess water-soluble vitamins are excreted from your body, and surplus amounts generally aren't stored. Some vitamins, such as vitamins E and C, as well as the mineral selenium, flavonoids, and carotenoids, act as antioxidants because they help counteract the damaging effects of oxygen-containing molecules called free radicals. If free radicals accumulate faster than your body can neutralize them, their damaging effects can contribute to chronic diseases and conditions. Fruits, vegetables, and whole grains are robust sources of antioxidants. Many vitamins in foods can be destroyed or lost by exposure to air, water, and heat. The overconsumption of some vitamins can be toxic. Provitamins can be converted to vitamins in the body.

NutriTools

Let's Go to Lunch: Fat-Soluble Vitamins

What fat-soluble vitamins are in your lunch? Visit www.pearsonhighered .com/blake and complete this interactive NutriTools activity.

preformed vitamins Substances that are found in active form in foods.

Vitamin A

What Is Vitamin A?

Vitamin A is actually a family of substances called **retinoids** that includes **retinol, retinal,** and **retinoic acid.** These are called **preformed vitamin A** because they are in a form that your body readily uses. Retinol is the most usable of the three forms and can be converted to both retinal and retinoic acid in your body.[1]

Preformed vitamin A is found only in foods from animal sources, such as liver and eggs, and is added to all processed milk. Plant food sources do not contain preformed vitamin A, but some do contain **provitamin A carotenoids,** which can be converted to retinol in your body. Carotenoids are the yellow-red pigments that give carrots, butternut squash, and cantaloupe their vibrant, deep orange color.

There are more than 600 different carotenoids, but only 3—beta-carotene (β-carotene), beta-cryptoxanthin (β-cryptoxanthin), and alpha-carotene (α-carotene)—can be converted to vitamin A. These three provide approximately 25 to 35 percent of the dietary vitamin A consumed by adults in the United States, with the majority of it coming from beta-

carotene.[2] Other nutritionally significant carotenoids, including lycopene, lutein, and zeaxanthin, may function as antioxidants or provide health benefits, but cannot be converted to vitamin A.

Light → [figure a — eye diagram]

a

Cornea
Light →
Lens

Macula
Retina
Optic nerve (signal to brain)

b

Retina

Light →

Rod responsible for black and white vision (contains rhodopsin)

Cone responsible for color vision (contains iodopsin)

to the macula (which is located in the retina, as shown in the figure (a) and allows you to see fine details and things that are straight in front of you).

Vitamin A is a component of two light-sensitive proteins that are essential for vision. The two proteins, **rhodopsin** and **iodopsin,** are in the tips of light-absorbing cells in the retina called **rods** and **cones,** respectively (b).

As rhodopsin absorbs incoming light, the shape of vitamin A is altered, and it detaches from its protein. This causes a cascade of events that transmits visual messages through your optic nerve to your brain. This change in rhodopsin is called **bleaching.** Although the breakdown of iodopsin is similar, rhodopsin is more sensitive to light than iodopsin and is more likely to become bleached. After bleaching, the vitamin A returns to its original shape and becomes part of the protein again, regenerating the eye's light-absorbing capabilities. This regeneration process can take a few moments.

Have you ever been outside on a sunny day without sunglasses and then entered a dark building? Was it difficult for you initially to see the objects in the room? In this situation, your eyes needed an adjustment period because much of your rhodopsin had been bleached in the bright outdoor sun and your eyes needed to regenerate it once you were in the dark room. Luckily, there is a pool of vitamin A in your retina to immediately help with this regeneration.

Functions of Vitamin A

Vitamin A Is Essential for Vision

Rays of light are bouncing off this page. For you to read this sentence, your eyes receive this reflection of light and begin the process of translating the light into visible images. After light enters your eye through the cornea, it travels to the back of your eye

The carotenoid lycopene, found in tomatoes and tomato products, functions as an antioxidant in the body.

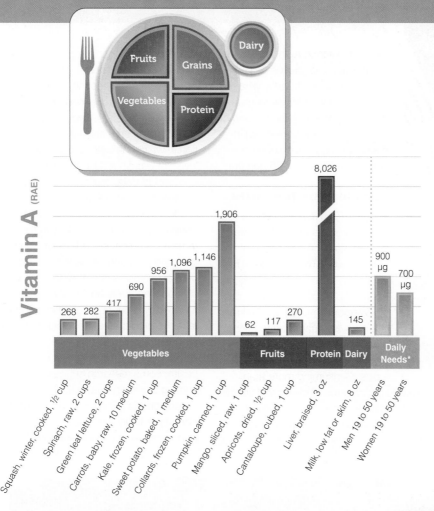

Vitamin A (RAE)

Vegetables:
- Squash, winter, cooked, ½ cup: 268
- Spinach, raw, 2 cups: 282
- Green leaf lettuce, 2 cups: 417
- Carrots, baby, raw, 10 medium: 690
- Kale, frozen, cooked, 1 cup: 956
- Sweet potato, baked, 1 medium: 1,096
- Collards, frozen, cooked, 1 cup: 1,146
- Pumpkin, canned, 1 cup: 1,906

Fruits:
- Mango, sliced, raw, 1 cup: 62
- Apricots, dried, ½ cup: 117
- Cantaloupe, cubed, 1 cup: 270

Protein:
- Liver, braised, 3 oz: 8,026

Dairy:
- Milk, low fat or skim, 8 oz: 145

Daily Needs*:
- Men 19 to 50 years: 900 µg
- Women 19 to 50 years: 700 µg

pression. Too much vitamin A, however, can negatively affect healthy bones.

Vitamin A is important for keeping your skin and the mucous membranes of your lungs, intestinal tract, and kidneys healthy and structurally sound. If these linings are weakened or damaged, bacteria and viruses can infiltrate your body and make you sick.

Vitamin A helps keep your skin, which acts as another barrier to infections, healthy to prevent harmful bacteria from entering your body. Vitamin A also works with your immune system to create white blood cells that fight pathogens that enter your bloodstream.

Daily Needs*

Vitamin A in foods and supplements can be measured in two ways: in micrograms (µg) of **retinol activity equivalents (RAE)** and in **international units (IU).**

Because retinol is the most usable form of vitamin A and because provitamin A carotenoids can be converted to retinol, the preferred way to measure vitamin A in foods is its conversion to RAE. However, some vitamin supplements and food

Vitamin A Is Involved in Cell Differentiation, Reproduction, Bone Health, and Immunity

Vitamin A plays an important role in cell division and **cell differentiation,** the processes that determine what a cell becomes in your body.[3]

Vitamin A affects cell division by prompting gene expression, a process that uses genetic information to make the proteins needed to begin the process of cell division. As cells divide and cluster together, changes occur that cause them to become different from their initiating cells. This differentiation determines what they become in your body. When immature skin cells differentiate into mature skin cells, for example, vitamin A acts as a signal to turn on the genes to create the proteins needed to make healthy skin.

This role of vitamin A is one reason dermatologists prescribe retinoid-containing medicines, such as Retin-A or Accutane, to treat acne (see photo). Retin-A is a topi-

cal medication that works by enhancing the turnover of skin cells and inhibiting the formation of acne. Accutane is a medication taken orally that affects cell differentiation by manipulating the gene expression of acne-producing cells to alter their development in the skin.[4]

During the early stages of pregnancy, vitamin A signals cells to differentiate into tissues that form the baby's body. Vitamin A plays a particularly important role in the development of the limbs, heart, eyes, and ears.[5]

Vitamin A may help regulate the cells involved in bone growth through gene ex-

Vitamin A can aid in the treatment of acne.

*Throughout this book, the amount of each nutrient that is needed daily is based on adults age 19 to 50. If you are younger than 19, your needs may be different. See the inside cover of this textbook for the specific amount of each nutrient you need daily based on your age and gender.

labels use the older measure, IU, on their products. (One RAE in micrograms is the equivalent of 3.3 IU.)

Adult females need 700 micrograms RAE of vitamin A daily, whereas adult males need 900 micrograms RAE daily. This is the average amount needed to maintain adequate stores in your body to keep it healthy.[6]

A daily recommendation for beta-carotene hasn't been established, but the Institute of Medicine suggests consuming 3 to 6 milligrams of beta-carotene every day from foods.[7] (Beta-carotene is measured in milligrams.) You can obtain this easily by eating five or more servings of fruits and vegetables. This amount will provide about 50 percent of the recommended vitamin A intake.

Vegetarians who eat no animal foods, including vitamin A–rich milk and eggs, need to be especially conscientious about eating carotenoids and beta-carotene–rich foods to meet their daily vitamin A needs.

Food Sources

Organ meats (liver), milk, and eggs are the most popular sources of preformed vitamin A in the U.S. diet.

Carrots, spinach, and sweet potatoes are American favorites for provitamin A carotenoids, including beta-carotene.

Similar to vitamin A and other fat-soluble vitamins, carotenoids are absorbed more efficiently when fat is present in your intestinal tract. Adding as little as 1 tablespoon of vegetable oil to your diet can increase the absorption of carotenoids by as much as 25 percent.[8]

Too Much or Too Little

Because vitamin A is stored in your body, excessive amounts of preformed vitamin A can accumulate to toxic levels. The upper level for adults has been set at 3,000 micrograms of preformed vitamin A daily.

Overconsumption of preformed vitamin A is usually due to taking supplements and is less likely to occur from overeating vitamin A in foods. Consuming more than 15,000 micrograms of preformed vitamin A at one time or over a short period of time can lead to nausea, vomiting, headaches, dizziness, and blurred vision.[9]

Chronic daily consumption of more than 30,000 micrograms of vitamin A (more than 300 times the amount that adults need daily) can lead to **hypervitaminosis A** (*hyper* = over, *osis* = condition), an extremely serious condition in which the liver accumulates toxic levels of vitamin A. Hypervitaminosis A can lead to deterioration and scarring of the liver and even death.[10]

High intake of preformed vitamin A during pregnancy, particularly in the first trimester, can cause birth defects in the face and skull and damage the child's central nervous system. All women of childbearing age who are using retinoids for acne or other skin conditions should take the proper steps to avoid becoming pregnant.[11]

Although vitamin A is needed for bone health, some research suggests that consuming too much may lead to **osteoporosis** (*osteo* = bone, *porosis* = porous) or thinning of the bone, which in turn increases the risk of fractures.

The hand on the right exhibits the orange-tinged skin characteristic of carotenodermia.

Osteoporosis-related hip fractures appear to be prevalent in Swedes and Norwegians, who tend to have high consumption of vitamin-A–rich cod-liver oil and specialty dairy products that have been heavily fortified with vitamin A.[12] As little as 1,500 micrograms (3,000 IU) of retinol, which is slightly more than twice the RDA recommended for women, has been shown to be unhealthy for bones.[13]

The upper level applies *only* to preformed vitamin A from foods, fortified foods, and supplements. Provitamin A carotenoids in foods are not toxic and do not pose serious health problems. Your body has a built-in safeguard to prevent provitamin A carotenoids from contributing to vitamin A toxicity, birth defects, or bone damage. If you consume more carotenoids than you need to meet your vitamin A needs, your body will decrease their conversion to retinol. Extra amounts of carotenoids are stored in your liver and in the fat under your skin.[14]

Eating too many carotenoids can cause a nonthreatening condition called **carotenodermia** (*carotene* = carotene, *dermia* = skin) which results in orange-tinged skin, particularly on the palms of the hands and soles of the feet. Because these areas are cushioned with fat, they become more concentrated with the pigments and more visibly orange in color (right hand in photo). Cutting back on carotenoid-rich foods will reverse carotenodermia.

Though a diet abundant in carotenoid-rich foods is not dangerous, carotenoid supplements may be. In a study of adult male smokers, those who consumed beta-carotene supplements were shown to have significantly higher rates of lung cancer than those who didn't take the supplements. However, when these research findings were further analyzed, it appeared that only the men in the study who drank one alcoholic drink daily and consumed the beta-carotene supplement experienced the higher incidences of lung cancer.[15] There is no known benefit associated with taking beta-carotene supplements. Eating a variety of fruits and vegetables is the safest and most healthful way to meet your vitamin A needs.

A chronic vitamin A deficiency can lead to an inability to regenerate rhodopsin, causing **night blindness.** Individuals with night blindness have difficulty seeing at dusk, because they can't adjust from daylight to dark, and may not be able to drive a car during this time of the day. If diagnosed early, night blindness can be reversed by taking vitamin A.

A prolonged vitamin A deficiency can also lead to dryness and permanent damage to the cornea, a condition called **xerophthalmia** (*xero* = dry, *ophthalm* = eye). Up to 10 million children, mostly in developing countries, suffer from xerophthalmia annually, and as many as 500,000 of these children go blind every year because they don't consume enough vitamin A. Vitamin A deficiency is the number-one cause of preventable blindness in children.[16]

A deficiency of vitamin A is also associated with **stunting** of bones.

Table Tips
Score an A

Dunk baby carrots in a tablespoon of low-fat ranch dressing for a healthy snack.

Keep dried apricots in your backpack for a sweet treat.

Add baby spinach to a lunchtime salad.

Bake sweet potatoes rather than white potatoes at dinner.

Buy frozen mango chunks for a ready-to-thaw beta-carotene–rich addition to cottage cheese or yogurt.

Terms to Know

retinoids ∘ retinol ∘ retinal ∘ retinoic acid ∘ preformed vitamin A ∘ provitamin A carotenoids ∘ rhodopsin ∘ iodopsin ∘ rods ∘ cones ∘ bleaching ∘ cell differentiation ∘ retinol activity equivalents (RAE) ∘ international units (IU) ∘ hypervitaminosis A ∘ osteoporosis ∘ carotenodermia ∘ night blindness ∘ xerophthalmia ∘ stunting

Vitamin E

What Is Vitamin E?

Vitamin E is sometimes referred to as a vitamin in need of a disease to cure. For almost 40 years after its discovery, scientists searched unsuccessfully for a curative role for vitamin E. They now have shifted their focus and begun valuing the vitamin's importance as an effective antioxidant.[17]

There are eight different forms of naturally occurring vitamin E, but one form, **alpha-tocopherol (α-tocopherol)**, is most active in your body. The synthetic form of vitamin E found in dietary supplements is only half as active as the natural form.[18]

Functions of Vitamin E

Vitamin E as an Antioxidant

Vitamin E's nutritional claim to fame is its role as a powerful antioxidant. This role is extremely important in protecting cell membranes and preventing oxidation of the "bad" LDL cholesterol carrier.

As you recall from Chapter 5, phospholipids (lipids that contain phosphorus and two fatty acids) are critical components of cell membranes. Many phospholipids contain unsaturated fatty acids, which are vulnerable to the damaging effects of free radicals. As an antioxidant, vitamin E neutralizes free radicals before they can harm cell membranes (see figure below).

When the bad LDL cholesterol carrier is oxidized, it contributes to the buildup of artery-clogging plaque. Antioxidants, including vitamin E, help protect the LDL cholesterol carrier from being oxidized and reduce the buildup in the arteries, called atherosclerosis.[19]

Other Functions of Vitamin E

Vitamin E is an **anticoagulant** (*anti* = against, *coagulant* = causes clotting), which means that it inhibits platelets (fragments of cells used in blood clotting) from unnecessarily clumping together and creating a damaging clot in your bloodstream. Vitamin E also alters the stickiness of the cells that line your lymph and blood vessels. This decreases the ability of blood components to stick to these walls and clog these passageways.

Studies are still under way to assess if the long-term use of vitamin E supplements could play a protective role against heart disease.[20]

Daily Needs

Adults need to consume 15 milligrams of vitamin E daily. Because alpha-tocopherol is the most active form of vitamin E in your body, your vitamin E needs are in alpha-tocopherol equivalents.

Researchers speculate that healthy Americans, on average, are falling short of their dietary vitamin E needs (see Table 7.4) on page 266.[21]

Food Sources

Because vitamin E is fat soluble, vegetable oils, foods that contain these oils, nuts, and seeds are good sources. Some green leafy vegetables, avocado, and fortified cereals can also contribute to your daily needs.

Too Much or Too Little

There isn't any known risk of consuming too much vitamin E from natural food sources. However, overconsumption of the synthetic form that is found in supplements and/or fortified foods could pose risks.

Because vitamin E can act as an anticoagulant and interfere with blood clotting, excess amounts in your body increase the risk of **hemorrhage.** Because of this, the upper level from supplements and/or fortified foods is 1,000 milligrams for adults. This applies only to healthy individuals consuming adequate amounts of vitamin K. (Vitamin K also plays a

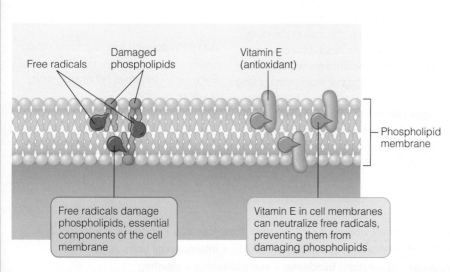

Free radicals | Damaged phospholipids | Vitamin E (antioxidant)

Phospholipid membrane

Free radicals damage phospholipids, essential components of the cell membrane

Vitamin E in cell membranes can neutralize free radicals, preventing them from damaging phospholipids

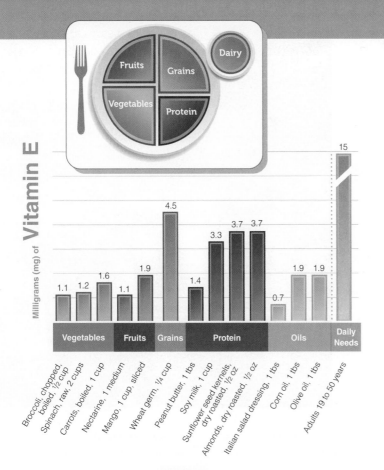

Vitamin E

Milligrams (mg) of

Food	mg
Vegetables	
Broccoli, chopped, boiled, 1/2 cup	1.1
Spinach, raw, 2 cups	1.2
Carrots, boiled, 1 cup	1.6
Fruits	
Nectarine, 1 medium	1.1
Mango, 1 cup, sliced	1.9
Grains	
Wheat germ, 1/4 cup	4.5
Protein	
Peanut butter, 1 tbs	1.4
Soy milk, 1 cup	3.3
Sunflower seed kernels, dry roasted, 1/2 oz	3.7
Almonds, dry roasted, 1/2 oz	3.7
Oils	
Italian salad dressing, 1 tbs	0.7
Corn oil, 1 tbs	1.9
Olive oil, 1 tbs	1.9
Daily Needs	
Adults 19 to 50 years	15

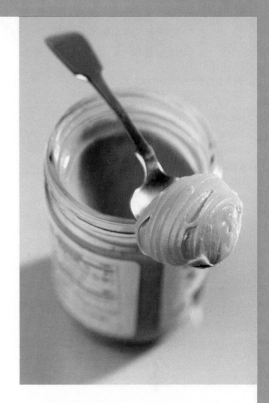

role in blood clotting. A deficiency of vitamin K can exacerbate the anticoagulant effects of vitamin E.) Individuals taking anticoagulant medication and vitamin E supplements should be monitored by their physician to avoid the serious situation in which the blood can't clot quickly enough to stop the bleeding from a wound.

Although the upper level of 1,000 milligrams was set to keep you safe, it may actually be too high. A study showed that those at risk of heart disease who took 400 IU (265 milligrams) or more of vitamin E daily for at least one year had an overall higher risk of dying. One theory is that too much vitamin E may disrupt the balance of other antioxidants in the body, causing more harm than good.[22]

Though rare, a chronic deficiency can cause nerve problems, muscle weakness, and uncontrolled movement of body parts. Because vitamin E is an antioxidant and is found in the membranes of red blood cells, a deficiency can also increase the susceptibility of cell membranes to damage by free radicals.

Individuals who can't absorb fat properly may fall short of their vitamin E needs.

Terms to Know

alpha-tocopherol (α-tocopherol) • anticoagulant • hemorrhage

Vitamin K

What Is Vitamin K?

There are two forms of vitamin K: **menaquinone** and **phylloquinone.** Menaquinone is synthesized by the bacteria that exist naturally in your intestinal tract. Phylloquinone is found in green plants, and is the primary source of vitamin K in your diet.

Bacteria in your GI tract synthesizes one form of vitamin K.

Functions of Vitamin K

Vitamin K Is Essential for Blood Clotting

An easy way to remember vitamin K's major function is to associate the letter *K* with "klotting."

Vitamin K plays a major role in blood **coagulation,** or clotting. Blood clotting is a complex chain of events involving substances in your blood, many of which are proteins, called clotting factors. Vitamin K plays a role in synthesizing four of these **clotting factors.** Without vitamin K, a simple cut on your finger would cause uncontrollable bleeding.

Vitamin K Is Important to Bone Health

Acting as a coenzyme, vitamin K aids an enzyme that alters the bone protein **osteocalcin.** Vitamin K enables osteocalcin to bind with the bone-strengthening mineral calcium.

Chronic inadequate amounts of dietary vitamin K may be a factor in osteoporosis. In a study of women over a ten-year period, researchers found that a low dietary intake of vitamin K was associated with an increased risk of hip fractures.[23] Research continues in the area of vitamin K and bone health.

Daily Needs

Currently, it is not known how much of the vitamin K made from bacteria in your intestinal tract truly contributes to meeting your daily needs. Because of this, it is hard to pinpoint the exact amount you need to consume daily in your foods. Therefore, the recommendation for dietary vitamin K is based on the current amount that is consumed, on average, by healthy Americans.[24]

Adult women need 90 micrograms of vitamin K per day, and men need 120 micrograms daily.

Food Sources

When it comes to meeting your vitamin K needs, think green. Vegetables like broccoli, spinach, salad greens, brussels sprouts, and cabbage are all rich in vitamin K. Vegetable oils and margarine are the second largest source of vitamin K in the diet.

Vitamin K

Microgram (μg) of

Coleslaw, 1 cup	75
Romaine lettuce, raw, 2 cups	96
Green cabbage, raw, 2 cups	107
Broccoli, cooked, 1 cup	110
Brussels sprouts, raw, 1 cup	156
Spinach, raw, 2 cups	290
Collards, raw, 2 cups	368
Kale, raw, 2 cups	1,095
Olive oil, 1 tsp	3
Margarine, regular, 80% fat, 1 tsp	4
Canola oil, 1 tsp	6
Soybean oil, 1 tsp	9
Men 19 to 50 years	120
Women 19 to 50 years	90

Vegetables · **Oils** · **Daily Needs**

A green salad with oil and vinegar dressing at lunch and ¾ cup broccoli at dinner will meet your vitamin K needs for the entire day.

Too Much or Too Little

There are no known adverse effects of consuming too much vitamin K from foods or supplements, so an upper intake level hasn't been set for healthy people.

Individuals taking anticoagulant (anticlotting) medications such as **warfarin** (also known as Coumadin) need to keep a consistent intake of vitamin K. This medication decreases the activity of vitamin K and prolongs the time it takes for blood to clot. If these individuals suddenly increase the vitamin K in their diets, the vitamin can override the effect of the

drug, enabling the blood to clot too quickly. In contrast, a sudden decline in dietary vitamin K can enhance the effectiveness of the drug.[25]

A vitamin K deficiency severe enough to affect blood clotting is extremely rare in healthy individuals.[26] People with illnesses affecting absorption of fat in the intestinal tract, which is necessary to absorb fat-soluble vitamin K, may be at risk of not meeting their vitamin K needs.

Table Tips

Getting Your Ks

Have a green salad daily.

Cook with soybean oil.

Add shredded cabbage to your salad, or top it with a scoop of coleslaw.

Add a tad of margarine to your steamed spinach. Both will provide some vitamin K.

Dunk raw broccoli florets in salad dressing for two sources of vitamin K.

Terms to Know

menaquinone ● phylloquinone ● coagulation ● clotting factors ● osteocalcin ● warfarin

Vitamin D

What Is Vitamin D?

Vitamin D is called the "sunshine vitamin" because it is made in your body with the help of **ultraviolet (UV) rays** from sunlight. In fact, most healthy people can synthesize all the vitamin D they need as long as they receive adequate sun exposure.[27] People who don't obtain enough sun exposure must meet their needs through their diets.

Whether from food or sunlight, vitamin D enters your body in an inactive form. The ultraviolet rays of the sun convert a cholesterol-containing compound in your skin to previtamin D, which is then converted to an inactive form of vitamin D in your blood. The vitamin D in your foods is also in this inactive form.

This inactive form travels in your blood to your liver, where it is changed into a circulating form of vitamin D and is released back into your blood. Once in your kidneys, it is converted to an active form of vitamin D.

Functions of Vitamin D

Vitamin D Helps Bone Health by Regulating Calcium and Phosphorus

Once in an active form, vitamin D acts as a hormone and regulates two important bone minerals, calcium and phosphorus. Vitamin D stimulates the absorption of calcium and phosphorus in the intestinal tract, helping to keep the levels of these minerals within a healthy range in your blood. Because of its role in regulating these minerals, vitamin D helps to build and maintain your bones.

Although phosphorus deficiency is very rare, dietary calcium deficiencies do occur, causing blood levels of calcium to drop. When this happens, vitamin D and **parathyroid hormone** cause calcium to leave your bones to maintain the necessary levels in your blood. Vitamin D then signals your kidneys to decrease the amount of calcium excreted in the urine. All of these actions help to regulate the amount of calcium in your blood.

Vitamin D May Prevent Some Cancers and Diabetes

Research studies have shown that breast, colon, and prostate cancers are more prominent in individuals living in sun-poor areas of the world than in those living in sunny regions. Vitamin D helps regulate the growth and differentiation of certain cells. Researchers speculate that an inadequate amount of vitamin D in the body may reduce the proliferation of the healthy cells, and allow cancer cells to flourish.[28]

Vitamin D may also help prevent diabetes mellitus. Many individuals with type 2 diabetes mellitus have low blood levels of vitamin D. One study revealed that insulin resistance, the inability of the cells to effectively use insulin in the blood, was greater among those with low blood levels of vitamin D, suggesting that the vitamin plays a role in insulin sensitivity.[29]

Vitamin D May Help Regulate the Immune System and Blood Pressure

Vitamin D may also reduce the risk of developing certain autoimmune disorders, such as inflammatory bowel syndrome. Most cells in the immune system have

a receptor for vitamin D. The role of vitamin D is still not understood, but some researchers suggest that it may affect the function of the immune system and inhibit the development of autoimmune diseases.[30] Vitamin D may help reduce high blood pressure by acting on the gene that is involved in regulating blood pressure.[31] Blood pressure readings tend to be higher during the winter, when people are exposed to less sunlight, than in the summer. People with mild hypertension may be able to lower their blood pressure by consuming adequate vitamin D.

Daily Needs

Not everyone can rely on the sun to meet their daily vitamin D needs. During the winter months in areas above latitudes of approximately 40 degrees north (Boston, Toronto, Salt Lake City) and below approximately 40 degrees south (Melbourne, Australia), sun exposure isn't strong enough to synthesize vitamin D in the skin.

Individuals with darker skin, such as African-Americans, have a higher amount of the skin pigment melanin, which reduces vitamin D production from sunlight. These individuals need a longer period of sun exposure, compared to a person with less melanin, to derive the same amount

IU of Vitamin D

Food	IU
Total Corn Flakes, 1 cup	26
Total Raisin Bran, 1 cup	40
Egg, fried, 1 large	17
Soy milk, fortified, 1 cup	126
Tuna fish, light, canned in oil, 3 oz	201
Salmon, cooked, 3 oz	309
Cheese, cheddar, 1½ oz	5
Tapioca pudding, prepared from mix and made with whole milk, ½ cup	49
Pudding, prepared with vitamin-D-fortified milk, ½ cup	50
Yogurt, fortified with vitamin D, 8 oz	100
Milk, nonfat, vitamin-D-fortified, 1 cup	102
Milk, 1% milk fat, vitamin-D-fortified, 1 cup	127
Margarine, fortified, 1 tbs	60
Adults 19 to 50 years (Daily Needs)	600

(Grouped as: Grains, Protein, Dairy, Oils, Daily Needs)

of vitamin D. The use of sunscreen can also block the body's ability to synthesize vitamin D by more than 95 percent.[32]

Because of these variables involving sun exposure, your daily vitamin D needs are based on the amount you would need to eat in foods and are not based on the synthesis of vitamin D in your skin from sunlight.

Based on the important roles that vitamin D plays in your body, it is currently recommended that adults ages 19 to 70 consume 15 micrograms, or 600 IU, of vitamin D daily. This is a significant increase from previously recommended daily amounts. Also, based on revised Dietary Reference Intakes, adults over the age of 70 should incorporate 20 micrograms, or 800 IU, into their daily consumption.[33]

When you are reading labels to assess the amount of vitamin D in your foods, keep in mind that the Daily Value (DV) on the Nutrition Facts panel is set at 400 IU, less than the current amount recommended for adults.

Food Sources

One of the easiest ways to get your vitamin D from food is to drink fortified milk, which provides 100 IU, or 2½ micrograms, of vitamin D per cup. Other than fatty fish (such as sardines and salmon) and fortified milk, breakfast cereals, juice, and yogurt, very few foods provide ample amounts of vitamin D. With this scarcity of naturally occurring vitamin D–rich sources, it isn't surprising that many Americans are not meeting their daily dietary vitamin D needs.[34]

Too Much or Too Little

Consuming too much vitamin D can cause loss of appetite, nausea, vomiting, and constipation. The upper level for vitamin D has been set at 4,000 IU (100 micrograms), which is five

to six times higher than recommended daily.

As with the other fat-soluble vitamins, excess amounts of vitamin D are stored in the fat cells, and an accumulation can reach toxic levels, causing **hypervitaminosis D.** This condition causes overabsorption of calcium from the intestines as well as calcium loss from bones. When both of these symptoms occur, blood calcium levels can become dangerously high.

A chronically high amount of calcium in the blood, or **hypercalcemia** (*hyper* = over, *calc* = calcium, *emia* = blood), can cause damaging calcium deposits in the tissues of your kidneys, lungs, blood vessels, and heart. Excess vitamin D can also affect your nervous system and cause severe depression.[35]

The good news is that it is highly unlikely that you will get hypervitaminosis D from foods, even fortified foods. The only exception is fish oils, specifically cod-liver oil, which provides 1,360 IU of vitamin D per tablespoon. Luckily, the less-than-pleasant taste of this oil is a safeguard against overconsumption. A more likely culprit behind hypervitaminosis D is the overuse of vitamin D supplements.

Sun worshippers don't have to worry about getting hypervitaminosis D from the sun (although they should be concerned about the risk of skin cancer). Overexposing the skin to UV rays will eventually destroy the inactive form of vitamin D in the skin, causing the body to shut down production of vitamin D.

Rickets on the Rise

Rickets is a vitamin D deficiency disease that occurs in children. The bones of children with rickets aren't adequately mineralized with calcium and phosphorus, and this causes them to weaken. Because of their "soft bones," these children develop bowed legs, as they are unable to hold up their own body weight when they are standing upright.[36]

Since milk became fortified with vitamin D in the 1930s, rickets has been considered a rare disease among children in the United States. However, the disease has once again become a public health concern. In the late 1990s, a review of hospital records in Georgia suggested that as many as five out of every 1 million children between 6 months and 5 years of age were hospitalized with rickets associated with a vitamin D deficiency. This probably underestimates the prevalence of rickets in the state, as only hospitalized children were investigated. Similarly, more than 20 percent of more than 300 adolescents at a Boston-based hospital clinic were recently found to be deficient in vitamin D.[37]

A child with rickets.

Changes in the diets and lifestyles of children provide clues as to why rickets is on the rise in America. One factor may be the increased consumption of soft drinks. A U.S. Department of Agriculture (USDA) report found that the number of children who drank soft drinks, in and outside of school, has more than doubled over a 20-year period.[38] This displacement of milk (a good source of vitamin D) with soft drinks (a poor source) is causing many children to come up short in their vitamin D intake.

Increased concern over skin cancer may be another factor. Skin cancer is the most common form of cancer in the United States, and childhood sun exposure appears to increase the risk of skin cancer in later years. Because of this, organizations such as the Centers for Disease Control and the American Cancer Society have run campaigns that recommend limiting exposure to ultraviolet light. People are encouraged to use sunscreen, wear protective clothing when outdoors, and minimize activities in the sun. The American Association of Pediatricians also recommends that infants younger than 6 months not be exposed to direct sunlight and that children use sunscreen before going outside.[39] With less exposure to UV light, many children aren't able to synthesize vitamin D in adequate amounts to meet their needs, thereby increasing their risk of developing rickets. The increased use of child day-care facilities, which may limit outdoor activities during the day, may also play a role in this increased prevalence of rickets.[40]

Finally, air pollution reduces the ultraviolet rays of the sun by as much as 60 percent—another factor limiting the production of vitamin D in the skin. In fact, children living in an industrial, polluted region of India were shown to have less vitamin D in their blood than children living in a less polluted area of the country.[41]

Other Vitamin D Deficiency Disorders

Osteomalacia is the adult equivalent of rickets and can cause muscle and bone weakness and pain. The bones can't mineralize properly because there isn't enough calcium and phosphorus available in the blood.[42] Although there may be adequate amounts of these minerals in the diet, the deficiency of vitamin D hampers their absorption.

Vitamin D deficiency and its subsequent effect on decreased calcium absorption can lead to **osteoporosis,** a condition in which the bones can mineralize properly, but there isn't enough calcium in the diet to maximize the bone density, or mass.

Table Tips

Dynamite Ways to Get Vitamin D

Use low-fat milk, not cream, in your hot or iced coffee.

Buy vitamin-D–fortified yogurts and have one daily as a snack. Top it with a vitamin-D–fortified cereal for another boost of "D."

Start your morning with cereal, and douse it with plenty of low-fat or skim milk.

Flake canned salmon over your lunchtime salad.

Make instant hot cocoa with hot milk rather than water.

Terms to Know

ultraviolet (UV) rays • parathyroid hormone • hypervitaminosis D • hypercalcemia • rickets • osteomalacia • osteoporosis

The B Vitamins and Vitamin C Are Water Soluble

There are nine water-soluble vitamins, and eight of them belong to the vitamin B complex. When initially discovered in the early 1900s, the "water-soluble B" was thought to be one vitamin. After years of research, it became apparent that this was not a single substance but rather many vitamins—thiamin, riboflavin, niacin, vitamin B_6, folate, vitamin B_{12}, pantothenic acid, and biotin—known collectively as the B vitamins. The ninth water-soluble vitamin is vitamin C.

Water-soluble vitamins are different from fat-soluble vitamins in that they dissolve in water, are generally not stored in the body, and are often excreted through the urine. Consumers who take large amounts of water-soluble vitamins in an attempt to "beef up" their vitamin stores literally end up flushing their vitamins, and their money, down the toilet. Because excess amounts are not stored, most water-soluble vitamins are not toxic. However, routine intakes of excessive amounts can be harmful. In fact, Brendan's illness, described at the beginning of the chapter, wasn't due to a vitamin deficiency but to overconsumption of the water-soluble vitamin C.

Underconsuming the water-soluble vitamins can lead to deficiency symptoms, and because many B vitamins are found in similar food sources, an individual experiencing a deficiency of one B vitamin is likely also deficient in others.

Water-soluble vitamins serve numerous similar functions in the body. The B vitamins share a common role as **coenzymes** (see **Figure 7.6**), helping numerous enzymes produce reactions in your cells. Although vitamins don't provide calories and thus aren't sources of energy, you need many of the B vitamins to use the three energy-yielding nutrients (carbohydrates, proteins, and fat). The roles of the B vitamins don't end here. Each vitamin has other important functions in your body. Vitamin C plays important roles in the immune system and in bone health, in addition to its other functions. Take the Self-Assessment to see if you are consuming foods that are rich in the B vitamins and vitamin C.

a Two compounds approach the enzyme, but a coenzyme is needed for the reaction to occur.

b Once the coenzyme is present, the compounds can interact with the enzyme.

c The enzyme changes shape.

d The reaction occurs, and the product is released.

Figure 7.6 How B Vitamins Function as Coenzymes

Self-Assessment

Are You Getting Enough Water-Soluble Vitamins in Your Diet?

Take this brief self-assessment to see if your diet is rich in the water-soluble B vitamins and vitamin C.

1. Do you eat at least 1 cup of a ready-to-eat cereal or hot cereal every day? **Yes ☐ No ☐**
2. Do you enjoy a citrus fruit or fruit juice, such as an orange, a grapefruit, or orange juice, every day? **Yes ☐ No ☐**
3. Do you have at least one slice of bread, a bagel, or a muffin daily? **Yes ☐ No ☐**
4. Do you have at least a cup of vegetables throughout your day? **Yes ☐ No ☐**
5. Do you consume at least ½ cup of pasta daily? **Yes ☐ No ☐**

Answers

Yes answers to all of these questions, make you a vitamin superstar! Rice, pasta, cereals, and bread and bread products are all excellent sources of B vitamins. Citrus fruits are a ringer for vitamin C. In fact, all vegetables can contribute to meeting your daily vitamin C needs. If you answered no more than yes, read on to learn how to add more Bs and C to your diet.

coenzymes Substances needed by enzymes to perform many chemical reactions in your body. Many vitamins act as coenzymes.

Thiamin (B₁)

What Is Thiamin?

Thiamin, or vitamin B_1, was the first B vitamin to be discovered. The path to its discovery began in the 1890s in East Asia. A Dutch doctor, Christiann Eijkman, noticed that chickens and pigeons that ate polished rice (rice with the nutrient- and thiamin-rich outer layer and germ stripped away) developed **polyneuritis** (*poly* = many, *neur* = nerves, *itis* = inflammation). This debilitating nerve condition resulted in the birds not being able to fly or stand up. Eijkman noted that polyneuritis was also a symptom of beriberi, a similar disease that had been observed in humans.

When Eijkman changed the birds' diet to unpolished rice, with the outer layer and germ intact, the birds were cured.[43] Though Eijkman realized that the unpolished rice eliminated the symptoms, he didn't know why. Finally, in 1911, Casimir Funk identified thiamin as the curative factor in the unpolished rice.

Functions of Thiamin

Thiamin Is Needed for Nerve Function and Energy Metabolism

Thiamin plays a role in the transmission of nerve impulses and so helps keep nerves healthy and functioning properly.

You also need thiamin for the metabolism of carbohydrates and certain amino acids. Thiamin also plays a role in breaking down alcohol in the body.

Daily Needs

The RDA for thiamin for adults is 1.1 milligrams for women and 1.2 milligrams for men. Currently, adult American men consume close to 2 milligrams of thiamin daily, whereas women, on average, eat approximately 1.2 milligrams daily, so both groups are meeting their daily needs.[44]

Food Sources

Enriched and whole-grain foods, such as bread and bread products, ready-to-eat cereals, pasta, and rice, and combined foods, such as sandwiches, are the biggest contributors of thiamin in the American diet. A medium-sized bowl of ready-to-eat cereal in the morning and a

sandwich at lunch will just about meet your daily thiamin requirement.

Pork is the richest source of naturally occurring thiamin.

Too Much or Too Little

There are no known toxicity symptoms from consuming too much thiamin from food or supplements, so no upper level has been set.

The disease that occurs in humans who are deficient in thiamin is **beriberi.** There are two types of beriberi. Wet beriberi affects the cardiovascular system, so symptoms often include a rapid heartbeat, shortness of breath, and edema (swelling) in a person's calves and feet. Dry beriberi affects the nervous system, so symptoms may include difficulty in walking, tingling in the hands and feet,

Berberi

Milligrams (mg) of Thiamin

Food	mg
Peas, boiled, 1 cup	0.41
Rice, brown, cooked, ½ cup	0.10
Wheat bread, 1 slice	0.10
Oatmeal, cooked, ½ cup	0.13
Pasta (spaghetti), enriched, cooked, ½ cup	0.14
Wheat crackers, 1 oz	0.14
Bagel, medium, ½	0.24
Pretzels, hard, 10 pretzels	0.27
Ready-to-eat cereal, whole wheat, ¾ cup	0.4
Ham, extra lean, 2 oz	0.05
Lentils, boiled, 1 cup	0.33
Pork, center loin, lean, broiled, 3 oz	0.8
Men 19 to 50 years	1.2
Women 19 to 50 years	1.1

can cause beriberi, and chronic alcohol abuse can lead to an advanced form of thiamin deficiency called **Wernicke-Korsakoff syndrome.** The syndrome is a progressively damaging brain disorder that can cause mental confusion and memory loss, difficulty seeing clearly, low blood pressure, uncontrolled movement of the arms and legs, and even coma. Although some of these symptoms can be reversed after the person is medically treated with thiamin, some of the memory loss may be permanent.[46]

and problems with coordination.[45] Other symptoms of beriberi include loss of appetite and weight loss, memory loss, and confusion.

The populations of poor countries with an inadequate food supply rely heavily on refined grains that are not enriched (recall that enriched grains have the B vitamins thiamin, riboflavin, niacin, and folic acid, as well as the mineral iron, added to them). These people are more susceptible to a thiamin deficiency and the side effects of beriberi.

In the United States, widespread use of enriched grains means that instances of beriberi are rare. Americans, however, are not completely immune to thiamin deficiencies. Those who chronically abuse alcohol tend to have a poor diet that is probably deficient in thiamin. Alcohol consumption also interferes with the absorption of the small amounts of thiamin that may be in the diet, accelerating its loss from the body. Alcoholics may find themselves battling a thiamin deficiency that

Table Tips

Thrive on Thiamin

Sprinkle cereal on your yogurt.

Toss pasta with peas. Both foods will boost your thiamin.

Add cooked rice to soups.

Have a sandwich daily.

Enjoy oatmeal for breakfast.

Terms to Know
polyneuritis • beriberi • Wernicke-Korsakoff syndrome

Riboflavin (B$_2$)

What Is Riboflavin?

Riboflavin, also known as vitamin B$_2$, is a light-sensitive B vitamin that is abundant in milk. One of the reasons that milk is packaged in opaque bottles or cardboard containers is to prevent its riboflavin content from being destroyed by light.

Not so long ago, milk made its way to a household not via the grocery store cooler, but by way of a daily visit from a milkman in the early hours of the morning. At each delivery, the milkman placed the clear glass milk bottles inside a covered "milk box" outside the home. The milk box helped protect the light-sensitive riboflavin in the milk from being destroyed by the morning sunlight. Sunlight destroys riboflavin quickly. In fact, just 30 minutes of midday summer sun will destroy more than 30 percent of the riboflavin in glass-bottled milk.[47]

Daily Needs

You need to consume a little over 1 milligram of riboflavin daily to be healthy. Adult males should consume 1.3 milligrams and females, 1.1 milligrams of riboflavin every day. Americans, on average, typically exceed their daily needs.

Food Sources

Milk and yogurt are the most popular sources of riboflavin in the diets of American adults, followed by enriched cereals and grains. A breakfast of cereal and milk and a lunchtime pita sandwich and yogurt will meet your riboflavin needs for the day.

Too Much or Too Little

Your body has a limited ability to absorb riboflavin, so excessive amounts are ex-

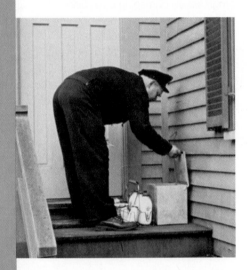

Functions of Riboflavin

Riboflavin Is Important for Energy Metabolism and Healthy Cells

Your body needs riboflavin to turn the carbohydrates, proteins, and fats that you eat into energy, and to keep the cells in your body healthy.[48] Riboflavin also enhances the functions of other B vitamins, such as niacin and B$_{12}$.

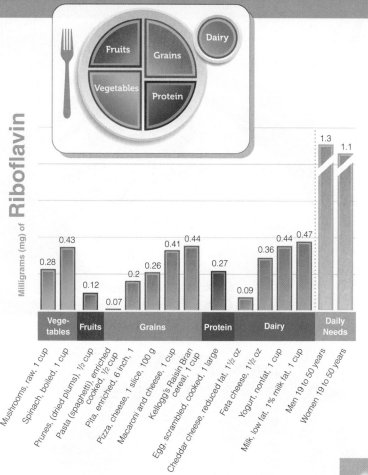

Riboflavin

Milligrams (mg) of Riboflavin

Vege-tables	Fruits	Grains	Protein	Dairy	Daily Needs

Values: 0.28, 0.43, 0.12, 0.07, 0.2, 0.26, 0.41, 0.44, 0.27, 0.09, 0.36, 0.44, 0.47, 1.3, 1.1

- Mushrooms, raw, 1 cup — 0.28
- Spinach, boiled, 1 cup — 0.43
- Prunes, (dried plums), ½ cup — 0.12
- Pasta (spaghetti), enriched, cooked, ½ cup — 0.07
- Pita, enriched, 6 inch, 1 — 0.2
- Pizza, cheese, 1 slice, 100 g — 0.26
- Macaroni and cheese, 1 cup — 0.41
- Kellogg's Raisin Bran cereal, 1 cup — 0.44
- Egg, scrambled, cooked, 1 large — 0.27
- Cheddar cheese, reduced fat, 1½ oz — 0.09
- Feta cheese, 1½ oz — 0.36
- Yogurt, nonfat, 1 cup — 0.44
- Milk, low fat, 1% milk fat, 1 cup — 0.47
- Men 19 to 50 years — 1.3
- Women 19 to 50 years — 1.1

Table Tips
Rally Your Riboflavin

Have a glass of milk with your meals.

A yogurt snack is a riboflavin snack.

Add spinach to your salad for a riboflavin bonus.

Enriched pasta will enrich your meal with riboflavin.

Macaroni and cheese provides a double source of riboflavin from the pasta and the cheese.

creted in urine. No upper level for riboflavin has been determined. However, because riboflavin is a bright yellow compound, consuming large amounts through supplements will turn urine as yellow as a school bus. While this isn't dangerous to your health, it isn't beneficial either, so you should skip the supplements and pour yourself a glass of milk instead.

If you don't consume enough of this B vitamin, the cells in the tissues that line your throat, mouth, tongue, and lips will be the first to signal a deficiency. Your throat would be sore, the inside of your mouth would swell, your tongue would be inflamed and look purplish red, and your lips would be dry and scaly. Deficiencies are rarely seen in healthy individuals who eat a balanced diet.

An inflamed tongue (glossitis) is one symptom of a riboflavin deficiency.

Niacin (B₃)

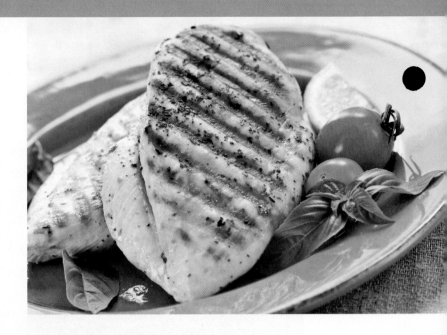

What Is Niacin?

Niacin, or vitamin B_3, is the generic term for **nicotinic acid** and **nicotinamide,** which are the two active forms of niacin that are derived from foods.

Functions of Niacin

Niacin Is Needed to Use the Energy in Your Food

Niacin is another nutrient your body needs in order to use carbohydrates, proteins, and fats. Without niacin, you wouldn't be able to create energy from the foods that you eat. Niacin is also needed to synthesize fat and cholesterol.

Other Functions of Niacin

Niacin is needed to keep your skin cells healthy and your digestive system functioning properly.

Niacin has been shown to lower the total amount of cholesterol in the blood and the "bad" LDL cholesterol carrier. It can also lower high levels of fat (triglycerides) in the blood and simultaneously raise the level of the "good" HDL cholesterol carrier. The nicotinic acid form of niacin is sometimes prescribed by physicians for patients with high blood cholesterol levels. When niacin is used to treat high blood cholesterol, it is considered a drug. The amount prescribed by a physician is often more than 40 times the upper level for niacin. Note that you should *never* consume high amounts of niacin unless a physician is monitoring you.

Daily Needs

The recommended daily amount for adults is 14 milligrams for women and 16 milligrams for men, an amount set to prevent the deficiency disease pellagra. American adults, on average, far exceed their daily niacin needs.[49]

Niacin is found in many foods, but it can also be synthesized in the body from the amino acid **tryptophan.** For this reason, your daily niacin needs are measured in **niacin equivalents (NE).** It is estimated that 60 milligrams of tryptophan can be converted to 1 milligram of niacin or 1 milligram NE.

Food Sources

Niacin is found in meat, fish, poultry, enriched whole-grain breads and bread products, and fortified cereals. Protein-rich foods, particularly animal foods such as meat, are good sources of tryptophan and thus of niacin. However, if you are falling short of both your dietary protein and niacin, tryptophan will first be used to make protein in your body, at the expense of your niacin needs.[50]

As with thiamin, your niacin needs are probably met after you eat your breakfast and lunch, especially since similar foods contain both vitamins.

Too Much or Too Little

As with most water-soluble vitamins, there isn't any known danger from consuming too much niacin from foods such as meat and enriched grains. However,

Niacin

Milligrams (mg) of Niacin

Food	mg
Peppers, raw, 1 cup	0.7
Potatoes, mashed, 1/2 cup	1.1
Sweet potato, baked in skin, 1	2.1
Corn, canned, 1 cup	2.5
Pasta (spaghetti) enriched, cooked, 1/2 cup	1.2
Rice, brown, cooked, 1 cup	3.0
Cheerios, 1 cup	5.8
Peanuts, dry roasted, 1/2 oz	1.9
Turkey, light meat, roasted, 3 oz	5.6
Sirloin steak, lean, broiled, 3 oz	6.6
Salmon, cooked, 3 oz	7.2
Tuna fish, light, canned in water, 3 oz	11.3
Chicken breast, skinless, roasted, 3 oz	11.7
Men 19 to 50 years	16
Women 19 to 50 years	14

Categories: Vegetables, Grains, Protein, Daily Needs

Inflamed skin (dermatitis) can result from pellagra.

overconsuming niacin by taking supplements or eating too many overly fortified foods can cause **flushing,** a reddish coloring of the face, arms, and chest. Too much niacin consumption can also cause nausea and vomiting, be toxic to your liver, and raise your blood glucose levels.

The upper level for niacin for adults is 35 milligrams to prevent flushing, the first side effect to be observed when too much niacin is consumed. This upper level applies only to healthy individuals. It may be too high for those with certain medical conditions, such as diabetes mellitus and liver disease.[51]

Too little niacin in the diet can result in the deficiency disease called **pellagra.** In the early 1900s, pellagra was widespread among the poor living in the southern United States, where people relied on corn—a poor source of niacin—as a dietary staple. The symptoms of pellagra—**dermatitis** (inflammation or irritation of the skin), **dementia** (loss of memory along with confusion and disorientation), and **d**iarrhea—led to its being known as the disease of the three Ds. A fourth D, **d**eath, was often associated with the disease.

Once other cereal grains were available, pellagra disappeared as a widespread disease in the United States. The niacin in the grains was later identified as the curative factor for pellagra. Although no longer common in the United States, pellagra does occur among individuals who abuse alcohol and have a very poor diet.

Table Tips

Nail Your Niacin

Have a serving of enriched cereal in the morning.

Dip niacin-rich peppers in hummus.

Enjoy a lean chicken breast at dinner.

Snack on peanuts.

Put tuna fish flakes on your salad.

Terms to Know

nicotinic acid • nicotinamide • tryptophan • niacin equivalents (NE) • flushing • pellagra • dermatitis • dementia

Vitamin B₆

What Is Vitamin B₆?

Vitamin B₆ is a collective name for several related compounds, including **pyridoxine,** the major form found in plant foods and the form used in supplements and fortified foods.[52] Two other forms, **pyridoxal** and **pyridoxamine,** are found in animal food sources such as chicken and meat.

Functions of Vitamin B₆

Vitamin B₆ Is an Active Coenzyme

Vitamin B₆ acts as a coenzyme with more than 100 enzymes involved in the metabolism of proteins. It is needed to create nonessential amino acids and to convert the amino acid tryptophan to niacin.[53] Vitamin B₆ also helps your body metabolize fats and carbohydrates and break down glycogen, the storage form of glucose.

Other Functions of B₆

Vitamin B₆ is needed to make the oxygen-carrying hemoglobin in your red blood cells and to keep your immune and nervous systems healthy.[54]

Finally, recent research indicates that vitamin B₆, along with two other water-soluble vitamins, folate and vitamin B₁₂, may help reduce the risk of heart disease (see the "B Vitamins for Your Heart" feature box on page 230).

Daily Needs

Adult women need 1.3 to 1.5 milligrams and men need 1.3 to 1.7 milligrams of vitamin B₆ daily, depending on their age.

Food Sources

Because vitamin B₆ is found in so many foods, including ready-to-eat cereals, meat, fish, poultry, many vegetables and fruits, nuts, peanut butter, and other legumes, Americans on average easily meet their daily needs.

Too Much or Too Little

To protect against potential nerve damage, the upper level for vitamin B₆ is set at 100 milligrams daily for adults over the age of 19. Luckily, it would be extremely difficult to take in a dangerous level of vitamin B₆ from food alone.

However, taking vitamin B₆ in supplement form can be harmful. Over the years, vitamin B₆ has been touted to aid a variety of ailments, including **carpal tunnel syndrome** and **premenstrual syndrome (PMS).** But research studies have failed to show any significant clinical benefit of taking vitamin B₆ supplements for either of these syndromes.

In fact, taking large amounts of vitamin B₆ through supplements may be

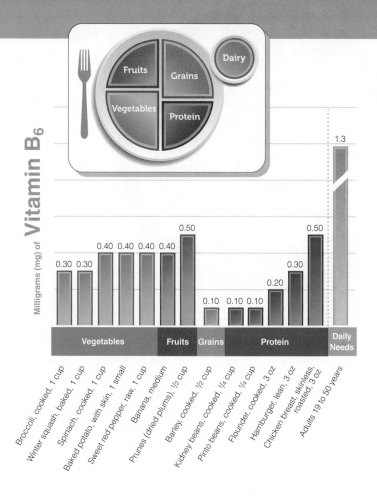

Vitamin B₆

Milligrams (mg) of **Vitamin B₆**

| Vegetables | Fruits | Grains | Protein | Daily Needs |

- 0.30 — Broccoli, cooked, 1 cup
- 0.30 — Winter squash, baked, 1 cup
- 0.40 — Spinach, cooked, 1 cup
- 0.40 — Baked potato, with skin, 1 small
- 0.40 — Sweet red pepper, raw, 1 cup
- 0.40 — Banana, medium
- 0.50 — Prunes (dried plums), ½ cup
- 0.10 — Barley, cooked, ½ cup
- 0.10 — Kidney beans, cooked, ¼ cup
- 0.10 — Pinto beans, cooked, ¼ cup
- 0.20 — Flounder, cooked, 3 oz
- 0.30 — Hamburger, lean, 3 oz
- 0.50 — Chicken breast, skinless, roasted, 3 oz
- 1.3 — Adults 19 to 50 years

associated with a variety of ill effects, including nerve damage. Individuals taking as little as 500 milligrams and as much as 6,000 milligrams of vitamin B₆ daily for two months experienced difficulty walking and tingling sensations in their legs and feet. These symptoms subsided once supplement consumption stopped.[55]

The telltale signs of a vitamin B₆ deficiency are a sore tongue, inflammation of the skin, depression, confusion, and possibly **anemia.**

Those who consume too much alcohol are more likely to fall short of their needs. Not only does alcohol cause your body to lose vitamin B₆, but those suffering from alcoholism are likely to have an unbalanced diet, with little variety.

Table Tips

Beam with B₆

Have a stuffed baked potato with steamed broccoli and grilled chicken for lunch.

Grab a banana for a midmorning snack.

Add cooked barley to your soup.

Snack on prunes.

Add kidney beans to your chili or salad.

Terms to Know

pyridoxine • pyridoxal • pyridoxamine • carpal tunnel syndrome • premenstrual syndrome (PMS) • anemia

Folate

What Is Folate?

There are two forms of the vitamin **folate:** the naturally occurring folate in foods and the synthetic form, **folic acid,** which is added to foods (such as ready-to-eat cereals and grains) and found in supplements. (A very small amount of folic acid can occur naturally in foods. But, for practical purposes in this book, *folic acid* always refers to the synthetic variety.)

Functions of Folate

Folate Is Vital for DNA Synthesis

Folate is vital to making the DNA in your cells. If the synthesis of DNA is disrupted, your body's ability to create and maintain new cells is impaired.[56] For this reason, folate plays many important roles, from maintaining healthy blood cells and preventing birth defects to possibly fighting cancer and heart disease. Folate also helps your body use amino acids and is needed to help red blood cells divide and increase in adequate numbers.

(T)(F) Folate Prevents Birth Defects

Folate plays an extremely important role during pregnancy, particularly in the first few weeks after conception, often before the mother knows she is pregnant. Folate

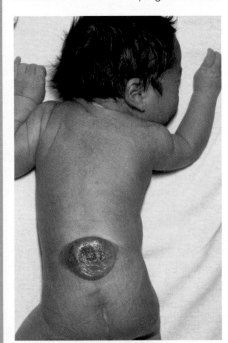

Infant with spina bifida.

is needed to create new cells so that the baby can grow and develop. A deficiency during pregnancy can result in birth defects called **neural tube defects.** The neural tube forms the baby's spine, brain, and skull. If the neural tube doesn't develop properly, two common birth defects, **anencephaly** and **spina bifida,** can occur. In anencephaly, the brain doesn't completely form so the baby can't move, hear, think, or function. An infant with anencephaly dies soon after birth. In spina bifida (see photo), the baby's spinal cord and backbone aren't properly developed, causing learning and physical disabilities, such as the inability to walk.[57] Folic acid reduces the risk of these birth defects by 50 to 70 percent if consumed at least the month prior to conception and during the early part of pregnancy.[58]

Research studies to date suggest that synthetic folic acid has a stronger protective effect than the folate found naturally in foods.

Folate Reduces Some Cancer Risks

Inadequate amounts of folate in the body can disrupt the cell's DNA, potentially triggering the development of cancer,[59] and adequate intake of folate has been shown to help reduce the risk of certain cancers, specifically colon cancer. Studies show that men and women taking a multivitamin supplement or otherwise consuming the recommended amounts of folate have

a lower risk of developing colon cancer. Other studies show an association between diets low in folate and an increased risk of breast and pancreatic cancers.

Daily Needs

Your body absorbs the synthetic folic acid more easily than it absorbs naturally occurring folate. In fact, synthetic folic acid is absorbed 1.7 times more efficiently than most folate that is found naturally in foods.[60] Because of this, your folate needs are measured in **dietary folate equivalents (DFE).** Most adults should consume 400 micrograms DFE of folate daily.

While the foods in your diet analysis program database list the micrograms of folate as DFE, the Nutrition Facts panel on the food label doesn't make this distinction. To convert the micrograms of folic acid found on the food labels of foods with folic acid added, such as enriched pasta, rice, cereals, and bread, to dietary folate equivalents, multiply the amount listed on the label by 1.7:

$$100 \ \mu g \times 1.7 = 170 \ \mu g \ DFE$$

Because 50 percent of pregnancies in the United States are unplanned, women at risk of becoming pregnant should consume 400 micrograms of synthetic folic acid daily from fortified foods or supplements, along with a diet high in naturally occurring folate. Women with a family history of neural tube defects should, under the guidance of their physicians, take even larger amounts.[61]

Food Sources

Since 1998, the FDA has mandated that folic acid be added to all enriched grains and cereal products. This enrichment program has reduced the incidence of neural tube defects by more than 25 percent.[62] Enriched pasta, rice, breads and cereals, legumes (dried peas and beans), leafy green vegetables (spinach, lettuce, collards), broccoli, asparagus, and orange juice are all good sources of this vitamin.

Too Much or Too Little

There isn't any danger in consuming excessive amounts of naturally occurring folate in foods. However, consuming too much folic acid, either through supplements or fortified foods, can be harmful for individuals who are deficient in vitamin B_{12}. A vitamin B_{12} deficiency can cause anemia and, more dangerous, crippling and irreversible nerve damage. Too much folate in the diet masks the symptoms of B_{12}-deficiency anemia. Though the folate can correct anemia, the nerve damage due to the vitamin B_{12} deficiency persists. This delays a proper diagnosis and corrective therapy with vitamin B_{12}. By the time the person is given the vitamin B_{12}, irreversible nerve damage may have occurred. While, as you read, low folate intake may be associated with increased cancer risk, studies suggest that folate consumption double the DRI or even

higher may increase the risk of cancer.[63] When it comes to folic acid, some is essential, but more may not be better.

A folate deficiency can also result in abnormally large and immature cells known as **megaloblasts** (*megalo = large*). These megaloblasts develop into abnormally large red blood cells, or **macrocytes,** that have a diminished oxygen-carrying capacity. Eventually, **macrocytic anemia** causes a person to feel tired, weak, and irritable and to experience shortness of breath. Because folate acts with vitamin B_{12} to produce healthy red blood cells, a defi-

ciency of either vitamin can lead to macrocytic anemia.

An upper level of 1,000 micrograms has been set for folic acid from enriched and fortified foods and supplements to safeguard those who may be unknowingly deficient in vitamin B_{12}.

Table Tips

Fulfill Your Folate Needs

Have a bowl of cereal in the morning.

Add chickpeas to your salad.

Enjoy a tossed salad with your lunch.

Add fresh spinach leaves to your sandwich.

Have a handful of crackers as a late afternoon snack.

Folate

Micrograms (mcg) of DFE of Folate

Food	mcg
Iceberg lettuce, raw, 2 cups	42
Cauliflower, cooked, 1 cup	55
Spinach, raw, 2 cups	116
Asparagus, boiled, 1 cup	268
Orange juice, 1 cup	45
Wheat bread, 1 slice	32
Pasta (spaghetti), enriched, cooked, ½ cup	86
White rice, long-grain, cooked, ½ cup	111
Bran flakes, 1 cup	216
Kidney beans, canned, 1 cup	35
Chickpeas, cooked, ¼ cup	66
Daily Needs: Adults 19 to 50 years	400 µg

Categories: Vegetables, Fruits, Grains, Protein, Daily Needs

Pre-red blood cell

a Folate adequate
Normal cell division
Healthy red blood cells

b Folate deficient*
Immature megaloblast
Macrocyte

*A vitamin B_{12} deficiency can also cause the formation of macrocytes

Terms to Know

folate • folic acid • neural tube defects • anencephaly • spina bifida • dietary folate equivalents (DFE) • megaloblasts • macrocytes • macrocytic anemia

Vitamin B$_{12}$

What Is Vitamin B$_{12}$?

The family of compounds referred to as vitamin B$_{12}$ is also called cobalamin because it contains the metal cobalt.[64] Vitamin B$_{12}$ is the only water-soluble vitamin that can be stored in your body, primarily in your liver.

B$_{12}$ Needs Intrinsic Factor to Be Absorbed

A protein produced in your stomach called **intrinsic factor** is needed to promote vitamin B$_{12}$ absorption. Intrinsic factor binds with vitamin B$_{12}$ in your small intestine, where the vitamin is absorbed. Individuals who cannot produce intrinsic factor are unable to absorb vitamin B$_{12}$ and are diagnosed with **pernicious anemia** (*pernicious* = harmful). Individuals with this condition must be given regular shots of vitamin B$_{12}$, which injects the vitamin directly into the blood, bypassing the intestine.

Because your body stores plenty of vitamin B$_{12}$ in the liver, the symptoms of pernicious anemia can take years to develop.

Functions of Vitamin B$_{12}$

Vitamin B$_{12}$ Is Vital for Healthy Nerves and Red Blood Cells

Your body needs vitamin B$_{12}$ to use certain fatty acids and amino acids and to make the DNA in your cells. Vitamin B$_{12}$ is also needed for healthy nerves and tissues. Like folate, vitamin B$_{12}$ plays an important role in keeping your cells, particularly your red blood cells, healthy.[65] It is also one of the three B vitamins that collectively could be heart healthy (see the feature box "B Vitamins for Your Heart" on p. 230).

Daily Needs

Adults need 2.4 micrograms of vitamin B$_{12}$ daily. American adults, on average, consume more than 4 micrograms daily.

The body's ability to absorb naturally occurring vitamin B$_{12}$ from foods diminishes with age. This decline appears to be due to a reduction in the acidic juices

in the stomach, which are needed to break the bonds that bind the B$_{12}$ to the proteins in food. If the bonds aren't broken, the vitamin can't be released. Up to 30 percent of individuals over the age of 50 experience this decline in acidic juices in their stomachs. Not surprisingly, the pernicious anemia associated with a vitamin B$_{12}$ deficiency occurs in about 2 percent of individuals over the age of 60.[66]

With less acid juice present, the bacteria normally found in the intestines aren't properly destroyed and so tend to overgrow. This abundance of bacteria feed on vitamin B$_{12}$, diminishing the amount of the vitamin that may be available. Luckily, the synthetic form of vitamin B$_{12}$ that is used in fortified foods and supplements isn't bound to a protein, so it doesn't depend on your stomach secretions to be absorbed. (Synthetic vitamin B$_{12}$ still needs intrinsic factor to be absorbed.)

Because the synthetic variety is a more reliable source, individuals over the age of 50 should meet their vitamin B$_{12}$ needs primarily from fortified foods or a supplement.[67]

Food Sources

Naturally occurring vitamin B$_{12}$ is found only in foods from animal sources, such as meat, fish, poultry, and dairy products. A varied diet that includes the minimum recommended servings of these food groups will easily meet your daily needs.

Synthetic vitamin B$_{12}$ is found in fortified soy milk and some ready-to-eat cereals, which are ideal sources for older adults and strict vegetarians, who avoid all foods from animal sources.

Vitamin B₁₂

Micrograms (µg) of Vitamin B₁₂

| Protein | Dairy | Daily Needs |

- Turkey breast, 3 oz — 0.08
- Chicken, dark meat, without skin, cooked, 3 oz — 0.3
- Hamburger, 90% lean, broiled, 3 oz — 2.2
- Salmon, cooked, 3 oz — 2.4
- Tuna, light, canned in water, 3 oz — 2.5
- Soy milk, calcium fortified, 1 cup — 3.0
- Mozzarella cheese, part skim, 1½ oz — 0.4
- Cottage cheese, low fat, 1% milk fat, ½ cup — 0.7
- Feta cheese, 1½ oz — 0.7
- Milk, low fat, 1% milk fat, 1 cup — 1.1
- Yogurt, nonfat, plain, 8 oz — 1.4
- Adults 19 to 50 years — 2.4

If you are relying solely on fortified foods to meet your vitamin B₁₂ needs, continually check the labels on these products to make sure they haven't unexpectedly been reformulated to exclude the vitamin.

Too Much or Too Little

At present, there are no known risks of consuming too much vitamin B₁₂ from foods, fortified foods, or supplements, and no upper level has been set. There is also no known benefit from taking B₁₂ supplements if your diet contains foods from animal sources and/or fortified foods.

A Vitamin B₁₂ Deficiency Can Cause Macrocytic Anemia

Because vitamin B₁₂ and folate work closely together to make healthy red blood cells, a vitamin B₁₂

deficiency can cause macrocytic anemia, the same type of anemia caused by a folate deficiency. In macrocytic anemia due to a vitamin B₁₂ deficiency, there is enough folate available for red blood cells to divide, but the folate can't be utilized properly because there isn't enough vitamin B₁₂ available. In fact, the true cause of macrocytic anemia is more likely a B₁₂ deficiency than a folate deficiency.

Because pernicious anemia (caused by a lack of intrinsic factor) is a type of macrocytic anemia, its initial symptoms are the same as those seen in folate deficiency: fatigue and shortness of breath.

Vitamin B₁₂ is needed to protect nerve cells, including those in your brain and spine, so one long-term consequence of pernicious anemia is nerve damage marked by tingling and numbness in the arms and legs and problems walking. If diagnosed early enough, these symptoms can be reversed with treatments of vitamin B₁₂.

Table Tips

Boost Your B₁₂

Enjoy heart-healthy fish at least twice a week.

Sprinkle your steamed vegetables with reduced-fat shredded cheese.

Drink milk or fortified soy milk.

Try a cottage cheese and fruit snack in the afternoon.

Enjoy a grilled chicken breast on a bun for lunch.

Terms to Know
intrinsic factor • pernicious anemia

Vitamin C

You don't have to go out of your way to ensure that your dog's daily chow contains enough vitamin C. Dogs and many other animals possess an enzyme that can synthesize vitamin C from glucose. Humans, however, lack the necessary enzyme for this conversion, and have to rely on food to meet their daily vitamin C needs.[68]

Functions of Vitamin C

Vitamin C Acts as a Coenzyme

Vitamin C, also known as **ascorbic acid,** acts as a coenzyme that is needed to synthesize and use certain amino acids. In particular, vitamin C is needed to make collagen, the most abundant protein in your body. Collagen is plentiful in your connective tissue, which supports and connects all your body parts, so this protein is needed for healthy bones, teeth, skin, and blood vessels.[69] Thus, a vitamin-C–deficient diet would affect your entire body.

Vitamin C Acts as an Antioxidant

Like beta-carotene and vitamin E, vitamin C acts an antioxidant that may help reduce the risk of chronic diseases such

as heart disease and cancer. It also helps you absorb the iron in plant foods such as grains and cereals and break down histamine, the component behind the inflammation seen in many allergic reactions.[70]

White blood cells

Vitamin C Boosts Your Immune System

Vitamin C helps keep your immune system healthy by enabling your body to make white blood cells, like the ones shown in the photo above. These blood cells fight infections, and this immune-boosting role has fostered the belief that high doses of vitamin C can cure the common cold. (The "Gesundheit! Myths and Facts about the Common Cold" box on page 261 takes a look at this theory.)

Daily Needs

Women need to consume 75 milligrams of vitamin C daily, and men need to consume 90 milligrams daily to meet their needs.

Smoking accelerates the breakdown and elimination of vitamin C from the body, so smokers need to consume an additional 35 milligrams of vitamin C every day to make up for these losses.[71]

Food Sources

Americans meet about 90 percent of their vitamin C needs by consuming fruits and vegetables, with orange and/or grapefruit juice being the most popular source in the diet. One serving of either juice will just about meet an adult's daily needs. Tomatoes, peppers, potatoes, broccoli, oranges, and cantaloupe are also excellent sources.

Too Much or Too Little

Brendan, the track athlete introduced at the beginning of this chapter, attempted to ward off a cold by taking vitamin C supplements. His attempt to solve one medical dilemma created another one that impeded his training more than his sniffling and sneezing.

Though excessive amounts of vitamin C aren't known to be toxic, consuming more than 3,000 milligrams daily through the use of supplements has been shown to cause nausea, stomach cramps, and diarrhea. Brendan can attribute the diarrhea he experienced to his daily 3,500-milligram supplement of vitamin C. Once he stopped taking the supplement, his diarrhea ceased.

Vitamin C

Milligrams (mg) of

Food	mg
Tomato, ½ medium	8
Baked potato, with skin, 1 small	13
Sweet potato, boiled, 1	20
Peas, frozen, low sodium, cooked, 1 cup	35
Vegetable juice, low sodium, 1 cup	67
Tomato soup, 1 cup	68
Broccoli, boiled, 1 cup	101
Red pepper, 1 raw	226
Pineapple, canned, 1 cup	24
Cantaloupe, 1 cup	59
Orange, 1 medium	70
Kiwi, 1	71
Grapefruit, sections, 1	79
Strawberries, raw, 1 cup	89
Men 19 to 50 years	90
Women 19 to 50 years	75

Vegetables · Fruits · Daily Needs

The upper level for vitamin C for adults is set at 2,000 milligrams to avoid the intestinal discomfort that excessive amounts of the vitamin can cause. Too much vitamin C can also lead to the formation of kidney stones in individuals with a history of kidney disease.

Vitamin C–deficiency skin hemorrhages.

Because vitamin C helps to absorb the form of iron found in plant foods, those with a rare disorder called **hemochromatosis** (*hemo* = blood; *chroma* = color; *osis* = condition), which causes the body to store too much iron, should avoid excessive amounts of vitamin C. Iron toxicity is extremely dangerous and can damage many organs in your body, including the liver and heart.

For centuries, **scurvy,** the disease of a vitamin C deficiency, was the affliction of sailors on long voyages. After many weeks at sea, sailors would run out of vitamin-C–rich produce and then develop the telltale signs of scurvy: swollen and bleeding gums, a rough rash on the skin, coiled or curly arm hairs, and wounds that wouldn't heal. Because vitamin C is needed for healthy blood vessels, a deficiency also often causes purple colored spots, a sign of skin hemorrhages, to appear on the skin and in mucus mem-

branes of the body such as the lining of the mouth.

In 1753, a British naval surgeon discovered that orange and lemon juice prevented scurvy. Decades later, the British government added lemon or lime juice to their standard rations for sailors to thwart scurvy. In 1919, vitamin C was discovered as the curative factor in these juices.[72]

Table Tips

Juicy Ways to Get Vitamin C

Have at least one citrus fruit (such as an orange or grapefruit) daily.

Put sliced tomatoes on your sandwich.

Enjoy a fruit cup for dessert.

Drink low-sodium vegetable juice for an afternoon refresher.

Add strawberries to your low-fat frozen yogurt.

Terms to Know

ascorbic acid · hemochromatosis · scurvy

Pantothenic Acid and Biotin

What Are Pantothenic Acid and Biotin?

Pantothenic acid and biotin are B vitamins.

Functions of Pantothenic Acid and Biotin

Pantothenic acid and biotin aid in the metabolism of the nutrients that provide you with energy: carbohydrates, proteins, and fats.

Daily Needs

Adults need 5 milligrams of pantothenic acid and 30 micrograms of biotin daily.

Food Sources

Both pantothenic acid and biotin are widely available in foods, including whole grains and whole-grain cereals, nuts and legumes, broccoli, peanut butter, meat, milk, and eggs. Most Americans easily meet their needs.[73]

Biotin deficiency is so rare that an accurate list of the amount in foods is hard to find. In addition to its abundance in foods, biotin can be synthesized by the bacteria in your intestinal tract, providing yet another avenue to meet your needs. Eating a healthy diet to meet all of your other B vitamin needs will ensure that you meet your needs for pantothenic acid and biotin.

Too Much or Too Little

Like many of the other B vitamins, there are no known adverse effects from consuming too much pantothenic acid or biotin. An upper level has not been determined for either of these vitamins.

Although a pantothenic acid deficiency is rare, if you do fall short of your needs, your symptoms might include fatigue, nausea, vomiting, numbness, muscle cramps, and difficulties walking.

During World War II, prisoners of war in Asia experienced a "burning feet" syndrome. The symptoms ranged from heat sensations and tingling on the soles of their feet to a painful burning intense enough to disrupt sleep. Their diet consisted predominantly of nutrient-poor polished rice. A doctor in India who was studying an identical phenomenon in his patients discovered that when he gave them supplements of pantothenic acid, the condition stopped.[74] In both cases, the syndrome was later attributed to a diet deficient in pantothenic acid.

Consuming inadequate amounts of biotin can cause hair loss, skin rash, and feelings of depression, fatigue, and nausea.[75] Though deficiencies are rare, they can occur if you eat a lot of raw egg whites. The protein avidin, found in egg whites, binds with biotin and blocks it from being absorbed in your intestine. Cooking the egg denatures and inactivates the protein, eliminating the problem.[76]

Gesundheit! Myths and Facts about the Common Cold

You probably know the symptoms well. Your nose runs like a leaky faucet and turns beet red from constant wiping. Your head seems stuffed with cotton, and it feels like someone is playing bongo drums under your scalp. Between coughing and sneezing, you can't get the rest you need to relieve what feels like constant fatigue. The diagnosis? At least one of the more than 200 varieties of cold virus has invaded your body, and you have a cold that could last as long as two weeks.

You're never alone if you have a case of the common cold. Colds are the leading cause of doctor visits in the United States, and Americans will suffer a billion of them this year alone.[4] Students miss more than 20 million school days every year battling the common cold.[5]

The Truth about Catching a Cold

Contrary to popular belief, you can't catch a cold from being outside on a cold day without a coat or hat. Rather, the only way to catch a cold is to come into contact with a cold virus. Contact can be direct, such as when you hug or shake hands with someone who is carrying the virus; or indirect, such as when you touch an object like a keyboard or telephone contaminated with a cold virus. The next time you touch your nose or rub your eyes, you transfer these germs from your hands into your body. You can also catch a cold virus by inhaling virus-carrying droplets from a cough or sneeze of someone with the cold.

The increased frequency of colds during the fall and winter is likely due to people spending more time indoors in the close quarters of classrooms, dorm rooms, and the workplace, which makes the sharing of germs easier. The low humidity of the winter air can also cause the inside of your nose to be drier and more permeable to the invasion of these viruses.

Vitamin C and the Common Cold

In the 1970s, a scientist named Linus Pauling theorized that consuming at least 1,000 milligrams of vitamin C would prevent the common cold. Since then, study after study has shown that megadoses of vitamin C are not effective in preventing colds. One large analysis of more than 30 studies with more than 11,000 participants did not show any benefit of taking vitamin C for either preventing a cold or reducing the duration of a cold once it was contracted.[6]

Other Cold Remedies: The Jury Is Still Out

Recently, other dietary substances, such as the herb echinacea and the mineral zinc, have emerged as popular treatment strategies for the common cold. Echinacea had been used centuries ago by some Native American populations to treat coughs and sore throats. Studies have shown that the herb comes up short in preventing or affecting the duration or severity of a cold and may contribute to side effects such as a rash and intestinal discomfort. The results of a review of more than 300 studies on use of echinacea were inconclusive. More research must be done to establish whether echinacea can help prevent or treat the common cold.[7]

Studies of zinc have also had mixed results. Too much zinc can be toxic and can actually suppress your immune system. You will learn more about zinc and its role in the immune system in Chapter 8.

What You Can Do

One of the best ways to reduce your chances of catching a cold is to wash your hands frequently with soap and water. This will lower the likelihood of germs being transmitted from your hands to your mouth, nose, or eyes. One study found that children who washed their hands four times a day had 20 percent fewer sick days from school than those who washed their hands less frequently. When soap and water aren't available, gel sanitizers or disposable alcohol-containing hand wipes can be an effective alternative.[8] Covering your mouth and nose when you cough or sneeze and then immediately washing your hands will help you keep from contaminating the people around you.

Finally, the Centers for Disease Control recommends the following steps if you do get a cold:

➤ Get plenty of rest.
➤ Drink plenty of fluids. (Chicken soup and juices are considered fluids.)
➤ Gargle with warm salt water or use throat lozenges for a sore throat.
➤ Dab petroleum jelly on a raw nose to relieve irritation.
➤ Take aspirin* or acetaminophen (Tylenol) for headache or fever.

*The American Academy of Pediatrics recommends that children and teenagers avoid consuming aspirin or medicine containing aspirin when they have a viral illness, as it can lead to a rare but serious illness called Reye's syndrome. This syndrome can cause brain damage or death.

Are There Other Important Nutrients?

Choline Is an Essential Nutrient

Choline is an essential nutrient that your body needs for healthy cells and nerves, but it is not classified as a vitamin. Although your body can synthesize it, a study has shown that males given choline-deficient diets weren't able to synthesize enough of it to meet their needs and experienced liver damage. Research has not yet determined whether this would occur in women, infants, children, and older adults.[13] To be safe, the current recommendation of 425 milligrams for women and 550 milligrams for men is based on the amount needed to protect the liver.

Although choline is widely available in foods, especially milk, liver, eggs, and peanuts, Americans' diets appear to be falling short of this nutrient (see Table 7.4 on page 266). Too much choline from supplements can cause sweating and vomiting as well as **hypotension** (*hypo* = low), or low blood pressure. Too much choline can also cause a person to emit an unpleasant fishy odor as the body tries to get rid of the excess. The upper level of 3,500 milligrams for choline has been set to prevent your blood pressure from dropping too low and to keep you from smelling like a fish.

Carnitine, Lipoic Acid, and Inositol Are Vitamin-Like Substances

Certain vitamin-like substances are needed for overall health and important body functions, but they are not considered essential nutrients because your body can synthesize them in adequate amounts without consuming them in foods, and deficiency symptoms are not known to occur in humans.

Carnitine (*carnus* = flesh) is needed to properly utilize fat. It is abundant in foods from animal sources, such as meat and dairy products. Although there is no research to support the claim, carnitine supplements are sometimes advertised to promote weight loss and help athletes improve their performance.[14]

Similar to many B vitamins, **lipoic acid** helps your cells generate energy, and it was in fact initially thought to be a vitamin.[15] Lipoic acid is also being studied for its potential role as an antioxidant that could help reduce the risk of certain chronic diseases, such as diabetes mellitus and cataracts.

Lastly, **inositol** is needed to keep cell membranes healthy. Inositol can be found in foods from plant sources. As with the other important vitamin-like substances, healthy individuals can synthesize enough inositol to meet their needs, so supplements are not necessary.

The "Vitamins at a Glance" chart in Table 7.3 provides you with a quick guide to your vitamin needs.

The Take-Home Message Choline, carnitine, lipoic acid, and inositol are vitamin-like substances. Choline is an essential nutrient that is needed for healthy cells and nerves. Americans' diets may be falling short of choline. Carnitine, lipoic acid, and inositol are needed for important body functions and overall health, but are not essential nutrients. Your body can synthesize these substances in adequate amounts, and there are no known deficiency symptoms.

choline A vitamin-like substance needed for healthy cells and nerves.

hypotension Low blood pressure.

carnitine A vitamin-like substance needed to properly utilize fat.

lipoic acid A vitamin-like substance that your body needs for energy production; it may also act as an antioxidant.

inositol A vitamin-like substance synthesized in your body that helps to keep your cells and their membranes healthy.

Table 7.3

Vitamins at a Glance

	Major Functions	Adult DRI, Ages 19 to 50 Years	Food Sources	Toxicity Symptoms/UL	Deficiency Symptoms/Conditions
Fat-Soluble Vitamins					
Vitamin A	Vision, cell differentiation, reproduction, bone health, immune function	700–900 µg RAE/day	Beef liver, fortified dairy products	Compromised bone health, birth defects during pregnancy	Night blindness, xerophthalmia, stunting of bones
Beta-carotene	Provitamin A carotenoid, antioxidant		Sweet potatoes, carrots, winter squash, cantaloupe	Carotenodermia	
Vitamin D	Calcium balance, bone health, cell differentiation, immune system	15 µg (600 IU)/day	Fatty fish (salmon, tuna, sardines) Fortified foods (dairy products, orange juice, cereals)	Hypercalcemia	Rickets and osteomalacia
Vitamin E	Antioxidant, health of cell membranes, heart health	15 mg alpha-tocopherol/day	Vegetable and seed oils, nuts, seeds, fortified cereals, green leafy vegetables	Interference with blood clotting and increased risk of hemorrhage UL: 1,000 mg from supplements and/or fortified foods	Nerve problems, muscle weakness, and uncontrolled movement of body parts
Vitamin K	Blood clotting, bone health	90–120 µg/day	Green leafy vegetables, soybeans, canola and soybean oils, beef liver	None known	Excessive bleeding
Water-Soluble Vitamins					
Thiamin (B₁)	Coenzyme, needed for nerve function and energy metabolism	1.1 mg–1.2 mg/day	Pork Enriched and fortified foods, whole grains	None known	Beriberi, Wernicke-Korsakoff syndrome
Riboflavin (B₂)	Coenzyme in energy metabolism, enhances function of other B vitamins	1.1–1.3 mg/day	Milk, enriched and fortified grains, whole grains	Can turn urine bright yellow	Sore throat, inflammation of the mouth, tongue, and lips

continued

Table 7.3 continued

Vitamins at a Glance

	Major Functions	Adult DRI, Ages 19 to 50 Years	Food Sources	Toxicity Symptoms/UL	Deficiency Symptoms/ Conditions
Water-Soluble Vitamins					
Niacin (B$_3$)	Coenzyme in energy metabolism, needed to synthesize fat and cholesterol	14–16 mg/ day	Lean meats, fish, poultry, enriched and fortified grains and cereals, whole grains, corn, sweet potatoes	Flushing, nausea, vomiting, toxic to liver, may raise blood glucose levels UL: 35 mg/day	Pellagra, characterized by dermatitis, diarrhea, and dementia
Vitamin B$_6$	Coenzyme in energy metabolism, hemoglobin, healthy immune and nervous systems, homocysteine metabolism	1.3–1.7 mg/ day	Fortified cereals, meat, fish, poultry, many vegetables and fruits, nuts, peanut butter, and other legumes	Nerve damage, tingling in hands and feet UL: 100 mg/day	Sore tongue, inflammation of skin, depression, possible anemia, confusion
Folate	DNA and red blood cell formation, prevention of specific birth defects, homocysteine metabolism	400 µg/day	Dark green leafy vegetables, enriched pasta, rice, breads and cereals, legumes, orange juice, asparagus, spinach	Masks vitamin B$_{12}$ deficiency UL: 1,000 µg/day	Macrocytic anemia
Vitamin B$_{12}$	Synthesis of new cells, especially red blood cells, healthy nerves and tissues Activates folate	2.4 µg/day	Animal products, including lean meats, fish, poultry, eggs, cheese, fortified foods	None known	Pernicious anemia, macrocytic anemia, nerve damage as indicated by tingling and numbness in the hands and feet
Vitamin C	Collagen formation, antioxidant, enhanced iron absorption, healthy immune system	75–90 mg/day (an additional 35 mg if a smoker)	Citrus fruit, tomatoes, peppers, potatoes, broccoli, cantaloupe	Nausea, diarrhea, stomach cramps UL: 2,000 mg/ day	Scurvy; characterized by bleeding gums, skin hemorrhages, coiled or curly arm hairs
Biotin and Pantothenic Acid	Aid in the metabolism of the energy nutrients	Pantothenic Acid: 5 mg/ day Biotin: 30 µg/day	Both are widespread in foods	No known adverse effects UL has not been set	For pantothenic acid: fatigue, nausea, vomiting, numbness, muscle cramps, and difficulty walking For biotin: hair loss, skin rash, depression, fatigue, nausea

How Should You Get Your Vitamins?

Natural food sources, like fruits and vegetables, have long been advocated as an excellent way to get your vitamins. With advances in fortified foods and supplements, new options became available for meeting your nutrient needs. Let's look next at the pros and cons of each of these.

Foods Are Still the Best Way to Meet Your Vitamin Needs

Because foods provide more than just vitamins (many are also rich in disease-fighting phytochemicals, antioxidants, and fiber), they are the best way to meet your vitamin needs. The substances and nutrients in foods all work together to keep you healthy. For example, the fat in your salad dressing helps you absorb the carotenoids in the carrots in your salad. The vitamin-C–rich tomatoes on your sandwich help you absorb the iron in the wheat bread. The whole is indeed greater than the sum of its parts when it comes to eating a balanced diet to meet your vitamin needs.

The *Dietary Guidelines for Americans* recommend eating a wide variety of foods from each food group with ample amounts of vitamin-rich fruits, vegetables, whole grains, and lean dairy foods. Table 7.4 shows the estimated intake of each nutrient that a 2,000-calorie diet based on the *Dietary Guidelines* will provide. As you can see from the table, it may be challenging to get enough of vitamins E and D to meet your needs.[16] Refer to the Table Tips for these vitamins on pages 239 and 244 for more suggestions on meeting your vitamin needs for the day.

If you are falling short of some vitamins in your diet, fortified foods can help make up the difference.

Store vitamin-B–rich whole-wheat flour in an airtight container in your refrigerator or freezer. Because whole-wheat flour contains the germ of the wheat kernel, which is rich in unsaturated fatty acids, it is more susceptible to becoming rancid than refined white flour.

Fortified Foods Can Provide Additional Nutrients, but at a Price

When you pour your morning glass of orange juice, you know that you are getting a significant splash of vitamin C. However, depending on the brand of orange juice, you may also be meeting your vitamin E and vitamin D needs—two nutrients that are not (and never have been) naturally found in oranges. Welcome to the world of fortified foods.

Fortified foods—that is, foods that have nutrients added to them—can be a valuable option for individuals whose diets fall short of some nutrients. For instance, someone who doesn't drink milk, such as a strict vegetarian or an individual who is lactose intolerant, would benefit from drinking vitamin D- and calcium-fortified soy milk. Older adults who are inactive, and thus, have lower calorie needs may choose fortified foods to add nutrients, such as vitamins B_{12} and E, to their limited dietary selections. Women in their childbearing years may look to folic-acid–fortified cereals to help them meet their daily needs of this B vitamin.

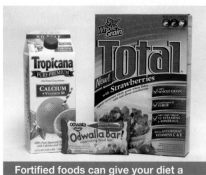

Fortified foods can give your diet a vitamin boost.

fortified foods Foods with added nutrients.

Table 7.4

You Can Meet Your Vitamin Needs with Healthy Food Choices

Nutrient	USDA Food Intake Pattern, 2,000 Calories	Institute of Medicine Recommendations RDA/AI*
Vitamin A, µg RAE	851	700–900
Vitamin D, IU	258	600
Vitamin E, mg AT	8.3	15
Vitamin K, µg	140	90–120
Thiamin, mg	1.8	1.1–1.2
Riboflavin, mg	2.2	1.1–1.3
Niacin, mg	23	14–16.0
Vitamin B_6, mg	2.3	1.3–1.7
Vitamin B_{12}, µg	6.5	2.4
Folate, µg	628	400
Vitamin C, mg	126	75–90
Choline, mg	340	425–550

Note: RDA = Recommended Dietary Allowance; AI = Adequate Intakes; RAE = retinol activity equivalents; AT = α-tocopherol; mg = milligrams; µg = micrograms
*The recommended intake level for adult men or women, age 19–50 years old, is stated.

Source: U.S. Department of Agriculture. 2010. *Report of the Dietary Guidelines Advisory Committee on the Dietary Guidelines for Americans, 2010.* Available at www.cnpp.usda.gov/DGAs2010-DGACReport.htm; Institute of Medicine. 2011. Dietary Reference Intakes for Calcium and Vitamin D. Available at www.iom.edu/Reports/2010/Dietary-Reference-Intakes-for-Calcium-and-Vitamin-D/DRI-Values.aspx.

Fortified foods can do a disservice in the diet if they displace other vitamin- and mineral-rich foods. For example, a sugary orange drink that has vitamin C added to it should not replace vitamin-C–rich orange juice. Although the vitamin C content of the two beverages may be the same, the orange-flavored drink doesn't compare well to the juice when it comes to providing other nutrients and phytochemicals. As you can see from **Figure 7.7**, the orange drink is basically orange-flavored water sweetened with 7 teaspoons of sugar and enriched with vitamin C.

A diet containing numerous fortified foods can put you at risk of overconsuming some nutrients. If a heavily fortified food, like some cereals, snack bars, and beverages, claims to contain "100% of the vitamins needed daily," then eating several servings of the food or a combination of several fortified foods is similar to taking several multivitamin supplements. You are more likely to overconsume vitamins from fortified foods than from whole foods.

eLearn

Do I Shake the Cantaloupe to Tell If It's Ripe?

Fruits are loaded with vitamins and antioxidants, but how do you spot Mother Nature's tastiest gems? To learn how to find the ripest fruit at the supermarket, visit www.pearsonhighered.com/blake.

Vitamin Supplements Are Not a Substitute for Healthy Eating

Americans spend more than $11 billion on vitamin and mineral supplements annually and are expected to spend more than $15 billion by 2014. The aging of the population appears to be driving this increase in the use of supplements—older people may use vitamins and minerals in an attempt to mitigate ongoing medical issues.[17]

Vitamin supplements are called supplements for a reason: A vitamin pill or a combined multivitamin and mineral pill may be used to *supplement* your diet. Supplements should never be used to replace a healthy diet. A consistent diet of nonnutritious foods

Added sugar = 0

Added sugar =

a Pure orange juice is an excellent source of the mineral potassium and doesn't contain any added sugar.

b Orange drink is basically sugar water with vitamin C added to it. A glass will contain the equivalent of 7 teaspoons of added sugar.

= 1 tsp of added sugar

followed by a daily supplement won't transform your less-than-desirable eating habits into a healthy diet. The disease-fighting phytochemicals, fiber, and other substances that your body needs are all missing from a bottle of supplements.

Who Might Benefit from a Supplement?

Supplements are useful for people who cannot meet their nutrient needs through a regular, varied diet. Among those who may benefit from taking a dietary supplement are:[18]

> Women of childbearing age who may become pregnant, as they need to consume adequate amounts of folic acid to prevent certain birth defects
> Pregnant and lactating women who can't meet their nutrient needs with foods
> Older individuals, who need adequate amounts of vitamin D and synthetic vitamin B_{12}
> Individuals who do not drink enough milk and/or do not have adequate sun exposure to meet their vitamin D needs
> Individuals on low-calorie diets that limit the amount of vitamins and minerals they can consume through food
> Strict vegetarians, who have limited dietary options for vitamins B_{12} and D and other nutrients

- Individuals with food allergies or lactose intolerance that limit food choices
- Individuals who abuse alcohol, have a poor appetite, have medical conditions such as intestinal disorders, or are taking medications that may increase their need of certain vitamins
- Individuals who are food insecure and those who are eliminating food groups from their diet
- Infants who are breast-fed should receive 400 IU of vitamin D daily until they are consuming at least 1 quart of formula daily. Children age one and older should receive 400 IU of vitamin D daily if they consume less than one quart of milk per day. Adolescents who consume less than 400 IU of vitamin D daily from their diet would also benefit from a supplement.

Always talk to your health care professional or a registered dietitian (RD) before taking a vitamin or mineral supplement to make sure it is appropriate based on your medical history, especially if you are taking prescription medications. Supplements can interact or interfere with certain medications. If you regularly eat many fortified foods, the addition of a supplement could cause you to overconsume some nutrients. A meeting with a RD for a diet "checkup" can help you decide if a supplement is needed.

See Table 7.5 for a brief consideration of the pros and cons of relying on foods, supplements, and fortified foods to meet your vitamin needs.

Who's Minding the Vitamin Store?

Dietary supplements, a category that includes vitamins, minerals, and herbs, are regulated less stringently by the Food and Drug Administration (FDA) than are drugs. In 1994, Congress passed the Dietary Supplement Health and Education Act, which shifted the responsibility for determining the quality, effectiveness, and safety of dietary supplements from the FDA to the manufacturers. Unlike drugs, dietary supplements do not require FDA approval before they can be marketed to the public, unless they contain a new ingredient that hadn't been used prior to 1994. Recall from Chapter 2 that supplement manufacturers are legally permitted to make structure/function claims on the labels of dietary supplements. The FDA cannot remove a supplement from the marketplace unless it has been shown to be unsafe or harmful to the consumer.[19]

The FDA is trying to tighten its regulation of dietary supplements to better safeguard the public against harmful products and misleading claims. One way it plans to do this is to improve the criteria that it uses to make enforcement decisions about dietary supplements. The FDA is also trying to improve its process for evaluating potential safety concerns and adverse reports that may arise from a variety of sources, including consumers, media reports, consumer groups, and experts.

There is an organization that provides some guidance for consumers when it comes to labeling dietary supplements. The **U.S. Pharmacopoeia (USP)** is a nonprofit organization that sets standards for dietary supplements.[20] Although it does *not* endorse or validate health claims that the supplement manufacturers make, it will test a supplement to ensure that it:

- Contains the ingredients in the amounts stated on the label
- Will disintegrate and dissolve in a reasonable amount of time in the body for proper absorption

U.S. Pharmacopeia (USP) A nonprofit organization that sets purity and reliability standards for dietary supplements.

Table 7.5 Foods, Fortified Foods, and Supplements

There are a variety of ways to meet your vitamin needs. Consider the pros and cons to find out the best combination for you.

Foods

Pros: Sources of other nutrients and energy; can supply phytochemicals, antioxidants, and fiber; delicious and satisfying

Cons: Need to shop for and prepare meals; need to plan for in diet

Fortified Foods

Pros: Easy to obtain a specific nutrient; can be delicious and satisfying

Cons: Often more expensive than regular variety; risk of overconsumption of nutrients; can displace a more nutrient-dense food

Supplements

Pros: Easy to obtain; no planning or preparation involved

Cons: Can be expensive; risk of overconsumption of nutrients; lack of antioxidants, phytochemicals, and fiber found naturally in foods; not satisfying

---

➤ Is free of contaminants

➤ Has been manufactured using safe and sanitary procedures

Supplement manufacturers can voluntarily submit their products to the USP's staff of scientists for review. Products that meet the preceding criteria can display USP's seal on their labels.

What's a Consumer to Do?

With hundreds of bottles of vitamin and mineral supplements available on the store shelves, you could get dizzy trying to find one that's right for you. The best place to start when picking a supplement is to carefully read the label. The FDA has strict guidelines for the information that must appear on any supplement label. For example, the term "high potency" can be used only if at least two-thirds of the nutrients in the supplement contain at least 100 percent of the daily value (**Figure 7.8**). The label must also clearly identify the contents of the bottle. While a supplement may have the USP seal of approval for quality and purity, it doesn't have the FDA's approval, even if it makes a claim. Supplements must contain a panel that lists the serving size, the number of tablets in the bottle, the amount of the vitamin in each capsule, and the percentage of the Daily Value. All the ingredients must also be listed.

When you need to perform your best, take vitamin C. It's a smart choice to help your immune system.

DIRECTIONS FOR USE: Take one capsule daily.

Supplement Facts

Serving Size 1 Capsule		%DV
Amount Per Capsule		
Vitamin C	60mg	100%

Other ingredients: Gelatin, water, and ascorbic acid.

XYZ Company
Some Place, NJ 00001

Figure 7.8 Supplement Smarts
The FDA has strict guidelines for the information that must appear on any supplement label. **(a)** The FDA allows the term "high potency" to be used as long as at least two-thirds of the nutrients contain at least 100 percent of the daily value. **(b)** All supplements must clearly identify what is in the bottle. **(c)** Always look for the USP seal of approval for quality and purity. Choose the cheapest supplement with the seal to save a few dollars. **(d)** The FDA disclaimer is a reminder that this product doesn't have the FDA seal of approval for effectiveness. **(e)** The structure/function claim explains that vitamin C is beneficial for your immune system. **(f)** The net quantity of contents must be listed. The Supplement Facts panel lists the serving size, the vitamins in the supplement, and the amount of the vitamin in each capsule. **(g)** The amount of each supplement is also given as a percentage of the Daily Value. Remember, the Daily Value may be higher than you actually need. **(h)** All the ingredients must be listed in descending order by weight. **(i)** The name and address of the manufacturer or distributor must be provided.

The Take-Home Message A well-balanced diet that provides adequate calories can meet most individuals' daily vitamin needs. Fortified foods, as part of a healthy diet, can provide extra nutrients for those whose diets fall short. A vitamin supplement is another option for individuals unable to meet their daily vitamin needs. The consumer needs to take care when selecting a dietary supplement and should seek advice and guidance from a qualified health professional.

Made Over, Made Better

Including vegetables in your diet is a good step in the right direction, but sometimes there are improvements that can be made to increase the vitamin content in your meals and snacks.

Here are some typical vitamin-rich foods made over and made nutritionally better!

Source: USDA National Nutrient Database for Standard Reference; food manufacturers.

If you like this. . .	Try this instead!

Creamed Spinach
1 cup: 180 calories
Vitamin A: 2,000 IU

Steamed Spinach
1 cup: 54 calories
Vitamin A: 14,790 IU

Fried, Breaded Onion Rings
10 rings: 244 calories
Vitamin C: 1 gram

Sautèed Onions
1 onion: 115 calories
Vitamin C: 2 grams

Cheese & Bacon Stuffed Baked Potato
1 loaded potato: 451 calories
Folate: 30 micrograms

Baked Potato
1 plain potato: 161 calories
Folate: 49 micrograms

Broccoli with Cheese Sauce
1 cup: 113 calories
Vitamin C: 59 milligrams

Broccoli, Steamed
1 cup: 52 calories
Vitamin C: 74 milligrams

Two Points of View

Is Sun Exposure Necessary to Ensure Adequate Vitamin D Intake?

Vitamin D is essential for optimal function of all cells and tissues, so having adequate amounts in the body is essential to overall health. Although vitamin D is added to some foods, notably milk, some researchers contend that it is best produced by the body after exposure to sunlight. This exposure, however, leads to increased risk of skin cancer.

Is synthesizing vitamin D in the skin after sun exposure preferable to consuming it in foods or supplements? What are the potential pitfalls of sun exposure? After you've read the arguments for each side, read the critical thinking questions and decide for yourself.

Yes

- Osteoporosis, heart disease, hypertension, autoimmune diseases, certain cancers, depression, chronic fatigue, and chronic pain are all associated with vitamin D deficiency.[1]

- Obtaining sufficient vitamin D from natural food sources alone can be difficult, and taking vitamin D supplements carries the risk of consuming too much and experiencing toxicity symptoms.[2]

- Controlled exposure to sunlight is the safest way to replenish vitamin D stores. It eliminates the risk of toxicity because your body produces only a limited amount of vitamin D from sun exposure.[3]

- Some sensible exposure of your skin to the sun for several minutes every day could meet your daily vitamin D needs without significantly increasing the risk of skin cancer.[4]

No

- UV radiation is a carcinogen responsible for most of the estimated 1.5 million skin cancers and the 8,000 deaths due to metastatic melanoma that occur annually in the United States.[5] It is not known whether a desirable level of regular sun exposure exists that imposes no (or minimal) risk of skin cancer over time.

- The American Academy of Dermatology advises that appropriate measures, including the use of sunscreen, hats, and clothing, be taken whenever one is exposed to the sun.[6]

- Even the modest amount of recommended exposure—exposing the arms and legs or hands, arms, and face to the sun for 5 to 15 minutes, two to three times per week, between 10 A.M. and 3 P.M. without sunscreen protection—would result in damage to the skin and increase the risk of skin cancer.[7]

- Dietary supplements can be tailored to individual needs, and do not result in skin damage.

What do you think?

1. Which is more compelling—that some sun exposure is necessary for adequate vitamin D synthesis, or that all unprotected sun exposure should be avoided because of the risk of skin cancer? **2.** Should kids be exposed to sunlight, or should they be given vitamin D via supplements? **3.** What is the best way to increase your vitamin D intake?

Chapter Review

Be a Nutrition Sleuth

Deciphering the Food Label

As mentioned in Chapter 2, the current Daily Values (DVs) for vitamins and minerals that appear on food labels are based on reference values introduced in the 1970s! Consequently, these values may be higher or lower than the *latest* amounts recommended for each vitamin that you read about in this chapter.

Go to www.pearsonhighered.com/blake to see if you can figure out how much of vitamins A, D, and C are in typical breakfast cereals and milk. You may be surprised!

Get Real!

Are You Meeting Your Vitamin Needs?

Let's get real and find out if you are getting an adequate amount of vitamins in your diet. Go to www.pearsonhighered.com/blake and use the food chart to enter a typical daily diet. Don't forget to put in any vitamin supplements or fortified foods that you consume.

Use the Food Composition Table supplement or the MyDietAnalysis program to complete the chart to see how you fare with these specific vitamins. You may discover that there are vitamins you are getting too much or too little of in your diet.

The Top Ten Points to Remember

1. Vitamins are essential nutrients needed by your body to grow, reproduce, and maintain good health. They are found naturally in foods, added to foods, or in pill form in dietary supplements.

2. Fat-soluble vitamins are stored in your body and require fat for absorption. They can accumulate to the point of toxicity if your intake is excessive. Water-soluble vitamins are absorbed with water and typically aren't stored for extended periods. Excess amounts of water-soluble vitamins do not accumulate to toxic levels, but can be harmful if you routinely consume too much.

3. Antioxidants, such as vitamins E and C, and beta-carotene, suppress harmful oxygen-containing molecules called free radicals that can damage cells. Free radicals can contribute to chronic diseases such as cancer and heart disease and accelerate the aging process. Diets abundant in antioxidant-rich fruits, vegetables, and whole grains are associated with a lower incidence of many diseases.

4. Vitamin A is needed for strong vision, reproduction, and healthy fetal development. Carotenoids are yellow-reddish pigments that give some fruits and vegetables their vibrant yellow-red color. The carotenoid beta-carotene is a common provitamin that can be converted to vitamin A in your body. Two other carotenoids, lutein and zeaxanthin, are being investigated for their potential role in eye health. The carotenoid lycopene acts as an antioxidant in the body.

5. Vitamin D is necessary for absorption of calcium and phosphorus. Although vitamin D can be made in your body with the help of ultraviolet rays from the sun, some individuals are not exposed to enough sunlight to meet their needs. A deficiency of vitamin D can cause rickets in children and osteomalacia in adults. Milk and fortified yogurts are excellent sources of vitamin D.

6. Vitamin E is an antioxidant that protects your cells' membranes. It plays an important role in helping prevent the "bad" LDL cholesterol carrier from being oxidized. High levels of artery-clogging, oxidized LDL cholesterol are a risk factor for heart disease. Vitamin K helps your blood to clot and to synthesize proteins that keep bones healthy.

7. The B vitamins thiamin, riboflavin, niacin, vitamin B_6, pantothenic acid, and biotin are all coenzymes that assist in numerous energy-producing reactions.

8. The B vitamins folate and vitamin B_{12} are needed for healthy red blood cells. A deficiency of either can cause macrocytic anemia. Adequate amounts of folic acid can reduce the risk of certain birth defects, including spina bifida and anencephaly. A prolonged vitamin B_{12} deficiency can cause nerve damage.

9. Vitamin C is needed for healthy bones, teeth, skin, and blood vessels, and for a healthy immune system. Excessive amounts can cause intestinal discomfort. Vitamin C doesn't prevent the common cold, but may

reduce the duration and severity of a cold in some people once it is contracted.

10. Fortified foods and vitamin supplements can help individuals with inadequate diets to meet their nutrient needs. However, supplements should never replace a healthy diet. The U.S. Pharmacopoeia (USP) seal on a supplement label indicates that the supplement has been tested and meets the criteria for purity and accuracy.

Test Your Knowledge

1. Which of the following vitamins are water soluble? (Circle all that apply.)
   a. vitamin A
   b. vitamin C
   c. vitamin B_6
   d. vitamin K
   e. folic acid

2. The most usable form of vitamin A in your body is
   a. retinol.
   b. retinal.
   c. retinoic acid.
   d. retinoids.
   e. none of the above.

3. Vitamin D is
   a. a hormone.
   b. made in your body with the help of sunlight.
   c. found in fortified milk.
   d. all of the above.
   e. a and b only.

4. You are enjoying a salad bar lunch (good choice!). You want to top your greens with vitamin-E–rich foods. You could choose
   a. olive oil and vinegar.
   b. chopped nuts.
   c. avocado slices.
   d. all of the above.
   e. none of the above.

5. A deficiency of thiamin can cause
   a. rickets.
   b. beriberi.
   c. scurvy.
   d. osteomalacia.

6. Which of the following are considered antioxidants?
   a. vitamin E
   b. vitamin K
   c. beta-carotene
   d. all of the above
   e. a and c only

7. Adam Craig is 55 years old. Which of the following might his body have difficulty absorbing?
   a. the vitamin B_{12} in a piece of steak
   b. the vitamin B_6 in liver
   c. the folate in spinach
   d. the riboflavin in milk
   e. the thiamin in bread

8. You are enjoying a lovely breakfast of raisin bran cereal doused in skim milk and a glass of orange juice. The vitamin C in the orange juice will enhance the absorption of
   a. the calcium in the milk.
   b. the vitamin D in fortified milk.
   c. the iron in the cereal.
   d. none of the above.
   e. a and b only.

9. Folic acid can help reduce the risk of
   a. acne.
   b. neural tube defects.
   c. night blindness.
   d. pellagra.
   e. none of the above.

10. The USP seal on the vitamin label means that the dietary supplement has been tested and shown to
    a. be free of any contaminants.
    b. be manufactured using safe and sanitary procedures.
    c. contain the amount of the substance that is stated on the label.
    d. meet all of the above criteria.
    e. a and b only.

Answers

1. (b, c, e) Vitamins C, B_6, and folic acid are water soluble, whereas vitamins A and K are fat soluble.

2. (a) Retinol is the most usable form of vitamin A in your body. Retinoids include all three forms of preformed vitamin A: retinol, retinal, and retinoic acid.

3. (d) Vitamin D is a hormone and can be made in your body with the help of adequate exposure to the sun's ultraviolet rays. You can also obtain it by drinking fortified milk.

4. (d) Go for all of them. Olive oil, nuts, and avocados are all excellent sources of vitamin E.

5. (b) A chronic deficiency of thiamin can cause beriberi. A vitamin D deficiency can cause rickets in children and osteomalacia in adults. Scurvy is the result of a vitamin C deficiency.

6. (e) Both vitamin E and beta-carotene function as antioxidants in your body. Although vitamin K isn't an antioxidant, it helps your blood clot.

7. (a) Approximately 10 to 30 percent of adults over the age of 50 have reduced secretions of acidic stomach juices, which affects the absorption of the vitamin B_{12} that is found naturally in food. The other B vitamins should be absorbed regardless of Adam's age.

8. (c) Vitamin C will help your body absorb the iron in grain products and cereals. Vitamin C does not affect the absorption of calcium or vitamin D. However, the vitamin D in the milk will help you absorb the mineral calcium.

9. (b) If consumed prior to and during the first several weeks of pregnancy, adequate amounts of folic acid can reduce the risk of neural tube defects, including spina bifida and anencephaly. Vitamin-A–containing medication may be used to treat acne. Vitamin A can also help prevent night blindness. Consuming adequate amounts of niacin prevents pellagra.

10. (d) Manufacturers of dietary supplements can voluntarily have their products tested for all of the above. The U.S. Pharmacopoeia (USP) seal also signifies that the supplement has been tested for its ability to dissolve in a reasonable amount of time in your body so that it can be properly absorbed.

Web Resources

➥ To learn more about fulfilling your needs for fruits and vegetables, visit www.fruitsandveggiesmorematters.org/

➥ For more information on the disease-fighting capabilities of fruits and vegetables, visit www.fruitsandveggiesmatter.gov/

➥ To find out the latest recommendations for vitamins, visit http://ods.od.nih.gov/factsheets/list-VitaminsMinerals/

➥ To learn more about preparing and cooking vitamin-rich foods and vegetables, visit http://apps.nccd.cdc.gov/dnparecipe/recipesearch.aspx

Answers to Myths and Misperceptions

1. **False.** Although vitamins perform numerous functions in your body, they don't provide energy, as do carbohydrates, proteins, and fats. To find out more, turn to page 226.

2. **False.** Some vitamins are stored in the body and can build up to toxic levels if taken in excess. To find out more, turn to page 228.

3. **True.** Deep orange vegetables and some green vegetables are good sources of the vitamin A precursor beta-carotene, which is converted to vitamin A in your body. To find out more about beta-carotene and vitamin A, turn to page 235.

4. **True.** Vitamin E functions as an antioxidant in your body. To learn more about antioxidants, turn to page 238.

5. **True.** Vitamin K helps a protein in your bones bind with the bone-strengthening mineral calcium. To learn about other functions of vitamin K, turn to page 240.

6. **True.** However, some people are unable to meet their vitamin D needs through sunlight exposure alone. To find out if you are at risk, turn to page 242.

7. **True.** Folate can lower the risk of some birth defects during pregnancy. However, timing is everything. To find out when a pregnant woman needs to be taking this B vitamin, turn to page 254.

8. **False.** There is no clear evidence that taking megadoses of vitamin C, such as from supplements, protects you from the common cold. To find out what role it does play in combating colds, turn to page 261.

9. **True.** However, fortified foods are not always healthy foods. To find out how to tell the difference, turn to page 265.

10. **False.** While foods are an excellent source of vitamins, some individuals may need extra vitamin support from a supplement. To find out who would benefit from a supplement, turn to page 267.

8

True or False?

1. Your morning mug of **coffee** counts toward fulfilling your daily water needs. (T|F) p. 284

2. Enhanced waters are **healthier** than plain water. (T|F) p. 287

3. Minerals are more **bioavailable** in plant foods than in animal foods. (T|F) p. 288

4. Most of your dietary sodium comes from the **salt** that you shake on your foods. (T|F) p. 290

5. Magnesium can help lower your **blood pressure**. (T|F) p. 293

6. A serving of **milk** will provide about one-third of an adult's daily calcium needs. (T|F) p. 296

7. **Trace minerals** are not as important to your body as major minerals. (T|F) p. 305

8. Meat is the major source of **iron** in the American diet. (T|F) p. 307

9. **Fluoride** has been added to most bottled water. (T|F) p. 314

10. Chromium can help weight lifters build **bigger muscles** and stay lean. (T|F) p. 316

See page 329 for answers to these Myths and Misperceptions.

Minerals and Water

Desiree, a college sophomore, stops off at the campus convenience store every morning to buy a bottle of water to take to her classes and her part-time job. Later in the day, she purchases another bottle before heading for the gym. Her mother sent her a reusable water bottle that she could fill at numerous on-campus water fountains, but Desiree scoffed at her mom's suggestion to drink tap water instead of bottled water. Desiree believes that bottled water is pure and safer to drink than tap water.

Do you think Desiree's perceptions about bottled water being better than tap water are accurate? What are the potential disadvantages to consuming only bottled water? In this chapter, we'll discuss the essential roles that water plays in the body, as well as the daily needs for and best sources of water. We'll also discuss the individual minerals, and explore the health implications of consuming them in deficient or toxic amounts.

Chapter Objectives

After reading this chapter, you will be able to:

1. Explain the functions of water in the body.

2. Describe the daily recommended intake for water consumption.

3. Describe the difference between dehydration and water intoxication.

4. List at least one food source for each major mineral.

5. Identify the role of sodium in your body.

6. Name at least three lifestyle habits that can increase the risk for high blood pressure.

7. Describe osteoporosis and the factors that influence the risk of developing the disease.

8. List at least one major food source for each trace mineral.

9. Compare and contrast heme and nonheme iron.

10. Explain the role of fluoride in tooth and bone structure.

Why Is Water So Important?

The average healthy adult is about 60 percent water, which makes water the most abundant substance in your body. However, individuals vary in the exact amount of water they carry, because factors such as age, gender, and the body's amount of fat and muscle tissue affect body water (**Figure 8.1**). Muscle tissue is approximately 65 percent water, whereas fat tissue is only 10 to 40 percent water.[1] Men have a higher percentage of muscle mass and a lower percentage of fat tissue than women of the same age, so men have more body water. For the same reason, muscular athletes have a higher percentage of body water than do sedentary individuals.

You could survive for weeks without food, but only a few days without water. This is in part because of water's role in allowing chemical reactions, including those that provide you with energy, to take place within your cells.

Water is also essential for maintaining the fluid balance inside your body. Think about it: Your body cells are plump with fluid, and they float in the fluid that surrounds them. As part of your body fluid, water is essential for maintaining fluid balance. You learned in Chapter 6 that fluid balance refers to the equal distribution of fluid among several compartments in your body. The fluid inside your cells is in the **intracellular fluid compartment,**

~5% minerals and other nutrients

~14% protein

29% fat

52% water

~5% minerals and other nutrients

~17% protein

20% fat

59% water

Female, 137 lbs.   Male, 168 lbs.

Figure 8.1 Your Body Is Mostly Water
More than 50 percent of your body is made up of water. Protein, fat, and minerals make up most of the rest of you.

whereas the fluid in the space outside your cells is in the **extracellular fluid compartment.** The extracellular fluids are further broken down into (1) **interstitial fluids,** which are in the space immediately outside your cells, and (2) the fluids in your blood (see **Figure 8.2**). The interstitial fluids act as an area of exchange between your blood fluids and your cells.

Maintaining the equal distribution of all this body fluid is crucial to health, and water and dissolved minerals play key roles. The minerals important in fluid balance are called **electrolytes** (*electro* = electricity, *lytes* = soluble). They include sodium, potassium, phosphate, magnesium, calcium, and chloride. Water in your body is drawn into and out of your cells by the "pull" of electrolytes. When cells have more electrolytes than the fluid outside them, water flows in, and vice versa. We will talk more about the movement of fluids later in this chapter.

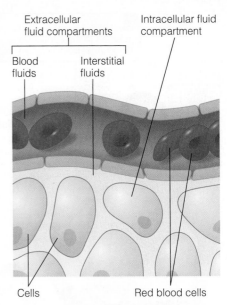

Water Is the Universal Solvent

Water is a wonderful **solvent,** a liquid in which substances dissolve. In fact, water is commonly known as the universal solvent. As a solvent, water is part of the medium in which molecules come in contact with each other. This contact between molecules allows chemical reactions to take place. For example, the combining of specific amino acids to synthesize a protein occurs in the watery medium inside your cells.

Figure 8.2 Water as Part of Body Fluids
Water is a key component of the fluid compartments both inside and outside cells.

Water Is a Transport Medium

The water in blood and lymph helps transport substances throughout your body. Did you know that only about 45 percent of your blood is red blood cells? Most of the rest is water. As part of blood, water helps transport oxygen, nutrients, and other important substances to your cells. It also helps transport waste products away from cells to be excreted in urine and stool. Like the fluid in blood, lymph fluid is almost entirely water. Lymph transports proteins back to the bloodstream, and it is important in the absorption of fats. Lymph also transports wastes and microbes through "cleaning stations" called *lymph nodes,* where defensive cells consume these harmful substances before the lymph returns to the blood.

Water Helps Maintain Body Temperature

The water in your blood is like the coolant that runs through a car. They both absorb, carry, and ultimately release heat in order to keep a running machine from overheating. In a car, the coolant absorbs the heat from a running engine and carries it to the radiator for release. In your body, the water in your circulating blood absorbs the heat from your internal core—the center of your body, where your most important organs are located—and carries it to the skin for release (**Figure 8.3**). Water works so well as a coolant in both your car and your body because it has a unique ability to absorb and release a tremendous amount of heat. Like a car, your body sometimes gets overheated. For instance, if you were to go jogging on a hot summer day, the enormous amount of internal heat that would be generated would probably overwhelm the heat-absorbing capacity of your body's water. The increasing heat would break apart the molecules of water on your skin, transforming them from a liquid (sweat) to a vapor. The evaporation of sweat from your skin would release the heat and cool you down, enabling you to maintain a safe body temperature. When you are cold, less

intracellular fluid compartment The fluid located inside your cells.

extracellular fluid compartment The fluid located outside your cells. Interstitial fluids and fluids in the blood are extracellular fluids.

interstitial fluids Fluids located between cells.

electrolytes Charged ions that conduct an electrical current in a solvent such as water. Sodium, potassium, and chloride are examples of electrolytes in the body.

solvent A liquid that acts as a medium in which substances dissolve. Water is considered the universal solvent.

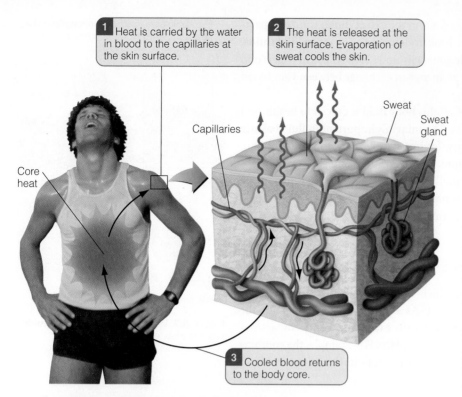

1 Heat is carried by the water in blood to the capillaries at the skin surface.

2 The heat is released at the skin surface. Evaporation of sweat cools the skin.

Sweat

Sweat gland

Capillaries

Core heat

3 Cooled blood returns to the body core.

Figure 8.3 Water Helps Regulate Your Body Temperature

A developing fetus is cushioned in a sac of watery amniotic fluid to protect it from physical harm during pregnancy.

blood flows to your body surface, so that your core stays warm. That's why your hands, feet, and face can become so cool to the touch on a cold day.

Water Is a Lubricant and a Protective Cushion

Water, combined with other molecules, acts as a lubricant for your joints, helping to promote easy, friction-free movement. The water in tears lubricates your eyes and helps flush out dust and other debris. Water is also part of the saliva that moistens your mouth and foods and the mucus that lubricates your intestinal tract. Water is the main part of the fluid that surrounds certain organs, including your brain; thus, it acts as a cushion to protect them from injury during a fall or other trauma. During pregnancy, a developing fetus is surrounded by a sac of watery amniotic fluid, which helps protect it from physical harm.

The Take-Home Message Your body is mostly water. Muscle tissue has more water than does fat tissue. The water inside your body cells is balanced by the water outside your cells. Electrolytes help maintain fluid balance. Water is a universal solvent that helps transport oxygen and nutrients throughout your body. It also absorbs and releases heat to regulate your body temperature, acts as a lubricant through saliva and mucus, and provides a protective cushion for your brain and other organs.

What Is Water Balance and How Do You Maintain It?

water balance The state whereby an equal amount of water is lost and replenished daily in the body.

When the amount of water you consume is equal to the amount you lose daily, you are in **water balance**. When you are not in water balance—that is, having too much or too little water in your system—health problems can occur. Thus, maintaining water balance is very important.

There are several ways in which water is lost from your body and several mechanisms that help you replenish those losses. Let's look at this next.

Figure 8.4 The Concept of Water Balance: Intake Equals Output
You get most of your water from foods and beverages, though a small amount is also generated through the process of metabolism. You lose water in your urine, stool, sweat, and exhaled breath. The amount of water that you take in is balanced with the amount that you excrete every day.

You Take in Water through Beverages and Food

The first aspect of being in water balance is consuming enough water. You get most of your daily water from beverages such as tap or bottled water, milk, juices, and soft drinks. You also get some water from the foods that you eat, although much less in comparison (**Figure 8.4**). Even the driest foods, like oatmeal and bread, provide some water. A small amount of water is also generated during metabolism.

You Lose Water through Your Kidneys, Large Intestine, Lungs, and Skin

The other aspect of water balance is excreting excess water so that you don't have too much in your body. You normally lose water daily through these four routes:

➤ Via your kidneys in the form of urine
➤ Via intestinal fluids in your stool (unless you are experiencing diarrhea, the amount of water lost in stool is normally small)
➤ Via the water that evaporates when you exhale
➤ Via your skin when you release the heat produced in your body core

The water that evaporates when you exhale and the water lost through your skin when you release the heat generated during normal reactions is called **insensible water loss,** as it occurs without your noticing it. An individual living in a moderate or temperate climate and doing little physical activity loses between one-half and one quart of water daily through insensible water loss.[2]

Insensible water loss doesn't include the water lost in sweat. Sweating is your body's way of releasing a higher than normal amount of heat. The amount of water lost during sweating varies greatly and depends upon many environmental factors, such as the temperature, the humidity, the wind, the sun's intensity, clothing worn, and the amount of physical activity you are doing.[3] For example, if you jump rope in

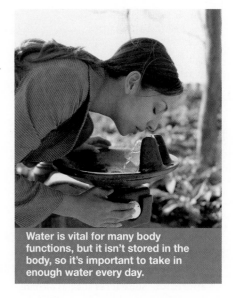

Water is vital for many body functions, but it isn't stored in the body, so it's important to take in enough water every day.

insensible water loss The water that is lost from the body daily through exhalation from the lungs and evaporation off the skin.

Drink low-fat or skim milk with each meal to add calcium as you meet your fluid needs.

Freeze grapes for a juicy and refreshing snack.

Add a vegetable soup to your lunch for a fluid-packed meal.

Cool down with a sweet treat by spooning slightly thawed frozen strawberries onto low-fat vanilla ice cream.

Add zip to your water by adding a slice of fresh lemon or lime.

dehydration The state whereby there is too little water in the body due to too much water being lost, too little being consumed, or a combination of both.

diuretics Substances such as alcohol and some medications that cause the body to lose water.

thirst mechanism Various bodily reactions caused by dehydration that signal you to drink fluids.

osmosis The movement of a solvent, such as water, from an area of lower concentration of solutes across a membrane to an area of higher concentration of solutes. It balances the concentration of solutes between the compartments.

antidiuretic hormone (ADH) A hormone that directs the kidneys to concentrate urine and reduce urine production in order to reduce water loss from the body.

the noontime sun on a summer day wearing a winter coat, you'll soon be losing a lot of water as sweat. In contrast, little or no sweat will leave your body if you sit under a shady tree on a dry, cool day wearing shorts and a light tee shirt.

Losing Too Much Water Can Cause Dehydration

Dehydration is a state in which you've lost too much, or aren't taking in enough, water. Dehydration can result from not drinking enough fluids and/or from conditions that result in too much water (and sodium) being lost from the body, such as diarrhea, vomiting, high fever, and the use of **diuretics.** If dehydration persists, a person can experience weight loss, dizziness, and confusion, as well as impaired physical coordination, and, in extreme situations, death.[4]

Have you ever been outside for a while on a hot day and noticed that your mouth was as dry as the Sahara Desert? The dry mouth is part of your **thirst mechanism,** and is your body's way of telling you to find a water source—you are on the road to dehydration. The thirst mechanism plays an important role in helping you avoid dehydration and restore the water balance in your body.

Your Thirst Mechanism Signals Dehydration

The dry mouth that makes you thirsty when you are dehydrated is due to the increased concentration of electrolytes in your blood. As the concentration of these minerals increases, less water is available to your salivary glands to make saliva.[5] Thus, your mouth feels very dry.

When you are dehydrated, the fluid volume in your blood decreases, resulting in a higher concentration of sodium in the blood. To restore balance, the fluid inside your cells will move through the membrane to the outside of the cell and into your blood to balance the concentration of sodium between these compartments. This movement of water across the cell membrane is called **osmosis** (see **Figure 8.5**).

Your brain detects the increased concentration of sodium in your blood and triggers your thirst mechanism, reminding you to drink fluids. Your brain will also trigger the secretion of **antidiuretic hormone (ADH)** from the pituitary gland. ADH causes your kidneys to decrease further loss of water and thus concentrate your urine.[6] These mechanisms work together to keep your body in water balance.

Other Ways to Tell If You Are Dehydrated

Just quenching your thirst will not typically provide enough fluids to remedy dehydration. This isn't a concern for moderately active individuals eating a balanced diet, as fluids from beverages and food throughout the day will eventually restore water balance.[7] However, older adults, and individuals who are very physically active and/or who have physically vigorous jobs, such as firefighters, are at higher risk of dehydration because they don't take in enough fluid, or they lose body water copiously through sweating. These individuals need to take additional steps to ensure that they are properly hydrated.

One way to monitor hydration is the cornerstone method, which involves measuring body weight before and after long bouts of intense physical activity or labor and noting any changes. If a person weighs less after an activity than before, the weight change is due to loss of body water, and that water must be replenished. (Alternatively, if a weight gain is noted, overhydration is likely, and you need to drink less before your next activity.)

Urine color can also be used to assess hydration. When you are dehydrated, you produce less urine due to the release of ADH. The urine you do produce is more concentrated, as it contains a higher proportion of compounds to the smaller volume of

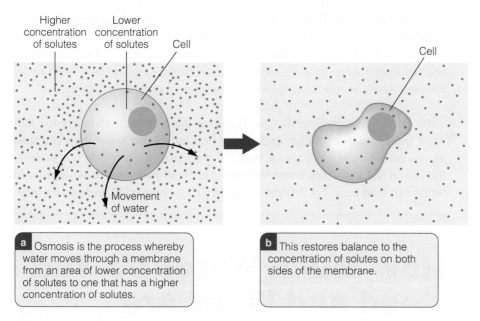

a Osmosis is the process whereby water moves through a membrane from an area of lower concentration of solutes to one that has a higher concentration of solutes.

b This restores balance to the concentration of solutes on both sides of the membrane.

Figure 8.5 Osmosis

water. This causes the urine to be darker in color.[8] The National Athletic Trainers Association has created a chart to help individuals assess if they are drinking enough fluids to offset the amount of water lost through sweating (see **Figure 8.6**).[9] If you are very physically active and the color of your urine darkens during the day, to the point where it resembles the shade of a "yield" sign or darker, you likely need to increase the amount of fluids in your diet. (Note: Other factors, such as consuming excessive amounts of the B vitamin, riboflavin, and certain medications can also affect the color of urine.)

Consuming Too Much Water Can Cause Hyponatremia

For healthy individuals who consume a balanced diet, it's hard to consume too much water, because the body will just produce more urine to eliminate the excess. However, some individuals, particularly soldiers during military training and athletes who participate in endurance events such as marathons, have experienced water toxicity in certain circumstances.[10]

In April 2002, 28-year-old Cynthia Lucero was running the Boston Marathon. About five miles from the finish line, Lucero began to feel wobbly and mentioned to a friend that she felt dehydrated even though she had been consuming fluids throughout her run. She suddenly collapsed and was taken to a nearby hospital. She died the next day, not of dehydration, but of overhydration. In January 2007, 28-year-old Jennifer Strange collapsed after competing in a California radio contest to see who could drink the most water without using the restroom. She was found dead in her home a few hours after completing the contest.[11] The cause of death for both of these individuals was swelling of the brain brought on by **hyponatremia** (*hypo* = under, *natrium* = sodium, *emia* = blood), caused by overconsumption of fluids. In both cases, drinking too much fluid diluted the blood to the point where sodium levels were too low, which in turn resulted in the swelling of body tissues. When swelling occurs in the brain, the person can experience symptoms similar to those of dehydration—fatigue, confusion, and disorientation.[12] Mistakenly treating these symptoms by consuming more fluids will only make matters worse.

Figure 8.6 Urine Color Can Signal Dehydration
If you collect your urine in a cup and it looks like the color of 1 through 3 on the chart, you are well hydrated. If it resembles color 7 or is darker, you are dehydrated and need to drink more fluids.

hyponatremia A condition of too little sodium in the blood.

Even though dehydration is more common and a bigger challenge to physically active individuals than overhydration, the seriousness of overhydration has prompted the USA Track & Field association to revise its hydration guidelines for long-distance and marathon runners to avoid hyponatremia. Chapter 11 will provide these guidelines and show you how to calculate how much fluid you need during exercise.

The Take-Home Message You lose water daily through your kidneys, intestinal tract, lungs, and skin. If you lose more water than you take in, you will become dehydrated. Your thirst mechanism reminds you to drink fluids and helps restore water balance. Although rare, overconsumption of fluids can lead to an electrolyte imbalance (hyponatremia) and can be fatal.

How Much Water Do You Need and What Are the Best Sources?

Your daily water requirements may be different from those of your grandparents, parents, siblings, and even the classmate sitting next to you. The amount of water a person needs depends on his or her physical activity, environmental factors such as air temperature, and diet. (Recall from Chapter 4 that increasing the fiber in your diet should be accompanied by an increase in water consumption.)

The current recommendation for the amount of water you should consume daily is based on the reported total water intake (from both beverages and food) of healthy Americans.[13] Currently, healthy female adults consume about 12 cups, whereas men consume about 16 cups of water daily. About 80 percent of this intake is from beverages. Therefore, adult women should ingest about 9 cups (~80 percent of 12 cups) and adult males approximately 13 cups (~80 percent of 16 cups) of beverages daily. People who are very active will have higher water requirements because they lose more water by sweating. Complete the Self-Assessment to see if you are meeting your daily fluid needs.

If you think that sounds like a lot, keep in mind that a well-balanced, 2,200-calorie diet that includes beverages at all meals and snacks will provide about 12 cups of water.[14] Drinking water (either from the tap or from a bottle), milk, and juices throughout the day can help you meet your needs. The feature box "Tap Water or Bottled Water: Is Bottled Better?" discusses the differences and similarities between tap water and bottled water.

The remaining 20 percent of your water can come from foods. All foods contain some water. Cooked hot cereals and many fruits and vegetables are robust sources of water (see **Figure 8.7**).

Contrary to popular belief, beverages like caffeinated coffee, tea, and soft drinks ⓣⒻ will contribute to your daily water needs. Caffeine is a diuretic, so it causes water to be excreted, but the water loss it causes is short lived. In other words, the caffeine doesn't cause a significant loss of body water over the course of a day compared with noncaffeinated beverages. In fact, research suggests that individuals who routinely consume caffeinated beverages actually develop a tolerance to its diuretic effect and experience less water loss over time.[15]

Even though caffeinated beverages can count as a water source, this doesn't mean you should start guzzling caffeinated colas and other soft drinks. Their high calorie and sugar

Figure 8.7 Water Content of Foods
Approximately 20 percent of the water you consume comes from foods. Fruits, vegetables, and cooked grains all contain a high percentage of water by weight.

Source: A. Grandjean and S. Campbell, *Hydration: Fluids for Life*. (Washington, D.C.: ILSI Press, 2004). Available at www.ilsi.org.

contents can quickly have you drinking your way into a very unbalanced, high-calorie diet. These soft drinks also contain acids that can contribute to erosion of tooth enamel. See **Figure 8.8** on page 288 for a list of the healthiest fluids to drink to meet your daily water needs.

The Take-Home Message Adult women should ingest about 9 cups of water daily, whereas adult men should drink about 13 cups daily. Those who are very active will need more water to avoid dehydration. Foods and caffeinated beverages contribute to your daily water needs.

What Are Minerals and Why Do You Need Them?

What do a cast-iron skillet, the salt on an icy road, and the copper pipes in some houses all have in common? They're made from some of the same **minerals** that play essential roles in your body. From iron to sodium to copper, these rocky substances occur as part of the earthen world around you and are necessary for your day-to-day functioning. You already read that electrolytes (minerals that are charged ions in your body fluids) help maintain fluid balance. Minerals can also, like vitamins, be part of enzymes, work with your immune system, and play an invaluable role in structural growth. They help chemical reactions take place in your cells, help your muscles contract, and keep your heart beating. In short, they are essential to your overall health and well-being.

minerals Inorganic elements essential to the nutrition of humans.

Tap Water or Bottled Water: Is Bottled Better?

What items do you *have* to have when you walk out the door in the morning? Your keys? Your student ID? Your wallet? What about a bottle of water? Would you never leave home without it? Are you one of the many individuals, like Desiree from the beginning of this chapter, who drinks *only* bottled water because you think it is superior to tap water? If you are, you're certainly not alone. But is bottled water really better or safer for you than tap water?

Desiree is wrong in her assumption that her bottled water is "pure." In fact, drinking 100 percent *pure* water is impossible. Whether you fill your reusable water bottle from the tap or purchase bottled water, the water will contain some impurities. However, this does not mean that the water is unsafe for most individuals to drink. (Note that individuals with a weakened immune system, such as those with HIV/AIDS, undergoing chemotherapy, and/or taking steroids, should speak with their health care provider prior to drinking any water. These individuals may need to take precautions such as boiling their water—no matter the source—before consuming it.[1])

The source of any water will vary from faucet to faucet and bottle to bottle, so it is virtually impossible to make a direct comparison. There are some basic points to understand about each type, though. Let's look at how tap and bottled water compare in terms of regulation, cost, and safety.

Turn on the Tap

Most Americans obtain their drinking water from a community water system. The source of this municipal water can be underground wells or springs, or rivers, lakes, or reservoirs. Regardless of the source, all municipal water is sent to a treatment plant where any dirt and debris are filtered out, bacteria are killed, and other contaminants are removed. The Environmental Protection Agency (EPA) oversees the safety of public drinking water with national standards that set limits for more than 80 contaminants, either naturally occurring ones, such as bacteria, or man-made ones, such as chemicals, that may find their way into your drinking water. Hundreds of billions of dollars have been invested in these treatment systems to ensure that the public water is safe to drink.[2]

Each year, the water supplier in your community must provide you with an annual report about the quality and source of your tap water. In fact, many of these regional reports can be accessed online at www.epa.gov. Even with these precautions, some individuals, who may not like the taste of their tap water or have health concerns, use an in-home water treatment device to further filter their water. Filter devices can range from a less costly pitcher (see photo) or device mounted on the kitchen faucet to a more costly, larger system that treats all the water that enters the home. Depending upon the device, it can filter contaminants such as bacteria, viruses, lead, nitrates, and pesticides. Whatever the device used, it is important that it be maintained regularly to ensure that it is working effectively.

You may have heard the terms "hard" or "soft" water used to describe tap water. The "hardness" refers to the amount of metals—specifically, calcium and magnesium—in the water. The higher the amount, the harder the water. There aren't any health concerns from drinking hard water. In fact, there may be a benefit, as hard water may contribute small amounts of these minerals to your daily diet. Whether your water is hard or soft is less important than meeting your daily needs for enough water.

Another benefit of consuming tap water is that many municipalities add fluoride to

A Well of Sources for Bottled Water

Water can be classified according to its source or how it is treated prior to bottling.

Mineral water	Water derived from an underground source that contains a specific amount of naturally occurring minerals and trace elements. The minerals and elements cannot be added to the water after bottling.
Spring water	Water that is obtained from underground water that flows naturally to the surface. The water is collected at the spring or the site of the well purposefully drilled to obtain this water.
Sparkling water	Spring water that has carbon dioxide gas added to supply "bubbles" before bottling. Also sold as seltzer water or club soda. *Note:* This is technically considered a soft drink and does not have to adhere to FDA bottled water regulations.
Distilled water	Water that has been boiled and processed to remove most, but not all, contaminants.
Flavored water	Water that has a flavor such as lemon or lime added. It may also contain added sugars and calories.
Vitamin or enhanced waters	Water that has vitamins, protein, herbs, and/or caffeine added to it. Such water may also contain added sugars and calories.

Source: A. Bullers, 2002. Bottled Water: Better Than Tap? *FDA Consumer Magazine,* Food and Drug Administration; Center for Science in the Public Interest, Water, Water . . . Everywhere. In *Nutrition Action Health Letter* (June 2000).

their water. About 70 percent of Americans who drink from public systems have fluoride in their water (see the map on page 315).[3] Fluoridation of public water has had a positive impact on the nation's dental health, reducing the incidence of dental caries.

Lastly, tap water costs less than a penny a gallon, making it a very affordable way to stay hydrated.

Bottling Boom

Bottled water is second only to carbonated soft drinks in popularity among Americans. Bottled water that is sold through interstate commerce is regulated by the FDA. Thus, as with other food products, manufacturers must adhere to specific FDA regulations, such as standards of identity. In other words, if the label on the bottle states that it is "spring water," the manufacturer must derive the water from a very specific source (see table). Interestingly, some bottled water may actually be from a municipal water source. (In fact, Desiree may be drinking municipal water in the bottled water that she purchases daily.) The bottled water must also adhere to a standard of quality set forth by the FDA, which specifies the maximum amount of contaminants that can be in the water for it still to be considered safe for consumption. The FDA sets its standards for bottled water based on the EPA's standards for public drinking water. However, water that is bottled and sold in the same state is not regulated by the FDA.[4]

The price of bottled water can be hefty, ranging from $1 to $4 a gallon. Desiree pays $1.50 per bottle and buys two bottles daily, so she is shelling out more than $20 a week and $80 monthly buying bottled water. Over the course of a nine-month term at college, she is spending more than $750 on a beverage that she can get free from the campus water fountains. Finally, many bottled waters are not fluoridated, so bottled water drinkers may be losing out on this important cavity fighter if this is their predominant source of drinking water.[5]

Another costly bottled beverage option is the newer "designer" drinks such as vitamin waters and enhanced waters. Although bottled plain water has become increasingly popular in the past few decades, it seems to be losing ground to these new types of waters. These drinks often advertise health benefits beyond just keeping you hydrated. Sold under brand names such as Aquafina Alive and Dasani Plus, they have been "enhanced" or fortified with additional compounds such as vitamins, sugar, caffeine, and protein, though most Americans typically consume enough or even too much of these in their diet. These designer waters can cost more than $2.50 for a 20-ounce bottle, more than $10 a gallon!

Keep in mind that reusing the bottles from bottled water is not advised. The plastic containers cannot withstand repeated washing and the plastic can actually break down, causing chemicals to leach into the water. Sturdier water bottles that are designed for reuse must be thoroughly cleaned with hot soapy water after each use to kill germs.

The bottom line is that both tap water and bottled water can be safe to drink. Your choice is likely to come down to personal preference and costs. Consider your choice carefully using the Bottled vs. Tap Water table here.

Bottled vs. Tap Water: A Summary

Bottled Water	Tap Water
Cost to Consumers	
➤ About $1.00–$4.00 per gallon (plain water)	➤ About $0.003 per gallon
➤ Designer waters can cost more than $10 per gallon and may contain added sugar and calories	
Safety	
➤ Generally safe	➤ Municipal water is regulated by EPA, state, and local regulations
➤ Some bottled water is not tested for contaminants	
➤ Only bottled water sold across state lines is regulated by the FDA; bottled water not sold across state lines is regulated by state and local guidelines	➤ EPA guidelines require that the public have access to water quality reports and be notified if water quality is outside established bounds
Benefits to Consumers	
➤ Packaging of bottled water may make it more convenient than tap water	➤ Available at the faucet
➤ May taste better than tap water	➤ Often contains fluoride, which helps to prevent tooth decay
	➤ Doesn't contain any added sugar or calories

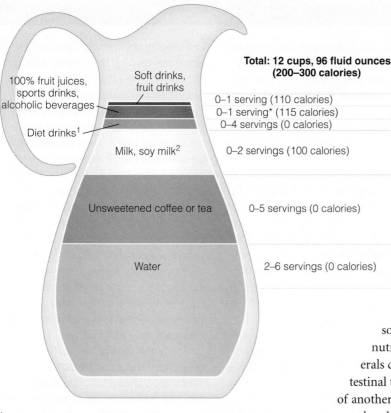

Total: 12 cups, 96 fluid ounces (200–300 calories)

100% fruit juices, sports drinks, alcoholic beverages — 0–1 serving (110 calories)

Soft drinks, fruit drinks — 0–1 serving* (115 calories)

Diet drinks[1] — 0–4 servings (0 calories)

Milk, soy milk[2] — 0–2 servings (100 calories)

Unsweetened coffee or tea — 0–5 servings (0 calories)

Water — 2–6 servings (0 calories)

[1] Includes diet soft drinks and tea or coffee with sugar substitutes.
[2] Includes fat-free or 1% milk and unsweetened fortified soy milk.
* 0–2 servings of alcohol are okay for men.

Figure 8.8 The Best Way to Meet Your Daily Water Needs

inorganic Compounds that do not contain carbon and are not formed by living things.

bioavailability The degree to which a nutrient from foods is available for absorption by the body.

major minerals Minerals needed from your diet and in your body in amounts greater than 100 milligrams per day. These include sodium, chloride, potassium, calcium, phosphorus, magnesium, and sulfur.

trace minerals Minerals needed from your diet and in your body in small amounts, less than 20 milligrams daily. These include iron, zinc, selenium, fluoride, chromium, copper, manganese, and molybdenum.

Your body needs these **inorganic** elements in relatively small amounts. Like vitamins, minerals don't provide calories, so they aren't a source of energy themselves, but they work with other nutrients, such as protein and carbohydrates, to enable your body to function properly.

Mineral Absorption Depends on Bioavailability

Minerals are found in both plant and animal foods, but the best food sources, as you will soon see, tend to be vegetables, legumes, milk, and meats. Absorption of minerals from your foods can vary depending upon their **bioavailability.** The mineral content of plants reflects the soil in which they are grown, as plants must derive nutrients from the soil through their roots. Some minerals compete with each other for absorption in your intestinal tract, and too much of one can cause an imbalance of another. For example, too much zinc in your diet can decrease the absorption of copper. Minerals are also sometimes bound to other substances and your body cannot absorb them (they are eliminated from your body in your stool). An example of this is the calcium in spinach. Spinach is technically high in calcium, but is a poor source of this nutrient because it contains oxalates, which bind with the calcium and render most of it unavailable for absorption. Recall from Chapter 6 that phytates, compounds in fibrous plant foods, can bind to both iron and zinc and inhibit their absorption. This is why the DRI for both zinc and iron is increased for vegans, who consume only plant-based foods. Similarly, the polyphenols in tea and coffee can inhibit your body's absorption of iron, reducing its bioavailability. In contrast, vitamin C will enhance the absorption of iron that is found in plant foods. Protein from animal foods will enhance the absorption of zinc and iron, and (as you read in Chapter 7), vitamin D enhances the absorption of calcium. All these factors affect the bioavailability of these nutrients.

You Need Major Minerals in Larger Amounts

Minerals are categorized into two groups, depending on how much of them you need. The **major minerals,** known also as *macrominerals,* are needed in amounts greater than 100 milligrams per day, and the **trace minerals,** known also as *microminerals,* are needed in amounts less than 20 milligrams per day. The major minerals are major because you need more of them in your body, and thus, you need more of them in your diet (**Figure 8.9**).[16] Your daily needs for the major minerals range from hundreds of milligrams daily to more than a thousand. The major minerals include sodium, chloride, potassium, calcium, phosphorus, magnesium, and sulfur.

Many of these minerals work closely together to perform major body functions. For example, the sodium and chloride located mainly outside your cells, and the potassium, calcium, magnesium, and sulfur, which are mostly inside your cells, all play a key role in maintaining fluid balance. Calcium, phosphorus, and magnesium work together to strengthen your bones and teeth.

Overconsumption of Minerals Can Be Toxic

As with many other nutrients, consuming large amounts of some minerals, particularly the trace minerals, including iron and copper, can have toxic effects. In fact, for some minerals such as magnesium, there isn't a huge difference between the amount that is recommended daily for good health and the excessive amount that can cause gastrointestinal problems such as diarrhea and cramps. The good news is that foods alone rarely provide excessive amounts of any of the minerals; toxicities are usually the result of the use of supplements. This is one more reason why you should try to eat a wide variety of foods to meet your daily needs. **Figure 8.10** gives examples of minerals that are often obtained by following the MyPlate plan.

The Take-Home Message
Minerals are essential nutrients needed in relatively small amounts to enable your body to function properly. All minerals are inorganic elements. The body's absorption of minerals from foods varies, depending on their bioavailability. The seven major minerals are needed in amounts greater than 100 milligrams per day, and the nine trace minerals are needed in amounts less than 20 milligrams per day. Several minerals, particularly the trace minerals, can be toxic if consumed in high amounts.

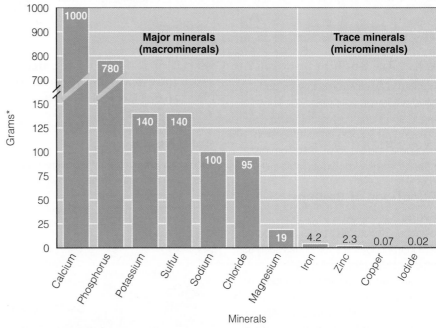

* Based on a 154-pound person

Figure 8.9 The Minerals in Your Body
The major minerals are present in larger amounts than the trace minerals. However, all are equally important to your health.

Vegetables	Fruit	Grains	Protein	Dairy
Potassium	Potassium	Sodium	Sodium	Potassium
Calcium	Calcium	Phosphorus	Phosphorus	Calcium
Magnesium	(fortified juice)	Magnesium	Magnesium	Phosphorus
Chromium	Manganese	Iron	Iron	
Manganese	Boron	Zinc	Copper	
		Selenium	Zinc	
		Chromium	Selenium	
		Manganese		

Figure 8.10 Minerals Are Found Widely in MyPlate
Eating a variety of foods from all food groups is the best strategy to meet your daily mineral needs.

The following pages contain visual summaries of the major minerals you need to stay healthy.

Sodium

What Are Sodium and Salt?

Sodium is an electrolyte in your body. Most sodium in your body is in your blood and in the fluid surrounding your cells. About 90 percent of the sodium you consume is in the form of sodium chloride, commonly known as table salt.

Functions of Sodium

Sodium's chief role is regulation of fluid balance. Sodium also plays an important role in transporting substances such as amino acids across cell membranes.

Salt is frequently added to foods to enhance flavor and as a preservative. It is also added to yeast breads to help the dough rise and to reduce the growth of bacteria and mold in many bread products and deli meats. Sodium phosphate, sodium carbonate, and sodium bicarbonate (baking soda) are food additives and preservatives that perform similar functions in foods.

Monosodium glutamate (MSG) is a common additive in Asian cuisines that is used to intensify the flavor of foods.

Sodium Balance in Your Body

The amount of sodium in your body is maintained at a precise level. When your body needs more sodium, your kidneys reduce the amount that is excreted in your urine. Likewise, when you take in too much sodium, you excrete the excess. For example, when you eat salty pretzels or potato chips, your kidneys will excrete the extra sodium you take in from these snacks.

Smaller amounts of sodium are lost in your stool and through daily perspiration. The amount of sodium lost through perspiration depends upon the rate at which you are sweating, the amount of sodium you have consumed (the more sodium in your diet, the higher the loss), and the intensity of heat in the environment. As you get acclimated to environmental heat,

less sodium will be lost over time in your sweat. This built-in protective mechanism helps to prevent the loss of too much sodium from your body.

Daily Needs

The penny shown below is covered with about 180 milligrams of sodium. This is the bare minimum you need daily. It is based on the amount of sodium needed by individuals who live in temperate climates and those who have become acclimated to hotter environments.[1]

Planning a balanced diet with such a small amount of sodium is virtually impossible, so the recommended sodium intake for adults up to 51 years of age is set at 1,500 milligrams daily. This sodium recommendation allows you to eat a variety of foods from all the food groups so that you can meet your other nutrient needs. It also covers any sodium that is lost in sweat by moderately active individuals, or those who are not acclimated to the environmental temperature. Those who are very physically active and/or not acclimated to the heat will likely need to consume a higher amount of sodium. This can easily be obtained in the diet.

Americans currently consume more than double the recommended amount, or more than 3,400 milligrams of sodium daily, on average.

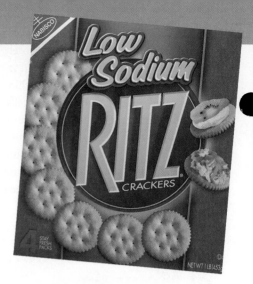

Food Sources

Sodium is so widely available in foods that you don't have to go out of your way to meet your needs.

About 12 percent of Americans' consumption of sodium is from foods in which it occurs naturally, such as fruits, vegetables, milk, meat, fish, poultry, and legumes. Another 5 percent gets added during cooking and another 6 percent is used to season foods at the table.

Processed foods contribute a hefty 77 percent of the sodium in the diet of Americans. Comparing the amount of sodium in a fresh tomato (11 milligrams) with the amount found in a cup of canned tomatoes (355 milligrams) aptly illustrates just how much more sodium is found in processed foods.

Because the majority of your sodium comes from processed foods, and a fair amount comes from the salt that you add to your foods, cutting back on these two sources is the best way to lower your intake. When you buy processed foods, look for the terms "low," "reduced," or "sodium free" on the labels. Further, bypass the salt shaker at the table and

3,500 — American adult daily consumption (>3,400 mg)
3,000
2,500 — Adult upper level (2,300 mg)
2,000
1,500 — Adult recommended daily (1,500 mg)
1,000
500
0 — Adult needed daily (180 mg)

Milligrams of Sodium

Milligrams (mg) of **Sodium**

Food	mg
Green beans, fresh, 1 cup	7
Green beans, frozen, cooked, 1 cup	12
Green beans, canned, cooked, 1 cup	354
Tomato, raw, 1 medium	6
Tomato juice, canned, 1 cup	654
Cucumber, 1 cup	2
Pickles, 1 cup	1,987
Apple, raw, slices with skin, 1 cup	1
Applesauce, canned, sweetened, 1 cup	71
Rice, long-grain white rice, cooked without salt, ½ cup	1
Rice pilaf, cooked, ½ cup	390
Pretzels, unsalted, 1 oz	82
Pretzels, 1 oz	486
Bagel, plain, 2 oz (½ of a large)	254
Bagel, salted, 2 oz (½ of a large)	770
Chicken breast, roasted, without skin, 3 oz	63
Chicken nuggets, 6 pieces (3.4 oz)	671
Turkey breast, roasted, without skin, 3 oz	44
Turkey breast, lunchmeat, 3 oz	1,013
Pork loin, roasted, 3 oz	56
Ham, extra lean, roasted, 3 oz	1,177
Cheese, cheddar, low sodium, 1 oz	6
Cheese, cheddar, 1 oz	176
Cottage cheese, low fat, 1 cup	918
Adults 19 to 50 years (Daily Needs)	1,500

Categories: Vegetables, Fruits, Grains, Protein, Dairy, Daily Needs

season foods with black pepper, Tabasco sauce, lemon juice, or a no-salt seasoning blend.

Too Much or Too Little

There is a direct relationship between sodium and blood pressure in many people. In general, as a person's intake of sodium increases, so does his or her blood pressure. Blood pressure that becomes too high, known as **hypertension,** increases the risk for heart disease, stroke, and kidney disease (see the boxed feature "You and Your Blood Pressure" for more about hypertension). Unfortunately, many Americans will develop hypertension sometime during their lives. Researchers estimate that if Americans reduced their sodium intake by a mere 400 milligrams daily, there would be 1.5 million fewer cases of high blood pressure annually, which could save more than $2 billion in health care costs.[2] To help reduce the risk of high blood pressure, the upper level for adults for sodium is set at 2,300 milligrams. Many Americans exceed this upper limit daily.

Sodium deficiency is rare in healthy individuals consuming a balanced diet.

Table Tips

Shake Your Habit

When buying canned soups, look for the reduced-sodium or low-sodium versions. Add some cooked, frozen vegetables for an even healthier meal.

Keep your portions of deli meats to no more than 3 ounces and build a "meaty" sandwich by adding naturally low-sodium tomatoes, lettuce, cucumbers, and shredded cabbage. Remember to skip the high-sodium pickles!

Nibble on low-sodium dried fruits (apricots, raisins) and unsalted walnut pieces for a sweet and crunchy snack.

Skip the salty french fries and potato chips and enjoy the sodium-free baked potato at dinner.

Use olive oil and balsamic vinegar for a salad dressing with less sodium than is in bottled dressings. Or, dilute equal portions of regular salad dressing with vinegar to cut the sodium.

Terms to Know
hypertension

You and Your Blood Pressure

High blood pressure, or hypertension, is an increasing problem in the United States. In fact, if you were sitting in a room with three other adults, there is a good chance that one of you would have high blood pressure. High blood pressure increases the risk of heart disease, stroke, and kidney damage.[6]

What Is Blood Pressure?

Your blood pressure is a measure of the force your blood exerts against the walls of your arteries. With every beat, your heart pumps blood into your arteries, and thus to all the areas in your body. Blood pressure is highest at the moment of the heart beat. This is known as your **systolic pressure.** Pressure is lower when your heart is at rest between beats. This is called your **diastolic pressure.** Your blood pressure is expressed using these two measurements: systolic pressure/diastolic pressure. Blood pressure of less than 120/80 mm Hg (millimeters of mercury) is considered normal. Your blood pressure rises naturally as you age, which is believed to be due in part to the increased stiffness of the arteries.[7] However, if it rises too much, serious medical problems may occur.

Why Is Hypertension a Silent Killer?

Hypertension happens gradually. As blood pressure begins to rise above normal—that is, systolic is 120 or above and diastolic is 80 or above—it is classified as prehypertension. Many individuals with prehypertension will develop hypertension if they don't lower their blood pressure. A blood pressure of 140/90 mm Hg or above is called **hypertension.**

> **systolic pressure** The force of your blood against the artery walls when your heart beats.
>
> **diastolic pressure** The pressure of your blood against the artery walls when the heart is at rest between beats.
>
> **hypertension** High blood pressure.

Hypertension is referred to as the "silent killer" because there aren't any outward symptoms that your pressure is dangerously elevated; people can have it for years without knowing it. The only way to be sure you don't have it is to have your blood pressure checked regularly.

Individuals with chronic high blood pressure have a higher than normal force pounding against the walls of their arteries, which makes the walls thicker and stiffer, and contributes to atherosclerosis. The heart becomes enlarged and weakened, as it has to work harder to pump enough oxygen- and nutrient-laden blood throughout the body. This can lead to fatigue, shortness of breath, and possibly heart attack. Hypertension can also damage the arteries leading to the brain, kidneys, and legs, which increases the risk of stroke, kidney failure, and partial amputation of a leg.[8]

Can You Control Your Hypertension?

There are factors that increase the chances of developing hypertension, some of which you can control and others you cannot.

Your family history, the aging process, and your race all affect the likelihood that you will develop high blood pressure. These are the risk factors that you can't control.

If your parents, siblings, and/or grandparents have or had hypertension, you are at a higher risk of developing it yourself. Typically, the risk of hypertension increases with age. It is more likely to occur after the age of 35 for men, and women generally experience it after menopause. Hypertension is more prevalent in African-Americans, and tends to occur earlier and be more severe than in Caucasians.[9]

The good news is that there are more risk factors that you *can* control than those that you can't. You can change several dietary and lifestyle habits to help reduce your risk. Among these are your weight and your physical activity level. Individuals who are obese are twice as likely to have hypertension as those at a healthy weight. Even a modest weight loss can have an impact. Losing as little as 10 pounds can reduce a person's blood pressure, and may actually prevent hypertension in overweight individuals even if they haven't yet reached a healthy weight. Additional weight loss can have an even more dramatic effect on blood pressure. Regular physical activity can lower blood pressure even if weight loss hasn't occurred.[10]

You can also control your alcohol consumption, which affects your risk of developing high blood pressure. Studies have shown that

Sweets (5 or less per week)

Beans, nuts, seeds (4–5 per week)

Oils, salad dressing, mayonnaise (2–3 per day)

Low-fat dairy (2–3 per day)

Seafood, poultry, lean meat (0–2 per day)

Grains (preferably whole) (6–8 per day)

Vegetables and fruit (8–10 per day)

The DASH diet, which is rich in whole grains, fruits, vegetables, and low-fat dairy foods, can help lower blood pressure.

drinkers who consumed 3 to 6 drinks daily and then reduced their alcohol consumption by 67 percent, on average, were able to reduce their systolic pressure by more than 3 mm Hg and their diastolic pressure by 2 mm Hg.[11] Less drinking and more physical activity is the name of the game when it comes to keeping high blood pressure at bay.

Lastly, eating a balanced diet is a proven strategy to lower your blood pressure. A large research study, called the DASH (Dietary Approaches to Stop Hypertension) study, followed individuals on three different diets. One diet was a typical American diet: low in fruits, vegetables, and dairy products and high in fat, saturated fat, and cholesterol. A second was rich in just fruits and vegetables, and a third, the DASH diet, was a balanced diet that was lower in fat, saturated fat, cholesterol, and sweets, and high in whole grains, fruits, vegetables, and low-fat dairy products (see figure).

The individuals in the study who followed the DASH diet experienced a significant reduction in blood pressure compared with those who followed the other two diets. Because the sodium content of all three diets was the same,

about 3,000 milligrams, which is the approximate amount that Americans consume daily, on average, the blood pressure lowering effect was attributed to some other substance, or a combination of nutrients working together. For example, due to its abundance of fruits and vegetables, the DASH diet provides healthy doses of potassium and magnesium, and because of its numerous servings of dairy foods, it is also rich in calcium. Dietary potassium, magnesium, and calcium can all play a role in lowering blood pressure.[12]

A follow-up to the DASH study, called the DASH-Sodium study, went one step further and investigated whether reducing the amount of dietary sodium in each of the three diets could also help lower blood pressure. Not surprisingly, it did. We know that, in general, as a person's sodium intake increases, so does the blood pressure. Although this study showed that reducing dietary sodium from about 3,300 milligrams to 2,400 milligrams daily lowered blood pressure, the biggest reduction occurred when sodium intake was limited to only 1,500 milligrams daily. Most importantly, the overall best diet combination for lowering blood

pressure was the DASH diet plus consuming only 1,500 milligrams of sodium daily.[13] *The Dietary Guidelines for Americans, 2010* recommend that Americans should reduce their sodium to less than 2,300 mg daily. Other populations should reduce their sodium even further, to 1,500 mg daily; this lower recommendation applies to about half of the U.S. population, including children and those looking to fight hypertension (see Chapter 2 for more on the *Dietary Guidelines*).[14]

Calculating Your Risk for Hypertension

Would you like to find out *your* risk for developing high blood pressure and learn how lifestyle changes can affect your personal risk? Visit the American Heart Association website and click on the High Blood Pressure Health Risk Calculator at www.americanheart.org/beatyourrisk/en_US/main.html.

Take Charge of Your Blood Pressure!

Diet and lifestyle changes help reduce blood pressure and help prevent hypertension.

If You	By	Your Systolic Blood Pressure* May Be Reduced by
Reduce your sodium intake	Keeping dietary sodium consumption to less than 2,400 mg daily	8–14 mm Hg
Lose excess weight	An amount that allows you to maintain a normal, healthy body weight	5–20 mm Hg for every 22 lbs of weight loss
Stay physically active	Partaking in 30 minutes of aerobic activity (brisk walking) on most days of the week	4–9 mm Hg
Drink alcohol only in moderation	Limiting consumption to no more than 2 drinks daily for men and 1 drink daily for women	2–4 mm Hg
Follow the DASH diet	Consuming this diet, which is abundant in fruits and vegetables and low-fat dairy products	8–14 mm Hg

*Controlling the systolic pressure is more difficult than controlling the diastolic pressure, especially for individuals 50 years of age and older. Therefore, it is the primary focus for lowering blood pressure. Typically, as systolic pressure goes down with diet and lifestyle changes, the diastolic pressure will follow.

Source: Adapted from A. V. Chobanian, et al., "The Seventh Report of the Joint National Committee on Prevention, Detection, Evaluation, and Treatment of High Blood Pressure," *Journal of the American Medical Association* 289 (2003): 2560–2572.

Potassium

What Is Potassium?

Potassium is an important mineral with numerous functions in your body. Luckily, it is also found in numerous foods, so it's not difficult to meet your needs for it.

Functions of Potassium

Potassium Is Needed for Fluid Balance and as a Blood Buffer

More than 95 percent of the potassium in your body is inside your cells, with the remainder in the fluids outside your cells, including your blood. As with other electrolytes, potassium helps maintain fluid balance and keeps your blood pH and acid-base balance correct.

Potassium Is Needed for Muscle Contraction and Nerve Impulse Conduction

Potassium plays a role in the contraction of your muscles, including your heart, and the conduction of nerve impulses. Because of this, a dramatic increase of potassium in your body can lead to irregular heart beats or heart attack, whereas dangerously low levels could cause paralysis. Thus, potassium is tightly controlled and balanced in your body with the help of your kidneys.

Potassium Can Help Lower High Blood Pressure

A diet with plentiful potassium has been shown to help lower blood pressure, especially in salt-sensitive individuals who respond more intensely to sodium's blood pressure–raising capabilities. Potassium causes the kidneys to excrete excess sodium from the body, and keeping sodium levels low can help lower blood pressure. The DASH diet is abundant in foods with potassium.

Potassium Aids in Bone Health and Reduces Kidney Stones

Because potassium plays a buffering role in your blood, it helps keep the bone-strengthening minerals, calcium and phosphorus, from being lost from the bones and kidneys.[3] Numerous studies suggest that having plenty of potassium in your diet helps increase the density, and thus the strength, of your bones.

Potassium also helps reduce the risk of **kidney stones** by causing the body to excrete citrate, a compound that binds with calcium to form kidney stones, shown in the photo below.

Daily Needs

Adults should consume 4,700 milligrams of potassium daily. This amount is recommended to help reduce the risk of high blood pressure. Potassium can also help lower the risk of developing kidney stones and preserve bone health.

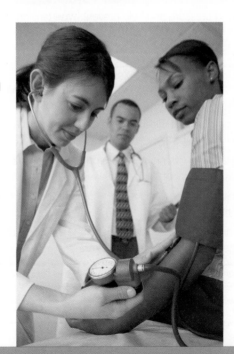

Because Americans fall short of their servings of fruits, vegetables, and lean dairy, they are also falling short of their daily potassium needs. Adult females are consuming only about 2,400 milligrams of potassium, and adult males are consuming only about 3,200 milligrams daily, on average.[4]

Food Sources

The *Dietary Guidelines for Americans, 2010*, recommend consuming an abundance of fruits and vegetables so as to meet your potassium needs. A diet rich in at least 4½ cups of fruits and vegetables, especially leafy greens, which is the *minimum* amount you should be consuming daily, can help you meet your potassium needs. Dairy foods, nuts, and legumes are also good sources (see figure).

Too Much or Too Little

There isn't any known danger from consuming too much potassium that occurs naturally in foods. These excesses will be excreted in your urine. However, consuming too much from supplements or salt substitutes (the sodium in some salt substitutes is replaced with potassium) can cause **hyperkalemia** (*hyper* = too much, *kalemia* = potassium in the blood) for some individuals. Hyperkalemia can cause irregular heartbeats, damage the heart, and be life-threatening.[5]

Those at a higher risk for hyperkalemia include individuals with impaired kidneys, such as people with type 1 diabetes mellitus, those with kidney dis-

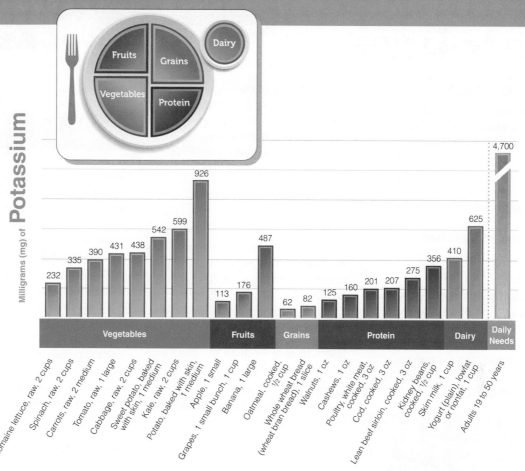

Milligrams (mg) of Potassium

Food	mg
Romaine lettuce, raw, 2 cups	232
Spinach, raw, 2 cups	335
Carrots, raw, 2 medium	390
Tomato, raw, 1 large	431
Cabbage, raw, 2 cups	438
Sweet potato, baked with skin, 1 medium	542
Kale, raw, 2 cups	599
Potato, baked with skin, 1 medium	926
Apple, 1 small	113
Grapes, 1 small bunch, 1 cup	176
Banana, 1 large	487
Oatmeal, cooked, ½ cup	62
Whole wheat bread (wheat bran bread), 1 slice	82
Walnuts, 1 oz	125
Cashews, 1 oz	160
Poultry, white meat, cooked, 3 oz	201
Cod, cooked, 3 oz	207
Lean beef sirloin, cooked, 3 oz	275
Kidney beans, cooked, ½ cup	356
Skim milk, 1 cup	410
Yogurt (plain), lowfat or nonfat, 1 cup	625
Adults 19 to 50 years (Daily Needs)	4,700

ease, and individuals taking medications for heart disease or diuretics that cause the kidneys to block the excretion of potassium. These individuals may also need to consume less than the recommended amount of potassium daily, as advised by their health care professional.

Although a deficiency of dietary potassium is rare, too little potassium can cause **hypokalemia** *(hypo* = too little, *kalemia* = potassium in the blood). This may occur during bouts of vomiting and/or diarrhea. It has been seen in individuals who have anorexia nervosa and/or bulimia nervosa. Hypokalemia can cause muscle weakness, cramps, and, in severe situations, irregular heart beats and paralysis.[6]

Individuals who consume high-protein diets that contain few fruits and vegetables may be depriving themselves of the buffering actions of potassium. The breakdown of excessive amounts of dietary protein causes the formation of acids that are balanced by the buffering action of potassium. A diet too low in fruits and vegetables is setting the stage for an imbalance of acids and bases in the blood and the increased risk of kidney stones, loss of bone mass, and high blood pressure.

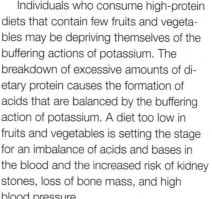

Table Tips
Potassium Power!

Slice a banana on your oatmeal at breakfast to begin the day with a potassium boost.

Add leafy greens to all your sandwiches. Spinach in particular is a potassium dynamo!

Add a spoonful of walnuts to your mid-morning yogurt for a one-two (nuts and dairy) potassium punch.

Have bean soup with your lunchtime sandwich for a warm way to enjoy your potassium.

Baked regular or sweet potatoes are potassium powerhouses on your dinner plate.

Terms to Know
kidney stones • hyperkalemia • hypokalemia

Calcium

What Is Calcium?

Calcium is one of the most abundant minerals in nature and is found in everything from pearls to seashells to eggshells. Calcium is also the most abundant mineral in your body. More than 99 percent of your body's calcium is located in your bones and teeth.

Functions of Calcium

Calcium Helps Build Strong Bones and Teeth

Calcium couples with phosphorus to form *hydroxyapatite*, providing strength and structure in your bones and the enamel on your teeth. Adequate dietary calcium is needed to build and maintain bone mass. Calcium makes up almost 40 percent of the weight of your bones.[7]

Healthy bone (left) vs weakened bone (right)

Calcium Plays a Role in Your Muscles, Nerves, and Blood

The remaining 1 percent of calcium is in your blood, in the fluids that surround your cells, in your muscles, and in other tissues. Calcium is needed for muscle contraction, and to help your nervous system transmit messages. Calcium is also involved in the dilation and contraction of blood vessels, and it helps your blood clot. Finally, calcium is necessary for the secretion of some hormones and enzymes. It must be maintained at a constant level for your body to function properly.[8]

Calcium May Help Lower High Blood Pressure

Studies have shown that a heart-healthy diet rich in calcium, potassium, magnesium, fruits, vegetables, and low-fat dairy products can help lower blood pressure. One example of such a diet, the DASH diet, contains three servings of lean dairy foods, the minimum amount of servings recommended to obtain this protective effect[9] (see the boxed feature "You and Your Blood Pressure" on page 292).

Calcium May Help Prevent Colon Cancer

A diet with plenty of calcium has been shown to help reduce the risk of developing benign tumors in the colon that may eventually lead to cancer. Calcium may protect the lining of the colon from damaging bile acids and cancer-promoting substances.[10]

Calcium May Reduce the Risk of Kidney Stones

Approximately 2 million American adults visit their doctors annually with kidney stones. Most of these stones are composed mainly of calcium oxalate.[11] Although health professionals in the past often warned those who suffer with kidney stones to minimize their dietary calcium, this advice has since been reversed. Research has shown that a balanced diet, along with adequate amounts of dietary calcium, may actually reduce the risk of developing kidney stones. Calcium binds with the oxalates in foods in the intestines and prevents their absorption. With fewer oxalates filtering through the kidneys, fewer stones are formed.[12]

Calcium May Reduce the Risk of Obesity

Some preliminary research suggests that low-calcium diets may trigger several responses that stimulate fat production and its storage in cells, which increases the risk for obesity.[13] When dietary calcium is inadequate, the active form of vitamin D increases in the body in order to enhance calcium absorption from the diet. Parathyroid hormone is also increased, which causes less calcium to be lost from the body. These hormone responses may also cause a shift of calcium into fat cells, which is the mechanism that stimulates fat production and storage.[14] The opposite also appears to be true. When the diet is high in calcium, less calcium is stored in fat cells and more fat is burned for energy. Preliminary results suggest that high dietary calcium intake may increase the amount of fat excreted in the feces and increase core body temperature.[15] However, more research is needed to confirm this relationship.

Daily Needs

Adults age 19 to 50 need 1,000 milligrams of calcium daily. Women older than 50, and men aged 70 and beyond, should increase their daily intake to 1,200 mg. Most women and many older males do not meet their daily calcium needs.[16]

Food Sources

Milk, yogurt, and cheese are the major sources of calcium in the American diet. Each serving from the dairy group will provide approximately 300 milligrams of calcium. (Choose nonfat, low- or reduced-fat, or skim milk versions to reduce the amount of saturated fat in these foods.) Although three servings of dairy foods will just about meet many adults' daily needs, Americans consume only about 1½ servings of dairy daily, on average.[17]

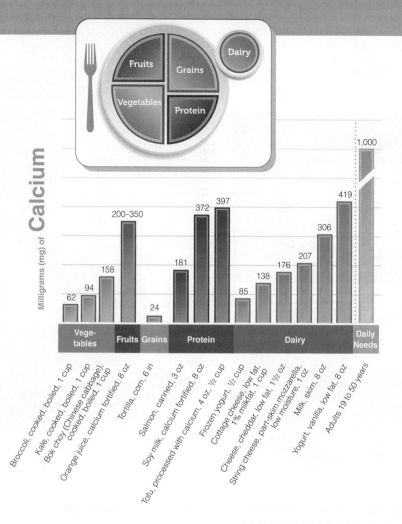

Milligrams (mg) of Calcium

Category	Food	mg
Vegetables	Broccoli, cooked, boiled, 1 cup	62
Vegetables	Kale, cooked, boiled, 1 cup	94
Vegetables	Bok choy (Chinese cabbage), cooked, boiled, 1 cup	158
Fruits	Orange juice, calcium fortified, 8 oz	200–350
Grains	Tortilla, corn, 6 in	24
Protein	Salmon, canned, 3 oz	181
Protein	Soy milk, calcium fortified, 8 oz	372
Protein	Tofu, processed with calcium, 4 oz, 1/2 cup	397
Dairy	Frozen yogurt, 1/2 cup	85
Dairy	Cottage cheese, low fat, 1% milkfat, 1 cup	138
Dairy	Cheese, cheddar, low fat, 1 1/2 oz	176
Dairy	String cheese, part-skim mozzarella, low moisture, 1 oz	207
Dairy	Milk, skim, 8 oz	306
Dairy	Yogurt, vanilla, low fat, 8 oz	419
Daily Needs	Adults 19 to 50 years	1,000

Broccoli, kale, canned salmon with bones (the calcium is in the bones), and tofu that is processed with calcium can also add calcium to the diet. Calcium-fortified foods, such as juices and cereals, are also excellent sources. Spinach, rhubarb, and okra also contain calcium, but these foods are also high in calcium-binding oxalates, so less than 10 percent of the mineral is absorbed in the body (see figure below).

<10%
Spinach
Rhubarb
Okra

20–30%
Milk   Salmon
Cheese   OJ with
Yogurt   calcium
Tofu   Almonds
Soy milk   Beans

>40%
Kale
Broccoli
Chinese mustard
   greens
Turnip greens
Green cabbage

Less ← **Percent Calcium Absorption** → More

Terms to Know
hypercalcemia • osteoporosis

Too Much or Too Little

The upper level for calcium has been set at 2,500 milligrams daily for adults age 19 to 50, and at 2,000 mg for those age 51 and beyond, to avoid **hypercalcemia,** or too much calcium in the blood, subsequent impaired kidneys, and calcium deposits in the body. Too much dietary calcium can also cause constipation and interfere with the absorption of other minerals, such as iron, zinc, magnesium, and phosphorus.

If your diet is low in calcium, calcium leaves your bones in order to maintain a constant level in your blood. A chronic deficiency of dietary calcium can lead to less dense, weakened, and brittle bones and increased risk for **osteoporosis** and bone fractures. See the boxed feature "Osteoporosis: Not Just Your Grandmother's Problem" on page 303.

Calcium Supplements

Some individuals are advised by their health care provider to take a calcium supplement. The calcium in supplements is part of a compound, typically either calcium carbonate or calcium citrate. Calcium carbonate tends to be the form of calcium most commonly purchased. It is most effective when consumed with a meal, as the acidic juices in your stomach help with its absorption.[18] Calcium citrate can be taken any time throughout the day, as it doesn't need the help of acidic juices to be absorbed.

Regardless of the form, all calcium, whether from supplements or from fortified or naturally occurring foods, should be consumed in doses of 500 milligrams or less, as this is the maximum that your body can absorb efficiently at one time.[19]

Calcium from unrefined oyster shell, bone meal, or dolomite (a rock rich in calcium) may also contain lead and other toxic metals. Supplements from these sources should state on the label that they are "purified" or carry the USP symbol to ensure purity. Because calcium can interfere with and reduce the absorption of iron, a calcium supplement shouldn't be taken along with an iron supplement.

Be cautious about adding a calcium supplement to your diet if you are already consuming plenty of lean dairy foods and/or calcium-fortified foods.

Table Tips
Calcium Counts!

Make cereal doused with skim or low-fat milk a morning habit.

Spoon a few chunks of tofu onto your salad bar lunch for extra calcium.

Use low-fat pudding or yogurt to satisfy a sweet tooth and obtain tooth-friendly calcium to boot.

Phosphorus

What Is Phosphorus?

Phosphorus is the second most abundant mineral in your body. The majority of phosphorus—about 85 percent—is in your bones. The remainder is in your cells and fluids outside your cells, including your blood.

Functions of Phosphorus

Phosphorus Is Needed for Bones and Teeth and Is an Important Component of Cells

As mentioned, phosphorus combines with calcium to form hydroxyapatite, the strengthening material found in bones and teeth.

Phosphorus is part of phospholipids, which give your cell membranes their structure (see figure). Phospholipids act as a barrier to keep specific substances out of the cells, while letting others in.

Phosphorus in phospholipid head

Phospholipid

Phosphorus Is Needed during Metabolism

Phosphorus helps store, for later use, energy generated from the metabolism of carbohydrates, protein, and fat from food. Your body can draw upon these stores as needed.

Phosphorus Acts as a Buffer and Is Part of the DNA and RNA of Every Cell

If your blood becomes too acidic or too basic, phosphorus can act as a buffer to help return your blood pH to normal. Your blood pH must stay within a very narrow range to prevent damage to your tissues.

Phosphorus is part of your DNA and RNA. The instructions for your genes are coded in your DNA and transcribed in your RNA to make the proteins needed in your body.

Daily Needs

Adults, both male and female, need 700 milligrams of phosphorus daily. Americans, on average, consume more than 1,000 milligrams of phosphorus daily.[20]

Food Sources

A balanced, varied diet will easily meet your phosphorus needs. Foods from animal sources such as meat, fish, poultry, and dairy products are excellent sources of phosphorus. Phosphorus is also part of many food additives.

Too Much or Too Little

Typically, consuming too much dietary phosphorus and its subsequent effect, **hyperphosphatemia,** is an issue only for individuals with kidney problems who cannot excrete excess phosphorus.

Constantly high phosphorus and low calcium intake can cause the loss of cal-

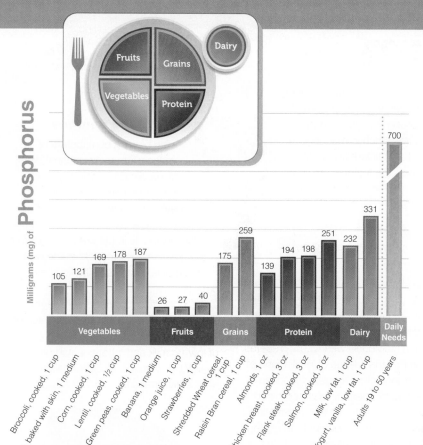

Phosphorus

Milligrams (mg) of Phosphorus

Vegetables		
Broccoli, cooked, 1 cup	105	
Potato, baked with skin, 1 medium	121	
Corn, cooked, 1 cup	169	
Lentil, cooked, 1/2 cup	178	
Green peas, cooked, 1 cup	187	
Fruits		
Banana 1 medium	26	
Orange juice, 1 cup	27	
Strawberries, 1 cup	40	
Grains		
Shredded Wheat cereal, 1 cup	175	
Raisin Bran cereal, 1 cup	259	
Protein		
Almonds, 1 oz	139	
Chicken breast, cooked, 3 oz	194	
Flank steak, cooked, 3 oz	198	
Salmon, cooked, 3 oz	251	
Dairy		
Milk, low fat, 1 cup	232	
Yogurt, vanilla, low fat, 1 cup	331	
Daily Needs		
Adults 19 to 50 years	700	

cium from your bones and a subsequent decrease in bone mass. Loss of bone mass increases the risk of osteoporosis. Hyperphosphatemia can also lead to calcification of tissues in the body. To protect against this, the upper level for phosphorus has been set at 4,000 milligrams daily for adults age 19 to 50 and 3,000 milligrams for those 50 years of age and older.

Too little phosphorus in the diet can cause its level in your blood to drop dangerously low and result in muscle weakness, bone pain, rickets, confusion, and, at the extreme, death. Because phosphorus is so abundant in the diet, a deficiency is rare. In fact, a person would have to be in a state of near starvation before experiencing a phosphorus deficiency.[21]

Table Tips
Fabulous Phosphorus

Layer sliced bananas, yogurt, and raisin bran cereal for a high-phosphorus breakfast that tastes like a dessert.

Blend together orange juice and slightly thawed frozen strawberries for a refreshing smoothie.

Skip the butter and sprinkle sliced almonds over your dinner vegetables for a crunchy topping.

Dunk raw broccoli florets in a spicy salsa for a snack with a kick.

Combine shredded wheat cereal, mixed nuts, and raisins for a sweet and crunchy snack mix.

Terms to Know
hyperphosphatemia

Magnesium

What Is Magnesium?

Magnesium is another abundant mineral in your body. While about half of the magnesium is in your bones, most of the remaining magnesium is inside the cells. A mere 1 percent is found in your blood and, like calcium, this amount must be maintained at a constant level.

Functions of Magnesium

Magnesium Is Needed for Metabolism and to Maintain Healthy Muscles, Nerves, Bones, and Heart

Magnesium helps more than 300 enzymes produce reactions inside your cells. It is needed for the metabolism of carbohydrates, proteins, and fats. Magnesium is used during the synthesis of protein and to help your muscles and nerves function properly. It is also needed to help you maintain healthy bones and a regular heart beat.[22]

Magnesium May Help Lower High Blood Pressure

Studies have shown that magnesium may help regulate blood pressure and that a plant-based diet abundant in fruits and vegetables, which are rich in magnesium as well as other minerals, lowered blood pressure.[23]

The blood-pressure-lowering DASH diet, which has been clinically proven to lower blood pressure, is rich in magnesium as well as calcium and potassium (see the feature box "You and Your Blood Pressure" on page 292).[24]

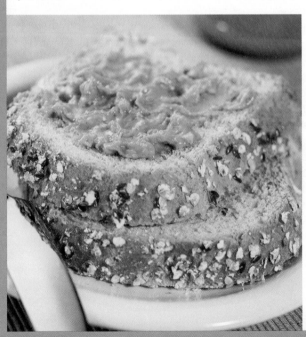

Magnesium May Help Reduce the Risk of Diabetes Mellitus

Some studies suggest that a diet abundant in magnesium may help decrease the risk of type 2 diabetes mellitus. Low blood levels of magnesium, which often occur in individuals with type 2 diabetes, may impair the release of insulin, one of the hormones that regulate blood glucose. This may lead to elevated blood glucose levels in those with preexisting diabetes, and may contribute to higher than normal blood glucose levels in those at risk for type 2 diabetes.[25]

Daily Needs

Adult females age 19 to 30 need 310 milligrams of magnesium, whereas men of the same age need 400 milligrams daily. Females age 31 and over need 320 milligrams; men of this age need 420 milligrams of magnesium daily.

Currently, many Americans fall short of their magnesium needs. Women consume only about 85 percent of their needs, or about 265 milligrams daily, on average. Men consume approximately 350 milligrams daily, on average, which is only about 80 percent of the amount recommended daily.[26] Because older adults tend to consume fewer calories, and thus less dietary magnesium, elders are at an even higher risk of falling short of their needs.

Food Sources

The biggest contributors of magnesium to Americans' diets are vegetables, whole grains, nuts, and fruits. Milk, yogurt, meat, and eggs are also good sources. Because the majority of the magnesium is in the bran and germ of the grain kernel, products made with refined grains, such as white flour, are poor sources.

It's not difficult to meet your magnesium needs. A peanut butter sandwich on whole-wheat bread, chased with a glass of low-fat milk and a banana, will provide over 200 milligrams, or about half of an adult's daily needs.

Too Much or Too Little

There isn't any known risk in consuming too much magnesium from food sources. However, consuming large amounts from supplements has been shown to cause intestinal problems such as diarrhea, cramps, and nausea. In fact, some laxatives purposefully contain magnesium because of its known cathartic effect. Because of this distress on the intestinal system, the upper level for magnesium from supplements, not foods, is set at 350 milligrams for adults. This level is

Magnesium

Milligrams (mg) of **Magnesium**

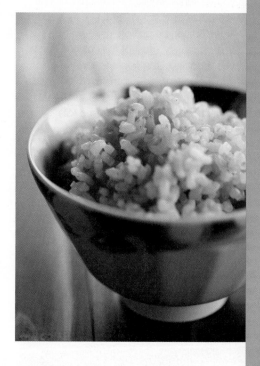

Category	Food	mg
Vegetables	Romaine lettuce, 2 cups	13
Vegetables	Spinach, fresh, 2 cups	47
Fruits	Pineapple, diced, 1 cup	19
Fruits	Banana, 1 medium	32
Grains	Brown rice, cooked, 1/2 cup	42
Grains	Wheat germ, 2 tbs (approx. 1/8 cup)	45
Protein	Kidney beans, cooked, 1/2 cup	37
Protein	Chickpeas, cooked, 1/2 cup	39
Protein	Peanut butter, 2 tbs	49
Protein	Almonds, 1 oz	81
Dairy	Milk, low fat, 1 cup	27
Dairy	Yogurt, low fat, strawberry, 1 cup	37
Daily Needs	Men 19 to 30 years	400
Daily Needs	Men 31 to 50 years	420
Daily Needs	Women 19 to 30 years	310
Daily Needs	Women 31 to 50 years	320

to prevent diarrhea, the first symptom that typically arises when too much magnesium is consumed.[27] As mentioned earlier in this chapter, the difference between consuming enough and getting too much magnesium is rather narrow. Look to food to meet your magnesium needs rather than supplements, which can quickly cause you to consume too much.

Even though many Americans don't meet their magnesium needs, deficiencies are rare in healthy individuals because the kidneys compensate for low magnesium intake by excreting less of it. However, some medications may cause magnesium deficiency. Certain diuretics can cause the body to lose too much magnesium, and some antibiotics, such as tetracycline, can inhibit the absorption of magnesium, both of which can lead to a deficiency. Individuals with poorly controlled diabetes or who abuse alcohol can experience excessive losses of

magnesium in the urine, which could also cause a deficiency. A severe magnesium deficiency can cause muscle weakness, seizures, fatigue, depression, and irregular heartbeats.

Table Tips

Magnificent Magnesium

Sprinkle chopped almonds over your morning whole-grain cereal for two crunchy sources of magnesium.

Add baby spinach to your salad.

Add rinsed, canned beans to salsa for a veggie dip with a magnesium punch.

Spread peanut butter on whole-wheat crackers for a satisfying afternoon snack.

Try precooked brown rice for an easy way to add whole grains to your dinner!

Chloride

What Is Chloride?

Chloride is a form of chlorine, a mineral you've surely smelled in bleach. Chlorine is a powerful disinfectant that if inhaled or ingested can be poisonous.

Fortunately, most of the chlorine in your body is in the nontoxic form of chloride (Cl^-). Chloride is part of hydrochloric acid, a strong acid in your stomach that enhances protein digestion and kills harmful bacteria that may be consumed with your foods·

Functions of Chloride

Chloride Helps Maintain Fluid Balance and Acid-Base Balance

Sodium and chloride are the major electrolytes outside your cells and in your blood. They help maintain fluid balance between these two compartments.

Chloride also acts as a buffer to help keep your blood at a normal pH.

Daily Needs and Food Sources

Adults age 19 to 50 should consume 2,300 milligrams of chloride a day. Sodium chloride, which is 60 percent

chloride, is the main source of chloride in your diet, so the food sources for it are the same as those for sodium.

Because Americans consume plenty of salt, it is estimated that they are consuming, on average, 3,400 milligrams to just over 7,000 milligrams of dietary chloride daily.

Too Much or Too Little

Because sodium chloride is the major source of chloride in the diet, the upper level for adults for chloride is set at 3,600 milligrams to coincide with the upper level for sodium.[28]

A chloride deficiency rarely occurs in healthy individuals. Individuals who experience significant bouts of vomiting and diarrhea may become deficient as chloride is lost from the body.

Sulfur

What Is Sulfur?

Sulfur is typically found in your body as part of other compounds. For example, sulfur is part of the vitamins thiamin, biotin, and pantothenic acid.

Functions of Sulfur

Sulfur Helps Shape Some Amino Acids

The amino acids methionine, cystine, and cysteine all contain sulfur. The sulfur part of these amino acids helps give some proteins their three-dimensional shape. This enables these proteins to perform effectively as enzymes and hormones.[29]

Sulfites Are Preservatives

Sulfur-based substances called *sulfites* are often used as a preservative by food

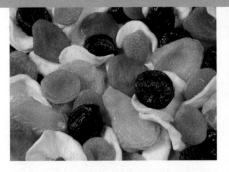

manufacturers. They help prevent food spoilage and discoloration. (We discuss sulfites further in Chapter 13.)

Food Sources

Foods that contain the two amino acids mentioned above are the major dietary sources of sulfur. A varied diet that contains meat, poultry, fish, eggs, legumes, dairy foods, fruits, and vegetables will provide sulfur.

Daily Needs and Too Much or Too Little

There isn't any recommendation for the amount of sulfur to be consumed daily, nor are there any known toxicity or deficiency symptoms. Most people get plenty of sulfur in their diet.

Osteoporosis: Not Just Your Grandmother's Problem

If you are fortunate enough to have elders, such as grandparents, in your life, you may have heard them comment that they are "shrinking" as they age. Of course, they aren't really shrinking, but they may be losing height as the tissues supporting their spine lose mass and elasticity and the joint capsules between the bones (or vertebrae) of the spine lose their cushion of fluid. This is normal. In many older adults, however, the vertebrae themselves lose mass and begin to collapse, so that it becomes more difficult for the spine to hold the weight of the head and upper body. This leads to a gradual curvature of the spine, which affects their posture (see figure). As older individuals begin to hunch over, they can lose as much as a foot in height.[15]

Bones Are Constantly Changing

Bones are a dynamic, living tissue. Older layers of bones are constantly removed, and new bone is constantly added. In

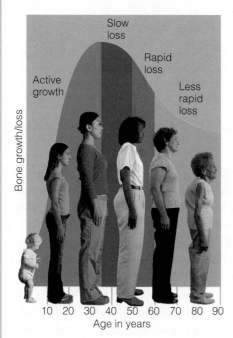

In your early years, more bone mass is added than lost in your body. In their mid-30s, women begin to slowly lose bone mass until menopause, when the rate of loss is accelerated for several years. Bone loss continues after age 60 but at a slower rate. Bone loss also occurs in men as they age.

fact, your entire skeleton is replaced with new bone about every decade. During childhood and adolescence, more bone is added than is removed, as the bones grow in length and mass. Although growth of bone length typically ceases during the teenage years, bone mass will continue to accumulate into the early years of young adulthood. **Peak bone mass,** which is the genetically determined maximum amount of bone mass an individual can build up, typically occurs when a person is in his or her 20s. Some additional bone mass can be added when an individual is in his or her 30s. After peak bone mass is reached, the loss of bone mass begins to slowly exceed the rate at which new bone is added.[16]

As bones lose mass, they become porous, and **osteoporosis** (*osteo* = bone, *porosis* = porous) can develop. The weakened, fragile bones are prone to fractures. A minor stumble while walking can result in a broken ankle, rib cage, or arm bone as the result of an ensuing fall. Shopping for groceries, showering, dressing, and even brushing one's teeth become challenges for many older people with osteoporosis.

Hip fractures can be devastating because they often render a person immobile, which quickly affects quality of life. Feelings of helplessness and depression often ensue. Up to two-thirds of all individuals with hip fractures are never able to regain the quality of life they had prior to the injury, and about 20 percent die within a year due to complications from the injury.[17] It is estimated that by the year 2020, one out of every two Americans will either have or be at risk for hip fractures due to osteoporosis, and even more will be at risk for fractures of other bones.[18]

Weak bones cause the spine to collapse over time.

ual's bone. The denser the bones, the stronger the bones. A low test score indicates **osteopenia** (*penia* = poverty), which signals low bone mass. A very low test score indicates osteoporosis.

Ironically, though osteoporosis is often thought of as a condition of the elderly, it has its roots in childhood and must be prevented throughout adulthood. Saving up bone mass is like saving money for retirement. The more you save when you are young and preserve throughout your adulthood, the more you will have for your later years. Conversely, if you don't save enough early in life, you may end up with little to fall back on when you need it later.

It's never too late to try to reduce your risk of osteoporosis. To take a look at the risk factors involved, see the Self-Assessment.

Adults can have a bone test done by their doctors to assess how their **bone mineral density (BMD)** compares with that of a healthy 30-year-old. BMD refers to the amount of minerals, in particular calcium, per volume in an individ-

peak bone mass The genetically determined maximum amount of bone mass an individual can build up.

osteoporosis A condition in which the bones are less dense, increasing the risk of fractures.

bone mineral density (BMD) The amount of minerals, in particular calcium, per volume in an individual's bone. The denser the bones, the stronger the bones.

osteopenia A condition whereby the bones are less dense, increasing the risk of fractures.

(continued)

Are You at Risk for Osteoporosis?

Answer the following questions to determine how many risk factors you have for osteoporosis. Shade in each part of the skeleton based on your answers.

1. *Gender:* Are you female?

   Yes ☐ **No** ☐ (If you answered no, shade in the left arm of the skeleton.)

   Females are at higher risk for osteoporosis than males because they have smaller bones, and thus less bone mass. Also, bone mass is lost at a faster rate right after menopause due to the decline of estrogen in women's bodies. However, men can suffer from osteoporosis and can experience it at a fairly young age.[19]

2. *Ethnicity:* Are you a Caucasian or Asian-American female?

   Yes ☐ **No** ☐ (If no, shade in the right arm of the skeleton.)

   Caucasian and Asian women typically have lower bone mass than other women.

3. *Age:* Are you over 30 years of age?

   Yes ☐ **No** ☐ (If no, shade in the left hand of the skeleton.)

   You begin to lose bone mass after about age 30, which increases your risk of osteoporosis and fractures.

4. *Body Type:* Are you a small-boned or petite woman?

   Yes ☐ **No** ☐ (If no, shade in the right hand of the skeleton.)

   Thin women have lower bone mass and increased risk of fractures. A higher body weight puts more weight-bearing, mechanical stress on bones, helping them to stay healthy. A healthy body weight also means you'll have some padding should a fall occur. Also, since most of the estrogen produced in menopausal women's bodies is formed in fat tissue, thinner women have less bone-protecting estrogen.[20]

 NutriTools

Know Your Calcium Food Sources

Which foods are the richest sources of calcium? Visit www.pearsonhighered .com/blake and complete this interactive NutriTools activity to find out.

After you have completed the self-assessment, look at the skeleton. If it has mostly shaded areas, you have fewer risk factors for osteoporosis; the less shaded the skeleton, the more risk factors you have, and the higher your risk of developing osteoporosis. Many of these risk factors can be reduced by a healthy diet and lifestyle.

Although you cannot control the first five risk factors (your gender, ethnicity, age, body type, and family history), you can control the remaining six risk factors. If your sex hormone levels are lower than they should be and/or if you are taking medications that may increase your risk of osteoporosis, talk to your doctor. Quitting smoking, exercising regularly, and limiting or avoiding alcohol will help reduce your risk. Lastly, make sure that you consume adequate amounts of vitamin D (Chapter 7) and calcium (see the Visual Summary Table for calcium on page 296). If you can't meet your calcium needs through food, a supplement may be necessary.

5. *Family History of Fractures:* Have your parents or grandparents ever experienced any bone fractures in their golden years?
   Yes ☐ **No** ☐ (If no, shade in the left leg of the skeleton.)
   A family history of bone fractures in your relatives' later years increases your risk of osteoporosis.

6. *Level of Sex Hormones:* Are you a premenopausal woman who has stopped menstruating, a menopausal woman, or a male with low testosterone levels?
   Yes ☐ **No** ☐ (If no, shade in the right leg area of the skeleton.)
   Women with amenorrhea (the absence of menstrual periods) experience hormonal imbalances, especially if they are at a dangerously low body weight.[21] Menopausal women, or men with low levels of sex hormones, which are protective against bone loss, are also at a higher risk.

7. *Medications:* Are you taking certain medications such as glucocorticoids (prednisone), antiseizure medications (phenytoin), aluminum-containing antacids, and/or excessive amounts of thyroid replacement hormones?
   Yes ☐ **No** ☐ (If no, shade in the torso of the skeleton.)
   The long-term use of glucocorticoids, antiseizure medicines, certain antacids, or too much thyroid hormone–replacing medication can lead to a loss of bone mass and increase the risk of fractures.[22] Certain cancer treatments can also cause bone loss. Though you shouldn't stop taking any prescribed medications, you should speak to your doctor regarding your bone health.

8. *Smoking:* Do you smoke?
   Yes ☐ **No** ☐ (If no, shade in the left foot of the skeleton.)
   Smokers absorb less calcium than do nonsmokers. Women smokers have lower levels of estrogen in their bodies and begin menopause earlier than do nonsmokers.

9. *Physical Activity:* Do you spend less than 30 minutes exercising daily?
   Yes ☐ **No** ☐ (If no, shade in the left hip of the skeleton.)
   Regular physical activity contributes to higher peak bone mass in a person's early years, and strength and weight-bearing activities such as walking, hiking, and tennis help maintain bone mass during adulthood. These activities cause you to work against gravity, which helps strengthen your bones. Regular exercise also helps you maintain healthy muscles and improves your coordination and balance, which can help prevent falls.[23]

10. *Alcohol:* Do you consume more than one alcoholic drink a day if you are a woman or consume more than two alcoholic drinks daily if you are a man?
    Yes ☐ **No** ☐ (If no, shade in the right hip of the skeleton.)
    Heavy consumption of alcohol can reduce bone mass by inhibiting the formation of new bone, preventing the activation of vitamin D, and increasing the loss of calcium. It can also increase the risk of stumbling and falling.[24]

11. *Inadequate Amounts of Calcium and Vitamin D:* Do you consume less than 3 cups daily of milk or yogurt that has been fortified with vitamin D?
    Yes ☐ **No** ☐ (If no, shade in the right foot of the skeleton.)
    Because calcium is needed to build and maintain bone mass, and vitamin D is needed for your body to absorb this mineral, having inadequate amounts of either or both of these nutrients increases your risk of low bone mass, bone loss, and bone fractures.

The Trace Minerals Are Needed in Small Amounts

The trace minerals—iron, zinc, selenium, fluoride, chromium, copper, iodine, manganese, and molybdenum—are needed in much smaller amounts, less than 20 milligrams daily, compared with the major minerals.[17] However, don't assume that this diminishes their importance. Trace minerals play essential roles that are as important as those of the major minerals. Some (chromium, iodine) help certain hormones, such as insulin and thyroid hormones, function. They are indispensable for maintaining healthy red blood cells (iron) and protecting your teeth (fluoride), and can be cofactors (iron, zinc, copper, manganese, and molybdenum) that work with enzymes to ensure that numerous critical reactions occur. Let's look at each of these essential trace minerals.

Iron

What Is Iron?

Iron is the most abundant mineral on Earth, and the most abundant trace mineral in your body. A 130-pound female has more than 2,300 milligrams of iron in her body—about the weight of a dime—whereas a 165-pound male will have 4,000 milligrams of iron in his body—slightly less than two dimes.

As a key component of blood, iron is highly valuable to the body and is treated accordingly. For the most part, iron is not excreted in the urine or stool, so once absorbed very little of it leaves the body. Approximately 95 percent of your iron is recycled and reused.[30] Whereas some iron is shed in hair, skin, and sloughed-off intestinal cells, most iron loss is due to bleeding.

Iron Occurs in Two Forms: Heme and Nonheme

Foods from animal sources, such as meat, poultry, and fish, provide heme iron in your diet. Heme iron (see figure) is part of the protein **hemoglobin** in your red blood cells and the protein **myoglobin** in your muscles. Heme iron is easily absorbed by your body.

Heme

Plant foods such as grains and vegetables are the main sources of nonheme iron in your diet. Nonheme iron is not as easily absorbed as heme iron. This is because other compounds in foods, such as phytates in legumes, rice, and grains, the polyphenols in tea, and the protein in soy products, all inhibit its absorption.

In general, your body absorbs only about 10 to 15 percent of the iron you eat. However, if your body stores are low, the amount you absorb from foods will increase.

You can enhance your nonheme iron absorption by eating a food that's high in vitamin C along with iron-rich foods. Vitamin C and the acids in your stomach change the configuration of nonheme iron, which improves its absorption. As little as 25 milligrams of vitamin C—the amount in about one-quarter cup of orange juice—can double the amount of nonheme iron you absorb from your meal and 50 milligrams of vitamin C can increase the amount absorbed about sixfold.[31] Keep this in mind when you make your next peanut butter-on-whole-wheat sandwich and have an orange for dessert.

Another way to enhance nonheme iron absorption from foods is to eat meat, fish, or poultry at the same meal. The peptides in these animal-derived foods are thought to be the enhancing factors. The meat in your next turkey sandwich will help enhance the absorption of the nonheme iron in the whole-wheat bread.

Functions of Iron

Hemoglobin and Myoglobin Transport Oxygen

Approximately two-thirds of the iron in your body is in hemoglobin, the oxygen-carrying transport protein in your red blood cells. The iron-containing heme group binds with oxygen from your lungs and is transported to your tissues for their use. Hemoglobin also picks up carbon dioxide waste products from your cells and brings them to your lungs to be exhaled from your body.

Similarly, iron is part of the myoglobin that transports and stores oxygen in your muscles.

Iron Is Needed for Brain Function

Iron helps enzymes that are involved in the synthesis of neurotransmitters in your brain send messages to the rest of your body. A deficiency of iron in children can reduce their ability to learn and retain information. Studies have shown that children with iron-deficiency anemia in their early years can have persistent, decreased cognitive ability during their later school years.[32]

Daily Needs

Adult females, age 19 to 50, need 18 milligrams daily to cover the iron lost during menstruation. During pregnancy, a woman's iron needs increase to 27 milligrams per day to support her growing fetus. After a woman stops menstruating, usually around age 50, her daily iron needs drop to 8 milligrams because she is no longer losing blood monthly.

Adult males need 8 milligrams of dietary iron daily. These recommendations

Iron — Milligrams (mg) of Iron

Category	Food	mg
Vegetables	Baked potato with skin, 1 small	1.5
Fruits	Raisins, 1/2 cup	1.4
Fruits	Dried apricots, 1/2 cup	1.7
Grains	Brown rice, cooked, 1/2 cup	0.5
Grains	Whole wheat or white bread, 1 slice	0.8
Grains	Spaghetti (enriched), cooked, 1/2 cup	0.9
Grains	Oatmeal, cooked, 1/2 cup	5.1
Grains	Total cereal, 3/4 cup	22.4
Protein	Chicken breast, skinless, 3 oz	0.9
Protein	Black beans, cooked, 1/4 cup	0.9
Protein	Kidney beans, cooked, 1/4 cup	1.0
Protein	Tofu, firm, 2 oz, 1/4 cup	1.0
Protein	Chickpeas, cooked, 1/4 cup	1.2
Protein	Tuna, light, canned, 3 oz	1.3
Protein	Sirloin steak, cooked, 3 oz	1.8
Protein	Turkey, dark meat, cooked, skinless, 3 oz	2.0
Protein	Shrimp, 3 oz	2.6
Daily Needs	Men 19 to 50 years	8
Daily Needs	Women 19 to 50 years	18

for women and men take into account a typical American diet, which includes both heme and nonheme iron sources.

Adult men consume more than twice their recommended iron needs—more than 16 milligrams, on average, daily. Adult premenopausal women consume only about 70 percent of their daily need, or approximately 14 milligrams, on average. Postmenopausal women consume approximately 13 milligrams of iron daily, so, like men, they are meeting their needs.

The iron needs of vegetarians are 1.8 times higher than those of nonvegetarians due to components in plant foods that inhibit iron absorption.[33]

Food Sources

(T|F) About half of Americans' dietary iron intake comes from iron-enriched bread and other grain foods such as cereals. Heme iron in meat, fish, and poultry contributes only 12 percent of the dietary iron needs of males and females. Cooking foods in iron pans and skillets can increase their

nonheme iron content, as foods absorb iron from the pan.[34]

Too Much or Too Little

Consuming too much iron from supplements can cause constipation, nausea, vomiting, and diarrhea. The upper level for iron for adults is set at 45 milligrams daily, as this level is slightly less than the amount known to cause these intestinal symptoms. This upper level doesn't apply to individuals with liver disease or other diseases, such as hemochromatosis, which can affect iron stores in the body. It is too high for these individuals.

In the United States, the accidental consumption of supplements containing iron is a leading cause of poisoning deaths in children under age 6. Ingestion of as little as 200 milligrams of iron has been shown to be fatal. Children who swallow iron supplements can experience symptoms such as nausea, vomiting, and diarrhea within minutes. Intestinal bleeding can also occur, which can lead to

 NutriTools

Know Your Iron Sources

Can you identify the sources of iron in your diet? Visit www.pearsonhighered .com/blake and complete this interactive NutriTools activity.

shock, coma, and even death. The FDA has mandated that a warning statement about the risk of iron poisoning in small children be put on every iron supplement label.[35]

Undetected excessive storing of iron in the body over several years is called iron overload and can damage a person's tissues and organs, including the heart, kidneys, liver, and nervous system. **Hemochromatosis,** a genetic disorder in which individuals absorb too much dietary iron, can cause iron overload. Though this condition is congenital, its symptoms often aren't manifested until adulthood. If not diagnosed and treated early enough, organ damage can occur. These individuals need to avoid iron supplements throughout their lives, as well as large amounts of vitamin C supplements, which enhance iron absorption.

Iron overload from consuming too much dietary iron has occurred in South Africans and Zimbabwean natives who consume large amounts of beer. The iron content in the particular beer that they drink is high: 80 milligrams per liter. However, these individuals may also have a genetic disorder that contributes to excessive iron storage in the body. It is not known if excessive amounts of dietary iron alone in healthy individuals could cause iron overload.

The jury is still out about the role of iron in heart disease. Some studies suggest that iron can stimulate free radical production in the body, which can damage the arteries leading to the heart. Though this association is not definite, unless you are medically diagnosed with iron deficiency, it doesn't make any sense to consume excessive amounts of iron.

Normal red blood cells

Blood cells affected by anemia

Iron deficiency is the most common nutritional disorder in the world. If your diet is deficient in iron, your body stores will be slowly depleted so as to keep your blood hemoglobin in a normal range. **Iron-deficiency anemia** occurs when your stores are so depleted that your hemoglobin levels decrease. This will diminish the delivery of oxygen through the body, causing fatigue and weakness. Premenopausal females, menstruating women and teenage girls (especially those with heavy blood losses), pregnant women (because of their increased iron needs), preterm and low-birth-weight infants, and older infants and toddlers are at risk of developing iron-deficiency anemia because they often fall short of the recommended dietary amounts.[36] (This is discussed further in Chapters 15 and 16.)

Table Tips

Ironing Out Your Iron Needs

Enjoy an iron-enriched whole-grain cereal along with a glass of vitamin-C–rich orange juice to boost the nonheme iron absorption from your bowl of cereal.

Add plenty of salsa (vitamin C) to your bean burritos to enhance the absorption of the nonheme iron in both the beans and the flour tortilla.

Stuff a cooked baked potato (nonheme iron, vitamin C) with shredded cooked chicken (heme iron) and broccoli (vitamin C) and top it with melted low-fat cheese for a delicious dinner.

Eat a small box of raisins (nonheme iron) and a clementine or tangerine (vitamin C) as a sweet, iron-rich afternoon snack.

Add chickpeas (nonheme iron) to your salad greens (vitamin C). Don't forget the tomato wedges for another source of iron-enhancing vitamin C.

Terms to Know
hemoglobin • myoglobin • hemochromatosis • iron-deficiency anemia

Copper

What Is Copper?

Copper may bring to mind ancient tools, great sculptures, or American pennies (although pennies are no longer made of solid copper), but it is also associated with several key body functions.

Functions of Copper

Copper is part of many enzymes and proteins. It is important for iron absorption and transfer and the synthesis of hemoglobin and red blood cells.

Copper helps generate energy in your cells, synthesize melanin (the dark pigment found in skin), and link the proteins collagen and elastin together in connective tissue. It works with enzymes to protect your cells from free radicals.

Copper also plays an important role in blood clotting and in maintaining a healthy immune system.[37]

Daily Needs

Both adult women and men need 900 micrograms of copper daily. American women consume 1,200 micrograms, whereas men consume 1,600 micrograms daily, on average.

Food Sources

Organ meats such as liver, seafood, nuts, and seeds are abundant in copper. Bran cereals, whole-grain products, and cocoa are also good sources. Whereas potatoes, milk, and chicken are low in copper, they are consumed in such abundant amounts that they contribute a fair amount of copper to Americans' diets.

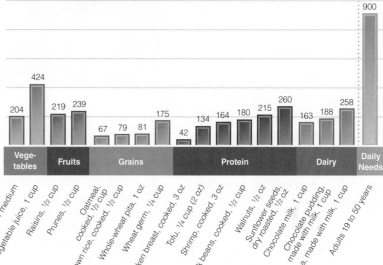

Microgams (µg) of **Copper**

Food	µg
Baked potato w/skin, 1 medium	204
Vegetable juice, 1 cup	424
Raisins, 1/2 cup	219
Prunes, 1/2 cup	239
Oatmeal, cooked, 1/2 cup	67
Brown rice, cooked, 1/2 cup	79
Whole-wheat pita, 1 oz	81
Wheat germ, 1/4 cup	175
Chicken breast, cooked, 3 oz	42
Tofu, 1/4 cup (2 oz)	134
Shrimp, cooked, 3 oz	164
Black beans, cooked, 1/2 cup	180
Walnuts, 1/2 cup	215
Sunflower seeds, dry roasted 1/2 oz	260
Chocolate milk, 1 cup	163
Chocolate pudding, made with milk, 1 cup	188
Hot cocoa, made with milk, 1 cup	258
Daily Needs: Adults 19 to 50 years	900

Too Much or Too Little

Too much copper can cause stomach pains and cramps, nausea, diarrhea, vomiting, and even liver damage. The upper level for copper for adults is set at 10,000 micrograms daily.

Copper deficiency is rare in the United States. It has occurred in premature babies fed milk formulas, malnourished infants fed cow's milk, and individuals given intravenous feedings that lacked adequate amounts of copper.

Zinc

What Is Zinc?

Zinc is found in almost every cell of your body. It is involved in the function of more than 100 enzymes, including those used for protein synthesis. As important as it is, it was not considered an essential nutrient until 1974.

Functions of Zinc

Zinc Is Needed for DNA Synthesis and Growth and Development

Zinc plays a role in the structure of both RNA and DNA in your cells and in gene expression.

Zinc is needed for adequate growth in developing infants and throughout the adolescent years.[38]

Zinc Helps Keep Your Immune System Healthy and Helps Wounds Heal

Zinc is needed for production of white blood cells, so it helps keep your immune system healthy. It helps reduce the inflammation that can accompany skin wounds. Zinc also helps in wound healing by being part of enzymes and proteins that repair and enhance the proliferation of skin cells.[39]

Zinc Brings Out the Best in Your Taste Buds

One lick of a chocolate ice cream cone or a forkful of cherry cheesecake will make you appreciate the role that zinc plays in taste acuity, which is the ability to savor the flavors of your foods. A deficiency of zinc has been shown to alter taste perceptions.[40]

Zinc and the Common Cold

A recent review of 15 randomly controlled studies of healthy individuals has shown promise that zinc can affect the common cold. In these studies, those who consumed zinc lozenges or syrup within 24 hours of the onset of the first sniffle or sneeze appeared to somewhat benefit from a reduction in the duration and severity of a cold. These were healthy individuals so it is too early to say if these results would occur in people with chronic illness or a compromised immune system. Also, those who took zinc lozenges were more likely to experience side effects such as nausea. More studies are needed to determine if zinc could be safely used in the general population to treat the common cold, and to determine a safe dose and appropriate duration without adverse effects.[41]

Zinc May Help Fight AMD

Research studies do support the assertion that zinc may play a role in reducing the risk of age-related macular degeneration (AMD), a condition that hampers central vision. Zinc may work with an enzyme in your eyes that's needed to properly utilize vitamin A for vision. Zinc may also help mobilize vitamin A from the liver to ensure adequate blood levels of this vitamin. Supplements that contain antioxidants along with zinc have been shown to reduce the risk of AMD.[42] (See the section on antioxidants in Chapter 7.)

Daily Needs

Adult males need 11 milligrams of zinc, whereas women need 8 milligrams daily. American adults, on average, are meeting their daily zinc needs. Men are consuming approximately 15 milligrams and women are consuming 10 milligrams of zinc daily, on average.

Vegetarians, especially strict vegetarians, can have as much as a 50 percent higher need for zinc. Phytates in grains and legumes, which are staples of vegan diets, can bind with zinc, reducing its absorption in the intestinal tract.

Food Sources

Red meat, some seafood, and whole grains are excellent sources of zinc. Because zinc is found in the germ and bran portion of the grain, refined grains stripped of these components have as much as 80 percent less zinc than whole grains.

Too Much or Too Little

The upper level for zinc in food and/or supplements for adults is set at 40 milligrams daily. Consuming too much zinc, as little as 50 milligrams, can cause stomach pains, nausea, vomiting, and diarrhea. Approximately 60 milligrams of zinc daily has been shown to lower the level of copper in your body by competing with this mineral for absorption in the intestinal tract. This is an excellent example of how

Skin rash is one of the symptoms of zinc deficiency.

Milligrams (mg) of **Zinc**

Chart data (Milligrams of Zinc):

Vegetables
- Mushrooms, cooked, 1 cup: 1.4
- Spinach, cooked, 1 cup: 1.4
- Green peas, cooked, 1 cup: 1.9

Fruits
- Watermelon, raw, 1 cup: 0.2
- Cantaloupe, 1 cup: 0.3

Grains
- Whole-wheat bread, 1 slice: 0.3
- Wheat germ, 1/4 cup: 4.7
- Total cereal, 3/4 cup: 17.5

Protein
- Light tuna, water, 3 oz: 0.7
- Mixed nuts, 1 oz: 1.0
- Shrimp, cooked, 3 oz: 1.3
- Red kidney beans, cooked, 1/2 cup: 2.0
- Chicken, dark meat, cooked, 3 oz: 2.4
- Beef, flank steak, lean, cooked, 3 oz: 6.3
- Oyster, cooked, 3 oz: 38.4

Dairy
- Skim milk, 1 cup: 1.0
- Swiss cheese, reduced fat, 1½ oz: 1.6
- Yogurt, plain, nonfat, 1 cup: 2.4

Daily Needs
- Men 19 to 50 years: 11
- Women 19 to 50 years: 8

the overconsumption of one mineral can compromise the benefits of another.

Excessive amounts, such as 300 milligrams of zinc daily, have been shown to suppress the immune system and lower the HDL ("good") cholesterol.[43]

A deficiency of zinc can cause hair loss, loss of appetite, impaired taste of foods, diarrhea, and delayed sexual maturation, as well as impotence and skin rashes.

Because zinc is needed during development, a deficiency can slow and impair growth. Classic studies of groups of people in the Middle East showed that people who consumed a diet mainly of unleavened bread, which is high in zinc-binding phytates, experienced impaired growth and dwarfism.[44]

Table Tips
Zapping Your Zinc Needs!

Enjoy a tuna fish sandwich on whole-wheat bread at lunch for a double serving (fish and bread) of zinc.

Add kidney beans to your cup of soup. (These beans are often at cafeteria salad bars, so add a spoonful to your soup and salad lunch.)

Pack a small handful of mixed nuts and raisins in a zip-closed bag for a snack on the run.

Top your breakfast yogurt with cereal for two servings of zinc in one bowl!

Add cooked green peas to casseroles, stews, soups, and salads.

Selenium

What Is Selenium?

The mineral selenium is part of a class of proteins called selenoproteins, many of which are enzymes. Selenoproteins have important functions in your body.

Functions of Selenium

Selenium Is Needed by Your Thyroid

Selenium-containing enzymes help regulate thyroid hormones in your body.

Selenium Plays an Antioxidant Role

Selenoproteins can also function as antioxidants that protect your cells from free radicals. (See the section on antioxidants in Chapter 7.) As you recall, free radicals are natural by-products of metabolism and can also result from exposure to chemicals in the environment. If free radicals accumulate faster than your body can neutralize them, their damaging effects can contribute to chronic diseases, such as heart disease.[45]

Selenium May Help Fight Cancer

Research studies have suggested that deaths from cancers, such as lung, colon, and prostate cancers, are lower in groups of people that consume more selenium. Selenium's antioxidant capabilities, and its ability to potentially slow the growth of tumors, are thought to be the mechanism behind its anticancer effects.

The FDA now allows a Qualified Health Claim on food labels and dietary supplements stating that "selenium may reduce the risk of certain cancers but the evidence is limited and not conclusive to date."[46]

Daily Needs

Both adult females and males need 55 micrograms of selenium daily. American adults are more than meeting their needs—they consume about 92 micrograms to 134 micrograms daily, on average.

Food Sources

Meat, seafood, pasta, grains, dairy foods, and fruits and vegetables can all contribute to dietary selenium. However, the amount of selenium in the foods you eat depends upon the soil where the plants were grown and the animals grazed. For example, wheat grown in selenium-rich soil can have more than ten times as much selenium as an identical wheat grown in selenium-poor soil.

Too Much or Too Little

Too much selenium can cause toxicity and a condition called **selenosis.** A person with selenosis will have brittle

nails and hair, both of which may fall out. Other symptoms include stomach and intestinal discomfort, a skin rash, garlicky breath, fatigue, and damage to the nervous system. The upper level for selenium for adults is set at 400 micrograms to prevent the loss and brittleness of nails and hair, which is the most common symptom of selenosis.

Though rare in the United States, a selenium deficiency can cause **Keshan disease,** which damages the heart. This disease typically only occurs in children who live in rural areas that have selenium-

Selenium

Microgram (µg) of **Selenium**

Food	µg
Vegetables	
Green beans, frozen, boiled, 1 cup	0.5
Baked potato, with skin, 1 medium	0.7
Broccoli, frozen spears, boiled, 1 cup	3.5
Fruits	
Apple, 1 medium	0
Pear, 1 medium	0.2
Watermelon, 1 cup diced	0.6
Banana, 1 medium	1.2
Grains	
Wheat crackers, 5 crackers, 1 oz	1.8
Frozen waffle, 1	4.2
Brown rice, long-grain, cooked, ½ cup	9.6
Whole-wheat bread, 1 slice	11.2
Spaghetti, cooked, ½ cup	19
Protein	
Walnuts, ½ oz	0.7
Peanut butter, 1 tbls	0.9
Egg, hard-boiled, 1 large	15.4
Chicken breast, cooked, 3 oz	23.5
Roast beef, 3 oz	23.8
Salmon, cooked, 3 oz	48.6
Tuna, light, canned in water, 3 oz	68.3
Brazil nuts, ½ oz	271
Dairy	
Milk, skim, 1 cup	5.2
Cheddar cheese, reduced fat, 1½ oz	6.5
Cottage cheese, low fat, 2 cups	40.7
Daily Needs	
Adults 19 to 50 years	55

poor soil. However, some researchers speculate that selenium deficiency alone may not cause Keshan disease; the selenium-deficient individual may also be exposed to a virus, which, together with the selenium deficiency, leads to the damaged heart.[47]

Terms to Know

selenosis • Keshan disease

Table Tips
Seeking Out Selenium

Top a toasted whole-wheat bagel with a slice of reduced-fat cheddar cheese for a hot way to start the day.

Spread peanut butter on whole-wheat crackers and top with a slice of banana.

Top your dinner pasta with broccoli for a selenium-smart meal.

Zap sliced apples, sprinkled with a little apple juice and cinnamon, in the microwave and top with vanilla yogurt.

Spoon a serving of low-fat cottage cheese into a bowl and top with canned sliced pears and walnuts for a fabulous dessert.

Fluoride

What Is Fluoride?

Fluoride is the safe ion form of fluorine, a poisonous gas. Calcium fluoride is the form that is found in your bones and teeth.

Functions of Fluoride

Fluoride Protects against Dental Caries

The best known function of fluoride is its role in keeping teeth healthy. Your teeth have an outer layer called enamel (see figure), which can become eroded over time by acids and result in dental caries. The acids are produced by the bacteria in your mouth when they feast on the carbohydrates that you eat. Continual exposure of your teeth to these acids can cause erosion and create a cavity.

Enamel
Gum
Bone

Fluoride from food, beverages, and dental products, such as toothpaste, helps protect your teeth in several ways. It helps to repair the enamel that has already started to erode, and it interferes with the ability of the bacteria to metabolize carbohydrates, thus reducing the amount of acid they produce. Finally, fluoride provides a protective barrier between your tooth and the destructive acids. As a component of saliva, it provides a continual fluoride bath to your teeth's surfaces.[48]

Consuming adequate amounts of fluoride is extremely important during infancy and childhood, when teeth are developing, and for maintenance of healthy teeth throughout your life.

Fluoride in Drinking Water Has Improved the Nation's Dental Health

In the 1930s, scientists noticed lower rates of dental caries among individuals whose community water systems contained significant amounts of fluoride. Studies confirmed that the fluoride was the protective factor in the water that helped fight dental decay. Since 1945, most communities have fluoridated their water, and today, almost 70 percent of Americans live in communities that have a fluoridated water supply (see map).

The increase in access to fluoridated water is one of the major reasons why there has been a decline in dental caries in the United States, and fluoridation of water is considered one of the ten greatest public health advances of the twentieth century.[49]

To find out if your community water is fluoridated and how much fluoride is added, visit the Centers for Disease Control and Prevention's website, My Water's Fluoride, at http://apps.nccd.cdc.gov/MWF/Index.asp.

Daily Needs

Adult men should consume 3.8 milligrams and women 3.1 milligrams of fluoride daily to meet their needs. If the tap water in your community is fluoridated at 0.7 milligram/liter, you would have to consume more than 15 cups of water daily, through either beverages or cooking, to meet your fluoride needs (1 liter = 4.2 cups).

The toothpaste that you use to brush your teeth can also be a source of fluoride.[50]

Food Sources

Foods in general are not a good source of fluoride. The best sources are fluoridated water and beverages and foods made with this water, such as coffee, tea, and soups. Another source of fluoride can be juices made from concentrate using fluoridated tap water.

Water and processed beverages, such as soft drinks, account for up to 75 percent of Americans' fluoride intake.

Tea is also a good source of fluoride, as tea leaves accumulate fluoride. Note that decaffeinated tea has twice the amount of fluoride as the caffeinated variety.[51]

If you shy away from tap water and drink and cook predominantly with bottled water, you may be robbing yourself of some cavity protection. Most bottled waters sold in the United States have less than the optimal amount of fluoride. It is difficult to determine the fluoride content of many bottled waters because currently, the amount of fluoride in bottled water has to be listed on the label only if fluoride has been specifically added. Check the label to see if your bottled water contains added fluoride. For more information about the differences between bottled and tap water, and their advantages and disadvantages, see the boxed feature "Tap Water or Bottled Water: Is Bottled Better?" on page 286.

Too Much or Too Little

Because of fluoride's protective qualities, too little exposure to or consumption of fluoride increases the risk of dental caries.

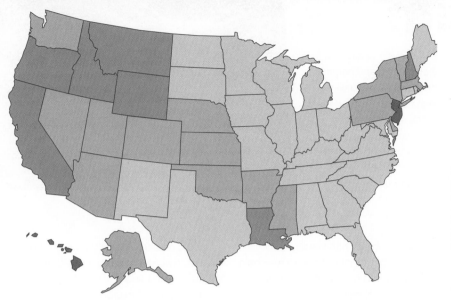

Key*
- ■ 0 – 24
- ■ 25 – 49
- ■ 50 – 74
- □ 75 – 100

Teeth pitted by fluorosis

The upper level for adults has been set at 10 milligrams to reduce the risk of fluorosis in the bones. (Note, however, that the upper level for infants and children is much lower, to prevent fluorosis in teeth. See the inside cover of the textbook for this upper level.)

Having some fluoride is important for healthy teeth, but too much can cause **fluorosis,** a condition whereby the teeth become mottled (pitted) and develop white patches or stains on the surface. Fluorosis creates teeth that are extremely resistant to caries but cosmetically unappealing (see photo).

Fluorosis occurs when teeth are forming, so only infants and children up to 8 years of age are at risk. Once teeth break through the gums, fluorosis can't occur. Fluorosis results from overfluoridation of water, swallowing toothpaste, or excessive use of dental products that contain fluoride. Some research suggests that fluorosis may be reversible, but more studies are needed to determine this.

Skeletal fluorosis can occur in bones when a person consumes at least 10 milligrams of fluoride daily for 10 or more years. This is a rare situation that occurs when water is mistakenly overfluoridated. This can cause bone concentrations of fluoride that are up to five times higher than normal and result in stiffness or pain in joints, osteoporosis, and calcification of the ligaments.

Table Tips

Fabulous Ways to Get Fluoride

Pour orange juice into ice cube trays and pop a couple of frozen cubes into a glass of tap water for a refreshing and flavorful beverage.

Use tap water when making coffee, tea, or juice from concentrate, and for food preparation.

Brew a mug of flavored decaffeinated tea, such as French vanilla or gingerbread, to keep you warm while you're hitting the books.

Terms to Know
fluorosis

Chromium

What Is Chromium?

The most recent mineral to be found necessary in humans, chromium was identified as an essential mineral in 1977, although researchers have had an interest in chromium and its roles in the metabolism of glucose since the 1950s.[52]

Functions of Chromium

Chromium Helps Insulin in Your Body

The main function of this mineral is to increase insulin's effectiveness in cells. The hormone insulin plays an important role in the metabolism and storage of carbohydrates, fats, and protein in your body. Individuals who were intravenously fed a chromium-free diet experienced high blood levels of glucose, weight loss, and nerve problems—all telltale signs of uncontrolled diabetes and poor blood glucose control. The problems were corrected when chromium was provided.[53]

Chromium May Reduce Prediabetes

Because it works with insulin, some researchers think that chromium may help individuals who have diabetes mellitus or prediabetes (glucose intolerance) improve their blood glucose control. There has yet to be a large research study in the United States that confirms this theory.

One small study suggests that a chromium supplement may reduce the risk of insulin resistance, and therefore, favorably affect the handling of glucose in the body. Improving the body's sensitivity to insulin and maintaining a normal blood glucose level can possibly lower the incidence of type 2 diabetes in individuals at risk.

Based on this one study, the FDA has allowed a Qualified Health Claim on chromium supplements. However, the supplement label must state that the evidence regarding the relationship between chromium supplements and either insulin resistance or type 2 diabetes is not certain at this time.[54]

Chromium Does Not Help Build Muscle Mass

Although advertisements have sometimes touted chromium supplements as an aid to losing weight and building lean muscle, the research doesn't support the claim. A review of more than 20 research studies didn't find any benefits from taking up to 1,000 micrograms of chromium daily.[55] If you are trying to become lean and mean, taking chromium supplements isn't going to help.

Daily Needs

Adult men age 19 to 50 need 30 to 35 micrograms of chromium daily, whereas women of the same age need 20 to 25 micrograms daily, on average, depending upon their age. It is estimated that American men consume 33 micrograms of chromium from foods, and women consume 25 micrograms, on average, daily.[56]

Food Sources

Grains are good sources of chromium. Meat, eggs, and poultry and some fruits and vegetables can also provide chromium, whereas dairy foods are low in the mineral.

Micrograms (μg) of Chromium

Food	μg
Vegetables	
Peas, 1 cup	0.8
Green beans, 1 cup	2.2
Potatoes, mashed, 1 cup	2.7
Broccoli, 1 cup	22
Fruits	
Tomato, 1 medium	1.0
Apple with skin, 1 medium	1.4
Orange juice, 1 cup	2.2
Grape juice, 1 cup	7.5
Grains	
Whole-wheat bread, 1 slice	1.0
Whole-wheat English muffin, 1/2	1.8
Protein	
Egg, 1	0.2
Chicken breast, 3 oz	0.5
Turkey breast, 3 oz	1.7
Ham, 3 oz	3.6
Daily Needs	
Men 19 to 50 years	35
Women 19 to 50 years	25

Too Much or Too Little

As yet, there is no known risk from consuming excessive amounts of chromium from food or supplements, so no upper level has been set.

A chromium deficiency is very rare in the United States. The jury is still out on whether individuals with diabetes who did not have a chromium deficiency would benefit by taking a supplement. More research is needed in this area.[57]

Table Tips

Cram in the Chromium

Toast a whole-wheat English muffin and top it with a slice of lean ham for a meaty, chromium-laden breakfast.

Add broccoli florets to your salad for a chromium-packed lunch.

Try an afternoon glass of cold grape juice for a refreshing break. Add an apple for a double dose of chromium.

Combine mashed potatoes and peas for a sweet and starchy addition to your dinner plate and your chromium count.

Slice tomatoes on your sandwich for a chromium-rich lunch.

Iodine

What Is Iodine?

Like the fluoridation of community drinking water, the iodization of salt was a significant advance for public health in the United States. Prior to the 1920s, many Americans suffered from the iodine-deficiency disease, goiter. Once salt manufacturers began adding iodine to their product, incidence of the disease dropped. Today, rates of the disease are very low in the United States, though not in other parts of the world.

Functions of Iodine

Iodine is an essential mineral for your thyroid, a butterfly-shaped gland located in your neck. The thyroid needs iodine to make some essential hormones. In fact, approximately 60 percent of your thyroid hormones are comprised of iodine.

Thyroid hormones affect the majority of your cells, regulate your metabolic rate, and help your heart, nerves, muscles, and intestines function properly. Children need thyroid hormones for normal bone growth and brain development.[58]

Daily Needs

Adult men and women need 150 micrograms of iodine daily to meet their needs. Americans currently consume 230 micrograms to 410 micrograms of iodine daily, on average, depending upon their age and gender.

Food Sources

The amount of iodine that occurs naturally in foods is typically low, approximately 3 to 75 micrograms in a serving, and is influenced by the amount of iodine in the

Goiter

soil, water, and fertilizers used to grow foods.

Fish can provide higher amounts of iodine, as they concentrate it from seawater. Iodized salt provides 400 micrograms of iodine per teaspoon. Note that not all salt has added iodine. Kosher salt, for example, has no additives, including iodine. Processed foods that use iodized salt or iodine-containing preservatives are also a source.

Too Much or Too Little

Consuming too much iodine can challenge the thyroid, impairing its function and reducing the synthesis and release of thyroid hormones. Because of this, the upper level for adults for iodine is 1,100 micrograms.

An early sign of iodine deficiency is **goiter,** which is an enlarged thyroid gland (see photo above). An iodine-deficient thyroid has to work harder to make the thyroid hormones, causing it to become enlarged.[59]

A deficiency of iodine during the early stages of fetal development can damage the brain of the developing baby, causing mental retardation. Inadequate iodine during this critical time can cause lower IQ scores. Depending upon the severity of the iodine deficiency, **cretinism,** also known as **congenital hypothyroidism** (*congenital* = born with, *hypo* = under, *ism* = condition), can occur. Individuals with cretinism can experience abnormal sexual development, mental retardation, and dwarfism (see photo).

Early detection of an iodine deficiency and treatment in children is critical to avoiding irreversible damage.

Micrograms (µg) of **Iodine**

Food	µg
Tuna, canned in oil, (½ can) 3 oz	17
Egg, large, 1	29
Turkey breast, 3 oz	34
Navy beans, cooked, ½ cup	35
Shrimp, 3 oz	35
Cod, 3 oz	99
Daily Needs Adults 19 to 50 years	150

Cretinism

Table Tips
Iodine Impact

Add a hard-cooked egg to your breakfast.

Add beans to your lunchtime soup.

Sprinkle tuna fish flakes on your dinner salad.

Terms to Know
goiter • cretinism (congenital hypothyroidism)

Manganese

What Is Manganese?

Manganese is either part of, or activates, many enzymes in your body.

Functions of Manganese

Manganese Is Needed in Metabolism and for Healthy Bones

This mineral is involved in the metabolism of carbohydrates, fats, and amino acids. Manganese is needed for the formation of bone.

Daily Needs

Adult women need 1.8 milligrams, whereas men need 2.3 milligrams, of manganese daily. Americans are easily meeting their manganese needs. Adult women consume more than 2 milligrams of manganese daily, and adult men consume more than 2.8 milligrams daily, on average, from the foods in their diet.[60]

Food Sources

When it comes to meeting your manganese needs, look to whole grains, nuts, legumes, tea, vegetables, and fruits such as pineapples, strawberries, and bananas. A teaspoon of ground cinnamon provides just under 0.5 milligram of manganese.

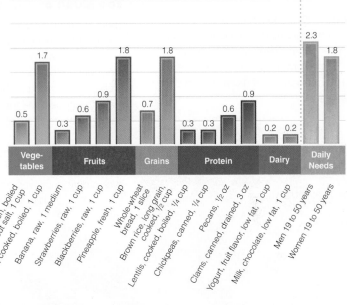

Milligrams (mg) of **Manganese**

Food	mg
Vegetables	
Peas, green, frozen, boiled without salt, 1 cup	0.5
Spinach, cooked, boiled, 1 cup	1.7
Fruits	
Banana, raw, 1 medium	0.3
Strawberries, raw, 1 cup	0.6
Blackberries, raw, 1 cup	0.9
Pineapple, fresh, 1 cup	1.8
Grains	
Whole-wheat bread, 1 slice	0.7
Brown rice, long grain, cooked, 1/2 cup	1.8
Protein	
Lentils, cooked, boiled, 1/4 cup	0.3
Chickpeas, canned, 1/4 cup	0.3
Pecans, 1/2 oz	0.6
Clams, canned, drained, 3 oz	0.9
Dairy	
Yogurt, fruit flavor, low fat, 1 cup	0.2
Milk, chocolate, low fat, 1 cup	0.2
Daily Needs	
Men 19 to 50 years	2.3
Women 19 to 50 years	1.8

Too Much or Too Little

Manganese toxicity, which has occurred in miners who have inhaled manganese dust, can cause damage to the nervous system and symptoms that resemble Parkinson's disease.[61] A study of individuals who drank water with high levels of manganese showed that they also experienced Parkinson's-disease–like symptoms.

To protect against this toxicity, the upper level has been set at 11 milligrams daily.

A deficiency of manganese is rare in healthy individuals who have a balanced diet. Individuals fed a manganese-deficient diet developed a rash and scaly skin.

Table Tips
Managing Your Manganese

Sprinkle your whole-wheat toast with a dusting of cinnamon to spice up your morning.

Combine cooked brown rice, canned and rinsed lentils, and chickpeas for a dinner in a snap.

Spoon vanilla yogurt over canned crushed pineapples and sliced bananas for a tropical treat.

Molybdenum

What Is Molybdenum?

Molybdenum is part of several enzymes involved in the breakdown of certain amino acids and other compounds.

Daily Needs

Adult men and women need to consume 45 micrograms of molybdenum daily. American women currently consume 76 micrograms and men consume 109 micrograms of molybdenum daily, on average.

Food Sources

Legumes are excellent sources of molybdenum. Grains and nuts are also good sources.[62]

Too Much or Too Little

There is limited research on the adverse effects of too much dietary molybdenum in humans. In animal studies, too much molybdenum can cause reproductive problems. Because of this finding in animals, the upper level for molybdenum in humans has been set at 2 milligrams for adults.

A deficiency of molybdenum has not been seen in healthy individuals. However, a deficiency was observed in an individual who was fed

intravenously for years and developed symptoms that included rapid heartbeats, headaches, and night blindness.

Other Minerals: Arsenic, Boron, Nickel, Silicon, and Vanadium

A few other minerals exist in your body, but their nutritional importance in humans has not yet been established. These minerals include arsenic, boron, nickel, silicon, and vanadium. Although limited research suggests that these may have a function in animals, there isn't enough data to confirm an essential role in humans.[18]

Table 8.1 summarizes these minerals, their potential role in animal health, their food sources, and the levels of deficiency and toxicity, if known, in humans.

NutriTools

Vitamin or Mineral?

Is it a vitamin? Is it a mineral? Do you know the difference? Visit www.pearsonhighered.com/blake and complete this interactive NutriTools activity.

Table 8.1

Additional Minerals

Mineral	Potential Role and Deficiency Symptoms	Food Sources	Potential Toxicity
Arsenic	May be needed in the metabolism of a specific amino acid in rats. A deficiency may impair growth and reproduction in animals.	Dairy products, meat, poultry, fish, grains, and cereal products	No known adverse effect in humans from the organic form of arsenic found in foods. The inorganic form is poisonous to humans.
Boron	A deficiency may be associated with reproductive abnormalities in certain fish and frogs, which suggests a possible role in normal development in animals.	Grape juice, legumes, potatoes, pecans, peanut butter, apples, and milk	No known adverse effect from boron in food. Some research suggests that high amounts of boron may cause reproductive and developmental problems in animals. Because of this, the upper limit for human adults has been set at 20 mg daily, which is more than 10 times the amount American adults consume daily, on average.
Nickel	May be needed by specific enzymes in the body. It is considered an essential mineral in animals.	Grains and grain products, vegetables, legumes, nuts, and chocolate	No known toxicity of nickel in humans when consuming a normal diet. In rats, large exposure to nickel salts can cause toxicity, with symptoms such as lethargy, irregular breathing, and lower than normal weight gain. Because of this, the upper limit for adults is set at 1 mg daily for nickel salts.
Silicon	May be needed for bone formation in animals.	Grains, grain products, and vegetables	No known risk of silicon toxicity in humans from food sources.
Vanadium	In animals, vanadium has insulin-like actions and a deficiency increases the risk of abortion.	Mushrooms, shellfish, parsley, and black pepper	No known risk of toxicity in humans from vanadium in foods. Too much has been shown to cause kidney damage in animals. Vanadium can be purchased as supplements. Because of the known toxicity in animals, the upper limit for adults is set at 1.8 mg daily.

Source: Institute of Medicine. *Dietary Reference Intakes: Vitamin A, Vitamin K, Arsenic, Boron, Chromium, Copper, Iodine, Iron, Manganese, Molybdenum, Nickel, Silicon, Vanadium, and Zinc.* (Washington, D.C.: The National Academies Press, 2001). Available at www.nap.edu.

Let's Go to Lunch: Minerals

What minerals are in your lunch? Visit www.pearsonhighered.com/blake and complete this interactive NutriTools activity.

Putting Together All the Major Nutrients

Table 8.2 provides you with a visual summary of all the minerals and your needs.

Currently Americans, on average, meet many of their nutrient needs. As Table 8.3 shows, however, our diets could still use a little fine-tuning to meet all of the recommendations for a healthy diet. Consuming a wide variety of foods from all the food groups, with an emphasis on whole grains, whole fruits, and vegetables along with adequate amounts of lean dairy and meat, poultry, and plenty of fluids, is the best diet prescription to meet your needs for carbohydrates, protein, fat, vitamins, minerals, and water. The Table Tips in the preceding chapters can help you with your diet fine-tuning.

Table 8.2

Minerals at a Glance: Major Minerals

Major Minerals	Major Functions	Adult DRI, 19 to 50 years	Food Sources	Excessive/Toxicity Symptoms/UL	Deficiency Symptoms/ Conditions
Sodium	Major electrolyte outside the cell; helps regulate body water and blood pressure	1,500 mg/day	Processed foods, table salt, meat, seafood, milk, cheese, eggs	Hypertension UL: 2,300 mg	Rare in individuals consuming a healthy diet
Potassium	Major mineral inside the cell, needed for muscle contraction and nerve impulses; regulates body water and blood pressure	4,700 mg/day	Potatoes, melons, citrus fruits, most fruits and vegetables, meat, milk, legumes	Hyperkalemia	Hypokalemia
Calcium	Formation of bones and teeth, muscle contraction and relaxation, blood clotting, heart and nerve function	1,000 mg/day	Milk and dairy products, leafy greens, broccoli, salmon, sardines, tofu	Hypercalcemia UL: 2,500 mg	Osteoporosis
Phosphorus	Formation of bones and teeth	700 mg/day	Meat, fish, poultry, eggs, dairy, cereals	Hyperphosphatemia UL: 3,000 to 4,000 mg	Muscle weakness, bone pain, rickets, confusion, and death
Magnesium	Participates in muscle contraction and nerve conduction	310 to 420 mg/day	Meat, seafood, nuts, legumes, dairy, whole grains	Large intakes from supplements can cause diarrhea, cramps, and nausea	Rare
Chloride	Helps maintain fluid and acid-base balance	2,300 mg/day	Found as sodium chloride in foods	UL: 3,600 mg	Rare
Sulfur	A part of other compounds in body; helps give some amino acids their three-dimensional shape	None	Meats, fish, poultry, eggs, dairy foods, fruits, vegetables	None	None

Table 8.2   continued

Minerals at a Glance: Trace Minerals

Trace Minerals	Major Functions	Adult DRI, 19 to 50 years	Food Sources	Excessive/Toxicity Symptoms/UL	Deficiency Symptoms/ Conditions
Iron	As a major component of hemoglobin and myoglobin, helps transport oxygen throughout the body; enhances brain function	8 to 18 mg/day	Meat, fish, poultry, enriched and fortified breads and cereals	Vomiting, nausea, diarrhea, constipation, organ damage including the kidney and liver UL: 45 mg	Fatigue, iron-deficiency anemia, growth retardation in infants
Copper	A component of several enzymes; involved in iron transport; needed for healthy connective tissue enzymes; role in blood clotting and a healthy immune system	900 µg/day	Organ meats, nuts, seeds, cocoa, whole grains, legumes, and shellfish	Vomiting, abdominal pain, nausea, diarrhea, liver damage UL: 10,000 µg	Impaired growth and development
Zinc	Cofactor for several enzymes; DNA and RNA synthesis; needed for a healthy immune system, wound healing, and taste acuity	8 to 11 mg /day	Meat, poultry, seafood, whole grains	Nausea, vomiting, cramps, diarrhea, impaired immune function UL: 40 mg	Skin rash and hair loss, diarrhea, loss of taste and smell
Selenium	A component of enzymes; antioxidant	55 µg/day	Meat, seafood, fish, eggs, whole grains	Selenosis, brittle hair and nails, skin rash, garlic breath odor, fatigue UL: 400 µg	Keshan disease
Fluoride	Makes teeth stronger	3 to 4 mg/day	Fluoridated water, tea	Fluorosis in teeth and skeletal fluorosis UL: 10 mg	Increased susceptibility to dental caries
Chromium	Improves insulin response	20–35 µg/day	Pork, egg yolks, whole grains, nuts	Unconfirmed toxicity effects	Potential increase of insulin resistance
Iodine	Component of a thyroid hormone	150 µg/day	Iodized salt, seafood, dairy products	Impaired functioning of thyroid UL: 1,000 µg	Goiter, cretinism
Manganese	Cofactor involved in metabolism	1.8 to 2.3 mg/day	Beans, oats, nuts, tea	Abnormal central nervous system effects UL: 11 mg	Deficiency rare; rash and scaly skin
Molybdenum	Cofactor for a variety of enzymes	45 µg/day	Legumes, nuts, leafy vegetables, dairy, cereals	Unknown in humans UL: 2 mg	Unknown in humans

Table 8.3

Putting It All Together: Making Better Choices

American Adults Typically Consume Enough:	But Could Fine-Tune Their Dietary Choices to Include More:
Saturated fat	Unsaturated fat in place of saturated fat
Carbohydrates	Fiber-rich foods and less added sugars
Vitamins A, E, and K	Vitamin D if not exposed to adequate sunlight
B vitamins and vitamin C	Synthetic folic acid (premenopausal women only) Synthetic vitamin B_{12} (individuals 51+ years; vegans)
Sodium, phosphorus, zinc, selenium, chromium, copper, iodine, manganese, molybdenum	Potassium, calcium, magnesium, iron (premenopausal women; vegans), zinc (vegans), fluoride (if not consuming fluoridated water)
Fluids with added sugar	Fluids (water)

Fresh fruits and vegetables can be natural sources of multiple nutrients. Jicama (shown here) can add potassium, calcium, folate, and phosphorus to an afternoon snack.

Made Over, Made Better!

Snacks can be a great way to give your diet a mineral boost. Bananas, for example, are packed with potassium, raisins are naturally high in iron, peanuts are rich in magnesium, and cheese is a ringer for calcium. However, depending upon how these foods are processed, they may be higher in calories, fat, and saturated fat than you bargained for.

Here are some typical mineral-rich snacks made over and made nutritionally better!

If you like this. . .

Banana Chips
Serving size: 1/2 cup
Calories: 300
Fat: 14 grams
Saturated Fat: 12 grams

Yogurt Covered Raisins
Serving size: 1/2 cup
Calories: 280
Fat: 12 grams
Saturated Fat: 9 grams

Trail Mix
Serving size: 1/2 cup
Calories: 300
Fat: 20 grams
Saturated Fat: 4 grams

Cheddar Cheese
Serving size: 1 ounce
Calories: 120
Fat: 10 grams
Saturated Fat: 6 grams

Try this healthy alternative!

Banana
1 small
Calories: 90
Fat: <0.5 grams
Saturated Fat: 0 grams

Raisins
Serving size: 1/2 cup
Calories: 123
Fat: 0 grams
Saturated Fat: 0 grams

Peanuts in Shell
Serving size: 1/2 cup
Calories: 170
Fat: 13 grams
Saturated Fat: 2 grams

String Cheese
Serving size: 1 ounce
Calories: 80
Fat: 6 grams
Saturated Fat: 3 grams

Source: USDA National Nutrient Database for Standard Reference.

Two Points of View

Is Fluoridation of the Water Supply Only a Good Thing?
About 180 million people receive fluoridated water through their municipal water supply. "Optimally fluoridated" water, which has a fluoride concentration of 0.7 to 1.2 parts per million, has been credited with reducing tooth decay.[1] But overconsuming fluoride can result in toxicity symptoms, and some groups oppose the addition of fluoride to drinking water.

Do the drawbacks of fluoridated water outweigh the benefits? Read the arguments on both sides of the issue and decide for yourself.

Yes

- Tooth decay is one of the most common childhood diseases: It is five times more common than asthma and seven times more common than hay fever in children aged 5 to 17. Considering that every $1 spent per community saves $38 in dental costs, fluoridated water is the most efficient way to prevent this disease.[2]

- Water fluoridation is effective in reducing dental decay by 20 to 40 percent, even now, in an era where other sources of fluoride, such as toothpaste, are widely available.[3]

- Fluoridation of the public water supply benefits Americans of all ages and socioeconomic status.[4]

- In 1960, the town of Antigo, Wisconsin stopped fluoridating its water after 11 years of doing so. By 1965, second-graders in the town had 200 percent more tooth decay than second-graders in 1960, fourth-graders had 70 percent more, and sixth-graders 90 percent more.[5]

- A lethal one-time dose of fluoride would be 5 to 10 grams for a 155-pound man—more than 10,000 to 20,000 times the concentration of fluoride in an eight-ounce glass of fluoridated water.[6]

No

- Chronic, high-level exposure to fluoride can lead to skeletal fluorosis, which can result in changes to bone structure and hardened ligaments. Ingesting a large amount of fluoride, while rare, causes abdominal pain, nausea, and vomiting, with possible seizures and muscle spasms.[7]

- In children, overconsumption of fluoride can lead to dental fluorosis, which leads to staining and/or pitting of the teeth.

- The Environmental Protection Agency, which officially neither opposes nor endorses fluoridated drinking water, reports that drinking water with more than 4 milligrams of fluoride per liter can lead to skeletal fluorosis. The EPA sets a maximum contaminant level (MCL) of 4.0 milligrams per liter.[8]

- Some environmental organizations oppose mandatory fluoridation, or at least would like the MCL level lowered, because of fluoride's impact on aquatic life and ecosystems, and human health.[9]

What do you think?

1. Which side do you think has the more compelling argument? Why? **2.** Does the public benefit (lower rates of tooth decay) outweigh the rights of individual choice? Why or why not? **3.** Do you think that you would consume adequate amounts of fluoride without consuming the nutrient in drinking water?

Chapter Review

Be a Nutrition Sleuth

Where's the Sodium in Your Foods?

Go online to **www.pearsonhighered.com/blake** and take a virtual trip down the supermarket aisle to find the sodium content of some of your favorite foods. (Beware: If you're a ramen fan, click with caution.)

Get Real!

Calcium Counter

Are you falling short of your calcium needs? Or are you enjoying too many calcium-fortified food products, possibly exceeding the upper limit? Visit the Calcium Counter at **www.pearsonhighered.com/blake** and get a ballpark estimate of your current calcium intake.

The Top Ten Points to Remember

1. Water is an important solvent that helps transport oxygen, nutrients, and other substances throughout your body and waste products away from your cells. It helps regulate body temperature and cushion organs. Combined with other substances to form saliva and mucus, it acts as a lubricant in your mouth and intestines. Adult women should consume 9 cups of water, and adult men should drink approximately 13 cups of water, daily. Caffeinated beverages, juices, and milk can all count toward meeting your water needs. Many foods are also a good source of water.

2. Minerals are micronutrients that play many roles in the body. Many are part of enzymes. Minerals help maintain fluid and acid-base balance; play a role in nerve transmission and muscle contractions; help strengthen bones, teeth, and the immune system; and are involved in growth. Minerals are found in both plant and animal foods, but often vary in bioavailability due to binding agents (oxalates, phytates) or competition with other minerals for absorption in the intestinal tract.

3. Sodium plays an important role in balancing the fluid between your blood and cells. Americans currently consume more than double the sodium recommended daily, predominantly as sodium chloride (table salt). Processed foods are the major source of sodium chloride in the diet. Reducing dietary sodium and following the DASH diet, which is abundant in foods rich in potassium, magnesium, and calcium, can help lower blood pressure. Losing excess weight, being physically active, and limiting alcohol can also lower blood pressure.

4. Potassium helps keep your heart, muscles, nerves, and bones healthy. The current recommendations to increase the fruits and vegetables in your diet will help you meet your potassium needs.

5. Calcium, along with phosphorus, forms hydroxyapatite, which provides strength and structure for bones and teeth. A diet adequate in protein, vitamin K, calcium, and vitamin D, along with regular physical activity, is needed to build and maintain healthy bones. Dairy foods can be a good source of both calcium and phosphorus. Osteoporosis is a condition caused by frail bones. A chronic deficiency of dietary calcium and/or vitamin D, excess alcohol consumption, and smoking can all increase the risk of osteoporosis.

6. Iron is part of the oxygen-carrying transport proteins—hemoglobin in your red blood cells and myoglobin in your muscles. Heme iron is found in meat, poultry, and fish. Nonheme iron is found in plant foods, such as grains and vegetables. Nonheme iron is the predominant source of the iron in your diet but isn't absorbed as readily as heme iron. A deficiency of iron in children can reduce their ability to learn and retain information. Iron-deficiency anemia can cause fatigue and weakness.

7. More than 100 enzymes in your cells need zinc to function properly. Zinc plays a role in the structure of both RNA and DNA, in your taste acuity, and in helping fight age-related macular degeneration (AMD). Meat, fish, and whole grains are good sources of zinc. More research is needed in order to confirm whether zinc can help fight the common cold.

8. Selenium acts as an antioxidant in your body and may help fight cancer. Chromium helps the hormone insulin function, but has not been proven to enhance weight loss or build muscle mass during exercise. Iodine is essential to make thyroid hormones, which affect the majority of the cells and help regulate metabolic rate.

9. Copper is part of many enzymes and proteins that are involved in the absorption and transfer of iron and the synthesis of hemoglobin and red blood cells. Both manganese and molybdenum also help enzymes function in your body.

10. Both tap and bottled waters can be safe to drink. Fluoride is often added to water that comes from the tap, whereas bottled water typically does not contain added fluoride. In the United States, bottled water is not safer or purer than tap water.

Test Your Knowledge

1. The most abundant substance in your body is
   a. magnesium.
   b. iron.
   c. sodium.
   d. water.

2. All bottled water is regulated by the FDA.
   a. true
   b. false

3. In your body, minerals can
   a. help maintain fluid balance.
   b. be part of enzymes.
   c. work with your immune system.
   d. do all of the above.

4. The daily recommendation for dietary sodium intake for adults up to age 51 is
   a. 3,400 milligrams.
   b. 2,300 milligrams.
   c. 1,500 milligrams.
   d. 180 milligrams.

5. Which food groups are good sources of potassium?
   a. Fruits and vegetables
   b. Vegetables and grains
   c. Dairy and protein
   d. all of the above

6. Which of the following can increase the risk for hypertension?
   a. a family history of high blood pressure
   b. consuming excessive amounts of alcohol
   c. being inactive
   d. all of the above

7. One cup of skim milk, 8 ounces of low-fat yogurt, and 1½ ounces of reduced-fat cheddar cheese *each* provide
   a. 100 milligrams of calcium.
   b. 200 milligrams of calcium.
   c. 300 milligrams of calcium.
   d. 400 milligrams of calcium.

8. You are having pasta for dinner. You want to enhance your absorption of the nonheme iron in the pasta. To do that, you could top your spaghetti with
   a. butter.
   b. olive oil.
   c. tomato sauce.
   d. nothing; eat it plain.

9. Chromium increases the effectiveness of
   a. thyroid hormones.
   b. the hormone insulin.
   c. antidiuretic hormone (ADH).

10. Fluoride will help strengthen and repair the enamel on your teeth. What other mineral strengthens your teeth?
    a. chloride
    b. phosphorus
    c. sulfur
    d. zinc

Answers

1. (d) Your body is about 60 percent water. Water bathes the trillions of cells in your body and is part of the fluid inside your cells where reactions take place. Iron, though part of hemoglobin, is a trace mineral, so you only have small amounts in your body. Both magnesium and sodium are major minerals used in your body but are not as abundant as water.

2. (b) False. The FDA only regulates bottled water that is sold through interstate commerce. Bottled water that is manufactured and sold within the same state is not regulated by the FDA.

3. (d) Although you need only small amounts of minerals in your diet, they play enormously important roles in your body, such as helping to maintain fluid balance, being part of enzymes, and working with your immune system to keep you healthy.

4. (c) The daily recommended amount of sodium for adults up to age 51 is 1,500 milligrams. The upper level for sodium daily is 2,300 milligrams, whereas the absolute minimum that should be consumed is 180 milligrams per day. Unfortunately, Americans far exceed these recommendations and consume more than 3,400 milligrams of sodium daily, on average.

5. (d) Eating foods from the five food groups can help you to meet your potassium needs.

6. (d) They all can increase the risk of hypertension. People can't change their family history, but they can become more physically active, lose excess weight, and limit their alcohol consumption, all of which will help them to better manage their blood pressure.

7. (c) Each of these servings of dairy foods provides 300 milligrams of calcium. Consuming the recommended three servings of lean dairy products daily will just about meet the amount of calcium recommended daily (1,000 milligrams) for many adults.

8. (c) Ladle the tomato sauce on your pasta—the vitamin C in it can enhance nonheme iron absorption. Though the butter and olive oil will give your spaghetti flavor, they won't help you absorb iron.

9. (b) Chromium increases insulin's effectiveness in your cells. Iodine is needed to make thyroid hormones, and ADH is the hormone that directs kidneys to minimize water loss and concentrate urine.

10. (b) Phosphorus, along with calcium, forms hydroxyapatite, which is the strengthening material found in your teeth. Chloride is one of the electrolytes in your blood that helps maintain fluid and acid-base balance. Sulfur plays an important role as part of many compounds in your body, such as certain amino acids. Zinc helps with wound healing and maintaining a healthy immune system.

Web Resources

➡ To learn more about the safety of your local water supply, visit the EPA's website at www.epa.gov/enviro/html/sdwis/sdwis_query.html#geography

➡ For more on the DASH diet, visit DASH for Health at www.dashforhealth.com

➡ For more on osteoporosis, visit the National Osteoporosis Foundation at www.nof.org

➡ For more on high blood pressure, visit www.nhlbi.nih.gov/hbp/

Answers to Myths and Misperceptions

1. **True.** Your mug of java does contribute to meeting your daily water needs, even though it may contain caffeine, a diuretic. Turn to page 284 to find out why.

2. **False.** Enhanced waters such as vitamin waters contain additional calories. To improve your fluid intake, plain water is just as healthy and much cheaper. Turn to page 287 to learn more about these waters.

3. **False.** Both plant and animal products are bioavailable sources of minerals. Turn to page 288 to find out more.

4. **False.** Although seasoning your food with salt adds sodium, it is not the major culprit in sodium overload. Turn to page 290 to find out what is.

5. **True.** Magnesium, along with calcium and potassium, is part of a diet that has been shown to substantially lower blood pressure. To find out more, turn to page 293.

6. **True.** In fact, the recommended three servings of dairy foods, including milk, yogurt, and/or cheese, will almost nail your calcium needs for the day. Unfortunately, most Americans' diets fall short in regard to this food group. To find out how to meet your needs, turn to page 296.

7. **False.** Although needed in much smaller amounts, trace minerals are as indispensable as major minerals. See why on page 305.

8. **False.** Although meat, fish, and poultry are fabulous sources of iron, they are not the main sources in Americans' diets. Turn to page 307 to find out what contributes the most iron to our diets.

9. **False.** Most bottled water sold in the United States does not contain fluoride. Turn to page 314 to find out why this could be bad news for your teeth.

10. **False.** Dream on. Turn to page 316 to learn the truth.

9

True or False?

1. Alcohol is an **essential** nutrient. ⓉⒻ p. 332

2. A shot of **whiskey** contains more alcohol than a can of beer. ⓉⒻ p. 334

3. Red wine contains **phytochemicals** that are good for your heart. ⓉⒻ p. 334

4. If you **passed out** from heavy drinking, your blood alcohol level would stabilize and gradually return to normal. ⓉⒻ p. 337

5. **Women** feel the effects of alcohol sooner than **men**. ⓉⒻ p. 338

6. The best way to cure a **hangover** is to drink a Bloody Mary (tomato juice and vodka) the next morning. ⓉⒻ p. 341

7. Alcohol provides **7 calories** per gram. ⓉⒻ p. 341

8. Drinking too much alcohol can lead to **malnutrition**. ⓉⒻ p. 343

9. Some states in the United States have lowered the **legal drinking age** to 18. ⓉⒻ p. 350

10. **Alcoholism** can be cured through counseling. ⓉⒻ p. 351

See page 357 for answers to these Myths and Misperceptions.

Alcohol

Twenty-one-year-old Leah has a brother, Steve, who craves alcohol. Steve says he needs to have "a few" drinks daily to relax. When he arrives home from work, he is often anxious or grouchy but becomes "human" again, as Leah puts it, after several beers. Sometimes he drinks his dinner, eating very little food, making a meal out of a second six-pack. His girlfriend broke up with him because he drank too much. Steve has tried to cut back on the amount of beer he drinks, but once he gets started he can't seem to stop. When he tried to give up drinking cold turkey, he became anxious, shaky, and nauseous, and broke out in cold sweats. He has become dependent on alcohol to "steady his nerves." Leah knows these symptoms all too well, as Steve's drinking patterns and behaviors mimic her father's, who died of cirrhosis of the liver when he was 62, and her grandfather's, who "drank himself to his grave," according to her mother.

Though Leah doesn't consider herself a heavy drinker, she does have a beer after dinner on most nights of the week. She is afraid that the beer she consumes on weeknights, as well as during her weekend partying with friends, is becoming a habit that she can't stop.

Do you think Leah is right to be worried—is she at a higher risk of following in her brother's footsteps? Why should she be concerned about her alcohol intake? In this chapter, we discuss the nature of alcohol, including its various forms, how it is digested and absorbed in the body, and its potential short-term and long-term health effects. We also explore alcohol use and abuse, and steps you can take if you suspect that you or someone close to you is abusing alcohol.

Chapter Objectives

After reading this chapter, you will be able to:

1. List at least one reason why people drink alcohol.

2. Explain how the body absorbs alcohol.

3. Describe how alcohol is circulated throughout the body.

4. Explain the role of the liver and enzymes in the metabolism of alcohol.

5. Describe how men and women metabolize alcohol differently.

6. Explain the effects of alcohol on the brain.

7. Define the term *moderate drinking* and discuss the benefits of moderate alcohol consumption.

8. Describe how alcohol can be harmful.

9. List at least two red flags for alcohol abuse.

10. Name the four classic symptoms of alcoholism.

What Is Alcohol and How Is It Made?

Your body doesn't need alcohol to survive. Therefore, alcohol is not an essential nutrient. You don't gain any nutrition from drinking it, other than calories. Ounce for ounce, it can cost 100 times more than bottled water. It's legally sold in the United States, but supposedly off limits to those who aren't adults, even though teenagers often feel under social pressure to consume it. Some medical reports say that in moderation, it can be good for you, while others tell you that drinking too much of it can kill you.

A bottle of beer, a glass of wine, or a rum and cola are all drinks that might come to mind when we consider the term **alcohol.** Technically, these beverages aren't alcohol by themselves, but they all contain a type of alcohol called **ethanol.**

Ethanol is one of three similar compounds in the chemical category of alcohol. The other two compounds, methanol (used in antifreeze) and isopropanol (used in rubbing alcohol), are both poisonous when ingested. Ethanol is considered safe for consumption, but it is not harmless. Consuming excessive amounts of ethanol can be toxic and damage your body. Too much can even kill you.

Ethanol is made through the **fermentation** of yeast and the natural sugars in grains (glucose and maltose) and fruits (fructose and glucose). The yeast breaks down the sugar into ethanol and carbon dioxide. The carbon dioxide evaporates, leaving an alcohol-containing beverage. Grapes provide the sugar for making wine, whereas the starch from grains provides the sugar when producing beer.

Liquors, such as rum, scotch, and whiskey, are made through a process called **distillation** and are more accurately called distilled spirits.[1] In this process, an alcoholic beverage is heated, causing the ethanol to vaporize. The vapor is collected, cooled, and condensed into a very concentrated liquid called liquor.

Although ethanol is the scientific name for the alcohol found in beverages, we will use the more common term *alcohol* throughout this chapter.

The Take-Home Message Ethanol is the type of alcohol consumed in alcoholic beverages. Alcoholic beverages are made by the processes of fermentation or distillation. Alcohol is not an essential nutrient because your body does not need it to survive.

Why Do People Drink Alcohol?

People around the world drink alcohol in many different forms and for many different reasons. The sake (rice wine) of Japan is used during tea and Shinto ceremonies, while the dark beer of the Irish is consumed by many pub patrons celebrating their favorite sport. The vodka of Russia and the chardonnay of Napa Valley are consumed in the pursuit of relaxation and pleasure. Globally, wine is part of many religious traditions, including the Catholic Mass and the Jewish Sabbath, and in some cultures, it's the beverage of choice during the main meal of the day. For parts of human history, wine and beer were safer to drink than water.

In the United States, more than half of adults consume at least one alcoholic beverage per month.[2] Americans drink alcohol for many of the same reasons people in other parts of the world do. We use it to relax, celebrate, and socialize. Lately, we have also found that it may provide health benefits. Let's explore these motives for drinking alcohol more closely.

Beer is made from the fermentation of yeast and the natural sugars from grains.

People Drink to Relax, Celebrate, and Socialize

Alcohol is a drug that alters your conscious mind. Within minutes of sipping an alcoholic beverage, a person will feel more relaxed. After a few more sips, a mild, pleasant euphoria sets in and inhibitions begin to loosen. By the end of the first or second drink, a person will often feel more outgoing, happy, and social. This anxiety-reducing, upbeat initial effect is why people seek out and continue to drink alcohol.[3]

Having a drink with another person symbolizes social bonding. When it comes to mingling with others or celebrating a special occasion, whether it's with friends, coworkers, or even strangers, pubs and parties are common gathering spots, and alcoholic drinks are commonly served. This is considered **social drinking,** which is defined as drinking patterns that are considered acceptable by society.[4] Social drinking is not the same as moderate drinking (see the next section), as consuming too much alcohol, even in socially acceptable situations, can be harmful, even if it is only done on the weekends. Later in this chapter we discuss binge drinking, which often occurs in social settings.

Moderate Alcohol Consumption May Have Health Benefits

Some people drink alcohol because of its health benefits. That's right. Some studies have suggested that moderate alcohol consumption may reduce the risk of heart disease, and the risk of dying in general, for middle-aged and older adults.[5] **Moderate alcohol consumption** is defined as an average daily consumption of up to one drink

alcohol A chemical class of substances that contain ethanol, methanol, and isopropanol.

ethanol The type of alcohol in alcoholic beverages such as wine, beer, and liquor.

fermentation The process by which yeast converts sugars in grains or fruits into ethanol and carbon dioxide, resulting in an alcoholic beverage.

distillation The evaporation and then collection of a liquid by condensation. Liquors are made using distillation.

social drinking Drinking patterns that are considered acceptable by society.

moderate alcohol consumption An average daily consumption of up to one drink per day for women and up to two drinks per day for men, as well as no more than three drinks in any single day for women and no more than four drinks in a single day for men.

Figure 9.1 What Is a Standard Drink?
One standard drink of beer (12 ounces), wine (5 ounces), or liquor (1½ ounces) contains the same amount of alcohol.

12 oz
(1 drink)

16 oz
(1⅓ drink)

5 oz
(1 drink)

8 oz
(1½ drink)

Figure 9.2 When a Drink Is More Than a Drink . . .
Depending on the size, one drink may actually be the equivalent of 1⅓ to 2 drinks or more.

per day for women and up to two drinks per day for men, as well as no more than three drinks in any single day for women and no more than four drinks in a single day for men.

A standard drink is any one of the following:

➤ One 12-ounce serving of beer
➤ One 1.5-ounce shot of liquor
➤ One 5-ounce glass of wine

Each of these contains about half an ounce of alcohol (**Figure 9.1**).

On November 17, 1991, the television news show *60 Minutes* aired a segment called "The French Paradox," touting the benefits of modest amounts of red wine to help reduce the risk of heart disease. The French Paradox is so called because the people of France have lower rates of heart disease even though their saturated fat intake mimics that of Americans. They also drink more red wine than Americans do, which is thought to be the differentiating factor. (However, the French also consume fewer *trans* fats and have a less stressful lifestyle and better developed social networks, which can also contribute to their impressively lower risk of heart disease.) In the four weeks after the segment was aired, sales of red wine increased by about 45 percent.[6] Suddenly, instead of thinking that "an apple a day keeps the doctor away," people were hoping that "a drink a day keeps the cardiologist at bay." Were these people on the right track?

Red wine contains resveratrol, a flavonoid and type of phytochemical, which acts as an antioxidant. (Dark beer also contains flavonoids.) Antioxidants help prevent the "bad" LDL cholesterol from becoming oxidized, which leads to its accumulation in the artery wall and atherosclerosis. Flavonoids help inhibit the stickiness of platelets in the blood. Alcohol also helps inhibit the stickiness of platelets in the blood, just like flavonoids, but also increases the level of heart-protective "good" HDL cholesterol. Because of these potential heart-healthy attributes, alcohol and red wine have been in the media limelight since the 1990s.

There isn't enough evidence to support the theory that wine, whether red, white, or rosé, has any health superiority over beer and distilled spirits. In fact, some studies comparing various alcohol sources have found that the majority of heart-protective effects are attributable to the alcohol content regardless of the source.[7] In other words, a beer, a glass of cabernet, or a shot of scotch all appear to have similar heart-protective effects. When it comes to the health benefits of alcohol, the source is unlikely to make much of a difference.

Before you crack open a beer to celebrate though, be aware that the people who gain the health benefits from moderate alcohol consumption are women age 55 and older and men age 45 and older. Alcohol consumption by younger people has not been shown to provide many—if any—health benefits. In fact, drinking alcohol during your younger years increases the risk of injuries and violent, traumatic deaths, which offsets any possible health benefits from the alcohol.[8]

All individuals who choose to drink alcohol need to stick to moderate drinking, and even then they need to carefully monitor their intake. Moderate drinkers need to watch out for (1) the size of their drinks and (2) the frequency of their drinking. As mentioned earlier, a standard drink contains about 0.5 ounce of alcohol. If your 8-ounce wine glass gets filled to the brim, or you chug an oversized mug of beer, you could consume close to two standard drinks in one glass or mug (**Figure 9.2**). A 750-milliliter bottle of wine contains five, 5-ounce glasses of wine. If you split a bottle with a friend, you are consuming the equivalent of 2½ glasses of wine. One rum and cola can provide the equivalent of more than 2½ alcoholic drinks. Another important point to remember is that abstaining from drinking through the week and then having seven drinks on a single Friday night does not count as moderate drinking. When it comes to alcohol, no "banking" is allowed.

The Take-Home Message People drink alcohol to relax, celebrate, and socialize. Moderate alcohol consumption, which means 1 to 2 drinks per day for men and 1 drink per day for women, may provide health benefits in some older adults. While the flavonoids in red wine and dark beer are thought to be beneficial compounds, the alcohol itself may also provide protective benefits, such as increasing "good" HDL cholesterol levels. Individuals who choose to drink alcohol need to do so in moderation and monitor both the size of their drinks and the frequency of their drinking.

What Happens to Alcohol in the Body?

Your body treats alcohol differently from any other substance. Unlike the other energy-containing nutrients, such as carbohydrates and fats, your body cannot store alcohol. Because alcohol is a toxin, the body quickly works to metabolize and eliminate it.

Many factors, including your gender, your body type, the amount of food in your stomach, and the amount of alcohol you drink, will affect how quickly you absorb and metabolize it.[9] Alcohol travels through the body in the blood, and is distributed throughout the watery tissues, including the brain. Let's follow a swallow of beer through your digestive system and see how it's handled along the way (**Figure 9.3**).

Blood vessels

Alcohol

Alcohol dehydrogenase

Liver

4 Most alcohol is metabolized in the liver.

5 Alcohol that is not metabolized will return to the blood and circulate throughout the body, including the brain.

1 Some alcohol is metabolized in the stomach by the enzyme alcohol dehydrogenase.

2 Some alcohol is absorbed through the stomach. Food in the stomach slows the absorption of alcohol.

3 Most alcohol is absorbed in the small intestine.

Stomach

Small intestine

Figure 9.3 The Metabolism of Alcohol

You Absorb Alcohol in Your Stomach and Small Intestine

Within seconds of the first sip of the beer, about 20 percent of the alcohol will be directly absorbed through the stomach and into your blood. Some alcohol is also metabolized in the stomach by an enzyme called **alcohol dehydrogenase** before it is absorbed. The majority of alcohol, about 80 percent, is absorbed in the small intestine.

Light beer has about the same amount of alcohol as regular beer.

The amount and type of food in the stomach determine how long alcohol lingers there before entering the small intestine. If your swallow of beer chases a bacon cheeseburger and fries, the alcohol will take longer to leave the stomach than if the beer was consumed without food after a period of fasting. One study showed that an alcoholic drink consumed after a meal was absorbed about three times more slowly than if it was consumed on an empty stomach.[10] This is why you should always try to avoid drinking alcohol on an empty stomach. Fat also slows down the departure of food from the stomach, so a large amount of fat in the food, as in this burger meal, will help delay the arrival of the alcohol into the small intestine.

Keep in mind, however, that though a stomach full of high-fat food will delay the arrival of alcohol in the small intestine, the alcohol will still eventually arrive there. If a person drinks several glasses of beer with dinner, the alcohol will be absorbed once the stomach starts emptying. Intoxication could be an unexpected postdinner surprise.

You Metabolize Alcohol Primarily in Your Liver

Once in your blood, alcohol travels to the liver, where the majority of it is metabolized. Enzymes in the liver, most importantly alcohol dehydrogenase, convert the alcohol to **acetaldehyde,** which is eventually metabolized to carbon dioxide and water.[11] A healthy liver can metabolize about one alcoholic drink in about 1½ to 2 hours. Regardless of the amount consumed, the metabolism of alcohol occurs at a steady rate in your body.

There is a second major enzyme system in the liver that metabolizes alcohol: the **microsomal ethanol-oxidizing system (MEOS).** Individuals who consume a lot of alcohol will have a somewhat more active MEOS because this system is revved up when chronically high levels of alcohol are present in the liver.

Alcohol Circulates in Your Blood

If your liver cannot handle the amount of alcohol all at once, the extra alcohol reenters the blood and is distributed in the watery tissues in your body. Your **blood alcohol concentration (BAC)** is the amount of alcohol in your blood, measured in grams of alcohol per deciliter of blood, usually expressed as a percentage.[12] Table 9.1 gives you a ballpark idea of how your BAC is affected by the number of alcoholic beverages you consume. As you can see, the more you drink, the higher your BAC. Because alcohol infiltrates your brain, as your BAC increases so does your level of mental impairment and intoxication.

Though the liver will eventually metabolize most of the alcohol that is consumed, a small amount will leave your body intact through your breath and urine. Because the amount of alcohol in your breath correlates with the amount of alcohol in your blood, a Breathalyzer test can be used to measure your BAC. Police officers often use this device when they suspect that a person has consumed too much alcohol.

alcohol dehydrogenase One of the alcohol-metabolizing enzymes found in the stomach and the liver.

acetaldehyde An intermediary by-product of the breakdown of ethanol in the liver.

microsomal ethanol-oxidizing system (MEOS) The other major enzyme system in the liver that metabolizes alcohol.

blood alcohol concentration (BAC) The measurement of the amount of alcohol in your blood. BAC is measured in grams of alcohol per deciliter of blood, usually expressed as a percentage.

Table 9.1
Blood Alcohol Concentration Tables

For Women

Body Weight in Pounds

Drinks per Hour	100	120	140	160	180	200
1	0.05	0.04	0.03	0.03	0.03	0.02
2	0.09	0.08	0.07	0.06	0.05	0.05
3	0.14	0.11	0.10	0.09	0.08	0.07
4	0.18	0.15	0.13	0.11	0.10	0.09
5	0.23	0.19	0.16	0.14	0.13	0.11
6	0.27	0.23	0.19	0.17	0.15	0.14
7	0.32	0.27	0.23	0.20	0.18	0.16
8	0.36	0.30	0.26	0.23	0.20	0.18
9	0.41	0.34	0.29	0.26	0.30	0.20
10	0.45	0.38	0.32	0.28	0.25	0.23

For Men

Body Weight in Pounds

Drinks per Hour	100	120	140	160	180	200
1	0.04	0.03	0.03	0.02	0.02	0.02
2	0.08	0.06	0.05	0.05	0.04	0.04
3	0.11	0.09	0.08	0.07	0.06	0.06
4	0.15	0.12	0.11	0.09	0.08	0.08
5	0.19	0.16	0.13	0.12	0.11	0.09
6	0.23	0.19	0.16	0.14	0.13	0.11
7	0.26	0.22	0.19	0.16	0.15	0.13
8	0.30	0.25	0.21	0.19	0.17	0.15
9	0.34	0.28	0.24	0.21	0.19	0.17
10	0.38	0.31	0.27	0.23	0.21	0.19

Tables are adapted from those of the Pennsylvania Liquor Control Board, Harrisburg.
Notes: Gray shaded area indicates legal intoxication.
Blood alcohol concentrations are expressed as percent, meaning grams of alcohol per 10 milliliters (per deciliter) of blood.

The Effects of Alcohol on Your Brain

Alcohol is a *depressant,* a substance that slows the transmission of nerve impulses. Your brain is very sensitive to the depressant effect of alcohol. For instance, alcohol slows down your reaction time to stimuli (such as a car coming toward you on the road), confuses your thoughts, impairs your judgment, and induces sleepiness. The more you drink, the more areas of the brain are affected. Table 9.2 and **Figure 9.4** show how increasing BAC levels affect specific areas of the brain, and how body movements and behaviors are affected. (*Note:* A person's BAC can continue to rise even after unconsciousness.) If enough alcohol has been consumed, the activities of the brainstem, which controls breathing and heart rate, can be suppressed, and ultimately cause death. Excessive amounts of alcohol can cause "brain shrinkage," which can impair memory and

A Breathalyzer is used to measure a person's blood alcohol concentration (BAC).

Table 9.2

Progressive Effects of Alcohol

Blood Alcohol Concentration	Changes in Feelings and Personality	Brain Regions Affected	Impaired Functions (continuum)
0.01–0.05	Relaxation, sense of well-being, loss of inhibition	Cerebral cortex	Alertness; judgment
0.06–0.10	Pleasure, numbing of feelings, nausea, sleepiness, emotional arousal	Cerebral cortex and forebrain	Coordination (especially fine motor skills); visual tracking
0.11–0.20	Mood swings, anger, sadness, mania	Cerebral cortex, forebrain, and cerebellum	Reasoning and depth perception; appropriate social behavior
0.21–0.30	Aggression, reduced sensations, depression, stupor	Cerebral cortex, forebrain, cerebellum, and brainstem	Speech; balance; temperature regulation
0.31–0.40	Unconsciousness, coma, death possible	Entire brain	Bladder control; breathing
0.41 and greater	Death		Heart rate

Source: National Institute on Alcohol Abuse and Alcoholism. 2003. Understanding Alcohol: Investigations into Biology and Behavior. Available at http://science.education.nih.gov/supplements/nih3/alcohol/default.htm.

Cerebral cortex

Forebrain

Cerebellum

Brainstem

Figure 9.4 The Brain and Alcohol
As you consume more alcohol, additional areas of your brain are affected. Your cerebral cortex is affected first, followed by your forebrain, cerebellum, and brainstem. The greater the alcohol intake, the greater the physical and behavioral changes in your body.

learning as well as coordination and balance. Heavy drinking also reduces blood flow to the brain, which can similarly impair balance and coordination such as for walking.[13]

Because alcohol is a depressant, it can be very unhealthy, and even dangerous, to mix it with a stimulant, such as the high amounts of caffeine found in energy drinks. In a study of more than 4,000 college students, research found that those who consumed alcohol mixed with caffeinated energy drinks were twice as likely to be injured, require medical attention, ride with an intoxicated driver, and either take sexual advantage of someone or be the victim of sexual aggressiveness.[14] Because energy drinks can reduce the symptoms of alcohol intoxication, such as tiredness, individuals may continue drinking to the point where the BAC increases to dangerous levels, affecting both the body's mental and physical functions.[15]

Women Are More Susceptible to the Effects of Alcohol Than Men

In essence, every alcoholic beverage that a male consumes is equivalent to about ⓣⓕ 1⅓ alcoholic beverages for a woman. Two factors contribute to women's greater susceptibility to alcohol:

➤ Women have about 20 to 30 percent less alcohol dehydrogenase in their stomachs than men, so more alcohol will enter the blood immediately through women's stomachs.[16]
➤ Women have less muscle mass, and thus less body water, than men. (Recall from Chapter 8 that muscle tissue has a higher percentage of water than fat.) Because alcohol mixes in water, people with more muscle are able to distribute more of the alcohol throughout their body than people who have more fat.

Because of these factors, women will feel alcohol's effects sooner than men. Women take note: It's dangerous to try to keep up, drink for drink, with male companions. You will begin to feel the effects of alcohol long before a man will.

Finally, Asian women also need to be aware of a potential lower tolerance to alcohol. About 50 percent of Asians experience "alcohol flush," a reddish skin reaction that occurs because of an enzyme deficiency. Symptoms include facial flushing, nausea, and rapid heartbeat, and one study has shown that people who experience this condition, particularly East Asians, are at higher risk of esophageal cancer.[17]

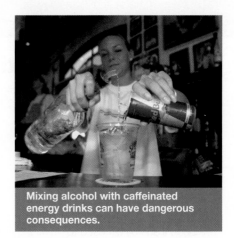

Mixing alcohol with caffeinated energy drinks can have dangerous consequences.

The Take-Home Message Alcohol is absorbed in the stomach and small intestine and is metabolized primarily in the liver. Your sex, body type, the amount of food in your stomach, and the quantity of alcohol consumed will affect the rate of absorption and metabolism in your body. The blood alcohol concentration (BAC) is the measurement of alcohol in your blood. Alcohol is a central nervous system depressant. Because your brain is sensitive to alcohol, alcohol affects your behavior. Because of having less alcohol dehydrogenase in the stomach and less body water, women will feel the effects of the same amount of alcohol before men will.

How Can Alcohol Be Harmful?

Although alcohol is often advertised in magazines, billboards, and television commercials as a trendy and sexy way to relax and socialize (see the boxed feature "Alcohol and Advertising"), it can cause a number of problems for those who abuse it. Some of these problems merely cause temporary discomfort, but other long-term effects can be extremely damaging to health.

Alcohol Can Disrupt Sleep and Cause Hangovers

Many people wrongly think that a drink before bed will help them sleep better, but it will actually have the opposite effect. Whereas having a drink within an hour before bed may help you to fall asleep sooner, it will disrupt your sleep cycle, cause you to awaken in the middle of the night, and make returning to sleep a challenge.[18] You will feel tired the next morning, which will make it harder for you to pay attention to what you are learning in class, and you may doze off by the end of the lecture. Even a moderate amount of alcohol consumed at dinner—or even late in the afternoon during happy hour—can disrupt that night's sleep.

If you have a bad night's sleep, it's a bad idea to drink alcohol the next day. Studies have shown that a night of sleep disruption followed by even small amounts of alcohol the next day reduces the reaction time and alertness in individuals performing a simulated driving test. Being tired and then drinking alcohol exacerbates alcohol's sedating effect.[19]

A **hangover** is your body's way of saying, "don't do that to me again." After a bout of heavy drinking, individuals can experience hangover symptoms ranging from a pounding headache, fatigue, nausea, and increased thirst to a rapid heartbeat,

eLearn

How Much Alcohol Is Too Much?

If you drink alcohol, take the short, ten-question survey based on the World Health Organization's Alcohol Use Disorders Identification Test (AUDIT), which will help you analyze your current drinking habits and provide information on what to do if you drink too much. To access the survey, log on to www.alcoholscreening.org/Home.aspx.

hangover A collective term for the unpleasant symptoms, such as a headache and dizziness, that occur after drinking an excessive amount of alcohol.

Alcohol and Advertising

Advertising for alcoholic beverages is pervasive and persuasive. You need only drive down a major highway or turn on your television to see billboards and commercials for a beer or liquor brand. In some media, including popular magazines like *Rolling Stone* and *Sports Illustrated*, alcohol ads can outnumber non–alcohol ads by almost 3 to 1.[1]

Companies that make alcoholic beverages pay large sums of money to create and show these ads for one reason: They work. Studies have shown that advertisements for alcoholic beverages are associated with an increase in drinking among adolescents. Many ads tend to emphasize sexual and social stereotypes. When targeted to underage drinkers, this type of message has been shown to increase adolescents' desire to emulate those portrayed in the advertisements.[2]

Alcohol ads should be viewed with caution, as the messages in them are often misleading and in some cases blatantly false. Let's take a look at the messages and realities in a typical alcohol advertisement that might appear in a magazine.

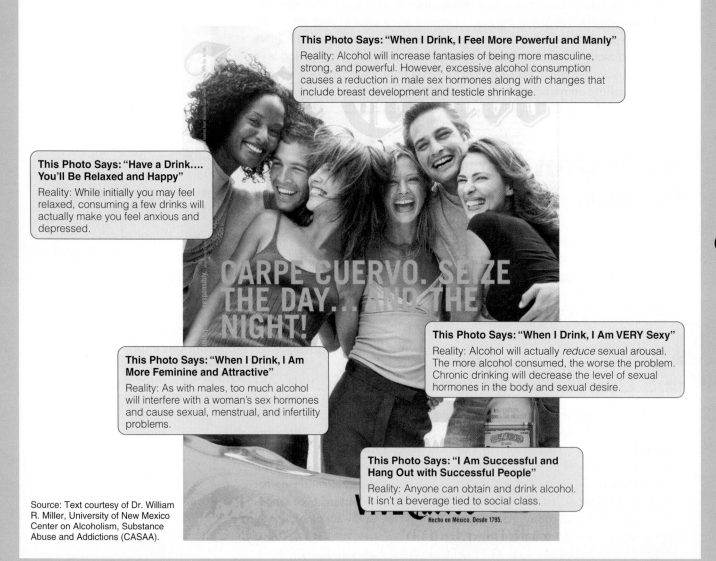

This Photo Says: "When I Drink, I Feel More Powerful and Manly"
Reality: Alcohol will increase fantasies of being more masculine, strong, and powerful. However, excessive alcohol consumption causes a reduction in male sex hormones along with changes that include breast development and testicle shrinkage.

This Photo Says: "Have a Drink…. You'll Be Relaxed and Happy"
Reality: While initially you may feel relaxed, consuming a few drinks will actually make you feel anxious and depressed.

This Photo Says: "When I Drink, I Am More Feminine and Attractive"
Reality: As with males, too much alcohol will interfere with a woman's sex hormones and cause sexual, menstrual, and infertility problems.

This Photo Says: "When I Drink, I Am VERY Sexy"
Reality: Alcohol will actually *reduce* sexual arousal. The more alcohol consumed, the worse the problem. Chronic drinking will decrease the level of sexual hormones in the body and sexual desire.

This Photo Says: "I Am Successful and Hang Out with Successful People"
Reality: Anyone can obtain and drink alcohol. It isn't a beverage tied to social class.

CARPE CUERVO. SEIZE THE DAY… AND THE NIGHT!

Hecho en México. Desde 1795.

Source: Text courtesy of Dr. William R. Miller, University of New Mexico Center on Alcoholism, Substance Abuse and Addictions (CASAA).

tremors, sweating, dizziness, depression, anxiety, and irritability. A hangover begins within hours of your last drink, as your BAC begins to drop. The symptoms will appear in full force once all the alcohol is gone from your blood, and these symptoms can linger for up to an additional 24 hours.[20] In other words, a few hours of excessive alcohol consumption on a Saturday night can not only ruin your entire Sunday but even disrupt part of your Monday morning.

There are several ways that alcohol contributes to the symptoms of a hangover. Alcohol is a diuretic, so it can cause dehydration, and thus, electrolyte imbalances. It inhibits the release of antidiuretic hormone from your pituitary gland, which in turn causes your kidneys to excrete water, as well as electrolytes, in your urine. Vomiting and sweating during or after excessive drinking will further contribute to dehydration and electrolyte loss. Dehydration also increases your thirst and can make you feel lightheaded, dizzy, and weak. Increased acid production in the stomach and secretions from the pancreas and intestines can cause stomach pain, nausea, and vomiting.

Coffee will not sober you up. An intoxicated person who drinks coffee will end up being a stimulated drunk. It takes time to sober up because your liver has to metabolize all the alcohol that you consumed.

Lastly, alcoholic beverages often contain compounds called **congeners,** which enhance their taste and appearance but may contribute to hangover symptoms. Congeners can be produced during the fermentation process or be added during production of the alcoholic beverages. The large number of congeners in red wine can cause headaches in some people.[21]

Forget the old wives' tale of consuming an alcoholic beverage to "cure" a hangover. Drinking more alcohol, even if it is mixed with tomato or orange juice, during a hangover only prolongs the recovery time. In fact, time is the only true remedy for hangover symptoms. Whereas aspirin and other nonsteroidal anti-inflammatory medications, such as ibuprofen, can ease a headache, these medications can also contribute to stomachache and nausea. Taking acetaminophen (Tylenol) during and after alcohol consumption, when the alcohol is being metabolized, has been shown to intensify this pain reliever's toxicity to the liver and may cause liver damage in some cases.[22] The best strategy for dealing with a hangover is to avoid it by limiting the amount of alcohol consumed.

Alcohol Can Interact with Hormones

Many individuals who overindulge in alcohol tend not to eat enough while they are drinking, which causes their body's glucose stores to become depleted and their blood glucose levels to fall. Typically, the hormones insulin and glucagon would automatically be released to make glucose, but alcohol interferes with this process. Because the brain needs glucose to function properly, a low blood glucose level can contribute to the feelings of fatigue, weakness, mood changes, irritability, and anxiety often experienced during a hangover.

In addition to the hormones that regulate your blood glucose level, alcohol can interfere with other hormones. Alcohol negatively affects parathyroid hormone and other bone-strengthening hormones, which can increase the risk of osteoporosis.[23] Alcohol can also increase estrogen levels in women, which may increase the risk of breast cancer. Drinking alcohol can affect reproductive hormones and is associated with both male and female sexual dysfunction, and alcohol abuse has been associated with infertility.[24]

Alcohol May Lead to Overnutrition and Malnutrition

At 7 calories per gram, alcohol provides fewer calories than fat (9 calories per gram) but more than either carbohydrates or protein (4 calories per gram each). However, unless you are drinking a straight shot of liquor, your alcoholic beverages will contain additional calories (see Table 9.3). For example, a rum and cola contains the calories

congeners Compounds in alcohol that enhance the taste but may contribute to hangover symptoms.

Table 9.3 Calories in Selected Alcoholic Drinks

Beer

Serving size: 12 oz
Alcohol serving: 1
Calories per drink: 150

Light Beer

Serving size: 12 oz
Alcohol serving: 1
Calories per drink: 110

Distilled Spirits (whiskey, vodka, gin, rum)

Serving size: 1.5 oz
Alcohol serving: 1
Calories per drink: 100

Wine (white or red)

Serving size: 5 oz
Alcohol serving: 1
Calories per drink: 100–105

Cosmopolitan

Serving size: 2.5 oz
Alcohol servings: 1.7
Calories per drink: 131

Mudslide

Serving size: 12 oz
Alcohol servings: 4
Calories per drink: 820

Bloody Mary

Serving size: 5.5 oz
Alcohol serving: 1
Calories per drink: 97

Margarita

Serving size: 6.3 oz
Alcohol servings: 3
Calories per drink: 327

Rum and Cola

Serving size: 12 oz
Alcohol servings: 2.7
Calories per drink: 361

Note: Alcohol servings are per beverage.

from both the rum and the cola, making the drink more than three times as high in calories as the rum itself. Depending on the mixers and ingredients added to your beverage, the calorie count in your drink can escalate to that of a meal. A mudslide, for example, made with vodka, Irish cream, coffee liqueur, ice cream, and cream, should be ordered from the dessert menu and served with a spoon.

If you consistently add extra calories from alcoholic beverages—or any food or beverage source—to a diet that is already meeting your daily calorie needs, you will gain weight. Excessive consumption of alcohol has also been shown to increase fat and weight around the stomach. Though this is usually referred to as a "beer" belly, extra calories from any type of alcoholic beverage can contribute to a paunch. If high-

Dinner 1

5 12-oz beers
1719 total calories

8 BBQ chicken wings

1 handful goldfish crackers

1 large serving nachos with cheese

Total fat (g)	**51**	
Saturated fat (g)	**16**	
Cholesterol (mg)	**154**	

Dinner 2

724 total calories

2 oz whole wheat dinner roll
4 tsp soft margarine

1 cup fat-free milk

4 oz grilled chicken breast
3/4 cup mashed potatoes
1 1/2 cup steamed carrots

28	Total fat (g)	
8	Saturated fat (g)	
89	Cholesterol (mg)	

Figure 9.5 Too Much Alcohol Costs You Good Nutrition
A dinner of several alcoholic beverages and bar foods not only adds calories, fat, and saturated fat to your diet, but also displaces healthier foods that would provide better nutrition.

calorie "bar foods" are consumed with the drinks, the calories can add up rapidly (**Figure 9.5**).

Compensating for calories in alcoholic beverages by cutting out more nutritious foods will cause you to fall short of your nutrient needs. If you drink a daily glass of beer instead of an equal amount of low-fat milk, your waist may not suffer, but your bones could. You will rob yourself of an excellent source of calcium and vitamin D that the milk, but not the beer, provides. A chronic substitution of excessive amounts (T|F) of alcohol for nutritious foods in the diet can lead to malnutrition.

Individuals who drink excessively often eat diets inadequate in nutrients, especially vitamins and minerals. Often, they drink too much and don't eat enough. Those who consume more than 30 percent of their daily calories from alcohol tend to consume less protein, fiber, vitamins A, C, D, riboflavin, and thiamin, and the minerals calcium and iron.[25] This isn't surprising once you consider that if a person consuming 2,000 calories daily devotes 600 (30 percent) of these calories to alcohol, there would only be 1,400 calories left to meet all of his or her nutrient needs. When you're routinely limited to a diet of 1,400 calories daily, you're bound to have nutrient deficiencies.

Excessive alcohol consumption can also affect how the body handles the essential nutrients it actually gets. Routinely drinking too much alcohol can interfere with the absorption and/or use of protein, zinc, magnesium, the B vitamins thiamin, folate, and B_{12}, and the fat-soluble vitamins A, D, E, and K. As you have read in previous chapters, a chronic deficiency of nutrients can cause a cascade of ill health conditions and diseases. In particular, a thiamin deficiency can affect brain function, including memory loss, and increase the risk of Wernicke-Korsakoff syndrome, which includes mental confusion and uncontrolled muscle movement (see Chapter 7).

Figure 9.6 The Stages of Alcohol Liver Disease

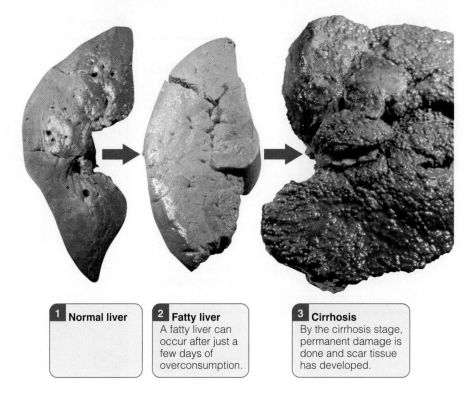

1 Normal liver

2 Fatty liver
A fatty liver can occur after just a few days of overconsumption.

3 Cirrhosis
By the cirrhosis stage, permanent damage is done and scar tissue has developed.

Alcohol Can Harm Your Digestive Organs, Heart, and Liver

Chronically drinking too much alcohol can lead to an inflamed esophagus. Alcohol inhibits the ability of the esophagus to contract. This enables the acid juices in the stomach to flow back up into the esophagus, causing inflammation. Chronic inflammation can be a stepping stone to esophageal cancer. If you smoke when you drink, your chances of developing esophageal cancer, as well as mouth and throat cancer, are even higher.[26] Individuals who are heavy drinkers also have increased incidences of **gastritis** (*gastr* = stomach, *itis* = inflammation) and stomach ulcers.[27]

Excessive amounts of alcohol can also affect the beating and rhythm of the heart, which likely plays a role in the sudden deaths of some alcoholics.[28] It can damage heart tissue and increase the risk of hypertension. Hypertension is a risk factor for both heart disease and stroke.

Alcohol can also damage your liver and cause **alcoholic liver disease.** The disease develops in three stages, although some stages can occur simultaneously (**Figure 9.6**). The first stage of the disease is **fatty liver,** which can result from just a weekend or a few days of excessive drinking. Because alcohol metabolism takes top priority in the liver, the metabolism of other nutrients, including fats, will take a back seat to alcohol. Thus, the liver isn't able to metabolize all the fat that arrives in the liver, causing a buildup in this organ. Simultaneously, the liver uses some of the by-products of alcohol metabolism to make even more fat. The net effect is a liver that has cells that are full of fat.[29] A fatty liver can reverse itself *if* the alcohol consumption is stopped.

If the drinking doesn't stop, the second stage of liver disease, **alcoholic hepatitis,** can develop. In alcoholic hepatitis, the liver basically becomes irritated by various by-products of alcohol metabolism. Some by-products, namely acetaldehyde, are toxic to the liver. Free radicals, another by-product of alcohol metabolism, react with the proteins, lipids, and DNA in your cells, causing damage. Nausea, vomiting, fever, jaundice, and loss of appetite are signs of alcoholic hepatitis. Chronic, excessive amounts

gastritis Inflammation of the stomach.

alcohol liver disease A degenerative liver condition that occurs in three stages: (1) fatty liver, (2) alcoholic hepatitis, and (3) cirrhosis.

fatty liver Stage 1 of alcohol liver disease.

alcohol hepatitis Stage 2 of alcohol liver disease; due to chronic inflammation.

of alcohol may also impair your immune system, which can contribute to liver damage and increase the susceptibility to pneumonia and other infectious diseases.

Heavy drinking can also cause the increased passage of destructive **endotoxin,** which is released from bacteria in your intestines into your blood. Once endotoxin arrives in your liver, it can cause the release of substances called *cytokines* that further damage healthy liver cells and perpetuate scarring.[30]

As bouts of heavy drinking continue, chronic inflammation further injures the liver cells and can cause scarring. **Cirrhosis** is the third and final stage of alcoholic liver disease. In cirrhosis, the cells of the liver die and form scar tissue, which prevents this organ from performing critical metabolic roles, such as filtering toxins and waste products in the blood and out of the body. If these toxins and waste products build up, it can lead to mental confusion, nausea, tremors or shakiness, and even coma.

As many as 70 percent of individuals with alcoholic hepatitis end up developing cirrhosis.[31] More than 12,000 die from alcoholic liver disease each year.[32] **Figure 9.7** summarizes the many harmful effects of excessive drinking.

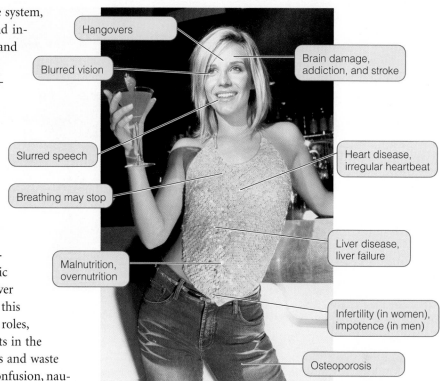

Figure 9.7 **Effects of Alcohol on the Body**

Labels in figure:
Hangovers
Blurred vision
Slurred speech
Breathing may stop
Malnutrition, overnutrition
Brain damage, addiction, and stroke
Heart disease, irregular heartbeat
Liver disease, liver failure
Infertility (in women), impotence (in men)
Osteoporosis

Alcohol Can Put a Healthy Pregnancy at Risk

More than 30 years ago, Drs. David Smith and Kenneth Jones noticed an interesting trait among children in their clinic at the University of Washington School of Medicine. Some children looked alike even though they weren't related. Many had facial abnormalities such as eyes with very small openings and thin upper lips (**Figure 9.8**). These children also weren't physically growing as normally as other children their age, and they seemed to have some mental and behavioral difficulties, such as reduced attention span and memory, and learning disabilities. The scientists discovered that these children were all born to women who drank alcohol during their pregnancy. The doctors coined the term "fetal alcohol syndrome" (FAS) to describe these physical, mental, and behavioral abnormalities.[33]

When a pregnant woman drinks, she is never drinking alone—her fetus becomes her drinking partner. Because the baby is developing, the alcohol isn't broken down as quickly as in the mother's body. The baby's BAC can become higher and stay higher longer than the mother's, causing serious damage to its central nervous system, particularly the brain. FAS is the leading cause of mental retardation and birth defects in the United States. Children with FAS often have problems in school and interacting socially with others, poor coordination, low IQ, and problems with everyday living.[34] Approximately 4 million infants each year in the United States have experienced prenatal exposure to alcohol, and an estimated 6,000 babies are born with FAS.

Recently a newer term, **fetal alcohol spectrum disorders (FASDs),** which includes FAS, has been adopted by major health organizations to describe a wide range of

endotoxin A damaging product produced by intestinal bacteria that travels in the blood to the liver and initiates the release of cytokines that damage liver cells, leading to scarring.

cirrhosis Stage 3 of alcohol liver disease in which liver cells die, causing severe scarring.

fetal alcohol spectrum disorders (FASDs) A range of conditions that can occur in children who are exposed to alcohol in utero. Fetal alcohol syndrome (FAS) is the most severe of the FASDs; children with FAS will display physical, mental, and behavioral abnormalities.

Skin folds over the eyes

Low nasal bridge

Short turned up nose

Indistinct philtrum (groove between nose and upper lip)

Small head circumference

Small eye opening

Small midface

Flattened face

Thin upper lip

Figure 9.8 Fetal Alcohol Syndrome
Children born with fetal alcohol syndrome often have facial abnormalities.

eLearn

What Are Those Drinks Costing You?

Did you ever consider how much you're spending on alcohol in a given year? Use the alcohol calculator at www.collegedrinkingprevention.gov/CollegeStudents/calculator to see how quickly a few drinks will add up.

alcohol abuse The continuation of alcohol consumption even though this behavior has created social, legal, and/or health problems.

alcoholism Chronic disease with genetic, psychological, and environmental components; also referred to as *alcohol dependence*. Alcoholics crave alcohol, can't control their intake, and develop a higher tolerance for it. Alcoholics also exhibit a dependency on alcohol, as abstaining from drinking will cause withdrawal symptoms.

conditions that can occur in children exposed to alcohol prenatally. For example, not all children exposed to alcohol during pregnancy may experience *all* of the physical, mental, and behavioral abnormalities seen in FAS, which is the severe end of the FASDs. However, no matter the degree of abnormalities, FASDs are permanent. The only proven, safe amount of alcohol a pregnant woman can consume is *none*. Women should avoid alcohol if they think they are, or could become, pregnant.

The Take-Home Message Excessive drinking can disrupt your sleep, cause hangovers, and add extra calories to your diet, which can lead to weight gain. Drinking too much alcohol can also cause hormone imbalances; lead to malnutrition; harm your digestive organs, heart, and liver; and cause irreversible damage to a developing fetus during pregnancy. Individuals with alcoholic liver disease can experience a fatty liver and deterioration of the liver that develops into alcohol-related hepatitis and cirrhosis.

What Are Alcohol Abuse and Alcoholism?

When people choose not to drink alcohol responsibly, they often end up abusing alcohol, or suffering from a full-blown addiction. **Alcohol abuse** begins when a person allows alcohol to interfere with his or her life. He may have to call in sick to work or school due to a hangover, or he may have blank spots in his memory due to intoxication. At the extreme end of the spectrum is the disease of **alcoholism**. By the time a person is addicted to alcohol, she is no longer in control of her drinking habits and is at serious risk of suffering long-term health damage. Approximately 17 percent of regular drinkers either abuse or are addicted to alcohol.[35]

Let's take a closer look at both of these categories of alcohol dysfunction.

Binge Drinking, Drinking and Driving, and Underage Drinking Are Forms of Alcohol Abuse

When people continue to consume alcohol even though the behavior has created social, legal, and/or health problems for them, they are abusing alcohol. Binge drinking and drunk driving are situations in which alcohol is being abused. Because 21 is the legal drinking age in the United States, anyone under this age who consumes alcohol is abusing it.

Binge Drinking

Binge drinking occurs when a male consumes 5 or more drinks or when a woman consumes 4 or more drinks in a very short time. Approximately 1 in 3 American adults who drink alcohol have fallen into this category during the past month. College students who binge-drink are more likely to miss classes, have hangovers, and experience unintentional injuries, such as falling, motor vehicle accidents, and drowning, and may even die (**Figure 9.9**).

Research also indicates that binge drinkers engage in more unplanned sexual activity and fail to use safe sex strategies more frequently than nonbinge drinkers.[37] Sexual aggression and assaults on campus increase when drinking enters the picture. Alcohol is involved in more than 70 percent of the reported rapes on college campuses. Victims are often too drunk to consent to or refuse the actions of the other person.

Binge drinking is associated with many other health problems, such as hypertension, heart attack, sexually transmitted disease, suicide, homicide, and child abuse.[38] Binge drinking can also cause **blackouts,** which are periods of time that a person cannot remember, even though he or she may have been conscious. A research study of more than 700 college students found that more than half of them had blacked out at least once in their lives, and many found out after the fact that they had taken part in activities such as vandalism, unprotected sex, and driving a motor vehicle during the blackout period.[39]

Research shows that college students often have exaggerated perceptions of the amount of alcohol their peers consume. Many college-aged binge drinkers think that everyone is drinking all the time, but this isn't always the case. Binge drinking was found to occur at rates ranging from almost never to nearly 70 percent of the students on a college campus.[40] Those who think binge drinking is just a normal part of the college experience often have a circle of like-minded buddies who reinforce their misperceptions.

Drinking in groups is associated with an increased intake of alcohol. Joining a fraternity or sorority tends to increase alcohol consumption among college students and frequenting frat parties raises the bar as to what is the normal amount and frequency of alcohol consumption during college life. The boxed feature "Smashed: Story of a Drunken Girlhood" describes the true story of Koren Zailckas and her struggles with alcohol abuse. The Self-Assessment will help you recognize some red flags of alcohol abuse.

Binge drinking can lead to **alcohol poisoning,** which can have devastating results. Bradley was a junior at Michigan State University. At midnight on the eve of Brad's twenty-first birthday, he and a group of friends went to a bar to celebrate his birthday. A birthday tradition around campus was to "drink your age" in shots of liquor. Brad not only drank 21 shots but gulped down another three for a grand total

Figure 9.9 Consequences of College Binge Drinking
Alcohol use by college students results in numerous assaults, injuries, and deaths each year.

Source: National Institute on Alcohol Abuse and Alcoholism, based on information from Hingson, R., et al. 2005. Magnitude of Alcohol-Related Mortality and Morbidity Among U.S. College Students Ages 18–24: Changes from 1998 to 2001. *Annual Review of Public Health* 26: 259–279.

binge drinking The consumption of 5 or more alcoholic drinks by men, or 4 or more drinks by women, in a very short time.

blackouts Periods of time when an intoxicated person cannot recall part or all of an event.

alcohol poisoning When the BAC rises to such an extreme level that a person's central nervous system is affected and his or her breathing and heart rate are interrupted.

Smashed: Story of a Drunken Girlhood

Koren Zailckas was a shy, insecure girl raised in an upscale town in the Boston suburbs. She started drinking at the age of 14, and almost from her first sip, there was no turning back. During a socially awkward adolescence, Koren found it difficult to be at ease around other people, particularly girls her own age. When she drank, she became assertive and friendly. She bonded with other girls and met tons of guys. Throughout her high school and college years, alcohol was her crutch and best pal.

Koren didn't think of herself as an alcoholic, but she was a binge drinker. She drank herself into her first blackout with a thermos full of vodka at the age of 16. She woke up in her bedroom

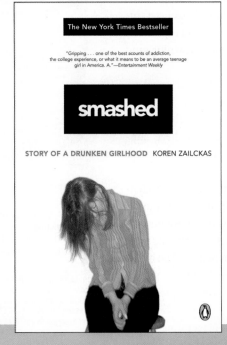

The New York Times Bestseller

"Gripping . . . one of the best acounts of addiction, the college experience, or what it means to be an average teenage girl in America. A."—*Entertainment Weekly*

smashed

STORY OF A DRUNKEN GIRLHOOD   KOREN ZAILCKAS

wearing a hospital Johnny and a pink plastic bracelet on her wrist. The bracelet was compliments of her local hospital emergency room. The Johnny had replaced her vomit-covered clothes from the night before. Her stomach had been pumped. Her parents had carried her from the back seat of the family car to her bedroom in the middle of the night. They were devastated.

As a freshman entering college, Koren used beer and liquor to make friends and be accepted. She pledged a sorority for the sisterhood and booze. She frequently drank herself into a state of numbness and allowed sorority sisters and male friends to make many of her decisions. She was often the last girl to leave the party be-

cause she was too drunk to know that she should have left an hour before.

After college graduation, Koren continued her drunken lifestyle in New York City. She worked hard during the day and drank hard at night. One morning she woke up in a strange bed, in a strange condo, next to a stranger from the cab ride the night before. For Koren, this was rock bottom. She realized that her chronic drinking was a magnet for like-minded people who similarly abused alcohol and were as damaged in life as she. But she wanted a good life. She wanted sound friendships and self-confidence, and she recognized that she wasn't going to achieve these goals with alcohol. At that moment, she decided to get help.

Through guidance from an addiction counselor and her own drive to quit drinking, Koren stopped her destructive behavior and began surrounding herself with a healthier circle of friends. Today, she is sober, and has a new lease on life.

You can read more about Koren's struggles and triumphs in her best-selling book, *Smashed* (Penguin, 2006), and on her website, www.korenzailckas.com.

---

of 24 shots in less than two hours. On the way out of the bar, Brad passed out. His friend brought him home and put him in his bed to "sleep it off." Unfortunately, because he had drunk an enormous amount of alcohol, his BAC level continued to rise to a lethal level, even though he was unconscious and no longer taking in alcohol. Brad stopped breathing and died before the sun came up on his twenty-first birthday.[41]

Chronic drinking can lead to **alcohol tolerance,** which occurs over time as the body adjusts to long-term alcohol use. As the brain becomes less sensitive to alcohol, more is needed to get the same intoxicating effect.[42] People who've developed an alcohol tolerance should not think they can drink more without damaging the body. The harmful effects that you read about in the previous section still occur.

Many health professionals use a four-question screening tool called CAGE to assess if their patients have a problem controlling their alcohol consumption (Table 9.4). If a person is experiencing two or more of the responses, this is a sign that alcohol abuse may be a problem for that individual.

alcohol tolerance When the body adjusts to long-term alcohol use by becoming less sensitive to the alcohol. You need to consume more alcohol in order to get the same effect.

Red Flags for Alcohol Abuse

Complete the following self-assessment to see if you may be at increased risk for alcohol abuse.

1. Do you fail to fulfill major work, school, or home responsibilities because of your consumption of alcohol?
   Yes ☐   No ☐

2. Do you drink in situations that are potentially dangerous, such as while driving a car or operating heavy machinery?
   Yes ☐   No ☐

3. Do you experience repeated alcohol-related legal problems, such as being arrested for driving while intoxicated?
   Yes ☐   No ☐

4. Do you have relationship problems that are caused or made worse by alcohol?
   Yes ☐   No ☐

5. Do you try to hide your alcohol consumption from family or friends because you know they will tell you to stop?
   Yes ☐   No ☐

Answers

If you answered yes to any of these questions, you should speak with your health care provider for insight and guidance.

Source: Adapted from National Institute on Alcohol Abuse and Alcoholism. 2003. Understanding Alcohol: Investigations into Biology and Behavior. Available at http://science.education.nih.gov/supplements/nih3/alcohol/default.htm. Accessed June 2010; U.S. Department of Health and Human Services. 1997. Ninth Special Report of the U.S. Congress on Alcohol and Health. Bethesda, MD: National Institute on Alcohol Abuse and Alcoholism.

Drinking and Driving

If you have spent any time behind a steering wheel, you know that you can't *just* drive. You have to drive defensively. Driving involves multitasking. You need to keep the car within your lane, stay within the speed limit, make constant quick decisions, and, of course, maneuver the car based on these decisions. Alcohol intake impairs all of these skills. It is illegal to drive in the United States with a BAC of 0.08 (some states in the United States have set their legal limit even lower), but the level of alcohol in the blood doesn't have to get that high to impair your driving. As we saw in Table 9.1, even the lowest level of BAC, the level that occurs after one alcoholic beverage, will impair alertness, judgment, and coordination. In 2008, more than 11,000 people died in automobile accidents that involved a driver with a BAC of 0.01 or higher.[43]

The latest data regarding the alcohol intake of Americans shows that more than 2 percent of adults in the United States admitted to driving while alcohol impaired within the last 30 days. Even more astounding, 1.4 million Americans were arrested for driving under the influence (DUI) of alcohol or drugs. This translates to 1 out of every 137 licensed drivers being arrested for DUI and putting your life at risk if you are on the road at the same time with them.[44] Legal penalties for DUI can be severe, ranging from stiff fines and loss of license to jail time in some states.

People who ride with drunk drivers put themselves at high risk of being involved in an accident. To educate the public about the risks of drinking and driving, the Ad Council and the United States Department of Transportation launched a campaign in the early 1980s to promote the Designated Driver Program. The concept of the program was to designate a sober driver at social gatherings to ensure that people who choose to drink have a safe ride home. The "Friends Don't Let Friends Drive Drunk" tagline has been instrumental in reducing the annual number of alcohol-related automobile fatalities since its inception in 1983. Unfortunately, many people think they can still drive safely as long as they consume "only a few" drinks. But because even one alcoholic beverage can affect the skills needed when driving, the only sober driver is one who abstains from drinking alcohol.

Another campaign, entitled "Buzzed Driving Is Drunk Driving," has been launched to reinforce the concept that the designated driver shouldn't be the least drunk member of the group, but rather the one who hasn't consumed any alcohol.

Table 9.4

The CAGE Screening Tool

C	Have you ever felt that you should **c**ut down on your drinking?
A	Have people **a**nnoyed you by criticizing your drinking?
G	Have you ever felt **g**uilty about your drinking?
E	Have you ever had a drink first thing in the morning (**e**ye opener) to steady your nerves or get rid of a hangover?

Source: National Institute on Alcohol Abuse and Alcoholism. 2003. Understanding Alcohol: Investigations into Biology and Behavior. Available at http://science.education.nih.gov/supplements/nih3/alcohol/default.htm. Accessed June 2010.

Underage Drinking

The average age of the first drink for Americans from 12 to 20 years of age is 14 years old.[45] That means that many American youth are drinking alcohol when they are not even tall enough to see over the bar. By high school, more than 30 percent of teenagers are binge-drinking at least one time a month.[46] Underage drinking not only increases the risk of violence, injuries, and other health risks, as discussed earlier, but alcohol consumption at this age can also interfere with brain development and lead to permanent cognitive and memory damage in teenagers.

Underage drinking, coupled with driving, is a disaster waiting to happen. Adolescent drivers are inexperienced behind the wheel to begin with, so it isn't surprising that automobile accidents are the number-one cause of death of young people between the ages of 15 and 20. Those between the ages of 16 and 20 who drink and drive are twice as likely to die in automobile accidents as those 21 years of age and older who drink before getting behind the wheel.[47] In fact, this is why the minimum legal drinking age in the United States is 21. Studies conducted between 1970 and 1975, when several states had lowered the legal drinking age to under 21, showed that the rate of motor vehicle crashes and fatalities increased among teenagers.[48] Since 1984, all states have adopted 21 as the minimum legal drinking age and prohibited the sale of alcohol to underage individuals. ⓉⒻ

There is another danger in consuming alcohol at a young age. The earlier in life a person starts drinking, the higher the chances that alcohol will become a problem later in life. A person who starts drinking at age 15 is four times more likely to suffer from alcoholism than an individual who doesn't start drinking until age 20.[49]

Drinking and driving can be deadly.

As the price of beer goes up, the number of people involved in fatal traffic accidents goes down.

The "It's Only Another Beer"
Black and Tan

8 oz. pilsner lager
8 oz. stout lager
1 frosty mug
1 icy road
1 pick-up truck
1 10-hour day
1 tired worker
A few rounds with the guys

Mix ingredients.
Add 1 totaled vehicle.

Never underestimate 'just a few.'
Buzzed driving is drunk driving.

Council.org

U.S. Department of Transportation

"Buzzed driving is drunk driving" was a successful ad campaign that underscored the dangers of drinking and driving.

Alcoholism Is a Disease

In the beginning of the chapter, you read that Leah is concerned about her daily alcohol habit. Her brother Steve currently suffers from alcoholism, which is often referred to as *alcohol dependence.* Her father and grandfather both died of cirrhosis due to alcoholism.

Steve exhibits the four classic symptoms of alcoholism: (1) he craves alcohol; (2) he has developed a higher tolerance for alcohol; (3) he can't control or limit his intake once he starts drinking; and (4) he has developed a dependency on alcohol because, if he stops drinking, his body reacts to the withdrawal. An alcoholic's craving, loss of control, and physical dependency distinguish him or her as an "alcoholic" rather than a person who abuses alcohol but doesn't have these three other characteristics.[50]

Because the disease runs in her family, Leah is at a higher than average risk for alcoholism. Research has shown that children of alcoholics are about four times more likely to develop alcohol-related problems than those who do not have parents with alcoholism.[51] However, this genetic risk alone does not mean that Leah is destined to become an alcoholic. Her risk for alcoholism is also influenced by her environment. Her home life, the drinking habits of her family and friends, social pressures, and access to alcohol will all affect whether she develops the disease. If Leah's roommate and friends drink heavily, and she works part-time as a bartender, she will be at greater risk of developing alcoholism. If she chooses to surround herself with friends and a lifestyle that don't focus on alcohol, she can reduce her risk of following in her brother's footsteps.

There is no cure for alcoholism. However, it can be treated using a physical and psychological approach. The physical symptoms, such as the severe craving for alcohol, can be treated with medication that helps reduce the craving. Psychologically, self-help therapies and support groups can be invaluable to an alcoholic on the road to recovery. Because alcoholics can't limit their consumption once they start drinking, reducing the amount of alcohol consumed will not work for them. They must eliminate alcohol entirely from their lifestyle to have a successful recovery.

Alcoholics Anonymous (AA), the first support group devoted to helping those who suffer with alcoholism, was created in 1935 by Bill Wilson, a stockbroker, and Dr. Robert Smith, a surgeon, who together declared themselves hopeless drunks. They founded AA to help themselves and others stay sober. With more than 2 million members in 150 countries, AA is a worldwide fellowship of men and women with various backgrounds, lifestyles, and educational levels who meet, bond, and support each other, with the sole purpose of remaining sober. AA's 12 steps for recovery and supportive group meetings help individuals maintain sobriety.[52]

If you are interested in learning more about AA or finding a group in your area, look in your local telephone directory or online at www.alcoholics-anonymous.org. Everyone is welcomed at their meetings, including family members, friends, and coworkers.

Alcohol abusers and alcoholics should avoid alcohol. But they're not the only ones. According to the latest *Dietary Guidelines for Americans*, the following people should also abstain from alcohol:[53]

➤ Women of childbearing age who may become pregnant
➤ Pregnant and lactating women
➤ Children and adolescents
➤ Those taking medications that can interact with alcohol, which include prescription and over-the-counter medications
➤ Those with specific medical conditions, such as liver disease
➤ Those engaging in activities that require attention, skill, or coordination, such as driving or operating machinery
➤ Those who cannot restrict their alcohol intake

For these individuals, abstinence is the best option, as even modest amounts of alcohol can have detrimental health effects.

The Take-Home Message Individuals who abuse alcohol by binge-drinking, drinking and driving, and underage drinking are putting themselves and others at risk of injuries, violence, and even death. Alcoholism is a disease that can't be cured, but it can be treated with medical help and psychological support. People who are addicted to alcohol need to abstain from drinking it entirely. Other individuals who need to avoid alcohol include pregnant and lactating women; women who may become pregnant; anyone who is under the legal drinking age; those with specific medical conditions or taking certain medications; people who operate heavy machinery; those who plan to drive, operate machinery, or take part in activities, (such as swimming or climbing a ladder) where impaired judgment could provoke an injury; and those who cannot control their intake.

Table Tips

Keeping Your Drinking to a Moderate Amount

Never drink on an empty stomach. The alcohol will be absorbed too quickly, which will impair your judgment and lower your willpower to decline the next drink.

Make your first—and even your second—drink at a party a tall glass of water. This will allow you to pace yourself and eliminate the chance that you will guzzle your first alcoholic drink because you are thirsty. Also, have a glass of water before you have a second alcoholic drink. By the time you drink all this water, it will be time to go home.

Drink fun nonalcoholic drinks. Try a Virgin Mary (a Bloody Mary without the vodka), a tame margarita (use the mix and don't add the tequila), or a Tom Collins without the gin (club soda, lemon, and sugar).

Be an alcohol snob. Rather than consume excessive amounts of cheap beer or jug wine at parties, wait until you get home and have a better quality micro-brewed beer or a glass of nice wine. Don't drink a lot of junk; drink a little of the good stuff.

Become the standing Designated Driver among your friends and make your passengers reimburse you for the cost of the gasoline. You'll be everyone's best friend and have the money to buy the good stuff to drink when you're off duty.

Made Over, Made Better!

Trendy "mocktails" are increasing in popularity. These non-alcoholic beverages can be a caloric bargain in comparison with traditional cocktails.

Here are some typical cocktails made over and made nutritionally better!

Instead of this cocktail. . .	Try this mocktail!
Pomegranate Cosmo (vodka, Triple Sec, pomegranate juice, lime juice) **Calories: 124**	**Virgin Pomegranate Cosmo** (pomegranate juice, club soda, lime juice) **Calories 20**
Grey Goose L'Orange (Grey Goose L'Orange, Cointreau, cranberry juice, lime) **Calories: 110**	**Maui Punch** (pineapple juice, orange juice, soda water, grenadine) **Calories: 33**
Vodka Tonic (vodka, tonic, lime) **Calories: 114**	**Tonic with a Twist** (diet tonic, lime) **Calories: 2**
Beer **Calories: 140**	**Nonalcoholic Beer** **Calories: 67**

Two Points of View

Are There Health Benefits to Drinking Alcohol? Many people have heard about the supposed health benefits of moderate alcohol consumption, but the potential negative health effects of drinking alcohol in excess—alcoholism, cirrhosis, and behavioral issues—are still very big problems in the United States.

Should young adults drink alcohol for its health benefits? Or do the risks associated with alcohol consumption outweigh those benefits? After you've read the arguments for and against, answer the critical thinking questions and decide for yourself.

Yes

- There is ample evidence that moderate alcohol consumption reduces the risk of heart attack and stroke.[1]

- Moderate alcohol consumption may also lead to fewer gallstones, fewer kidney stones, and improved cognitive function in the elderly.[2]

- People who drink alcohol in moderation have been shown to have greater longevity than those who abstain or those who abuse alcohol.[3]

- Beer and wine can provide some nutrients, including soluble fiber, vitamins, antioxidants, and minerals.[4]

No

- Alcohol consumption is disproportionately risky for college students, for whom binge drinking is often an issue.[5] Alcohol is involved in more than 50 percent of on-campus property damage, violent behavior, diminished academic performance, and acquaintance rape.[6]

- Among young people, drinking alcohol greatly increases the risk for unintentional injuries.[7]

- Because the brain is not fully developed until the early twenties, underage consumption of alcohol can compromise the development of the brain.[8]

- People who start drinking at an early age are more likely to become addicted.[9]

What do you think?

1. Are the benefits of alcohol consumption worth the risks? **2.** How are those risks different for you and your peers as opposed to the general population? **3.** Why do you think overconsumption of alcohol is so prevalent among college students? **4.** Do you think some people really drink alcohol strictly for the potential health benefits? **5.** Aside from abstaining from alcohol entirely, how can some of the potential risks associated with drinking be avoided?

Chapter Review

Be a Nutrition Sleuth

Is Your Friend Too Drunk to Drive?

You be the judge. Go to **www.pearsonhighered.com/ blake** to view two driving simulations, one through the eyes of a sober driver, the other through the eyes of a driver who has consumed alcohol. You'll see the impairment caused by alcohol, which the affected driver may not even recognize.

Get Real!

Step Up to the Virtual Bar

Go to **www.pearsonhighered.com/blake** to learn how drinking a variety of beverages will affect *your* blood alcohol concentration (BAC). You can see how your BAC changes based on your gender, weight, type of drink, speed at which you're drinking, and food you have eaten.

The Top Ten Points to Remember

1. Alcohol is not an essential nutrient. Ethanol is the type of alcohol in alcoholic beverages. Unlike other types of alcohol, ethanol isn't poisonous when ingested. However, it can be toxic if too much is consumed. Alcoholic beverages are made via the processes of fermentation (turning sugars into alcohol and carbon dioxide; examples include beer and wine) or distillation (causing alcohol to vaporize and then collecting and condensing the vapor; examples include distilled spirits).

2. Alcohol produces an initial euphoric, pleasurable state of mind. For adults who choose to drink, moderate alcohol consumption is considered up to one drink for women daily and up to two drinks a day for men. A standard drink is 12 ounces of beer, 5 ounces of wine, or 1.5 ounces of liquor. Drinking alcohol in moderation may help reduce the risk of heart disease in older adults.

3. About 20 percent of the alcohol you drink is absorbed in the stomach. The rest is absorbed in the small intestine. The presence of food will slow the departure of alcohol from your stomach to your intestines. This is why drinking on an empty stomach is not a good idea.

4. Alcohol dehydrogenase begins to metabolize some of the alcohol in the stomach before it reaches your blood. Women have less of this enzyme in their stomachs than men. Alcohol mixes with water and is distributed in the watery tissues of the body. Women have less body water than men. Both of these factors cause women to feel the narcotic effects of alcohol sooner than men do.

5. The majority of the alcohol you consume is metabolized in your liver. Some alcohol is lost from your body in your breath and urine. Your liver can only metabolize about one standard drink in about 1½ to 2 hours. As you drink more alcohol, your BAC goes up, as does your level of impairment and intoxication.

6. Whereas alcohol is often thought of as a stimulant, it is actually a central nervous system depressant. Your brain is sensitive to the effects of alcohol, and depending on the amount you consume, alcohol can cause numerous mental, behavioral, and physical changes in your body. Your alertness, judgment, and coordination will initially be affected. As you drink more alcohol, your vision, speech, reasoning, and balance will be altered. An excessive amount of alcohol can interfere with your breathing and heart rate.

7. Alcohol can disrupt your sleep, cause hangovers, interfere with hormones, and add excess calories and/or displace healthier food choices from your diet. Chronically consuming excessive amounts of alcohol can harm your digestive organs, heart, and liver. It can also do long-term damage to the brain. The three stages of alcoholic liver disease are fatty liver, alcoholic hepatitis, and cirrhosis. Many individuals die annually of alcohol-related liver disease. Alcohol can put a fetus at risk for fetal alcohol spectrum disorders.

8. Alcohol abuse occurs when people continue to consume alcohol even though this behavior negatively affects their lives. Binge drinking, underage drinking, and drinking and driving are examples of alcohol abuse.

Individuals who binge-drink, many of whom are also underage, are at risk for blackouts and alcohol poisoning. Individuals who chronically drink alcohol often develop alcohol tolerance, which occurs when the brain becomes less sensitive to alcohol. Because alcohol affects alertness and judgment, the only safe amount of alcohol to consume when driving is none.

9. Alcoholism, also called alcohol dependence, is a disease characterized by four symptoms: a craving for alcohol, a higher tolerance for alcohol, the inability to control or limit one's intake, and a physical dependence on it. Genetics plays a role in increasing certain people's risk of developing alcoholism. Though alcoholism can't be cured, it can be treated with medical and psychological support.

10. Alcohol should be avoided by women of childbearing age who may become pregnant, or who are pregnant or lactating; anyone under the age of 21; those engaging in activities that require attention, skill, or coordination, such as driving or operating machinery; those taking certain medications or with specific medical conditions; and those who cannot restrict or limit their intake of alcohol.

Test Your Knowledge

1. Alcohol provides
   a. 9 calories per gram.
   b. 7 calories per gram.
   c. 4 calories per gram.
   d. 0 calories per gram.
   e. none of the above.

2. A standard drink is considered
   a. a 12-ounce can of beer.
   b. a 5-ounce glass of white wine.
   c. a shot (1.5 ounces) of liquor.
   d. any of the above.
   e. none of the above.

3. The major site of alcohol metabolism in your body is your
   a. kidneys.
   b. lungs.
   c. liver.
   d. stomach.
   e. none of the above

4. Which of the following factors affect(s) your rate of absorption and the metabolism of alcohol?
   a. whether you're male or female
   b. the amount of food in your stomach
   c. the time of day you drink
   d. the individuals you are drinking with
   e. a and b only

5. Blood alcohol concentration (BAC) is the
   a. minimum amount of alcohol needed in your blood daily.
   b. amount of alcohol in your blood, measured in grams of alcohol per deciliter of blood.
   c. number of drinks you consumed in an hour.
   d. grams of alcohol per liter of beverage.
   e. none of the above.

6. The *best* cure for a hangover is
   a. chicken soup.
   b. a light beer.
   c. time and abstinence.
   d. taking acetaminophen (Tylenol).
   e. none of the above.

7. Individuals who chronically drink excessively are at increased risk for
   a. malnutrition.
   b. gastritis.
   c. inflammation of the esophagus.
   d. fatty liver.
   e. all of the above.

8. The four characteristics of alcoholism are (1) a craving for alcohol, (2) the development of a higher tolerance for alcohol, (3) the inability to control or limit the intake of alcohol, and (4) _____.
   a. the inability to keep a stable job
   b. the inability to maintain social relationships
   c. the tendency to become violent
   d. the development of a dependency on alcohol
   e. the revocation of the person's driver's license

9. Of the following list, who shouldn't drink alcohol?
   a. your pregnant aunt
   b. your high-school–aged brother
   c. your uncle who has a stomach ulcer
   d. your father while he is riding the lawn mower
   e. all of the above

10. Drinking 4 to 5 alcoholic beverages on one occasion in a very short time is called
   a. alcoholism.
   b. drunk driving.
   c. blackout.
   d. binge drinking.
   e. none of the above.

Answers

1. (b) Alcohol serves up 7 calories per gram, which is less than fat at 9 calories per gram, and more than carbohydrates and protein, which each provide 4 calories per gram. Alcohol isn't an essential nutrient—your body doesn't need it to survive—and it's not calorie free.

2. (d) All of these drinks contain ½ ounce of alcohol, so each is considered a standard drink.

3. (c) Most alcohol in the body is metabolized in the liver. A small amount of alcohol is lost in your urine (kidneys) and in your breath (your lungs). Some alcohol is also metabolized in your stomach, though substantially less than in your liver.

4. (e) Both your sex and the amount of food in your stomach will affect the rate of absorption and the metabolism of alcohol. Women have less of the enzyme alcohol dehydrogenase in their stomachs, which means they metabolize less alcohol in the stomach and more alcohol will be absorbed into the blood. Drinking on a full stomach will delay the arrival of alcohol in your small intestine, which is the primary site of absorption. The time of day doesn't have any effect on the absorption and metabolism of alcohol. Your drinking partners also won't alter the absorption and metabolism of alcohol. Of course, they could influence the *amount* of alcohol you consume.

5. (b) Your BAC is the concentration of alcohol in your blood. It is measured in grams of alcohol per deciliter of blood. Your body doesn't need a minimum intake of alcohol daily. The number of drinks that you consume in an hour will affect your BAC; the more you drink, the higher the concentration of alcohol in your blood. BAC has nothing to do with the concentration of alcohol in a drink.

6. (c) The best cure is to stop drinking and let your body have the time it needs to recover from consuming too much alcohol. Neither chicken soup nor coffee nor any other food or beverage will cure the fatigue and other ill effects of drinking alcohol. Taking acetaminophen is not recommended, as its toxicity to your liver is enhanced if it is consumed while alcohol is being metabolized. The worst thing you can do for a hangover is to have another alcoholic beverage.

7. (e) All of the above. When too much alcohol is chronically consumed, more nutritious foods are often displaced in the diet, increasing the risk of malnutrition. A constant intake of alcohol will cause irritation and inflammation of both the esophagus and your stomach. A fatty liver can occur after only a few days of excessive drinking.

8. (d) The last characteristic of alcoholism is the development of a dependency on alcohol, such that a withdrawal will cause symptoms in the body. Although alcoholism can have financial consequences such as job instability, interfere with personal relationships, and increase the risk of violence, not all individuals with alcoholism have these experiences.

9. (e) All pregnant women should avoid alcohol, as drinking during pregnancy will increase the risk of fetal alcohol spectrum disorders (FASDs). Unless your brother is 21 years old, he shouldn't be drinking alcohol. Because alcohol causes gastritis, your uncle would benefit from avoiding alcohol. Your father should wait until he has finished mowing the lawn before having a drink, as this chore involves operating machinery that requires attention, skill, and coordination.

10. (d) Consuming that much alcohol in a very short time is considered binge drinking. Binge drinking can lead to alcoholism. Individuals who binge-drink may experience blackouts or may drive while drunk.

Web Resources

- For more information about drinking at college, visit www.collegedrinkingprevention.gov/
- For more information about alcohol and your health, visit the National Institute on Alcohol Abuse and Alcoholism (NIAAA) at www.niaaa.nih.gov/
- For more information about alcohol consumption and its consequences, visit the National Center for Chronic Disease Prevention and Health Promotion, Alcohol and Public Health, at www.cdc.gov/alcohol/index.htm

Answers to Myths and Misperceptions

1. **False.** Although alcohol provides calories, it's not an essential nutrient. See page 332 to find out why.

2. **False.** A straight shot of liquor may look and taste more potent than a can of beer, but it isn't. To learn more, turn to page 334.

3. **True.** Red wine does contain heart-healthy compounds. To find out more about them, turn to page 334.

4. **False.** The alcohol in your stomach and small intestine would continue to be absorbed, your blood alcohol concentration would continue to rise, and you could die from alcohol poisoning. See page 337 for more.

5. **True.** Women respond more quickly to the narcotic effects of alcohol than do men. To find out why, turn to page 338.

6. **False.** Drinking more alcohol isn't going to take away the ill effects of a hangover. To find out what will, turn to page 341.

7. **True.** However, not all alcoholic beverages contain equal amounts of calories. For an eye-opener as to the amount of calories in some common alcoholic drinks, turn to page 341.

8. **True.** You're darn right it can. If you're puzzled as to how that can happen, turn to page 343.

9. **False.** Decades ago, some states lowered their legal drinking age, but today you have to be 21 to legally purchase and consume alcohol in the United States. Turn to page 350 to learn more.

10. **False.** Although counseling is an important component of alcoholism recovery, it will not cure it. Page 351 explains why.

10

Weight
Manage
Energy

True or False?

1. **Overweight** people have a harder time sleeping. ⓉⒻ p. 361

2. Being **skinny** is always healthy. ⓉⒻ p. 361

3. One of the best ways to tell if you are at a **healthy weight** is to compare yourself to celebrities. ⓉⒻ p. 362

4. **Fat** around the hips is as unhealthy as fat stored around the waist. ⓉⒻ p. 364

5. The number of **calories** you burn daily is affected by your body size. ⓉⒻ p. 368

6. Your body weight is affected by your genes and your **environment**. ⓉⒻ p. 373

7. Eating *more* **vegetables** and fruits can help you lose weight. ⓉⒻ p. 377

8. The nutrient that has the most effect on **satiety** is fat. ⓉⒻ p. 382

9. **Disordered** eating and eating disorders are the same thing. ⓉⒻ p. 392

10. Eating disorders can be **fatal**. ⓉⒻ p. 394

See page 405 for answers to these Myths and Misperceptions.

ment and Balance

ighteen-year-old Hannah is more nervous about the "freshman 15" than about her course load during her first year at college. After years of struggle, she was able to maintain a healthy weight during her senior year of high school by changing her eating habits and exercising regularly. However, now that she's away at school, she's less likely to eat the fresh fruits and vegetables her parents always had on hand, and finding the time to exercise has become more of a challenge. To help ensure that she doesn't gain weight, she's taken to skipping breakfast, which she assumes will help her keep her calorie intake low. However, she's usually starving before lunchtime and needs a snack from the vending machine to get through an 11 A.M. class.

Do you think Hannah is likely to gain the 15 pounds she's trying to avoid? Why do you think so many college freshman are worried about weight gain? Are their concerns justified? In this chapter, you will learn the truth about the "freshman 15," as well as the keys to successful weight management and healthy strategies for weight loss. We will also discuss the disordered eating patterns that sometimes occur among young men and women.

Chapter Objectives

After reading this chapter, you will be able to:

1. Explain the concept of a healthy weight, and differentiate between the conditions of underweight, overweight, and obesity.

2. Define and describe the concept of energy balance.

3. Discuss what happens to the body if too many or too few calories are consumed.

4. Define and describe the concepts of hunger, appetite, and satiety.

5. Explain how the body regulates hunger.

6. List three environmental factors that often contribute to higher body weight.

7. Describe a basic plan for healthy weight loss and/or weight gain.

8. Define the terms disordered eating and eating disorder, and give two examples of each.

lip through a magazine, watch a little television, or spend some time online, and before long you'll find someone talking about weight loss. You may be used to so much coverage of weight management, but it hasn't always been that way. In the early 1960s, fewer than 32 percent of Americans were overweight, so weight didn't receive much media attention. Today, the majority of Americans are overweight, so it's a much hotter topic.[1] In fact, obesity is one of the most frequently covered health stories in the media.[2]

Americans currently spend more than $45 billion—the highest amount ever—on everything from over-the-counter diet pills to books, magazines, online support groups, and commercial dieting centers to help shed excess weight.[3] Unfortunately, these programs usually aren't successful, and the U.S. health care system bears more than $92 billion in costs of treating the medical complications associated with being overweight.[4] No matter what you personally weigh, some of your tax dollars are supporting these costs. Despite spending so much money on the battle of the bulge, we are not winning the war on weight control.

What is causing this trend, and how unhealthy is it? What does it mean to manage your weight, and what are the best strategies for doing so? Lastly, should we strive to be thin at all costs—or can this be equally unhealthy?

Let's try to figure this all out.

What Is a Healthy Weight and Why Is Maintaining It Important?

A **healthy weight** is considered a body weight that doesn't increase your risk of developing weight-related health problems or diseases. Rather than a single number, it's a range of weight that is appropriate for your gender, height, and muscle mass, a weight at which you feel energetic and fit. A healthy weight is also a *realistic* weight, one that you can maintain naturally through consuming a nourishing diet and engaging in regular physical activity. As the U.S. Centers for Disease Control and Prevention (CDC) puts it, a healthy weight is not a diet; it's a healthy lifestyle![5]

Weight management, then, means maintaining your weight within a healthy range. Either extreme—being very overweight or very underweight—can be unhealthy, a red flag for undernutrition of some nutrients, overnutrition of others, and impending health problems. Being **overweight,** or weighing 10 to 15 pounds more than your healthy weight, tends to be a stepping stone to **obesity.** A person with 25 to 40 or more pounds of weight above his or her healthy weight is considered obese. Currently, 68 percent of Americans are overweight, with 34 percent of those obese.[6]

In addition to potentially leading to obesity, being overweight can increase your risk of numerous other health problems, including:

➤ Hypertension and stroke
➤ Heart disease
➤ Gallbladder disease
➤ Type 2 diabetes
➤ Osteoarthritis
➤ Some cancers
➤ Sleep apnea

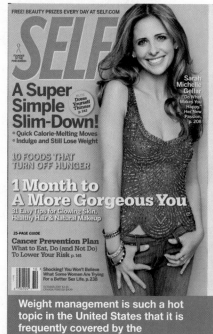

Weight management is such a hot topic in the United States that it is frequently covered by the mainstream media.

Generally, as a person's weight increases, so does his or her blood pressure. Overweight individuals can experience increased retention of sodium, which causes both increased blood volume and resistance in the blood vessels. This and additional demands on the heart all likely contribute to high blood pressure.[7] High blood pressure increases the risk of stroke and heart disease. Overweight people also tend to have high blood levels of both fat and the "bad" LDL cholesterol, and less of the "good" HDL cholesterol, which is an unhealthy combination for the heart. High blood cholesterol levels increase the risk for gallstones and gallbladder disease. They are also more likely to contribute to an enlarged gallbladder, impeding its function.

More than 80 percent of those with type 2 diabetes are overweight. Excess weight causes the body's cells to become insulin resistant. Over time, this resistance causes the pancreas to work harder to produce more insulin and can eventually cause the pancreas to stop producing it altogether. Incidences of cancers of the colon, uterus, and breast (in postmenopausal women) are also higher. Excess weight means extra stress on joints, especially in the knees, hips, and lower back, and contributes to osteoarthritis. Sleep apnea, a condition in which breathing stops for brief periods during sleep, disrupts a person's ability to obtain a restful slumber. The fat stored around the neck, as well as fat-induced inflammation in that area, may contribute to a smaller airway and interfere with breathing.[8]

American people aren't the only ones getting bigger—American pets are also putting on pounds. According to the National Academy of Sciences, there has been an epidemic of obesity among pet dogs and cats.

Although being overweight can lead to many unhealthy conditions and diseases, the good news is that losing as little as 10 to 20 pounds can reduce a person's risk of all these conditions.[9]

While overweight and obesity are currently far more prevalent among Americans, being **underweight** is also of concern, especially among teens and young adults, because of the potential negative health effects that are associated with it. Being underweight means that a person doesn't have enough weight on his or her body for his or her height. For some, being very slender is their natural, healthy body shape, but for others, it's a sign of malnutrition. Excessive calorie restriction and/or physical activity, emotional stress, or an underlying medical condition such as cancer or an intestinal disorder can often cause someone to be underweight.[10] Young adults who are underweight often face health challenges, including nutrient deficiencies, electrolyte imbalance, low energy levels, and decreased concentration. Over time, more serious health effects can arise, such as heart complications that can be fatal. For older adults (those over age 65), being undernourished means an increased risk for low body protein and

healthy weight A body weight in relationship to your height that doesn't increase the risk of developing any weight-related health problems or diseases.

weight management Maintaining your weight within a healthy range.

overweight Weighing about 10 to 15 pounds more than a healthy weight for your height.

obesity Carrying an excessive amount of body fat above the level of being overweight.

underweight Weighing too little for your height.

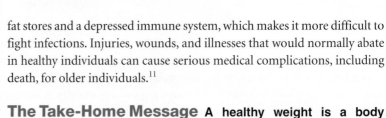

fat stores and a depressed immune system, which makes it more difficult to fight infections. Injuries, wounds, and illnesses that would normally abate in healthy individuals can cause serious medical complications, including death, for older individuals.[11]

The Take-Home Message A healthy weight is a body weight that doesn't increase your risk of developing weight-related health problems or diseases. It's realistic for your build and can be attained with a nourishing diet and regular exercise. Weight management means maintaining a healthy weight to reduce your risk for specific health problems. Being overweight, obese, or underweight can be unhealthy.

How Do You Know If You're at a Healthy Weight?

Over the years, varying body shapes have trended in and out of the media spotlight. In the 1980s, fashion models were 8 percent thinner than the average woman. Today, the typical cover girl is more than 20 percent thinner. The male physique is being held to a similarly unattainable standard. Witness the change from scrawny to beefy in toy action figures over the years.[12] Although models, celebrities, and dolls may reflect the "in" look, they don't necessarily correlate with good health, nor should they be your reference for the body weight that *you* should strive to obtain.

So, how can you determine if your body weight is within a healthy range? Following are a few methods that can be helpful.

Over the years, the idealized model look has gone from curvy to stick thin to sporty and back to waiflike again. Today, superslender women are the norm in magazines and movies.

The male physique depicted in popular action figures in the 1970s, like Luke Skywalker and Han Solo from *Star Wars*, was more realistic than the bulked-up versions of the late 1990s.

BMI Measurements Can Provide a General Guideline

One of the most common and inexpensive ways to assess a healthy weight is to measure **body mass index (BMI)**. BMI is a calculation of weight in relationship to height using the following formula:

$$BMI = \frac{weight\ (pounds) \times 703}{height\ squared\ (inches^2)}$$

Here's how to interpret your BMI:

➤ *Underweight.* If your BMI falls in the first part of the graph (shaded orange in **Figure 10.1**), it is below 18.5 and you are considered underweight. Although people who are underweight are at reduced risk for the chronic diseases associated with obesity, they are at increased risk for infection, and their overall risk of mortality is higher than for people of normal weight.

➤ *Healthy weight.* If your BMI falls between 18.5 and 24.9 (the green part of the graph), it is considered healthy.

➤ *Overweight.* If your BMI falls between 25 and 29.9 (the blue area of the graph), you are considered overweight. As the amount you are overweight increases, so does your risk of dying from certain chronic diseases, although research shows that the risk is modest until a person reaches a BMI of closer to 30.

➤ *Obese.* If your BMI is 30 or over (the purple part of the graph), you are considered obese. Obese individuals have a 50 to 100 percent higher risk of dying prematurely, compared with those at a healthy weight.[13]

body mass index (BMI) A calculation of your weight in relationship to your height. A BMI between 18.5 and 24.9 is considered healthy.

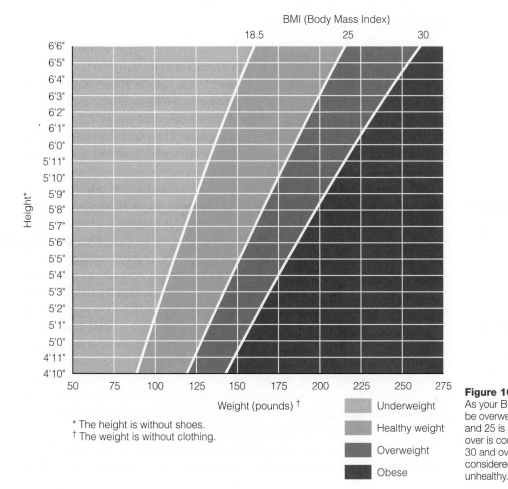

* The height is without shoes.
† The weight is without clothing.

Underweight

Healthy weight

Overweight

Obese

Figure 10.1 What's Your BMI?
As your BMI increases, you are more likely to be overweight or obese. A BMI between 18.5 and 25 is considered healthy. A BMI of 25 and over is considered overweight, and a BMI of 30 and over is obese. A BMI under 18.5 is considered underweight, and can also be unhealthy.

Determining Your BMI

Want to know your exact BMI based on your height and weight? Use the BMI calculator at www.nhlbisupport .com/bmi/.

BMI is used as a screening tool to identify potential weight problems and should not be used as a diagnostic tool for specific medical conditions. Also, because BMI is not a direct measure of percentage body fat, it may not be accurate for everyone. This is particularly true for athletes. Many, many athletes have a BMI that should put them in the "unhealthy" category, but they aren't because their body weight is predominantly muscle, not fat. For example, Tom Brady, the New England Patriots quarterback, and Peyton Manning, the quarterback for the Indianapolis Colts, both have a BMI of 27. They are not "overfat" and unhealthy, and their muscular weight does not increase their health risk. Therefore, athletes and other people with a high percentage of muscle mass may have a BMI over 25 yet still be healthy, as they have a low percentage of body fat. Many young, athletic adults may also have BMI results similar to these celebrity athletes, but once again, they are not considered "unhealthy" or at risk for other health conditions because of their muscular physique.

In contrast, a person may be in a healthy weight range, but may have been steadily losing weight due to an unbalanced diet or poor health. This chronic weight loss is a sign of loss of muscle mass and the depletion of nutrient stores in the body, which increases health risks even though the BMI seems healthy. Lastly, because height is factored into the BMI, individuals who are very short—under 5 feet—may have a high BMI, but, similarly to athletes, may not be unhealthy.[14] In general, BMI is best used to assess overweight and obesity for populations rather than individuals. If someone is classified as underweight, overweight, or obese according to BMI, further assessments by a health care provider will determine health risks or present medical conditions associated with weight.

Measure Your Body Fat and Its Location

According to the American College of Sports Medicine, the average healthy adult male between the ages of 20 and 49 carries 16 to 21 percent of his weight as body fat. The average woman of the same age range carries 22 to 26 percent of her weight as body fat. There are several techniques you can use to measure total body fat, including skinfold thickness measurements, bioelectrical impedance, dual-energy X-ray absorptiometry, underwater weighing, and air displacement. These tests must be conducted by trained technicians and some of them can be expensive. Table 10.1 describes the ways to measure body fat.

How much fat you carry isn't the only determinant of health risk—where you carry it also matters. **Central obesity,** that is, carrying excess fat around the waist (sometimes referred to as an "apple" body shape) versus carrying it around the buttocks, hips, and thighs (a "pear" body shape), has been shown to increase the risk of heart disease, diabetes, and hypertension.[15] Central obesity is due to storing too much **visceral fat** (the fat that surrounds organs in your chest and stomach and above your hips) around your waist. (Another type of fat, called **subcutaneous fat,** is the fat sandwiched between your skin and your muscles.) (See **Figure 10.2.**) On average, men tend to be apple shaped and women more pear shaped, because of the female hormone estrogen. This hormone is made by the ovaries and is responsible for prompting ovulation every menstrual cycle. The presence of estrogen causes more fat to be stored in the lower body than the abdomen, resulting in women of childbearing age being more pear shaped. However, keep in mind that women being more likely to have a pear shape is a generalization, not an absolute. People of both genders can be of either shape and develop health risks associated with it.

Because visceral fat is located near the liver, it is believed that fatty acids released from the fat storage area travel to the liver and can lead to insulin resistance, high

Figure 10.2 Visceral and Subcutaneous Fat Storage in the Body
Visceral fat stored around the waist is more likely to lead to health problems than subcutaneous fat stored elsewhere in the body.

— Liver
— Abdominal muscle
— Subcutaneous fat
— Visceral fat

central obesity An excess storage of visceral fat in the abdominal area, which increases the risk of heart disease, diabetes, and hypertension.

visceral fat The fat stored in the abdominal area.

subcutaneous fat The fat located under the skin and between the muscles.

Table 10.1 Ways to Measure Percentage of Body Fat

Skinfold Thickness Measurements

How It Is Done: Calipers are used to measure the thickness of fat that is located just under the skin in the arm, in the back, on the upper thigh, and in the waist area. From these measurements, percent body fat can be determined.

Cost: $

Bioelectrical Impedance

How It Is Done: An electric current flows through the body and its resistance is measured. Lean tissue is highly conductive and less resistant than fat mass. Based on the current flow, the volume of lean tissue can be estimated. From this information, the percentage of body fat can be determined.

Cost: $

Dual-Energy X-Ray Absorptiometry (DXA)

How It Is Done An X-ray is used to measure bone, fat, and lean tissue. The type of tissue that the X-ray passes through will absorb different amounts of energy. The amount of energy lost will allow the percentage of body fat to be determined.

Cost: $$$

Underwater Weighing

How It Is Done A person is weighed on land and also suspended in a water tank. This is done to determine the density of the body. Fat is less dense and weighs less than muscle mass and will be reflected as such when the person is weighed in the water. The difference of a person's weight in water and on land is then used to calculate the percentage of body fat.

Cost: $$

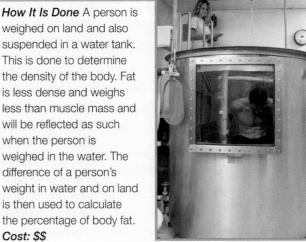

Air Displacement Using a BodPod

How It Is Done A person's body volume is determined by measuring air displacement from a chamber. The person sits in a special chamber (called the Bod-Pod) and the air displacement in the chamber is measured. From this measurement, the percentage of body fat can be estimated.

Cost: $$$

$ = very affordable
$$ = less affordable
$$$ = expensive

Figure 10.3 Your waist circumference should be measured around your bare abdomen just above your hip bone.

levels of fat, low levels of the good HDL cholesterol, and high levels of LDL cholesterol in the blood, which all increase the risk of heart disease and diabetes. Insulin resistance also increases the risk for hypertension. Men, postmenopausal women, and obese people tend to have more visceral fat than young adults and lean individuals.

Measuring a person's waist circumference can quickly reveal whether he or she is at risk. (**Figure 10.3** shows how to make this measurement accurately.) A woman with a waist measurement of more than 35 inches or a man with a belly that's more than 40 inches around is at a higher health risk than people with slimmer middles. Carrying extra fat around your waist can increase health risks even if you are not overweight. In other words, a person who may be at a healthy weight according to BMI, but who has excess fat around the middle, is at a higher health risk. A person who has both a BMI $\geq$ 25 and a large waist circumference is considered at a higher risk for health problems than if he or she only had a high BMI (**Figure 10.4**).

The Take-Home Message Body mass index (BMI) is a calculation of weight in relationship to height and can be used to assess if weight increases health risks. It is not a direct measure of body fat and may be inaccurate for people who are muscular or who are frail due to illness. Skinfold thickness measurements using calipers, bioelectrical impedance, dual-energy X-ray absorptiometry, underwater weighing, and air displacement are all techniques that can be used to measure the percentage of body fat. Individuals with central obesity, who carry excess fat around the middle, have an increased risk of several chronic diseases, regardless of BMI.

Extremely High Risk
BMI 40+ and high waist circumference

Very High Risk
BMI 30–39.9 and high waist circumference

High Risk
BMI 25–29.9 and high waist circumference
or
BMI 30–34.9 and low waist circumference

Increased Risk
BMI 25–29.9 and low waist circumference

Low Risk
BMI under 25

Figure 10.4 How at Risk Are You?
Considering both your BMI and your waist circumference can give you a good idea of your level of risk for health problems.

energy balance The state at which energy (calorie) intake and energy (calorie) output in the body are equal.

positive energy balance The state whereby you store more energy than you expend. Over time, this results in weight gain.

What Is Energy Balance and What Determines Energy Needs?

To maintain your weight, you need to make sure that you don't consume more calories than you expend daily. Spending as many calories as you take in is the concept behind energy balance.

Energy Balance Is Calories in versus Calories Out

Energy balance is the state at which your energy intake and your energy expenditure, both measured in calories, are equal (**Figure 10.5a**). When you consume more calories than you expend, you are in **positive energy balance** (**Figure 10.5b**). Routinely eating more calories than you expend will cause the storage of fat. When your calorie intake falls short of your needs, you are in **negative energy balance** (**Figure 10.5c**). Imbalances that occur over a long time period, such as weeks and months, are what change body weight.

You can determine whether you are in positive or negative energy balance by comparing the number of calories you take in to the number of calories you expend on a given day. Figuring out how many calories you take in is fairly straightforward. You can use the food label or a diet analysis program (like the one available with this book) to find out how many calories are in the foods and beverages you eat and drink.

Figure 10.5 Energy Balance and Imbalances

a **Energy balance:** When the calories that you consume meet your needs, you are in energy balance. Your weight will be stable.

Calories in → Energy balance → Calories out

Calories in → Positive energy balance → Calories out

b **Positive energy balance:** When you take in more calories than you need, the surplus calories will be stored as fat. You will gain weight.

Calories in → Negative energy balance → Calories out

c **Negative energy balance:** When you consume fewer calories than you expend, your body will draw upon your stored energy to meet its needs. You will lose weight.

You can also use the grams of macronutrients in foods to calculate the number of total calories they contain. Recall from Chapter 1 that carbohydrates and protein each contain 4 calories/gram and fat contains 9 calories/gram. (Note that alcohol, at 7 calories/gram, can also contribute calories.) Multiplying the number of grams of carbohydrates, protein, or fat by the calories per gram and then adding up these numbers will provide the total amount of calories in the food.

Calculating the number of calories you expend daily is a little more complicated.

Energy Needs Are Different for Everyone

Energy needs are unique to every individual, and your energy needs are different from those of your 80-year-old grandparents, your 50-year-old parents, and your marathon-running roommate. Your energy needs are comprised of your basal metabolism, the thermic effect of food (TEF), and the calories needed to fuel your physical activities. (See **Figure 10.6.**)

Your BMR Is the Minimum Amount of Energy You Need to Function

Even when you're not at the gym or sprinting to class, your body is using energy. Pumping your blood, expanding your lungs, and using your brain all require energy every moment of your life. **Basal metabolism** is the amount of energy expended to meet the basic physiological needs that enable your organs and cells to function. Also referred to as your **basal metabolic rate (BMR),** it is the minimum energy needed to keep you alive.

Figure 10.6 The Three Components of Energy Needs
The "calories out" side of the energy balance equation includes BMR, the thermic effect of food (TEF), and the energy you use to fuel physical activity.

negative energy balance The state in which you expend more energy than you consume. Over time, this results in weight loss.

basal metabolism The amount of energy the body expends to meet its basic physiological needs. Also referred to as **basal metabolic rate (BMR).**

Table 10.2

Factors That Affect Your Basal Metabolic Rate

Factor	Explanation
Lean body mass	Lean body mass, which is mostly muscle mass, is more metabolically active than fat tissue, so more calories are needed to maintain it. Athletes who have a large percentage of lean body mass due to their increased muscle mass will have a higher BMR than individuals who aren't athletic.
Age	For adults, BMR declines about 1 to 2 percent per decade after the early adult years, but it increases by 15 percent during pregnancy. For children, BMR increases during times of rapid growth such as infancy and adolescence.
Gender	Women have less lean body mass, and typically have a higher percentage of body fat than men. This results in women having up to a 10 percent lower BMR. Women also tend to have a smaller body size.
Body size	Taller individuals will have a higher BMR due to increased surface area compared with shorter individuals. More surface area means more heat lost from the body, which causes the metabolism rate to increase to maintain the body's temperature.
Genes	Research suggests that genes may affect BMR, as individuals within families have similar metabolic rates.
Ethnicity	African-Americans have BMRs that are about 10 percent lower than that of Caucasians.
Stress	Hormones such as epinephrine, which are released during emotional stress, increase BMR. Physiological stress on the body caused by injury, fever, burns, and infections also causes the release of hormones that raise BMR. Heat lost from the body through wounds, as well as the response of the immune system during infection, increase BMR.
Hormones	An increase in thyroid hormone increases BMR, whereas too little of this hormone lowers BMR. Hormone fluctuations during a woman's menstrual cycle lower BMR during the phase before ovulation.
Starvation	Both starvation and fasting for more than about 48 hours lower BMR.
Environmental temperature	Being very cold or very hot can increase BMR, but the change is minimal if you make adjustments in your clothing or in the temperature of your surroundings.
Caffeine	Caffeine can raise BMR but only slightly when consumed regularly in moderate amounts.
Drugs	Nicotine may increase BMR. Drugs such as amphetamines and ephedrine increase BMR.

*Note: Smoking is not a weight-management strategy. Some people may think that replacing snacks with cigarettes helps them stay slim, but the health risks associated with smoking, such as lung cancer, heart disease, and stroke, make it a foolish habit. Anyone concerned about weight gain when quitting smoking can minimize the chances of this with exercise (plus, you'll be able to run farther and faster with your cleaner lungs!).
Source: Institute of Medicine. 2002. *Dietary Reference Intakes for Energy, Carbohydrate, Fiber, Fat, Fatty Acids, Cholesterol, Protein, and Amino Acids.* Available at www.iom.edu.

Approximately 60 percent of your daily energy needs is determined by your BMR. The factor that most affects your BMR, **lean body mass,** accounts for about 70 percent of your BMR. Age, gender, body size, genes, ethnicity, emotional and physical stress, thyroid hormone, nutritional state, and environmental temperature, as well as your caffeine and nicotine intake, affect your BMR. Table 10.2 explains each of these factors.

The Thermic Effect of Food Is the Energy Your Body Needs to Process Food

lean body mass The body mass once the fat mass has been subtracted. It contains mostly muscle but also organs and fluids. Lean body mass is the metabolically active tissue in the body.

thermic effect of food (TEF) The amount of calories the body uses to digest, absorb, metabolize, and store food.

Your body uses energy to extract the calories from the foods that you consume. The **thermic effect of food (TEF)** is the amount of calories you expend to digest, absorb, metabolize, and store your food. Approximately 10 percent of calories in the food consumed is used for TEF. In other words, if you eat a 100-calorie cookie, about 10 calories will be used to metabolize the cookie. The TEF varies by the type of food

What's Your Estimated Energy Requirement (EER)?

Calculating your EER is a two-step process.

1. First, complete the information below.

   a. My age is ⬚

   b. My physical activity during the day based on the chart below is ⬚

Physical Activity	Male	Female
Sedentary (no exercise)	1.00	1.00
Low active (walks about 2 miles daily at 3–4 mph)	1.11	1.12
Active (walks about 7 miles daily at 3–4 mph)	1.26	1.27
Very active (walks about 17 miles daily at 3–4 mph)	1.48	1.45

   c. My weight in pounds is _____ divided by 2.2 = ⬚ kg

   d. My height in inches is _____ divided by 39.4 = ⬚ meters

2. Using your answers in each box in step 1, complete the following calculation based on your gender and age.

   Males, 19+ years old, use this calculation:

   662 − (9.53 × _____) + _____ × (15.9 × _____ + 539.6 × _____) = _____
              a   b   c   d   EER

   Females, 19+ years old, use this calculation:

   354 − (6.91 × _____) + _____ × (9.36 × _____ + 726 × _____) = _____
              a   b   c   d   EER

you eat. Protein and carbohydrate have a higher TEF than dietary fat. This is because your body requires more energy to digest, absorb, and metabolize amino acids, starches, and sugar into stored body fat than to use and store dietary fat into body fat.

Physical Activity Will Increase Your Energy Needs

If you are very physically active, you're going to need more energy than someone who is sedentary. For sedentary people, the amount of energy expended in physical activity is less than half of their BMR. For very physically active individuals, such as athletes, it can be as much as double their BMR. The more physical activity you routinely incorporate into your day, the more calories you will need to eat to meet your energy needs. The amount of energy expended during physical activity goes beyond the activity itself. Exercise causes a small increase in energy expenditure for some time after the activity has stopped.[16]

Calculating Your Energy Needs

Recall Table 2.1 from Chapter 2, which helped you estimate your energy needs. This table was derived from the DRIs' **estimated energy requirement (EER).** The EER is the average calorie intake that is estimated to maintain energy balance based on a person's gender, age, height, body weight, and level of physical activity. (The physical activity levels are separated into categories ranging from sedentary to very active.) While Table 2.1 used a reference height and weight for each age grouping, you can calculate your own EER using your specific height and weight with the Self-Assessment "What's Your Estimated Energy Requirement (EER)?"

eLearn

An Estimated Energy Requirement Online Tool

To calculate a more precise EER, you need to record all of your daily physical activity. Visit the interactive tracker tool at www.ChooseMyPlate.gov and enter your gender, height, weight, age, and all the activities you do in a 24-hour period. The Tracker will then calculate your EER.

estimated energy requirement (EER) The amount of daily energy needed to maintain a healthy body weight and meet energy (calorie) needs based on age, gender, height, weight, and activity level.

The Take-Home Message Energy balance is the relationship between your energy intake and your energy expenditure, which are both measured in calories. Your basal metabolism, the thermic effect of food (TEF), and your physical activities all determine your daily energy needs.

What Are the Effects of an Energy Imbalance?

The handful of cheese curls that Pam eats every night while watching television is adding about 100 more calories than she needs daily. After three months, she's gained a little over two pounds. Bryan, in contrast, is so busy juggling studying with tennis practice that he consumes about 50 calories fewer daily than he expends. After four months, he has dropped about 1½ pounds from his already light frame. Over time, a chronic energy imbalance results in a change in body weight. Let's look at what is happening inside your body when an energy imbalance occurs.

Reducing Calories Can Lead to Weight Loss

Consuming fewer calories than you need daily will cause your body to draw upon its energy stores to overcome the deficit. Like Bryan, you will lose weight. In Chapter 4, you learned that when you don't eat for a period of time, glycogen and fat are used as fuel sources to meet your body's glucose and energy needs until your next meal or snack. Amino acids from the breakdown of body protein, particularly muscle, can also be used to make glucose.

In prolonged fasting, all of the glycogen in your liver is depleted. The breakdown of body fat contributes to your energy needs, while the breakdown of muscle provides materials to meet your glucose needs. Ketone bodies are also generated through the incomplete breakdown of fat, and these are used as an energy source. People at a healthy weight can't live much beyond 60 days of fasting, as their fat stores, as well as about one-third of their lean tissue mass, will be depleted by this time.[17]

Excess Calories Can Lead to Weight Gain

Eating more calories than you need, regardless of the foods they come from, will result in your body storing the excess as fat. Recall from Chapters 4 and 6 that you have limited capacity to store glucose as glycogen and that you can't store extra protein. However, you have unlimited capacity to store fat.

Although the relationship between eating too many calories and gaining weight appears straightforward, this isn't necessarily the case. The causes of overweight and obesity and the ability to prevent them can be complex, as there is more to eating than just nourishing the body. Let's look at this next.

Your body contains about 35 billion fat cells, which can expand to accommodate a surplus of calories.

The Take-Home Message When you don't eat enough calories to meet your needs, your glycogen and fat stores, as well as muscle mass, will be broken down for fuel. A chronic deficit of calories will produce weight loss. When you chronically consume more calories than you need, the excess will be stored as fat, and weight gain will occur.

What Factors Are Likely to Affect Body Weight?

Numerous factors influence weight management, starting with what and how often you eat. Physiology, genetics, and your environment also play a role. Let's look at how each of these can affect your body weight.

Hunger and Appetite Affect What You Eat

Recall from Chapter 3 that there is a difference between your physiological need for food (or hunger) and the psychological factors that prompt you to eat (your appetite.) Hunger is the physical need for nourishment that drives you to consume food. Once you start eating, hunger will subside as the feeling of **satiation** begins to set in. Satiation will determine how long and how much you eat. **Satiety** is the sensation that you feel when you have had enough to eat. Satiety determines the length of time between eating episodes.[18] An increase in satiety will delay the start of your next meal or snack.

> Being sleep deprived can increase your appetite by lowering the levels of leptin and increasing the amount of ghrelin in your body.

Your appetite is affected by hunger, as well as environmental factors, like seeing or smelling something that you think will taste good, your social setting, your stress level, and so forth. Hunger, in turn, is affected by many physiological mechanisms, as well as genetics. Both hunger and appetite ultimately affect what you eat.

Physiological Mechanisms Help Regulate Hunger

Various physiologic feedback mechanisms involving the mouth, stomach, intestines, and brain all work together to increase or decrease your hunger. For example, many hormones play a role. When your stomach is empty, the hormone **ghrelin,** which is produced mainly in the stomach, signals your brain that you need to take in food. Your body produces more ghrelin during fasting (such as between meals) in order to stimulate hunger, and it produces less after food is consumed. Another hormone, **leptin,** which is produced in fat tissue, helps regulate your body fat by affecting hunger. As your fat stores increase, leptin signals the brain to decrease your level of hunger and food intake.

Once food enters your mouth, sensory signals are sent to the brain that tell you whether or not to continue eating. The feedback mechanism is very much affected by your prior experience of tasting that food.[19] For example, a spoonful of your favorite ice cream is a pleasant stimulus, and your brain would encourage you to keep eating it. However, if you took a sip of sour milk, this stimulus would be unacceptable to the

satiation The feeling during eating that determines how long and how much you eat.

satiety The sensation that you feel when you have had enough to eat. It determines how long you will go between meals and/or snacks.

ghrelin A hormone produced mainly in the stomach that increases hunger.

leptin A hormone produced in fat tissue that helps regulate body fat by signaling the reduction of food intake in the brain and interfering with the storage of fat in the cells.

brain, especially if the last time you drank sour milk it made you sick. Your brain will instruct you to spit out the sour milk so that you don't swallow it.

Once food is in your stomach, other factors, such as the size of the meal, come into play. After you eat a large meal, your stomach becomes distended. This will signal the brain to decrease your hunger, and you will stop eating. A distended stomach also causes the release of **cholecystokinin,** a hormone that is associated with the feeling of satiation. Cholecystokinin will also decrease your hunger.[20]

When the food reaches your small intestine, the nutrients, protein, fatty acids, and monosaccharides all stimulate feedback to the brain to decrease your hunger. Once these nutrients are absorbed, the hormone insulin is released, which also causes the brain to decrease your hunger.[21]

Changes in your food intake can also cause changes in your hunger cues. If you suddenly decrease the size of your meals, you may feel an initial increase in hunger. If you continue eating smaller meals, your stomach adapts to the reduced quantity and the feelings of extreme hunger will diminish over time. After a while, a larger meal can make you feel extremely full and uncomfortable because your stomach has gotten used to smaller meals.[22] People sometimes refer to this effect as the "shrinking" of the stomach, but the organ itself does not get smaller.

In a perfect world, all these physiologic mechanisms, when recognized and responded to appropriately, would keep you in perfect energy balance. When you are hungry, you eat, and when you are satiated, you stop. The reality, however, is that many people override these mechanisms and end up in energy imbalance. Factors like genetics and the environment also affect how much energy you consume and expend.

Genetics Partially Determine Body Weight

Genetics has such a strong influence on your body weight that if your mother and father are overweight (BMI ≥ 25), your risk of becoming obese approximately doubles, and your risk triples if they are obese (BMI ≥ 30). If your parents are severely obese (BMI > 40), your risk increases fivefold.[23] Studies on separated identical twins raised in different home environments confirm this, as both twins showed similar weight gain and body fat distribution.[24]

Research suggests that genetic differences in the level or the functioning of some hormones can influence a person's body weight and appetite. For example, genetically high levels of ghrelin may cause some people to overeat and become obese.[25] Individuals who are genetically prone to being leptin deficient become massively obese, yet when they are given leptin, their appetite decreases and their weight falls to within a healthy range.[26] Ironically, many obese people have adequate amounts of leptin but the brain has developed a resistance to it, rendering its appetite control ineffective.[27] For these individuals, other mechanisms are coming into play that prevent leptin from functioning as a regulator of their appetite.

Genetics may also affect how calories are expended in the body by affecting **thermogenesis** (*thermo* = heat, *genesis* = origin), which is the production of heat in body cells. Genes may cause different rates of **nonexercise-associated thermogenesis (NEAT),** which is the energy you expend during fidgeting, standing, chewing gum, getting up and turning off the television, and other nonexercise movement throughout the day. When some individuals overeat, they are able to rev up their NEAT to expend some of the excess calories and are thus better able to manage their energy

People who share genes will often have similar body weights.

cholecystokinin A hormone released when the stomach is distended. It is associated with the feeling of satiation.

thermogenesis The production of heat in body cells.

nonexercise-associated thermogenesis (NEAT) The energy expenditure that occurs during nonexercise movements, such as fidgeting, standing, and chewing gum.

balance.[28] Many overweight individuals don't appear to have this compensatory mechanism.

Some researchers have described a genetic "set point" that determines body weight. This theory holds that the body fights to remain at a specific body weight and opposes attempts at weight loss. The body may even enable very easy weight gain in order to get back to this "set point" when weight is lost. In other words, a person's weight remains fairly constant because the body "has a mind of its own." Given that the weight of Americans has disproportionately increased over the last few decades relative to previous decades, this theory either isn't true or the set point can be overridden.[29]

Research also suggests that people with a genetic propensity to become overweight experience greater challenges to preventing obesity in an environment that is conducive to gaining weight. This relationship is referred to as a **gene-environment interaction.** To explain how these two entities interact with each other, researchers have used the analogy that genes load the gun but an obesity-promoting environment pulls the trigger.[30] For instance, if a person's lifestyle stays the same, his or her weight should remain fairly stable. However, if the environment shifts to make it easier to gain weight, the body will also shift, but it will shift upward. This means that an environment in which people can easily and cheaply obtain endless amounts of energy-dense food may be one of the biggest culprits in the current obesity epidemic. In one study, rats, which should genetically be able to maintain a healthy body weight, were shown to overeat and become fat when they had access to unlimited fatty foods and sweets.[31]

The same effect has been observed in human populations. For instance, Pima Indians of the southwestern United States have a high rate of obesity. Research comparing Pimas in Mexico with Pimas living in Arizona suggested that the environment promoted weight gain in this weight-susceptible population. The traditional Mexican Pimas whom the researchers studied lived an active lifestyle and ate a diet rich in complex carbohydrates and lower in animal fats than that of the "Americanized" Pimas in Arizona, who had a more sedentary lifestyle and fatty diet. The overweight Mexican Pimas, on average, had a BMI of about 25, compared with the obese Arizona Pimas, who had, on average, a BMI of over 33.[32] The traditional Pimas had a better chance of avoiding obesity because they lived in a healthier environment. As this study suggests, even if you have a genetic predisposition to being overweight, it's not a done deal. If you are determined to make healthy dietary choices and engage in regular physical activity, you can "outsmart" your genes.

Environmental Factors Can Increase Appetite and Decrease Physical Activity

How many times have you eaten a satisfying meal before going to the movies, but bought a bucket of popcorn at the theater anyway? You didn't buy the popcorn because you were hungry. You just couldn't resist the buttery smell and the allure of munching during the film. Environmental factors don't just affect people who are genetically prone to being overweight—anyone can fall prey to an environment that encourages them to eat! In fact, there are many stimuli in the environment that can drive your appetite. In addition to aromas and certain venues such as movie theatres, events such as holidays and sporting events, people such as your friends and family, and even the convenience of obtaining food can all encourage you to eat even when you're not hungry.

gene-environment interaction
The interaction of genetics and the environment that increases the risk of obesity in some people.

Does Your Environment Affect Your Energy Balance?

1. Do you eat out at least once a day?
   Yes ☐ No ☐

2. Do you often buy snacks at convenience stores, coffee shops, vending machines, sandwich shops, or other eateries?
   Yes ☐ No ☐

3. Do you buy the largest portions of fast foods or snacks because you think you're getting more for your money?
   Yes ☐ No ☐

4. When you order pizza, do you have it delivered?
   Yes ☐ No ☐

5. Do you drive around the parking lot to get the closest parking space to the entrance?
   Yes ☐ No ☐

6. Do you get off at the subway or bus stop that is nearest to your destination?
   Yes ☐ No ☐

7. Do you take the elevator when stairs are available in a building?
   Yes ☐ No ☐

8. Do you e-mail or call your friends and neighbors rather than walk next door to talk to them in person?
   Yes ☐ No ☐

Answers

All of the habits listed above contribute to an obesity-promoting environment. If you answered yes to more than half, you should think about how you can improve your lifestyle habits.

The size of the average dinner plate has increased by more than 35 percent since 1960. The larger the plate, the more food it will hold, and the more food you will likely consume.

Over the past few decades, the environment around us has changed in ways that have made it easier for many of us to incur an energy imbalance and a propensity to gain weight. Take the Self-Assessment "Does Your Environment Affect Your Energy Balance?" to reflect upon how your environment may influence the lifestyle decisions that you make throughout your day.

Let's look at some environmental issues that are feeding Americans' energy imbalance.

We Work More and Cook Less

One reason Americans are getting larger is that they often aren't eating at home. Research shows that adults today spend more time traveling to work and devote more of their daily hours to work than in previous decades.[33] This longer workday means there is less time to devote to everyday activities, such as food preparation.

Today, almost one-third of Americans' daily calories come from ready-to-eat foods that are prepared outside the home.[34] Between 1972 and 1995, the prevalence of eating out in the United States increased by almost 90 percent, a trend that is expected to increase steadily to the year 2020.[35] To accommodate this demand, the number of eateries in the United States has almost doubled, to nearly 900,000 food-service establishments, during the last three decades.[36]

Dining out frequently is associated with a higher BMI.[37] The top three foods selected when eating out, especially among college-aged diners, are energy-dense french fries, hamburgers, and pizza. Less energy-dense, waist-friendly vegetables, fruits, and salads didn't even make the top five choices on the list among college-aged diners. For many people, dining out often is harming their diet by making energy-dense foods too readily available and displacing less-energy-dense vegetables and fruits.

We Eat More (and More)

In the United States food is easy to get, there's a lot to choose from, and portion sizes are generous. All of these factors are associated with consuming too many calories.[38]

Years ago, people went to a bookstore for the sole purpose of buying a book. Now they go to a bookstore to sip a mocha latte and nibble on biscotti while they ponder which book to buy. Americans can grab breakfast at a hamburger drive-through, lunch at a fast-food court, a sub sandwich at many gas stations, and a three-course meal of nachos, pizza, and ice cream at a movie theater. At any given moment of your day, you can probably easily find a bundle of calories to consume.

This access to a variety of foods is problematic for weight-conscious individuals. While the appeal of a food diminishes as it continues to be eaten (that is, the first bite will taste the best, but each subsequent bite loses some of that initial pleasure), having a variety of foods available allows the eater to move on to another food once boredom sets in.[39] The more good-tasting foods that are available, the more a person will eat. For example, during that three-course meal at the movie theater, once you're tired of the nachos, you can move on to the pizza, and when that loses its appeal, you can dig into the ice cream. If the pizza and ice cream weren't available, you would have stopped after the nachos and consumed fewer calories.

As you learned from Chapter 2, the portion sizes of many foods, such as french fries and sodas, have doubled, if not tripled, compared with the portions listed on food labels. Because the larger portions often cost only slightly more than the regular size, they are perceived as bargains by the consumer. Research shows that people tend to eat more of a food, and thus more calories, when larger portions are served.[40]

When serving yourself at home, the size of the serving bowl or package of food influences the amount of the food you put on your plate. Serving yourself from a large bowl or package has been shown to increase the serving size by more than 20 percent.[41] This means that you are more likely to scoop out (and eat) a bigger serving of ice cream from a half-gallon container than from a pint container. To make matters worse, most people don't compensate for these extra calories by reducing the portions at the next meal.[42]

Research has shown that women who dine out five or more times weekly consume close to 300 calories more on dining-out days than do women who eat at home.

We Sit More and Move Less

Americans are not only eating more calories—about 300 calories more daily since 1985—but they are expending less energy during their day.[43] The resulting increase in "calories in" and decrease in "calories out" is a recipe for an energy imbalance and weight gain. Compared with years past, Americans are expending less energy both at work and during their leisure time.

When your great-grandparents went to work in the morning, chances are good they headed out to the fields or off to the factory. Your parents and older siblings, though, are more likely to go to an office and sit in front of a computer, and you yourself probably sit at a desk for much of your day. This shift in work from jobs that required manual labor to jobs that are more sedentary has been shown to increase the risk of becoming overweight or obese.[44] One study found that men who sit for more than 6 hours during their workday are at higher risk of being overweight than those who sit for less than an hour daily.[45] Technology in the workplace now allows us to communicate with everyone without having to leave our desks. This means that people no longer have to get up and walk to see the colleague down the hall or the client across town. Researchers estimate that a 145-pound person expends 3.9 calories for each minute of walking, compared with 1.8 calories per minute sitting. Thus, walking 10 minutes during each workday to communicate in person with coworkers would expend 10,000 calories annually, yet only about 5,000 calories would be expended if the person sat in the office sending e-mails or calling colleagues on the phone.[46]

Labor-saving devices have also affected energy expenditure outside of work. Driving short distances is now the norm, while walking and biking have decreased over the years.[47] Dishes aren't washed by hand but are stacked in a dishwasher.[48] The labor saved by these devices adds up, and the cumulative daily savings of energy expenditure can be more than 100 calories (about the amount in that handful of cheese curls Pam likes to eat).[49] As technology continues to advance and allows you to become more energy efficient in your work and lifestyle habits, you need to offset this conservation of energy with *planned* physical activity at another time of the day.

More than half of Americans do not accumulate even the recommended minimum of 30 minutes of moderate-intensity activity on most days weekly.[50] In fact, more than 20 percent of Americans report no leisure-time physical activity daily, due partly to the fact that leisure and social activities have become more sedentary.[51] Americans are spending more time than ever with their televisions, computers, and mobile phones, with television remaining the dominant screen, watched more than 142 hours a month.[52] Young adults in particular have increased their "screen time," due in part to a growing trend for watching videos on handheld mobile devices.[53]

Increased amounts of "screen time" are contributing to decreased amounts of physical activity.

We are moving less during both work and play. With less energy being expended, weight gain is becoming easier and the need for weight loss even greater. Combine

**Less in-home food preparation
More dining out**

**Larger portion sizes
More energy-dense foods**

Higher calorie intake

Lack of physical activity

**Weight gain
Higher BMI**

Figure 10.7 Environmental Factors of Weight Gain
This flowchart shows how eating out more often leads to consuming larger portion sizes of energy-dense foods, which leads to intake of excess calories. Combine this with less physical activity and the result is weight gain and a higher BMI.

this with an environment that is conducive to eating and with the genetic makeup of many Americans, and it's not difficult to see why many people are becoming overweight or obese (**Figure 10.7**). Many Americans have to begin making conscious diet and lifestyle changes that will help them lose weight, or at the very least, prevent further weight gain.

Let's look at what is a realistic amount of weight to lose and how to do it healthfully.

The Take-Home Message Your appetite is your desire to eat and is affected by hunger, satiation, and satiety. It is influenced by physiologic mechanisms, your genes, and your environment. Physiological mechanisms, such as hormones, signal your brain to increase your hunger when you are hungry and decrease it after you have eaten. Genetics can make it more difficult for some individuals to manage their weight. The current environment—which provides easy access to a variety of excessive amounts of energy-dense foods and at the same time decreases energy expenditure—encourages obesity.

How Can You Lose Weight Healthfully?

According to the National Institutes of Health, overweight individuals should aim to lose about 10 percent of their body weight over a six-month period.[54] This means that the goal for an overweight 180-pound person should be to shed 18 pounds over six months, about 3 pounds a month, or ¾ pound weekly. Because a person must have an energy deficit of approximately 3,500 calories over time to lose a pound of fat, a deficit of 250 to 500 calories daily will result in a weight loss of about ½ to 1 pound weekly. This is a healthy rate of weight loss that you can sustain. Although fad diets promise dramatic weight loss "overnight," don't be fooled. These plans are not based on legitimate science, and some can endanger your health. We'll talk more about fad diets in the feature box "Fad Diets Are the Latest Fad."

Although there is no single diet approach that has been universally embraced, many health experts agree that a person needs to adjust three areas of life for successful, long-term weight loss (**Figure 10.8**):

➤ Diet
➤ Physical activity
➤ Behavior modification

Let's start with the diet.

Eat Smart, Because Calories Count

When it comes to losing weight, you need to remember two important words: *calories count*—no matter where they come from. Because an energy imbalance of too many calories in and not enough calories out causes weight gain, reversing the imbalance will cause the opposite. That is, taking in fewer calories and burning off

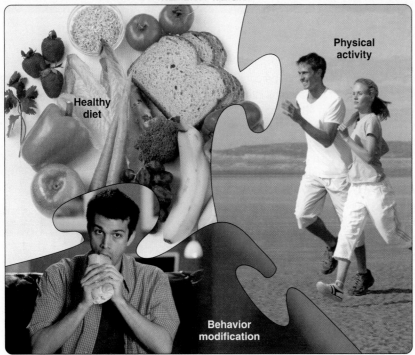

Figure 10.8 Three Pieces of the Long-Term Weight-Loss Puzzle
Diet, physical activity, and behavior modification are all necessary for long-term weight management.

more will result in weight loss. However, cutting back too drastically on calories often results in a failed weight-loss attempt. If a person skips meals or isn't satiated at each meal because of skimpy portions, the person will experience hunger between meals and be more inclined to snack on energy-dense foods. Thus, a key strategy during the weight-loss process is for the person to eat a healthy, balanced diet that is not only lower in calories, but is also *satisfying*. One way you can add heft and satiation to your lower calorie meals is by including higher-volume foods.

Eat More Vegetables, Fruit, and Fiber

People tend to eat the same amount of food regardless of its energy density—that is, the amount of calories in the meal.[55] In other words, you need a certain volume of food in order to feel full. As you learned in Chapter 4, it is very easy to overeat energy-dense, low-volume foods such as candy, which can easily fill you *out* before they fill you *up*. You'll overeat them before you become satiated. The reverse of this— eating high-volume, low-energy-density foods that fill you up before they fill you out—can help in weight management. High-volume foods include fruits and vegetables, which are bulked up because of their water content, and whole grains, which contain a lot of fiber. These foods are also low in fat (which contains 9 calories/gram) and high in carbohydrate (which contains only 4 calories/gram.) Research shows that these foods are associated with increased satiety and reduced feelings of hunger and calorie intake.[56]

In fact, consuming a large, high-volume, low-energy-density salad before a meal can reduce the calories eaten at that meal by more than 10 percent.[57] Adding vegetables to sandwiches and soups will increase both the volume of food consumed and

Fad Diets Are the Latest Fad

Americans spend more than $30 billion annually on weight-loss programs, products, and pills, and are more than willing to keep reaching into their wallets for the next quick diet fix.[1] Though it may seem that there is a new fad diet around every corner, many of these diets have actually been around for years.

The low-carbohydrate, high-protein and -fat diets of the 1970s (Dr. Atkins' Diet Revolution) were replaced by the very high-carbohydrate and very low-fat diets of the 1980s (Pritikin diets) and continued into the early 1990s (Dr. Ornish's diet). These diets led the way to the more carbohydrate-restricted, moderate protein and fat diets of the late 1990s (The Zone diet), only to flip back to the low-carbohydrate, high-protein and -fat diets in the early part of 2000s (Dr. Atkins' New Diet Revolution, South Beach). In the later part of the last decade, portion sizes and an emphasis on increasing whole grains, fruits, and vegetables in the diet became the talk of the diet scene. The tables "What's in the Fad Diets?" "The Cost of Dieting for a Week," and "Battle of the Diet Books" summarize how these diets compare with the DRIs, what they will cost you, and how they compare with each other.

After decades of clashing diet books, does one emerge as the clear winner in the battle of the bulge? The answer is no. Researchers who analyzed close to 200 weight-loss studies using a variety of these diets concluded that it's the calories, not the composition of the diet, that count when it comes to losing weight.[2] In fact, a study comparing the Atkins, Ornish, Weight Watchers, and Zone diets showed that no matter what diet the individuals followed, they all lost about the same amount of weight, on average, by the end of one year. Whereas each of these diets provides a different percentage of carbohydrates, protein, and fat, they all had one important thing in common: They all reduced calories.

A very interesting point emerged from this study: People who were most diligent about adhering to the diet—no matter which one—experienced the most weight loss. However, more than 20 percent of the dieters quit just two months into the study, and more than 40 percent of them dropped out after one year. The highest dropout rates occurred among followers of the Atkins or Ornish diets. The researchers speculate that the rigidity of these extreme diets may have caused the higher dropout rates.[3] Thus, the problem with many fad diets is that people give up on them long before they meet their weight-loss goals. A fad diet doesn't fix anything in the long term. If it did, there wouldn't be new (or recycled) fad diets continually appearing on the market. Some extreme diets may also be unhealthy in the long term. In fact, the high dropout rate for some fad diets has probably protected many individuals from serious ill health effects and long-term nutrient deficiencies.

Another problem with many commercial and fad diets is that they can be expensive. See the table on the next page for a comparison of the weekly food cost for several diet plans.

Marketers often make sensational claims about fad diets and weight-loss

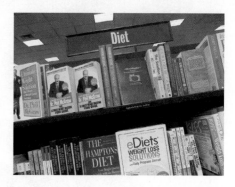

products. These red flags can often tell you if a diet is questionable.

Red Flags for Diet Hype

⚑ It's the Carbs, Not the Calories, That Make You Fat!

Many fad diet ads claim that you can eat as much protein and fat as you want as long as you keep away from the carbs. These diets claim that your consumption of pasta, breads, rice, and many fruits and vegetables should be limited, but fatty meats such as ribs, salami, bologna, and poultry with skin, as well as butter,

What's in the Fad Diets?			
	Percent of Calories from		
Type of Diet	**Carbohydrates**	**Protein**	**Fat**
Low carbohydrate, higher protein, high fat	<20	25–30	55–65
Example: Atkins diet			
Very high carbohydrate, moderate protein, very low fat	>65	10–20	<10–19
Example: Dr. Ornish's diet, Pritikin diet			
Carbohydrate-restricted, higher protein, moderate fat	40	30	30
Example: The Zone diet			
Compared to the DRI Recommendations	**45–65**	**10–35**	**20–35**

Source: Adapted from M. Freedman, J. King, and E. Kennedy, "Popular Diets: A Scientific Review," *Obesity Research* 9 (2001): 1S–40S.

The Cost of Dieting for a Week

Diet	Weekly Menu Cost ($)*
Jenny Craig	137.65
NutriSystem	113.52
Atkins Diet	100.52
Weight Watchers	96.64
Zone Diet	92.84
Ornish Diet	78.74
South Beach Diet	78.61
Slim-Fast	77.73
Sugar Busters	69.62
Subway sandwich	68.60
No diet	54.44

Source: Forbes, Fresh Direct, Amazon, Bureau of Labor Statistics.

*Includes the cost of associated book, if applicable, and any membership fees associated with the diet, averaged over a six-month period.

bacon, and cheeses should be on the menu often.

The Truth Behind the Hype

Diets that severely limit carbohydrates (<130 grams daily) eliminate so many foods, as well as sweets and treats, that it is impossible for a person not to consume at least 500 fewer calories daily. This will theoretically produce about one pound of weight loss per week.[4] When you curtail the carbohydrates, you likely will also be cutting back on fat.[5] When you stop eating the bagel (carbs), you'll also eliminate the cream cheese (fat) you slather on each half. Also, the monotonous nature of these diets causes people to become bored with eating, so they stop. Because the bread, mashed potatoes, and corn are off limits at dinner, the dieter is limited to fatty steak and not much else. Most people can only eat so much of this before it loses its appeal, so they're likely to stop eating sooner. As always, putting down the fork will cut calorie consumption.

Buyer Beware

A diet high in saturated fat and low in fiber and phytochemicals because it is low in whole grains, fruits, and vegetables is a recipe for heart disease, cancer, constipation, elevated blood cholesterol levels, and deficiencies in many vitamins and minerals, such as vitamins A, E, and B_6, folate, calcium, iron, zinc, and potassium.[6] So each time you follow a diet low in whole grains, fruits, and vegetables and high in animal fats, you are robbing your body of the protection of plant foods and overfeeding it the wrong type of fat. The high protein content of these diets may also cause the loss of calcium, and thus increase the risk of osteoporosis, as well as kidney stones (see Chapter 6).

🏳 Lose Seven Pounds in One Week!

Many diets guarantee rapid weight loss. This may happen on a low-carbohydrate diet—but only during the first few days, and only temporarily.

The Truth Behind the Hype

The 4- to 7-pound weight loss during the first week of low-carbohydrate dieting is due to loss of body water that results from two physiological processes. First, because the reduced amount of carbohydrates can't support the body's need for glucose, the stored glycogen in the liver and muscle will be broken down. Each gram of glycogen removed from storage causes the loss of 2 grams of water with it. Because you store about 500 grams of glycogen in your body, you can expect to lose approximately 2 pounds of water weight during the first week of a low-carbohydrate diet. Secondly, the ketone bodies generated by the breakdown of fat are lost from the body through the kidneys. This will also cause the body to lose sodium. As you know from Chapter 8, where sodium goes, water follows. Therefore, the ketone bodies that cause you to lose sodium will also cause you to lose water.[7]

Buyer Beware

Though water weight may be lost during the first week, the rate of weight loss after

that will be determined by the energy imbalance in the body, as in any calorie-reducing diet. As soon as carbohydrates are added back to the diet, the body will retain water and some water weight will come back on. When it comes to shedding weight, quick loss usually means quick regain.

🏳 Celebrity-Endorsed Miracle Weight-Loss Products with a Money-Back Guarantee!

Just because a celebrity actor or model tries to sell you a product doesn't mean that the product is valid. It just means that the celebrity is being paid to do what he or she does best: act.

The Truth Behind the Hype

No cream, shake, or potion will magically melt away body fat, and many marketers who claim that their products do this end up paying millions of dollars in fines to the Federal Trade Commission (FTC) for public deception.[8]

Buyer Beware

Forget about getting your money back. The FTC has received numerous complaints from dissatisfied customers who have unsuccessfully tried to get a refund. The more miraculous the claim, the more likely you are to lose (money, that is, not weight).

🏳 Naturally Occurring Plants, Herbs, and Other Substances Will Help You Lose Weight Without Risk!

"Natural" substances, such as glucomannan, guar gum, chitosan, and bitter orange are not necessarily safer or more effective for weight loss.

The Truth Behind the Hype

Glucomannan is a compound found in the root of the starchy konjac plant, and guar gum is a type of dietary fiber found in a specific bean. Both are ineffective in weight loss. Chitosan is produced from a substance found in shellfish. Though the claim is that these substances decrease

(continued)

Fad Diets Are the Latest Fad (continued)

Battle of the Diet Books

Name	Claim	What You Eat
South Beach Diet Super-charged (2008) by Arthur Agatston, MD, with Joseph Signorile, PhD	It will help you burn more calories and fat in less time to lose weight (especially belly fat), decrease cravings for sugary and starchy carbs, lower blood sugar and cholesterol levels, and improve overall health. Like the original *South Beach Diet*, this version guides readers to choose high-fiber carbohydrates found in vegetables, fruits, and whole grains, healthy unsaturated fats, lean sources of protein, and low-fat dairy.	Yes: Seafood, chicken breast, lean meat, low-fat cheese, most veggies, nuts, oils; (later) whole grains, most fruits, low-fat milk or yogurt, beans Less: Fatty meats, full-fat cheese, refined grains, sweets, juice, potatoes
The New Atkins for a New You (2010) by Eric C. Westman, MD, Ph.D., Jeff S. Volek, and Eric C. Westman.	A low-carb diet is the key to weight loss (and good health) because carbs cause high insulin levels.	Yes: Seafood, poultry, meat, eggs, cheese, salad veggies, oils, butter, cream; limited amounts of nuts, fruits, wine, beans, veggies, whole grains Less: Sweets, refined grains, milk, yogurt
Enter the Zone (1995) by Barry Sears	Eating the right mix of the right fats, carbs, and protein keeps you trim and healthy by lowering insulin.	Yes: Seafood, poultry, lean meat, fruits, most veggies, low-fat dairy, nuts Less: Fatty meats, full-fat dairy, butter, shortening, grains (limited), sweets, potatoes, carrots, bananas
The Flat Belly Diet (2008) by Liz Vaccariello and Cynthia Sass	Eat certain foods and get a flat belly, along with weight loss of up to 15 pounds in 32 days.	1,600 calories per day broken down into four 400-calorie meals spaced out every four hours. Each meal contains a monounsaturated fat, which is the diet's "secret food" for melting away belly fat. Meals and snacks emphasize whole grains, fruits, vegetables, nuts, seeds, beans, and lean protein similar to a Mediterranean-style diet.
You, On a Diet (2007) by Michael F. Roizen, MD, and Mehmet C. Oz, MD	By understanding how the body works in terms of fat burning and fat storage, you can shave inches off your waistline and learn how to "diet smart and not hard." The diet also claims that a two-week rebooting program will help you lose up to two inches within two weeks.	Approximately 1,700 calories via three meals a day, plus two to three snacks and dessert every other day. Yes: Whole grains, nuts, lean meats and fish; for beverages, water, seltzer, skim milk, tea, and up to two diet sodas a day are allowed, as well as up to eight ounces of fruit or vegetable juice fortified with calcium and vitamin D and up to one alcoholic beverage a day. Less: Foods that contain high-fructose corn syrup and other simple sugars (using some table sugar, maple sugar, and honey in recipes is allowed), saturated fats such as butter and tropical oils, *trans* fats, and enriched and other flours that are not 100 percent whole grain or whole wheat.

the absorption of fat in the body, research doesn't back up the claim. Bitter orange is a plant that is being touted as a substitute for ephedra (see the medications listed in the box "Extreme Measures for Extreme Obesity" on page 388, yet the research is not definitive on its ability to stimulate weight loss.[9]

Buyer Beware

Guar gum has been shown to cause diarrhea, flatulence, and gastrointestinal dis-

Is the Science Solid?	Is the Diet Healthy?	Worst Feature	Most Preposterous Claim
Healthier version of Atkins diet that's backed by solid evidence on fats and heart disease.	Pro: Mostly healthy foods.	Restricts carrots, bananas, pineapple, and watermelon.	You won't ever be hungry (despite menus that average just 1,200 calories a day).
Low-carb "bible" overstates the results of some studies and doesn't mention studies that show people lost more weight after 6—but not 12—months on Atkins than on a typical diet. Doesn't mention high dropout rate of followers or small studies.	Con: Too much red meat may raise risk of colon or prostate cancer. Con: Lack of enough fiber, vegetables, and fruits may raise risk of heart disease, stroke, cancer, diverticulosis, and constipation.	Long-term safety not established.	Recommends approximately a pound of protein-rich foods such as meat, poultry, and fish, daily.
Exaggerates evidence that the Zone diet is the key to weight loss and implies that the diet can cure virtually every disease.	Pro: Mostly healthy foods. Con: Few recipes or menus.	May convince people to use the diet to treat cancer, AIDS, chronic pain, impotence, depression, and arthritis.	"I believe that the hormonal benefits gained from a Zone-favorable diet will be considered the primary treatment for all chronic disease states, with drugs being used as secondary backup."
No solid research to prove that monounsaturated fats, stress, or sleep are linked to a reduction in belly fat as this diet claims.	Pro: Mostly healthy foods. Con: While calories of meals are controlled at 400, nutrient content can vary. Fat can contribute up to 40% of your intake, exceeding the recommended 20–35% calories from fat.	Before starting the 28-day diet, a 1,200–1,400-calorie anti-bloating, jump-start diet is required for 4 days to "help you feel better and get rid of that sluggish feeling."	Losing 15 pounds in 32 days is likely not achievable for most people, except when most of the weight loss is water and not primarily body fat. To lose 15 pounds of body fat, you would have to burn off nearly 1,700 calories per day! Most people would not achieve this, especially when exercise is *optional* on this diet.
Successfully simplifies much of the science about how the body works as well as the health perils of having too much body fat (especially in the abdominal region). In addition to outlining a sensible dietary pattern, the authors also acknowledge the importance of exercise to achieve and maintain a healthy body weight.	Pros: Encourages a healthful, albeit idealistic way of eating that can promote both weight loss and improved overall health. Cons: Because the menu plans do not include many of the refined foods people in America commonly consume, following the plan may make people feel they have to eat very differently than they normally do to lose weight. This can make following the program a challenge over the long term.	Includes few low-fat dairy foods and other nondairy sources of calcium, which can make it tough for many people to meet their calcium and vitamin D needs without supplementation.	None

Source: D. Schardt. Adapted from *Nutrition Action Healthletter* (January/February 2004): 6–7, American Dietetic Association, Consumer Diet and Lifestyle Book Reviews. Available at www.eatright.org/Media/content.aspx?id=264&terms=diet+book. Accessed and updated July 2010.

turbances. Chitosan may cause nausea and flatulence.[10] Bitter orange can increase blood pressure and interfere with the metabolism of other drugs in the body.[11] Naturally occurring substances are not necessarily safe to consume, and there's no evidence that they help you lose weight.

3/4 cup chicken broth: **29** calories
1/2 cup chicken (white meat): **106** calories
1 cup noodle: **212** calories

347
total calories

2 slices whole wheat bread: **138** calories
4 oz ham: **125** calories
2 oz American cheese: **213** calories

476
total calories

3/4 cup chicken broth: **29** calories
1/2 cup chicken (white meat): **106** calories
1/2 cup noodles: **106** calories
1/2 cup mixed vegetables: **59** calories

300
total calories

2 slices whole wheat bread: **138** calories
2 oz ham: **63** calories
1 oz American cheese: **106** calories
2 slices tomato: **7** calories
2 leaves Romaine lettuce: **10** calories

324
total calories

Figure 10.9 Adding Volume to Your Meals
Adding high-volume foods like fruits and vegetables to your sandwiches, soups, and meals can add to satiety and displace higher-calorie foods, two factors that can help in weight management.

meal satisfaction and help displace higher calorie items (**Figure 10.9**). If you are full after eating a sandwich loaded with vegetables, you'll eat less from the bag of energy-dense chips. This is important because you don't need to eliminate chips from your diet if you enjoy them. Any food—from chocolate to chips—can be modest in calories if you eat modest amounts. Table 10.3 on page 383 provides examples of low-, moderate-, and high-energy-density foods. See the Table Tips for ways to increase the volume of foods you consume, while decreasing your overall caloric intake.

Fiber also contributes to the bulk of vegetables and fruits and their ability to prolong satiety.[58] Overweight individuals have been shown to consume less dietary fiber and fruit than normal-weight people.[59] For these reasons, high-fiber foods, such as vegetables, fruit, and whole grains, are a key part of a weight-loss diet.

Include Some Protein and Fat in Your Meals

Of all the dietary substances that increase satiety, protein will have the most dramatic effect. Even though the mechanism is unknown, this is likely one of the reasons why high-protein diets tend to reduce hunger and can help in weight loss.[60] Because fat slows the movement of food out of the stomach into the intestines, it can also prolong satiety. Therefore, including some lean protein and fat in all meals and even with snacks can help increase satiety between meals.

However, you don't want to add high-saturated-fat foods such as whole milk and/or whole-milk cheese, fatty cuts of meat, and butter, because eating these foods to feel full will come at the expense of your heart. It would be better to add lean meat, skinless chicken, fish, nuts, and oils, which are kinder to a person's waist and heart. (Note: Unsaturated fat still contains 9 calories per gram, so excessive amounts of nuts and oils, even though these are heart healthy, can quickly add excess calories to the diet.)

Table 10.3 The Energy Density of Foods

Low

These foods provide 0.7 to 1.5 calories per gram and are high in water and fiber. Examples include most vegetables and fruits—tomatoes, cantaloupe, strawberries, broccoli, cauliflower— as well as broth-based soups, fat-free yogurt, and cottage cheese.

Medium

These foods have 1.5 to 4 calories per gram and contain less water. They include bagels, hard-cooked eggs, dried fruits, lean sirloin steak, hummus, whole-wheat bread, and part-skim mozzarella cheese.

High

These foods provide 4 to 9 calories per gram, are low in moisture, and include chips, cookies, crackers, cakes, pastries, butter, oil, and bacon.

Source: Adapted from the Centers for Disease Control and Prevention, "Can Eating Fruits and Vegetables Help People to Manage Their Weight?" 2005. Available at www.cdc.gov/nccdphp/dnpa/nutrition/pdf/rtp_practitioner_10_07.pdf. Accessed March 2010.

Look at the difference between the foods shown in **Figure 10.10**. The snack and dinner on the left are low in volume, but high in calories. The foods on the right are high in volume but have almost 500 fewer calories combined! These higher volume foods will be more satisfying for fewer calories.

Use MyPlate as a Weight-Loss Guide

Meals that contain a high volume of fruits and vegetables, whole grains, some lean protein, and modest amounts of fat are a smart combination for weight loss, so a diet that contains all the five food groups can be used to lose weight. Most importantly, this type of diet is well balanced and will meet your daily nutrient needs.

Reducing caloric intake a little at a time can add up to healthy weight loss. A 180-pound, overweight person who consumes 2,800 calories daily can reduce his or her intake to 2,400 to 2,600 calories for a calorie deficit of 200–400 calories per day. He or she will then lose 10 pounds in about three months. Small changes, like switching from full-fat to nonfat dairy products or replacing the afternoon soda with a glass of water, will contribute to this calorie reduction. Following the recommendations at ChooseMyPlate.gov to eat a variety of foods, but replacing higher-calorie foods with lower-calorie options within each food group, results in a satisfying diet while losing weight.

If this person added some extra physical activity, he or she could further increase that daily calorie deficit. Let's now look at the other side of the energy equation: energy expenditure.

Table Tips

Eat More to Weigh Less

Eat more whole fruit and drink less juice at breakfast. The orange will have more fiber and bulk than the OJ.

Make the vegetable portions on your dinner plate twice the size of your meat portion.

Have a side salad with low-fat dressing with your lunchtime sandwich instead of a snack bag of chips.

Order your next pizza with less pepperoni and more peppers, onions, and tomatoes. A veggie pizza can have 25 percent fewer calories and about 50 percent less fat and saturated fat than a meat pie.

Cook up a whole-wheat blend pasta instead of enriched pasta for your next Italian dinner. Ladle on plenty of tomato sauce and don't forget the big tossed salad as the appetizer.

Low-volume, high-calorie

16 oz Dunkin Donuts Coffee Coolata® with cream: **350** calories

460 total calories

Dunkin Donuts chocolate chunk cookie: **110** calories

Pizza Hut Pepperoni Lover's® Pizza 2 slices, large pizza: **570** calories

890 total calories

Cheese breadstick **320** calories

High-volume, low-calorie

Pop Secret Snack popcorn, 94% fat free, butter: **110** calories

180 total calories

16 oz Dunkin Donuts Hot Latte Lite made with skim milk: **70** calories

Pizza Hut Veggie Lover's® Pizza 3 slices, large pizza: **610** calories

676 total calories

1 cup Romaine lettuce: **8** calories
½ cup cherry tomatoes: **13** calories
½ cup sliced cucumbers: **7** calories
1 tsp light ranch dressing: **38** calories

Figure 10.10 The Volume of Food You Eat
Low-volume, high-calorie foods can be much less satisfying than higher-volume, lower-calorie foods.

Table Tips
Get UP and MOVE

The next time you want to chat with your dorm mate, skip the text message and go knock on his door.

Don't go to the closest coffee shop for your morning latte. Walk to the java joint that is a few blocks farther away.

Take a five-minute walk at least twice a day. A little jolt of exercise can help break the monotony of studying and work off some stress.

Accomplish two goals at once by scrubbing down your dorm room or apartment. A 150-pound person will burn about 4 calories for every minute spent cleaning. Scrub for 30 minutes and you could work off about 120 calories.

Offer to walk your neighbor's pet daily.

Move to Lose

Research shows that regular physical activity is associated with a healthier body weight. Some individuals may need to devote 45 minutes or more to participation in moderate-intensity activities daily to prevent overweight or to aid in weight loss for those who need to lose weight.[61] Moderately intense physical activity would be the equivalent of walking 3.5 miles per hour (Table 10.4). Regular physical activity can also displace sedentary activity such as watching television, which often leads to mindless snacking on energy-dense foods.[62] Going for a walk and expending calories rather than watching television while snacking on a bag of chips will provide caloric benefits beyond the exercise alone.

A way to assess if you are incorporating enough physical activity into your day is to count your steps (such as with a pedometer). Research suggests that accumulating 10,000 steps daily, which is the equivalent of walking 5 miles, can help reduce the risk of becoming overweight.[63] Americans, on average, accumulate only 900 to 3,000 steps daily.[64] To reach 10,000 steps, a conscious effort is needed by most people to keep moving. See the Table Tips for some ideas for fun ways to expend more energy during the day.

Break Bad Habits

Hannah, the freshman you read about at the beginning of the chapter, will be relieved to find out that a 15-pound weight gain is not inevitable for college freshmen. In fact,

Table 10.4

Calories Used During Activities

Moderate Physical Activity	Approximate Calories/Hour for a 154-lb Person*	Vigorous Physical Activity	Approximate Calories/Hour for a 154-lb Person*
Hiking	370	Running/jogging (5 mph)	590
Light gardening/yard work	330	Bicycling (> 10 mph)	590
Dancing	330	Swimming (slow freestyle laps)	510
Golf (walking and carrying clubs)	330	Aerobics	480
Bicycling (< 10 mph)	290	Walking (4.5 mph)	460
Walking (3.5 mph)	280	Heavy yard work (chopping wood)	440
Weight lifting (general light workout)	220	Weight lifting (vigorous effort)	440
Stretching	180	Basketball (vigorous)	440

*Calories burned per hour will be higher for persons who weigh more than 154 lbs (70 kg) and lower for persons who weigh less.
Source: Adapted from Centers for Disease Control and Prevention, *Dietary Guidelines for Americans 2005.*

research to support the "freshman 15" is rather slim. Some research has found that weight gain didn't occur at all or didn't occur in the majority of the students during the first semester (the length of the study) or the entire first year.[65] Other studies found that students gained less than 5 pounds, on average, and one of these studies showed that certain behaviors such as snacking in the evening, consumption of junk foods, and the number of meals eaten on weekends were associated with weight gain.[66]

If Hannah continues her new bad habits, however, including skipping breakfast and hitting the vending machine for a midmorning snack, she may find weight management during her freshman year to be an uphill struggle. She would benefit from some behavior modification.

Behavior modification focuses on changing the behaviors that contribute to weight gain or impede weight loss. Several behavior modification techniques can be used to identify and change poor eating behaviors. These techniques include self-monitoring the behaviors by keeping a food log, controlling environmental cues that trigger eating when not hungry, and learning how to better manage stress.[67]

Do you really know when, why, and what you eat? Understanding the habits and emotions that drive your eating patterns can help you change your less-than-healthy behaviors. Keeping a food log is one way to track the kinds of foods you eat during the day, when and where you eat them, your moods, and hunger ratings. You can use this information to minimize or eliminate the eating behaviors that interfere with weight management.

For example, if Hannah were to keep a food record, a typical day's log might be similar to the one in **Figure 10.11**. Her habits are common to people who struggle with their weight. A study of overweight women who typically skipped breakfast showed that once they started consuming cereal for breakfast, they indulged in less impulsive snacking.[68] Eating a bowl of high-fiber whole-grain cereal (approximately 200 calories) will likely appease Hannah's morning hunger and help her bypass her 11 A.M. vending machine snack of 270-calorie cookies and a 210-calorie sports drink. This one behavior change would not only save her 280 calories in the morning, but also reduce her added sugar intake and add more nutrition to her day. Similarly, adding a less-energy-dense salad

Wearing a pedometer, like the one shown here, can help you track your steps. Remember to aim for 10,000 steps per day.

The average weight gain between Thanksgiving and New Year's Day is about a pound. But many people don't lose this extra weight and add to it every year.

behavior modification Changing behaviors to improve health. Identifying and altering eating patterns that contribute to weight gain or impede weight loss is behavior modification.

Figure 10.11 Food Log

Keeping track of when, where, and what you eat, as well as why you ate it, can yield some surprising information. Do you think you sometimes eat out of boredom or stress, rather than because you're hungry?

Food Log

For: Jenna

Date: Monday, September 6

Food and drink	Time eaten	What I ate/ Where I ate it	Hunger level*	Mood †
Breakfast		Skipped it	3	G
Snack	11 a.m	Oreo cookies, PowerAde from vending machine during morning class.	5	E
Lunch	1:30 p.m.	Ham and cheese sandwich, 2 large M&M cookies in student union cafeteria.	4	B
Snack				
Dinner	6:30 p.m.	Hamburger, French fries, salad at kitchen table	4	F
Snack	7 p.m. to 10 p.m.	Large bag of tortilla chips and entire bag of Pepperidge Farm Milano cookies while studying at kitchen table	1	I

*Hunger levels (1–5): 1 = not hungry; 5 = super hungry

† Moods:
A = Happy; B = Content; C = Bored; D = Depressed; E = Rushed; F = Stressed; G = Tired; H = Lonely; I = Anxious; J = Angry

Table Tips

Adopt Some Healthy Habits

Don't eat out of boredom; go for a jog instead. If we ate only when hungry, we would probably be a lot leaner.

Food shop with a full stomach and a grocery list. Walking around aimlessly while hungry means you are more likely to grab items on a whim.

When you feel wound up or stressed, lace up those sneakers and go for a walk.

The next time you pass a difficult course, or get that long-awaited raise, reward yourself with something other than food. Instead of a celebratory dinner, buy a new book or some music, or spend time with friends.

Declare a vending machine–free day at least once a week and stop the impulsive snacking. On that day, pack two pieces of fruit as satisfying snacks.

at lunch could help increase her satiety and displace at least one of the cookies that she often eats with her sandwich.

Because studying for exams stresses her out and causes her to munch even though she isn't hungry, Hannah shouldn't study in her dorm, where she is surrounded by snacks, but should go to the campus library, an environment where eating is prohibited. Exercising before or after studying would be a healthier way to relieve her stress than eating her way through a bag of snacks.

Changing behaviors that have become unhealthy habits is another important piece of improving weight management. Individuals who eat "out of habit" and in response to their emotions need to replace this unnecessary eating to better manage their weight. The Table Tips lists some healthy behaviors that can easily be incorporated into your life.

The Take-Home Message For successful, long-term weight loss, people need to reduce their daily calorie intake, increase their physical activity, and change their behavior. Adding low-energy-density, high-volume vegetables, fruit, and fiber along with some lean protein and healthy oils to the diet can help in satiety and reduce unplanned snacking. Incorporating approximately 60 minutes of physical activity daily can help with weight loss. Changing unhealthy habits by restructuring the environment to minimize or eliminate the eating behaviors that interfere with weight loss can also help shed extra pounds.

How Can You Maintain Weight Loss?

You, or someone you know, may be familiar with the typical fad diet experience: the triumphant rush associated with the dropping of 10 pounds, the disappointment that sets in when 15 pounds is regained, then a new round of hope when 10 of them are re-shed. An estimated 90 to 95 percent of individuals who lose weight regain it within several years.[69] This fluctuation is known as **weight cycling,** and some research suggests that it can lead to problems such as hypertension, gallbladder disease, and elevated blood cholesterol levels, not to mention depression and feelings of frustration.[70]

Research suggests that weight cycling may not be as common as previously thought. A study of 800 people who lost weight showed that they were able to keep off at least 30 pounds for 5 years. These people were successful because they maintained their physical activity habits and positive behavior changes after they reached their weight goal.[71] They commonly limited the intake of fatty foods, monitored their calorie intake, and ate nearly five times a day, on average. (For many people, eating smaller meals allows them to avoid becoming ravenous and overeating at the next meal.) The majority of them weighed themselves weekly and maintained a high level of daily physical activity, expending the energy equivalent of walking four miles a day.[72] This suggests that weight loss can be maintained as long as the individual doesn't abandon the healthy habits that promoted the weight loss and revert to the unhealthy habits that caused the excess weight in the first place.

Physical activity can also help those who've lost weight close the "energy gap." After weight loss, a person will have lower overall energy needs, as there is less body weight to maintain. The **energy gap** is the difference in daily calories that are needed for weight maintenance before and after weight loss.[73] Researchers have estimated that the energy gap is about 8 calories per pound of lost weight.[74]

For example, someone who lost 30 pounds would need approximately 240 fewer calories a day to maintain the new, lower body weight. This person can eat 240 fewer calories, expend this amount of calories through added physical activity, or do a combination of both. Because the environment we live in seems to encourage eating more than discourage it, researchers feel that increasing daily physical activity is likely the easier way to close the energy gap.[75] *Adding* something (physical activity) to your lifestyle is often easier than *removing* something (calories). Individuals who lose weight are advised to engage in 60 to 90 minutes of moderate physical activity daily to maintain their weight loss.[76] Note that formerly obese individuals who've lost weight will still have more fat cells than lean individuals, and will always have a propensity for weight gain. Unfortunately, their metabolism is much more efficient in restoring fat deposits, and the large number of fat cells that shrank during weight loss are still there, ready to restore excess energy stores.

Some individuals are candidates for extreme treatment to help them shed their unhealthy excess weight. The feature box "Extreme Measures for Extreme Obesity" discusses treatment options for those with BMIs of greater than 40.

The Take-Home Message People who lose weight are most likely to keep it off if they maintain the positive diet and lifestyle habits that helped them lose the weight. Eating less and/or exercising more will help close the energy gap after weight loss.

eLearn

52 Steps (Tips) to Lose Weight

Want more diet, physical activity, and behavior modification tips? Visit Lose Weight in 52 Steps at http://people.bu.edu/SALGE/52_small_steps/weight_loss/index.html. The site provides weekly lifestyle tips to help you lose weight.

weight cycling The repeated gain and loss of body weight.

energy gap The difference between the numbers of calories needed to maintain weight before and after weight loss.

Extreme Measures for Extreme Obesity

People with a BMI greater than 40 fall into the category of **extreme obesity.** They are at such a high risk for conditions such as heart disease and stroke, and even of dying, that an aggressive weight-loss treatment is necessary. Treatments that go beyond eating less and exercising more, such as a very low-calorie diet, medications, and/or surgery, are often recommended. Let's look at each of these options.

A Very Low-Calorie Diet

On her television show in 1988, a very petite Oprah Winfrey beamed with joy after having lost 67 pounds using a **very low-calorie diet.** Oprah achieved her weight loss by consuming a liquid protein diet or *protein-sparing modified fast.* Such protein-rich diets provide fewer than 800 calories daily, are very low in or devoid of carbohydrates, and have minimal amounts of fat. They are designed to help individuals at high risk of disease drop a substantial amount of weight in a short amount of time. However, they are not a long-term solution. After consuming the diet for 12 to 16 weeks, the dieter is switched over to a well-balanced, low-calorie diet.

Very low-calorie diets have to be supplemented with vitamins and minerals

extreme obesity Having a BMI > 40.

very low-calorie diet or protein-sparing modified fast A diet of fewer than 800 calories per day and high in protein. These diets are very low in or devoid of carbohydrates and have a minimal amount of fat.

bariatric surgery Surgical procedures that reduce the functional volume of the stomach so that less food is eaten. Such surgeries are sometimes used to treat extreme obesity.

gastric banding A type of gastric surgery that uses a silicone band to reduce the size of the stomach so that less food is needed to feel full.

and must be supervised by a medical doctor, as they can cause dangerous electrolyte imbalances as well as gallstones, constipation, fatigue, hair loss, and other side effects. The National Institutes of Health doesn't recommend very low-calorie diets because well-balanced low-calorie diets are just as effective in producing a similar amount of weight loss after one year and are less dangerous.[12]

After all that effort, Oprah ultimately regretted her very low-calorie diet. "I had literally starved myself for four months—not a morsel of food—to get into a pair of size 10 Calvin Klein jeans," claims Oprah. "Two hours after that show, I started eating to celebrate—of course, within two days those jeans no longer fit!"[98] In 2005, Oprah reached her goal weight of 160 pounds and was convinced she knew how to maintain her new weight. Two years later her life started to become "unbalanced," which resulted in weight gain once again. By 2009, she had regained 40 pounds, putting her back up to the 200-pound mark.

Medication

Some prescription medications can help a person lose weight. The drugs either suppress the appetite or inhibit the absorption of fat in the intestinal tract. For example, the drug sibutramine (trade name Meridia) reduces hunger and increases thermogenesis, which increases energy expenditure. The drug can also increase a person's heart rate and blood pressure. Therefore, it may not be appropriate for those who have hypertension, which tends to occur often in overweight individuals. In fact, because all drugs have side effects, their use must be monitored by a doctor.

Orlistat (trade name Xenical; recall that this drug is discussed in Chapter 3) inhibits an intestinal enzyme that is needed to break down fat. If it isn't broken down, the fat (and calories) will not be absorbed by the body. Up to about one-third of the dietary fat will be blocked and expelled in the stool. Orlistat has to be taken at each

In the 1980s Oprah Winfrey reached her goal weight by consuming a very low-calorie, liquid protein diet. She has since regained the weight, and often publicly discusses the challenges of maintaining a stable, healthy weight.

meal and should accompany a diet that provides no more than about 30 percent of its calories from fat. Because fat is lost in the stool, the drug can cause oily and more frequent stools, flatulence, and oily discharge.[13] Ironically, these side effects may help an individual adhere to a low-fat diet, as these effects are more pronounced if a high-fat meal is consumed. Today, a reduced-strength version of orlistat (trade name Alli) is approved for over-the-counter sale for adults 18 years and older. It is intended to be used in conjunction with a low-fat, low-calorie meal and regular exercise to treat obesity, and can have the same unpleasant side effects as the full-strength version. Because of the recent reports of rare, but serious, cases of liver damage in individuals using Xenical and Alli, both of these drugs must now carry warnings on their labels.[14]

Sometimes the side effects of weight-loss medications can be so serious that the medication must be withdrawn from the market. For instance, the FDA has prohibited the sale of supplements that contain ephedra (also called Ma huang), the plant source for ephedrine. Ephedrine has been shown to cause chest pains, palpitations, hypertension, and an accelerated heart rate. In 2003, baseball player Steve Bechler died at age 23 after taking a weight-loss supplement containing ephedrine during spring training. Ephedrine was determined to have contributed to his death.

Whereas individuals who take prescription medications to lose weight have been shown to lose as much as 20 pounds, these drugs should be coupled with, and can't replace, a lower-calorie diet, regular physical activity, and behavior modification for long-term weight loss.

Surgery

In 1998, approximately 13,000 obese patients went under the knife to reduce the size of their stomachs. By 2008, an estimated 220,000 people in the United Stated had **bariatric surgery.**[15] In one version of this surgery, the majority of the stomach is stapled shut. This reduces the size of the stomach so that it holds about ¼ cup of fluid. Food consumed leaves the small stomach pouch through a surgically

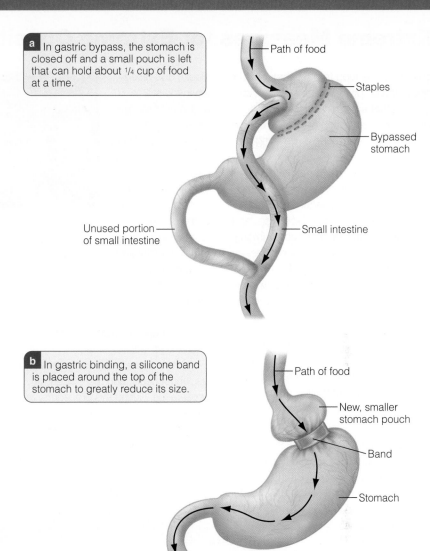

a In gastric bypass, the stomach is closed off and a small pouch is left that can hold about ¼ cup of food at a time.

Path of food

Staples

Bypassed stomach

Unused portion of small intestine

Small intestine

b In gastric binding, a silicone band is placed around the top of the stomach to greatly reduce its size.

Path of food

New, smaller stomach pouch

Band

Stomach

Gastric bypass and gastric banding.

Al Roker, NBC's *Today Show* weather man, lost approximately 140 pounds after gastric bypass surgery.

added intestinal loop that bypasses the original stomach and attaches directly to the small intestine. After the surgery, these individuals need to consume small, frequent meals because the stomach pouch can only expand to a maximum of about 5 ounces, the size of a woman's fist. Individuals not only eat less because of their smaller stomachs, but have higher levels of satiety and lower levels of hunger after the surgery. This effect on their appetite is thought to be associated with lower levels of ghrelin due to the loss of stomach area after the surgery.[16]

Because both the majority of the stomach and the upper part of the small

intestine are bypassed after the surgery, individuals can experience deficiencies of vitamin B_{12}, iron, and calcium. (Vitamin B_{12} needs intrinsic factor from the stomach to be absorbed, which is missing after surgery. Iron and calcium are typically absorbed in the upper part of the small intestine, which is now bypassed.) Supplements must be given because of these deficiencies.

A type of bariatric surgery that's becoming more popular is **gastric banding,** in which a silicone band is placed around the top of the stomach to create a small pouch with a very narrow opening at the

(continued)

Extreme Measures for Extreme Obesity (continued)

bottom for the food to pass through. This delays the emptying of the stomach contents so that a person will feel fuller longer. The doctor can adjust the opening of the pouch by inflating or deflating the band.

Although dramatic amounts of weight loss can occur and research has shown that incidences of hypertension, diabetes, high blood cholesterol levels, and sleep apnea have been reduced among people who've had the surgery, there are also risks involved. About 10 percent of those undergoing bariatric surgery experience complications such as gallstones,

ulcers, and bleeding in the stomach and intestines. Approximately 1 to 2 percent die.[17] After surgery, individuals need to be monitored long term by medical and nutrition professionals to ensure that they remain healthy and meet their nutritional needs. (See the Two Points of View at the end of this chapter for a discussion about the increasing trend of surgical weight loss methods for adolescents.)

Another type of surgery, **liposuction,** is less about health and more about physical appearance. During this procedure, a doctor removes subcutaneous fat from the abdomen, hips, or thighs (and sometimes other areas of the body) by suctioning it out with a penlike instrument. People often undergo liposuction to get rid of **cellulite,** which isn't a medical term, but refers to

Liposuction is a surgical procedure that removes subcutaneous fat. Unlike gastric banding or bypass surgeries, liposuction is purely cosmetic and does not result in health benefits.

the fat cells that give the skin a dimpled appearance. Complications such as infections, scars, and swelling can arise after liposuction. Fat can also reappear at the site where it was removed, so the results of liposuction may not be permanent.

liposuction The surgical removal of subcutaneous fat with a penlike instrument. Usually performed on the abdomen, hips, and thighs, and/or other areas of the body.

cellulite A nonmedical term that refers to fat cells under the skin that give it a ripplelike appearance. Contrary to popular belief, cellulite is no different from other fat in the body.

The Bottom Line

Very low-calorie diets, medications, and surgery may be viable options for those with extreme obesity, but they are not without risks. For those who are overweight, the safest route to a healthy weight is to make incremental diet and lifestyle changes to take in fewer calories and expend more calories. Of course, the best overall strategy for weight management is to avoid becoming overweight in the first place.

How Can You Gain Weight Healthfully?

For people who are underweight, weight gain can be as challenging and frustrating as losing weight is for an overweight individual. The major difference is that the thin person rarely gets sympathy from others. Like overweight individuals, those who are underweight experience an energy imbalance. In their case, however, they consume fewer calories than they expend.

People who want to gain weight need to do the opposite of those who are trying to lose weight. Whereas waist watchers hunt for the lower-calorie foods, individuals seeking to gain weight should make each bite more energy dense. These individuals need to add at least 500 calories to their daily energy intake. This will enable them to add about a pound of extra body weight weekly.

Of course, someone who wants to gain weight should not just load up on high-fat, high-calorie foods. The quality of the extra calories is very important. Snacking on an extra 500 calories of jelly beans will add 500 calories of sugar and little nutrition. Rather, these individuals should make energy-dense, nutritious choices from a variety of foods within each food group. For example, instead of eating a slice of toast

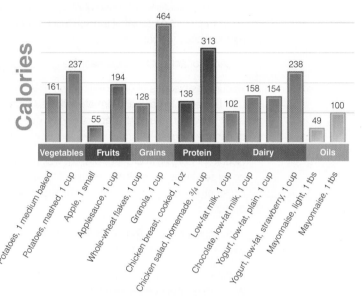

in the morning, they should choose a waffle. Adding coleslaw rather than cabbage will increase the calories in a salad-bar lunch more than tenfold. **Figure 10.12** contrasts more- and less-energy-dense foods within each food group. Eating snacks during the day will also add calories. The Table Tips provides easy and portable snack ideas.

The Take-Home Message People who want to gain weight need to add energy-dense foods to their diet so that they take in more energy than they expend. Adding nutrient-dense snacks between meals is an easy way to increase the number of calories consumed daily.

What Is Disordered Eating and What Are the Warning Signs?

Attaining a healthy weight, whether it means gaining or losing a few pounds, is a worthwhile goal that can result in lowered risk of disease and a more productive life. However, it's important to maintain your weight in a healthy way. Patterns of eating that involve severe calorie restriction, purging, or other abnormal behaviors can be severely damaging to health. Whereas disordered eating and eating disorders are sometimes thought of as psychological rather than nutrition-related topics, it's important to be aware of them and recognize their symptoms.

Table Tips

Healthy Snacks for Healthy Weight Gain

For healthy snacks that travel well and don't need refrigeration, try this: Stash an 8-ounce can or box of 100 percent fruit juice (about 100 calories) in your bag along with one of the 150-calorie snacks listed below for a quick 250-calorie snack (food and juice combined) between meals.

- Graham crackers, 5 crackers (2½ inches square)

- Mixed nuts, 1 oz

- Fig bars, 2-oz package

- Pudding, individual serving sizes, 4 oz

- Peanut butter on whole-wheat crackers (1 tbs peanut butter on 6 crackers)

Table 10.5

Diagnostic Criteria for Eating Disorders

Eating Disorder	Diagnostic Criteria
Anorexia nervosa	• Consistent body weight under the minimally normal weight for age and height (less than 85% of expected)
	• Intense fear of gaining weight or becoming fat, even though underweight
	• Disturbance in the way one's body weight or shape is experienced, excessive influence of body weight or shape on self-esteem, or denial of the seriousness of the current low body weight
	• Absence of at least three consecutive menstrual cycles
Bulimia nervosa	• Recurrent episodes of binge eating, which is characterized by eating larger than normal amounts of food in a short period of time, and a lack of control over eating during the binge
	• Recurrent purging in order to prevent weight gain, such as by self-induced vomiting, misuse of laxatives, diuretics, enemas, or other medications; fasting; or excessive exercise
	• The binging and purging occur, on average, at least twice a week for three months
	• Persistent overconcern with body shape and weight, which may influence self-esteem
Eating disorder not otherwise specified	• Disordered eating behaviors that do not meet the criteria for anorexia nervosa or bulimia nervosa, including binge eating disorder and night eating syndrome

Source: Adapted from the American Psychiatric Association, *Diagnostic and Statistical Manual of Mental Disorders,* 4th ed. (Washington, D.C.: American Psychiatric Association, 1994).

The term **disordered eating** is used to describe a variety of eating patterns considered abnormal and potentially harmful. Refusing to eat, compulsive eating, binge eating, restrictive eating, vomiting after eating, and abusing diet pills, laxatives, or diuretics are all examples of disordered eating behaviors. **Eating disorders,** in contrast, are diagnosed by meeting specific criteria that include disordered eating behaviors as well other factors (see Table 10.5). It is possible for someone to engage in disordered eating patterns without having an actual eating disorder. (T|F)

There are several different types of eating disorders that someone could develop, including anorexia nervosa, bulimia nervosa, binge eating disorder, and night eating syndrome. In the United States, approximately 11 million people struggle with eating disorders.[77] Adolescent and young adult females in predominantly white upper-middle- and middle-class families are the population with highest prevalence. However, eating disorders and disordered eating among males, minorities, and other age groups are increasing.[78] In fact, about 10 percent of all cases of anorexia nervosa and bulimia nervosa occur in men. And this may be an underestimate, as many men, as well as women, feel ashamed or embarrassed and may hide their problem. The prevalence of eating disorders among both males and females is probably higher than reported. Anyone can develop one of these conditions regardless of gender, age, race, ethnicity, or social status.

disordered eating Abnormal and potentially harmful eating behaviors that do not meet specific criteria for anorexia nervosa or bulimia nervosa.

eating disorders The term used to describe psychological illnesses that involve specific abnormal eating behaviors: anorexia nervosa (self-starvation), bulimia nervosa (bingeing and purging), binge eating disorder, and night eating syndrome.

No Single Factor Causes Eating Disorders

Although there is typically no one cause of disordered eating and eating disorders, there are certain factors that may increase one's risk for developing these conditions. Current research suggests that eating disorders are prompted by a complex network of sociocultural, genetic, and preexisting psychological factors (**Figure 10.13**).

Sociocultural Factors

Some researchers theorize that the higher prevalence of eating disorders in females is due in part to the greater societal pressure they experience to be thin and have a "perfect" figure. Thinness is too often associated with beauty, success, and happiness in our society, as evidenced by images in magazines and on billboards of fashion models and celebrities with abnormally low body weights. Many young women don't realize that these images have been digitally enhanced and do not depict the people as they appear in real life. Instead, they come to believe that extreme thinness is both possible and desirable and that they cannot be beautiful, successful, or happy unless they achieve it. These young women may feel such extreme body dissatisfaction that they try to lose weight at any cost, including engaging in disordered eating behaviors.

Genetic Factors

Researchers have not found a gene or genes that promote eating disorders; however, they theorize that a combination of genetic predisposition and environmental factors can increase an individual's risk. Certainly, eating disorders have been observed to "run in families." For example, an adolescent female has a greatly increased risk of developing an eating disorder if she has a sibling with an eating disorder, even if she does not live with that sibling.[79]

Psychological Factors

Depression and anxiety are common in people with an eating disorder, as is obsessive-compulsive disorder (OCD), a psychiatric illness characterized by intrusive thoughts that something bad will happen if a certain behavior is not repeated in a certain way. OCD is also more common in family members of people with an eating disorder.[80]

Although the highest rates of disordered eating patterns occur among females, males are not immune. Adolescents in particular can feel pressure to achieve a certain body image.

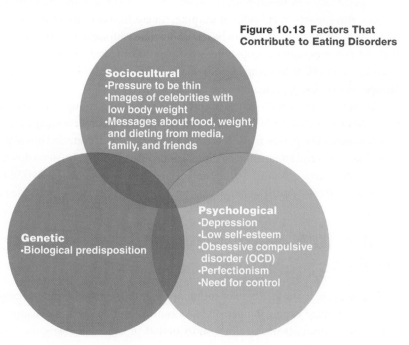

Figure 10.13 Factors That Contribute to Eating Disorders

Sociocultural
- Pressure to be thin
- Images of celebrities with low body weight
- Messages about food, weight, and dieting from media, family, and friends

Genetic
- Biological predisposition

Psychological
- Depression
- Low self-esteem
- Obsessive compulsive disorder (OCD)
- Perfectionism
- Need for control

Not only women but men diagnosed with eating disorders have higher rates of other psychiatric illness, compared with men who do not have eating disorders.[81]

A personality trait that can contribute to eating disorders is perfectionism, as an inability to reach unrealistic standards (such as in school or in athletic competition) can lead to a sense of failure and lowered self-worth. Many people who struggle with eating disorders are trying to gain some control in their lives. When external factors feel out of control, the person with an eating disorder gets a sense of security from being able to control food intake and body weight. Other common psychological factors include lack of self-esteem, high family expectations, and family dysfunction.

The most common eating disorders are anorexia nervosa, bulimia nervosa, binge eating disorder, and night eating syndrome. Let's take a look at each type of disorder and the characteristics that make each one unique.

Anorexia Nervosa Results from Severe Calorie Restriction

Anorexia nervosa is a serious, potentially life-threatening eating disorder that is characterized by self-starvation and excessive weight loss. People who suffer from anorexia nervosa have an intense fear of gaining weight or being fat. This fear causes them to control their food intake by restricting the amount of food they consume, resulting in significant weight loss.

Many people with anorexia nervosa have a distorted sense of body image and usually see themselves as fat even though they are underweight (you can read more about the concept of body image in the feature box "A Closer Look at Body Image"). This misperception of body size contributes to the behavior of restricting food intake in order to lose (more) weight. For instance, someone with anorexia nervosa might eat only a piece of fruit and a small container of yogurt during an entire day. They may also have a fear of eating certain foods, such as those that contain fat and sugar. They believe that these foods will make them fat, regardless of how much they eat. Some may also exercise excessively as a means of controlling their weight.

There are numerous health consequences that can occur with anorexia nervosa, and some can be fatal. One of the most serious health effects is an electrolyte imbalance, specifically low blood potassium, which can occur if someone with anorexia nervosa also engages in episodes of purging. An electrolyte imbalance can lead to an irregular heart rhythm, which can be fatal. Someone who's lost an extreme amount of body fat may experience a drop in body temperature and feel cold even when it is hot outside. In an effort to regulate body temperature, their body may begin to grow **lanugo** (downy hair), particularly on the face and arms.

Because someone with anorexia nervosa is not getting enough calories, the body begins to slow or shut down some processes in an effort to conserve energy for its most vital functions. The person may experience a decrease in heart rate and blood pressure, overall weakness and fatigue, and hair loss. The digestive process also slows down, which often results in constipation, bloating, and delayed gastric emptying. Dehydration, iron deficiency, and osteoporosis are also negative health effects caused by anorexia nervosa.

Bulimia Nervosa Involves Cycles of Binge Eating and Purging

lanugo Very fine, soft hair on the face and arms of people with anorexia nervosa.

Bulimia nervosa is another type of eating disorder that can be life-threatening. During times of binge eating, the person lacks control over eating and consumes larger than normal amounts of food in a short period of time. Following the binge, the

A Closer Look at Body Image

What Is Body Image?

Body image refers to the way that you perceive and what you believe about your physical appearance, whether you are looking in the mirror or picturing yourself in your mind.[18] Most people think of body image as being about body weight and shape, but it actually refers to any physical attribute such as skin color, hair texture, or height.

Body image can be further defined as having positive or negative characteristics. People with a positive body image view themselves as they truly are (no distortion) and overall feel comfortable and confident in and about their body. They engage in healthy eating and exercise behaviors and don't spend a lot of time worrying about weight, dieting, or changing their looks using extreme measures. They accept their body and don't define their self-worth based on physical appearances.[19] In contrast, those with a negative body image often have distorted views of the way they look and may view their shape as larger than they actually

are. This is especially true of people with anorexia nervosa. Additionally, they are ashamed, uncomfortable, or self-conscious about their physical appearance and spend a large amount of time focusing on their weight or looks that they perceive as unattractive. They often believe that only others are attractive.[20] A negative body image can contribute to the development or continuation of unhealthy behaviors, like eating disorders, in many individuals.

What Is Body Dysmorphic Disorder?

Body dysmorphic disorder (BDD) is a mental illness in which a person's preoccupation with minor or imaginary physical flaws causes significant distress or impairment in work, school, or other areas of functioning. BDD is estimated to affect slightly more than 2 percent of the U.S. population and frequently occurs along with other psychiatric disorders, such as obsessive-compulsive disorder, anorexia nervosa, and clinical depression.[21]

Muscle dysmorphia, also referred to as "bigorexia" or "reverse anorexia," is a specific type of BDD that typically occurs in males who have a well-defined muscular build but view themselves as being small or weak.[22] Symptoms of muscle dysmorphia include extreme exercise (especially weight lifting) and attention to diet, anxiety when missing a workout, constant mirror checking, use of anabolic steroids to enhance muscle mass, and neglecting family, friends, or work in order to exercise. Media influence on men and their muscle mass and size is thought to

be a major contributing factor in the increasing prevalence of muscle dysmorphia. Anyone with these symptoms should seek professional help and treatment, as they can get worse over time.

How Can You Attain a Positive Body Image?

Many factors can influence your body image, including family, friends, peers, media, and culture. We live in a society where certain images are labeled "ideal," yet are not achievable by most. Nonetheless, we strive to get the "perfect" body through any means necessary. Comparing our bodies to those of friends, models, and celebrities that we view as more attractive only leads to lowered self-esteem and feeling "not good enough."

The following are strategies to help you attain a positive body image:[23]

➤ Know and accept what determines your physical characteristics (genetics, stage of life, nutritional intake, activity levels)
➤ Avoid dieting and eat normally by responding to hunger and fullness cues
➤ Avoid comparing yourself to others, especially models and celebrities
➤ Recognize that you are a whole person and not just individual parts
➤ Respect yourself and others

body dysmorphic disorder
A mental illness in which a person is excessively concerned about and preoccupied by a perceived defect in his or her body.

Both men and women can experience issues with body image.

---

person counters the binge with some type of **purging.** Many people assume that bulimics purge by vomiting, but self-induced vomiting is only one form. Purging can be described as any behavior that assists in "getting rid" of food to prevent weight gain or to promote weight loss. This can include excessive exercise; abuse of diet pills, laxatives, or diuretics; and strict dieting or fasting.

Most of the health consequences that occur with bulimia nervosa are associated with self-induced vomiting, such as tears in the esophagus, swollen parotid glands,

purging Measures taken to prevent weight gain or lose weight after consuming food; examples include self-induced vomiting, laxatives, diuretics (water pills), excessive exercise, and/or fasting.

People with binge eating disorder often eat in secret.

tooth decay and gum disease (due to stomach acid), and broken blood vessels in the eyes (due to pressure from vomiting). Electrolyte imbalance also occurs with bulimia nervosa and can be fatal. People with bulimia nervosa may also experience dehydration and constipation due to frequent episodes of binge eating and purging.

Laxative abuse can also cause serious medical complications depending on the type, amount, and length of time the person has used them. Laxatives used repeatedly can cause constipation, dehydration due to fluid loss in the intestines, electrolyte imbalances, fluid retention, bloody stools, and impaired bowel function.

Binge Eating Disorder Involves Compulsive Overeating

Binge eating disorder is characterized by recurrent episodes of binge eating without purging. People who have binge eating disorder eat without regard to physiological cues. They may eat for emotional reasons, and feel out-of-control while eating. The overeating results in physical and psychological discomfort. Many people who struggle with this type of eating disorder will often eat in secret and feel ashamed about their behaviors.

The health effects of binge eating disorder are commonly those that are associated with obesity, because most people who struggle with binge eating disorder are of normal or heavier-than-average weight. Health effects may include high blood pressure, high cholesterol levels, heart disease, type 2 diabetes, and gallbladder disease.

Binge eating disorder has specific signs and symptoms. However, it does not have its own diagnostic criteria like anorexia nervosa and bulimia nervosa. Because binge eating disorder does not meet the diagnostic criteria for anorexia nervosa or bulimia nervosa, but still requires treatment, it falls into the diagnostic category of "Eating Disorders Not Otherwise Specified." Other behaviors in this category include purging without binging, restrictive eating by people who are in a normal weight range despite having significant weight loss, binging and purging but not frequently enough to meet criteria for bulimia, and chewing and spitting out food instead of swallowing it.

Night Eating Syndrome Is a Type of Eating, Sleeping, and Mood Disorder

People with night eating syndrome may consume more than half their day's calories between 8 P.M. and 6 A.M.

Night eating syndrome is described as an abnormal eating pattern in which a person consumes the majority of daily calories after the evening meal, as well as wakes up during the night, possibly even several times, to eat. In addition, the person typically does not have an appetite during the morning hours and consumes very little throughout the day. One study found that people with night eating syndrome consume 56 percent of their 24-hour calorie intake between the hours of 8:00 P.M. and 6:00 A.M. This study also found that people with night eating syndrome generally do not binge-eat with each awakening; rather, they eat smaller portions of food on several occasions throughout the night.[82] This disorder is most common among obese individuals, though people of normal weight can also develop night eating syndrome.[83]

Night eating syndrome appears to be a unique combination of disordered eating, a sleep disorder, and a mood disorder (see Table 10.6).[84] Research has shown that night eating syndrome is associated with low self-esteem, depression, reduced daytime hunger, and less weight loss among obese patients.[85] Stress also appears to be a contributing factor in the development and continuation of night eating syndrome.[86]

Table 10.6

Signs of Night Eating Syndrome

Sign	Explanation/Example
Morning anorexia	Not hungry in the morning, even if breakfast is eaten; eats very minimal amounts during morning and early afternoon hours
Eating during the night	Awakens to eat at least once a night, at least three nights a week, for at least three months; frequently consumes high-calorie snacks during awakenings
Eating after the last evening meal	At least 50% of daily caloric intake is consumed in snacks after the last evening meal

Someone may feel guilty, ashamed, or embarrassed while they are eating during the night, as well as the next morning.

There Are Some Common Signs of Disordered Eating

There are both physical and behavioral warning signs of eating disorders and disordered eating (Table 10.7). Hair loss is very common among people with anorexia nervosa and bulimia nervosa, as the body does not receive adequate nutrients for hair maintenance and growth. You may also notice significant weight changes, such as sudden weight loss in anorexia nervosa, and sudden weight gain in bulimia nervosa, binge eating disorder, or night eating syndrome. *Russell's sign,* which is scar tissue on the knuckles of fingers used to induce vomiting, is one indicator of bulimia nervosa. This is caused by scraping the knuckles when removing the fingers from the mouth during purging.

Self-Assessment

Are You at Risk for an Eating Disorder?

Check the appropriate box in the following statements to help you find out.

1. I constantly think about eating, weight, and body size. Yes ☐ No ☐
2. I'm terrified of being overweight. Yes ☐ No ☐
3. I binge-eat and can't stop until I feel sick. Yes ☐ No ☐
4. I weigh myself several times each day. Yes ☐ No ☐
5. I exercise too much or get very rigid about my exercise plan. Yes ☐ No ☐
6. I have taken laxatives or forced myself to vomit after eating. Yes ☐ No ☐
7. I believe food controls my life. Yes ☐ No ☐
8. I feel extremely guilty after eating. Yes ☐ No ☐
9. I eat when I am nervous, anxious, lonely, or depressed. Yes ☐ No ☐
10. I believe my weight controls what I do. Yes ☐ No ☐

Answers

These statements are designed to help you identify potentially problematic eating behavior. These statements do *not* tell you if you have an eating disorder. Look carefully at any statement you marked as yes and decide if this behavior prevents you from enjoying life or makes you unhealthy. Changing these behaviors should be done gradually, making small changes one at a time. Contact your student health services center or your health care provider if you suspect you need help.

Table 10.7

Warning Signs for Eating Disorders

Symptom	Explanation/Example
Weight is below 85% of ideal body weight	Refusal to accept and maintain body weight (even if it is within normal range).
Exercise excessively	Often exercise daily for long periods of time to burn calories and prevent weight gain. May skip work or class to exercise.
Preoccupation with food, weight, and diet	Constantly worry about amount and type of food eaten. May weigh themselves daily or several times per day.
Distorted body image	Do not see themselves as they truly are. May comment on being fat even if underweight.
Refusing to eat	Will avoid food in order to lose weight or prevent weight gain. May avoid only certain foods, such as those with fat and sugar.
Loss of menstrual period	Periods become irregular or completely absent.
Diet pill use or laxative use	Evidence of pill bottles, boxes, or packaging.
Changes in mood	May become more withdrawn, depressed, or anxious, especially around food.
Hair loss	Hair becomes thinner and falls out in large quantities.
Avoid eating around others	Want to eat alone. Make excuses to avoid eating with others.

People with disordered eating often avoid social situations because they know food will be present and do not feel comfortable eating around others. Preoccupation with food and body weight is also present among people with eating disorders, such as weighing several times each day or obsessively counting calories. They may also deny unusual eating behaviors if confronted about them.

What Can You Do If You Suspect a Friend Has an Eating Disorder?

Many people may know someone with an eating disorder, but may not know how to help them. Learning about eating disorders will help you understand why a friend or loved one can have destructive eating behaviors and be seemingly unaware of the damage, pain, or danger they can cause. You also need to know the warning signs so you can identify disordered eating behaviors that could progress into more serious eating disorders.

If you are concerned about someone, find a good time and place to gently express your concerns without criticism or judgment. Realize that you may be rejected or your friend may deny the problem. Be supportive and let these persons know that you are available if they want to talk to you at another time. You should also realize that there are many things that you cannot do to help a loved one or friend get better. You cannot force an anorexic to eat, keep a bulimic from purging, or make a binge eater stop overeating. It is up to the individual to decide when he or she is ready to deal with the issues in life that led to the eating disorder.

The best thing you can do is learn to listen. Find out about resources in your area for treating eating disorders so that you can refer someone there when that person is ready to get help. Some Web-based resources are listed on page 405.

The Take-Home Message Disordered eating is characterized by an abnormal eating pattern. Eating disorders include disordered eating behaviors and other specific criteria. Approximately 11 million people, including females, males, minorities, and predominantly upper- and middle-class individuals of all age groups, struggle with eating disorders. Eating disorders are prompted by a complex network of factors, including sociocultural, genetic, and preexisting psychological factors. The most common eating disorders include anorexia nervosa, bulimia nervosa, binge eating or compulsive overeating, and night eating syndrome. There are both physical and behavioral warning signs of eating disorders.

How Are Eating Disorders Treated?

The most effective treatment for eating disorders is a multidisciplinary team approach including psychological, medical, and nutrition professionals. All members of the team must be knowledgeable and experienced with eating disorders because it is a complex area that some health care professionals do not feel comfortable treating. A psychologist can help the person deal with emotional and other psychological issues that may be contributing to the eating disorder. Anyone who struggles with an eating disorder should be closely monitored by a physician or other medical professional, as some eating disorders can be life-threatening. A registered dietitian can help someone with an eating disorder establish normal eating behaviors.

Some nutritional approaches to eating disorders include identifying binge triggers, safe and unsafe foods, and hunger and fullness cues. Food journals are often helpful to identify eating patterns, food choices, moods, eating disorder triggers, eating cues, and timing of meals and snacks. Meals plans are also used in some instances to ensure intake of adequate calories and nutrients among those with anorexia nervosa, and to help avoid overeating among those with bulimia nervosa or binge eating disorder.

Most people can recover from eating disorders and may not have to struggle with it for the rest of their lives. When treatment is sought in the early stages, there is a better chance that the person will recover fully and have a shorter recovery process than someone who begins treatment after many years. Some people continue to have the desire to engage in disordered eating behaviors; however, they are able to refrain from actually doing these behaviors. Unfortunately, some individuals may never fully recover from an eating disorder. Caregivers must recognize that recovery is a process that often takes years and has no quick fix.

The Take-Home Message Eating disorders are most effectively treated with a multidisciplinary team of psychologists, physicians, and registered dietitians. Understanding food triggers and using food journals and nutritious food plans are key strategies in the treatment of eating disorders. A full recovery takes time but is possible, especially if the disorder is treated in the early stages.

Made Over, Made Better!

Eating on the run doesn't have to ruin your health. Many eateries are now offering a wide range of options for the health-conscious consumer—if you make the right selection. Try these options the next time you're eating on the fly!

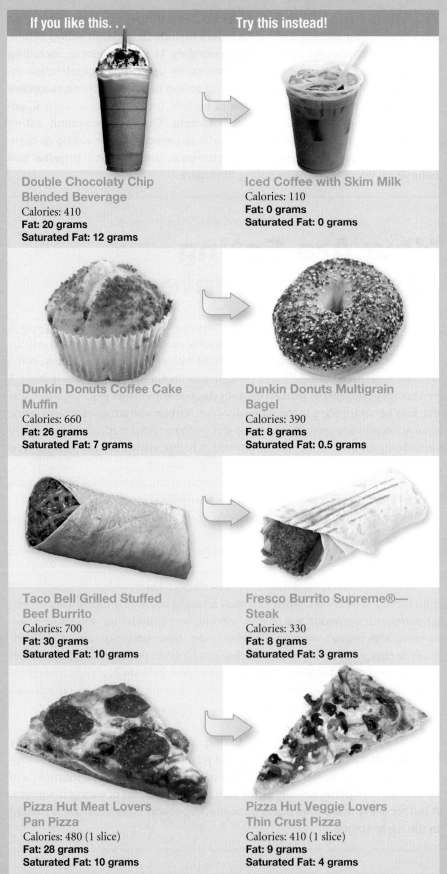

If you like this. . .

Double Chocolaty Chip Blended Beverage
Calories: 410
Fat: 20 grams
Saturated Fat: 12 grams

Dunkin Donuts Coffee Cake Muffin
Calories: 660
Fat: 26 grams
Saturated Fat: 7 grams

Taco Bell Grilled Stuffed Beef Burrito
Calories: 700
Fat: 30 grams
Saturated Fat: 10 grams

Pizza Hut Meat Lovers Pan Pizza
Calories: 480 (1 slice)
Fat: 28 grams
Saturated Fat: 10 grams

Try this instead!

Iced Coffee with Skim Milk
Calories: 110
Fat: 0 grams
Saturated Fat: 0 grams

Dunkin Donuts Multigrain Bagel
Calories: 390
Fat: 8 grams
Saturated Fat: 0.5 grams

Fresco Burrito Supreme®— Steak
Calories: 330
Fat: 8 grams
Saturated Fat: 3 grams

Pizza Hut Veggie Lovers Thin Crust Pizza
Calories: 410 (1 slice)
Fat: 9 grams
Saturated Fat: 4 grams

Source: USDA National Nutrient Database for Standard Reference.

Two Points of View

Is Gastric Bypass Surgery a Healthy Weight-Loss Measure for Obese Adolescents?

Gastric bypass surgery is the most commonly performed bariatric surgery in the United States.[1] By changing the digestive system, it limits the amount of food a person can eat.[2] In recent years, this type of surgery has been increasingly performed not just on adults, but also on adolescents[3].

Is this type of surgery a healthy weight-loss measure for young people? Or are the risks too great? Take a close look at the arguments for both sides and see what you think.

Yes

- The rate of childhood obesity has more than tripled in the last 30 years, leaving children at greater risk for a host of diseases, including cardiovascular disease and diabetes, at earlier ages.[4] Childhood obesity can also lead to depression and increased tendency toward risk-taking behaviors.[5]

- As with adults, gastric bypass surgery does have risks, and as a result is not for everyone. Only severely obese children, with a BMI in the 95th percentile and with other medical complications as a result of obesity, should be considered, and then only after all other weight-loss measures have failed.[6]

- A study has shown that gastric bypass did result in significant weight loss among adolescents with no negative effects on metabolism or growth.[7]

- Another study showed that surgery could actually reverse the effects of type 2 diabetes in obese adolescents.[8]

- As gastric banding becomes more commonly used among adolescents, outcomes are even better. One study found that 24 of 25 adolescent patients who underwent gastric banding lost more than 50 percent of their excess weight.[9]

No

- Children who are still growing run an increased risk of complications from gastric bypass surgery.[10]

- Because of the drastically reduced amount of food their bodies are taking in, adolescents are at a heightened risk of nutritional deficiencies, especially iron, which is normally absorbed through the duodenum, a section of the digestive tract that is bypassed in the surgery.[11]

- While children tend to dramatically shed excess weight during the first year after surgery, as with adults, the weight loss tends to slow over time; their BMI tends to level off in Year 2 at a point that remains above normal.[12]

- Some researchers fear that as weight-loss surgery for teenagers becomes more popular, some doctors—because they are either tempted by a potentially lucrative market or motivated by a sincere desire to help—will operate on patients who should not have the surgery.[13]

- Few studies have followed patients for more than about two years after surgery, and little research is available on the long-term outcomes of bariatric surgery in adolescents. Some patients are likely to have later complications that are not yet apparent.[14]

What do you think?

1. Imagine you had an obese child whom doctors recommended for surgery. What factors would come into play for you in deciding whether or not your child should have it? **2.** Do you think rates of gastric surgery among adolescents are likely to increase or decrease in the future? Explain your answer.

Chapter Review

Be a Nutrition Sleuth

Which Snacks Are the Highest in Calories?

Do you know how to avoid high-calorie snacks when you need a quick bite to eat? Go to **www .pearsonhighered.com/blake** to learn about a variety of satisfying snacks that are kind to your waist.

Get Real!

How to Order Healthy Food at a Restaurant

Visit the Nutrition and You Virtual Restaurant Menu at **www.pearsonhighered.com/blake** and learn how to order a complete healthy meal, from appetizer to dessert. No tipping necessary!

The Top Ten Points to Remember

1. A healthy body weight is considered a body weight that doesn't increase the risk of developing any weight-related health problems. Being very underweight increases the risk of nutritional deficiencies and related health problems. Being overweight increases the risk of chronic diseases such as heart disease, cancer, and type 2 diabetes. Weight management means maintaining your weight within a healthy range.

2. To assess if you are at a healthy weight, you can consider your BMI, which is your weight in relationship to your height. A BMI of 18.5 to 24.9 is considered healthy. A BMI of 25 up to 29.9 is considered overweight. A BMI of 30 or higher is considered obese. As your BMI increases above 25, so does your risk of dying from many chronic diseases. However, some individuals, such as athletes, may have a high BMI but their weight doesn't put them at a health risk because they are not overfat. In contrast, some individuals who have unintentionally lost weight may have a healthy BMI but be at nutrition risk. In general, BMI is best used to assess overweight and obesity for populations rather than individuals. Excess weight around the middle, measured by your waist circumference, could put you at a higher health risk, regardless of your BMI.

3. When your energy (calories) intake equals your energy (calories) expenditure, you are in energy balance. When you consume more energy than you expend, you are in positive energy balance and weight gain occurs. When your calories fall short of your needs and/or you expend more energy, you are in negative energy balance and lose weight. Your basal metabolic rate (BMR), the thermic effect of food (TEF), and your physical activities all factor into your daily energy needs. Your BMR is influenced mainly by your lean body mass, but also by your age, gender, body size, genes, ethnicity, emotional and physical stress, thyroid hormone, nutritional state, and environmental temperature. Your caffeine intake and use of nicotine can also affect your BMR.

4. Appetite is your psychological desire for food and is affected by hunger, satiety, and satiation, as well as your emotions and your environment. Hunger prompts you to eat, and it will subside as the feeling of satiation sets in after you start eating. Satiety is the feeling you experience when you have had enough to eat and determines the length of time between meals or snacks. Physiological mechanisms such as hormones, sensory signals, and a distended stomach, as well as the size of the meal and the nutrients in your foods, all influence your appetite. Genetics and your environment also play a role in your appetite and weight. If your parents were overweight, you are at a higher risk of developing obesity. An environment that enables easy access to a variety of large portions of foods, and encourages you to be sedentary, will also promote obesity.

5. Losing 10 percent of your body weight over a six-month period is considered a reasonable rate of weight loss. Losing weight rapidly can cause a person to fall short of meeting nutrient needs. Many fad diets promise quick results but can be unhealthy for the long term.

6. Eating more low-energy-density, high-volume foods, such as vegetables and fruit, can help you lose weight because you will feel full for fewer calories. Fiber also promotes satiation. Because protein has the most dramatic effect on satiety, eating high-protein lean meats, chicken, and fish at meals can help reduce hunger between meals. Because fat slows the movement of food out of the stomach into the intestines, it can also prolong satiety.

7. Routine physical activity can add to the daily energy deficit needed for weight loss. To aid in weight loss, overweight individuals should partake in 60 minutes of moderate-intensity exercise daily and continue at least this amount of activity daily to maintain the weight loss.

8. Changing the eating behaviors that contribute to weight gain or impede weight loss is necessary for long-term weight-loss success. Self-monitoring of these behaviors by keeping a food record, controlling environmental cues that trigger eating when not hungry, and learning how to better manage stress are all behavior modification techniques that can be used by individuals who eat out of habit and in response to their environment.

9. Disordered eating describes a variety of abnormal eating patterns, such as restrictive eating, binge eating, vomiting after eating, and abusing laxatives or diet pills. Eating disorders are diagnosed by meeting specific criteria that include disordered eating behaviors. Anorexia nervosa is characterized by self-starvation and excessive weight loss. Bulimia nervosa involves repeated cycles of binge eating and purging. Binge eating disorders are characterized by binge eating without purging. Night eating syndrome is described as excessive calorie intake in the evening and waking up during the night to eat.

10. Numerous health consequences can occur with eating disorders, such as hair loss, digestive problems, electrolyte imbalances, changes in heart rate and blood pressure, dehydration, and nutrient deficiencies. The most effective treatment for eating disorders involves a multidisciplinary team approach including psychological, nutrition, and medical professionals.

Test Your Knowledge

1. Being overweight can increase your risk of
   a. heart disease.
   b. osteoarthritis.
   c. gallbladder disease.
   d. all of the above.

2. Kyle has a BMI of 27. He is considered
   a. underweight.
   b. overweight.
   c. at a healthy weight.
   d. obese.

3. Central obesity refers to
   a. the accumulation of excess fat in your hips and thighs.
   b. the accumulation of excess fat in your stomach area.
   c. the accumulation of excess fat in your arms and legs.
   d. none of these.

4. Your basal metabolic rate (BMR) refers to
   a. the amount of energy you expend during physical activity.
   b. the amount of energy you expend digesting your food.
   c. the amount of energy (calories) that you consume daily.
   d. the amount of energy expended to meet your basic physiological needs.

5. You just ate a large plate of pasta and tomato sauce, so your stomach is full and distended. Which hormone is released because of the distention of your stomach?
   a. cholecystokinin
   b. insulin
   c. thyroid hormone
   d. none of the above

6. Which of the following can increase your risk of becoming overweight?
   a. having a mother who is overweight
   b. having a father who is obese
   c. having a sedentary lifestyle
   d. living on your own away from home
   e. a, b, and c only

7. Which are examples of low-energy-density, high-volume foods that can aid in weight loss?
   a. raw vegetables and salsa
   b. tomato soup
   c. olive oil
   d. fruit salad
   e. a, b, and d only

8. Mary Ellen was obese and lost 30 pounds during the last year by eating a well-balanced, calorie-reduced diet and being physically active daily. To maintain her weight loss, she should continue to eat a healthy diet, monitor her eating behaviors, and
   a. accumulate 10 minutes of moderate-intensity physical activity daily.
   b. accumulate 45 minutes or more of moderate-intensity physical activity daily.
   c. accumulate 20 minutes of moderate-intensity physical activity daily.
   d. do none of the above.
9. A form of purging in bulimia nervosa includes
   a. self-induced vomiting.
   b. fasting.
   c. exercise.
   d. all of the above.
10. Lanugo, or downy hair growth, is common in what type of eating disorder?
    a. anorexia nervosa
    b. bulimia nervosa
    c. binge eating disorder
    d. night eating syndrome

Answers

1. (d) Being overweight increases your risk of all these diseases and conditions, as well as type 2 diabetes, some cancers, and sleep apnea.
2. (b) Because Kyle's BMI falls between 25 and 29.9, he is considered overweight. If his BMI was under 18.5, he would be underweight, whereas a BMI of 18.5 to 24.9 would put him in the healthy weight category. A BMI of 30 and higher is considered obese.
3. (b) Central obesity refers to the accumulation of excess fat in the stomach area and can be determined by measuring a person's waist circumference. Central obesity increases the risk of heart disease, diabetes, and hypertension.
4. (d) Your BMR refers to the bare minimum amount of energy (calories) needed to keep your blood circulating and lungs breathing so that you can stay alive. The amount of energy or calories that you expend during physical activity is not factored into your BMR. The energy that you expend digesting, absorbing, and processing food is called the thermic effect of food (TEF) and is also not part of your BMR. The amount of energy or calories that you consume daily doesn't factor into your BMR.
5. (a) A distended stomach causes the release of cholecystokinin, which is associated with the feeling of satiation and the ending of eating. Insulin will be released once this carbohydrate-heavy meal is digested and absorbed into the blood. Thyroid hormone affects your BMR and is not associated with your stomach being distended.
6. (e) Having parents who are overweight and/or obese and not engaging in regular physical activity can all increase your risk of becoming overweight. Moving out of your home and living on your own won't necessarily cause you to gain weight unless you consume more calories than you need daily.
7. (e) Vegetables, including salsa and vegetable soups, and fruit are all low-energy-density, high-volume foods. These foods will increase satiation, contain few calories per bite, and can displace more energy-dense foods in the diet, all of which can help promote weight loss. Even though olive oil is a good source of heart-healthy unsaturated fat, it is very energy dense.
8. (b) If Mary Ellen would like to keep the weight off, she should try to accumulate 45 minutes or more of moderate-intensity physical activity daily.
9. (d) Self-induced vomiting, fasting, and exercise are all forms of purging, as they assist in "getting rid" of food.
10. (a) Lanugo grows typically on the face and arms of people with anorexia nervosa as a way of regulating body temperature.

Web Resources

➡ For more on overweight and obesity, visit the Centers for Disease Control and Prevention at www.cdc.gov/nccdphp/dnpa/obesity/index.htm

➡ For more information on weight control and physical activity, visit the Weight-control Information Network (WIN) at http://win.niddk.nih.gov/index.htm

➡ For more weight-loss shopping tips, recipes, and menu makeovers, visit the USDA's Nutrition and Weight Management website at www.nutrition.gov

➡ For more on eating disorders, visit the National Eating Disorders Association at www.nationaleatingdisorders.org

Answers to Myths and Misperceptions

1. **True.** Overweight people can suffer from a condition called sleep apnea. To find out what this is and why being overweight contributes to it, turn to page 361.

2. **False.** Being underweight due to a poor diet can have serious health risks. Turn to page 361 to find out why.

3. **False.** Celebrities and models in magazine photos may reflect social trends, but they often don't reflect a healthy body weight. Turn to page 362 to find out more.

4. **False.** Fat around the belly puts a person at a higher health risk than fat stored on the hips and thighs. To find out why, turn to page 364.

5. **True.** But this isn't the only factor. Turn to page 368 to find out the others.

6. **True.** To find out why and how these factors interact with each other, turn to page 373.

7. **True.** Surprising as it may be, eating *more* of certain foods can help you lose weight. To find out why, turn to page 377.

8. **False.** Whereas fat makes food stay in the stomach longer, which slows its digestion and absorption, it isn't the nutrient that provides the greatest level of satiety. You may be surprised to learn what is. Turn to page 382 to find out.

9. **False.** Technically, disordered eating describes abnormal eating behaviors, whereas eating disorders are clinically diagnosed illnesses. Turn to page 392 to learn more about these behaviors and illnesses.

10. **True.** Some eating disorders can be life-threatening. Turn to page 394 to learn about the health effects of eating disorders.

11

True or False?

See page 443 for answers to these Myths and Misperceptions.

Nutrition and Fitness

When they moved from Costa Rica to the United States to work in the high-tech industry, Darla's parents were both slender. Now, nine years later, both are overweight, and Darla's mother was recently diagnosed with type 2 diabetes. Determined to stay fit, Darla starts each day with a 90-minute workout in her school's fitness center. She runs on the treadmill, then switches to the stair-climber, and finishes with a circuit on the weight-training machines.

Although she's maintained her program for months, Darla is disappointed that her strength hasn't improved, and she still experiences muscle soreness.

Do you see any potential problems with Darla's fitness strategy? Why do you think she hasn't gained the muscle strength she's after? What exactly is physical fitness, and what does it take to attain it? In this chapter, we'll explore these questions and help you design a fitness program that's right for you.

What Is Physical Fitness and Why Is It Important?

Physical fitness is simply defined as good health or physical condition, primarily as the result of exercise and proper nutrition. Some people think of exercise and physical activity as the same thing, but this isn't technically the case. **Physical activity** refers to body movement that results in expending calories. Activities such as gardening, walking the dog, and playing with children can all be regarded as physical activity. **Exercise** is defined as formalized training or structured activity, like step aerobics, running, or weight lifting. For the purpose of this chapter, though, the terms *exercise* and *physical activity* are used interchangeably.

Being physically active and consuming a healthy diet are the two most important components of overall health and fitness. You will not achieve optimal fitness if you ignore either of these areas.

Physical Fitness Has Five Basic Components

The five basic components of fitness include cardiorespiratory endurance, muscular strength, muscular endurance, flexibility, and body composition. Most strength training programs blend muscular strength and muscular endurance, which is generally referred to as *muscular fitness*. To be physically fit, one must consider all five variables.

Cardiorespiratory endurance is the ability to sustain cardiorespiratory exercise, such as running and biking, for an extended length of time. This requires that the body's cardiovascular and respiratory systems provide enough oxygen and energy to the working muscles without becoming overly fatigued or exhausted. Someone who can run a leisurely mile without being too out of breath to talk has good cardiorespiratory endurance. Someone who is out of breath after climbing one flight of stairs, in contrast, does not.

Muscle strength is the ability to produce force for a brief period of time, while **muscle endurance** is the ability to exert force over a long period of time without fatigue. Increasing muscle strength and muscle endurance is best achieved with **strength training.** You probably associate muscle strength with bodybuilders or weight lifters, and it's true that these people train to be particularly strong. However, other athletes, such as cheerleaders and ballet dancers, also work hard to strengthen their muscles. Consider the strength it takes to lift another person above your head. If you could hold the person up for several minutes, that would show exceptional muscle endurance.

Flexibility is the range of motion around a joint and is improved with stretching. Athletic performance and joint and muscular function are all enhanced with improved flexibility, which also reduces the likelihood of injury. A gymnast exhibits high flexibility when performing stunts and dance routines. In contrast, someone with low flexibility would not be able to bend over and touch his toes from a standing or sitting position.

Finally, **body composition** is the proportion of muscle, fat, water, and other tissues in the body. Together, these tissues make up your total body weight. Your body composition can change without your total body weight changing, due to the fact that muscle takes up less space (per pound) than does body fat. This is why you can lose inches on your body without losing pounds of weight when you increase your lean muscle mass and decrease body fat.

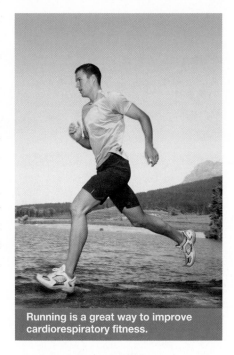
Running is a great way to improve cardiorespiratory fitness.

Physical Fitness Provides Numerous Benefits

We have long heard that eating a balanced diet and exercising regularly maintains good health. We also know that even modest amounts of exercise will provide health benefits, and the more you exercise, the more fit you'll be. However, despite knowing the benefits that exercise brings, more than half of the adults living in the United States do not meet the recommendations for regular physical activity.[1]

So, how does physical activity improve and maintain good health? One of the most obvious roles is that it helps you achieve or maintain a healthy body weight, which in turn helps reduce the risk of developing chronic diseases like type 2 diabetes mellitus and heart disease. In addition, being physically fit can improve overall health in other ways, like helping you get restful sleep and reducing stress. Table 11.1 lists some of the numerous health benefits that result from being physically active on a regular basis. You have to be cautious, however, not to overexercise and increase your risk of injury.

To improve the health of American adults and children through regular physical activity, the U.S. Department of Health and Human Services developed the *2008 Physical Activity Guidelines for Americans.* This publication gives information and guidance on the types and amounts of physical activity that provide substantial health benefits for Americans ages 6 years and older. The recommendations are based on a review of scientific research on the benefits of physical activity, and conclude with the main idea that regular physical activity over time can produce long-term health benefits.[2]

The Take-Home Message Physical fitness is the state of being in good physical condition through proper nutrition and regular physical activity. The five components of physical fitness are cardiorespiratory endurance, muscle strength, muscle endurance, flexibility, and body composition. To achieve optimal fitness, all five components must be considered. The numerous health benefits of physical activity include higher likelihood of a healthy body weight, as well as reduced risk of several chronic diseases, including type 2 diabetes and heart disease; improved body composition, bone health, and immune function; more restful sleep; and reduced stress.

physical fitness The ability to perform physical activities requiring cardiorespiratory endurance, muscle endurance, and strength and/or flexibility; physical fitness is acquired through physical activity and adequate nutrition.

physical activity Voluntary movement that results in energy expenditure (burning calories).

exercise Any type of structured or planned physical activity.

cardiorespiratory endurance The body's ability to sustain prolonged exercise.

muscle strength The greatest amount of force exerted by the muscle at one time.

muscle endurance The ability of the muscle to produce prolonged effort.

strength training Exercising with weights or other resistance to build, strengthen, and tone muscle to improve or maintain overall fitness; also called *resistance training*.

flexibility The joints' ability to move freely through a full and normal range of motion.

body composition The relative proportion of muscle, fat, water, and other tissues in the body.

Table 11.1 The Benefits of Physical Fitness

Reduced Risk of Heart Disease

How It Works: Research has shown that moderate physical activity lowers blood pressure.[1] In addition, exercise is positively associated with high-density lipoprotein (HDL) cholesterol.[2]

Improved Body Composition

How It Works: Exercise helps burn excess stored body fat and builds muscle, resulting in a leaner body mass. Individuals with moderate cardiorespiratory fitness have less total fat and abdominal fat compared with people with low cardiorespiratory fitness.[3]

Reduced Risk of Type 2 Diabetes

How It Works: Exercise helps control blood glucose levels by increasing insulin sensitivity.[4] This not only reduces risk for type 2 diabetes, but also improves blood glucose control for those who have been diagnosed with type 2 diabetes.

Improved Bone Health

How It Works: Bone density has been shown to improve with weight-bearing exercise and resistance training, thereby reducing the risk for osteoporosis.[5]

Improved Immune System

How It Works: Regular moderate exercise can enhance the immune system by increasing immunoglobulins in the body. Immunoglobulins function like antibodies, protecting against colds and other infectious diseases.[6]

Improved Sleep

How It Works: People who engage in regular exercise often have better quality of sleep due to anxiety reduction, antidepressant effect, and changes in body temperature that promote sleep.[7]

What Does a Physical Fitness Program Look Like?

Physical fitness programs are generally based on the five components of fitness, and include aerobic exercise, resistance training, and stretching. A successful fitness program should be tailored to meet the needs of the individual and performed consistently so that any gains in physical fitness are not lost. It is also important to incorporate activities that are enjoyable so that they become a regular part of your lifestyle. If you dislike jogging, for example, you won't be likely to consistently work a daily run into your schedule.

Resistance training improves muscle strength and endurance.

Cardiorespiratory Exercise Can Improve Cardiorespiratory Endurance and Body Composition

Cardiorespiratory exercise often involves continuous activities that use large muscle groups, such as high-impact aerobics, stair climbing, and brisk walking. This type of exercise is predominantly **aerobic** because it uses oxygen. During cardiorespiratory exercise, your heart beats faster and more oxygen-carrying blood is delivered to your tissues. How does this work? As you begin to exercise, your body requires more oxygen to break down nutrients for energy, so it increases blood flow (volume) to the working muscles. It accomplishes this by increasing your heart rate and **stroke volume.** Your body also redistributes blood from your internal organs to maximize the volume of blood that is delivered to the muscles during exercise.

> Between birth and old age, you will walk about 70,000 miles. Walking is one of the best activities you can do to improve cardiovascular health and maintain a healthy weight. Plus, it's free!

Your level of cardiorespiratory fitness can be measured by the maximum amount of oxygen your muscles can consume during exercise, or **VO₂max.** People who are more physically fit have a higher VO₂max and can exercise at a higher intensity without fatigue than someone who is not as fit.

Cardiorespiratory exercise provides the most benefits to your cardiovascular system (heart, blood, and blood vessels), which improves your cardiorespiratory endurance. In addition, it reduces stress and lowers your risk of heart disease by maintaining normal cholesterol levels, heart rate, and blood pressure. Cardiorespiratory exercise also helps you maintain a healthy weight and improve your body composition by burning excess calories, leading to a reduction of body fat.

Strength Training Can Improve Muscle Strength, Muscle Endurance, and Body Composition

Strength (or resistance) training has long been associated with gaining muscle mass, strength, and endurance. Maintaining adequate muscle mass and strength is important for everyone. Just because you engage in resistance training does not mean that you will develop large, bulky muscles. Many females, as well as males,

aerobic With oxygen.

stroke volume The amount of blood pumped by the heart with each heartbeat.

VO₂max The maximum amount of oxygen (ml) a person uses in one minute per kilogram of body weight.

use resistance training to tone and define their muscles to improve their physical appearance and body composition.

To increase muscle strength, you should perform a low number of repetitions using heavy weights or other resistance. If you want to increase muscle endurance, you should perform a high number of repetitions using lighter resistance. However, heavier resistance can also be used to improve muscle endurance by allowing short rest intervals between repetition sets.

Rest periods between sets of an exercise and between workouts are important so that you do not overwork your muscles and increase your risk of muscle strains or other injury. If you don't allow time for your muscles to rest, your muscles may break down and not recover, leading to a loss of muscle mass. The amount of rest depends on your fitness goals and level of **conditioning.** If increasing strength is your goal, you should allow long rest periods of 2 to 3 minutes between sets. If increasing muscle endurance is your goal, shorter rest periods of 30 seconds or less are recommended.

Between workouts, the general guideline to reduce the risk of injury is to allow 48 hours between sets that use the same muscle groups. However, strength training can be done daily as long as different muscles are used on consecutive days. If Darla from the beginning of the chapter isn't changing her strength training routine from day to day, she could be setting herself up for injury.

Stretching Can Improve Flexibility

When you think about your flexibility, you are likely considering how far you can stretch in a particular way without feeling pain or discomfort. Improving flexibility can improve balance, posture, and circulation of blood and nutrients throughout your body. The most common exercise used to improve flexibility is stretching.

There are several types of stretching. The most common form is *static stretching*, which consists of relaxing a muscle, then extending it to a point of mild discomfort for about 10 to 30 seconds, and then relaxing it again. You can use static stretching exercises to stretch one muscle at a time, or you can stretch more than one muscle or muscle group simultaneously.

A form of stretching used by many professional athletes as a pre-event warm-up is *dynamic stretching*, which stretches muscles while moving, for example, by performing arm swings, kicks, or lunges. A form of exercise called *yoga* incorporates aspects of both static and dynamic stretching, and individuals who perform yoga on a regular basis can significantly improve their flexibility. Note that when you perform these stretches for the first time, you'll need to consult a qualified trainer, coach, or physician on proper techniques to reduce your risk of injury.

Another form of stretching, called *ballistic stretching*, involves a repetitive, bouncing motion while you are stretching. Some believe that ballistic stretching increases your risk for pulling a muscle; therefore, it is less favored than static and dynamic stretching. Other, less common forms of stretching are types that involve a partner or machine to create the force needed to stretch the muscle, and controlled stretches that use momentum to create the force needed to extend the muscle.

Recommendations about stretching often conflict and the research to sort it out is limited. Some researchers have concluded that stretching before exercise does not prevent muscle soreness after exercise, nor does it prevent acute sports injuries.[3] However, stretching afterward has been shown to relax and reduce tension on muscles that were just exercised.[4]

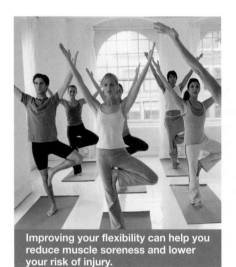

Improving your flexibility can help you reduce muscle soreness and lower your risk of injury.

conditioning The process of improving physical fitness through repeated activity.

The FITT Principle Can Help You Design a Fitness Program

One easy way to design a successful physical fitness program is to follow the FITT principle. FITT is an acronym for frequency, intensity, time, and type. Let's take a closer look at each of these components:

➤ **F**requency is how often you do the activity, such as the number of times per week.

➤ **Intensity** refers to the degree of difficulty at which you perform the activity. Common terms used to describe intensity are low, moderate, and vigorous (high). One measure of intensity for cardiorespiratory exercise is **rate of perceived exertion (RPE),** in which the person performing the activity self-assesses the level of intensity (see Table 11.2). For strength training, intensity is referred to as **repetitions of maximum (RM).** For example, 1 RM is the maximum amount of weight that can be lifted at one time.

➤ **T**ime, or **duration,** is how long you performed the activity, such as a 30-minute run.

➤ **T**ype means the specific activity that you are doing, such as step aerobics or cycling.

The frequency, intensity, time (duration), and type of exercise that are right for you depend partly on what goal you are trying to achieve. For some health benefits, the *2008 Physical Activity Guidelines* state that as little as 60 minutes a week of moderate-intensity activity, such as brisk walking or dancing, will help you achieve that goal. However, adults who wish to see substantial health benefits, including a reduced risk of many chronic diseases, need a total amount of 150 minutes (2 hours and 30 minutes) of moderate-intensity aerobic activity per week. Additionally, resistance training, such as by lifting weights, at a moderate or high intensity, should be performed two or more days per week. Anyone who wants to maintain body weight and prevent gradual

Table 11.2

Rating of Perceived Exertion (RPE)

Scale	Perceived Exertion	Physical Signs
6 7	Very, very light	No perceptible sign
8 9	Very light	No perceptible sign
10 11	Fairly light	Feeling of motion
12 13	Somewhat hard	Warmth on a cool day, slight sweat on warm days
14 15	Hard	Sweating, but can still talk without difficulty
16 17	Very hard	Heavy sweating, difficulty talking
18 19 20	Very, very hard	Feeling of near exhaustion

Source: Rating of Perceived Exertion (RPE) from G. V. Borg in *Medicine and Science in Sports and Exercise,* Vol. 14, pp. 377–378. © 1982 Wolters Kluwer, Lippincott Williams and Wilkins. Used with permission.

intensity The level of difficulty of an activity.

rate of perceived exertion (RPE) A subjective measure of the intensity level of an activity using a numerical scale.

repetitions of maximum (RM) The maximum amount of weight that can be lifted for a specified number of repetitions.

duration The length of time of performing an activity.

Do you feel like you don't have a 30-minute block of time to exercise? The good news is that you don't have to do an activity for 30 consecutive minutes to get health benefits. You can break this time up into three 10-minute bouts of activity and still receive the same benefits as if you were to do it all at one time.

weight gain should participate in approximately 60 minutes of moderate- to vigorous-intensity activity on most days of the week while not consuming excess calories. Those wishing to lose weight need to participate in at least 60 to 90 minutes of daily moderate-intensity physical activity and make calorie adjustments to their diet. You can use the Physical Activity Pyramid to help you become more physically active or improve your current level of fitness (**Figure 11.1**). People with diabetes, high blood pressure, and other types of heart disease should consult with a health care provider before participating in any exercise program, especially one to be performed at a vigorous intensity.

The key to being physically active is to find activities that you enjoy so that you continue to do them on a regular basis. If you don't like jogging, you don't have to do it! Just find other activities that you like. Maybe you enjoy playing basketball, going for a walk, or hiking. It doesn't really matter what the activity is, as long as you take pleasure in what you are doing and do it regularly.

You can use the FITT approach to meet the American College of Sports Medicine's guidelines for cardiorespiratory endurance, muscular fitness, and flexibility for healthy adults, which are summarized in Table 11.3. For example, on your FITT program, you may want to jog three days a week for 30 minutes on Tuesday, Thursday, and Friday to attain your cardiorespiratory fitness. On Monday and Wednesday, you may want to lift weights for muscular fitness and make sure that you stretch beforehand to improve your flexibility.

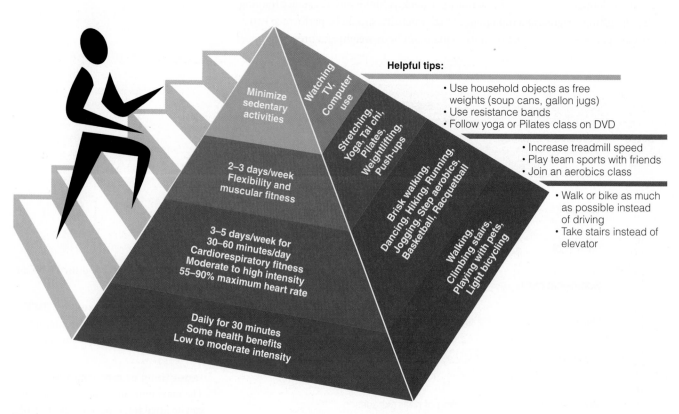

Figure 11.1 Physical Activity Pyramid
Participating in a variety of activities, such as those shown in this Physical Activity Pyramid, will have you on your way to physical fitness.

Table 11.3

Using FITT to Improve Fitness

	Cardiorespiratory Fitness	Muscular Fitness	Flexibility
Frequency	3–5 days per week	2–3 days per week	2–3 days per week
Intensity	55–90% of maximum heart rate	8–12 RM	Enough to develop and maintain range of motion
Time	20–60 minutes, continuous or intermittent (minimum of 10-minute bouts)	8–10 different exercises performed in 1–3 sets	At least 4 repetitions for each muscle group; hold static stretch for 10–30 seconds
Type	Brisk walking, jogging, biking, step aerobics	Weight training, Pilates, push-ups, pull-ups	Stretching, yoga

Source: Adapted from American College of Sports Medicine, June 1998. Position Stand: The Recommended Quantity and Quality of Exercise for Developing and Maintaining Cardiorespiratory and Muscular Fitness and Flexibility in Healthy Adults, Vol. 30, No. 6. Copyright © 1998 Wolters Kluwer, Lippincott Williams and Wilkins. Used with permission.

The Progressive Overload Principle Can Help Improve Fitness over Time

During conditioning, the body gradually adapts to the activities that are being performed. Over time, if the activity is kept exactly the same, the body doesn't have to work as hard and fitness levels will plateau as a result. To continue to improve your fitness level, you must challenge your body by using the **progressive overload principle.** Modifying one or more of the FITT principles so that you gradually increase exercise demands on the body will improve fitness. For example, if you are trying to improve cardiorespiratory endurance, you might gradually increase the duration of a run. To increase muscle strength, you may gradually increase the amount of weight being lifted.

As your body responds to the work that it is being asked to do, physical fitness will be attained. Muscles will increase in size, endurance, and strength and you will notice increased cardiorespiratory endurance and improved flexibility. However, if conditioning is executed improperly or nutrient intake is inadequate for physical activity, muscles can lose mass, endurance, and strength, and cardiorespiratory fitness levels will suffer.

The Take-Home Message Cardiorespiratory exercise improves cardiorespiratory endurance and body composition. Strength training can improve muscle strength and endurance as well as body composition. Flexibility can be enhanced by stretching. An effective training program can be designed using the FITT principle, which stands for frequency, intensity, time, and type of activity. Most people should aim for 60 minutes of moderate activity per week for some health benefits; greater amounts of exercise are needed for substantial health benefits, weight management, and physical fitness improvement. Applying the progressive overload principle to workouts will help you achieve optimal fitness levels.

Fitness Tips

Get Moving!

Schedule physical activity into your day, just like you would schedule a meeting, class, or work.

Find activities that you enjoy. Make exercise something you look forward to, so that you're more likely to keep it up.

Ask a friend or coworker to exercise with you. Many people are more likely to exercise if they have a partner to motivate them.

Track your exercise in a log or journal so you see how much you are getting and note your improvements over time.

Be adventurous and try new activities. If you're used to jogging or going to the gym, try hiking or racquetball. Mixing up your routine will help prevent boredom.

progressive overload principle
A gradual increase in exercise demands resulting from modifications to the frequency, intensity, time, or type of activity.

How Are Carbohydrate, Fat, and Protein Used during Exercise?

In addition to regular physical activity, you need the right foods and fluids in order to be physically fit. When you eat and drink, you meet your nutrient needs for physical activity in two ways: (1) You supply the energy, particularly from carbohydrate and fat, that your body needs for the activity; and (2) you provide the nutrients, particularly carbohydrate and protein, that will help you recover properly so that you can repeat the activity.

We mentioned earlier in the chapter that much energy production during cardiorespiratory exercise is aerobic because it uses oxygen. But during the first few minutes of exercise, energy production occurs under **anaerobic** conditions, or without oxygen. For the anaerobic production of energy, the body relies heavily on two high-energy molecules in muscle cells:

Figure 11.2 Energy Metabolism
During anaerobic metabolism, energy is derived from the breakdown of ATP and creatine phosphate.

➤ **Adenosine triphosphate** (ATP) is a compound composed of a molecule called adenosine attached to a "tail" of three phosphates (*tri* = three). When one of these phosphates is removed from ATP, energy is released as a by-product (**Figure 11.2**). The remaining compound is called adenosine diphosphate (ADP), because it contains only two phosphates (*di* = two). The amount of ATP (energy) in cells is limited, so its breakdown can support only a few seconds of intense exercise.

➤ **Creatine phosphate** is a compound containing the molecule creatine attached to a single phosphate. Your body produces creatine with the help of the liver and kidneys and then stores it in skeletal muscle and other tissues. Your body also gets some creatine from foods, including meat and fish. Direct energy is produced when the phosphate is split off from the creatine, and indirect energy is produced when the phosphate is donated to ADP, thereby regenerating ATP. The amount of creatine that can be stored in the muscles is very limited and becomes depleted after about 10 seconds of high-intensity activity.

As you continue exercising beyond a few minutes, you will breathe more heavily and take in an increased amount of oxygen. At this point your body begins to rely more on aerobic energy production because the amount of ATP needed to support your activity cannot be generated fast enough by anaerobic energy production to meet the energy demands. To supply your body with the energy it needs, you begin to oxidize carbohydrate (glucose), fat (fatty acids), and, to a minimal extent, protein (amino acids) to produce energy in the form of ATP.

Your body relies on carbohydrate, fat, and protein for energy during exercise, but the type and amount of energy that is used depends highly on the intensity and duration of the exercise, your nutritional status, and your level of physical fitness. Carbohydrate and fat contribute most of the energy needed for activity, while protein is best used to promote muscle growth and recovery. The following section discusses the roles of carbohydrate, fat, and protein during exercise.

anaerobic Without oxygen.

adenosine triphosphate (ATP) A compound that is broken down to produce energy for working muscles and other tissues.

creatine phosphate A compound stored in the muscles that is broken down to replenish ATP stores.

Carbohydrate Is the Primary Energy Source during High-Intensity Exercise

During exercise, you obtain energy from carbohydrate through blood glucose and stored glycogen in the muscles and the liver. In an average-sized man, about 525 grams of glycogen are stored in the muscle, 100 grams of glycogen are stored in the liver, and 25 grams of glucose are in the blood.

The total amount of energy stored as carbohydrate in the body is about 2,600 calories (650 grams multiplied by 4 calories per gram), of which 2,000 calories can be used. This is enough energy to perform about 2 hours of moderate exercise, and then glycogen stores are almost completely depleted.

Glucose derived from stored muscle glycogen is the preferred carbohydrate source for energy during exercise. However, liver glycogen stores are just as important to your body during activity. Glycogen provided by the liver is converted into glucose and delivered to the bloodstream in order to maintain normal blood glucose levels, both during times of activity and while you are at rest.

While muscle glycogen provides energy for the muscles during activity, blood glucose is the energy source for your brain. If you are not supplying your brain with the energy it needs, you may feel a lack of coordination or lack of concentration—two things you especially *don't* want to experience during exercise or a sport competition.

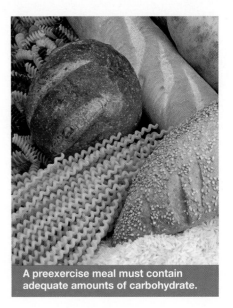

A preexercise meal must contain adequate amounts of carbohydrate.

Intensity Affects How Much Glucose and Glycogen You Use

Your muscles will use carbohydrates for energy no matter how intense the exercise. However, the *amount* of carbohydrate used is affected by intensity, as well as your level of fitness, initial muscle glycogen stores, and whether you're consuming carbohydrates during exercise. Research shows that as the intensity of exercise increases, so does the use of glucose and glycogen for energy.[5] At very high intensities (85% VO_2max), most of the energy is supplied by carbohydrates in the form of muscle glycogen. During exercise of moderate intensity (65% VO_2max), carbohydrate (in the form of blood glucose and muscle glycogen) contributes to approximately half of the energy needed, with the other half coming from fat (more on this in a later section). Although carbohydrates are not the main energy source during exercise of low intensity (25% VO_2max), they still provide some energy for the working muscles from glucose in the bloodstream. Additionally, if carbohydrates are consumed before or during exercise, the use of carbohydrates as an energy source would be greater, even at lower intensities.

When glucose is broken down at a very high rate and there is not enough oxygen, the muscles produce a by-product called **lactate**. Lactate is continuously produced and removed from the body at all times, even at rest. When produced at a low rate, the muscles can effectively clear lactate from the blood and use it directly as an energy source or convert it to glucose (which can also be used for energy). For example, during low-intensity exercise, the body is able to oxidize the lactate that is produced by the muscle for energy and therefore it does not accumulate in the working muscle tissue. This makes it an important fuel source for exercise. The body also shuttles excess lactate to other tissues, such as the brain, heart, and liver, to prevent excessive accumulation.

As exercise intensity increases, the body relies more heavily on breaking down glucose as an energy source, which occurs at a faster rate, and less oxygen becomes available. As a result, more lactate is formed and begins to accumulate in the muscles faster than it can be used for energy or shuttled out of the body. This can potentially

One of the first athletic shoe ideas came from waffles. The cofounder of the company Nike poured rubber into his waffle iron to create ridges for the bottom of shoes that would increase traction and improve athletic performance, especially among runners.

lactate A by-product of rapid glucose metabolism.

negatively affect exercise performance due to a reduction in pH in the muscle cell, thereby causing fatigue. The good news is that the ability of the muscles to effectively use and shuttle lactate to other tissues improves with training.

Duration Affects How Much Glucose and Glycogen You Use

In addition to intensity, the duration of exercise also affects the source and amount of carbohydrate that you use to fuel physical activity. At the start of low- to moderate-intensity exercise, stored muscle glycogen is the main carbohydrate source of energy, although fat contributes most of the total energy at lower intensities. After about 20 minutes, as low- to moderate-intensity exercise continues, muscle glycogen stores diminish and your muscles rely more on fat for fuel (more on this in a later discussion). As your muscle glycogen stores diminish, the liver also contributes its glycogen to be converted to glucose for energy and to prevent hypoglycemia.

Remember that your body will always use glycogen for energy during exercise, and if the intensity and duration of the exercise last long enough, muscle and liver glycogen stores become depleted and the activity that you are doing can no longer be sustained. Many endurance runners refer to this as "hitting the wall."

Conditioning Affects How Much Glucose and Glycogen You Use

Research has shown that the amount of glycogen that muscles can hold can be affected by training.[6] When your muscles are well trained, they have the ability to store 20 to 50 percent more glycogen than untrained muscles. More stored glycogen means more fuel for your working muscles, which means you can exercise for a longer period of time and increase your endurance. Just eating a high-carbohydrate meal before an exercise session or athletic competition will not optimize your performance. You need to train your muscles *and* eat a high-carbohydrate diet regularly to improve endurance.

How Much Carbohydrate Do I Need for Exercise?

Recall that most adults should be getting 45 to 55 percent of their daily energy intake from carbohydrates. Glycogen stores are continuously being depleted and replenished. If you exercise often, eating carbohydrate-rich foods on a regular basis is important to provide your muscles with adequate glycogen. When glycogen stores are inadequate, the muscles have only a limited amount of energy available to support activity, which has been shown to reduce performance and promote fatigue.[7] Keep in mind that the glycogen storage capacity of both the muscles and the liver is limited. Once your muscles and liver have stored all of the glycogen possible, any excess glucose will be converted into fatty acids and stored in the form of body fat.

The best types of carbohydrates to eat during and/or immediately after exercise are simple carbohydrates such as sports drinks, bars, and gels, bananas, bagels, or corn flakes because they are quickly absorbed and enter the bloodstream, and therefore can be used immediately for energy (glucose) or to replenish glycogen stores. Complex carbohydrates like whole grains, rice, pasta, oatmeal, and corn are ideal a couple of hours before exercise because they take longer to digest than simple carbohydrates and enter the bloodstream much more slowly, thereby providing a sustained source of energy. Remember, however, that complex carbohydrates are generally high in fiber, and too much fiber can cause bloating, gas, and diarrhea.

You will learn more about timing your nutrient intake in a later section of this chapter. Table 11.4 shows the amount of carbohydrate needed for different durations of physical activity.[8] Carbohydrate loading is one training strategy that athletes use to build up muscle glycogen stores before a competition (see the feature box "Carbohydrate Loading").

Table 11.4
Carbohydrate Needs for Activity

Duration of Activity (per Day)	Grams Carbohydrate/ Kg Body Weight (per Day)
1 hour	6–7
2 hours	8
3 hours	10
4 hours or more	12–13

Source: From *Sports Nutrition: A Guide for the Professional Working with Active People.* Third Edition. Copyright © 2000 American Dietetic Association. Adapted with permission.

Carbohydrate Loading

The goal of **carbohydrate loading** before an endurance event is to maximize the storage capacity of muscle glycogen. Increasing the amount of stored muscle glycogen can improve an athlete's endurance performance by giving the energy to fuel activity at an optimal pace for a longer period of time.

Not all athletes or physically active people will have improved performance with carbohydrate loading. The people who are likely to benefit the most from this strategy are those who participate in endurance events or exercise that lasts more than 90 minutes. Examples of endurance events include marathons, triathlons, cross-country skiing, and long-distance cycling and swimming. If you exercise or train for less than 90 minutes, you should follow the standard recommendations for carbohydrate intake for athletes to ensure that you have adequate muscle glycogen stores. Research has also shown that women are less likely

carbohydrate loading A diet and training strategy that maximizes glycogen stores in the body before an endurance event.

than men to have improved performance with carbohydrate loading because women oxidize significantly more fat and less carbohydrate and protein compared with men during endurance exercise.[41] Additionally, recall that when the muscles store more glycogen, they also hold more water (3 grams per 1 gram of glycogen). This additional water causes an increase in weight and potential decrease in flexibility, therefore making this method less desirable for some athletes.

So how do athletes start carbohydrate loading? When this concept was first recognized by athletes, they began by training very hard for three to four days in addition to eating a low-carbohydrate diet (less than 5 to 10 percent of total calories). This period was called the depletion phase and was thought to be necessary to increase glycogen stores during the next phase, called the loading phase. The loading phase involved three to four days of minimal or no training while eating a

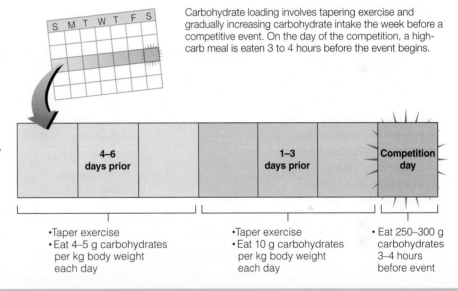

Carbohydrate loading involves tapering exercise and gradually increasing carbohydrate intake the week before a competitive event. On the day of the competition, a high-carb meal is eaten 3 to 4 hours before the event begins.

| 4–6 days prior | 1–3 days prior | Competition day |

- •Taper exercise
- •Eat 4–5 g carbohydrates per kg body weight each day

- •Taper exercise
- •Eat 10 g carbohydrates per kg body weight each day

- •Eat 250–300 g carbohydrates 3–4 hours before event

(continued)

Fat Is the Primary Energy Source during Low-Intensity Exercise

Fat supplies nearly all of the energy required during prolonged low-intensity activity. Even at rest, your body uses fat as its main energy source. Unlike glycogen, fat does not contain water, so the amount of energy stored in the form of body fat is far greater, and more concentrated, than the amount of energy that is stored as glycogen.

Fat is supplied as an energy source during exercise in two forms: fatty acids in the bloodstream (derived from food and triglycerides released from adipose tissue) and fatty acids in muscle tissue (also in the form of triglycerides). When the body uses stored fat in adipose tissue for energy, it is broken down into fatty acids and then supplied to the muscles via the bloodstream, where it is converted into energy (ATP). Muscle triglycerides are directly oxidized to provide energy to the working muscles in which they are stored.

Carbohydrate Loading   (continued)

diet high in carbohydrates. This resulted in higher muscle glycogen stores and better endurance performance.

Many people found the depletion phase hard to endure and would often experience irritability, hypoglycemia, and fatigue. In fact, today, many endurance athletes have modified this training strategy to exclude the depletion phase. Research has shown that depleting muscle glycogen stores is not necessary to increase the amount of stored muscle glycogen. However, there will be greater increases in muscle glycogen by initially depleting muscle glycogen stores.[42]

To begin a modified carbohydrate loading regimen, you should taper your exercise about seven days prior to the event by doing a little bit less activity each day. This is often the hardest recommendation to follow because many athletes feel that they will be out of shape if they stop training before competition. But tapering your exercise is necessary to increase muscle glycogen; otherwise, you will continue to burn glycogen for fuel rather than storing it to be used for energy during the upcoming event. One study showed that you can decrease your training by 70 percent of your normal training schedule about one week prior to an

endurance event without negatively affecting your performance.[43]

In addition to tapering your exercise, you should eat a high-carbohydrate diet that provides about 4 to 5 grams of carbohydrate per kilogram of body weight for the first three to four days. During the last three days of tapering exercise, increase your intake of carbohydrates to 10 grams per kilogram of body weight. Lastly, a meal that is high in carbohydrate (providing about 250 to 300 grams of carbohydrate), moderate in protein, and low in fat should be consumed about 3 to

4 hours prior to the start of the event to further maximize glycogen stores.

Despite the emphasis on carbohydrates, you do not want to compromise your intake of protein and fat by eating too much carbohydrate. Remember to include at least 0.8 grams of protein per kilogram of body weight (some athletes may require more protein) in your training diet, as well as about 20 to 25 percent of calories coming from fat, preferably unsaturated fats. The following is a sample one-day menu that is high in carbohydrate, adequate in protein, and low in fat.

Breakfast	Lunch	Dinner	Snack
1 cup orange juice	2 slices oatmeal bread	3 cups spaghetti (6 ounces uncooked)	1 cup vanilla yogurt
½ cup Grape-Nuts	3 oz turkey breast with lettuce, tomato	1 cup tomato sauce	6 fig bars
1 medium banana			
1 cup 2% milk		2 oz ground turkey	
1 English muffin	8 oz apple juice	¼ loaf multigrain bread (4 ounces)	
1 tbs jelly	1 cup frozen yogurt		
750 calories	750 calories	1,300 calories	500 calories
85% carbohydrates	65% carbohydrates	70% carbohydrates	80% carbohydrates
Total: 3,300 calories: 75% carbohydrates (610 g), 15% protein (125 g), 10% fat (40 g)			

Source: N. Clark, *Nancy Clark's Sports Nutrition Guidebook*, 3rd ed. (Champaign, IL: Human Kinetics, 2003).

Intensity, Duration, and Training Affect How Much Fat You Use

For low-intensity exercise, your body uses mostly fat for energy in the form of free fatty acids in the blood rather than fatty acids stored in muscles. Oxidation of fat from adipose tissue typically occurs after 15 to 20 minutes of aerobic exercise. When exercising at a low intensity for a period of up to 2 hours, fatty acids in the bloodstream that are used for energy are replaced by fatty acids from adipose tissue to sustain energy levels. During moderate exercise, approximately half of the energy needed is supplied by fat and the other half is supplied by carbohydrates. For moderate-intensity exercise lasting for up to 3 hours, your body begins to use equal amounts of fatty acids from muscle triglycerides and fatty acids in the bloodstream (derived from adipose tissue). This, in turn, results in an increase in total fat oxidation compared to a lower intensity at which muscle triglycerides were not significantly used. At high levels of activity, fatty acids cannot be converted into energy fast enough to meet the demand; therefore, fat use decreases and carbohydrates become the preferred energy source. Also note that your body requires more oxygen to convert fat into energy compared with carbohydrate, which creates more stress for the cardiovascular system.

Your level of training can affect how much fat your body will use for energy. Muscles that are well trained will burn more fat than muscles that are not as well trained. This is thought to be caused by an increase in enzymes that are necessary to burn fat for energy. As a result, the body uses less glycogen for energy and more fat, thereby having the potential to increase endurance by "saving" your glycogen stores for later energy use. So, if you are trying to lose weight and body fat, should you reduce the intensity of your workout? The feature box "The Truth about the Fat-Burning Zone" on page 422 addresses this interesting question.

How Much Fat Do I Need for Exercise?

Dietary recommendations for fat intake are generally the same for active people as for the average adult population, with 25 to 30 percent of calories coming from fat.[9] Recall from Chapter 5 that high intakes of saturated and *trans* fats have been linked to high cholesterol levels and heart disease. Physically active people sometimes assume that because they're in shape, they don't have to worry about these diseases. While it is true that physical activity grants some protection against heart disease, athletes and other fit people can also have high cholesterol, heart attacks, and strokes. Everyone, regardless of activity level, should limit saturated fat to no more than 10 percent of total calories, and consume unsaturated fats in foods to meet the body's need for dietary fat.[10]

Some athletes, such as endurance runners and those in sports in which low body weight is important, like gymnasts and figure skaters, may feel they can benefit from a very low-fat diet (less than 20 percent). Though consuming too much dietary fat is a concern, you don't want to limit your fat intake too much. When you consume less than adequate amounts of fat, you are more likely at risk for consuming inadequate calories, essential fatty acids, and fat-soluble vitamins, which can negatively affect exercise performance.[11]

Protein Is Primarily Needed to Build and Repair Muscle

Amino acids obtained from protein are the main nutrients needed to promote muscle growth and recovery. Muscle damage is one of the most significant physiological effects of exercise, especially in weight or strength training. You need to supply your muscles with protein so that this muscle damage does not result in decreased muscle mass and strength. Not all muscle damage is bad, however. It can stimulate remodeling of the muscle cells, which increases muscle strength and mass.

The Body Can Use Protein for Energy

Your body prefers to use carbohydrate and fat as its main energy sources during exercise (see **Figure 11.3**). Small amounts of protein are used for energy, but greater amounts are used when calorie intake and carbohydrate stores are insufficient. When needed, proteins can be broken down into amino acids and oxidized to provide energy directly to the working muscles in the form of ATP. Excess protein that is not used by your body for its normal functions is converted into glycogen or fatty acids, which can provide energy at a later time.

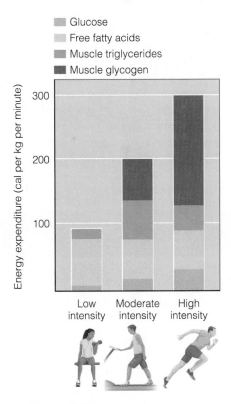

Figure 11.3 Energy Use during Varying Intensities of Exercise
During exercise, your body prefers to use carbohydrate and fat for energy. The intensity of the exercise will determine how much of each of these is used.

Source: Adapted from J. A. Romijn et al., "Regulation of Endogenous Fat and Carbohydrate Metabolism in Relation to Exercise Intensity and Duration," *American Journal of Physiology–Endocrinology and Metabolism* 265 (September 1993): E380–E391.

The Truth about the Fat-Burning Zone

Many people recognize the importance of exercise, especially of the cardiovascular system, for weight loss. They head off to the gym and jump on an exercise machine to start their workout. Once on the machine, they hook up to a device that monitors their heart rate, which lets them know if they are in the "fat-burning" zone (65 to 73 percent of one's maximum heart rate) or the "cardio" zone (more than 73 percent of one's maximum heart rate). Because most people seek to lose body fat, they exercise in the fat-burning zone because they believe that this is the most effective way to lose weight. After all, it is true that the body will burn more fat at lower intensities and will burn more carbohydrate as the intensity increases. So, is staying in the fat-burning zone the best advice to follow if you are trying to lose weight? The simple answer is no. Let's look at some calculations to better understand why.

If you are trying to lose weight, you need to burn more calories than you consume. Working out is an excellent way to do this, but you need to be aware of how many calories you are burning, and aim to work off as many as possible. In the fat-burning zone at 65 percent of maximum heart rate, a moderately fit person

will burn an average of 220 calories during 30 minutes of exercise. Also at this same intensity, fat supplies about 50 percent of the total calories burned for energy. This means that the person is burning an average of 110 fat calories (50 percent of 220). As the intensity increases to about 85 percent of maximum heart rate, this same person burns an average of 330 calories during 30 minutes

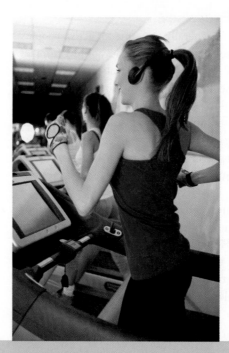

of exercise, with fat supplying only about 33 percent of the total calories burned. Guess what? The person still burns the same number of fat calories (33 percent of 330), but is burning more total calories (330 calories) at a higher intensity, which will help meet the weight loss goal sooner than exercising at a lower intensity (burning 220 calories). The bottom line is, you don't need to stay in the fat-burning zone to effectively lose body fat. You just need to burn calories so that there is an overall calorie deficit.

If you prefer not to exercise at a high intensity, there is an advantage to exercising at a lower intensity. If you have time for a long workout, you can probably exercise at a lower intensity for a longer period of time without getting tired. In other words, if you are jogging (high intensity) you may get tired after you cover 3 miles. However, if you are walking briskly (lower intensity), you may be able to cover 4 miles because you aren't as fatigued. Covering that extra mile will allow you to expend more overall calories during your outing. But if you have a busy lifestyle and feel pressed for time to exercise, don't be afraid to go out of the fat-burning zone to get the most out of your workout and effectively lose weight!

Muscle protein can also be an energy source by being broken down into amino acids that are then released into the bloodstream. These amino acids are carried to the liver, where they get converted into glucose, which supplies the working muscles with energy. If the body has to use a significant amount of protein for energy, including muscle protein, that protein is not available to build and repair tissues. If this occurs too often, a loss of muscle mass will likely result.

How Much Protein Do I Need for Exercise?

Many athletes and exercisers assume that they need substantially more protein than nonexercisers need. It is true that those who are fit and physically active need more protein than those who are sedentary, but those needs are not significantly higher. Recall from Chapter 6 that the RDA for protein for most healthy adults is 0.8 gram per kilogram of body weight per day, and most people, including athletes, far exceed this.

People who are recreational exercisers can meet their needs for protein with a balanced diet. The increased protein needs of competitive and elite athletes, as well as bodybuilders, can also be met with a balanced diet. Endurance athletes are advised to consume 1.2 to 1.4 grams of protein per kilogram of body weight. People who primarily participate in resistance and strength activities may need to consume as much as 1.6 to 1.7 grams of protein per kilogram of body weight.[12]

Total Calorie Needs Depend on the Type and Schedule of Exercise

Your daily calorie needs depend on the type of exercise (swimming, volleyball, tennis, etc.) you choose and your training schedule. Playing an hour of Frisbee with your friends will use a little over 200 calories (based on a 150-pound person). Compare that with an hour of downhill skiing, which will burn over 500 calories. When eight-time Olympic gold medal champion Michael Phelps is training, he needs to consume more than 10,000 calories daily to fuel his activities and maintain his weight. However, if the average jogger were to adopt this eating pattern, he would quickly gain a lot of body fat. The best way to determine if you are consuming enough calories is to monitor your weight. If your weight doesn't decrease, you are consuming enough calories. If your weight *increases*, and it's not due to an increase in muscle mass, you are consuming too many calories.

Unfortunately, some female athletes in certain "lean-build" sports are under pressure to maintain a low weight that's not conducive to good health. As discussed in the feature box, this pressure can contribute to a complex condition known as the female athlete triad.

Timing of Meals Affects Fitness and Athletic Performance

Timing the foods that you eat around exercise has a significant impact on energy levels and recovery time. Recall from Chapter 6 that inadequate calorie intake leads to muscles being broken down for energy. This in turn can lead to loss of muscle mass and strength, and lack of energy, which can negatively affect exercise performance.

During exercise, especially weight training, muscles are under a great deal of stress, which can result in overstretching and tearing of proteins and potential inflammation. After exercise, the body is in a catabolic (breaking down) state: Muscle and liver glycogen stores are low or depleted, muscle protein is broken down, and the immune system is suppressed. Therefore, supplying the body with the nutrients needed to reverse this catabolic state into an anabolic state (building up) is crucial and necessary for optimal fitness.

What Should I Eat before Exercise?

You need to eat before exercise or a competition so that you have enough energy for optimal performance. However, one of the most important considerations about eating before exercise is allowing sufficient time for the food to be digested so that it doesn't negatively affect your performance. In general, larger meals (making you feel quite full) may take 3 to 4 hours to digest, whereas smaller meals (making you feel satisfied but not overly full) may take only 2 to 3 hours to digest. If you are drinking a liquid supplement or having a small snack, you should allow about 30 minutes to 1 hour for digestion. These are general guidelines and may not apply to everyone, so

What Is the Female Athlete Triad?

Christy Henrich joined the U.S. gymnastics team in 1986 weighing 95 pounds at 4 feet, 11 inches tall. Christy soon succeeded as a gymnast, but after a judge told her she needed to lose weight, she developed anorexia nervosa. Sadly, her weight plummeted to 47 pounds, and she died from multiple organ failure at the age of 22.

The anorexia that Christy battled is one part of the *female athlete triad,* a combination of disordered eating, amenorrhea, and osteoporosis. Female athletes are often pressured to reach or maintain an unrealistically low body weight and/or level of body fat. This pressure contributes to the development of disordered eating, which helps to initiate the triad. Of major concern with this disorder is that it not only reduces the performance of the athlete, but may have serious medical and psychological consequences later in life.

The major components of the triad are discussed here.

Disordered Eating

Athletes who have disordered eating may engage in abnormal, and often harmful, eating behaviors in order to lose weight or maintain a low body weight. At one extreme are those who fulfill the diagnostic criteria for anorexia nervosa or bulimia nervosa. At the other are those who unintentionally take in fewer calories than they

need. They may appear to be eating a healthy diet—one that would be adequate for a sedentary individual—but their caloric needs are higher due to their level of physical activity. Many athletes mistakenly believe that losing weight by any method enhances performance, and that disordered eating is harmless. Disordered eating is most common among athletes in sports where appearance is important, such as figure skating, gymnastics, and ballet, but can occur in athletes in all types of sports.

Amenorrhea

Amenorrhea, the absence of three to six consecutive menstrual cycles, is the most recognizable component of the triad. This

Disordered eating

Female athletes for whom body size or appearance is an issue, such as dancers, gymnasts, and skaters, are often particularly vulnerable to the female athlete triad.

menstrual disorder is caused by a failure to consume enough energy to compensate for the "energy cost" of the exercise. Unfortunately, many females welcome the convenience of not menstruating and do not report it. However, this may put them at risk for reduced bone mass and a faster rate of bone loss caused by decreased levels of estrogen in the body.

Osteoporosis

Osteoporosis is the loss of bone mineral density and the inadequate formation of bone. Premature osteoporosis, which is perpetuated by poor nutrition and amenorrhea, puts the athlete at risk for stress fractures, hip and vertebral fractures, and the loss of bone mass, which may be irreplaceable.

All individuals, including friends, teachers, and coaches, involved with such athletes should be aware of the warning signs because the triad components are very often not recognized, not reported, or denied. Warning signs include menstrual changes, weight changes, disordered eating patterns, cardiac arrhythmia, depression, and stress fractures. People working with these athletes should provide a training environment in which athletes are not pressured to lose weight and should be able to recommend appropriate nutritional, medical, and/or psychological resources if needed.

---

be sure that you experiment with your own eating and exercise schedule well before a workout or competition so that you know how long you need to wait before starting your activity.

You just learned that carbohydrates are one of the main sources of energy during exercise. Thus, your preexercise meal should contain adequate amounts of carbohydrate so that you maximize muscle and liver glycogen stores and maintain normal blood glucose levels. In general, your preexercise meal should contain 1 to 4.5 grams of carbohydrate per kilogram of body weight and be consumed 1 to 4 hours prior to exercise.

Consuming carbohydrate immediately before exercise (about 15 to 30 minutes prior to the start) provides an advantage because it gives your muscles an immediate source of energy (glucose) and spares your glycogen stores so that you can exercise for a longer period or at a higher intensity without becoming tired as quickly.[13] Carbohydrate intake prior to the start of exercise can also help reduce muscle damage by causing the release of insulin, which promotes muscle protein synthesis.

Just as your body needs a continuous supply of carbohydrate, it also needs moderate amounts of protein throughout the day. Timing your protein intake around activity will have a significant impact on muscle preservation, growth, and recovery.

The consumption of foods with both protein *and* carbohydrate before exercise, such as fruit and yogurt, benefits the body by causing a greater increase in muscle glycogen synthesis than consuming carbohydrate alone. With more glycogen in your muscles, you can increase endurance. Another benefit of consuming both protein and carbohydrate before exercise is that it results in greater protein synthesis after the exercise is over compared with either protein or carbohydrate alone.[14] The making of new proteins, including muscles, is necessary for optimal fitness and muscle preservation, repair, and growth.

Foods with a higher fat content take longer to digest than foods that are higher in carbohydrate and protein. For this reason, high-fat foods should generally be avoided several hours before exercise. If you eat high-fat foods before exercise, you may feel sluggish or have stomach discomfort, which can impair your performance. Of course this is a general guideline, and not all active people have difficulty during exercise if they consume higher-fat foods before starting to exercise.

Crackers are commonly consumed before and during endurance exercise to help prevent early fatigue.

What Should I Eat during Exercise?

For exercise lasting longer than 1 hour, carbohydrate intake should begin shortly after the start of exercise and continue at 15- 20-minute intervals throughout. For long-lasting endurance activities, a total of 30 to 60 grams of carbohydrate should be consumed per hour to prevent early fatigue. Sports drinks and gels are one way to take in carbohydrate immediately before and/or during activity, but foods such as crackers and sports bars are also commonly eaten.

The best types of carbohydrate to consume during exercise are glucose, sucrose, and maltodextrin because they are absorbed by the body more quickly than other carbohydrates. Fructose, the sugar found in fruit and fruit juice, should generally be avoided because it may cause gastrointestinal problems or stomach discomfort.

Many sports drinks and gels contain only carbohydrate and electrolytes; others also contain protein. For endurance athletes, consuming both carbohydrate and protein during exercise has been shown to improve net protein balance at rest as well as during exercise and postexercise recovery.[15] This will, in turn, have an effect on muscle maintenance and growth.

Sports drinks can be a good source of carbohydrate during exercise.

What Should I Eat after Exercise?

What you eat after exercise will affect how fast you recover, which may affect how soon you're ready for your next workout or training session. This is especially important for competitive athletes who train more than once per day. Some people who load up on high-fat foods after a workout or competition experience fatigue that often results in less-than-optimal performance during the next workout.

The best postexercise meal is consumed quickly and contains both carbohydrate and protein. The muscles are most receptive to storing new glycogen within the first 30 to 45 minutes after you have finished exercising, so this is a crucial time period in which to provide the body with carbohydrate.[16] Research shows that consuming carbohydrate immediately after exercise also results in a more positive body protein balance.[17] In addition, protein intake immediately after exercise rather than several hours later results in greater muscle protein synthesis. Finally, the consumption of protein with carbohydrate causes an even greater increase in glycogen synthesis than

Low-fat chocolate milk is a low-cost option for providing the whey protein and carbohydrate that help with muscle and glycogen synthesis after exercise.

carbohydrate or protein alone.[18] In short, both nutrients should be consumed soon after exercise.

What is the best way to get these two nutrients? Studies have shown that consumption of carbohydrate and protein in a ratio of approximately 3:1 (in grams) is ideal to promote muscle glycogen synthesis, protein synthesis, and faster recovery time.[19] Whey protein (such as in milk) is the preferred protein source because it is rapidly absorbed and contains all of the essential amino acids that your body needs. You can use commercial shakes and drinks, but they can be expensive. A cheaper alternative is low-fat chocolate milk, which will provide you with adequate amounts of carbohydrate and protein to assist in recovery after exercise.[20] If you consume a liquid supplement or small snack after exercise, this should be followed by a high-carbohydrate, moderate-protein, low-fat meal within the next 2 hours. An old-fashioned peanut butter and jelly sandwich or a slice of cheese pizza are inexpensive and can help you recover after exercise too.

If you are a competitive athlete, always experiment with timing your nutrient intake and consuming new foods and beverages during practice, not on the day of competition. You don't want to be unpleasantly surprised to find that a particular food doesn't agree with you a few hours before an important race or other event.

In addition to consuming adequate protein and carbohydrate, drinking adequate fluids is important for exercise performance and recovery. You will learn more about hydration in a later section of this chapter.

The Take-Home Message Carbohydrate and fat are the primary sources of fuel during exercise. Carbohydrates provide energy in the form of blood glucose and muscle and liver glycogen, and are the main energy source during high-intensity exercise. Fat is the main energy source during low-intensity exercise. Carbohydrate and fat contribute equally as energy sources during moderate-intensity exercise. Protein provides amino acids that are necessary to promote muscle growth and repair muscle damage caused by exercise. Consuming the right balance of nutrients at the right time can improve exercise performance and recovery time.

What Vitamins and Minerals Are Important for Fitness?

In addition to several other important functions, vitamins and minerals play a major role in the metabolism of carbohydrate, fat, and protein for energy during exercise. Some also act as antioxidants and help protect cells from the oxidative stress that can occur with exercise.

Antioxidants Can Help Protect Cells from Damage Caused by Exercise

Your muscles use more oxygen during exercise than while you are at rest. Because of this, your body increases its production of free radicals that damage cells, especially during intense, prolonged exercise. Antioxidants, such as vitamins E and C, are known to protect cells from the damage of free radicals. Vitamin C also assists in the production of collagen, which provides most of the structure of connective tissues like bone, tendons, and ligaments. This, in turn, can affect your likelihood of developing strains, sprains, and fractures that may occur as a result of exercise.

Research has not proven that supplementation with vitamins E or C improves athletic performance, nor that it decreases oxidative stress in highly trained athletes.[21] Therefore, you do not need to consume more than the RDA of these vitamins, but you do need to be sure to consume adequate amounts from foods like nuts, vegetable oils, broccoli, and citrus fruits to meet your needs.

Some Minerals Can Be of Concern in Highly Active People

You learned in Chapter 8 that minerals have important roles in normal body functions and health. Minerals are also essential to physical fitness and athletic performance. Though active people do not need more minerals than less active individuals, there are two minerals that they must be careful to consume in adequate amounts.

Iron

Iron is important to exercise because it is necessary for energy metabolism and transporting oxygen throughout the body and within muscle cells. Iron is a structural component of hemoglobin and myoglobin, two proteins that carry and store oxygen in the blood and muscle, respectively. If iron levels are low, hemoglobin levels can also fall, diminishing the blood's ability to carry oxygen to the cells. If this occurs during exercise, you will experience early fatigue. (You can also feel tired if iron levels are low and you are not exercising.) Iron supplementation can improve aerobic performance for people with depleted iron stores.[22]

Many athletes and physically fit people are prone to iron-deficiency anemia. Although iron-deficiency anemia can occur in both females and males, female athletes are at a greater risk. Long-distance runners, as well as athletes in sports where they must "make weight," have also been noted to be at higher risk for iron-deficiency anemia. Athletes in other sports such as basketball, tennis, softball, and swimming also have been shown to have suboptimal iron status.[23]

Low iron levels can be a result of poor dietary intake or increased iron losses. Women can lose a lot of iron during menstruation, depending on their iron status and menstrual blood flow. Iron is also lost in sweat, but not in amounts significant enough to lead to iron deficiency.

Another effect of exercise on iron is intravascular hemolysis (*hemo* = blood, *lysis* = breaking down), which is the bursting of red blood cells. This happens when you are running and your feet repeatedly hit the ground (a hard surface), causing red blood cells to burst and release iron. This iron is recycled by the body and not lost, and therefore does not typically contribute to iron deficiency.

Some people experience decreased levels of hemoglobin because of training, especially when the training is quite strenuous. During exercise your blood volume increases, which in turn causes lower concentrations of hemoglobin in the blood. This is often referred to as sports anemia, or pseudoanemia, and is not the same as iron-deficiency anemia. Iron-deficiency anemia typically has to be treated with iron supplementation. Sports anemia can be corrected on its own because the body can adapt to training and produce more red blood cells, which restores normal hemoglobin levels.

Whether you exercise or not, you can maintain your iron status by consuming adequate amounts of iron-rich foods, and supplements if necessary. However, many female athletes do not consume enough iron to meet their needs, which often leads to

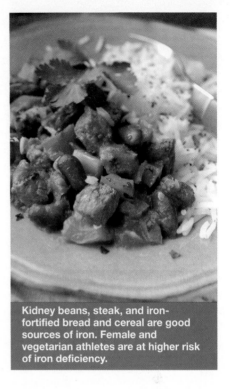

Kidney beans, steak, and iron-fortified bread and cereal are good sources of iron. Female and vegetarian athletes are at higher risk of iron deficiency.

Eating calcium-rich foods daily assists with bone health, muscle contraction, and blood clotting.

low iron levels. Vegetarian athletes are especially susceptible to iron deficiency and need to plan their diets appropriately so they consume adequate amounts of foods plentiful in iron.

Calcium

Most people know about the importance of calcium to maintain bone health, but athletes are particularly susceptible to broken bones and fractures. Therefore, they need to consume enough calcium in their diets to reduce their risk of developing these types of injuries. Calcium affects both skeletal and heart muscle contraction, and hormone and neurotransmitter activity during exercise. It also assists in blood clotting when you have a cut or other minor hemorrhage, which may occur during exercise or competition.

Many people may not be aware that calcium is lost in sweat, and the more you sweat the more calcium you lose. One study concluded that bone loss is related to dietary calcium, and that exercise can increase bone mineral content (the mass of all minerals in bone) only when calcium intake is sufficient to compensate for what is lost through sweating.[24]

Calcium supplements are not recommended unless your intake from food and beverages is inadequate and you are not meeting your daily needs. Choosing foods that are high in calcium, including fortified foods, can ensure that athletes meet their needs for calcium.

Vitamin and Mineral Supplements Are Generally Not Necessary

Active people generally do not need more vitamins than sedentary people, because vitamins can be used repeatedly in metabolic reactions. Many athletes mistakenly believe that vitamins and minerals themselves supply energy, and often consume extra vitamins and minerals so that they can perform better. In fact, studies have shown that multivitamin and mineral supplements are the supplements most commonly used by college athletes.[25] As you know by now, vitamins and minerals themselves don't provide energy. But can taking these supplements improve athletic performance for other reasons? The answer is: not unless you are experiencing a deficiency. For people who consume enough vitamins and minerals in their diet, taking more than the RDA will not result in improved performance during exercise.[26]

Everyone, not just athletes, should obtain vitamins and minerals through nutrient-dense foods before considering the use of supplements. Eating a wide variety of foods that meets your calorie needs will likely provide your body with plenty of vitamins and minerals. Thus, it is probably a waste of money to use vitamin and mineral supplements.

The Take-Home Message Athletes need to pay special attention to their intakes of certain vitamins and minerals. Antioxidants such as vitamins E and C are not needed in excessive amounts, as they have not been proven to reduce oxidative damage to cells from exercise. Iron is important because of its role in transporting oxygen in blood and muscle, and deficiency is prevalent among athletes, especially females and vegetarians. Calcium intake is important for bone health and muscle contraction. Adequate amounts of all nutrients can be consumed in foods, so supplements are not usually necessary.

How Does Fluid Intake Affect Fitness?

As basic as it sounds, water is one of the most important nutrients during physical activity. When you drink too little fluid, or you lose too much fluid and electrolytes through sweating, this causes physiological changes that can negatively affect exercise performance and health. You may experience early fatigue or weakness when your body doesn't have sufficient amounts of water. Consuming adequate fluids on a regular basis, as well as monitoring fluid losses during physical activity, are key to maintaining optimal performance and preventing **dehydration** and electrolyte imbalance.

Fluid and Electrolyte Balance and Body Temperature Are Affected by Exercise

You learned in Chapter 8 that water and some electrolytes are necessary to maintain the fluid balance in your body. When you are physically active, your body will lose more water via sweat and exhalation of water vapor than when you are less active, so you need to replace water lost during exercise to maintain normal fluid balance.

Sodium and chloride are the two primary electrolytes that are lost in sweat. Potassium is also lost in sweat, but to a lesser extent than sodium and chloride. An electrolyte imbalance can cause heat cramps, as well as nausea, lowered blood pressure, and edema in the hands and feet, all of which can hinder your performance. When electrolyte losses are within the range of normal daily dietary intake, they can easily be recovered by consuming a balanced meal within 24 hours after exercise. Electrolytes can also be replaced by beverages that contain them, such as sports drinks, if food is not available.

The sweat you produce during exercise releases heat and helps keep your body temperature normal. The amount of fluid lost through sweating depends on the type, intensity, and duration of exercise and varies from person to person. Some people sweat heavily, while others may sweat very little. Regardless of how much you sweat, it is important that you don't allow your body to lose too much fluid without replacing it with water or other beverages.

Exercising in hot, humid weather results in more fluid being lost in breathing in addition to sweating, which will increase your body's need for fluids. However, if the air outside is very humid (that is, it contains a lot of water), sweat may not evaporate off the skin, and the body won't cool down. This can cause heat to build up in your body, placing you at risk for heat exhaustion or heat stroke. One significant warning sign of heat stroke is if you are *not* sweating when you should be. This happens when you are extremely dehydrated and cannot produce sweat, which prevents the release of heat and causes your body temperature to rise. Other warnings signs of heat exhaustion and heat stroke are shown in Table 11.5.

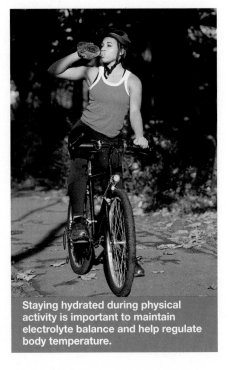

Staying hydrated during physical activity is important to maintain electrolyte balance and help regulate body temperature.

You Need Fluids before, during, and after Exercise

Many active people are aware that it's important to stay hydrated during exercise, but your need for water doesn't begin with your first sit-up or lap around the track.

dehydration Loss of water in the body as a result of inadequate fluid intake or excess fluid loss, such as through sweating.

Table 11.5

Warning Signs of Heat Exhaustion and Heat Stroke

Heat Exhaustion	Heat Stroke
Profuse sweating	Extremely high body temperature (above 103°F [39.4°C], orally)
Fatigue	
Thirst	Red, hot, and dry skin (no sweating)
Muscle cramps	Rapid, strong pulse
Headache	Rapid, shallow breathing
Dizziness or light-headedness	Throbbing headache
Weakness	Dizziness
Nausea and vomiting	Nausea
Cool, moist skin	Extreme confusion
	Unconsciousness

Meeting your fluid needs before and after activity is also important to maintain fluid and electrolyte balance and optimize performance.

Consuming adequate fluid every day is important for everyone, from sedentary individuals to competitive athletes. Recall from Chapter 8 that most healthy adult women need approximately 9 cups of beverages daily, while most healthy adult men need about 13 cups. This is a general guideline to follow for adequate hydration. Another way to determine your estimated daily fluid needs is to divide your body weight by 2. This tells you the number of ounces of fluid you need (8 ounces = 1 cup) on a daily basis, not including the additional needs associated with exercising.

For active individuals, preexercise hydration is essential to replace sweat losses. As you learned in Chapter 8, you can determine your fluid needs during exercise by weighing yourself both before and after an activity. Because the amount of weight that is lost is mainly due to losses in body water, you should consume 16 to 24 fluid ounces (about 2 to 3 cups) of fluid for every pound of body weight lost.[27] The American College of Sports Medicine (ACSM) has specific recommendations for how much fluid to drink before and during exercise. See Table 11.6 for these recommendations.

Some Beverages Are Better than Others

Beverages like tea, coffee, soft drinks, fruit juice, and, of course, water contribute to your daily fluid needs. But what is the best type of fluid for preventing dehydration

Table 11.6

ACSM Hydration Recommendations

When?	How Much?
2 to 3 hours before exercise	14–22 fluid ounces (2–3 cups)
5 to 10 minutes before exercise	4–8 fluid ounces (½–1 cup) as tolerated
At 15- to 20-minute intervals after exercise has begun	6–12 fluid ounces (¾–1½ cups)

prior to and during activity? What about for rehydrating your body after activity? For these purposes, not all beverages are equal.

Sports drinks are popular in the fitness world and are often marketed as tasty beverages to all groups of people, not just athletes. They typically contain 6 to 8 percent carbohydrate as well as sodium and potassium, two electrolytes that are critical in muscle contraction and maintaining fluid balance. One purpose of sports drinks is to replace fluid and electrolytes that are lost through sweating. These drinks have been shown to be superior to water for rehydration, mostly because their flavor causes people to drink more than they would of just plain water.[28]

Sports drinks also provide additional carbohydrate to prevent glycogen depletion. This is beneficial if you engage in long endurance events or exercise when glycogen stores may be running low. When you consume a sports drink during exercise, you provide your body with glucose to be used as an immediate energy source and prevent further decline in muscle glycogen stores.

However, not everyone actually needs sports drinks in order to stay adequately hydrated, and at about 60 calories per 8-ounce cup, they can be a source of unwanted extra calories. For exercise that lasts less than 60 minutes, water is sufficient to replace fluids lost through sweating and food consumption following exercise will adequately replace electrolytes. A sports drink is most appropriate when physical activity lasts longer than 60 minutes.[29]

Other beverages may be suboptimal for hydration during physical activity. Fruit juice and juice drinks contain a larger concentration of carbohydrate and do not hydrate the body as quickly as beverages with a lower concentration of carbohydrates (like sports drinks). Carbonated drinks contain a large amount of water; however, the air bubbles from the carbonation can cause stomach bloating and may limit the amount of fluid consumed.

Though alcohol may seem like an unlikely choice for rehydration, some people may drink alcoholic beverages, such as beer, in order to quench thirst. But because alcohol is a diuretic, it can actually contribute to dehydration. Alcohol during performance can also impair your judgment and reasoning, which can lead to injuries not only for you, but for those around you.

Another diuretic, the caffeine found in coffee and some soft drinks, should only be consumed in moderate amounts, because excessive intake can cause increased heart rate, nausea, vomiting, excessive urination, restlessness, anxiety, and difficulty sleeping. Moderate caffeine intake is about 250 milligrams (the amount found in about three cups of coffee) per day.[30]

For most people, water will provide adequate hydration before, during, and after exercise, and it's cheaper in both calories and cost than sports drinks.

Consuming Too Little or Too Much Fluid Can Be Harmful

As your body loses fluid through sweating and exhalation during physical activity, it will let you know that you need to replace these fluids by sending a signal of thirst. However, by the time you're thirsty, you may already be dehydrated. **Figure 11.4** shows the effect of dehydration on exercise performance. As you can see from the figure, thirst is not a good indicator of fluid needs for most athletes and physically active people. Knowing the warning signs of dehydration so that you can respond by drinking adequate fluids will help prevent health consequences and impaired exercise performance.

If you become dehydrated over a short period of time, such as during a single exercise session or sport competition, **acute dehydration** may set in. Acute dehydration most commonly occurs if you are not adequately hydrated before beginning a hard exercise session, especially if you have been sick, if it is extremely hot and humid, or

acute dehydration Dehydration starting after a short period of time.

Figure 11.4 Effects of Dehydration on Exercise Performance
Failing to stay hydrated during exercise or competition can result in fatigue and cramps and, in extreme cases, heat exhaustion. Because the thirst mechanism doesn't kick in until after dehydration has begun, replacing fluids throughout physical activity is important.

Source: Adapted from E. Burke and J. Berning, *Training Nutrition*. (Travers City, MI: Cooper Publishing Group, 1996).

Impaired aerobic performance

Reduced muscle endurance

Reduced muscle strength

Heat cramps, heat exhaustion

Sensation of thirst

High

Athletic Performance

Low

Fully hydrated · 2% · 4% · 6% · 8%

Water loss as percentage of body weight

if the temperature is significantly different from what you are used to. To prevent acute dehydration, follow a regimented hydration schedule using water or sports drinks to hydrate before, during, and after exercise sessions and/or competition.

Chronic dehydration refers to when you are not adequately hydrated over an extended period of time, such as during several sport practices or games. The most common warning signs of chronic dehydration include fatigue, muscle soreness, poor recovery from a workout, headaches, and nausea. If your urine is very dark and you do not need to go to the bathroom every 3 or 4 hours, then you could be experiencing chronic dehydration. As with acute dehydration, following a regimented hydration schedule throughout the day will help prevent chronic dehydration.

When speaking of hydration and physical activity, we are usually concerned about consuming *enough* fluids so that we do not become dehydrated. As you recall from Chapter 8, consuming too much fluid can also be harmful. Taking in too much water without sufficient electrolytes can result in **hyponatremia.** Symptoms of severe hyponatremia may include rapid weight gain, bloated stomach, nausea, vomiting, swollen hands and feet, headache, dizziness, confusion, disorientation, and lack of coordination. Hyponatremia is more likely to occur in those who participate in endurance sports or prolonged exercise periods (greater than 4 hours), in which fluid and sodium loss is more likely.

Drinking as much fluid as possible and "staying ahead of thirst" has been the recommendation for hydration among long-distance runners for quite some time. Due to the growing concern about overhydration and hyponatremia, USA Track & Field (USATF) revised its guidelines on hydration in order to lower the risk of hyponatremia among long-distance runners. The USATF recommends consuming 100 percent of fluids lost due to sweat while exercising, and to be sensitive to the onset of thirst as the signal to drink, rather than "staying ahead of thirst."

chronic dehydration Dehydration over a long period of time.

hyponatremia Dangerously low levels of sodium in the blood.

Calculating Your Fluid Needs for Endurance Exercise

The next time you take a 1-hour training run, use the following process to determine your fluid needs.

1. Make sure that you are properly hydrated before the workout. Your urine should be clear.
2. Do a warm-up run to the point where you start to sweat, then stop. Urinate if necessary.
3. Weigh yourself on an accurate scale.
4. Run for one hour at an intensity similar to your targeted race.
5. Drink a measured amount of a beverage of your choice during the run to quench your thirst. Be sure to keep track of how much you drink.
6. Do not urinate during the run.
7. After you have finished the run, weigh yourself again on the same scale you used in Step 3.
8. Calculate your fluid needs using the following formula:

   a. Enter your body weight from Step 3 in pounds _____
   b. Enter your body weight from Step 7 in pounds − _____
   c. Subtract b from a = _____

   × 15.3

   d. Convert the pounds of weight in c to fluid ounces by multiplying by 15.3 _____
   e. Enter the amount of fluid you consumed during the run in ounces + _____
   f. Add e to d = _____

The final figure is the number of ounces of fluid that you must consume per hour to remain well hydrated.

Source: Adapted from D. Casa. 2003. *USA Track & Field Self-Testing Program for Optimal Hydration for Distance Running.* Available at http://www.usatf.org/groups/Coaches/library/2007/hydration/USATFSelfTestingProgramForOptimalHydration.pdf.

If you are a distance runner, take the Self-Assessment to determine your fluid needs during long-distance races.[31] Keep in mind that you should perform this hydration test well before a competition or event, and perform the test again if your level of fitness improves or if the climate changes from when you initially determined your fluid needs.

The Take-Home Message Being adequately hydrated before, during, and after exercise is important to sustain fluid and electrolyte balance and a normal body temperature. Inadequate hydration can impair performance. Water is the preferred beverage for hydration, but sports drinks can be beneficial during moderate- or vigorous-intensity exercise that lasts longer than 60 minutes. Too little fluid intake can result in acute or chronic dehydration, while consuming too much water can lead to hyponatremia.

Can Dietary Supplements Contribute to Fitness?

Competitive athletes are always looking for an edge, and many turn to supplements in the hope of improving their performance. The pill and powder manufacturers may claim that their products enhance immunity, boost metabolism, improve memory, or provide some other physical advancement. Because dietary supplements are not strictly regulated by the Food and Drug Administration, their manufacturers do not have to prove the purity, quality, safety, or efficacy of any of their products or claims. As a result, many athletes risk their health and, in some cases, eligibility for competition by taking supplements that can be ineffective, dangerous, or contain banned substances. Proper nutrition and exercise should be first and foremost in any training regimen. Once these requirements have been met, then supplementation can be considered to improve health and overall fitness. Meeting with a sports dietitian will help you determine if you need supplements and what risks you might be taking by consuming them.

Dietary Supplements and Ergogenic Aids May Improve Performance, but Can Have Side Effects

The term **ergogenic aid** describes any substance, including dietary supplements, used to improve athletic performance. Although the makers of dietary supplements do not have to prove their effectiveness, researchers have examined several supplements and their effects on athletic performance. Studies have indicated that some dietary supplements have a positive effect on performance, while others do not. Further, some ergogenic aids cause serious side effects. Let's take a closer look at some of the most popular dietary supplements and ergogenic aids in the fitness industry.

Creatine

Creatine is one of the best-known dietary supplements in the fitness industry today. In the early 1990s, research revealed that creatine supplementation increased creatine stores in the muscles (in the form of creatine phosphate), which increased the amount of ATP generated and improved performance during high-intensity, short-duration exercise.[32]

However, the data on whether creatine enhances performance are mixed. Studies have shown that creatine supplementation does improve athletic performance in high-intensity, short-duration activities such as weight training, when the body relies on anaerobic energy metabolism. Creatine supplementation has also been shown to increase muscle strength and muscle mass. But research yields mixed results as to whether creatine supplementation improves sprint running performance, with some studies showing improvement and others showing no benefit.[33]

To date, creatine has not been found to have negative effects on blood pressure, or kidney or liver function among healthy people.[34] Still, anyone considering taking creatine supplements should check with a health care provider first.

Caffeine

Caffeine used to be known mostly in the context of its negative effect on hydration (recall that caffeine is a diuretic). Today, caffeine has gained popularity as an ergogenic aid among athletes, trainers, and coaches. Caffeine may decrease perception of effort

Athletes sometimes take supplements, such as creatine phosphate or caffeine, to enhance their athletic performance. Supplements are not strictly regulated by the FDA, so their quality and effectiveness can vary widely.

ergogenic aid A substance, such as a dietary supplement, used to enhance athletic performance.

by stimulating the central nervous system, directly affect the breakdown of muscle glycogen, and increase the availability of fatty acids during exercise, therefore sparing glycogen stores. Studies on the effects of caffeine on exercise have shown that caffeine does enhance athletic performance, mostly during endurance events.[35] However, research has not proven that caffeine provides any benefit during short-duration activities, such as sprinting.[36] Caffeine is considered a banned substance by some athletic associations when consumed in high amounts. For example, the National Collegiate Athletic Association (NCAA) classifies caffeine as a banned substance when urine concentrations exceed 15 micrograms per milliliter. This would be the equivalent of drinking four or five cups of coffee.

Anabolic Steroids

Anabolic steroids (*anabolic* = to stimulate growth) are testosterone-based substances designed to mimic the bodybuilding traits of testosterone. There are two primary effects of anabolic steroids. The anabolic effect, which is the one users are seeking, results in the promotion of protein growth and muscle development, which leads to bigger muscles and greater strength. Most athletes want to be stronger and will often turn to anabolic steroids to build up muscle to a level that's not naturally possible.

Anabolic steroids are sometimes used by athletes seeking to bulk up. Because they are testosterone based, they can have unique effects on the body for both men and women.

The other, undesirable, effect of anabolic steroids is the androgenic effect (*andro* = testosterone promoting). Taking in testosterone causes the body to decrease its own production of the hormone, leading to a hormone imbalance. In men, this can cause shrinkage of the testicles, decreased sperm production, impotence, painful urination, severe acne (especially on the back), and changes in hair growth (an increase in facial hair and a decrease in hair on the head). Men may also experience psychiatric side effects such as extreme mood swings and aggressiveness, which can lead to violence.

Women who use anabolic steroids also experience androgenic effects. Just as with men using anabolic steroids, women experience severe acne, increased facial and body hair, and loss of hair on the head. Additionally, women may experience a lower voice, increased aggressiveness, **amenorrhea,** and increased sex drive.

Although anabolic steroids can increase muscle mass and strength, their use among collegiate and professional athletes is prohibited by most agencies. Abusing anabolic steroids, to improve performance or physical appearance, can lead to severe health consequences such as liver and kidney tumors, liver cancer, high blood pressure, trembling, and increases in LDL cholesterol.

Growth Hormone

Growth hormone has been promoted with claims that it will increase muscle mass and strength and decrease body fat, thereby improving performance. Some competitive athletes use growth hormone instead of anabolic steroids to build muscles because they believe it is less likely to be detected through current testing methods.

Growth hormone is naturally produced by the pituitary gland to stimulate growth in children. Synthetic, or manmade, growth hormone was originally created for children with growth hormone deficiency to enable them to grow to their full height. It targets numerous tissues, including bones, skeletal muscle, fat cells, immune cells, and liver cells. Growth hormone increases protein synthesis by increasing amino acid transport across cell membranes, causing an increase in muscle mass but not strength. This increased muscle mass but not strength could actually impair performance by reducing one's power, speed, and endurance.

Growth hormone also decreases glycogen synthesis and the use of glucose for energy, causing an increase in fat breakdown and the use of fatty acids for energy. This, in turn, can improve body composition by decreasing body fat. For these reasons, many people assume they can improve their performance with the use of growth hormone.

amenorrhea Absence of menstruation.

The hand on the left shows someone with acromegaly compared with the normal hand on the right.

Little research exists on the effectiveness of growth hormone on improving fitness and athletic performance, and the results of studies that have been done are mixed. Growth hormone has been shown to reduce body fat and increase fat-free mass in well-trained adults.[37] However, other studies show that it does not improve muscle strength or lean body mass in healthy adult athletes or the elderly.[38] It also appears to have no positive effect on cardiovascular performance in adults with growth hormone deficiency.[39]

Abuse of growth hormone can have serious health effects, including the development of diabetes, atherosclerosis (hardening of the arteries), and hypertension. Excess growth hormone can also cause **acromegaly,** a condition in which tissues, bones, and internal organs grow abnormally large.

Erythropoietin and Blood Doping

Erythropoietin is a hormone produced by the kidneys when there is a decrease in blood oxygen levels. The hormone travels to the bone marrow and stimulates the formation of red blood cells, which carry oxygen to tissues. Synthetic versions of erythropoietin are used as ergogenic aids by athletes because increasing the number of red blood cells increases the oxygen-carrying capacity of the blood. This results in the athlete's being able to train at a higher intensity without becoming fatigued as quickly,[40] thereby having the potential to improve performance and overall physical fitness. Despite its popularity among competitive athletes, synthetic erythropoietin is a banned substance in most athletic organizations.

Before synthetic erythropoietin was discovered, the most common way to increase the oxygen-carrying capacity of the blood was blood doping. Blood doping, or red blood cell reinfusion, involves removing 250 to 500 milliliters of an athlete's own blood, extracting the red blood cells, and storing them for a few weeks prior to competition. The stored red blood cells are reinfused as the competition day approaches, so that the athlete has a higher than normal number of blood cells in his or her body. This results in an increase in the amount of oxygen in the blood, which can increase aerobic endurance.

Synthetic erythropoietin and blood doping can be dangerous because they increase blood viscosity (thickness). If the blood becomes too thick, it moves slowly and can clog capillaries. If this occurs in the brain, it results in a stroke. If there is a blood clot in the heart, it causes a heart attack. Both of these can be life-threatening. Erythropoietin may also cause sudden death during sleep, which is believed to have been a contributing factor in numerous deaths among professional European cyclists.

Table 11.7 summarizes the supplements that are often used to enhance athletic performance.

Sports Bars, Shakes, and Meal Replacers May Provide Benefits

Sports bars and shakes are not considered dietary supplements because they are more like food and contain one or more macronutrients.

The main energy source in most sports bars and shakes is carbohydrate, with protein and fat contributing smaller amounts of energy. The ratio of the macronutrients in these foods varies depending on the purpose. Bars and shakes that are intended to provide energy for and recovery from exercise have a greater proportion of energy supplied by carbohydrates. Those that are promoted for muscle protein synthesis typically contain more protein than carbohydrate and fat. Bars and shakes that are high in protein are often used by vegetarians and some athletes who may think that they need additional sources of protein in their diet. Most bars and shakes also contain a variety of vitamins and minerals. Of course, these vitamins and minerals may not be

acromegaly A condition caused by excess growth hormone in which tissues, bones, and internal organs grow abnormally large.

Table 11.7

The Truth about Supplements and Ergogenic Aids

Supplement/Ergogenic Aid	Belief or Claim	Evidence/Potential Side Effects
Multivitamin/mineral (most common among college athletes)	Improves overall health and performance; provides energy	Will improve health and performance only when deficiencies exist. Avoid multivitamin/mineral supplements containing more than 100% RDA of contents. Vitamins and minerals do not directly supply energy, but assist with the breakdown of carbohydrate, fat, and protein to use for energy.
Creatine	Increases muscle mass and strength; makes athlete faster and stronger	Mixed results in clinical trials. Has been shown to increase muscle mass and strength and improve performance in high-intensity, short-duration exercise by increasing ATP. Mixed results in improving performance in exercise of longer duration. No negative effects seen in healthy individuals.
Caffeine	Improves endurance	Has been shown to improve endurance in some athletes, but no improvement shown in short-duration activities. NCAA lists caffeine as a banned substance when urine concentrations exceed 15 mcg/ml (about 4–5 cups of coffee).
Anabolic steroids	Increase muscle mass, size, and strength	Have been shown to increase muscle mass, size, and strength, but also contribute many negative side effects such as hormone imbalance, changes in hair growth, shrinkage of testicles and decreased sperm count in men, and psychiatric effects like extreme mood swings and aggressiveness. Steroids are illegal in the United States unless prescribed by a physician.
Growth hormone	Increases muscle mass and strength, decreases body fat	Mixed results in clinical trials regarding improved athletic performance. May improve body composition in well-trained adults, but not others. Can have negative side effects such as acromegaly, and the development of diabetes, atherosclerosis, and hypertension. NCAA lists GH as a banned substance.
Erythropoietin	Improves cardiorespiratory fitness and endurance	Has been shown to improve cardiorespiratory fitness and endurance in athletes, but can be dangerous by increasing blood thickness and possibly forming blood clots. Has been linked to sudden death during sleep among European cyclists. NCAA lists erythropoietin as a banned substance.
Glucosamine/chondroitin	Prevents deterioration of joint cartilage caused by heavy training	Has not been shown to effectively preserve/restore joint cartilage in anyone, including athletes. Chondroitin can cause bleeding in people who have a bleeding disorder or take a blood-thinning drug. Synthetic glucosamine is made from shellfish and should be avoided by those with shellfish allergies.

Table 11.8

Bulking Up on Protein to Bulk Up?

Probably one of the biggest dietary misconceptions related to fitness is that to bulk up your muscles, you need to bulk up the protein or amino acids in your diet. Although athletes need more dietary protein than less active folks, their diets are likely supplying more than enough to build muscle. Expensive protein supplements are not only unnecessary, but may actually provide undesirable results.

The following chart will help you separate fact from fiction:

Fact	Fiction
You need weight resistance training to build muscle mass. The purpose of resistance training is to stress the muscle tissue so it increases its bulk. This is the only process that will result in increased muscle strength.	**Protein intake is more important than weight resistance training to build muscle.** This is pure fiction, as regularly scheduled weight resistance exercises are a key component to building muscle. No matter how much protein you consume, you won't build muscle without proper training.
Consuming adequate daily calories, especially from carbohydrates and fat, are vital to building muscle. A diet adequate in all three nutrients—carbohydrates, fat, and protein—is a muscle must! You need adequate carbohydrates and fats to fuel your workouts so that your dietary protein will be preserved to build and repair your muscles.	**There isn't any downside to eating a lot of protein.** Excessive amounts of protein, beyond your daily calorie needs, will be stored as body fat. Also, excessive protein burdens the kidneys to excrete the excess nitrogen as urea in urine.
The best recovery snack after your workout is one that will supply both carbohydrates and protein. Carbohydrates are needed for post-workout recovery to replenish your glycogen stores. Protein is also needed to aid in muscle repair and growth. Peanut butter on crackers with a glass of milk, yogurt and fruit, or chocolate milk all make excellent post-workout snacks.	**The protein and amino acids in supplements are more easily used by the body.** Your body doesn't distinguish between sources of protein and amino acids, but your wallet does. A supplement can cost more than $25 for 12 servings. Whole foods not only provide all three nutrients needed to build muscle, but they are also less expensive than overpriced supplements.
For best results, your recovery snack or meal should occur within 30 minutes of your workout. It's a fact!	**It doesn't matter when you eat after your workout.** Wrong again. Timing is everything, and waiting too long will diminish the body's ability to use the newly consumed carbohydrate and protein for glycogen replacement and muscle repair.

Sources: SCAN. 2009. Eating for Recovery, Nutrition Fact Sheet. Available at: http://www.scandpg.org/files/2009/SD-USA_Fact_Sheet_Eating_for_Recovery_Apr09.pdf; SCAN, 2010. Gaining Weight and Building Muscle. Available at: http://www.scandpg.org/files/2010/SD-USA_Fact_Sheet_Gaining_Weight_Building_Muscle_Jan_2010.pdf; Skinner, R. 2008. Nutrition for Muscle Mass. Gatorade Sports Science Institute. Available at: http://www.gssiweb.com/Article_Detail.aspx?articleid=753

necessary if you are consuming balanced meals regularly or taking a daily multivitamin. Table 11.8 separates fact from fiction when it comes to using protein supplements to bulk up.

If you're a supremely busy person, these products may be a convenient alternative to meals or snacks prepared at home. However, keep in mind that these items are often expensive. An energy bar may be trendy and easy to stash in your book bag, but an old-fashioned peanut butter sandwich on whole-grain bread would cost less and be just as easy to carry. Alternatively, you could even make your own energy bars for much less than it costs to buy them (see **Figure 11.5**).

Are You Meeting Your Fitness Recommendations and Eating for Exercise?

Now that you know how to plan an effective fitness strategy and eat for optimal fitness and performance, think about your current dietary and exercise habits. Take this brief assessment to find out if your daily habits are as healthful as they could be:

1. Do you participate in 30 minutes of moderately intense physical activity most days of the week?
   Yes ☐ **No** ☐

2. Do you participate in weight training 2 to 3 times per week?
   Yes ☐ **No** ☐

3. Do you drink 6 to 12 ounces of fluid every 15 to 20 minutes during exercise?
   Yes ☐ **No** ☐

4. Do you drink a sports beverage after moderate- or high-intensity exercise lasting longer than 1 hour?
   Yes ☐ **No** ☐

5. Do you consume carbohydrate and protein within 30 to 45 minutes after stopping exercise?
   Yes ☐ **No** ☐

Answer

If you answered yes to all of the questions, you are well on your way to optimal fitness. Participating in regular exercise, including aerobic exercise and strength training, helps you maintain optimal health and improves your level of fitness. Eating and drinking adequate nutrients also improves fitness. If you answered no to any of the questions, review this chapter to learn more on fitness and eating for exercise.

No Oven Needed Energy Bars

Ingredients:
5 Tablespoons natural peanut butter
6 scoops chocolate whey protein (~130 grams protein)
1 cup dry oats
1 cup non-fat dry milk
1 teaspoon vanilla
1/2 cup water

Directions:
Spray an 8x8 inch baking dish with non-stick cooking spray. Mix oats, whey protein, and non-fat dry milk in a bowl. Stir in peanut butter (mixture will look crumbly and dry). Add water and vanilla to mixture and stir until it forms a dough. Spray a clean spatula with non-stick cooking spray and use it to spread dough in baking dish. Refrigerate for a few hours, then cut into squares. Wrap bars individually in plastic wrap and keep in refrigerator until you are ready to eat them!

Figure 11.5 "No Oven Needed" Energy Bars
Try this recipe as an inexpensive alternative to commercial energy bars.

The Take-Home Message Dietary supplements and ergogenic aids, such as creatine, caffeine, anabolic steroids, growth hormone, erythropoietin, and blood doping, may enhance performance, but can have serious health effects. Sports bars and shakes are convenient sources of energy, but are more expensive than whole foods and should only be included as a minor part of an overall healthy diet.

Two Points of View

Are Personal Trainers a Credible Source of Nutrition Information?

For anyone belonging to a gym or recreational facility, personal trainers are often available to help you meet your fitness goals, whether it's weight loss, athletic training, or just wanting to be in better health. The main role of personal trainers is usually to help set up an individualized exercise routine, but many also offer diet and supplement advice. Are they qualified to discuss this subject with their clients? After you've read the arguments for and against, answer the critical thinking questions and decide for yourself.

Yes, Sometimes

- The primary goal of a personal trainer is to work with an individual to assess, design, and support a personal exercise program.[1]

- Qualified personal trainers are certified by groups like the American College of Sports Medicine (ACSM) or the American Council on Exercise (ACE). To qualify for a reputable certification, individuals have to pass rigorous exams. The ACE certification, for example, involves an intensive three-hour, 150-question exam and written simulation that covers exercise science and programming knowledge, including anatomy, kinesiology, health screening, basic nutrition, and instructional methods.[2]

- Some trainers do have advanced degrees or licenses in nutrition and thus talk to their clients about dietary habits and meal planning. The key is for the client to make sure the trainer is also an RD and/or, if you're an athlete seeking to improve your sport performance, a board certified sports dietitian (CSSD).[3]

No

- Most personal trainers simply haven't undergone enough nutrition education to prescribe diet plans, and in 29 states and Washington, D.C., it's actually illegal for them to do so unless they're also licensed as a registered dietitian.[4]

- Some personal trainer certification programs offer a certification in sports nutrition using their certification materials rather than requiring a degree in nutrition.[5] Such a training program is likely to be inadequate.

- Reputable certification programs advise their personal trainers *not* to dispense nutrition advice unless they have additional training. For example, the ACSM says its trainers should discuss no more than the most basic nutrition guidelines found on the government's food pyramid.[6]

- Inappropriate nutritional counseling can have severe consequences. In the 1999 case Capati vs Crunch Fitness, Anne Marie Capati, 37, died from a brain hemorrhage after a physical trainer advised her to take herbal supplements despite knowing that she had high blood pressure that required medication.[7]

What do you think?

1. Which side has the stronger evidence to support its argument? **2.** Do you think personal trainers should be government regulated rather than just certified? **3.** Have you or someone you know ever taken advice from a trainer at the gym? Knowing what you know now, do you think the advice was valid?

Chapter Review

Be a Nutrition Sleuth

Stay Hydrated for Fitness

How much fluid should you drink before, during, and after your workout? Go to **www.pearsonhighered.com/blake** to find out.

Get Real!

Get Ready to Get FITT!

Are you ready to incorporate more "FITTness" into your physical activity program? Go to **www.pearsonhighered.com/blake** and use the FITT worksheet to assess your regular physical activities for frequency, intensity, time, and type. Track your activities for a week, and see where you need to make adjustments to optimize your workouts.

The Top Ten Points to Remember

1. Physical fitness is defined as good health or physical condition, especially as the result of exercise and proper nutrition. There are five basic components of physical fitness: cardiorespiratory endurance, muscle strength, muscle endurance, flexibility, and body composition.

2. Engaging in regular physical activity provides several health benefits, such as reducing the risk of chronic diseases like cardiovascular disease and type 2 diabetes; and improving body composition, immunity, and bone health. As little as 60 minutes a week of moderate-intensity activity will provide health benefits, with more activity providing greater benefits.

3. The source of energy needed to fuel exercise depends on the intensity of the activity. Carbohydrate, specifically muscle glycogen, is the main energy source for high-intensity activity. Fat is the preferred source of energy during low-intensity activity. Carbohydrate and fat contribute equally to the energy needs incurred during exercise of moderate intensity.

4. Protein is important to fitness because it functions to maintain, build, and repair tissues, including muscle tissue. Only small amounts of protein are used for energy during exercise.

5. Vitamins and minerals assist in energy metabolism and are necessary for fitness. Athletes do not have greater needs for vitamins and minerals than do nonathletes, and intakes of vitamins and minerals above the RDA do not improve athletic performance.

6. Female and vegetarian athletes are at greater risk of developing iron deficiency and should consume iron-rich foods regularly. Athletes also need to be sure their calcium intake is adequate to help reduce their risk of bone fractures during physical activity.

7. Being adequately hydrated before, during, and after exercise is important to both health and athletic performance. Staying hydrated helps maintain fluid and electrolyte balance and normal body temperature. Water is the best fluid for hydration during exercise, though sports drinks can be beneficial for moderate- to vigorous-intensity exercise that lasts longer than 60 minutes.

8. Dietary supplements are not strictly regulated for their safety and efficacy; those who choose to use them may be placing their health at risk. Some dietary supplements are used as ergogenic aids to improve athletic performance.

9. Creatine has been shown to increase both muscle strength and mass, but research is mixed on its role in athletic performance. Caffeine has been shown to improve endurance performance, but has not shown any benefit in activities of short duration. Anabolic steroids can increase muscle mass and strength, but will also cause undesirable androgenic side effects for both men and women. Growth hormone may increase muscle mass and decrease body fat, but also has serious health effects. Synthetic erythropoietin and blood

doping can improve endurance, but can also thicken the blood, which may lead to a stroke or heart attack.

10. All athletes and physically active people must consume adequate calories, carbohydrate, protein, fat, vitamins, and minerals to achieve optimal fitness and athletic performance. Well-balanced meals and snacks consisting of whole foods should be the basis of an athlete's diet, with sports bars, shakes, and other supplements used only when necessary.

Test Your Knowledge

1. Which of the following is *not* a component of physical fitness?
   a. muscle strength
   b. cardiorespiratory endurance
   c. stress
   d. body composition

2. If you are able to do 100 consecutive push-ups without taking a break, you are exhibiting great
   a. cardiorespiratory endurance.
   b. muscle endurance.
   c. flexibility.
   d. muscle strength.

3. Well-trained muscles have the ability to store an unlimited amount of glycogen.
   a. True
   b. False

4. During low-intensity activity, your body obtains most of its energy from
   a. muscle glycogen.
   b. liver glycogen.
   c. muscle protein.
   d. fatty acids.

5. Under what conditions will the body use significant amounts of protein for energy during exercise?
   a. inadequate calorie intake
   b. inadequate carbohydrate stores
   c. inadequate fluid intake
   d. both a and b

6. A pregame meal should be
   a. high in carbohydrate, low in fat.
   b. high in carbohydrate and high in fat.
   c. low in carbohydrate, high in fat.
   d. low in protein, high in fat.

7. A condition that occurs when too much water is consumed or too much sodium is lost in sweating, resulting in abnormally low levels of sodium in the blood, is called
   a. acute dehydration.
   b. chronic dehydration.
   c. hyponatremia.

8. A commercial sports drink might be beneficial after 60 minutes or more of exercise because it
   a. contributes to hydration.
   b. provides electrolytes.
   c. provides carbohydrate.
   d. does all of the above.

9. An appropriate exercise recovery beverage would be
   a. a soft drink.
   b. coffee.
   c. low-fat chocolate milk.
   d. orange juice.

10. Acromegaly can be caused by abuse of which ergogenic aid?
    a. creatine
    b. growth hormone
    c. anabolic steroids
    d. erythropoietin

Answers

1. (c) Muscle strength, cardiorespiratory endurance, and body composition, along with muscle endurance and flexibility, are the five basic components of physical fitness. Stress is not a component of physical fitness.

2. (b) Performing 100 consecutive push-ups without resting shows great muscle endurance because you are able to exert the force needed to push yourself up over a long period of time without getting tired.

3. (b) Muscles that are well trained have the ability to store about 20 to 50 percent more glycogen than normal; however, the storage capacity of muscle glycogen is limited.

4. (d) Fatty acids are the main source of energy during low-intensity activity. As the intensity increases, the body will use less fatty acids and more glycogen for energy.

5. (d) The body will use larger amounts of protein for energy if overall calorie intake is inadequate and if carbohydrate stores are low.

6. (a) A meal before a game or workout should be high in carbohydrate to maximize glycogen stores and low in fat to prevent feelings of fatigue or discomfort.

7. (c) Hyponatremia occurs when blood levels of sodium become abnormally low as a result of drinking too much water or not replacing sodium lost through sweating. Long-distance runners are at higher risk for developing hyponatremia.

8. (d) Sports drinks supply fluids to rehydrate the body during and after exercise, electrolytes to replace those lost during sweating, and carbohydrate, which acts as an immediate source of energy that can potentially improve performance.

9. (c) Low-fat chocolate milk is a good exercise recovery beverage because it contains an appropriate ratio of carbohydrate and protein that is necessary for optimal recovery. Soft drinks, coffee, and orange juice will provide your body with fluids, but lack other nutrients that are ideal for recovery after exercise.

10. (b) Abusing growth hormone causes acromegaly, a disease in which tissues, bones, and internal organs grow abnormally large in size.

Web Resources

For more on nutrition and fitness, visit:
➡ The President's Council on Physical Fitness and Sports, www.fitness.gov
➡ American Council on Exercise, www.acefitness.org
➡ American College of Sports Medicine, www.acsm.org
➡ American Dietetic Association, www.eatright.org
➡ Sports, Cardiovascular, and Wellness Nutritionists: A Dietetics Practice Group of the American Dietetic Association, www.scandpg.org
➡ Gatorade Sports Science Institute, www.gssiweb.org
➡ For information on independent testing and product reviews about dietary supplements, visit www.ConsumerLab.com

Answers to Myths and Misperceptions

1. **False.** Less than half of all Americans meet recommendations for physical activity. Check out the potential drawbacks of this on page 409.

2. **True.** You don't have to be an Olympian to enjoy the health benefits of exercise. With as little as 60 minutes per week, you can burn more calories and lower your risk of certain diseases. Turn to page 413 for more information.

3. **True.** The body does use carbohydrate, fat, and protein for energy during exercise, but the amount that is used partly depends on the intensity of the exercise. Turn to page 416 to learn about energy sources during exercise.

4. **True.** Muscles adapt to training by storing more glycogen and using more body fat as fuel, which can increase endurance. Turn to page 418 to learn more.

5. **True.** Consumption of nutrients immediately after stopping exercise will improve recovery. Find out more on page 425.

6. **False.** Taking vitamin and/or mineral supplements will only improve performance if you're deficient in vitamins or minerals in the first place. Turn to page 427 to learn more about the roles of vitamins and minerals during exercise.

7. **True.** Female and vegetarian athletes are at higher risk for iron deficiency. Turn to page 427 to find out why this is the case.

8. **False.** Sports drinks are generally beneficial only when you exercise for longer than one hour. Find out more about fluid needs during exercise on page 431.

9. **False.** Drinking too much water can dilute your blood and alter the delicate fluid and electrolyte balance of your body. Turn to page 432 to learn more about proper hydration during exercise.

10. **True.** You may be surprised to learn that just a few cups of coffee can supply excessive amounts of caffeine. To learn more, turn to page 435.

12

True or False?

1. Food **advertising** probably has no effect on you. ⓉⒻ p. 446

2. Food comes from the **grocery store**. ⓉⒻ p. 447

3. Most farms in the United States are **small family farms**. ⓉⒻ p. 449

4. Coffee and bananas are **major crops** grown in the United States. ⓉⒻ p. 453

5. **Locally grown** foods usually require fewer natural resources to produce. ⓉⒻ p. 456

6. Eating in season can help reduce the **"food miles"** of a particular food. ⓉⒻ p. 457

7. Food **policy** is not tightly regulated in the United States. ⓉⒻ p. 469

8. The food industry has little influence on the **regulation** of food policy. ⓉⒻ p. 472

9. Organic foods are never produced with the use of **pesticides**. ⓉⒻ p. 474

10. **Organic foods** are always preferable to nonorganic foods. ⓉⒻ p. 475

See page 479 for answers to these Myths and Misperceptions.

Consumer From Farm

**ism:
to Table**

David, a 20-year-old junior, is studying to be an environmental engineer and shares an off-campus apartment with three business-major classmates. To save money, the four of them take turns making dinner. One evening, his roommate Bryan walked into the apartment and found a dark kitchen. "Who's cooking tonight?" asked Bryan. "David," another roommate called from the living room. "Where is he?" shouted Bryan. "You know David . . . he went to the farmers' market across town to get some stuff for dinner." Exasperated, Bryan said, "Why does David need to be a locavore? I'm starving. Can't he just get food from the supermarket down the street like everyone else?"

Do you know what a *locavore* is? Why do you think David goes to the farmers' market rather than the more convenient supermarket? As you have read thus far in this textbook, when it comes to good nutrition, "you are what you eat." It is also important that as a consumer you understand where you get what you eat. In this chapter, we will explore what it means to be a food consumer, where your food comes from, and how you can make informed decisions about purchasing your food.

Chapter Objectives

After reading this chapter, you will be able to:

1. Describe how advertising and marketing affect your food choices.

2. Define what constitutes a U.S. farm.

3. Explain the role of agribusiness in the United States and the world.

4. Name at least three internal resources that are used to produce food.

5. Name at least three external resources that are used to produce food.

6. Describe what constitutes a sustainable food system.

7. Understand the role that hormones, antibiotics, and pesticides play in food production.

8. Explain how food policy affects the foods that are available to you.

9. Describe how a food lobbyist may influence your food choices.

What Does It Mean to Be a Food Consumer?

The fact that we buy food, whether at the dining hall, mini mart, grocery store, or a restaurant, makes us all **food consumers.** As such, we command a great deal of influence on the **food industry,** which is a global, $4 *trillion* a year business.[1] We literally speak with our food dollars. The foods we choose to buy, where we choose to buy them, and how often we make these purchases are decisions that are tremendously important to the people who grow, process, market, distribute, and sell our food products. Although you may think that you are in the "driver's seat" when choosing the foods you eat, this isn't entirely the case. In fact, there are many outside factors that influence the foods that you have access to and end up purchasing.

The Take-Home Message Anyone who buys food is a food consumer. As a food consumer, you influence the behaviors of the farmers, processors, marketers, distributors, and retailers of the food industry by choosing what, where, and when to buy. The food industry, however, ultimately controls what products are available.

How Do Advertising and Marketing Influence Your Food Choices?

Every year, vast amounts of money are spent by food companies to persuade you to buy their products. Whether they are advertised on television, radio, magazines, or the Internet, or placed in movies, these products' manufacturers spend more than $10 billion annually to promote them. Much of the promotion is for nutritionally dubious products. In fact, more than $2 billion alone is spent on the marketing of breakfast cereals, candy, and gum. Another $500 million is spent on advertising carbonated soft drinks.[2] You can probably think of an ad campaign you've seen recently for a particular brand of soda or fast-food chain. In comparison, when was the last time you saw an advertisement for broccoli? Have you *ever* seen an ad for broccoli?

A growing trend in food advertising is to market heavily to college-aged and young adults by targeting college campuses and social venues that are popular with this age group. For example, one marketing strategy for Red Bull, a caffeinated energy drink, was to give away free samples on college campuses, at sports events, and in trendy clubs and bars. And it worked like a charm. Within three years of rolling out this product in the United States, Red Bull sparked a booming trend in energy beverage consumption. In 2008, Red Bull enjoyed $1 billion in sales.[3] Why did this advertising and marketing strategy work? Red Bull astutely identified where its target audience hangs out, and then the beverage company hung out with them.

More recently, Red Bull has followed its target audience online to social media sites, including Facebook, MySpace, and Twitter.[4] Facebook users can "like" Red Bull, and those on MySpace can add the drink to their list of "friends." While you may think you are immune to the influence of these techniques, companies like Red Bull put a lot of thought and effort into keeping you excited about their brand, and they do it because they think it works. Wherever you, and your wallet, go, they will follow.

In contrast, advertising for fruits and vegetables is almost nonexistent, which is a shame because healthy foods can be successfully marketed. When the dairy industry noted a decline in milk consumption among Americans in the early 1990s, it launched the *Got Milk?* ad campaign, which featured celebrities wearing milk mustaches. This campaign strove to make drinking milk sexy, and it worked. Milk sales increased by nearly 1.5 billion pounds, the equivalent of about 45 million pounds of milk being sold for each ad dollar spent.[5]

The Take-Home Message The food industry spends large amounts of money on marketing and advertising its products, often to target audiences. The most heavily advertised foods are often the least nutritious.

Red Bull uses strategies that help it target college-aged, young-adult consumers.

Where Does Your Food Come From?

Most people don't think too much about where their food comes from before it appears on the supermarket shelf. Have you ever considered where the ingredients in your morning cereal and orange juice, for example, originate? Unless you're growing wheat and oranges and keeping a cow in your backyard, you're depending on the work of numerous individuals, from the farmer to the food distributor, to transform raw milk and stalks of wheat into the foods that you have available to you. No matter what you're eating, it started out on a farm (see **Figure 12.1**).[6]

Much of Your Food Comes from Small, Family-Run American Farms

In the United States, a **farm** is considered an establishment that produces and sells at least $1,000 of agricultural products annually. By this definition, there are just over

food consumers The role that individuals play when they are making decisions about which food to buy and which to avoid.

food industry The collective efforts of various businesses, including farms, food processors, food marketers, wholesalers, and retailers, that provide food to consumers.

farm An establishment that produces and sells at least $1,000 worth of agricultural products annually.

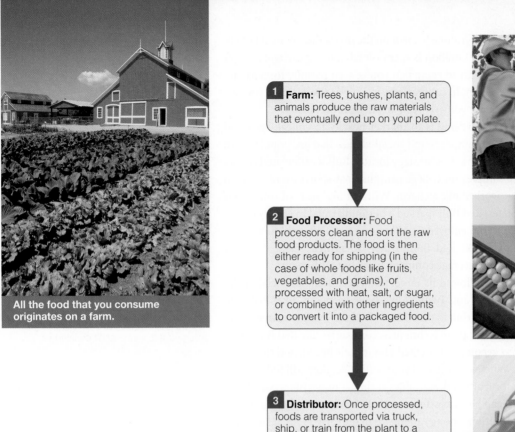

All the food that you consume originates on a farm.

1 **Farm:** Trees, bushes, plants, and animals produce the raw materials that eventually end up on your plate.

2 **Food Processor:** Food processors clean and sort the raw food products. The food is then either ready for shipping (in the case of whole foods like fruits, vegetables, and grains), or processed with heat, salt, or sugar, or combined with other ingredients to convert it into a packaged food.

3 **Distributor:** Once processed, foods are transported via truck, ship, or train from the plant to a retail outlet, where consumers can buy them.

4 **Seller:** While people buy food from several sources, including restaurants, farmers' markets, and convenience stores, most food shopping takes place at the grocery store.

5 **Consumer:** You, the consumer, are the final step in the process.

Figure 12.1 From Farm to Consumer
Many individuals make it easier for you to obtain the foods you consume and enjoy.

2 million farms in the United States, and they're largely concentrated in the Midwest, Great Plains, and California (**Figure 12.2**). Although 2 million may sound like a lot of farms, it's actually many fewer than in the past. In 1935, there were more than 6.5 million farms feeding approximately 127 million Americans.[7] Currently, fewer than 960,000 hard-working Americans—less than 1 percent of the population—produce enough food to feed the country's 300 million people. This lopsided scenario, with

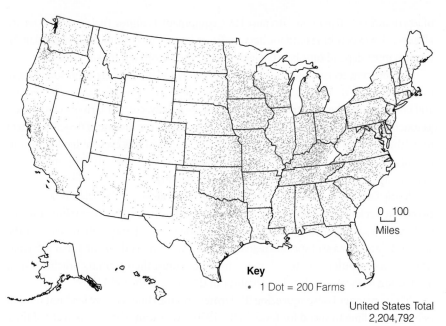

Figure 12.2 The Location and Number of Farms in the United States, 2007

Source: United States Department of Agriculture, "2007 Census of Agriculture." 2009. Available at www.agcensus.usda.gov/Publications/2007/index.asp.

0 100
Miles

Key
• 1 Dot = 200 Farms

United States Total
2,204,792

Table 12.1
Types of Farms in the United States

Farm Type	Number of Farms	Percent of Total Farms
Small		
(annual sales less than $250,000)	1,869,200	90.5
Large		
(annual sales greater than $250,000)	195,500	9.5
Nonfamily	42,300	2.0
Large family	153,200	7.5
Total farms in the U.S.	2,064,700	100

Source: United States Environmental Protection Agency, "Ag 101: Demographics." 2009. Available at www.epa.gov/oecaagct/ag101/demographics.html. Accessed May 2010.

fewer farms but more people, has forced farmers to become more efficient in the ways they produce food. We will read more about this later in the chapter.

You probably think that to feed all these people, farms must be mammoth, but most American farms are actually small farms (see Table 12.1). Further, 90 percent of U.S. farms, both large and small, are owned and operated by families. However, these families are not necessarily passing the business on to the next generation, and the age of the average farmer is increasing.[8]

What Are Some of the Challenges of Farming?

While running a family farm may sound like a desirable career path—after all, you'd spend much of your time outside and, if you're working for your family, would probably enjoy a flexible schedule—the challenges farmers face are actually quite steep. High costs, a demand for low food prices, competition, and a dependence on the cooperation of Mother Nature can all derail a farmer's bottom line. In fact, more than 75 percent of American farms generate gross revenues (this is revenue before expenses)

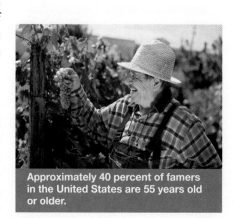

Approximately 40 percent of famers in the United States are 55 years old or older.

Modern machinery has helped farmers increase yields.

Table 12.2

Major Agricultural Crops Produced in the United States

Crop	Harvested Area (millions of acres)
Corn (grain)	72.7
Soybeans	72.7
Hay	59.9
Wheat	53.0
Cotton	13.1
Sorghum (grain)	7.7
Rice	3.0

Source: United States Environmental Protection Agency, "Ag 101: Crop Systems." 2009. Available at www.epa.gov/oecaagct/ag101/cropsystems.html. Accessed May 2010.

precision agriculture A cost-efficient, precise farming method that uses new technologies to collect data about variations in field soil to better manage the use of appropriate seeds, fertilizer, water, and pesticides for the growing of crops with less waste.

commodity crops Crop products such as corn and soybeans that can be used for commerce.

agribusiness The businesses collectively associated with the production, processing, and distribution of agricultural products, including food.

Corn Belt The parts of the United States where corn is grown in abundance. This includes Iowa, Indiana, most of Illinois, and parts of Kansas, Missouri, Nebraska, South Dakota, Minnesota, Ohio, and Wisconsin.

of less than $50,000 per year.[9] Because land, equipment, facilities, fuel, and fertilizer are all expensive (a combine used for harvest, for example, can cost upwards of $200,000), farmers must depend on a hearty yield to cover their costs and make a profit.[10]

Fortunately, technology and machinery allow today's farmers to produce more food on less land. Whereas a farmer in the 1930s could expect to harvest about 100 bushels (1 bushel is equal to 32 quarts) of corn daily, current farmers can harvest as much as 900 bushels of corn every hour.[11] But again, the machines that allow them to do this are very expensive. Thus, farmers are caught in this cycle of having to continually invest in new machines and technology to ensure a hearty crop in order to make enough money to pay for the expense of farming.

Some farmers use computers and the Internet to farm more efficiently. Known as **precision agriculture,** these farmers use a Global Positioning System (similar to the GPS in a car) along with other technologies to help collect and evaluate data on the soil, pests, and disease at specific field locations. The farmers then enter that information into a computer and, based on the findings, adjust their farming practices, such as by using less water and/or less fertilizer in that area of the field.[12]

The consumer is also squeezing the farmer's bottom line, as there is a limit to what people are willing to spend for food. In the 1930s, Americans spent 25 percent of their disposable income on food. Today, Americans allocate only 10 percent of their earnings to what they eat.[13] Once again, farmers are forced to produce large volumes in order to keep foods affordable for consumers, cover their expenses, and still make a profit.[14]

To try to offset their rising costs, many farmers take advantage of government-sponsored financial subsidies that are available to raise **commodity crops,** such as corn and soybeans. To obtain this financial support, these crops must also be grown in accordance with conservation plans that protect the environment.[15] Unfortunately, even with this support, there has been a trend toward larger farms, which are sometimes owned by giant corporations, producing large amounts of agricultural products in America. This can make it more difficult for small farms to stay in business.[16]

The Role of Agribusiness

All farming, large and small, is part of a wider field known as **agribusiness**—the blending of agricultural and business entities that affect how food, as well as the clothes in your closet and the furnishings in your home, are developed, processed, distributed, and purchased in the United States. The food component of agribusiness includes not only food production but also agricultural chemicals, agricultural finance and trade, farm management, environmental considerations, and land development. In essence, it involves all of the major elements needed in the efficient meshing of agriculture and the food business.[17]

The agriculture sector employs just over one-sixth of the U.S. population, or over 18 million Americans.[18] *Food-processing companies*, which take raw fruits, vegetables, grains, meats, and dairy products and convert them into edible food, comprise a large segment of those employed in agriculture (**Figure 12.3**). While agribusiness is "big business" because it employs many individuals, this doesn't mean that it consists only of enormous conglomerates. In fact, two-thirds of the more than 20,000 processing operations in the United States have fewer than 20 employees.[19]

What Crops Are Grown for Food?

The top three agricultural food crops grown in the United States are corn, soybeans, and wheat (see Table 12.2). The United States is the largest producer of corn in the world, with 10 billion bushels harvested on more than 400,000 farms spread out over almost 73 million acres in the **Corn Belt** (**Figure 12.4**). Most of that corn, however, isn't consumed as cornflakes, corn syrup, cornmeal, or other human food products. Rather, about 80 percent ends up as feed for livestock, poultry, and fish.

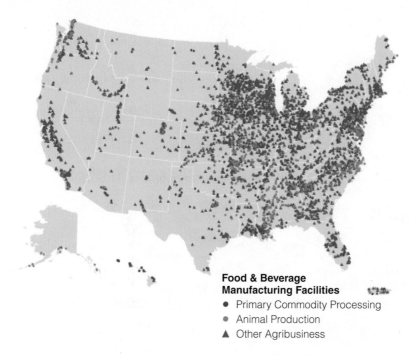

Food & Beverage Manufacturing Facilities
- Primary Commodity Processing
- Animal Production
- ▲ Other Agribusiness

Figure 12.3 The Location and Number of Food- and Beverage-Processing Facilities, 2007
Food- and beverage-processing facilities employ many of the 26 million people who work in the American agriculture sector.

Source: United States Environmental Protection Agency, "Location of U.S. Facilities." Available at www.epa.gov/sectors/sectorinfo/sectorprofiles/agribusiness.html. Accessed May 2010.

Fifty percent of the world's soybean production occurs on about 350,000 U.S. farms (see Figure 12.4). In addition to products like tofu, soy sauce, and edamame, soy is used to produce soybean oil, the number-one oil consumed by Americans. More than 30 million tons of soybean meal (the part of the soybean left after the oil is extracted) are used to feed livestock annually.[20]

The United States produces about 13 percent of the world's wheat, which is harvested from more than 240,000 farms clustered in the Great Plains from Texas to Montana (see Figure 12.4). More than 70 percent of this wheat is used for food products, such as bread and cereal; about 22 percent is used for animal feed; and the rest is left for seeds to replenish the crops.[21]

As you can tell from these statistics, most of the staple crops grown in the United States are used not to feed humans, but to feed animals that will themselves later enter our food supply. Does it surprise you to learn that livestock in the United States consume a substantial amount of the crops that are grown in the United States? Should we be growing crops to feed animals, or should we be eating fewer animal foods and eating more crops? Later on in the chapter we will look at this important issue.

What Animals Are Raised for Food?

By far, the dominant food animals in the United States are cows, pigs, and chickens. Beef products such as steaks, roasts, and hamburger originate from animals raised on more than 800,000 beef farms, concentrated in Texas, Colorado, Nebraska, Kansas, Iowa, California, Missouri, and Oklahoma (see Figure 12.4). Calves (young cattle) typically graze on croplands after harvest or in open grass pasturelands until they reach a certain weight. They are then confined to **feedlots,** where they are fed roughage (inedible hay and plant parts such as cornstalks and grasses) and grains as a complete feed or meal, so that they will grow to 1,000 pounds or more before being slaughtered.[22]

Soy is used to make numerous food products, including soybean oil, which is the number-one oil used by Americans.

feedlot A facility where cattle are fed grain and other foods before being slaughtered.

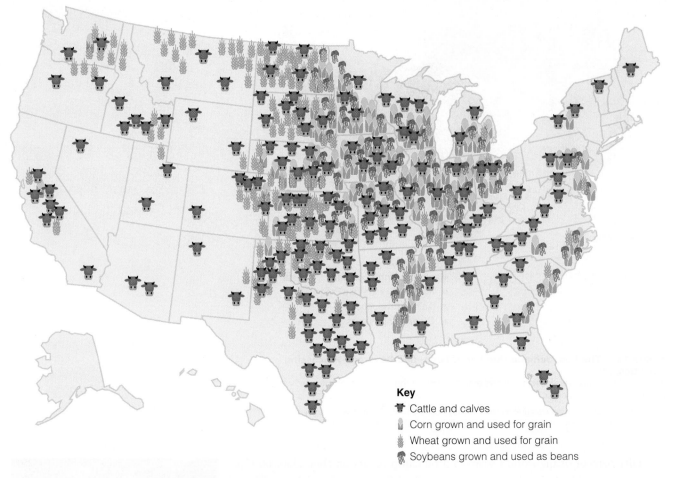

Key

🐄 Cattle and calves

🌽 Corn grown and used for grain

🌾 Wheat grown and used for grain

🌿 Soybeans grown and used as beans

Figure 12.4 Major U.S. Centers of Cattle, Corn, Wheat, and Soybean Production

Source: United States Department of Agriculture, "2007 Census of Agriculture." 2009. Available at www
.agcensus.usda.gov/Publications/2007/index.asp.

Pork by-products can be used
to make insulin for managing
diabetes and valves for heart
surgery in humans.

There are about 100,000 U.S. pig farms, concentrated in the Corn Belt and in North Carolina, producing pork products such as bacon, pork chops, and ham. Unlike their ancestors, most of today's hogs are raised indoors to protect them from weather, predators, and the spread of disease. They're also leaner and meatier than ever, with a 250-pound animal producing 150 pounds of pork.[23] However, the reduced price that you are used to paying for pork has forced smaller pork farmers out of business. They can't compete with larger-scale farms to produce the volume of product necessary to make a profit.

If you enjoy eggs with your bacon, you can thank the more than 99,000 poultry farms located in the Corn Belt, North Carolina, and the southern United States that focus on poultry and egg production.[24] Americans eat more poultry products than either beef or pork.[25] As with pork, raising poultry indoors has increased production and reduced labor, and thus has resulted in lower poultry prices.

Exporting Foods: The Good and Bad News

In addition to producing enough food to feed Americans, U.S. farmers help feed the world. An estimated 30 percent of the income from a U.S. farm is derived from trading with other countries.[26] Since the mid-1940s, the United States has exported more agricultural products than it has imported.[27] In 2010, agricultural exports were predicted to top $100 billion, an increase of more than a billion dollars from

Americans eat more poultry than
either beef or pork.

the previous year.[28] Grains (corn, soybeans, and wheat) and oilseeds (seeds used to make oils such as corn oil and soybean oil) are the most popular exports from the United States.

We are also exporting many of our unhealthy eating habits, including the consumption of large amounts of high-calorie, high-fat, processed foods. According to the Economic Research Service, the globalization of the food industry has caused the "Americanization" of many food cultures around the world. As the income of individuals in countries such as Mexico, Poland, Brazil, and China has increased, so has their desire for an American-like diet. As these affluent individuals shift their food choices from native grains and other carbohydrate-rich staples to more expensive meats, dairy foods, confectionery products, soft drinks, convenience foods, and fast foods,[29] they experience the same shift in body weight as we are seeing in the United States. That is, they also experience a growing problem with obesity.

Globesity, or the rapidly growing incidence of obesity worldwide, is becoming a global threat. For example, in the late 1980s, less than 10 percent of Mexicans were overweight. Currently, more than 65 percent of citizens in Mexico are overweight, which, not coincidentally, is the same percentage as of Americans who are battling the bathroom scale.[30] It is now estimated that more than 115 million people worldwide suffer health problems related to being overweight and obese.[31]

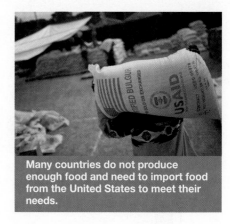

Many countries do not produce enough food and need to import food from the United States to meet their needs.

Food Production outside the United States

So, if we are exporting so much food and we are producing plenty of food here at home, does that mean we don't import foods from other countries? In a word, no. The next time you are in a supermarket, look beyond the colorful fruits and vegetables in the produce aisle, and read the signs posted alongside these foods. It's not uncommon for those juicy green grapes to be from Chile, the vibrant red peppers from Mexico, the fresh shrimp from Canada, and the nuts from Costa Rica. You may feel as though you are traveling around the world rather than around the grocery aisles.

Americans' plates are filled with more imported foods than ever before. In fact, most fish and shellfish eaten in the United States is now imported from other countries, including China and Thailand, and about 32 percent of the fruit and nuts that we buy originate outside the United States (see **Figure 12.5**). The United States currently imports close to $1 billion worth of bananas annually from Guatemala, Ecuador, Costa Rica, Colombia, and Honduras.[32] Vegetable imports have doubled, and importation of fruits, juices, and nuts has increased by 20 percent from decades ago.[33] The majority of our coffee comes from Colombia and Brazil. All told, approximately 13 percent of your food comes from outside the United States.[34]

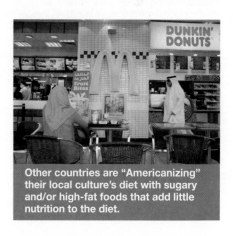

Other countries are "Americanizing" their local culture's diet with sugary and/or high-fat foods that add little nutrition to the diet.

Importing Foods: The Good and Bad News

Why do we get so much of our food from other countries? Two primary reasons are our demand for a diverse array of products year round, regardless of U.S. growing seasons, and our demand for cheap food.

Americans have lost their patience for waiting. Even with a foot of snow on the ground, Northerners in the United States still want to wake up to fresh cantaloupe for breakfast, so retailers have the fruit shipped in from Mexico. The novelty of waiting until the summer to enjoy melons is, well, a novelty.

Also, as already mentioned, farming in the United States is an expensive endeavor. This opens the door to the outsourcing of agricultural production to poorer,

globesity A blend of the words *global* and *obesity,* coined by the World Health Organization, which refers to the worldwide obesity epidemic.

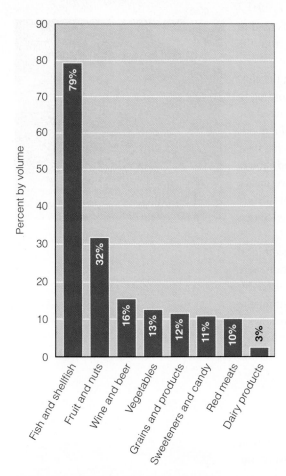

Figure 12.5 Percent of Selected Foods and Beverages Consumed in the United States That Are Imported, by Volume
America is importing foods such as seafood now more than ever before.

Source: A. Jerardo, "What Share of U.S. Consumed Food Is Imported?" *Amber Waves* (2008). Available at www.ers.usda.gov/amberwaves/february08/datafeature.

developing nations that have lower overhead costs, and hence, can provide cheaper food to the consumer.[35] Although this outsourcing can provide jobs and income for developing countries (good news), you will learn in the next section that there are environmental costs (bad news) of shipping these foods long distance to the United States and ultimately to your plate.

In addition to the environmental costs, the other downside to importing foods is the potential for contamination. There have been reports of imported foods containing excessive amounts of pesticides and foodborne pathogens compared with similar domestic products.[36] This increased risk of contamination places an increased burden on the FDA, the agency that polices the safety of the domestic food supply. In the past, the FDA has had to block contaminated farm-raised fish imported from China because the fish contained additives that have been shown to cause cancer in animals.[37] The globalization of the food supply is going to require that uniform, global food-safety standards be developed and implemented to keep imported foods safe.[38] This will entail an enormous, unified effort among many countries.

Let's now look at how all of this modernization and globalization affect the environment.

The Take-Home Message The food that you consume originates on a farm. Most farms in the United States are small and family operated. Agribusiness is a blending of agriculture and business and affects how foods are developed, processed, distributed, and purchased. The major crops grown in the United States are corn, soybeans, and wheat, and the major animals raised for food are cows, pigs, and chickens. Some of the foods you consume are grown in the United States and some are imported from other countries. Many countries rely on the United States for part of their food supply.

How Does Food Production Impact the Environment?

All agriculture affects the environment in some way.[39] From the water required for irrigation to the fuel needed to run the tractors to the animal wastes produced in feedlots, the processes of growing, harvesting, slaughtering, and transporting food products require the use, depletion, and potential contamination of natural resources.

Food Production Requires the Use of Internal and External Resources

Numerous natural resources are used when growing crops and raising animals for foods. Both natural and man made by-products that are produced during these proc-

Table 12.3

Environmental Effects of Food Production

	The Challenge	How Can We Minimize the Environmental Impact?
Land overuse	Excessive use of farming equipment, overtilling, and livestock overgrazing can all damage soil.	Proper land management and conservation methods of tilling can help preserve the land and replenish soil nutrients.
Soil erosion	Wind and rain can cause more than 1.5 billion tons of nutrient-rich topsoil to be blown and washed away each year. When fertile topsoil is lost, crop yield declines.	Proper crop covering and shielding from wind as well as proper tillage of the soil can dramatically reduce erosion.
Water depletion	Irrigation accounts for 80 percent of water consumption in the United States; hence, excessive irrigation can deplete naturally occurring groundwater.	Precision farming and the conscious reduction of overwatering can help preserve water.
Water runoff	After a rainfall (and the watering of the crops), the water runoff from farms can spread pesticides from crops and pathogens in animal manure to other fields, surface water, and downfield rivers and streams, contaminating these ecosystems.	Basins can be installed to collect the runoff water to prevent this contamination prior to discharge to streams and rivers.
Airborne emissions	Emissions of ammonia and nitrogen (see below) in manure are released into the air. The ammonia released from these airborne emissions can settle on water surfaces, killing fish and encouraging the growth of toxic algae, both of which disrupt the natural ecosystem.	The proper handling of manure (see below) mitigates this problem.
Nitrate production	The production of nitrates from the nitrogen in the manure can pollute our surface water and groundwater that is used as drinking water.	Proper collection, stockpiling, and disposal of manure to minimize the leaching of nitrates into runoff and groundwater, as proposed in the latest EPA regulations, will help concentrated animal feeding operations (CAFOs) to safely manage manure.

Source: Harmon, A. H., and B. L. Gerald, "Position of the American Dietetic Association: Food and Nutrition Professionals Can Implement Practices to Conserve Natural Resources and Support Ecological Sustainability," *Journal of the American Dietetic Association* 107 (2007): 1033–1043; Department of Agriculture Economics Research Service, "Irrigation and Water Use." 2004. Available at www.ers.usda.gov/briefing/WaterUse. Accessed January 2010; U.S. Environmental Protection Agency, "Ag 101: Crop Production." 2009. Available at www.epa.gov/oecaagct/ag101/cropmajor.html. Accessed January 2010; U.S. Environmental Protection Agency, "Ag 101: Beef Production." 2009. Available at www.epa.gov/oecaagct/ag101/beef.html. Accessed January 2010.

esses can affect the environment. Natural resources are used "internally" to produce foods and "externally" to move these food products from the farm to the consumer. Table 12.3 describes several of the challenges associated with using internal resources, including land and water, to produce food, and various strategies that can be employed to protect the environment.

External resources, or those not used in the actual growing of the food, also contribute to the environmental costs of food production. For example, the use of fossil fuels to grow, process, and transport food contributes to the release of *carbon dioxide gas emissions*. The carbon dioxide and other gases released when fossil fuels are burned

Figure 12.6 How Far Did Your Food Travel?
You might be surprised to learn just how far some of your food travels to get to your local supermarket.

Source: Adapted from R. Pirog, et al., "Food, Fuel, and Freeways: An Iowa Perspective on How Far Food Travels, Fuel Usage, and Greenhouse Gas Emissions," Leopold Center for Sustainable Agriculture. 2002. Available at www.leopold.iastate.edu/pubs/staff/ppp.

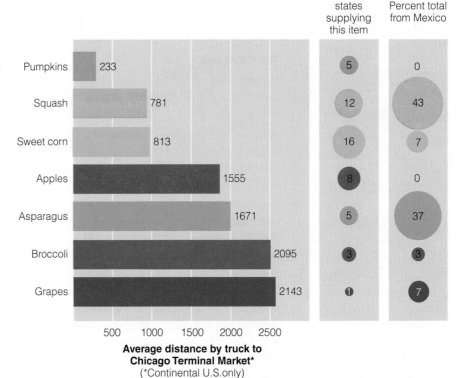

for energy are referred to as **greenhouse gases,** as these gases absorb and trap the heat in the air and re-radiate that heat downward. It is estimated that global temperatures could increase by 35 to 39 degrees Fahrenheit by 2100 due to these greenhouse gases.[40]

The carbon emissions associated with the transport of food from farm to supermarket are substantial, and you use additional fuel to drive to the supermarket and to prepare your food at home. The lettuce, orange, or cantaloupe that you put in your grocery cart during the winter may have traveled 1,400 to 2,400 miles to reach you.[41] Produce trucked to Chicago has traveled an average of slightly over 1,500 miles, which is more than a 20 percent increase since the early 1980s (see **Figure 12.6**).[42] The amount of fossil fuel used to transport that produce all those miles, coupled with the increase in carbon dioxide gas emissions into the air from burning that fuel, has enormous environmental costs.[43] A study conducted in Iowa showed that produce made available from national sources and shipped in from various distances used 4 to 17 times more fuel and released 5 to 17 times more carbon dioxide gas emissions than produce that was locally produced.[44]

Natural resources aside, these fuel costs are also factored into the price of the food, so they affect your financial resources. An estimated 12 percent of your food dollars go toward the cost of getting the food from the farm to your plate. Consequently, as the price of oil increases, the price that you pay for your food will also increase.[45] Thus, the farther your food has to travel, the more resources will be used, which not only has a negative effect on the environment, but is also a drain on your wallet. Because of these reasons, many people are trying to buy more and more of their food from locally grown sources.

Locally Grown Food Requires Fewer Natural Resources

David, the student whom you read about in the opening of this chapter, is a **locavore,** a person who attempts to eat locally grown food whenever possible. Locavores try to frequent local farms, farmers' markets, and roadside stands rather than buy similar

greenhouse gases Gases that absorb and "trap" the heat in the air and re-radiate that heat downward.

locavore A person who eats locally grown food whenever possible.

foods at supermarkets, that were shipped farther distances. Depending upon where they live, it may be very difficult for locavores to consume 100 percent of their diet from local sources year-round. Although Vermonters have access to fresh dairy foods 365 days a year, robust crops are hard to find under a foot of snow in the dead of winter. Like David, many locavores try to eat foods grown locally and then supplement their meals with foods from the supermarket.

The movement for "eating locally" has gained momentum for numerous reasons. Among these is that most people perceive locally grown foods as tasting better. A locally grown summer tomato, for example, is usually much more flavorful than one that has been shipped in a refrigerated truck for 2,000 miles. Similarly, a New England Macintosh apple tastes much better picked off a tree at the height of apple season than after sitting in a cold storage room for three months. Eating locally also has environmental benefits, because the less your food travels, the less energy is being used to get it to you.

In addition, local, small farms are typically run by farmers who not only farm the land but also live on it. They harvest foods at peak ripeness, tend to use little packaging, and travel fewer miles to distribute their goods, all of which can potentially reduce negative effects on the environment. The "food miles" saved can be eye-opening. Table 12.4 shows the distance travelled for the ingredients in a meal that was obtained locally or from conventional sources. A meal consisting of foods obtained at a local supermarket can travel as much as 60 times the miles as the same meal made from locally grown foods.

Home gardening can reduce food miles to food "steps." The feature box "You as a Sustainable Farmer" on page 458 shows you how to grow your own vegetables even if you don't have a backyard.

Many large supermarkets now sell locally grown produce. This combining of locally grown foods with conventionally grown foods allows the consumer to do "one-stop shopping" rather than having to drive to the farmers' markets, farm stands, and **community-supported agriculture (CSA)** pick-ups in addition to the supermarket. Corporate America is also making it easier to eat locally. Some large corporations and industrial complexes have weekly farmers' markets on their premises. Employees can shop for locally grown foods during the day and head home with the fixings for dinner.[46] The USDA recently awarded more than $5 million in grants to support local food connections between farmers and consumers, even in large cities, with its "Know Your Farmer, Know Your Food" initiative.[47]

Some individuals wrongfully assume that locally grown food is the same as sustainably grown food. A *sustainable diet* contains foods that meet your nutrient and health needs but can be sustained for a long time without negatively impacting the environment.[48] Buying food from small local farms doesn't guarantee that the foods

Locally grown, seasonal New England apples are crisp and full of flavor.

The *Oxford American Dictionary* declared the word *locavore* the 2007 Word of the Year!

community-supported agriculture (CSA) An arrangement where individuals pay a fee to support a local farm, and in exchange receive a weekly or biweekly box of fresh produce from the farm.

Table 12.4				
Food Miles in a Meal				
Food item	Local Source	Distance Traveled from Local Source	Conventional Source	Distance Traveled through Conventional Channels
Chuck roast	Local grass-fed beef farm	75 miles	Colorado	675 miles
Potatoes	Farmers' market	10–15 miles	Idaho	1,300 miles
Carrots	Backyard garden	40 feet	California	1,700 miles
Green beans	Backyard garden	40 feet	California	1,700 miles

You as a Sustainable Farmer: Growing Vegetables in a Container

You might think you need a yard, a hoe, and a shovel to have a garden, but this isn't necessarily the case. Edible plants can grow in all kinds of environments and containers, and for those living in dorms or apartments, a sunny window sill, a balcony, or your front step will provide enough space to create your own garden. All you need are a container, potting soil, water, a plant, and sun. In fact, there are even advantages to growing plants in containers rather than in the ground. There won't be any weeds to pull, and you'll have fewer pests to damage your plants. Your garden is also transportable so you can move it if you need to.

Here's what you need to get started:[1]

The Container

Most any container, such as a ceramic pot, planter box, one- to five-gallon tubs, or even the plastic trash container under your desk, will do. The size of the container will depend on what you want to grow (see table). Drainage is key to growing a hearty plant. So, your container must have two important elements: 1) ¼-inch drilled holes, evenly spaced along the bottom of the container, and 2) an inch-thick layer of coarse gravel, pebbles, or broken pieces of a clay pot in the bottom of the container. This layer will allow excess water to drain from the plant.

The Potting Mixture

In place of soil, potting mixtures, which may be a combination of several compounds such as sawdust, peat moss, and vermiculite (a mineral that puffs up when exposed to heat such as from the sun), can be purchased at most garden centers, many hardware stores, and even on Amazon.com. The amount of potting mixture that you need will depend on the type of vegetables you want to grow and the size of your container (see table).

The Plant

Many of the vegetables that grow in a backyard garden will also sprout quite nicely in a container garden. The table provides a list of the easier-to-grow vegetables for first-time gardeners that are ideal for containers. Transplants (small plants that you transfer to the container) can be purchased at garden centers, farmers' markets, local farm stands, and even some supermarkets. When these

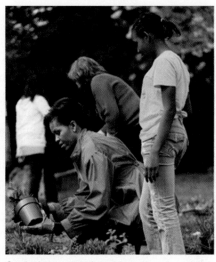

Gardening can be done at any home, even the White House, as Michelle Obama demonstrates.

Cows are often confined to feedlots until they reach 1,000 pounds.

were grown in a sustainable way, nor does being from a distant farm mean that those farmers didn't practice sustainable agriculture. The feature box "What's a Sustainable Food System?" looks at the issue of sustainable diets and how farms, both small and large, are implementing sustainable farming practices.

Hormones, Antibiotics, and Pesticides Can Improve Food Production but May Have Environmental Consequences

In addition to the use of fossil fuels and other natural resources, compounds widely used to enhance the food supply, such as hormones, antibiotics, and pesticides, also sometimes present environmental concerns. Let's look at why these compounds are added and the benefits, risks, and environmental implications of having them in the food supply.

Vegetables: From Plant to Plate

Vegetable	Minimum Container Size	Number of Plants	Amount of Sunlight	Approximate Number of Days to Harvest
Cabbage	1 gallon	1 plant	Partial shade	48–53
Cucumbers	1 gallon	2 plants	Full sun	46–66
Green beans	1 gallon	2–3 plants	Full sun	37–58
Lettuce	1 gallon	4–6 plants	Partial shade	41–56
Peppers	2 gallon	2 plants	Full sun	82–112
Tomatoes	3 gallon	1 plant	Full sun	84–124

Source: Adapted from S. Cotner and J. Masabni, "Vegetable Gardening in Containers." AgriLife Extension, Texas A&M System (March 2009). Available at http://repository.tamu.edu/bitstream/handle/1969.1/87590/pdf_2695.pdf?sequence=1. Accessed April 2010; Iowa State University Extension, "Container Vegetable Gardening." (2005). Available at www.extension.iastate.edu/publications/prn870b.pdf. Accessed April 2010.

transplants become available in your area, it is time to begin your vegetable garden.

Fertilizing

Because the rejuvenating, nutrient-rich soil of a backyard is missing in a container garden, you will need to routinely fertilize your plants. You can purchase a powdered fertilizer at your local supermarket, garden center, or hardware store and dilute it with water as directed on the package. Pour this diluted nourishment around the plant once a week or every other week.

Watering

Container plants tend to dry out more quickly than plants grown in outdoor gardens. Depending on the plant, you may need to water daily. Avoid waiting until the soil is completely dried out. Pour enough water so that some liquid will drain out the bottom of the container. (Put a foil pan under your plant if you are growing it inside your home to catch any excess water.) Avoid overwatering, which can be as damaging to a grown plant as underwatering. If your plant becomes waterlogged, the roots won't be able to "breathe" and receive the oxygen the plant needs to grow. You'll end up with root rot.

Harvesting

This is the fun part, as you get to eat your bounty. The table will give you a ballpark idea as to how long it will take from planting your vegetables until you can enjoy them on your plate.

Hormones

Scientists and dairy farmers have known for years that cows injected with a naturally occurring bovine **growth hormone,** also known as bovine somatotropin, produce more milk. Cows injected with a synthetic version of the hormone, **recombinant bovine somatotropin (rbST),** can produce more milk than untreated cows. Though consumer groups and Health Canada (the FDA equivalent in Canada) have questioned the long-term safety of rbST, the FDA's extensive review of rbST has found no evidence that it poses any long-term health threat to humans.[49] Other hormones are sometimes used to increase the amount of weight that cattle gain and the amount of meat that they produce.[50] Runoff from sewage sludge containing these hormones can reach surface waters and interfere with the reproductive cycle of wildlife.[51]

Antibiotics

Antibiotics, whether injected into food-producing animals or given via feed, are used for three purposes: (1) to treat animals that are sick; (2) to preventively treat animals that may be at risk of being sick (for example, if one animal becomes ill, the entire herd may be given antibiotics); and (3) to promote growth by keeping the gut and

growth hormone A protein-based hormone that stimulates cell growth and reproduction in humans and animals.

recombinant bovine somatotropin (rbST) A synthetically made hormone identical to a cow's natural growth hormone, somatotropin, that stimulates milk production. Also known as rbGH (recombinant bovine growth hormone).

antibiotics Drugs that kill or slow the growth of bacteria.

What Is a Sustainable Food System?

"Eat Green" or "Eat Sustainably"? If you have seen these phrases in the media lately and are not sure what they mean, you're among friends. According to a recent survey, more than half of American adults are not familiar with the concept of producing food in a sustainable way.[2]

To be *sustainable* means being able to be maintained indefinitely. A **sustainable food system,** then, is one that will survive over the long term so that you, and future generations, can be confident that the foods you need for good health will always be available. To maintain a sustainable food system, the natural resources used to produce, transport, and distribute the food are conserved, not destroyed or depleted.[3] That is, minimal natural resources, including soil and water, were depleted to grow the food and minimal energy use and food miles were incurred to transport the food. A **sustainable diet** contains foods that are produced in a way that is ecologically neutral.

You may not worry too much about being able to obtain all your favorite foods tomorrow, next week, and in the years to come. But you should. According to research, America's industrialized agriculture system is using topsoil, fossil fuel, and water—all precious natural resources—at unsustainable rates. We are also degrading the environment, reducing **biodiversity,** and polluting our air and water.[4] Business as usual can't continue as usual if we want the next genera-

tion to enjoy the bountiful diet and healthy environment that we have been taking for granted.

To address this issue, the American Dietetic Association (ADA) recently developed a sustainable food system model (see figure) that illustrates the factors needed to support a sustainable food system.[5] True sustainability involves every sector in the food system, from the farm to the consumer. Starting at the bottom of the food system model and reading upward, the "inputs" or the natural and human resources and economics, are considered the foundation of the model. These "inputs" are important because a sustainable food system should be:[6]

➤ *Naturally or Ecologically Sound:* The components of the natural resources have to be conserved, regen-

erated, or recycled, and protect the natural resources with little waste and pollution. When something is removed from the environment, it must be replenished. Diversity among species and ecosystems also has to be maintained.

➤ *Socially Acceptable and Humane:* The foods produced should be healthy, culturally and socially acceptable, affordable, and sustainable for future generations. Individuals producing the foods are to be treated with respect.

➤ *Economical:* All aspects of the system are economically viable for all participants working within the system.

Moving higher up on the model, you will notice that there are factors that influence and impact the food system. They are:[7]

➤ Social/cultural values and trends
  ➤ Economic factors
    ➤ Policy (local, federal, and international)

> **Americans, on average, waste close to 15 percent of the food they purchase.**

sustainable food system A system that conserves the natural resources and can be maintained indefinitely.

sustainable diet A diet containing foods that meet your health needs and are produced in an ecologically sustainable way.

biodiversity Having a wide variety of plant and animal species within an environment.

Sustainable Food Systems Model

Source: Harmon, A. H., and B. L. Gerald, "Position of the American Dietetic Association: Food and Nutrition Professionals Can Implement Practices to Conserve Natural Resources and Support Ecological Sustainability," *Journal of the American Dietetic Association* 107 (2007): 1033–1043.

- Education and research
- Outcomes (adequate foods produced and preservation of resources used)

All of these factors are constantly changing as new trends, financial resources, research, and outcomes continue to emerge and impact the food system. Note that policy is smack in the middle of the system. Policies that encourage agriculturally friendly practices are needed for sustainability.[8]

Abuse of any of the natural resources required to grow foods can prevent sustainability. Soil, fuel, and water are key natural resources that must be preserved in a sustainable food system.

The Soil Web

More than 99 percent of the food you eat is produced on land, compared to less than one percent that comes from the sea. All land crops are dependent upon the thin layer of topsoil that sits atop the earth's crust.[9] It's not surprising, then, that numerous experts are concerned about soil degradation.[10]

Looking at the figure of the "soil food web" below, you can see that all organisms depend upon the earth's soil. Organisms within the soil, such as bacteria and other microorganisms, feed on the nutrients provided by animal waste products and decaying plant and animal matter. Plants use nutrients in the soil to grow, and to produce fruit, vegetables, nuts, and seeds. Humans and animals later obtain these same nutrients when they eat the plants and plant products.

Just as all organisms depend on healthy soil for survival, healthy soil depends on the organisms to anchor it in place and to keep it well oxygenated. Plant roots help hold soil in place, which protects it from water and wind erosion, and they also break up the soil to allow the dispersal of oxygen. As topsoil is formed and regenerated from decaying plants, organisms, animals, and rocks, a perfect, perpetual web is formed.

Problems arise when the topsoil can't be regenerated and/or is less fertile. When this happens plants cannot grow, the web is severed, and nourishment for all—the animals, organisms, and *you*—suffers.[11] Unfortunately, the natural process of regenerating *one inch* of nutrient-rich topsoil takes more than 500 years.[12] Improper agricultural practices that facilitate soil erosion faster that it can be regenerated disrupt the entire web and food system.[13]

The average layer of topsoil is only as thick as a dime.

The Importance of Biodiversity

As you can deduce from the soil web, achieving and maintaining **biodiversity** is

(continued)

The Soil Food Web

Source: Bureau of Land Management, "The Soil Food Web." Available at www.blm.gov/nstc/soil/foodweb/index.html. Accessed May 2010.

What Is a Sustainable Food System? (continued)

an important part of a sustainable food system, and the extinction of even one member of the web can have dramatic consequences. For example, the 70 percent decline in the honeybee population of more than 20 U.S. states could impact the pollination, and therefore the availability, of certain foods (consider that an estimated 30 percent of the foods that you eat need pollination to flourish).[14] Lack of biodiversity among aquatic systems is also a potential problem. More than 70 percent of commerical fisheries are overharvested, endangering the existence of more than 30 percent of native fish in North America.[15] As biodiversity is reduced, so will be the variety and nutritional quality of your diet.[16]

Energy

Research suggests that almost 16 percent of the total energy consumption in the United States is used in the production, processing, transport, and prepara-

tion of our food.[17] As you have read, the use of fossil fuel is costly and the release of carbon dixoide from the burning of it harms the environment. Eating a sustainable diet can both reduce the reliance on fossil fuel and reduce pollution.

Did you know that more energy (as well as land and water) is required to produce a meat-based diet than to produce a plant-based diet?[18] Every pound of animal protein generated from livestock requires approximately 6 pounds of plant protein in the form of feed.[19] Allowing livestock to graze on pasture rather than feeding them a grain diet would cut the amount of fuel needed to produce and transport feed grain in half.[20]

Even better, organically and locally grown meat has been shown to use fewer

> Energy-conserving refrigerators, stoves, and other household appliances can reduce energy consumption up to about 60 percent. Visit www.energystar.com for information.

natural resources and be better for the environment than produce (plants) that has to be transported long distances.[21]

Does all this mean you should avoid eating meat that isn't locally grown? No. Meat is a wonderful, nutritious, and delicious food. However, decreasing the *amount* you eat, the frequency with which you eat it, and/or purchasing grass-fed and locally raised meat when available could help the food system.

Producing chemical fertilizers and pesticides for crops also requires large amounts of fossil fuels.[22] Avoiding these chemicals and using natural fertilizers, such as animal manure, not only cuts the use of fossil fuel, but can also can make soil more fertile.[23] Research also shows that crop rotation and other aspects of

---

Self-Assessment

How Sustainable Is Your Food Shopping?

Use the following checklist to assess a food or beverage product before you purchase it. Circle the check mark next to each statement that is true of the product you are considering. The more check marks, the greater contribution the food product makes to a sustainable food system.

✓ The producer or farmer who grew the food is known.

✓ The location of where the food originated is known.

✓ The food traveled the least distance possible.

✓ The food is fresh, seasonal, and grown without harming soil, water, or air quality.

✓ The food was raised humanely without synthetic hormones or antibiotics.

✓ The process used to produce the food conserves genetic biodiversity and ecological integrity.

✓ The farm workers, processors, or food-service workers earned a fair wage, worked in safe conditions, and were not exploited in the making of this food.

✓ The nutritional value of the food is maintained and it is free of artificial ingredients.

✓ There were no or low environmental impacts as a result of processing and transporting the food.

✓ The food packaging is minimal, made from renewable resources, and is recyclable.

✓ The label on the food product directs you to find more information. Product labeling is transparent.

✓ The name and any claims of the food product are specific, meaningful, and logical.

✓ The food product has a legitimate and reputable third-party seal or certification.

✓ The local, national, and global implications of this food product are known.

Adapted from A. Tagtow, MS, RD, LD, "Shades of Green: Looking at the Food System with a Critical Eye." In Tagtow, A., and A. Harmon. 2009. *Healthy Land, Healthy Food & Healthy Eaters.* Available at www.uwyo.edu/winwyoming/Pubs/HealthyLand%20HealthyFood%20HealthyEaters.pdf. Accessed February 2010.

organic farming result in less soil erosion than nonorganic methods.[24]

Water

According to the EPA, since the 1950s, the population in America has nearly doubled while our water consumption has more than tripled.[25] Americans, on average, use 100 gallons—about 1,600 full glasses—of water each day.[26] By 2013, it is estimated that more than 35 states will experience water shortages.[27]

This heightened demand for water is not only a danger to the environment but also to your health. You need water to survive; therefore, conserving water now to ensure a healthy supply in the future makes sense. There are several steps you and/or your family can take to conserve water. Installing water-efficient appliances, including washing machines and dishwashers, helps cut down on water used for daily chores. If all households installed water-efficient appliances, the United States would save more than 3 trillion gallons annually.[28] Low-flow toilets and shower heads can also help save water, as can turning off the tap while washing dishes or brushing your teeth. When it comes to individual water conservation, think of saving water "one gallon at a time."

Being a More Sustainable Food Consumer

If each American set a goal to incorporate three "greener" habits in his/her daily life (see table) over the next year, the reduction in natural resources could be dramatic. The "How Sustainable Is Your Food Shopping?" food assessment can help you determine if the foods that you purchase were made in a sustainable way. Think about these questions as you plan, shop for, and prepare your next meal and consider following some of the suggestions in the "Go Green" table.

Go Green

What You Can Do	How You Can Do It
Purchase locally grown, seasonal foods when possible	Visit the Natural Resources Defense Council for an interactive guide to the seasonal foods available in your area at www.nrdc.org/health/foodmiles/default.asp.
Waste not, want not	Don't buy excessive amounts of food at one time. If you can't eat the food that you purchased before it goes bad, consider donating it to a food pantry and/or shelter. Your excess is someone else's dinner.
Eat more plant protein	Go meatless at least one meal a week. For delicious meatless ideas, visit www.meatlessmonday.com.
Plant your own garden	For the ultimate reduction in food miles, plant your produce in your backyard or in containers. To help you develop a green thumb, visit the National Gardening Association's Food Gardening Guide, the ultimate source for information on growing your favorite vegetables, fruits, and herbs, at www.garden.org/foodguide/browse.
Buy from local farm stands, farmers' markets, and community supported agriculture (CSA) farms	Shop at local farmers' markets and roadside farm stands to find just-picked fruits and veggies (which will be at their peak nutritional value) for minimal food miles. You can also join a CSA to enjoy weekly or monthly boxes of farm-fresh produce delivered to your doorstep or a local pick-up site. Find local farmers' markets and community-supported farms in your area at http://apps.ams.usda.gov/FarmersMarkets and www.localharvest.org/csa/.
Conserve water in your home	—Only run the dishwasher when it is full. —Recycle cooled cooking water to water your plants and garden. —Defrost food in your refrigerator rather than under running water. —Scrape rather than rinse your plates before putting them in the dishwasher. Visit the EPA's WaterSense for more ways to conserve water at www.epa.gov/watersense/water_efficiency/index.html.
Conserve energy in your home	—Use pots with lids for a shorter cooking time. —Turn off an electric stovetop before the food is cooked and let the residual heat finish the dish.
Buy foods with less packaging	—To reduce the waste you throw in the garbage, buy foods in bulk, with less packaging. —Use reusable cloth bags to carry your food home from the market or grocery store. —Recycle food containers. For more tips, visit CalRecycle at www.calrecycle.ca.gov/ReduceWaste/Home/#Reuse.

intestines healthy. When antibiotics are used for the first two purposes, they are used for a relatively short period of time. This isn't true when antibiotics are used for the third purpose. Low-dose antibiotics are sometimes put in animal feed, because animals that consume this feed gain more weight than animals fed antibiotic-free feed.[52] While many livestock producers practice prudent use of antibiotics to reduce risks to the environment and food supply, medical and veterinary professional organizations are working to promote the appropriate use of antibiotics in animal agriculture.

Pathogenic bacteria such as *Campylobacter, E. coli* O157:H7, and *Salmonella* are commonly found in the gastrointestinal tracts of animals without making them sick. However, when animals are chronically given antibiotics, **antibiotic-resistant bacteria** strains can sometimes grow in their intestinal tracts. If a human contracts a foodborne illness from this animal food source, treatment with the same antibiotic that was used in the feed, which killed the bacteria in the past, may no longer be effective. One example of this occurred as follows: In the late 1980s, the antibiotic fluoroquinolone was successfully used to treat *Campylobacter,* which is commonly found in chickens. In 1995, this antibiotic began to be used regularly in poultry. Shortly after, doctors began seeing patients with *Campylobacter*-induced foodborne illness whose infections were resistant to treatments with fluoroquinolone.[53]

The National Antimicrobial Resistance Monitoring System–Enteric Bacteria (NARMS) has been established, which is a joint effort between the Food and Drug Administration's Center for Veterinary Medicine (FDA CVM), the U.S. Department of Agriculture (USDA), and the Centers for Disease Control and Prevention (CDC), to monitor this important issue of preventing antibiotic-resistant bacteria strains in animals and humans.[54] The Center for Veterinary Medicine has developed guidelines for the judicious use of antibiotics in food-producing animals in order to minimize the development of antibiotic-resistant bacteria.[55]

Pesticides

You have probably been handling **pesticides** for years and not even realizing it. If you use a disinfectant to control the mold in your shower, bug spray to ward off flesh biters on muggy summer nights, or a flea collar to keep your pet itch free, you're making use of chemicals that destroy or mitigate pests. These chemicals are collectively known as pesticides. Whereas pesticides can cause harm, some more so than others, they are needed to control disease-causing organisms and pests that threaten or affect the food supply. By using pesticides on agricultural crops, food plants can flourish and produce a hearty bounty. This enables farmers to offer affordable crops to consumers.

Types of Pesticides

Several different types of pests can diminish or destroy crop yields, including insects, microorganisms (bacteria, viruses), fungi (mold), and rodents (rats and mice). Pesticides used to kill weeds are called **herbicides,** whereas those used on microorganisms are **antimicrobials. Fungicides** are used to destroy fungi.

Pesticides can be chemically or biologically based. Biologically based pesticides, such as **biopesticides** and sex pheromones, use materials from animals, plants, bacteria, and some minerals. Unlike chemically based pesticides, biopesticides only curtail a specific pest, and thus are not harmful to birds and other animals that may come into contact with them. For example, baking soda (sodium bicarbonate) can be diluted with water and sprayed onto plants to inhibit the growth of fungi without any known risk to humans. Another type of biopesticide uses strains of the bacterium *Bacillus thuringiensis*, or *Bt*, which kills developing insects.[56] Insect **sex pheromones** can be used to interfere with the mating of pests. Scented extracts from plants can also be used to lure and then trap insects. Biopesticides are typically safer than chemical pesticides.[57]

---

antibiotic-resistant bacteria Bacteria that have developed a resistance to an antibiotic such that they are no longer affected by antibiotic medication.

pesticides Substances that kill or repel pests such as insects, weeds, microorganisms, rodents, or fungi.

herbicides Substances that are used to kill and control weeds.

antimicrobials Substances or a combination of substances, such as disinfectants and sanitizers, that control the spread of bacteria and viruses on non-living surfaces or objects.

fungicides Chemicals used to kill mold.

biopesticides Substances derived from natural materials such as animals, plants, bacteria, and certain minerals to control pests.

sex pheromones Naturally occurring chemicals secreted by one organism to attract another; used as a biopesticide to control pests by interfering with their mating.

Chemically based **organophosphates** make up about half of all the insecticides used in the United States and are used on fruits, nuts, vegetables, corn, wheat, and other crops, as well as commercial and residential lawns and plants.[58] These pesticides affect the nervous systems of the pests they destroy. Some organophosphates have been removed from the market because of their ill effects on human health and the environment. All pesticides are continually re-reviewed by the EPA to ensure their safety.

Farmers use pesticides on food crops to diminish the damage from pests.

Risks and Regulation of Pesticides

The problem with pesticides, especially chemically based pesticides, is that they can cause unintended harm to animals, the environment, and even humans. The American bald eagle almost became extinct due to a now-banned pesticide that was ingested by the eagles. Research has shown that some pesticides, depending upon their level of toxicity and how much is consumed, may cause serious health problems, such as cancer, birth defects, and nerve damage, in humans.[59]

To prevent potential harm to consumers, pesticide use is heavily regulated in the United States. The EPA evaluates all food pesticides with a four-part **risk assessment** to ensure that they can be used with "a reasonable certainty of no harm." The risk assessment process includes:

1. *Hazard identification* identifies the potential hazards or ill effects that may develop after exposure to a specific pesticide in animals.
2. *Dose-response assessment* determines the dose at which these ill effects occur in animals and then uses this information to identify a potentially equal dose in humans.
3. *Exposure assessment* determines all the ways that a person could typically be exposed to that pesticide. Exposure could occur orally when you eat food or drink water, or by inhalation or absorption through your skin when you are using household disinfectants or gardening pesticides around your home.
4. *Risk characterization* uses the information obtained in the first three steps to determine the overall risk of the pesticide.[60]

Because there are potential differences between the effects of a pesticide on animals and its effect on humans, as well as differences among humans, the EPA builds in a margin of safety when determining the health risk. An extra tenfold safety factor is added (unless there is evidence that a lesser margin of safety is adequate) to protect the most vulnerable groups, such as infants and children, who could be exposed to the pesticide. Before a pesticide can be registered by the EPA, the manufacturer must submit it to more than 100 health and environmental tests, at a cost of over $150 million, and it takes approximately nine years before being approved.[61] Thus, much effort goes into ensuring that the foods you eat are safe, yet affordable, in order for you to reap their health benefits and minimize any known risks. **Figure 12.7** shows you how to reduce the pesticides on the foods that you consume.

The EPA also conducts environmental risk assessments to make sure that a pesticide doesn't pose any risk to wildlife and the environment. If it does, or is even thought to hurt the environment, acceptable levels are determined to prevent any known harm.[62]

Alternatives to Pesticides

Rather than use pesticides, some growers use an approach called **integrated pest management (IPM)** to manage pests in their crops. The goal of this approach is to use the most economical methods to control pests while causing the least risk of harm to the consumer, the crops, or the environment. The IPM method includes preventive measures, such as rotating crops and choosing pest-resistant strains of crops, to

organophosphates A group of synthetic pesticides that adversely affect the nervous systems of pests.

risk assessment The process of determining the potential human health risks posed by exposure to substances such as pesticides.

integrated pest management (IPM) Alternative to pesticides that uses the most economical and the least harmful methods of pest control to minimize risk to consumers, crops, and the environment.

Figure 12.7 Reducing Pesticides in Food

Wash: Thoroughly wash and scrub all fresh fruits and vegetables with a vegetable brush with sturdy surfaces under running water to dislodge bacteria and some of the pesticide residue. Running water is more effective for this purpose than soaking the fruit and vegetables.

Peel and trim: Peeling fruits and vegetables and tossing the outer leaves of leafy vegetables helps reduce pesticides. Trimming the visible fat from meat and the fatty skin from poultry and fish helps reduce some of the pesticide residue that remains in the fatty tissue of the animal.

Eat a variety of foods: Eating a variety of foods reduces your chances of being overexposed to any particular pesticide.

reduce the likelihood of attracting pests. When these measures aren't adequate to control pests, biologically based alternatives, such as biopesticides or the introduction of natural predators (specific insects that eat the unwanted pests), may be used to curtail an infestation. If all these methods don't control the spread of the pests, targeted spraying of chemically based pesticides is then considered.[63] Note that foods grown using IPM methods typically aren't labeled, so the consumer can't easily spot them in the supermarket.

Biotechnology Can Help Produce Hardier Crops but Is Not Embraced by Everyone

Another strategy of the food industry to maximize food production is the use of **biotechnology.** Although this sounds like a high-tech term, humans have actually been manipulating the genes of food products for generations. In years past, they did this through selective breeding. In fact, the fresh apples that you eat today look nothing like their small, sour Asian ancestors. Because apples have been intentionally grown (or cultivated) by humans for thousands of years, apple farmers have had plenty of time to crossbreed different versions of the tree to produce more desirable offspring. For example, if one tree produced large, fleshy apples with thinner skins, and another produced smaller, sour apples with thicker skins, an ancient apple farmer might have bred the two in the hope of producing a tree with large, fleshy, hardy fruit. This process is a form of **plant breeding.**

Historically, farmers have crossbred plants by trial and error, hoping for the best results and using the best offspring to further breed more desirable plants. In the past two centuries, however, as scientists learned more about DNA and its workings, and how to manipulate it, the process has become faster and more controlled. Today, farmers in the United States and around the world routinely use selectively bred, **genetically modified** plants to create bigger and better produce and disease-resistant crops, and to increase crop yields. In fact, you would be hard pressed to find many fruits and vegetables today that aren't a product of plant breeding.

biotechnology The application of biological techniques to living cells, which alters their genetic makeup.

plant breeding A type of biotechnology in which two plants are crossbred to produce offspring with desired traits from both.

genetically modified A cell that has its genetic makeup altered.

Genetic Engineering

Today's versions of bioengineered foods include new techniques, such as **genetic engineering (GE),** to alter the genetic makeup of an organism. In this type of bioengineering, the exact gene or genes from the DNA of a plant cell are isolated and inserted into the DNA of another cell to create the genetically modified product (**Figure 12.8**). This cutting and splicing of genes into the DNA of another cell is called *recombinant DNA* (rDNA) technology. Organisms that have been genetically engineered to contain both original and foreign genes are called **genetically modified organisms (GMOs).** These GMOs are used to grow GE plants that produce GE foods.

Genetically modified crops were first grown in the early 1990s, and in 2007, the United States planted 140 million acres of bioengineered crops, including corn, cotton, canola, and soybeans. Bioengineered crops are being cultivated in more than 20 countries globally.[64] While some individuals and groups have expressed concern about the use of genetically modified foods (sometimes calling them "frankenfoods"), proponents believe that GMOs can be good for the environment, help feed countries that have an inadequate food supply, improve the quality and quantity of foods available all year round, and create new uses for plants in industries such as pharmaceuticals and manufacturing. In the words of former President Jimmy Carter, "biotechnology is not the enemy . . . hunger is."[65]

The original purpose of using biotechnology in plants was to reduce the amount of pesticides used on food crops. For example, the bacterium *Bacillus thuringiensis*, mentioned previously and found naturally in soil, produces a toxin that is poisonous to certain pests but not to humans or other animals. When the gene for this toxin is inserted into a crop plant, the plant becomes resistant to these pests. Some corn crops in the United States contain the *Bt* gene, which makes them resistant to some insect pests. The use of biotechnology to reduce the use of pesticides is working—the total amount of pesticides has declined by 2.5 million pounds by using this method.[66]

First-generation bioengingeered products were also created to improve a crop's tolerance to herbicides. With an herbicide-resistant version of a desired crop, a farmer can spray herbicide over a field to kill a variety of weeds without harming the crop. Approximately 68 percent of soybeans grown in the United States have been genetically modified to be herbicide resistant.[67]

The second-generation bioengineered products were designed to provide consumers with added nutritional value as well as other attributes, such as increasing the crop's shelf life. For example, "golden" rice contains foreign gene segments that encode the rice grain to make beta-carotene and to stockpile extra iron. This "super" rice, if planted by farmers and accepted by consumers in Southeast Asia, could help eliminate the epidemic of vitamin A and iron deficiency in children there.[68] Bioengineered, high-oleic-acid soybean oil is less prone to becoming rancid, and thus is more stable when used for frying foods.

Third-generation bioengineered products hold promise in the pharmaceutical, environmental, and industrial arenas. In fact, the first such bioengineered product created for commercial use was human insulin (needed by diabetics) produced by genetically engineered *E. coli*.

a Traditional plant breeding involved crossing two plants of the same species to produce DNA with more desirable traits. The process was imprecise, however, and achieving the desired result could take years.

b Today, genetic engineering allows scientists to precisely manipulate the DNA from plants and impart desirable qualities from one plant to its offspring much more quickly.

Figure 12.8 Plant Breeding versus Genetic Engineering

Bt **corn has been genetically engineered to be resistant to the corn borer.**

genetic engineering (GE)
A biological technique that isolates and manipulates the genes of organisms to produce a targeted, modified product.

genetically modified organisms (GMOs) Organisms that have been genetically engineered to contain both original and foreign genes.

Concerns and Regulations Associated with GE Foods

While many professional organizations, such as the American Medical Association, the National Academy of Sciences, the World Health Organization, and the Society of Toxicology, have all supported agricultural and biotechnology, some opponents of bioengineered foods fear that biotechnology can cause the creation of "Frankenstein" foods.[69] If you are concerned about "frankenfoods," you should know that the risk of an abnormal plant is smaller in bioengineered foods than in foods cultivated through plant breeding. In fact, because genetic engineering involves precise cutting and splicing of specific genes, its end products are less likely to have undesirable traits. Bioengineering in agriculture is also more tightly regulated than any other technology, so there are safeguards in place to halt or prevent undesirable outcomes.

Other concerns have arisen about the production of plant toxins, changes in the nutrient content and substances in foods, and the production of unsafe animal feed. Table 12.5 lists the safeguards that are in place to address these issues.

Bioengineered foods in the United States are regulated by the same three government agencies that regulate pesticides: the FDA, USDA, and EPA. The FDA ensures that foods are safe to eat. The USDA ensures that the plants are safe to grow, while the EPA makes certain that the gene for any pesticide, such as that for *Bt* toxin, inserted into a plant is safe and won't hurt the environment. Though these agencies work together to ensure the safety of these foods, the FDA has the overall authority to remove any food that doesn't meet the same high safety standards that are set for its conventionally grown equivalent.[70]

Table 12.5

Concerns and Regulations for GE Foods

Concern	FDA Regulation
Undesirable genetic modification	To avoid the creation of undesirable products, all genes used must not have prior evidence of encoding any harmful substances. The genes must also be stably inserted into the plant in order to avoid any rearranging of genetic information that would produce an undesirable substance.
Introduction of allergens	GE foods must be monitored for food allergens. Protein encoded from common allergen food sources (such as milk, eggs, fish, tree nuts, and legumes) should be presumed to be allergens and should be labeled as such on the GE food.
Excessive level of toxins	GE foods should not contain natural toxins at levels that are higher than those found naturally in plants.
Changes in nutrients	All GE foods should be monitored to assess unintentional changes in the nutrient levels in the plants and their ability to be utilized in the human body as compared with their conventional counterparts.
Creation of new substances	If the genes that are introduced into plants encode substances that are different in structure and function than those normally found in foods, these substances would have to be approved by the FDA, as would any other food additive. However, if these substances are GRAS or "substantially equivalent" to substances that already exist in foods, they do not require premarket approval from the FDA.
Unsafe animal feeds	Because a single plant may be the predominant food source in an animal feed, all GE animal feeds must meet the same strict safety standards that are in place for food that is grown for humans.

Source: FDA. 1995 "Policy for Food Developed by Biotechnology." Available at http://vm.cfsan.fda.gov/~lrd/bioeme.htm; J. H. Maryanski. 1997. "Bioengineered Foods: Will They Cause Allergic Reactions?" Center for Food Safety and Applied Nutrition. Available at www.cfsan.fda.gov/~dms/pubalrgy.html; FDA. 2009. "Plant Biotechnology for Food and Feed. FDA's Biotechnology Policy." Available at www.fda.gov/Food/Biotechnology/default.htm. Accessed January 2010; C. Bruh. 2006. "Position of the American Dietetic Association: Agricultural and Food Biotechnology." *Journal of the American Dietetic Association* 106: 285–293.

The public seems to be warming up to bioengineered foods because of their health benefits and improved quality. In a survey of 1,000 Americans, almost 50 percent of them stated that they would likely purchase bioengineered foods if the food provided less unhealthy saturated fat and *trans* fats as well as fewer pesticides.[71]

The Take-Home Message Numerous natural resources are used when growing crops and raising animals for foods. Natural resources are used internally to produce foods and externally to move these food products from the farm to the consumer. By-products that are produced during food processing can affect the environment. Locally grown foods use fewer natural resources. Hormones, antibiotics, and pesticides are used to increase food production, but can impact the environment. Both plant breeding and genetic engineering are types of biotechnology that alter the genetic makeup of an organism's cells to create a new plant with more desirable traits.

How Can Food Policy Affect the Foods We Buy?

Farmers and food companies aren't the only ones responsible for keeping food safe, healthy, and available, and producing it in an environmentally friendly way. Several government agencies, from the USDA and the FDA to the Environmental Protection Agency (EPA) and the Federal Trade Commission (FTC), regulate the food industry and set national food and nutrition policy (see Table 12.6). These policies can have a dramatic effect on the foods available to you to purchase and consume. Sometimes policy drives the production of healthier foods and sometimes it doesn't.

Food Policy Can Help Encourage Food Producers to Create Healthier Products

In 2005, the Department of Health and Human Services (DHHS) and USDA's *Dietary Guidelines for Americans* not only encouraged the public to eat more whole grains, but for the first time in history made a specific recommendation that at least half of daily grain servings should come from whole grains. This policy released a tidal wave of reaction in the food industry. Manufacturers quickly scrambled to increase the production of good-tasting whole-grain products to keep up with consumer demand. In 2006, soon after the release of the *Dietary Guidelines*, whole-grain bread sales increased more than 200 percent.[72] This increased demand caused a change in crop production at the farm level, as farmers switched from growing crops such as red winter wheat to a different variety that can be used in processed whole-grain food products.[73] In essence, the farmers had to catch up to the demands of consumers.

Interestingly, this industry shift of offering more whole-grain products to the consumer had an even larger impact on the American diet. The availability of a slew

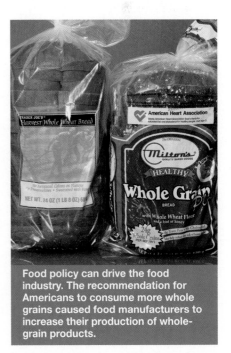

Food policy can drive the food industry. The recommendation for Americans to consume more whole grains caused food manufacturers to increase their production of whole-grain products.

Table 12.6

Who Oversees the Food Supply?

Agency	Responsible for
United States Department of Agriculture (USDA)	Monitoring agriculture and food production and ensuring safe and accurately labeled meat, poultry, and eggs. The USDA enforces tolerances for pesticide residues in meat, poultry, and eggs set forth by the EPA.
Food and Drug Administration (FDA)	Overseeing domestic and imported foods except for meat and poultry products. Ensures that these foods are safe, sanitary, nutritious, wholesome, and honestly and adequately labeled. Overseeing food-processing plants and has responsibility for approval and surveillance of food-animal drugs, feed additives, and all food additives. FDA enforces tolerances for pesticide residues that are set by the EPA.
Environmental Protection Agency (EPA)	Protecting you and the environment from harmful pesticides. EPA is responsible for the safe use of pesticides and fertilizers, as well as food-plant detergents and sanitizers on foods and in the environment. It establishes the safe tolerances for pesticide residues in or on food commodities and animal feed.
Animal and Plant Health Inspection Service (APHIS)	Protecting against plant and animal pests and disease
National Marine Fisheries Service (NMFS)	Overseeing a voluntary seafood inspection for quality and grading program
Centers for Disease Control and Prevention (CDC)	Surveillance and investigation of human and animal diseases
Federal Trade Commission (FTC)	Regulating food advertising
Department of Health and Human Services (DHHS)	Protecting the health of and providing essential human services to Americans, including those who are less able

Source: Committee to Ensure Safe Food from Production to Consumption, Institute of Medicine and National Research Council. 1998. "Ensuring Safe Food: From Production to Consumption." Washington, D.C., The National Academies Press. Available at www.nap.edu/catalog.php?record_id=6163#toc. Accessed March 2010.

of new whole-grain products enabled even the less motivated, less health-conscious consumers to more easily incorporate this recommendation into their lives. In fact, according to research, Americans have dramatically increased their consumption of whole-grain foods, not necessarily by personal choice, but because so many food manufacturers reformulated their products to include more whole grains. Many food consumers increased the whole grains in their diet without even realizing it, as their favorite reformulated products continued to taste good.[74] This is an example of how food policy and food production can work together to make it easier for the food consumer to consume healthy foods.

Food Policy Can Lead to Relabeling and Reformulating without Providing a Healthier Food Product

Unfortunately, changes in nutrition and food policy can also sometimes result in less-than-healthy consequences. For example, the food labeling policy on *trans* fats caused some manufacturers to reformulate their products in ways that did not benefit the consumer. In 2003, based on the research documenting the heart-unhealthy attributes of *trans* fat, the FDA issued a policy for the mandatory labeling of *trans* fats on the Nutrition Facts panel on the food label. Major food manufactures, such as Kraft, Campbell's, and Frito-Lay, reformulated some of their cookies, crackers, chips, and bakery items to remove *trans* fat. While some of these products were reformulated to replace the *trans* fats with healthy vegetable oils, others were reformulated using heart-unhealthy saturated fats, such as butter and palm oil.[75] As a result, the products ended up containing fats that were just as unhealthy as the *trans* fat versions they replaced. Also, the removal of the *trans* fats from the cookies, crackers, chips, and other bakery items enabled manufacturers to boast "0 grams *trans* fats" on the food label. This kind of labeling can lead to a "halo effect" on these foods, encouraging consumers to eat them without worrying about the consequences.[76] Let's face it, when you take the *trans* fats out of the doughnut, you are still left with a doughnut. The doughnut didn't magically morph into an apple. No matter what type of fat is in the bakery item, few Americans have room in their diets for a lot of cookies or pastries, especially when they displace much-needed fruit or vegetables.

The Take-Home Message Many government agencies regulate the food supply. Food policy can have an impact on the types of foods that are available to you as a food consumer.

What Are the Politics of the Food Industry?

The intersection of food policy (set by various government agencies) and the interests of the food industry (made up of hundreds of companies that produce, distribute, and sell food) can often yield interesting results. The National School Lunch Program, which you will learn more about in Chapter 16, is one example. This program supplies American children with reduced-price, nutritionally regulated lunches via the standard school cafeteria. Who supplies the schools with the massive amounts of food needed for this nationwide program? The answer is the federal government, the nation's biggest food consumer.

Government Programs Are Food Consumers

In addition to the $8 billion the government provides to help cover the costs of the meals for the National School Lunch Program, about $1 billion in free food commodities, including poultry, eggs, fruits, vegetables, peanut butter, and dairy products, also make their way to school cafeterias. School districts can request these commodities to help keep the cost of the school lunch at an affordable rate. Where do these commodities come from? They are the surplus, unsold foods grown and raised on our U.S. farms. The government buys these foods from the farmers and gives them to schools.[77]

In addition to the National School Lunch Program, other U.S. programs, such as the Summer Food Service Program, the Emergency Food Assistance Program, and the Child and Adult Care Food Program, all have access to these commodities.[78] In 2008, the U.S. Congress passed a Farm Bill, which, among other things, reauthorized the distribution of surplus commodities to these special nutrition projects. The advantage of this arrangement is twofold: The government provides a market for farmers' surplus foods while ensuring that American citizens get fed.

The Food Lobby Exerts Influence

(T|F) Food companies and other members of the food industry often voice their preferences to government agencies and politicians via individuals known as *lobbyists*. A lobbyist is paid to meet with and persuade politicians to vote on pending legislation in a direction that would favor the interests of the party the lobbyist represents.[79] All lobbyists must be registered, make the parties that they represent publicly known, and report how they are funded.[80]

Sometimes research can prompt food companies and businesses to spring food lobbyists into action. In 2009, a report published in the *New England Journal of Medicine* by a group of prominent researchers claimed that the consumption of sugar-sweetened beverages was linked to an increased risk of obesity, diabetes, and heart disease among Americans. The researchers' solution: to tax these beverages to dissuade consumption.[81] They also recommended that monies generated from the tax could be used to support childhood nutrition and obesity prevention programs, and fund health care in general. The makers of these sweetened beverages, supermarket companies, fast-food restaurants, and other organizations with a vested interest in maintaining high sales of sugary beverages such as the National Corn Growers Association (whose products create high-fructose corn syrup, the main sweetener found in soft drinks), spent more than $20 million on lobbying efforts to convince Congress to block this not-so-sweet proposal.[82] Will sweetened beverages be taxed? Only time will tell. But you can be sure that businesses that will be impacted by this tax aren't going to leave Washington, D.C., without a fight.

The Take-Home Message The U.S. government is also a food consumer, and it purchases large amounts of surplus commodities that are used in various food and nutrition programs. The food industry uses lobbyists to influence national food policy.

How Can You Be an Informed Food Consumer?

As you just read, many factors, including decisions made by farmers, food companies, grocery stores, and government agencies, will affect the foods that are available to you. At the end of the day, though, you get to choose which food products to buy. Knowing and understanding the terms found on food labels or posted near foods can help you select the healthiest, most environmentally friendly options.

Know the Label Terms That Indicate How Animal Foods Are Produced

The term "natural," when used on the packaging of meat and poultry, indicates that no artificial ingredients were added and that the product is minimally processed.

Both the FDA and USDA are the consumer watchdogs for food labeling, and labeling of animal food products is essential when it comes to determining how the animals were fed, raised, and treated. The label terms for meat and poultry are determined and defined by the USDA. The following list includes terms often found on prepackaged meat products:[83]

- ➤ *Certified.* Indicates that the USDA has evaluated a meat product for class, grade, or other quality characteristics (for example, "Certified Angus Beef").
- ➤ *Fresh Poultry.* Poultry that has never had an internal temperature below 26°F.
- ➤ *Free Range.* Producers must demonstrate that the animal has been allowed access to the outdoors.
- ➤ *Kosher.* Meat and poultry products that were prepared under the supervision of a rabbi.
- ➤ *Natural.* The food contains no artificial ingredient or added color and is only minimally processed; that is, using processes that do not fundamentally alter the raw product. The label must explain the use of the term natural (such as "no added colorings or artificial ingredients").
- ➤ *No Hormones (pork or poultry).* Hormones are not allowed in raising hogs or poultry. Therefore, the claim "no hormones added" cannot be used on the labels of pork or poultry unless it is followed by a statement that says "Federal regulations prohibit the use of hormones."
- ➤ *No Hormones (beef).* The phrase "no hormones administered" may be approved for use on the label of beef products if no hormones have been used in raising the animals.
- ➤ *No Antibiotics.* May be used on labels for meat or poultry products if the animals were raised without antibiotics.

In addition to these common terms, the use of the term "organic" is appearing on increasing numbers of products on supermarket shelves.

Understand the Meaning of the Term *Organic*

As more consumers become concerned about how their food is grown and raised, the popularity of **organic** foods has increased, with sales rising from $3.6 billion in 1997 to slightly over $21 billion in 2008.[84] In fact, more than two-thirds of Americans buy organic products at least occasionally, and over 25 percent buy organic products weekly.[85]

This growing interest in organic foods prompted the USDA to develop National Organic Standards (NOS) in 2002. The NOS provide specific criteria that food producers must meet during production, handling, and processing to label their products organic. As a result of these standards, you can be confident that if the food is labeled as organic, it was produced and handled using specific guidelines and certified by a USDA-accredited inspector.[86]

Organic farming involves growing crops without the use of *some* synthetic pesticides, synthetic fertilizers, bioengineering, or irradiation. Contrary to popular belief,

organic Being free of chemical-based pesticides, synthetic fertilizers, irradiation, and bioengineering. A USDA-accredited certifying inspector must certify organic foods.

Figure 12.9 The USDA Organic Seal
Foods that are labeled or advertised with the USDA Organic seal must contain at least 95 percent organic ingredients.

organic foods are not necessarily free of all pesticides. Organically grown crops may come into contact with chemicals due to drift from wind and rainwater. Also, though organic farmers use IPM, and grow more disease- and pest-resistant plants, sometimes synthetic pesticides and biopesticides may still be needed. The National Organic Program has created the National List of Allowed and Prohibited Substances that identifies substances that can and cannot be used in organic crop production. According to the list, several synthetic pesticides, such as insecticidal soaps, are allowed, while some natural substances, such as ash from the burning of manure, cannot be used in organic farming.[87]

For animal food products, only antibiotic-free or growth hormone–free animals can be used to produce organic meat, poultry, eggs, and dairy foods.[88]

You can identify organically produced foods in your supermarket by looking for the USDA Organic seal (**Figure 12.9**). Foods that display this seal or otherwise state that they are organic must contain at least 95 percent organic ingredients. However, organic food producers can choose whether or not to display this seal, so it may not be on all such products. There are other label claims and standards for foods that are 100 percent organic, or that use organic ingredients. Table 12.7 describes the standards that organic label claims must meet.

Research studies are mixed, so the jury is still out on whether or not organic foods are nutritionally superior to those grown in a conventional manner.[89] Studies have

Table 12.7 Various Levels of Organic

If the label

Says "100% Organic"
Then: the food must be composed entirely of organic ingredients.
Note: These foods cannot contain sulfites and must declare the certifying agent. The USDA Organic seal may be displayed.

If the label

Says "Made with Organic Ingredients"
Then: The food contains at least 70 percent organic ingredients.

If the label

Says "Organic" and/or displays the USDA Organic seal
Then: The food contains at least 95 percent organic ingredients.

If the label

Makes no organic claims
Then: The food contains less than 70 percent organic ingredients.

shown that organic farming can help the environment by reducing pesticide use, energy use, and greenhouse emissions, and by increasing biodiversity in fields.[90] Unfortunately, organic foods tend to cost more than those that are conventionally grown. For example, organic produce can cost anywhere from 5 to 70 percent more than conventional foods. The price isn't likely to decline any time soon, as the demand for organic food is currently higher than the supply. Another issue to consider when choosing organic foods is where they were grown. In 2007, the USDA certified 27,000 producers and handlers of organic foods to help keep up with consumer demand. However, 11,000 of them were in foreign countries.[91] Keep in mind that if your organic food has to travel from Turkey and Mexico, the food miles that it travels may negate some of the environmental benefits described earlier.[92] Finally, organic foods are not always healthy foods. There are plenty of processed foods that contain high amounts of salt, sugar, and fat that are made with some organic ingredients, and therefore bear the organic label.

The Take-Home Message Labeling terms can provide information that can help you select the best foods. Organic foods are grown without the use of some synthetic pesticides, synthetic fertilizers, bioengineering, or irradiation. Organically produced animal foods are produced without antibiotics or hormones. The National Organic Standards provide specific criteria and guidelines for the production, handling, processing, and labeling of organic foods, as well as mandatory certification by an accredited inspector. Organic foods usually cost more than conventionally grown foods, and there is no conclusive evidence that they are more nutritious than conventionally grown foods.

Two Points of View

Can Organic Go Large Scale? More and more people are seeking out and purchasing organic foods, and the increasing demand for organic products has motivated numerous large retailers to stock and sell these items. But is organic food from your local farmers' market the same as organic food from large grocery stores like Wal-Mart or Whole Foods? Does "organic" mean different things to different people? Take a look at both sides of the issue and decide for yourself.

Yes

- According to federal legislation, all foods that carry the USDA Organic label must meet strict standards that are set and enforced by the USDA.[1]

- Consumers now have more choice when it comes to organic products. Market growth in the organic sector averaged 17 percent a year between 1995 and 2006, dramatically increasing the number of organic food products flowing along the supply chain.[2]

- Organic foods are usually more expensive than their nonorganic counterparts, and national retailers can use their large-scale buying power to make such products more affordable to more people. For example, an informal survey of organic milk at Denver area grocery stores found that Wal-Mart's label was 8 percent to 35 percent cheaper than other brands.[3]

- Hundreds of thousands of pounds of agricultural chemicals are *not* being used because of the large shifts to organic production.[4]

- Interest in organic food has also led to growth in small cooperative farms and farmers' markets, and more interest in buying local.[5] As this trend continues, it will hopefully yield improved dietary habits as well as environmental benefits.

No

- Large-scale retailers may sometimes misuse the organic label. Wal-Mart's store brand organic milk, for example, comes from Aurora Dairy in Boulder, Colorado. In 2007, federal investigators found that Aurora had "willfully" violated 14 tenets of the organic standards, including confining their cattle to feedlots, instead of grazing, and bringing thousands of illegal conventional cows into their organic operation.[6]

- Taking organic large scale means making it more industrial. Big supermarket chains find it easier, and therefore, more profitable to buy from big farms selling lots of one thing (monoculture). This trend comes at the expense of small farmers and of some of the founding principles of organic farming, including its commitment to polyculture and to social and economic sustainability.[7]

- Not all organic foods are healthy foods. Processed foods like tortilla chips and cookies may be labeled organic, but they are still nutritionally dubious.[8]

- Organic foods, or the resources needed to produce them, are often shipped in from overseas, where they are produced more cheaply. This threatens the business of small, local, organic producers who may not be able to compete on price.[9]

What do you think?

1. Has the large-scale growth of the organic food industry been helpful or harmful to consumers in general? What about to the environment? **2.** Does the term "organic" mean the same thing today that it did a decade ago? **3.** What is the likely difference between an organic food purchased at a farmers' market and one purchased at a large grocery store?

Chapter Review

 Be a Nutrition Sleuth

Eating Green Calculator

Want to know what effect your diet might have on your health and the health of your planet? Visit the student companion website at **www.pearsonhighered.com/blake** for a fun and interactive tool to calculate how green your food choices are.

 Get Real!

Season Your Plate

Don't know what foods are in season in your area? Visit **www.pearsonhighered.com/blake** for a handy tool that will tell you the fruits and vegetables that are in season throughout the year in your neighborhood.

The Top Ten Points to Remember

1. As a food consumer, your food choices influence the foods grown and products developed and sold by farmers and food processors, marketers, distributors, and retailers. Food advertisers and marketing influence your food choices.

2. Agribusiness is a blend of agriculture and business. While some of the foods that you eat are grown in the United States, many are imported from other countries. Many countries depend on the United States to meet their food and nutrition needs.

3. All types of agriculture impact the environment. Numerous natural resources are used when growing crops and raising animals for food. Land overuse, soil erosion, water depletion and runoff, airborne emissions, nitrate production, the handling of manure, and greenhouse emissions are by-products of agriculture and negatively affect the environment. Locally grown food uses fewer natural resources.

4. The use of antibiotics, hormones, and pesticides in the production of food can improve food production but can negatively impact the environment. Integrated pest management is an alternative to using pesticides. Biotechnology can also reduce pesticide use.

5. A sustainable diet is comprised of foods that not only meet your nutrient and health needs but also can be sustained for a long time without negatively affecting the environment. A sustainable food system is one that is designed so future generations will have access to the foods needed for good health.

6. Food policy can affect the foods that are available for you to buy and consume. The government is also a food consumer, because it purchases commodities and distributes them to numerous government-sponsored programs, such as the National School Lunch Program and the Emergency Food Assistance Program. Lobbyists attempt to influence food policy.

7. Labeling terms—such as certified, fresh poultry, free range, kosher, natural, no hormones, and no antibiotics—on food labels can provide information that can help you with your food selections.

8. Organic foods are grown without the use of some synthetic pesticides, synthetic fertilizers, bioengineering, or irradiation. Organically produced animal foods are produced without antibiotics or hormones. There is no conclusive evidence that organic foods are more nutritious than conventionally grown foods.

9. The National Organic Standards provide specific criteria and guidelines for the production, handling, processing, and labeling of organic foods, as well as mandatory certification by an accredited inspector.

10. You can be a sustainable farmer by growing your own vegetables in and/or outside your home.

Test Your Knowledge

1. The majority of farms in the United States are run by
   a. families.
   b. the United States government.
   c. large United States companies.
   d. large overseas companies.
2. Agribusiness is
   a. a food business that occurs only in the Corn Belt section of the United States.
   b. a very large business entity.
   c. the combination of agricultural and business entities that impacts how foods are developed, processed, distributed, and purchased.
   d. only comprised of large conglomerates.
3. Americans eat more _____ than any other animal food.
   a. poultry
   b. beef
   c. pork
   d. soy
4. Globesity refers to
   a. the rise in greenhouse gases globally.
   b. the rise in the number of foods being exported from the United States.
   c. the rise in famine in underdeveloped countries.
   d. the rise and rapid growth of the incidence of obesity globally.
5. Which of the following is an example of a challenge that can deplete internal natural resource(s) in the production of food?
   a. land overuse
   b. soil erosion
   c. carbon dioxide gas emission from trucks transporting food from the farm to the supermarket
   d. all of the above
   e. a and b only
6. Food miles are
   a. the number of miles shoppers have to drive to get their food.
   b. the number of miles the food travels from where it was to grown to the location where the consumer purchases it.
   c. the amount of food that can be transported per mile.
   d. none of these.
7. A sustainable diet is
   a. a diet that can sustain your life.
   b. a diet that is financially sustainable.
   c. a diet that contains foods that meet your nutrient and health needs and can be sustained for a long time without negatively impacting the environment for future generations.
   d. a diet that a family can sustain.
8. A food lobbyist works for
   a. the government.
   b. the interests of all food consumers.
   c. a food company or organization that has a vested interest in the outcome of food policy.
   d. only those in health care.
9. You are in the supermarket shopping for cereal and find a package of raisin bran that bears the USDA Organic seal. You can be assured that this cereal is made with
   a. at least 95 percent organic ingredients.
   b. 70 percent organic ingredients.
   c. 60 percent organic ingredients.
   d. 50 percent organic ingredients.
10. The process of applying biological techniques to a living cell in order to alter its DNA and create a desired trait is called
    a. biology.
    b. biotechnology.
    c. bioterrorism.
    d. biochemistry.

Answers

1. (a) The majority of farms in the United States are family farms.
2. (c) Agribusiness refers to the entire industry of agricultural and business entities that produce most of our food supply. Small farms and small food companies are part of agribusiness, as are large corporate farms and food company conglomerates.
3. (a) Poultry is the predominant type of animal food consumed by Americans. Soy is a plant food.
4. (d) The term globesity has been coined to reflect the rise of obesity that is occurring globally due to an upward shift of body weights; the shift largely results from an international desire to eat an American-like diet.

5. (e) Both land overuse and soil erosion deplete internal natural resources to produce food. Carbon emission from trucks that transport food is considered an external natural resource.

6. (b) Food miles account for the distance food travels from where it is grown to where you, the consumer, buy it.

7. (c) A sustainable diet is a healthy diet for you and for future generations.

8. (c) While it would be nice to think that a food lobbyist works for the interests of all food consumers, in reality the lobbyist works for a company or organization that has an interest in the outcome of food policy. A lobbyist's job is to persuade government officials to vote in a direction favorable to the companies or organizations the lobbyist represents.

9. (a) Only foods made with at least 95 percent organic ingredients can display the USDA Organic seal. If a product is made with at least 70 percent organic ingredients, an organic statement can be made, but the seal cannot be displayed.

10. (b) Biotechnology, through either plant breeding or bioengineering, can alter a cell's genetic makeup to create a desirable trait and genetically modified product.

Web Resources

➡ Looking to help the environment? Pick five easy changes you can make that are environmentally friendly, by visiting www.epa.gov/pick5/

➡ For more on living green, visit www.epa.gov/epahome/learn.htm

➡ To help you pick environmental products while shopping, visit www.epa.gov/epahome/shopping.htm

➡ For help in finding local farms, visit www.localharvest.org/about.jsp

Answers to Myths and Misperceptions

1. **False.** Although you may think you are indifferent to food advertising, it likely has a significant impact on your food decisions. See page 446 to find out more.

2. **False.** Would you be surprised to learn that food doesn't originate in your grocer's freezer? Turn to page 447 to find out where it really comes from.

3. **True.** Small family farms comprise the majority of farms in the United States. Turn to page 449 to learn more.

4. **False.** Although the United States produces numerous food crops, these two popular staples are almost always imported from other countries. Find out where we get these foods on page 453.

5. **True.** Food that's produced locally will require less fossil fuel for distribution and transport than food that's shipped a great distance from farm or processing plant to grocery store. To find out more, turn to page 456.

6. **True.** Buying foods that are in season can save thousands of "food miles." To find out more, turn to page 457.

7. **False.** Many government agencies are involved in forming and enforcing American food policy. To learn how this is done, turn to page 469.

8. **False.** You may be surprised to learn how much time and effort are invested by the food industry to sway food policy. Turn to page 472 to learn more.

9. **False.** Organic foods are not necessarily pesticide free. To learn more, turn to page 474.

10. **False.** Although organic foods do have some advantages when it comes to preserving the environment, there are times when they may not be the best choice. Turn to page 475 to learn more.

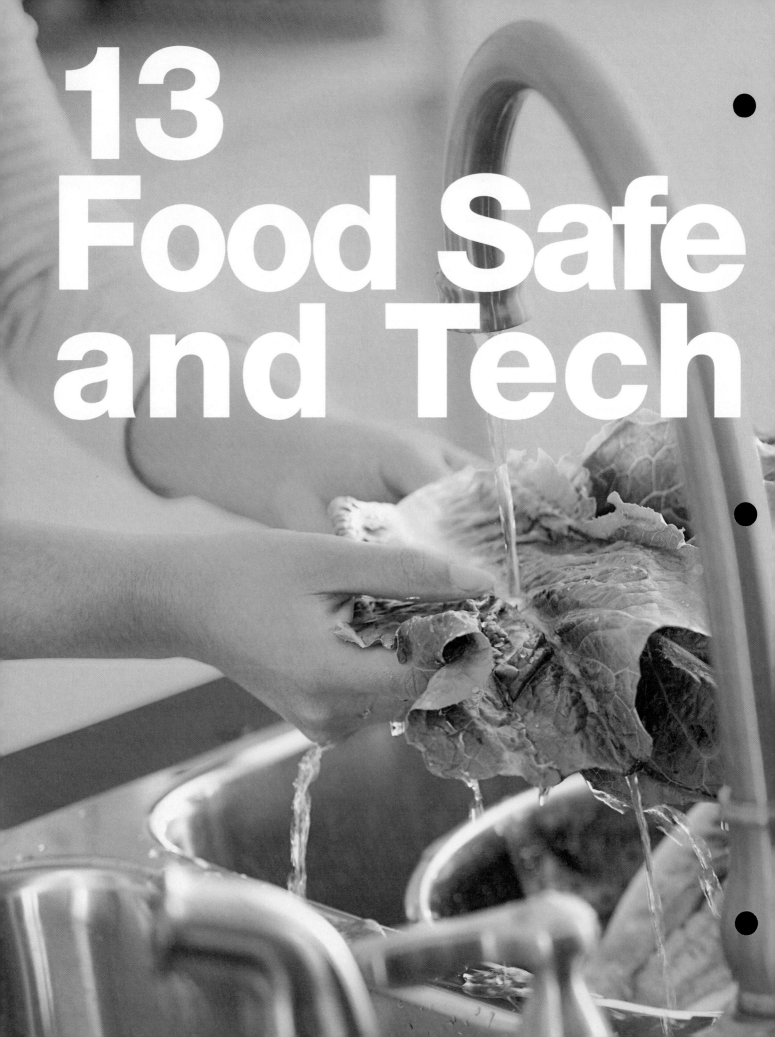

13
Food Safe and Tech

ty
nology
True or False?

1. Foods that can make you **sick** always smell bad. (T)(F) p. 488

2. Hand washing is a key part of practicing food safety. (T)(F) p. 493

3. Cross-contamination can occur as **raw food** is being handled and prepared in the kitchen. (T)(F) p. 494

4. The **temperature** for your refrigerator should be set at 40°F or below. (T)(F) p. 497

5. Freezing foods kills **bacteria.** (T)(F) p. 497

6. Leftovers that have been stored in the fridge for a week will still be safe to eat. (T)(F) p. 497

7. Food irradiation makes food radioactive. (T)(F) p. 503

8. As long as the **expiration date** hasn't passed, packaged food is always safe to eat. (T)(F) p. 504

9. There are no benefits to using **food additives.** (T)(F) p. 505

10. Bioterrorism is a concern in the United States today. (T)(F) p. 511

See page 515 for answers to these Myths and Misperceptions.

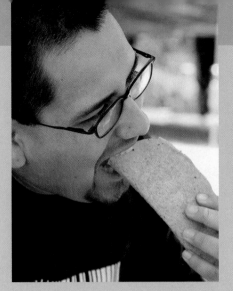

The summer after his sophomore year in college, 20-year-old Miguel decided to take advantage of his school's semester-abroad program and spend some time in Mexico. One night in Mexico City, he bought a fish taco from a street vendor near the campus where he was staying. Several hours later, he woke up with horrible cramps. After running to the bathroom and experiencing a painful bout of diarrhea, he headed to a local clinic to seek some help.

Can you guess the cause of Miguel's unfortunate illness? Have you heard warnings about traveler's diarrhea, and do you know how to avoid it? In this chapter, we'll explore the causes of this and other foodborne illnesses, and find out how they can be prevented.

Chapter Objectives

After reading this chapter, you will be able to:

1. Describe what food safety is and why it is important.

2. Name the pathogens that cause foodborne illness.

3. Identify those individuals who are at a higher risk for foodborne illness.

4. Distinguish between food spoilage and foodborne illness.

5. Identify the four C's that can prevent foodborne illness.

6. Explain the "Danger Zone" and identify the temperature ranges that define this zone.

7. Discuss how the food supply is protected in the United States.

8. Explain the role that food additives play in food production.

9. Name at least two naturally occurring toxins that could be found in foods.

10. Explain how food can play a role in bioterrorism.

What Is Food Safety and Why Is It Important?

Although the United States enjoys one of the safest food supplies in the world, millions of Americans still suffer annually from some type of **foodborne illness.** In fact, cases of foodborne illness cause about 76 million illnesses, 325,000 hospitalizations, and 5,000 deaths per year, and the medical costs and lost wages associated with just one type of illness, that due to the bacterium *Salmonella,* are estimated to top $1 billion per year.[1] These illnesses often result in distressing gastrointestinal symptoms such as cramps, diarrhea, and vomiting.

Efforts to prevent foodborne illnesses have led to the development of extensive **food safety** practices and guidelines. Several government agencies work together to ensure the safety of foods from the farm to the table. Food safety is also the practice of minimizing your risk of contaminating foods as you store and prepare them in your kitchen. There are several strategies consumers can use to make sure the foods they eat and serve are safe. We'll find out more about all of these in this chapter.

What Causes Foodborne Illness?

Most people do not question the safety of the foods they eat until there is a national food-safety recall or they experience firsthand the effects of foodborne illness. A classic example of emerging public awareness occurred in 1906 with the publication of *The Jungle,* by Upton Sinclair. The descriptions of the unsanitary conditions in the Chicago meat-packing plants,[2] which among other atrocities included rodent droppings and body parts making their way into consumer-bound meat products, horrified the public. Meat sales plummeted as a result of consumer fear about eating contaminated foods. Due to the enormous public health risks associated with these unsanitary practices, President Theodore Roosevelt incited the United States Congress to pass the Meat Inspection Act.[3] The act demanded a continuous inspection of all meat-processing plants by the United States Department of Agriculture.[4]

Other improvements in food safety, such as pasteurization of milk, safe canning, and disinfection of water supplies, conquered the common foodborne illnesses of the era. Before long, these food-safety precautions resulted in positive effects on the nation's health. By 1920, instances of one foodborne illness, typhoid fever, had declined by about two-thirds, and by the 1950s it had virtually disappeared in the United States.[5]

Today, advances in production and distribution, new food sources, and the growing volume of food imports continue to present challenges to maintaining a safe food supply. Prior to the advent of convenience foods like bagged lettuce, a contaminated head of lettuce might have affected only one family. Now, however, contaminated lettuce may be processed with thousands of other heads and placed into bags that end up in thousands of homes. This could lead to large outbreaks, making the source difficult to pinpoint.[6] Prevention of such outbreaks remains a public health priority for governmental agencies.

Even with stringent regulations in place, however, bouts of foodborne illness still happen. Let's take a look at the causes of foodborne illness.

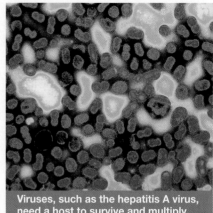

Viruses, such as the hepatitis A virus, need a host to survive and multiply.

Foodborne Illnesses Are Often Caused by Pathogens

To contract a foodborne illness, you must eat foods or beverages that contain one or more harmful agents. The agents can be disease-causing microbes, also known as **pathogens,** such as viruses, bacteria, parasites, fungal agents, or prions. Pathogens can be found in the stool or droppings of infected humans and/or animals. Drinking water that has been contaminated with infected droppings, or putting anything in your mouth (such as food or your hands) that has been in contact with fecal matter, are common ways to become infected. This route of transmission is known as **fecal-to-oral transmission,** and this is why people should always wash their hands after using the bathroom and before preparing foods. Eating raw or undercooked meat, poultry, or fish from an infected animal can also expose you to pathogens.

Pathogenic viruses and bacteria are the most common causes of foodborne illness in the United States. Parasites, fungi, and prions are less common causes. Let's begin with the various viruses that can make you sick.

Viruses

The term **virus** denotes a microscopic infectious agent that contains chromosomes that carry genetic information (DNA or RNA) for their own replication. Viruses must have a living **host,** such as a plant or an animal, to survive. When an individual eats a contaminated plant or animal as food, the pathogen can invade the cells of the stomach and intestinal walls. The virus can then cause the cells' genetic material to start producing more viruses, ultimately leading to illness.[7]

The most common type of virus that causes foodborne illness is the **norovirus.** Noroviruses are named after the original strain of the virus, Norwalk virus, which was the cause of **gastroenteritis** (*gastro* = stomach, *entero* = intestines, *itis* = inflammation), or the "stomach flu," in a school in Norwalk, Ohio, in 1968.[8] (Note: The stomach flu is not the same as influenza (flu), which is a respiratory illness caused by the influenza virus.) About half of all the foodborne illness outbreaks in the United States may be due to noroviruses, making this the single most common cause of foodborne illness (see Table 13.1).[9]

Another foodborne virus, hepatitis A, caused a multistate outbreak among young concertgoers in 2003. The concerts were often multiday events at campgrounds that had less than optimal sanitary conditions. The unofficial food vendors were the attendees

foodborne illness Sickness caused by consuming contaminated food or beverages. Also known as foodborne disease or food poisoning.

food safety Guidelines and procedures that help keep foods free from contaminants.

pathogens Collective term for disease-causing microorganisms (microbes). Includes viruses, bacteria, and parasites. The most common source of foodborne illness.

fecal-to-oral transmission The spread of pathogens by putting something in the mouth that has been in contact with infected stool. Poor hygiene, such as not washing hands after using the bathroom, can be a cause of this contamination.

virus A microscopic organism that carries genetic information for its own replication; can infect a host and cause illness.

host A living plant or animal (including a human) that a virus infects for the sake of reproducing.

norovirus The most common type of virus that causes foodborne illness. Noroviruses can cause gastroenteritis, or the "stomach flu." Also known as Norwalk-like viruses.

gastroenteritis Inflammation of the stomach and intestines.

Table 13.1

Pathogens That Cause Foodborne Illness

Microbe	Where You Find It	How You Can Get It	What You May Experience	Treatment
Viruses				
Noroviruses	In the stool or vomit of infected individuals	Fecal-to-oral transmission; eating ready-to-eat foods or drinking liquids contaminated by an infected person; eating contaminated shellfish; touching contaminated objects and then putting hands in mouth.	Watery diarrhea, nausea, vomiting, flulike symptoms; possible fever. Can appear 24–48 hours after onset and last 24–60 hours. Typically not serious.	Symptoms usually abate without treatment; fluid replacement may be necessary to treat dehydration due to vomiting and/or diarrhea.
Hepatitis A (HAV)	In the stool of infected individuals	Fecal-to-oral transmission; eating raw produce irrigated with contaminated water; eating raw or undercooked foods that have not been properly reheated; drinking contaminated water.	Diarrhea, dark urine, jaundice, flulike symptoms that can appear 30 days after incubation. Can last 2 weeks to 3 months.	Treatment of symptoms only. Vaccination is the most effective means of preventing HAV transmission among persons at risk for infection.
Bacteria				
Campylobacter jejuni	Intestinal tracts of animals and birds, raw milk, untreated water, and sewage.	Drinking contaminated water or raw milk; eating raw or undercooked meat, poultry, or shellfish.	Fever, headache, and muscle pain followed by diarrhea (sometimes bloody), abdominal pain, and nausea. Appears 2 to 5 days after eating; may last 7 to 10 days. Guillain-Barré syndrome may occur.	Almost all persons infected with *Campylobacter* recover without any specific treatment. Patients should drink extra fluids as long as the diarrhea lasts. In more severe cases, antibiotics such as azithromycin or erythromycin can shorten the duration of symptoms if given early in the illness.
Clostridium botulinum	Widely distributed in nature in soil, water, on plants, and in the intestinal tracts of animals and fish. Grows only in environments with little or no oxygen.	Eating improperly canned foods, garlic in oil, vacuum-packaged and tightly wrapped food.	Bacteria produce a toxin that causes illness by affecting the nervous system. Symptoms usually appear after 18 to 36 hours. May experience double vision, droopy eyelids, trouble speaking and swallowing, and difficulty breathing. Fatal in 3 to 10 days if not treated.	The respiratory failure and paralysis that occur with severe botulism may require a patient to be on a breathing machine (ventilator) for weeks, plus intensive medical and nursing care. After several weeks, the paralysis slowly improves. If diagnosed early, foodborne and wound botulism can be treated with an equine antitoxin which blocks the action of toxin circulating in the blood. This can prevent patients from worsening, but recovery still takes many weeks.

Table 13.1   continued

Pathogens That Cause Foodborne Illness

Microbe	Where You Find It	How You Can Get It	What You May Experience	Treatment
Clostridium perfringens	Soil, dust, sewage, and intestinal tracts of animals and humans. Grows only in little or no oxygen.	Called "the cafeteria germ" because many outbreaks result from eating food left for long periods in steam tables at improper temperatures or at room temperature. Bacteria are destroyed by cooking, but some spores may survive.	Diarrhea and gas pains may appear 8 to 24 hours after eating; usually last about 1 day, but less severe symptoms may persist for 1 to 2 weeks.	Supportive care. Avoid dehydration.
Escherichia coli O157:H7	Intestinal tracts of some mammals, raw milk, unchlorinated water; one of several strains of *E. coli* that can cause human illness.	Drinking contaminated water, unpasteurized apple juice or cider, or raw milk, or eating raw or rare ground beef or uncooked fruits and vegetables.	Diarrhea or bloody diarrhea, abdominal cramps, nausea, and weakness Can begin 2 to 5 days after food is eaten, lasting about 8 days Small children and elderly adults may develop hemolytic uremic syndrome (HUS) that causes acute kidney failure. A similar illness, thrombotic thrombocytopenic purpura (TTP), may occur in adults.	Supportive care and avoidance of dehydration. Antibiotics should not be used to treat this infection. There is no evidence that treatment with antibiotics is helpful, and taking antibiotics may increase the risk of HUS.
Enterotoxigenic *Escherichia coli* (major cause of traveler's diarrhea)	Intestinal tracts of some mammals and unpasteurized dairy products. More common in developing countries.	Fecal-to-oral transmission. Consuming stool-contaminated water and foods from unsanitary water supplies and food establishments.	Diarrhea, nausea, vomiting, stomach cramping, bloating, fever, and weakness.	Traveler's diarrhea often resolves without specific treatment; however, oral rehydration is often beneficial to replace lost fluids and electrolytes. Travelers who develop three or more loose stools in an 8-hour period—especially if associated with nausea, vomiting, abdominal cramps, fever, or blood in stools—may benefit from antimicrobial therapy. Antibiotics usually are given for 3 to 5 days.

(continued)

Table 13.1   continued

Pathogens That Cause Foodborne Illness

Microbe	Where You Find It	How You Can Get It	What You May Experience	Treatment
Listeria monocytogenes	Intestinal tracts of humans and animals, milk, soil, leafy vegetables; can grow slowly at refrigerator temperatures.	Eating ready-to-eat foods such as hot dogs, luncheon meats, cold cuts, fermented or dry sausage, other deli-style meat and poultry, or soft cheeses; drinking unpasteurized milk.	Fever, chills, headache, backache, sometimes upset stomach, abdominal pain, and diarrhea; may take up to 3 weeks to become ill; may later develop more serious illness in high-risk individuals.	When infection occurs during pregnancy, antibiotics given promptly to the pregnant woman can often prevent infection of the fetus or newborn. Babies with listeriosis receive the same antibiotics as adults. Even with prompt treatment, some infections result in death.
Salmonella (more than 2,300 types)	Intestinal tracts and feces of animals; *Salmonella enteritidis* in eggs.	Eating raw or undercooked eggs, poultry, and meat, raw milk and dairy products, and seafood. Can also be spread by infected food handlers.	Stomach pain, diarrhea, nausea, chills, fever, and headache usually appear 8 to 72 hours after eating; may last 1 to 2 days.	*Salmonella* infections usually resolve in 5 to 7 days and often do not require treatment other than oral fluids. Persons with severe diarrhea may require rehydration with intravenous fluids. Antibiotics are not usually necessary unless the infection spreads from the intestines. Some *Salmonella* bacteria have become resistant to antibiotics, largely as a result of the use of antibiotics to promote the growth of food animals.
Shigella (more than 30 types)	Human intestinal tract; rarely found in other animals.	Fecal-to-oral transmission by consuming contaminated food and water. Most outbreaks result from eating food, especially salads, prepared and handled by workers with poor personal hygiene.	Disease referred to as "shigellosis" or bacillary dysentery. Diarrhea containing blood and mucus, fever, abdominal cramps, chills, and vomiting begins 12 to 50 hours from ingestion of bacteria; can last a few days to 2 weeks.	Persons with mild infections usually recover quickly without antibiotic treatment. However, appropriate antibiotic treatment kills *Shigella* bacteria, and may shorten the illness by a few days. Some *Shigella* bacteria have become resistant to antibiotics.

Table 13.1 continued

Pathogens That Cause Foodborne Illness

Microbe	Where You Find It	How You Can Get It	What You May Experience	Treatment
Staphylo-coccus aureus	On humans (skin, infected cuts, pimples, noses, and throats).	Consuming foods that were contaminated by being improperly handled. Bacteria multiply rapidly at room temperature.	Severe nausea, abdominal cramps, vomiting, and diarrhea occur 1 to 6 hours after eating; recovery within 2 to 3 days, longer if severe dehydration occurs.	For most patients, staphylococcal food poisoning will cause a brief illness of 1 to 3 days. The best treatments are rest, plenty of fluids, and medicines to calm the stomach. Antibiotics are not useful in treating this illness.
Parasites				
Crypto-sporidium parvum	In the intestines of humans and animals.	Fecal-to-oral transmission. Drinking contaminated water, eating contaminated vegetables and fruits.	Stomach pains, diarrhea, cramps, fever, and vomiting.	The illness usually goes away without medical intervention in 3 to 4 days. For individuals with weakened immune systems, cryptosporidiosis can be serious, long-lasting, and sometimes fatal.
Cyclospora cayetanensis	Human stool.	Fecal-to-oral transmission. Drinking contaminated water, eating contaminated produce.	Diarrhea, flatulence, stomach cramps, vomiting, fatigue.	Can be treated with antibiotics.
Giardia lamblia	In the intestines of humans and animals.	Fecal-to-oral transmission. Drinking contaminated water, eating contaminated produce.	Diarrhea, stomach pains, flatulence.	Several prescription drugs are available to treat *Giardia* infection. Although *Giardia* can infect all people, young children and pregnant women might be more susceptible to dehydration resulting from diarrhea and should, therefore, drink plenty of fluids while ill.
Trichinella spiralis	In undercooked or raw meats containing *Trichinella* worms.	Raw or undercooked contaminated meat, usually pork or game meats.	Nausea, vomiting, diarrhea, fever, aching joints and muscles.	Several safe and effective prescription drugs are available to treat trichinellosis. Treatment should begin as soon as possible.

Sources: Centers for Disease Control and Prevention (CDC), "Diagnosis and Management of Foodborne Illness: A Primer for Physicians" (2004); CDC, "Norovirus: Food Handlers," (2010); CDC, "Viral Hepatitis A" (2003); CDC, "Travelers' Diarrhea" (2004); MMWR, "Recommendations and Reports" 50 (January 2001): 1–69; CDC, "Parasitic Disease Information" (2004). All available at www.cdc.gov. Food Safety and Inspection Service, "Foodborne Illness: What Consumers Need to Know" (2006); Food Safety and Inspection Service, "Parasites and Foodborne Illness" (2001). Both available at www.fsis.usda.gov.

themselves. Many of the concert attendees traveled from concert to concert. This type of living environment, in which people are living, cooking, and eating in unsanitary conditions, practicing poor hand washing and hygiene, and traveling from state to state, can create a breeding ground for an outbreak. Approximately 300 attendees had to be vaccinated against hepatitis A.[10]

Bacteria

E. coli O157:H7 is the strain of bacteria that causes most foodborne illness. Most forms of *E. coli* are harmless.

If you were to swab your kitchen sink right now and look at the results under a microscope, you would find that there are about 16 million bacteria living on each square centimeter (less than half an inch) of your sink. Whereas viruses need a host to survive, bacteria can flourish on both living and nonliving surfaces. They live on your computer mouse, keyboard, body, clothing, and in every room of your house. In fact, there are hundreds of different types of bacteria on your skin alone.[11] The majority of bacteria around you are harmless, and some are even essential, such as the ones in your intestine that synthesize biotin and vitamin K. Bacteria are also used to make some of the foods we enjoy, like yogurt, cheese, and buttermilk.

A few bacteria are harmful, however, and can cause food spoilage or illness. The bacteria that cause food spoilage are not the same as those that cause foodborne illness. Food spoilage bacteria cause the deterioration of the quality of food. For example, a carton of sour milk and that forgotten Chinese takeout in the back of your refrigerator have gone "bad" because of food spoilage bacteria. Though most individuals will not become seriously ill after eating spoiled foods, these items can cause nausea and shouldn't be eaten. (Luckily, the less-than-pleasant odor of sour milk or spoiled food usually leads to it being thrown away.) In contrast to spoiled foods, contaminated foods that contain bacterial pathogens may look and smell perfectly fine. Pathogenic bacteria can cause illness in several ways: 1) by directly invading the intestinal wall and multiplying, 2) by producing an infection via a toxin that is absorbed into your blood, and 3) by invading deeper body tissues.[12]

Reptiles (lizards, snakes, and turtles) often carry *Salmonella*. You should always wash your hands after touching a reptile, and keep reptiles away from small children.

The most common bacteria that cause foodborne illness are *Campylobacter*, *Escherichia coli* (*E. coli*) O157:H7, and *Salmonella* (see Table 13.1). Another bacterium, *Listeria monocytogenes*, a less prevalent cause of foodborne illness, is still of concern for individuals most likely to get foodborne illness, especially pregnant women and newborns (see the feature box, "The Lowdown on *Listeria*," on page 489).

Campylobacter is the most common cause of bacteria-related diarrhea in the United States.[13] Over two million people[14] are infected annually with the *Campylobacter jejuni* species, the most prevalent variety in the United States. It is found mostly in contaminated water, raw milk, and raw meat products, particularly poultry. Some individuals may develop a rare nerve disease called **Guillain-Barré syndrome** after contracting a *Campylobacter* infection, which causes a person's immune system to attack its own nerves and results in temporary paralysis.[15]

Guillain-Barré syndrome A condition that can result from a *Campylobacter* infection. It causes the immune system to attack its own nerves and can lead to paralysis for several weeks.

hemolytic uremic syndrome A rare condition that can be caused by *E. coli* O157:H7 and results in the destruction of red blood cells and kidney failure.

Though most strains of *E. coli* are harmless, *E. coli* O157:H7 is estimated to cause more than 70,000 cases of foodborne illness[16] and 60 deaths in the United States annually. Contaminated ground beef has been the culprit behind most cases of foodborne illness caused by *E. coli* O157:H7. Because bacteria live in the gastrointestinal tract of healthy cattle, they can easily come into contact with the meat of the animal during the slaughtering process and then get mixed in when making ground beef. Proper cooking can destroy these bacteria. In people at highest risk for foodborne illness (the very young and the elderly), *E. coli* O157:H7 can cause **hemolytic uremic syndrome** (HUS; *hemo* = blood, *lyti* = destroyed, *uremic* = too much urea in blood),

The Lowdown on *Listeria*

Listeriosis, the illness caused by the bacterium *Listeria monocytogenes,* seriously affects approximately 2,500 individuals annually, with pregnant women being 20 times more likely than other people to become infected. *Listeria* can reach the fetus through the placenta, be transmitted to the newborn, and lead to severe illness, premature delivery, miscarriage, and stillbirth. Older adults and those with a weakened immune system are also at risk for becoming very sick or even dying.

Animals can harbor *Listeria,* which leads to contamination of meat and dairy foods. Pasteurization will kill *Listeria,* so unpasteurized soft cheeses, such as Camembert, Brie, and blue cheeses, carry a higher risk of containing *Listeria.* Compared to hard cheeses such as Parmesan, these soft cheeses are less acidic and contain more moisture, two conditions that enhance bacterial growth. Even though cooking can also destroy *Listeria,* the lower cooking temperature used during the processing of soft cheeses isn't high enough to destroy this bacterium. Because contamination can occur after processing, many outbreaks have been associated with foods such as hot dogs, deli-style luncheon meats, Brie cheese, salami, and paté. *Listeria* can

also continue to multiply at refrigerated temperatures.

The following tips can help pregnant women and other higher risk individuals reduce their likelihood of contracting *Listeria:*

➤ Reheat ready-to-eat luncheon meats, cold cuts, fermented and dry sausage, deli-style meat and poultry products, and hot dogs until they are steamy hot (165 if you are using a thermometer) to kill any existing bacteria before you eat them. Pregnant women should avoid cold luncheon meats.

➤ Don't allow the fluid from hot dog packages to drip on other foods, utensils, and food preparation surfaces. Always wash your hands after handling hot dogs, luncheon meats, and deli meats.

➤ Wash your hands with hot, soapy water after touching these types of ready-to-eat foods, or any foods, for that matter. Thoroughly wash cutting boards, dishes, and utensils to avoid cross-contamination.

➤ Avoid soft cheeses such as feta, Brie, Camembert, blue-veined (blue) cheese, and Mexican-style cheeses

unless they are made with pasteurized milk. (Read the ingredients list to see if pasteurized milk was used.) You can safely eat hard cheeses, semi-soft cheese such as mozzarella, pasteurized processed cheeses, cream cheese, and cottage cheese.

➤ Avoid unpasteurized milk and foods made from unpasteurized milk.

➤ Avoid refrigerated smoked seafood such as smoked salmon (lox or nova style), trout, whitefish, cod, tuna, or mackerel unless they are used in an entrée such as in a heated casserole. You can safely eat canned fish and shelf-stable smoked seafood.

➤ Avoid refrigerated paté or meat spreads. You can safely eat canned or shelf-stable varieties.

➤ Eat precooked or ready-to-eat perishable items before the expiration date on the food label.

Source: Centers for Disease Control. 2008. Listeriosis. Available at www.cdc.gov/ncczved/divisions/dfbmd/diseases/listeriosis/; USDA. 2006. Protect Your Baby and Yourself from Listeriosis. Available at http://origin-www.fsis.usda.gov/Fact_Sheets/Protect_Your_Baby/index.asp.

---

which results in the destruction of red blood cells and damage to and eventual failure of the kidneys.[17]

Another type of *E. coli*, called enterotoxigenic (*entero* = intestines, *toxi* = toxin, *genic* = forming) *E. coli*, is a common cause of **traveler's diarrhea.** Each year, up to 50 percent of international travelers, like Miguel from the beginning of the chapter, have their trips interrupted by unpleasant intestinal side effects. Traveler's diarrhea is primarily caused by consuming contaminated food or water. People visiting countries where proper sanitation is in question, including some developing countries in Latin America, Africa, the Middle East, and Asia, are at a higher risk of contracting it.[18] See the Table Tips on page 492 for suggestions on how to avoid traveler's diarrhea.

There are several types of *Salmonella* bacteria. *Salmonella enteritidis* is one of the most common varieties found in the United States. An estimated 40,000 incidences of

> The bacterium *E. coli* that is in your intestinal tract helps to make vitamin K. This is not the same as *E. coli* O157:H7, the pathogen that can cause foodborne illness.

traveler's diarrhea A common pathogen-induced intestinal disorder experienced by some travelers who visit areas with unsanitary conditions.

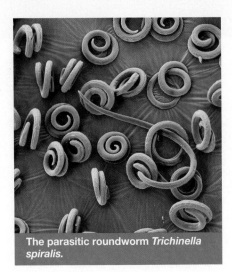

The parasitic roundworm *Trichinella spiralis.*

Salmonella-related foodborne illness occur annually, and about 400 individuals die yearly due to this bacterium.[19] *S. enteritidis* is most commonly found in raw eggs, so foods that contain raw eggs, such as the dressing on homemade Caesar salad, raw cookie dough, or cake batter, can potentially cause illness.

Parasites

Parasites are microscopic animals that, like viruses, take their nourishment from hosts. They can be found in food and water and are often transmitted through the fecal-to-oral route.[20] The most common parasitic illness outbreaks in the United States have been caused by just a few types: *Crytosporidium parvum, Cyclospora cayatenensis, Giardia lamblia,* and *Trichinella spiralis.*[21]

Both *Crytosporidium parvum* and *Cyclospora cayatenensis* can be found in contaminated water or food sources, while *Giardia lamblia* is one of the most common sources of waterborne illness and can be a serious cause of traveler's diarrhea. *Trichinella spiralis* (see photo below) is an intestinal worm whose larvae (hatched eggs) can travel from the digestive tract to the muscles of the body. *Trichinella spiralis* is typically transmitted by eating undercooked or raw meat or fish. Some steps can be taken to eliminate or control the risk of parasitic infection; see the feature box "Sushi: A Cautionary Tale." Refer again to Table 13.1 for a summary of these parasites and the foodborne illnesses they cause.

Prions

Prions are an extremely rare but deadly infectious agent. **Bovine spongiform encephalopathy (BSE)** is a slow, degenerative, and deadly disease caused by an unusual protein called a **prion** that attacks the central nervous system of cattle. Cattle can become infected by consuming feed that is contaminated with BSE.[22] Individuals who are exposed to BSE by eating beef from infected cattle experience neurological symptoms and damage.

Meat and bone meal given to young calves and cattle that was rendered from contaminated tissues, such as the brain or spinal cord of infected bovines, may have played a role in an outbreak of BSE that occurred in the United Kingdom in the early 1980s.[23] The outbreak also may have been caused by feeding cattle meat and bone meal made from sheep infested with *scrapie,* a prion disease related to BSE.[24] In January 1993, the outbreak peaked in the United Kingdom, when approximately 1,000 new cases of BSE were reported weekly in cows.[25] By the end of November 2003, more than 180,000 cases of BSE were confirmed, involving more than 35,000 different herds in the United Kingdom. Other countries, including the Republic of Ireland, France, Portugal, Holland, and Switzerland, have also been affected by BSE.[26]

The contaminant that causes BSE in animals is thought to cause a similar disease, called *variant Creutzfeldt-Jakob Disease (vCJD),* in humans. Three cases of vCJD have been confirmed in the United States, though in all cases, patients were exposed to the prion in another country before moving to the United States.[27]

Although no one has acquired vCJD from cattle in the United States, a cow that tested positive for BSE was slaughtered in a meat plant in the state of Washington in 2003. Trace-back investigations confirmed that this BSE-infected cow was imported from Canada. A recall was made of all the meat plant's production for that day, and the affected animal's herd was quarantined. Since then, two additional U.S. cattle, one in Texas and one in Alabama, have been found with the disease.[28]

Since the late 1980s, the United States has taken specific steps to protect the public against beef contaminated with BSE. First and foremost, **ruminant animals** such as cattle and sheep, meat and meat products from ruminant animals, and animal feed that contains animal protein derived from countries that are at risk for BSE can no

parasites Organisms that live on or in another organism. Parasites obtain their nourishment from their hosts.

bovine spongiform encephalopathy (BSE) A slow, degenerative, and deadly disease that attacks the central nervous system of cattle. Also known as **mad cow disease.**

prion Cellular proteins. An abnormal prion protein is the cause of mad cow disease.

ruminant animals Animals that have four chambers in their stomachs for digesting coarse food such as plants.

Sushi: A Cautionary Tale

Are you looking for a delicious meal that's typically low in calories, high in nutrients, and a good source of omega-3 fatty acids? Well, then, sushi may be for you! But before we declare sushi the next great superfood, we need a reality check. When improperly handled, some types of sushi can be a significant harbor for organisms that cause foodborne illness.

Sushi is a traditional Japanese food that contains vinegared rice, seaweed (*nori*), vegetables (such as cucumber, radish, or avocado), and seafood (for example, tuna, yellowtail, salmon, squid, octopus, shrimp, eel, or roe, among many others). Some types of sushi are made with vegetables and rice only, or use cooked fish or other seafood, and therefore create less risk of harm. However, sushi that specifically contains raw fish, including the type of sushi known as **sashimi,** carries a greater potential risk.

sushi A Japanese dish of cooked, vinegared rice served with fish or other seafood, vegetables, and/or seaweed.

sashimi A type of sushi that primarily consists of raw seafood, sliced into thin pieces and served with a dipping sauce (soy sauce with wasabi paste) or other condiments (such as fresh ginger).

Raw-fish versions of sushi can sometimes carry illness-inducing parasites, including nematodes (roundworms), tapeworms, and flukes, in the flesh or organs of the fish. The parasites can only be killed with heat (by cooking) or cold (by freezing). In fact, despite the common wisdom that "fresh" sushi is better than frozen, all seafood (with the exception of tuna) that's slated for raw consumption in the United States is commercially frozen, per FDA regulations. This means that it is held at a temperature of 4°F—a temperature below that of most home freezers—for at least three days. When buying fish at the grocery store, the terms "sushi grade" or "sashimi grade" on a product's packaging indicate that it's been commercially frozen.

Once it's been thawed and prepared, leftover sushi must be kept refrigerated to avoid the growth of harmful microorganisms. If you make sushi at home, always wash your hands thoroughly before and after handling it to avoid cross-contamination. Remember that even the rice that has come into contact with sushi or sashimi can make you sick if you don't keep it refrigerated.

Pregnant women, young children, and older adults are more susceptible to foodborne illness and should avoid raw seafood—as should anyone with a compromised immune system, including those being treated for cancer, AIDS, diabetes, or kidney disease.

Sources: FDA, "Parasites: A Biological Hazard," *Fish and Fisheries Products Hazards and Controls Guidance* 3 (November 2009). Available at www.fda.gov/Food/GuidanceComplianceRegulatoryInformation/GuidanceDocuments/Seafood/FishandFisheriesProductsHazardsandControlsGuide/ucm091704.htm. Accessed August 2010. Moskin, Julia, "Sushi Fresh from the Deep . . . The Deep Freeze," *The New York Times*, April 8, 2004. Available at www.nytimes.com/2004/04/08/nyregion/sushi-fresh-from-the-deep-the-deep-freeze.html. Accessed August 2010.

---

longer be imported into the United States. Also, feed for ruminant animals that is sold in North America is banned from containing any ruminant protein. This type of feed has been identified as a major route of BSE transmission.[29]

Chemical Agents and Toxins Can Also Cause Illness

Foodborne illnesses can also be caused by **toxins** and chemical agents that occur naturally in foods, such as those found in certain fungi (including poisonous mushrooms) and some fish. Chemical agents, such as antibiotics and pesticides that are intentionally added to foods, can also cause foodborne illness. We'll discuss specific toxins and chemicals later in the chapter.

toxins Poisons that can be produced by living organisms.

Some People Are at Higher Risk for Foodborne Illness

Some individuals are at greater risk of developing foodborne illness than others. Older adults, young children, and those with a compromised immune system are more susceptible to the adverse effects of foodborne illness.

In older adults, the age-related deterioration of the immune system increases the risk for foodborne illness. Also, because less acidic gastric juice is produced in the stomach as you age, fewer foodborne pathogens are destroyed during digestion, resulting in greater risk of gastrointestinal infections and their complications. In fact, the elderly are at higher risk of dying of gastroenteritis, which is a severe complication of foodborne illness.[30]

Young children, because of their underdeveloped immune systems, are also more vulnerable to foodborne illness. Children are also smaller and weigh less than adults, and can become sickened by exposure to a smaller quantity of pathogens. About a third of the $6.9 billion spent on medical costs and lost job productivity associated with foodborne disease is due to illnesses that occur in children under 10 years of age.[31]

Any condition that weakens a person's immune system can increase his or her risk of contracting foodborne illness. This applies to individuals with HIV, AIDS, cancer, and diabetes.[32] The hormonal shifts seen during pregnancy can affect a pregnant woman's immune system, making her more vulnerable to certain foodborne illnesses such as listeriosis. Often in cases of foodborne illness in pregnancy, the mother is mildly sick, but the risk to the fetus can be great and often can lead to death of the baby.

Individuals in institutional settings (such as nursing homes, hospitals, and schools), where groups of people eat foods from the same source, are also at higher risk of foodborne illness. Improper handling of foods and poor hygiene practices of food-service workers are often the cause of foodborne disease outbreaks in institutional settings. Luckily, there are many ways to reduce your risk of contracting such an illness.

The Take-Home Message Foodborne illness is caused by consuming pathogens in contaminated food or drinks. Viruses and bacteria are the most common causes in the United States, though parasites, prions, and fungal agents can cause some foodborne illness as well. Natural toxins and chemical agents can cause illness as well. Certain populations, including the elderly, children, and those with compromised immune systems, are at higher risk of contracting foodborne illness.

What Can You Do to Prevent Foodborne Illness?

Because foods may harbor some contamination even when you bring them home from the store, the best way to fight foodborne illness is to take action in your kitchen to kill any disease-causing microbes and to prevent them from flourishing. Bacteria, for instance, thrive and multiply in an environment with the following characteristics (see **Figure 13.1**):

Figure 13.1 A Bulk Recipe for Bacteria

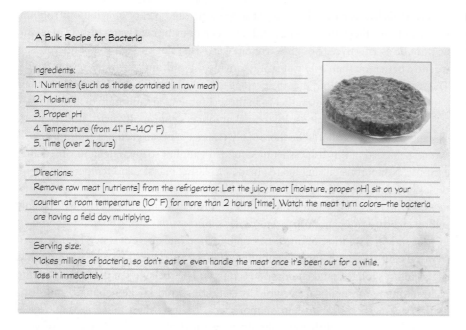

A Bulk Recipe for Bacteria

Ingredients:
1. Nutrients (such as those contained in raw meat)
2. Moisture
3. Proper pH
4. Temperature (from 41° F–140° F)
5. Time (over 2 hours)

Directions:
Remove raw meat [nutrients] from the refrigerator. Let the juicy meat [moisture, proper pH] sit on your counter at room temperature (10° F) for more than 2 hours [time]. Watch the meat turn colors—the bacteria are having a field day multiplying.

Serving size:
Makes millions of bacteria, so don't eat or even handle the meat once it's been out for a while. Toss it immediately.

> *Adequate nutrients.* Protein- and nutrient-rich animal foods, such as raw and undercooked meat, poultry, seafood, eggs, and unpasteurized milk, are the most common havens for bacterial growth.
> *Moisture.* Bacteria thrive in moist environments, such as in raw chicken that is sitting in its own juices.
> *A low level of acidity (pH).* Most bacteria don't thrive in acidic foods, such as citrus fruits, but can flourish in less acidic foods, such as meat, fish, and poultry.
> *The correct temperature.* Bacteria multiply most abundantly between the temperatures of about 40°F and 140°F.[33]
> *Time.* At body temperature, 98.6°F, bacteria can divide and double within 30 minutes, and they multiply to millions in about 12 hours.[34] Perishable food, such as raw meat, left at room temperature for an extended period can become a feast for bacterial growth.

You can reduce your risk for foodborne illness by practicing proper food handling and storage strategies. They're easy to remember as the "four *C*s" of food safety: cleaning, combating cross-contamination, cooking, and chilling (**Figure 13.2**). Let's look at each of these four steps individually.

Figure 13.2 Fight BAC!
The Fight BAC! symbol sums up the four Cs of keeping food safe in your kitchen: clean, combat cross-contamination (separate raw meats from ready-to-eat foods), cook thoroughly, and chill to a cold enough temperature.

Clean Your Hands and Produce

You were probably taught as a child to wash your hands before eating, and guess what? Your parents were right. Hand washing is one of the most important strategies for preventing foodborne illness. However, washing your hands *thoroughly*—that is, making sure to scrub both sides of the hands, between the fingers, and under the fingernails—is just as important as washing your hands regularly, and this is where many people fall short. In a study conducted at Utah State University, more than 100 participants were videotaped to observe their food handling practices. After reviewing the video, the researchers found that only 2 percent of the participants had

One study involving more than 300 school-aged children found that those who washed their hands four times a day had almost 25 percent fewer sick days due to respiratory illnesses and more than 50 percent fewer sick days due to stomachaches.

Scrub Away Pathogens

Wash your hands before eating, before and during cooking, and especially after visiting the bathroom or changing diapers.

Wash your hands with hot, soapy water for at least 20 seconds and use plenty of agitation. (Recite the alphabet or sing "Happy Birthday" twice, which will take you approximately 20 seconds.) Dry with a clean towel, or better yet, a paper towel, which lets you toss away the germs.

Wash sponges and dishcloths at least weekly in the hot water cycle of the washing machine or put in the microwave until dry (2 to 3 minutes). Sponges can also be run through the dishwasher cycle.

Wash all fruits and vegetables under cold running tap water to remove dirt and microbes. Use a vegetable brush for firmer produce, such as apples, cucumbers, and potatoes. Do not use detergents or soaps, as these can leave a residue on or be absorbed into the produce. (Detergents and soaps are not approved for human consumption.)

You don't need to wash meat, poultry, fish, or eggs. Proper cooking will destroy foodborne pathogens in these foods.

washed their hands correctly, with hot soapy water and plenty of agitation (rubbing your hands together). Just rinsing hands in water, or using cold water instead of warm, will not be as effective. Though warm tap water isn't hot enough to kill microbes, it will do a better job than cold water of removing dirt, oil, and germs from your hands. The researchers also found that the average time the participants spent washing their hands was a mere 7 seconds, rather than the recommended minimum of 20 seconds.[35]

In addition to your hands, anything that touches your food, such as knives, utensils, and countertops, should be thoroughly cleaned between each use. Cutting boards should be placed in the dishwasher or scrubbed with hot soapy water and rinsed after each use. Nonporous cutting boards made of plastic, marble, and tempered glass are typically easier to keep clean than the more porous wood cutting boards or wooden surfaces. Cracks in a cutting board can become a hideaway for microbes, so try to keep only unbroken boards on hand. You can routinely sanitize your cutting board by flooding it in your sink in a solution of one teaspoon bleach in one quart of water. Let the board sit in the sanitizing liquid for a few minutes to kill the microbes, then rinse it thoroughly.

A moist sponge that contains food scraps and has been left at room temperature is an ideal environment for bacteria. In fact, household kitchen sponges and dishcloths have been shown to harbor more fecal bacteria than toilet seats.[36] Consequently, sponges and dishcloths should be washed often in the hot cycle of your washing machine, preferably with bleach in addition to the soap. Sponges can also be put in your dishwasher or microwave.

Fruits and vegetables should be thoroughly washed under cold running tap water before eating. This will help remove any dirt or microbes on their surfaces. Produce with a firm surface can be scrubbed with a vegetable brush. The Table Tips summarize the cleaning strategies you should apply when preparing food.

You should also keep your refrigerator clean. Research shows that many Americans, especially young adults, neglect to properly clean their refrigerators adequately and often enough.[37] Interestingly, research has shown that the vegetable drawer was found to harbor more bacteria than the meat drawer.[38] The interior of your refrigerator should be cleaned weekly with hot, soapy water and then thoroughly rinsed. Toss out leftovers and perishable foods that are no longer safe to eat.[39]

Combat Cross-Contamination

Produce, especially if it's going to be eaten raw, should never come in contact with raw meat, poultry, or fish during the food preparation process. If these items do come in contact, they could **cross-contaminate** each other, meaning that microbes from one could move to the other and vice versa. Microbe-containing raw meat, poultry, and fish should be kept separate from ready-to-eat foods during food preparation, and stored separately in your refrigerator. You should even keep these products apart on the trip home from the grocery store.

Marinades that are used to tenderize and flavor meats, poultry, or fish shouldn't be used as a serving sauce unless they have been boiled for several minutes to kill any pathogens; instead of reusing, set aside an amount for sauces before marinating.

The knife and cutting board used to cut and prepare raw meat, poultry, or fish shouldn't be used to slice vegetables or bread unless both have been thoroughly cleaned. Your best bet is to use separate cutting boards for meat and nonmeat foods to avoid cross-contamination. Keep one board for slicing raw meats, poultry, and fish, and use another one for cutting fresh produce, breads, rolls, and other ready-to-eat foods. All plates and bowls that have contained raw meats, poultry, and fish should be thoroughly washed before they are reused. For example, at a barbecue, the plate that held the raw hamburgers should *never* be used to serve the cooked burgers unless it

Do separate raw meats from produce in the refrigerator.

Do sanitize sponges and cutting boards with chlorine bleach solution.

Do wash utensils, countertops, and cutting boards thoroughly with hot soapy water after they touch raw meat, fish, or poultry.

Do marinate raw meat in refrigerator in sealed containers.

Don't use dirty towels to dry clean dishes.

Don't reuse the marinade unless it has been boiled.

Do discard worn cutting boards with lots of cuts and scratches.

Figure 13.3 The Do's and Don'ts of Cross-Contamination

has been thoroughly washed between each use. In addition, the tongs that you use to handle the raw meat should be either cleaned or exchanged for a clean pair as the meat cooks.

Soiled dishtowels shouldn't be used to dry clean dishes or utensils. A towel that was used to wipe up raw meat juices from a counter or your hands can transfer any microbes from the juices to your clean dishes or utensils. You could easily coat those clean surfaces with a layer of germs. Dishes and utensils should air-dry for the least contamination. **Figure 13.3** provides more ways to combat cross-contamination when you prepare food.

Cook Foods Thoroughly

Though you may assume that brown meat is cooked meat, this is often not the case. Look at the two hamburger patties in the photos here. Which one do you think looks safe to eat? The answer may surprise you. The patty on the bottom looks as though it is more thoroughly cooked than the patty on the top, but it's actually not. Color is not always a proper indication that meat is safe to eat; some lean varieties of beef can remain pink even though they have reached an internal temperature of 160°F, high enough to kill any potential pathogens.

The color of beef is largely determined by *myoglobin,* a protein that provides the purplish-red pigment in meat (and poultry). Whereas meat typically turns from pink to brown during cooking, if it starts out brown, this color change won't occur. Thus, the burger could look "done" when it may still be raw in places. Research has shown that hamburgers can look "well done" while having reached an internal temperature of only approximately 135°F.[40]

A hamburger needs to reach an internal temperature of 160°F to ensure that all foodborne pathogens are killed. Can you tell which of these two hamburgers is safe to eat? (If you answered "a," you're right!)

cross-contaminate Transfer pathogens from a food, utensil, cutting board, kitchen surface, and/or hands to another food.

Thermocouple digital food thermometer displays the temperature of the food within 6 seconds after placement.

Thermometer fork combination thermometers allow you to stab and check. A device that measures the temperature in the food is located in the tines of the fork.

Thermistor digital food thermometers take approximately 10 seconds to display the temperature of the food on the dial.

Oven-safe bimetallic-coil thermometers are most useful when cooking thick foods such as roasts and turkeys. They are unique, as they can stay in the food during cooking.

Packaging materials like zip-close bags, egg cartons, and takeout containers should be thrown away after use. Even if you clean them, pathogens can cling to these items and contaminate other foods.

Poultry can also remain pink after thorough cooking. Gases in your oven can cause a chemical reaction in the poultry that will give the meat a pink tinge. Because younger birds have thin skins, the gases can react with their flesh more easily and make the meat look pinker than that of older birds. Also, if nitrates and nitrites are added as a preservative, these can give poultry a pink tinge (see the discussion of food additives later in the chapter).[41]

With so many variables in fresh meat and poultry, color is not a reliable indicator that food is safe to eat. The only way to determine if your food has reached an appropriate internal temperature, high enough to kill pathogens, is to use a food thermometer. **Figure 13.4** shows several types of food thermometers you can use when cooking.

When it comes to foodborne pathogens, always remember that though eating raw meats, poultry, and fish can make you *ill*, cooking to the proper temperature will *kill* the pathogens. Table 13.2 provides a list of the internal temperatures that your foods should reach to ensure that they are safe to eat.

Chill Foods at a Low Enough Temperature

Just as cooking foods to a high enough temperature to kill pathogens is essential, chilling foods at a low enough temperature to inhibit pathogenic growth is also important. Foodborne bacteria multiply most rapidly in temperatures between 40°F and 140°F (or 5°C to 60°C), a range known as the **danger zone.** To keep foods out of the danger zone, make sure that you keep hot foods *hot*, above 140°F, and cold foods *cold*, 40°F or below (**Figure 13.5**). In other words, the lasagna on a buffet table should be sitting on a hot plate or other heat source that keeps its temperature above 140°F, while the potato salad should be sitting on ice that will keep it chilled and at 40°F or below at all times.

Cold temperatures will slow down microbes' ability to multiply to dangerous levels. (The only exception to this is *Listeria*, which can multiply at refrigerator temperatures.) Because of this, the temperature in your refrigerator should be set at or below

danger zone The range of temperatures (between 40°F and 140°F) at which foodborne bacteria multiply most rapidly. Room temperature falls within the danger zone.

Table 13.2
Cook It Until It's Done!

If You Are Cooking (Food)	The Food Thermometer Should Reach (°F)*
Ground Meat and Meat Mixtures	
Beef, pork, veal, lamb	160
Turkey, chicken	165
Fresh Beef, Veal, Lamb	145**
Poultry	
Chicken, turkey, whole or parts	165
Duck and goose	165
Fresh Pork	145**
Ham, raw	145**
Ham, precooked (to reheat)	140
Eggs and Egg Dishes	
Eggs	Cook until yolk and white are firm
Egg dishes	160
Leftovers and Casseroles	165

Source: Food Safety and Inspection Service. 2011. Available at www.foodsafety.gov.

*The thermometer should be placed in the thickest part of the food item.

**Meat should rest for 3 minutes before consumption to ensure that pathogens are destroyed.

Figure 13.5 The Danger Zone
Bacteria multiply rapidly in the "danger zone," between temperatures of 40°F and 140°F.

40°F. The only way to know if the temperature in your refrigerator or freezer is low enough is to use a thermometer.

The temperature for the freezer should be set at 0°F or below. Food will stay safe in the freezer indefinitely, though its quality may deteriorate. (For example, freezer burn may occur if frozen food is not tightly wrapped and gets exposed to air. Freezer burn causes food to dry out and taste less pleasant, but it isn't harmful.) Most microbes become dormant and are unable to multiply when they are frozen, but they aren't destroyed. In fact, once the frozen foods are defrosted, many microbes can "thaw out" and thrive if given the proper conditions.

Perishables such as raw meat and poultry shouldn't be left out at room temperature (a temperature within the danger zone) for more than two hours. If the air temperature is above 90°F, foods shouldn't be left out for more than one hour.[42] Leftovers should be refrigerated within two hours of being served. Large roasts and pots of soup or stews should be divided into smaller batches in order to cool down more quickly in the refrigerator. If these items have been left in the danger zone for too long or have been mishandled, bacteria can not only grow but can also produce toxins that are heat resistant. These toxins won't be destroyed even if the food is cooked to a proper internal temperature, and could make you sick if consumed.[43]

Even stored at a proper temperature, foods shouldn't remain in the refrigerator for more than a few days. The rule of thumb is that leftovers can be in the refrigerator at 40°F or below for no more than four days. Here's an easy way to remember this:

Raw eggs and other perishables should not be stored on your refrigerator door as temperature swings are more likely. Store perishables in the back of the refrigerator, for a colder and more constant temperature.

After *four* days in the refrigerator, leftovers are ready *for* disposal. Raw meats and poultry can be kept for a maximum of two days in the refrigerator. Table 13.3 provides a listing of the storage times for various foods. If you are unsure about the safety of a food, remember this: *When in doubt, throw it out.*

Now that you've read about how cleaning, cooking, chilling, and avoiding cross-contamination can help keep your foods safe, think about how many of these strategies you use in your own kitchen. The Self-Assessment will help you identify areas in which you may need to improve your food-safety habits.

Table 13.3
Keeping It Cool!

Follow these guidelines to keep your perishable foods safe.

Product	Storage Time after Purchase*	
For Raw Foods		
Poultry	1 or 2 days	
Beef, veal, pork, and lamb	3 to 5 days	
Ground meat and ground poultry	1 or 2 days	
Fresh variety meats (liver, tongue, brain, kidneys, heart, intestines)	1 or 2 days	
Cured ham, cook-before-eating	5 to 7 days	
Sausage from pork, beef or turkey, uncooked	1 or 2 days	
Eggs	3 to 5 weeks	
	Unopened, after Purchase*	**after Opening***
For Processed Product Sealed at Plant		
Cooked poultry	3 to 4 days	3 to 4 days
Cooked sausage	3 to 4 days	3 to 4 days
Sausage, hard/dry, shelf-stable	6 weeks/pantry	3 weeks
Corned beef, uncooked, in pouch with pickling juices	5 to 7 days	3 to 4 days
Vacuum-packed dinners, commercial brand with USDA seal	2 weeks	3 to 4 days
Bacon	2 weeks	1 week
Hot dogs	2 weeks	1 week
Luncheon meat	2 weeks	3 to 5 days
Ham, fully cooked, whole	7 days	3 days
Ham, canned, labeled "keep refrigerated"	9 months	3 to 4 days
Ham, canned, shelf-stable	2 years/pantry	3 to 5 days
Canned meat and poultry, shelf-stable	2 to 5 years/pantry	3 to 4 days
Leftovers		3 to 4 days

Source: Food Safety and Inspection Service, "Keep Foods Safe! Food Safety Basics" (2007). Available at www.fsis.usda.gov/PDF/Keep_Food_Safe_Food_Safety_Basics.pdf.

*Based on refrigerator home storage (at 40°F or below).

How Do Your Food-Safety Habits Stack Up?

Take the following quiz to find out.

How Often Do You	Always	Sometimes	Never
Wash your hands before preparing food?			
Scrub your fruits and vegetables under cold, running water before eating them?			
Use an insulated pouch and an ice pack to transport your perishable lunches and snacks?			
Wash your hands after using the bathroom?			
Throw out refrigerated leftovers after four days?			
Chop raw vegetables on a clean chopping board rather than the one you just used for raw meat, fish, or poultry?			
Use a thermometer to determine if the meat or poultry is done cooking?			

Answers

If you answered "Always" to all of the above, you are a food-safety superstar. If you didn't, there's more you can do to reduce your chances of contracting a foodborne illness. This chapter will help!

The Take-Home Message **Proper food handling and storage strategies, particularly cleaning, combating cross-contamination, cooking, and chilling, can help reduce your risk of foodborne illness. Anything that comes in contact with your foods, including your hands, should be thoroughly washed. You should always wash produce before eating it, and separate raw meats, poultry, and fish, plus any utensils that touch them, from ready-to-eat foods to prevent cross-contamination. A food thermometer is the only accurate way to tell if your cooked food is safe to eat. Perishables should be properly and promptly chilled to minimize the growth of bacteria.**

Who Protects Your Food and How Do They Do It?

Foods don't originate in the grocery store. Whether in a bag, box, or bin, every food you buy starts life on a farm. Keeping food safe from the time it's harvested until you buy it is the responsibility of farmers, food manufacturers, and several government agencies. In this section, we'll look at the regulations, food preservation techniques, product dating, and irradiation that are done during various steps between the farm and the table. We'll start by looking at the government agencies that keep an eye on the food supply.

Several Government Agencies Police the Food Supply

Today, several federal agencies share responsibility for food safety in the United States.[44] Table 13.4 lists these agencies and summarizes the roles they each play in safeguarding your foods. This shared responsibility has paid off. There was a 16 percent decline in foodborne illness from 1996 to 2002.[45] Much of this decline can be attributed to the **Food Safety Initiative (FSI),** which was begun in 1997. The FSI coordinates the research, inspection, outbreak response, and educational activities of the various government agencies. The goal of the FSI is to make sure that government agencies work collaboratively.[46]

One FSI program is FoodNet, a combined effort among the Centers for Disease Control and Prevention (CDC), the United States Department of Agriculture (USDA), the Food and Drug Administration (FDA), and other health departments to conduct ongoing active monitoring of specific foodborne illnesses when they arise in the United States. Improved reporting and monitoring systems, as well as outbreak investigations, have helped to quickly identify and trace the causes of foodborne illness.

PulseNet, another foodborne disease watchdog, is a network of government and public health laboratories that specializes in detecting foodborne diseases using **DNA fingerprinting.** Finding similar strains of a bacterium in both a person and a food suggests a common source and potential connection.[47] Once these patterns are determined, they are entered into an electronic database at a local or state health department, maintaining an ongoing collection of DNA fingerprints. These patterns are also sent to the CDC's central computer. If similar patterns emerge at the same time in different states, this could indicate a potential outbreak. Once a suspicious foodborne illness outbreak is reported, several government agencies work together to contain the disease.

The *E. coli* O157:H7 outbreak in spinach that occurred in the fall of 2006 provides one example of how these multiple agencies work together to identify and contain an outbreak. First, the CDC alerted the FDA of an outbreak of illness due to *E. coli* O157:H7 that spanned 26 states in the United States. PulseNet used DNA fingerprinting to determine that the strain of *E. coli* was the same in all those infected. The suspected food was bagged raw spinach grown in California. The CDC issued an official health alert about the outbreak, and the FDA advised consumers to stop eating raw spinach. Before it was over, more than 200 people were infected, and more than half of them were hospitalized. Three individuals died and 31 developed hemolytic uremic syndrome from the outbreak. However, the swift, coordinated action of these federal and state agencies helped curtail the outbreak and kept it from being much worse.[48] Investigators from the FDA, CDC, and USDA worked with the state of California to conclude that the infected spinach came from one grower and most likely occurred

Food Safety Initiative (FSI) Coordinates the research, surveillance, inspection, outbreak response, and educational activities of the various government agencies that work together to safeguard food.

DNA fingerprinting A technique in which bacterial DNA "gene patterns" (or "fingerprints") are detected and analyzed to distinguish between different strains of a bacterium.

Table 13.4

Who's Policing the Food Supply?

Agency	Responsible for
USDA Food Safety and Inspection Service (FSIS)	Ensuring safe and accurately labeled meat, poultry, and eggs
Food and Drug Administration (FDA)	Ensuring the safety of all other foods besides meat, poultry, and eggs
Environmental Protection Agency (EPA)	Protecting you and the environment from harmful pesticides
Animal and Plant Health Inspection Service (APHIS)	Protecting against plant and animal pests and disease

Source: Food and Drug Administration and the U.S. Department of Agriculture, "A Description of the U.S. Food Safety System" (2000). Available at www.fsis.usda.gov/OA/codex/system.htm.

because of cross-contamination of infected water and animals with the produce in the field. The same strain of *E. coli* was found in a nearby stream and in the feces of cattle on a neighboring farm.

The FDA and USDA have also adopted a food-safety program called Hazard Analysis and Critical Control Points (HACCP) (pronounced "hassip") that is used to identify and control foodborne hazards that may occur in all the stages of the food production process.[49] HACCP procedures are in place for food manufacturers and transporters to help safeguard food. Manufacturers also apply food preservation techniques to some foods to make them safer when you buy them. These techniques will be discussed in the next section.

Once the food arrives at retail and food-service establishments such as grocery stores and restaurants, these outlets use the Food Code, a reference document published by the FDA. The Food Code provides practical, science-based guidance, including HACCP guidelines, and provisions to help purveyors minimize foodborne illness.[50] The FDA updates the Food Code periodically to keep pace with emerging science, and states use the FDA Food Code to present their food codes and laws. The Partnership for Food Safety Education (PFSE) is a program designed to educate the public about safe food handling after purchase.

From the farmer to the consumer, everyone involved in the production and preparation of food plays a role in making sure the food we eat is safe. The **farm-to-table continuum** is a visual tool that shows how farmers, food manufacturers, transporters of food, retailers, and you, the consumer, can help ensure a safe food supply. **Figure 13.6** on the next page shows the steps in this continuum.

In addition to government efforts to help prevent foodborne illness, food manufacturers also work to safeguard food. Food processing, preservation techniques, and irradiation help destroy contaminants and/or maintain a food's color and freshness, and product dating can help you know when a food is past its prime and should be tossed.

Food Manufacturers Use Preservation Techniques to Destroy Contaminants

One way to control foodborne hazards is to use **food preservation** methods. Pickling (adding an acidic substance such as vinegar to the food), salting, drying, heating, freezing, and newer techniques such as irradiation and the use of food additives are all methods of food preservation. You use some of these yourself when you cook (apply heat to) or freeze (apply cold to) foods. Pickling, drying, and canning (a form of heating) have been in use for centuries, though today they're more often done by food manufacturers than home cooks.

Pasteurization is a technique that involves heating foods and liquids to a high enough temperature to kill pathogens. The process kills *E. coli* O157:H7 as well as other bacteria. In addition to dairy foods, most juices (about 98 percent) consumed in the United State are pasteurized. Juices that aren't pasteurized must display a warning on the label.[51] Another method of pasteurization is ultra-high temperature (UHT) pasteurization, which is often used to aseptically package juice and some milks in "boxes." These are shelf-stable until opened, which saves manufacturers (and you) a lot of money because the products don't have to be shipped and stored under expensive refrigeration. Once they are opened, they do have to be refrigerated.

Pasteurizing milk and dairy foods improves their quality and helps them stay fresh longer. Though raw (unpasteurized) milk and cheese are sometimes touted as being more healthful, this is an unfounded claim and can be dangerous, as raw milk

farm-to-table continuum Illustrates the roles that farmers, food manufacturers, food transporters, retailers, and consumers play in ensuring that the food supply, from the farm to the plate, remains safe.

food preservation The treatment of foods to reduce deterioration and spoilage, and help prevent the multiplication of pathogens that can cause foodborne illness.

pasteurization The process of heating liquids or food at high temperatures to destroy foodborne pathogens.

1 **Farm: Use good agricultural practices.** Farmers grow, harvest, sort, pack, and store their crops in ways that help reduce food safety hazards.

2 **Processing: Monitor at critical control points.** During processing, HACCP measures are implemented.

3 **Transportation: Use clean vehicles and maintain the proper temperature.** Food is kept at a proper temperature during transportation to reduce the growth of foodborne microbes.

4 **Retail: Follow the Food Code guidelines.** Retail outlets, including restaurants, grocery stores, and institutions (such as hospitals) use the Food Code guidelines to reduce the risk of foodborne illness.

5 **Consumer: Always follow the four Cs of food safety (clean, combat cross-contamination, cook, chill).** The consumer uses the four Cs to reduce the risk of foodborne illness.

Figure 13.6 The Farm-to-Table Continuum
Every step in the farm-to-table continuum plays an important role in reducing microbes and the spread of foodborne illness.

can contain *Salmonella, E. coli* O157:H7, and *Listeria monocytogenes.*

Canning goes a step beyond pasteurization by packing food in airtight containers after heating it to a temperature high enough to kill most bacteria. Though this preserves the safety of most foods, botulism is one illness that can still result from improperly canned foods. The bacterium *Clostridium botulinum* can survive environments without air, such as sealed cans, and creates **spores** that are not destroyed at normal cooking temperatures; a temperature higher than boiling (212°F) is needed to kill these spores.[52] **Retort canning** has eliminated botulism from commercially canned foods. Because of the success of retort canning, the very rare cases of botulism typically result from products that have been home canned. This is a great reason to make sure you are using modern canning methods at home. If you have an old recipe from Grandma, you need to modify Grandma's instructions to make the product safe.

Many people were initially resistant to the processes of pasteurization and canning because they thought the techniques would promote the use of inferior ingredients. The federal government helped address such fears by putting formal food grading processes in place to reassure consumers that only quality foods would be used. Both of these preservation methods are now widely used and generally regarded as effective to thwart foodborne illness.

Two newer preservation methods used to keep foods fresh are MAP and HPP. **Modified atmosphere packaging (MAP)** is a process during which the manufacturer changes the composition of the air surrounding the food in a package. Usually, the amount of oxygen is reduced, which delays the decay of packaged fruits and vegetables. MAP is used in such foods to extend their shelf life and preserve their quality.[53] **High-pressure processing (HPP)** is a newer method in which foods are exposed to pulses of high pressure, which destroys microorganisms. If bacterial spores are present on the food, heat may also have to be applied along with the HPP. Foods such as jams, fruit juices, fish, vacuum-packed meat products, fruits, and vegetables can be treated with HPP.[54]

There is another method of food preservation that manufacturers and growers use to keep food safe: food irradiation.

Irradiation

After foods have been packaged by a manufacturer, they may undergo **irradiation,** at either the manufacturing plant or another facility. During this process, foods are subjected to a radiant energy source within a protective, shielded chamber called an **irradiator.** Most of the energy passes through the food and the packaging without leaving any residue behind.[55] This level of energy damages the DNA of the harmful organisms, either killing them all or greatly reducing their numbers, thus reducing the risk of foodborne disease.[56]

Foods that have been irradiated are not radioactive and don't undergo any harmful or dangerous chemical changes.[57] The temperature of the food isn't significantly raised during irradiation, which helps prevent nutrient losses. In fact, heat pasteurization, canning, and drying often destroy more nutrients, such as certain vitamins, than does irradiation.[58]

Irradiation destroys bacteria such as *Campylobacter, E. coli* O157:H7, and *Salmonella* and helps control insects and parasites.[59] It does not destroy viruses such as norovirus and hepatitis A, however, because the higher radiation levels needed to destroy the DNA of these smaller microbes have not yet been approved by the FDA. Irradiation can also stop the ripening process in some fruits and vegetables and reduce the number of food spoilage bacteria. Irradiated strawberries can last up to three weeks before spoiling, whereas nonirradiated strawberries typically stay fresh for three to five days.[60]

Food irradiation has been studied and tested for more than 50 years and remains the most researched food-related technology ever approved in the United States.[61] Irradiation has been used for years to sterilize surgical instruments and implants. Hospitals have used irradiation to destroy disease-promoting microbes in foods served to patients with cancer and others who have weakened immune systems.

Foods that are irradiated must bear the "radura" logo, along with the phrase "treated by irradiation" or "treated with radiation" on the package (**Figure 13.7**). If a product such as sausage contains irradiated meat or poultry, it must be listed as "irradiated pork" or "irradiated chicken" on the food label.[62] A label is not required if a minor ingredient, such as a spice, has been irradiated and used in the product.

Some foods can't be irradiated, as their quality will be altered. Egg whites tend to become milky and liquid, fatty meats may develop an odor, and grapefruits can get soft and mushy after irradiation. Foods that are currently approved for irradiation in the United States include:[63]

> Fruits and vegetables
> Herbs and spices
> Fresh meat, pork, and poultry
> Wheat flour
> White potatoes

Though irradiation has many advantages, it doesn't guarantee that a food is safe, and some foods should still not be eaten raw, even if they have been irradiated. Steak tartare (a dish that contains raw ground beef) isn't a safe menu option even if it is made with irradiated ground beef, because the beef could be recontaminated after irradiation. Proper food handling, preparation, and cooking techniques must still be used for foods that have been irradiated.

Once foods are preserved as appropriate, many manufacturers stamp them with a food product dating code. A date on a product can help you determine if it's fresh, or if it will still be fresh, by the time you consume it. Let's look at the specifics of food product dating.

Product Dating Can Help You Determine Peak Quality

Although food product dating isn't federally mandated, except for infant formula and some baby foods, more than 20 states in the United States require some form of food product dating. There are two types of food product dating: closed dating and open

Figure 13.7 The International Radura Symbol
The radura symbol must appear on all irradiated foods.

canning The process of heating food to a temperature high enough to kill bacteria and then packing the food in airtight containers.

spores Hardy reproductive structures that are produced by certain bacteria. Some bacterial spores can survive boiling temperature (212°F).

retort canning The process of subjecting already-canned foods to an additional high-temperature heat source to destroy potential pathogens.

modified atmosphere packaging (MAP) A food preservation technique that changes the composition of the air surrounding the food in a package to extend its shelf life.

high-pressure processing (HPP) A method used to pasteurize foods by exposing the items to pulses of high pressure, which destroys the microorganisms that are present.

irradiation A process in which foods are placed in a shielded chamber, called an **irradiator,** and subjected to a radiant energy source. This kills specific pathogens in food by breaking up the cells' DNA.

Figure 13.8 Closed and Open Food Product Dating.

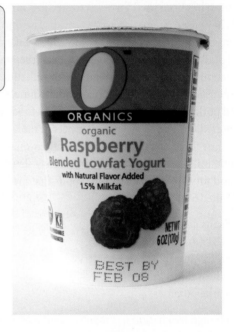

b Open food product dating must contain a calendar date and is used on perishable food items along with information on how to use the date.

dating. **Closed (or "coded") dating** refers to the packing numbers used by manufacturers that are often found on nonperishable, shelf-stable foods, such as cans of soup and fruit (see **Figure 13.8**). This type of dating is used by the manufacturer to keep track of product inventory, rotate stock, and identify products that may be involved in a recall.[64]

Open dating is typically found on perishable items such as meat, poultry, eggs, and dairy foods, and is more useful for the consumer. Open dating must contain a calendar date that includes at least a month and day. (If the product is shelf-stable or frozen and a calendar date is used, the year must also be included in the date.) You can use open dating to help you decide when to buy and consume a product while it is at its peak quality. Note: This date does not refer to food safety, but to the *quality* of the food. For example, a carton of yogurt that has been mishandled and not refrigerated for several hours may be unsafe to eat even though the date on the container hasn't passed.

When open dating is used, there must be a phrase next to the date that tells you how to interpret it. If there is "Sell By" next to the date, you should purchase the product on or before that date. If there is "Best if Used By" or "Use By" next to it, this refers

closed or "coded" dating Refers to the packing numbers that are decodable only by manufacturers and are often found on nonperishable, shelf-stable foods.

open dating Typically found on perishable items such as meat, poultry, eggs, and dairy foods; must contain a calendar date.

to the date by which you should consume the product in order to enjoy it at its best.[65] If you don't plan to consume a product by its Use By date, you can freeze it; once frozen, the Use By date doesn't apply.

In addition to preservation techniques, irradiation, and product dating, food manufacturers sometimes use food additives to enhance the safety, but more often the quality, of foods.

What Are Food Additives and How Are They Used?

Food manufacturers use **food additives** for numerous reasons, including to increase the shelf life of products, enrich nutrient content, and improve the flavor and texture of foods. Commonly used additives include preservatives (such as antioxidants and sulfites), nutrients, and flavor enhancers (such as MSG).

Preservatives Prevent Spoilage and Increase Shelf Life

Most additives are *preservatives* that are added to foods to prevent spoilage (usually by (T|F) destroying microbes) and increase shelf life. The most common antimicrobial preservatives are salt and sugar. Salt has been used for centuries, particularly in meat and fish, to create a dry environment in which bacteria cannot multiply. Sugar is used for the same preserving effect in products such as canned and frozen fruits and condiments.

Nitrites and **nitrates** are salts that are added to foods to prevent microbial growth and are used in cured meats such as hot dogs and hams to prevent the growth of *Clostridium botulinum.* They are also the chemical that gives these foods their pink color. The use of these salts has been controversial due to the fact that they form **carcinogenic** nitrosamines in the digestive tract of animals.

The addition of antioxidants to foods can prevent an off taste or off color in a product that's vulnerable to damage by oxidation. Currently two vitamins have been approved for use as food additives due to their actions as antioxidants: vitamin E and vitamin C. Vitamin E is added to oils and cereals to prevent the fats in them from becoming rancid, and vitamin C is often added to cut fruit to prevent premature browning. Butylated hydroxyanisole (BHA) and butylated hydroxytoluene (BHT) are two chemical antioxidants that are also used as preservatives.

Sulfites are a group of antioxidants that are used as preservatives to help prevent the oxidation and browning of some foods and to inhibit the growth of microbes.[66] Sulfites are often found in dried fruits and vegetables, packaged and prepared potatoes, wine, beer, bottled lemon and lime juice, and pickled foods.

For most people, sulfites pose no risk, but there are people who experience adverse reactions. Individuals who are sensitive to sulfites may experience symptoms ranging from chest tightness, difficulty breathing, and hives to the more serious and potentially fatal anaphylactic shock. Studies suggest that the sulphur dioxide in the sulfites appears to cause these symptoms.[67] People at highest risk for negative reactions include people who suffer from asthma, those who are taking steroids, and those who have extremely sensitive airways.

Due to the risk of adverse reactions in people who are sulfite sensitive, the FDA has prohibited the use of sulfites on fruits and vegetables that are served raw, such as in a salad bar, or are advertised as "fresh." Foods that contain sulfite additives or

food additives Substances added to food that affect its quality, flavor, freshness, and/or safety.

nitrates (nitrites) Substances that can be added to foods to function as a preservative and to give meats such as hot dogs and luncheon meats a pink color.

carcinogenic A substance thought to cause cancer.

sulfites Preservatives used to help prevent foods from turning brown and to inhibit the growth of microbes. Often used in wine and dried fruit products.

ingredients treated with sulfites must declare "added sulfites" in the ingredients listing on the label. Food sold in bulk, such as dried fruit treated with sulfites, must display the ingredients on a sign near the food. Because sulfites destroy the B vitamin thiamine, the FDA prohibits their use in enriched grain products and other foods that are good sources of the vitamin.[68]

Some Additives Enhance Texture and Consistency

Food additives can improve food quality in a number of ways. Gums and pectins are used to improve consistency and texture and are added to thicken yogurts and puddings. Emulsifiers improve the stability, consistency, and homogeneity of products like mayonnaise and ice cream. Lecithin is an example of an emulsifier that is added to some salad dressing. Leavening agents are added to breads to incorporate gases that cause them to rise. Anti-caking agents prevent products like powdered sugar that are crystalline in nature from absorbing moisture and lumping. Humectants such as propylene glycol are added to increase moisture in products so that they stay fresh.

Some Additives Improve Nutrient Content

Additives can be used to enhance a product's nutrition content, such as when refined grains are enriched with added B vitamins and iron. In some cases, such additions are mandated. This was the case in 1996 when the FDA published regulations requiring the addition of folic acid to enriched breads, cereal, and other grain products in order to help decrease the risk of neural tube defects in newborns.

Color and Flavor Enhancers Improve the Appeal of Foods

Additives can be used to enhance the color of foods. Two main categories make up the FDA's list of permitted colors. "Certifiable" color additives are man-made and are derived primarily from petroleum and coal sources. You can recognize these types of additives by the prefixes FD&C, D&C, or Ext. An example is FD&C Yellow, which is often found in cereals and baked goods. The second main category of color additives includes those obtained largely from plant, animal, or mineral sources. Examples include caramel color and grape color extract. Reactions to color additives are rare, though FD&C Yellow No. 5 may cause itching and hives in some people. This additive is found in beverages, desserts, and processed vegetables and is required to be listed on food labels. Table 13.5 provides a list of commonly used additives and their functions in foods.

monosodium glutamate (MSG)
A flavor enhancer.

GRAS (generally recognized as safe) A substance that is believed to be safe to consume based on a long history of use by humans or a substantial amount of research that documents its safety.

MSG Is a Common Flavor Enhancer
Monosodium glutamate (MSG) is often used as a flavor enhancer in Asian foods, canned vegetables and soups, and processed meats. Consumers can buy it in a form that is similar in texture to salt; although it doesn't have a strong taste of its own, it enhances sweet, salty, sour, and bitter tastes in other foods. Because of its long history of safe use, MSG is **generally recognized as safe (GRAS).** However, the FDA has received numerous consumer complaints that it can cause symptoms such as headaches and

Table 13.5

Commonly Used Food Additives

Additive(s)	Function(s)	Where You'll Find Them
Alginates, carrageenan, glyceride, guar gum, lecithin, mono- and diglycerides, methyl cellulose, pectin, sodium aluminosilicate	Impart/maintain desired consistency	Baked goods, cake mixes, coconut, ice cream, processed cheese, salad dressings, table salt
Ascorbic acid (vitamin C), calcium carbonate, folic acid, thiamine (B_1), iron, niacin, pyridoxine (B_6), riboflavin (B_2), vitamins A and D, zinc oxide	Improve/maintain nutritive value	Biscuits, bread, breakfast cereals, desserts, flour, gelatin, iodized margarine, milk, pasta, salt
Ascorbic acid, benzoates, butylated hydroxyanisole (BHA), butylated hydroxytoluene (BHT), citric acid, propionic acid and its salts, sodium nitrite	Maintain palatability and wholesomeness	Bread, cake mixes, cheese, crackers, frozen and dried fruit, lard, margarine, meat, potato chips
Citric acid, fumaric acid, lactic acid, phosphoric acid, sodium bicarbonate, tartrates, yeast	Produce light texture and control acidity/alkalinity	Butter, cakes, cookies, chocolates, crackers, quick breads, soft drinks
Annatto, aspartame, caramel, cloves, FD&C Red No. 40, FD&C Blue No. 1, fructose, ginger, limonene, MSG, saccharin, turmeric	Enhance flavor or provide desired color	Baked goods, cheeses, confections, gum, spice cake, gingerbread, jams, soft drinks, soup, yogurt

Source: FDA, "Food Additives" (2010). Available at www.fda.gov/Food/FoodIngredientsPackaging/FoodAdditives/default.htm.

nausea, along with concerns that it can contribute to Alzheimer's disease, brain tumors, and nerve cell damage.[69]

After an extensive review, the FDA confirmed that MSG is safe to consume in the amounts typically used in processed foods and cooking (a typical meal that contains MSG has less than 0.5 gram). However, when consumed in large quantities such as 3 or more grams at a time, it may cause short-term reactions in people who are sensitive to it.[70] These reactions, which are called the **MSG symptom complex,** can include numbness, burning sensation, facial pressure or tightness, chest pain, rapid heart-beat, and drowsiness. In addition, people with asthma may have difficulty breathing after consuming MSG. For these reasons, the FDA requires that all foods containing MSG declare this ingredient on the food label.

Food Additives Are Closely Regulated by the FDA

Food additives are under strict regulation by the FDA, with consumer safety a top priority. The Federal Food, Drug and Cosmetic Act of 1938 gave the FDA authority to regulate food and food ingredients, including the use of food additives. The 1958 Food Additives Amendment further mandated that manufacturers document the safety of a food additive and obtain FDA approval before using it in a food.[71]

Two categories of food additives were exempted from this amendment. The first category includes substances that were known to be safe before 1958 and were given **prior-sanctioned** status. For example, because nitrates were used to preserve meats before 1958, they have prior-sanctioned status, but *only* for their use in meats. They cannot be used in other foods, such as vegetables, without FDA approval.[72] The second category includes substances that have a long history of being safe for consumption, such as salt, sugar, and spices, or have extensive research documenting that they are safe to consume, such as vitamins. These additives are exempt from FDA approval because they are "generally recognized as safe" (GRAS).[73]

MSG symptom complex A series of reactions such as numbness, burning sensation, facial pressure or tightness, chest pain, rapid heart-beat, and drowsiness that can occur in some individuals after they consume MSG.

prior sanctioned Having previous approval.

The FDA continually monitors both prior-sanctioned additives and those with GRAS status to ensure that current research continues to support their safety. To remain on the GRAS list, an additive must not have been found to be cancer-causing in animals or humans. The 1958 Food Additives Amendment also included the *DeLaney Clause,* which was created to protect consumers from additives found to cause cancer. The clause states that no substances that have been shown to cause cancer in animals or humans at any dosage may be added to foods. However, with the present increases in technology and the ability to detect substances at very low levels, the clause is considered outdated. To address this issue, the FDA deems additives safe if lifetime use presents no more than a one-in-a-million risk of cancer in human beings. If an additive is suddenly called into question, the FDA can prohibit its use or require that the food manufacturer conduct additional studies to ensure its safety.[74]

Even with these safeguards in place, some additives, such as MSG and sulfites, may cause adverse reactions in some people and should be avoided by those who are sensitive to them.

Some Food Additives Are Unintentional

The food additives already discussed are all *intentional food additives* used to improve the quality of food products. However, *unintentional food additives* may sometimes be added indirectly to a food. For example, very small amounts of substances used during packaging or processing may inadvertently end up in the food. The safety of packaging must therefore be determined by manufacturers to ensure that packing substances aren't harmful to the consumer. Unintentional additives may also include chemicals from processing, including compounds used during the process of decaffeinating coffee, and *dioxins* used during the manufacture of bleached paper such as coffee filters. Dioxins can accumulate in the food chain and cause cancer in animals. The FDA requires that dioxin levels in products present no health risks to people.[75]

The Take-Home Message Food additives are often used by manufacturers to preserve foods, enhance their color or flavor, or add to their nutrient content. Some additives, such as MSG and sulfites, may cause unpleasant symptoms in sensitive individuals, but all additives are strictly regulated by the FDA. All intentional food additives must be listed on food labels. Some additives may be added unintentionally during processing or cause adverse reactions in sensitive individuals.

What Are Toxins and Chemical Agents?

In addition to pathogens, naturally occurring toxins can contaminate foods, and chemicals can accumulate in foods. In this section we'll discuss these toxins and some of the chemical agents.

Level 1 Dinoflagellates produce toxin and/or other microscopic organisms become contaminated with toxins.

Level 2 Small fish eat the dinoflagellates. Over time, the toxins accumulate and become more concentrated in their bodies.

Level 3 Large, predatory fish consume the smaller contaminated fish, which increases their toxin concentration.

Level 4 Fishermen catch the larger fish for human consumption.

Increasing accumulation of biotoxins →

Figure 13.9 Bioaccumulation of Toxins

Toxins Occur Naturally

Toxins frequently occur in nature to help a plant or animal fend off predators or capture its meals. In many cases, toxins in food animals exist in amounts too small to harm humans, but there are instances in which the toxins found in plant and animal foods can make a person ill, or worse.

Marine Toxins

Although there are numerous reasons to include fish and seafood in your diet (recall their omega-3 fatty acid and low saturated fat content from Chapter 5), you should be aware of the risks involved. Some seafood, such as some of the raw fish used in sushi, can contain pathogens, and some can harbor naturally occurring **marine toxins.** Thorough cooking will kill many harmful bacteria and viruses found in seafood, but it won't destroy any of the marine toxins.

Spoiled finfish, such as tuna and mackerel, can cause **scombrotoxic fish poisoning,** in which the spoilage bacteria break down proteins in the fish and generate histamine. Other by-products are created that block the breakdown of histamine. Consuming fish that contain large amounts of histamine can cause symptoms such as diarrhea, flushing, sweating, and vomiting within 2 minutes to 2 hours.[76]

Eating large, predatory reef fish, such as barracuda and grouper, can sometimes result in **ciguatera poisoning,** which is caused by ciguatoxins. These toxins originate in microscopic sea organisms called *dinoflagellates*, which are then eaten by small tropical fish. As larger fish eat the smaller fish, the toxins **bioaccumulate** and become more concentrated in the larger fish.[77] **Figure 13.9** shows how these toxins can accumulate in the food chain. In addition to experiencing various gastrointestinal discomforts, individuals infected with ciguatera may have temperature sensation reversal in the mouth when they eat.[78] To them, ice cream feels hot and hot coffee feels cold.

Certain shellfish, such as mussels, clams, scallops, oysters, crabs, and lobsters, that typically live in the coastal waters of New England and the Pacific states can be contaminated with **neurotoxins** (*neuro* = nerve, *toxin* = toxic). Neurotoxins are also produced by dinoflagellates, and the particular reddish-brown-colored dinoflagellates that contain them can become so abundant that the ocean appears to have red streaks, also known as "red tides." Eating contaminated shellfish can lead to **paralytic shellfish poisoning.** Symptoms include mild numbness or tingling in the face, arms, and legs, as well as headaches and dizziness. Muscle paralysis, inability to breathe, and, in severe cases, death could result.[79]

marine toxins Chemicals that occur naturally and contaminate some fish.

scombrotoxic fish poisoning A condition caused by consuming spoiled fish that contain large amounts of histamines. Also referred to as histamine fish poisoning.

ciguatera poisoning A condition caused by marine toxins produced by *dinoflagellates* (microscopic sea organisms). Small fish eat dinoflagellates and larger fish consume the small fish. The toxins then bioaccumulate in the fish.

bioaccumulate When a substance or chemical builds up in an organism over time, so that the concentration of the chemical is higher than would be found naturally in the environment.

neurotoxins Toxins that affect the nerves and can cause symptoms including mild numbness or tingling in the face, arms, and legs, as well as headaches and dizziness. Severe cases could result in death.

paralytic shellfish poisoning A condition caused by a reddish-brown-colored dinoflagellate that contains neurotoxins.

Warning signs like this one are often posted when local waters have been found to contain high amounts of pollutants. Fish caught in such waters should never be eaten.

Toxins in Other Foods

Many plant foods naturally contain toxins in small amounts, so though they're generally safe to eat, consuming them in very large amounts could be harmful. Potatoes that have been exposed to light and turned green, for example, contain increased amounts of solanine, a toxin that can cause fever, diarrhea, paralysis, and shock. (Luckily, peeling potatoes usually removes the green layer and the potato can be safely eaten. If it tastes bitter, however, throw it out.) Wild lima beans contain high amounts of cyanogenic glycosides, which can be converted to the poison cyanide. (The variety of lima beans sold commercially have minimal, nonthreatening amounts of this substance, so are safe to eat.) Cassava also contains cyanogenic glycosides and has been known to cause cyanide poisoning in people who eat large amounts of this root vegetable. Raw soybeans contain amylase inhibitors, which are inactivated when cooked or fermented.[80]

Other foods contain toxins that are harmful even in trace amounts, and so should be avoided altogether. Certain wild mushrooms, for example, are poisonous; they contain toxins that can cause nausea, vomiting, liver damage, and death.

Contamination Is Sometimes Due to Pollution

One person's trash can become another person's illness. Although industrial and household chemicals have useful purposes, if traces of these substances end up in the food supply, they can have negative health effects. Two pollutants of concern are PCBs and methylmercury.

Polychlorinated biphenyls (PCBs) are chemicals that occur in the food supply due to industrial pollution. A few decades ago, these chemicals were used as coolants and lubricants because they are good insulators and don't burn easily. They were banned in 1977 due to concerns about their toxicity.[81] For example, they may be responsible for promoting cancer in humans. Although PCBs are no longer manufactured in the United States, they can still make their way into the environment through hazardous waste sites, the burning of wastes, and the improper disposal of consumer products, such as old television sets and other electrical fixtures and devices.[82] PCBs have been shown to contaminate the sediments in rivers and lakes. Because PCBs don't break down over time, they bioaccumulate in small organisms and fish. In fact, PCBs are the major chemical risk associated with eating fish.[83]

Mercury occurs in nature, but it is also a by-product of industrial pollution. An airborne form of mercury can accumulate on the surface of streams and oceans and be transformed by the bacteria in the water into the toxic form of methylmercury. As fish either absorb the methylmercury from the water or eat smaller fish that contain methylmercury, they can bioaccumulate the substance to high levels.

The Take-Home Message Toxins can occur naturally in foods and can cause harm to humans. Marine toxins can occur in certain varieties of spoiled fish and bioaccumulate in fish that feed on toxin-containing sea organisms. Chemicals can also get into the food supply as a result of environmental contamination. Polychlorinated biphenyls (PCBs) and methylmercury have been shown to bioaccumulate in fish.

polychlorinated biphenyls (PCBs) Synthetic chemicals that have been shown to cause cancer and other adverse effects on the immune, reproductive, nervous, and endocrine systems in animals. PCBs may cause cancer in humans.

What Is Bioterrorism and How Can You Protect Yourself?

Food and water supplies are potential targets for **bioterrorism.** Agents such as the bacterium that causes anthrax and the virus that causes smallpox are examples of possible bioterrorist weapons. Until recently, scenarios of human-caused outbreaks of these diseases were thought to exist only in Hollywood movies. Today, Americans face the real threat of someone using plant or animal food supplies, or drinking water sources, to cause harm.[84]

Food can be the primary agent of bioterrorism by being contaminated with a biological or chemical toxin. In fact, the CDC lists several foodborne pathogens, such as botulism, *Salmonella, E. coli* O157:H7, and *Shigella* as potential bioterrorism agents.[85]

Food and water can also be used as secondary agents of bioterrorism by disrupting the availability of adequate safe amounts of these necessities and by limiting the fuel needed to safely cook and refrigerate perishable foods. Several years ago, London police arrested individuals involved in a plot to add poison to the food served at a British military base, and in Jerusalem, people were arrested for planning to poison customers at a local restaurant.[86] Tainted foods, or even the threat of such contamination, could cause a mandatory or self-imposed avoidance of a particular category of food and/or eating establishment and contribute to social disarray.[87]

To combat these threats, governmental agencies have made bioterrorism a national priority. Under the direction of the Department of Homeland Security, numerous local, state, and federal agencies, such as the Federal Emergency Management Agency (FEMA), FDA, and USDA, work together at each stage of the food continuum—from the farm to the table—to protect your foods.

As a consumer, you also play an important role in **food biosecurity,** and there are strategies you can employ if you should come into contact with suspicious-looking food items. Although food tampering is rare in the United States, a watchful consumer can spot it and avoid it. The Table Tips list ways you can identify food items that may have been tampered with, and where to report suspicious items if you find them.

The Take-Home Message
Food and water can be primary agents of bioterrorism by being contaminated with a biological or chemical toxin. These necessities can also be used as secondary agents if a terrorist act disrupts their availability, or limits access to the fuel needed to safely cook and refrigerate perishable foods. If you come into contact with a tampered food, you should report the suspicious items to the appropriate authorities.

Table Tips

Avoid Potentially Tampered Foods

Don't purchase a food product if the outer seal is broken, the package is torn, dented, or otherwise damaged, and/or if the safety button on the jar lid is up.

Purchase your foods by the "Sell By" dates.

Don't buy canned items that are bulging or leaking.

Don't purchase frozen items if they look as though they have been thawed and re-frozen. Cardboard will be distorted or wet or stained if this has happened.

Report any suspicious store items to the store manager.

Source: FDA. 2003. Food Tampering. Available at www.fda.gov/Food/ResourcesForYou/Consumers/ucm079137.htm.

---

bioterrorism The use of a biological or chemical agent to frighten, threaten, coerce, injure, and/or kill individuals.

food biosecurity Protecting the food supply from bioterrorist attacks.

Two Points of View

Are Plastics Safe for Our Food? You may have heard warnings to avoid plastic containers because they can break down when exposed to heat (for example, during microwaving) and release chemicals, such as bisphenol A (BPA) and phthalates, that can leach into food.[1] How valid is this concern, particularly for infants and small children? Is it safe to eat food or drink beverages that are stored in, or consumed from, plastic containers? Take a look at the evidence on both sides of the issue, consider the questions posed, and decide for yourself.

Yes

- Bisphenol A has been in use for more than 50 years, and is largely credited with reducing the incidence of foodborne illness.[2]

- In 2008, the FDA issued a draft report stating that bisphenol A is safe at typical exposure levels from food and drink.[3]

- As chemical analysis techniques become more sophisticated, they can find one part per trillion. Chemicals found in such trace amounts are not necessarily harmful.[4]

No

- After originally claiming that BPA was safe, the FDA updated its recommendations to support efforts to make BPA-free baby bottles and recommend the development of BPA-free can liners.[5]

- The U.S. National Toxicology Program found that there is "some concern" about the effects of BPA on infants and children. It had lower levels of concern for other groups and concluded that more research is needed to determine just what the risks of BPA exposure might be.[6]

- Prenatal exposure to phthalates has been associated with behavioral disorders in children.[7]

- Prenatal exposure to even small amounts of other chemicals has proven to result in lower IQ for children.[8]

What do you think?

1. Which side do you think has the more compelling argument? Why? **2.** Do you think warnings to avoid plastic food and beverage containers are justified? Why or why not? **3.** Is BPA contamination only a concern for parents of small children? **4.** Are there other concerns aside from potential BPA contamination that should be considered when using plastic containers to store or prepare food? **5.** Are you likely to alter your habits based on the evidence provided?

Chapter Review

Be a Nutrition Sleuth

What's Wrong with This Picture?

Can you spot the food-safety hazards in an online kitchen? Go to **www.pearsonhighered.com/blake** to find out.

Get Real!

Real Food-Safety Decisions

Now that you've read about how you can minimize exposure to foodborne illness, let's put your newfound knowledge to the test. Go to **www.pearsonhighered.com/blake** to test your food-safety savvy in five real-world scenarios.

The Top Ten Points to Remember

1. Pathogens (viruses, bacteria, and parasites, as well as prions and fungal agents) are the primary causes of foodborne illness. Noroviruses are the single largest cause of foodborne illness. The most common bacteria that cause foodborne illness are *Campylobacter, E. coli* O157:H7, and *Salmonella.*

2. Bacteria multiply rapidly in a moist, protein- and nutrient-rich, nonacidic, and warm environment. The "danger zone" for rapid bacterial growth is between 40 and 140 degrees Fahrenheit.

3. Older adults, young children, pregnant women, and those with liver disease or a compromised immune system are at a higher risk for foodborne illness.

4. Animal foods, such as raw and undercooked meat, poultry, seafood, eggs, and unpasteurized milk and cheese, are the most common havens for bacterial growth.

5. Proper food handling techniques during four critical steps—cleaning, combating cross-contamination, cooking, and chilling—can help reduce your risk of foodborne illness. Separate cutting boards should be used for meat and nonmeat foods, and utensils and serving dishes that touch raw meat should not be used to handle cooked meat.

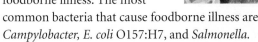

6. When serving foods, hot foods should be kept hot and cold foods should be kept cold. Leftovers should be divided and refrigerated quickly (within 1 to 2 hours), and frozen foods should never be thawed at room temperature. Refrigerators should always be set at 40°F or below and freezers should always be set at 0°F or below. The only way to tell if a meat product has been thoroughly cooked is to check its temperature with a meat thermometer.

7. Through the coordinated effort of the Food Safety Initiative, numerous United States government agencies work together to safeguard America's food supply against foodborne illness. Everyone, from the farmer to the consumer, plays an important role in food safety. Food irradiation exposes a food item to a radiant energy source that kills or greatly reduces some pathogens.

8. Food additives are used as preservatives, antioxidants, flavoring, coloring, and leavening agents; to maintain a food's consistency; and to add nutrients. The FDA must approve most additives before they can be used in foods, and all additives must be listed on the food label. Some additives are exempted from obtaining FDA approval by having attained GRAS or prior-sanctioned status based on their long history of safe consumption.

9. In addition to pathogens, toxins and chemical agents can also cause foodborne illness. Naturally occurring toxins include marine toxins and chemical agents include polychlorinated biphenyls.

10. Because food and water are basic necessities, they are targets for bioterrorism. The Department of Homeland Security coordinates the efforts of numerous local, state, and federal agencies to protect the United States, which includes safeguarding your food and water supply.

Test Your Knowledge

1. Which of the following is *not* a potential cause of food-borne illness?
   a. parasites
   b. viruses
   c. bacteria
   d. food additives
   e. naturally occurring chemicals and toxins
2. Which group is at greatest risk of contracting a food-borne illness?
   a. a 70-year-old grandmother, a 2-year-old toddler, and a teenage boy
   b. a 35-year-old basketball coach, a 70-year-old grandmother, and a 45-year-old professor
   c. a 70-year-old grandmother, a 2-year-old toddler, and a middle-aged woman who has diabetes
   d. a 45-year-old professor, a middle-aged woman who has diabetes, and a teenage boy
3. Bacteria need a "host"—a living plant or animal—to survive.
   a. True
   b. False
4. Foodborne pathogens cause the quality of a food, such as its taste, to deteriorate.
   a. True
   b. False
5. For bacteria to multiply, they need nutrients, moisture, the correct temperature, and
   a. sunlight and the proper pH.
   b. the proper pH and plenty of time.
   c. heat and plenty of time.
   d. water and heat.
   e. water and sunlight.
6. The danger zone is the temperature at which bacteria will multiply most rapidly. The temperature range of the danger zone is
   a. 40°F to 140°F.
   b. 45°F to 140°F.
   c. 40°F to 145°F.
   d. 50°F to 150°F.
   e. 50°F to 140°F.
7. There are four critical steps in the food handling process that you need to take to help prevent foodborne illness. These four steps are
   a. cutting, cleaning, chopping, and chilling.
   b. cleaning, combating cross-contamination, cutting, and chilling.
   c. clearing, combating cross-contamination, cutting, and chilling.
   d. cleaning, combating cross-contamination, cooking, and chilling.
   e. cooking, combating cross-contamination, cutting, and chilling.
8. Though most bacteria will grow more slowly in a refrigerator set at 40°F and below, one of the following does not. Which one?
   a. *E. coli* O157:H7
   b. *Salmonella*
   c. Norwalk virus
   d. *Campylobacter*
   e. *Listeria*
9. Two intentional food additives that some people might be sensitive to are
   a. *Salmonella* and antioxidants.
   b. heat and lemon juice.
   c. sulfites and MSG.
   d. dioxins and MSG.
10. PCBs can bioaccumulate in marine organisms and are the major chemical risk associated with eating fish.
    a. True
    b. False

Answers

1. (d) Parasites, viruses, bacteria, and naturally occurring toxins and chemicals can cause foodborne illness. Food additives do not. In fact, they are either approved by the FDA prior to use or have GRAS or prior-sanctioned status based on a history of safe consumption.
2. (c) Older adults, young children, and individuals with a compromised immune system, such as those with diabetes, are at a higher risk of contracting foodborne illness. A healthy teenager and a professor (even a tired one around exam time) aren't at an increased risk for foodborne disease.
3. (b) False. Bacteria can grow or multiply on any living or nonliving surface or object.
4. (b) False. Food spoilage bacteria, not foodborne pathogens, cause your food to go "bad," or deteriorate in quality. Foodborne pathogens can be in a food without affecting its taste or quality. Consequently, you should never taste foods that you suspect may be contaminated with foodborne pathogens. Even a small amount of a contaminated food might be enough to make you ill.
5. (b) In addition to nutrients, moisture, and the correct temperature, bacteria also need the proper pH and plenty of time (2 hours or more) to multiply to potentially dangerous levels. Sunlight isn't needed and high

heat can actually destroy bacteria. Water is an additional source of moisture.

6. (a) The danger zone is 40°F to 140°F.

7. (d) To prevent foodborne illness, it's important to employ proper food handling strategies when cleaning, combating cross-contamination, cooking, and chilling the foods in your meal.

8. (e) The bacterium *Listeria* can multiply at refrigerator temperatures of 40°F or below. *Salmonella* and *Campylobacter* bacteria will not. Norwalk virus is a virus, not a bacterium.

9. (c) Sulfites and MSG are fine for most people but can cause unpleasant symptoms in people who are sensitive to them. *Salmonella*, heat, and lemon juice are not food additives. Antioxidants can be used as food additives but are generally not harmful. Dioxins in foods are considered unintentional food additives.

10. (a) True. Along with methylmercury, PCBs are a significant environmental pollutant and can sometimes be found in fish.

Web Resources

➡ For food safety education, visit www.fightbac.org

➡ For food safety tips for college students, visit www.fsis .usda.gov/News_&_Events/NR_082405_01/index.asp

➡ For foodborne illness fact sheets, visit www.fsis.usda.gov/ Fact_Sheets/Foodborne_Illness_What_Consumers_Need_ to_Know/index.asp

➡ For information about safe home canning methods, visit http://uwacadweb.uwyo.edu/cesnutrition/Food_Preserve/ usda_home_canning.htm

Answers to Myths and Misperceptions

1. **False.** A food can contain disease-causing bacteria that can make you sick, yet smell perfectly fine. An off smell in food is more likely a sign of *spoilage*. Turn to page 488 to find out more.

2. **True.** As simple as it sounds, thorough hand washing is one of the best defenses against foodborne illness. The key is to hand wash well. Find out why on page 493.

3. **True.** Cross-contamination refers to the transfer of foodborne pathogens from one food to another via plates, containers, utensils, cutting boards, or any other implement used to handle and prepare raw food. You can find out how to prevent cross-contamination on page 494.

4. **True.** To be effective at keeping food safe, the temperature in your refrigerator should be 40°F or below. To find out why, turn to page 497.

5. **False.** Freezing doesn't kill bacteria, but only puts them in a dormant state. Find out what happens once the food is thawed on page 497.

6. **False.** Leftovers should be thrown out if they're not consumed within 3 to 5 days. To find out more about safe food storage, turn to page 497.

7. **False.** Irradiated food is treated with gamma rays that interrupt DNA and make cells unable to reproduce, thus killing harmful pathogens. It does not make foods radioactive. Learn more about food irradiation on page 503.

8. **False.** Package dates refer to food quality, not safety. To find out why consuming a food before the expiration date can't guarantee that the item is safe to eat, turn to page 504.

9. **False.** From keeping bread fresh to enhancing flavors, food additives serve a variety of useful functions in foods. Learn more about specific additives on page 505.

10. **True.** There are a couple of ways that the food and water supplies in the United States could be affected by bioterrorism. To learn more, turn to page 511.

14

True or False?

1. **Food insecurity** is a nonissue in the United States. ⓉⒻ p. 519

2. Food insecurity in the developing world is primarily due to **poverty**. ⓉⒻ p. 520

3. People who are **obese** don't experience food insecurity. ⓉⒻ p. 523

4. Not enough food is **produced** in the world to feed everyone. ⓉⒻ p. 525

5. **Children** are at higher risk for food insecurity than are healthy adults. ⓉⒻ p. 528

6. **Older adults** who are financially secure can still sometimes experience low food security and under nutrition. ⓉⒻ p. 528

7. Consuming **inadequate nutrients** won't affect mental development. ⓉⒻ p. 528

8. There is nothing **you** can do to help eradicate food insecurity. ⓉⒻ p. 532

9. **Agricultural** advances can help increase food production. ⓉⒻ p. 534

10. **Fortifying** foods is an effective strategy to ensure that some populations receive adequate nutrients. ⓉⒻ p. 534

See page 539 for answers to these Myths and Misperceptions.

Hunger at Home and Abroad

Anna is in her early 30s, single, and has a four-year-old son named Greg. She is going back to school to become a nurse, and attends classes at her local community college during the morning and early afternoon four days a week. To support herself and her son, she works part-time at a local restaurant every evening. Anna has permission to eat one daily meal at the restaurant at a reasonable cost. With her limited income and time constraints, Anna finds herself frequently unable to buy enough food, or prepare nutritious meals, for herself and her son to eat.

Greg, meanwhile, is at day care during the day and spends his evenings with his grandmother. Greg's noon meal at the day-care center is well-balanced and nutritious, but his evening intake usually consists of snacks, like potato chips, dips, sodas, and sweets, that his grandmother eats. Greg doesn't eat anything nourishing while he is at his grandmother's house because Anna cannot afford to bring his meals to her mother's. Anna doesn't want to complain about her mother's food habits. Naturally, she is thankful for the free child care.

Do you think Anna is compromising her and her son's nutritional health? Which of her habits do you think might be harmful? What suggestions would you make to help Anna improve her situation? In this chapter, we'll explore the conditions of food insecurity and malnutrition, their causes and effects, and steps you can take to help the hungry in your own community, and around the world.

Chapter Objectives

After reading this chapter, you will be able to:

1. Define hunger, food security, and food insecurity.

2. Summarize the extent of food insecurity in the United States and worldwide.

3. List and describe three causes of food insecurity and poverty in the United States.

4. List and describe three causes of food insecurity and poverty worldwide.

5. List three populations at highest risk for experiencing food insecurity.

6. Describe the consequences of food insecurity.

7. Describe two steps you can take to help eradicate food insecurity.

What Is Food Insecurity and Why Does It Exist?

The U.S. Department of Agriculture (USDA) describes an American household as *food secure* if it has access at all times to enough food for an active, healthy life for all household members.[1] In contrast, **food insecurity** is a situation in which members of a household are uncertain whether they will have the resources they need to get adequate amounts of nutritious food. Thus, people who experience food insecurity may be at risk for undernutrition due to insufficient calories and nutrients in the diet. (You can see the range of definitions for high to very low food security in Table 14.1.)

Because the United States is the wealthiest country in the world, it seems unlikely that some of its citizens would be unable to visit a local grocery store and buy an ad-

Table 14.1

Ranges of Food Security

Level of Food Security	Description of Conditions in the Household
High food security	No reported indications of food-access problems or limitations
Marginal food security	One or two reported indications—typically of anxiety over food sufficiency or shortage of food in the house. Little or no indication of changes in diets or food intake.
Low food security	Reports of reduced quality, variety, or desirability of diet. Little or no indication of reduced food intake.
Very low food security	Reports of multiple indications of disrupted eating patterns and reduced food intake

Source: Adapted from USDA Economic Research Service. 2009. Available at www.ers.usda.gov/Briefing/FoodSecurity/measurement.htm. Accessed April 2010.

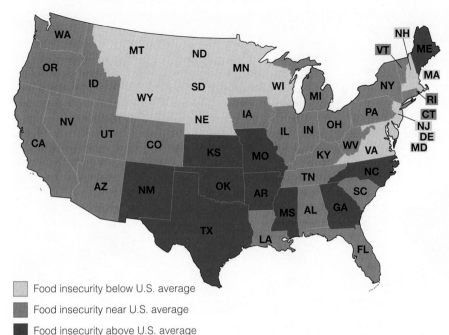

Figure 14.1 Prevalence of Food Insecurity in the United States
Though some areas of the United States have higher rates of food insecurity, these conditions can happen anywhere.

Source: Household Food Security in the United States. 2008. Available at www.ers.usda.gov/Briefing/FoodSecurity/stats_graphs.htm#food_secure.

■ Food insecurity below U.S. average

■ Food insecurity near U.S. average

■ Food insecurity above U.S. average

equate supply of healthy foods. However, food insecurity in the United States is a major problem: In 2008, 14.6 percent of American households—representing 49.1 million people—were food insecure at least sometime during the year. This is an increase of 3.5 percent from 2007, and is the highest rate of food insecurity since 1995, when the first food security survey was conducted.[2] **Figure 14.1** illustrates the prevalence of food insecurity in the United States.

Also in 2008, 12.1 million adults and 5.2 million children lived in households with *very low food security*, meaning that the food intake of one or more adults was reduced and their eating patterns were disrupted at times during the year.[3] People who have very low food security are at significant risk for **hunger.** Prolonged hunger can lead to **starvation,** a state in which the body breaks down its own tissues for fuel. As shown in **Figure 14.2,** you can think of these states—from food security to starvation and death—as occurring along a continuum.

Although the percentage of Americans who experience food insecurity might surprise you, it is much lower than in many countries of the world. That's because the United States is a **developed country** with a high rate of industrial capacity, technological sophistication, and economic productivity. In contrast, in **developing** and **underdeveloped countries** where there are low levels of economic productivity, the rates of food insecurity and very low food security are higher. **Figure 14.3**

> Enough food is available to provide at least 4.3 pounds of food per person per day worldwide.

food insecurity The inability to satisfy basic food needs due to lack of financial resources or other problems. The USDA further defines food insecurity as falling into the categories of either *low food security* or *very low food security.*

hunger Physical discomfort that results from the lack of food associated with food insecurity.

starvation To suffer severely from lack of food; a state in which the body breaks down its own tissue for fuel.

developed country A nation advanced in industrial capability, technological sophistication, and economic productivity.

developing country A nation having a relatively low level of industrial capability, technological sophistication, or economic productivity.

underdeveloped country A nation having a low level of economic productivity and technological sophistication within the contemporary range of possibility.

| Food security | Food insecurity | Malnutrition | Hunger | Starvation | Death |

Figure 14.2 Spectrum of Food Security
Food insecurity and hunger are points along the continuum between being food secure and dying from starvation.

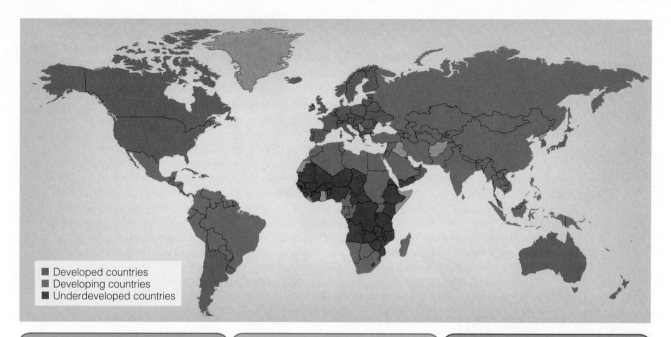

- Developed countries
- Developing countries
- Underdeveloped countries

Examples of developed countries	Examples of developing countries	Examples of underdeveloped countries
United States	China	Ethiopia
Canada	India	Sudan
Japan	Mexico	Angola
Australia	Brazil	Haiti
New Zealand	Mongolia	Sierra Leone
Most Western European nations	Saudi Arabia	Yemen

Figure 14.3 Developed, Developing, and Underdeveloped Countries around the World
Food insecurity and hunger are global problems. In developed countries, such as the United States, Canada, and the countries of Western Europe, people often experience food insecurity due to disability, periods of unemployment, and poverty. In underdeveloped countries, like many in central Africa, war, civil conflict, and natural disasters can lead to chronic hunger.

Source: United Nations Development Programme. 2010. *United Nations Human Development Report.* Available at http://hdr.undp.org/en/reports/global/hdr2010. Accessed April 2010.

Thanks to agricultural advances, the world's farmers can grow plenty of food. However, distribution problems and other factors keep some people from getting enough to stave off hunger.

identifies developed, developing, and underdeveloped countries around the world, and **Figure 14.4** illustrates rates of food insecurity in developing and underdeveloped countries. Worldwide, the Food and Agriculture Organization of the United Nations (FAO) estimates that, in 2009, 1.02 billion people, or one-seventh of the world's population, were hungry.[4] In underdeveloped countries, such as those in central Africa, more than 50 percent of the population is undernourished.[5] As of 2008 (2004 statistics), the World Bank has estimated that 982 million poor people in developing countries live on $1.25 a day or less.[6]

In developed countries, food insecurity typically results from factors affecting individuals, such as **poverty** or poor health. In developing and underdeveloped countries, regional problems, such as discrimination, armed conflict, natural disasters, and population overgrowth, can be as significant as individual hardships. Let's take a closer look at these factors, beginning with those contributing to food insecurity in the United States.

In the United States, Food Insecurity Is Often Caused by Poverty

poverty Lacking the means to provide for material or comfort needs.

Poverty levels in the United States are defined according to strict guidelines. A family of four is considered impoverished if its annual income is at or below $22,050. In

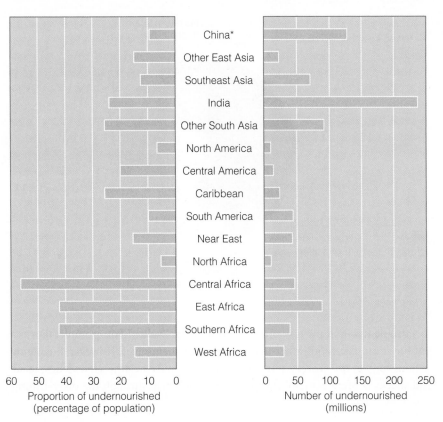

Figure 14.4 Number and Proportion of Undernourished People
Many developing and underdeveloped nations have high rates of food insecurity.

China*
Other East Asia
Southeast Asia
India
Other South Asia
North America
Central America
Caribbean
South America
Near East
North Africa
Central Africa
East Africa
Southern Africa
West Africa

60 50 40 30 20 10 0
Proportion of undernourished
(percentage of population)

0 50 100 150 200 250
Number of undernourished
(millions)

*Including Taiwan Province of China

2008, about 13.2 percent of the U.S. population lived at or below the poverty level, including 14.1 million children.[7]

According to the U.S. Census Bureau, those at the greatest risk of experiencing poverty and food insecurity are people living in the following households:[8]

➤ Households headed by a single woman
➤ Households with children
➤ Households with members in a minority group
➤ Households located in the inner city

These circumstances contribute to poverty because they contribute to disadvantages, such as increased exposure to crime and fewer employment opportunities. For example, single mothers may feel "trapped," with very few options to explore different career paths, because of obligations to their children. Also, arranging for child care can prompt additional stress and drain an already tight budget.

Anna, the single mom you read about at the beginning of this chapter, has a less than ideal child-care arrangement but can't afford to change the situation because of her limited employment options. Single mothers are more likely to experience times without adequate amounts of food than are families headed by a married couple.[9]

You may be surprised to learn that steady employment does not guarantee that an individual or a family won't experience food insecurity. Even people with an excellent job may experience food insecurity if they are laid off. Additionally, people can be steadily employed in a low-wage full-time job, in a series of seasonal jobs, or in several part-time jobs and still experience food insecurity. In fact, in 2003, about 7.4 million individuals were classified among the **working poor.** In these households, once the monthly expenses are paid, there is often too little money available to feed everyone adequately (see **Figure 14.5**).

In the United States, poor single parents and their children can experience food insecurity due to unemployment, low wages, or other circumstances that lead to financial hardship.

working poor Individuals or families who are steadily employed but still experience poverty due to low wages or high dependent expenses.

Figure 14.5 Employment Status of Food-Insecure Households

Almost half of households with the greatest difficulty putting adequate food on the table include an employed adult.

Source: USDA Economic Research Service, "Economic Information Bulletin," 2009. www.ers .usda.gov/Publications/eib48/spreads/3/index.htm. Accessed June 2010.

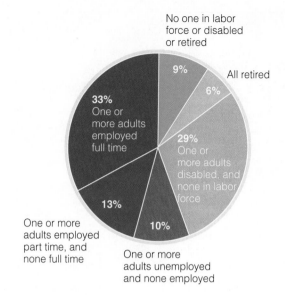

No one in labor force or disabled or retired
9%

All retired
6%

33% One or more adults employed full time

29% One or more adults disabled, and none in labor force

13% One or more adults employed part time, and none full time

10% One or more adults unemployed and none employed

People living in poverty often try to shop for "value." For example, they may opt for cheap fast food rather than cooking for themselves. However, buying nutritious food at the grocery store and using it to make healthy sandwiches, salads, and snacks is often actually cheaper than a daily trip through the drive-through (see Table 14.2).

Table 14.2

Eating Healthy Can Cost Less

Lunch Item	Total Calories	Total Fat (grams)	Cost
Fast-Food Burger Meal			
Fast-food burger: 2 beef patties on a sesame seed bun with lettuce, cheese, "special sauce," pickles, and onions	540	29	$4.05
Medium order of french fries	380	19	$1.72
Cost of a fast-food burger meal	**920**	**48**	**$5.77**
Homemade Packed Lunch			
Homemade turkey sandwich: 3 ounces oven-roasted turkey on 2 pieces of whole-wheat bread with 1 slice tomato, 1 leaf lettuce, and 1 tsp mustard	350	5	$1.46
Baby carrots, 3 oz	30	0	$.40
Granola bar, 1 Oat & Honey	100	3	$.60
Cost of a homemade packed lunch	**480**	**8**	**$2.46**

Data from: USDA National Nutrient Database for Standard Reference; McDonald's Web Site; Bureau of Labor Consumer Price Index. Accessed February 2010.

The Paradox of Being Overweight and Undernourished—A Typical Scenario

Recall that in Chapter 10, we addressed the paradox of obesity—that is, the counterintuitive idea that those with the most limited food budgets are often overweight or obese—and the factors most often involved. Now, let's consider a scenario in which this paradox might occur.

Maria, a mother of two school-aged children, works full-time for minimum wage at a fast-food restaurant, and is considered one of the "working poor." She has difficulty making ends meet, especially during the winter months, when the cost of heating her one-bedroom apartment cuts into her monthly food budget. Maria eats breakfast and lunch at her job. She purposely fills up on french fries before she leaves work so that she can skip dinner without feeling hungry. With one less mouth to feed at supper, she can stretch her limited household food budget to feed her children and husband. Not surprisingly, Maria is obese.

Studies have shown that adults in situations similar to Maria's are at risk for being overweight.[1] Minority women with low income have the greatest likelihood of being overweight. For example, Mexican-American women living below the poverty line are approximately 13 percent more likely to be overweight or obese than those who live above the poverty line.[2] Studies have also shown that the percentage of teenagers who are overweight is 50 percent higher in low-income families and that the prevalence of obesity in low-income two- to four-year-olds is increasing, from 12.4 percent in 1998 to 14.6 percent in 2008.[3]

These higher rates of overweight and obesity among people of lower socioeconomic status is thought to result from an interaction of several contributing factors, including cultural factors that influence diet and exercise behaviors.[4] Other factors include lack of access to healthy food in communities where supermarkets are not available (the so-called "food deserts"); lack of safe areas in which to exercise or for children to play; lack of access to basic health care; poor housing; low-wage work and long working hours; and increased stress that can lead to central adiposity and emotional eating.

What do you think Maria can do to improve the nutritional status of herself and her family? What government or community programs are most likely to help? What other steps could be taken to address the problems of limited access to healthier, nutrient-dense foods and adequate physical activity?

People in poor, urban areas often find themselves in "food deserts," with little access to the fresh, healthy food found in supermarkets, and easy access to fast foods and snack foods like those found in drive-through restaurants and liquor or convenience stores.

Health Problems Contribute to Food Insecurity among Americans

A variety of health issues can also set the stage for food insecurity:

➤ *Chronic illness.* Adults who are chronically ill are less likely to earn a steady income and therefore are at risk of having a poor diet. Chronic illness in an elderly person can reduce mobility, making it difficult to get to a grocery store or to prepare nourishing meals.

➤ *Disability.* Many adults who are disabled lead highly productive lives, but others are limited to low-skilled, low-wage jobs. Some cannot work at all and must depend on disability income, which may not provide adequate money for nourishing food. Similar to chronic illness, disability can make it difficult for a person to shop for food and prepare meals.

Are You at Risk for Food Insecurity?

Take this quiz to find out if you are at risk for food insecurity and/or hunger.

In the past 12 months:

1. Have you ever run out of money to buy food?
   Yes ☐ **No** ☐

2. Have you ever eaten less than you felt you should because there was not enough money to buy food or enough food to eat?
   Yes ☐ **No** ☐

3. Have you ever completely depleted your food supply because there was not enough money to buy replacement groceries?
   Yes ☐ **No** ☐

4. Have you ever gone to bed hungry because there was not enough food to eat?
   Yes ☐ **No** ☐

5. Have you ever skipped meals because there was not enough money to buy food?
   Yes ☐ **No** ☐

6. Have you ever relied on a limited number of foods to feed yourself because you were running out of money to buy food?
   Yes ☐ **No** ☐

Answers

If there are zero "yes" replies, you are food secure. If there are one to three "yes" replies, you are at risk for food insecurity. If there are four or more "yes" replies, you are classified as "hungry."

Source: Adapted from The Community Childhood Hunger Identification Project Survey, July 1995; R. E. Kleinman, et al., "Hunger in Children in the United States: Potential Behavioral and Emotional Correlates," *Pediatrics* 101 (1998): 3–10.

➤ *Substance abuse.* Drug and alcohol abuse are common causes of food insecurity, in part because of the challenge these problems create in maintaining steady employment. Many people who abuse substances become unable to keep up their mortgage or rent, and they descend into homelessness. In fact, an estimated 85 percent of all homeless men and women in urban areas abuse substances and/or have a mental illness.

➤ *Mental illness.* Many mentally ill people, often including the **homeless,** are forced to rely on charity, church meals, or public assistance programs for most of their food. Even people with homes and jobs who suffer from mental illness can lose interest in eating or have decreased ability to prepare meals. For example, clinical depression among mothers, particularly those in low-income families, has been associated with food insecurity in households.[10]

Now that you've learned about the factors contributing to food insecurity in the United States, you may be wondering if you're at risk. If so, take the Self-Assessment to find out.

homeless Individuals who are either "crashing" with friends or family members, or residing on the street or in their automobiles.

Global Food Insecurity Is Caused by Regional Issues

Worldwide, food insecurity persists despite the fact that global food production exceeds the needs of the world's population. This sobering reality tells us that agricultural production is not the problem, and increasing it is not the sole solution. What are the real culprits in global hunger?

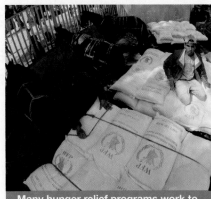

Many hunger relief programs work to provide food aid to needy nations. However, successfully delivering the food to those who need it is often challenging.

Discrimination

Various forms of discrimination, including racial, gender, and ethnic discrimination, contribute to reduced employment, lower educational achievement, and fewer business opportunities in some cultures.[11] Vulnerable groups include women, the elderly, people with disabilities, refugees, orphans, migrant workers, and people who are illiterate. In many countries, such as Sudan, Afghanistan, Angola, and Ethiopia, discrimination exists at both the national and local levels. For example, at the national level, control over land and other assets is often unequal. At the local or household level, access to food is influenced by factors such as gender, control over income, education, birth order, and age.[12] Much of the inequity is due to educational inequalities between boys and girls. Two-thirds of the almost 900 million illiterate adults in the world are women. Thus, it's not surprising that, worldwide, 70 percent of the 1.2 billion people who live in extreme poverty are female.[13]

Political Sanctions and Armed Conflicts

Political **sanctions,** such as boycotts and trade embargoes, may be used by one government or country to force political change on another. Sometimes the goal of sanctions is to postpone or replace possible military actions. Other goals include restoring democracy, condemning the abuse of human rights, and punishing groups that protect terrorists or international criminals. Although the goals of the sanctions may be noble, the outcomes—such as shortages in food, fuel, or medicine—often harm innocent people, affecting "the poor, not the powerful."[14] Agricultural embargoes create food shortages by decreasing access to agricultural supplies, fuel, or crops. As with sanctions, embargoes are more likely to hurt the average citizen than affect government authorities.[15]

War, armed conflict, and civil unrest cause hunger because of the disruption to agriculture, food distribution, and normal community activities. During wars and regional conflicts, government money is often diverted from nutrition programs and food distribution efforts and redirected toward weapons and military support. Conflicts have caused increases in hunger and overwhelmed the humanitarian safety network. Political turbulence can compromise food distribution programs.[16]

Crop Failure, Natural Disasters, and Wasteful Agricultural Practices

Natural disasters, such as drought, floods, crop diseases, and insect infestations, can occur in any country, on any continent. However, the impact of natural disasters is much greater on underdeveloped countries than on developed countries. There are several reasons for this, including the population's inability to relocate away from disaster-prone areas and people's inability to make their homes and farms less vulnerable to destructive natural forces. Additionally, the local economy and infrastructure tend to be unstable in underdeveloped areas, so a natural disaster can quickly become devastating.[17] (See the feature box "Natural Disasters and Food Insecurity" for a closer examination of efforts conducted to feed the hungry in the wake of severe natural disasters.)

> Eighty percent of people who experience hunger around the world make their living from the land, and 50 percent are actually farmers.

sanctions Boycotts or trade embargoes used by one country or international group to apply political pressure on another.

Natural Disasters and Food Insecurity: A Dire Combination

Natural disasters, including earthquakes, hurricanes, tsunamis, and floods, can be disastrous no matter where they occur, but when they strike a country or region that's particularly ill-prepared or impoverished, the results can be devastating.

In 2008, 231 worldwide natural disasters, including one major (7.9) earthquake in the Sichuan province of China, killed almost 236,000 people and cost an estimated $181 billion.[5] In February 2010, a sizable (7.0) earthquake rocked the small, impoverished nation of Haiti, where more than 2 million people—over half the population—were already food insecure or undernourished. The earthquake resulted in more than 200,000 deaths, 300,000 injuries, and a million people being left homeless.[6] As people's homes

and possessions were destroyed, they were often left wandering and destitute. They were afraid to reenter damaged housing for fear of aftershocks or further collapse. Those who sustained injuries were often untreated for days, without food and water, as relief workers struggled to find and rescue them.

Those lucky individuals who escaped the initial encounter were faced with a second crisis: looking for food, water, and shelter. Aid workers rushed in with supplies, such as nutritious biscuits and bottled water, only to find that remote sites were largely inaccessible due to difficult terrain, extensive damage, or lack of infrastructure. Thus, widespread food insecurity developed. While some farmers were still producing food, damage to in-

frastructure such as roads and bridges prevented many of them from reaching markets. The food that did end up in the marketplace was often too expensive even for those who had a bit of money.[7]

As the situation stabilized and people returned home or left the cities to find shelter with families or friends in rural areas, the long-term consequences of the disaster began to be addressed. In the case of Haiti, 62 percent of the country's population lives in rural areas, and 80 percent relies on agriculture for its livelihood, including small-scale production in the form of backyard gardening and small animal rearing in urban areas.[8] International relief efforts therefore focused on:[9]

➤ Rapidly restoring food production through input distribution and technical support to small-scale urban and rural farmers in time for the planting season

➤ Reestablishing the livelihoods of about 1 million people living in urban and rural areas that were directly or indirectly hit by the earthquake, by supporting field-based and backyard food production, and providing assistance for small-scale agricultural and livestock production, including seeds, fertilizers, seedlings, and small animals

➤ Rehabilitating basic rural infrastructure in the affected areas, such as rural roads, irrigation facilities, food storage, and farm infrastructure, for about 1 million people

These efforts were not cheap, and the international relief community relied heavily on monetary and other assistance from nations, organizations, and charities to facilitate the repair and rebuilding necessary to restore a basic quality of life.

The distribution of high-energy, nutritious biscuits was a lifeline in the first days after the disaster in Haiti.

Drought is the leading cause of severe food shortages in developing and underdeveloped countries. Because of water's essential role in growing crops, water and food security are closely linked. Lack of water is a major cause of **famine** and undernutrition. However, floods can also destroy food crops, and are major causes of food shortages.

Wasteful agricultural practices also threaten limited resources. The depletion of natural resources through practices such as improper land plowing, overgrazing of livestock, aggressive timber harvesting, and the misuse of fertilizers, pesticides, and water may increase yield in the short term but inhibit production in the long term.[18]

Lack of irrigation also contributes to crop failures and low yields. The proper use of irrigation can increase crop yield by 100 to 400 percent. Surprisingly, only 17 percent of the world's land is irrigated, yet this small amount disproportionately produces 40 percent of the world's food.[19]

> Irrigation is not a new practice. Evidence shows that Mesopotamians were irrigating crops as early as 5400 BC.

Population Overgrowth

The human population is growing by more than 80 million people per year, and the projected world population for 2020 is 7.7 billion people.[20] By 2050, the United Nations estimates, the world population will reach 8 to 12 billion people. Most of this growth is occurring in developing and underdeveloped countries. Whenever rapid population growth occurs in areas that are strained for food production, the resulting **overpopulation** can take a toll on the local people's nutritional status.

The Take-Home Message The causes of food insecurity in the United States include individual hardships, such as poverty and health problems. Food insecurity is particularly prevalent in households headed by a single mother, households with children, minority households, and households in inner cities. The causes of hunger in other parts of the world also include poverty, as well as discrimination, political sanctions and conflicts, crop failures, natural disasters, wasteful agricultural practices, and overpopulation.

As the world's population continues to grow, demands on limited resources for food production will increase.

Who Is at Increased Risk for Undernutrition?

The following populations are at increased risk for undernutrition:

➤ *Pregnant and lactating women.* Pregnant women need extra calories and nutrients—in particular, protein, vitamins, and minerals—to support their own health and their growing baby. Many inadequately nourished pregnant women give birth to undernourished infants. Lactating women need even more calories than pregnant women if they are to maintain their weight and produce an adequate, nourishing milk supply. The global recommendation is for women to nurse their babies for the first six months and to continue nursing with supplemental foods into the second year of life.[21]

➤ *Infants.* Infants are vulnerable to undernutrition because they are growing rapidly, have high nutrient requirements (per unit of body weight), and may be breast-fed by mothers who are undernourished themselves. Because they are dependent on their caregivers to give them adequate breast milk, formula, or foods, they are particularly vulnerable to neglect. From 6 to 12 months of age, as an infant transitions from breast milk to a diet of breast milk plus solid

famine A severe shortage of food caused by crop destruction due to weather problems or poor agricultural practices so that the food supply is destroyed or severely diminished. This can also be caused by pestilence and/or war.

overpopulation When a region has more people than its natural resources can support.

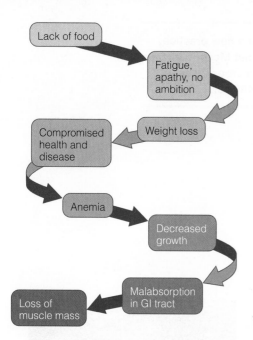

Figure 14.6 Downward Spiral of Poverty and Hunger
Lack of food can lead to numerous other symptoms that compound the problem of hunger.

foods, inadequate feeding can lead to diminished growth and the potential for severe undernutrition during the second year of life.[22]

➤ *Children.* The risk for undernutrition continues into childhood if the family experiences food shortages or chronic disease. For example, AIDS can result in the death, and loss of income, of one or both parents. An estimated 13 million children worldwide have become orphaned by AIDS.[23] (T)(F)

➤ *The critically ill.* Liver and kidney disease can impair the body's ability to process and use some nutrients. Some cancer patients, and most people with AIDS, experience loss of appetite, which further complicates their treatment and their ability to eat.[24]

➤ *Older adults.* Older adults are at increased risk for undernutrition because of a decreased sense of taste and smell, dental problems, immobility, malabsorption, or chronic illnesses.[25] In addition, loneliness, isolation, confusion, or depression can diminish appetite or cause a person to lose interest in cooking and eating. (T)(F)

What Are the Effects of Chronic Malnutrition?

Once people move along the continuum from food insecurity to malnutrition and hunger, it can be extremely difficult to get ahead again. That's because lack of food can lead to physical problems that interfere with a person's ability to earn an adequate income, a situation that leads to continued poverty and lack of adequate food (**Figure 14.6**).

In general, whenever the body experiences fasting, famine, serious disease, or severe malnutrition, it attempts to conserve energy and preserve body tissues. Over an extended period of time, however, the body breaks down its own tissue as a source of energy. This results in the deterioration of internal organs and muscle mass, and the reduction of stored fat. In prolonged starvation, adults can lose up to 50 percent of their body weight. The greatest amount of deterioration occurs in the intestinal tract and the liver. The loss is moderate in the heart and kidneys, and the least damage occurs in the brain and nervous system.[26]

Let's look at some individual effects of chronic malnutrition.

Impaired Growth and Development

When children do not receive the nutrients they need to grow and develop properly, they are likely to experience both physical and mental problems, including insufficient weight gain, improper muscle development, lowered resistance to infection, growth **stunting**, and impaired brain development (**Figure 14.7**).[27] Their bodies attempt to compensate for a lack of food by decreasing physical and intellectual growth. Children are more likely to show behavioral, emotional, and academic problems if they come from families that experience hunger and food insufficiency rather than families that do not report hunger experiences.[28] In particular, long-term undernutrition is associated with increased anxiety, irritability, attention problems, and increased prevalence of school absence and tardiness rates.[29]

If hunger persists or occurs at early, crucial times of brain development, cognitive development is impaired.[30] This could result in permanent lower intelligence and hindered learning ability. As a result, malnourished children may have a difficult time (T)(F)

stunting Primarily manifested in early childhood and includes malnutrition during fetal development. Once growth stunting occurs, it is usually permanent. It can affect the vital body organs and cause premature death.

Figure 14.7 Effects of Undernutrition
As hunger persists, physical symptoms set in and lead to further complications.

completing their basic elementary education. This is particularly unfortunate because school attendance has a measurable impact on earning ability later in life. Research demonstrates that underweight and malnourished children complete fewer years of school compared with well-nourished children.[31]

Even if the children are healthy enough to regularly attend school, hunger and malnutrition impair learning ability. For example, iron deficiency is associated with reduced attention span and decreased memory capacity.[32] Malnourished children also seem to be fatigued, inattentive, and unresponsive to their learning environment. An isolated child who does not respond to or interact with others tends to be neglected by peers, teachers, and adult caregivers.

Globally, an estimated 225 million children experience height stunting because of deficiencies in protein and other nutrients. About 33 percent of children under 5 years of age living in developing countries are physically stunted (decreased height for age), and about 27 percent of these children between 3 and 5 years old show physical **wasting** (decreased weight for age).[33] Growth stunting has also been associated with long-term detrimental effects on physical work capacity and fertility.[34]

Impaired Immunity and Disease

A malnourished individual has a weakened immune system, which increases his or her vulnerability to various infections. Fever, parasitic disease, pneumonia, measles, and malaria are examples of conditions that occur because of weakened immune systems and chronic malnutrition.

The World Health Organization estimates that 60 percent of all childhood deaths in developing countries are associated with chronic hunger and malnutrition. Many

wasting A condition caused by extremely low energy intake from too little food. It is sometimes referred to as acute malnutrition. Infections, high energy use, or nutrient loss can cause wasting.

of the deaths can be attributed to one of the following five causes or a combination thereof.[35]

1. Diarrhea
2. Acute respiratory infection
3. Measles
4. Malaria
5. Malnutrition

Diarrhea—caused by viruses, parasites, and other harmful microorganisms—can result in severe dehydration (loss of fluids and electrolytes). More than 2 million children die each year from severe dehydration caused by diarrhea. Contaminated water worsens the situation. An ill, malnourished child lacks the physical strength and nutrient reserves to survive a severe case of diarrhea, dehydration, and electrolyte imbalance.[36]

Acute respiratory infection is caused by either viruses or bacteria in the respiratory tract. Pneumonia is the most serious respiratory infection and can be successfully treated with oral antibiotics. Children experiencing measles or malnutrition are especially vulnerable to respiratory problems.[37] Malaria is caused by a parasite-infected mosquito. Table 14.3 summarizes the ramifications of these illnesses.

Vitamin and mineral deficiencies and their resulting diseases are serious concerns for people living in developing countries and in the United States. For example, more than 2 billion people, or greater than one-third of the world's population, live with vitamin A, iron, or iodine deficiency. These micronutrient deficiencies are referred to as "hidden hunger." Table 14.4 lists the most common vitamin and mineral deficiencies observed in those who are malnourished.

Increased Rates of Infant and Child Mortality

As mentioned, malnutrition is part of a vicious cycle that passes hunger from one generation to the next. Unfortunately, many young women experience undernutrition during their own infancy and childhood. Girls who were low birth weight ba-

Table 14.3

Common Illnesses in Malnourished Children

Disease/Condition	Cause	Effect
Diarrhea	Pathogenic infections	Severe dehydration
Acute respiratory infection	Virus or bacteria	Pneumonia, bronchitis, colds, fast breathing, coughing, and fever
Malaria	Parasite (transmitted by a mosquito)	Fever, weakness, sweating, shivering, shaking, nausea, liver failure, infected red blood cells, kidney failure or bleeding in the kidneys
Measles	Respiratory illness caused by a highly contagious virus, from airborne droplets (coughing/sneezing)	Pneumonia, brain inflammation, infection, diarrhea, and seizures

Table 14.4

Most Common Vitamin and Mineral Deficiencies among the Malnourished

Vitamin or Mineral	Effects	Incidence
Vitamin A	Eye disease; blindness	Vitamin A deficiency is the leading cause of preventable blindness in children in developing countries.
Iron	Iron-deficiency anemia	Extremely common worldwide. Anemia is most common among 7- to 12-month-old infants; toddlers and young children (<8 years of age); women of reproductive age; and anyone who has lost large amounts of blood.
Iodine	Goiter, cretinism	Up to 790 million people (13% of the world's population) have some form of iodine deficiency, goiter, or mental impairment caused by lack of iodine.
B vitamins (folic acid, B_{12})	Folic acid: macrocytic anemia	Folic acid deficiency is common among women of reproductive age; individuals with limited diets and reduced vegetable consumption; individuals who abuse alcohol; and obese individuals.
	Vitamin B_{12}: pernicious anemia	B_{12} deficiency is common among elderly men and women (>50 years of age); African-American adults; individuals who have malabsorption syndromes; and persons who practice extreme vegetarianism.

Source: World Health Organization. 2010. Micronutrient Deficiencies. Available at www.who.int/nutrition/topics/micronutrients/en/index.html.

bies or were undernourished and ill during the first five years of life may be physically stunted and less able to support a healthy pregnancy when they become adults. The infants born to malnourished women are more likely to be malnourished, experience chronic illness, and have an increased risk of premature death. Premature babies who do reach adulthood are more likely to have malnourished children of their own. Approximately 12 million children younger than 5 years of age die each year in developing countries from preventable causes, such as diarrhea, measles, and malaria, mentioned earlier. Malnutrition is linked to more than half of these childhood deaths.[38]

The Take-Home Message Pregnant and lactating women, infants and children, and the ill and elderly are particularly vulnerable to the effects of malnutrition. If malnutrition occurs during adulthood, the body will try to conserve nutrients and preserve its own organs, but eventually there could be irreversible organ damage. Physical effects of malnutrition include stunted growth, impaired mental development and immunity, and higher likelihood of disease. Other mental effects include anxiety, irritability, and attention problems. Vitamin and mineral deficiency diseases can occur, and the impairment of the immune system increases vulnerability to infectious disease.

How Can We Reduce Food Insecurity?

Global hunger harms all of us. When citizens of your community experience hunger, you are likely to see increased disease incidence, low ambition, poverty, and general apathy among the individuals affected. Additionally, from a humanitarian perspective, the painful physical symptoms of hunger are unacceptable when you consider that a surplus of food is grown each year.

Everyone—from children to adults— can help eradicate hunger.

At the local level, individuals, families, churches, and community relief agencies seek out and assist people who have insufficient resources. From providing free food and meals to education and job training, there are numerous ways such organizations can help alleviate hunger. Similarly, corporations and governments can help solve the hunger problem by providing food aid and creating economic opportunity for people who want to improve their life position. See Table 14.5 for examples of programs that help combat hunger in the United States. If you are wondering how you can contribute to reducing food insecurity, see the feature box ⒯⒡ "Food Insecurity among Us—and How You Can Help!"

Table 14.5

Food Assistance Programs in the United States

Program	Eligibility	Description	Prevalence
Supplemental Nutrition Assistance Program (SNAP), (formerly the Food Stamp Program)	Low income (for a family of four, the net monthly income cannot exceed $1,883)	Individuals who are eligible for food stamps are issued a debit card to purchase specified foods, such as fruit, vegetables, cereals, meats, and dairy products, at their local authorized supermarket. (Items such as alcohol, tobacco products, and household items are not covered.)	In 2009, more than 31 million people per month in the United States
Special Supplemental Nutrition Program for Women, Infants and Children (WIC)	At-risk low-income pregnant and lactating women, infants, and children less than 5 years old	The program provides nutritious, culturally appropriate food, including tortillas, brown rice, soy-based beverages, and a wide choice of fruits and vegetables, to supplement the diet. There are even some organic forms of WIC-eligible foods. The program also emphasizes nutrition education and offers referrals to health care professionals.	9.3 million women, infants, and children per month
National School Lunch Program	Children with families with incomes at or below 130% of the poverty level are eligible for free meals and those with incomes between 130% and 185% of the poverty level are eligible for reduced-price meals	Eligible children receive free or reduced-price lunches each year. A subsidized breakfast is sometimes also available at schools.	More than 30.5 million American children per year
Summer Food Service Program	Available to communities based on income data	Federal program that combines a meal or feeding program with a summer activity program for children	Almost 2 million children at 31,000 sites
Child and Adult Care Food Program	Available to communities based on income data	Program provides nutritious meals to low-income children and senior adults who receive day care or adult care outside the home. There are income guidelines and specific menu requirements for program participation.	3 million children and 90,000 adults receive meals and snacks each day as part of this program
Congregate Meals for the Elderly and Meals on Wheels	Age 60 or over	The programs provide meals at a community site or delivered to the home.	More than 250 million meals served at sites across the country

Food Insecurity among Us—and How You Can Help!

Food insecurity may be closer than you think. In fact, you may have friends, relatives, or neighbors who've experienced hunger sometime in their lives.

Here's a true account of one young man's experience with hunger.

I grew up poor. My mother, who was single, worked two jobs to support us AND pay her way through college. I was never hungry then, but when I got to college I realized how little wiggle room there can be in a food budget!

It was my first week at LSU in Baton Rouge. We started classes a few days before Labor Day weekend, then got a four-day break before classes really went into full swing the following Monday.

I was enrolled in the 3-squares-a-day university meal plan, but the program was run Monday through Friday only. The dining halls weren't open until after the Labor Day weekend anyway. My mom had given me as much money as she could spare at the time, $20.00. Since I did not have cooking facilities at the dormitory, I was forced to go "out" to eat, and pay for the public transportation to get to places to eat, for the first 3 days of class.

Then the worst happened. My mother was going to pick me up on Friday evening to bring me back home to New Orleans for the weekend. But Friday morning her car got stolen. She had to spend all of her money on the insurance deductible, and didn't have any extra to get me a bus ticket home.

I was stuck on campus, and everyone I knew there had already left for the extended weekend. I had no money, no job to earn money, no food, and the dining halls were closed.

I lived on Celestial Seasonings herbal tea and Ovaltine (made with water, and appropriated from my roommate) for 4 days. I was a wreck because I was so hungry. I couldn't concentrate on anything, I had no patience at all, and I lost over 10 pounds, which I really could not afford to lose since I weighed about 115 pounds at the time.

The good part is that this situation was only temporary for me. I skipped my first class on Monday morning to go eat a mammoth breakfast at the dining hall. But this sort of catch-22 situation can, and does, happen to people everywhere. For most, it isn't a temporary situation at all.

You'd think that this would never happen to someone like me—I'm a middle-class college student. It certainly opened my eyes to what numerous Americans have to face every day. It also made me understand the problems my mother was facing when she was in nursing school when I was little and couldn't chip in at all.

I would have gone to a food bank if I had known about them then. Please,

PLEASE volunteer your time at your local shelters, and donate food and money whenever you are able to. The next person that has to go to a food bank might be me, or you!

Feeding America, formerly called Second Harvest, is the nation's leading domestic hunger-relief charity. It is a national network of individuals, local food banks, and offices, as well as corporate and government partners, that helps distribute excess and donated food and grocery items annually to those who are hungry. Its mission is to feed America's hungry through a network of more than 200 member food banks and to continue the fight to end food insecurity in this country.

Feeding America collects surplus food from national food companies and other large donors and stores it in a centralized location. The food is then moved to local food pantries in order to reach those who need it.

When it comes to fighting hunger in America, everyone needs to pitch in. You can help your needy neighbors in three ways: give funds, give food, and/or give time. Funds can be donated online at www.feedingamerica.org. Every dollar donated can provide seven meals for those in need. You can also donate food by hosting a food drive. Finally, you can volunteer your time by helping out in your local community, perhaps tutoring children at a local Kids Cafe, repackaging donated food, stocking shelves at a local food pantry, or transporting food to the hungry.

To find out where you can help, visit the Feeding America website and search for opportunities using the Volunteer Match service (www.feedingamerica.org).

Better land and water management and appropriate crop selection can all help eliminate hunger.

In addition to the human (person-to-person) help provided by people and organizations, technology is also playing a role in alleviating malnutrition. As research and development provide new ways to pack more nutrition into food crops, hunger may be reduced. Enriched crops will ultimately benefit hungry people by providing some of the common nutrients (iron, vitamin A, and iodine) that are in low supply in current crops.

Better Land Management and Proper Sanitation

Proper land management and appropriate crop selection can help increase agricultural production. For example, productive land is frequently used for nonconsumable crops, such as tobacco or flowers, for sale to industrialized nations. Raising edible, nutritious plants such as high-protein beans, vegetables, grains, seeds, nuts, or fruit instead of planting export crops like tea, coffee, and cocoa, or raising animal feed for livestock, would help eliminate hunger.[39]

Food security and land access are directly related, even if the land is not irrigated or of the highest quality. Ownership of even a few acres provides incentive for improved land decisions regarding irrigation, crop rotation, land fallowing (plowed, but unplanted, land), and appropriate soil management.[40] Landownership is part of a long-term solution to a very complex problem. However, in the short term, remarkable progress is being made by providing access to land for women and their families for the purpose of growing food and planting gardens.

Most people think providing food is the primary means of reducing hunger, but safe water is equally important. The World Health Organization estimates that 88 percent of all diarrheal illnesses in the world are attributable to inadequate water or sanitation.[41] More than 2.6 billion people (40 percent of the world's population) lack basic sanitation facilities, and over 1 billion people drink unsafe water.[42] The consequences of unsanitary conditions are enormous. Thousands of children become ill or die each month from dehydration-related diseases, and adult workers are less productive when they are ill themselves or caring for family members. Entire communities are often at risk for health problems from drinking contaminated water.

Some innovative solutions are being proposed to alleviate the world's water problems. For example, in some African villages, solar energy is used to thermally purify the water supply. Water is poured into plastic jugs, then the jugs are placed on black-covered roofs and allowed to heat for several hours. If the temperature of the water exceeds 50°C (122°F), it becomes safe to drink. The heat from solar radiation effectively destroys common waterborne bacteria such as cholera, typhoid, and dysentery.[43] This example of technology is available, inexpensive, and accessible in many countries with a warm climate.

Other water sanitation solutions are more complex. They include chlorination of water, irrigation technology, river diversion projects, piped water systems, and the presence of community wells. Sustained economic development for a country or a community depends on a reliable, sanitary water supply.

Fortification of Foods

Food fortification can help alleviate micronutrient deficiencies. Because they are the most commonly deficient (see Table 14.4), iodine, iron, and vitamin A are the three nutrients most often added to foods. For food fortification to work, the foods chosen to carry these extra nutrients must be a staple in the community's food supply (and therefore eaten often) and consistently available. The food should also be shelf stable

Access to clean drinking water is just as important as adequate nutrition for human health.

and affordable. Rice, cereals, flours, salt, and even sugar are examples of foods that can be successfully fortified.

Because food fortification is inexpensive, yet enormously beneficial, fortification programs are being developed and implemented worldwide. Countries from China and Vietnam to South Africa and Morocco are fortifying foods such as salt, flour, oil, sugar, and soy sauce with iron, iodine, and vitamin A.[44]

Education Is Key

Education plays an important role in ensuring food security. Educated people are more likely to have increased economic and career opportunities, and less likely to fall into the trap of poverty. Literacy and education also build self-esteem and self-confidence, two qualities that help people overcome life's challenges.

Education also reduces poverty in other ways. For example, one study found that societies with a more educated population enjoyed:[45]

➤ Higher earning potential
➤ Improved sanitation
➤ More small businesses/rural enterprises
➤ Lower rates of infant mortality and improved child welfare
➤ Higher likelihood of technological advancement

The curriculum and format for international education are somewhat different in the developing world than in the developed world. International education that aims to improve rates of food security ought to focus on literacy, technical knowledge, agricultural skills, horticulture, health education, and the development of natural resources. Agricultural education and increased agricultural production in developing countries help create jobs, which increases income, which then lifts people out of poverty.[46]

Meanwhile, education in the developed world should focus on land management, improved crop yields, boosting nutrient levels within crops, and continued development of drought-resistant and insect-repelling plants.

The Take-Home Message Eradicating hunger benefits everyone, and local charities and community groups, including faith-based organizations, as well as corporations and governments, can provide aid and organize programs to alleviate hunger. Education of the world's population is also important, along with proper land management and proper crop selection.

Two Points of View

Food Aid vs Monetary Aid: Which Is More Effective for Alleviating Hunger?

As discussed in this chapter, food insecurity and hunger are major issues both in the United States and around the world. Numerous government agencies and nonprofit organizations attempt to remedy food insecurity with both food and monetary aid. However, experts differ as to which of these strategies is more effective.

Is the disbursement of food aid effective for alleviating hunger? Are cash payments more likely to be misused or abused? Read the two sets of arguments presented below, and then answer the questions to draw your own conclusions.

Food Aid

- Food aid has clearly had a significant role in reducing the loss of life during food emergencies in such countries as Ethiopia, Sudan, Somalia, Afghanistan, Rwanda, and Haiti.[1]

- Giving people money instead of food can upset local economies, fuel conflicts, and exclude the most needy.[2] For example, cash transfers can cause local food prices to rise, which can cause additional hardship for those who don't directly receive food aid.[3]

- Cash can be physically risky for those handling the money, and may disadvantage women who are less able to keep control of it.[4] In contrast, food aid that's given to women and children tends to be consumed by women and children.

- Food aid may be less vulnerable to corruption. Bags of maize cannot easily be swapped for cigarettes or beer, and stories of food being turned into fleets of Mercedes Benzes are few and far between.[5]

- Cash is not useful when there is nothing to buy. Refugees fleeing war and living in camps or earthquake victims living amid rubble are better benefited by receiving food directly.[6]

Monetary Aid

- Cash aid has larger positive effects on household welfare, and benefits extended family members and not just the direct recipients of aid.[7]

- In cases where food is locally available, monetary donations are more cost effective than food donations, because the cost of shipping food internationally usually exceeds the cost of purchasing food locally.[8]

- Flooding a market with food can drive down the price for local farmers and therefore provide a disincentive to local food production.[9]

- In the case of emergency food aid, it often arrives too late, it fails to be properly and efficiently distributed to the neediest regions and groups, and/or it often consists of the wrong commodities.[10]

- In the United States, political considerations can influence which types of food are sent and which companies provide it. U.S. law mandates that all food aid be grown by American farmers. More than half the $700 million in food provided through USAid in 2004 came from just four large food corporations.[11]

What do you think?

1. What are the underlying causes of food insecurity in many countries around the world? **2.** Which approach do you think is likely to yield greater benefits—food aid or monetary aid? **3.** Why is food aid currently the preferred method of the U.S. government? Is this likely to change?

Chapter Review

 Be a Nutrition Sleuth

The State of Food Insecurity in the United States

Do you know which U.S. states experience the highest rates of hunger and food insecurity? You can go to **www.pearsonhighered.com/blake** and complete the Nutrition Sleuth activity to find out!

 Get Real!

Making Good Decisions to Stay Food Secure

Would you know what to do in a situation where you faced a few days (or more) of being food insecure? Consider the scenarios in the Get Real! activity at **www.pearsonhighered.com/blake** and put your nutrition knowledge to work.

The Top Ten Points to Remember

1. Food security is the access by all people at all times to enough food for an active, healthy life. Food insecurity is the inability to secure adequate amounts of nutritious foods to meet one's need due to lack of available resources. Malnutrition is the state of being under- or overnourished, and chronic hunger leads to undernutrition. Despite abundant food production, many people in the United States and around the world suffer from food insecurity and malnutrition.

2. Causes of food insecurity in the United States include poverty, disease or disability, lack of education, and inadequate wages. Mental illness and/or drug and alcohol abuse sometimes lead to homelessness, which in turn often results in hunger. Individuals who are employed but still fall below the poverty line are sometimes referred to as the working poor.

3. Political sanctions, armed conflicts, crop failure, wasteful agricultural practices, and overpopulation factor into rates of food insecurity in many countries. When a country's economy is dependent on agriculture, natural disasters such as drought, floods, diseases, and insect infestations can have a dire impact on food production and levels of food insecurity.

4. Less than one-sixth of the world's population lives in developed nations that have a high standard of living. Many of the world's residents live in developing or underdeveloped countries and have access to fewer resources. Overpopulation in developing and underdeveloped countries can strain limited food resources.

5. Populations at increased risk of food insecurity and hunger include pregnant and lactating women, infants and children, the ill, and the elderly.

6. Effects of chronic hunger include stunted growth, wasting, impaired immune function, infections, anemia, and nutrient deficiencies. A nutrient deficiency can lead to serious, permanent health damage in both children and adults.

7. The "paradox of obesity" refers to the higher rates of obesity in certain age, race, and gender groups in the population of people who are food insecure. While there is no single cause, food insecurity could lead to overweight due to a lack of nutrition education; lack of available healthy foods; the low cost of calorie-dense, low-nutrient foods; overcompensation when food is plentiful; and lack of safe areas to be physically active.

8. Community and faith-based organizations can help end food insecurity by providing free food and meals and assistance programs to help people overcome poverty. Corporations and governments can invest in education programs that increase economic opportunity.

9. Food assistance programs such as SNAP, WIC, and the National School Lunch program, among others, provide assistance to those who experience food insecurity in the United States.

10. Local and national organizations, such as Feeding America, provide opportunities and food for those in their communities who are food insecure.

Test Your Knowledge

1. Food insecurity exists because
   a. not enough food is produced in the world to feed everyone adequately.
   b. food distribution is uneven, and some people do not have access to enough food.
   c. some people choose not to eat.
   d. none of the above are true.

2. What causes famine?
   a. poverty
   b. lack of education and economic opportunity
   c. war, natural disaster, or civil unrest
   d. using inappropriate farm machinery

3. In which of the following countries does food insecurity not exist?
   a. the United States and Canada
   b. Brazil and Argentina
   c. France and Germany
   d. Somalia and Ethiopia
   e. none of the above

4. What is the name of the common condition whereby vitamin A, iron, or iodine are consistently deficient in the diet?
   a. concealed concern
   b. hidden hunger
   c. dangerous dilemma
   d. neglected nutrition

5. Which of the following groups are especially vulnerable to food insecurity–related illness because of immature immune systems?
   a. infants and young children
   b. adolescents
   c. adult men
   d. adult women

6. Which of the following is a nutritional risk factor for older adults?
   a. increased metabolic rate
   b. rapid cell growth and turnover
   c. decreased sense of taste and smell
   d. increased energy needs

7. Which of these factors does *not* contribute to the "obesity paradox"?
   a. lack of access to lower-calorie, nutrient-dense foods, such as fresh fruits and vegetables
   b. genetic predisposition of impoverished individuals to being overweight or obese
   c. lack of outdoor space to play or exercise safely
   d. lack of education about what constitutes a healthy diet

8. Who are the "working poor"?
   a. all individuals classified as low income by the United States Department of Labor
   b. all individuals who fall outside the middle-class range of income
   c. individuals who are employed but have incomes that fall below the poverty line
   d. all minimum-wage workers

9. Which nutrients are most likely to be used to fortify food?
   a. vitamins D, E, and K
   b. sodium, potassium, and chloride
   c. magnesium, phosphorus, and sulfur
   d. iron, iodine, and vitamin A

10. Which of the following programs helps decrease food insecurity in the United States?
    a. Meals on Wheels
    b. soup kitchens
    c. Feeding America
    d. the National School Lunch program
    e. all of the above

Answers

1. (b) Although enough food is produced to feed everyone in the world, the distribution of the world's food supply is uneven, and people in some parts of the world do not have access to, or cannot afford, adequate food. Everyone needs to eat to survive.

2. (c) Famine is an extreme situation in which food crops cannot be produced because of war, civil unrest, or a natural disaster. Poverty and lack of education are factors that can lead to individual hunger, but don't generally cause crop failure.

3. (e) Whereas the developed nations of North America (the United States and Canada) and Western Europe have a higher standard of living and lower rates of food insecurity, many people in these countries are still poor, hungry, and/or malnourished. Citizens of the developing countries of South America and the underdeveloped countries of Africa are more likely to be poor and experience hunger.

4. (b) Hidden hunger refers to vitamin A, iron, or iodine deficiency. This condition affects more than 2 billion people in the world.

5. (a) Infants and young children have immature immune systems. Adolescents and adults have stronger (mature), better-functioning immune systems.

6. (c) Older adults sometimes lose interest in food or have a diminished appetite because they cannot enjoy food's smells or tastes. Older people have a decreased basal metabolic rate and experience slower cell growth and decreased energy requirements.

7. (b) Although a number of conditions contribute to rates of overweight and obesity among individuals who are food insecure, including lack of access to healthy foods, outdoor space, and nutrition education, poor individuals are not genetically more likely than their wealthier counterparts to be overweight or obese. Lifestyle factors, not genetics, are the predominant factors when it comes to gaining weight.

8. (c) The working poor includes individuals who are employed 27 or more weeks of each year, yet still have incomes below the official poverty line.

9. (d) Iron, iodine, and vitamin A are frequently used to fortify food because deficiencies of them are linked to many common and serious illnesses. Many of the other nutrients listed are important, but are not generally incorporated into food fortification programs.

10. (e) While soup kitchens, Meals on Wheels, Feeding America, and the National School Lunch Program are funded and run by different groups (including the government and private organizations), they all exist for the same purpose: to help alleviate food insecurity and hunger in the United States.

Web Resources

➡ For more on the state of food insecurity and hunger in the United States and around the world, visit the Bread for the World Institute at www.bread.org

➡ To learn more about one organization that is fighting global poverty, visit CARE at www.care.org

➡ To find out how the Food and Agriculture Organization of the United Nations leads international efforts to defeat hunger, visit www.fao.org

➡ To learn more about the efforts of the Global Health Council, visit the National Council for International Health website at www.globalhealth.org/

➡ To learn more about an international children's group, visit the UNICEF website at www.unicef.org

➡ For more about the World Health Organization, visit www.who.int/en/

Answers to Myths and Misperceptions

1. **False.** Despite living in a wealthy nation, many people in the United States grapple with food insecurity. Turn to page 519 to find out why.

2. **True.** Poverty does play a significant role in food insecurity around the world. Additional factors like war, overpopulation, and disease can also affect people's access to sufficient food. Find out more on page 520.

3. **False.** An overweight or obese individual can also be experiencing a chronic shortage of food. To learn more, turn to page 523.

4. **False.** The world's agricultural producers grow enough food to nourish every man, woman, and child on the planet. The challenge lies in distributing their products evenly. Learn more on page 525.

5. **True.** Children are dependent on the adults around them for adequate food, and therefore are more susceptible to food insecurity. Children are also more prone to long-term consequences of nutrient deficiencies. Find out more on page 528.

6. **True.** Older adults may have sufficient funds for food, but may experience food insecurity due to mobility issues or emotional problems. Learn more on page 528.

7. **False.** Poor nutrition affects *both* physical and mental development. Turn to page 528 to learn more.

8. **False.** You can help the hungry in your own backyard by volunteering your time or making a donation to your local food bank. Learn more on page 532.

9. **True.** Advances in agricultural processes are increasing the amount of food grown per acre of farmland. Find out more on page 534.

10. **True.** Fortifying foods can provide numerous nutrients that some populations wouldn't otherwise obtain. Learn which foods are being fortified on page 534.

15

True or False?

1. A **father's** health has no impact on the health of a developing fetus. ⓣⒻ p. 542

2. Women who are **obese** may have more trouble becoming pregnant than women who are normal weight or only somewhat overweight. ⓣⒻ p. 543

3. Drinking **red wine** is fine during pregnancy. ⓣⒻ p. 544

4. **Morning sickness** only happens between 8 A.M. and noon during the first trimester. ⓣⒻ p. 545

5. Pregnant women shouldn't **exercise**. ⓣⒻ p. 552

6. **Formula** is better for babies than breast milk. ⓣⒻ p. 556

7. Chubby babies should be put on **diets**. ⓣⒻ p. 565

8. Infants never need **supplements**. ⓣⒻ p. 565

9. Commercial **baby food** is always less healthy than homemade. ⓣⒻ p. 567

10. **Raw carrots** are a great way for an infant to get vitamin A. ⓣⒻ p. 567

See page 577 for answers to these Myths and Misperceptions.

Life Cycle

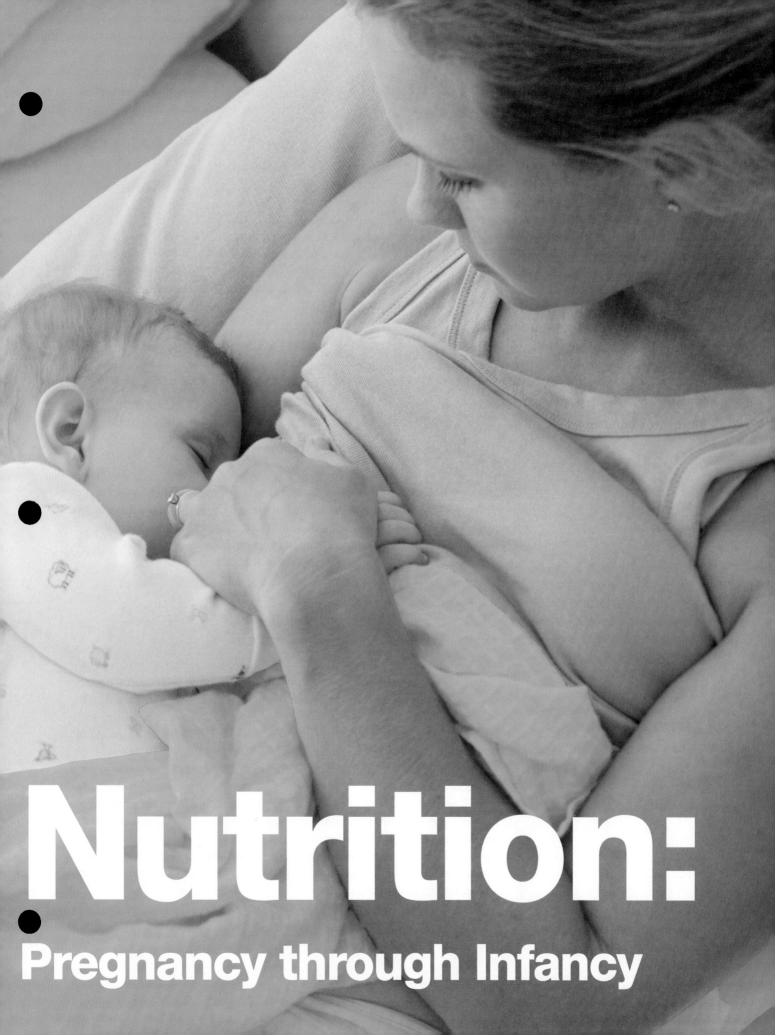

Nutrition:
Pregnancy through Infancy

Kathy is 28 years old and in the midst of a career change. Though she enjoys her job in social work, she's decided that technology is more exciting and has enrolled in several computer science classes at her local community college. Kathy and her husband had expected to start their family once she finished her degree, but were thrilled when she unexpectedly became pregnant. She delivered her bouncing baby boy during the middle of spring semester.

Kathy wants to finish the semester so that she can get a part-time job in a high-tech company. She also wants to breast-feed while attending morning classes on campus. How can Kathy ensure that her newborn will receive adequate nutrition? How can she overcome the challenges of nursing while attending classes? In this chapter, we discuss the importance of good nutrition and a healthy lifestyle both before and throughout a pregnancy. We also explore the nutritional needs of infants, and the best way to meet those needs.

Chapter Objectives

After reading this chapter, you will be able to:

1. Explain the diet and lifestyle factors for both men and women that most commonly affect the likelihood of conception.

2. Describe the key diet and lifestyle factors associated with a successful pregnancy.

3. Discuss the optimal weight gain for normal weight, overweight, and obese women during pregnancy.

4. Identify the supplements a pregnant woman might need to take to meet her increased nutrient needs.

5. Explain how potential complications of pregnancy, such as gestational diabetes and hypertension, are managed.

6. List special concerns of young and older mothers-to-be.

7. Describe the benefits of breast-feeding.

8. Explain the nutritional needs of infants.

What Nutrients and Behaviors Are Important Before Attempting a Healthy Pregnancy?

You're probably aware of at least a few things that women shouldn't do during pregnancy to support the baby's health. For instance, you probably know that pregnant women shouldn't smoke or drink alcohol. But it might surprise you to learn that, even before a couple attempt to get pregnant, they should both adopt some healthy behaviors, including several by the father-to-be. Let's review these now.

A Man's Diet and Lifestyle Affect the Health of His Sperm

The moment when a sperm fertilizes an egg is called **conception.** For conception to occur, the male's sperm has to be plentiful and motile: able to swim against obstacles to reach the waiting egg. Thus, men who hope to father a child should take note: Their lifestyle and dietary habits may affect the number and motility of their sperm. Smoking, alcohol and drug abuse, and obesity have been associated with decreased production and function of sperm.[1] Stopping smoking, striving for a healthy body weight, and abstaining from alcohol and other drugs or drinking only in moderation are all beneficial behaviors.

An adequate intake of zinc and folate has been associated with the production of healthy sperm. In addition, antioxidants, such as vitamins E and C and carotenoids, may help protect sperm from damage by free radicals.[2] Men should make sure to eat a balanced diet that contains adequate amounts of fruits and vegetables (containing antioxidants and folate), as well as whole grains, lean meats and dairy foods, legumes, and nuts (containing zinc).[3]

Are You Nutritionally Ready for a Healthy Pregnancy?

Both men and women should have healthy habits before becoming parents. Take the following self-assessment to see if you need some diet and lifestyle fine-tuning before trying to get pregnant.

For Both Men and Women

1. Are you overweight?
   Yes ☐ **No** ☐
2. Do you smoke?
   Yes ☐ **No** ☐
3. Do you abuse alcohol?
   Yes ☐ **No** ☐
4. Do you consume less than 400 micrograms of folic acid daily?
   Yes ☐ **No** ☐
5. Do you use any illicit drugs such as marijuana, cocaine, and/or Ecstasy?
   Yes ☐ **No** ☐

Additional Questions for Women Only

1. Do you drink alcohol?
   Yes ☐ **No** ☐
2. Do you take herbs or use herbal teas?
   Yes ☐ **No** ☐
3. Do you drink more than 12 ounce of caffeinated coffee or energy drinks or four cans of caffeinated soft drinks daily?
   Yes ☐ **No** ☐
4. Do you eat albacore tuna, swordfish, mackerel, tilefish, and/or shark?
   Yes ☐ **No** ☐

Answers

If you answered yes to any of these questions, read on to find out how these diet and lifestyle habits can negatively affect a pregnancy.

Women Need to Adopt a Healthy Lifestyle before Conception

If you have ever run a marathon or know someone who has, you know that a tremendous amount of effort and diligence goes into training for the event. Your commitment doesn't begin on the day of the race, but as far as a year in advance. In fact, the more time and effort the runner puts into preparing for the race, the better the results are likely to be.

Ask any woman who has had a baby and she will tell you that planning, carrying, and delivering a healthy child was the marathon of her life. The commitment to change not-so-healthy behaviors is an extremely important part of prepregnancy preparation.

Let's look at the specific nutritional and lifestyle adjustments a woman needs to make to improve her chances of conceiving a healthy baby.

Attain a Healthy Weight

Women who want to get pregnant should strive for a healthy weight *before* conception. Women who begin pregnancy at a healthy weight are likely to conceive more easily, have an uncomplicated pregnancy, and have an easier time nursing the baby.[4] In contrast, both women who are obese and women who are underweight may have a ⓣⒻ harder time getting pregnant, possibly because of irregular menstrual cycles. When they do become pregnant, they are at increased risk for a variety of health problems, some of which can affect the baby.

Get Plenty of Folic Acid

Folic acid is needed to create new cells and help the baby grow and develop properly. To reduce the risk for neural tube birth defects in infants, the mother-to-be should consume adequate amounts of folic acid at least one month prior to conception and during the early weeks of pregnancy. These birth defects occur very early in the pregnancy, typically three to four weeks after conception—a time when few women even know they are pregnant. For this reason, women who are capable of

conception The moment when a sperm fertilizes an egg.

Table 15.1

Fishing for a Healthy Baby

Pregnant and nursing women and women of childbearing age who may become pregnant should follow these guidelines for eating fish:

Do Not Eat	Limit	Enjoy
Shark Swordfish King mackerel Tilefish (golden bass or golden snapper)	• Albacore (white) tuna to no more than 6 oz weekly • Locally caught fish from nearby lakes, rivers, and coastal areas. Check local advisories regarding its safety before consuming it. If no advice is available, eat up to 6 oz weekly. Don't consume any other fish during that week.	Up to 12 oz weekly of fish with low levels of methylmercury, such as: Canned light tuna Cod Catfish Crab Pollack Salmon Scallops Shrimp

becoming pregnant and are planning to conceive should consume 400 micrograms of folic acid through supplements or fortified foods.

Moderate Fish and Caffeine Consumption

The Food and Drug Administration (FDA) recommends that women of childbearing age who may become pregnant avoid certain fish that may contain high amounts of the toxin *methylmercury*. This form of mercury can harm the nervous system of a developing fetus, especially during the first trimester of pregnancy. All fish contain some methylmercury, and Table 15.1 summarizes the fish consumption guidelines for prepregnant, pregnant, and lactating women.

Caffeine consumption may affect a woman's fertility. Research suggests that consuming 500 milligrams or more of caffeine daily may delay conception.[5] Although the mechanism by which caffeine affects fertility is unknown, to be safe, women who are trying to get pregnant should consume less than 200 milligrams of caffeine per day.[6] This means limiting brewed coffee and energy drinks to no more than about 12 ounces a day—or better yet, switching to decaffeinated versions of these drinks. See Table 15.2 for other common sources of caffeine in the diet.

Avoid Cigarettes and Other Toxic Substances

Cigarette smoking increases the risk of infertility, making conception more difficult.[7] If a female smoker is able to conceive, she'll face the difficulty of needing to quit smoking along with the many other challenges of pregnancy. The risks of maternal smoking are discussed later in this chapter.

Alcohol can affect a baby within weeks of conception, before a woman is aware that she is pregnant. For this reason, the surgeon general has recommended that all (T|F) women who may become pregnant abstain from alcohol.[8]

Smoking marijuana can reduce fertility in both men and women. Women who use it should speak with their health care provider about how to stop. They can also visit the National Drug and Alcohol Treatment Referral Routing Service at the website listed in the "Web Resources" section at the end of this chapter.

Now that you've learned which health habits are important to establish before trying to become parents, the next step is to learn what is needed for a healthy pregnancy.

Table 15.2

A Jolt of Caffeine

Beverage	Caffeine (mg)
Coffee (8 oz)	
Brewed, drip	85
Brewed, decaffeinated	3
Espresso (1 oz)	40
Tea (8 oz)	
Brewed	40
Iced	25
Soft drinks (8 oz)	24
"Energy drinks" (8 oz)	80
Hot cocoa (8 oz)	6
Chocolate milk (8 oz)	5
Milk chocolate (1 oz)	6

Source: National Toxicology Program, Department of Health and Human Services, www.cerhr.niehs.nih .gov; the International Food Information Council (IFIC), www.ific.org.

The Take-Home Message Good nutrition and healthy lifestyle habits are important for both men and women before conception. Smoking, alcohol abuse, and obesity are associated with the decreased production and function of sperm. Conception is easier for women when they are at a healthy weight. Women should consume adequate amounts of folic acid prior to getting pregnant and continue to take it during pregnancy. Women should also avoid consuming fish that may contain high amounts of methylmercury and should consume caffeine only in moderation. They should not smoke, drink alcohol, or take recreational drugs.

eLearn

Virtual Stages of Pregnancy

For a summary of the developments during each stage of pregnancy, visit www.womenshealth.gov/pregnancy/you-are-pregnant/stages-of-pregnancy.cfm.

What Nutrients and Behaviors Are Important in the First Trimester?

When a woman is pregnant, her diet must not only maintain her own health, but also foster the health and growth of her baby. She is truly eating for two. To help you appreciate the increased nutrient needs during pregnancy, let's examine how a pregnancy begins and how the developing child obtains nutrients from the mother.

During the First Trimester, the Fertilized Egg Develops into a Fetus

A full-term pregnancy is approximately 40 weeks long and is divided into three **trimesters.** The moment of conception marks the beginning of the first trimester. During the first few days of this 13-week period, the fertilized egg travels down the fallopian tube to embed itself in the lining of the woman's uterus (**Figure 15.1**). This enables the developing **embryo** to obtain nutrients via the **placenta,** an organ of common tissue between the mother and the growing embryo that develops in the mother's uterus (**Figure 15.2**). The placenta is attached to the growing baby via the **umbilical cord.** After the eighth week of pregnancy, the developing embryo is called a **fetus.** As the fetus develops, the mother's diet and lifestyle habits are critical in supporting and nurturing it.

By the end of the first trimester, the baby's liver is already forming red blood cells, the heart is pumping blood, the limbs are taking shape, and the brain is growing rapidly. With all this activity taking place, the fetus still weighs just ½ ounce and measures about 3 inches long. It has a lot more growing to do before being born.

Morning Sickness and Cravings Are Common

During the first trimester, the mother's body is also changing rapidly. She's beginning to notice some breast tenderness, a newly heightened sense of taste or smell, and perhaps some morning sickness or food cravings. One of the biggest myths of pregnancy is that morning sickness happens only in the morning. Ask any of the 80 percent of women who experience nausea and vomiting during pregnancy and many will tell you that they wish their symptoms ended by noon. The causes of morning sickness

trimesters The three time periods of pregnancy.

embryo Term that refers to a fertilized egg during the third through the eighth week of pregnancy. After the eighth week, the developing baby is called a fetus.

placenta The site of common tissue between the mother and growing embryo. The placenta is attached to the fetus with the **umbilical cord.**

fetus A developing embryo that is at least eight weeks old.

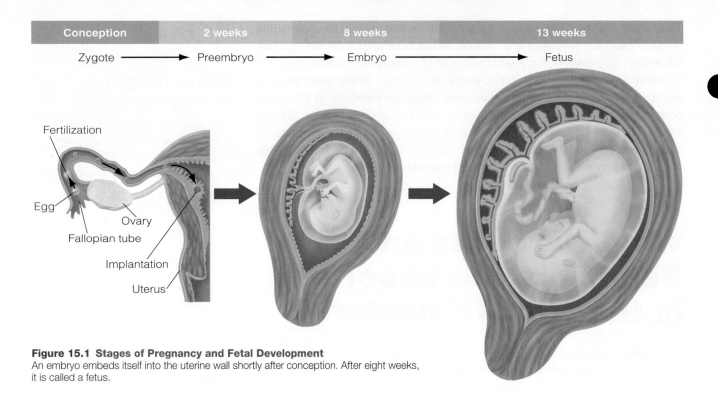

Figure 15.1 Stages of Pregnancy and Fetal Development
An embryo embeds itself into the uterine wall shortly after conception. After eight weeks, it is called a fetus.

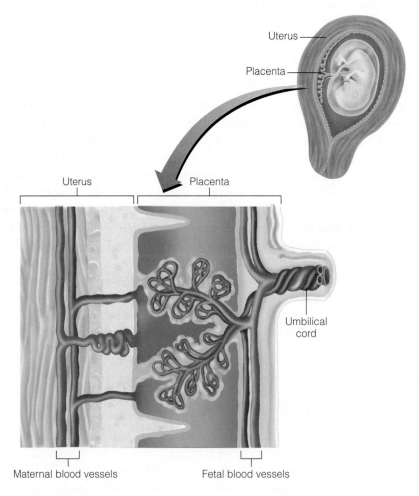

Figure 15.2 The Placenta
The placenta is the site of common tissue between the mother and the embryo where nutrients, oxygen, and waste products are exchanged.

are unknown, but fluctuating hormone levels may play a role.[9] There are no known dietary deficiencies that cause morning sickness, or diet changes that can prevent it. However, there are some behaviors that might help reduce it (see the Table Tips).

While some pregnant women develop an aversion to certain foods, such as coffee, tea, or fried or spicy foods, other women may have cravings for specific foods. Chocolate, citrus fruits, pickles, chips, and ice cream are foods that women commonly want when they are pregnant.[10] Sometimes women even crave and consume nonfood substances, such as cornstarch, clay, dirt, or baking soda. This condition, called *pica*, can lead to iron deficiency or the ingestion of toxic substances, such as lead.

Adequate Weight Gain Supports the Baby's Growth

Healthy women gain, on average, 27.5 pounds during the entire pregnancy.[11] This is the approximate amount of weight needed to support the growth of the baby (**Figure 15.3**). The amount of weight an individual woman gains should be enough to ensure a healthy 6.5- to 8.5-pound baby, but not so much that she increases her risk for complications during delivery (see Table 15.3).[12] Gaining excess weight will also make it more difficult to lose the weight once the baby is born, increases the likelihood of the mother's remaining overweight many years after childbirth, and also increases the risk that the baby will be obese later in life.[13] Because pregnant women typically gain only about 2 pounds in the entire first trimester, they do not yet need an increased intake of calories. However, a pregnant woman does have an increased need for certain nutrients immediately after conception.

The Need for Certain Nutrients Increases

From the moment of conception, a pregnant woman needs certain vitamins and minerals in higher quantities. Luckily, her body adjusts somewhat to help make this happen, by increasing absorption of certain nutrients and slowing down digestion to allow for the increased absorption. Many of the increased nutrient needs can be met easily through a healthy diet. However, the need for some nutrients, including folate, iron, zinc, copper, and calcium, is high enough (up to 50 percent higher) that it may not be met through food or increased absorption.

First trimester   Second trimester   Third trimester

Total weight gain ~30 lbs

- Maternal fat stores (~7 lbs)
- Uterus and breast (4 lbs)
- Blood (3–4 lbs)
- Fetus (~7 lbs)
- Placenta, amniotic fluid, and other fluids (~8 lbs)

Figure 15.3 Components of Weight Gain during Pregnancy
Healthy-weight women gain 25 to 35 pounds, on average, during pregnancy.

Table 15.3

Recommended Weight Gain during Pregnancy

Body Mass Index (BMI)	Recommended Weight Gain (in Pounds)
<18.5	28–40
18.5-24.9	25–35
25.0-29.9	15–25
>30.0	at least 15

Source: Institute of Medicine. 2009. Weight Gain during Pregnancy: Reexamining the Guidelines. www.iom.edu/Reports/2009/Weight-gain-during-pregnancy-reexamining-the-guidelines.aspx; L. Kaiser and L. Allen, "Position of the American Dietetic Association: Nutrition and Lifestyle for a Healthy Pregnancy Outcome," *Journal of the American Dietetic Association* 108 no. 3 (2008): 553–561.

Let's examine these specific nutrients individually:

> *Folate.* If a woman is conscientious about taking folic acid prior to conception and continues to take a supplement and/or consume folic-acid–fortified foods, she should be able to meet her increased needs for this vitamin. Foods high in folate include green leafy vegetables, citrus fruits and juices, and whole-grain products.

> *Iron.* Pregnant women need extra iron to make additional red blood cells, prevent anemia, and provide for fetal growth and development.[14] Although meat, fish, poultry, and enriched grains supply iron, the amount recommended during pregnancy is unlikely to be met from food alone, so a supplement is needed.[15] Many women are prescribed a prenatal supplement to help them meet their iron and other increased nutrient needs.

> *Zinc and copper.* Because iron can interfere with the absorption of other minerals, if a woman is taking more than 30 milligrams of iron daily, she should also take 15 milligrams of zinc and 2 milligrams of copper.[16] Both of these minerals are key to a growing baby's cell growth and development.

> *Calcium and vitamin D.* A pregnant woman will absorb more calcium from foods during pregnancy to offset the amount of calcium needed by the growing fetus, but she still needs to meet her own daily needs for calcium, as well as for vitamin D, to preserve bone mass and prevent osteoporosis later in life. One way to ensure an adequate calcium and vitamin D intake is to drink nutrient-dense milk as the beverage of choice, rather than nutritionally empty sodas.

Other nutrients are also of concern during pregnancy, especially if the mother is a vegetarian or vegan. Pregnant women, especially vegetarians, should be mindful about meeting their need for essential fatty acids, which are important in the formation of new tissues, particularly those of the central nervous system. Choline intake is important during pregnancy and when nursing the baby. Choline is needed for healthy cells to divide and grow, especially in the brain.[17] Vegans who don't consume any animal products need to make sure that they are getting a reliable source of vitamin B_{12}.

While it's important that pregnant women meet their nutrient needs, it is equally important that they not consume too much of some nutrients. Too much vitamin A can be toxic and increase the risk for birth defects, especially when taken during the first trimester. Pregnant women who take a supplement should consume no more than 5,000 IU (1,500 micrograms) of preformed vitamin A daily, which is 100 percent of the Daily Value (DV) listed on the label. Most prenatal supplements have higher levels of folate, iron, and calcium than regular supplements and may be a good option for women who are in high-risk groups such as teens, women carrying multiple fetuses, older women, and women who do not eat an adequate diet.

To assist women in having healthy pregnancies, the USDA has created Daily Food Plans for Pregnancy and Breastfeeding (available at ChooseMyPlate.gov).[18] The site includes menu-planning tools that can be used to show how much and what women need to eat and provides links to additional topics and advice.

Figure 15.4 summarizes the nutrient needs of pregnant women and compares them with a well-balanced diet. As you can see, a balanced diet can meet the majority of a pregnant woman's nutrient needs.

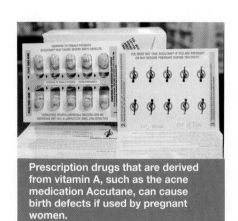

Prescription drugs that are derived from vitamin A, such as the acne medication Accutane, can cause birth defects if used by pregnant women.

Figure 15.4 Nutrient Needs during Pregnancy
A balanced 2,000-calorie diet can meet most of a pregnant woman's increased nutrient needs even before she adds calories in her second and third trimesters.

Vegetables	Fruits	Grains	Protein	Dairy	Oils
2.5 cups	2 cups	6 oz eq	5.5 oz eq	3 cups	6 tsp

Nutrient	Recommended DRI for Nonpregnant Women Age 19–50 Years	Recommended Nutrient Intake During Pregnancy
Protein	46 g	71 g
Carbohydrates	130 g	175 g (minimum)
Linoleic acid	12 g	13 g
Alpha-linolenic acid	1.1 g	1.4 g
Dietary folate equivalents	400 mcg	600 mcg*
Thiamin	1.1 mg	1.4 mg
Riboflavin	1.1 mg	1.4 mg
Niacin equivalents	14 mg	18 mg
Vitamin B_6	1.3–1.5 mg	1.9 mg
Vitamin B_{12}	2.4 mg	2.6 mg
Vitamin C	75 mg	85 mg
Vitamin E	15 mg	15 mg
Vitamin A	700 mcg	770 mcg
Calcium	1,000 mg	1,000 mg
Magnesium	310–320 mg	350–360 mg
Copper	0.9 mg	1.0 mg
Iron	18 mg	27 mg†
Phosphorus	700 mg	700 mg
Zinc	8 mg	11 mg
Calories	**2,000–2,200‡**	**§**

* Supplemented and/or fortified foods are recommended.
† A supplement is recommended.
‡ Varies depending upon activity level and weight.
§ Doesn't increase until second and third trimester.

Pregnancy Increases the Risk for Foodborne Illness

During pregnancy, a woman's immune system is weakened and the fetus's immune system is undeveloped, both of which set the stage for potential difficulties in fighting off pathogens that can cross the placenta. The bacterium *Listeria monocytogenes,* for example, may cause miscarriages, premature labor, low birth weight, developmental problems, and even infant death. Meat and dairy foods are most likely to be contaminated. Pasteurization kills *Listeria,* but unpasteurized soft cheeses, such as Camembert, Brie, and blue cheeses, may be contaminated. Deli-style luncheon meats, salami, and paté may also harbor bacteria. Thus, pregnant women should avoid these foods.

Raw meats and fish are more likely to carry pathogens and should be handled with care or avoided during pregnancy. Sushi and sashimi, for example, contain raw fish and are more likely to contain parasites or bacteria. Pregnant women should also avoid undercooked meat, fish, or poultry; unpasteurized milk, cheese, and juices; and raw sprouts.

Food that may carry pathogens, such as sashimi, should be avoided by pregnant women for their own safety and the safety of the fetus.

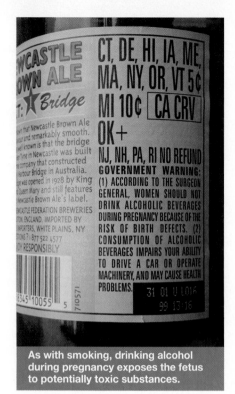

As with smoking, drinking alcohol during pregnancy exposes the fetus to potentially toxic substances.

Pregnant Women Should Avoid Many Other Substances

We noted earlier that smoking decreases the chance that a woman will conceive. When a woman continues smoking during pregnancy, her infant will weigh a half-pound less, on average, than infants of nonsmokers, and will be at an increased risk of being born prematurely or dying. Prenatal exposure to smoke can also increase the risk for sudden infant death syndrome (SIDS)—the unexplained death of an infant less than 1 year of age—and may stunt the infant's growth. Even secondhand smoke can affect the health of a mom-to-be and her infant. Exposure to passive smoke can affect the infant's ability to grow properly.[19] Thus, pregnant women and new mothers should avoid work, home, or social environments where they are exposed to secondhand smoke.

As you read in Chapter 9, drinking alcohol during pregnancy can lead to fetal alcohol syndrome (FAS) in the baby. Children exposed to even low levels of alcohol during pregnancy can be born with learning and behavioral disabilities. Because there is no known safe level of alcohol consumption, pregnant women need to abstain completely to eliminate the chance of harming the baby.

When used during pregnancy, illicit drugs can increase the risk for miscarriage, preterm labor, a **low birth weight baby,** and birth defects.[20] After birth, the baby may experience drug withdrawal symptoms, such as excessive crying, trembling, and seizures, as well as long-term problems, such as heart defects and behavioral and learning problems.

Pregnant women should restrict their intake of caffeine, which can be passed on to the fetus (as can anything else consumed). Research studies to date suggest that caffeine intake of less than 150 milligrams daily, or the amount in 12 ounces (1½ cups) of coffee, doesn't increase the risk for miscarriage or birth defects. However, some studies suggest that intakes greater than 200 milligrams (found in about two cups of coffee) daily, especially if the pregnant woman is also smoking and/or drinking alcohol, may increase the risk for miscarriages.[21]

The Importance of Critical Periods

Because the early part of pregnancy is when the main body systems and major organs are forming, it is the most critical time for the health of the fetus. Cells multiply, differentiate, and establish functional tissues and organs during various **critical periods** in the first trimester of pregnancy. These periods of rapid cellular activity are highly vulnerable to nutritional deficiencies, toxins, and other potentially harmful factors (or insults) and are when the risk for spontaneous termination is the greatest.

The harm that results from the influence of a toxin or deficiency during a critical period is often irreversible, and can affect future developmental stages (see **Figure 15.5**). For example, persons conceived during periods of famine not only have a higher cumulative incidence of heart disease, but also an earlier onset of the disease. Inadequate fetal growth may have later, long-term effects on hypertension, glucose tolerance, and lipid metabolism. Both micronutrient and macronutrient malnutrition may contribute to the onset of heart disease.[22] Inadequate iron intake in early pregnancy during the critical period for the central nervous system may cause poor cognitive development.[23]

The mother's optimal nutrition during critical periods of pregnancy may also prevent or delay a child's risk of chronic diseases, such as heart disease and diabetes, later in life. There is growing evidence that maternal nutrition can alter how genes

low birth weight baby A baby weighing less than 5½ pounds at birth.

critical periods Developmental stages during which cells and tissue rapidly grow and differentiate to form body structures.

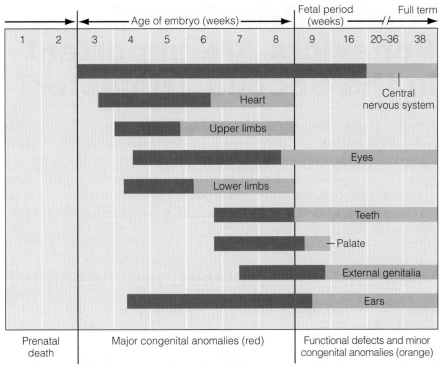

| 1 | 2 | 3 | 4 | 5 | 6 | 7 | 8 | 9 | 16 | 20–36 | 38 |

Age of embryo (weeks)

Fetal period (weeks)

Full term

Heart

Upper limbs

Eyes

Lower limbs

Teeth

Palate

External genitalia

Ears

Central nervous system

Prenatal death

Major congenital anomalies (red)

Functional defects and minor congenital anomalies (orange)

*Red indicates highly sensitive periods when major anomalies can occur.

Figure 15.5 Critical Periods of Development
The damage caused by toxins or lack of nutrients during pregnancy can vary according to the stage of fetal development. Damage done during critical periods may be irreversible.

are expressed, and adverse events during critical periods of gestation can persist into adulthood.[24] This phenomenon is part of an emerging area of research into metabolic or fetal programming. The relationship between maternal nutrition, metabolic fetal programming, and adult-onset chronic disease is supported by studies showing that inadequate nutrient intake during pregnancy predisposes the child to metabolic diseases in adulthood.[25] These impacts may even extend to the child's future children.

The Take-Home Message A pregnancy is divided into trimesters. During the first trimester, the fertilized egg develops into an embryo and eventually into a fetus. The placenta is the site of common tissue between the fetus and the mother, and is attached to the baby via the umbilical cord. Many women experience morning sickness and cravings during the first trimester. The average woman should gain from 25 to 35 pounds during pregnancy, depending on her prepregnancy weight. The needs for folate, iron, zinc, and calcium increase significantly during pregnancy. Pregnant women should avoid excess amounts of preformed vitamin A. They also need to avoid foods that may contain pathogens. Caffeine intake should be limited to no more than 150 milligrams daily. Tobacco, alcohol, and illicit drugs should be avoided throughout pregnancy but particularly in the first trimester. Potentially harmful toxins and other substances can cause irreversible damage to the fetus, especially during critical periods.

1 whole-wheat English muffin
2 tbs peanut butter
5 baby carrots

340
total calories

The extra calorie and nutrient needs of the second and third trimesters can be met with nutrient-dense diet additions.

What Nutrients and Behaviors Are Important in the Second Trimester?

For many pregnant women, the nausea and fatigue of the first trimester subside during the second trimester, and the appetite begins to increase. The baby is growing rapidly, and the mother's body is changing to accommodate this growth (see Figure 15.3 on page 547). The fetus is just under 2 pounds and about 13 inches long by the end of this trimester. During this period of growth, the mother needs to focus on consuming adequate calories and nutrients; to exercise, if possible; and to be aware of potential complications.

Pregnant Women Need to Consume Adequate Calories, Carbohydrate, and Protein to Support Growth

Pregnant women should consume an additional 340 calories daily during the second trimester and gain slightly less than a pound per week. A whole-wheat English muffin topped with peanut butter and a few baby carrots fits these requirements nutritiously, as do many other meal combinations. This combination of foods also provides plenty of essential fatty acids, carbohydrates, fiber, zinc, iron, and protein—the nutrients that a woman needs more of during pregnancy.

Pregnant women need a minimum of 175 grams of carbohydrates per day (versus 130 grams for nonpregnant women) to cover the amount of glucose needed for both the developing brain and the energy needs of the fetus. Protein needs also increase by about 35 percent, to about 71 grams daily, during the second and third trimesters. As you can see from Figure 15.4 on page 549, women usually meet this higher protein demand by eating a balanced diet.

Daily Exercise Is Important

Daily exercise during pregnancy can help improve sleep, lower the risk of ⓉⒻ hypertension and diabetes, prevent backaches, help relieve constipation, shorten labor, and allow women to return more quickly to their prepregnancy weight after delivery. Exercise can also help provide an emotional boost by reducing stress, depression, and anxiety.[26]

The American College of Obstetricians and Gynecologists recommends 30 minutes or more of moderate exercise on most, if not all, days of the week, as long as the woman doesn't have any medical issues or complications.[27] Pregnant women should check with their health care providers before exercising to see if it is appropriate. Low-impact activities, such as walking, swimming, and stationary cycling, are recommended (Table 15.4). See the Table Tips for more on exercising while pregnant.

Table 15.4

Safe and Unsafe Exercises during Pregnancy

Safe Activities	Unsafe Activities (Contact Sports and High-Impact Activities)
Walking	Hockey (field and ice)
Stationary cycling	Basketball
Low-impact aerobics	Football
Swimming	Soccer
Dancing	Gymnastics
	Horseback riding
	Skating
	Skiing (snow and water)
	Vigorous racquet sports
	Weight lifting

Source: T. Wang, and B. Apgar, "Recommendations for Sports Activities during Pregnancy," *American Family Physician* 57 (1998): 1846–1856. Used by permission of the American Academy of Family Physicians.

Potential Complications: Gestational Diabetes and Hypertension

Sometimes a pregnant woman develops high blood glucose levels and is diagnosed with **gestational diabetes** (*gestation* = pregnancy-related). This type of diabetes occurs in about 7 percent of pregnancies in the United States and manifests after approximately the twentieth week.[28] A pregnant woman should be tested for gestational diabetes during her second trimester.

Though the cause of gestational diabetes is still unknown, hormones from the placenta appear to lead to insulin resistance in the mother, which in turn causes hyperglycemia. This elevated blood glucose crosses the placenta, stimulating the baby's pancreas to make more insulin, which leads to the storage of excess glucose as fat and can result in **macrosomia** (*macro* = large, *somia* = body), or a large baby.[29] A larger-than-normal baby can increase the risk of injury to the baby's shoulders during delivery or of having to have a cesarean delivery.[30] Gestational diabetes also increases the risk of the baby developing **jaundice,** breathing problems, and birth defects.[31] Because the baby is producing extra insulin during pregnancy, this hormone is elevated after birth, causing a rapid drop in blood glucose levels, which can cause hypoglycemia.[32]

Certain factors can increase a woman's risk for gestational diabetes:

➤ Being overweight
➤ Being over 25 years old
➤ Having a history of higher-than-normal blood glucose levels
➤ Having a family history of diabetes
➤ Being of Hispanic, African-American, Native American, or Pacific Islander descent
➤ Having previously given birth to a very large baby or a stillborn baby
➤ Having had gestational diabetes in the past

According to the National Institute of Child Health and Human Development, if a woman has two or more of these risk factors, she is at high risk for developing gestational diabetes. If she has one risk factor, she is at an average risk, whereas if she doesn't have any of these, she is at low risk.[33] Eating healthfully, maintaining a healthy weight, and exercising regularly can help reduce the risk of developing diabetes during pregnancy.

Hypertension (high blood pressure) during pregnancy can damage the woman's kidneys and other organs and increase the risk for low birth weight and premature delivery.[34] It occurs in about 6 to 8 percent of pregnancies in the United States.[35] Some women have hypertension prior to conceiving, but others develop it during their pregnancy.

Pregnancy-induced hypertension includes *gestational hypertension, preeclampsia,* and *eclampsia,* each progressively more medically serious. Gestational hypertension is more likely to occur halfway through pregnancy and be a sign of preeclampsia. Preeclampsia (also known as toxemia) occurs when the pregnant woman has hypertension and severe edema, and her urine contains protein, which is a signal of damage to her kidneys.[36] *Note:* Though some swelling or edema in a woman's feet and ankles is normal during pregnancy, the dramatic edema seen in preeclampsia is visible in her face and hands and can cause weight gain of more than 2 pounds a week.[37] The cause of preeclampsia is not known, but it is dangerous to the baby because less oxygen- and nutrient-rich blood is reaching the placenta.[38] Women who have hypertension prior to pregnancy or develop it during pregnancy, are overweight, under the age of 20 or over the age of 40, are carrying more than one baby, or have diabetes are at higher risk of developing preeclampsia.[39] If left untreated, preeclampsia can lead to

gestational diabetes Diabetes that occurs in women during pregnancy.

macrosomia A large baby, weighing more than 8 pounds, 13 oz.

jaundice A yellowish coloring of the skin due to the presence of bile pigments in the blood.

pregnancy-induced hypertension A category of hypertension that includes *gestational hypertension* (occurs in pregnancy in a woman without a prior history of high blood pressure), *preeclampsia* (hypertension, severe edema, and protein loss occur), and *eclampsia* (can result in seizures; may be extremely dangerous for mother and baby).

eclampsia, which can cause seizures in the mother and is a major cause of death of women during pregnancy.[40] The only cure for preeclampsia and eclampsia is to deliver the baby. However, delivery too early (before 32 weeks) is unsafe for the baby. Women are often confined to bed rest, managed with medications, and even hospitalized to treat preeclampsia until the baby can be safely born.[41] Calcium supplements had been proposed to prevent preeclampsia, but research doesn't support that it reduces the risk, especially if the mother's diet is adequate in this mineral.[42] Some research suggests that antioxidants, specifically vitamins C and E, may reduce the risk, but more research is needed.[43]

The Take-Home Message Pregnant women need to consume an additional 340 calories daily during the second trimester. A varied selection of nutrient-dense foods will easily meet increased calorie needs. Exercise can provide numerous benefits during pregnancy. Some women develop gestational diabetes and pregnancy-induced high blood pressure and need to be monitored closely by a health care professional.

What Nutrients and Behaviors Are Important in the Third Trimester?

By the end of the third trimester, a pregnant woman should be taking in an extra 450 calories daily and be gaining about one pound per week (adding a banana to the English muffin, peanut butter, and carrot snack will increase this to about 450 calories). At the end of the third trimester, the baby will weigh approximately 7 pounds. The mother is likely to have a harder time getting around due to her expanding body. As the growing baby exerts pressure on her intestines and stomach, and hormonal changes slow the movement of food through the gastrointestinal (GI) tract, she may experience **heartburn.** To minimize heartburn, pregnant women should eat frequent, small meals and avoid foods that may irritate the esophagus, such as spicy or highly seasoned foods. They also shouldn't lie down after meals, and they should elevate their heads during sleep.[44]

Constipation is also common near the end of pregnancy. The slower movement of food through the GI tract and a tendency toward less physical activity are factors. The large amount of iron in prenatal supplements can also contribute to constipation.[45] Eating more fiber-rich foods, such as oatmeal, bran cereals, beans, whole grains, fruits, and vegetables, along with drinking plenty of fluids, can help keep things moving along.

Pregnancy also makes a woman more prone to hemorrhoids, because the growing uterus puts pressure on the pelvic veins and the large vein on the right side of the body that receives blood from the lower limbs. The increased pressure can slow the return of blood from the lower half of the body, which causes the veins below the uterus to become swollen.

The Take-Home Message During the third trimester, a woman needs an additional 450 calories per day and should continue gaining about a pound per week. Heartburn and constipation commonly occur during the third trimester. Eating smaller meals and consuming more fiber can help.

Walking is one form of exercise that is safe for both mother and baby.

heartburn A burning sensation in the esophagus. Heartburn is usually caused by the reflux of gastric contents from the stomach into the esophagus.

What Special Concerns Might Younger or Older Mothers-to-Be Face?

Pregnancy and childbirth place demands on the body of a mother-to-be no matter what her age, but women who become pregnant during their teenage years face particular challenges. Women over the age of 35 also face some additional challenges.

More than 435,000 babies are born to young girls annually.[46] Because a teenage girl's body is still growing, she has higher nutrient needs than does an adult woman. In addition, teenage girls, like many adolescents, are more likely to eat on the run, skip meals, eat less-nutrient-dense snacks, and consume inadequate amounts of whole grains, fruits, vegetables, and lean dairy products. Add this unbalanced diet to the increased needs of pregnancy, and these young girls are likely to fall short of many of their nutrient requirements, especially iron, folic acid, calcium, and potentially even calories. In some cases, a teenage girl may delay prenatal care because she is in denial of the pregnancy or fears telling others. She may also restrict her calorie intake to avoid weight gain as she attempts to hide her pregnancy.

Teenage mothers are also more likely to develop pregnancy-induced hypertension and deliver premature and low birth weight babies, putting the baby at risk for health problems. They are more likely to engage in unhealthy lifestyle habits such as smoking, drinking alcohol, and taking illicit drugs, all of which can compromise the baby's health.[47]

Women who delay pregnancy until their 30s or beyond, as many now do (in fact, the number of births for women over age 35 has risen 40 percent since 1990), may also face additional challenges.[48] Fertility typically begins to decline starting in a woman's early 30s, so conception may take longer. Women are not only at higher risk of having diabetes and high blood pressure after the age of 35, but also are at a higher risk of developing these conditions during pregnancy. Older mothers are also more physiologically likely to conceive multiples and use fertility-enhancing techniques. With multiple births comes a set of increased risks. Multiples are more likely to be born prematurely, and, as a result, are more likely to experience complications and low birth weight. Siblings who are born in close succession, less than a year apart, are also more likely to be born with a low birth weight than are those who are born a year or more apart.

Older mothers should try to achieve a healthy body weight prior to conception, avoid smoking, eat a balanced diet before and during pregnancy, and consume adequate amounts of folic acid. As with all pregnant women, they should limit their caffeine intake and avoid alcohol and illicit drugs.

Regardless of her age, as her due date draws near, an expectant mother needs to decide how to nourish her newborn after delivery: should she breast-feed or use formula? Let's look at both of these options next.

Due to additional steps taken to ensure pregnancy, older mothers often deliver multiples—twins, triplets, or quads.

The Take-Home Message Teens who become pregnant are at higher risk of developing hypertension and delivering a premature and low birth weight baby. Because a teen is still growing, she will likely have a hard time meeting both her own nutrient needs and her baby's unless she is diligent about eating a well-balanced diet. Women over age 35 may have a harder time conceiving and are at higher risk for high blood pressure and diabetes during pregnancy.

What Is Breast-Feeding and Why Is It Beneficial?

A woman who has just given birth will begin a period of **lactation;** that is, her body will produce milk to nourish her new infant. Milk production is stimulated by the infant's suckling at the mother's nipple. Signals sent from the nipple to the hypothalamus in the mother's brain prompt the pituitary gland to release two hormones: prolactin and oxytocin. Prolactin causes milk to be produced in the breast, while oxytocin causes the milk to be released, or **let down,** so the infant can receive it through the nipple (see **Figure 15.6**).[49]

The old adage "breast is best" when it comes to nourishing (T)(F) an infant is still true. Through **breast-feeding,** or nursing, mothers provide food that is uniquely tailored to meet their infant's nutritional needs in an easily digestible form. Breast-feeding also provides many other advantages for both the mother and the baby.

Newborn babies may eat as often as 12 times a day!

Breast-Feeding Provides Physical, Emotional, and Financial Benefits for Mothers

Breast-feeding provides short- and long-term benefits for both mother and child. During infancy, breast-feeding can be cheaper, safer, and more convenient than bottle-feeding. The long-term health and emotional benefits can last for years after infancy.

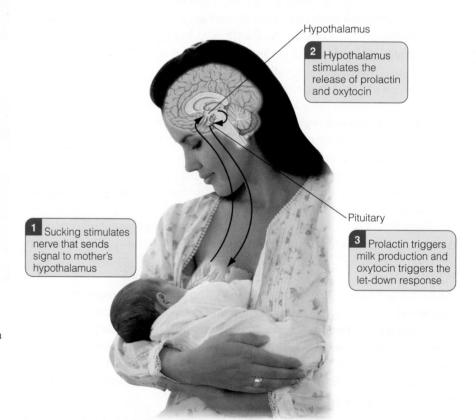

Hypothalamus

2 Hypothalamus stimulates the release of prolactin and oxytocin

1 Sucking stimulates nerve that sends signal to mother's hypothalamus

Pituitary

3 Prolactin triggers milk production and oxytocin triggers the let-down response

Figure 15.6 The Let-Down Response

lactation The production of milk in a woman's body after childbirth, and the period during which it occurs. The baby receives the milk through **breast-feeding**.

let-down The release of milk from the mother's breast to feed the baby.

Breast-Feeding Helps with Pregnancy Recovery and Reduces the Risk of Some Chronic Diseases

In addition to stimulating the release of breast milk, the hormone oxytocin stimulates contractions in the uterus, which helps the organ return to its prepregnancy size and shape. Breast-feeding also reduces blood loss in the mother after delivery.[50] Breast-feeding may help some women return to their prepregnancy weight and manage their postpregnancy weight.

Breast-feeding, especially if it is done exclusively (not combining it with formula-feeding), can also help delay the return of the menstrual cycle, which may decrease fertility. However, this does not mean that women who breast-feed their newborns should assume they won't get pregnant. They still need to take precautions if they wish to avoid pregnancy.

Women in their 20s who breast-feed for up to two years may reduce the risk of breast and ovarian cancer. Breast-feeding has also been shown to reduce the risk of hip fractures later in life, increase bone density, and reduce the risk of type 2 diabetes.[51]

Breast Milk Is Less Expensive and More Convenient than Formula

A new mother who opts to buy formula rather than breast-feed her baby will spend an estimated $1,200 for the first year's worth of powdered formula (more if she buys the ready-to-feed variety). The costs associated with breast-feeding, in contrast, are primarily associated with buying the extra food a woman needs to produce breast milk, and come in at about $300 for the first year.[52] In other words, making breast milk is about 75 percent cheaper than buying powdered formula. One study concluded that the national cost of *not* breast-feeding infants in their first year of life is as much as $13 billion dollars.[53]

There are other costs associated with formula-feeding beyond the price of the product. For example, there are substantial environmental costs of dealing with the 550 million formula cans and 800,000 pounds of paper packaging and waste that are disposed of in landfills each year, as well as costs associated with the energy needed to properly clean the feeding bottles. In addition, the United States Department of Agriculture estimates that $36 billion dollars in health care costs could be saved per year if breast-feeding rates were increased to the levels recommended by the Surgeon General.[54] For the family, the environment, and society as a whole, breast-feeding is cheaper than formula-feeding.

Finally, feeding from the breast is more convenient than bottle-feeding because the milk is always sterile and at the right temperature, and there isn't any need to prepare bottles. The mother also doesn't need to prepare the milk before feeding, and she has less cleanup to do afterward.

Breast-Feeding Promotes Bonding

The close interaction between mother and child during nursing promotes a unique bonding experience. The physical contact helps the baby feel safe, secure, and emotionally attached to the mother.[55] Breast-feeding may also play a role in reducing incidences of infants being abandoned by their mothers.[56]

Breast-Feeding Provides Nutritional and Health Benefits for Infants

There are more than 200 compounds in breast milk that benefit infants. Numerous research studies have indicated that breast-feeding provides nutritional and health advantages that can last years beyond infancy.[57] It is one of the most important strategies for improving an infant's long-term health.

Infant formula is available in several forms and varies in cost and ingredients. Infant formula is highly regulated by the FDA, so any formula on the market in the United States can be considered safe.

Breast Milk Is Best for an Infant's Unique Nutritional Needs

The nutritional composition of breast milk changes as the infant grows. Right after birth, a new mother produces a carotenoid-rich, yellowish fluid called **colostrum** that has little fat but a lot of protein, vitamin A, and minerals. Colostrum also contains antibodies that help protect the infant from infections, particularly in the digestive tract.

Four to seven days later, actual breast milk begins to flow. Breast milk is high in lactose, fat, and B vitamins, and lower in fat-soluble vitamins, sodium, and other minerals. These nutrients are proportionally balanced to enhance their absorption.[58] Breast milk is low in protein so as not to stress the infant's immature kidneys with excessive amounts of nitrogen waste products. The protein is also mostly in the form of alpha-lactalbumin, which is easier for the infant to digest.[59] The nutrient composition of breast milk continues to change as the baby grows and his or her needs change.[60] By the time the infant has breast-fed for six months, the mother's milk will contain less protein than it did during the first month.[61]

Breast-Feeding Protects Against Infections, Allergies, and Chronic Diseases and May Enhance Brain Development

Breast milk provides the infant with a disease-fighting boost until the baby's own immune system matures. Research supports that breast-feeding decreases the risk and severity of diarrhea and other intestinal disorders, respiratory infections, meningitis, ear infections, and urinary tract infections.[62]

One protein in breast milk, lactoferrin, protects the infant against bacteria, viruses, fungi, and inflammation by binding with iron, and making it unavailable to the bacteria that need it to flourish.[63] Lactoferrin also inhibits the ability of bacteria to stick to the walls of the intestines. Bacteria must adhere to the intestinal wall to flourish.

Breast milk provides other beneficial compounds, such as antioxidants, hormones, enzymes, and growth factors that play a role in the development of the infant and protect the baby from pathogens, inflammation, diseases, and allergies.[64] Some research suggests that breast milk may also protect against SIDS, asthma, leukemia, heart disease, and diabetes mellitus.[65]

Breast-feeding, especially if continued beyond six months, may help reduce the risk of childhood obesity. The reason for this isn't clear, but could be associated with the tendency of breast-fed infants to gain less weight during the first year of life than formula-fed infants. The lower weight gain may be due to breast-fed infants having more control over when they start and stop eating than their bottle-fed counterparts.[66] Babies at the breast will rely on their internal cues to eat until they are full, and then stop eating. Bottle-fed babies, in contrast, may find their internal cues overruled as the parent or caregiver feeds them until the bottle is empty.[67] This relationship, whereby the caregiver controls how much food is consumed, rather than relying on the child's internal cues, could lead to chronic overfeeding.[68]

Lastly, breast milk may help infants with their intellectual development. Breast milk is rich in two unsaturated fatty acids, docosahexaenoic acid (DHA) and arachidonic acid (AA), which are important for the development of the central nervous system, particularly the brain (see Chapter 5). Research suggests that breast-fed infants may have greater cognitive function, measured by IQ and academic success in school, than formula-fed babies, which may be due in part to these two fatty acids.[69] DHA and AA have been added to some infant formulas.

Because of all of these benefits, the American Academy of Pediatrics (AAP) and the American Dietetic Association (ADA) recommend that women exclusively breast-feed for the first six months and then use a combination of appropriate foods and breast-feeding during at least the first year. The recent White House Task Force on

Women can express breast milk using a breast pump and store the milk in the refrigerator or freezer for later use.

colostrum The fluid that is expressed from the mother's breast after birth and before the development of breast milk.

Childhood Obesity also recommends that women be educated, empowered, and supported in their efforts to increase breast-feeding practices.[70]

The breast-fed infant doesn't always have to consume breast milk directly from the breast. Milk can be pumped, or expressed, with a breast pump, refrigerated, and fed to the baby in a bottle by another caregiver at another time. This allows the mother to work outside the home or enjoy a few hours "off duty." The feature box "Breast-Feeding at Work Can Work" addresses the dilemma of moms who want to breast-feed but who want or have to return to work.

Expressed breast milk should be used within 24 hours, or it can be stored in the freezer for three to six months. Kathy, the college student you read about in the beginning of the chapter, can pump and express her milk before she leaves for class. She can refrigerate the milk so that her baby can be fed while she is on campus.

> Breast milk should be stored in the back of the freezer, where there is less temperature fluctuation and it is less likely to defrost. Premature defrosting increases the risk of harmful bacteria multiplying.

The Take-Home Message Breast-feeding provides numerous benefits for women and babies. It can help mothers return to their prepregnancy weight and reduce the risk of certain cancers, osteoporosis, and type 2 diabetes. Breast-feeding is the least expensive and most convenient way to nourish an infant, and helps the mother and baby to bond. Human milk is rich in nutrients, antibodies, and other compounds that can protect the baby against infections, allergies, and chronic diseases and may enhance the child's cognitive development. Women are advised to breast-feed exclusively for the first six months, and then breast-feed to supplement solid food through the rest of the first year.

What Are the Best Dietary and Lifestyle Habits for a Breast-Feeding Mother?

During the first six months of breast-feeding, the mother produces about three-quarters of a quart of breast milk daily and she produces a little over half a quart daily in the second six months of feeding. During this period, her body needs additional amounts of fluid and nutrients.

To meet her increased fluid needs, a breast-feeding woman should drink about 13 cups of water and beverages daily. She also needs 500 extra calories daily during the first six months of lactation. However, not all of these calories have to come from the diet. Approximately 170 calories are mobilized daily from fat that was stored during pregnancy. Therefore, only 330 extra calories have to come from her foods. This use of fat stores allows a potential weight loss of about 2 pounds a month.

During the second six months of breast-feeding, fewer calories are available from stored body fat, so a lactating woman needs to consume about 400 extra calories daily to meet her needs.[71] Interestingly, these amounts of extra calories are very similar to the needs of pregnant women during the second and third trimesters. Although a breast-feeding woman's dietary carbohydrate, vitamin, and mineral requirements increase slightly, a well-balanced diet similar to the one she consumed during pregnancy

Breast-Feeding at Work Can Work

For many women, the decision to breast-feed their infants is an easy one. The bigger challenge is how to juggle breast-feeding with returning to work or school.

Many women feel uncomfortable about breast-feeding outside the home, especially at their job. Consider that about 50 percent of working mothers have babies that are one year of age or younger, and you can see that this reluctance is a big issue.[1] The hesitation isn't just one-sided: Research shows that most companies don't offer support for working mothers, even though employer support for breast-feeding can extend the duration that a mother nurses her baby, which would benefit both mothers and babies.[2] Many women have to choose between breast-feeding and a paycheck.

But this may be slowly changing. In 1998, the state of Minnesota mandated that its companies aid and support breast-feeding moms. From 1998 to 2002, the percentage of women still breast-feeding at 6 months more than doubled within the state.[3] Currently, 10 states in the United States have laws about breast-feeding in the workplace.[4]

Worksite support is not only healthy for the infant but, in many ways, healthy for the corporate bottom line. Because breast-fed infants are sick less often than formula-fed babies, annual health care costs are approximately $400 lower for breast-fed than for non-breast-fed babies.[5] Employees who are able to breast-feed are also happier, have improved productivity, and show greater loyalty to the employer. It is estimated that each $1 invested in a corporate breast-feeding program saves the company $3.[6]

Women who return to work while lactating need only minimal worksite resources to accommodate their breast-feeding. First, they need adequate break times and access to a private, comfortable room with an electrical outlet in order to pump their breast milk. They need a sink in which to wash their hands and the pumping equipment, and a refrigerator for storing the milk.[7]

Some companies, such as Johnson & Johnson, have gone beyond these minimum requirements and initiated a company-wide breast-feeding program called Nurture Space. Employees who are new parents receive a lactation education kit, a discount on a portable breast pump, and free telephone consultations with a certified lactation consultant. At many Johnson & Johnson corporate locations, there are Nurture Space rooms where breast-feeding mothers can comfortably express their milk during the workday.

Johnson & Johnson is committed to this program because there are many benefits to supporting nursing mothers upon their return to work. Breast-fed babies have fewer allergies and illnesses. Working mothers enjoy greater peace of mind and job satisfaction when they can choose to continue to nurse. The company then benefits from fewer absences, faster return-to-work rates, lower health care costs, and improved productivity, loyalty, and corporate image.

will meet her needs. Lactating women who are vegans should make sure that they consume adequate amounts of vitamin B_{12} and zinc.

Anything that goes into a breast-feeding mother's body can potentially pass into her breast milk, and ultimately to her baby. Illicit drugs, such as cocaine, heroin, and marijuana, for example, can be transferred to a breast-fed infant and cause harm. Methylmercury, which a mother can overconsume if she doesn't avoid certain fish, can also be harmful, so nursing mothers should adhere to the FDA's guidelines about fish to minimize the infant's exposure (see Table 15.1 on page 544).

Coffee should be limited to two to three cups daily because the caffeine can interfere with the baby's sleep and cause crankiness. Alcohol can not only appear in breast milk, it can also inhibit milk production, and so should be avoided by women who are nursing. Finally, inhaling tobacco smoke is associated with a decrease in milk production and smaller weight gains in the baby, and nicotine can be passed on to the baby in breast milk, so nursing women should not smoke.[72]

Breast milk can also reflect the foods a mother eats, and babies can become fussy if the mother has consumed certain spicy or gassy foods. The mother can stop eating the food, wait a few days, and then try it again in her diet. If the infant reacts the same way, it's best to stop eating that food while nursing.

The Take-Home Message **A nursing mother needs to consume an extra 330 calories daily during the first six months of lactation and an extra 400 calories daily during the second six months. She needs to increase her fluid and nutrient intake to help her body produce breast milk. Anything a woman consumes can be passed on to her baby in breast milk, so nursing mothers should avoid all illicit drugs, caffeine, alcohol, and smoking.**

When Is Formula a Healthy Alternative to Breast Milk?

If the infant isn't going to be breast-fed, the only other healthy option is formula. For some women, the choice is a personal preference. For others, breast-feeding may not be possible due to illness or other circumstances, and formula-feeding is necessary.

Some Women May Not Be Able to Breast-Feed

Women who are infected with HIV (human immunodeficiency virus), the virus that causes AIDS (acquired immune deficiency syndrome), should not breast-feed, as this virus can be transmitted to the child through breast milk. Women who have AIDS, human T-cell leukemia, active tuberculosis, are receiving chemotherapy and/or radiation, or use illegal drugs should not breast-feed either.[73] (*Note:* For HIV-infected women living in countries where there is inadequate food, an unsafe food supply, and/or frequent incidences of nutritional deficiencies and infectious diseases, the benefits of providing the infant with nutrient- and immune-rich breast milk may outweigh the risks of HIV infection for the baby.)

An infant born with a genetic disorder called galactosemia can't metabolize lactose and shouldn't be breast-fed.[74] Lastly, any woman taking prescribed medications should check with her health care provider to ensure that they are safe to consume while breast-feeding.

Formula Can Be a Healthy Alternative to Breast-Feeding

The best alternative to breast-feeding is to feed an infant with a commercially made formula. Cow's milk cannot be used, as it won't meet the baby's nutritional needs. It contains too much protein, mainly in the form of casein, which is difficult for the infant to digest.[75] Cow's milk, even whole milk, is also too low in fat and linoleic acid, and too high in sodium and potassium.[76] Also, the iron in cow's milk is poorly

Table 15.5

Nutritional Similarities between Infant Formula and Breast Milk

Nutrient	Amount in Breast Milk	Amount in Formula
Protein (g/100 ml)	1.8	1.4
Fat (g/100 ml)	4	4.8
Carbohydrate (g/100 ml)	7	7.3
Sodium (mg/100 ml)	1.3	0.7
Calcium (mg/100 ml)	22	53
Phosphorus (mg/100)	14	38
Iron (mg/100 ml)	0.03	0.1
Zinc (mg/100 ml)	3.2	5.1
Vitamin D (IU/100ml)	4	41

absorbed, and to make matters worse, cow's milk can cause intestinal blood loss in infants, which will cause iron loss and, possibly, anemia.[77] Feeding infants cow's milk can also increase their risk of developing an allergy to cow's milk.[78]

Infant formula is developed to be as similar as possible to breast milk (see Table 15.5), so formula-fed infants can grow and develop quite normally. The FDA regulates all infant formulas sold in the United States and has set specific requirements for the nutrients that the formula must contain.

Formula is typically made from cow's milk that has been altered to improve its nutrient content and digestibility. Soy-protein–based formulas are free of cow's protein and lactose and can be used for infants who can't tolerate cow-milk protein-based formula or who are vegetarians. **Hypoallergenic infant formulas** are available for infants who can't consume cow's milk or soy formulas. The AAP recommends that all formula-fed infants consume iron-fortified formulas to reduce the risk of iron deficiency during infancy.[79]

Formula can be purchased as powder, as a concentrated liquid, or in ready-to-use forms. Powdered formula is the cheapest and the ready-to-use form tends to be the most expensive. Care should be taken to mix the powdered or concentrated liquid with the correct amount of water so the formula will not be too diluted or too concentrated.

If the infant doesn't finish the bottle, the formula should be discarded, rather than saved for another feeding. The bacteria in the infant's mouth can contaminate the formula and multiply to levels that could be harmful even if the formula is reheated. Constant reheating of the formula can destroy some of the heat-sensitive nutrients.[80] Also, formula should not be left out at room temperature for more than two hours, as bacteria can multiply to unhealthy levels.

Note that infants should not be allowed to sleep with a bottle containing milk, formula, or other sugary liquids (such as fruit juice, soda, or other sweetened drinks), as this practice can potentially lead to **nursing bottle tooth decay** (see **Figure 15.7**) and ear infections. Liquids from bottles tend to pool in the mouth during sleep. The normal bacteria in the mouth change the sugar to an acid, which gradually dissolves the immature enamel and allows tooth decay to occur.[81] Drinking from the bottle while lying down also prevents liquid from fully draining from the ear tubes. The liquid buildup increases the risk of ear infections. The American Academy of Pediatric Dentistry recommends avoiding putting infants to sleep with bottles and sweetened pacifiers.[82]

Figure 15.7 Nursing Bottle Tooth Decay When infants are given a bottle shortly before sleep, the sugary beverage can pool in the mouth and dissolve immature tooth enamel.

hypoallergenic infant formulas Specially developed formulas for infants who have food allergies and cannot tolerate regular formula.

nursing bottle tooth decay Tooth decay from prolonged contact with formula, milk, fruit juice, or other sugar-rich liquid offered to an infant in a bottle.

The Take-Home Message If a woman doesn't breast-feed, formula is the only other healthy option. Cow's milk should not be given before age 1, as it is too high in protein and some minerals and too low in fat. Powdered and concentrated formulas must be mixed carefully so they are not too diluted or concentrated for the baby's digestive system. Infants should never be given a bottle as they are put down to sleep, as this can lead to tooth decay and ear infections.

What Are the Nutrient Needs of an Infant and Why Are They So High?

Whereas parents and caregivers can be confident that breast milk and commercial formulas are meeting their infants' unique nutritional needs, they would benefit from knowing exactly what those nutrient needs are, and what causes them to be so high. Let's explore these topics next.

Infants Grow at an Accelerated Rate

During a child's **infancy,** or first year of life, he experiences a tremendous amount of growth. In fact, an infant doubles his birth weight by about 6 months of age, and triples it by the age of 12 months. Length will double around the end of the first year as well. Let's try to imagine the physical growth of an infant in adult terms. On January first, you weigh 100 pounds. Around the month of June, you have grown to 200 pounds. By New Year's Eve, you would weigh 300 pounds! You would have to eat an enormous amount of food every day to actually make this happen. For an infant, though, this is a normal growth rate.

Infants are doing much more than just getting heavier and longer. Intellectual and social developments are also under way. As time goes by, infant communication skills go beyond crying, and at around three months of age a baby usually starts to smile. Preferences also become clearer: for particular people (such as the mom), for specific activities (getting kisses or being held), and for certain foods (such as mashed bananas).[83]

An infant should reach certain stages of physical development within a distinct time frame. If an infant is not growing in the expected fashion, this may be a sign that something is wrong. Parents, caregivers, and health care providers need to be alert to infants who miss the mark, and then look more deeply into the situation. The child may not be receiving sufficient nutrition (see **Figure 15.8**). Perhaps an infant has a poor appetite, and the new mom has no idea that the child should be eating more frequently. Maybe an infant is having some digestive problems, and the new day care provider does not mention the frequency of dirty diapers.

Of course, optimal infant nutrition is sometimes hindered by circumstance. In less developed countries where poverty is the norm and food is scarce, problems such as protein-energy malnutrition (see Chapter 6) are common. Even in developed countries, such as the United States, there are problems with poor infant nutrition that may affect growth. For example, iron-deficiency anemia (see Chapter 8) is sometimes seen in infants when caregivers substitute juice or cow's milk for breast milk or formula.[84] Or, if a breast-fed infant does not begin consuming iron in solid foods by around 6 months, his or her iron stores are depleted, paving the way for anemia.

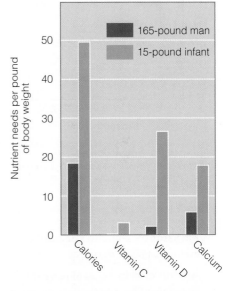

Figure 15.8 Nutrient Needs per Pound of Body Weight
Nutrient recommendations for a 5-month-old infant and an adult male compared on the basis of body weight.

Source: USDA, Dietary Reference Intakes: Recomended Intakes for Individuals, www.usda.gov.

infancy The age range from birth to 12 months.

Figure 15.9 Foods for Baby's First Year
During the first year after birth, as developmental milestones are being met, an infant's diet will progress from breast milk or formula to age-appropriate versions of family meals.

Figure 15.10 Growth Chart
Growth charts can help determine if a child is growing at a healthy rate for his or her age.

milestones Objectives or significant events that occur during development.

growth charts Series of percentile curves that illustrate the distribution of selected body measurements in U.S. children.

percentile The most commonly used clinical indicator to assess the size and growth patterns of children in the United States. An individual child is ranked according to the percentage of the reference population he equals or exceeds.

Monitoring Infant Growth

An infant who does not receive adequate nutrition (whether in terms of quantity or quality) may have difficulty reaching developmental **milestones** (**Figure 15.9**). Think of these as checkpoints, which can be physical, social, or intellectual. While most parents do not know the specific nutrient needs of their infant, it's important that the infant attain the specific milestones at the appropriate time. This assures parents that they are providing the right amount and type of nourishment.

If a child doesn't reach the appropriate milestones, he or she may eventually develop a condition called failure to thrive (FTT). A child with FTT is delayed in physical growth or size or does not gain enough weight. Poor appetite, an unbalanced diet, or a medical problem that has not yet been diagnosed can all be causes of FTT. Sometimes, FTT results from inappropriate care or neglect. Caregivers and health care providers need to be aware of the signs of this condition and watch for those signs in their children and patients.

In addition to milestones, parents and health care providers can use **growth charts** to track physical development progress. Typically, measures of head circumference, length, weight, and weight for length are used to assess growth. These measures are taken at each "well-check" visit to the health care provider, about once a month for the first year. The information obtained from the measurements is plotted on the growth chart, placing the child into a **percentile**. Percentiles rank the infant with regard to other infants of the same age in a reference group. For example, a four-month-old who is in the 25th percentile for weight for age weighs less than 75 percent of the four-month-olds and weighs the same as or more than 25 percent (see **Figure 15.10**).[85]

Infants Have Specific Calorie, Iron, and Other Nutrient Needs

Though one size does not fit all, when it comes to feeding infants there are certain guidelines to follow so that they can meet their nutrient needs. For example, an average of 108 calories per kilogram (kg) of body weight is recommended for the first six months of life.[86] Again, imagine a similar proportion of calories at that scale for an adult who weighs 150 pounds (68 kg)—it would work out to 7,344 (68 kg × 108) calories. That's the equivalent of 13 large chocolate milkshakes!

Carbohydrate, protein, and fat needs all change with age. Infants 0 to 6 months should consume 60 grams of carbohydrate per day, which increases to 95 grams daily at 7 to 12 months. Infants need 9.1 grams of protein per day during the first six months of life, which increases to 11 grams daily in the second six months. (*Note:* The DRIs for infants are listed in the inside front cover of this textbook.) Fat should not be limited at this stage of the life cycle, as this practice could negatively affect growth. In fact, healthy babies should never be put on weight-loss diets, as this can severely retard their physical or mental development.

Three nutrients must be added to an infant's diet: vitamin K, vitamin D, and iron. As you recall from Chapter 7, all infants should receive an injection of vitamin K to ensure that their blood will clot. This is necessary because infants are born with a sterile gut, and vitamin K is partially produced from intestinal bacteria.[87]

The amount of vitamin D in breast milk is not enough to prevent rickets, so infants should also receive 400 IU of vitamin D drops daily. Once they reach age 1, they can drink vitamin-D–fortified milk at meals. If vitamin-D–fortified formula is introduced before age 1, vitamin D supplementation isn't necessary if they are drinking adequate amounts to meet their vitamin D needs. Even though vitamin D can be obtained through exposure of the infant's skin to sunlight, this isn't recommended because it can cause sunburns and increases the risk of skin cancer.[88]

Iron-rich foods, such as enriched cereals, should be introduced at around 6 months, as the infant's stores of iron are depleted at about this time. Premature infants, who were born early and thus have lower iron stores, may need iron supplementation before 6 months.[89]

Because vitamin B_{12} is naturally found only in animal foods, supplementation may also be recommended if the infant is being breast-fed by a strict vegan mother. If the child's water supply is nonfluoridated or if bottled water is used for mixing formula, a fluoride supplement may also be necessary.[90]

Water (or, more correctly, fluid) needs generally are met with breast milk or formula. Extra fluid is only necessary in hot climates or to replenish stores following episodes of diarrhea, fever, or vomiting when the body loses fluid and electrolytes. Even in these circumstances extra fluid should still be limited, as filling up on water might keep the baby from being hungry for needed, nutrient-rich breast milk or formula.[91]

"Colic" involves an infant's chronic, inconsolable crying, often for long periods of time. Though the cause of colic is not known, some possible nutrition-related contributors include an immature digestive tract, cow's milk allergies or intolerance, food backup into the esophagus, increased intestinal gas, or the breast-feeding mother's diet.

The Take-Home Message Infants grow at a dramatic rate during the first year of life. Caregivers and health care providers can monitor infant growth by making sure the child achieves appropriate developmental milestones and by using growth charts. Nutrient needs during the first year of life are substantial, and supplements may be needed in some circumstances.

When Are Solid Foods Safe?

Often, proud parents can hardly wait to show off how their baby is eating "real food." It is an exciting time, because eating **solid foods** represents maturing skills in the baby. Typically, solid foods are introduced around 6 months of age.[92] However, parents should not suddenly decide to serve their baby steak! The infant must be nutritionally, physiologically, and physically ready to eat solid foods. Let's take a look at what we mean by this.

Solid Foods May Be Introduced Once Certain Milestones Are Met

First, the infant needs to be nutritionally ready for solid foods. At about 6 months old, an infant has depleted his or her stored iron and will need to begin consuming it in foods. Also, common sense tells us that as babies get bigger in size, they need more nutrients. Thus, an older, larger infant has higher nutrient needs than a younger, smaller one. Though breast milk can technically still provide most nutrients, introducing solid foods will further meet the infant's needs and help her develop feeding skills.

The infant also needs to be physiologically ready; that is, his body systems must be able to process solid foods. At birth, and in early infancy, the GI tract and organs such as the kidneys cannot process solid foods. Introducing solid foods too early can increase a child's risk of allergic reactions to common allergy-causing foods (see the feature box on page 568, "A Taste Could Be Dangerous: Food Allergies").

These next questions are very specific to the individual child. Is the infant physically ready? Has he or she met the necessary developmental milestones? To determine this, caretakers need to answer the following questions:

> Has the **tongue-thrust reflex** faded? This is a reflex infants have to protect against choking. The tongue automatically pushes outward when a substance is placed on it. The reflex fades at around 4 to 6 months of age.
> Does the infant have head and neck control? Without control, the infant is at greater risk for choking on solids.
> Have the infant's swallowing skills matured enough?
> Is the infant able to sit with support?
> Does the infant have the ability to turn his or her head to indicate "I'm full!"?

All of these questions should be answered with a "Yes" to know that it is safe and realistic to begin offering solid foods. If not, parents and caregivers would be wise to wait until the infant does develop these skills.[93] Still nervous about feeding an infant? See the feature box "Feeding the Baby" on page 570 for more information.

solid foods Foods other than breast milk or formula given to an infant, usually around 6 months of age.

tongue-thrust reflex A forceful protrusion of the tongue in response to an oral stimulus, such as a spoon.

Solid Foods Should Be Introduced Gradually

Once an infant is ready for solids, foods should be introduced gradually to make sure the child isn't allergic or intolerant. The best suggestion is to introduce only one new food per week.[94] Parents and caregivers should be mindful of how the infant reacts to new foods. If she develops hives or a rash, or starts sneezing or vomiting, the food may be the culprit. The least allergy-causing food—rice cereal—is a great first food. It is best offered to the infant when it is heavily diluted with breast milk or formula so there is a familiar taste mixed in with the new taste. This will promote the infant's acceptance of the new food. Whole milk shouldn't be given to an infant until after one year of age.

After several days to a week of feeding the infant rice cereal (assuming there has been no negative reaction), a suggested next step is to proceed with other single-grain cereals, such as barley or oats. Once all of these have been fed to the infant without difficulty, then multigrain cereals (rice, barley, and oats) can be offered.

The next step is to offer puréed vegetables, so that the infant will become familiar with the more bitter taste of these foods; then fruits in the same manner; then meats. All of these foods should be introduced one at a time. Phasing in solid foods should take place over a period of several months. The food should initially be served puréed; eventually it can be served not puréed, but cooked so that the texture is soft, as the infant's chewing and swallowing skills are sharpened with practice. Rather than deciding that the infant does not like sweet potatoes because he spits it out upon the first taste, parents and caregivers should offer a given food more than once, over several days, to give the infant opportunity to accept the food.[95]

(T|F) Many motivated parents wonder if they should try making homemade baby food. This is an admirable idea, and certainly gives the child exposure to fresh, unprocessed meals. However, commercially made baby foods are of high quality and often comparable to homemade. The choice is really up to the parent or caregiver. One benefit of homemade food that everyone might agree upon is the financial savings—there are no added costs for fancy packaging and labels. (See "Two Points of View" at the end of this chapter for more on this topic.)

Refer again to Figure 15.9 on page 564 for suggested foods for a baby's first year of life.

Solid foods like rice cereal and oatmeal can be introduced between 4 and 6 months of age.

Some Foods Are Dangerous and Should Be Avoided

In spite of all the new skills an infant develops during the first year, becoming stronger, smarter, and more independent, parents and caregivers still need to "baby the baby" when it comes to eating. Many foods are just not appropriate for a baby. For example, (T|F) some foods, like hot dog rounds or raw carrot slices, present a choking hazard; they should be cut into very small pieces or avoided altogether. Because infants have few teeth, foods should be soft textured so they do not require excessive chewing, and ideally should easily "melt" in the mouth, like a cracker. No matter what they are eating, infants should always be supervised.

Parents and caregivers should also avoid feeding common allergens, such as chocolate, fish, and strawberries, to infants. Reactions may range from a very mild tingling sensation in the mouth or swelling of the tongue and the throat to difficulty breathing, hives, vomiting, abdominal cramps, diarrhea, a drop in blood pressure, and loss of consciousness or death. Waiting a few months until the infant's digestive system has matured is a smart way to keep the infant safe.[96] Other common allergens, like egg whites, cow's milk, and peanut butter, should not be offered before the child is a year old.

Some foods are so dangerous as to be potentially fatal. Honey has been known to carry *Clostridium botulinum*, which can lead to a fatal disease called **botulism.**

botulism A rare but serious paralytic illness caused by the bacterium *Clostridium botulinum*. Infant botulism is caused by consuming the spores of the bacteria, which then grow in the intestines and release toxin. It can be fatal.

A Taste Could Be Dangerous: Food Allergies

One-year-old Adam was playing in the sandbox at the neighborhood playground, when his babysitter pulled a peanut butter cookie from her backpack. She broke off a small bite of the cookie and handed it to Adam, knowing that he must be hungry for his afternoon snack. After a minute of chewing, Adam started to wheeze and have difficulty breathing. Then he vomited. The sitter quickly used her cell phone to call for emergency help. She gave the rest of the cookie to one of the paramedics who rushed Adam to the hospital. Unbeknownst to the sitter, Adam was allergic to peanuts.

A **food allergy** is an abnormal physical reaction of the immune system in response to the consumption of a particular food allergen. **Food allergens** are proteins that are not broken down during cooking or by the gastric juices and enzymes in the body during digestion. Because they are not degraded, they enter the body intact, and can cause an adverse immune reaction if the allergen is perceived as a foreign invader.

food allergy An abnormal reaction by the immune system to a particular food.

food allergens Proteins that are not broken down by cooking or digestion and enter the body intact, causing an adverse reaction by the immune system.

mast cells Cells in connective tissue to which antibodies attach, setting the stage for potential future allergic reactions.

anaphylactic reactions Severe, life-threatening reactions that cause constriction of the airways in the lungs, which inhibits the ability to breathe.

food intolerance Adverse reaction to a food that does not involve an immune response. Lactose intolerance is one example.

A food allergy reaction occurs in two stages, the "sensitization stage" followed by the actual response or "allergic reaction stage." In the first stage (see the figure on the next page), the food allergens don't provoke a reaction, but rather introduce themselves to the person's immune system. In response, the immune system creates an army of antibodies that enter the blood. The antibodies attach to **mast cells,** setting the stage for a potential future allergic reaction.

The second stage, the reaction stage, occurs when a person eats the food allergens for the second and subsequent times. After they are consumed, the food allergens come in contact with the mast cells. The mast cells release chemicals such as histamine that trigger reactions in the body. The areas in the body that manifest a food allergy reaction are the areas where mast cells are prevalent. In very sensitive individuals, a minute exposure of a food allergen—$\frac{1}{44,000}$ of a peanut, for example—can trigger an allergic reaction.[8]

Reactions can appear as quickly as a few minutes after eating the food. In fact, an itchiness in the mouth may occur as soon as the food touches the tongue. After the food reaches the stomach and begins to be digested, vomiting and/or diarrhea may result. When they enter the blood, the food allergens can cause a drop in blood pressure. When the allergens are near the skin, hives can develop, and as the allergens make their way to the lungs, asthma can ensue.[9]

Individuals with allergies, or their caretakers, often carry a syringe injector of epinephrine (adrenaline) to be self-administered when severe reactions occur, to help treat these symptoms. Epinephrine constricts blood vessels, relaxes the muscles in the

lungs to help with breathing, and decreases swelling and hives.

Eggs, milk, and peanuts are the most common sources of food allergens in children. Some allergens, such as strawberries, chocolate, and fish, should be avoided for infants. In adults, shellfish, peanuts, tree nuts, fish, wheat, soy, and eggs are the most common sources of food allergens. These foods together cause 90 percent of all reactions to food allergens. Some children will outgrow their reactions to milk, and up to 20 percent of them will outgrow a peanut allergy.[10] In contrast, adults are rarely able to rid themselves of a food allergy once it is established.

In the United States, food allergies are the cause of 2,000 admittances to the hospital, approximately 30,000 **anaphylactic** (*ana* = without, no, *phylaxis* = protection) **reactions** (severe, life-threatening allergic reactions), and almost 200 deaths annually.[11] An anaphylactic reaction can cause vomiting and constriction or narrowing of the airways in the lungs, which inhibits breathing.

The symptoms of a **food intolerance** may mimic a food allergy, but they are different responses. A food intolerance does not involve the immune system. Recall from Chapter 4 that one common food intolerance, lactose intolerance, is caused by inadequate amounts of the enzyme lactase in the body.

The FDA requires that virtually all food ingredients be listed on the food label, and that the food label state whether the product contains protein from any of the major foods known to cause an allergic reaction: milk, egg, fish, shellfish, tree nuts, peanuts, soybeans, or wheat.[12]

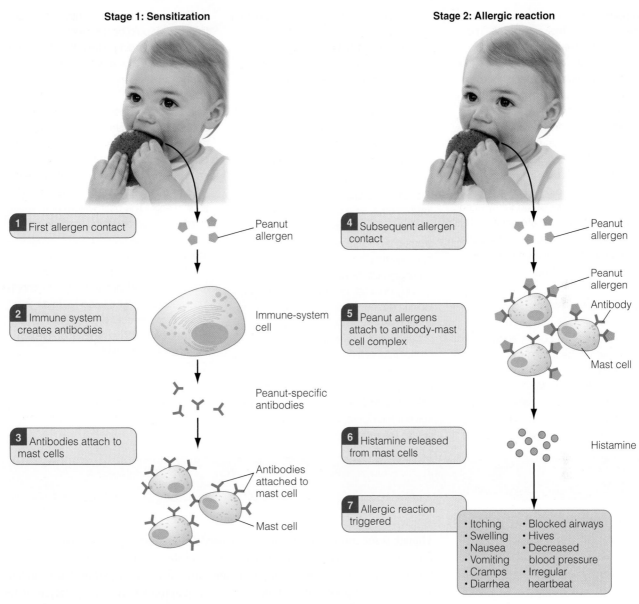

Stage 1: Sensitization

1 First allergen contact

Peanut allergen

2 Immune system creates antibodies

Immune-system cell

Peanut-specific antibodies

3 Antibodies attach to mast cells

Antibodies attached to mast cell

Mast cell

Immune Response to a Food Allergy

Stage 2: Allergic reaction

4 Subsequent allergen contact

Peanut allergen

Peanut allergen

Antibody

5 Peanut allergens attach to antibody-mast cell complex

Mast cell

6 Histamine released from mast cells

Histamine

7 Allergic reaction triggered

- Itching
- Swelling
- Nausea
- Vomiting
- Cramps
- Diarrhea
- Blocked airways
- Hives
- Decreased blood pressure
- Irregular heartbeat

Feeding the Baby

New parents are often nervous when it comes to feeding their newborns. They may wonder if their baby is eating too much or too little, or swallowing too much air, and, if they are bottle-feeding, they may be worried about nipple confusion or other concerns they have heard about from well-meaning friends and relatives. The good news is that most parents can relax when it comes to feeding baby, as Mother Nature has built in numerous mechanisms to help babies healthfully consume the amount of food they need.

For example, infants are equipped with several reflexes that help them take in adequate amounts of breast milk (or formula) and avoid choking. Among these reflexes are:

➤ Rooting reflex—When a baby's mouth, lips, cheek, or chin are touched by an object, such as a nipple, the head and mouth turn toward it.

➤ Suck/swallow reflex—After opening the mouth when a baby's lips and mouth area are touched, suckling movements begin and the tongue moves to the back of the mouth for swallowing.

➤ Tongue-thrust reflex—When the lips are touched, the baby's tongue moves out of the mouth.

➤ Gag reflex—When an object such as a spoon or solid is placed in the mouth, it is pushed back out by the tongue.

Note that a baby should be fed when he indicates that he is hungry, rather than on a set schedule. Newborns may need to feed as often as every ½ to 2 hours, whereas older infants, who have larger stomachs, may taper off to 3 to 4 hours between feedings. Some cues that a baby is hungry include waking and tossing, sucking on a fist, crying or fussing, and looking like he is going to cry. Caregivers should respond early to the signs of hunger rather than waiting until the baby is crying. Infants are usually very clear about when they are ready to stop feeding, and use several techniques to communicate this to a caregiver. For example, they may spit out the nipple, close their lips, and decrease the rate of suckling.

When feeding an infant from a bottle, the baby should be gently and slowly positioned for feeding. The baby should be held upright in the cradle of the arm with the head higher than the rest of the body to avoid choking. The bottle should be held and not propped during feeding because propping can cause choking or baby bottle tooth decay, and deprives the baby of human contact. To expel any excess swallowed air and alleviate potential gassiness, a baby needs to be burped after she eats. The best way to burp a baby is to gently pat or rub her back while she is resting on the caregiver's shoulder or sitting on the lap.

All babies develop at their own rate and each individual baby's developmental readiness should be used to determine which foods should be fed, what texture the foods should be, and what feeding styles should be used.

Source: USDA (2002). Feeding Infants: A Guide for Use in Child Nutrition Programs. www.fns.usda.gov/tn/resources/feeding_infants.html.

Though some cultures and families have used honey-dipped pacifiers to calm infants for generations, this is a dangerous practice and should never be done. Infants with botulism become lethargic, feed poorly, and suffer from constipation. They will have a weak cry and poor muscle tone. Untreated symptoms may cause paralysis of the arms, legs, trunk, and respiratory muscles. The resulting respiratory failure is what makes this food potentially deadly. Older children and adults can consume honey without these concerns, as they have adequate amounts of intestinal microorganisms that compete with botulism and inhibit its growth in the intestines.[97]

Herbal tea may also pose a risk to infants. Even though the label says "natural," that does not always mean it is safe, because herbal remedies are not regulated. Many herbs are not well researched, and the effectiveness and potential dangers are not always known.

Parents and caregivers also need to think before adding seasonings such as salt, sugar, and butter to their infants' foods. Restaurants, processed foods, and our own habits have taught us to think that food only tastes "right" if it is salty, sweet, or buttery. Infants do not care if something is bland, and there is no nutritional benefit to enhancing the taste of foods with additional flavors. At this stage of the life cycle, infants can learn to find the natural flavors in whole foods satisfying, without added sugar or salt.

What about all those benefits of fiber the experts tell us about? Do babies need "roughage" to keep them "regular" like adults? Though fiber is useful for many reasons, too much can actually be harmful to an infant because it can pull nutrients through the GI tract before they have a chance to be absorbed. As the infant gets older, more fiber is suitable.

Beverages, such as apple juice, are a popular component of infant diets. In fact, 100 percent juice is considered one of the major sources of infants' calories.[98] Although juice can provide some nutrients, it also may provide so many calories that the infant will prefer to drink rather than to eat food, displacing necessary nutrients.

Overabundance of breast milk and formula is not always suitable, either. This is important at the end of the first year, as the infant will likely be learning to use solid food to obtain calories, rather than relying on milk or formula. If an infant spends too much time drinking, he may not be interested in the foods that will help expand his feeding skills. Of course, breast milk or formula will still be the primary source of calories, and some parents and caregivers prefer not to start solid foods until after the first year. See **Figure 15.11** for recommended nutritional guidelines for mothers, fathers, and infants.

The Take-Home Message An infant must be physically, physiologically, and nutritionally ready before being introduced to solid foods. Solid foods should be introduced gradually and cautiously. Parents and caregivers must educate themselves about foods that are appropriate and those that are not in order to keep the infant safe and healthy.

	Prior to conception	First trimester	Second trimester	Third trimester	First year
Father	• Stop smoking • Limit alcohol • Maintain a healthy weight • Consume a balanced diet • Avoid illicit drugs				
Mother	• Consume a balanced diet • Maintain a healthy weight • Add folic acid to diet • Limit caffeine • Avoid certain fish with high levels of methylmercury • Avoid alcohol, herbs, illicit drugs, and smoking • Exercise regularly	• Consume a balanced diet • Continue getting folic acid • Take an iron-rich supplement • Limit caffeine • Avoid too much vitamin A • Avoid foodborne illness • Continue exercising	• Consume a balanced diet with adequate calories for growth • Continue exercising	• Consume a balanced diet with adequate calories for growth • Eat frequent small meals if more comfortable • Choose high-fiber foods • Drink plenty of fluids • Continue nonimpact exercises	• Consume a balanced diet with adequate calories and fluids for breast-feeding • Avoid illicit drugs, smoking, and alcohol • Limit caffeine • Avoid certain fish with high levels of methylmercury
Baby					• Supplement diet with vitamins K and D and sources of iron or iron-fortified foods • Avoid common food allergens, honey, and herbal tea • Consume breast milk or formula as primary source of calories • Do not start drinking cow's milk until after this year • Introduce solid foods gradually and one at a time • Avoid too much fiber and excessive amounts of juice

Figure 15.11 Summary of Nutritional Guidelines
Nutritional guidelines for both parents and infants.

Two Points of View

Do Parents Need to Make Their Own Baby Food? Many anxious parents worry about the foods they feed their babies, and when it comes to introducing solid foods, they often struggle with the question of whether to make their own homemade baby food, buy organic versions of commercially made products, or buy regular, nonorganic (and usually less expensive) jarred baby foods.

What concerns do parents have when it comes to commercially made baby food, and are those concerns valid? What other options are available? Are there advantages other than nutrition to making homemade baby food, or buying only organic products? Read through the arguments on both sides of the issue, and then consider the critical thinking questions to decide for yourself!

Yes

- Homemade baby foods are usually more nutrient dense. Commercial baby foods often contain more water, starch, and sugar than homemade baby foods. The addition of these additives dilutes the nutrient content of commercial foods.[1]

- Commercially made baby foods are often processed with high heat during jarring, which can destroy some of the vitamins and other nutrients.[2]

- The average baby in the United States will consume 600 jars of baby food. Parents who use processed baby food spend an average of $300 during their infant's first year of life. On average, baby food prepared at home can cost as little as $55 in the first year.[3]

- Providing babies with homemade baby food made of fresh fruits and vegetables can help instill taste and preference for these healthy food choices. Babies will get used to the fresher tastes, and be less interested in the tastes of highly processed foods later on in life.[4]

No

- Pesticide levels in commercial baby foods are tightly regulated by U.S. law and include a safety factor that is ten times the levels known to be safe.[5]

- Homemade baby foods may spoil more quickly and require refrigeration, which will take up room in the fridge or freezer if a lot of servings are made ahead of time. Prepackaged baby foods don't have to be refrigerated until they've been opened.[6]

- In preparing homemade food, adults may season it to their own tastes, adding enough salt or sugar to raise pediatric concerns.[7]

- Certain vegetables, particularly spinach, beets, and carrots, may contain high levels of nitrates, which can be harmful to young babies. There seems to be little or no risk of nitrate poisoning from commercially prepared infant foods in the United States. However, reports of nitrate poisoning from home-prepared vegetable foods for infants indicate that this does occur.[8]

What do you think?

1. Which side has the overall stronger argument? Why?
2. Why might parents need to choose commercially prepared food over homemade food? **3.** Do you think making homemade baby food is worth the extra time and effort? Why or why not?

Chapter Review

The Top Ten Points to Remember

1. Both the father and the mother should make healthy diet and lifestyle changes if needed prior to pregnancy. For healthy sperm, men should stop smoking, abstain from alcohol or drink only in moderation, strive for a healthy body weight, and consume a well-balanced diet with adequate amounts of fruits and vegetables, whole grains, lean meats, dairy foods, and legumes. Women should consume adequate amounts of folic acid prior to conception to reduce the risk of neural tube defects.

2. Women who begin pregnancy at a healthy weight are more likely to conceive more easily, have an uncomplicated pregnancy, and have an easier time nursing their babies. Children born to obese women are at greater risk for being born larger than normal, having more difficulties breathing, having a slower heart rate, and having an increased risk of both heart defects and certain birth defects. These children are also more likely to develop childhood obesity.

3. Pregnant women should abstain from alcohol, herbs, and illicit drugs, as these can all harm fetal growth and development. They should avoid fish that contain high amounts of methylmercury and consume caffeine only in moderation.

4. To alleviate symptoms of morning sickness, women should eat small, frequent meals that are high in carbohydrates. Salty foods may also help, and tart beverages such as lemonade. Healthy women should gain approximately 25 to 35 pounds during pregnancy. Most of a pregnant woman's increased nutrient needs can be met through a nutrient-dense, balanced diet. A supplement is needed for iron, but care should be taken to avoid consuming too much preformed vitamin A, which can cause birth defects.

5. Awareness of food safety is important, as bacteria such as *Listeria monocytogenes* may cause miscarriages, premature labor, delivery of a low birth weight infant, developmental problems, or even infant death. Pregnant women should handle raw meats and fish with care and avoid consuming raw or undercooked meat, fish, or poultry; unpasteurized milk, cheese, and juices; and raw sprouts.

Total weight gain ~30 lbs

- Maternal fat stores (~7 lbs)
- Uterus and breast (4 lbs)
- Blood (3–4 lbs)
- Fetus (~7 lbs)
- Placenta, amniotic fluid, and other fluids (~8 lbs)

Third trimester

6. A pregnant woman should consume an additional 340 calories daily during the second trimester and an extra 450 calories daily during the third trimester. This will enable her to gain slightly less than a pound per week until delivery. Exercise during pregnancy can help improve sleep, lower the risk of hypertension and diabetes, prevent backaches, help relieve constipation, shorten labor, reduce stress and depression, and allow women to return more quickly to their prepregnancy weight after delivery. Low-impact activities such as walking, swimming, and stationary cycling are recommended to prevent injury to both mother and baby.

7. Sometimes a woman develops gestational diabetes and/or hypertension during pregnancy. Gestational diabetes increases the risk of delivering a larger-than-normal baby who may also be at risk for developing jaundice, breathing problems, and birth defects. Pregnancy-induced hypertension includes gestational hypertension, preeclampsia, and eclampsia, each

progressively more medically serious. Gestational hypertension is often a sign of preeclampsia. During preeclampsia, less oxygen- and nutrient-rich blood is reaching the placenta. Eclampsia can cause seizures in the mother and is a major cause of death of women during pregnancy.

8. Breast-feeding is the gold standard for feeding an infant. It provides physical, emotional, convenience, and financial benefits for the mother and nutritional and health benefits for the infant. Breast-feeding mothers need to consume 330 to 400 extra calories daily to produce breast milk. If an infant isn't breast-fed, formula is the only healthy alternative.

9. An infant doubles his or her birth weight by around 6 months of age, and triples it by 12 months. With proper nutrition, an infant should reach certain stages of physical development within a distinct time frame. Poor infant nutrition (whether in quality or quantity) will likely prevent ideal growth and the ability of the child to reach milestones on time. Infants need approximately 108 calories per kilogram of body weight during the first six months of life. All infants should receive a vitamin K injection at birth, and breast-fed infants need vitamin D supplements until one year of age. Infants older than 6 months need to begin taking in iron through food sources, as their stored iron supply is depleted around this time.

10. Infants need to be nutritionally, physiologically, and physically ready before they begin eating solid foods. Foods should be introduced gradually and one at a time to monitor possible allergies or intolerances. Certain foods can be dangerous and should be avoided. Parents and caregivers should avoid adding heavy seasoning (such as sugar or salt), too much fiber, or fruit juice (which can lead to overconsumption of calories) to their infants' diets.

Test Your Knowledge

1. To prevent neural tube birth defects, a woman should start taking 400 micrograms of folic acid
   a. during the first trimester.
   b. during the second trimester.
   c. at least one month prior to conception and during the early weeks of pregnancy.
   d. during the last trimester.

2. The production and function of sperm in males may decrease because of
   a. antioxidants.
   b. smoking.
   c. obesity.
   d. alcohol abuse.
   e. b, c, and d only.

3. A low birth weight baby is a baby who is born weighing
   a. more than 5½ pounds.
   b. less than 5½ pounds.
   c. more than 6 pounds.
   d. more than 7 pounds.

4. Two potential complications of pregnancy that must be closely monitored by a health care provider are
   a. cravings and morning sickness.
   b. gestational diabetes and preeclampsia.
   c. weight gain and exercise.
   d. constipation and heartburn.

5. A woman at a healthy weight should gain _____ pounds during pregnancy.
   a. 20 to 30 pounds
   b. 15 to 25 pounds
   c. 50 to 60 pounds
   d. 25 to 35 pounds

6. During pregnancy a woman's need for many nutrients increases. Which mineral requirement is unlikely to be met through her diet alone?
   a. iron
   b. potassium
   c. sodium
   d. calcium

7. During the second trimester of pregnancy, a woman should increase her daily calorie intake by
   a. 450 calories.
   b. 340 calories.
   c. 500 calories.
   d. No increase is needed.

8. Breast-feeding can
   a. help women reduce their risk of breast cancer.
   b. reduce women's risk of type 2 diabetes.
   c. decrease the risk of the baby developing respiratory and ear infections.
   d. do all of the above.

9. Andy is a healthy 3-month-old baby boy who is being breast-fed by his mother. Which of the following nutrients should be added to his diet?
   a. vitamin D
   b. potassium
   c. vitamin C
   d. all of the above
10. Six-month-old Cathy is ready to take on solid foods. The first food that should be introduced in her diet is
    a. oatmeal.
    b. iron-fortified cooked rice cereal.
    c. whole milk.
    d. none of the above.

Answers

1. (c) To reduce the risk of these birth defects, folic acid should be consumed prior to conception and continue during the early weeks of pregnancy. Waiting until pregnancy occurs will be too late. Because pregnancy increases the need for this vitamin, the mother should continue to make sure that folate intake is adequate throughout her pregnancy.

2. (e) Smoking, alcohol abuse, and obesity have all been associated with the decreased production and functioning of sperm. Antioxidants, in particular vitamins E and C and carotenoids, may help protect sperm.

3. (b) A baby born weighing less than 5½ pounds is considered a low birth weight baby.

4. (b) Gestational diabetes and preeclampsia are both potentially life-threatening complications that can be brought on by pregnancy and should be closely monitored by a physician. Cravings, morning sickness, constipation, and heartburn can all occur during pregnancy, but are not considered serious unless they are severe. Weight gain and exercise are not complications of pregnancy.

5. (d) A woman at a healthy weight should gain 25 to 35 pounds during pregnancy.

6. (a) Because a pregnant woman's increased iron needs cannot be easily met through the diet, she will likely need a supplement. She can get the potassium, sodium, and calcium she needs through a well-balanced diet.

7. (b) A pregnant woman needs 340 extra calories daily during the second trimester to meet her needs. During the third trimester, she needs an extra 450 calories every day. She doesn't need additional daily calories during the first trimester, but does have additional nutrient needs, so she should be sure to eat nutrient-dense foods.

8. (d) Breast-feeding provides health advantages to both the mother and the baby. Breast-feeding reduces the risk of breast cancer and diabetes in the mother and the incidences of respiratory and ear infections in the baby.

9. (a) Although breast milk is an ideal food for baby Andy, it doesn't contain enough vitamin D, so Andy should receive daily drops in his diet. He doesn't need to be supplemented with vitamin C or the mineral potassium.

10. (b) Cooked rice cereal is the perfect choice, as it is the least likely to cause an allergic reaction. If Cathy tolerates the rice cereal well, oatmeal could be the next grain added to her diet. Milk shouldn't be introduced into Cathy's diet until she turns one year of age.

Web Resources

- For more information on breast-feeding, visit the La Leche League International website at www.llli.org/
- For more food safety guidance for moms-to-be during pregnancy and after the baby is born, visit the FDA's Center for Food Safety and Applied Nutrition website at www.fda.gov/Food/ResourcesForYou/HealthEducators/ucm081785.htm
- For more on infant nutrition, visit the USDA's Food and Nutrition Center website at www.nal.usda.gov/fnic
- For more information on children and their dietary needs, visit the American Academy of Pediatrics at www.aap.org
- For more information on food allergies, visit the Food Allergy and Anaphylaxis Network at www.foodallergy.org

Answers to Myths and Misperceptions

1. **False.** Fathers need to eat healthy diets and avoid certain substances to help produce a healthy baby. Turn to page 542 to find out why this is the case.

2. **True.** Obese women may have more difficulty conceiving, possibly because of irregular menstrual cycles. Turn to page 543 to find out more.

3. **False.** Any type of alcohol, including red wine, can harm a growing fetus. To find out what other substances can be harmful during pregnancy, turn to page 544.

4. **False.** Though it's called morning sickness, nausea can happen at any time of day, and sometimes occurs after the first trimester. To learn more about conditions during pregnancy, turn to page 545.

5. **False.** Physical activity can be good for mothers-to-be, though some activities should be avoided. To find out which activities are safe, turn to page 552.

6. **False.** Formula can be a healthy alternative, but breast milk is best for a baby. Turn to page 556 to find out why.

7. **False.** Infants should never be put on a weight-loss diet. Babies need calories and fat to support their rapid growth and development. To find out more about the demands of infant growth, turn to page 565.

8. **False.** Most infants receive an injection of vitamin K at birth, and there are other nutrients that infants may need to supplement their diet. Find out why this is the case on page 565.

9. **False.** Although there's probably nothing as delicious as fresh and homemade, most brands of jarred baby foods are just as healthy. Read more about commercially made versus homemade baby foods on page 567.

10. **False.** Although they're a good source of vitamin A, raw carrots are a potential choking hazard for an infant. For more on potentially dangerous foods, turn to page 567.

16
Life Cycle
Toddlers through the Later Years

Nutrition:

True or False?

1. Toddlers and preschoolers are often **too busy** to eat. Ⓣ/Ⓕ p. 580

2. Young children tend to eat too much chicken, which often leads to an **iron deficiency**. Ⓣ/Ⓕ p. 582

3. Once a child **refuses** a food, there is no point in offering it again. Ⓣ/Ⓕ p. 582

4. Young children are often **picky eaters.** Ⓣ/Ⓕ p. 583

5. The rise in **childhood obesity** is due entirely to fast food. Ⓣ/Ⓕ p. 587

6. Lunches served under the National **School Lunch** Program have to follow certain nutritional regulations. Ⓣ/Ⓕ p. 590

7. As long as teens drink **diet soda**, they don't have to worry about negative health effects. Ⓣ/Ⓕ p. 593

8. Older adults don't need as many **calories** daily as they did in their youth. Ⓣ/Ⓕ p. 595

9. **Food insecurity** among elders is a nonissue in the United States. Ⓣ/Ⓕ p. 608

10. **Alcohol abuse** is extremely rare among older adults. Ⓣ/Ⓕ p. 609

See page 613 for answers to these Myths and Misperceptions.

Two-and-a-half-year-old Cara has a very busy life. When she gets up in the morning, her mom seats her at the kitchen table to eat a few pieces of banana and some whole-grain cereal, but she usually loses interest after just a few bites. Once she's dressed, she spends at least 8 or 9 minutes playing with her dog, Murphy, before running outside to grab her shovel and dig in her sandbox. When she gets bored with shoveling, she shouts for her mom to push her on the swing, or dashes over to investigate an anthill on the sidewalk. Then, she's zipping up to her room in urgent need of her toy trains. By lunchtime, her mom is saying it's time to come to the kitchen and eat, but Cara isn't interested. There's too much to see, do, and explore before she has to lie down for her afternoon nap.

Cara's parents are worried that Cara may be eating too little and missing some essential nutrients from her diet, but they're not sure how to get their daughter to slow down and eat when she should. Do you have any advice for Cara's mom and dad? What do you think is the best strategy for ensuring that a toddler like Cara gets all the nutrients she needs, without putting her at risk for obesity? In this chapter, we'll explore the answers to these questions, as well as the unique nutrition needs of toddlers, preschoolers, school-aged children, adolescents, and older adults.

Chapter Objectives

After reading this chapter, you will be able to:

1. Describe the potential nutritional issues that can affect young children and adolescents.

2. Define the concept of food aversions and explain how caregivers can address them.

3. Identify factors that contribute to childhood obesity.

4. Describe how lifestyle choices can affect how people age.

5. Summarize the most common changes in nutrient needs of older adults.

6. Describe how and why lifelong dietary choices can help prevent chronic disease.

7. Summarize the social, economic, and environmental factors that contribute to food insecurity in older adults.

8. List and describe the community nutrition programs available for older adults.

What Are the Nutritional Needs and Issues of Young Children?

There are two distinct age categories during early childhood: **toddlers** (1- to 3-year-olds) and **preschoolers** (ages 3 to 5 years). Toddlers and preschoolers are still growing, but their growth rates have slowed significantly, especially compared with those of infants. During the second year of life, the average weight gain is only about 3 to 5 pounds, and the average height or length gain is about 3 to 5 inches a year.[1] As a result of this slowed growth, the nutritional needs and appetites of toddlers diminish, relative to the needs of infants.

Whereas parents spend their child's first year tending to the infant's constant desire for food, they often spend the toddler and preschool years trying to make sure their busy child takes enough time to eat.[2] Toddlers and preschoolers need the same nutrients as older people, but they need them in different amounts due to their lower energy needs (calories per kilogram of body weight), smaller appetites, and smaller stomachs. As a toddler's appetite diminishes, caregivers may grow concerned that the child isn't eating enough. As long as parents monitor growth and stay alert for anything that seems suspicious (such as changes in the child's energy level, diarrhea, nausea, and/or vomiting, or changes in the quality of the child's hair, skin, or nails), it is likely that the child's food intake will be sufficient.

Young Children Need to Eat Frequent, Small Meals and Nutrient-Dense Foods

Toddlers are extremely active, and they have small stomachs, so the key to ensuring that a toddler obtains adequate nutrients is to feed him nutrient-dense foods at small

Table 16.1

Calorie Needs for Children and Adolescents

| Age | Gender | Activity Level* | | |
		Sedentary	Moderately Active	Active
2–3 years (toddlers)	Male and Female	1,000	1,000–1,400	1,000–1,400
4–8 years (preschoolers and school aged)	Female	1,200	1,400–1,600	1,400–1,800
4–8 years (preschoolers and school aged)	Male	1,400	1,400–1,600	1,600–2,000
9–13 years (school aged)	Female	1,600	1,600–2,000	1,800–2,200
9–13 years (school aged)	Male	1,800	1,800–2,200	2,000–2,600
14–18 years (adolescent)	Female	1,800	2,000	2,400
14–18 years (adolescent)	Male	2,200	2,400–2,800	2,800–3,200

*These levels are based on Estimated Energy Requirements (EER) from the Institute of Medicine's *Dietary Reference Intakes Macronutrients Report*, 2002, calculated by gender, age, and activity level for reference-sized individuals. "Reference size," as determined by the IOM, is based on median height and weight for ages up to 18 years.

Source: HHS/USDA, *Dietary Guidelines for Americans* (2009). Available at http://iom.edu/Activities/Nutrition/SummaryDRIs/~/media/Files/Activity%20Files/Nutrition/DRIs/DRISummaryListing3.ashx. Accessed September 2010.

meals and snacks throughout the day. Because they are always on the go, they need between 1,000 and 1,400 calories per day (see Table 16.1). Meals and snacks should consist of small portions of meat and beans, fruits, vegetables, milk, and whole grains rather than items like chicken nuggets, french fries, sugary drinks, cookies, and crackers.[3] (You can use the Daily Food Plans For Preschoolers and Kids, discussed later in this chapter, for specific numbers of servings for young children.)

Parents must be mindful about portion sizes for young children and avoid pushing children to eat more than they need. One way to help ensure proper portion sizes is to use child-sized plates and cups, which are usually a size more appropriate for the quantity of food that a child can fit into his or her stomach. The rule of thumb is to serve one tablespoon of food at a time per year of age. A two-year-old, for example, would receive two tablespoons of food. Of course, caregivers looking after children with larger or smaller appetites need to tailor portion sizes to each child's individual needs.

Whenever young children are given solid foods, it is important that the food not pose a choking hazard. All foods should be cut into bite-sized pieces. The American Academy of Pediatrics recommends keeping hot dogs, nuts and seeds, chunks of meat or cheese, whole grapes, hard candy, popcorn, chunks of peanut butter, raw vegetables, raisins, and chewing gum away from children younger than age 4.[4] Having the child sit when eating rather than running around will lessen the likelihood of food becoming lodged in the windpipe during a trip or fall. The Table Tips provide some ideas for healthy, toddler-friendly snacks.

Children who attend day care often receive a substantial portion of their daily calories from a day-care provider. Parents should know what is being offered at the day-care site and provide alternative foods for their child if the day-care provider's meals and snacks are insufficient or unhealthy. This is especially important for children who have food allergies or intolerances. Parents should ask day-care providers to alert them of special occasions, such as birthday parties, so they can bring in a treat for their own child if their child is allergic to certain foods. Even if children do not have special dietary concerns, parents have the right to be firm about what their child eats. In some cases, day-care providers may offer menu items or snacks that are superior to what is given at home.

Table Tips

Tasty Treats for Toddlers

Peel and cut (into very small bites) fresh pear, peach, or plum

Mini bagel (not toasted, cut into small bites)

Whole-grain pumpkin or bran muffin

Natural (no added sugar) applesauce

Yogurt with sliced bananas

Remember: Young children should always be supervised while eating!

toddlers Children aged 1 to 3 years old.

preschoolers Children aged 3 to 5 years old.

Using child-sized dishes at mealtimes can help caregivers monitor portion sizes.

Table Tips

Kid-Friendly, Iron-Rich Foods

Stir raisins into warm cereal, or provide a small box of raisins for a snack (for children aged 4 and older).

Add cooked chickpeas to tossed salads for an iron boost.

Tote a baggie of an enriched breakfast cereal on car trips and errands for an iron-rich snack.

Use iron-enriched pastas such as macaroni or spaghetti. Toss in some lean meatballs for a double dose of iron.

Mix enriched rice with dinnertime veggies for a nutrient-dense side dish.

Young Children Have Unique Nutrient Needs

The following nutrients are of special concern in the diets of young children:

➤ *Calcium.* Young children need calcium to develop healthy bones. Children between 1 and 3 years of age should consume 500 milligrams of calcium per day, and children age 4 and 5 should consume 800 milligrams.[5] They can easily meet their needs with milk, as each 8-ounce glass provides 300 milligrams of calcium.

➤ *Iron.* Young children are at particular risk for iron deficiency, which can lead to developmental delays, such as diminished mental, motor, and behavioral functioning.[6] In the United States, an estimated 9 percent of children aged 1 to 2 years old, and 4 percent of children aged 3 to 4 years old, experience iron deficiency.[7] Parents and caregivers must include good sources of iron, such as lean meats and iron-fortified cereals, in children's diets (see the Table Tips for more ideas for iron-rich foods). Although iron deficiency is a concern, iron toxicity is a leading cause of death in children under age 6. Because so little iron is excreted from the body, it can build up to toxic levels in the tissues and organs. Children have died from ingesting as little as 200 milligrams of iron.[8] To protect children from accidental iron poisoning, the Food and Drug Administration (FDA) requires warning labels on iron-containing drugs, supplements, and other products.[9]

➤ *Vitamin D.* To build healthy bones, children ages 1 to 8 should consume 10 micrograms (or 400 IU) of vitamin D daily, which is the latest recommendation by the American Academy of Pediatrics. Because consuming 2 cups of milk daily will meet only half of a child's daily vitamin D needs, fortified cereals and/or a supplement is needed.[10]

➤ *Fiber.* The recommended daily intake for fiber is 19 grams for children ages 1 to 3 and 25 grams for 4- to 8-year olds.[11] Like adults, toddlers need fiber to promote bowel regularity and prevent constipation. A balanced diet that contains whole fruits, vegetables, and whole grains can easily meet a young person's daily fiber needs.

➤ *Fluids.* Daily fluid recommendations are based on a child's weight. For example, a 7-pound child needs about 2 cups of fluid per day; a 21-pound child needs 5 cups; and a 44-pound child needs 8 cups. Caregivers need to monitor a child's beverage intake and provide water, milk, and possibly some 100 percent juice, while avoiding soda and sugary drinks.

Picky Eating and Food Jags Are Common in Small Children

As a young child grows and develops increasingly independent feeding skills (see Table 16.2), the variety of healthy food choices in his or her diet should also increase. If a child's first encounter with cooked peas results in the peas ending up on the floor, this doesn't mean that peas should be permanently off the menu. Research shows that a child may need to be exposed to a food 10 times or more before accepting it.[12] Par- ents also should not remove healthy foods, like broccoli or green beans, from a child's diet because they themselves don't like those foods. Children will often adapt to the foods made available to them.

According to Ellyn Satter, an expert on child feeding and nutrition, there is a division of responsibility when it comes to control of feeding. The adult is responsible

Table 16.2

Food Skills of Young Children

Age	Developmental Feeding Skill
1–2	Child uses the big muscles of the arm and can tear and snap vegetables, help scrub, drink from a cup, and help feed self.
3	Child uses the medium muscles of the hand and can help pour, mix, shake, and spread foods. Child can crack nuts with supervision and feed self independently.
4	Child uses the small muscles of the fingers and can peel, juice, crack raw eggs, and use all utensils and napkins.
5	Child uses eye-hand coordination and can measure, cut with supervision, grind, and grate.

Source: A. Hertzler, 1989 "Preschoolers' Food Handling Skills and Motor Development," *Journal of Nutrition Education* 21:100B-100C

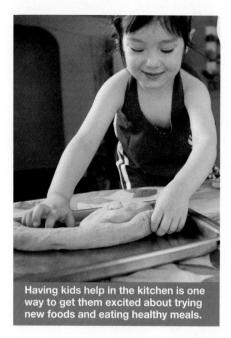

Having kids help in the kitchen is one way to get them excited about trying new foods and eating healthy meals.

for what the child is offered to eat, as well as when and where the food is offered. The child, however, is responsible for whether he or she eats, and how much.[13] Food and power struggles can occur when adults think that their job is not only to provide the food but also to make sure that the child eats it. Often, parents encourage their children to "clean their plates," even though the children may have indicated that they are finished eating. This is a risky habit that encourages overconsumption of calories, which can ultimately lead to obesity. Children should be allowed to stop eating once they are full.

Young children have more taste buds than adults, so foods can taste stronger to them. This can sometimes seem to narrow their food preferences. Parents may think, "My child only eats chicken nuggets and fries," or "She hates vegetables." Though it's true that toddlers often demonstrate **picky eating,** parents should not give up on encouraging them to try and accept new foods.

One way to help small children accept a varied diet is to eat a varied diet yourself. Research suggests that adults' vegetable consumption should serve as a model for younger diners.[14] That is, adults should load up their own plates with a variety of vegetables, and snack on items like carrot sticks and apple slices between meals, so that children will be more likely to follow suit. Children often mimic adults' behaviors, including the unhealthy ones. A mom who only drinks diet soda for dinner, or a dad who insists that his 3-year-old eat asparagus but never puts it on his own plate, may send confusing messages. Involving children in the food shopping, menu selection, and preparation of meals is another way to encourage them to enjoy a variety of foods.

When five-year-old girls (many of whom had dieting moms) were asked, "What do people do when they are on a diet?" their responses included, "Eat more good things," "Can't eat any more snacks; smoke instead," and "Cook for the kids but don't eat the food they make." Caretakers need to model healthy eating habits for all in view.

Whereas picky eating involves not wanting to try new foods, **food jags** are a child's tendency to want to eat only a limited selection of foods. Did your parents ever mention that when you were small, all you wanted to eat was macaroni and cheese or peanut butter? This behavior of getting "stuck" on a small selection of foods is quite common and normal in young children. Luckily, food jags are usually temporary. A child who only wants to eat pretzels and oranges, or refuses to eat anything green, will likely emerge from the phase within a few days or weeks.

If a parent or caregiver senses that the food jag is not going away, then it might be more serious than the natural tendency for a child to assert some independence. At that point, it is helpful to pay careful attention to what the child is eating as well as

picky eating Unwillingness to eat unfamiliar foods.

food jags When a child will only eat the same food meal after meal.

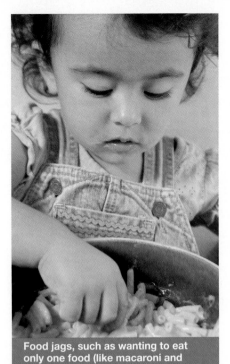

Food jags, such as wanting to eat only one food (like macaroni and cheese), or avoiding certain foods, are common among toddlers.

what he or she is avoiding. Is the child really "eating only goldfish crackers," or is the parent forgetting that the child is also drinking milk and eating green beans and orange slices when they are offered? A parent or caregiver can keep a food diary of everything the child eats and drinks for a few days to help identify any major problems. Sharing concerns (and the food diary) with the child's health care provider and asking for advice may prevent serious nutrient deficiencies in the long run.

In some cases, indulging the food jag may be a means to an end. For example, if a child really does stay stuck on something like pasta, a parent or caregiver can offer a variety of foods within that category (for example, serving different shapes of pasta, and using different accompanying ingredients). Another, braver tactic is to gradually wean the child from a particular food. Parents and caregivers must remember that they have ultimate authority. While this should not be license to have dinner table wars, it does mean that the adult needs to control the situation in a healthy manner for the sake of the child.

Young Children and Vegetarianism

Young children can grow and develop normally on a vegetarian diet, as long as their dietary patterns are well planned and include good sources of calcium, iron, and zinc. Children on vegan diets also need a reliable source of B_{12}. Vegetarian diets should be rich in whole grains, vegetables, and fruits, the very foods that are encouraged for the general population. Because many vegetarian foods are high in fiber, the amount of foods needed to meet nutrient requirements may exceed what young children can eat, since their small stomachs cannot hold too much food at one time.[15]

The Take-Home Message Toddlers grow at a much slower rate than infants, and have reduced appetites. Caregivers need to be sure that toddlers get adequate amounts of calcium, iron, vitamin D, and fiber. Caregivers also need to monitor a child's beverage intake and provide water, milk, and 100 percent juice while avoiding soda and sugary drinks. Adults should be sure to offer children appropriate portion sizes. Toddlers and preschoolers will stop eating when full and shouldn't be forced to clean their plates. Caregivers should be good role models when it comes to getting children to try new foods, which may need to be offered 10 times or more before they are accepted. Food jags are normal and usually temporary. Young children can grow and thrive on vegetarian diets as long as the diets are carefully planned.

What Are the Nutritional Needs and Issues of School-Aged Children?

school-aged children Children between the ages of 6 and 10 to 12.

School-aged children, usually considered those between the ages of 6 and 10 to 12, still have plenty of growing to do, and the quality of their diet affects their growth. (See Table 16.1 on page 581 for the range of calorie needs for children in this age

Table 16.3

TASTE: Increasing Fruits and Vegetables in the Family Meal

T: Try something new at every eating occasion	Add shredded carrots to casseroles, chili, lasagna, meatloaf, or soup.
	Drop berries into cereal, pancakes, or yogurt.
	Make fruit smoothies and veggie burritos.
	Use leftover veggies for salad, or add them to a can of soup.
	Keep grab-and-go snacks handy, such as boxes of raisins, dried fruit trail mix, frozen 100% fruit juice bars. Cherry tomatoes and carrot sticks with hummus can be a tasty and refreshing veggie treat.
A: All forms of fruits and veggies count!	Consider fresh, frozen, 100% juice, canned, and dried.
	Cook fruits and veggies in different ways, including steamed, slow-cooked, sautéed, stir-fried, grilled, and microwaved.
S: Shop smart	Fresh produce in season is more affordable. Look for specials.
	Clean and cut up the produce so it will be ready to use.
	At a restaurant, substitute vegetables for high-fat side orders.
T: Turn it into a family activity	Let kids skewer a shish-kabob or make a pizza.
	Farmer's markets can be a fun trip for kids.
E: Explore the bountiful variety	Use salad bars or buffets to try new flavors.
	On a shopping trip, let kids pick out a new produce item for the family meal.

Source: Adapted from Fruits & Veggies—More Matters, "T.A.S.T.E. Tips and Information for Moms." Available at www.fruitsandveggiesmorematters.org.

group.) Gross and fine motor skills become more refined. Due to the routine of school and being away from home, school-aged children do not eat as many times throughout the day as do toddlers and preschoolers.

Although children of school age have developed skills such as tying their own shoes or buckling their own seat belts, there are still several nutrition-related issues that parents and caregivers need to keep in mind. At this point in the life cycle, children are learning habits that they may keep for life, so encouraging a healthy lifestyle is essential. Parents and caregivers should capitalize on their role model status, as children are watching and learning from the habits and actions of adults. See Table 16.3 for ideas on encouraging healthy eating habits among children in this age group. Note that some parents have linked diet to certain developmental disabilities. The boxed feature "Nutrition and Developmental Disabilities" explores whether there is evidence of a connection.

Nutrition and Developmental Disabilities

Many young children are diagnosed with behavior-related conditions such as **attention deficit hyperactivity disorder (ADHD)** (sometimes still called attention deficit disorder, or ADD). ADHD is a condition in which children are inattentive, hyperactive, and impulsive.[1] It generally emerges in early childhood, and those with ADHD have difficulty controlling their behavior. An estimated 3 to 5 percent of children (about 2 million) in the United States have ADHD. Given the common characteristics of the condition, it can be difficult and frustrating to manage. Parents often wonder if dietary factors, like sugar intake or food additives, are responsible for their children's behavior.

Although the myth that sugar contributes to ADHD persists, there isn't any research to support this. In a study, children whose mothers felt they were sugar sensitive were given aspartame as a substitute for sugar. Half of the mothers were told their children were given sugar, half that their children were given aspartame. The mothers who thought their children had received sugar rated them as more hyperactive than the other children and were more critical of their behavior.[2]

Currently, the American Dietetic Association has concluded that sugar doesn't have an effect on behavior or learning. The American Academy of Pediatrics has also confirmed that there is no evidence that ADHD is caused by eating too much sugar, or by food additives, allergies, or immunizations.[3]

With so many children and families affected by ADHD, more theories about the cause of ADHD have emerged in recent years. There have been studies citing a possible connection between cigarette and alcohol use during pregnancy and increased risk for the child to have ADHD. Other studies have noted a higher risk of ADHD with high levels of lead in the bodies of preschoolers. Attention disorders often run in families, so there are likely to be genetic influences.[4]

Although there are no definitive answers about the root cause, there are a range of treatments for ADHD. Medication, psychotherapy, and behavioral therapies, as well as diet restrictions, are among the many methods used to address the condition. Parents of children with ADHD may want to consult with a registered dietitian to help their child with nutritional issues, such as underweight due to side effects of certain medications that decrease appetite. Disruptive mealtimes may also be a concern (if untreated). Organizations such as the National Institute of Mental Health (www.nimh.nih.gov) and the American Academy of Child and Adolescent Psychiatry (www.aacap.org) provide information for families with children who have ADHD.

Autism spectrum disorder (ASD) is another developmental disorder that appears in the first three years of life and affects the brain's normal development of social and communication skills. The symptoms and severity of autism vary greatly. However, all autism disorders affect a child's ability to communicate and interact with others. There is no cure for ASD; the ideal treatment includes educational and behavioral interventions that meet the specific needs of the child.[5]

Because autism is incurable, many parents seek out alternative therapies, including specialized diets. Although research is limited and results vary, several diet strategies have been suggested as possible treatments for autism. One of the most popular diets eliminates gluten (a protein found in most grains, including wheat) as well as casein (a milk protein). Other dietary interventions include restricting food allergens; including probiotics in the diet; following a yeast-free diet; and supplementing the diet with vitamin A, vitamin C, vitamin B_6, magnesium, folic acid, vitamin B_{12}, and omega-3 fatty acids.[6] Because more research is needed to determine the efficacy of these interventions, parents of autistic children are encouraged to work with a registered dietitian with expertise in this field.

attention deficit hyperactivity disorder (ADHD) Previously known as attention deficit disorder (ADD). A condition in which an individual may be easily distracted, and have difficulty listening and following directions, difficulty focusing and sustaining attention, difficulty concentrating and staying on task, and/or inconsistent performance in school.

autism spectrum disorder
A brain disorder that makes it hard to communicate and relate to others due to failure of different parts of the brain to work together.

School-Aged Children Are Experiencing Higher Rates of Obesity and Diabetes

childhood obesity The condition of a child's having too much body weight for his height.

In recent decades, overweight and obesity among both children and adults have increased dramatically (see **Figure 16.1**) and recent data show that almost 20 percent of U.S. school-aged children are obese.[16] The reason for the increase in **childhood obesity**

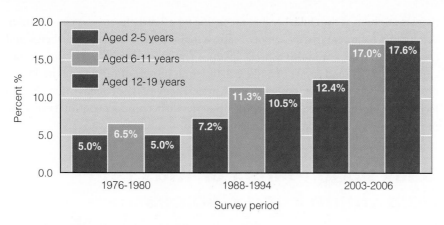

Figure 16.1 **Increase in Obesity among U.S. Children and Adolescents**

is likely a combination of several factors, including too many calories and too little physical activity.

Children Are Overeating

Children are taking in excess calories from several sources, including sodas, candy, and snack items like chips. Food is everywhere, including in places where it was previously unavailable, such as at gas stations and bookshops. Portion sizes, both in restaurants and at home, are bigger than they used to be.[17] American children, on the whole, eat a diet higher in fat, sodium, and added sugars, and lower in whole grains, fruits, vegetables, and lean dairy products, than they should be consuming.[18]

Children Are Not Getting Enough Physical Activity

Children are not getting enough physical activity to balance the energy they're consuming. The following are two of the multiple factors contributing to the decreased level of physical activity in recent years:

➤ *Increased screen time.* Research shows that 8- to 18-year-olds devote an average of 7½ hours daily to entertainment media, including television, computer time, video games, and movies. Further more, because they spend so much of that time "media multitasking" (using more than one medium at a time), they actually manage to pack a total of 10 hours and 45 minutes worth of media content into those 7½ hours.[19] Screen time should be limited to no more than 2 hours daily.

➤ *Decreased physical activity at school.* Children are getting less physical activity while at school and during other parts of their day. Only 8 percent of U.S. elementary schools and 6.4 percent of middle schools provide daily physical education to students.[20] In addition, 20 percent of U.S. elementary schools have abolished recess, and less than 25 percent of children engage in 30 minutes of any kind of physical activity daily.[21] To reduce children's risk of becoming overweight or obese, the American Academy of Pediatrics recommends that parents and caregivers serve as role models for healthy eating coupled with physical activity.[22]

Obesity Contributes to Diabetes

One result of increased obesity among children is an associated increase in rates of type 2 diabetes, which used to be seen solely in adulthood. For children diagnosed with type 2 diabetes, early intervention and treatment are a must. The sooner the family learns what the child needs to eat and how to manage all other aspects of the disease, the better off the child will be. In fact, the entire family should consider eating in

We Can!

Want to learn more about programs that help families battle obesity? Visit www.nhlbi.nih.gov/health/public/heart/obesity/wecan to learn about the We Can! program (Ways to Enhance Children's Activity & Nutrition) from the National Institutes of Health, which helps parents and caregivers prevent overweight and obesity in children.

the same fashion as the child, because managing type 2 diabetes involves moderation, variety, and balance. Physical activity is also a major part of managing diabetes, and everyone can take part in this as well. Taking a family walk or bike ride after dinner and enjoying weekend games of basketball or tennis instead of turning on the TV are excellent ways to teach the importance of physical activity. The child is more likely to feel supported and succeed with keeping his or her diabetes under control if everyone in the family is educated about what to do to help.

Daily Food Plans For Kids Can Help Guide Food Choices

Because most parents are not nutrition experts, the idea of trying to meet all of the nutrient needs of children can be overwhelming and confusing. Fortunately, child-friendly (and, therefore, parent-friendly) versions of the Daily Food Plans and the new 10 tips Nutrition Education Series (see **Figure 16.2**) available at ChooseMyPlate.gov can help guide their choices.

Cut back on kid's sweet treats

1 Serve small portions

2 Offer healthy drinks

3 Use the check-out lane that does not display candy

4 Chose not to offer sweets as rewards

5 Make fruit the everyday dessert

6 Make food fun

7 Encourage kids to invent new snacks

8 Play detective in the cereal aisle

9 Make treats "treats," not everyday foods

10 If kids don't eat their meal, they don't need sweet "extras"

Be a healthy role model for children

1 Show by example

2 Go food shopping together

3 Get creative in the kitchen

4 Offer the same foods for everyone

5 Reward with attention, not food

6 Focus on each other at the table

7 Listen to your child

8 Limit screen time

9 Encourage physical activity

10 Be a good food role model

Figure 16.2 Tips and Daily Food Plans from ChooseMyPlate.gov

Source: USDA, 10 tips Nutrition Education Series. 2011. Available at www.choosemyplate.gov

The portions of the ChooseMyPlate.gov website for children encourages kids to:

➤ *Be physically active every day.*
➤ *Choose healthier foods from each group.* Every food group has foods that should be eaten more often than others. Choices from the vegetables, fruits, grains, protein, and dairy groups should be varied.
➤ *Eat more of some food groups than others.* The sizes of the food groups as high-lighted in MyPlate indicates suggested relative proportionality.
➤ *Eat foods from every food group every day.* The different colors of the food groups shown in MyPlate represent the five different food groups (and don't forget healthy oils!).
➤ *Make the right choices for you.* ChooseMyPlate.gov gives everyone in the family personal ideas on how to eat better and exercise more.
➤ *Take it one step at a time.* Start with one new, good thing a day, and continue to add another new one every day.

Children who have special health-related issues or chronic diseases may not nec-essarily be able to follow the Daily Food Plans for Preschoolers and for Kids. For example, children with autism may become especially fixated on specific foods or be reluctant to try new foods. Overcoming these issues generally requires intervention and support from professionals who work with children with special needs, such as a health care provider or a registered dietitian.

The Importance of Breakfast

For both cognitive and health reasons, it's hard to overstate the importance of a nutritious morning meal for school-aged children. Breakfast can positively bene-fit mental function (especially memory), academic performance, school atten-dance rates, psychosocial function, and mood. If a child is hungry during the midmorning hours, it will affect his or her learning during this time period. Eating breakfast also improves blood glucose levels, which in turn leads to improvements in both comprehension and memory. Studies conducted by the USDA on the school breakfast program have found that children who received a school breakfast did better on standardized tests than children who did not eat breakfast.[23]

Research has also shown that eating breakfast may be associated with healthier body weight in children and adolescents and reduce the risk of obesity in this age group. Breakfast eaters tend to have better overall nutrient intakes and consume less fat and cholesterol and more fiber over the course of the day than non–breakfast eaters. Nutrients missed at breakfast—calcium, fiber, and certain vitamins and minerals—are rarely made up for during the day. The habit of skipping breakfast is often seen in children and adolescents who are overweight.[24] Those who miss break-fast are less likely to engage in physical activity.

Optimally, children should eat breakfast at home before school. Fortified cereals that are low in sugar can be a quick and nutritious choice, as they are a good source of iron, folic acid, zinc, and B vitamins. Many of these cereals also contain added vi-tamin A, thiamin, niacin, calcium, phosphorus, and magnesium. Choosing whole-grain cereals contributes to fiber intake and, when paired with fortified milk, provides for a nutrient-dense breakfast. If children don't have time to eat breakfast at home, and aren't receiving school breakfast, caregivers can also provide quick, nutritious morning meals that can be eaten on the way to school. See the Table Tips for some on-the-go breakfast ideas.

Table Tips
Breakfast on the Go

Mix some dry, unsweetened, whole-grain cereal with an individual-sized container of low-fat yogurt. Throw in some banana slices, berries, or dried fruit to make it even more nutritious.

Sprinkle reduced-fat cheese on a corn tortilla and melt it in the oven or mi-crowave. Add some salsa and corn and roll it up into a portable tortilla tube.

Spread a thin layer of natural peanut but-ter or all-fruit preserves on a toasted whole-wheat waffle, and pair it with a travel cup of skim milk.

School Lunches Contribute to Children's Nutritional Status

The National School Lunch Program provides breakfast and noontime meals for millions of school-aged children.

The National School Lunch Program (NSLP) provides nutritionally balanced, low-cost or free lunches to more than 30 million children each school day. The NSLP meals are designed to meet certain nutrient guidelines, including minimum levels for calories, protein, calcium, iron, vitamin A, and vitamin C. There are maximum levels for the percent of calories from fat as well as other specific nutrient and portion recommendations (see Tables 16.4 and 16.5).[25]

Imagine that you are a school food-service director running a school cafeteria. On the one hand, you are running a business. You need to make money for payroll, to keep the ovens heated, to purchase paper goods on which to serve the food, and so forth. On the other hand, you must meet the nutritional requirements set up by the USDA while satisfying your hungry customers who have distinct preferences and dislikes. The USDA donates certain foods, which helps keep prices down, but you have to stick to the regulations in order to receive these foods. You may also have the competition of nearby fast-food restaurants or vending machines vying for your customers' attention. In order to serve healthy school lunches, the director has to plan a balanced meal, using a variety of food groups, in the right portions, depending on the age of the student. Many times, further healthy substitutions can be made that will improve the quality of the meal.

As you can see, the school food-service director has quite a few people to satisfy, and much to consider when deciding what to serve. For some children, the food that they eat at school is the healthiest meal—perhaps the only meal—they eat all day.

Table Tips

Tips for Packing School Lunches

Get children excited about their lunches by having them pick out a fun lunch box or decorate a brown paper bag with stickers.

Involve the child in planning lunches and then shop for the items together.

Make a lunch calendar and go over the specific days the child will eat a school-provided lunch and the days he or she will pack lunch. On packing days, be sure to give the child food options.

Select new foods that the child likes and ask if there are new items he or she wants to try.

Be mindful of what the child is actually eating and what might be left behind or thrown away. If, for example, the apple keeps coming back day after day, it's time to try an orange.

Table 16.4

Minimum Nutrient and Calorie Levels for School Lunches (School Week Averages)

Nutrients and Energy Allowances	Minimum Requirements*		
	Preschool	Grades K–6	Grades 7–12
Energy allowances (calories)	517	664	825
Total fat (g)†	17 g	22 g	28 g
Saturated fat (g)‡	6 g	7 g	9 g
RDA for protein (g)	7 g	10 g	16 g
RDA for calcium (mg)	267 mg	286 mg	400 mg
RDA for iron (mg)	3.3 mg	3.5 mg	4.5 mg
RDA for vitamin A (RE)	150 RE	224 RE	300 RE
RDA for vitamin C (mg)	14 mg	15 mg	18 mg

Source: USDA Food and Nutrition Service. Available at http://www.fns.usda.gov/cnd/menu/menu.planning.NSLP.htm. Accessed September, 2010.

*Based on the enhanced menu approach, maximizing low-fat alternatives and increasing calorie intake of fruits, vegetables, and grains/breads. Alternative menu planning options are available, including optional grade K-3 enhanced menu planning.
†Total fat not to exceed 30 percent of total calories; grams of fat will vary depending on the actual level of calories offered.
‡Saturated fat to be less than 10 percent of total calories; grams of fat will vary depending on the actual level of calories offered.

Table 16.5

Food and Beverages That Meet Recommended School Standards

Preferred Foods for All Students (Tiers 1 and 2)

Tier 1 Foods

Recommended for students of all grade levels during the school day, and include fresh or minimally processed foods such as fruits, vegetables, whole grains, and nonfat dairy products. Limited to:

- 200 calories or less per portion
- No more than 35% of total calories from fat
- Less than 10% of total calories from saturated fats
- Zero *trans* fat
- 35% or less of calories from total sugars, except for yogurt with no more than 30 g of total sugars, per 8-oz portion as packaged
- Sodium content of 200 mg or less per portion as packaged

- Individual fruits: apples, pears, oranges
- Fruit cups packed in juice or water
- Vegetables: baby carrots, broccoli
- Dehydrated or dried fruits
- 100% fruit juice or low-sodium 100% vegetable juice
- Whole-grain, low-sugar cereals
- 100% whole-grain mini bagels
- 8-oz servings of low-fat fruit-flavored yogurt with <30 grams of sugar per serving

Tier 1 Beverages

Low in calories and sugar, nutrient dense, and caffeine free, with the exception of trace amounts of naturally occurring caffeine substances.

- Water without flavoring, additives, or carbonation
- Low-fat (1%) and nonfat milk in 8-oz portions
- 100% juice in 4-oz portion as packaged for elementary/middle school and 8 oz (2 portions) for high school

Tier 2 Foods

Designed only for high school students after the end of the school day and do not necessarily provide a serving of fruits, vegetables, whole grains, or low-fat or nonfat dairy; however, they do meet the food composition recommendations for calories, fat, sugar, and sodium.

- Same as above
- May also include processed foods such as certain baked potato chips, whole-wheat crackers, animal cracker cookies, graham crackers, and pretzels

Tier 2 Beverages

These are Tier 1 beverages that are sold after school and are low in calories and sugar, nutrient dense, and caffeine free, with the exception of trace amounts of naturally occurring caffeine substances.

- Same as above

Source: Institute of Medicine, "Nutrition Standards for Foods in Schools: Leading the Way toward Healthier Youth" (2007). Available at www8.nationalacademies.org/onpinews/newsitem.aspx?RecordID=04252007. Accessed July 2010.

If children are not eating the school lunches, it's up to the parents and care-givers to come up with a healthy substitute. Simply giving the child money may lead to a candy-bar-and-soda lunch, which will shortchange him of about one-third of his nutrition for the day. Rather, it makes nutritional sense for the parent *and* the child to use the Daily Food Plans at ChooseMyPlate.gov as a guide to put together a mutually agreeable healthy lunch for the child to take to school. A lunch that the child has helped to plan has a better chance of being eaten. Without the child's input, the "healthy lunch" may end up being swapped for unhealthy foods, or worse, tossed in the trash can. The Table Tips provide some useful ideas to improve the likelihood that a child will eat his packed lunch.

The Take-Home Message Increasing obesity rates are contributing to rising rates of type 2 diabetes in school-aged children. Parents and care-givers need to be sure children limit their empty-calorie foods and get enough physical activity. Daily Food Plans available at ChooseMyPlate.gov address the nutritional needs of preschool and school-aged children. Children who eat breakfast tend to have better concentration in class and better overall dietary habits, among other benefits, than those who do not eat breakfast. School meals provide nourishment for children. For children who refuse to eat school lunches, parents and caregivers need to provide a healthy alternative.

What Are the Nutritional Needs and Issues of Adolescents?

Adolescence is the stage of the life cycle between the start of puberty and adulthood. With adolescence come many hormonal, physical, and emotional changes, including:

➤ *Hormonal changes.* Under the influence of hormones, adolescents develop secondary sex characteristics, such as pubic hair and, for boys, a lower speaking voice. Girls experience breast development and their first menstrual period (called *menarche*). Adolescents of either sex can experience their first outbreak of acne.

➤ *Physical changes.* Among the physical changes are a rapid **growth spurt,** which must be supported with appropriate quantities of nutrients, and adequate calories (energy) and protein. Adolescents attain about 15 percent of their adult height during this stage, and about 50 percent of their ideal adult weight. Bones grow significantly, and lean muscle mass and body fat stores also increase. Thus, calcium, vitamin D, and iron are particularly important at this stage. As with younger age groups, the rate of obesity is increasing among adolescents, and approximately 18 percent are considered obese.[26]

➤ *Emotional changes.* Some nutrition-related issues that arise during adolescence may be indirectly caused by the emotional growth that is occurring. Adolescents experience a strong desire for independence and individuality, and most want to make their own food choices, which may be less nutritious than what is being served at home.

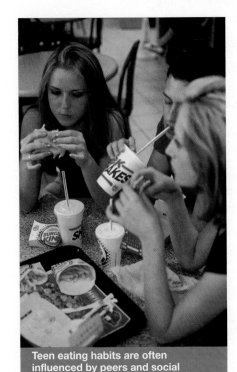
Teen eating habits are often influenced by peers and social settings.

Peer Pressure and Social Eating

When children are young, their parents and families have greater control over what they eat. As they get older, however, what their friends eat in the school environment and what is available to them in school and elsewhere will have an impact on their choices. Fitting in is very important to teens; if a soft drink and a burger are what everyone else is eating, then a teen may be less likely to opt for a salad and a bottle of water. Some teens may defy authority by adopting more rigid dietary choices than their parents, such as insisting on organically grown foods or adopting a vegan diet. Young people within a group tend to take into account what, when, and how their

adolescence The developmental period between childhood and early adulthood.

growth spurt A rapid increase in height and weight.

peers eat and then make decisions about whether or not they fit into this "norm." This can be particularly difficult for teens who struggle to make or maintain friendships.

The influence of peers, the media, and other nonparental role models may also prompt adolescents to adopt damaging habits, such as smoking to lose weight or drinking alcohol to gain acceptance as one of the "in crowd." Unfortunately, these habits not only are unhealthy, but also can contribute to low self-esteem when the outcomes do not meet expectations.

Finally, time (or lack of it) has an influence on the food choices of teens. Unstructured meals and choosing to snack or graze is part of a growing culture and is commonplace among adolescents. Many teens skip breakfast because they don't have time or they want to lose weight, and they rely on snacks of junk food for nourishment. These snacks are often high in calories, sugar, and saturated fat and low in vitamins, minerals, and fiber. The fact that teenagers often do not have much money to spend or do not like to spend it on food often leads them to fast-food restaurants where social determinants come into play. Due to the increased reliance on convenience, the number of overweight teens continues to grow, increasing their risk for multiple health issues.

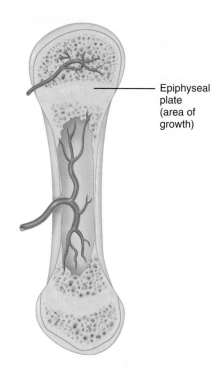

Epiphyseal plate (area of growth)

Figure 16.3 Epiphyseal Plate in Long Bone
Adolescent bone growth takes place along the epiphyseal plate. Once the plates close, lengthening of the bone stops.

Adolescents Need Calcium and Vitamin D for Bone Growth

Adolescents experience rapid bone growth. Most of the growth occurs in the **epiphyseal plate** (**Figure 16.3**), the area of tissue near the end of the long bones in children and adolescents. The growth plate determines the future length and shape of the mature bone. At some point during adolescence, bone growth is complete. The plates close and are replaced by solid bone.[27] (In contrast, **bone mineral density** increases through early adulthood, and **peak bone mass** may not be reached until age 30.) Inadequate intakes of calcium and vitamin D during adolescence are factors that can lead to low peak bone mass and increase the risk for osteoporosis. As with young children, the recommendation for vitamin D has recently been increased to 400 IU daily.[28]

Inadequate intakes of calcium and vitamin D among adolescents are common. One reason for this trend is teens' increased preference for soft drinks instead of milk or other beverages providing calcium and vitamin D (see **Figure 16.4** on the next page). Research suggests that 13- to 18-year-old boys, on average, consume the equivalent of 2 12-ounce cans of soda a day and girls, on average, consume 1⅓ cans per day.[29] Sodas and other empty-calorie beverages, such as energy drinks and sports drinks, may taste good and be popular with peers, but they lack the nutrients that are so crucial for developing bones.

Teenagers Need More Iron

Adolescents need additional iron to support muscle growth and increased blood volume. Adolescent girls also need more iron to support the onset of menstruation. Many adolescents, especially those who are dieting, have an inadequate iron intake. In a large study, iron deficiency was found in more than 14 percent of the girls aged 15 to 18 and in 12 percent of the boys aged 11 to 14 in the United States.[30] Iron deficiency has been shown to exist in both male and female teens of all races and socioeconomic levels.[31] Teens who limit enriched grains, lean meats, and legumes in their diet are running the risk of failing to meet their daily iron needs.

epiphyseal plate The growth plate of the bone. In puberty, growth in this area leads to increases in height.

bone mineral density (BMD) The amount of minerals, in particular calcium, per volume in an individual's bone. The denser the bones, the stronger the bones.

peak bone mass The genetically determined maximum amount of bone mass an individual can build up.

Figure 16.4 Increased Consumption of Soft Drinks among Children and Adolescents
Over the past several decades, young Americans have been drinking more soda and less milk, which isn't a healthy combination for their growing bones.

Table Tips

Teen Table Tips

Encourage teens to read labels on soda to find out how many empty calories are in a serving.

Talk to them about real-life stories of people using weight-loss pills, steroids, or other quick fixes to lose weight rather than eating in a healthy way to get results.

Direct them to credible websites for information, such as www.kidshealth.org/teen/food_fitness/ or www.win.niddk.nih.gov/publications/take_charge.htm

Be a role model! Eat well, get enough rest, exercise, be realistic about dieting, and don't smoke.

Teach teens to look for healthy options, such as salads and granola bars, at fast-food restaurants and in vending machines so they can still do what they like without compromising health.

Adolescents Are Sometimes at Risk for Disordered Eating

Teens must adjust to new bodies, new thoughts, new experiences, and new social networks. These changes, along with the typical adolescent feeling of immortality, increase the potential for an adolescent to engage in risky tactics to reach and maintain a desired weight, and can ultimately lead to disordered eating behaviors. These can include eating very little food, using a food substitute, skipping meals, smoking cigarettes, taking diet pills, engaging in self-induced vomiting, and/or using laxatives or diuretics. These behaviors typically fail. A study found that, compared with teens who did not use any weight-control methods, adolescents who engaged in unhealthful behaviors to control their weight exhibited a slightly higher body mass index and a greater risk of being overweight, binge eating, or extreme dieting five years later.[32] In essence, the teen ends up with two problems: the feeling of failure as well as the health consequences associated with the risky tactic used to try to change his or her weight.

The Take-Home Message Adolescents face hormonal, physical, and emotional changes. They typically want to have control over their food and lifestyle decisions, and peers and the media exert a tremendous amount of influence. Calcium, vitamin D, and iron intakes are particularly important during adolescence to ensure adequate bone and muscle growth. Increased consumption of soft drinks and decreased milk consumption can compromise bone health. Adolescents are sometimes at risk of developing disordered eating patterns due to poor body image, emotional issues, and peer pressure. Because many adolescents live in the "here and now," they may not realize the long-term health consequences of the poor diet and lifestyle habits they adopt during their teenage years.

What Are the Nutritional Issues of Older Adults?

At about age 50, a person is considered an older adult. Reaching this age wasn't always a given. If you were born in 1900, you would have been lucky to see your fiftieth birthday, as the average **life expectancy** at the time was 47 years. Your relatives born in the 1960s can expect to live to about age 70, while those born in the 1990s are expected to live past age 75.[33] Currently, there are more than 50,000 centenarians, people who are 100 years of age or older, living in the United States.[34]

Adults Are Living Longer

What happened in the past 100-plus years to so dramatically increase the average life expectancy? Advances in research and health care, coupled with public health promotion programs, have all contributed to Americans' longer lives. For example, the infectious and deadly diseases of the 1900s, such as tuberculosis, pneumonia, polio, mumps, and measles, have been dramatically reduced, if not eradicated, due to better vaccinations and medical care. For decades, ongoing public education campaigns have emphasized a healthy diet and lifestyle to prevent and manage conditions such as high blood pressure and blood cholesterol levels before they develop into the more crippling and sometimes deadly stroke and heart disease.

All of these efforts will benefit the generation of "baby boomers" born between 1946 and 1964. Those at the tail end of this group, ages 55 to 64, are expected to be the fastest growing segment of the population over the next decade. The number of individuals 65 years of age and older is projected to increase to more than 80 million in 2050. The number of those living beyond the age of 80 will also rise (**Figure 16.5**).[35]

Good nutrition continues to play a key role in healthful aging. Nutrient needs, and the way the body uses some nutrients, change as you age.[36]

People are living longer today than in previous decades.

Older Adults Need Fewer Calories, Not Less Nutrition

Because a person's metabolic rate naturally declines with age, older adults need fewer calories. The decline in their metabolism is a combination of the natural loss of muscle mass (muscle mass requires more energy to be maintained than fat mass) and the

life expectancy The number of years that a person will live.

Figure 16.5 Aging of the Baby Boomers
The number of older adults in the United States is expected to increase dramatically over the next several decades.

Source: Federal Interagency Forum on Aging-Related Statistics, www.agingstats.gov.

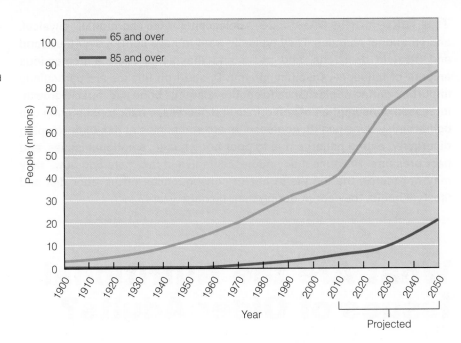

tendency toward less daily physical activity. This decline amounts to approximately 10 calories a year for men and 7 calories yearly for women.[37] In other words, a man at age 60 needs 300 fewer daily calories—about the amount in a turkey sandwich—than he needed at age 30. Some research has even suggested that at 80 years of age, calorie intake may be reduced by as much as 1,000 calories daily in some men and by 600 calories daily in some women compared to when they were in their 20s.[38]

Though calorie needs may be reduced, the need for many nutrients and phytochemicals isn't. In fact, the requirement for some nutrients actually increases in older adults, making nutrient-dense food selections even more important. Because phytochemicals, especially antioxidants, have possible roles in helping to reduce the risk of certain cancers, heart disease, cataracts, and age-related macular degeneration, foods should be both nutrient dense and phytochemical dense.

Older Adults Need to Get Enough Fiber and Fluids

Because they are consuming fewer calories, older adults need to eat high-fiber foods, such as whole grains, fruits, and vegetables at each meal. Though their dietary fiber needs actually decrease slightly, more than 70 percent of Americans over age 50, on average, are still not meeting their daily needs.[39] Recall from Chapter 4 that fiber may help reduce the risk of diverticulosis, heart disease, type 2 diabetes mellitus, obesity, and certain cancers, which are all more common during the older years. Older adults' requirements for dietary protein, fat, and carbohydrates don't change from their younger years, and research shows that these three nutrient needs can be easily met by a balanced diet.[40]

Consuming adequate amounts of fluid is important, as the kidneys' ability to concentrate urine declines with age, which can lead to dehydration. An older person's thirst mechanism also becomes blunted, further increasing the risk of becoming dehydrated. Certain medications may cause the body to lose water and/or further blunt the thirst mechanism.[41]

Though older adults have the same fluid recommendations as younger people, the fear of frequent trips to the bathroom, especially when they are away from home, often causes them to deliberately consume less fluid. Incidences of urinary incontinence (the loss of control of the bladder) also increase with age due to prostate prob-

Table 16.6

Dietary Changes Needed as You Age

What Older Adults Need	Why Older Adults Need It	How They Can Get It
More nutrient-dense foods	Lower metabolic rate, which reduces their daily calorie needs	Choose foods in each food group that are low in added sugar and saturated fat.
More fiber	Consumption of fewer daily calories, which decreases their fiber intake	Choose whole-wheat bread, whole-grain cereals, brown rice, vegetables, and whole fruit.
More water and nutrient-dense fluids. Less sugary, low-nutrient soft drinks	Decreased ability of their kidneys to concentrate urine and a blunted thirst mechanism, which can both increase risk of dehydration	Drink low-fat or skim milk and water with and between meals.
More foods high in beta-carotene to meet vitamin A needs and less vitamin A supplements and heavily fortified foods	Higher excess amounts of stored pre-formed vitamin A in the body, which can be unhealthy for bones	Choose carrots, cantaloupe, sweet potatoes, broccoli, and winter squash.
More vitamin D–fortified foods	Decreased ability to make the active form of vitamin D, which decreases the absorption of calcium and phosphorus and increases the risk of osteoporosis	Choose vitamin D–fortified milk, yogurt, and cereals. Add a supplement if needed.
More synthetic form of vitamin B_{12}	Fewer acidic stomach juices, which will lessen the absorption of vitamin B_{12} in foods	Choose vitamin B_{12}–fortified cereals and soy milk. Add a supplement if needed.
More iron-rich foods	Higher prevalence of anemia in aging people	Choose lean meat, fish, and poultry. Enjoy enriched grains and cereals along with vitamin C–rich foods (citrus fruits) to enhance absorption.
More zinc-rich foods	Suppressed immune system and appetite in aging people due to a zinc deficiency	Choose fortified cereals, lean meats, poultry, legumes, and nuts.
More calcium-rich foods	Higher risk of osteoporosis and dietary calcium deficiency	Consume 3 servings of dairy foods daily, plus a serving of a calcium-fortified food. Add a supplement if needed.

lems in men and weakened bladder muscles in many women after pregnancy. This may further reduce the enthusiasm for consuming fluids during the day and cause many older people to become dehydrated. Dehydration can also lead to constipation, another common condition in older adults, as the stool becomes hard and compacted in the colon.

Because of the need for nutrient-dense foods, there is little room in an older adult's diet for sugar-laden soft drinks that are high in calories and low in nutrients. Water and milk are better beverages for meeting their fluid needs and avoiding dehydration. Table 16.6 summarizes these dietary changes.

Older Adults Need to Monitor Micronutrient Intake

Appropriate intakes of certain micronutrients become a concern as we age:

➤ *Vitamin A.* Although the recommended daily amount of vitamin A doesn't change for people over the age of 50, too much preformed vitamin A (derived from animal sources), which is stored in the body, may increase the risk for osteoporosis and fractures. Older adults should be cautious when choosing supplements and fortified foods so as to prevent overconsuming this form of vitamin A.[42] However, beta-carotene, a vitamin A precursor, is not of concern and is actually beneficial because of its role as an antioxidant in the body.

➤ *Vitamin D.* The skin's ability to make vitamin D from sunlight declines with age. Further, the intestines and kidneys lose some ability to absorb and convert vitamin D into its active form. Because of these changes, the need for vitamin D in the diet increases to 800 IU at age 70.[43]

➤ *Vitamin B_{12}.* In up to 30 percent of people over the age of 50, the stomach secretes less hydrochloric acid. One role of hydrochloric acid is to separate the vitamin B_{12} from the proteins in foods of animal origin. Thus, low acid production means that we cannot free up and absorb enough of the vitamin B_{12} that naturally occurs in foods. The synthetic form of B_{12} found in fortified foods and supplements is not affected, so these sources should be added to an older adult's diet. Vitamin B_{12}, along with adequate amounts of folate and vitamin B_6, may also help lower homocysteine levels, decreasing the risk for heart disease.

➤ *Iron.* Iron deficiency is common in older adults; more than 10 percent of adults 65 years or older, and more than 20 percent of those 85 or older, experience iron-deficiency anemia.[44] Although iron deficiency can occur from intestinal blood loss, an estimated one-third of the anemia in older adults stems from inadequate iron consumption and/or from insufficient folate and vitamin B_{12} in the diet.[45]

➤ *Zinc.* Zinc affects our ability to taste things, and a deficiency can depress a person's appetite, and hence, her desire to eat nutritious foods. About 25 percent of older Americans don't meet their needs for daily dietary zinc and would benefit from adding more zinc to their diets through foods such as cereals and legumes (dried beans and peas).[46]

➤ *Calcium.* The need for calcium increases 20 percent—to 1,200 milligrams daily—for women over the age of 50 and beyond, and for men over the age of 70. More than 70 percent of older Americans fall short of their dietary calcium needs.[47] Older adults should eat at least three servings of dairy foods daily and should add a serving of a calcium-fortified food or a supplement, to cover their increased calcium needs.

The Take-Home Message Life expectancy has increased in the last century due to improved research and health care, as well as dietary and lifestyle changes. Older adults need fewer calories but not less nutrition as they age. Nutrient-dense food selections are important to meet their fiber, fluid, vitamin, mineral, and phytochemical needs.

What Additional Challenges May Older Adults Face?

As adults approach their leisure years, life should get easier, not harder. However, the physical and emotional changes that accompany older age can make eating and exercising regularly a challenge.

Eating Right for Good Health and Disease Prevention

According to the World Health Organization (WHO), the best dietary strategy for aging adults in order to maintain good health and to prevent chronic diseases is to consume a varied, nutrient- and phytochemical-dense, heart-healthy diet.[48] This is the same dietary advice that is recommended in the *Dietary Guidelines for Americans*. (The graphic in Figure 16.6 addresses the unique nutritional needs of older Americans.)

The majority of older Americans aren't heeding this advice. When the diets of Americans 65 years of age and older were assessed to see if they were following these guidelines, only 19 percent of those studied had diets that could be rated as "good." More than 65 percent of older Americans were eating diets that needed improvement and 13 percent were consuming diets rated as "poor."[49] In fact, this research showed that less than 30 percent of those studied consumed the recommended servings from the fruit and milk groups, which reduces their dietary sources of phytochemicals, fiber, calcium, and vitamin D. These compounds can help fight certain cancers, heart disease, osteoporosis, cataracts, and age-related macular degeneration. Many older adults have inadequate servings of vegetables and whole grains, limiting dietary sources of zinc, iron, folate, and antioxidants, which can help reduce the risk of diabetes, stroke, certain diseases, and an impaired immune system.[50]

Antioxidants can also help protect the body against free radicals, which damage the brain and lead to the reduced cognitive ability

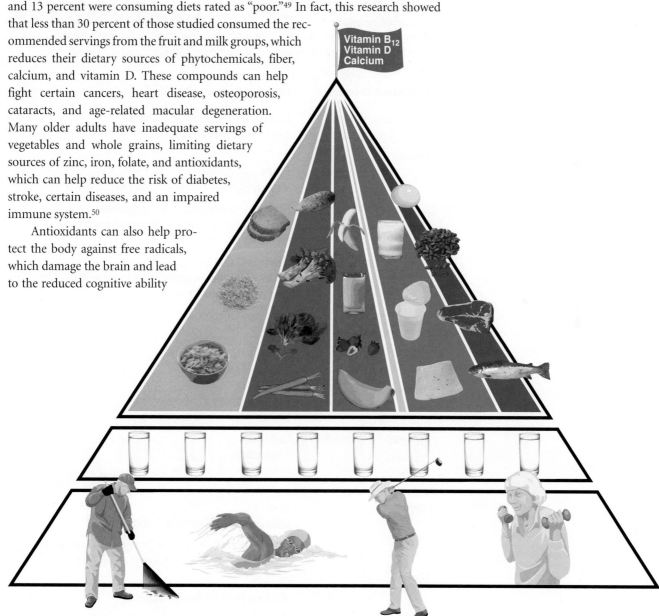

Figure 16.6 Older Adults Benefit from Good Nutrition and Physical Activity
Older adults need to focus on nutrient-dense foods that contain adequate fiber, calcium, vitamin B₁₂, and vitamin D. They also need to ensure adequate fluid intake and regular participation in physical activity.

seen in those with Alzheimer's disease and Parkinson's disease.[51] The diets of many older adults have also been shown to be too high in saturated fat, cholesterol, and sodium, increasing their risk of heart disease, hypertension, and stroke.[52]

Eating right is important in every stage of the life cycle, especially in older adults. Table 16.7 summarizes the many diseases and conditions that a healthy diet can affect as you age. Of particular concern to many older adults and their families is the possibility of developing cancer. The boxed feature "Fighting Cancer with a Knife and Fork" provides more information about the ways that good nutrition can potentially help reduce your risk.

Table 16.7

Eating Right to Fight Age-Related Diseases and Conditions

A varied, plant-based diet with plenty of phytochemicals, fiber, and essential nutrients is the best diet defense against the conditions and chronic diseases associated with aging.

Condition/Disease	Disease-Fighting Compounds
Alzheimer's disease Parkinson's disease	Antioxidants, vitamins E and C, and carotenoids (see Chapter 7)
Anemia	Iron Folate Vitamin B_{12} (see Chapters 7 and 8)
Cancer (colon, prostate, breast)	Fiber in whole grains, fruits, vegetables Phytochemicals (phenols, indoles, lycopene, beta-carotene) (see Chapters 2 and 4)
Cataracts, age-related macular disease	Vitamins C and E Phytochemicals (lycopene, lutein, zeaxanthin) Zinc (see Chapter 7)
Constipation, diverticulosis	Fiber (see Chapter 4)
Heart disease	Vitamins B_6, B_{12}, and folate Omega-3 fatty acids Soluble fiber Phytochemicals in whole grains (see Chapters 4, 5, and 7)
Hypertension, stroke	Calcium Magnesium Potassium (see Chapter 8)
Impaired immune response	Iron Zinc Vitamin B_6 (see Chapters 7 and 8)
Obesity	Fiber as part of low-calorie, high-satiety fruits and vegetables (see Chapters 4 and 10)
Osteoporosis	Calcium Vitamins D and K (see Chapter 8)
Type 2 diabetes	Chromium Fiber Phytochemicals (see Chapters 4 and 8)

Fighting Cancer with a Knife and Fork

The risk for one disease that afflicts many older adults can be significantly reduced by a lifetime of healthy habits. **Cancer** is the term used to identify a group of more than 100 diseases that are all characterized by the uncontrolled growth and spread of abnormal cells. Normally, a healthy body will quickly repair or destroy a cell whose DNA has been altered or damaged, so that it cannot reproduce (Figure a). Cancer begins when a small number of abnormal cells don't follow this process. Instead, the abnormal cells multiply, and, if they're not stopped, form a tumor (Figure b). Sometimes cells break off from the tumor and spread to other parts of the body.

The most common cancers are prostate cancer (among men) and breast cancer (among women). The second most common cancer in both men and women is lung cancer.[7]

Carcinogens Are Thought to Cause Most Cancers

Only about 5 to 10 percent of cancers are thought to be related to the presence of a specific "cancer gene."[8] More often, external factors, such as long-term exposure to carcinogens, lead to DNA mutations. Some of the most common carcinogens include:

➤ *Tobacco.* At least 80 chemicals in tobacco are carcinogens. Smoking is the primary cause of lung cancer, and tobacco is the culprit behind 20 percent of all cancer deaths worldwide.[9] In addition, each year, about 3,400 nonsmoking adults die of lung cancer as a result of breathing secondhand smoke.[10]

➤ *Radiation.* Excessive exposure to UV radiation is associated with an increased risk for skin cancer, and frequent exposure to other types of radiation—for instance, from X-rays—has long been associated with an increased risk for certain types of cancer.

➤ *Industrial chemicals.* Certain metals (such as nickel), some pesticides, and some chemical compounds (such as benzene) can act as carcinogens. Workers exposed for long periods are at greatest risk.

➤ *Cancer-causing agents in foods and beverages.* These include chemicals that form in charred portions of barbecued meat, poultry, and fish; molds, especially in stored foods; pollutants that enter foods from the environment; and excessive alcohol.

You Can Reduce Your Risk for Cancer with a Healthy Diet

Some compounds, found largely in fruits and vegetables, can help reduce your risk for numerous cancers:

➤ Certain *phytochemicals* can help reduce cancer risk. For example, the phytochemical lycopene, abundant in tomatoes and tomato products, is thought to help prevent certain cancers, including prostate cancer.

➤ *Antioxidants,* including carotenoids, the vitamins C and E, and the mineral selenium, neutralize free radicals, which can damage cellular DNA. They may also help prevent cancer from spreading to nearby tissues.

➤ *Retinoids* (vitamin A), *vitamin D,* and *folate* can stop the development of cancer by inhibiting the progression of damaged cells.

➤ *Omega-3 fatty acids,* found in fatty fish and some oils, may help reduce cancer cell growth.

(continued)

a Normal cell division

Damaged cell is destroyed or repaired; no reproduction

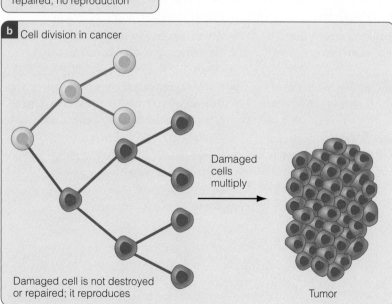

b Cell division in cancer

Damaged cells multiply

Damaged cell is not destroyed or repaired; it reproduces

Tumor

Cancer Occurs When Abnormal Cells Reproduce

cancer Type of diseases characterized by the uncontrolled growth and spread of abnormal cells.

Fighting Cancer with a Knife and Fork (continued)

➤ *Fiber* helps dilute waste products, which may contain cancer-promoting agents, in your intestinal tract and quickly move these out of your body. Also, the healthy bacteria that live in your colon feast on the fiber, creating a by-product that may also help in the fight against cancer, especially colorectal cancer.

Avoid Foods and Beverages That May Increase Your Risk for Cancer

Some foods and beverages, when consumed in excessive amounts, may increase your risk:

➤ A diet high in red and/or processed meats can increase your risk for cancer. *Nitrite,* which is commonly used to preserve processed meats, can react with the amino acids in the meat or in your stomach to form potential cancer-promoting compounds called nitrosamines and nitroamides.

➤ Alcohol, especially when consumed in excess, can increase the risk for cancer of the mouth, pharynx, larynx, and esophagus, as well as breast cancer in women and colorectal cancer in men. The more you drink, the higher your risk.

➤ High salt consumption can damage the lining of the stomach, paving the way for stomach cancer.

➤ Overweight and obesity are thought to increase the risk for many types of cancer and contribute to 14 to 20 percent of all cancer-related deaths.[11]

The best strategy to reduce your risk for cancer is to follow the cancer-fighting recommendations listed in the table below.

Recommendations for Preventing Cancer

Recommendation	What to Do	How to Do It
1. Be as lean as possible within the normal range of body weight.	➤ Maintain a BMI between 21 and 23.* ➤ Avoid weight gain, especially around your middle, as you age.	➤ Your pants are your best predictor of weight gain. If they begin to feel snug, assess your diet. Is your diet heavy in the junk food? ➤ See recommendation 3. ➤ Review Chapters 10 and 11 for strategies to obtain and maintain a healthy BMI.
2. Be physically active as a part of everyday life.	➤ Incorporate at least 30 to 60 minutes of physical activity into your day. ➤ Reduce the amount of screen time (TV, DVDs, computer, video games) spent daily.	➤ Set a timer at your computer and get up and move for at least 5 minutes every hour. ➤ Watch one less TV show or play one less computer game daily. Spend that time cleaning, doing laundry, or running errands.
3. Limit consumption of energy-dense foods. Avoid sugary drinks.	➤ Cut back on sweets and treats that are energy (calorie) dense and serve up little nutrition. ➤ Don't drink your calories by guzzling sodas, sports and energy drinks, fruit juices, or sweetened coffee beverages.	➤ If you want to snack on goodies, eat no more than about 100 calories of the item. That's typically a small handful of chips, cookies, and candy. ➤ Drink one less sweetened beverage and one more glass of water daily.

Recommendations for Preventing Cancer

Recommendation	What to Do	How to Do It
4. Eat mostly foods of plant origin.	➤ Eat at least 5 cups of a variety of colorful fruits and veggies for phytochemicals, fiber, and nutrients. ➤ At least half of your daily grain choices should be whole grains. ➤ Eat dried peas and beans (legumes) as often as you can.	➤ Eat at least one salad with a minimum of three different colored veggies daily. ➤ Choose only whole-grain cereals, such as raisin bran, oatmeal, and shredded wheat, in the morning. ➤ Add kidney beans and/or chickpeas to the daily salad that you are now going to be eating.
5. Limit intake of red meat and avoid processed meat.	➤ Limit beef, lamb, and pork to no more than 18 ounces a week. ➤ Avoid processed meats, such as ham, bacon, salami, hot dogs, and sausages.	➤ Eat red meat only at lunch in a sandwich, as the portion size will be only about 3 ounces. ➤ Try veggie or turkey sausages.
6. Limit alcoholic drinks.	If you choose to drink, ➤ Women should consume no more than one alcoholic drink daily. ➤ Men should consume no more than two alcoholic drinks daily.	➤ Make a glass of water the first drink, rather than alcohol, when you are socializing. ➤ Alternate alcoholic beverages with nonalcoholic drinks to pace your evening. Make the nonalcoholic drink twice as big as the one containing the booze.
7. Limit salt consumption.	➤ Avoid salt, salt-preserved, and salty foods. ➤ Limit sodium to no more than 2,400 mg daily.	➤ Remove the salt from your salt shaker and fill it with a no-salt seasoning blend, such as Mrs. Dash, to accompany the pepper shaker.
8. Aim to meet nutritional needs through diet alone.	➤ Look to food, not supplements, to fight cancer. ➤ Eat at least three meals a day to increase the variety and all the potential cancer-fighting compounds in food.	➤ Don't skip meals. ➤ Eat at least three pieces of fruit daily. Use a stoplight as your guide. Choose one fruit from each of the following colors: (1) **red** (apple, watermelon, red grapes), (2) **yellow** (banana, pineapple, citrus fruit), and (3) **green** (green grapes, Granny Smith apple, kiwi).

Other Recommendations

➤ If you are pregnant, plan to breast-feed exclusively for up to six months and continue with complementary breast-feeding afterward to reduce your risk for breast cancer. Being breast-fed may also protect your child from becoming overweight.

➤ Cancer survivors should obtain nutritional recommendations from an appropriately trained professional, such as a registered dietitian, and should eat a healthy diet, maintain a healthy weight, and be as physically active as they are able.

Data adapted from: World Cancer Research Fund/American Institute for Cancer Research (AICR), *Food, Nutrition, Physical Activity, and the Prevention of Cancer: A Global Perspective* (Washington, D.C.: AICR, 2007).

*See Chapter 10 to determine your BMI.

Staying Physically Active in Spite of Physical and Mental Challenges

Although the cross sections of the thigh are similar in size, note the greatly reduced muscle area (in yellow) of the older, sedentary adult in the bottom image compared to that of a younger, more active adult. Most people lose a significant amount of muscle as they age, which could be prevented by engaging in regular physical activity.

eLearn

Exercise for Life!

Want to learn more about how to help an older relative or friend stay active and healthy? Visit www.asaging.org/cdc/module6/home.cfm to find information about how to increase physical activity in older people's lives.

arthritis Inflammation in the joints that can cause pain, stiffness, and swelling in joints, muscles, tendons, ligaments, and bones.

Joan skis both downhill and cross-country in the winter and has been attending aerobics class six days a week for the past decade—a rather active schedule for a 76-year-old. Robert attends weekly fitness classes and skates in a hockey league three days a week. At age 78, he only skates in nonchecking leagues, but admits that collisions are part of the game.

No one is too old to exercise, and physical activity is not a luxury for older adults; it's a necessity. Routine physical activity can help lower the risk of heart disease, colon and breast cancer, diabetes, hypertension, osteoporosis, arthritis, and obesity. It can help maintain healthy bones, muscles, and joints, and reduce anxiety, stress, and depression. Routine exercise improves sleep, flexibility, and range of motion, and can help postpone the decline in cognitive ability that naturally occurs in aging.[53] Elders in good physical shape are also able to live independently longer, reducing the need for assistance with everyday functions.

Despite the many health benefits of being physically active, only 16 percent of those aged 64 to 74 and only 12 percent of those 75 years of age and older engage in at least 30 minutes of moderate activity five days a week. Lifestyle activities such as working in the garden, mowing the lawn, raking leaves, and even dancing will all provide health benefits. Older adults would also benefit from strength-training activities such as lifting weights and calisthenics at least twice a week to help maintain muscle strength.[54]

Arthritis

Getting out of bed, trying to open up a jar of mustard, or climbing stairs can all be challenging for anyone with **arthritis** (*arthr* = joint, *itis* = inflammation). Arthritis can cause pain, stiffness, and swelling in joints, muscles, tendons, ligaments, and bones. While there are more than 100 types of arthritis, osteoarthritis and rheumatoid arthritis commonly occur in older adults.

More than 20 million Americans suffer with osteoarthritis and more than half of adults age 65 and older have this type of arthritis in at least one joint.[55] Osteoarthritis occurs when the cartilage, which covers the ends of the bones at the joints, wears down, causing the bones to rub together. This constant friction between the bones causes swelling, loss of motion, and pain. Osteoarthritis commonly occurs in the fingers, neck, lower back, knees, and hips, which can interfere with the normal activities of daily living. Exercises that increase flexibility, keep joints limber, and improve the range of motion can help with osteoarthritis. Losing excess weight will also help relieve some of the stress at the hip and knee joints that bear the weight of the body.[56]

Research has shown that the dietary supplements glucosamine and chondroitin sulfate, which are naturally found in cartilage, may provide some pain relief for some individuals with moderate to severe knee pain due to osteoarthritis. It doesn't appear to help those with mild knee pain.[57] Individuals with osteoarthritis should speak with their health care provider to assess whether they would benefit from using this supplement. For safety's sake, they should also discuss the use of all supplements, including herbs, with a health care provider prior to consuming them. The boxed feature "Drug, Food, and Drug-Herb Interactions" on page 606 discusses the potentially harmful interactions between certain herbs, nutrients, and drugs.

Rheumatoid arthritis, which occurs in about 2 million U.S. adults, is an inflammatory disease of the joints.[58] Research suggests that numerous compounds in a Mediterranean-type diet, which is rich in fish, vegetables, and olive oil, may help protect against and manage rheumatoid arthritis (see Chapter 5). The omega-3 fatty acids in fish have anti-inflammatory effects and may help reduce the stiffness and joint tenderness of rheumatoid arthritis.[59] The current recommendation to eat two fish meals weekly to protect against heart disease may also be helpful to those who suffer with this type of arthritis. Compounds in cooked vegetables have been shown to possibly lower the risk of rheumatoid arthritis, and the fatty acids in olive oil may also help reduce the inflammation.[60]

Alzheimer's Disease

Although it's normal for older adults to experience some cognitive changes, such as taking longer to learn new information, a more serious mental decline can be cause for concern. Some adults begin to forget where they live, become increasingly disoriented, have difficulty speaking, and/or become emotionally unstable. These individuals may be experiencing **dementia,** due to changes in their brain function, which interferes with their ability to remember, speak, and "be themselves." **Alzheimer's disease** is the most common form of dementia in older adults. This irreversible disease slowly damages the brain tissues and can progress over the years to severe brain damage. An estimated 5 million Americans have Alzheimer's disease, with approximately 5 percent of adults showing signs of it as early as age 65.[61]

Research suggests that free radicals and inflammation may contribute to the brain damage observed in Alzheimer's disease and that antioxidants, such as vitamins E and C and selenium, may help slow its progression.[62] Studies are currently under way to determine the role these antioxidants may play in preventing Alzheimer's disease or at least helping to slow the loss of cognitive function. A diet adequate in the B vitamins and folate, which may help lower homocysteine levels in the body, could also play a role. A high blood level of homocysteine may damage the blood vessels in the brain, affecting its function;[63] consuming adequate amounts of these vitamins may help prevent the damage.

Some research suggests that the anti-inflammatory activities of omega-3 fatty acids may reduce the risk of Alzheimer's disease.[64] Studies are also being done to determine whether the herb ginkgo biloba, which has been purported to improve memory, could play a role in preventing dementia.[65]

Older adults with dementia likely need full-time care and shouldn't be allowed to take walks, jogs, or bike rides alone. However, accompanying an elder during any of these activities is a great way for both of you to get some exercise. While those with dementia experience mental deterioration, they should not be allowed to also experience physical deterioration.

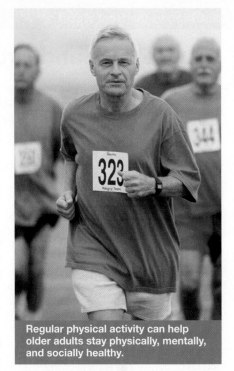

Regular physical activity can help older adults stay physically, mentally, and socially healthy.

Economic and Emotional Conditions Can Affect Nutritional Health

Staying physically active and coping with arthritis or Alzheimer's are common challenges that older adults face when it comes to their health. Conditions like food insecurity, depression, grief, or even drug and alcohol abuse may also enter the picture.

Food Insecurity

Between his medical and pharmaceutical costs and basic living expenses, Joe Powers exhausts his entire Social Security check by the twentieth day of each month. For the 10 days until he gets his next check, Joe is relegated to a stark menu of oatmeal and eggs. Though technically he's not starving, his limited diet is depriving him of many basic nutrients.

Severe arthritis can make everyday activities, like writing, typing, and handling objects, a challenge.

dementia A disorder of the brain that interferes with a person's memory, learning, and mental stability.

Alzheimer's disease A type of dementia.

Drug, Food, and Drug-Herb Interactions

Seventy-nine-year-old Donald David uses a seven-day plastic pill box to remind him to take his four daily prescriptions. Because Donald takes pills for heart disease, high blood pressure, and diabetes, his local pharmacist works with him to make sure that the drugs do not interact with each other in a way that could harm his health. The pharmacist also reminds Donald that he needs to keep his dietary vitamin K intake at an even keel, as major fluctuations can affect his blood thinner medication, and warns him about taking certain herbs that could also interfere with this drug.

Donald is lucky to have his pharmacist in his life to remind him how drugs, food, and herbs can all interact and produce unhealthy side effects. Some older adults aren't so lucky. About 80 percent of older

Daily pill containers like this one are often used by the elderly to remind them to take various medications.

adults take both prescription and nonprescription medications at the same time, but use more than one pharmacy or order their medications online or through the mail, so they lack this personal guidance. In addition, few clinical studies have sys-

tematically assessed the potential interactions between prescription drugs, food, and herbal remedies, and most patients do not readily disclose their use of non-prescription drugs and herbal supplements to their health care providers.[12] When patients are not fully informed about the potential interactions between their diets and their medication or herbal supplements, the results can be dangerous.

Food can interact with medications in several ways. For example, it can delay or increase the absorption of a drug. Calcium, for instance, can bind with tetracycline (an antibiotic), decreasing its absorption. For this reason, this drug shouldn't be taken with milk or calcium-fortified foods. In contrast, grapefruit and grapefruit juice will increase the absorption of calcium channel blocking agents,

Potential Side Effects of Selected Herbs and Nutrients

Herb/ Nutrient	Purported Use	Potential Side Effects	Drug Interactions
Aconite	Reduces pain by acting as a natural anesthetic	May cause atrial or ventricular fibrillation	None listed
Black cohosh	Reduce hot flashes and other menopausal symptoms	Possible headache and stomach discomfort	May exert estrogen activity and affect breast tissue
Calcium	Prevent osteoporosis	Constipation; calcium deposits in body	Decreases the absorption of tetracycline, thyroid medication, iron, zinc, and magnesium
Danshen	Treatment of coronary heart disease and menstrual abnormalities	Increases bleeding	Increases side effects of digoxin
Dong quai root	Relieve menopausal symptoms	Excessive bleeding due to blood thinning	Blood-thinning drugs and aspirin. Enhances the blood-thinning actions of vitamin E, garlic, and ginkgo biloba
Echinacea	Treat the common cold	Skin inflammation in sensitive individuals	May decrease effectiveness of immune-suppressing drugs (cyclosporine, corticosteroids)
Fish oil	Reduce the risk of heart disease	Excessive amounts could raise both blood glucose and LDL cholesterol levels, increase the risk of excessive bleeding, and cause a fishy aftertaste in mouth	Blood-thinning drugs and aspirin
Garlic, garlic supplements	Lower blood cholesterol levels	Possible stomach and intestinal discomfort	Blood-thinning drugs and aspirin. Enhances the blood-thinning actions of vitamin E, garlic, and ginkgo biloba
Ginkgo biloba	Reduce memory loss, dementia	Possible stomach and intestinal discomfort	Blood-thinning drugs and aspirin. Enhances the blood-thinning actions of vitamin E and garlic

which are a type of medication often used to treat heart disease.[13]

Drugs can also interfere with the metabolism of certain substances in foods. The compound tyramine, which is abundant in aged cheese, smoked fish, yogurt, and red wine, is metabolized by an enzyme called monoamine oxidase. Certain medications called monoamine oxidase inhibitors, which may be prescribed to treat depression, prevent tyramine from being properly metabolized. High levels of tyramine in the blood can result in dangerously high blood pressure.

Herbs can also interact with medications (see the table). Herbs are regulated as food and not as drugs under the Dietary Supplement Health and Education Act of 1994. This act allowed manufacturers to be exempt from premarket safety and efficacy testing. Herbal remedies are falsely assumed to be safe because they are natural, although dangerous interactions can occur when they are combined with prescription medications. For example, ginkgo biloba can interfere with blood clotting and shouldn't be consumed with

the blood-thinning drug Coumadin, or with aspirin, which also thins the blood. Consuming ginkgo with either or both of these medications can increase the risk of bleeding as well as stroke.[14]

The best way to avoid an interaction is to make sure a health care provider and/or a pharmacist is aware of all the prescribed and over-the-counter medications, herbs, and supplements that are being consumed. See the accompanying table for a list of potential interactions.

Potential Side Effects of Selected Herbs and Nutrients

Herb/ Nutrient	Purported Use	Potential Side Effects	Drug Interactions
Ginseng	Reduce fatigue, stress	None known at this time	May interfere with MAO inhibitors, diabetes medication, heart medication (digoxin), blood-thinning drugs, aspirin Enhances the blood-thinning actions of vitamin E, garlic, and ginkgo biloba
Grapefruit, grapefruit juice	Source of vitamin C	None known at this time	Potentiates certain heart medications (calcium channel blocking agents), corticosteroids, immunosuppressants
Gynura	Improve circulation and reduce pain	Hypotension	None listed
Hawthorn	Hypertension, congestive heart failure	Increased risk of bleeding	Increases effect of nitrates and cardiac glycosides
Licorice	Used as expectorant	Hypokalemia, hypotension, edema	May reduce effectiveness of antihypertensive drugs
Motherwort	Acts as a sedative and decreases platelet aggregation	Increased risk of bleeding	Blood thinners
Kava kava	Reduce anxiety, stress	Possible stomach and intestinal discomfort	Potentiates the effects of alcohol and anti-anxiety medications
Saw palmetto	Treatment for benign prostatic hypertrophy	Increased risk of bleeding	Blood thinners
St. John's wort	Reduce depression	Excessive amounts may cause an allergic reaction in some individuals	Avoid when taking antidepressants Can decrease the effect of certain heart medications (digoxin), oral contraceptives, cyclosporine
Tetrandrine	Treatment for hypertension and angina	Lowers plasma glucose	Competes with calcium channel blockers
Vitamin E	Reduce the risk of heart disease	Excessive amounts can interfere with blood clotting, increasing the risk of hemorrhage	Blood-thinning drugs
Yohimbine	Treatment of sexual disorders and exhaustion	Increases blood pressure	Antihypertensive drugs

Are You at Nutritional Risk?

Circle the number in the right column for the statements that apply to you (or someone you know if you are taking the assessment for a friend or relative). Add up the circled numbers to determine your score.

I have an illness or condition that has made me change the kind and/or amount of food I eat.	2
I eat fewer than two meals per day.	3
I eat few fruits or vegetables or milk products.	2
I have three or more drinks of beer, liquor, or wine almost every day.	2
I have tooth or mouth problems that make it hard for me to eat.	2
I don't always have enough money to buy food.	4
I eat alone most of the time.	1
I take three or more different prescribed or over-the-counter drugs a day.	1
Without wanting to, I have lost or gained 10 pounds in the last six months.	2
I am not always physically able to shop, cook, and/or feed myself.	2
Total =	

Answers

If your score is

0–2 good! Your diet and lifestyle don't appear to put you at risk of not meeting your nutritional needs.

3–5 You are at moderate nutritional risk. Your local office on aging, senior citizens' center, or health department can help you improve your nutritional health.

6 or over You are at high nutritional risk. Bring this checklist the next time you see your doctor, dietitian, or other qualified health or social service professional. Ask for help to improve your nutritional health.

Source: American Academy of Family Physicians, American Dietetic Association, and National Council on Aging, Inc., 2002. The Nutrition Screening Initiative is available at www.aafp.org/afp/980301ap/edits.html. Accessed July 2010.

Programs such as Meals On Wheels provide hot meals to elderly adults who cannot leave their homes.

food insecurity The chronic lack of sufficient food to nutritiously feed oneself.

congregate meals Meals served at churches, synagogues, or other community sites where older adults can receive a nutritious meal and socialize.

Joe is not alone. Almost 7 percent of households with older adults in the United States experience **food insecurity**.[66] Research has shown that elders who consistently experience food insecurity not only have more than double the risk of not meeting their daily nutritional needs, but also tend to be in only fair to poor health.[67]

Limited finances aren't always the cause of food insecurity. Some elders may be able to afford food but lack the physical means to obtain it, prepare it, or, because of health issues such as tooth loss, consume it.[68] A quick and easy assessment of an older adult's diet can help screen if he or she is at risk for food insecurity (see the Self-Assessment).

Because America is "the land of plenty," it is unacceptable that older adults should want for food. In 1965, the Older Americans Act was passed to provide support and services, including nutritious meals and nutrition education, to those age 60 and older to help them maintain good health, an adequate quality of life, and an acceptable level of independence.[69] **Congregate meals** are one type of available service. These nutritious hot meals are served at specified sites in the community, such as churches and synagogues. This guarantees that older adults receive a nutritious daily meal and provides an opportunity for them to socialize. Often, transportation to these meals is also available.

For those who are homebound, a healthy meal can be delivered to the home.[70] The Meals On Wheels Association of America is the largest organization in the United States providing meals to the homes of older adults who need them.

Young people in the community can help make sure that older adults are aware of and take advantage of the numerous services available to them. Consider "adopting" an older adult in your neighborhood or a family member and, if need be, help him or her locate these services. Visit First. Gov for Seniors at www.seniors.gov to locate these resources.

Depression and Grief

When Laura lost her husband at the age of 78, she stopped cooking a nightly dinner and took to opening a can of chicken soup for most of her evening meals. Her energy level dropped dramatically after his death, and on many days, she didn't even bother to get out of her pajamas. Like many elders who lose a spouse, Laura became depressed.

Up to 20 percent of older adults can suffer from depression, ranging from mild to major depressive disorders.[71] The loss of significant others and friends as well as chronic pain and concerns about their own health can add to feelings of grief, sadness, and isolation. Depression can interfere with an elder's motivation to eat, be physically active, and socialize—all of which can impact a person's mental and physical health.

Alcohol Abuse

Alcohol abuse isn't uncommon among elders, as the bodily changes and emotional swings caused by aging sometimes induce them to turn to alcohol.

As they age, adults become more sensitive to the intoxicating effects of alcohol. This is due in part to the decline of their body water. Individuals with a lower percentage of body water will have a higher blood alcohol concentration (BAC), and thus, feel its effects sooner. Adults' tolerance for alcohol also declines with aging, so the beer that one could manage easily at age 65 may have a narcotic effect at age 75.[72]

Prescription and nonprescription medications, which are commonly taken by those over age 65, can interact with alcohol by intensifying its effects, diminishing the effects of the medication, or both. (On average, people over age 65 are taking two to seven prescription medications daily.[73]) Someone who is taking anticoagulants to reduce the risk of blood clots, for example, may interfere with the drugs' effectiveness if he or she chronically consumes alcohol.[74]

An elderly person's increased alcohol consumption could be a way of self-medicating. Chronic health problems, loss of friends and loved ones, and/or financial stress could make alcohol an appealing sedative to temporarily ease discomfort or depression. As usual, though, consuming alcohol only makes things worse. Heavy drinking can exacerbate depression, which can lead to more drinking.[75] Also, because alcohol impairs one's judgment and interferes with coordination and reaction time, elders who have been drinking are at a higher risk for stumbling, falling, and fracturing bones.

Health care providers sometimes misdiagnose alcohol abuse in elders as the forgetfulness and disorientation associated with "normal aging."[76] **Figure 16.7** lists the red flags from the National Institute of Aging that may signal alcohol abuse in an older adult. Because of these numerous potential interactions with alcohol, the National Institute on Alcohol Abuse and Alcoholism recommends that adults over 65 who choose to drink should consume no more than one alcoholic drink daily.[77]

The Take-Home Message Older adults should consume a varied, nutrient- and phytochemical-dense diet to meet their needs and help prevent many of the chronic diseases associated with aging. They also benefit from regular physical activity. Arthritis, Alzheimer's disease, food insecurity, depression, and alcohol abuse can challenge the abilities of older adults to maintain healthy diets and lifestyles.

Red Flags for Alcohol Abuse in Older Adults

Drinks to calm nerves, reduce stress or depression, or forget his or her troubles.

Gulps drinks.

Frequently has more than one drink a day.

Lies about or tries to hide his or her drinking habits.

Hurts self or others when drinking.

Needs increased amounts of alcohol to get high.

Feels irritable, resentful, or unreasonable when not drinking.

Has medical, social, or financial worries caused by drinking.

Figure 16.7 Red Flags for Alcohol Abuse in Older Adults

Source: National Institute on Aging, "Alcohol Use and Abuse." Available at www.niaPublications.org/agepages/alcohol.asp. Accessed July 2010.

Two Points of View

Are School Lunches as Healthy and Effective as They Need to Be?

The National School Lunch Program feeds millions of schoolchildren each year, many at no or low cost.[1] But how nutritious are these lunches, and are they the optimal strategy for making sure schoolchildren receive a healthy midday meal? Read through the arguments on both sides, and then decide what you think.

Yes

- School lunches provided under the NSLP must provide no more than 30 percent of daily calories from fat, and less than 10 percent from saturated fat. These lunches must also provide one-third of the Recommended Dietary Allowances of protein, vitamin A, vitamin C, iron, calcium, and calories.[2]

- Studies have shown that children in the school lunch program consume more milk and vegetables at lunch and fewer sweets, sweetened beverages, and snack foods than nonparticipants.[3]

- Among high-school students, those who do not eat school lunch are more likely to eat something from a vending machine, or, if going off campus is an option, something from a local fast-food restaurant. Many of those choices are higher in fat and/or sugar.[4]

- Individuals who eat school meals are more likely to consume vegetables and milk products, not just during school, but throughout the day. They learn to eat correctly from their meals at school.[5]

No

- Children who eat school lunches consume more sodium and slightly more calories than those who bring lunch from home, and are at higher risk for being overweight.[6]

- Meeting the nutrition and health needs of children is not the only purpose of the NSLP. It is also set up to help meet the economic needs of farmers by purchasing their surplus commodities. The program is therefore highly political, and has strong support from agriculture interests and powerful backing from members of Congress from farm states or districts.[7]

- As noted above, the NSLP obtains a substantial amount of its food products as commodities through the USDA. Unfortunately, commodities like beef and cheese, which are high in saturated fat, are more frequently ordered and available than are fruits and vegetables.[8]

- As budgets for kitchen equipment have been cut, the NSLP has shifted from emphasizing preparation of whole foods in the school kitchen to having processed foods such as nuggets and french fries delivered directly to the schools.[9]

What do you think?

1. What is the greatest strength of the current school lunch program? What is its greatest weakness? **2.** How could the school lunch program best be improved? **3.** What actions could teachers, administrators, and/or cafeteria workers take to use school lunch to teach students about healthy eating?

Chapter Review

Be a Nutrition Sleuth

Junior Nutrition Sleuth

Do you have a younger sibling or family member who would like to be a nutrition detective and find out what nutrients may be missing in his or her diet? Visit **http://exhibits.pacsci.org/** nutrition and help this person be a nutrient sleuth by uncovering the missing nutrient in various sample meals!

Get Real!

Blast Off with Good Nutrition and Physical Activity

Visit **www.ChooseMyPlate.gov/kids** for a fun, interactive computer game in which children can learn how to fuel their bodies with good food and a healthy amount of physical activity.

The Top Ten Points to Remember

1. Toddlers and preschoolers grow less rapidly than infants, but need to eat small, frequent, nutrient-dense meals and snacks to fuel their busy lifestyles. Young children may be picky eaters and go on food jags, but these behaviors are normal and usually temporary. Caregivers may need to offer a new food up to 10 times before the child accepts it.

2. Iron deficiency is likely with young children who consume large quantities of milk in place of food. Young children need enough calcium, vitamin D, and fiber to ensure healthy bone growth and bowel regularity. Milk, water, and diluted juices are better beverage choices than sweetened, flavored drinks.

3. Obesity and type 2 diabetes are occurring at higher rates in children. Poor dietary choices and insufficient exercise are two of the key culprits of this problem. Parents and caregivers must provide healthy foods and encourage physical activity to combat a child's likelihood of developing these conditions.

4. The Daily Food Plans and 10 tips series available at ChooseMyPlate.gov provide guidance for planning healthy meals and snacks for children. Breakfast is an important meal for school-aged children for both mental and physical reasons. The National School Lunch Program must meet certain guidelines set by the USDA. Children with packed school lunches should be involved in the planning and preparation of the lunch so they are more likely to eat it.

5. Adolescents are heavily influenced by peers, media, and other nonparental role models, which may lead them to adopt unhealthy eating and lifestyle habits, such as skipping meals, choosing unhealthy foods, dieting, or smoking. Because adolescent bones are still growing, teens need to consume enough calcium, and increased soda consumption may interfere with this if it displaces milk in the diet. Iron is also important for growth of lean muscle, and for girls' onset of menstruation. Some teens may be at risk for disordered eating patterns.

6. Metabolism slows with age, so older adults need fewer calories than their younger counterparts. Older adults need to be sure to consume enough fiber, fluid, vitamins D and B_{12}, and the minerals iron, calcium, and zinc. Too much preformed vitamin A, in contrast, may increase an elder's risk of osteoporosis and bone fractures, so should be avoided.

7. Staying physically active is important during the older years, though sometimes this is challenging due to arthritis, Alzheimer's, or other diseases and conditions.

8. Older adults sometimes suffer from food insecurity, due to decreased mobility, financial hardship, or health conditions such as tooth loss. Social programs can help ensure the proper nourishment of homebound adults by delivering precooked meals. Alcohol abuse is sometimes an issue with older adults.

9. There is no conclusive evidence that sugar causes hyperactivity or ADHD in children. However, some

caregivers claim that making certain dietary changes helps their child's behavior.

10. Prescription medications and herbs can reduce or accelerate nutrient absorption, or interact with foods, so those taking drugs or herbs should check with a pharmacist or health care provider to ensure that they don't suffer any unfortunate side effects.

Test Your Knowledge

1. Because they are still growing but have diminished appetites (compared with infants), toddlers and preschoolers should
   a. consume large meals.
   b. consume nutrient-dense foods.
   c. consume foods high in fat.
   d. consume foods high in sugar.
   e. do all of the above.

2. The key message(s) for children at ChooseMyPlate.gov include
   a. Be physically active every day.
   b. Choose healthier foods from each group.
   c. Eat more of some food groups than others.
   d. Eat foods from every food group every day.
   e. all of the above.

3. Breakfast is important for school-aged children because
   a. it helps them slow down in the morning.
   b. it improves alertness and ability to concentrate throughout the day.
   c. it may decrease their risk for childhood obesity.
   d. b and c only

4. There appears to be a relationship between the rise in childhood obesity and the increase in
   a. childhood cancers.
   b. ADHD.
   c. type 2 diabetes in children.
   d. childhood cavities.
   e. all of these.

5. The National School Lunch Program must meet strict guidelines set by the USDA.
   a. true.
   b. false

6. Which mineral supports healthy bone development and is particularly important during adolescence?
   a. calcium
   b. iron
   c. vitamin D
   d. copper
   e. all of these

7. Adolescent eating patterns can be influenced by
   a. a growing desire to assert their independence.
   b. social pressure and a desire to "fit in" with peers.
   c. lack of time.
   d. all of the above.

8. Which of the following two nutrient needs increase with age?
   a. water and lead
   b. calcium and vitamin D
   c. protein and lipids
   d. vitamin K and biotin

9. Which of the following can influence an older adult's ability to consume a nutritious diet?
   a. living on a fixed income
   b. loss of teeth
   c. alcohol abuse
   d. all of the above
   e. a and c only

10. Congregate meals are
    a. meals delivered to the homes of older adults who are homebound.
    b. frozen meals that adults can purchase at the supermarket.
    c. hot meals that are served at a site in the community, such as at churches and synagogues.
    d. none of the above.

Answers

1. (b) Toddlers need to eat nutrient-dense foods in order to obtain all the nutrients they need. Their reduced appetites mean they aren't likely to eat large meals, and foods high in fat and sugar may add significant calories without contributing many nutrients.

2. (e) The ChooseMyPlate.gov website encourages physical activity and healthy food choices from a variety of food groups for children.

3. (d) School-aged children who eat breakfast have been shown to perform better in school and to have higher rates of physical activity and lower rates of obesity. Breakfast doesn't have to be eaten at the table, as caregivers can provide "to go" foods for children if they are in a hurry.

4. (c) Rates of type 2 diabetes among children have risen along with rates of overweight and obesity.

5. (a) The Food and Nutrition Service, part of the USDA, provides guidelines that direct the minimum amounts of some nutrients, and the maximum amounts of calories and saturated fat, that school lunches can contain.

6. (a) Adolescents need adequate amounts of calcium to support their growing bones. Iron is also important during adolescence to support development of lean muscle mass and offset the iron lost by girls as they begin menstruating. Vitamin D is not a mineral, but is also very important for bone growth. Copper is a trace mineral that most people consume in adequate amounts.

7. (d) Teen eating patterns can change based on a variety of physical, emotional, and social factors, including a need to assert their independence, the influence of peers, and a busier schedule.

8. (b) The need for both vitamin D and calcium is increased in older adults. Protein, fat, and water needs don't change with aging. Lead is a toxin and should never be consumed. Vitamin K and biotin are necessary for health, but you don't need them in higher amounts as you age.

9. (d) Older adults who may have a limited income may not be able to purchase adequate amounts of healthy foods to meet their nutrient needs. If they lose their teeth or have other dental problems, they may limit their food choices based on their inability to chew certain foods. An alcohol-heavy diet will not only displace nutritious foods, but can also increase the risk of falls and injuries.

10. (c) Congregate meals allow older adults in a community to meet and eat hot meals together. Older adults who are homebound can request that a healthy meal be delivered to their home. A variety of frozen meals can be purchased at the grocery store by adults of all ages.

Web Resources

➡ For more information on nutrition during the younger years, visit www.cdc.gov/HealthyYouth/nutrition/index.htm

➡ For more information on children's and teens' health, visit www.kidshealth.org

➡ For more about ADHD, search for "ADHD" at www.nimh.nih.gov

➡ For more about the USDA's School Lunch Program, visit www.fns.usda.gov/cnd/lunch

➡ For more nutrition information for older adults, visit www.cdc.gov/aging/aginginfo/index.htm

➡ For more information on herbs, visit the National Center for Complementary and Alternative Medicine, National Institutes of Health, at http://nccam.nih.gov

Answers to Myths and Misperceptions

1. **True.** Between the ages of 1 and 4, small children are extremely active and may forget to eat. Turn to page 580 to find out how to make sure children get the nutrients they need.

2. **False.** Iron deficiency is often caused by a limited diet that relies too heavily on milk or other iron-poor food sources. Read more about this condition on page 582.

3. **False.** Parents and caregivers may need to offer foods several times before a child accepts the food. This topic is covered in more detail on page 582.

4. **True.** Young children often go on food "jags" or may get hooked on a particular food and eat only that item for a while. Learn more about these short-term habits and how to cope with them on page 583.

5. **False.** Fast food is only part of the problem. Too little exercise and too much screen time also contribute. Read more about the obesity epidemic among children on page 587.

6. **True.** The school lunch and breakfast programs must meet specific requirements established by the USDA. Details are found on page 590.

7. **False.** Sodas, including diet sodas, are nutritionally empty beverages. Turn to page 593 to find which beverages will help adolescents achieve healthy adult bodies.

8. **True.** Because a person's metabolism slows naturally with age, older adults need fewer calories than their younger counterparts. Learn more about the altered energy and nutrient needs associated with aging on page 595.

9. **False.** Financial circumstances or reduced mobility can cause older adults to experience food insecurity. Turn to page 608 to find out how this happens.

10. **False.** Older adults sometimes turn to alcohol to deal with discomfort, loneliness, or boredom. Find out more on page 609.

Appendices

Appendix A Calculations and Conversions

Calculation and Conversion Aids

Commonly Used Metric Units

millimeter (mm): one-thousandth of a meter (0.001)
centimeter (cm): one-hundredth of a meter (0.01)
kilometer (km): one-thousand times a meter (1000)
kilogram (kg): one-thousand times a gram (1000)
milligram (mg): one-thousandth of a gram (0.001)
microgram (µg): one-millionth of a gram (0.000001)
milliliter (ml): one-thousandth of a liter (0.001)

International Units

Some vitamin supplements may report vitamin content as International Units (IU).

To convert IU to:

- Micrograms of vitamin D (cholecalciferol), divide the IU value by 40 or multiply by 0.025.
- Milligrams of vitamin E (alpha-tocopherol), divide the IU value by 1.5 if vitamin E is from natural sources. Divide the IU value by 2.22 if vitamin E is from synthetic sources.
- Vitamin A: 1 IU = 0.3 µg retinol or 3.6 µg beta-carotene

Retinol Activity Equivalents

Retinol Activity Equivalents (RAE) are a standardized unit of measure for vitamin A. RAE account for the various differences in bioavailability from sources of vitamin A. Many supplements will report vitamin A content in IU, as shown above, or in Retinol Equivalents (RE).

1 RAE = 1 µg retinol
      12 µg beta-carotene
      24 µg other vitamin A carotenoids

To calculate RAE from the RE value of vitamin carotenoids in foods, divide RE by 2.

For vitamin A supplements and foods fortified with vitamin A, 1 RE = 1 RAE.

Folate

Folate is measured as Dietary Folate Equivalents (DFE). DFE account for the different factors affecting bioavailability of folate sources.

1 DFE = 1 µg food folate
      0.6 µg folate from fortified foods
      0.5 µg folate supplement taken on an empty stomach
      0.6 µg folate as a supplement consumed with a meal

To convert micrograms of synthetic folate, such as that found in supplements or fortified foods, to DFE:

$$\text{µg synthetic folate} \times 1.7 = \text{µg DFE}$$

For naturally occurring food folate, such as spinach, each microgram of folate equals 1 microgram DFE:

$$\text{µg folate} = \text{µg DFE}$$

Conversion Factors

Use the following table to convert U.S. measurements to metric equivalents:

Original Unit	Multiply By	To Get
ounces avdp	28.3495	grams
ounces	0.0625	pounds
pounds	0.4536	kilograms
pounds	16	ounces
grams	0.0353	ounces
grams	0.002205	pounds
kilograms	2.2046	pounds
liters	1.8162	pints (dry)
liters	2.1134	pints (liquid)
liters	0.9081	quarts (dry)
liters	1.0567	quarts (liquid)
liters	0.2642	gallons (U.S.)
pints (dry)	0.5506	liters
pints (liquid)	0.4732	liters
quarts (dry)	1.1012	liters
quarts (liquid)	0.9463	liters
gallons (U.S.)	3.7853	liters
millimeters	0.0394	inches
centimeters	0.3937	inches
centimeters	0.03281	feet
inches	25.4000	millimeters
inches	2.5400	centimeters
inches	0.0254	meters
feet	0.3048	meters
meters	3.2808	feet
meters	1.0936	yards
cubic feet	0.0283	cubic meters
cubic meters	35.3145	cubic feet
cubic meters	1.3079	cubic yards
cubic yards	0.7646	cubic meters

Length: U.S. and Metric Equivalents

¼ inch = 0.6 centimeter
1 inch = 2.5 centimeters
1 foot = 0.3048 meter
      30.48 centimeters
1 yard = 0.91144 meter
1 millimeter = 0.03937 inch
1 centimeter = 0.3937 inch
1 decimeter = 3.937 inches
1 meter = 39.37 inches
      1.094 yards
1 micrometer = 0.00003937 inch

Weights and Measures

Food Measurement Equivalencies from U.S. to Metric

Capacity

⅛ teaspoon = 1 milliliter
¼ teaspoon = 1.25 milliliters
½ teaspoon = 2.5 milliliters
1 teaspoon = 5 milliliters
1 tablespoon = 15 milliliters
1 fluid ounce = 28.4 milliliters
¼ cup = 60 milliliters
⅓ cup = 80 milliliters
½ cup = 120 milliliters
1 cup = 225 milliliters
1 pint (2 cups) = 473 milliliters
1 quart (4 cups) = 0.95 liter
1 liter (1.06 quarts) = 1,000 milliliters
1 gallon (4 quarts) = 3.84 liters

Weight

0.035 ounce = 1 gram
1 ounce = 28 grams
¼ pound (4 ounces) = 114 grams
1 pound (16 ounces) = 454 grams
2.2 pounds (35 ounces) = 1 kilogram

U.S. Food Measurement Equivalents

3 teaspoons = 1 tablespoon
½ tablespoon = 1½ teaspoons
2 tablespoons = ⅛ cup
4 tablespoons = ¼ cup
5 tablespoons + 1 teaspoon = ⅓ cup
8 tablespoons = ½ cup
10 tablespoons + 2 teaspoons = ⅔ cup
12 tablespoons = ¾ cup
16 tablespoons = 1 cup
2 cups = 1 pint
4 cups = 1 quart
2 pints = 1 quart
4 quarts = 1 gallon

Volumes and Capacities

1 cup = 8 fluid ounces
½ liquid pint
1 milliliter = 0.061 cubic inch
1 liter = 1.057 liquid quarts
0.908 dry quart
61.024 cubic inches
1 U.S. gallon = 231 cubic inches
3.785 liters
0.833 British gallon
128 U.S. fluid ounces

1 British Imperial gallon = 277.42 cubic inches
1.201 U.S. gallons
4.546 liters
160 British fluid ounces
1 U.S. ounce, liquid or fluid = 1.805 cubic inches
29.574 milliliters
1.041 British fluid ounces
1 pint, dry = 33.600 cubic inches
0.551 liter
1 pint, liquid = 28.875 cubic inches
0.473 liter
1 U.S. quart, dry = 67.201 cubic inches
1.101 liters
1 U.S. quart, liquid = 57.75 cubic inches
0.946 liter
1 British quart = 69.354 cubic inches
1.032 U.S. quarts, dry
1.201 U.S. quarts, liquid

Energy Units

1 kilocalorie (kcal) = 4.2 kilojoules
1 millijoule (MJ) = 240 kilocalories
1 kilojoule (kJ) = 0.24 kcal
1 gram carbohydrate = 4 kcal
1 gram fat = 9 kcal
1 gram protein = 4 kcal

Temperature Standards

	°Fahrenheit	°Celsius
Body temperature	98.6°	37°
Comfortable room temperature	65–75°	18–24°
Boiling point of water	212°	100°
Freezing point of water	32°	0°

Temperature Scales

To Convert Fahrenheit to Celsius
$[(°F - 32) \times 5]/9$

1. Subtract 32 from °F
2. Multiply (°F – 32) by 5, then divide by 9

To Convert Celsius to Fahrenheit
$[(°C \times 9)/5] + 32$

1. Multiply °C by 9, then divide by 5
2. Add 32 to (°C × 9/5)

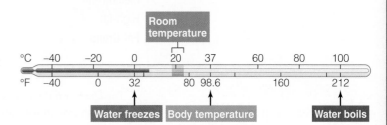

Appendix B U.S. Exchange Lists for Meal Planning

The "Exchange Lists for Meal Planning" group foods together according to their carbohydrate, protein, and fat composition. There are three main groups: the Carbohydrate Group, the Meat and Meat Substitutes Group, and the Fat Group. As you will see in the charts on the following pages, the Carbohydrate Group contains starchy foods such as bread and other grain products, as well as fruit, milk, and vegetables; the Meat and Meat Substitutes Group includes meat, fish, poultry, eggs, luncheon meats, and legumes; and the Fat Group contains oils, nuts, and other spreads. Also note that two of these main groups (specifically, the Carbohydrate Group and the Meat and Meat Substitutes Group) also contain subgroups.

Specific portion sizes are provided for each of the foods within each group. This ensures that all the foods in each subgroup contain relatively the same amount of carbohydrates, protein, and fats, and thus, will have a similar amount of calories per serving. Because any food within a food subgroup will have similar amounts of these nutrients, they can be exchanged or swapped with each other at meals and snacks. This flexible meal plan is a useful tool to help individuals, such as those with diabetes and/or those who want to lose weight, better control the amount of nutrients and calories at all meals and snacks. A diet with a set amount of nutrients, such as carbohydrates and calories, can help individuals with diabetes better control their blood glucose levels and calories throughout the day. Calorie control is important for those who are trying to improve or manage their body weight.

The following chart shows the amount of nutrients in one serving from each of the three main groups.

Group/List	Carbohydrate (grams)	Protein (grams)	Fat (grams)	Calories
Carbohydrate Group				
Starch	15	3	0–1	80
Fruit	15	—	—	60
Milk				
Fat-free, low-fat	12	8	0–3	90
Reduced-fat	12	8	5	120
Whole	12	8	8	150
Other carbohydrates	15	varies	varies	varies
Nonstarchy vegetables	5	2	—	25
Meat and Meat Substitutes Group				
Very lean	—	7	0–1	35
Lean	—	7	3	55
Medium-fat	—	7	5	75
High-fat	—	7	8	100
Fat Group				
	—	—	5	45

The charts on the following pages show the exchange lists for each of the subgroups shown above (i.e., Starch, Fruit, Milk, etc.).

Starch List

Food	Serving Size	Food	Serving Size
Bread		Squash, winter (acorn, butternut, pumpkin)	1 cup
Bagel, 4 oz	¼ (1 oz)	Yam, sweet potato, plain	½ cup
Bread, white, whole-wheat, pumpernickel, rye	1 slice (1 oz)	**Crackers and Snacks**	
English muffin	½	Animal crackers	8
Hot dog bun or hamburger bun	½	Graham crackers, 2½" square	3
Pancake, 4" across, ¼" thick	1	Popcorn (popped, no fat added or low-fat microwave)	3 cups
Pita, 6" across	½	Pretzels	¾ oz
Roll, plain, small	1 (1 oz)	Rice cakes, 4" across	2
Tortilla, flour, 6" across	1	Saltine-type crackers	6
Cereals and Grains		Snack chips, fat-free or baked (tortilla, potato)	15–20 (¾ oz)
Bran cereals	½ cup	Whole-wheat crackers, no fat added	2–5 (¾ oz)
Bulgur	½ cup	**Beans, Peas, and Lentils**	
Cereals, cooked	½ cup	*(Count as 1 starch exchange, plus 1 very lean meat exchange)*	
Cereals, unsweetened, ready-to-eat	¾ cup	Beans and peas (garbanzo, pinto,	
Couscous	⅓ cup	kidney, white, split, black-eyed)	½ cup
Oats	½ cup	Lima beans	⅔ cup
Pasta	⅓ cup	**Starchy Foods Prepared with Fat**	
Puffed cereal	1½ cup	*(Count as 1 starch exchange plus 1 fat exchange)*	
Rice, white or brown	⅓ cup	Biscuit, 2½" across	1
Shredded wheat	½ cup	Crackers, round butter type	6
Sugar-frosted cereal	½ cup	Croutons	1 cup
Starchy Vegetables		French-fried potatoes (oven-baked) (see also the fast foods list)	1 cup (2 oz)
Baked beans	⅓ cup		
Corn	½ cup		
Peas, green	½ cup	Muffin, 5 oz	⅕ (1 oz)
Potato, mashed	½ cup	Popcorn, microwaved	3 cups

Source: © American Dietetic Association. Used with permission.

Fruit List

Food	Serving Size	Food	Serving Size
Apples, unpeeled, small	1 (4 oz)	Pineapple, fresh	¾ cup
Applesauce, unsweetened	½ cup	Plums, small	2 (5 oz)
Apricots, dried	8 halves	Raisins	2 tbs
Banana, small	1 (4 oz)	Raspberries	1 cup
Blueberries	¾ cup	Strawberries	1¼ cup whole berries
Cantaloupe, small or 1 cup cubes	⅓ melon (11 oz)	Watermelon	1 slice (13½ oz) or 1¼ cup cubes
Cherries, sweet, fresh	12 (3 oz)		
Dates	3	**Fruit Juice, Unsweetened**	
Figs, dried	1½	Apple juice/cider	½ cup
Grapefruit, large	½ (11 oz)	Cranberry juice cocktail	⅓ cup
Grapes, small	17 (3 oz)	Cranberry juice cocktail, reduced-calorie	1 cup
Honeydew melon or 1 cup cubes	1 slice (10 oz)		
Kiwi	1 (3½ oz)	Fruit juice blends, 100% juice	⅓ cup
Mango, small	½ (5½ oz) or ½ cup	Grape juice	⅓ cup
Orange, small	1 (6½ oz)	Grapefruit juice	½ cup
Peach, medium, fresh	1 (4 oz)	Orange juice	½ cup
Pear, large, fresh	½ (4 oz)	Pineapple juice	½ cup

Milk List

Food	Serving Size	Food	Serving Size
Fat-Free and Low-Fat Milk		**Reduced-Fat Milk**	
(0–3 g fat per serving)		*(5 g fat per serving)*	
Fat-free milk	1 cup	2% milk	1 cup
½% milk	1 cup	Soy milk	1 cup
1% milk	1 cup	**Whole Milk**	
Buttermilk, low-fat or fat-free	1 cup	*(8 g fat per serving)*	
Soy milk, low-fat or fat-free	1 cup	Whole milk	1 cup
Yogurt, plain, fat-free	6 oz	Yogurt, plain (made from whole milk)	8 oz
Yogurt, fat-free, flavored, sweetened with nonnutritive sweetener and fructose	1 cup		

Other Carbohydrates List

These carbohydrate-rich foods can be substituted for a starch, fruit, or milk choice.

Food	Serving Size	Exchanges per Serving
Angel food cake, unfrosted	½₂ cake (about 2 oz)	2 carbohydrates
Brownies, small, unfrosted	2" square (about 1 oz)	1 carbohydrate, 1 fat
Cake, frosted	2" square (about 2 oz)	2 carbohydrates, 1 fat
Cookie or sandwich cookie with creme filling	2 small (about ⅔ oz)	1 carbohydrate, 1 fat
Cranberry sauce, jellied	¼ cup	1½ carbohydrates
Doughnut, plain cake	1 medium (1½ oz)	1½ carbohydrates, 2 fats
Energy, sport, or breakfast bar	1 bar (2 oz)	2 carbohydrates, 1 fat
Fruit juice bars, frozen, 100% juice	1 bar (3 oz)	1 carbohydrate
Granola or snack bar, regular or low-fat	1 bar (1 oz)	1½ carbohydrates
Ice cream	½ cup	1 carbohydrate, 2 fats
Ice cream, light	½ cup	1 carbohydrate, 1 fat
Milk, chocolate, whole	1 cup	2 carbohydrates, 1 fat
Pudding, regular (made with reduced-fat milk)	½ cup	2 carbohydrates
Pudding, sugar-free, or sugar-free and fat-free (made with fat-free milk)	½ cup	1 carbohydrate
Sherbet, sorbet	½ cup	2 carbohydrates
Sports drink	8 oz (1 cup)	1 carbohydrate
Yogurt, frozen, fat-free	⅓ cup	1 carbohydrate
Yogurt, frozen, fat-free, no sugar added	½ cup	1 carbohydrate, 0–1 fat

Vegetable List

Serving size = ½ c cooked vegetables or vegetable juice or 1 c raw vegetables

Asparagus
Beans (green, wax, Italian)
Broccoli
Brussels sprouts
Cabbage
Carrots
Cauliflower
Celery
Cucumber
Eggplant
Mushrooms
Okra
Onions
Pea pods
Peppers (all varieties)
Radishes
Salad greens (endive, escarole, lettuce, romaine, spinach)
Spinach
Summer squash
Tomato
Tomatoes, canned
Tomato sauce*
Tomato/vegetable juice*
Zucchini

= 400 mg or more sodium per exchange.

Meat and Meat Substitutes List

Food	Serving Size
Very Lean Meat and Substitutes	
Poultry: Chicken or turkey (white meat, no skin)	1 oz
Fish: Fresh or frozen cod, flounder, haddock, halibut, trout, lox (smoked salmon)*; tuna, fresh or canned in water	1 oz
Shellfish: Clams, crab, lobster, scallops, shrimp, imitation shellfish	1 oz
Cheese with 1 g fat/oz:	
Fat-free or low-fat cottage cheese	¼ cup
Fat-free cheese	1 oz
Other:	
Processed sandwich meats with 1 g fat/oz (such as deli thin, shaved meats, chipped beef*, turkey ham)	1 oz
Egg whites	2
Hot dogs with 1 g fat/oz*	1 oz
Sausage with 1 g fat/oz	1 oz
Count as one very lean meat and one starch exchange:	
Beans, peas, lentils (cooked)	½ cup
Lean Meat and Substitutes	
Beef: USDA Select or Choice grades of lean beef trimmed of fat (round, sirloin); tenderloin; roast; steak; ground round	1 oz
Pork: Lean pork (fresh ham); canned, cured, or boiled ham; Canadian bacon*; tenderloin, center loin chop	1 oz
Lamb: Roast, chop, leg	1 oz
Veal: Lean chop, roast	1 oz
Poultry: Chicken, turkey (dark meat, no skin), chicken white meat (with skin)	1 oz
Fish:	
Oysters	6 medium
Salmon (fresh or canned), catfish	1 oz
Tuna (canned in oil, drained)	1 oz
Cheese:	
4.5% fat cottage cheese	¼ cup
Grated Parmesan	2 tbs
Cheeses with 3 g fat/oz	1 oz

Food	Serving Size
Other:	
Hot dogs with 3 g fat/oz*	1½ oz
Processed sandwich meat with 3 g fat/oz (turkey, pastrami, or kielbasa)	1 oz
Medium-Fat Meat and Substitutes	
Beef: Most beef products (ground beef, meatloaf, corned beef, short ribs, Prime grades of meat trimmed of fat, such as prime rib)	1 oz
Pork: Top loin, chop, cutlet	1 oz
Lamb: Rib roast, ground	1 oz
Veal: Cutlet (ground or cubed, unbreaded)	1 oz
Poultry: Chicken dark meat (with skin), ground turkey or ground chicken, fried chicken (with skin)	1 oz
Fish: Any fried fish product	1 oz
Cheese with 5 g fat/oz:	
Feta	1 oz
Mozzarella	1 oz
Ricotta	¼ cup (2 oz)
Other:	
Egg (high in cholesterol; limit to 3/week)	1
Sausage with 5 g fat/oz	1 oz
Tempeh	¼ cup
Tofu	4 oz or ½ cup
High-Fat Meat and Substitutes	
Pork: Spareribs, ground pork, pork sausage	1 oz
Cheese: All regular cheeses (American* cheddar, Monterey Jack, Swiss)	1 oz
Other:	
Processed sandwich meats with 8 g fat/oz (bologna, salami)	1 oz
Sausage (bratwurst, Italian, knockwurst, Polish, smoked)	1 oz
Hot dog (turkey or chicken)*	1 (10/lb)
Bacon	3 slices
Peanut butter (contains unsaturated fat)	1 tbs
Count as one high-fat meat plus one fat exchange:	
Hot dog (beef, pork, or combination)*	1 (10/lb)

* = 400 mg or more of sodium per serving.

Fat List

Food	Serving Size
Monounsaturated Fats	
Avocado, medium	2 tbs (1 oz)
Oil (canola, olive, peanut)	1 tsp
Olives, ripe (black)	8 large
Olives, green, stuffed*	10 large
Almonds, cashews	6 nuts
Peanuts	10 nuts
Pecans	4 halves
Peanut butter, smooth or crunchy	½ tbs
Sesame seeds	1 tbs
Polyunsaturated Fats	
Margarine, stick, tub, or squeeze	1 tsp
Margarine, lower-fat (30 to 50% vegetable oil)	1 tbs
Mayonnaise, regular	1 tsp
Mayonnaise, reduced-fat	1 tbs
Nuts, walnuts, English	4 halves
Oil (corn, safflower, soybean)	1 tsp
Salad dressing, regular*	1 tbs
Salad dressing, reduced-fat	2 tbs
Seeds, pumpkin, sunflower	1 tbs
Saturated Fats	
Bacon, cooked	1 slice (20 slices/lb)
Butter, stick	1 tsp
Butter, whipped	2 tsp
Butter, reduced-fat	1 tbs
Cream, half and half	2 tbs
Cream cheese, regular	1 tbs (½ oz)
Cream cheese, reduced-fat	1½ tbs (¾ oz)
Sour cream, regular	2 tbs
Sour cream, reduced-fat	3 tbs

= 400 mg or more sodium per exchange.

Free Foods List

A free food is any food that contains less than 20 calories or less than 5 grams of carbohydrate per serving. Free foods should be limited to three servings per day.

Fat-Free or Reduced-Fat Foods

Cream cheese, fat-free	1 tbs (½ oz)
Creamers, nondairy, liquid	1 tbs
Mayonnaise, fat-free	1 tbs
Mayonnaise, reduced-fat	1 tsp
Margarine, spread, fat-free	4 tbs
Nonstick cooking spray	
Salad dressing, fat-free or low-fat	1 tbs
Sour cream, fat-free, reduced-fat	1 tbs

Sugar-Free Foods

Candy, hard, sugar-free	1 candy
Gelatin dessert, sugar-free	
Gum, sugar-free	1 stick
Jam or jelly, light	2 tsp
Syrup, sugar-free	2 tbs

Drinks

Bouillon, broth, consommé*
Bouillon or broth, low-sodium
Carbonated or mineral water
Club soda
Cocoa powder, unsweetened . . . . 1 tbs
Coffee
Diet soft drinks, sugar-free
Drink mixes, sugar-free
Tea
Tonic water, sugar-free

Condiments

Catsup	1 tbs
Horseradish	
Lemon juice	
Lime juice	
Mustard	
Salsa	¼ cup
Soy sauce, regular or light*	1 tbs
Taco sauce	1 tbs
Vinegar	
Yogurt	2 tbs

= 400 mg or more sodium per choice.

Combination Foods List

Food	Serving Size	Exchanges per Serving
Entrées		
Tuna noodle casserole, lasagna, spaghetti with meatballs, chili with beans, macaroni and cheese*	1 cup (8 oz)	2 carbohydrates, 2 medium-fat meats
Tuna or chicken salad	½ cup (3½ oz)	½ carbohydrate, 2 lean meats, 1 fat
Frozen Entrées		
Dinner-type meal*	generally 14–17 oz	3 carbohydrates, 3 medium-fat meats, 3 fats
Meatless burger, soy based	3 oz	½ carbohydrate, 2 lean meats
Meatless burger, vegetable and starch based	3 oz	1 carbohydrate, 1 lean meat
Pizza, cheese, thin crust* (5 oz)	¼ of 12" (6 oz)	2 carbohydrates, 2 medium-fat meats
Pizza, meat topping, thin crust* (5 oz)	¼ of 12" (6 oz)	2 carbohydrates, 2 medium-fat meats, 1½ fats
Entrée with less than 340 calories*	about 8–11 oz	2–3 carbohydrates, 1–2 lean meats
Soups		
Bean*	1 cup (8 oz)	1 carbohydrate, 1 very lean meat
Cream (made with water)*	1 cup (8 oz)	1 carbohydrate, 1 fat
Split pea (made with water)*	½ cup (4 oz)	1 carbohydrate
Tomato (made with water)*	1 cup (8 oz)	1 carbohydrate
Vegetable beef, chicken noodle, or other broth-type*	1 cup (8 oz)	1 carbohydrate

* = 400 mg or more sodium per exchange.

Fast-Foods List[a]

Food	Serving Size	Exchanges per Serving
Burrito with beef*	1 (5–7 oz)	3 carbohydrates, 1 medium-fat meat, 1 fat
Chicken nuggets*	6	1 carbohydrate, 2 medium-fat meats, 1 fat
Chicken breast and wing, breaded and fried*	1 each	1 carbohydrate, 4 medium-fat meats, 2 fats
Chicken sandwich, grilled*	1	2 carbohydrates, 3 very lean meats
Chicken wings, hot*	6 (5 oz)	1 carbohydrate, 3 medium-fat meats, 4 fats
Fish sandwich/tartar sauce*	1	3 carbohydrates, 1 medium-fat meat, 3 fats
French fries, thin	20–25	2 carbohydrates, 2 fats
Hamburger, regular	1	2 carbohydrates, 2 medium-fat meats
Hamburger, large*	1	2 carbohydrates, 3 medium-fat meats, 1 fat
Hot dog with bun*	1	1 carbohydrate, 1 high-fat meat, 1 fat
Individual pan pizza*	1	5 carbohydrates, 3 medium-fat meats, 3 fats
Pizza, cheese, thin crust*	¼ of 12" (about 6 oz)	2½ carbohydrates, 2 medium-fat meats, 1½ fats
Pizza, meat, thin crust*	¼ of 12" (about 6 oz)	2½ carbohydrates, 2 medium-fat meats, 2 fats
Soft serve ice cream cone	1 medium	2 carbohydrates, 1 fat
Submarine sandwich*	1 (6")	3 carbohydrates, 1 vegetable, 2 medium-fat meats, 1 fat
Taco, hard shell*	1 (6 oz)	2 carbohydrates, 2 medium-fat meats, 2 fats
Taco, soft shell*	1 (3 oz)	1 carbohydrate, 1 medium-fat meat, 1 fat

[a]Ask at your fast-food restaurant for nutrition information about your favorite fast foods or check Web sites.

* = 400 mg or more sodium per exchange.

The following charts show a possible distribution of exchanges for an individual consuming 2,000 calories. This set amount of exchanges can help you plan meals and snacks for a day, such as shown in the "One-Day Sample Meal Plan."

Daily Meal Pattern

Targets:
Total kcal = 2,000/day

	Percent of Kcal	Amount in Grams
Carbohydrate	50–55	250–275
Protein	15–20	75–100
Fat	25–30	60–67

Exchanges	Number of Exchanges	Protein (g)	Fat (g)	Carbohydrate (g)
Milk, low-fat	3	24	9	36
Fruit	4	0	0	60
Vegetable	6	12	0	30
Starch/Bread/Cereal	9	27	0	135
Meat, lean	6	42	18	0
Fat	6	0	30	0
Total		105	57	261
Total kcals	1,977	420	513	1,044
% kcals		21	26	53

Distribution of Exchanges at Meals and Snacks

Exchanges	Total Number	Breakfast	AM Snack	Lunch	PM Snack	Dinner	Night Snack
Milk	3	1	1	0	0	1	0
Fruit	4	1	1	1	0	0	1
Vegetable	6	0	0	2	1	3	0
Starch/Bread/Cereal	9	2	1	2	2	2	0
Meat	6	0	0	3	0	3	0
Fat	6	2	0	2	1	1	0
Total	34	6	3	10	4	10	1
Total carbohydrate (g)	261	57	42	55	35	57	15
% Total Carb.		22	16	21	13	22	6

One-Day Sample Meal Plan

Breakfast

1% milk (8-oz glass)	1 milk exchange
Honeydew melon (1 cup cubes)	1 fruit exchange
Whole-wheat English muffin (1)	2 starch exchanges
Peanut butter (1 tbs)	2 fat exchanges

Morning Snack

Low-fat plain yogurt (6 oz)	1 milk exchange
Strawberries (1¼ cup whole berries)	1 fruit exchange
Low-fat granola (¼ cup)	1 starch exchange

Lunch

2 slices whole-wheat bread	2 starch exchanges
Canned light tuna (3 oz)	3 meat exchanges
Reduced-fat mayonnaise (1 tbs)	1 fat exchange
Small tossed salad (1 c romain lettuce, 1 c raw veggies)	2 vegetable exchanges
Reduced-fat Italian dressing (2 tbs)	1 fat exchange
Apple (1 small)	1 fruit exchange
Unsweetened ice tea	Free food

Afternoon Snack

Baby carrots (1 cup raw)	1 vegetable exchange
4 whole-wheat crackers, no fat added	1 starch exchange
Hummus (⅓ cup)	1 starch exchange, 1 fat exchange

Dinner

1% milk (8-oz glass)	1 milk exchange
3 oz grilled chicken breast	3 meat exchanges
2/3 c rice pilaf (prepared with reduced-fat butter)	2 starch exchanges, 1 fat exchange
¾ c steamed broccoli	1½ vegetable exchanges
1½ c baby salad greens	1½ vegetable exchanges
Low-fat salad dressing (1 tbs)	Free food

Night Snack

Reduced-calorie cranberry juice cocktail (8 oz)	1 fruit exchange

Appendix C Organizations and Resources

Academic Journals

International Journal of Sport Nutrition and Exercise Metabolism
Human Kinetics
P.O. Box 5076
Champaign, IL 61825-5076
(800) 747-4457
www.humankinetics.com/IJSNEM

Journal of Nutrition
A. Catharine Ross, Editor
Department of Nutrition
Pennsylvania State University
126-S Henderson Building
University Park, PA 16802-6504
(814) 865-4721
www.nutrition.org

Nutrition Research
Elsevier: Journals Customer Service
6277 Sea Harbor Drive
Orlando, FL 32887
(877) 839-7126
www.journals.elsevierhealth.com/periodicals/NTR

Nutrition
Elsevier: Journals Customer Service
6277 Sea Harbor Drive
Orlando, FL 32887
(877) 839-7126
www.journals.elsevierhealth.com/periodicals/NUT

Nutrition Reviews
International Life Sciences Institute
Subscription Office
P.O. Box 830430
Birmingham, AL 35283
(800) 633-4931
www.ingentaconnect.com/content/ilsi/nure

Obesity Research
North American Association for the Study of Obesity (NAASO)
8630 Fenton Street, Suite 918
Silver Spring, MD 20910
(301) 563-6526
www.obesityresearch.org

International Journal of Obesity
Journal of the International Association for the Study of Obesity
Nature Publishing Group
The Macmillan Building
4 Crinan Street
London N1 9XW
United Kingdom
www.nature.com/ijo

Journal of the American Medical Association
American Medical Association
P.O. Box 10946
Chicago, IL 60610-0946
(800) 262-2350
http://jama.ama-assn.org

New England Journal of Medicine
10 Shattuck Street
Boston, MA 02115-6094
(617) 734-9800
http://content.nejm.org/

American Journal of Clinical Nutrition
The American Journal of Clinical Nutrition
9650 Rockville Pike
Bethesda, MD 20814-3998
(301) 634-7038
www.ajcn.org

Journal of the American Dietetic Association
Elsevier: Health Sciences Division
Subscription Customer Service
6277 Sea Harbor Drive
Orlando, FL 32887
(800) 654-2452
www.adajournal.org

Aging

Administration on Aging
U.S. Health & Human Services
200 Independence Avenue, SW
Washington, DC 20201
(877) 696-6775
www.aoa.gov

American Association of Retired Persons (AARP)
601 E. Street, NW
Washington, DC 20049
(888) 687-2277
www.aarp.org

Health and Age
Sponsored by the Novartis Foundation for Gerontology &
The Web-Based Health Education Foundation
Robert Griffith, MD
Executive Director
573 Vista de la Ciudad
Santa Fe, NM 87501
www.healthandage.com

National Council on the Aging
300 D Street, SW, Suite 801
Washington, DC 20024
(202) 479-1200
www.ncoa.org

International Osteoporosis Foundation
5 Rue Perdtemps
1260 Nyon
Switzerland
41 22 994 01 00
www.osteofound.org

National Institute on Aging
Building 31, Room 5C27
31 Center Drive, MSC 2292
Bethesda, MD 20892
(301) 496-1752
www.nia.nih.gov

Osteoporosis and Related Bone Diseases National Resource Center
2 AMS Circle
Bethesda, MD 20892-3676
(800) 624-BONE
www.osteo.org

American Geriatrics Society
The Empire State Building
350 Fifth Avenue, Suite 801
New York, NY 10118
(212) 308-1414
www.americangeriatrics.org

National Osteoporosis Foundation
1232 22nd Street, NW
Washington, DC 20037-1292
(202) 223-2226
www.nof.org/

Alcohol and Drug Abuse

National Institute on Drug Abuse
6001 Executive Boulevard, Room 5213
Bethesda, MD 20892-9561
(301) 443-1124
www.nida.nih.gov

National Institute on Alcohol Abuse and Alcoholism
5635 Fishers Lane, MSC 9304
Bethesda, MD 20892-9304
www.niaaa.nih.gov

Alcoholics Anonymous
Grand Central Station
P.O. Box 459
New York, NY 10163
www.alcoholics-anonymous.org

Narcotics Anonymous
P.O. Box 9999
Van Nuys, California 91409
(818) 773-9999
www.na.org

National Council on Alcoholism and Drug Dependence
20 Exchange Place, Suite 2902
New York, NY 10005
(212) 269-7797
www.ncadd.org

National Clearinghouse for Alcohol and Drug Information
11420 Rockville Pike
Rockville, MD 20852
(800) 729-6686
http://ncadi.samhsa.gov

Canadian Government

Health Canada
A.L. 0900C2
Ottawa, ON K1A 0K9
(613) 957-2991
www.hc-sc.gc.ca/english

National Institute of Nutrition
408 Queen Street, 3rd Floor
Ottawa, ON K1R 5A7
(613) 235-3355
www.nin.ca/public_html/index.html

Agricultural and Agri-Food Canada
Public Information Request Service
Sir John Carling Building
930 Carling Avenue
Ottawa, ON K1A 0C5
(613) 759-1000
www.arg.gc.ca

Bureau of Nutritional Sciences
Sir Frederick G. Banting Research Centre
Tunney's Pasture (2203A)
Ottawa, ON K1A 0L2
(613) 957-0352
www.hc-sc.gc.ca/food-aliment/ns-sc/e_nutrition.html

Canadian Food Inspection Agency
59 Camelot Drive
Ottawa, ON K1A 0Y9
(613) 225-2342
www.inspection.gc.ca/english/toce.shtml

Canadian Institute for Health Information
CIHI Ottawa
377 Dalhousie Street, Suite 200
Ottawa, ON K1N 9N8
(613) 241-7860
www.cihi.ca

Canadian Public Health Association
1565 Carling Avenue, Suite 400
Ottawa, ON K1Z 8R1
(613) 725-3769
www.cpha.ca

Canadian Nutrition and Professional Organizations

Dietitians of Canada, Canadian Dietetic Association
480 University Avenue, Suite 604
Toronto, ON M5G 1V2
(416) 596-0857
www.dietitians.ca

Canadian Diabetes Association
National Life Building
1400-522 University Avenue
Toronto, ON M5G 2R5
(800) 226-8464
www.diabetes.ca

National Eating Disorder Information Centre
CW 1-211, 200 Elizabeth Street
Toronto, ON M5G 2C4
(866) NEDIC-20
www.nedic.ca

Canadian Pediatric Society
100-2204 Walkley Road
Ottawa, ON K1G 4G8
(613) 526-9397
www.cps.ca

Disordered Eating/ Eating Disorders

American Psychiatric Association
1000 Wilson Boulevard, Suite 1825
Arlington, VA 22209
(703) 907-7300
www.psych.org

Harvard Eating Disorders Center
WACC 725
15 Parkman Street
Boston, MA 02114
(617) 236-7766
www.hedc.org

National Institute of Mental Health
Office of Communications
6001 Executive Boulevard, Room 8184, MSC 9663
Bethesda, MD 20892
(866) 615-6464
www.nimh.nih.gov

National Association of Anorexia Nervosa and Associated Disorders (ANAD)
P.O. Box 7
Highland Park, IL 60035
(847) 831-3438
www.anad.org

National Eating Disorders Association
603 Stewart Street, Suite 803
Seattle, WA 98101
(206) 382-3587
www.nationaleatingdisorders.org

Eating Disorder Referral and Information Center
2923 Sandy Pointe, Suite 6
Del Mar, CA 92014
(858) 792-7463
www.edreferral.com

Anorexia Nervosa and Related Eating Disorders, Inc. (ANRED)
E-mail: jarinor@rio.com
www.anred.com

Overeaters Anonymous
P.O. Box 44020
Rio Rancho, NM 87174
(505) 891-2664
www.oa.org

Exercise, Physical Activity, and Sports

American College of Sports Medicine (ACSM)
P.O. Box 1440
Indianapolis, IN 46206-1440
(317) 637-9200
www.acsm.org

American Physical Therapy Association (APTA)
1111 North Fairfax Street
Alexandria, VA 22314
(800) 999-APTA
www.apta.org

Gatorade Sports Science Institute (GSSI)
617 West Main Street
Barrington, IL 60010
(800) 616-GSSI
www.gssiweb.com

National Coalition for Promoting Physical Activity (NCPPA)
1010 Massachusetts Avenue, Suite 350
Washington, DC 20001
(202) 454-7518
www.ncppa.org

Sports, Cardiovascular, and Wellness Nutrition (SCAN)
P.O. Box 60820
Colorado Springs, CO 80960
(719) 635-6005
www.scandpg.org

President's Council on Physical Fitness and Sports
Department W
200 Independence Avenue, SW
Room 738-H
Washington, DC 20201-0004
(202) 690-9000
www.fitness.gov

American Council on Exercise
4851 Paramount Drive
San Diego, CA 92123
(858) 279-8227
www.acefitness.org

IDEA Health and Fitness Association
10455 Pacific Center Court
San Diego, CA 92121
(800) 999-4332, ext. 7
www.ideafit.com

Food Safety

Food Marketing Institute
655 15th Street, NW
Washington, DC 20005
(202) 452-8444
www.fmi.org

Agency for Toxic Substances and Disease Registry (ATSDR)
ORO Washington Office
Ariel Rios Building
1200 Pennsylvania Avenue, NW
M/C 5204G
Washington, DC 20460
(888) 422-8737
www.atsdr.cdc.gov

Food Allergy and Anaphylaxis Network
11781 Lee Jackson Highway, Suite 160
Fairfax, VA 22033-3309
(800) 929-4040
www.foodallergy.org

Foodsafety.gov
www.foodsafety.gov

The USDA Food Safety and Inspection Service
Food Safety and Inspection Service
United States Department of Agriculture
Washington, DC 20250
www.fsis.usda.gov

Consumer Reports
Web Site Customer Relations Department
101 Truman Avenue
Yonkers, NY 10703
www.consumerreports.org

Center for Science in the Public Interest: Food Safety
1875 Connecticut Avenue, NW
Washington, DC 20009
(202) 332-9110
www.cspinet.org/foodsafety/index.html

Center for Food Safety and Applied Nutrition
5100 Paint Branch Parkway
College Park, MD 20740
(888) SAFEFOOD
www.cfsan.fda.gov

Food Safety Project
Dan Henroid, MS, RD, CFSP
HRIM Extension Specialist and Website Coordinator
Hotel, Restaurant and Institution Management
9e MacKay Hall
Iowa State University
Ames, IA 50011
(515) 294-3527
www.extension.iastate.edu/foodsafety

Organic Consumers Association
6101 Cliff Estate Road
Little Marais, MN 55614
(218) 226-4164
www.organicconsumers.org

Infancy and Childhood

Administration for Children and Families
370 L'Enfant Promenade, SW
Washington, DC 20447
www.acf.dhhs.gov

The American Academy of Pediatrics
141 Northwest Point Boulevard
Elk Grove Village, IL 60007
(847) 434-4000
www.aap.org

Kidshealth: The Nemours Foundation
1600 Rockland Road
Wilmington, DE 19803
(302) 651-4046
www.kidshealth.org

National Center for Education in Maternal and Child Health
Georgetown University
Box 571272
Washington, DC 20057
(202) 784-9770
www.ncemch.org

Birth Defects Research for Children, Inc.
930 Woodcock Road, Suite 225
Orlando, FL 32803
(407) 895-0802
www.birthdefects.org

USDA/ARS Children's Nutrition Research Center at Baylor College of Medicine
1100 Bates Street
Houston, TX 77030
www.kidsnutrition.org

Centers for Disease Control—Healthy Youth
www.cdc.gov/healthyyouth

International Agencies

UNICEF
3 United Nations Plaza
New York, NY 10017
(212) 326-7000
www.unicef.org

World Health Organization
Avenue Appia 20
1211 Geneva 27
Switzerland
41 22 791 21 11
www.who.int/en

The Stockholm Convention on Persistent Organic Pollutants
11–13 Chemin des Anémones
1219 Châtelaine
Geneva, Switzerland
41 22 917 8191
www.pops.int

Food and Agriculture Organization of the United Nations
Viale delle Terme di Caracalla
00100 Rome, Italy
39 06 57051
www.fao.org

International Food Information Council
1100 Connecticut Avenue, NW
Suite 430
Washington, DC 20036
(202) 296-6540
www.ific.org

Pregnancy and Lactation

San Diego County Breastfeeding Coalition
c/o Children's Hospital and Health Center
3020 Children's Way, MC 5073
San Diego, CA 92123
(800) 371-MILK
www.breastfeeding.org

National Alliance for Breastfeeding Advocacy
Barbara Heiser, Executive Director
9684 Oak Hill Drive
Ellicott City, MD 21042-6321
OR
Marsha Walker, Executive Director
254 Conant Road
Weston, MA 02493-1756
www.naba-breastfeeding.org

American College of Obstetricians and Gynecologists
409 12th Street, SW, P.O. Box 96920
Washington, DC 20090
www.acog.org

La Leche League
1400 N. Meacham Road
Schaumburg, IL 60173
(847) 519-7730
www.lalecheleague.org

National Organization on Fetal Alcohol Syndrome
900 17th Street, NW
Suite 910
Washington, DC 20006
(800) 66 NOFAS
www.nofas.org

March of Dimes Birth Defects Foundation
1275 Mamaroneck Avenue
White Plains, NY 10605
(888) 663-4637
http://modimes.org

Professional Nutrition Organizations

North American Association for the Study of Obesity (NAASO)
8630 Fenton Street, Suite 918
Silver Spring, MD 20910
(301) 563-6526
www.naaso.org

American Dental Association
211 East Chicago Avenue
Chicago, IL 60611-2678
(312) 440-2500
www.ada.org

American Heart Association
National Center
7272 Greenville Avenue
Dallas, TX 75231
(800) 242-8721
www.americanheart.org

American Dietetic Association (ADA)
120 South Riverside Plaza, Suite 2000
Chicago, IL 60606-6995
(800) 877-1600
www.eatright.org

The American Society for Nutrition (ASN)
9650 Rockville Pike, Suite L-4500
Bethesda, MD 20814-3998
(301) 634-7050
www.nutrition.org

The Society for Nutrition Education
7150 Winton Drive, Suite 300
Indianapolis, IN 46268
(800) 235-6690
www.sne.org

American College of Nutrition
300 S. Duncan Avenue, Suite 225
Clearwater, FL 33755
(727) 446-6086
www.amcollnutr.org

American Obesity Association
1250 24th Street, NW, Suite 300
Washington, DC 20037
(800) 98-OBESE
www.obesity.org

American Council on Science and Health
1995 Broadway
Second Floor
New York, NY 10023
(212) 362-7044
www.acsh.org

American Diabetes Association
ATTN: National Call Center
1701 North Beauregard Street
Alexandria, VA 22311
(800) 342-2383
www.diabetes.org

Institute of Food Technologies
525 W. Van Buren, Suite 1000
Chicago, IL 60607
(312) 782-8424
www.ift.org

ILSI Human Nutrition Institute
One Thomas Circle, Ninth Floor
Washington, DC 20005
(202) 659-0524
http://hni.ilsi.org

Trade Organizations

American Meat Institute
1700 North Moore Street
Suite 1600
Arlington, VA 22209
(703) 841-2400
www.meatami.com

National Dairy Council
10255 W. Higgins Road, Suite 900
Rosemont, IL 60018
(312) 240-2880
www.nationaldairycouncil.org

United Fresh Fruit and Vegetable Association
1901 Pennsylvania Ave., NW, Suite 1100
Washington, DC 20006
(202) 303-3400
www.uffva.org

U.S.A. Rice Federation
4301 North Fairfax Drive, Suite 425
Arlington, VA 22203
(703) 236-2300
www.usarice.com

U.S. Government

The USDA National Organic Program
Agricultural Marketing Service
USDA-AMS-TMP-NOP
Room 4008-South Building
1400 Independence Avenue, SW
Washington, DC 20250-0020
(202) 720-3252
www.ams.usda.gov

U.S. Department of Health and Human Services
200 Independence Avenue, SW
Washington, DC 20201
(877) 696-6775
www.hhs.gov

Food and Drug Administration (FDA)
5600 Fishers Lane
Rockville, MD 20857
(888) 463-6332
www.fda.gov

Environmental Protection Agency
Ariel Rios Building
1200 Pennsylvania Avenue, NW
Washington, DC 20460
(202) 272-0167
www.epa.gov

Federal Trade Commission
600 Pennsylvania Avenue, NW
Washington, DC 20580
(202) 326-2222
www.ftc.gov

Partnership for Healthy Weight Management
www.consumer.gov/weightloss

Office of Dietary Supplements
National Institutes of Health
6100 Executive Boulevard, Room 3B01, MSC 7517
Bethesda, MD 20892
(301) 435-2920
http://dietary-supplements.info.nih.gov

Nutrient Data Laboratory Homepage
Beltsville Human Nutrition Center
10300 Baltimore Avenue
Building 307-C, Room 117
BARC-East
Beltsville, MD 20705
(301) 504-8157
www.nal.usda.gov/fnic/foodcomp

National Digestive Diseases Information Clearinghouse
2 Information Way
Bethesda, MD 20892-3570
(800) 891-5389
http://digestive.niddk.nih.gov

The National Cancer Institute
NCI Public Inquiries Office
Suite 3036A
6116 Executive Boulevard, MSC 8322
Bethesda, MD 20892-8322
(800) 4-CANCER
www.cancer.gov

The National Eye Institute
31 Center Drive, MSC 2510
Bethesda, MD 20892-2510
(301) 496-5248
www.nei.nih.gov

The National Heart, Lung, and Blood Institute
Building 31, Room 5A52
31 Center Drive, MSC 2486
Bethesda, MD 20892
(301) 592-8573
www.nhlbi.nih.gov/index.htm

National Institute of Diabetes and Digestive and Kidney Diseases
Office of Communications and Public Liaison
NIDDK, NIH, Building 31, Room 9A04
Center Drive, MSC 2560
Bethesda, MD 20892
(301) 496-4000
http://www2.niddk.nih.gov/

National Center for Complementary and Alternative Medicine
NCCAM Clearinghouse
P.O. Box 7923
Gaithersburg, MD 20898
(888) 644-6226
http://nccam.nih.gov

U.S. Department of Agriculture (USDA)
1400 Independence Avenue, SW
Washington, DC 20250
(202) 720-2791
www.usda.gov

Centers for Disease Control and Prevention (CDC)
1600 Clifton Road
Atlanta, GA 30333
(404) 639-3311 / Public Inquiries: (800) 311-3435
www.cdc.gov

National Institutes of Health (NIH)
9000 Rockville Pike
Bethesda, MD 20892
(301) 496-4000
www.nih.gov

Food and Nutrition Information Center
Agricultural Research Service, USDA
National Agricultural Library, Room 105
10301 Baltimore Avenue
Beltsville, MD 20705-2351
(301) 504-5719
www.nal.usda.gov/fnic

National Institute of Allergy and Infectious Diseases
NIAID Office of Communications and Public Liaison
6610 Rockledge Drive, MSC 6612
Bethesda, MD 20892
(301) 496-5717
www.niaid.nih.gov

Weight and Health Management

The Vegetarian Resource Group
P.O. Box 1463, Dept. IN
Baltimore, MD 21203
(410) 366-VEGE
www.vrg.org

American Obesity Association
1250 24th Street, NW
Suite 300
Washington, DC 20037
(202) 776-7711
www.obesity.org

Anemia Lifeline
(888) 722-4407
www.anemia.com

The Arc
(301) 565-3842
E-mail: info@thearc.org
www.thearc.org

Bottled Water Web
P.O. Box 5658
Santa Barbara, CA 93150
(805) 879-1564
www.bottledwaterweb.com

The Food and Nutrition Board
Institute of Medicine
500 Fifth Street, NW
Washington, DC 20001
(202) 334-2352
www.iom.edu/board.asp?id-3788

The Calorie Control Council
www.caloriecontrol.org

TOPS (Take Off Pounds Sensibly)
4575 South Fifth Street
P.O. Box 07360
Milwaukee, WI 53207
(800) 932-8677
www.tops.org

Shape Up America!
15009 Native Dancer Road
N. Potomac, MD 20878
www.shapeup.org

World Hunger

Center on Hunger, Poverty, and Nutrition Policy
Tufts University
Medford, MA 02155
(617) 627-3020
www.tufts.edu/nutrition

Freedom from Hunger
1644 DaVinci Court
Davis, CA 95616
(800) 708-2555
www.freefromhunger.org

Oxfam International
1112 16th Street, NW, Suite 600
Washington, DC 20036
(202) 496-1170
www.oxfam.org

WorldWatch Institute
1776 Massachusetts Avenue, NW
Washington, DC 20036
(202) 452-1999
www.worldwatch.org

The Hunger Project
15 East 26th Street
New York, NY 10010
(212) 251-9100
www.thp.org

U.S. Agency for International Development
Information Center
Ronald Reagan Building
Washington, DC 20523
(202) 712-4810
www.usaid.gov

America's Second Harvest
35 E. Wacker Drive #2000
Chicago, IL 60601
www.secondharvest.org

Glossary

A

absorption The process by which digested nutrients move into the tissues where they can be transported and used by the body's cells.

Acceptable Macronutrient Distribution Range (AMDR) A healthy range of intakes for the energy-containing nutrients—carbohydrates, proteins, and fats—in your diet, designed to meet your nutrient needs and help reduce the risk of chronic diseases.

acetaldehyde An intermediary by-product of the breakdown of ethanol in the liver.

acid group The COOH group that is part of every amino acid; also called the *carboxyl group*.

acromegaly A condition caused by excess growth hormone in which tissues, bones, and internal organs grow abnormally large.

acute dehydration Dehydration starting after a short period of time.

added sugars Sugars that are added to processed foods and sweets.

adenosine triphosphate (ATP) A compound that is broken down to produce energy for working muscles and other tissues.

Adequate Intake (AI) The *approximate* amount of a nutrient that groups of similar individuals are consuming to maintain good health.

adolescence The developmental period between childhood and early adulthood.

aerobic With oxygen.

age-related macular degeneration (AMD) A disease that affects the macula of the retina, causing blurry vision.

agribusiness The businesses collectively associated with the production, processing, and distribution of agricultural products, including food.

alcohol A chemical class of substances that contain ethanol, methanol, and isopropanol.

alcohol abuse The continuation of alcohol consumption even though this behavior has created social, legal, and/or health problems.

alcohol dehydrogenase One of the alcohol-metabolizing enzymes found in the stomach and the liver.

alcohol hepatitis Stage 2 of alcohol liver disease; due to chronic inflammation.

alcohol liver disease A degenerative liver condition that occurs in three stages: (1) fatty liver, (2) alcoholic hepatitis, and (3) cirrhosis.

alcohol poisoning When the BAC rises to such an extreme level that a person's central nervous system is affected and his or her breathing and heart rate are interrupted.

alcohol tolerance When the body adjusts to long-term alcohol use by becoming less sensitive to the alcohol. You need to consume more alcohol in order to get the same effect.

alcoholism Chronic disease with genetic, psychological, and environmental components; also referred to as *alcohol dependence*. Alcoholics crave alcohol, can't control their intake, and develop a higher tolerance for it. Alcoholics also exhibit a dependency on alcohol, as abstaining from drinking will cause withdrawal symptoms.

alpha-linolenic acid A polyunsaturated essential fatty acid; part of the omega-3 fatty acid family.

Alzheimer's disease A type of dementia.

amenorrhea Absence of menstruation.

amine group The nitrogen-containing part (NH_2) of an amino acid.

amino acid pools A limited supply of amino acids stored in your blood and cells and used to build new proteins.

amino acid profile The types and amounts of amino acids in a protein.

amino acids The building blocks of protein. Amino acids contain carbon, hydrogen, oxygen, and nitrogen. All amino acids are composed of an acid group, an amine group, and a unique side chain.

anaerobic Without oxygen.

anaphylactic reactions Severe, life-threatening reactions that cause constriction of the airways in the lungs, which inhibits the ability to breathe.

antibiotic-resistant bacteria Bacteria that have developed a resistance to an antibiotic such that they are no longer affected by antibiotic medication.

antibiotics Drugs that kill or slow the growth of bacteria.

antibodies Proteins made by your body to bind to and neutralize foreign invaders, such as harmful bacteria, fungi, and viruses, as part of the body's immune response.

antidiuretic hormone (ADH) A hormone that directs the kidneys to concentrate urine and reduce urine production in order to reduce water loss from the body.

antimicrobials Substances or a combination of substances, such as disinfectants and sanitizers, that control the spread of bacteria and viruses on nonliving surfaces or objects.

antioxidants Substances that neutralize free radicals. Vitamins A, C, and E and beta-carotene are antioxidants.

appetite The psychological desire to eat or drink.

arthritis Inflammation in the joints that can cause pain, stiffness, and swelling in joints, muscles, tendons, ligaments, and bones.

atherosclerosis Narrowing of the coronary arteries due to buildup of debris along the artery walls.

attention deficit hyperactivity disorder (ADHD) Previously known as attention deficit disorder (ADD). A condition in which an individual may be easily distracted, and have difficulty listening and following directions, difficulty focusing and sustaining attention, difficulty concentrating and staying on task, and/or inconsistent performance in school.

autism spectrum disorder A brain disorder that makes it hard to communicate and relate to others due to failure of different parts of the brain to work together.

B

baby bottle tooth decay The decay of baby teeth in children due to continual exposure to fermentable sugary liquids.

bariatric surgery Surgical procedures that reduce the functional volume of the stomach so that less food is eaten. Such surgeries are sometimes used to treat extreme obesity.

basal metabolism The amount of energy the body expends to meet its basic physiological needs. Also referred to as **basal metabolic rate (BMR)**.

behavior modification Changing behaviors to improve health. Identifying and altering eating patterns that contribute to weight gain or impede weight loss is behavior modification.

bile A greenish-yellow fluid made in the liver and concentrated and stored in the gallbladder. It helps emulsify fat and prepare it for digestion.

binge drinking The consumption of 5 or more alcoholic drinks by men, or 4 or more drinks by women, in a very short time.

bioaccumulate When a substance or chemical builds up in an organism over time, so that the concentration of the chemical is higher than would be found naturally in the environment.

bioavailability The degree to which a nutrient is absorbed from foods and used in the body.

biodiversity Having a wide variety of plant and animal species within an environment.

biopesticides Substances derived from natural materials such as animals, plants, bacteria, and certain minerals to control pests.

biotechnology The application of biological techniques to living cells, which alters their genetic makeup.

bioterrorism The use of a biological or chemical agent to frighten, threaten, coerce, injure, and/or kill individuals.

blackouts Periods of time when an intoxicated person cannot recall part or all of an event.

blood alcohol concentration (BAC) The measurement of the amount of alcohol in your blood. BAC is measured in grams of alcohol per deciliter of blood, usually expressed as a percentage.

body composition The relative proportion of muscle, fat, water, and other tissues in the body.

body dysmorphic disorder A mental illness in which a person is excessively concerned about and preoccupied by a perceived defect in his or her body.

body mass index (BMI) A calculation of your weight in relationship to your height. A BMI between 18.5 and 24.9 is considered healthy.

bolus Chewed mass of food.

bone mineral density (BMD) The amount of minerals, in particular calcium, per volume in an individual's bone. The denser the bones, the stronger the bones.

botulism A rare but serious paralytic illness caused by the bacterium *Clostridium botulinum*. Infant botulism is caused by consuming the spores of the bacteria, which then grow in the intestines and release toxin. It can be fatal.

bovine spongiform encephalopathy (BSE) A slow, degenerative, and deadly disease that attacks the central nervous system of cattle. Also known as **mad cow disease.**

bran The indigestible outer shell of the grain kernel.

buffers Substances that help maintain the proper pH in a solution by attracting or donating hydrogen ions.

C

cancer Type of diseases characterized by the uncontrolled growth and spread of abnormal cells.

canning The process of heating food to a temperature high enough to kill bacteria and then packing the food in airtight containers.

carbohydrate loading A diet and training strategy that maximizes glycogen stores in the body before an endurance event.

carcinogenic A substance thought to cause cancer.

cardiorespiratory endurance The body's ability to sustain prolonged exercise.

carnitine A vitamin-like substance needed to properly utilize fat.

catalysts Substances that aid and speed up reactions without being changed, damaged, or used up in the process.

cataract A common eye disorder that occurs when the lens of the eye becomes cloudy.

celiac disease An illness of the small intestine that involves the inability to digest the protein gluten.

cellulite A nonmedical term that refers to fat cells under the skin that give it a ripplelike appearance. Contrary to popular belief, cellulite is no different from other fat in the body.

central obesity An excess storage of visceral fat in the abdominal area, which increases the risk of heart disease, diabetes, and hypertension.

chemical digestion Breaking down food with enzymes or digestive juices.

childhood obesity The condition of a child's having too much body weight for his height.

chlorophyll The green pigment in plants that absorbs energy from sunlight to begin the process of photosynthesis.

cholecystokinin A hormone released when the stomach is distended. It is associated with the feeling of satiation.

choline A vitamin-like substance needed for healthy cells and nerves.

chronic dehydration Dehydration over a long period of time.

chylomicron A type of lipoprotein that carries digested fat and other lipids through the lymph system into the blood.

chyme A liquid combination of partially digested food, water, HCl, and digestive enzymes.

ciguatera poisoning A condition caused by marine toxins produced by *dinoflagellates* (microscopic sea organisms). Small fish eat dinoflagellates and larger fish consume the small fish. The toxins then bioaccumulate in the fish.

cirrhosis Stage 3 of alcohol liver disease in which liver cells die, causing severe scarring.

closed or "coded" dating Refers to the packing numbers that are decodable only by manufacturers and are often found on nonperishable, shelf-stable foods.

coenzyme Substances, often vitamins, that are needed by enzymes to perform many chemical reactions in your body.

collagen A ropelike, fibrous protein that is the most abundant protein in your body.

colostrum The fluid that is expressed from the mother's breast after birth and before the development of breast milk.

commodity crops Crop products such as corn and soybeans that can be used for commerce.

community-supported agriculture (CSA) An arrangement where individuals pay a fee to support a local farm, and in exchange receive a weekly or biweekly box of fresh produce from the farm.

complemented proteins Incomplete proteins that are combined with modest amounts of animal or soy proteins or with other plant proteins that are rich in the limiting amino acids to create a complete protein.

complete protein A protein that provides all the essential amino acids that your body needs, along with some nonessential amino acids. Soy protein and protein from animal sources, in general, are complete.

complex carbohydrates A category of carbohydrates that contain many sugar units combined. A polysaccharide is a complex carbohydrate.

conception The moment when a sperm fertilizes an egg.

conditionally essential amino acids Nonessential amino acids that become essential if the body cannot make them, such as during bouts of illness.

conditioning The process of improving physical fitness through repeated activity.

congeners Compounds in alcohol that enhance the taste but may contribute to hangover symptoms.

congregate meals Meals served at churches, synagogues, or other community sites where older adults can receive a nutritious meal and socialize.

connective tissue The most abundant tissue type in the body. Made up primarily of collagen, it supports and connects body parts as well as providing protection and insulation.

consensus The opinion of a group of experts based on a collection of information.

constipation Difficulty in passing stools.

control group The group given a placebo.

Corn Belt The parts of the United States where corn is grown in abundance. This includes Iowa, Indiana, most of Illinois, and parts of Kansas, Missouri, Nebraska, South Dakota, Minnesota, Ohio, and Wisconsin.

creatine phosphate A compound stored in the muscles that is broken down to replenish ATP stores.

critical periods Developmental stages during which cells and tissue rapidly grow and differentiate to form body structures.

Crohn's disease An inflammatory bowel disease.

cross-contaminate Transfer pathogens from a food, utensil, cutting board, kitchen surface, and/or hands to another food.

D

Daily Values (DVs) Established reference levels of nutrients, based on a 2,000-calorie diet, that are used on food labels.

danger zone The range of temperatures (between 40°F and 140°F) at which foodborne bacteria multiply most rapidly. Room temperature falls within the danger zone.

dehydration The state whereby there is too little water in the body due to too much water being lost, too little being consumed, or a combination of both.

dementia A disorder of the brain that interferes with a person's memory, learning, and mental stability.

denaturation The alteration of a protein's shape, which changes the structure and function of the protein.

dental caries The decay or erosion of teeth.

deoxyribonucleic acid (DNA) Genetic material within cells that directs the synthesis of proteins in the body.

developed country A nation advanced in industrial capability, technological sophistication, and economic productivity.

developing country A nation having a relatively low level of industrial capability, technological sophistication, or economic productivity.

diabetes mellitus A medical condition whereby an individual either doesn't have enough insulin or is resistant to the insulin available. This will cause the blood glucose level to rise. Diabetes mellitus is often called diabetes. **Type 1 diabetes** is an autoimmune disease and is rarer than **type 2 diabetes**, which is seen in those with insulin resistance.

diarrhea Frequent, loose, watery stools.

diastolic pressure The pressure of your blood against the artery walls when the heart is at rest between beats.

dietary fiber Nondigestible polysaccharides found in foods.

Dietary Guidelines for Americans Guidelines published every five years that provide dietary and lifestyle advice to healthy individuals aged 2 and older to maintain good health and prevent chronic diseases.

Dietary Reference Intakes (DRIs) Reference values for the essential nutrients needed to maintain good health, to prevent chronic diseases, and to avoid unhealthy excesses.

digestibility A food's capacity to be broken down so that it can be absorbed.

digestive process The breakdown of foods into absorbable components using mechanical and chemical means.

diglyceride A glycerol with only two attached fatty acids.

disaccharide Two sugar units combined. There are three disaccharides: sucrose, lactose, and maltose.

discretionary calorie allowance Calories left over in the diet once all nutrient needs have been met from the basic food groups.

disordered eating Abnormal and potentially harmful eating behaviors that do not meet specific criteria for anorexia nervosa or bulimia nervosa.

distillation The evaporation and then collection of a liquid by condensation. Liquors are made using distillation.

diuretics Substances such as alcohol and some medications that cause the body to lose water.

diverticula Small bulges at weak spots in the colon wall.

diverticulitis Infection of the diverticula.

diverticulosis The existence of diverticula in the lining of your intestine.

DNA The blueprint in cells that stores all genetic information. DNA remains in the nucleus of the cell and directs the synthesis of proteins.

DNA fingerprinting A technique in which bacterial DNA "gene patterns" (or "fingerprints") are detected and analyzed to distinguish between different strains of a bacterium.

double-blind placebo-controlled study When the scientists and subjects in a research experiment can't distinguish between the treatments given to the subjects and don't know which group of subjects received which treatment.

duration The length of time of performing an activity.

dysphagia Difficult swallowing.

E

eating disorders The term used to describe psychological illnesses that involve specific abnormal eating behaviors: anorexia nervosa (self-starvation), bulimia nervosa (bingeing and purging), binge eating disorder, and night eating syndrome.

edema The accumulation of excess fluid in the spaces surrounding your cells, which causes swelling of the body tissue.

eicosanoids Hormone-like substances in the body. Prostaglandins, thromboxanes, and leukotrienes are all eicosanoids.

eicosapentaenoic acid (EPA) and docosahexaenoic acid (DHA) Two omega-3 fatty acids that are heart healthy. Fatty fish such as salmon are good sources.

electrolytes Charged ions that conduct an electrical current in a solvent such as water. Sodium, potassium, and chloride are examples of electrolytes in the body. Vomiting and diarrhea cause the loss of electrolytes from your body.

embryo Term that refers to a fertilized egg during the third through the eighth week of pregnancy. After the eighth week, the developing baby is called a fetus.

empty calories Calories that come with little nutrition. Jelly beans are an example of a food that provides lots of calories from sugar but few nutrients.

emulsifier A compound that keeps two incompatible substances, such as oil and water, mixed together.

endosperm The starchy part of the grain kernel.

endotoxin A damaging product produced by intestinal bacteria that travels in the blood to the liver and initiates the release of cytokines that damage liver cells, leading to scarring.

energy balance The state at which energy (calorie) intake and energy (calorie) output in the body are equal.

energy density A measurement of the calories in a food compared with the weight (grams) of the food.

energy gap The difference between the numbers of calories needed to maintain weight before and after weight loss.

enriched grains Refined grain foods that have folic acid, thiamin, niacin, riboflavin, and iron added.

enzymes Substances that produce chemical changes or catalyze chemical reactions.

epidemiological research Research that looks at populations of people; it is often observational.

epiglottis Flap of tissue that protects the trachea while swallowing.

epiphyseal plate The growth plate of the bone. In puberty, growth in this area leads to increases in height.

ergogenic aid A substance, such as a dietary supplement, used to enhance athletic performance.

esophagus Tube that extends from the throat to the stomach.

essential amino acids The nine amino acids that the body cannot synthesize; they must be obtained through dietary sources.

essential fatty acids The two polyunsaturated fatty acids that the body cannot make and therefore must be eaten in foods: linoleic acid and alpha-linolenic acid.

Estimated Average Requirement (EAR) The average amount of a nutrient that is known to meet the needs of 50 percent of the individuals in a similar age and gender group.

Estimated Energy Requirement (EER) The amount of daily energy needed to maintain a healthy body weight and meet energy (calorie) needs based on age, gender, height, weight, and activity level.

estrogen The hormone responsible for female sex characteristics.

ethanol The type of alcohol in alcoholic beverages such as wine, beer, and liquor.

Exchange Lists for Meal Planning A grouping of foods, in specific portions, according to their carbohydrate, protein, and fat composition to ensure that each food in the group contributes a similar amount of calories per serving.

exercise Any type of structured or planned physical activity.

experimental group The group given a specific treatment.

experimental research Research involving at least two groups of subjects.

extracellular fluid compartment The fluid located outside your cells. Interstitial fluids and fluids in the blood are extracellular fluids.

extreme obesity Having a BMI > 40.

F

famine A severe shortage of food caused by crop destruction due to weather problems or poor agricultural practices so that the food supply is destroyed or severely diminished. This can also be caused by pestilence and/or war.

farm An establishment that produces and sells at least $1,000 worth of agricultural products annually.

farm-to-table continuum Illustrates the roles that farmers, food manufacturers, food transporters, retailers, and consumers play in ensuring that the food supply, from the farm to the plate, remains safe.

fat substitutes Substances that replace added fat in foods by providing the creamy properties of fat for fewer calories and fewer total fat grams.

fatty acid The basic unit of triglycerides and phospholipids.

fatty liver Stage 1 of alcohol liver disease.

fecal-to-oral transmission The spread of pathogens by putting something in the mouth that has been in contact with infected stool. Poor hygiene, such as not washing hands after using the bathroom, can be a cause of this contamination.

feedlot A facility where cattle are fed grain and other foods before being slaughtered.

fermentation The process by which yeast converts sugars in grains or fruits into ethanol and carbon dioxide, resulting in an alcoholic beverage.

fetal alcohol spectrum disorders (FASDs) A range of conditions that can occur in children who are exposed to alcohol in utero. Fetal alcohol syndrome (FAS) is the most severe of the FASDs; children with FAS will display physical, mental, and behavioral abnormalities.

fetus A developing embryo that is at least eight weeks old.

fiber The portion of plant foods that isn't digested in the small intestine.

flatulence Production of excessive gas in the stomach or the intestines.

flavonoids Phytochemicals found in fruits, vegetables, tea, nuts, and seeds.

flexibility The joints' ability to move freely through a full and normal range of motion.

fluid balance The equal distribution of water throughout your body and within and between cells.

food additives Substances added to food that affect its quality, flavor, freshness, and/or safety.

food allergens Proteins that are not broken down by cooking or digestion and enter the body intact, causing an adverse reaction by the immune system.

food allergy An abnormal reaction by the immune system to a particular food.

food biosecurity Protecting the food supply from bioterrorist attacks.

food consumers The role that individuals play when they are making decisions about which food to buy and which to avoid.

food guidance systems Visual diagrams that provide a variety of food recommendations to help create a well-balanced diet.

food industry The collective efforts of various businesses, including farms, food processors, food marketers, wholesalers, and retailers, that provide food to consumers.

food insecurity The inability to satisfy basic food needs due to lack of financial resources or other problems.

food intolerance Adverse reaction to a food that does not involve an immune response. Lactose intolerance is one example.

food jags When a child will only eat the same food meal after meal.

food preservation The treatment of foods to reduce deterioration and spoilage, and help prevent the multiplication of pathogens that can cause foodborne illness.

food safety Guidelines and procedures that help keep foods free from contaminants.

Food Safety Initiative (FSI) Coordinates the research, surveillance, inspection, outbreak response, and educational activities of the various government agencies that work together to safeguard food.

foodborne illness Sickness caused by consuming contaminated food or beverages. Also known as foodborne disease or food poisoning.

fortified foods Foods with added nutrients.

free radicals Unstable oxygen-containing molecules that can damage the cells of the body and possibly contribute to the increased risk of chronic diseases.

fructose The sweetest of the monosaccharides; also known as fruit sugar.

functional fiber The nondigestible polysaccharides that are added to foods because of a specific desired effect on health.

functional foods Foods that have a positive effect on health beyond providing basic nutrients.

fungicides Chemicals used to kill mold.

G

galactose A monosaccharide that links with glucose to create the sugar found in dairy foods.

gallstones Small, hard, crystalline structures formed in the gallbladder or bile duct due to abnormally thick bile.

gastric banding A type of gastric surgery that uses a silicone band to reduce the size of the stomach so that less food is needed to feel full.

gastrin A digestive hormone produced in the stomach that stimulates digestive activities and increases motility and emptying.

gastritis Inflammation of the stomach.

gastroenteritis Formal term for "stomach flu." Caused by a virus or bacteria and results in inflammation of the stomach and/or intestines.

gastrointestinal (GI) tract Body area containing the organs of the digestive tract. It extends from the mouth to the anus.

gene A DNA segment that codes for a specific protein.

gene-environment interaction The interaction of genetics and the environment that increases the risk of obesity in some people.

genetic engineering (GE) A biological technique that isolates and manipulates the genes of organisms to produce a targeted, modified product.

gene expression The processing of genetic information to create a specific protein.

genetically modified A cell that has its genetic makeup altered.

genetically modified organisms (GMOs) Organisms that have been genetically engineered to contain both original and foreign genes.

germ In grains, the seed of the grain kernel.

gestational diabetes Diabetes that occurs in women during pregnancy.

ghrelin A hormone produced mainly in the stomach that increases hunger.

globesity A blend of the words *global* and *obesity,* coined by the World Health Organization, which refers to the worldwide obesity epidemic.

glucagon The hormone that directs glycogenolysis and gluconeogenesis to increase glucose in the blood. Glucagon is produced in and released from the pancreas.

gluconeogenesis The creation of glucose from noncarbohydrate sources, predominantly protein.

glucose The most abundant sugar in foods and the primary energy source for your body.

gluten intolerance A sensitivity to the protein gluten, which is found in wheat and other grains. Symptoms incude stomachaches, diarrhea, bloating, and tiredness.

glycerol The three-carbon backbone of a triglyceride.

glycogen The storage form of glucose in humans and animals.

glycogenesis The process of converting excess glucose into glycogen in your liver and muscle.

glycogenolysis The breakdown of glycogen to release glucose.

GRAS (generally recognized as safe) A substance that is believed to be safe to consume based on a long history of use by humans or a substantial amount of research that documents its safety.

greenhouse gases Gases that absorb and "trap" the heat in the air and re-radiate that heat downward.

growth charts Series of percentile curves that illustrate the distribution of selected body measurements in U.S. children.

growth hormone A protein-based hormone that stimulates cell growth and reproduction in humans and animals.

growth spurt A rapid increase in height and weight.

Guillain-Barré syndrome A condition that can result from a *Campylobacter* infection. It causes the immune system to attack its own nerves and can lead to paralysis for several weeks.

H

hangover A collective term for the unpleasant symptoms, such as a headache and dizziness, that occur after drinking an excessive amount of alcohol.

health claims Claims on the label that describe a relationship between a food or dietary compound and a disease or health-related condition.

Healthy People 2020 A set of disease prevention and health promotion objectives for Americans to meet during the second decade of the new millennium.

healthy weight A body weight in relationship to your height that doesn't increase the risk of developing any weight-related health problems or diseases.

heart attack Permanent damage to the heart muscle that results from a sudden lack of oxygen-rich blood.

heartburn A burning sensation originating in the esophagus. Heartburn is usually caused by the reflux of gastric contents from the stomach into the esophagus. Chronic heartburn can lead to **gastroesophageal reflux disease (GERD).**

hemolytic uremic syndrome A rare condition that can be caused by *E. coli* O157:H7 and results in the destruction of red blood cells and kidney failure.

hemorrhoids Swelling in the veins of the rectum and anus.

herbicides Substances that are used to kill and control weeds.

high-density lipoprotein (HDL) A lipoprotein that removes cholesterol from the tissues and delivers it to the liver to be used as part of bile and/or to be excreted from the body. Because of this, it is known as the *good* cholesterol carrier.

high-pressure processing (HPP) A method used to pasteurize foods by exposing the items to pulses of high pressure, which destroys the microorganisms that are present.

homeless Individuals who are either "crashing" with friends or family members, or residing on the street or in their automobiles.

hormones Protein- or lipid-based chemical messengers that initiate or direct a specific action. Insulin, glucagon, and estrogen are examples of hormones.

host A living plant or animal (including a human) that a virus infects for the sake of reproducing.

Human Genome Project A project sponsored by the United States government to determine the complete set and sequencing of DNA in human cells and identify all human genes.

hunger The physical need for food.

hydrochloric acid (HCl) A powerful acid made in the stomach that has digestive functions. It also helps to kill microorganisms and lowers the pH in the stomach.

hydrogenation Adding hydrogen to an unsaturated fatty acid to make it more saturated and solid at room temperature.

hydrophobic Having an aversion to water.

hypertension High blood pressure.

hypoallergenic infant formulas Specially developed formulas for infants who have food allergies and cannot tolerate regular formula.

hypoglycemia A blood glucose level that drops to lower than 70 mg/dl. Hunger, shakiness, dizziness, perspiration, and light-headedness are some signs of hypoglycemia.

hyponatremia A condition of too little sodium in the blood.

hypotension Low blood pressure.

hypothesis An idea generated by scientists based on their observations.

I

ileocecal sphincter Gateway between the end of the small intestine and the beginning of the large intestine. The sphincter prevents backflow of fecal contents from the large intestine into the small intestine.

immunity The state of having built up antibodies to a particular foreign substance so that when particles of the substance enter the body, they are destroyed by the antibodies.

impaired glucose tolerance A condition whereby a fasting blood glucose level is higher than normal (>100 mg/dl), but not high enough ($\leq$126 mg/dl) to be classified as diabetes mellitus. Also called prediabetes.

incomplete protein A protein that is low in one or more of the essential amino acids. Protein from plant sources tends to be incomplete.

infancy The age range from birth to 12 months.

inorganic Compounds that do not contain carbon and are not formed by living things. Inorganic compounds include minerals, water, and salts.

inositol A vitamin-like substance synthesized in your body that helps to keep your cells and their membranes healthy.

insensible water loss The water that is lost from the body daily through exhalation from the lungs and evaporation off the skin.

insoluble fiber A type of fiber that doesn't dissolve in water and is not fermented by intestinal bacteria.

insulin The hormone, produced in and released from the pancreas, that directs the glucose from the blood into cells.

insulin resistance The inability of the cells to respond to insulin.

integrated pest management (IPM) Alternative to pesticides that uses the most economical and the least harmful methods of pest control to minimize risk to consumers, crops, and the environment.

intensity The level of difficulty of an activity.

interstitial fluids Fluids located between cells.

intracellular fluid compartment The fluid located inside your cells.

irradiation A process in which foods are placed in a shielded chamber, called an **irradiator,** and subjected to a radiant energy source. This kills specific pathogens in food by breaking up the cells' DNA.

irritable bowel syndrome (IBS) A functional disorder that involves changes in colon rhythm.

isoflavones Naturally occurring phytoestrogens, or weak plant estrogens, that function in a fashion similar to the hormone estrogen in the human body.

J

jaundice A yellowish coloring of the skin due to the presence of bile pigments in the blood.

K

ketoacidosis The buildup of ketone bodies to dangerous levels, which can result in coma or death.

ketone bodies The by-products of the incomplete breakdown of fat.

ketosis The condition of increased ketone bodies in the blood.

kilocalories The measurement of energy in foods. Commonly referred to as *calories.*

kwashiorkor A state of PEM where there is a severe deficiency of dietary protein.

L

laboratory experiment A scientific experiment conducted in a laboratory. Some laboratory experiments involve animals.

lactate A by-product of rapid glucose metabolism.

lactation The production of milk in a woman's body after childbirth, and the period during which it occurs. The baby receives the milk through **breast-feeding**.

lactose A disaccharide composed of glucose and galactose; also known as milk sugar.

lactose intolerant When maldigestion of lactose results in symptoms such as nausea, cramps, bloating, flatulence, and diarrhea.

lactose maldigestion The inability to digest lactose in foods due to low levels of the enzyme lactase.

lanugo Very fine, soft hair on the face and arms of people with anorexia nervosa.

large intestine Final organ of the GI tract. It consists of the cecum, appendix, colon, and rectum.

lean body mass The body mass once the fat mass has been subtracted. It contains mostly muscle but also organs and fluids. Lean body mass is the metabolically active tissue in the body.

leptin A hormone produced in fat tissue that helps regulate body fat by signaling the reduction of food intake in the brain and interfering with the storage of fat in the cells.

let-down The release of milk from the mother's breast to feed the baby.

licensed dietitian (LD) An individual who has met specified educational and experience criteria deemed necessary by a state licensing board to be considered an expert in the field of nutrition. An RD would meet all the qualifications to be an LD.

life expectancy The number of years that a person will live.

limiting amino acid The amino acid that is in the shortest supply in an incomplete protein.

linoleic acid A polyunsaturated essential fatty acid; part of the omega-6 fatty acid family.

lipid A category of carbon, hydrogen, and oxygen compounds that are insoluble in water.

lipoic acid A vitamin-like substance that your body needs for energy production; it may also act as an antioxidant.

lipoproteins Capsule-shaped transport carriers that enable fat and cholesterol to travel through the lymph and blood.

liposuction The surgical removal of subcutaneous fat with a penlike instrument. Usually performed on the abdomen, hips, and thighs, and/or other areas of the body.

liver The largest gland of the body. It aids in digestive activity and is responsible for metabolism of nutrients, detoxification of alcohol, and some nutrient storage.

locavore A person who eats locally grown food whenever possible.

low birth weight baby A baby weighing less than 5½ pounds at birth.

low-density lipoprotein (LDL) A lipoprotein that deposits cholesterol in the walls of the arteries. Because this can lead to heart disease, LDL is referred to as the *bad* cholesterol carrier.

lower esophageal sphincter (LES) A circular band of muscle between the esophagus and the stomach that opens and closes to allow food to enter the stomach.

lumen The interior of the digestive tract, through which food passes.

lymph Watery fluid that circulates through the body in lymph vessels and eventually enters the blood.

M

macronutrients The energy-containing essential nutrients that you need in higher amounts: carbohydrates, lipids (fats), and proteins.

macrosomia A large baby, weighing more than 8 pounds, 13 oz.

major minerals Minerals needed from your diet and in your body in amounts greater than 100 milligrams per day. These include sodium, chloride, potassium, calcium, phosphorus, magnesium, and sulfur.

malnourished The long-term outcome of consuming a diet that doesn't meet nutrient needs.

maltose A disaccharide composed of two glucose units joined together.

marasmus A state of PEM where there is a severe deficiency of calories that perpetuates wasting; also called starvation.

marine toxins Chemicals that occur naturally and contaminate some fish.

mast cells Cells in connective tissue to which antibodies attach, setting the stage for potential future allergic reactions.

mechanical digestion Breaking food down through chewing and grinding, or moving it through the GI tract with peristalsis.

medical nutrition therapy The integration of nutrition counseling and dietary changes based on an individual's medical and health needs to treat a patient's medical condition.

megadose A very large dose or amount.

messenger RNA (mRNA) A type of RNA that copies the genetic information encoded in DNA and carries it out of the nucleus of the cell to synthesize the protein.

metabolism The numerous reactions that occur within the cell. The calories in foods are converted to energy in the cells of the body.

micelles Small transport carriers in the intestine that enable fatty acids and other compounds to be absorbed.

micronutrients Essential nutrients that you need in smaller amounts: vitamins and minerals.

microsomal ethanol-oxidizing system (MEOS) The other major enzyme system in the liver that metabolizes alcohol.

milestones Objectives or significant events that occur during development.

minerals Inorganic elements essential to the nutrition of humans.

moderate alcohol consumption An average daily consumption of up to one drink per day for women and up to two drinks per day for men, as well as no more than three drinks in any single day for women and no more than four drinks in a single day for men.

modified atmosphere packaging (MAP) A food preservation technique that changes the composition of the air surrounding the food in a package to extend its shelf life.

monoglyceride A glycerol with only one attached fatty acid.

monosaccharide One sugar unit. There are three monosaccharides: glucose, fructose, and galactose.

monosodium glutamate (MSG) A flavor enhancer.

monounsaturated fatty acid (MUFA) A fatty acid that has one double bond.

MSG symptom complex A series of reactions such as numbness, burning sensation, facial pressure or tightness, chest pain, rapid heartbeat, and drowsiness that can occur in some individuals after they consume MSG.

mucus Viscous, slippery secretions found in saliva and other digestive juices.

muscle endurance The ability of the muscle to produce prolonged effort.

muscle strength The greatest amount of force exerted by the muscle at one time.

MyPlate Depicts five food groups using the familiar mealtime visual of a place setting. It represents recommendations given in the *Dietary Guidelines for Americans*.

N

naturally occurring sugars Sugars such as fructose and lactose that are found naturally in fruit and dairy foods.

negative energy balance The state in which you expend more energy than you consume. Over time, this results in weight loss.

neurotoxins Toxins that affect the nerves and can cause symptoms including mild numbness or tingling in the face, arms, and legs, as well as headaches and dizziness. Severe cases could result in death.

nitrates (nitrites) Substances that can be added to foods to function as a preservative and to give meats such as hot dogs and luncheon meats a pink color.

nitrogen balance The state in which an individual is consuming the same amount of nitrogen (from protein) in the diet as he or she is excreting in the urine.

nonessential amino acids The 11 amino acids that the body can synthesize.

nonexercise-associated thermogenesis (NEAT) The energy expenditure that occurs during nonexercise movements, such as fidgeting, standing, and chewing gum.

normal blood pressure Less than 120 mm Hg (systolic—the top number) and less than 80 mm Hg (diastolic—the bottom number). Referred to as 120/80.

norovirus The most common type of virus that causes foodborne illness. Noroviruses can cause gastroenteritis, or the "stomach flu." Also known as Norwalk-like viruses.

nursing bottle tooth decay Tooth decay from prolonged contact with formula, milk, fruit juice, or other sugar-rich liquid offered to an infant in a bottle.

nutrient content claims Claims on the label that describe the level or amount of a nutrient in a food product.

nutrient density The amount of nutrients per calorie in a given food. Nutrient-dense foods provide more nutrients per calorie than less nutrient-dense foods.

nutrients Compounds in foods that sustain your body processes. There are six classes of nutrients: carbohydrates, fats (lipids), proteins, vitamins, minerals, and water.

Nutrition Facts panel The area on the food label that provides a uniform listing of specific nutrients obtained in one serving of the food.

nutrition The science that studies how the nutrients and compounds in foods that you eat nourish and affect your body functions and health.

nutritional genomics A field of study that researches the relationship between nutrition and genomics (the study of genes and gene expression).

nutritionist A generic term with no recognized legal or professional meaning. Some people may call themselves nutritionists without having any credible training in nutrition.

O

obesity Carrying an excessive amount of body fat above the level of being overweight.

observational research Research that involves looking at factors in two or more groups of subjects to see if there is a relationship to certain outcomes.

oils Lipids that are liquid at room temperature.

open dating Typically found on perishable items such as meat, poultry, eggs, and dairy foods; must contain a calendar date.

organic Being free of chemical-based pesticides, synthetic fertilizers, irradiation, and bioengineering. A USDA-accredited certifying inspector must certify organic foods.

organophosphates A group of synthetic pesticides that adversely affect the nervous systems of pests.

osmosis The movement of a solvent, such as water, from an area of lower concentration of solutes across a membrane to an area of higher concentration of solutes. It balances the concentration of solutes between the compartments.

osteopenia A condition whereby the bones are less dense, increasing the risk of fractures.

osteoporosis A condition in which the bones are less dense, increasing the risk of fractures.

overnutrition A state of excess nutrients and calories in the diet.

overpopulation When a region has more people than its natural resources can support.

overweight Carrying extra weight on your body in relation to your height.

oxidation The process during which oxygen combines with other molecules.

P

pancreas Accessory organ of digestion that produces hormones and enzymes. It's connected to the duodenum via the bile duct.

paralytic shellfish poisoning A condition caused by a reddish-brown-colored dinoflagellate that contains neurotoxins.

parasites Organisms that live on or in another organism. Parasites obtain their nourishment from their hosts.

pasteurization The process of heating liquids or food at high temperatures to destroy foodborne pathogens.

pathogens Collective term for disease-causing microorganisms (microbes). Includes viruses, bacteria, and parasites. The most common source of foodborne illness.

peak bone mass The genetically determined maximum amount of bone mass an individual can build up.

Peak bone mass The genetically determined maximum amount of bone mass an individual can build up.

peer-reviewed journal A research journal in which fellow scientists (peers) review studies to assess if they are accurate and sound before they are published.

pendular movement A constrictive wave that involves both forward and reverse movements of chyme and enhances nutrient absorption.

pepsin A digestive enzyme produced in the stomach that breaks down protein.

peptic ulcers Sores, erosions, or breaks in the mucosal lining of the stomach.

peptide bonds The bonds that connect amino acids, created when the acid group of one amino acid is joined with the nitrogen-containing amine group of another amino acid.

percentile The most commonly used clinical indicator to assess the size and growth patterns of children in the United States. An individual child is ranked according to the percentage of the reference population he equals or exceeds.

peristalsis The forward, rhythmic motion that moves food through the digestive system. Peristalsis is a form of mechanical digestion because it influences motion, but it does not add chemical secretions.

pesticides Substances that kill or repel pests such as insects, weeds, microorganisms, rodents, or fungi.

pharynx The throat. Passageway for the respiratory (air) and digestive tracts (food and beverages).

phospholipids Lipids made up of two fatty acids and a phosphate group attached to a glycerol backbone.

photosynthesis A process by which green plants create carbohydrates using the energy from sunlight.

physical activity Voluntary movement that results in energy expenditure (burning calories).

physical fitness The ability to perform physical activities requiring cardiorespiratory endurance, muscle endurance, and strength and/or flexibility; physical fitness is acquired through physical activity and adequate nutrition.

phytochemicals Plant chemicals that have been shown to reduce the risk of certain diseases such as cancer and heart disease. Beta-carotene is a phytochemical.

phytosterols Naturally occurring sterols found in plants. Phytosterols lower LDL cholesterol levels by competing with cholesterol for absorption in the intestinal tract.

picky eating Unwillingness to eat unfamiliar foods.

placebo A sugar pill that has no impact on the individual's health when ingested.

placenta The site of common tissue between the mother and growing embryo. The placenta is attached to the fetus with the **umbilical cord.**

plant breeding A type of biotechnology in which two plants are crossbred to produce offspring with desired traits from both.

plaque The hardened buildup of cholesterol-laden foam cells, platelets, cellular waste products, and calcium in the arteries that results in atherosclerosis.

polychlorinated biphenyls (PCBs) Synthetic chemicals that have been shown to cause cancer and other adverse effects on the immune, reproductive, nervous, and endocrine systems in animals. PCBs may cause cancer in humans.

polysaccharide Many sugar units combined. Starch, glycogen, and fiber are all polysaccharides.

polyunsaturated fatty acid (PUFA) A fatty acid with two or more double bonds.

positive energy balance The state whereby you store more energy than you expend. Over time, this results in weight gain.

poverty Lacking the means to provide for material or comfort needs.

precision agriculture A cost-efficient, precise farming method that uses new technologies to collect data about variations in field soil to better manage the use of appropriate seeds, fertilizer, water, and pesticides for the growing of crops with less waste.

precursor A substance that is converted into or leads to the formation of another substance.

preformed vitamins Substances that are found in active form in foods.

pregnancy-induced hypertension A category of hypertension that includes *gestational hypertension* (occurs in pregnancy in a woman without a prior history of high blood pressure), *preeclampsia* (hypertension, severe edema, and protein loss occur), and *eclampsia* (can result in seizures; may be extremely dangerous for mother and baby).

preschoolers Children aged 3 to 5 years old.

prion Cellular proteins. An abnormal prion protein is the cause of mad cow disease.

prior sanctioned Having previous approval.

progressive overload principle A gradual increase in exercise demands resulting from modifications to the frequency, intensity, time, or type of activity.

proportionality The relationship of one entity to another. Grains, fruits, and vegetables should be consumed in a higher proportion than oils and meats in the diet.

protein digestibility corrected amino acid score (PDCAAS) A score measured as a percentage that takes into account both digestibility and amino acid profile and gives a good indication of the quality of a protein.

protein-energy malnutrition (PEM) A lack of sufficient dietary protein and/or calories.

protein quality The measure of a protein's digestibility and how its amino acid pattern compares with your body's needs. Proteins that are more easily digested and have a complete set of amino acids are of higher quality.

protein turnover The continual process of degrading and synthesizing protein. When the daily amount of degraded protein is equivalent to the amount that is synthesized, you are in protein balance.

proteins Compounds in your body that consist of numerous amino acids and are found in all living cells.

provitamins Substances found in foods that can be converted into an active form once they are absorbed.

public health nutritionist An individual who may have an undergraduate degree in nutrition but isn't an RD.

purging Measures taken to prevent weight gain or lose weight after consuming food; examples include self-induced vomiting, laxatives, diuretics (water pills), excessive exercise, and/or fasting.

pyloric sphincter Sphincter in the bottom of the stomach that separates the pylorus from the duodenum of the small intestine.

Q

quackery The promotion and selling of health products and services of questionable validity. A quack is a person who promotes these products and services in order to make money.

R

rancidity The decomposition, or spoiling, of fats through oxidation.

rate of perceived exertion (RPE) A subjective measure of the intensity level of an activity using a numerical scale.

recombinant bovine somatotropin (rbST) A synthetically made hormone identical to a cow's natural growth hormone, somatotropin, that stimulates milk production. Also known as rbGH (recombinant bovine growth hormone).

Recommended Dietary Allowance (RDA) The average amount of a nutrient that meets the needs of 97 to 98 percent of individuals in a similar age and gender group. The RDA is higher than the EAR.

rectum The lowest part of the large intestine, continuous with the sigmoid colon and the **anus.**

refined grains Grain foods that are made with only the endosperm of the kernel. The bran and germ are not included.

registered dietitian (RD) A health professional who has completed at least a bachelor's degree in nutrition from an accredited university or college in the United States, completed a supervised practice, and passed an exam administered by the American Dietetic Association (ADA).

remineralization The repairing of teeth by adding back the minerals lost during tooth decay. Saliva can help remineralize teeth.

repetitions of maximum (RM) The maximum amount of weight that can be lifted for a specified number of repetitions.

retort canning The process of subjecting already-canned foods to an additional high-temperature heat source to destroy potential pathogens.

risk assessment The process of determining the potential human health risks posed by exposure to substances such as pesticides.

RNA A molecule that carries out the orders of DNA.

ruminant animals Animals that have four chambers in their stomachs for digesting coarse food such as plants.

S

saliva Watery fluid secreted by the salivary glands in the mouth. Saliva moistens food and makes it easier to swallow.

sanctions Boycotts or trade embargoes used by one country or international group to apply political pressure on another.

sashimi A type of sushi that primarily consists of raw seafood, sliced into thin pieces and served with a dipping sauce (soy sauce with wasabi paste) or other condiments (such as fresh ginger).

satiation The feeling during eating that determines how long and how much you eat.

satiety The sensation that you feel when you have had enough to eat. It determines how long you will go between meals and/or snacks.

saturated fats Fats that contain mostly saturated fatty acids.

saturated fatty acid A fatty acid that has all of its carbons bound with hydrogen.

school-aged children Children between the ages of 6 and 10 to 12.

scientific method A stepwise process used by scientists to generate sound research findings.

scombrotoxic fish poisoning A condition caused by consuming spoiled fish that contain large amounts of histamines. Also referred to as histamine fish poisoning.

segmentation A "sloshing" motion that thoroughly mixes chyme with the chemical secretions of the intestine.

sex pheromones Naturally occurring chemicals secreted by one organism to attract another; used as a biopesticide to control pests by interfering with their mating.

sickle-cell anemia A blood disorder caused by a genetic defect in the development of hemoglobin. Sickle-cell anemia causes the red blood cells to distort into a sickle shape and can damage organs and tissues.

side chain The side group of an amino acid that provides it with its unique qualities; also referred to as the R group.

simple carbohydrates A category of carbohydrates that contain a single sugar unit or two sugar units combined. Monosaccharides and disaccharides are simple carbohydrates.

small intestine Comprised of the duodenum, jejunum, and ileum, the small intestine is the longest part of the GI tract. Most of the digestion and absorption of food occurs in the small intestine.

social drinking Drinking patterns that are considered acceptable by society.

solid foods Foods other than breast milk or formula given to an infant, usually around 6 months of age.

soluble fiber A type of fiber that dissolves in water and is fermented by intestinal bacteria. Many soluble fibers are viscous and have gummy or thickening properties.

solvent A liquid that acts as a medium in which substances dissolve. Water is considered the universal solvent.

spores Hardy reproductive structures that are produced by certain bacteria. Some bacterial spores can survive boiling temperature (212°F).

starch The storage form of glucose in plants.

starvation To suffer severely from lack of food; a state in which the body breaks down its own tissue for fuel.

sterol A lipid that contains four connecting rings of carbon and hydrogen.

stomach Digestive organ that holds food after it's moved down the esophagus and before it is propelled into the small intestine.

stool (feces) Waste products that are stored in the large intestine and then excreted from the body. Consists mostly of bacteria, sloughed-off gastrointestinal cells, inorganic matter, water, unabsorbed nutrients, food residue, undigested fibers, fatty acids, mucus, and remnants of digestive fluids.

strength training Exercising with weights or other resistance to build, strengthen, and tone muscle to improve or maintain overall fitness; also called *resistance training*.

stroke A condition caused by a lack of oxygen to the brain that could result in paralysis and possibly death.

stroke volume The amount of blood pumped by the heart with each heartbeat.

structure/function claims Claims on the label that describe how a nutrient or dietary compound affects the structure or function of the human body.

stunting Primarily manifested in early childhood and includes malnutrition during fetal development. Once growth stunting occurs, it is usually permanent. It can affect the vital body organs and cause premature death.

subcutaneous fat The fat located under the skin and between the muscles.

sucrose A disaccharide composed of glucose and fructose. Also known as table sugar.

sugar substitutes Alternatives to table sugar that sweeten foods for fewer calories.

sulfites Preservatives used to help prevent foods from turning brown and to inhibit the growth of microbes. Often used in wine and dried fruit products.

sushi A Japanese dish of cooked, vinegared rice served with fish or other seafood, vegetables, and/or seaweed.

sustainable diet A diet containing foods that meet your health needs and are produced in an ecologically sustainable way.

sustainable food system A system that conserves the natural resources and can be maintained indefinitely.

systolic pressure The force of your blood against the artery walls when your heart beats.

T

thermic effect of food (TEF) The amount of calories the body uses to digest, absorb, metabolize, and store food.

thermogenesis The production of heat in body cells.

thirst The physical need for water.

thirst mechanism Various bodily reactions caused by dehydration that signal you to drink fluids.

toddlers Children aged 1 to 3 years old.

Tolerable Upper Intake Level (UL) The highest amount of a nutrient that can be consumed daily without harm in a similar age and group of individuals.

tongue-thrust reflex A forceful protrusion of the tongue in response to an oral stimulus, such as a spoon.

toxicity The level at which exposure to a substance becomes harmful.

toxins Poisons that can be produced by living organisms.

trace minerals Minerals needed from your diet and in your body in small amounts, less than 20 milligrams daily. These include iron, zinc, selenium, fluoride, chromium, copper, manganese, and molybdenum.

***trans* fat** Substance that contains mostly *trans* fatty acids.

***trans* fatty acids** Substances that result from the hydrogenating of an unsaturated fatty acid, causing a reconfiguring of some of its double bonds. A small amount of *trans* fatty acids occurs naturally in animal foods.

transfer RNA (tRNA) A type of RNA that collects the amino acids within the cell that are needed to make a specific protein.

transport proteins Proteins that carry lipids (fat and cholesterol), oxygen, waste products, and vitamins through the blood to various organs and tissues. Proteins can also act as channels through which some substances enter cells.

traveler's diarrhea A common pathogen-induced intestinal disorder experienced by some travelers who visit areas with unsanitary conditions.

triglyceride Three fatty acids that are attached to a glycerol backbone. Also known as fat.

trimesters The three time periods of pregnancy.

U

U.S. Pharmacopeia (USP) A nonprofit organization that sets purity and reliability standards for dietary supplements.

underdeveloped country A nation having a low level of economic productivity and technological sophistication within the contemporary range of possibility.

undernutrition A state of inadequate nutrition whereby a person's nutrient and/or calorie needs aren't met through the diet.

underweight Weighing too little for your height.

unsaturated fats Fats that contain mostly unsaturated fatty acids.

unsaturated fatty acid A fatty acid that has one or more double bonds between carbons.

urea A nitrogen-containing waste product that is excreted in urine.

V

vegetarian A person who doesn't eat meat, fish, or poultry or (sometimes) foods made from these animal sources.

very low-calorie diet or protein-sparing modified fast A diet of fewer than 800 calories per day and high in protein. These diets are very low in or devoid of carbohydrates and have a minimal amount of fat.

very low-density lipoprotein (VLDL) A lipoprotein that delivers fat made in the liver to the tissues. VLDL remnants are converted into LDLs.

villi Projections on the walls of the small intestine that increase the surface area over which nutrients can be absorbed. Villi are in turn covered with microvilli, which increase the surface area even more.

virus A microscopic organism that carries genetic information for its own replication; can infect a host and cause illness.

visceral fat The fat stored in the abdominal area.

vitamins Essential nutrients that your body needs in small amounts to grow, reproduce, and maintain good health.

VO$_2$max The maximum amount of oxygen (ml) a person uses in one minute per kilogram of body weight.

W

wasting A condition caused by extremely low energy intake from too little food. It is sometimes referred to as acute malnutrition. Infections, high energy use, or nutrient loss can cause wasting.

water balance The state whereby an equal amount of water is lost and replenished daily in the body.

weight cycling The repeated gain and loss of body weight.

weight management Maintaining your weight within a healthy range.

whole grains Grain foods that are made with the entire edible grain kernel: the bran, the endosperm, and the germ.

working poor Individuals or families who are steadily employed but still experience poverty due to low wages or high dependent expenses.

Z

zoochemicals Compounds in animal food products that are beneficial to human health. Omega-3 fatty acids are an example of zoochemicals.

References

Chapter 1

1. Glanz, K., M. Basil, E. Maibach, J. Goldberg, and D. Snyder. 1998. Why Americans Eat What They Do: Taste, Nutrition, Cost, Convenience, and Weight Control Concerns as Influences on Food Consumption. *Journal of the American Dietetic Association* 98: 1118–1126.
2. National Turkey Federation. 2004. Turkey Facts and Trivia. Available at www.eatturkey.com/consumer/history/history.html. Accessed October 2010.
3. Freeland-Graves, J., and S. Nitzke. 2002. Total Diet Approach to Communicating Food and Nutrition Information. *Journal of the American Dietetic Association* 102: 100–108.
4. Coomes, S. Pizza Marketplace. Personal communication. February 2006.
5. Mintel International Group. 2005. Cinemas and Movie Theaters-United States, Mintel Reports-USA, Leisure-USA. Available at www.reports.mintel.com. Accessed March 2006.
6. Nord, M., M. Andrews, and S. Carlson. 2009. Food Security in the United States. Economic Research Report No. 83. Available at www.ers.usda.gov/Publications/ERR83/ERR83fm.pdf. Accessed October 2010.
7. French, S. A. 2003. Pricing Effects on Food Choices. *Journal of Nutrition* 133: 841S–843S.
8. Freeland-Graves. Total Diet Approach.
9. Specialty Coffee Association. 2006. Retail in the USA 2004–2007. Available at www.scaa.org. Accessed March 2006.
10. Mintel International Group. 2004. Breakfast Foods: The Consumer-US, Mintel Reports-USA, Food and Food Service-USA. Available at www.reports.mintel.com. Accessed February 2006.
11. U.S. Department of Agriculture, Agricultural Research Service. 2008. Nutrient Intakes from Food: Mean Amounts Consumed per Individual, One Day, 2005–2006. Available at www.ars.usda.gov/ba/bhnrc.fsrg. Accessed March 2011.
12. U.S. Department of Agriculture, U.S. Department of Health and Human Services. 2010. *Dietary Guidelines for Americans, 2010.* 7th ed. Washington, D.C.: U.S. Government Printing Office.
13. U.S. Department of Agriculture, Agricultural Research Service. 2008.
14. U.S. Department of Agriculture, U.S. Department of Health and Human Services, Marra, M., and A. Boyar. 2009. Position of the American Dietetic Association: Nutrient Supplement. *Journal of the American Dietetic Association* 109: 2073–2085.
15. Todd, J., L. Mancino, and B. Lin. 2010. The Impact of Food Away from Home on Adult Diet Quality, ERR-90, U.S. Department of Agriculture, Economic Research Service.
16. Ibid.
17. United States Department of Agriculture. 2010. *Report of the Dietary Guideline Advisory Committee on the Dietary Guidelines for Americans,* 2010. Available at www.cnpp.usda.gov/DGAs2010-DGAC Report.htm. Accessed March 2011.
18. Ibid.
19. Centers for Disease Control. 2010. Obesity and Overweight. Available at www.cdc.gov/nchs/fastats/overwt.htm. Accessed March 2011.
20. Healthy People 2020. 2010. Nutrition and Weight Status. Available at www.healthypeople.gov/2020/topicsobjectives2020/objectiveslist.aspx?to picid=29. Accessed March 2011.
21. U.S. Department of Health and Preventative Services. 2010. *Healthy People 2020.* Available at www.healthypeople.gov/2020/about/default.aspx. Accessed March 2011.
22. Krane, D. 2005. Number of "Cyberchondriacs"—U.S. Adults Who Go Online for Health Information—Increases to Estimated 117 Million. Harris Interactive Healthcare Research. Available at www.harrisinteractive.com. Accessed October 2010.
23. National Center for Complementary and Alternative Medicine. 10 Things to Know About Evaluating Medical Resources on the Web. Updated 2006. Available at www.nccam.nih.gov. Accessed March 2006.

Feature Box References

1. Drewnowski, A., and S. E. Specter. 2004. Poverty and Obesity: The Role of Energy Density and Energy Costs. *American Journal of Clinical Nutrition* 79:6–16. © 2004 American Society for Clinical Nutrition.
2. Scheier, L. M. What Is the Hunger-Obesity Paradox? *Journal of the American Dietetic Association.* Practice Applications: Beyond the Headlines. Pages 883–886. © 2005 American Dietetic Association.
3. Scheier. What Is the Hunger-Obesity Paradox?
4. Drewnowski and Specter. Poverty and Obesity: The Role of Energy Density and Energy Costs.
5. Scheier. What Is the Hunger-Obesity Paradox?
6. Debusk, R.M., C. P. Fogarty, J. M. Ordovas, and K. S. Kornman. 2005. Nutritional Genomics in Practice: Where Do We Begin? *Journal of the American Dietetic Association* 105: 589–598.

Two Points of View References

1. A. E. Gallo, "Food Advertising in the United States." USDA, Economic Research Service. Available at www.ers.usda.gov/publications/aib750/aib750i.pdf. Accessed August 2010; Federal Trade Commission, "FTC Report Sheds New Light on Food Marketing to Children and Adolescents." (July 2008)Available at www.ftc.gov/opa/2008/07/foodmkting.shtm. Accessed August 2010.
2. Ibid.
3. Federal Trade Commission. "Bureau of Economics Staff Report: Children's Exposure to TV Advertising in 1977 and 2004."(2007) Available at www.ftc.gov/bcp/workshops/childobesity/presentations/ippolito.pdf. Accessed August 2010.
4. L. M. Powell, G. Szczpka, F. J. Chaloupka, and C. L. Braunschweig, "Nutritional Content of Television Food Advertisements Seen by Children and Adolescents," *Pediatrics* 120 (2007): 576–583; J. Harris, J. Bargh, and K. Brownell, "Priming Effects of Television Food Advertising on Eating Behavior," *Health Psychology* 28, no. 4 (2009): 404–413. Available at www.yale.edu/acmelab/articles/Harris_Bargh_Brownell_Health_Psych.pdf. Accessed August 2010.
5. G. Cairns, K. Angus, and G. Hastings, "The Extent, Nature and Effects of Food Promotion to Children: A Review of the Evidence to December 2008." Prepared for the World Health Organization. Available at http://whqlibdoc.who.int/publications/2009/9789241598835_eng.pdf. Accessed August 2010.
6. J. L. Veerman, E. Van Beeck, et al., "By How Much Would Limiting TV Food Advertising Reduce Childhood Obesity?" *European Journal of Public Health* 19 no. 4 (August 2009): 365–369. Available at www.ncbi.nlm.nih.gov/pmc/articles/PMC2712920/. Accessed August 2010.
7. Harris. Priming Effects of Television Food Advertising.
8. B. Young, "Food Advertising, Food Choice and Obesity: A Survey of Existing Research." Advertising Education Forum (2003). Available at http://www.eaca.be/_upload/documents/research/obesity.pdf. Accessed August 2010.
9. D. Toops, "Right to Defend Our Rights: The Alliance for American Advertising Plans to Change the Perception that Advertising Makes Children Obese," *Food Processing* (March 2005). Available at www.allbusiness.com/marketing-advertising/advertising/383404-1.html. Accessed August 2010.
10. J. Q. Xu K. D. Kochanek S. L. Murphy, and B. Tejada-Vera. "Deaths: Final Data for 2007." *National Vital Statistics Reports Web Release* 58 no. 19. Hyattsville, Maryland: National Center for Health Statistics. Released May 2010. Available at http://www.cdc.gov/NCHS/data/nvsr/nvsr58/nvsr58_19.pdf. Accessed August 2010.
11. E. Edelson, "Deaths from Heart Disease, Stroke, Down 30%," *Washington Post* (December 2008). Available at www.washingtonpost.com/wp-dyn/content/article/2008/12/15/AR2008121502201.html. Accessed August 2010; American Cancer Society, "Cancer Facts and Figures

2010." Available at www.cancer.org/acs/groups/content/@nho/documents/document/acspc-024113.pdf. Accessed August 2010.

12. UK Advertising Association, Food Advertising Unit, "Interim Review of the Media Landscape: Food Advertising Changes in Context" (September 2007). Available at http://www.adassoc.org.uk/Media%20Landscape%20FAU.pdf. Accessed August 2010.

Chapter 2

1. Institute of Medicine. 2003. *Dietary Reference Intakes: Applications in Dietary Planning.* Washington, D.C.: The National Academies Press.
2. Davis, C., and E. Saltos. 1999. Chapter 2: Dietary Recommendations and How They Have Changed Over Time. In E. Frazo, ed., *America's Eating Habits: Changes and Consequences.* Agriculture Information Bulletin No. AIB750. Available at www.ers.usda.gov/publications/aib750. Accessed September 2005.
3. Lee, P. R. 1978. Nutrition Policy: From Neglect and Uncertainty to Debate and Action. *Journal of the American Dietetics Association* 72: 581–588.
4. U.S. Department of Agriculture. 2005. *2005 Report of the Dietary Guidelines Advisory Committee.* Available at www.health.gov/dietaryguidelines/dga2005/report. Accessed February 2005.
5. Ibid.
6. Painter, J., J. Rah, and Y. Lee. 2002. Comparison of International Food Guide Pictorial Representations. *Journal of the American Dietetic Association* 102: 483–489.
7. Center for Food Safety and Applied Nutrition. 2008. A Food Labeling Guide. Available at www.fda.gov/Food/GuidanceComplianceRegulatoryInformation/GuidanceDocuments/FoodLabelingNutrition/FoodLabelingGuide/default.htm. Accessed April 2010.
8. Food Safety and Inspection Service. 2010. A Guide to Federal Food Labeling Requirements for Meat and Poultry Products. Available at www.fsis.usda.gov/PDF/Labeling_Requirements_Guide.pdf. Accessed April 2010.
9. Center for Food Safety and Applied Nutrition. A Food Labeling Guide.
10. Food Safety and Inspection Service. A Guide to Federal Food Labeling Requirements for Meat and Poultry Products.
11. Ibid.
12. Ibid.
13. Farley, D. 1993. Look for "Legit" Health Claims on Foods. *FDA Consumer Magazine;* 27: 21–28.
14. Center for Food Safety and Applied Nutrition. 2003. Claims That Can Be Made for Conventional Foods and Dietary Supplements. Available at www.cfsan.fda.gov/∼dms/hclaims.html. Accessed October 2010.
15. Hasler, C. M., A. S. Bloch, C. A. Thomson, E. Enrione, and C. Manning. 2004. Position of the American Dietetic Association: Functional Foods. *Journal of the American Dietetic Association* 104: 814–826.
16. Institute of Food Technologists. 2005. Expert Report on Functional Foods: Opportunities and Challenges, Executive Summary. Available at http://www.ift.org/knowledge-center/read-ift-publications/science-reports/expert-reports.aspx. Accessed October 2010.

Feature Box References

1. Nutrition Insights. 2000. Servings Sizes in the Food Guide Pyramid and on the Nutrition Facts Label: What's Different and Why? United States Department of Agriculture. Available at www.cnpp.usda.gov/Publications/NutritionInsights/Insight22.pdf. Accessed May 2010.
2. Young, L. R., and M. Nestle. 2003. Expanding Portion Sizes in the U. S. Marketplace: Implications for Nutrition Counseling. *Journal of the American Dietetic Association* 103: 231–234; Diliberti, N., P. L. Bordi, M. T. Conklin, and B. J. Rolls. 2004. Increased Portion Size Leads to Increased Energy Intake in a Restaurant Meal. *Obesity Research* 12: 562–568.
3. Smiciklas-Wright, H., D. C. Mitchell, S. Mickle, J. Goldman, and A. Cook. 2003. Foods Commonly Eaten in the United States, 1989–1991 and 1994–1996: Are Portion Sizes Changing? *Journal of the American Dietetic Association* 103: 41–47.
4. Rolls, B. 2003. The Supersizing of America: Portion Size and the Obesity Epidemic. *Nutrition Today* 38: 42–53.
5. Rolls, B., L. S. Roe, and J. S. Meengs. 2006. Larger Portion Sizes Lead to a Sustained Increase in Energy Intake Over 2 Days. *Journal of the American Dietetic Association* 106: 543–549.
6. Centers for Disease Control. 2005. Overweight and Obesity: Obesity Trends. Available at www.cdc.gov.
7. Hasler, C., and A. Brown. 2009. Position of the American Dietetic Association: Functional Foods. *Journal of the American Dietetic Association* 109: 735–746; IFIC. 2007. Functional Foods. Available at www.ific.org. Accessed April 2010.

8. IFIC. 2007. Functional Foods.
9. Progressive Grocers. 2009. Healthy Consumers Drive Functional Foods Market: Study. Available at www.packagedfacts.com/about/inthenews.asp?id=1406. Accessed April 2010.
10. IFIC. 2009. The 2009 Food and Health Survey. Available at www.ific.org. Accessed April 2010.
11. Hasler. Position of the American Dietetic Association: Functional Foods; IFIC. Functional Foods.
12. Riediger, N., R. Othman, M. Suh, and M. Moghadasian. 2009. A Systemic Review of the Roles of n-3 Fatty Acids in Health and Disease. *Journal of the American Dietetic Association* 109: 668–679.
13. American Dietetic Association. 2008. Hot Topics: Functional Beverages. Available at www.eatright.org. Accessed April 2010.

Two Points of View References

1. Food and Drink Weekly, "Critics and Supporters Weigh in on MyPyramid Nutrition Guide." April 2005. Available at http://findarticles.com/p/articles/mi_m0EUY/is_16_11/ai_n13828779/?tag=content;col1. Accessed August 2010.
2. W. D. McArdle, F. I. Katch, and V. L. Katch, *Essentials of Exercise Physiology* (Baltimore, MD, Lippincott Williams & Wilkins via Google Books, 2005), 103.
3. C. Johnston, "Uncle Sam's Diet Sensation: MyPyramid—An Overview and Commentary," *Medscape General Medicine* 7 no. 3 (August 2005): 78. Available at http://www.ncbi.nlm.nih.gov/pmc/articles/PMC1681673/. Accessed August 2010.
4. Center for Science in the Public Interest, "Dietary Guidelines Committee Criticized." 2003. Available at http://www.cspinet.org/new/200308191.html. Accessed August 2010.
5. Johnston. "Uncle Sam's Diet Sensation."
6. J. Haven, MS, RDa, A. Burns, MPPb, D. Herring, MSc, P. Britten, PhD, "MyPyramid.gov Provides Consumers with Practical Nutrition Information at Their Fingertips," *Journal of Nutrition Education and Behavior,* 38 no. 6, supplement (November 2006): S153–S154. Available at http://download.journals.elsevierhealth.com/pdfs/journals/1499-4046/PIIS1499404606005793.pdf. Accessed August 2010.
7. Food and Drink Weekly. "Critics and Supporters Weigh in on MyPyramid Nutrition Guide."
8. USDA, "Research Summary Report for MyPyramid Food Guidance System Development." August 2005. Available at www.cnpp.usda.gov/Publications/MyPyramid/DevelopmentMaterials/ConsumerResearch/ResearchSummaryReport.pdf. Accessed August 2010.
9. Ibid.

Chapter 3

1. Mennella, J. A., and G. K. Beauchamp. 1994. Early Flavor Experiences: When Do They Start? *Nutrition Today* 29 (5): 25.
2. De Roos, K. B. 1997. How Lipids Influence Food Flavor. *Food Technology* 51 (5): 60–62.
3. Bodyfelt, F. W., J. Tobias, and G. M. Trout. 1988. *The Sensory Evaluation of Dairy Products.* New York: Van Nostrand Reinhold.
4. Nagodawithana, T. 1994. Flavor Enhancers: Their Probable Mode of Action. *Food Technology* 48 (4): 79–85.
5. De Roos. How Lipids Influence Food Flavor.
6. Mahan, K., and S. Escott-Stump. 2008. *Krause's Food & Nutrition Therapy.* 12th ed. St. Louis: Saunders Elsevier.
7. Ibid.
8. Marieb, E. N. 2009. *Human Anatomy and Physiology.* 8th ed. San Francisco: Benjamin Cummings.
9. Ganong, W. F. 1977. *Review of Medical Physiology.* 8th ed. Los Altos, CA: Lange Medical Publications.
10. Mahan. *Krause's Food & Nutrition Therapy.*
11. Gropper, S. S., J. L. Smith, and J. L. Groff. 2005. *Advanced Nutrition and Human Metabolism.* 4th ed. Belmont, CA: Thomson Wadsworth.
12. Tortora, G. J., and N. P. Anagnostakos. 1990. *Principles of Anatomy and Physiology.* 6th ed. New York: Harper & Row Publishers.
13. Hole, J. W. 1984. *Human Anatomy and Physiology.* 3rd ed. Dubuque, IA: WC Brown Publishers.
14. Guyton, A. C. 1981. *Textbook of Medical Physiology.* 6th ed. Philadelphia: Saunders.
15. Ganong. *Review of Medical Physiology.*
16. Gropper. *Advanced Nutrition and Human Metabolism.*
17. Guyton. *Textbook of Medical Physiology.*
18. Mahan. *Krause's Food & Nutrition Therapy.*
19. Marieb. *Human Anatomy and Physiology.*

20. Gropper. *Advanced Nutrition and Human Metabolism*.

21. U.S. Department of Health and Human Services. Oral Health. Available at www.womenshealth.gov/faq/oral-health.cfm. Accessed October 2010.

22. Ibid.

23. Nelson, J. K., K. E. Moxness, M. D. Jensen, and C. F. Gastineau. 1994. *Mayo Clinic Diet Manual.* 7th ed. St. Louis: Mosby.

24. American Cancer Society. www.cancer.org.

25. Anderson, D. M. 2002. *Mosby's Medical, Nursing and Allied Health Dictionary.* 6th ed. St. Louis: Mosby.

26. Nelson, et al. *Mayo Clinic Diet Manual.*

27. National Digestive Diseases Information Clearinghouse, National Institute of Diabetes and Digestive and Kidney Diseases (NIDDK). 2007. Irritable Bowel Syndrome. Available at: http://digestive.niddk.nih.gov/ddiseases/pubs/ibs/. Accessed November 2009.

28. National Digestive Diseases Information Clearinghouse, National Institute of Diabetes and Digestive and Kidney Diseases (NIDDK). 2006. Crohn's Disease. Available at: http://digestive.niddk.nih.gov/ddiseases/pubs/crohns/. Accessed November 2009.

Two Points of View References

1. National Center for Complementary and Alternative Medicine. 2008. "Get the Facts: An Introduction to Probiotics." Available at http://nccam.nih.gov/health/probiotics/. Accessed July 2010.

2. Marteau P., P. Seksik, and R. Jian. 2002. "Probiotics and Intestinal Health Effects: A Clinical Perspective." *British Journal of Nutrition* 88 Suppl 1: S51–S57. Available at www.ncbi.nlm.nih.gov/pubmed/12215185. Accessed July 2010.

3. Douglas, L.C, and M. E. Sanders. 2008. "Probiotics and Probiotics in Dietetics Practice." *Journal of the American Dietetic Association* 108: 510–521.

4. American Gastroenterological Association, Patient Center., August 2008, "Probiotics: What They Are and What They Can Do For You." Available at www.gastro.org/patient-center/diet-medications/probiotics#Are% 20Probiotics%20Safe?. Accessed May 2010.

5. FDA. December 2006. "Guidance for Industry on Complementary and Alternative Medicine Products and Their Regulation by the Food and Drug Administration." Available at www.fda.gov/downloads/RegulatoryInformation/Guidances/UCM145405.pdf. Accessed July 2010; McGee, E. 2009. "Answers to Your Questions About Probiotics." Available at www.webmd.com/diet/features/answers-to-your-questions-about-probiotics. Accessed July 2010.

6. American Dietetic Association. 2009. "Hot Topics Sheet on Probiotics and Digestion." Available at www.eatright.org. Accessed May 2010.

7. National Center for Complementary and Alternative Medicine, "An Introduction to Probiotics." Available at http://nccam.nih.gov/health/probiotics. Accessed May 2010.

8. Joint FAO/WHO Working Group Report on Drafting Guidelines for the Evaluation of Probiotics in Food, London, Ontario, Canada, April 30 and May 1, 2002. Available at www.who.int/foodsafety/fs_management/en/probiotic_guidelines.pdf. Accessed July 2010.

Chapter 4

1. Painter, J., J. Rah, and Y. Lee. 2002. Comparison of International Food Guide Pictorial Representations. *Journal of the American Dietetic Association* 102: 483–489; Gifford, K. D. 2009. The Asian Diet Pyramid. *Oldways Preservation and Exchange Trust.* Available at www.oldwayspt.org/asian-diet-pyramid. Accessed October 2010.

2. Johnson, M. 2003. *Human Biology: Concepts and Current Issues.* 2nd ed. San Francisco: Benjamin Cummings.

3. McBean, L., and G. Miller. 1998. Allaying Fears and Fallacies About Lactose Intolerance. *Journal of the American Dietetic Association* 98: 671–676; Suarez, M. D., D. Savaiano, and M. Levitt. 1995. A Comparison of Symptoms After the Consumption of Milk or Lactose-Hydrolyzed Milk by People with Self-Reported Severe Lactose Intolerance. *New England Journal of Medicine* 333: 1–4.

4. Suarez. A Comparison of Symptoms; Johnson, A., J. Semenya, M. Buchowski, C. Enownwu, and N. Scrimshaw. 1993. Correlation of Lactose Maldigestion, Lactose Intolerance, and Milk Intolerance. *American Journal of Clinical Nutrition* 57: 399–401.

5. U.S. Department of Agriculture, U.S. Department of Health and Human Services. 2010. *Dietary Guidelines for Americans, 2010.* 7th ed. Washington, D.C.: U.S. Government Printing Office.

6. National Digestive Diseases Information Clearinghouse. June 2009. Lactose Intolerance. National Institutes of Health Publication No. 09-2751.

7. Suarez, F., and M. Levitt. 1996. Abdominal Symptoms and Lactose: The Discrepancy Between Patients' Claims and the Results of Blinded Trials. *American Journal of Clinical Nutrition* 64: 251–252; Suarez,

F. D. Savaiano, P. Arbisi, and M. Levitt. 1997. Tolerance to the Daily Ingestion of Two Cups of Milk by Individuals Claiming Lactose Intolerance. *American Journal of Clinical Nutrition* 65: 1502–1506.

8. Suarez. Tolerance to the Daily Ingestion; Dehkordi, N., D. R. Rao, A. P. Warren, and C. B. Chawan. 1995. Lactose Malabsorption as Influenced by Chocolate Milk, Skim Milk, Sucrose, Whole Milk, and Lactic Cultures. *Journal of the American Dietetic Association* 95: 484–486.

9. National Medical Association. 2009. Lactose Intolerance and African Americans: Implications for the Consumption of Appropriate Intake Levels of Key Nutrients. *Journal of the National Medical Association.* 101 (10 Suppl): 5S–23S.

10. Lee, C., and C. Hardy. 1989. Cocoa Feeding and Human Lactose Intolerance. *American Journal of Clinical Nutrition* 49: 840–844; Hertzler, S., B. Huynh, and D. Savaiano. 1996. How Much Lactose Is Low Lactose? *Journal of the American Dietetic Association* 96: 243–246.

11. Institute of Medicine. 2002. *Dietary Reference Intakes for Energy, Carbohydrate, Fiber, Fat, Fatty Acids, Cholesterol, Protein, and Amino Acids.* Washington, D.C.: The National Academies Press; U.S. Department of Agriculture, Agricultural Research Service. 2008. Nutrient Intakes from Food: Mean Amounts Consumed per Individual, One Day, 2005–2006. Available at www.ars.usda.gov/ba/bhnrc.fsrg. Accessed March 2011.

12. Ibid.

13. Lin, B., and R. Morrison. 2002. Higher Fruit Consumption Linked with Lower Body Mass Index. Economic Research Service, *FoodReview* 25: 28–32.

14. Wells, H. F., and J. C. Buzby. 2008. Dietary Assessment of Major Trends in U.S. Food Consumption, 1970–2005. Economic Information Bulletin No. 33. Economic Research Service, U.S. Dept. of Agriculture. Available at http://ers.usda.gov/Publications/EIB33/EIB33.pdf. Accessed January 2010.

15. Duffy, V., and M. Sigman-Grant. 2004. Position of the American Dietetic Association: Use of Nutritive and Nonnutritive Sweeteners. *Journal of the American Dietetic Association* 104: 255-275.

16. Horn, L., et al. 2010. Translation and Implementation of Added Sugars Consumption Recommendations. *Circulation* 122: 2470–2490; Howard, B., and J. Wylie-Rosett, 2002. Sugar and Cardiovascular Disease: A Statement for Healthcare Professionals from the Committee on Nutrition of the Council on Nutrition, Physical Activity, and Metabolism of the American Heart Association. *Circulation* 106: 523–527.

17. American Medical Association. 2008. The Health Effects of High-Fructose Syrup. Report 3 of the Council on Science and Public Health (A-08). Available at www.ama-assn.org/ama1/pub/upload/mm/443/csaph3a08-summary.pdf. Accessed January 2010; Duffy, V., and M. Sigman-Grant. 2008. Use of Nutritive and Nonnutritive Sweeteners. *Journal of the American Dietetic Association.* 104: 255–275.

18. Institute of Medicine. *Dietary Reference Intakes for Energy.*

19. World Health Organization and the Food and Agricultural Organization. 2003. Report of the Joint WHO/FAO Expert Consultation on Diet, Nutrition and the Prevention of Chronic Diseases. Available at www.who.int. Accessed May 2010.

20. Horn. Translation and Implementation of Added Sugars; Johnson, R. K., et al. 2009. Dietary Sugars Intake and Cardiovascular Health. A Scientific Statement from the American Heart Association. *Circulation* 120: 1011–1020. Available at http://circ.ahajournals.org/cgi/reprint/CIRCU-LATIONAHA.109.192627. Accessed January 2010.

21. United States Department of Agriculture, Economic Research Service. 2010. Taxing Caloric Sweetened Beverages to Curb Obesity. *Amber Waves.* Available at www.ers.usda.gov/AmberWaves/September10/Features/TaxingCaloricBeverages.htm. Accessed March 2011.

22. Duffy. Use of Nutritive and Nonnutritive Sweeteners.

23. Calorie Control Council. Reduced-Calorie Sweeteners: Hydrogenated Starch Hydrolysates. Available at www.caloriecontrol.org. Accessed March 2003.

24. Public Health Service, National Toxicology Program. 2000. Report on Carcinogens, 9th ed.

25. Ajinomoto USA, Inc. The History of Aspartame. Available at www.aspartame.net/. Accessed October 2010.

26. Council on Scientific Affairs. 1985. Aspartame: Review of Safety Issues. *Journal of the American Medical Association* 254: 400–402.

27. American Diabetes Association. 2008. Nutrition Recommendations and Interventions for Diabetes. *Diabetes Care* 31: S61–S78.; Hattan, D. G. 2002. Aspartame Limits. *FDA Consumer Magazine.* Available at www.cfsan.fda.gov. Accessed April 2010.

28. European Commission, Scientific Committee on Food. 2002. Opinion of the Scientific Committee on Food: Update on the Safety of Aspartame. Available at www.europa.eu.int. Accessed March 2003.

29. National Institutes of Health. 2000. Report of the NIH Consensus Development Conference on Phenylketonuria (PKU): Screening and Management. Available at www.nichd.nih.gov. Accessed May 2003.

30. The NutraSweet Company. Neotame: A Scientific Overview. Available at www.neotame.com. Accessed March 2003.

31. National Digestive Diseases Information Clearinghouse. 2007. Constipation. National Institutes of Health Publication No. 07-2754. Available at www.niddk.nih.gov. Accessed May 2010.

32. Ibid.

33. National Digestive Diseases Information Clearinghouse. 2008. Diverticulosis and Diverticulitis. National Institutes of Health Publication No. 08-1163. Available at www.niddk.nih.gov. Accessed May 2010.

34. Miller, W., M. Niederpruem, J. Wallace, and A. Lindeman. 1994. Dietary Fat, Sugar, and Fiber Predict Body Fat Content. *Journal of the American Dietetic Association* 94: 612–615; Appley, P., M. Thorogood, J. Mann, and T. Key. 1998. Low Body Mass Index in Non-Meat Eaters: The Possible Roles of Animal Fat, Dietary Fibre and Alcohol. *International Journal of Obesity-Related Metabolic Disorders* 22: 454–460.

35. Pietinen, P., E. Rimm, P. Korhonen, A. Hartman, W. Willett, D. Albanes, and J. Virtamo. 1996. Intake of Dietary Fiber and Risk of Coronary Heart Disease in a Cohort of Finnish Men: The Alpha-Tocopherol, Beta-Carotene Cancer Prevention Study. *Circulation* 94: 2720–2727; Rimm, E., A. Ascherio, E. Giovannucci, D. Spiegelman, M. Stampfer, and W. Willett. 1996. Vegetable, Fruit, and Cereal Fiber Intake and Risk of Coronary Heart Disease among Men. *Journal of the American Medical Association* 275: 447–451.

36. Wolk, A., J. Manson, M. Stampfer, G. Colditz, F. Hu, F. Speizer, C. Hennekens, and W. Willett. 1999. Long-Term Intake of Dietary Fiber and Decreased Risk of Coronary Heart Disease among Women. *Journal of the American Medical Association* 281: 1998–2004.

37. Chandalia, M., A. Garg, D. Lutjohann, K. von Bergmann, S. Grundy, and L. Brinkley. 2000. Beneficial Effects of High Fiber Intake in Patients with Type 2 Diabetes Mellitus. *New England Journal of Medicine* 342: 1392–1398; Vuksan, V., D. Jenkins, P. Spadafora, J. Sievenpiper, R. Owen, E. Vidgen, F. Brighenti, R. Josse, L. Leiter, and C. Bruce-Thompson. 1999. Konjac-Mannan (glucomannan) Improves Glycemia and Other Associated Risk Factors for Coronary Heart Disease in Type 2 Diabetes: A Randomized Controlled Metabolic Trial. *Diabetes Care* 22: 913–919; Anderson, J., L. Allgood, J. Turner, P. Oeltgen, and B. Daggy. 1999. Effects of Psyllium on Glucose and Serum Lipid Responses in Men with Type 2 Diabetes and Hypercholesterolemia. *American Journal of Clinical Nutrition* 70: 466–473; American Diabetes Association. 2008. Nutrition Recommendations and Interventions for Diabetes. *Diabetes Care* 31: S61–S78.

38. Slavin, J. 2008. Position of the American Dietetic Association: Health Implications of Dietary Fiber. *Journal of the American Dietetic Association* 108: 1716–1731.

39. Institute of Medicine. *Dietary Reference Intakes for Energy*.

40. National Cancer Institute. 2008. Colorectal Cancer Prevention (PDQ®). Available at www.cancer.gov. Accessed June 2008.

41. Bingham, S., N. Day, R. Luben, P. Ferrari, N. Slimani, T. Norat, et al. 2003. Dietary Fiber in Food and Protection Against Colorectal Cancer in the European Prospective Investigation into Cancer and Nutrition (EPIC): An Observation Study. *The Lancet* 361: 1496–1501; Ferguson, L., and P. Harris. 2003. The Dietary Fiber Debate: More Food for Thought. *The Lancet* 361: 1487–1488.

42. Ibid.

43. Slavin, J. 2008. Position of the American Dietetic Association: Health Implications of Dietary Fiber. *Journal of the American Dietetic Association* 108: 1716–1731.

44. National Digestive Diseases Information Clearinghouse. 2008. Diabetes Overview. National Institutes of Health Publication No. 09–3873. Available at http://diabetes.niddk.nih.gov/dm/pubs/overview/. Accessed January 2010.

45. American Diabetes Association. 2002. The Prevention or Delay of Type 2 Diabetes. *Diabetes Care* 25: 742–749.

46. National Digestive Diseases Information Clearinghouse. Diabetes Overview.

47. Ibid.

48. Ibid.

49. Centers for Disease Control and Prevention. 2009. Diabetes Successes and Opportunities for Population-Based Prevention and Control: At a Glance 2009. Available at www.cdc.gov/chronicdisease/resources/publications/AAG/ddt.htm. Accessed January 2010.

50. American Diabetes Association. 2003. Tests of Glycemia in Diabetes. *Diabetes Care* 26: S106–S108; National Diabetes Information Clearinghouse. 2001. Diabetes Control and Complications Trial (DCCT).

National Institutes of Health Publication No. 02-3874. Available at www.niddk.nih.gov. Accessed April 2003.

51. American Diabetes Association. 2008. Nutrition Recommendations and Interventions for Diabetes. *Diabetes Care* 31: S61–S78.

52. Sheard, N., N. Clark, J. Brand-Miller, M. Franz, F. Pi-Sunyer, E. Mayer-Davis, K. Kulkarni, and P. Geil. 2004. Dietary Carbohydrate (Amount and Type) in the Prevention and Management of Diabetes. *Diabetes Care* 27: 2266–2271.

53. Ludwig, D. 2002. The Glycemic Index: Physiological Mechanisms Relating to Obesity, Diabetes, and Cardiovascular Disease. *Journal of the American Medical Association* 287: 2414–2423.

54. Roberts, S. 2000. High-Glycemic-Index Foods, Hunger, and Obesity: Is There a Connection? *Nutrition Reviews* 58: 163–169; Foster-Powell, K., and J. Brand-Miller. 1995. International Tables of Glycemic Index. *American Journal of Clinical Nutrition* 62: 871S–893S.

55. American Diabetes Association. 2008. Nutrition Recommendations and Interventions for Diabetes. *Diabetes Care* 31: S61–S78.

56. Centers for Disease Control and Prevention. Diabetes Successes and Opportunities.

57. Ibid.

58. National Digestive Diseases Information Clearinghouse. Diabetes Overview; Centers for Disease Control and Prevention. Diabetes Successes and Opportunities; Centers for Disease Control and Prevention. 2009. Chronic Diseases and Health Promotion. Available at www.cdc.gov/chronicdisease/overview/index.htm. Accessed January 2010.

59. Centers for Disease Control and Prevention. Chronic Diseases and Health Promotion.

60. American Diabetes Association. 2004. Type 2 Diabetes in the Young: The Evolving Epidemic. *Diabetes Care* 27: 1798–1811.

61. Diabetes Prevention Program Research Group. 2002. Reduction in the Incidence of Type 2 Diabetes with Lifestyle Intervention or Metformin. *New England Journal of Medicine* 346: 393–403.

62. National Digestive Diseases Information Clearinghouse. 2003. Hypoglycemia. National Institutes of Health Publication No. 03-3926.

Feature Box References

1. Putnam, J., J. Allshouse, and L. Kantor. 2002. U.S. Per Capita Food Supply Trends: More Calories, Refined Carbohydrates, and Fats. Economic Research Service, *FoodReview* 25: 2–15.

2. Slavin, J., D. Jacobs, L. Marquart, and K. Wiemer. 2001. The Role of Whole Grains in Disease Prevention. *Journal of the American Dietetic Association* 101: 780–785.

3. Jacobs, D., K. Meyer, L. Kushi, and A. Folsom. 1999. Is Whole Grain Intake Associated with Reduced Total and Cause-Specific Death Rates in Older Women? The Iowa Women's Health Study. *American Journal of Public Health* 89: 322–329; Liu, S., J. Manson, M. Stampfer, K. Rexrode, F. Hu, E. Rimm, and W. Willett. 2000. Whole Grain Consumption and Risk of Ischemic Stroke in Women. *Journal of the American Medical Association* 284: 1534–1540.

4. Jorge, S., A. Ascherio, E. Rimm, G. Colditz, D. Spiegelman, D. Jenkins, M. Stampfer, A. Wing, and W. Willett. 1997. Dietary Fiber, Glycemic Load, and Risk of NIDDM in Men. *Diabetes Care* 20: 545–550; Salmeron, J., J. Manson, M. Stampfer, G. Colditz, A. Wing, and W. Willett. 1997. Dietary Fiber, Glycemic Load, and Risk of Non-Insulin-Dependent Diabetes Mellitus in Women. *Journal of the American Medical Association* 277: 472–477; Meyer, K., L. Kushi, D. Jacobs, J. Slavin, T. Seller, and A. Folsom. 2000. Carbohydrates, Dietary Fiber, and Incident Type 2 Diabetes in Older Women. *American Journal of Clinical Nutrition* 71: 921–930.

5. Slavin. The Role of Whole Grains.

6. Cook, A. J., and J. E. Friday. 2005. Pyramid Servings Intakes in the United States 1999–2002, 1 Day. USDA Agriculture Research Service, Community Nutrition Research Group, CNRG Table Set 3.0. Available at www.ba.ars.usda.gov/cnrg. Accessed January 2010.

7. Burt, A., and P. Satishchandra. 2001. Sugar Consumption and Caries Risk: A Systematic Review. *Journal of Dental Education* 65: 1017–1023.

8. NIH Consensus Statement. 2001. Diagnosis and Management of Dental Caries Throughout Life. Available at www.concensus.nih.gov. Accessed March 2003.

9. Heller, K., B. Burt, and S. Ekund. 2001. Sugared Soda Consumption and Dental Caries in the United States. *Journal of Dental Research* 80: 1949–1953; American Dental Association. 2002. Diet and Tooth Decay. *Journal of the American Dental Association* 133: 527; Joint Report of the American Dental Association Council on Access, Prevention and Interprofessional Relations and the Council on Scientific Affairs to the House of Delegates. 2001. Response to Resolution 73H-200. Available at www.ada.org. Accessed May 2003.

10. Academy of General Dentistry (2008). Popular Energy Drinks Cause Tooth Erosion, Study Shows. *ScienceDaily*. Available at http://www .sciencedaily.com/releases/2008/03/080312125606.htm. Accessed May 2010.

11. American Dental Association. 2003. Early Childhood Tooth Decay. Available at www.ada.org. Accessed May 2003.

12. Moynihan, P., S. Ferrier, and G. Jenkins. 1999. Eating Cheese: Does It Reduce Caries? *British Dental Journal* 187: 664–667; Kashket, S., and D. DePaola. 2002. Cheese Consumption and the Development and Progression of Dental Caries. *Nutrition Reviews* 60: 97–103.

13. Mandel, I. 1996. Caries Prevention: Current Strategies, New Directions. *Journal of the American Dental Association* 127: 1477–1488.

Two Points of View References

1. Retrieved from http://nutrition.gov, maintained by the U.S. Department of Agriculture and the Food and Nutrition Information Center, and the American Beverage Association: www.ameribev.org.

2. American Beverage Association. 2010. "Reducing Soda Consumption Is a Simplistic and Ineffective Solution to Public Health Challenges." Available at www.ameribev.org/nutrition—science/obesity/news-releases/more/199/. Accessed July 2010.

3. Ibid.

4. Ibid.

5. Zelman, K. 2007. "Can Soft Drinks Be Healthy?" WebMD. Available at www.webmd.com/diet/features/can-soft-drinks-be-healthy. Accessed July 2010.

6. Ibid.

7. Schulze, M.B., J. E. Manson, D. S. Ludwig, G. A. Colditz, M. J. Stampfer, W. C. Willett, and F. B. Hu. 2004. "Sugar-Sweetened Beverages, Weight Gain, and Incidence of Type 2 Diabetes in Young and Middle-Aged Women." *Journal of the American Medical Association* 292: 927–934.

8. Fung, T.T., V. Malik, K. M. Rexrode, J. E. Manson, W. C. Willett, and F. B. Hu. 2009. "Sweetened Beverage Consumption and Risk of Coronary Heart Disease in Women." *American Journal of Clinical Nutrition* 89: 1037–1042.

9. Harvard School of Public Health. 2010 "Sugar Drinks or Diet Drinks, What's the Best Choice?" Available at www.hsph.harvard.edu/nutritionsource/healthy-drinks/sugary-vs-diet-drinks/index.html. Accessed July 2010.

Chapter 5

1. Institute of Medicine. 2002. *Dietary Reference Intakes for Energy, Carbohydrate, Fiber, Fat, Fatty Acids, Cholesterol, Protein, and Amino Acids.* Washington, D.C.: The National Academies Press.

2. Kris-Etherton, P. M., W. S. Harris, and L. J. Appel. 2002. Fish Consumption, Fish Oil, Omega-3 Fatty Acids, and Cardiovascular Disease. *Circulation* 106: 2747–2757.

3. Kris-Etherton, P. M., and S. Innis. 2007. Position of the American Dietetic Association and Dietitians of Canada: Dietary Fatty Acids. *Journal of the American Dietetic Association;* 107: 1599–1611.

4. Stephen, A. M., and N. J. Wald. 1990. Trends in Individual Consumption of Dietary Fat in the United States, 1920–1984. *American Journal of Clinical Nutrition* 52: 457–469; U.S. Department of Agriculture, Agricultural Research Service. 2008. Nutrient Intakes from Food: Mean Amounts Consumed per Individual, One Day, 2005–2006. Available at www.ars.usda.gov/ba/bhnrc/fsrg. Accessed January 2010.

5. Institute of Medicine. *Dietary Reference Intakes for Energy.*

6. Ibid.

7. Ibid.

8. U.S. Department of Agriculture, U.S. Department of Health and Human Services. 2010. *Dietary Guidelines for Americans, 2010.* 7th ed. Washington, D.C.: U.S. Government Printing Office.

9. Food and Drug Administration. 2010. *Trans* Fat Now Listed with Saturated Fat and Cholesterol on the Nutrition Facts Label. Available at www.fda.gov/Food/LabelingNutrition/ConsumerInformation/ucm109832.htm. Accessed March 2011.

10. U.S. Department of Agriculture. *Dietary Guidelines for Americans.*

11. Ibid.

12. Calorie Control Council. Fat Replacers: Food Ingredients for Healthy Eating. Available at www.caloriecontrol.org/sweeteners-and-lite/fat-replacers. Accessed May 2010.

13. Mattes, R. D. 1998. Fat Replacers. *Journal of the American Dietetic Association* 98: 463–468.

14. Ibid.

15. Mattes. Fat Replacers; Wylie-Rosett, J. 2002. Fat Substitutes and Health: An Advisory from the Nutrition Committee of the American Heart Association. *Circulation* 105: 2800–2804.

16. Segal, M. Updated 1998. Fat Substitutes: A Taste of the Future? *FDA Consumer.* Available at www.vm.cfsan.fda.gov∼lrd/fats.html. Accessed August 2003.

17. Ibid.

18. Mattes. Fat Replacers.

19. Ibid.

20. Food and Drug Administration. August 5, 2003. 21 CFR Part 172. Food Additives Permitted for Direct Addition to Food for Human Consumption; Olestra; Final Rules. Federal Register. Available at www.fda.gov/OHRMS/DOCKETS/98fr/03-19508.pdf. Accessed January 2010.

21. Sandler. R. S., N. L. Zorich, T. G. Filloon, H. B. Wisman, D. J. Leitz, M. H. Brock, M. G. Royer, and R. K. Miday. 1999. Gastrointestinal Symptoms in 3,181 Volunteers Ingesting Snack Foods Containing Olestra or Triglycerides: A 6-Week Randomized, Placebo-Controlled Trial. *Annals of International Medicine* 130: 253–261; Cheskin, L. J., R. Miday, N. Zorich, and T. Filloon. 1998. Gastrointestinal Symptoms Following Consumption of Olestra or Regular Triglyceride Potato Chips: A Controlled Comparison. *Journal of the American Medical Association* 279: 150–152.

22. Patterson, R. E., A. R. Kristal, J. C. Peters, M. L. Neuhouser, C. L. Rock, L. J. Cheskin, D. Neumark-Sztainer, and M. D. Thornquist. 2000. Changes in Diet, Weight, and Serum Lipid Levels Associated with Olestra Consumption. *Archives of Internal Medicine* 160: 2600–2604.

23. American Heart Association. 2009. Heart Disease and Stroke Statistics—2009 Update. Available at www.aha.org. Accessed January 2010.

24. American Heart Association. 2010. Atherosclerosis. Available at www.aha.org. Accessed May 2010.

25. National Cholesterol Education Program. 2001. High Blood Cholesterol: What You Need to Know. National Institutes of Health, National Heart, Lung, and Blood Institute. NIH Publication No. 01-3290. Available at www.nhlbi.nih.gov/health/public/heart/chol/hbc_what.htm. Accessed July 2003.

26. Sandmaier, M. Revised 2007. The Healthy Heart Handbook for Women. National Institutes of Health, National Heart, Lung, and Blood Institute. NIH Publication No. 07-2720.

27. National Cholesterol Education Program. High Blood Cholesterol: What You Need to Know.

28. American Heart Association. Heart Disease and Stroke Statistics.

29. National Heart, Lung, and Blood Institute. 2010. Smoking and Your Heart. Available at www.nhlbi.nih.gov/health/dci/Diseases/smo/smo_risks.html. Accessed May 2010.

30. U.S. Department of Agriculture. *Dietary Guidelines for Americans;* U.S. Department of Agriculture, Agricultural Research Service. 2008. Nutrient Intakes from Food: Mean Amounts Consumed per Individual, One Day, 2005–2006. Available at www.ars.usda.gov/ba/bhnrc/fsrg. Accessed March 2011.

31. Sandmaier. The Healthy Heart Handbook for Women.

32. National Cholesterol Education Program. 2001. Detection, Evaluation, and Treatment of High Blood Cholesterol in Adults (Adult Treatment Panel III). National Institutes of Health Publication No. 01-3290; Grundy, S. A., N. Abate, and M. Chandalia. 2002. Diet Composition and the Metabolic Syndrome: What Is the Optimal Fat Intake? *American Journal of Medicine* 113 (9B): 25S–29S.

33. National Cholesterol Education Program. Detection, Evaluation, and Treatment of High Blood Cholesterol in Adults.

34. Institute of Medicine. *Dietary Reference Intakes for Energy.*

35. Center for Food Safety and Applied Nutrition. Questions and Answers About *Trans* Fat Nutrition Labeling.

36. Krauss, R. M., H. B. Eckel, and committee. 2000. 2000 AHA Dietary Guidelines. Revision 2000: A Statement for Healthcare Professionals from the Nutrition Committee of the American Heart Association. *Circulation* 102: 2296–2311.

37. U.S. Department of Agriculture. 2000. Nutrition and Your Health: Dietary Guidelines for Americans. *Home and Garden Bulletin* No. 232; Krauss. 2000 AHA Dietary Guidelines; Howell, W. H., D. J. McNamara, M. A. Tosca, B. T. Smith, and J. A. Gaines. 1997. Plasma Lipid and Lipoprotein Responses to Dietary Fat and Cholesterol: A Meta-Analysis. *American Journal of Clinical Nutrition* 65: 1747–1764.

38. Institute of Medicine. *Dietary Reference Intakes for Energy.*

39. Krauss. 2000 AHA Dietary Guidelines. Hu, F. B., M. J. Stampfer, E. B. Rimm, J. E. Manson, A. Ascherio, G. Colditz, B. Rosner, D. Spiegelman, F. E. Speizer, F. M. Sacks, C. H. Hennekens, and W. C. Willett. 1999. A Prospective Study of Egg Consumption and Risk of Cardiovascular Disease in Men and Women. *Journal of the American Medical Association* 281: 1387–1394.

40. Kramhout, D., E. B. Bosschieter, and C. Coulander. 1985. The Inverse Relation between Fish Consumption and 20-Year Mortality from Coronary Heart Disease. *New England Journal of Medicine* 312: 1205–1209.

41. Institute of Medicine. *Dietary Reference Intakes for Energy*; Kris-Etherton. Fish Consumption.
42. Daviglus, M. L., J. Stamler, A. J. Orencia, A. R. Dyer, K. Liu, P. H. Greenland, M. K. Walsh, D. Morris, and R. B. Shekelle. 1997. Fish Consumption and the 30-Year Risk of Fatal Myocardial Infarction. *New England Journal of Medicine* 336: 1046–1053; Albert, C. M., C. H. Hennekens, C. J. O'Donnell, U. A. Ajani, V. J. Carey, W. C. Willette, J. N. Ruskin, and J. E. Manson. 1998. Fish Consumption and Sudden Cardiac Death. *Journal of the American Medical Association* 279: 23–28.
43. Kris-Etherton. Fish Consumption.
44. Kris-Etherton. Fish Consumption; Center for Food Safety and Applied Nutrition. 2000. Letter Regarding Dietary Supplement Health Claim for Omega-3 Fatty Acids and Coronary Heart Disease. Docket No. 91N-0103. Available at http://vm.cfsan.fda.gov/∼dms/ds-ltr11.html. Accessed July 2003.
45. Center for Food Safety and Applied Nutrition. Letter Regarding Dietary Supplement Health Claim for Omega-3 Fatty Acids and Coronary Heart Disease.
46. Kris-Etherton, P. M., D. S. Taylor, S. Yu-Poth, P. Huth, K. Moriarty, V. Fishell, R. L. Hargrove, G. Zhao, and T. D. Etherton. 2000. Polyunsaturated Fatty Acids in the Food Chain in the United States. *American Journal of Clinical Nutrition* 71: 179S–188S.
47. Ibid.
48. Brown, L., B. Rosner, W. Willett, and F. Sacks. 1999. Cholesterol-Lowering Effects of Dietary Fiber: A Meta-Analysis. *American Journal of Clinical Nutrition* 69: 30–42.
49. National Cholesterol Education Program. Detection, Evaluation, and Treatment of High Blood Cholesterol in Adults.
50. Law, M. 2000. Plant Sterol and Stanol Margarines and Health. *British Medical Journal* 320: 861–864.
51. Food and Drug Administration. 2000. FDA Authorizes New Coronary Heart Disease Health Claim for Plant Sterol and Plant Stanol Esters. FDA Talk Paper. Available at www.cfsan.fda.gov/∼lrd/tpstero.html. Accessed July 2003.
52. Miettinen, T. A., P. Puska, H. Gylling, H. Vanhanen, and E. Vartiainen. 1995. Reduction of Serum Cholesterol with Sitostanol-Ester Margarine in a Mildly Hypercholesterolemic Population. *New England Journal of Medicine* 333: 1308–1312.
53. Tribble, D. L. 1999. AHA Science Advisory. Antioxidant Consumption and Risk of Coronary Heart Disease: Emphasis on Vitamin C, Vitamin E, and β-Carotene. *Circulation* 99: 591–595.
54. Hu, F. B., M. J. Stampfer, J. E. Manson, E. B. Rimm, G. A. Colditz, B. A. Rosner, F. E. Speizer, C. H. Hennekens, and W. C. Willett. 1998. Frequent Nut Consumption and Risk of Coronary Heart Disease in Women: Prospective Cohort Study. *British Medical Journal* 317: 1341–1345.
55. Feldman, E. B. 2002. LSRO Report: The Scientific Evidence of a Beneficial Health Relationship between Walnuts and Coronary Heart Disease. *Journal of Nutrition* 132: 1062S–1101S; Center for Food Safety and Applied Nutrition. 2003. Qualified Health Claims: Letter of Enforcement Discretion—Nuts and Coronary Heart Disease. Available at www.cfsan.fda/gov/∼dms/qhcnuts2.html. Accessed August 2003.
56. Howard, B. V., and D. Kritchevsky. 1997. Phytochemicals and Cardiovascular Disease. *Circulation* 95: 2591; Warshafsky, S., R. Kamer, and S. Sivak. 1993. Effect of Garlic on Total Serum Cholesterol: A Meta-Analysis. *Annals of Internal Medicine* 119: 599–605.
57. Warshafsky. Effect of Garlic on Total Serum Cholesterol; Spigelski, D., and P. J. Jones. 2001. Efficacy of Garlic Supplementation in Lowering Serum Cholesterol Levels. *Nutrition Reviews* 59: 236–244.
58. Hertog, M. G. L., E. J. M. Feskens, P. C. H. Hollman, M. B. Katan, and D. Kromhout. 1993. Dietary Antioxidant Flavonoids and Risk of Coronary Heart Disease: The Zutphen Elderly Study. *The Lancet* 342: 1007–1011.
59. Mukamal, K. J., M. Maclure, J. E. Muffer, J. B. Sherwood, and M. A. Mittleman. 2002. Tea Consumption and Mortality After Acute Myocardial Infarction. *Circulation* 105: 2476–2481.
60. National Cholesterol Education Program. Detection, Evaluation, and Treatment of High Blood Cholesterol in Adults.
61. Haskell, W., Lee, I., Pate, R., Powell, K., Blair, S., Franklin, B., Macera, C, G., Thompson, P., and Bauman, A. 2007. Physical Activity and Public Health, Updated Recommendation for Adults From the American College of Sports Medicine and the American Heart Association. *Circulation* 116: 1081–1093.
62. Ibid.
63. Rimm, E., A. Klatsky, D. Grobbee, and M. J. Stampfer. 1996. Review of Moderate Alcohol Consumption and Reduced Risk of Coronary Heart Disease: Is the Effect Due to Beer, Wine or Spirits? *British Medical Journal* 312: 731–736.

64. Goldberg, I. J., L. Mosca, M. R. Piano, and E. A. Fisher. 2001. Wine and Your Heart: A Science Advisory for Healthcare Professionals from the Nutrition Committee, Council on Epidemiology and Prevention, and Council on Cardiovascular Nursing of the American Heart Association. *Circulation* 103: 472–475.
65. Rimm, E., and R. C. Ellison. 1995. Alcohol in the Mediterranean Diet. *American Journal of Clinical Nutrition* 61: 1378S–1382S.
66. Mukamal, K. J., K. M. Conigrave, M. A. Mittleman, C. A. Camaro, M. J. Stampfer, W. C. Willett, and E. B. Rimm. 2003. Roles of Drinking Pattern and Type of Alcohol Consumed in Coronary Heart Disease in Men. *New England Journal of Medicine* 348:109–118.
67. Jenkins, D. J., C. W. Kendal, A. Marchie, D. A. Faulkner, J. M. Wong, R. de Souza, A. Emam, T. L. Parker, E. Vidgen, K. G. Lapsley, E. A. Trautwein, R. G. Josse, L. A. Leiter, and P. W. Connelly. 2003. Effects of a Dietary Portfolio of Cholesterol-Lowering Foods vs. Lovastatin on Serum Lipids and C-Reactive Protein. *Journal of the American Medical Association* 290: 502–510.
68. Anderson, J. W. 2003. Diet First, Then Medication of Hypercholesterolemia. *Journal of the American Medical Association* 290: 531–533.
69. Institute of Medicine. *Dietary Reference Intakes for Energy, Carbohydrate, Fiber, Fat, Fatty Acids, Cholesterol, Protein, and Amino Acids.*
70. Ibid.
71. U.S. Department of Agriculture. Nutrition and Your Health: Dietary Guidelines for Americans.

Feature Box References

1. Helsing, E. 1995. Traditional Diets and Disease Patterns of the Mediterranean, circa 1960. *American Journal of Clinical Nutrition* 61: 1329S–1337S.
2. Trichopoulou, A. N., T. Costacou, C. Bamia, and D. Trichopoulos. 2003. Adherence to a Mediterranean Diet and Survival in a Greek Population. *New England Journal of Medicine* 348: 2599–2608; de Lorgeril, M., P. Salen, J. L. Martin, I. Monjaud, J. Delaye, and N. Mamelle. 1999. Mediterranean Diet, Traditional Risk Factors, and the Rate of Cardiovascular Complications After Myocardial Infarction: Final Report of the Lyon Diet Heart Study. *Circulation* 99: 779–785; Kris-Etherton, P., R. H. Eckel, B. V. Howard, S. St. Jeor, and T. L. Bazzarre. 2001. Lyon Diet Heart Study. Benefits of a Mediterranean-Style, National Cholesterol Education Program/American Heart Association Step I Dietary Pattern on Cardiovascular Disease. *Circulation* 103: 1823–1825.
3. Willett, W. C., F. Sacks, A. N. Trichopoulou, G. Drescher, A. Ferro-Luzzi, E. Helsing, and D. Trichopoulos. 1995. Mediterranean Diet Pyramid: A Cultural Model for Healthy Eating. *American Journal of Clinical Nutrition* 61: 1402S–1406S.
4. Ibid.
5. de Lorgeril. Mediterranean Diet.
6. Willett. Mediterranean Diet Pyramid; Nestle, M. 1995. Mediterranean Diets: Historical and Research Overview. *American Journal of Clinical Nutrition* 61: 1313S–1320S.
7. Nestle. Mediterranean Diets: Historical and Research Overview.
8. Ibid.
9. Keys, A. 1995. Mediterranean Diet and Public Health: Personal Reflections. *American Journal of Clinical Nutrition* 61: 1321S–1323S.
10. Food and Drug Administration. April 2003. FDA's Advisory on Methylmercury in Fish. Available at www.fda.gov/bbs/topics/ANSWERS/2003/ANS01209.html. Accessed July 2003; Food and Drug Administration. Revised May 1995. Mercury in Fish: Cause for Concern? *FDA Consumer Magazine*. Available at www.fda.gov/fdac/reprints/mercury.html. Accessed July 2003.
11. Center for Food Safety and Applied Nutrition. March 2001. An Important Message for Pregnant Women and Women of Childbearing Age Who May Become Pregnant about the Risks of Mercury in Fish. Available at www.cfsan.fda.gov/∼acrobat/hgadv1.pdf. Accessed July 2003.
12. Food and Drug Administration. FDA's Advisory on Methylmercury in Fish; Food and Drug Administration. Mercury in Fish: Cause for Concern?
13. Environmental Protection Agency. Updated January 2003. Consumption Advice: EPA National Advice on Mercury in Freshwater Fish For Women Who Are or May Become Pregnant, Nursing Mothers, and Young Children. Available at www.epa.gov/waterscience/fishadvice/advice.html. Accessed July 2003.

Two Points of View References

1. Indiana University. 2004. "Farmed Salmon More Toxic Than Wild Salmon, Study Finds." *ScienceDaily*. Available at www.sciencedaily.com/releases/2004/01/040109072244.htm. Accessed July 2010.

2. Monterey Bay Aquarium. 2010 "Seafood Watch: Salmon Fact Sheet." Available at www.montereybayaquarium.org/cr/SeafoodWatch/web/sfw_factsheet.aspx?fid=133. Accessed July 2010.

3. The Cornucopia Institute. 2009. "How Farm-Raised Salmon Are Turning Our Oceans into Dangerous and Polluted Feedlots." Available at www.cornucopia.org/2009/09/how-farm-raised-salmon-are-turning-our-oceans-into-dangerous-and-polluted-feedlots/. Accessed July 2010.

4. Pew Environment Group. 2009. "Pew Environment Group Calls for a Crackdown on Unapproved Drug Use by Salmon Farms." Available at www.pewtrusts.org/news_room_detail.aspx?id=51366. Accessed June 2010.

5. Ziccarelli, V. 2009. "Nutritional Health Benefits of Salmon." Available at www.salmonfarmers.org/sites/default/files/Nutritional%20Benefits.pdf. Accessed July 2010.

6. Hites, R. and B. Hamilton. 2004. "Global Assessment of Organic Contaminants in Farmed Salmon." *Science* 303: Available at www.mindfully.org/Water/2004/Salmon-Farmed-Organochlorine9jan04.htm. Accessed July 2010.

7. Ziccarelli, V. "Nutritional Health Benefits of Salmon."

8. National Academy of Sciences (U.S.), Committee on the Implications of Dioxin in the Food Supply. 2003. *Dioxins and Dioxin-Like Compounds. Strategies to Decrease Exposure.* Washington, D.C.: National Academies Press

9. University of California Cooperative Extension. 2010. "Commercially Farmed and Wild-Caught Salmon—Bon Appetit!" Available at http://seafood.ucdavis.edu/pubs/farmed_and_wild_salmon.pdf. Accessed July 2010.

10. Ibid.

Chapter 6

1. Johnson, M. D. 2003. *Human Biology: Concepts and Current Issues.* 2nd ed. San Francisco: Benjamin Cummings.

2. Institute of Medicine. 2002. *Dietary Reference Intakes for Energy, Carbohydrate, Fiber, Fat, Fatty Acids, Cholesterol, Protein, and Amino Acids.* Washington, D.C.: The National Academies Press.

3. Bennion, M. 1980. *The Science of Food.* New York: Harper & Row.

4. Food Safety and Inspection Service. 1999. Poultry: Basting, Brining, and Marinating. Available at www.fsis.usda.gov/OA/pubs/bastebrine.htm. Accessed May 2004.

5. Institute of Medicine. *Dietary Reference Intakes for Energy.*

6. National Human Genome Research Institute. 2010. Learning about Sickle-Cell Disease. Available at www.genome.gov.; National Institutes of Health. Genes and Disease: Sickle-Cell Anemia. Available at www.ncbi.nlm.nih.gov/disease/sickle.html.

7. Marieb, E. N. 2004. *Human Anatomy and Physiology.* 6th ed. San Francisco: Benjamin Cummings.

8. Murray, R. K., D. K. Granner, P. A. Mayes, and V. W. Rodwell. 2006. *Harper's Illustrated Biochemistry.* 27th ed. New York: Lange Medical Books/McGraw-Hill.

9. National Institute of Allergy and Infectious Diseases. 2004. Food Allergy and Intolerances. Available at www.niaid.nih.gov/factsheets/food.htm. Accessed May 2004.

10. Astrup, A. 2006. Carbohydrates as Macronutrients in Relation to Protein and Fat for Body Weight Control. *International Journal of Obesity* 30: S4–S9.

11. Vedlhorst, M., A. Smeets, S. Soenen, A. Hochstenback-Waelen, R. Hursel, K. Diepvens, M. Lejeune, N. Luscombe-Marsh, and M. Westerterp-Plantenga. 2008. Protein-Induced Satiety: Effects and Mechanisms of Different Proteins. *Physiology & Behavior* 94: 300–307.

12. Stipanuk, M. 2006. *Biochemical and Physiological Aspects of Human Nutrition.* 2nd ed. Philadelphia: Saunders Elsevier.

13. Agricultural Research Service. 2008. Nutrient Intakes from Food: Mean Amounts Consumed per Individual, One Day, 2005–2006. Available at ars.usda.gov/ba/bhnrc/fsrg. Accessed May 2010.

14. Ibid.

15. American Dietetic Association, Dietitians of Canada, and the American College of Sports Medicine. 2009. Nutrition and Athletic Performance. *Journal of the American Dietetic Association* 109: 509–527

16. Economic Research Service (ERS). 2010. Food Availability Per Capita Data System. Available at www.ers.usda.gov/data/foodconsumption/. Accessed May 2010.

17. Ibid.

18. Allen, L. H., E. A. Oddoye, and S. Margen. 1979. Protein-Induced Calciuria: A Longer-Term Study. *American Journal of Clinical Nutrition* 32: 741–749; Lemann, J. 1999. Relationship between Urinary Calcium and Net Acid Excretion as Determined by Dietary Protein and Potassium: A Review. *Nephron* 81: 1–25; Reddy, S. T., C. Wang, K. Sahaee, L. Brinkley, and C. Pak. 2002. Effect of Low-Carbohydrate High-Protein Diets on Acid-Base Balance, Stone-Forming Propensity, and Calcium Metabolism. *American Journal of Kidney Diseases* 40: 265–274.

19. Institute of Medicine. *Dietary Reference Intakes for Energy.*

20. Heaney, R. P. 1998. Excess Dietary Protein May Not Adversely Affect Bone. *Journal of Nutrition* 128: 1054–1057.

21. Key, T. J., N. E. Allen, E. A. Spencer, and R. C. Travis. 2002. The Effect of Diet on Risk of Cancer. *The Lancet* 360: 861–868; World Cancer Research Fund/American Institute for Cancer Research. 2007. Food, Nutrition, Physical Activity, and the Prevention of Cancer: A Global Prospective. Available at www.dietandcancerreport.org/

22. Promislow, J. H. E., D. Goodman-Gruen, D. J. Slymen, and E. Barrett-Connor. 2002. Protein Consumption and Bone Mineral Density in the Elderly. The Rancho Bernardo Study. *American Journal of Epidemiology* 155: 636–644; Wengreen, H. J., R. G. Munger, N. A. West, D. R. Cutler, C. D. Corcoran, J. Zhang, and N. E. Sassano. 2004. Dietary Protein Intake and Risk of Osteoporotic Hip and Fracture in Elderly Residents of Utah. *Journal of Bone and Mineral Research* 19: 537–545.

23. Institute of Medicine. *Dietary Reference Intakes for Energy.*

24. Shils, M. E., J. A. Olson, M. Shike, and A. C. Ross. 1999. *Modern Nutrition in Health and Disease.* 9th ed. Baltimore: Williams and Wilkens; World Health Organization/Programme of Nutrition. WHO Global Database on Child Growth and Malnutrition: Introduction. Available at www.who.int/nutgrowthdb/about/introduction/en. Accessed June 2004.

25. Caulfield, L. E, M. de Onis, M. Blossner, and R. E. Black. 2004. Undernutrition as an Underlying Cause of Child Deaths Associated with Diarrhea, Pneumonia, Malaria, and Meals. *American Journal of Clinical Nutrition* 80: 193–198; de Onis, M., M. Blossner, E. Borghi, E. Frongillo, and R. Morris. 2004. Estimates of Global Prevalence of Childhood Underweight in 1990 and 2015. *Journal of the American Medical Association* 291: 2600–2606.

26. Shils. *Modern Nutrition.*

27. Ibid.

28. Ibid.

29. United Nations General Assembly. 2000. UN Resolution A/55/2. Available at www.un.org/millenium/declaration/ares552e.htm. Accessed June 2004; United Nations. 2002. The Millenium Development Goals: How Are We Doing? Available at www.un.org/milleniumgoals. Accessed June 2004.

30. American Dietetic Association and Dietitians of Canada. 2009. Position of the American Dietetic Association and Dietitians of Canada: Vegetarian Diets. *Journal of the American Dietetic Association* 109: 1266–1282.

31. The Vegetarian Resource Group. 2009. How Many Vegetarians Are There? Available at www.vrg.org/press/2009poll.htm. Accessed May 2010.

32. Mintel International Group, Limited. 2007. Vegetarian Foods, Processed, US, June 2007. Chicago: Mintel International Group, Limited.

33. Appleby, P. N., M. Thorogood, J. Mann, and T. J. Key. 1999. The Oxford Vegetarian Study: An Overview. *American Journal of Clinical Nutrition* 70: 525S–531S; Key, T. J., G. E. Fraser, M. Thorogood, P. N. Appleby, B. Beral, G. Reeves, M. L. Burr, J. Chang-Claude, R. Grentzel-Beyme, J. W. Kuzma, J. Mann, and K. McPherson. 1999. Mortality in Vegetarians and Nonvegetarians: Detailed Findings from a Collaborative Analysis of Five Prospective Studies. *American Journal of Clinical Nutrition* 70: 516S–524S.

34. Fraser, G. E. 1999. Associations between Diet and Cancer, Ischemic Heart Disease, and All-Cause Mortality in Non-Hispanic White California Seventh-Day Adventists. *American Journal of Clinical Nutrition* 70: 532S–538S.

35. Jenkins, D. J., C. Kendall, A. Marchie, A. L. Jenkins, L. Augustin, D. S. Ludwig, N. D. Barnard, and J. W. Anderson. 2003. Type 2 Diabetes and the Vegetarian Diet. *American Journal of Clinical Nutrition* 78: 610S–616S.

36. Fraser. Associations between Diet and Cancer.

Feature Box References

1. Consumer Reports. 2003. Energy Bars, Unwrapped. June: 19–21.

2. Soyfoods Association of North America. 2010. Sales and Trends. Available at www.soyfoods.org/products/sales-and-trends. Accessed May 2010.

3. United Soybean Board. 2009. Consumer Attitudes About Nutrition, Insights into Nutrition, Health, and Soyfoods. Available at www.soyfoods.org/wp/wp-content/uploads/2009/ConsumerAttitudes2009.pdf. Accessed May 2010.

4. Henkel, J. 2000. Soy Health Claims for Soy Protein, Questions about Other Components. *FDA Consumer Magazine.* Available at www.cfsan.fda.gov/∼dms/fdsoypr.html. Accessed July 2004.

5. Munro, I. C., M. Harwood, J. J. Hlywka, A. M. Stephen, J. Doull, W. G. Flammn, and H. Adlercrutz. 2003. Soy Isoflavones: A Safety Review. *Nutrition Reviews* 61: 1–33.

6. Ibid.

7. Maskarinec, G. 2005. Soy Foods for Breast Cancer Survivors and Women at High Risk for Breast Cancer. *Journal of the American Dietetic Association* 105: 1524–1528.

8. Anderson, J. W., B. M. Johnstone, and M. E. Cook-Newell. 1995. Meta-Analysis of the Effects of Soy Protein Intake on Serum Lipids. *New England Journal of Medicine* 333: 276–282.

9. Balk, E., M. Chung, P. Chew, S. Ip, G. Raman, B. Kupelnick, A. Tatsioni, Y. Sun, B. Wolk, D. Devine., and J. Lau. 2005. Effects of Soy on Health Outcomes, Summary, Evidence Report/Technology Assessment No.126. AHRQ Publication No. 05-E024-1. Rockville, MD: Agency for Healthcare Research and Quality; Sacks, F., A. Lichtenstein, L. Van Horn, W. Harris, P. Kris-Etherton, M. Winston, and the American Heart Association Nutrition Committee. 2006. Soy Protein, Isoflavones, and Cardiovascular Health: An American Heart Association Science Advisory for Professions from the Nutrition Committee. *Circulation* 113: 1034–1044.

10. Messina, M. J., V. Persky, K. D. R. Setchell, and S. Barnes. 1994. Soy Intake and Cancer Risk: A Review of the In Vitro and In Vivo Data. *Nutrition and Cancer* 21: 113–131; Messina, M. J., and C. L. Loprinzi. 2001. Soy for Breast Cancer Survivors: A Critical Review of the Literature. *Journal of Nutrition* 131: 3095S–3108S.

11. Shu, X. O., F. Jin, Q. Dai, W. Wen, J. D. Potter, L. H. Kushi, Z. Ruan, Y. Gao, and W. Zhenng. 2001. Soyfood Intake during Adolescence and Subsequent Risk of Breast Cancer among Chinese Women. *Cancer Epidemiology, Biomarkers & Prevention* 10: 483–488; Maskarinec. Soy Foods for Breast Cancer Survivors.

12. Maskarinec.Soy Foods for Breast Cancer Survivors; McMichael-Phillips, D. F., C. Harding, M. Morton, S. A. Roberts, A. Howell, C. S. Potten, and N. J. Bundred. 1998. Effects of Soy-Protein Supplementation on Epithelial Proliferation in the Histologically Normal Human Breast. *American Journal of Clinical Nutrition* 68: 1431S–1436S.

13. Munro. Soy Isoflavones.

14. American Cancer Society. 2008. Frequently Asked Questions about Nutrition and Physical Activity. Available at www.cancer.org/docroot/ped/content/ped_3_2x_common_questions_about_diet_and_cancer.asp. Accessed May 2010; McMichael-Phillips. Effects of Soy-Protein Supplementation.

Two Points of View References

1. Hays, M., H. Kim, A. Wells, et al. 2009. "Effects of Whey and Fortified Collagen Hydrolysate Protein Supplements on Nitrogen Balance and Body Composition in Older Women." *Journal of the American Dietetic Association* 109: 1082–1087. Available at www.adajournal.org/article/S0002-8223(09)00290-9/abstract. Accessed July 2010; Hospice and Palliative Nurses Association, Teaching Sheet. 2010 "Assisting Families to Manage Fatigue." Available at www.hpna.org/pdf/TeachingSheet_assistingfamiliestomanagefatigue.pdf?debugMode=false. Accessed July 2010.

2. Lemon, P.W., K. E. Yarasheski, and D. G. Dolny. 1984. "The Importance of Protein for Athletes." *Sports Medicine* 1(6): 474–484. Available at www.ncbi.nlm.nih.gov/pubmed/6390614. Accessed July 2010.

3. Ivy, J.L., Z. Ding, H. Hwang, L. C. Cialdella-Kam, and P. J. Morrison. 2008. "Postexercise Carbohydrate-Protein Supplementation: Phosphorylation of Muscle Proteins Involved in Glycogen Synthesis and Protein Translation." *Amino Acids* 35(1): 89–97. Epub 2007 Dec 28. Available at www.ncbi.nlm.nih.gov/pubmed/18163180. Accessed July 2010.

4. Anderson, J., L. Young, and S. Prior. May 2010 *Nutrition for the Athlete.* Colorado State University Extension. Available at www.ext.colostate.edu/pubs/foodnut/09362.html. Accessed July 2010.

5. Food and Drug Administration. 2007. "Dietary Supplements: What You Need to Know." Available at www.fda.gov/Food/ResourcesForYou/Consumers/ucm109760.htm. Accessed July 2010.

6. University of Illinois Extension. 2010. "Are High-Protein Diets Necessary for High School Athletes?" Available at http://urbanext.illinois.edu/hsnut/hsath3b.html. Accessed July 2010.

7. American Council on Exercise. 1999. "Fitness Q and A: Are There Any Risks Associated with Excess Protein Consumption?" Available at www.acefitness.org/fitnessqanda/fitnessqanda_display.aspx?itemid=272. Accessed July 2010.

8. Zeratsky, K. 2010. *Protein Shakes: Good for Weight Loss?* The Mayo Clinic. Available at www.mayoclinic.com/health/protein-shakes/AN01332. Accessed July 2010.

Chapter 7

1. Rosenfeld, L. 1997. Vitamine-Vitamin. The Early Years of Discovery. *Clinical Chemistry* 43: 680–685.

2. Young, I. S., and J. V. Woodside. 2001. Antioxidants in Health and Disease. *Journal of Clinical Pathology* 54: 176–186.

3. Dröge, W. 2002. Free Radicals in the Physiological Control of Cell Function. Physiology Review 82: 47–95; Traber, M. G. and H. Sies. 1996. Vitamin E in Humans: Demand and Delivery. Annual Review of Nutrition 16: 321–347; Young. Antioxidants in Health.

4. National Eye Institute, National Institutes of Health. 2004. Age-Related Macular Degeneration: What You Should Know. Updated June 2004. Available at www.nei.nih.gov/health/maculardegen/armd_facts.asp#1. Accessed September 2004.

5. Age-Related Eye Disease Study Research Group. 2001. A Randomized, Placebo-Controlled, Clinical Trial of High-Dose Supplementation with Vitamins C and E, Beta Carotene, and Zinc for Age-Related Macular Degeneration and Vision Loss: AREDS Report No. 8. Archives of Ophthalmology 119: 1417–1436; Brown, L., E. B. Rimm, J. M. Seddon, E. L. Giovannucci., L. Chasan-Tabar, D. Spiegelman, W. C. Willett, and S. E. Hankinson. 1999. A Prospective Study of Carotenoid Intake and Risk of Cataract Extraction in U.S. Men. *American Journal of Clinical Nutrition* 70: 517–524; Chasan-Tabar, L., W. C. Willett, J. M. Seddon, M. J. Stampfer, B. Rosner, G. A. Colditz, F. E. Speizer, and S. E. Hankinson. 1999. A Prospective Study of Carotenoid Intake and Risk of Cataract Extraction in U.S. Women. *American Journal of Clinical Nutrition* 70: 509–516; The National Eye Institute, National Institutes of Health. 2004. The AREDS Formulation and Age-Related Macular Degeneration: Are These High Levels of Antioxidants and Zinc Right for You? Updated June 2004. Available at www.nei.nih.gov/amd/summary.asp. Accessed September 2004.

6. Mares, J. A., T. L. La Rowe, and B. A. Blodi. 2004. Doctor, What Vitamins Should I Take for My Eyes? *Archives of Ophthalmology* 122: 628–635.

7. The National Eye Institute, National Institutes of Health. 2004. Cataract: What You Should Know. Updated August 2004. Available at www.nei.nih.gov/health/cataract/cataract_facts.asp. Accessed September 2004.

8. Craig, W. J. 1997. Phytochemicals: Guardians of Our Health. *Journal of the American Dietetic Association* 97: S199–S204.

9. U.S. Department of Agriculture, U.S. Department of Health and Human Services. 2010. *Dietary Guidelines for Americans, 2010.* 7th ed. Washington, D.C.: U.S. Government Printing Office; Kris-Etherton, P., A. H. Lichtenstein, B. V. Howard, D. Steinberg, J. L. Witztum. 2004. Antioxidant Vitamin Supplements and Cardiovascular Disease. *Circulation* 110: 637–641; U.S. Preventive Services Task Force. 2003. Routine Vitamin Supplementation to Prevent Cancer and Cardiovascular Disease: Recommendations and Rationale. *Annals of Internal Medicine* 139: 51–55.

10. U.S. Department of Agriculture. 2005. 2005 Report of the Dietary Guidelines Advisory Committee on the Dietary Guidelines for Americans. Available at www.health.gov/dietaryguidelines/dga2005/report. Accessed February 2005.

11. Lee, S. K., and A. A. Kader. 2000. Preharvest and Postharvest Factors Influencing Vitamin C Content of Horticultural Crops. *Postharvest Biology and Technology* 20: 207–220.

12. Pandrangi, S., and L. E. LaBorde. 2004. Retention of Folate, Carotenoid, and Other Quality Characteristics in Commercially Packaged Fresh Spinach. *Journal of Food Science* 69: C702-C707.

13. Institute of Medicine. Dietary Reference Intakes: Thiamin; Zeisel, S. H., K. H. Da Costa, P. D. Franklin, E. A. Alexander, J. T. Lamont, N. F. Sheard, and A. Beiser. 1991. Choline, an Essential Nutrient for Humans. Federation of American Societies for Experimental Biology 5: 2093–2098.

14. National Institutes of Health. 2004. Carnitine: The Science Behind a Conditionally Essential Nutrient. Available at http://ods.od.nih.gov/News/Carnitine_Conference_Summary.aspx. Accessed September 2004.

15. Packer, L., E. H. Witt, and H. J. Tritschler. 1994. Alpha-lipoic Acid as a Biological Antioxidant. *Free Radical Biology and Medicine* 19: 227–250.

16. U.S. Department of Agriculture. 2005. 2005 Report of the Dietary Guidelines Advisory Committee on the Dietary Guidelines for Americans. Available at www.health.gov/dietaryguidelines/dga2005/report. Accessed February 2005.

17. Mintel International Group Limited. September 2009. Vitamin and Supplement use. Market Size and Forecast – US. Available at http://academic.mintel.com/. Accessed May 2010.

18. Marra, M. and Boyar, A. 2009. Position of the American Dietetic Association: Nutrient Supplementation. *Journal of the American Dietetic Association* 109: 2073-2085.

19. Food and Drug Administration. 2004. FDA Announces Major Initiatives for Dietary Supplements. Available at www.cfsan.fda.gov/~lrd/fpsupp .html. Accessed March 2005; Food and Drug Administration, Center for Food Safety and Applied Nutrition. 2002. Overview of Dietary Supplements. Available at www.cfsan.fda.gov/~dms/supplmnt.html. Accessed May 2010.

20. United States Pharmacopoeia. USP's Dietary Supplement Verification Program. Available at www.www.usp.org/USPVerified/ dietarySupplements/. Accessed May 2010.

Visual Summary Tables

1. Institute of Medicine, Food and Nutrition Board. 2001. Dietary Reference Intakes: Vitamin A, Vitamin K, Arsenic, Boron, Chromium, Copper, Iodine, Iron, Manganese, Molybdenum, Nickel, Silicon, Vanadium, and Zinc. Washington, D.C.: The National Academies Press; Ross, A. C. 1999. Vitamin A and Retinoids. In M. E. Shils, J. Olson, M. Shike, A. C. Ross, eds., Modern Nutrition in Health and Disease. 9th ed. Baltimore: Williams and Wilkins.

2. Institute of Medicine. Dietary Reference Intakes: Vitamin A.

3. Office of Dietary Supplements, National Institutes of Health. 2003. Vitamin A and Caroteneids. Available at http://ods.od.nih.gov/factsheets/ vitamina.asp; Ross, A. C. 1993. Vitamin A as Hormone: Recent Advances in Understanding the Actions of Retinol, Retinoic Acid, and Beta Carotene. Journal of the American Dietetic Association 93: 1285–1290.

4. Bershad, S. V. 2001. The Modern Age of Acne Therapy: A Review of Current Treatment Options. Mount Sinai Journal of Medicine 68: 279–286.

5. Institute of Medicine. Dietary Reference Intakes: Vitamin A; Ross. Vitamin A as Hormone.

6. Institute of Medicine. Dietary Reference Intakes: Vitamin A.

7. Institute of Medicine, Food and Nutrition Board. 2000. Dietary Reference Intakes: Vitamin C, Vitamin E, Selenium, and Carotenoids. Washington, D.C.: The National Academies Press.

8. Giovannuci, E. 1999. Tomatoes, Tomato-Based Products, Lycopene, and Cancer: Review of the Epidemiologic Literature. Journal of the National Cancer Institute 91: 317–331.

9. Institute of Medicine. Dietary Reference Intakes: Vitamin A; Office of Dietary Supplements. Vitamin A.

10. Institute of Medicine. Dietary Reference Intakes: Vitamin A.

11. Office of Dietary Supplements. Vitamin A.

12. Brinkley, N., and D. Krueger. 2000. Hypervitaminosis A and Bone. Nutrition Reviews 58: 138–144; de Souza, P. G., and L. G. Martini. 2004. Vitamin A Supplementation and Risk of Skeletal Fracture. Mark, R. Berstrom, L. Holmber, H. Mallmin, A. Wolk, and S. Ljunghall. 1998. Excessive Dietary Intake of Vitamin A Is Associated with Reduced Bone Mineral Density and Increased Risk for Hip Fractures. Annals of Internal Medicine 129: 770–778; Office of Dietary Supplements. Vitamin A.

13. Feskanich, D., V. Singh, W. Willett, and G. Colditz. 2002. Vitamin A Intake and Hip Fractures among Postmenopausal Women. Journal of the American Medical Association 287: 47–54; Lips, P. 2003. Hypervitaminosis A and Fractures. New England Journal of Medicine 348: 347–349; Michaelsson, K., H. Lithell, B. Bvessby, and H. Melhus. 2003. Serum Retinol Levels and the Risk of Fractures. New England Journal of Medicine 348: 287–294.

14. Institute of Medicine. Dietary Reference Intakes: Vitamin C.

15. The Alpha-Tocopherol, Beta Carotene Cancer Prevention Study Group. 1994. The Effects of Vitamin E and Beta Carotene on the Incidence of Lung Cancer and Other Cancers in Male Smokers. New England Journal of Medicine 330: 1029–1035.

16. World Health Organization. 2004. Nutrition, Micronutrient Deficiencies. Available at www.who.int/nut/vad.htm. Accessed September 2004.

17. Mertz, W. 1994. A Balanced Approach to Nutrition for Health: The Need for Biologically Essential Minerals and Vitamins. Journal of the American Dietetic Association 94: 1259–1262.

18. Office of Dietary Supplements, National Institutes of Health. 2003. Vitamin E and Carotenoids. Available at http://ods.od.nih.gov/factsheets/ vitamine.asp. Accessed November 2004.

19. Young, I. S., and J. V. Woodside. 2001. Antioxidants in Health and Disease. Journal of Clinical Pathology 54: 176–186.

20. Office of Dietary Supplements. Vitamin E.

21. Institute of Medicine. Dietary Reference Intakes: Vitamin C.

22. Miller, E. R., R. Pastor-Barriso, D. Dalal, R. A. Riemersma, L. J. Appel, and E. Guallar. 2005. Meta-Analysis: High-Dosage Vitamin E Supplementation May Increase All-Cause Mortality. Annals of Internal Medicine 142: 37–46.

23. Feskanich, D., P. Weber, W. C. Willet, H. Rockett, S. L. Booth, and G. A. Colditz. 1999. Vitamin K Intake and Hip Fractures in Women: A Prospective Study. American Journal of Clinical Nutrition 69: 74–79.

24. Brinkley, N. C., and J. W. Suttie. 1995. Vitamin K Nutrition and Osteoporosis. Journal of Nutrition 125: 1812–1821. Institute of Medicine. Dietary Reference Intakes: Vitamin A.

25. National Institutes of Health. 2003. Coumadin and Vitamin K. Available at http://ods.od.nih.gov/factsheets/cc/coumadin1.pdf. Accessed March 2005.

26. Institute of Medicine. Dietary Reference Intakes: Vitamin A.

27. Institute of Medicine, Food and Nutrition Board. 1997. Dietary Reference Intakes for Calcium, Phosphorus, Magnesium, Vitamin D, and Fluoride. Washington, D.C: The National Academies Press.

28. Heaney, R. P. 2003. Long-latency Deficiency Disease: Insights from Calcium and Vitamin D. American Journal of Clinical Nutrition 78: 912–919; National Institutes of Health Conference. 2003. Vitamin D and Health in the 21st Century. Available at www.nichd.nih.gov/about/od/ prip/index.htm. Accessed October 2004.

29. U.S. Department of Agriculture. 2010. Report of the Dietary Guidelines Advisory Committee on the Dietary Guidelines for Americans, 2010. Available at www.cnpp.usda.gov/DGAs2010-DGACReport.htm. Accessed July 2010.

30. Cantorna, M. T., Y. Zhu, M. Froicu, and A. Wittke. 2004. Vitamin D Status, 1,25-dihydroxyvitamin D_3, and the Immune System. American Journal of Clinical Nutrition 80:1717S–1720S.

31. Li, Y. C. 2003. Vitamin D Regulation of the Renin-Angiotensin System. Journal of Cellular Biochemistry 88:327–331.

32. Institute of Medicine. Dietary Reference Intakes for Calcium.

33. Institute of Medicine. 2011. Dietary References Intakes for Calcium and Vitamin D. Available at www.iom.edu. Accessed March 2011.

34. Ibid.

35. Ibid.

36. National Institutes of Health. 2004. Dietary Supplement Fact Sheet: Vitamin D. Available at http://ods.od.nih.gov/factsheets/vitamind.asp. Accessed October 2004; Wharton, B., and N. Bishop. 2003. Rickets. The Lancet 362: 1389–1400.

37. Centers for Disease Control and Prevention. 2001. Severe Malnutrition among Young Children—Georgia, January 1997–June 1999. Morbidity and Mortality Weekly Report. Available at www.cdc.gov/mmwr/preview/ mmwrhtml/mm5012a3.htm. Accessed October 2004; Gordon, C. M., K. C. DePeter, H. A. Feldman, E. Grace, and S. J. Emans. 2004. Prevalence of Vitamin D Deficiency among Healthy Adolescents. Archives of Pediatric and Adolescent Medicine 158: 531–537; Weisberg, P., K. S. Scanlon, R. Li, and M. E. Cogswell. 2004. Nutritional Rickets among Children in the United States: Review of Cases Reported between 1986 and 2003. American Journal of Clinical Nutrition 80: 1697S–1705S.

38. Lin, B., and K. Ralston. 2003. Competitive Foods: Soft Drinks vs. Milk. Washington, D.C.: U.S. Department of Agriculture, Economic Research Service. Available at www.ers.usda.gov/publications/fanrr34/fanrr34-7. Accessed March 2010.

39. Wanger, C., Greer, F., and Section on Breastfeeding and Committee on Nutrition. 2008. Prevention of Rickets and Vitamin D Deficiency In Infants, Children, and Adolescents. Pediatric 122: 1142-1152; Scanlon, K. S. 2001. Vitamin D Expert Panel Meeting. Available at www.cdc.gov/ nccdphp/dnpa/nutrition/pdf/Vitamin_D_Expert_Panel_Meeting.pdf. Accessed October 2004.

40. Wharton. Rickets.

41. Agarwal, K. S., M. Z. Mughal, P. Upadhyay, J. L. Berry, E. B. Mawer, and J. M. Puliyel. 2002. The Impact of Atmospheric Pollution on Vitamin D Status of Infants and Toddlers in Delhi, India. Archives of Disease in Childhood 87: 111–113; Hanley, D., Cranney, A., Jones, G., Whiting, S., and Leslie, W. 2010. Vitamin D in adult health and disease: a review and guideline statement from Osteoporosis Canada – summary. Canadian Medical Association Journal.

42. Heaney. Long-Latency Deficiency Disease; Holick, M. F. 1999. Vitamin D. In M. E. Shils, J. Olson, M. Shike, A. C. Ross, eds., Modern Nutrition in Health and Disease. 9th ed. Baltimore: Williams and Wilkins.

43. Rosenfeld. Vitamine-Vitamin.

44. Institute of Medicine, Food, and Nutrition Board. 1998. Dietary Reference Intakes: Thiamin, Riboflavin, Niacin, Vitamin B_6, Folate, Vitamin B_{12} Pantothenic Acid, Biotin, and Choline. Washington, D.C.: The National Academies Press.

45. National Institutes of Health. 2008. Beriberi. Medline Plus. Available at: http://www.nlm.nih.gov/medlineplus/ency/article/000339.htm. Accessed May 2010.

46. National Institute of Neurological Disorders and Stroke (NINDS). 2004. NINDS Wernicke Korsakoff Syndrome Information Page. Available at

www.ninds.nih.gov/disorders/wernicke_korsakoff/wernicke-korsakoff .htm. Accessed December 2005.

47. Herreid, E. O., B. Ruskin, G. L. Clark, and T. B. Parks. 1952. Ascorbic Acid and Riboflavin Destruction and Flavor Development in Milk Exposed to the Sun in Amber, Clear, Paper, and Ruby Bottles. *Journal of Dairy Science* 35: 772–778.

48. Institute of Medicine. Dietary Reference Intakes: Thiamin.

49. Ibid.

50. Cervantes-Laurean, D., G. McElvaney, and J. Moss. Niacin. In M. E. Shils, J. Olson, M. Shike, A. C. Ross, eds., Modern Nutrition in Health and Disease. 9th ed. Baltimore: Williams and Wilkins.

51. Institute of Medicine. Dietary Reference Intakes: Thiamin.

52. Ibid.

53. National Institutes of Health. 2002. Vitamin B_6. Available at www.nih.gov. Accessed February 2005.

54. Leklem, J. M. 1999. Vitamin B_6. In M. E. Shils, J. Olson, M. Shike, A. C. Ross, eds., Modern Nutrition in Health and Disease. 9th ed. Baltimore: Williams and Wilkins.

55. American College of Obstetricians and Gynecologists. 2000. ACOG Practice Bulletin. Premenstrual Syndrome. No. 15; National Institute of Neurological Disorders and Stroke, National Institutes of Health. 2002. Carpal Tunnel Syndrome Fact Sheet. Available at www.ninds.nih.gov/ disorders/carpal_tunnel/detail_carpal_tunnel.htm. Accessed February 2005; National Women's Health Information Center, U.S. Department of Health and Human Services. 2002. Premenstrual Syndrome. Available at www.4woman.gov/faq/pms.htm. Accessed February 2005; Schaumburg, H., J. Kaplan, A. Windebran, N. Vick, S. Rasmus, D. Pleasure, and M. J. Brown. 1983. Sensory Neuropathy from Pyridoxine Abuse. *New England Journal of Medicine* 309: 445–448.

56. Institute of Medicine. Dietary Reference Intakes: Thiamin; Office of Dietary Supplements, National Institutes of Health. 2004. Dietary Supplement Fact Sheet: Folate. Available at http://ods.od.nih.gov/factsheets/ folate.asp. Accessed February 2005.

57. Centers for Disease Control and Prevention. 2003. Folic Acid Now Fact Sheet. Available at www.cdc.gov/doc.do/id/0900f3ec8000d615. Accessed February 2005.

58. Centers for Disease Control and Prevention. May 7, 2004. Spina Bifida and Anencephaly Before and After Folic Acid Mandate—United States, 1995–1996 and 1999–2000. Morbidity and Morality Weekly Reports 17: 362-365. Available at www.cdc.gov/mmwr/preview/mmwrhtml/ mm5317a3.htm. Accessed in February 2005; Centers for Disease Control and Prevention. 2003. Information for Health Professional— Recommendations. Available at www.cdc.gov/doc.do/id/ 0900f3ec800523d6. Accessed February 2005; Centers for Disease Control and Prevention. August 2, 1991. Effectiveness in Disease and Injury Prevention Use of Folic Acid for Prevention of Spina Bifida and Other Neural Tube Defects: 1983–1991. Morbidity and Morality Weekly Reports 40: 513–516. Available at www.cdc.gov/mmwr/preview/ mmwrhtml/00014915.htm. Accessed February 2005.

59. Giovannucci, E., M. J. Stampfer, G. A. Colditz, D. J. Hunter, C. Fuchs, B. A. Rosner, F. E. Speizer, and W. C. Willett. 1998. Multivitamin Use, Folate, and Colon Cancer in Women in the Nurses Health Study. *Annals of Internal Medicine* 129: 517–524.

60. Institute of Medicine. Dietary Reference Intakes: Thiamin.

61. Centers for Disease Control. Effectiveness in Disease; Centers for Disease Control. Information for Health Professionals.

62. Centers for Disease Control. Folic Acid Now; Institute of Medicine. Dietary Reference Intakes: Thiamin.

63. Ebbing, M., Bonaa, K., Nygard, O., Arnesen, E., Ueland, P., Nordrehaug, J., Rasmussen, K., Njolstad, I., Refsum., H., Nilsen, D., Tverdal, A., Meyer, K., and Vollset, S. 2009. Cancer Incidence and Mortality After Treatment with Folic Acid and Vitamin B12. *Journal of the American Medical Association*; 302: 2119-2126.; Cole, B., et. al., 2007. Folic Acid for the Prevention of Colorectal Adenomas. A Randomized Clinical Trial. *Journal of the American Medical Association*; 297:2351-2359.

64. Office of Dietary Supplements, National Institutes of Health. 2004. Dietary Supplement Fact Sheet: Vitamin B_{12}. Available at www.ods.od.nih .gov/factsheets/vitaminb12.asp. Accessed February 2005; Shane, B. 2000. Folic Acid, Vitamin B_{12}, and Vitamin B_6. In M. H. Stipanuk, ed., Biochemical and Physiological Aspects of Human Nutrition. Philadelphia: Saunders.

65. Institute of Medicine. Dietary Reference Intakes: Thiamin; Office of Dietary Supplements. Fact Sheet: Vitamin B_{12}.

66. Ibid.

67. Ibid.

68. Institute of Medicine. Dietary Reference Intakes: Vitamin C.

69. Iqbal, K., A. Khan, M. Khattak. 2004. Biological Significance of Ascorbic Acid (Vitamin C) in Human Health. *Pakistan Journal of Nutrition* 3: 5–13.

70. Ibid.

71. Institute of Medicine. Dietary Reference Intakes: Vitamin C.

72. Rosenfeld. Vitamine-Vitamin.

73. Ibid.

74. Glusman, M. 1947. The Syndrome of "Burning Feet" (Nutritional Melagia) as a Manifestation of Nutritional Deficiency. *American Journal of Medicine* 3: 211–223.

75. Sweetmna, L. 2000. Pantothenic Acid and Biotin. In M. H. Stipanuk, ed., Biochemical and Physiological Aspects of Human Nutrition. Philadelphia: Saunders.

76. Mock. D. M. 1999. Biotin. In M. E. Shils, J. Olson, M. Shike, A. C. Ross, eds., Modern Nutrition in Health and Disease. 9th ed. Baltimore: Williams and Wilkins.

Feature Box References

1. Appel, L. J., E. R. Miller, S. H. Jee, R. Stolzenberg-Solomon, P. Lin, T. Erlinger, M. R. Nadeau, and J. Selhub. 2000. Effect of Dietary Patterns on Serum Homocysteine: Results of a Randomized Controlled Feeding Study. Circulation 102: 852–857; Finklestein, J. D. 2000. Homocysteine: A History in Progress. *Nutrition Reviews* 58: 193–204; Institute of Medicine, Food, and Nutrition Board. 1998. Dietary Reference Intakes: Thiamin, Riboflavin, Niacin, Vitamin B_6, Folate, Vitamin B_{12} Pantothenic Acid, Biotin, and Choline. Washington, D.C.: National Academies Press.

2. Jacques, P. F., J. Selhum, A. G. Bostom, P. W. F. Wilson, and I. H. Rosenberg. 1999. The Effects of Folic Acid Fortification on Plasma Folate and Total Homocysteine Concentrations. *New England Journal of Medicine* 340: 1449–1454; Malinow, M. R., A. G. Bostom, and R. M. Krauss. 1999. Homocyst(e)ine, Diet and Cardiovascular Diseases. A Statement for Health Care Professionals from the Nutrition Committee. *Circulation* 99: 178–182; Miller, J. W. 2000. Does Lowering Plasma Homocysteine Reduce Vascular Disease Risk? *Nutrition Reviews* 59: 241–244.

3. Schnyder, G., M. Roffi, Y. Flammer, R. Pin, and O. M. Hess. 2002. Effect of Homocysteine-Lowering Therapy with Folic Acid, Vitamin B_{12}, and Vitamin B_6 on Clinical Outcome after Percutaneous Coronary Intervention. The Swiss Heart Study: A Randomized Controlled Trial. *Journal of the American Medical Association* 288:973–979; Cui, R., Iso, H., Date, C., Kikuchi, S., and Tamakoshi, A. 2010. Dietary Folate and Vitamin B6 and B12 Intake in Relation to Mortality From Cardiovascular Diseases. *Stroke* doi:10.1161/STROKEAHA.110.578906; Albert, C. M., N. R. Cook, J. M. Gaziano, E. Zaharris, J. MacFadyen, E. Danielson, J. E. Buring, and J. E. Manson. 2008. Effect of Folic Acid and B Vitamins on Risk of Cardiovascular Events and Total Mortality among Women at High Risk for Cardiovascular Disease: A Randomized Trial. *New England Journal of Medicine* 299: 2027–2036.

4. Roxas, M., and Jurenka, J. 2007. Colds and influenza: a review of diagnosis and conventional, botanical, and nutritional considerations. *Journal of Alternative Medicine and Review*; 12:25-48.

5. Centers for Disease Control. 2004. Stopping germs at home, work and school. Available at: http://www.cdc.gov/germstopper/home_work_ school.htm. Accessed June 2010.

6. Hemila, H, Chalker, E., Treacy, B., and Douglas, B. 2010. Vitamin C for Prevention and Treating the Common Cold (Review). Cochrane Database of Systematic Reviews. Available at http://www2.cochrane.org/ reviews/en/ab000980.html. Accessed May 2010; Chalmers, T. C. 1975. Effects of Ascorbic Acid on the Common Cold. An Evaluation of the Evidence. *American Journal of Medicine* 58: 532–536; Hemila, H., and Z. S. Herman. 1995. Vitamin C and the Common Cold: A Retrospective Analysis of Chalmers' Review. American College of Nutrition 14: 116–123; Institute of Medicine, Food, and Nutrition Board. 2001. Dietary Reference Intakes: Vitamin A, Vitamin K, Arsenic, Boron, Chromium, Copper, Iodine, Iron, Manganese, Molybdenum, Nickel, Silicon, Vanadium, and Zinc. Washington, D.C: National Academies Press; Institute of Medicine, Food, and Nutrition Board. 2000. Dietary Reference Intakes: Vitamin C, Vitamin E, Selenium, and Carotenoids. Washington, D.C: National Academies Press; Mossad, S. B. 2005. Treatment of the Common Cold. *British Medical Journal* 317: 33–36; National Institute of Allergy and Infectious Diseases, National Institutes of Health. 2004. The Common Cold. Available at www.niaid.nih. gov/factsheets/cold.htm. Accessed March 2005; Pauling, L. 1971. The Significance of the Evidence about Ascorbic Acid and the Common Cold. Proceedings from the National Academy of Science 68: 2678–2681.

7. Caruso, T. J., and J. M. Gwaltney. 2005. Treatment of the Common Cold with Echinacea: A Structured Review. *Clinical Infectious Diseases* 40: 807–810; Taylor, J. A., W. Weber, L. Standish, H. Quinn, J. Goesling, M. McGann, C. Calabrese. 2003. Efficacy and Safety of Echniacea in Treating Upper Respiratory Tract Infections in Children. *Journal of the American Medical Association* 290: 2824–2830; Turner, R. B., R. Bauer, K. Woelkart, T. C. Haulsey, and D. Gangemie. 2005. An Evaluation of Echniacea Angustifolia in Experimental Rhinovirus Infections. *New England Journal of Medicine* 353: 341–348.

8. Centers for Disease Control and Prevention, U.S. Department of Health and Human Services. 2004. Stopping Germs at Home, Work and School. Available at www.cdc.gov/germstopper/home_work_school.htm. Accessed March 2005; Food and Drug Administration Center for Foods Safety and Applied Nutrition, National Science Teachers Association. 2001. Hand Washing. Available at www.cfsan.fda.gov/~dms/a2z-h.html. Accessed March 2005.

Two Points of View References

1. Vitamin D Council, "Vitamin D Deficiency Syndrome."Available at www.vitamindcouncil.org/vdds.shtml. Accessed July 2010.

2. L. S. Nield, P. Mahajan, A. Joshi, et al. 2006, "Rickets: Not a Disease of the Past,"*American Family Physician* 74 no. 4: 619–626. Available at www.aafp.org/afp/2006/0815/p619.html. Accessed July 2010.

3. Office of Dietary Supplements, National Institutes of Health, *Dietary Supplement Fact Sheet: Vitamin D.* Available at http://ods.od.nih.gov/factsheets/vitamind.asp. Accessed July 2010; K. Zeratsky, "Vitamin D Toxicity: What If You Get Too Much?" Available at www.mayoclinic.com/health/vitamin-d-toxicity/AN02008. Accessed July 2010.

4. Vitamin D Council, "Vitamin D Deficiency Syndrome"; Zeratsky, "Vitamin D Toxicity: What If You Get Too Much?"

5. Medscape Today, "Experts Clash Over Sun Exposure to Boost Vitamin D."(May 2004). Available at www.medscape.com/viewarticle/537784. Accessed July 2010.

6. U.S. Department of Health and Human Services, Public Health Service, National Toxicology Program, "Report on Carcinogens," 11th ed. Available at http://ntp.niehs.nih.gov/ntp/roc/toc11.html. Accessed July 2010; D. Wolpowitz, and B. A. Gilchrest, "The Vitamin D Questions: How Much Do You Need and How Should You Get It?" *Journal of the American Academy of Dermatology* 54 (2006): 301–317. Available at www.direct-ms.org/pdf/VitDGenScience/Gilchrist%20Vit%20D.pdf. Accessed July 2010.

7. American Academy of Dermatology, "Sunscreens/Sunblocks, 2010." Available at www.aad.org/public/publications/pamphlets/sun_sunscreens.html. Accessed July 2010.

8. Centers for Disease Control and Prevention, "Skin Cancer: Prevention." (April 2010) Available at www.cdc.gov/cancer/skin/basic_info/prevention.htm. Accessed July 2010.

Chapter 8

1. Grandjean, A., and S. Campbell. 2004 *Hydration: Fluids for Life.* Washington, D.C.: ILSI Press. Available at www.ilsi.org. Accessed August 2005; Institute of Medicine. 2004. *Dietary Reference Intakes: Water, Potassium, Sodium, Chloride, and Sulfate.* Washington, D.C.: The National Academies Press. Available at www.nap.edu; Marieb, E. N. 2004. In *Human Anatomy and Physiology.* 6th ed. San Francisco: Pearson/Benjamin Cummings.

2. Sheng, H. 2000. Body fluids and water balance. In Stipanuk *Biochemical and Physiological Aspects of Human Nutrition.* Philadelphia: W. B. Saunders.

3. Institute of Medicine. *Dietary Reference Intakes: Water.*

4. Grandjean. *Hydration: Fluids for Life;* Institute of Medicine. *Dietary Reference Intakes: Water;* Marieb. *Human Anatomy and Physiology.*

5. Marieb. *Human Anatomy and Physiology.*

6. Sheng. Body fluids and water balance.

7. Institute of Medicine. *Dietary Reference Intakes: Water.*

8. Ibid.

9. Casa, D. J., L. E. Armstrong, S. K. Hillman, S. J. Montain, R. C. Reiff, B. S. E. Rich, W. O. Roberts, J. A. Stone. 2000. National Athletic Trainers Association Position Statement: Fluid Replacement for Athletes. *Journal of Athletic Training* 35: 212–224.

10. Institute of Medicine. *Dietary Reference Intakes: Water.*

11. Arnold, D. 2002. To the End, Marathon Was at Center of Student's Life. *The Boston Globe.* April 18, 2002; Aucoin, D. 2002. Tribute to a Fallen Champion of the Needs of the Afflicted. *The Boston Globe.* October 26, 2002; Noakes, T. D. 2003. Overconsumption of Fluids by Athletes. *British Medical Journal* 327: 113–114. Zeller, T. 2007. Too High a Price for a Wii. *The New York Times.* Available at http://thelede.blogs.nytimes.com/2007/01/15/too-high-a-price-for-a-wii/. Accessed June 2010.; Rosinski, J. Friends Remember Marathoner Who Died. Available at www.remembercynthia.com. Accessed August 2005; Smith, S. 2002. Marathon Runner's Death Linked to Excessive Fluid Intake. *The Boston Globe.* August 13, 2002.

12. Grandjean, A. C., K. J. Reimers, and M. E. Buyckx. 2003. Hydration: Issues for the 21st Century. *Nutrition Reviews* 61: 261–271.

13. Grandjean. *Hydration: Fluids for Life;* Institute of Medicine. *Dietary Reference Intakes: Water.*

14. Institute of Medicine. *Dietary Reference Intakes: Water.*

15. Grandjean et al. Hydration: Issues for the 21st Century; Institute of Medicine. *Dietary Reference Intakes: Water.*

16. Gallagher, M. 2008. The Nutrients and Their Metabolism. In *Krause's Food, Nutrition and Diet Therapy.* 12th ed. St. Louis: Saunders Elsevier.

17. Institute of Medicine. *Dietary Reference Intakes: Vitamin A. Molybdenum, Nickel, Silicon, Vanadium, and Zinc.* Washington, D.C.: The National Academies Press. Available at www.nap.edu.

18. Ibid.

Visual Summary Table References

1. Institute of Medicine. *Dietary Reference Intakes: Water.*

2. Dall, T., V. Fulgoni, Y. Zhang, K. Reimers, P. Packard, and J. Astwood. 2009. Potential Health Benefits and Medical Cost Savings from Calorie, Sodium, and Saturated Fat Reductions in the American Diet. *American Journal of Health Promotion* 23: 412–422.

3. Dietary Guidelines Advisory Committee. 2010. Report of the Dietary Guidelines Advisory Committee on the Dietary Guidelines for Americans, 2010. Available at: www.cnpp.usda.gov/DGAs2010-DGACReport.htm. Accessed August 2010.

4. U.S. Department of Agriculture, Agricultural Research Service. 2008. Nutrient Intakes from Food: Mean Amounts Consumed per Individual, One Day, 2005–2006. Available at www.ars.usda.gov/ba/bhnrc/fsrg. Accessed March 2011.

5. Sheng. Body fluids and water balance.

6. Ibid.

7. Institute of Medicine. 2011. *Dietary Reference Intakes for Calcium and Vitamin D.* Washington, D.C.: The National Academies Press. Available at www.nap.edu.

8. Institute of Medicine. *Dietary Reference Intakes: Calcium;* Office of Dietary Supplements. 2011. Dietary Supplement Fact Sheet: Calcium. Available at http://ods.od.nih.gov/factsheets/calcium.

9. Institute of Medicine, *Dietary Reference Intakes: Calcium;* Miller, G. D., G. D. DiRienzo, M. E. Reusser, and D. A. McCarron. 2000. Benefits of Dairy Product Consumption on Blood Pressure in Humans: A Summary of the Biomedical Literature. *Journal of the American College of Nutrition* 19: 147S–164S.

10. Office of Dietary Supplements; Baron, J. A., M. Beach, J. S. Mandel, R. U. van Stolk, R. W. Haile, R. S. Sandler, R. Rothstein, R. W. Summers, D. C. Snover, G. J. Beck, J. H. Bond, and E. R. Greenberg. 1999. Calcium Supplements for the Prevention of Colorectal Adenomas. *New England Journal of Medicine* 340: 101–107; Wu, K., W. C. Willet, C. S. Fuchs, G. A. Colditz, and E. L. Giovannucci. 2002. Calcium Intake and Risk of Colon Cancer in Women and Men. *Journal of the National Cancer Institute* 94: 437–446.

11. National Kidney and Urologic Diseases Information Clearinghouse. 2009. Kidney and Urologic Diseases Statistics for the United States. Available at http://kidney.niddk.nih.gov/kudiseases/pubs/kustats/index.htm. Accessed June 2010; Reynolds, T. M. 2005. Chemical Pathology Clinical Investigation and Management of Nephrolithiasis, *Journal of Clinical Pathology* 58: 134–140.

12. Office of Dietary Supplements; Borghi, L., R. Schianchi, T. Meschi, A. Guerra, U. Maggiore, and A. Novarini. 2002. Comparison of Two Diets for the Prevention of Recurrent Stones in Idiopathic Hypercalciuria. *New England Journal of Medicine* 346: 77–84; Bushinsky, D. A. 2002. Recurrent Hypercalciuric Nephrolithiasis: Does Diet Help? *New England Journal of Medicine* 346: 124–125; Curhan, G. C., W. C. Willett, E. B. Rimm, and M. J. Stampfer. 1993. A Prospective Study of Dietary Calcium and Other Nutrients and the Risk of Symptomatic Kidney Stones. *New England Journal of Medicine* 328: 833–838.

13. Zemel, M. B., W. Thompson, K. Morris, and P. Campbell. 2004. Calcium and Dairy Acceleration of Weight and Fat Loss During Energy Restriction in Obese Adults. *Obesity Research* 12: 582–590.

14. Parikh, S. J., and J. A. Yanovski. 2003. Calcium Intake and Adiposity. *American Journal of Clinical Nutrition* 77: 281–287.

15. Office of Dietary Supplements; Schrager, S. 2005. Dietary Calcium Intake and Obesity. *Journal of the American Board of Family Practice* 18: 205–210; Boon, N., G. B. J. Hul, J. H. C. H. Stegan, W. E. M. Sluijsmans, C. Valle, D.

Langin, N. Viguerie, and W. H. M. Saris. 2007. An Intervention Study of the Effects of Calcium Intake on Faecal Fat Excretion, Energy Metabolism, and Adipose Tissue mRNA Expression of Lipid-metabolism Related Proteins. *International Journal of Obesity* 31: 1704–1712.

16. Institute of Medicine. 2011. *Dietary Reference Intakes for Calcium and Vitamin D*. Washington, D.C.: The National Academies Press; U.S. Department of Agriculture, Agricultural Research Service. 2008. Nutrient Intakes from Food.

17. U.S. Department of Agriculture. Agricultural Research Service. 2008. Nutrient Intakes from Food: Mean Amounts Consumed per Individual, One Day; 2005-2006. Dietary Guidelines Advisory Committee. 2010. Report of the Dietary Guidelines Advisory Committee on the Dietary Guidelines for Americans, 2010. Available on: http://www.cnpp.usda .gov/DGAs2010-DGACReport.htm, Accessed August 2010.

18. National Institutes of Health. 2000. Osteoporosis Prevention, Diagnosis, and Therapy. NIH Consensus Statement Online. Available at http://consensus.nih.gov/2000/2000Osteoporosis111html.htm. Accessed October 2010.

19. Osteoporosis and Related Bone Diseases—National Resource Center. 2005. Calcium Supplements: What to Look For. Available at www.niams .nih.gov/bone/hi/calcium_supp.pdf. Accessed June 2010.

20. Institute of Medicine. 1997. *Dietary Reference Intakes: Calcium, Phosphorus, Magnesium, Vitamin D, and Fluoride*. Washington, D.C.: The National Academies Press. Available at www.nap.edu; United States Department of Agriculture. Nutrient Intakes from Food.

21. Institute of Medicine. *Dietary Reference Intakes: Calcium*.

22. Office of Dietary Supplements. Updated 2009. Magnesium. Available at http://ods.od.nih.gov. Accessed June 2010.

23. Appel, L. J., T. J. Moore, E. Obarzanek, W. M. Vollmer, L. P. Svetkey, F. M. Sacks, G. A. Bray, T. M. Vogt, J. A. Cutler, M. M. Windhauser, P. Lin, and N. Karanja. 1997. A Clinical Trial of the Effects of Dietary Patterns on Blood Pressure. *New England Journal of Medicine* 336: 1117–1124.

24. Harsha, D. W., P. Lin, E. Obarzanek, N. M. Karanja, T. J. Moore, and B. Caballero. 1999. Dietary Approaches to Stop Hypertension: A Summary of Study Results. *Journal of the American Dietetics Association* 99: S35–S39.

25. American Diabetes Association. 2008. Nutrition Recommendations and Intervention for Diabetes. *Diabetes Care* 31: S61-S78; Lopez-Ridaura, R., W. C. Willet, E. B. Rimm, S. Liu, M. J. Stampfer, J. E. Manson, and F. B. Hu. 2004. Magnesium Intake and Risk of Type 2 Diabetes in Men and Women. *Diabetes Care* 27: 134–140.

26. United States Department of Agriculture. Nutrient Intakes from Food.

27. Institute of Medicine, *Dietary Reference Intakes: Calcium*.

28. Institute of Medicine. *Dietary Reference Intakes: Water*.

29. Gallagher, M. The Nutrients and Their Metabolism.

30. Institute of Medicine. 2001. *Dietary Reference Intakes: Vitamin A, Vitamin K, Arsenic, Boron, Chromium, Copper, Iodine, Iron, Manganese, Molybdenum, Nickel, Silicon, Vanadium, and Zinc*. Washington, D.C.: The National Academies Press. Available at www.nap.edu.

31. Ibid

32. Beard, J. 2003. Iron Deficiency Alters Brain Development and Functioning. *Journal of Nutrition* 133: 1468S–1472S; Black, M. M. 2003. Micronutrient Deficiencies and Cognitive Function. *Journal of Nutrition* 133: 3972S–3931S.

33. Institute of Medicine. *Dietary Reference Intakes: Calcium*.

34. Britton, H. C., and C. E. Nossamn. 1986. Iron Content of Food Cooked in Iron Utensils. *Journal of the American Dietetic Association* 86: 897–901.

35. Federal Register Final Rule - 68 FR 59714, October 17, 2003: Iron-Containing Supplements and Drugs; Label Warning Statements and Unit-Dose Packaging Requirements; Removal of Regulations for Unit-Dose Packaging Requirements for Dietary Supplements and Drugs. Updated 2009. Available at www.fda.gov/Food/DietarySupplements/Guidance-ComplianceRegulatoryInformation/regulationsLaws/ucm107400.htm. Accessed March 2011.

36. Centers for Disease Control and Prevention. 2009. Iron Overload and Hemochromatosis: Causes and Risk Factors. Available at www.cdc.gov/ ncbddd/hemochromatosis/. Accessed June 2010; Centers for Disease Control and Prevention. 1998. Recommendations to Prevent and Control Iron Deficiency in the United States. *Morbidity and Mortality Weekly Report* 47: 1–29; Office of Dietary Supplements. Updated 2005. Dietary Supplement Fact Sheet: Iron. Available at http://ods.od.nih.gov/ factsheets/iron.asp. Accessed October 2005.

37. Institute of Medicine. 2001. *Dietary Reference Intakes: Vitamin A;* Turnlund, J. R. 2006. Copper. In Shils, M. E., M. Shike, A. C. Ross, B. Caballero, and R. J. Cousins, eds. *Modern Nutrition in Health and Disease*. 10th ed. Philadelphia: Lippincott Williams and Wilkins; Uaruy, R., M.

Olivares, and M. Gonzalez. 1998. Essentiality of Copper in Humans. *American Journal of Clinical Nutrition* 67: 952S–959S.

38. Institute of Medicine. *Dietary Reference Intakes: Vitamin A;* Office of Dietary Supplements. Updated 2011. Zinc. Available at http://ods.od.nih .gov/factsheets/cc/zinc.html. Accessed March 2011.

39. Ibs, K., and L. Rink. 2003. Zinc-altered Immune Function. *Journal of Nutrition* 133: 1452S–1456S; Schwartz, J. R., R. G. Marsh, and Z. D. Draelos. 2005. Zinc and Skin Health: Overview of Physiology and Pharmacology. *Dermatological Surgery* 31: 837–847; Walravens, P. A. 1979. Zinc Metabolism and Its Implications in Clinical Medicine. *Western Journal of Medicine* 130: 133–142.

40. Russell, R. M., M. E. Cox, and N. Solomons. 1983. Zinc and the Special Senses. *Annals of Internal Medicine* 99: 227–239.

41. Caruso, T., C. Prober, and J. Gwaltney. 2007. Treatment of Naturally Acquired Common Colds with Zinc: A Structured Review. *Clinical Infectious Diseases* 45: 569–574; Prasad, A., F. Beck, B. Bao, D. Snell, and J. Fitzgerald. 2008. Duration and Severity of Symptoms and Levels of Plasma Interleukin-1 Receptor Antagonist, Soluble Tumor Necrosis Factor Receptor, and Adhesion Molecules in Patients with Common Cold Treated with Zinc Acetate. *Journal of Infectious Diseases* 197: 795–802; Desbiens, M. A. 2000. Lessons Learned from Attempts to Establish the Blind in Placebo-controlled Trial of Zinc for the Common Cold. *Annals of Internal Medicine* 133: 302–303; Jackson, J. L., E. Lesho, and C. Peterson. 2000. Zinc and the Common Cold: A Meta-analysis Revisited. *Journal of Nutrition* 130: 1512S–1515S; Singh, M., and R. Das. 2011. Zinc for the Common Cold. Cochrane Database of Systematic Reviews. Issue 2. Art. No.: CD001364. DOI:10.1002/1465158.CD001364.pub3.

42. Office of Dietary Supplements, National Institutes of Health. 2011. Dietary Supplement Fact Sheet: Zinc. Available at http://ods.od.nih.gov/factsheets/Zinc-HealthProfessional/#about. Accessed March 2011.

43. Ibid.

44. Ibid.

45. Combs, G. F. 2005. Current Evidence and Research Needs to Support a Health Claim for Selenium and Cancer Prevention. *Journal of Nutrition* 135: 343–347; Institute of Medicine. 2000. *Dietary Reference Intakes: Vitamin C, Vitamin E, Selenium, and Carotenoids*. Washington, D.C.: The National Academies Press. Available at www.nap.edu; Office of Dietary Supplements. 2011. Selenium. Available at http://ods.od.nih .gov/factsheets/Selenium. Accessed March 2011.

46. Beck, M. A., O. A. Levander, and O. Handy. 2003. Selenium Deficiency and Viral Infection. *Journal of Nutrition* 133: 1463S–1467S; Li, H., M. J. Stampfer, E. L. Giovannucci, J. S. Morris, W. C. Willett, M. Gaziano, and J. Ma. 2004. A Prospective Study of Plasma Selenium Levels and Prostate Cancer Risk. *Journal of the National Cancer Institute* 96: 696–703; Sunde, R. A. 2000. Selenium. In Stipanuk, M. H. *Biochemical and Physiological Aspects of Human Nutrition*. Philadelphia: W. B. Saunders; Center for Food Safety and Applied Nutrition. 2005. Qualified Health Claims Subject to Enforcement Discretion. Available at www.cfsan.fda.gov/~dms/ qhc-sum.html. Accessed November 2005; Wei, W., C. C. Abnet, Y. Qiao, S. M. Dawsey, Z. Dong, X. Sun, J. Fan, E. Q. Gunter, P. R. Taylor, and S. D. Mark. 2004. Prospective Study of Serum Selenium Concentrations and Esophageal and Gastric Cardia Cancer, Heart Disease, Stroke, and Total Death. *American Journal of Nutrition* 79: 80–85; Office of Dietary Supplements. Selenium.

47. American Dental Association. 2005. Fluoridation Facts. Available at www.ada.org/sections/professionalResources/pdfs/fluoridation_facts .pdf. Accessed June 2010.

48. Centers for Disease Control and Prevention. 1999. Achievements in Public Health, 1900–1999: Fluoridation of Drinking Water to Prevent Dental Caries. *Morbidity and Mortality Weekly Report* 48(41): 933–940. Available at www.cdc.gov/mmwr/preview/mmwrhtml/mm4841a1.htm. Accessed November 2005; Centers for Disease Control and Prevention. 2011. Community Water Fluoridation: Questions and Answers. Available at www.cdc.gov/fluoridation/fact_sheets/CWF_qa.htm. Accessed March 2011.

49. Ibid

50. Centers for Disease Control and Prevention. Updated 2009. Water Fluoridation. Safety—Enamel Fluorosis. Available at www.cdc.gov/ fluoridation/safety/enamel_fluorosis.htm. Accessed June 2010.

51. Mertz, W. 1993. Chromium in Human Nutrition: A Review. *Journal of Nutrition* 123: 626–633.

52. American Diabetes Association. Nutrition Recommendations and Intervention for Diabetes; Hopkins, L. L., O. Ransome-Kuti, and A. S. Majaj. 1968. Improvement of Impaired Carbohydrate Metabolism by Chromium (III) in Malnourished Infants. *American Journal of Clinical*

Nutrition 21: 203–211; Jeejeebhoy, K. N., R. C. Clu, E. B. Marliss, G. R. Greenberg, and A. Bruce-Robertson. 1977. Chromium Deficiency, Glucose Intolerance, and Neuropathy Reversed by Chromium Supplementation in a Patient Receiving Long-term Total Parenteral Nutrition. *American Journal of Clinical Nutrition* 30: 531–538; Mertz, W. 1998. Interaction of Chromium with Insulin: A Progress Report. *Nutrition Reviews* 56: 174–177; Office of Dietary Supplements. Updated 2005. Chromium. Available at http://ods.od.nih.gov/factsheets/chromium.asp. Accessed June 2010.

53. Cefalu, W. T., and F. B. Hu. 2004. Role of Chromium in Human Health and in Diabetes. *Diabetes Care* 27: 2741–2751; Center for Food Safety and Applied Nutrition. 2005. Qualified Health Claims Subject to Enforcement Discretion: Chromium Picolinate and Insulin Resistance. Available at www.cfsan.fda.gov/~dms/qhccr.html. Accessed November 2005.

54. National Institutes of Health. Office of Dietary Supplements. 2005. Chromium. Available at: http://ods.od.nih.gov/factsheets/chromium .asp. Accessed August 2010.

55. Institute of Medicine. *Dietary Reference Intakes: Vitamin A.*

56. Office of Dietary Supplements. Updated 2005. Chromium. Available at http://ods.od.nih.gov/factsheets/chromium.asp. Accessed June 2010.

57. Freake, H. C. 2000. Iodine. In Stipanuk, M. H. *Biochemical and Physiological Aspects of Human Nutrition.* Philadelphia: W. B. Saunders; Stanbury, J. B., A. E. Ermans, P. Bourdoux, C. Todd, E. Oken, R. Tonglet, T. G. Vidor, L. E. Braverman, and G. Medeiros-Neto. 1998. Iodine-induced Hyperthyroidism: Occurrence and Epidemiology. *Thyroid* 8: 83–100; Institute of Medicine. *Dietary Reference Intakes: Vitamin A.*

58. Institute of Medicine. *Dietary Reference Intakes: Vitamin A.*

59. Ibid.

60. Barceloux, D. G. 1999. Manganese. *Clinical Toxicology* 37: 293–307.

61. Institute of Medicine. *Dietary Reference Intakes: Vitamin A.*

62. Ibid.

Feature Box References

1. U.S. Environmental Protection Agency. 2009. Ground Water and Drinking Water: Frequently Asked Questions. Available at www.epa.gov/safewater/faq/faq.html. Accessed June 2010.

2. Bullers, A. C. 2002. Bottled Water: Better than the Tap? *FDA Consumer Magazine.* Available at www.fda.gov/fdac/features/2002/402_h2o.html. Accessed August 2005; U.S. Environmental Protection Agency. 2010. Water on Tap: What You Need to Know. Available at www.epa.gov/safewater/wot/index.html. Accessed June 2010.

3. Centers for Disease Control and Prevention. 2009. Community Water Fluoridation: Statistics 2006. Available at www.cdc.gov/fluoridation/statistics.htm. Accessed June 2010.

4. Natural Resources Defense Council. 1999. Bottled Water: Pure Drink or Pure Hype? Available at www.nrdc.org. Accessed August 2005; San Francisco Department of Public Health, Environmental Health Section, and San Francisco Public Utilities Commission. 2004. Bottled Water vs. Tap Water: Making a Healthy Choice. Available at www.sfphes.org/water/FactSheets/bottled_water.pdf. Accessed June 2010.

5. Centers For Disease Control. Fluoride Recommendations Work Group. 2001. Recommendations for Using Fluoride to Prevent and Control Dental Caries in the United States. Morbidity and Mortality Weekly Report; 50 (RR14): 1–42. Available at www.cdc.gov/mmwr/preview/mmwrhtml/rr5014a1.htm Accessed August 2010.

6. American Heart Association. 2009. About High Blood Pressure. Available at www.americanheart.org/presenter.jhtml?identifier=468. Accessed June 2010.

7. Franklin, S. S., et al. 1997. Hemodynamic Patterns of Age-Related Changes in Blood Pressure. *Circulation* 96: 308–315. Available at www.circ.ahajournals.org/cgi/content/full/96/1/308. Accessed August 2005.

8. Chobanian, A. V., G. L. Bakris, H. R. Black, W. C. Cushman, L. A. Green, J. L. Izzo, D. W. Jones, B. J. Materson, S. Oparil, J. T. Wright, E. J. Roccella, and the National High Blood Pressure Education Program Coordinating Committee. 2003. The Seventh Report of the Joint National Committee on Prevention, Detection, Evaluation, and Treatment of High Blood Pressure. *Journal of the American Medical Association* 289: 2560–2572; National Heart, Lung, and Blood Institute. 2008. High Blood Pressure. Available at www.nhlbi.nih.gov/health/dci/Diseases/Hbp/HBP_WhatIs.html. Accessed June 2010.

9. American Heart Association. About High Blood Pressure.

10. U.S. Department of Health and Human Services. 2007. Overweight and Obesity: Health Consequences. Available at www.surgeongeneral.gov/topics/obesity/calltoaction/fact_consequences.htm. Accessed August 2010.; National Heart, Lung, and Blood Institute. 2004. The Seventh Report of the Joint National Committee on Prevention, Detection,

Evaluation, and Treatment of High Blood Pressure (JNC 7). Available at www.nhlbi.nih.gov/guidelines/hypertension/jnc7full.htm. Accessed September 2005; Wharton, S. P., A. Chin, X. Xin, and J. He. 2002. Effect of Aerobic Exercise on Blood Pressure: A Meta-analysis of Randomized Controlled Trials. *Annals of Internal Medicine* 136: 493–503.

11. Xin, X., J. He, M. G. Frontini, L. G. Ogden, O. I. Motsamai, and P. K. Whelton. 2001. Effects of Alcohol Reduction on Blood Pressure: A Meta-analysis of Randomized Controlled Trials. *Hypertension* 38: 1112–1117.

12. Harsha, D. W., P. Lin, E. Obarzanek, N. M. Karanja, T. J. Moore, and B. Caballero. 1999. Dietary Approaches to Stop Hypertension: A Summary of Study Results. *Journal of the American Dietetics Association* 99: S35–S39; Kotchen, T. A., and J. M. Kotchen. 2006. Nutrition, Diet, and Hypertension. In Shils, M. E., M. Shike, A. C. Ross, B. Caballero, and R. J. Cousins. *Modern Nutrition in Health and Disease.* 10th ed. Philadelphia, PA: Lippincott Williams and Wilkins; National Heart, Lung, and Blood Institute. 2002. Primary Prevention of Hypertension: Clinical and Public Health Advisory from the National Blood Pressure Education Program. Available at www.nhlbi.nih.gov/health/prof/heart/hbp/pphbp .pdf. Accessed September 2005.

13. National Heart, Lung, and Blood Institute. 2006. Your Guide to Lowering Your Blood Pressure with DASH. Available at www.nhlbi.nih.gov/health/public/heart/hbp/dash/new_dash.pdf. Accessed June 2010.

14. U.S. Department of Agriculture, U.S. Department of Health and Human Services. 2010. *Dietary Guidelines for Americans, 2010.* 7th ed. Washington, D.C.: U.S. Government Printing Office.

15. Patlak, M. 2001. Bone Builders: The Discoveries Behind Preventing and Treating Osteoporosis. *The FASEB Journal* 15: 1677.

16. Osteoporosis and Related Bone Diseases—National Resource Center. 2005. Osteoporosis Overview. Available at www.osteo.org/osteo.html. Accessed March 2011. U.S. Department of Health and Human Services. 2004. *Bone Health and Osteoporosis: A Report of the Surgeon General.* Washington, D.C.: U.S. Department of Health and Human Services, Office of the Surgeon General.

17. Ibid.

18. U.S. Department of Health and Human Services. *Bone Health and Osteoporosis.*

19. Office of Dietary Supplements. Updated 2009. Dietary Supplement Fact Sheet: Calcium. Available at http://ods.od.nih.gov/factsheets/calcium .asp. Accessed June 2010; U.S. Department of Health and Human Services. *Bone Health and Osteoporosis.*

20. U.S. Department of Health and Human Services. 2004. *Bone Health and Osteoporosis: Osteoporosis in Postmenopausal Women: Diagnosis and Monitoring Evidence.* Report/Technology Assessment No. 28. Agency for Healthcare Research and Quality; 2001. Publication No.: 01-E032.

21. Miller, K. K. 2003. Mechanisms by Which Nutritional Disorders Cause Reduced Bone Mass in Adults. *Journal of Women's Health* 12: 145–150.

22. Osteoporosis and Related Bone Diseases—National Resource Center. *Osteoporosis Overview.*

23. U.S. Department of Health and Human Services. *Bone Health and Osteoporosis.*

24. Ibid.

Two Points of View References

1. Centers for Disease Control and Prevention, "MMWR Report: Populations Receiving Optimally Fluoridated Public Drinking Water—United States, 1992–2006." Available at www.cdc.gov/mmwr/preview/mmwrhtml/mm5727a1.htm. Accessed July 2010.

2. American Dental Association, *Fluoridation Facts* (Chicago: American Dental Association, 2005.) Available at www.ada.org/sections/newsAndEvents/pdfs/fluoridation_facts.pdf. Accessed July 2010.

3. Ibid.

4. American Dental Hygienists Association, "Fluoride Facts." 2010. Available at www.adha.org/oralhealth/fluoride_facts.htm. Accessed July 2010.

5. American Dental Association, *Fluoridation Facts* (Chicago: American Dental Association, 2005.) Available at www.ada.org/sections/newsAndEvents/pdfs/fluoridation_facts.pdf. Accessed July 2010.

6. Ibid

7. World Health Organization, "Water-Related Diseases: Fluorosis."(2001) Available at www.who.int/water_sanitation_health/diseases/fluorosis/en. Accessed July 2010.

8. Environmental Protection Agency, "Fact Sheet: Fluoride in Drinking Water."Available at http://nlquery.epa.gov. Accessed July 2010.

9. Sierra Club, "Sierra Club Conservation Policies: Policy on Fluoride in Drinking Water." (2008) Available at www.sierraclub.org/policy/conservation/water_fluoridation.aspx. Accessed July 2010.

Chapter 9

1. Distilled Spirits Councils in the United States. 2007. Distilled Spirits Industry Primer. Available at www.discus.org/. Accessed June 2010.

2. Centers for Disease Control and Prevention. 2008. Alcohol and Public Health: General Alcohol Information. Available at www.cdc.gov/alcohol/index.htm. Accessed June 2010.

3. National Institute on Alcohol Abuse and Alcoholism. 2003. Understanding Alcohol: Investigations into Biology and Behavior. Available at http://science.education.nih.gov/supplements/nih3/alcohol/default.htm. Accessed June 2010.

4. Mandelbaum, D. G. 1965. Alcohol and Culture. *Current Anthropology* 6: 281–288; National Institute on Alcohol Abuse and Alcoholism. 1992. Moderate Drinking. Available at http://pubs.niaaa.nih.gov/publications/aa16.htm. Accessed June 2010.

5. U.S. Department of Agriculture. 2010. Report of the Dietary Guidelines Advisory Committee 2010. Available at www.cnpp.usda.gov/Publications/DietaryGuidelines/2010/DGAC/Report/D-7-Alcohol.pdf. Accessed June 2010; Goldberg, I. J., L. Mosca, M. R. Piano, and E. A. Fisher. 2001. Wine and Your Heart. A Science Advisory for Healthcare Professionals from the Nutrition Committee, Council on Epidemiology and Prevention, and Council on Cardiovascular Nursing of the American Heart Association. *Circulation* 103: 472–475.

6. Dodd, T. H., and S. Morse. 1994. The Impact of Media Stories Concerning Health Issues on Food Product Sales. *Journal of Consumer Marketing* 11: 17–24.

7. U.S. Department of Agriculture. Report of the Dietary Guidelines Advisory Committee; Goldberg, et al. Wine and Your Heart.

8. Andreasson, S., P. Allebeck, and A. Romelsjo. 1988. Alcohol and Mortality Among Young Men: Longitudinal Study of Swedish Conscripts. *British Medical Journal* 296: 1021–1025.

9. National Institute on Alcohol Abuse and Alcoholism. 2007. Alcohol Alert: Alcohol Metabolism. Available at http://pubs.niaaa.nih.gov/publications/AA72/AA72.htm. Accessed June 2010.

10. Jones, A. W., and K. A. Jonsson. 1994. Food-Induced Lowering of Blood-Ethanol Profiles and Increased Rate of Elimination Immediately After a Meal. *Journal of Forensic Sciences* 39: 1084–1093.

11. National Institute on Alcohol Abuse and Alcoholism. Alcohol Alert: Alcohol Metabolism.

12. Ibid.

13. National Institute on Alcohol Abuse and Alcoholism. 2004. Alcohol Alert: Alcohol's Damaging Effects on the Brain. Available at http://pubs.niaaa.nih.gov/publications/aa63/aa63.htm. Accessed June 2010; National Institute on Alcohol Abuse and Alcoholism. 2000. Alcohol Alert: Imaging and Alcoholism: A Window on the Brain. Available at http://pubs.niaaa.nih.gov/publications/aa47.htm. Accessed June 2010.

14. O'Brien, M., T. McCoy, S. Rhodes, A. Wagoner, and M. Wolfson. 2008. Caffeinated Cocktails: Energy Drink Consumption, High-Risk Drinking, and Alcohol-Related Consequences Among College Students. *Academy of Emergency Medicine* 15: 453–460.

15. Ferreira, S., T. deMello, S. Pompeia, and M. deSouza-Formigoni. 2006. Effects of Energy Drink Ingestion on Alcohol Intoxication. *Alcoholism: Clinical and Experimental Research* 30: 598–605.

16. Frezza, M., C. diPadova, G. Pozzato, M. Terpin, E. Baraona, and C. S. Lieber. 1990. High Blood Alcohol Levels in Women: The Role of Decreased Gastric Alcohol Dehydrogenase Activity and First-Pass Metabolism. *New England Journal of Medicine* 332: 95–99.

17. Brooks, P. J., M. A. Enoch, D. Goldman, T. K. Li, and A. Yokoyama. 2009. The Alcohol Flushing Response: An Unrecognized Risk Factor for Esophageal Cancer from Alcohol Consumption. *PLoS Medicine* 6: e1000050. doi:10.1371/journal.pmed.1000050. National Institute on Alcohol Abuse and Alcoholism. www.niaaa.nih.gov/NewsEvents/NewsReleases/alcohol_flush.htm. Accessed June 2010.

18. National Institute on Alcohol Abuse and Alcoholism. 1998. Alcohol Alert: Alcohol and Sleep. Available at www.niaaa.nih.gov/Publications/AlcoholAlerts. Accessed June 2010.

19. National Institute on Alcohol Abuse and Alcoholism. Alcohol Alert: Alcohol and Sleep; Roehrs, T., D. Beare, F. Zorick, and T. Roth. 1994. Sleepiness and Ethanol Effects on Simulated Driving. *Alcoholism: Clinical and Experimental Research* 18: 154–158.

20. Swift, R. S., and D. Davidson. 1998. Alcohol Hangover, Mechanisms and Mediators. *Alcohol Health & Research World* 22: 54–60. Available at http://pubs.niaaa.nih.gov/publications/arh22-1/54-60.pdf. Accessed June 2010.

21. Ibid.

22. National Institute on Alcohol Abuse and Alcoholism. Alcohol Alert: Alcohol Metabolism; Swift. Alcohol Hangover.

23. Ibid.

24. National Institute on Alcohol Abuse and Alcoholism. 2007. State of the Science Report on the Effects of Moderate Drinking. Available at http://pubs.niaaa.nih.gov/publications/ModerateDrinking-03.htm. Accessed June 2010; National Institute on Alcohol Abuse and Alcoholism. Updated 2000. Alcohol Alert: Alcohol and Cancer. Available at http://pubs.niaaa.nih.gov/publications/aa21.htm. Accessed June 2010; USDA. Report of the Dietary Guidelines Advisory Committee; National Institute on Alcohol Abuse and Alcoholism. 2004. Alcohol Alert: Alcohol—An Important Women's Health Issue. Available at http://pubs.niaaa.nih.gov/publications/aa62/aa62.htm. Accessed June 2010.

25. Lieber, C. S. 2000. Alcohol: Its Metabolism and Interaction with Nutrients. *Annual Review of Nutrition* 20: 394–430.

26. National Institute on Alcohol Abuse and Alcoholism. Alcohol Alert: Alcohol and Cancer; National Institute on Alcohol Abuse and Alcoholism. Alcohol Alert: Alcohol and Tobacco.

27. National Institute on Alcohol Abuse and Alcoholism. Understanding Alcohol.

28. Ibid.

29. Lieber, C. S. 2000. Alcohol: Its Metabolism and Interaction with Nutrients. *Annual Review of Nutrition* 20: 394–430.

30. National Institute on Alcohol Abuse and Alcoholism. 2000. Alcohol and the Liver: Research Update. Available at http://pubs.niaaa.nih.gov/publications/aa42.htm. Accessed January 2006.

31. National Institute on Alcohol Abuse and Alcoholism. 2005. Alcohol Alert: Alcohol and the Liver. Available at http://pubs.niaaa.nih.gov/publications/aa64/aa64.htm. Accessed June 2010.

32. Centers for Disease Control and Prevention. Alcohol and Public Health.

33. Jones, K., and D. Smith. 1973. Recognition of the Fetal Alcohol Syndrome in Early Infancy. *The Lancet* 2: 999–1001; Bertrand, J., R. L. Floyd, and M. K. Weber. 2005. Guidelines for Identifying and Referring Persons with Fetal Alcohol Syndrome. *Morbidity and Mortality Weekly Report* 54 (RR11): 1–10. Available at www.cdc.gov/mmwr/preview/mmwrhtml/rr5411a1.htm. Accessed January 2006; U.S. Department of Health and Human Services. Substance Abuse and Mental Health Services Administration. 2007. Effects of Alcohol on a Fetus. Available at http://fasdcenter.samhsa.gov/grabGo/factSheets.cfm. Accessed October 2010.

34. Bertrand, et al. Guidelines for Identifying and Referring Persons; Centers for Disease Control and Prevention. 2010. Fetal Alcohol Spectrum Disorders. Available at www.cdc.gov/ncbddd/fasd/index.html. Accessed June 2010.

35. National Institute on Alcohol Abuse and Alcoholism. Understanding Alcohol.

36. Henao, L. A. July 5, 2005. Obituary. *The Boston Globe*.

37. National Institute on Alcohol Abuse and Alcoholism. Understanding Alcohol.

38. Centers for Disease Control and Prevention. Alcohol and Public Health.

39. National Institute on Alcohol Abuse and Alcoholism. Alcohol Alert: Alcohol's Damaging Effects on the Brain; White, A. M., D. W. Jamieson-Drake, and H. S. Swartzwelder. 2002. Prevalence and Correlates of Alcohol-Induced Blackouts Among College Students: Results of an E-Mail Survey. *Journal of American College Health* 51: 117–131.

40. National Institute on Alcohol Abuse and Alcoholism. Publication No. 29 PH 357. The Genetics of Alcoholism Updated 2000. Available at http://pubs.niaaa.nih.gov/publications/aa18.htm. Accessed June 2010.

41. B.R.A.D. 21 website. Available at www.brad21.org/index.html.

42. National Institute on Alcohol Abuse and Alcoholism. Understanding Alcohol.

43. National Highway Traffic Safety Administration. 2009. Traffic Safety Facts: Crash Statistics on Alcohol-Related Fatalities in 2008. Available at http://www-nrd.nhtsa.dot.gov/pubs/811172.pdf. Accessed July 2010.

44. Centers for Disease Control and Prevention. Alcohol and Public Health.

45. National Institute on Alcohol Abuse and Alcoholism. 2006. Underage Drinking: A Major Public Health Challenge. Available at www.niaaa.nih.gov/Publications/AlcoholAlerts/default.htm. Accessed June 2010.

46. National Research Council. 2003. *Reducing Underage Drinking: A Collective Responsibility*. Washington, D.C.: The National Academies Press.

47. National Institute on Alcohol Abuse and Alcoholism. Underage Drinking; National Institute on Alcohol Abuse and Alcoholism. 2008. Research Findings on Underage Drinking and the Minimum Legal Drinking Age. Available at www.niaaa.nih.gov/AboutNIAAA/NIAAASponsoredPrograms/drinkingage.htm. Accessed June 2010.

48. American Medical Association. 2003. The Minimum Legal Drinking Age: Facts and Fallacies. Available at www.ama-assn.org. Accessed December 2005.

49. National Institute on Alcohol Abuse and Alcoholism. Underage Drinking.
50. Ibid.
51. National Institute on Alcohol Abuse and Alcoholism. 2007. College Drinking, Changing the Culture; FAQs on Alcohol Abuse and Alcoholism Available at: http://www.collegedrinkingprevention.gov/OtherAlcoholInformation/FAQsonAlcoholAbuseandAlcoholism.aspx#inherited. Accessed July 2010.
52. Alcoholics Anonymous. 2004. Membership Survey. Available at www.aa.org. Accessed January 2006.
53. U.S. Department of Agriculture. Report of the Dietary Guidelines Advisory Committee.

Feature Box References

1. Austin, E., and S. Hust. 2005. Targeting Adolescents? The Content and Frequency of Alcoholic and Nonalcoholic Beverage Ads in Magazine and Video Formats November 1999–April 2000. *Journal of Health Communications* 10: 769–785.
2. Austin, E., M. Chen, and J. Grube. 2006. How Does Alcohol Advertising Influence Underage Drinking? The Role of Desirability, Identification, and Skepticism. *Journal of Adolescent Health* 38: 376–384.

Two Points of View References

1. M. Maclure, "Demonstration of Deductive Meta-Analysis: Ethanol Intake and Risk of Myocardial Infarction," *Epidemilogic Reviews* 15 (1993): 328–351; J. M. Gaziano, J. E. Buring, J. L. Breslow, S. Z. Goldhaber, B. Rosner, M. VanDenburgh, W. Willett, and C. H. Hennekens, "Moderate Alcohol Intake, Increased Levels of High-Density Lipoprotein and Its Subfractions, and Decreased Risk of Myocardial Infarction," *New England Journal of Medicine* 329 (1993): 1829–1834; Mitchell S. V. Elkind, MD, MS, Robert Sciacca, DEngSc, et al., "Moderate Alcohol Consumption Reduces Risk of Ischemic Stroke," *Stroke* 37 (2006): 13. Available at http://stroke.ahajournals.org/cgi/content/full/37/1/13#R1-437806. Accessed July 2010.
2. D. J. Hanson, PhD, "Alcohol: Problems and Solutions," *Alcohol and Health.* Available at www2.potsdam.edu/hansondj/AlcoholAndHealth.html. Accessed July 2010.
3. Ibid.
4. C. Walker, "Vitamins in Beer," *Brewing Research International* (2008) Available at www.aim-digest.com/gateway/pages/general/articles/vitamins.htm. Accessed July 2010.
5. R. W. Hingson, T. Heeren, M. Winter, and H. Wechsler, "Magnitude of Alcohol-Related Mortality and Morbidity among U.S. College Students Ages 18–24: Changes from 1998 to 2001," *Annual Review of Public Health* 26 (2005): 259–79.
6. H. W. Perkins, "Surveying the Damage: A Review of Research on Consequences of Alcohol Misuse in College Populations" *Journal of Studies on Alcohol and Drug,* Supplement No. 14 (2002): 91-100. Available at www.collegedrinkingprevention.gov/supportingresearch/Journal/perkins.aspx. Accessed July 2010.
7. R. W. Hingson, T. Heeren, A. Jamanka, and J. Howland, "Age of Onset and Unintentional Injury Involvement after Drinking," *Journal of the American Medical Association* 284 (2000): 1527–1533.
8. A. Masten, V. Faden, and R. Zucker, *A Developmental Perspective on Underage Alcohol Use,* Vol. 32, no. 1 (2009). National Institute on Alcohol Abuse and Alcoholism. Available at http://pubs.niaaa.nih.gov/publications/arh321/3-15.htm. Accessed July 2010.
9. Ibid.

Chapter 10

1. Centers for Disease Control. 2010. Obesity and Overweight. Available at www.cdc.gov/nchs/fastats/overwt.htm. Accessed March 2011.
2. IFIC Foundation. 2005. Food for Thought VI, Reporting of Diet, Nutrition, and Food Safety News. Available at www.foodinsight.org.
3. Mintel Reports: USA, Health and Medical: USA, Health and Wellness: USA. 2005. Commercial Weight Loss Programs–U.S. Available at http://academic.mintel.com/sinatra/oxygen/display/id=121277. Accessed May 2010.
4. Centers for Disease Control and Prevention Economic Consequences of Overweight and Obesity. Available at www.cdc.gov/obesity/causes/economics.html. Accessed May 2010.
5. Centers for Disease Control and Prevention. 2008. Healthy Weight: Introduction. Available at www.cdc.gov/nccdphp/dnpa/healthyweight/index.htm. Accessed May 2010.
6. Centers for Disease Control and Prevention. 2010. Overweight and Obesity.

7. National Institutes of Health. 1998. Clinical Guidelines on the Identification, Evaluation, and Treatment of Overweight and Obesity in Adults. Available at http://www.nhlbi.nih.gov/guidelines/obesity/ob_gdlns.pdf. Accessed May 2010.
8. Ibid.
9. National Center for Health Statistics. 2010. Health, United States, 2009: With Special Feature on Medical Technology. Hyattsville, MD. Available at www.cdc.gov/nchs/data/hus/hus09.pdf#067. Accessed April 2010.
10. Gee, M., L. Mahan, and S. Escott-Stump. 2008. Weight Management. In L. Mahan and S. Escott-Stump, eds., *Krause's Food, Nutrition, and Diet Therapy.* 12th ed. Philadelphia: Saunders.
11. Hammond, K. 2008. Assessment: Dietary and Clinical Data. In L. Mahan and S. Escott-Stump, eds., *Krause's Food, Nutrition, and Diet Therapy.* 12th ed. Philadelphia: Saunders.
12. U.S. Department of Health and Human Services. 2002. A Century of Women's Health, 1900–2000. Available at www.womenshealth.gov/archive/owh/pub/century. Accessed March 2010.
13. National Institutes of Health. Clinical Guidelines on the Identification, Evaluation, and Treatment of Overweight and Obesity in Adults.
14. Ibid.
15. Ibid.
16. Institute of Medicine. 2002. *Dietary Reference Intakes for Energy, Carbohydrate, Fiber, Fat, Fatty Acids, Cholesterol, Protein, and Amino Acids.* Available at www.iom.edu. Accessed March 2010.
17. Hoffer, L. J. 2006. Metabolic Consequences of Starvation. In M. Shils, et al., eds., *Modern Nutrition in Health and Disease.* 10th ed. Philadelphia: Lippincott Williams & Wilkins.
18. Mattes, R., J. Hollis, D. Hayes, and A. Stunkard. 2005. Appetite: Measurement and Manipulations Misgivings. *Journal of the American Dietetic Association* 105 (supplement): S87–S97.
19. Smith, G. 2006. Controls of Food Intake. In M. Shils, et al., eds., *Modern Nutrition.*
20. Mattes. Appetite: Measurement and Manipulations Misgivings.
21. Smith. Controls of Food Intake.
22. Geliebter, A., S. Schachter, C. Lohmann-Walter, et al. 1996. Reduced Stomach Capacity in Obese Subjects After Dieting. *American Journal of Clinical Nutrition* 63: 170–173.
23. Center for Genomics and Public Health. 2004. Obesity and Current Topics in Genetics. Available at http://depts.washington.edu/cgph/Obesity.htm. Accessed March 2010.
24. Hill, J., V. Catenacci, and H. Wyatt. 2006. Obesity: Etiology. In M. Shils et al., eds., *Modern Nutrition.*
25. Hill. Obesity: Etiology.
26. Bray, G., and C. Champagne. 2005. Beyond Energy Balance: There Is More to Obesity than Kilocalories. *Journal of the American Dietetic Association* 105 (supplement): S17–S23.
27. Brodsky, I. 2006. Hormones and Growth Factors. In M. Shils et al., eds., *Modern Nutrition.*
28. Hill. Obesity: Etiology.
29. Ibid.
30. Bray. Beyond Energy Balance; Loos, R., and T. Rankinen. 2005. Gene-Diet Interactions on Body Weight Changes. *Journal of the American Dietetic Association* 105 (supplement): S29–S34.
31. Gale, S., T. Van Itallie, and I. Faust. 1981. Effects of Palatable Diets on Body Weight and Adipose Tissue Cellularity in the Adult Obese Female Zucker Rat (fa/fa). *Metabolism* 30: 105–110.
32. Ravussin, E., M. Valencia, J. Esparza, P. Bennett, and L. Schulz. 1994. Effects of a Traditional Lifestyle on Obesity in Pima Indians. *Diabetes Care* 17: 1067–1074; Wang, S., and K. Brownell. 2005. Public Policy and Obesity: The Need to Marry Science with Advocacy. *Psychiatric Clinics of North America* 28: 235–252.
33. The Keystone Group. 2006. The Keystone Forums on Away-From-Home Food, Opportunities for Preventing Weight Gain and Obesity. Available at http://keystone.org/files/file/about/publications/Forum_Report_FINAL_5-30-06.pdf. Accessed March 2010.
34. Ibid.
35. Wang. Public Policy and Obesity.
36. The Keystone Group. The Keystone Forums on Away-From-Home Food.
37. The Keystone Group. The Keystone Forums on Away-From-Home Food; Clemens, L., D. Slawson, and R. Klesges. 1999. The Effect of Eating Out on Quality of Diet in Premenopausal Women. *Journal of the American Dietetic Association* 99: 442–444.
38. The Keystone Group. The Keystone Forums on Away-From-Home Food; Meyers, A., A. Stunkard, and M. Coll. 1980. Food Accessibility and Food Choice. *Archives of General Psychiatry* 37: 1133–1135.

39. The Keystone Group. The Keystone Forums on Away-From-Home Food; Rolls, B. 1986. Sensory-Specific Satiety. *Nutrition Reviews* 44: 93–101.

40. Rolls, B. 2003. The Supersizing of America. *Nutrition Today* 38: 42–53.

41. Wansink, B. 1996. Can Package Size Accelerate Usage Volume? *Journal of Marketing* 60: 1–14.

42. Rolls, B., L. Roe, and J. Meengs. 2006. Larger Portion Sizes Lead to a Sustained Increase in Energy Intake over 2 Days. *Journal of the American Dietetic Association* 106: 543–549.

43. USDA Economic Research Service. 2010. Data Sets. Food Availability. Available at www.ers.usda.gov/data; Putnam, J., J. Allshouse, and L. Kantor. 2002. U.S. Per Capita Food Supply Trends: More Calories, Refined Carbohydrates, and Fats. Economic Research Service, USDA. *FoodReview* 25: 2–15; French, S., M. Story, and R. Jeffery. 2001. Environmental Influences on Eating and Physical Activity. *Annual Reviews of Public Health* 22: 309–335.

44. French. Environmental Influences on Eating.

45. Mummery, W., G. Schofield, R. Steele, E. Eakin, and B. Brown. 2005. Occupational Sitting Time and Overweight and Obesity in Australian Workers. *American Journal of Preventative Medicine* 29: 91–97.

46. French. Environmental Influences on Eating.

47. Wang. Public Policy and Obesity.

48. Lanningham-Foster, L., L. Nysse, and J. Levine. 2003. Labor Saved, Calories Lost: The Energetic Impact of Domestic Labor-Saving Devices. *Obesity Research* 11: 1178–1181.

49. Ibid.

50. Centers for Disease Control and Prevention. 2003. Prevalence of Physical Activity, Including Lifestyle Activities Among Adults—United States, 2000–2001. *Morbidity and Mortality Weekly Report* 52: 763–769. Available at www.cdc.gov/mmwr/preview/mmwrhtml/mm5232a2.htm. Accessed May 2010.

51. Centers for Disease Control and Prevention. 2005. Trends in Leisure-Time Physical Inactivity by Age, Sex, and Race/Ethnicity—United States, 1994–2004. *Morbidity and Mortality Weekly Report* 54: 991–994. Available at www.cdc.gov/mmwr/preview/mmwrhtml/mm5439a5htm. Accessed May 2010.

52. Nielsen Media Research. 2008. Americans Cannot Get Enough of Their Screen Time. Available at http://en-us.nielsen.com/main/news/news_releases/2008/november/americans_cannot_get. Accessed May 2010.

53. The Kaiser Family Foundation. 2010. Daily Media Use Among Children and Teens Up Dramatically from Five Years Ago. Available at www.kff.org/entmedia/entmedia012010nr.cfm. Accessed May 2010.

54. National Institutes of Health. Clinical Guidelines.

55. Mattes. Appetite: Measurement and Manipulations Misgivings; Lissner, L., D. Levitsky, B. Strupp, H. Kalkwarf, and D. Roe. 1987. Dietary Fat and the Regulation of Energy Intake in Human Subjects. *American Journal of Clinical Nutrition* 46: 886–892.

56. Tohill, B., J. Seymour, M. Serdula, L. Kettel-Khan, and B. Rolls. 2004. What Epidemiologic Studies Tell Us about the Relationship between Fruit and Vegetable Consumption and Body Weight. *Nutrition Reviews* 62: 365–374.

57. Rolls, B., E. Bell, and E. Thorwart. 1999. Water Incorporated into a Food but Not Served with a Food Decreases Energy Intake in Lean Women. *American Journal of Clinical Nutrition* 70: 448–455.

58. Burton-Freeman, B. 2000. Dietary Fiber and Energy Regulation. *Journal of Nutrition* 130: 272S–275S.

59. Davis, J., V. Hodges, and B. Gillham. 2006. Normal-Weight Adults Consume More Fiber and Fruit than Their Age- and Height-Matched Overweight/Obese Counterparts. *Journal of the American Dietetic Association* 106: 833–840.

60. Mattes. Appetite: Measurement and Manipulations Misgivings.

61. U.S. Department of Agriculture, U.S. Department of Health and Human Services. 2010. *Dietary Guidelines for Americans, 2010*. 7th ed. Washington, D.C.: U.S. Government Printing Office; Saries, W., S. Blair, M. van Baak, et al. 2003. How Much Physical Activity Is Enough to Prevent Unhealthy Weight Gain? Outcome of the IASO Stock Conference and Consensus Statement. *Obesity Reviews* 4: 101–114.

62. Keim, N., C. Blanton, and M. Kretsch. 2004. America's Obesity Epidemic: Measuring Physical Activity to Promote an Active Lifestyle. *Journal of the American Dietetic Association* 104: 1398–1409.

63. Jakicic, J., and A. Otto. 2005. Physical Activity Consideration for the Treatment and Prevention of Obesity. *American Journal of Clinical Nutrition* 82: 226S–229S.

64. Shape Up America! Not dated. 10,000 Steps. Available at www.shapeup.org/shape/steps.php. Accessed May 2010.

65. Edwards, J., and H. Meiselman. 2003. Changes in Dietary Habits during the First Year at University. *British Nutrition Foundation Nutrition Bulletin* 28: 21–34.

66. Graham, M., and A. Jones. 2002. Freshman 15: Valid Theory or Harmful Myth? *Journal of American College Health* 50: 171–173.

67. Poston, W., and J. Foreyt. 2000. Successful Management of the Obese Patient. *American Family Physician* 61: 3615–3622.

68. Schlundt, D., J. Hill, T. Sbrocco, J. Pope-Cordle, and T. Sharp. 1992. The Role of Breakfast in the Treatment of Obesity: A Randomized Clinical Trial. *American Journal of Clinical Nutrition* 55: 645–651.

69. Rosenbaum, M., R. Leibel, and J. Hirsch. 1997. Obesity. *New England Journal of Medicine* 337: 396–407.

70. National Institute of Diabetes and Digestive and Kidney Diseases. 2006. Weight Cycling. Available at http://win.niddk.nih.gov/publications/cycling.htm. Accessed May 2010.

71. Rosenbaum, M. Obesity; Klem, M. L., R. R. Wing, M. T. McGuire, H. M. Seagle, and J. O. Hill. 1997. A Descriptive Study of Individuals Successful at Long-Term Maintenance of Substantial Weight Loss. *American Journal of Clinical Nutrition* 66: 239–246.

72. Klem. A Descriptive Study of Individuals Successful at Long-Term Maintenance of Substantial Weight Loss.

73. Hill, J., H. Wyatt, G. Reed, and J. Peters. 2003. Obesity and the Environment: Where Do We Go from Here? *Science* 299: 853–897.

74. Hill, J., H. Thompson, and H. Wyatt. 2005. Weight Maintenance: What's Missing? *Journal of the American Dietetic Association* 105: S63–S66.

75. U.S. Department of Health and Human Services. 2005. Report of the Dietary Guidelines Advisory Committee on the *Dietary Guidelines for Americans 2005*. Available at www.health.gov/DietaryGuidelines/dga2005/report. Accessed May 2010.

76. Ibid.

77. National Eating Disorders Association. Information and Resources. Available at www.nationaleatingdisorders.org/information-resources/general-information.php#facts-statistics. Accessed May 2010.

78. Chamorro, R., and Y. Flores-Ortiz. 2000. Acculturation and Disordered Eating Patterns among Mexican American Women. *International Journal of Eating Disorders* 28: 125–129; Crago, M., C. M. Shisslak, and L. S. Estes. 1996. Eating Disturbances among American Minority Groups: A Review. *International Journal of Eating Disorders* 19: 239–248; Kjelsas, E., C. Bjornstrom, and K. G. Gotestam. 2004. Prevalence of Eating Disorders in Female and Male Adolescents (14–15 Years). *Eating Behaviors* 5: 13–25; O'Dea, J., and S. Abraham. 2002. Eating and Exercise Disorders in Young College Men. *Journal of American College Health* 50: 273–278.

79. Strober, M., and C. M. Bulik. 2002. Genetic Epidemiology of Eating Disorders. In D. G. Fairburn and K. D. Brownell, eds. *Eating Disorders and Obesity: A Comprehensive Handbook*. 2nd ed. New York: Guilford Press, 238–242.

80. Lilenfeld, L. R. R., S. Wonderlich, L. P. Riso, R. Crosby, and J. Mitchell. 2005. Eating Disorders and Personality: A Methodological and Empirical Review. *Clinical Psychology Review* 26: 299–320.

81. Woodside, D. B., P. E. Garfinkel, E. Lin, P. Goering, A. S. Kaplan, D. S. Goldbloom, and S. H. Kennedy. 2001. Comparisons of Men with Full or Partial Eating Disorders, Men without Eating Disorders, and Women with Eating Disorders in the Community. *American Journal of Psychiatry* 158: 570–574.

82. Birketvedt, G. S., J. Florholmen, J. Sundsfjord, B. Osterud, D. Dinges, W. Bilker, and A. Stunkard. 1999. Behavioral and Neuroendocrine Characteristics of the Night Eating Syndrome. *Journal of the American Medical Association* 282: 657–663.

83. Marshall, H. M., K. C. Allison, J. P. O'Reardon, G. Birketvedt, and A. J. Stunkard. 2004. Night Eating Syndrome among Nonobese Persons. *International Journal of Eating Disorders* 35: 217–222.

84. Birketvedt. Behavioral and Neuroendocrine Characteristics of the Night Eating Syndrome.

85. Gluck, M., A. Geliebter, and T. Satov. 2001. Night Eating Syndrome Is Associated with Depression, Low Self-Esteem, Reduced Daytime Hunger, and Less Weight Loss in Obese Outpatients. *Obesity Research* 9: 264–267.

86. Birketvedt, G. S., J. Sundsfjord, and J. R. Florholmen. 2002. Hypothalamic-Pituitary-Adrenal Axis in the Night Eating Syndrome. *American Journal of Physiology - Endocrinology and Metabolism* 282: E366–E369.

Feature Box References

1. Stein, K. 2000. High-Protein, Low-Carbohydrate Diets: Do They Work? *Journal of the American Dietetic Association* 100: 760–761.

2. Freedman, M., J. King, and E. Kennedy. 2001. Popular Diets: A Scientific Review. *Obesity Research* 9: 1S–40S.

3. Dansinger, M., J. Gleason, J. Griffith, H. Selker, and E. Schaefer. 2005. Comparison of the Atkins, Ornish, Weight Watchers, and Zone Diets for Weight Loss and Heart Disease Risk Reduction. *Journal of the American Medical Association* 293: 43–53.

4. Yudkin, J., and M. Carey. 1960. The Treatment of Obesity by the "High-fat" Diet: The Inevitability of Calories. *The Lancet* 2: 939–941.

5. Ornish, D. 2004. Was Dr. Atkins Right? *Journal of the American Dietetic Association* 104: 537–542.

6. Denke, M. 2001. Metabolic Effects of High-Protein, Low-Carbohydrate Diets. *The American Journal of Cardiology* 88: 59–61.

7. Ibid.

8. Federal Trade Commission. 2000. Marketers of "The Enforma System" Settle FTC Charges of Deceptive Advertising for Their Weight Loss Products. Available at www.quackwatch.org/02ConsumerProtection/FTCActions/enforma.html. Accessed May 2010; Federal Trade Commission. 2010. Marketers of Unproven Weight Loss Products Ordered to Pay Nearly $2 Million. Available at www.ftc.gov/opa/2010/01/diet.shtm. Accessed May 2010.

9. Dwyer, J., D. Allison, and P. Coates. 2005. Dietary Supplements in Weight Reduction. *Journal of the American Dietetic Association* 105: S80–S86; Pittler, M., and E. Ernst. 2004. Dietary Supplements for Body-Weight Reduction: A Systematic Review. *American Journal of Clinical Nutrition* 79: 529–536.

10. Pittler. Dietary Supplements for Body-Weight Reduction.

11. Dwyer. Dietary Supplements in Weight Reduction.

12. National Heart, Lung, and Blood Institute. 1998. Clinical Guidelines on the Identification, Evaluation, and Treatment of Overweight and Obesity in Adults. Available at www.nhlbi.nih.gov/guidelines/obesity/ob_gdlns.htm. Accessed May 2010.

13. Mariant, M. 2005. Oprah Regrets Her 1988 Liquid Diet. *USA Today* (November). Available at www.usatoday.com/life/people/2005-11-16-oprah-liquid-diet_x.htm. Accessed May 2010.

14. DeWald, T., L. Khaodhiar, M. Donahue, and G. Blackburn. 2006. Pharmacological and Surgical Treatments for Obesity. *American Heart Journal* 151: 604–624.

15. Food and Drug Administration. 2010. FDA Drug Safety Communication: Completed safety review of Senical/Alli (orlistat) and severe liver injury. Available at: http://www.fda.gov/Drugs/DrugSafety/PostmarketDrugSafetyInformationforPatientsandProviders/ucm213038.htm. Accessed June 2010.

16. National Institutes of Health, Weight Control Information Network. 2010. Longitudinal Assessment of Bariatric Surgery. Available at http://win.niddk.nih.gov/publications/labs.htm. Accessed May 2010.

17. Crookes, P. 2006. Surgical Treatment of Morbid Obesity. *Annual Review of Medicine* 57: 243–264.

18. DeWald. Pharmacological and Surgical Treatments for Obesity; Crookes. Surgical Treatment of Morbid Obesity.

19. National Eating Disorders Association. 2005. Handout on Body Image. Available at www.nationaleatingdisorders.org/nedaDir/files/documents/handouts/BodyImag.pdf. Accessed May 2010.

20. Ibid.

21. Ibid.

22. Koran, L. M., E. Abujaoude, M. D. Large, and R. T. Serpe. 2008. The Prevalence of Body Dysmorphic Disorder in the United States Adult Population. *CNS Spectrums* 13: 316–322. Abstract available at www.ncbi.nlm.nih.gov/pubmed/18408651?ordinalpos=19&itool=EntrezSystem2.PEntrez.Pubmed.Pubmed_ResultsPanel.Pubmed_RVDocSum. Accessed May 2010.

23. Pope, H. G. Jr., A. J. Gruber, P. Choi, R. Olivardia, and K. A. Phillips. 1997. Muscle Dysmorphia: An Under-Recognized Form of Body Dysmorphic Disorder. *Psychosomatics*. 38: 548–557. Abstract available at www.ncbi.nlm.nih.gov/pubmed/9427852. Accessed May 2010.

24. National Eating Disorders Association. 2005. Handout on Enhancing Male Body Image. Available at www.nationaleatingdisorders.org/nedaDir/files/documents/handouts/MalesEnh.pdf. Accessed May 2010.

Two Points of View References

1. Mayoclinic.com, "Definition of Gastric Bypass Surgery." Available at www.mayoclinic.com/health/gastric-bypass/my00825. Accessed August 2010.

2. Ibid.

3. Weight Control Information Network, "Bariatric Surgery for Severe Obesity." (March 2009) Available at http://win.niddk.nih.gov/publications/gastric.htm. Accessed August 2010.

4. CDC, "Health Topics: Childhood Obesity." October 2008. Available at www.cdc.gov/HealthyYouth/obesity/. Accessed August 2010.

5. R. Strauss, "Childhood Obesity and Self-Esteem," *Pediatrics* 105 no. 1 (January 2000): e15. Available at http://pediatrics.aappublications.org/cgi/content/abstract/105/1/e15. Accessed August 2010.

6. J. Han, D. Lawlor, and S. Kimm, "Childhood Obesity," *The Lancet* 375 no. 9727 (May 2010): 1737–1748. Abstract available at www.thelancet.com/journals/lancet/article/PIIS0140-6736%2810%2960171-7/abstract. Accessed August 2010.

7. R. T. Soper, E. E. Mason, K. J. Printen, and H. Zellweger, "Gastric Bypass for Morbid Obesity in Children and Adolescents," *Journal of Pediatric Surgery* 10 no. 1 (February 1975): 51–58. Available at www.ncbi.nlm.nih.gov/pubmed/1117394. Accessed August 2010.

8. T. Inge, J. Bean, et al., "Reversal of Type 2 Diabetes Mellitus and Improvements in Cardiovascular Risk Factors After Surgical Weight Loss in Adolescents," *Pediatrics* 123 no. 1 (January 2009): 214–222 (doi:10.1542/peds.2008-0522). Available at http://pediatrics.aappublications.org/cgi/content/abstract/123/1/214. Accessed August 2010.

9. P. O'Brien, S. Sawyer, et al., "Laparoscopic Adjustable Gastric Banding in Severely Obese Adolescents," *JAMA* 303 no. 6 (February 2010): 519–526. Abstract available at http://jama.ama-assn.org/cgi/content/abstract/303/6/519. Accessed August 2010.

10. Medline Plus, "Gastric Bypass Surgery." (updated May 2010). Available at www.nlm.nih.gov/medlineplus/ency/article/007199.htm. Accessed August 2010.

11. R Strauss, L. Bradley, and R. Brolin, "Gastric Bypass Surgery in Adolescents with Morbid Obesity," *Nutrition in Clinical Practice* no. 17 (February 2002): 43, Abstract available at http://ncp.sagepub.com/content/17/1/43.1.abstract. Accessed August 2010.

12. L. Beil, "Surgery for Obese Children?" *The New York Times* (February 2010). Available at www.nytimes.com/2010/02/16/health/16teen.html?pagewanted=1&_r=1. Accessed August 2010; H. Ippisch, T. Jenkins, T. Inge, and T. Kimball, "Do Acute Improvements in LV Mass and Diastolic Function Following Adolescent Bariatric Surgery Persist at Two Years Post-op?" *Circulation* 120 (2009): S474. Available at http://circ.ahajournals.org/cgi/content/meeting_abstract/120/18_MeetingAbstracts/S474-b?maxtoshow=&hits=10&RESULTFORMAT=&fulltext=Ippisch&searchid=1&FIRSTINDEX=0&resourcetype=HWCIT. Accessed August 2010.

13. Beil. "Surgery for Obese Children?"

14. Ibid.

Chapter 11

1. U.S. Department of Health and Human Services. 2011. *Healthy People 2020*. Available at www.healthypeople.gov/2020/topicsobjectives2020/objectiveslist.aspx?topicid=33. Accessed March 2011.

2. U.S. Department of Health and Human Services. 2008. *Physical Activity Guidelines for Americans*. Available at www.Health.gov/paguidelines/guidelines/default.aspx#toc. Accessed February 2010.

3. Herbert, R. D., and M. de Noronha. 2007. Stretching to Prevent or Reduce Muscle Soreness after Exercise. *Cochrane Database of Systematic Reviews* 4.

4. Thacker, Stephen B., et al. 2004. The Impact of Stretching on Sports Injury Risk: A Systematic Review of the Literature. *Medicine & Science in Sports & Exercise* 3: 371–378.

5. Romijn, J. A., E. F. Coyle, L. S. Sidossis, A. Gastaldelli, J. F. Horowitz, E. Endert, and R. R. Wolfe. 1993. Regulation of Endogenous Fat and Carbohydrate Metabolism in Relation to Exercise Intensity and Duration. *American Journal of Physiology - Endocrinology and Metabolism* 265: E380–E391.

6. Costill, D., R. Thomas, R. Robergs, D. Pascoe, C. Lambert, S. Barr, and W. Fink. 1991. Adaptations to Swimming Training: Influence of Training Volume. *Medicine & Science in Sports & Exercise* 23: 371–377; Sherman, W., M. Peden, and D. Wright. 1991 Carbohydrate Feedings 1 Hour Before Exercise Improves Cycling Performance. *American Journal of Clinical Nutrition* 54: 866–870.

7. Coyle, E. F., A. R. Coggan, M. K. Hemmert, and J. L. Ivy. 1986. Muscle Glycogen Utilization during Prolonged Strenuous Exercise When Fed Carbohydrate. *Journal of Applied Physiology* 61: 165–172; Hargreaves, M. 2004. Muscle Glycogen and Metabolic Regulation. *Proceedings of the Nutrition Society* 63: 217–220.

8. Rosenbloom, C., ed. 2000. *Sports Nutrition: A Guide for the Professional Working with Active People*. 3rd ed. Chicago: The American Dietetic Association, 16.

9. American College of Sports Medicine, American Dietetic Association, and Dietitians of Canada. 2000. Nutrition and Athletic Performance Joint Position Statement. *Medicine & Science in Sports & Exercise* 32: 2130–2145.

10. Ibid.

11. Brownell, K. D., S. N. Steen, and J. H. Wilmore. 1987. Weight Regulation Practices in Athletes: Analysis of Metabolic and Health Effects. *Medicine & Science in Sports & Exercise* 19: 546–556; Horvath, P. J., C. K. Eagen, S. D. Ryer-Calvin, and D. R. Pendergast. 2000. The Effects of Varying Dietary Fat on the Nutrient Intake in Male and Female Runners. *Journal of the American College of Nutrition* 19: 42–51.

12. American College of Sports Medicine, American Dietetic Association, and Dietitians of Canada. Nutrition and Athletic Performance Joint Position Statement.

13. Yaspelkis, B. B., J. G. Patterson, P. A. Anderla, Z. Ding, and J. L. Ivy. 1993. Carbohydrate Supplementation Spares Muscle Glycogen During Variable-Intensity Exercise. *Journal of Applied Physiology* 75: 1477–1485; Coyle, E. F., J. M. Hagberg, B. F. Hurley, W. H. Martin, A. A. Ehsani, and J. O. Holloszy. 1983. Carbohydrate Feeding During Prolonged Strenuous Exercise Can Delay Fatigue. *Journal of Applied Physiology* 55: 230–235.

14. Miller, S. L., K. D. Tipton, D. L. Chinkes, S. E. Wolf, and R. R. Wolfe. 2003. Independent and Combined Effects of Amino Acids and Glucose After Resistance Exercise. *Medicine & Science in Sports & Exercise* 35: 449–455.

15. Koopman, R., D. L. Pannemans, A. E. Jeukendrup, A. P. Gijsen, J. M. Senden, D. Halliday, W. H. Saris, L. J. van Loon, and A. J. Wagenmakers. 2004. Combined Ingestion of Protein and Carbohydrate Improves Protein Balance During Ultra-Endurance Exercise. *American Journal of Physiology - Endocrinology and Metabolism* 287: E712–E720.

16. Ivy, J. L., A. L. Katz, C. L. Cutler, W. M. Sherman, and E. F. Coyle. 1988. Muscle Glycogen Synthesis After Exercise: Effect of Time of Carbohydrate Ingestion. *Journal of Applied Physiology* 64: 1480–1485.

17. Roy, B. D., M. A. Tarnopolsky, J. D. MacDougall, J. Fowles, and K. E. Yarasheski. 1997. Effect of Glucose Supplement Timing on Protein Metabolism After Resistance Training. *Journal of Applied Physiology* 82: 1882–1888.

18. Rasmussen, B. B., K. D. Tipton, S. L. Miller, S. E. Wolf, and R. R. Wolfe. 2000. An Oral Essential Amino Acid-Carbohydrate Supplement Enhances Muscle Protein Anabolism after Resistance Exercise. *Journal of Applied Physiology* 88: 386–392; Zawadzki, K. M., B. B. Yaspelkis, and J. L. Ivy. 1992. Carbohydrate-Protein Complex Increases the Rate of Muscle Glycogen Storage after Exercise. *Journal of Applied Physiology* 72: 1854–1859.

19. Zawadzki. Carbohydrate-Protein Complex; Ivy, J. L., H. W. Goforth, B. M. Damon, T. R. McCauley, E. C. Parsons, and T. B. Price. 2002. Early Postexercise Muscle Glycogen Recovery Is Enhanced with a Carbohydrate-Protein Supplement. *Journal of Applied Physiology* 93: 1337–1344.

20. Karp, J. R., J. D. Johnston, S. Tecklenburg, T. D. Mickleborough, A. D. Fly, and J. M. Stager. 2006. Chocolate Milk as a Post-Exercise Recovery Aid. *International Journal of Sport Nutrition and Exercise Metabolism* 16: 78–91.

21. McAnulty, S. R., L. S. McAnulty, D. C. Nieman, J. D. Morrow, L. A. Shooter, S. Holmes, C. Heward, and D. A. Henson. 2005. Effect of Alpha-Tocopherol Supplementation on Plasma Homocysteine and Oxidative Stress in Highly Trained Athletes Before and After Exhaustive Exercise. *Journal of Nutritional Biochemistry* 16: 530–537; Nieman, D. C., D. A. Henson, S. R. McAnulty, L. S. McAnulty, N. S. Swick, A. C. Utter, D. M. Vinci, S. J. Opiela, and J. D. Morrow. 2002. Influence of Vitamin C Supplementation on Oxidative and Immune Changes After an Ultramarathon. *Journal of Applied Physiology* 92: 1970–1977.

22. Dubnov, G., and N. W. Constantini. 2004. Prevalence of Iron Depletion and Anemia in Top-Level Basketball Players. *International Journal of Sport Nutrition and Exercise Metabolism* 14: 30–37.

23. Gropper, S. S., D. Glessing, K. Dunham, and J. M. Barksdale. 2006. Iron Status of Female Collegiate Athletes Involved in Different Sports. *Biological Trace Element Research* 109: 1–14; Dubnov. Prevalence of Iron Depletion.

24. Klesges, R. C., K. D. Ward, M. L. Shelton, W. B. Applegate, E. D. Cantler, G. M. Palmieri, K. Harmon, and J. Davis. 1996. Changes in Bone Mineral Content in Male Athletes: Mechanisms of Action and Intervention Effects. *Journal of the American Medical Association* 276: 226–230.

25. Krumbach, C. J., D. R. Ellis, and J. A. Driskell. 1999. A Report of Vitamin and Mineral Supplement Use Among University Athletes in a Division I Institution. *International Journal of Sport Nutrition and Exercise Metabolism* 9: 416–425; Herbold, N. H., B. K. Visconti, S. Frates, and L. Bandini.

2004. Traditional and Nontraditional Supplement Use by Collegiate Female Varsity Athletes. *International Journal of Sport Nutrition and Exercise Metabolism* 14: 586–593.

26. Singh, A., F. M. Moses, and P. A. Deuster. 1992. Chronic Multivitamin-Mineral Supplementation Does Not Enhance Physical Performance. *Medicine & Science in Sports & Exercise* 24: 726–732.

27. C. Rosenbloom. *Sports Nutrition.*

28. Wilk, B., and O. Bar-Or. 1996. Effect of Drink Flavor and NaCl on Voluntary Drinking and Hydration in Boys Exercising in the Heat. *Journal of Applied Physiology* 80: 1112–1117.

29. American College of Sports Medicine. 1996. Position Stand on Exercise and Fluid Replacement. *Medicine & Science in Sports & Exercise* 28: i–vii.

30. McGee, W. 2005. Caffeine in the Diet. National Institutes of Health Medline Plus Medical Encyclopedia. Available at www.nlm.nih.gov/medlineplus/ency/article/002445.htm.

31. USA Track & Field. Press Release April 19, 2003. USATF Announces Major Change in Hydration Guidelines. Available at www.usatf.org/news/showRelease.asp?article=/news/releases/2003-04-19-2.xml.

32. Greenhaff, P. L., A. Casey, A. H. Short, R. Harris, K. Söderlund, and E. Hultman. 1993. Influence of Oral Creatine Supplementation on Muscle Torque During Repeated Bouts of Maximal Voluntary Exercise in Man. *Clinical Science* 84: 565–571.

33. Vandenberghe, K., M. Goris, P. Van Hecke, M. Van Leemputte, L. Vangerven, and P. Hespel. 1997. Long-Term Creatine Intake Is Beneficial to Muscle Performance During Resistance Training. *Journal of Applied Physiology* 83: 2055–2063; Kreider, R. B., M. Ferreira, M. Wilson, P. Grindstaff, S. Plisk, J. Reinardy, E. Cantler, and A. L. Almada. 1998. Effects of Creatine Supplementation on Body Composition, Strength, and Sprint Performance. *Medicine & Science in Sports & Exercise* 30: 73–82.

34. Mayhew, D. L., J. L. Mayhew, and J. S. Ware. 2002. Effects of Long-Term Creatine Supplementation on Liver and Kidney Functions in American College Football Players. *International Journal of Sport Nutrition and Exercise Metabolism* 12: 453–460; Kreider, R. B., C. Melton, C. J. Rasmussen, M. Greenwood, S. Lancaster, E. C. Cantler, P. Milnor, and A. L. Almada. 2003. Long-Term Creatine Supplementation Does Not Significantly Affect Clinical Markers of Health in Athletes. *Molecular and Cellular Biochemistry* 244: 95–104.

35. Wiles, J. D., S. R. Bird, J. Hopkins, and M. Riley. 1992. Effect of Caffeinated Coffee on Running Speed, Respiratory Factors, Blood Lactate and Perceived Exertion During 1500 M Treadmill Running. *British Journal of Sports Medicine* 26: 116–120; Spriet, L. L., D. A. MacLean, D. J. Dyck, E. Hultman, G. Cederblad, and T. E. Graham. 1992. Caffeine Ingestion and Muscle Metabolism During Prolonged Exercise in Humans. *American Journal of Physiology - Endocrinology and Metabolism* 262: E891–E898.

36. Paton, C. D., W. G. Hopkins, and L. Vollebregt. 2001. Little Effect of Caffeine Ingestion on Repeated Sprints in Team-Sport Athletes. *Medicine & Science in Sports & Exercise* 33: 822–825.

37. Crist, D. M., G. T. Peake, P. A. Egan, and D. L. Waters. 1988. Body Composition Responses to Exogenous GH During Training in Highly Conditioned Adults. *Journal of Applied Physiology* 65: 579–584; Foss, M., and S. Keteyian. 1998. *Physiological Basis for Exercise and Sport.* 6th ed. McGraw-Hill: 498.

38. Deyssig, R., H. Frisch, W. Blum, and T. Waldorf. 1993. Effect of Growth Hormone Treatment on Hormonal Parameters, Body Composition, and Strength in Athletes. *Acta Endocrinologica* 128: 313–318; Lange, K., J. Andersen, N. Beyer, F. Isaksson, B. Larsson, M. Rasmussen, A. Juul, J. Bülow, and M. Kjær. 2002. GH Administration Changes Myosin Heavy Chain Isoforms in Skeletal Muscle but Does Not Augment Muscle Strength or Hypertrophy, Either Alone or Combined with Resistance Exercise Training in Healthy Elderly Men. *Journal of Clinical Endocrinology & Metabolism* 87: 513–523.

39. Woodhouse, L. J., S. L. Asa, S. G. Thomas, and S. Ezzat. 1999. Measures of Submaximal Aerobic Performance Evaluate and Predict Functional Response to Growth Hormone (GH) Treatment in GH-Deficient Adults. *Journal of Clinical Endocrinology & Metabolism* 84: 4570–4577.

40. Ekblom, B., and B. Berglund. 1991. Effect of Erythropoietin Administration on Maximal Aerobic Power. *Scandinavian Journal of Medicine and Science in Sports* 1: 88–93.

Feature Box References

1. Tarnopolsky, M. A., S. A. Atkinson, S. M. Phillips, and J. D. MacDougall. 1995. Carbohydrate Loading and Metabolism During Exercise in Men and Women. *Journal of Applied Physiology* 78: 1360–1368.

2. Goforth, W. H., D. Laurent, W. K. Prusaczyk, K. E. Schneider, K. F. Peterson, and G. I. Shulman. 2003. Effects of Depletion Exercise and Light

Training on Muscle Glycogen Supercompensation in Men. *American Journal of Physiology - Endocrinology and Metabolism* 285: E1304–1311.

3. Houmard, J. A., D. L. Costill, J. B. Mitchell, S. H. Park, R. C. Hickner, and J. N. Roemmich. 1990. Reduced Training Maintains Performance in Distance Runners. *International Journal of Sports Medicine* 11: 46–52.

4. Whelton, S. P., A. Chin, X. Xin, J. He. 2002. Effect of Aerobic Exercise on Blood Pressure: A Meta-Analysis of Randomized, Controlled Trials. *Annals of Internal Medicine* 136: 493–503.

5. Alhassan S., K. A. Reese, J. Mahurin, E. P. Plaisance, B. D. Hilson, J. C. Garner, S. O. Wee, and P. W. Grandjean. 2006. Blood Lipid Responses to Plant Stanol Ester Supplementation and Aerobic Exercise Training. *Metabolism* 55: 541–549.

6. Janssen, I., P. T. Katzmarzyk, R. Ross, A. S. Leon, J. S. Skinner, D. C. Rao, J. H. Wilmore, T. Rankinen, and C. Bouchard. 2004. Fitness Alters the Associations of BMI and Waist Circumference with Total and Abdominal Fat. *Obesity* 12: 525–537.

7. O'Donovan, G., E. M. Kearney, A. M. Nevill, K. Woolf-May, and S. R. Bird. 2005. The Effects of 24 Weeks of Moderate- or High-Intensity Exercise on Insulin Resistance. *European Journal of Applied Physiology* 95: 522–528.

8. Kato, T., T. Terashima, T. Yamashita, Y. Hatanaka, A. Honda, and Y. Umemura. 2006. Effect of Low-Repetition Jump Training on Bone Mineral Density in Young Women. *Journal of Applied Physiology* 100: 839–843; Daly, R. M., D. W. Dunstan, N. Owen, D. Jolley, J. E. Shaw, P. Z. Zimmet. 2005. Does High-Intensity Resistance Training Maintain Bone Mass During Moderate Weight Loss in Older Overweight Adults with Type 2 Diabetes? *Osteoporosis International* 16: 1703–1712; Yung, P. S., Y. M. Lai, P. Y. Tung, H. T. Tsui, C. K. Wong, V. W. Hung, and L. Qin. 2005. Effects of Weight Bearing and Nonweight Bearing Exercises on Bone Properties Using Calcaneal Quantitative Ultrasound. *British Journal of Sports Medicine* 39: 547–551.

9. Karacabey, K., O. Saygin, R. Ozmerdivenli, E. Zorba, A. Godekmerdan, and V. Bulut. 2005. The Effects of Exercise on the Immune System and Stress Hormones in Sportswomen. *Neuroendocrinology Letters* 26: 361–366.

10. Youngstedt, S. D. 2005. Effects of Exercise on Sleep. *Clinics in Sports Medicine* 24: 355–365.

Two Points of View References

1. American College of Sports Medicine, *Certified Personal Trainer* (2007). Available at www.acsm.org/Content/NavigationMenu/Certification/GetCertified/CertifiedPersonalTrainer/ACSM_Certified_Pers1.htm. Accessed August 2010.

2. American Council on Exercise, *Personal Trainer Certification* (2010). Available at www.acefitness.org/getcertified/certification_pt.aspx. Accessed August 2010.

3. Sports, Cardiovascular, and Wellness Nutrition, A Dietetic Practice Group of the American Dietetic Association, *Sports Dietetics Certification* (March 2010). Available at www.scandpg.org/sports-nutrition/be-a-board-certified-sports-dietitian-cssd/. Accessed August 2010.

4. J. Stenson, "Nutrition Advice at the Gym?" MSNBC (September 2005) Available at www.msnbc.msn.com/id/8986850/. Accessed August 2010.

5. International Fitness Professionals Association, *Sports Nutrition Specialist Certification*. Available at www.ifpa-fitness.com/fitness_certification_sports_nutrition_specialist.php. Accessed August 2010.

6. Stenson. "Nutrition Advice at the Gym?"

7. S. Reents, "Personal Trainers Should Not Offer Nutrition Advice." May 2007. Available at www.athleteinme.com/ArticleView.aspx?id=264. Accessed August 2010.

Chapter 12

1. USDA Economic Research Service. 2009. Global Food Markets, Global Food Industry Structure. Available at www.ers.usda.gov/Briefing/GlobalFoodMarkets/Industry.htm. Accessed April 2010.

2. Gallo, A. 1999. Food Advertising in the United States. In *America's Eating Habits: Changes and Consequences*, ed. E Frazao, pp. 173-80. Washington, DC: United States Department of Agriculture.

3. SOS eMarketing. 2009. Red Bull: The Stuff of Beverage Marketing Legends. Available at www.sosemarketing.com/?p=351. Accessed March 2010.

4. Garner, J. 2009. Using Social Media to Market Your Products: The Case of Red Bull. ComputerWeekly.com. Available at www.computerweekly.com/blogs/editors-blog/2009/10/using-social-media-to-market-y.html. Accessed March 2010.

5. Blisard, N. 1999. Advertising and What We Eat: The Case of Dairy Products. *America's Eating Habits: Changes & Consequences*, USDA, ERS, Agricultural Information Bulletin No. 750.

6. Harmon, A. H., and B. L. Gerald. 2007. Position of the American Dietetic Association: Food and Nutrition Professionals Can Implement Practices to Conserve Natural Resources and Support Ecological Sustainability. *Journal of the American Dietetic Association* 107: 1033–1043; Sobal, J., L. Kahn, and C. Bisogni. 1998. A Conceptual Model of the Food and Nutrition System. *Social Science & Medicine* 47: 853–863.

7. U.S. Environmental Protection Agency. Ag 101: Demographics. Available at www.epa.gov/oecaagct/ag101/demographics.html. Accessed January 2010.

8. Ibid.

9. U.S. Environmental Protection Agency. 2009. Ag 101: Economic Overview. Available at www.epa.gov/oecaagct/ag101/economics.html. Accessed January 2010.

10. U.S. Environmental Protection Agency. Ag 101: Demographics.

11. International Food Information Council. 2009. Food Insight. Background on Agricultural Practices and Food Technologies. Available at www.foodinsight.org/Resources/Detail.aspx?topic=Background_on_Agricultural_Practices_and_Food_Technologies. Accessed January 2010.

12. Rickman, D., J. Luvall, J. Shaw, P. Mask, D. Kissel, and D. Sullivan. 2003. Precision Agriculture: Changing the Face of Farming. *GeoTimes*. Available at www.geotimes.org/nov03/feature_agric.html. Accessed January 2010.

13. International Food Information Council. 2009. Food Insight. From Farm to Fork: Questions and Answers About Modern Food Production. Available at www.foodinsight.org/Content/76/QandA-Mod%20Food%20Prod_9-1-09.pdf. Accessed January 2010.

14. U.S. Environmental Protection Agency. Ag 101: Economic Overview.

15. Ibid.

16. Ibid.

17. U.S. Environmental Protection Agency 2009. Agribusiness: Sectors Strategies Program, June 29, 2009. Available at www.epa.gov/sectors/sectorinfo/sectorprofiles/agribusiness.html. Accessed January 2010.

18. U.S. Environmental Protection Agency. Ag 101: Crop Production. Available at www.epa.gov/oecaagct/ag101/cropmajor.html. Accessed Janury 2010.

19. U.S. Environmental Protection Agency. Agribusiness.

20. U.S. Environmental Protection Agency. Ag 101: Crop Production.

21. Ibid.

22. U.S. Environmental Protection Agency. 2009. Ag 101: Beef Production. Available at www.epa.gov/oecaagct/ag101/beef.html. Accessed January 2010.

23. U.S. Environmental Protection Agency. 2009. Ag 101: Pork Production. Available at www.epa.gov/oecaagct/ag101/porknutrition.html. Accessed January 2010.

24. U.S. Environmental Protection Agency. 2009. Ag 101: Poultry Production. Available at www.epa.gov/oecaagct/ag101/poultry.html. Accessed January 2010.

25. Ibid.

26. International Food Information Council. Food Insight. Background on Agricultural Practices and Food Technologies.

27. Hendrickson, M., and H. James. 2008. Does the World Need U.S. Farmers Even If Americans Don't? *Journal of Agricultural and Environmental Ethics* 21: 311–328.

28. United States Department of Agriculture. 2009. Outlook for U.S. Agricultural Trade. Available at www.fas.usda.gov/cmp/outlook/2009/Nov-09/AES-11-30-2009.pdf. Accessed January 2010.

29. United States Department of Agriculture, Economic Research Service. 2009. Global Food Markets: International Consumer and Retail Trends. Available at www.ers.usda.gov/Briefing/GlobalFoodMarkets/consumer.htm. Accessed January 2010; Regmi, A., H. Takeshima, and L. Unnevehr. 2008. Convergence in Global Food Demand and Delivery. Economic Research Report No. ERR-56. Available at www.ers.usda.gov/publications/err56/. Accessed January 2010.

30. Popkin, B. 2007. The World Is Fat. *Scientific American*. Available at www.sciam.com. Accessed February 2010.

31. World Health Organization. 2010. Controlling the Global Obesity Epidemic. Available at www.who.int/nutrition/topics/obesity/en/index.html. Accessed January 2010.

32. United States Department of Agriculture, Economic Research Service. 2010. Value of U.S. Food Imports: Fruits and Fruit Preparations. Available at www.ers.usda.gov/Data/foodimports/. Accessed April 2010.

33. Hendrickson. Does the World Need U.S. Farmers?

34. Nucci, M., J. Dellava, C. Cuite, and W. Hallman. 2008. The U.S. Food Import System: Issues, Processes and Proposals. Working Paper RR-0208-001. Rutgers New Jersey Agricultural Experiment Station. Available at http://foodpolicy.rutgers.edu/docs/pubs/food_imports_%20addendum_0708.pdf. Accessed October 2010.

35. Hendrickson. Does the World Need U.S. Farmers?; Blank, S. 1998. *The End of Agriculture in the American Portfolio.* Westport, CT: Quorum Books.

36. Mundell, E. 2008. U.S. Food Safety: The Import Alarm Keeps Sounding. *U.S. News & World Report.* Available at http://health.usnews.com/usnews/health/healthday/080115/us-food-safety-the-import-alarm-keeps-sounding.htm. Accessed January 2010.

37. Martin, A. 2007. FDA Curbs Sale of 5 Seafoods Farmed in China. *The New York Times.* Available at www.nytimes.com/2007/06/29/business/worldbusiness/29fish.html?pagewanted=print. Accessed January 2010.

38. Regmi. Convergence in Global Food Demand and Delivery.

39. U.S. Environmental Protection Agency. Ag 101: Beef Production.

40. National Oceanic and Atmospheric Administration, National Climatic Data Center. 2008. Global Warming Frequently Asked Questions. Available at www.ncdc.noaa.gov/oa/climate/globalwarming.html#q1. Accessed January 2010.

41. Harmon. Position of the American Dietetic Association: Food and Nutrition Professionals Can Implement Practices.; Pirog, R., T. Van Pelt, K. Enshayan, and E. Cook. 2001. *Food, Fuel, and Freeways: An Iowa Perspective on How Far Food Travels, Fuel Usage, and Greenhouse Gas Emissions.* Leopold Center for Sustainable Agriculture. Available at www.leopold.iastate.edu/pubs/staff/ppp/food_mil.pdf. Accessed January 2010.

42. Pirog. *Food, Fuel, and Freeways;* Tompkins Country Relocalization Project. 2005. Implications of Fossil Fuel Dependence for the Food System. *Energy Bulletin.* Available at www.energybulletin.net. Accessed January 2010.

43. Pirog. *Food, Fuel, and Freeways.*

44. Ibid.

45. Tompkins Country Relocalization ProjectImplications of Fossil Fuel Dependence for the Food System; Hendrickson, J. 1996. Energy Use in the U.S. Food System: A Summary of Existing Research and Analysis. Center for Integrated Agricultural Systems, UW-Madison. Available at www.cias.wisc.edu/wp-content/uploads/2008/07/energyuse.pdf. Accessed January 2010.

46. Harmon. Position of the American Dietetic Association: Food and Nutrition Professionals Can Implement Practices.

47. United States Department of Agriculutre. 2009. USDA Awards More than $5 Million in Grants to Support Local Food Initiatives. Available at www.csrees.usda.gov/newsroom/news/2009news/11181_cfp.html. Accessed January 2010.

48. Harmon. Position of the American Dietetic Association: Food and Nutrition Professionals Can Implement Practices; Herremans, I., and R. Reid. 2002. Developing Awareness of the Sustainability Concept. *Journal of Environmental Education* 34: 16–20; Brundtland, G. 1987. *Our Common Future.* New York: Oxford University Press; Herrin, M., and J. D. Gussow. 1989. Designing a Sustainable Regional Diet. *Journal of Nutrition Education* 21: 270–275.

49. FDA, Center for Veterinary Medicine. 2009. Report on the Food and Drug Administration's Review of the Safety of Recombinant Bovine Somatotropin. Available at www.fda.gov/AnimalVeterinary/SafetyHealth/ProductSafetyInformation/ucm130321.htm. Accessed February 2010.

50. FDA, Center for Veterinary Medicine. Updated 2009. Steroid Hormones. Available at www.fda.gov/AnimalVeterinary/SafetyHealth/ProductSafetyInformation/ucm055436.htm. Accessed October 2010.

51. U.S. Environmental Protection Agency. Ag 101: Beef Production.

52. Centers for Disease Control and Prevention. 2005. Frequently Asked Questions about NARMS. Available at www.cdc.gov/NARMS/faq_pages/7.htm. Accessed February 2010.

53. Ibid.

54. FDA, Center for Veterinary Medicine. Updated 2009. National Antimicrobial Resistance Monitoring System. Available at www.fda.gov/AnimalVeterinary/SafetyHealth/AntimicrobialResistance/NationalAntimicrobialResistanceMonitoringSystem/default.htm. Accessed February 2010.

55. FDA, Center for Veterinary Medicine. Updated 2009. Judicious Use of Antimicrobials. Available at www.fda.gov/AnimalVeterinary/SafetyHealth/AntimicrobialResistance/JudiciousUseofAntimicrobials/default.htm. Accessed April 2010.

56. EPA. 2009. What Are Biopesticides? Available at www.epa.gov/opp00001/biopesticides/whatarebiopesticides.htm. Accessed April 2010.

57. Ibid.

58. Beseler, C., L. Stallones, J. Hoppin, M. Alavanja, A. Blair, T. Keefe, and F. Kamel. 2008. Depression and Pesticide Exposures among Private Pesticide Applicators Enrolled in the Agricultural Health Study. *Environmental Health Perspectives* 116: 1713–1719.

59. U.S. Environmental Protection Agency. 2007. Pesticides and Food: Health Problems Pesticides May Pose. Available at www.epa.gov/pesticides/food/risks.htm. Accessed January 2010.

60. U.S. Environmental Protection Agency. Updated 2007. Pesticides: Environmental Effects. Ecological Risk Assessments. Available at www.epa.gov/pesticides/ecosystem/ecorisk.htm. Accessed January 2010.

61. International Food Information Council. 2009. Food Insight. Background on Agricultural Practices and Food Technologies. Available at www.ific.org. Accessed January 2010.

62. U.S. Environmental Protection Agency. Updated 2007. Pesticides: Environmental Effects..

63. U.S. Environmental Protection Agency. Updated 2009. Pesticides: Topical and Chemical Fact Sheets. Integrated Pest Management (IPM) Principles. Available at www.epa.gov/pesticides/factsheets/ipm.htm. Accessed January 2010.

64. International Food Information Council. 2009. Food Insight. Questions and Answers about Food Biotechnology. Available at www.foodinsight.org. Accessed January 2010.

65. International Food Information Council. 2009. Food and Agricultural Biotechnology. Health Impacts in Developing Nations. Available at www.foodinsight.org/Resources/Detail.aspx?topic=Food_Agricultural_Biotechnology_Health_Impacts_in_Developing_Nations_CPE_Program. Accessed January 2010.

66. Fernandez-Cornejo, J., and W. McBride. 2002. Adoption of Bioengineered Crops. Available at www.ers.usda.gov/publications/aer810/. Agricultural Economic Report No. AER810. Accessed January 2010.

67. Ibid.

68. Bruh, C. 2006. Position of the American Dietetic Association: Agricultural and Food Biotechnology. *Journal of the American Dietetic Association* 106: 285–293.

69. Ibid.

70. Ibid.

71. International Food Information Council. 2008. 2008 Food Biotechnology: A Study of U.S. Consumer Trends. Available at www.ific.org. Accessed January 2010.

72. Golan, E., L. Mancino, and L. Unnevehr. 2009. Food Policy: Check the List of Ingredients. *Amber Waves.* Available at www.ers.usda.gov/AmberWaves/June09/Features/FoodPolicy.htm. Accessed March 2010.

73. Ibid.

74. Ibid.

75. Ibid.

76. Ibid.

77. Parker, L. 2008. *Commodity Foods and the Nutritional Quality of the National School Lunch Program: Historical Role, Current Operations, and Future Potential.* Washington, D.C.: Food Research and Action Center. Available at www.frac.org/pdf/commodities08.pdf. Accessed March 2010.

78. Ibid.

79. The Princeton Review. Lobbyist. Available at www.princetonreview.com/Careers.aspx?cid=88. Accessed March 2010.

80. Nestle, M. 2002. *Food Policy.* Berkeley: University of California Press.

81. Brownell, K., T. Farley, W. Willett, B. Popkin, F. Chaloupka, J. Thompson, and D. Ludwig. 2009. The Public Health and Economic Benefits to Taxing Sugar-Sweetened Beverages. *New England Journal of Medicine* 361: 1599–1605.

82. Eaton, J. 2009. The Food Lobby's War on a Soda Tax. The Center for Public Integrity. Available at www.publicintegrity.org/articles/entry/1805/. Accessed March 2010.

83. USDA. 2006. Meat and Poultry Labeling Terms. Available at www.fsis.usda.gov/FactSheets/Meat_&_Poultry_Labeling_Terms/index.asp. Accessed February 2010.

84. Greene, C., C. Dimitri, B. Lin, W. McBride, L. Oberholtzer, and T. Smith. 2009. Emerging Issues in the U.S. Organic Industry. United States Department of Agriculture, Economic Research Service, Bulletin No. 55. Available at www.ers.usda.gov/publications/eib55/eib55.pdf. Accessed February 2010.

85. Ibid.

86. Agricultural Marketing Service, National Organic Program. 2008. Background Information. Available at www.ams.usda.gov/AMSv1.0/getfile?dDocName=STELDEV3004443&acct=nopgeninfo. Accessed February 2010.

87. Agricultural Marketing Service, National Organic Program. 2007. National List of Allowed and Prohibited Substances. Available at http://www.ams.usda.gov/AMSv1.0/ams.fetchTemplateData.do?template=TemplateJ&navID=NationalOrganicProgram&leftNav=NationalOrganicProgram&page=NOPPetitionedSubstancesDatabase&

description=Petitioned%20Substances%20Database&acct=nopgeninfo. Accessed October 2010.

88. Agricultural Marketing Service, National Organic Program. Background Information.

89. Dangour, A., S. Dodhia, A. Hayter, E. Allen, K. Lock, and R. Uauy. 2009. Nutritional Quality of Organic Foods: A Systematic Review. *American Journal of Clinical Nutrition.*; Gold, M. 2008. Should I Purchase Organic Food? USDA AFSIC Research Guide. Available at www.nal.usda.gov/afsic/pubs/faq/BuyOrganicFoodsB.shtml#BuyB2. Accessed February 2010.

90. Greene. Emerging Issues in the U.S. Organic Industry.

91. Ibid.

92. Ibid.

Feature Box References

1. Cotner, S., and J. Masabni. 2009. Vegetable Gardening in Containers. AgriLife Extension, Texas A&M System. Available at http://repository.tamu.edu/bitstream/handle/1969.1/87590/pdf_2695.pdf?sequence=1. Accessed April 2010; Iowa State University Extension. 2005. Container Vegetable Gardening. Available at www.extension.iastate.edu/publications/pm870b.pdf. Accessed April 2010.

2. International Food Information Council. Sustainable Agriculture: Can Biotechnology Play a Role? Available at www.ific.org. Accessed February 2010.

3. Dahlberg, K. 1993. Regenerative food systems: Broadening the scope and agenda of sustainability. In P. Allen, ed. *Food for the Future: Conditions and Contradictions of Sustainability.* New York: John Wiley, 75–102.

4. Horrigan, L., R. Lawrence, and P. Walker. 2002. How Sustainable Agriculture Can Address the Environmental and Human Health Harms of Industrial Agriculture. *Environmental Health Perspectives* 110: 445–456.

5. Harmon. Position of the American Dietetic Association: Food and Nutrition Professionals Can Implement Practices to Conserve Natural Resources and Support Ecological Sustainability. *Journal of the American Dietetic Association* 107: 1033–1043.

6. Tagtow, A., and A. Harmon. 2009. Healthy Land, Healthy Food and Healthy Eaters. Available at www.uwyo.edu/winwyoming/Pubs/HealthyLand%20HealthyFood%20HealthyEaters.pdf. Accessed February 2010.

7. Ibid.

8. Ibid.

9. Brown, L. 2008. *Plan B 3.0. Mobilizing to Save Civilization.* New York: WW Norton & Company.

10. Pimentel, D., and M. Pimentel. 2003. Sustainability of Meat-Based and Plant-Based Diets and the Environment. *Journal of the American Dietetic Association* 78: 660S–663S.

11. Howard, A. 1940. *The Agricultural Testament.* London: Oxford University Press.

12. Environmental Protection Agency. 2009. What on Earth Is Soil? Available at www.epa.gov/gmpo/edresources/soil.html. Accessed February 2010.

13. Tagtow. Healthy Land, Healthy Food and Healthy Eaters.

14. Richards, A. 2001. Does Low Biodiversity Resulting from Modern Agriculture Practices Affect Crop Pollination and Yield? *Annals of Botany* 88: 165–172.

15. United Nations Food and Agriculture Organization. 2006. The State of World Fisheries and Aquaculture. Available at www.fao.org/docrep/009/A0699e/A0699E05.htm. Accessed February 2010; Hilborn, R., T. Quinn, D. Schindler, and D. Rogers. 2003. Biocomplexity and Fisheries Sustainability. *Proceedings of the National Academy of Sciences of the USA* 100: 4. Available at www.pnas.org/content/100/11/6564.full. Accessed February 2010.

16. Tagtow. Healthy Land, Healthy Food and Healthy Eaters.

17. Hendrickson, M., and H. James. 2008. Does the World Need U.S. Farmers Even If Americans Don't? *Journal of Agricultural and Environmental Ethics* 21: 311–328.

18. Pimentel. Sustainability of Meat-Based and Plant-Based Diets and the Environment.; Harmon. Position of the American Dietetic Association: Food and Nutrition Professionals Can Implement Practices.

19. Pimentel. Sustainability of Meat-Based and Plant-Based Diets and the Environment.

20. Ibid.

21. Heitschmidt, R., R. Short, and E. Gings. 1996. Ecosystems, Sustainability and Animal Agriculture. *Journal of Animal Science* 74: 1395–1405.

22. Heller, Martin C., and Gregory A. Keoleian. 2000. *Life Cycle-Based Sustainability Indicators for Assessment of the U.S. Food System.* Ann Arbor, MI: Center for Sustainable Systems, University of Michigan, 42; The Sustainable Table. 2009. Eat Local, Buy Local, Be Local. What Is Local?

Available at www.sustainabletable.org/issues/eatlocal/. Accessed February 2010.

23. Harmon. Position of the American Dietetic Association: Food and Nutrition Professionals Can Implement Practices.

24. Pimentel, D., P. Hepperly, J. Hanson, D. Douds, and R. Seidel. 2005. Environmental, Energetic, and Economic Comparisons of Organic and Conventional Farming Systems. *BioScience* 55: 573–582.

25. EPA. 2010. Watersense. Available at www.epa.gov/watersense/water_efficiency/index.html. Accessed February 2010.

26. Ibid.

27. Ibid.

28. Ibid.

Two Points of View References

1. United States Department of Agriculture, Agricultural Marketing Service, *National Organic Program* (2010). Available at www.ams.usda.gov/AMSv1.0/nop. Accessed July 2010.

2. C. Dimitri, and L. Oberholtzer, "The U.S. Organic Handling Sector in 2004: Baseline Findings of the Nationwide Survey of Organic Manufacturers, Processors, and Distributors," EIB-36, U.S. Department of Agriculture, Economic Research Service, April 2008.

3. Organic Consumers Association, "*New York Times* Exposes Wal-Mart's Ability to Sell Cheap Organic Milk—It's Coming from Factory Farms" (2006).Available at www.organicconsumers.org/articles/article_2404.cfm. Accessed July 2010.

4. S. Ritter, "Pinpointing Trends in Pesticide Use," *Chemical & Engineering News* 87, no. 07 (February 2009). Available at http://pubs.acs.org/cen/coverstory/87/8707cover1a.html. Accessed July 2010.

5. M. Roosevelt, "The Lure of the 100-Mile Diet," *Time Magazine* (Sunday June 11, 2006.) Available at www.time.com/time/magazine/article/0,9171,1200783,00.html. Accessed July 2010.

6. The Cornucopia Institute, "Wal-Mart in Trouble Again Over Organic Marketing Practices," (March 2010).Available at www.cornucopia.org/2010/03/wal-mart-in-trouble-again-over-organic-marketing-practices. Accessed July 2010.

7. M. Pollan, "Letters to Whole Foods CEO John Mackey: My Second Letter to Whole Foods,"(2006). Available at www.michaelpollan.com/article.php?id=80. Accessed July 2010.

8. Organic Consumers Association, "What Makes Food Organic? The Twinkie Problem," (2006). Available at www.organicconsumers.org/articles/article_716.cfm. Accessed July 2010.

9. Organic Consumers Association, "Grocery Chains Buying Organic Products from Overseas Undermine Standards and Hurt USA Organic Farmers." Available at www.organicconsumers.org/articles/article_2410.cfm. Accessed July 2010.

Chapter 13

1. U.S. Department of Agriculture, U.S. Department of Health and Human Services. 2010. *Dietary Guidelines for Americans, 2010.* 7th ed. Washington, D.C.: U.S. Government Printing Office.

2. Centers for Disease Control and Prevention. 1999. Safer and Healthier Foods: 1900–1999. *Journal of the American Medical Association* 48: 905–913; Young, J. H. 1981. Updated 1999. The Long Struggle for the 1906 Law. *FDA Consumer Magazine.* Available at http://web.archive.org/web/20080223170721/http://www.cfsan.fda.gov/~lrd/history2.html. Accessed July 2010.

3. Young. The Long Struggle for the 1906 Law.

4. Food Safety and Inspection Service. 1999. Origins of the Federal Food Safety System. *Food Safety Educator* 4: 3–4. Available at www.fsis.usda.gov/News_&_Events/food_safety_educator/index.asp. Accessed July 2010.

5. Centers for Disease Control and Prevention. Safer and Healthier Foods.

6. Food and Drug Administration. 2007. Food Protection Plan. Available at www.fda.gov/Food/FoodSafety/FoodSafetyPrograms/FoodProtectionPlan2007/default.htm. Accessed July 2010.

7. Center for Food Safety and Applied Nutrition. Updated 2002. Food Safety A to Z Reference Guide: Virus. Available at www.fda.gov/SiteIndex/default.htm. Accessed July 2010.

8. National Center for Infectious Diseases. Updated 2010. Norovirus: Technical Fact Sheet. Available at www.cdc.gov/ncidod/dvrd/revb/gastro/norovirus-factsheet.htm. Accessed July 2010.

9. Ibid.

10. Centers for Disease Control. September 9, 2003. Public Health Dispatch: Multistate Outbreak of Hepatitis A among Young Adult Concert Attendees, United States, 2003. *Morbidity and Mortality Weekly Report* 52: 844–845. Available at www.cdc.gov/mmwr/preview/mmwrhtml/mm5235a5.htm. Accessed July 2010.

11. Grice, E. A, H. H. Kong, G. Renaud, et al. 2008. A Diversity Profile of the Human Skin Microbiota. *Genome Research* 18: 1043–1050. Available at http://genome.cshlp.org/content/18/7/1043.long. Accessed July 2010.

12. Centers for Disease Control and Prevention. Foodborne Illness.

13. National Center for Zoonotic, Vector-Borne, and Enteric Diseases. 2010. General Information: *Campylobacter.* Available at www.cdc.gov/nczved/divisions/dfbmd/diseases/campylobacter/#how_common. Accessed July 2010.

14. Ibid.

15. Ibid.

16. National Center for Zoonotic, Vector-Borne, and Enteric Diseases. Updated July 2009. *E. coli.* Available at http://www.cdc.gov/nczved/divisions/dfbmd/diseases/ecoli_o157h7. Accessed July 2010.

17. Ibid.

18. National Center for Zoonotic, Vector-Borne, and Enteric Diseases. Updated November 2009. Traveler's Diarrhea. Available at www.cdc.gov/nczved/divisions/dfbmd/diseases/travelers_diarrhea. Accessed July 2010.

19. National Center for Zoonotic, Vector-Borne, and Enteric Diseases. Updated November 2009. Salmonellosis. Available at www.cdc.gov/nczved/divisions/dfbmd/diseases/salmonellosis. Accessed July 2010.

20. Food Safety and Inspection Service. 2010. Parasites and Foodborne Illness. Available at www.fsis.usda.gov/Fact_Sheets/Parasites_and_Foodborne_Illness/index.asp. Accessed July 2010.

21. Gerald, B. J., and J. E. Perkin. 2003. Position of the American Dietetic Association: Food and Water Safety. *Journal of the American Dietetic Association* 103: 1203–1218.

22. Animal and Plant Health Inspection Service. Revised December 2006. Bovine Spongiform Encephalopathy (BSE): An Overview. Available at www.aphis.usda.gov/publications/animal_health/content/printable_version/BSEbrochure12-2006.pdf. Accessed July 2010.

23. Centers for Disease Control and Prevention. 2003. Questions and Answers Regarding Bovine Spongiform Encephalopathy (BSE) and Creutzfeldt-Jakob Disease (CJD). Available at www.cdc.gov/ncidod/dvrd/bse. Accessed July 2010.

24. FDA. Updated June 2009. BSE Questions and Answers. Available at www.fda.gov/BiologicsBloodVaccines/SafetyAvailability/ucm111482.htm. Accessed July 2010.

25. Centers for Disease Control and Prevention. Questions and Answers.

26. Ibid.

27. Ibid.

28. Centers for Disease Control and Prevention. 2010. About BSE. Available at www.cdc.gov/ncidod/dvrd/bse. Accessed July 2010.

29. Centers for Disease Control and Prevention. Questions and Answers.

30. Buzby, J. C. 2003. Older Adults at Risk of Complications from Microbial Foodborne Illness. *Food Review* 25: 30–35.

31. Buzby, J. C. 2002. Children and Microbial Foodborne Illness. *Food Review* 24: 32–37.

32. Gerald. Position of the American Dietetic Association: Food and Water Safety.

33. National Restaurant Association Educational Foundation. 2010. *ServSafe® Coursebook.* 5th ed. Available at www.servsafe.com. Accessed July 2010.

34. Gerald. Position of the American Dietetic Association: Food and Water Safety.

35. Food Safety and Inspection Service. 2003. The Food Safety Educator: Thinking Globally, Working Locally. Available at www.fsis.usda.gov/Frame/FrameRedirect.asp?main=http://www.fsis.usda.gov/OA/educator/educator8-1.htm. Accessed July 2010.

36. Ibid.

37. U.S. Department of Agriculture. 2010. *Report of the Dietary Guidelines Advisory Committee on the Dietary Guidelines for Americans 2010.* Available at www.cnpp.usda.gov/DGAs2010-DGACReport.htm. Accessed July 2010.

38. Godwin, S., F. Chen, and R. Coppings. 2006. Correlation of Visual Perceptions of Cleanliness and Reported Cleaning Practices with Measures of Microbial Contamination in Home Refrigerators. *Food Protection Trends* 26: 474–480.

39. Food Safety and Inspection Service. 2010. Refrigeration and Food Safety. Available at www.fsis.usda.gov/factsheets/refrigeration_&_food_safety/index.asp#11. Accessed July 2010.

40. Food Safety and Inspection Service. 1998. Premature Browning of Cooked Ground Beef. Available at www.fsis.usda.gov/OPHS/prebrown.htm. Accessed July 2010.

41. Food Safety and Inspection Service. Updated 2006. The Color of Meat and Poultry. Available at http://origin-www.fsis.usda.gov/Fact_Sheets/Color_of_Meat_&_Poultry/index.asp. Accessed July 2010.

42. The Partnership for Food Safety Education. 2010. FightBacChill Fact Sheet. Available at www.fightbac.org/storage/documents/flyers/chill_fightbac_factsheet_2010_bw_pdf. Accessed July 2010.

43. Food Safety and Inspection Service. Updated August 2006. How Temperatures Affect Food. Available at www.fsis.usda.gov/Fact_Sheets/How_Temperatures_Affect_Food/index.asp. Accessed July 2010.

44. Food and Drug Administration and U.S. Department of Agriculture. 2000. A Description of the U.S. Food Safety System. Available at www.fsis.usda.gov/OA/codex/system.htm. Accessed July 2010.

45. Food Safety and Inspection Service. 2003. Enhancing Public Health: Strategies for the Future—2003 FSIS Food Safety Vision. Available at www.fsis.usda.gov/oa/programs/vision071003.htm. Accessed July 2010.

46. Food and Drug Administration and U.S. Department of Agriculture. A Description of the U.S. Food Safety System.

47. Centers for Disease Control. Updated 2003. PulseNet: The National Molecular Subtyping Network for Foodborne Disease Surveillance. Available at www.cdc.gov/pulsenet. Accessed July 2010.

48. Bracket, R. 2006. Statement before the Committee on Health, Education, Labor and Pensions, United States Senate. Ensuring Food Safety: FDA's Role in Tracking and Resolving the Recent E.coli Spinach Outbreak.Available at www.hhs.gov/asl/testify/t061115a.html. Accessed July 2010; Food and Drug Administration. 2006. FDA Statement on Foodborne *E. coli* O157:H7 Outbreak in Spinach. Available at www.fda.gov/NewsEvents/Newsroom/PressAnnouncements/2006/ucm108761.htm. Accessed July 2010.

49. Food and Drug Administration. 2009. Hazard Analysis and Critical Control Points (HACCP). Available at www.fda.gov/Food/FoodSafety/HazardAnalysisCriticalControlPointsHACCP/default.htm. Accessed July 2010.

50. Food and Drug Administration. Updated 2009. FDA Food Code. Available at www.fda.gov/Food/FoodSafety/RetailFoodProtection/FoodCode/default.htm. Accessed July 2010.

51. Food and Drug Administration. Updated 2010. Talking About Juice Safety: What You Need to Know. Available at www.fda.gov/Food/ResourcesForYou/Consumers/ucm110526.htm. Accessed July 2010.

52. Tauxe, R. B. 2001. Food Safety and Irradiation: Protecting the Public from Foodborne Infections. Centers for Disease Control and Prevention, Emerging Infectious Diseases. Available at www.cdc.gov/ncidod/eid/vol7no3_supp/tauxe.htm#Figure. Accessed July 2010.

53. Food and Drug Administration. 2009. Analysis and Evaluation of Preventive Control Measures for the Control and Reduction/Elimination of Microbial Hazards on Fresh and Fresh-Cut Produce. Available at www.fda.gov/Food/ScienceResearch/ResearchAreas/SafePracticesforFoodProcesses/ucm090977.htm. Accessed July 2010.

54. Finley, J., D. Deming, and R. Smith. 2006. Food Processing: Nutrition, Safety, and Quality. In Shils, M., M. Shike, A. Ross, B. Caballero, and R. Cousins. *Modern Nutrition in Health and Disease.* 10th ed. Philadelphia: Lippincott Williams & Wilkins.

55. Tauxe. Food Safety and Irradiation; Emmert, K., V. Duffy, and R. Earl. 2000. Position of the American Dietetic Association: Food Irradiation. *Journal of the American Dietetic Association* 100: 246–253.

56. Food and Drug Administration. 2009. Irradiated Food and Packaging: Consumer Information. Available at www.fda.gov/Food/FoodIngredientsPackaging/IrradiatedFoodPackaging/ucm135143.htm. Accessed July 2010.

57. Ibid.

58. Tauxe. Food Safety and Irradiation; Emmert. Position of the American Dietetic Association: Food Irradiation.

59. Tauxe. Food Safety and Irradiation; Food and Drug Administration. Irradiated Food and Packaging.

60. Ibid.

61. Emmert. Position of the American Dietetic Association: Food Irradiation.

62. Food and Drug Administration. Irradiated Food and Packaging.

63. Ibid.

64. Food Safety and Inspection Service. 2007. Food Product Dating. Available at www.fsis.usda.gov/factsheets/food_product_dating/index.asp. Accessed July 2010.

65. Food Safety and Inspection Service. Updated 2007. Food Product Dating. Available at http://origin-www.fsis.usda.gov/PDF/Food_Product_Dating.pdf. Accessed July 2010.

66. Grotheer, P. M. Marshall, and A. Simonne. 2005. Sulfites: Separating Fact from Fiction.Institute of Food and Agricultural Sciences, University

of Florida. Reviewed April 2008. Available at http://edis.ifas.ufl.edu/fy731. Accessed July 2010.

67. Papazian, R. 1996. Sulfites: Safe for Most, Dangerous for Some. Available at http://findarticles.com/p/articles/mi_m1370/is_n10_v30/ai_18979003/?tag=content;col1. Accessed July 2010.

68. Ibid.

69. Meadows, M. 2003. MSG: A Common Flavor Enhancer. *FDA Consumer* 37:35. Available at www.foodsafety.wisc.edu/assets/pdf_Files/MSG.pdf. Accessed July 2010.

70. Ibid.

71. FDA. Updated 2010. Food Additives. Available at www.fda.gov/Food/Food-IngredientsPackaging/FoodAdditives/default.htm. Accessed July 2010.

72. Rados, C. 2004. GRAS: Time Tested and Trusted Food Ingredients. *FDA Consumer* 38: 20. Available at www.foodsafety.wisc.edu/assets/pdf_Files/GRAS.pdf. Accessed July 2010.

73. FDA. Food Additives.

74. Rados, GRAS.

75. Food and Drug Administration. Updated 2010. Questions and Answers About Dioxins. Available at www.fda.gov/Food/FoodSafety/FoodContaminantsAdulteration/ChemicalContaminants/DioxinsPCBs/ucm077524.htm. Accessed July 2010.

76. Centers for Disease Control and Prevention. 2002. Marine Toxins. Available at www.cdc.gov/ncidod/dbmd/diseaseinfo/marinetoxins_g.htm. Accessed July 2010.

77. Ibid.; Centers for Disease Control and Prevention. 1998. Ciguatera Fish Poisoning: Texas 1997. *Morbidity and Mortality Weekly Report*, 47:692-694. Available at www.cdc.gov/mmwr/preview/mmwrhtml/00054548.htm. Accessed July 2010.

78. Centers for Disease Control and Prevention. Marine Toxins.

79. U.S. Environmental Protection Agency. Updated 2003. Polychlorinated Biphenyls (PCBs). Available at www.epa.gov/epawaste/hazard/tsd/pcbs/index.htm. Accessed July 2010.

80. Taylor, S. 2006. Food Additives, Contaminants, and Natural Toxicants and Their Risk Assessment. In Shils, M., M. Shike, A. Ross, B. Caballero, and R. Cousins. *Modern Nutrition in Health and Disease.* 10th ed. Philadelphia: Lippincott Williams & Wilkins.

81. U.S. Environmental Protection Agency. Polychlorinated Biphenyls (PCBs).

82. Persistent Bioaccumulative and Toxic (PBT) Chemical Program. Updated 2006. Polychlorinated Biphenyls (PCBs). www.epa.gov/pbt/pubs/pcbs.htm. Accessed July 2010.

83. Ibid.

84. Bruemmer, B. 2003. Food Biosecurity. *Journal of the American Dietetic Association* 203: 687–691.

85. Centers for Disease Control and Prevention. 2003. Food Safety Threats. Available at www.bt.cdc.gov/agent/food/index.asp. Accessed July 2010.

86. Meadows, M. 2004. The FDA and the Fight Against Terrorism. *FDA Consumer Magazine.* Available at www.nti.org/e_research/official_docs/other_us/fda012004_terrorism.pdf. Accessed July 2010.

87. Bruemmer. Food Biosecurity.

Two Points of View References

1. American Water Works Association, *Permeation and Leaching.* (Washington, D.C.: Environmental Protection Agency, 2002),1.

2. Gilbert Ross, MD, medical director, The American Council on Science and Health, a consumer advocacy group.

3. M. Hitti, "Bisphenol A Safe, Says FDA," *Web MD Health News* (2008). Available at www.webmd.com/parenting/news/20080815/bisphenol-a-safe-says-fda. Accessed July 2010.

4. J. DeVries, "Chasing "Zero" in Chemical Contaminant Analysis," *Food Safety Magazine* (August/September 2006). Available at www.foodsafetymagazine.com/article.asp?id=536&sub=sub. Accessed July 2010.

5. U.S. Food and Drug Administration, *Bisphenol A* (2010). Available at www.fda.gov/NewsEvents/PublicHealthFocus/ucm064437.htm. Accessed July 2010.

6. The American Cancer Society, News and Features, "Federal Report Looks at Risks from Plastics and Chemicals"(September 2008). Available at www.cancer.org/Cancer/news/News/federal-report-looks-at-risks-from-plastics-chemical. Accessed July 2010.

7. S. M. Engel, A. Miodovnik, R. L. Canfield, C. Zhu, M. J. Silva, A. M. Calafat, et al., "Prenatal Phthalate Exposure Is Associated with Childhood Behavior and Executive Functioning," *Environmental Health Perspectives* 118 (2010): 565–571. doi:10.1289/ehp.0901470. Available at http://ehsehplp03.niehs.nih.gov/article/info:doi%2F10.1289%2Fehp.0901470. Accessed July 2010.

8. F. P. Perera, Z. Li, et al., "Prenatal Airborne Polycyclic Aromatic Hydrocarbon Exposure and Child IQ at Age 5 Years," *Pediatrics* (July 2009). doi:10.1542/peds.2008-3506. July 2009, Available at http://pediatrics.aappublications.org/cgi/content/abstract/peds.2008-3506v1. Accessed July 2010.

Chapter 14

1. Nord, M., M. Andrews, and S. Carlson. 2008. Household Food Security in the United States, 2007. United States Department of Agriculture (USDA), Economic Research Report No. (ERR-66), November 2008. Available at www.ers.usda.gov/Publications/ERR66. Accessed January 2009.

2. Ibid.

3. Ibid.

4. Food and Agriculture Organization of the United Nations. 2010. Hunger. Available at www.fao.org/hunger/en/. Accessed April 2010.

5. Food and Agriculture Organization of the United Nations. 2004. Undernourished Population (2002–2004). Available at www.fao.org.es.ess.faostat/foodsecurity/FS%20Map/map14.htm. Accessed March 2010.

6. World Bank. 2010. Understanding Poverty. Available at www.worldbank.org/poverty. Accessed October 2010.

7. Hunger in the United States. 2007. Food Research and Action Center (FRAC). Available at www.frac.org/html/hunger_in_the_us/poverty.html. Accessed March 2010.

8. USDA. Food Security in the United States: Key Statistics and Graphics. Updated 2008. Available at www.ers.usda.gov/Briefing/FoodSecurity/stats_graphs.htm. Accessed April 2010.

9. United Nations Association of the United States of America and the Business Council for the United Nations. 2006. Millennium Development Goals—Goal 3: Gender Equity. Available at www.unausa.org/Page.aspx?pid=342. Accessed April 2010; Holben, D. H. 2010. Position of the American Dietetic Association: Food Insecurity and Hunger in the United States. *Journal of the American Dietetic Association* 110: 1368–1377.

10. Ibid.

11. U.S. Department of Health and Human Services. 2010. 2009 HHS Poverty Guidelines. *Federal Register* 74: 4199–4201. Available at http://aspe.hhs.gov/poverty/09poverty.shtml. Accessed April 2010.

12. Smith, L. C., and L. Haddad. 2000. *Explaining Child Malnutrition in Developing Countries: A Cross-Country Analysis of International Food Policy.* Washington, D.C.: International Food Policy Research Institute.

13. United Nations Association of the United States of America and the Business Council for the United Nations. Millennium Development Goals—Goal 3: Gender Equity.

14. Department of Foreign Affairs and International Trade, Canada. 2006. Statements on Humanitarian Affairs. Available at www.canadainternational.gc.ca/prmny-mponu/canada_un-canada_onu/statements-declarations/humanitarian-humanitaires/8272.aspx?lang=eng. Accessed April 2010.

15. United States Census. Historical Poverty Tables.

16. Struble, M. B., and L. Aomari. 2003. ADA Reports: Position of the American Dietetic Association. Addressing World Hunger. *Journal of the American Dietetic Association.*

17. Food and Agriculture Organization of the United Nations. 2008. The State of Food Insecurity in the World, 2008. Available at www.fao.org/docrep/011/i0291e/i0291e00.htm. Accessed April 2010.

18. Agriculture and Agri-Food Canada. 1997. The Pros and Cons of Pesticides. Available at www.ns.ec.gc.ca/epb/factsheets/pesticides/pro_con.html. Accessed April 2010.

19. Food and Agriculture Organization. The State of Food Insecurity in the World, 2008.

20. Bread for the World Institute. 2006. Hunger Basics: World Hunger and Hunger Facts. Available at www.bread.org/hunger/global/. Accessed October 2010; Rosegrant, M. W., and M. A. Sombilia. 1997. Critical Issues Suggested by Trends in Food, Population, and the Environment for the Year 2020. *American Journal of Agricultural Economics* 79: 1467–1471; Brown, L. R., G. Gardner, and B. Halweil. 1999. 16 Impacts of Population Growth. *Futurist* 33: 36–41.

21. Kramer, M. S., and R. Kakuma. 2004. The Optimal Duration of Exclusive Breast-Feeding: A Systematic Review. *Advanced Experimental Medical Biology* 554: 63–77.

22. King, F. S., and A. Burgess. 1993. *Nutrition for Developing Countries,* 2nd ed. Oxford, England: Oxford Medical Publications, Oxford University Press.

23. Struble. Addressing World Hunger.

24. Beers, M., R. Porter, T. Jones, J. Kaplan, and M. Berkwits, eds. 2006. Starvation. In *The Merck Manual of Diagnosis and Therapy*, Section 1—Nutritional Disorders, Chapter 2: Malnutrition Topics. Available at www.merck.com/mrkshared/mmanual/section1/chapter2/2b.jsp. Accessed April 2010.
25. Bureau of Labor Statistics. 2009. A Profile of the Working Poor, 2007. Available at www.bls.gov/cps/cpswp2007.pdf. Accessed April 2010.
26. Beers, et al. Starvation. In *The Merck Manual of Diagnosis and Therapy*.
27. SUSTAIN. 2010. Malnutrition Overview. Available at www.sustaintech.org/world.htm. Accessed April 2010.
28. Kleinman, R. E., et al. 1998. Hunger in Children in the United States: Potential Behavioral and Emotional Correlates. *Pediatrics* 101: 3–10.
29. Scanlon, K. S. 1989. (Thesis) Activity and Behavior Changes of Marginally Malnourished Mexican Pre-Schoolers. Storrs, CT: University of Connecticut; Mora, J. O. 1979. Nutritional Supplementation, Early Stimulation, and Child Development. In J. Brozek, ed. *Behavioral Effects of Energy and Protein Deficits*. Bethesda, MD: U.S. Department of Health, Education, and Welfare.
30. Uvin, P. 1994. The State of World Hunger. In P. Uvin, ed. *The Hunger Report, 1993*. Langhorne, PA: Gordon and Breach Science Publishers: 102.
31. U.S. Department of Health and Human Services. 2009 HHS Poverty Guidelines.
32. Food and Agriculture Organization. The State of Food Insecurity in the World, 2008.
33. U.S. Department of Health and Human Services. 2009 HHS Poverty Guidelines; United Nations Administrative Committee on Coordination Sub-Committee on Nutrition. 2010. *Sixth Report on the World Nutrition Situation*. Available at www.unscn.org/files/Publications/RWNS6/html/index.html. Accessed October 2010.
34. Martorell, R., J. Rivera, and H. Kaplowitz, 1992a. Consequences of Stunting in Early Childhood for Adult Body Size in Rural Guatemala. *Annales Nestle* 48: 85–92; Martorell, R., J. Rivera, H. Kaplowitz, and E. Pollit, 1992b. Proceedings of the VIth International Congress of Auxiology. Long-Term Consequences of Growth Retardation during Early Childhood. New York: Elsevier Science Publishers.
35. UNICEF Statistics. 2010. Integrated Management of Childhood Illness (IMCI). Available at www.who.int/child_adolescent_health/topics/prevention_care/child/imci/en/index.htm. Accessed April 2010.
36. U. S. Department of Health and Human Services. 2009 HHS Poverty Guidelines.
37. UNICEF Statistics. IMCI.
38. SUSTAIN. Malnutrition Overview.
39. Food and Agriculture Organization. The State of Food Insecurity in the World, 2008.
40. Agriculture and Agri-Food Canada. The Pros and Cons of Pesticides.
41. Struble. Addressing World Hunger.
42. Food and Agriculture Organization. The State of Food Insecurity in the World, 2008.
43. Bread for the World Institute. Hunger Basics; Rosegrant. Critical Issues Suggested by Trends in Food, Population, and the Environment for the Year 2020.; Brown. 16 Impacts of Population Growth.
44. Kramer. The Optimal Duration of Exclusive Breast-Feeding. www.ncbi.nlm.nih.gov/pubmed/15384567
45. King. *Nutrition for Developing Countries*.
46. Struble. Addressing World Hunger.

Feature Box References

1. ADA Reports. Position of the American Dietetic Association. Hunger.
2. American Obesity Association. 2005. Obesity Fact Sheets. Available at http://obesity1.tempdomainname.com/subs/fastfacts/Obesity_Minority_Pop.shtml; FRAC. 2010.
3. Miech, R. A., et al. 2006. Trends in the Association of Poverty with Overweight Among US Adolescents, 1971-2004. *Journal of the American Medical Association* Available at http://jama.ama-assn.org/cgi/content/abstract/295/20/2385?view=short&fp=2385&vol=295&lookupType=volpage. Accessed October 2010; Centers for Disease Control and Prevention. Overweight and Obesity Trends Among Adults. Available at http://cdc.gov/obesity/data/index.html. Accessed October 2010.
4. American Obesity Association.
5. World Health Organization. 2009. World Health Day 2009. Available at www.who.int/world-health-day/2009/emergencies_impact/en/. Accessed October 2010.
6. BBC News. 2010. Haiti Will Not Die, President Rene Preval Insists. Available at http://news.bbc.co.uk/2/hi/americas/8511997.stm. Accessed October 2010.
7. Friends of the World Food Program. 2010. Latest Assessment Reveals Widespread Food Insecurity in Haiti. Available at http://friendsofwfp.typepad.com/friends/2010/03/latest-assessment-reveals-widespread-food-insecurity-in-haiti.html. Accessed October 2010.
8. Food and Agriculture Organization of the United Nations (FAO). 2010. Haiti: Earthquake Flash Appeal, 2010. Available at http://www.fao.org/emergencies/tce-appfund/tce-appeals/appeals/emergency-detail0/en/item/39184/icode/?uidf=15446. Accessed October 2010.
9. Ibid.

Two Points of View References

1. United States Department of Agriculture, Economic Research Service, *Amber Waves: 50 Years of US Food Aid and Its Role in Reducing World Hunger* (2004) Available at www.ers.usda.gov/amberwaves/september04/features/usfoodaid.htm. Accessed August 2010.
2. UK Department for International Development, "Cash or Food?" *Developments* Available at. www.developments.org.uk/articles/cash-or-food/. Accessed August 2010.
3. Bretton Woods Project, "Farming Furor: World Bank Launches New Agriculture Fund." (February 2010) Available at www.brettonwoodsproject.org/art-565915. Accessed August 2010.
4. Ibid.
5. UK Department for International Development. "Cash or Food?"
6. Ibid.
7. A. Gelan, "Cash or Food Aid? A General Equilibrium Analysis for Ethiopia," *Development Policy Review* 24, no. 5 (September 2006): 601–624,. Available at http://ssrn.com/abstract=925064 or doi:10.1111/j.1467-7679.2006.00350. Accessed August 2010.
8. USAid Disaster Assistance, "How Can I Help? Advantages of Monetary Donations." Available at www.usaid.gov/our_work/humanitarian_assistance/disaster_assistance/help/advantages.html. Accessed August 2010.
9. Gelan. "Cash or Food Aid?"; H. Astier, BBC News, "Can Aid Do More Harm Than Good?" (February 2006) Available at http://news.bbc.co.uk/2/hi/africa/4185550.stm. Accessed August 2010.
10. H. W. Singer, "Food Aid: Pros and Cons," *Intereconomics* (March/April 1988) Available at http://resources.metapress.com/pdf-preview.axd?code=0601u35112210j75&size=largest. Accessed August 2010.
11. Food First, Institute for Food and Development Policy, "Famine in Africa Means the Poor Can't Buy Food." (January 2006) Available at www.foodfirst.org/node/1380. Accessed August 2010.

Chapter 15

1. Wong, W., C. Thomas, J. Merkus, G. Zielhuis, and R. Steegers-Theunissen. 2000. Male Factor Subfertility: Possible Causes and the Impact of Nutritional Factors. *Fertility and Sterility* 73: 435–442; Magnusdottir, E., T. Thorsteinsson, S. Thorsteinsdottir, M. Heimisdottir, and K. Olagsdottir. 2005. Persistent Organochlorines, Sedentary Occupation, Obesity, and Human Male Subfertility. *Human Reproduction* 20: 208–225.
2. Eskenazi, B., S. Kidd, A. Marks, E. Sloter, G. Block, and A. Wyrobek. 2005. Antioxidant Intake Is Associated with Semen Quality in Healthy Men. *Human Reproduction* 20: 1006–1012.
3. Wong. Male Factor Subfertility; Magnusdottir. Persistent Organochlorines, Sedentary Occupation, Obesity, and Human Male Subfertility; Eskenazi. Antioxidant Intake Is Associated with Semen Quality in Healthy Men.
4. Kaiser, L., and L. Allen. 2008. Position of the American Dietetic Association: Nutrition and Lifestyle for a Healthy Pregnancy Outcome. *Journal of the American Dietetic Association* 108:553–561.
5. Bolumar, F., J. Olsen, M. Rebagliato, L. Bisanti, and the European Study Group on Infertility and Subfecundity. 1997. Caffeine Intake and Delayed Conception: A European Multicenter Study on Infertility and Subfecundity. *American Journal of Epidemiology* 145: 324–334.
6. Weng, X., R. Odouli, and D. K. Li 2008. Maternal Caffeine Consumption during Pregnancy and the Risk of Miscarriage: A Prospective Cohort Study. *American Journal of Obstetrics and Gynecology* 198: 279.e1–e8 doi: 10.1136/bmj.c2331
7. U.S. Department of Health and Human Services. 2004. *The Health Consequences of Smoking: A Report of the Surgeon General*. Atlanta: National Center for Chronic Disease Prevention and Health Promotion, Office on Smoking and Health.
8. U.S. Department of Health and Human Services. 2005. U.S. Surgeon General Advisory on Alcohol Use in Pregnancy. Available at

www.cdc.gov/ncbddd/fas/documents/Released%20Advisory.pdf. Accessed July 2010.

9. Quilan. J. D, & Hill, D. A. Nausea and Vomiting of Pregnancy; Strong, T. 2001. Alternative Therapies of Morning Sickness. *Clinical Obstetrics and Gynecology* 44: 653–660.

10. Kaiser. Position of the American Dietetic Association: Nutrition and Lifestyle for a Healthy Pregnancy Outcome.

11. Institute of Medicine. 2009. Weight Gain during Pregnancy: Reexamining the Guidelines.Available at www.iom.edu/~/media/Files/Report%20Files/2009/Weight-Gain-During-Pregnancy-Reexamining-the-Guidelines/Report%20Brief%20-%20Weight%20Gain%20During%20Pregnancy.ashx. Accessed July 2010.

12. Ibid.

13. USDA. 2010. Report of the Dietary Guidelines Advisory Committee on the *Dietary Guidelines for Americans 2010*. Available at www.cnpp.usda.gov/DGAs2010-DGACReport.htm. Accessed June 2010.

14. Kaiser. Position of the American Dietetic Association: Nutrition and Lifestyle for a Healthy Pregnancy Outcome.

15. U.S. Department of Agriculture, U.S. Department of Health and Human Services. 2010. *Dietary Guidelines for Americans, 2010.* 7th ed. Washington, D.C.: U.S. Government Printing Office; Picciano, M. 2003. Pregnancy and Lactation: Physiological Adjustments, Nutritional Requirements and the Role of Dietary Supplements. *Journal of Nutrition* 133: 1997S–2002S.

16. Kaiser. Position of the American Dietetic Association: Nutrition and Lifestyle for a Healthy Pregnancy Outcome.

17. Hornstra, G. 2000. Essential Fatty Acids in Mothers and Their Neonates. *American Journal of Clinical Nutrition* 71: 1262S–1269S.; Hollenbeck, C. 2010. The Importance of Being Choline. *The Journal of the American Dietetic Association;* 110:1162-1165.

18. USDA. 2010. MyPyramid for Pregnancy and Breastfeeding. Available at www.mypyramid.gov/mypyramidmoms/. Accessed July 2010.

19. Kaiser. Position of the American Dietetic Association: Nutrition and Lifestyle for a Healthy Pregnancy Outcome.

20. Substance Abuse and Mental Health Services Administration. 2005. Results from the 2004 National Survey on Drug Use and Health: National Findings. Available at http://oas.samhsa.gov/nsduh/2k4nsduh/2k4Results/2k4Results.htm. Accessed July 2010.

21. Weng. Maternal Caffeine Consumption during Pregnancy.

22. Painter, R. C., S. R. de Rooij, P. M. Bossuyt, T. A. Simmers, C. Osmond, D. J. Barker, et al. 2006. Early Onset of Coronary Artery Disease after Prenatal Exposure to the Dutch Famine. *American Journal of Clinical Nutrition* 84: 322–327.

23. Ames, B. N. 2006. Low Micronutrient Intake May Accelerate the Degenerative Diseases of Aging through Allocation of Scarce Micronutrients by Triage. *Proceedings of the National Academy of Sciences* 103: 17589–17594.

24. Wu, G., F. W. Bazer, T. A. Cudd, C. J. Meininger, and T. E. Spencer. 2004. Recent Advances in Nutritional Sciences: Maternal Nutrition and Fetal Development. *Journal of Nutrition* 134: 2169–2172.

25. Stover, P. J., and M. A. Caudill. 2008. Genetic and Epigenetic Contributions to Human Nutrition and Health: Managing Genome-Diet Interactions. *Journal of the American Dietetic Association* 108: 1480–1487.

26. Wang, T., and B. Apgar. 1998. Exercise during Pregnancy. *American Family Physician* 57: 1846–1856; The National Women's Health Information Center. 2006. Healthy Pregnancy: Have a Fit Pregnancy. Available at www.4woman.org/pregnancy. Accessed July 2010.

27. ACOG Committee Obstetric Practice. 2002. ACOG Committee Opinion No. 267, Exercise during Pregnancy and the Postpartum Period. *Obstetrics and Gynecology* 99: 171–173.

28. American Diabetes Association. Gestational Diabetes. Available at www.diabetes.org/gestational-diabetes.jsp. Accessed July 2010.

29. Ibid.

30. National Institute of Child Health and Human Development. 2004. Will Gestational Diabetes Hurt My Baby? Available at www.nichd.nih.gov/publications/pubs/gdm/GDM2004_section2.pdf. Accessed July 2010.

31. Correa, A., L. Botto, Y. Liu, J. Mulinare, and J. Erickson. 2003. Do Multivitamin Supplements Attenuate the Risk of Diabetes-Associated Birth Defects? *Pediatrics 2003* 111: 1146–1151; National Institute of Child Health and Human Development. Will Gestational Diabetes Hurt My Baby?

32. American Diabetes Association. Gestational Diabetes.

33. National Institute of Child Health and Human Development. 2006. Am I at Risk for Gestational Diabetes? Available at http://diabetes.niddk.nih.gov/dm/pubs/gestational. Accessed July 2010.

34. Chobanian, A., G. Bakris, H. Black, W. Cushman, L. Green, J. Izzo, D. Jones, B. Materson, S. Oparil, J. Wright, E. Roccella, and the National High Blood Pressure Education Program Coordinating Committee. 2003. Seventh Report of the Joint National Committee on Prevention, Detection, Evaluation, and Treatment of High Blood Pressure. *Hypertension* 42: 1206–1252. Available at www.nhlbi.nih.gov/guidelines/hypertension/. Accessed July 2010.

35. National Heart, Lung, and Blood Institute. 2010. High Blood Pressure in Pregnancy. Available at www.nhlbi.nih.gov/health/public/heart/hbp/hbp_preg.htm. Accessed July 2010.

36. Ibid.

37. Ibid.

38. Ibid.

39. Ibid.

40. Ibid.

41. Kaiser. Position of the American Dietetic Association: Nutrition and Lifestyle for a Healthy Pregnancy Outcome.

42. Ibid.

43. Ibid.

44. Ibid.

45. Ibid.

46. Martin, J., B. Hamilton, P. Sutton, S. Ventura, F. Menacker, and M. Munson. 2005. Births: Final Data for 2003. *National Vital Statistics Reports,* Centers for Disease Control and Prevention. Available at www.cdc.gov/nchs/fastats/teenbrth.htm. Accessed June 2010.

47. Rees, J., and B. Worthington-Roberts. 1994. Position of the American Dietetic Association: Nutrition Care for Pregnant Adolescents. *Journal of the American Dietetic Association* 94: 449–450.

48. Martin, et al. Births: Final Data for 2003.

49. Shabert, J. 2000. Nutrition during pregnancy and lactation. In Krause, *Food, Nutrition, & Diet Therapy.* 11th ed. Philadelphia: Saunders.

50. U.S. Department of Health and Human Services (HSS). 2000. HHS Blueprint for Action on Breastfeeding. Available at www.womenshealth.gov/pub/hhs.cfm. Accessed July 2010.

51. Ibid.

52. Economic Research Service. 2001. Economic Benefits of Breastfeeding: A Review and Analysis. Available at www.ers.usda.gov/publications/fanrr13/fanrr13.pdf. Accessed July 2010.

53. Bartick, M., and Reinhold, A. 2010. The Burden of Suboptimal Breastfeeding in the United States. *Pediatrics* 125: e1048–e1056 Available at http://pediatrics.aappublications.org/cgi/content/abstract/125/5/e1048?maxtoshow=&hits=10&RESULTFORMAT=&fulltext=cost[plus]of[plus]breastfeeding&searchid=1&FIRSTINDEX=0&sortspec=relevance&resourcetype=HWCIT. Accessed June 2010.

54. Economic Research Service. Economic Benefits of Breastfeeding.

55. U.S. Breastfeeding Committee. 2002. Benefits of Breastfeeding. Available at www.ehd.org/pdf/sources/469.pdfwww.usbreastfeeding.org/Issue-Papers/Benefits.pdf. Accessed July 2010.

56. Klaus, K. 1998. Mother and Infant: Early Emotional Ties. *Pediatrics* 102: 1244–1246.

57. Institute of Medicine. 1992. *Nutrition during Lactation: Update to the Implementation Guide.* Washington, D.C.: National Academies Press. Available at www.mchlibrary.info/pubs/PDFs/nutritionupdate.pdf. Accessed July 1010.

58. James, D. C. S., and Lessen, R. 2009. Position of the American Dietetic Association: Promoting and Supporting Breastfeeding. *Journal of the American Dietetic Association* 109: 1926–1942.

59. Ibid.

60. Ibid.

61. Ibid.

62. Ibid.

63. Bidlack, W., and W. Wang. 2006. Designing Functional Foods. In Shils, M. *Modern Nutrition in Health and Disease.* 10th ed. Philadelphia: Lippincott Williams & Wilkins.

64. Picciano, M. 2006. Lactation. In Shils, M. *Modern Nutrition in Health and Disease.* 10th ed. Philadelphia: Lippincott Williams & Wilkins.

65. James. Position of the American Dietetic Association: Promoting and Supporting Breastfeeding.

66. Ibid.

67. U.S. Breastfeeding Committee. Benefits of Breastfeeding.; Fisher, J., L. Birch, H. Smiciklas-Wright, and M. Picciano. 2000. Breast-Feeding through the First Year Predicts Maternal Control in Feeding and Subsequent Toddler Energy Intakes. *Journal of the American Dietetic Association* 100: 641–646.

68. Grummer-Strawn, L., and Z. Mei. 2004. Does Breastfeeding Protect Against Pediatric Overweight? Analysis of Longitudinal Data from the Centers for Disease Control and Prevention Pediatric Nutrition Surveillance System. *Pediatrics* 113: e81–e86; Krebs, N., M. Jacobson, R. Baker, F. Greer, M. Heyman, T. Jaksic, and F. Lifshitz. 2003. Prevention of Pediatric Overweight and Obesity. *Pediatrics* 112: 424–430.

69. James. Position of the American Dietetic Association: Promoting and Supporting Breastfeeding. ; White House Task Force on Childhood Obesity. Report to the President. May 2010. Available at http://www.letsmove.gov/pdf/TaskForce_on_Childhood_Obesity_May2010_FullReport.pdf. Accessed August 2010.

70. Ibid.

71. Institute of Medicine. *Nutrition during Lactation: Update to the Implementation Guide.*

72. U.S. Department of Agriculture. *Dietary Guidelines for Americans;* Ward, R., B. Bates, W. Benitz, D. Burch?eld, J. Ring, J. Walls, and P. Walson. 2001. The Transfer of Drugs and Other Chemicals into Human Milk. *Pediatrics* 108: 776–784.

73. James. Position of the American Dietetic Association: Promoting and Supporting Breastfeeding.

74. Gartner, L., 2005. Breastfeeding and the Use of Human Milk. *Pediatrics* 115: 496–506.

75. Udall, J., and R. Suskind. 1999. Cow's Milk versus Formula in Older Infants: Consequences for Human Nutrition. *Acta paediatrica. Supplementum* 430: 61–70.

76. Udall. Cow's Milk versus Formula; Heird, W., and A. Cooper. 2006. Infancy and Childhood. In Shils, *Modern Nutrition in Health and Disease.* 10th ed. Philadelphia: Lippincott Williams & Wilkins.

77. Ibid.

78. Sarrinen, K., K. Juntunen-Backman, A. Jarvenpaa, P. Kuitunen, L. Lope, M. Renlund, M. Siivola, and E. Savilahti. 1999. Supplementary Feeding in Maternity Hospitals and the Risk of Cow's Milk Allergy: A Prospective Study of 6,209 Infants. *Journal of Allergy and Clinical Immunology* 104: 457–461.

79. American Academy of Pediatrics. Policy Statement: Iron Fortification of Infant Forumlas (1999). Available at www.aap.org. Accessed July 2010.

80. American Academy of Pediatrics. Iron Fortification of Infant Formulas; Food and Drug Administration. 2005. Food Safety for Moms-to-Be. Once Baby Arrives. Available at www.cfsan.fda.gov/~pregnant/pregnant.html. Accessed July 2010.

81. American Academy of Pediatrics. . Iron Fortification of Infant Formulas

82. Ibid.

83. Ibid.

84. Bogen, D. L., A. K. Duggan, G. J. Dover, and M. H. Wilson. 2000. Screening for Iron-Deficiency Anemia by Dietary History in a High-Risk Population. *Pediatrics* 105: 1254–1259.

85. National Center for Health Statistics. Centers for Disease Control and Prevention Growth Charts. Available at www.cdc.gov/nchs/about/major/nhanes/growthcharts/background.htm. Accessed July 2010.

86. Institute of Medicine, Food and Nutrition Board. 2002. *Dietary Reference Intakes for Energy, Carbohydrate, Fiber, Fat, Fatty Acids, Cholesterol, Protein, and Amino Acids.* Washington, D.C.: The National Academies Press.

87. Gartner. Breastfeeding and the Use of Human Milk.

88. American Academy of Pediatrics. 2008. Prevention of Rickets and Vitamin D Deficiency in Infants, Children, and Adolescents. Available at http://aappolicy.aappublications.org/cgi/content/abstract/pediatrics122/5/1142. Accessed July 2010.

89. American Academy of Pediatrics. 2005. Breastfeeding and the Use of Human Milk. Available at http://aappolicy.aappublications.org/cgi/content/abstract/pediatrics115/2/496. Accessed July 2010.

90. Ibid.

91. Ibid.

92. Butte, N., K. Cobb, J. Dwyer, L. Graney, W. Heird, and K. Rickard. 2004. The Start Healthy Feeding Guidelines for Infants and Toddlers. *Journal of the American Dietetic Association* 104: 442–454.

93. Ibid.

94. The Food Allergy and Anaphylaxis Network. 2004. Common Food Allergens. Available at www.foodallergy.org/section/allergens. Accessed July 2010.

95. Butte. The Start Healthy Feeding Guidelines for Infants and Toddlers.

96. Ibid.

97. Centers for Disease Control and Prevention. 2010. Botulism. Available at www.cdc.gov/ncidod/dbmd/diseaseinfo/botulism_g.htm. Accessed July 2010.

98. Briefel R., P. Ziegler, T. Novak, and M. Ponza. 2006. Feeding Infants and Toddlers Study: Characteristics and Usual Nutrient Intake of Hispanic and Non-Hispanic Infants and Toddlers. *Journal of the American Dietetic Association* 106 (supplement): S84–S95.

Feature Box References

1. Bureau of Labor Statistics. 2006. Table 6: Employment Status of Mothers with Own Children Under 3 Years Old by Single Year of Age of Youngest Child, and Marital Status, 2004–2005 Annual Averages. Available at www.bls.gov/news.release/famee.t06.htm. Accessed July 2010.

2. Slusser, W., L. Lange, V. Dickson, C. Hawkes, and R. Cohen. 2004. Breast Milk Expression in the Workplace: A Look at Frequency and Time. *Journal of Human Lactation* 20: 164–169.

3. Johnson, M. 2006. Letter to the Editor: Twentieth Anniversary Issue. *Journal of Human Lactation* 22: 14–15.

4. National Conference of State Legislatures. 2006. 50-State Summary of Breastfeeding Laws. Available at www.ncsl.org/programs/health/breast50.htm. Accessed July 2010.

5. U.S. Breastfeeding Committee. 2002. Workplace Breastfeeding Support. Available at www.usbreastfeeding.org/Issue-Papers/Workplace.pdf. Accessed July 2010.

6. Ibid.

7. Ibid.

8. National Institute of Allergy and Infectious Diseases. 2004. Food Allergy and Intolerances. Available at www.niaid.nih.gov/factsheets/food.htm. Accessed July 2010.

9. Ibid.

10. National Institute of Allergy and Infectious Diseases. Food Allergy and Intolerances; The Food Allergy and Anaphylaxis Network. 2004. Common Food Allergens. Available at www.foodallergy.org/allergens.html. Accessed July 2010.

11. Long, A. 2002. The Nuts and Bolts of Peanut Allergy. *New England Journal of Medicine* 346: 1320–1322.

12. Food and Drug Administration. 2006. Food Allergen Labeling and Consumer Protection Act of 2004 (Title II of Public Law 108–282). Report to the Committee on Health, Education, Labor, and Pensions, United States Senate, and the Committee on Energy and Commerce, United States House of Representatives. Available at www.cfsan.fda.gov/~acrobat/alrgrep.pdf. Accessed July 2010.

Two Points of View References

1. Health and Human Services Division, Municipality of Anchorage, Alaska, "Why Homemade?" Available at http://hhs.muni.org/wic/homemade_baby_food.aspx. Accessed August 2010; D. Stallone, and M. Jacobson, "Cheating Babies: Nutritional Quality and Cost of Baby Food," *CSPI Reports* Available at www.cspinet.org/reports/cheat1.html. Accessed August 2010.

2. Freshbaby.com, "Healthy Eating for Babies." Available at http://freshbaby.com/healthy_eating/healthyeating_featured_03.cfm. Accessed July 2010.

3. Municipality of Anchorage. "Why Homemade?"; Stallone. "Cheating Babies."; Freshbaby.com. "Healthy Eating for Babies."

4. B. Fountain, University of Mississippi Extension Service, "Homemade Baby Food Benefits Entire Family." (July 2010) Available at www.extension.org/pages/Homemade_Baby_Food_Benefits_Entire_Family. Accessed August 2010.

5. USDA, Agricultural Research Service, "The New Food Quality Protection Act, 2006." Available at www.ars.usda.gov/is/np/mba/april97/calepa.htm. Accessed August 2010.

6. G. Shaw, "Homemade Baby Food: Is it Right for You?" *Web MD* Available at www.webmd.com/parenting/baby/baby-food-nutrition-9/making-baby-food. Accessed July 2010.

7. E. Schaefer, and N. Fradgley, National Network for Child Care, "Feeding Your Baby." (1995) Available at www.nncc.org/Nutrition/feed.baby.html. Accessed August 2010.

8. F. Greer, and M. Shannon, "Infant Methemoglobinemia: The Role of Dietary Nitrate in Food and Water," *Pediatrics* 116 no. 3 (September 2005): 784–786 (doi:10.1542/peds.2005-1497). Available at http://pediatrics.aappublications.org/cgi/content/full/116/3/784. Accessed August 2010.

Chapter 16

1. National Center for Health Statistics. 2000. *NCHS Growth Curves for Children 0–19 Years.* U.S. Vital and Health Statistics, Health Resources Administration. Washington, D.C.: U.S. Government Printing Office.

2. American Academy of Pediatrics. "Promoting Healthy Nutrition," Available at http://brightfutures.aap.org/pdfs/Guidelines_PDF/6-Promoting_Healthy_Nutrition.pdf. Accessed July 2010.

3. Ziegler, P., C. Hanson, M. Ponza, T. Novak, and K. Hendricks. 2006. Feeding Infants and Toddlers Study: Meal and Snack Intakes of Hispanic and Non-Hispanic Infants and Toddlers. *Journal of the American Dietetic Association* 106 (supplement): 107–123.

4. American Academy of Pediatrics. "Parenting Corner Q & A: Choking Prevention. Available at www.aap.org. Accessed July 2010.

5. U.S. Department of Health and Human Services. 2004. *The 2004 Surgeon General's Report on Bone Health and Osteoporosis: What It Means to You.* Washington, D.C.: Office of the Surgeon General.

6. Kazal, L. A., Jr. 2002. Prevention of Iron Deficiency in Infants and Toddlers. *American Family Physician* 66: 1217–1224.

7. U.S. Dept. of Health & Human Services.*Healthy People 2010.* "Nutrition and Overweight." Available at www.healthypeople.gov. Accessed July 2010.

8. Corbett, J. V. 1995. Accidental Poisoning with Iron Supplements. *MCN: The American Journal of Maternal Child Nursing* 20: 234.

9. Food and Drug Administration. 1997. Preventing Iron Poisoning in Children. Available at http://vm.cfsan.fda.gov/~dms.bgiron.html. Accessed August 2009.

10. Wagner, C. L., F. R. Greer, and the Section on Breastfeeding and Committee on Nutrition. 2008. Prevention of Rickets and Vitamin D Deficiency in Infants, Children, and Adolescents. *Pediatrics* 122: 1142–1152.

11. Ibid.

12. American Academy of Pediatrics (AAP) Committee on Nutrition. 2003. *Pediatric Nutrition Handbook.* Elk Grove Village, IL: AAP.

13. Satter, E. 2003. *Child of Mine: Feeding with Love and Good Sense.* Boulder, CO: Bull Publishing.

14. Rolls, B. J., D. Engell, and L. L. Birch. 2000. Serving Portion Size Influences 5-Year-Old but Not 3-Year-Old Children's Food Intakes. *Journal of the American Dietetic Association* 100: 232–234.

15. American Dietetic Association, 2003. Position of the American Dietetic Association and Dietitians of Canada: Vegetarian Diets. *Journal of the American Dietetic Association* 103: 748–765.

16. National Center for Health Statistics (NCHS). 2010. Overweight Prevalence: National Health and Nutrition Examination Survey Data. Hyattsville, MD: Centers for Disease Control and Prevention. Available at www.cdc.gov/nchs/data/hestat/obesity_child_07_08/obesity_child_07_08.htm. Accessed June 2010.

17. National Institutes of Health. 2010. Obesity Education Initiative. Available at www.nhlbi.nih.gov/health/public/heart/obesity/wecan. Accessed June 2010.

18. Batada, A., M. Seitz., M. Wootan, and M. Story. 2008. Nine Out of 10 Food Advertisements Shown during Saturday Morning Children's Television Programming Are for Foods High in Fat, Sodium, or Added Sugars, or Low in Nutrients. *Journal of the American Dietetic Association* 108: 673–678.

19. Henry J. Kaiser Family Foundation. 2010. Generation M2: Media in the Lives of 8–18-Year-Olds: Report. Available at www.kff.org/entmedia/mh012010pkg.cfm. Accessed June 2010.

20. School Health Policies and Programs Study (SHPPS). 2006. Fact Sheet: Physical Education and Activity from SHPPS 2000. Available at www.cdc.gov/HealthyYouth/shpps. Accessed June 2010.

21. Satcher, D. 2005. Healthy and Ready to Learn: Research Shows That Nutrition and Physical Activity Affect Student Academic Achievement. *Educational Leadership* 63: 26–30.

22. American Academy of Pediatrics. 2003. Prevention of Pediatric Overweight and Obesity. *Pediatrics* 112: 424–430.

23. Rampersaud, G. C., M. A. Pereira, B. L. Girard, J. Adams, and J. D. Metzl. 2005. Breakfast Habits, Nutritional Status, Body Weight, and Academic Performance in Children and Adolescents. *Journal of the American Dietetic Association* 105:743-760.

24. U.S. Department of Agriculture, U.S. Department of Health and Human Services. 2010. *Dietary Guidelines for Americans, 2010.* 7th ed. Washington, D.C.: U.S. Government Printing Office.

25. U.S. Department of Agriculture. 2011. USDA Unveils Critical Upgrades to Nutritional Standards for School Meals. Available at http://usda.gov/wps/portal/usda/usdahome?contentidonly=true&contentid=2011/01/0010.xml; U.S. Department of Agriculture, Food and Nutrition Service. 2005. National School Lunch Program Fact Sheet. www.fns.usda.gov/cnd/lunch/aboutlunch/NSLPFactSheet.pdf.

26. Centers for Disease Control and Prevention. 2010. *Trends in Childhood Obesity.* Available at www.cdc.gov/obesity/childhood/trends.html. Accessed July 2010.

27. National Institute of Arthritis and Musculoskeletal and Skin Diseases. 2001. Growth Plate Injuries. Available at www.niams.nih.gov/Health_Info/Growth_Plate_Injuries/default.asp#1. Accessed June 2010.

28. Prevention of Rickets and Vitamin D Deficiency in Infants, Children, and Adolescents. *Pediatrics* 122:1142-1152.

29. U.S. Department of Agriculture. 2009. The Quality of Children's Diets as Measured by the Healthy Eating Index 2005. www.cnpp.usda.gov/Publications/NutritionInsights/Insight43.pdf. Accessed July 2010; Center for Science in the Public Interest. 2005. Liquid Candy. Available at www.cspinet.org/new/pdf/liquid_candy_final_w_new_supplement.pdf. Accessed July 2010.

30. Alaimo, K. 1994. *Dietary Intake of Vitamins, Minerals and Fiber of Persons Ages 2 Months and Over in the United States.* Hyattsville, MD: National Center for Health Statistics.

31. Johnson R. K., D. G. Johnson, M.Q.Wang, H. Smiciklas-Wright, and H. Guthrie. 1994. Characterizing Nutrient Intakes of Adolescents by Sociodemographic Factors. *Journal of Adolescent Health* 15: 149–152.

32. Neumark-Sztainer, D., M. Wall, J. Guo, M. Story, J. Haines, and M. Eisenberg. 2006. Obesity, Disordered Eating, and Eating Disorders in a Longitudinal Study of Adolescents: How Do Dieters Fare Five Years Later? *Journal of the American Dietetic Association* 106: 559–568.

33. Centers for Disease Control and Prevention. 2010. Health, United States, 2009, with Chartbook on Trends in the Health of Americans with Special Feature on Adults 55–64 Years. Available at www.cdc.gov/nchs/hus.htm. Accessed July 2010.

34. He, W., M. Sengupta, V. Velkoff, and K. Debarros. 2005. *65[plus] in the United States, Current Population Reports.* U.S. Census Bureau. Washington D.C.: U.S. Government Printing Office.

35. Centers for Disease Control and Prevention. 2003. Public Health and Aging: Trends in Aging—United States and Worldwide. *Morbidity and Mortality Weekly Report* 52: 101–106.

36. Bales, C., and C. Ritchie. 2006. The elderly. In Shils, M., M. Shike, A. Ross, B. Caballero, and R. Cousins. *Modern Nutrition in Health and Disease.* 10th ed. Philadelphia: Lippincott Williams & Wilkins.

37. Institute of Medicine. *Dietary Reference Intakes for Energy, Carbohydrates, Fiber, Fat, Protein, and Amino Acids.* Washington, D.C.: National Academies Press.

38. Kurczmarski, M., and D. Weddle. 2005. Position Paper of the American Dietetic Association: Nutrition across the Spectrum of Aging. *Journal of the American Dietetic Association* 105: 616–633; Wakimoto, P., and G. Block. 2001. Dietary Intake, Dietary Patterns, and Changes with Age: An Epidemiological Perspective. *Journals of Gerontology Series A: Biological Sciences and Medical Sciences* 56A: 65–80.

39. Moshfegh, A., J. Goldman, and L. Cleveland. 2005. What We Eat in America. NHANES 2001–2002: Usual Nutrient Intakes from Food Compared to Dietary Reference Intakes. Washington, D. C.: U.S. Department of Agriculture, Agricultural Research Service.

40. Ibid.

41. Kurczmarski. Position Paper of the American Dietetic Association: Nutrition across the Spectrum of Aging

42. Ibid.

43. Institute of Medicine. 2011. *Dietary Reference Intakes for Calcium and Vitamin D.* Available at www.iom.edu. Accessed March 2011.

44. Kurczmarski, M. Position Paper of the American Dietetic Association: Nutrition across the Spectrum of Aging; Wakimoto. Dietary Intake, Dietary Patterns, and Changes with Age: An Epidemiological Perspective.

45. Ibid.

46. Institute of Medicine. *Dietary Reference Intakes for Energy.*

47. Cooke, A., and J. Friday. 2005. Pyramid Servings Intakes in the United States 1999–2002: CNRG Table Set 3.0. Community Nutrition Research Group, Agricultural Research Service. Available at www.ba.ars.usda.gov/cnrg. Accessed May 2006.

48. World Health Organization. 2002. *Keep Fit for Life: Meeting the Nutritional Needs of Older Persons.* Geneva, Switzerland: WHO. Available at www.who.int/nutrition/publications/olderpersons/en/index.html. Accessed July 2010.

49. Juan, W., M. Lino, and P. Basiotis. 2008. Quality of Diet of Older Americans. *Nutrition Insight* 41. Center of Nutrition Policy and Promotion. Available at www.cnpp.usda.gov/Publications/NutritionInsights/Insight41.pdf. Accessed July 2010.

50. Cooke. Pyramid Servings Intakes in the United States 1999–2002.

51. World Health Organization. *Keep Fit for Life.*

52. Juan. Quality of Diet of Older Americans; Cooke. Pyramid Servings Intakes in the United States 1999–2002.

53. World Health Organization. *Keep Fit for Life.*

54. Agency for Healthcare Research and Quality and the Centers for Disease Control and Prevention. 2002. Physical Activity and Older Americans: Benefits and Strategies. Available at www.ahrq.gov/ppip/activity.htm. Accessed Accessed July 2010.

55. National Institute of Arthritis and Musculoskeletal and Skin Diseases. 2006. Osteoarthritis. Available at www.niams.nih.gov/Health_Info/Osteoarthritis/default.asp. Accessed July 2010.

56. Ibid.

57. Clegg, D., et al. 2006. Glucosamine, Chondroitin Sulfate, and the Two in Combination for Painful Knee Osteoarthritis. *New England Journal of Medicine* 354: 795–808.

58. National Institute of Arthritis and Musculoskeletal and Skin Diseases. 2009. Rheumatoid Arthritis. Available at www.niams.nih.gov/Health_Info/Rheumatic_Disease/default.asp. Accessed July 2010.

59. Choi, H. 2005. Dietary Risk Factors for Rheumatic Diseases. *Current Opinion in Rheumatology* 17: 141–146.

60. Linos, A., V. Kaklamani, E. Kaklamani, Y. Koumantaki, E. Giziaki, S. Papzoglou, and C. Mantzoros. 1999. Dietary Factors in Relation to Rheumatoid Arthritis: A Role for Olive Oil and Cooked Vegetables. *American Journal of Clinical Nutrition* 70: 1077–1082.

61. National Institute on Aging. 2010. Alzheimer's Fact Sheet. Available at www.nia.nih.gov/Alzheimers/Publications/adfact.htm. Accessed July 2010.

62. National Institute on Aging. Alzheimer's Fact Sheet; Nourhashemi, F., S. Gillette-Guyonnet, S. Andrieu, A. Ghisolfi, P. Ousset, H. Grandjean, A. Grand, J. Pous, B. Vellas, and J. Albarede. 2000. Alzheimer Disease: Protective Factors. *American Journal of Clinical Nutrition* 71: 643S–649S; Martin, A. 2003. Antioxidant Vitamins E and C and Risk of Alzheimer's Disease. *Nutrition Reviews* 61: 69–79.

63. Nourhashemi. Alzheimer Disease: Protective Factors.

64. Maclean, C., A. Iss, S. Newberry, W. Mojica, S. Morton, R. Garland, L. Hilton, S. Traina, and P. Shekell. 2005. Effects of Omega-3 Fatty Acids on Cognitive Function with Aging, Dementia, and Neurological Diseases. Summary, Evidence Report/Technology Assessment No. 114. Agency for Healthcare Research and Quality. Available at www.ahrq.gov/clinic/epcsums/o3cognsum.htm. Accessed July 2010.

65. National Institute on Aging. Alzheimer's Fact Sheet; U.S. Food and Drug Administration. 2009. Dietary Supplements: Tips for Older Dietary Supplement Users. Available at www.fda.gov/food/dietarysupplements/ConsumerInformation/ucm110493.htm. Accessed July 2010.

66. Nord, M., M. Andrews, and S. Carlson. 2008. Household Food Security in the United States, 2008. Economic Research Service. Available at www.ers.usda.gov/publications/err11. Accessed July 2010.

67. Lee, J., and E. Frongillo. 2001. Nutritional and Health Consequences Are Associated with Food Insecurity among U.S. Elderly Persons. *Journal of Nutrition* 131: 1503–1509.

68. Wolfe, W., E. Frongillo, and P. Valois. 2003. Understanding the Experience of Food Insecurity by Elders Suggests Ways to Improve Its Measurement. *Journal of Nutrition* 133: 2762–2769.

69. Administration on Aging. 2009. Older Americans Act. Available at www.aoa.gov/AoARoot/AoA_Programs/OAA/index.aspx. Accessed July 2010.

70. Kurczmarski. Position Paper of the American Dietetic Association: Nutrition across the Spectrum of Aging.

71. U.S. Department of Health and Human Services. 1999. *Mental Health: A Report of the Surgeon General—Executive Summary*. Rockville, MD: U.S. Department of Health and Human Services, Substance Abuse and Mental Health Services Administration, Center for Mental Health Services, National Institutes of Health, National Institute of Mental Health.

72. National Institute on Alcohol Abuse and Alcoholism. 1998. Alcohol and Aging. Available at http://pubs.niaaa.nih.gov/publications/aa40.htm. Accessed July 2010.

73. National Institute on Aging. 2005. Alcohol Use and Abuse. Available at www.niapublications.org/agepages/alcohol.asp. Accessed July 2010.

74. National Institute on Alcohol Abuse and Alcoholism. Alcohol and Aging.

75. Administration on Aging. Older Americans Act.

76. National Institute on Aging. Alcohol Use and Abuse.

77. National Institute on Alcohol Abuse and Alcoholism. Alcohol and Aging.

Feature Box References

1. National Institute of Mental Health. 2010. Attention Deficit Hyperactivity Disorder (ADHD). Available at www.nimh.nih.gov/health/topics/attention-deficit-hyperactivity-disorder-adhd/index.shtml. Accessed July 2010.

2. Consensus Development Panel. 1982. Defined Diets and Childhood Hyperactivity. National Institutes of Health Consensus Development Conference Summary, Volume 4, no. 3, National Institute of Mental Health. Available at www.nimh.nih.gov/health/topics/attention-deficit-hyperactivity-disorder-adhd/index.shtml. Accessed July 2010.

3. Position of the American Dietetic Association. 2004. Use of Nutritive and Nonnutritive Sweeteners. *Journal of the American Dietetic Association* 104: 255-275.

4. Biederman J., S. V. Faraone, K. Keenan, D. Knee, and M. F. Tsuang. 1990. Family-Genetic and Psychosocial Risk Factors in DSM-III Attention Deficit Disorder. *Journal of the American Academy of Child and Adolescent Psychiatry* 29: 526–533.

5. National Institute of Neurological Disorders and Stroke. 2010. Autism Fact Sheet. Available at www.ninds.nih.gov/disorders/autism/detail_autism.htm. Accessed June 2010.

6. Mayo Clinic. 2010. Autism. Available at www.mayoclinic.com/health/autism/DS00348. Accessed June 2010.

7. American Cancer Society. 2010. Cancer Facts and Figures 2010. Available at www.cancer.org/acs/groups/content/@nho/documents/document/acspc-024113.pdf. Accessed July 2010.

8. World Cancer Research Fund/American Institute for Cancer Research. 2007. *Food, Nutrition, Physical Activity, and the Prevention of Cancer: A Global Perspective*. Washington, D.C.: AICR.

9. Ibid.

10. American Cancer Society. Cancer Facts and Figures 2010.

11. Ibid.

12. Brown, C. 2000. Overview of Drug Interactions. *U.S. Pharmacist* 25: e1–e16.

13. Maskalyk, J. 2002. Grapefruit Juice: Potential Drug Interactions. *Canadian Medical Association Journal* 167: 279–280.

14. U.S. Food and Drug Administration. 2009. *Dietary Supplements: Tips for Older Dietary Supplement Users*. Available at www.fda.gov/food/dietarysupplements/ConsumerInformation/ucm110493.htm. Accessed July 2010.

Two Points of View References

1. USDA Food and Nutrition Service, "National School Lunch Program: Participation and Lunches Served." Available at www.fns.usda.gov/pd/slsummar.htm. Accessed August 2010.

2. USDA, "National School Lunch Program Fact Sheet" (August 2009) Available at www.fns.usda.gov/cnd/lunch/AboutLunch/NSLPFactSheet.pdf. Accessed August 2010.

3. K. Ralston, C. Newman, et al., "The National School Lunch Program: Background, Trends and Issues," USDA (July 2008) Available at www.ers.usda.gov/Publications/ERR61/ERR61.pdf. Accessed August 2010.

4. D. Neumark-Sztainer, S. French, et al., "School Lunch and Snacking Patterns Among High School Students: Associations with School Food Environment and Policies," *International Journal of Behavioral Nutrition and Physical Activity* (October 2005) Available at www.ijbnpa.org/content/2/1/14. Accessed August 2010.

5. J. Wardle, M. L. Herrera, L. Cooke, and E. L. Gibson, "Modifying Children's Food Preferences: The Effects of Exposure and Reward on Acceptance of an Unfamiliar Vegetable," *European Journal of Clinical Nutrition* 57 no. 2 (2003): 341–348.

6. Ralston. "The National School Lunch Program."

7. Ibid.

8. Food Research and Action Center, "Commodity Foods and the Nutritional Quality of the National School Lunch Program: Historical Role, Current Operations and Future Potential" (September 2008) Available at www.frac.org/pdf/commodities08.pdf. Accessed August 2010.

9. Ibid.

Index

Page references followed by *fig* indicate illustrated figures or photographs followed by *t* indicates a table.

Credits

iStockphoto; **p. 218, fourth right:** SoleilC/Shutterstock; **p. 218, second left:** ElliotKo/Shutterstock; **p. 218, second right:** a9photo/Shutterstock; **p. 218, third left:** Christopher Elwell/Shutterstock; **p. 218, third right:** Donald Erickson/iStockphoto; **p. 219:** Serghei Starus/iStockphoto; **p. 220:** Ariy/Shutterstock; **p. 220:** Brand X Pictures/age fotostock; **p. 221:** Dorling Kindersley; **p. 223:** Kristin Piljay

Chapter 7   **p. 224:** CLM/Shutterstock; **p. 226:** United States Pharmacopeia; **p. 227, bottom:** mtsyri/Shutterstock; **p. 227, left:** Photodisc/Getty Images; **p. 227, right:** Brand X Pictures/Getty Images; **p. 229, a:** National Eye Institute, National Institutes of Health; **p. 229, b:** National Eye Institute, National Institutes of Health; **p. 229, c:** National Eye Institute, National Institutes of Health; **p. 230:** Dorling Kindersley; **p. 232:** CarlssonInc/iStockphoto; **p. 234, bottom:** Dr. P. Marazzi/Photo Researchers, Inc.; **p. 234, top:** Dorling Kindersley; **p. 235:** Digital Vision/Getty Images; **p. 236, bottom:** Lew Robertson/Foodpix/Getty Images; **p. 236, top:** sarsmis/Shutterstock; **p. 237:** Envision/CORBIS; **p. 238, bottom:** Dal Canton Mazzone, The New England Journal of Medicine, Vol. 346, p. 821, 3/14/02; **p. 238, top:** Darren Robb/Getty Images; **p. 239, bottom:** Konmesa/Dreamstime.com; **p. 239, top:** Rachel Epstein/PhotoEdit Inc.; **p. 240, bottom left:** Eye of Science/Photo Researchers, Inc.; **p. 240, bottom right:** Ted Kinsman/Photo Researchers, Inc.; **p. 240, top left:** Brian Hagiwaraj/Foodpix/Getty Images; **p. 240, top right:** Cristina Pedrassini/Photo Researchers, Inc.; **p. 241, bottom:** CORBIS; **p. 241, top:** CORBIS; **p. 242, bottom:** Design Pics Inc./Alamy; **p. 242, top:** Suzannah Skelton/iStockphoto; **p. 243:** Pearson Education/PH College; **p. 244, left:** Jacek Chabraszewski/Shutterstock; **p. 244, right:** Zephyr Photography/Photo Researchers, Inc.; **p. 246, bottom left:** Biophoto Associates/Photo Researchers, Inc.; **p. 246, bottom right:** Ian Shaw/Alamy; **p. 246, top:** Isabelle Rozenbaum/AGE Fotostock; **p. 247, left:** NMSB/Custom Medical Stock Photo; **p. 247, right:** Foodmaniac/Dreamstime.com; **p. 248, bottom left:** Leigh Belsch/Foodpix/Getty Images; **p. 248, bottom right:** Johner/Getty Images; **p. 248, top:** Ralph Morse/Getty Images; **p. 249, left:** Markstout/Dreamstime.com; **p. 249, right:** SPL/Photo Researchers, Inc.; **p. 250, bottom:** Elena Elisseeva/Shutterstock; **p. 250, top:** JJAVA/Fotolia; **p. 251, left:** Lisa Thompson/Foodpix/Getty Images; **p. 251, right:** Dr. M.A. Ansary/Photo Researchers, Inc.; **p. 252, bottom left:** D. Hurst/Alamy; **p. 252, bottom right:** Photodisc Green/Getty Images; **p. 252, top:** CORBIS; **p. 253, left:** FoodCollection/Photolibrary; **p. 253, right:** Anthony-Masterson/Foodpix/Getty Images; **p. 254, bottom:** Cristina Cassinelli/Foodpix/Getty Images; **p. 254, top:** NMSB/Custom Medical Stock Photo; **p. 255:** Dorling Kindersley; **p. 256, :** Kristin Piljay; **p. 256, bottom left:** CORBIS; **p. 256, bottom right:** Rick Souders/Foodpix/Getty Images; **p. 257, bottom:** Martin Jacobs/Foodpix/Getty Images; **p. 257, top:** Lew Robertson/Foodpix/Getty Images; **p. 258, bottom left:** CORBIS; **p. 258, bottom right:** SPL/Photo Researchers, Inc.; **p. 258, middle:** Dimitri Vervits/Getty Images; **p. 258, top left:** Biophoto Associates/Photo Researchers, Inc.; **p. 258, top right:** Getty Images; **p. 259, bottom:** Edyta Pawlowska/Shutterstock; **p. 259, top:** CORBIS; **p. 260, bottom left:** Smileus/Shutterstock; **p. 260, bottom right:** Photodisc/Getty Images; **p. 260, middle:** Robin MacDougall/Getty Images; **p. 260, top:** David P. Smith/Shutterstock; **p. 261, bottom:** Dorling Kindersley; **p. 261, top:** Richard Radstone/Getty Images; **p. 263:** Cheryl Casey/Shutterstock; **p. 264, bottom:** Anna Sedneva/iStockphoto; **p. 264, top:** Brand X Pictures/age fotostock; **p. 265, bottom:** Mary Ellen Bartley/Foodpix/Getty Images; **p. 265, top:** CLM/Shutterstock; **p. 266:** Kristin Piljay; **p. 267, a:** Kristin Piljay; **p. 267, b:** Kristin Piljay; **p. 269, bottom:** Elizabeth Simpson/Getty Images; **p. 269, bottom:** Kristin Piljay; **p. 269, middle:** Julián Rovagnati/Shutterstock; **p. 269, top:** Brand X Pictures/age fotostock; **p. 271, first left:** Kristin Piljay; **p. 271, first right:** Helen Sessions/Alamy; **p. 271, fourth left:** Ciaran Griffin/Getty Images; **p. 271, fourth right:** Cathy Britcliffe/iStockphoto; **p. 271, second left:** foodfolio/Alamy; **p. 271, second right:** Smneedham/Foodpix/Getty Images; **p. 271, third left:** Maxim Pushkarev/Shutterstock; **p. 271, third right:** James Nesterwitz/Alamy; **p. 272:** Sally Scott/Shutterstock; **p. 275:** Tomasz Zachariasz/iStockphoto

Chapter 8   **p. 276:** Emma Rian/CORBIS; **p. 278:** Brand X Pictures/agefotostock; **p. 280:** Tony Anderson/Getty Images; **p. 280, top:** eyewave/iStockphoto; **p. 281:** Konmesa/Dreamstime.com; **p. 286:** Warren Morgan/CORBIS; **p. 287:** Olinchuk/Shutterstock; **p. 290, botom:** Stephen Beaudet/

zefa/Corbis; **p. 290, lert:** Kristin Piljay; **p. 290, middle:** J.Garcia/photocuisine/Corbis; **p. 290, top:** Kristin Piljay; **p. 291, bottom:** Kristin Piljay; **p. 291, top:** motorika/Fotolia; **p. 294, bottom:** Kristin Piljay; **p. 294, middle:** John Lund/Tiffany Schoepp/Getty Images; **p. 294, top:** Steve Sant/Alamy; **p. 295:** Mary Ellen Bartley/Foodpix/Getty Images; **p. 296, bottom:** Lehner/iStockphoto; **p. 296, middle:** D. Hurst/Alamy; **p. 296, top:** Joe Gough/Shutterstock; **p. 297, left:** J.Garcia/photocuisine/Corbis; **p. 297, middle:** Smit/Shutterstock; **p. 297, right:** Elena Schweitzer/Shutterstock; **p. 298, bottom:** Nayashkova Olga/Shutterstock; **p. 298, middle bottom:** Michael Pohuski/FoodPix/Getty Images; **p. 298, middle top:** Craig van der Lende/Getty Images; **p. 298, top right:** Michael Klein/Peter Arnold, Inc.; **p. 299, left:** Nitr/Shutterstock; **p. 299, right:** Dorling Kindersley; **p. 300, bottom:** Aprilphoto/Dreamstime.com; **p. 300, middle:** Nick Emm/Alamy; **p. 300, top:** BananaStock/Jupiter Images; **p. 301, bottom:** Ingram Publishing/Alamy; **p. 301, middle:** Suzannah Skelton/iStockphoto; **p. 301, top:** Stockbyte Gold/Alamy; **p. 302, bottom:** CORBIS; **p. 302, top left:** Sally Scott/Shutterstock; **p. 302, top right:** foodfolio/Alamy; **p. 303, bottom:** Office of the Surgeon General; **p. 303, top:** Office of the Surgeon General; **p. 306, bottom:** Steven Mark Needham/Foodpix/Getty Images; **p. 306, top:** Larry Korb/Shutterstock; **p. 307:** Tata/Shutterstock; **p. 308, bottom:** Eric Grave/Photo Researchers, Inc.; **p. 308, middle:** Comstock/Jupiter Images; **p. 308, top:** C Squared Studios/Getty Images; **p. 309, bottom left:** Robin MacDougall/Getty Images; **p. 309, bottom right:** Konmesa/Dreamstime.com; **p. 310, bottom:** Bon Appetit/Alamy; **p. 310, top:** Kevin Snair/iStockphoto; **p. 311, bottom:** Medical-on-Line/Alamy; **p. 311, top:** Joaquin Carrillo Farga/Photo Researchers, Inc.; **p. 312, bottom:** Corbis; **p. 312, middle left:** FoodCollection/age fotostock; **p. 312, middle right:** Image Source/Jupiter Images; **p. 312, top:** Foodcollection/Getty Images; **p. 313, bottom:** Bruce James/Foodpix/Getty Images; **p. 313, top:** Bill Aron/Photo Edit; **p. 314:** Getty Images; **p. 315, bottom:** Don Farrall/Getty Images; **p. 315, top:** John A Rizzo/age fotostock; **p. 316, bottom left:** Foodcollection.com/Alamy; **p. 316, bottom right:** Brand X Pictures/agefotostock; **p. 316, top:** National Institute of Dental Research; **p. 317, bottom:** shutterstock; **p. 317, middle:** FoodCollection/age fotostock; **p. 317, top:** Mary Ellen Bartley/Getty Images; **p. 318, middle:** Food Features/Alamy; **p. 318, bottom right:** Corbis/Bettmann; **p. 318, top:** Richard Megna/Fundamental Photographs, NYC; **p. 319, left:** John Paul Kay/Peter Arnold, Inc.; **p. 319, right:** Foodcollection/Getty Images; **p. 320, bottom:** Viktor/Fotolia; **p. 320, middle left:** Claude Edelmann/Photo Researchers, Inc.; **p. 320, middle right:** iStockphoto; **p. 320, top:** marco mayer/Shutterstock; **p. 324:** Brand X Pictures/agefotostock; **p. 325, first left:** Emma Rian/CORBIS; **p. 325, first right:** Blue Lemon Photo/Shutterstock; **p. 325, fourth left:** Melinda Fawver/Shutterstock; **p. 325, fourth right:** Maksymilian Skolik/Shutterstock; **p. 325, second left:** Imageman/Shutterstock; **p. 325, second right:** D. Hurst/Alamy; **p. 325, third left:** pdtnc/iStockphoto; **p. 325, third right:** Valentyn Volkov/Shutterstock; **p. 326:** Stockbyte Gold/Alamy; **p. 329:** Emma Rian/CORBIS

Chapter 9   **p. 330:** altrendo images/Getty Images; **p. 332:** AdCouncil.org/U.S. Dept. of Transportation; **p. 333:** LeS/Shutterstock; **p. 334, bottom left:** Foodcollection/Getty Images; **p. 334, bottom right:** Kristin Piljay; **p. 334, middle left:** Steve Gorton/Dorling Kindersley Media Library; **p. 334, middle right:** johnfoto18/Shutterstock; **p. 334, top:** AntiGerasim/Shutterstock; **p. 335:** Kristin Piljay; **p. 336:** Joe Atlas/CORBIS; **p. 337:** Adam Woolfitt/CORBIS; **p. 338:** Digital Vision/Getty Images; **p. 339:** Jim Varney/Photo Researchers, Inc.; **p. 340:** Fetal Alcohol & Drug Unit (FAS); **p. 342:** altrendo images/Getty Images; **p. 342, first left:** ol_vic/Shutterstock; **p. 342, first right:** iofoto/Shutterstock; **p. 342, fourth left:** Pali Rao/iStockphoto; **p. 342, fourth right:** Danny Hooks/Fotolia; **p. 342, second left:** Antonio Muñoz Palomares/iStockphoto; **p. 342, second right:** Joy Brown/Shutterstock; **p. 342, third left:** Dusanzidar/Dreamstime.com; **p. 342, third right:** unpict/Foltolia; **p. 343, left:** Corbis; **p. 343, right:** Richard Megna/Fundamental Photos; **p. 344, 1:** Richard Megna/Fundamental Photos; **p. 344, 2:** Arthur Glauberman/Photo Researchers, Inc.; **p. 344, 3:** Arthur Glauberman/Photo Researchers, Inc.; **p. 345:** Arthur Glauberman/Photo Researchers, Inc.; **p. 346:** Corbis; **p. 350, bottom:** The Image Works; **p. 350, top:** Joe Raedle/Getty Images; **p. 351:** ampFotoStudio.com/Fotolia; **p. 352, first left:** Paul Johnson/iStockphoto; **p. 352, first right:** Stockdisc Classic/Alamy; **p. 352, fourth left:** Paul Johnson/iStockphoto; **p. 352, fourth right:** Gabe Palmer/Alamy; **p. 352, second left:** Gpalmer/Dreamstime.com; **p. 352, second right:** Clive Streeter/Dorling

Kindersley Media Library; **p. 352, third left:** dibrova/Shutterstock; **p. 352, third right:** Gpalmer/Dreamstime.com; **p. 353:** ilian food & drink/Alamy; **p. 357:** altrendo images/Getty Images

Chapter 10 **p. 358:** pierre bourrier/Alamy; **p. 360:** D. Hurst/Alamy; **p. 361:** Joe Traver//Time Life Pictures/Getty Images; **p. 362, bottom right:** AP Photo/Women's Wear Daily; **p. 362, first left:** Bill Aron/PhotoEdit Inc.; **p. 362, fourth left:** AP photo/Remy de la Mauviniere; **p. 362, second left:** 20TH CENTURY FOX/THE KOBAL COLLECTION/SHAW, SAM; **p. 362, third left:** Bettmann/CORBIS; **p. 365, bottom left:** Mauro Fermariello/Photo Researchers, Inc.; **p. 365, bottom right:** David Young-Wolff/PhotoEdit; **p. 365, middle left:** Sean Aidan; Eye Ubiquitous/CORBIS; **p. 365, top left:** Foodcollection/Getty Images; **p. 365, top right:** Mauro Fermariello/Photo Researchers, Inc.; **p. 366:** George Doyle/Getty Images; **p. 367, a:** Sam Edwards/Getty Images; **p. 367, b:** Pixland/Corbis; **p. 367, c:** pintailpictures/Alamy; **p. 372:** Harrison G. Pope, Jr., MD; **p. 375, bottom:** Inmagine Asia/age fotostock; **p. 375, top:** Ilene MacDonald/Alamy; **p. 377, bottom left:** Image Source/Alamy; **p. 377, right:** Envision/Corbis; **p. 377, top left:** John Terence Turner/Getty Images; **p. 378:** Richard Megna/Fundamental Photos; **p. 382, bottom left:** US Department of Health and Human Services; **p. 382, bottom right:** US Department of Health and Human Services; **p. 382, top left:** Comstock Images/Jupiter Images; **p. 382, top right:** US Department of Health and Human Services; **p. 383, bottom:** Photolibrary/Alamy; **p. 383, middle:** Radius Images/Jupiter Images; **p. 383, top:** Julien Tromeur/Shutterstock; **p. 384, bottom left:** Richard Megna/Fundamental Photos; **p. 384, bottom right:** Richard Megna/Fundamental Photos; **p. 384, top left:** US Department of Health and Human Services; **p. 384, top right:** Richard Megna/Fundamental Photos; **p. 385:** GlowImages/Alamy; **p. 388:** Jerry Arcieri/CORBIS; **p. 389:** AP Photo/Charles Bennet; **p. 390:** Najlah Feanny/CORBIS; **p. 393:** Ruth Jenkinson/Dorling Kindersley Media Library; **p. 395:** LIU JIN/AFP/Getty Images; **p. 396, bottom:** image100/Jupiter Images; **p. 396, top:** Veit Mette/laif/Redux; **p. 400, first left:**. S. Department of Health and Human Services; **p. 400, first right:** Cabezonication/Dreamstime.com; **p. 400, fourth left:** Burke Triolo/Photolibrary; **p. 400, fourth right:** Denis Vrublevski/Shutterstock; **p. 400, second left:** Blueee/Dreamstime.com; **p. 400, second right:** James Pauls/iStockphoto; **p. 400, third left:** Sharon Day/Shutterstock; **p. 400, third right:** Juanmonino/iStockphoto; **p. 401:** Vasko Miokovic/iStockphoto; **p. 403:** pierre bourrier/Alamy; **p. 405:** Olivier Cadeaux/CORBIS

Chapter 11 **p. 406:** Thomas Barwick/Getty Images; **p. 408:** Image Source/Getty Images; **p. 409:** Stockbyte/Getty Images; **p. 410, fifth:** Photodisc/Getty Images; **p. 410, first:** Ivonne Wierink/Shutterstock; **p. 410, fourth:** Plattform/Getty Images; **p. 410, second:** Charles Thatcher/Getty Images; **p. 410, sixth:** Ryan McVay/Getty Images; **p. 410, third:** Tamara Lackey/Getty Images; **p. 411:** Dan Dalton/Getty Images; **p. 412:** BananaStock/Jupiter Images; **p. 417:** Creatas Images/Jupiter Images; **p. 422:** Bananastock/Jupiter Images; **p. 424:** webphotographeer/iStockphoto; **p. 425, bottom:** Marie C. Fields/Shutterstock; **p. 425, top:** Photo Network/Alamy; **p. 426:** Kristin Piljay; **p. 427:** Kristin Piljay; **p. 428:** Tim Hill/Alamy; **p. 429:** Kristin Piljay; **p. 431:** Image Source/Jupiter Images; **p. 434:** Danylchenko Iaroslav/Shutterstock; **p. 435:** Najlah Feanny/Corbis; **p. 436:** SPL/Photo Researchers, Inc.; **p. 440:** Photodisc/Getty Images; **p. 441:** Thomas Barwick/Getty Images; **p. 443:** Fuse/Getty Images

Chapter 12 **p. 444:** SamWirzba/age fotostock; **p. 446:** Brand X Pictures/agefotostock; **p. 447:** Beata Becla/iStockphoto; **p. 448:** Kristin Piljay;

p. 449: Russ Bishop/age fotostock; **p. 449, top:** Medical-on-Line/Alamy; **p. 450:** Zsolt Nyulaszi/age fotostock; **p. 451, bottom:** Terrance Klassen/Photolibrary; **p. 451, top:** USDA; **p. 452:** AGStockUSA/Alamy; **p. 453, bottom:** Benjamin J. Myers/CORBIS; **p. 453, top:** Michael Hanson/Getty Images; **p. 457:** peter dench/Alamy; **p. 458:** EPA; **p. 465:** Marc Hill/Alamy; **p. 467:** Dennis MacDonald/Photo Edit, Inc.; **p. 469:** DURAND FLORENCE/Sipa Press; **p. 473:** Bill Aron/Photo Edit Inc.; **p. 474, top left:** Sam Wirzba/age fotostock; **p. 475:** Josie Lepe/San Jose Mercury News/Newscom; **p. 479:** Michael Reynolds/epa/CORBIS

Chapter 13 **p. 480:** Jose Inc/Photolibrary; **p. 482:** Ambient Images Inc./Alamy; **p. 483:** Muellek Josef/Shutterstock; **p. 484:** Norma Jean Gargasz/Alamy; **p. 485:** wetnose1/Fotolia; **p. 486, bottom:** Foodcollection.com/Alamy; **p. 486, top:** E.G.Pors/Shutterstock; **p. 488, bottom:** Dr. Gary Gaugler/Phototake; **p. 488, top:** Phanie/Photo Researchers, Inc.; **p. 490:** Dr. Gary D. Gaugler/Photo Researchers, Inc.; **p. 491:** Foodcollection.com/Alamy; **p. 493:** Jose Inc/Photolibrary; **p. 494:** Eye of Science/Photo Researchers, Inc.; **p. 495, a:** piga&catalano/age fotostock; **p. 495, b:** USDA; **p. 496:** Angel Simon/Shutterstock; **p. 501:** USDA; **p. 504, a:** Brand X Pictures/age fotostock; **p. 504, b:** Kristin Piljay; **p. 510:** Kristin Piljay; **p. 512:** jathys/Shutterstock; **p. 513:** Photofusion Picture Library/Alamy; **p. 515:** Kate Kunz/Photolibrary

Chapter 14 **p. 516:** Viviane Moos/CORBIS; **p. 518:** Jon Jones/Sygma/Corbis; **p. 520:** Suzanne Tucker/Shutterstock; **p. 521:** David Cavagnaro/Peter Arnold, Inc.; **p. 523:** Peter Turnley/CORBIS; **p. 525:** Photofusion Picture Library/Alamy; **p. 526:** David Butow/CORBIS; **p. 527:** Abid Katib/Getty Images; **p. 529:** Michael Newman/PhotoEdit Inc.; **p. 531:** Ladi Kirn/Alamy; **p. 533:** Benjamin J. Myers/CORBIS; **p. 534, bottom:** Alan Evrard/Robert Harding World Imagery; **p. 534, top:** o44/ZUMA Press/Newscom; **p. 536:** Viviane Moos/CORBIS; **p. 539:** p71/ZUMA Press/Newscom

Chapter 15 **p. 540:** Brand X Pictures/age fotostock; **p. 542:** Laura Dwight/PhotoEdit Inc.; **p. 547, left:** A. Inden/zefa/Corbis; **p. 547, middle:** Dorling Kindersley; **p. 547, right:** Dorling Kindersley; **p. 548:** Kristin Piljay; **p. 549:** MICHAEL WIRTZ/MCT/Newscom; **p. 550:** Shutterstock; **p. 552:** Dan Peretz/Shutterstock; **p. 554:** Richard Megna/Fundamental Photographs, NYC; **p. 555:** Mango Productions/Corbis; **p. 556:** Dorling Kindersley; **p. 557:** Sally and Richard Greenhill/Alamy; **p. 558:** d75/ZUMA Press/Newscom; **p. 560:** American Images Inc/Getty Images; **p. 562:** Ariel Skelley/CORBIS; **p. 567:** Kayte M. Deioma/PhotoEdit; **p. 568:** Digital Vision/Getty Images; **p. 572, fifth:** Dorling Kindersley; **p. 572, first:** Dr. Martin S. Spiller, DMD; **p. 572, fourth:** Dorling Kindersley; **p. 572, second:** MedioImages/Getty Images; **p. 572, third:** Dorling Kindersley; **p. 573:** It Stock Free/age footstock

Chapter 16 **p. 578:** Red Chopsticks/age fotostock; **p. 580:** Tina Manley/Charity/Alamy; **p. 582:** Mike Flippo/Shutterstock; **p. 583:** Dorling Kindersley; **p. 584:** Creatas Images/Jupiter Images; **p. 588, bottom:** Wavebreakmedia Ltd/Dreamstime; **p. 588, top:** Gengberg/Dreamstime; **p. 590:** Skip Nall/Alamy; **p. 592:** Mike Booth/Alamy; **p. 595:** Bubbles Photolibrary/Alamy; **p. 604, bottom:** USDA, ARS; **p. 604, top:** Ariel Skelley/Thinkstock; **p. 605, bottom:** Ronnie Kaufman/CORBIS; **p. 605, top:** USDA, ARS; **p. 606:** USDA; **p. 608:** Sally and Richard Greenhill/Alamy; **p. 610:** Mike Flippo/Shutterstock; **p. 611:** Red Chopsticks/age fotostock; **p. 613:** Michael P. Gadomski/Photo Researchers, Inc.

Tolerable Upper Intake Levels (UL^a)

Vitamins

Life-Stage Group	Vitamin A (µg/d)^b	Vitamin C (mg/d)	Vitamin D (IU/d)	Vitamin E (mg/d)^{c,d}	Niacin (mg/d)^d	Vitamin B$_6$ (mg/d)^d	Folate (µg/d)^d	Choline (g/d)
Infants								
0–6 mo	600	ND^e	1,000	ND	ND	ND	ND	ND
6–12 mo	600	ND	1,500	ND	ND	ND	ND	ND
Children								
1–3 y	600	400	2,500	200	10	30	300	1.0
4–8 y	900	650	3,000	300	15	40	400	1.0
Males, Females								
9–13 y	1,700	1,200	4,000	600	20	60	600	2.0
14–18 y	2,800	1,800	4,000	800	30	80	800	3.0
19–70 y	3,000	2,000	4,000	1,000	35	100	1,000	3.5
>70 y	3,000	2,000	4,000	1,000	35	100	1,000	3.5
Pregnancy								
≤18 y	2,800	1,800	4,000	800	30	80	800	3.0
19–50 y	3,000	2,000	4,000	1,000	35	100	1,000	3.5
Lactation								
≤18 y	2,800	1,800	4,000	800	30	80	800	3.0
19–50 y	3,000	2,000	4,000	1,000	35	100	1,000	3.5

Elements

Life-Stage Group	Boron (mg/d)	Calcium (mg/d)	Copper (µg/d)	Fluoride (mg/d)	Iodine (µg/d)	Iron (mg/d)	Magnesium (mg/d)^f	Manganese (mg/d)	Molybdenum (µg/d)	Nickel (mg/d)	Phosphorus (g/d)	Selenium (µg/d)	Vanadium (mg/d)^g	Zinc (mg/d)
Infants														
0–6 mo	ND	1,000	ND	0.7	ND	40	ND	ND	ND	ND	ND	45	ND	4
6–12 mo	ND	1,500	ND	0.9	ND	40	ND	ND	ND	ND	ND	60	ND	5
Children														
1–3 y	3	2,500	1,000	1.3	200	40	65	2	300	0.2	3	90	ND	7
4–8 y	6	2,500	3,000	2.2	300	40	110	3	600	0.3	3	150	ND	12
Males, Females														
9–13 y	11	3,000	5,000	10	600	40	350	6	1,100	0.6	4	280	ND	23
14–18 y	17	3,000	8,000	10	900	45	350	9	1,700	1.0	4	400	ND	34
19–50 y	20	2,500	10,000	10	1,100	45	350	11	2,000	1.0	4	400	1.8	40
>50 y	20	2,000	10,000	10	1,100	45	350	11	2,000	1.0	3	400	1.8	40
Pregnancy														
≤18 y	17	3,000	8,000	10	900	45	350	9	1,700	1.0	3.5	400	ND	34
19–50 y	20	2,500	10,000	10	1,100	45	350	11	2,000	1.0	3.5	400	ND	40
Lactation														
≤18 y	17	3,000	8,000	10	900	45	350	9	1,700	1.0	4	400	ND	34
19–50 y	20	2,500	10,000	10	1,100	45	350	11	2,000	1.0	4	400	ND	40

Source: Adapted from the Dietary Reference Intakes series, National Academies Press. Copyright 1997, 1998, 2000, 2001, by the National Academy of Sciences. These reports may be accessed via www.nap.edu. Courtesy of the National Academies Press, Washington, D.C.

^{a} UL = The maximum level of daily nutrient intake that is likely to pose no risk of adverse effects. Unless otherwise specified, the UL represents total intake from food, water, and supplements. Due to lack of suitable data, ULs could not be established for vitamin K, thiamin, riboflavin, vitamin B$_{12}$, pantothenic acid, biotin, or carotenoids. In the absence of ULs, extra caution may be warranted in consuming levels above recommended intakes.

^{b} As preformed vitamin A only.

^{c} As α-tocopherol; applies to any form of supplemental α-tocopherol.

^{d} The ULs for vitamin E, niacin, and folate apply to synthetic forms obtained from supplements, fortified foods, or a combination of the two.

^{e} ND = Not determinable due to lack of data of adverse effects in this age group and concern with regard to lack of ability to handle excess amounts. Source of intake should be from food only to prevent high levels of intake.

^{f} The ULs for magnesium represent intake from a pharmacological agent only and do not include intake from food and water.

^{g} Although vanadium in food has not been shown to cause adverse effects in humans, there is no justification for adding vanadium to food, and vanadium supplements should be used with caution. The UL is based on adverse effects in laboratory animals, and this data could be used to set a UL for adults but not children and adolescents.

Daily Values for Food Labels

The Daily Values are standard values developed by the Food and Drug Administration (FDA) for use on food labels. The values are based on 2000 calories a day for adults and children over 4 years old.

Nutrient	Amount	Nutrient	Amount
Protein[a]	50 g	Vitamin K	80 μg
Thiamin	1.5 mg	Calcium	1000 mg
Riboflavin	1.7 mg	Iron	18 mg
Niacin	20 mg NE	Zinc	15 mg
Biotin	300 μg	Iodine	150 μg
Pantothenic acid	10 mg	Copper	2 mg
Vitamin B_6	2 mg	Chromium	120 μg
Folate	400 mcg	Selenium	70 μg
Vitamin B_{12}	6 mg	Molybdenum	75 μg
Vitamin C	60 mg	Manganese	2 mg
Vitamin A	5000 IU[b]	Chloride	3400 mg
Vitamin D	400 IU[b]	Magnesium	400 mg
Vitamin E	30 IU[b]	Phosphorus	1000 mg

Food Component	Amount	Calculation Factors
Fat	65 g	30% of calories
Saturated fat	20 g	10% of calories
Cholesterol	300 mg	Same regardless of calories
Carbohydrate (total)	300 g	60% of calories
Fiber	25 g	11.5 g per 1000 calories
Protein	50 g	10% of calories
Sodium	2400 mg	Same regardless of calories
Potassium	3500 mg	Same regardless of calories

[a] The Daily Values for protein vary for different groups: pregnant women, 60 g; nursing mothers, 65 g; infants under 1 year, 14 g; children 1 to 4 years, 16 g.

[b] Equivalent values for nutrients expressed as IU are: vitamin A, 1,500 RAE (assumes a mix of 40% retinol and 60% beta-carotene); vitamin D, 10 μg; vitamin E, 20 mg.